COMPACT

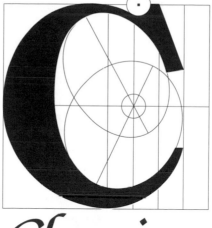

Classics™

YOUR PERSONAL PORTABLE LIBRARY

VOLUME I

Compact Classics, Inc.

1991

COMPACT

Classics™

First Printing, September 1991
Second Printing, May 1992
Third Printing, August 1992
Fourth Printing, October 1992

Lan C. England, Publisher
Stevens W. Anderson, Editor

Compact Classics, Inc.
P.O. Box 526145
Salt Lake City, Utah
84152-6145

ISBN 1-880184-01-X

Printed in the United States of America

COMPACT

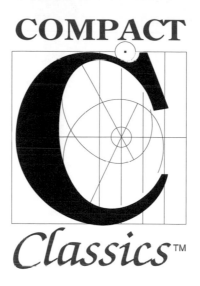

Classics™

Volume I

■ **INTRODUCTION:** Using Compact Classics

Compact Classics places concise, summary versions of important ideas and literature at your fingertips. A must addition to any busy person's home or office library, Compact Classics also comes available in its original seven-ring binder format, where pages can be removed and clipped into a 6-by-9 planning book for easy reading, anywhere, anytime.

In just minutes, you can become conversant and knowledgeable on any of hundreds of subjects – from business and life management principles, to classic and contemporary literature; from useful quotes and practical trivia, to information about your health; from notable historical figures to communication techniques and ideas. Brief commentary accompanies each book overview.

Compact Classics will introduce you to many great books. When you have time to sit down for a good long read, you'll know where to begin. But when you only have a few minutes, Compact Classics offers hundreds of reading adventures for your learning and enjoyment.

Invest in Yourself. Read the *Classics.*

■ **INVITATION:** We want to hear from you.

As you use the Compact Classics libraries, write down your suggestions for future books or articles on the form provided at the back. We'll pay for your original ideas. Your comments and questions are welcome.

Order Compact Classics as a valued gift for your friend, customer or family member. Call toll free 1 (800) 755-9777 for current price information.

■ INDEX: A Table of Contents

■ LIBRARY #1: Business and Leadership ■

Section A

1-A1   *Entrepreneurial Megabucks: The 100 Greatest Entrepreneurs of the Last Twenty-Five Years* by A. David Silver

1-A2   *Megatrends* by John Naisbitt

1-A3   *Megatrends 2000: Ten New Directions For the 1990's* by John Naisbitt and Patricia Aburdene

1-A4   *What They Don't Teach You at Harvard Business School: Notes From a Street-Smart Executive* by Mark H. McCormack

1-A5   *The Managerial Mystique: Restoring Leadership in Business* by Abraham Zaleznik

Section B

1-B1   *A Passion for Excellence* by Tom Peters and Nancy Austin

1-B2   *Leadership Secrets of Attila the Hun* by Wess Roberts

1-B3   *Thriving on Chaos: Handbook for a Management Revolution* by Tom Peters

1-B4   *The Greatest Management Principle in the World* by Micheal LeBoeuf

1-B5   *The One-Minute Manager* by Kenneth Blanchard and Spencer Johnson

Section C

1-C1   *The Greatest Salesman in the World* by Og Mandino

1-C2   *Swim With the Sharks (Without Being Eaten Alive)* by Harvey Mackay

1-C3   *How to Talk So People Listen* by Sonya Hamlin

1-C4   *A Whack on the Side of the Head: How You Can Be More Creative* by Roger von Oech

1-C5   *Developing Critical Thinkers: Challenging Adults to Explore Alternative Ways of Thinking* by Stephen D. Brookfield

Section D

1-D1   **Managing Conflict**

1-D2   **Maintaining Job Satisfaction**

1-D3   **Alleviating Worker Alienation**

1-D4   **Unlocking Your Workteam's Potential**

1-D5   **Attitudes at Work**

1-D6   **Dual-Career Couples**

Section E

1-E1   Situational Leadership

1-E2   Leadership: A Behavioral View

1-E3   What Do Managers Do . . . Really?

1-E4   Understanding Managerial Communication

1-E5   Communication Skills for Managers

1-E6   Psychological Contracts: Forces That Bind Managers and Employees

Section F

1-F1   Employee Recruitment and Selection

1-F2   Employee and Management Rights

1-F3   Incentives for Productivity

1-F4   The Performance Appraisal Process

1-F5   The Art of Group Decision-Making

1-F6   On Organizational Culture

LIBRARY #2: Personal Effectiveness

Section A: Personal Management

2-A1   *The Seven Habits of Highly Effective People* by Stephen R. Covey

2-A2   *Wishcraft: How to Get What You Really Want* by Barbara Sher

2-A3   *Peak Performance Principles for High Achievers* by John R. Noe

2-A4   *How to Get Control of Your Time and Your Life* by Alan Lakein

2-A5   *How to Put More Time in Your Life* by Dru Scott

2-A6   *Page-a-Minute Memory Book* by Harry Lorayne

Section B: Expanded Living

2-B1   *The Road Less Traveled* by M. Scott Peck

2-B2   *The Different Drum* by M. Scott Peck

2-B3   *Love is Letting Go of Fear* by Gerald G. Jampolsky

2-B4   *Psycho-cybernetics* by Maxwell Maltz

2-B5   *Understanding: Eliminating Stress and Finding Serenity in Life and Relationships* by Jane Nelsen

Section C: "Making It"

2-C1   *You Can Negotiate Anything: How To Get What You Want* by Herb Cohen

2-C2   *How to Prosper During the Coming Bad Years* by Howard J. Ruff

2-C3   *Wealth Without Risk: How to Develop a Personal Fortune Without Going Out On a Limb* by Charles J. Givens

2-C4   *The Richest Man in Babylon* by George S. Clason

2-C5   *Marshall Loeb's 1988 Money Guide* by Marshall Loeb

Section D: Tips and Techniques ─────────────────────────

2-D1   **Time-Saving Tips**

2-D2   **Business Gift-Giving Ideas**

2-D3   **Putting Spark in Your Relationships:** Activity Ideas

2-D4   **Dressing for Business**

2-D5   **Business and Executive Etiquette**

▰▰▰▰ LIBRARY #3: Quotes and Anecdotes ▰▰▰▰

Section A ──────────────────────────────────────

3-A1   **Work**

3-A2   **Adversity and Perseverance**

3-A3   **Achievement**

3-A4   **Leadership**

Section B ──────────────────────────────────────

3-B1   **Business**

3-B2   **Money**

3-B3   **Learning**

3-B4   **Problem Solving**

Section C ──────────────────────────────────────

3-C1   **Time and Life**

3-C2   **Relationships**

3-C3   **Communication**

3-C4   **Family Life**

Section D ──────────────────────────────────────

3-D1   **Integrity**

3-D2   **Happiness**

3-D3   **Health**

3-D4   **Thought Gems**

LIBRARY #4: Biographies

Section A: Pioneers in Science ——————————————

4-A1   Euclid

4-A2   Isaac Newton

4-A3   Galileo Galilei

4-A4   Nicolaus Copernicus

4-A5   Albert Einstein

Section B: Leaders in Crisis ——————————————

4-B1   Winston Churchill

4-B2   Benjamin Franklin

4-B3   Abraham Lincoln

4-B4   George Washington

4-B5   Thomas Jefferson

Section C: Artists and Philosophers ——————————

4-C1   William Shakespeare

4-C2   Leonardo da Vinci

4-C3   Ludwig van Beethoven

4-C4   Michelangelo

4-C5   Aristotle

Section D: Inventors and Innovators ——————————

4-D1   Thomas Alva Edison

4-D2   Marie Curie

4-D3   Orville and Wilbur Wright

4-D4   Louis Pasteur

4-D5   Antoine Lavoisier

Section E: Leaders of the Spirit ——————————————

4-E1   Martin Luther King, Jr.

4-E2   Mahatma Gandhi

4-E3   Florence Nightingale

4-E4   Christopher Columbus

4-E5   Confucius

Section F: A Medley of Books

4-F1   *My Life for the Poor: Mother Teresa of Calcutta*
by Jose Gonzalez-Balado and Janet N. Playfoot

4-F2   *Iacocca, An Autobiography* by Lee Iacocca, with William Novak

4-F3   *The Last Lion: Winston Spencer Churchill*
Vol. I: *Visions of Glory (1874-1932)* by William Manchester

4-F4   Vol. II: *Alone (1932-1940)* by William Manchester

4-F5   *The Autobiography of Malcolm X* by Malcolm X, with Alex Haley

▬▬▬▬▬ LIBRARY #5: Literary Classics ▬▬▬▬▬

Section A: Reflective Realism

5-A1   *The Scarlet Letter* by Nathaniel Hawthorne

5-A2   *A Farewell to Arms* by Ernest Hemingway

5-A3   *For Whom the Bell Tolls* by Ernest Hemingway

5-A4   *Anna Karenina* by Leo Tolstoy

5-A5   *Of Mice and Men* by John Steinbeck

Section B: Heroic Epic and Allegory

5-B1   *Paradise Lost* by John Milton

5-B2   *Beowulf* author unknown

5-B3   *Prometheus Bound* by Aeschylus

5-B4   *The Divine Comedy* by Dante Alighieri

5-B5   *El Cid* author unknown

Section C: Historical Fiction

5-C1   *A Tale of Two Cities* by Charles Dickens

5-C2   *The Lady of the Lake* by Sir Walter Scott

5-C3   *Henry VIII* by William Shakespeare

5-C4   *The Travels of Marco Polo* by Marco Polo

5-C5   *The Last of the Mohicans* by James Fenimore Cooper

Section D: Symbolic Characterization and Thought

5-D1   *The Rime of the Ancient Mariner* by Samuel Taylor Coleridge

5-D2   *Moby Dick* by Herman Melville

5-D3   *The Old Man and the Sea* by Ernest Hemingway

5-D4   *Don Quixote de la Mancha* by Miguel de Cervantes

5-D5   *Peer Gynt* by Henrik Ibsen

Section E: Adventure and Intrigue

5-E1   *The Maltese Falcon* by Dashiell Hammett

5-E2   *Call of the Wild* by Jack London

5-E3   *The Great Gatsby* by F. Scott Fitzgerald

5-E4   *Ben-Hur: A Tale of the Christ* by Lew Wallace

5-E5   *Robinson Crusoe* by Daniel Defoe

Section F: Science Fiction

5-F1   *The Picture of Dorian Gray* by Oscar Wilde

5-F2   *Frankenstein* by Mary Shelly

5-F3   *The Time Machine* by H. G. Wells

5-F4   *The Turn of the Screw* by Henry James

5-F5   *The Fall of the House of Usher* by Edgar Allan Poe

Section G: Social/Political Commentary

5-G1   *The Grapes of Wrath* by John Steinbeck

5-G2   *Candide* by Voltaire

5-G3   *A Connecticut Yankee in King Arthur's Court* by Mark Twain

5-G4   *1984* by George Orwell

5-G5   *The Prince and the Pauper* by Mark Twain

Section H: Shakespearean Tragedies

5-H1   *Hamlet, Prince of Denmark*

5-H2   *King Lear*

5-H3   *Romeo and Juliet*

5-H4   *Macbeth*

5-H5   *Othello*

Section I: Shakespearean Comedies

5-I1   *The Taming of the Shrew*

5-I2   *The Tempest*

5-I3   *As You Like It*

5-I4   *The Merchant of Venice*

5-I5   *Much Ado About Nothing*

Section J: Human Drama

5-J1   *The Courtship of Miles Standish* by Henry Wadsworth Longfellow

5-J2   *Our Town* by Thornton Wilder

5-J3   *Silas Marner* by George Eliot

5-J4   *Little Women* by Louisa May Alcott

5-J5   *Jane Eyre* by Charlotte Bronte

Section K: Philosophy

5-K1   *The Origin of Species* by Charles Darwin

5-K2   *Walden* by Henry David Thoreau

5-K3   *The Prince* by Machiavelli

5-K4   *Das Kapital* by Karl Marx

5-K5   *The Republic* by Plato

Section L: Examining Relationships

5-L1   *The Importance of Being Earnest* by Oscar Wilde

5-L2   *Babbit* by Sinclair Lewis

5-L3   *Death of a Salesman* by Arthur Miller

5-L4   *Pride and Prejudice* by Jane Austen

5-L5   *Far From the Madding Crowd* by Thomas Hardy

Section M: A Composite of Classics

5-M1   *Julius Caesar* by William Shakespeare

5-M2   *To Kill a Mockingbird* by Harper Lee

5-M3   *Oedipus Rex* by Sophocles I

5-M4   *Utopia* by Sir Thomas More

5-M5   *Faust* by Goethe

LIBRARY #6: Modern Literature

Section A: Popular Nonfiction

6-A1   *Life and Death in Shanghai* by Nien Cheng

6-A2   *The City of Joy* by Dominique Lapierre

6-A3   *Not Without My Daughter* by Betty Mahmoody, with William Hoffer

6-A4   *Blue Highways* by William Least Heat Moon

6-A5   *Hiroshima* by John Hersey

Section B: Worlds Away

6-B1   *One Hundred Years of Solitude* by Gabriel Garcia Marquez

6-B2   *The Painted Bird* by Jerzy Kosinski

6-B3   *Steppenwolf* by Hermann Hesse

6-B4   *The Handmaid's Tale* by Margaret Atwood

6-B5   *Lord of the Flies* by William Golding

Section C: Majorities of One

6-C1   *Henderson the Rain King* by Saul Bellow

6-C2   *My Name is Asher Lev* by Chaim Potok

6-C3   *Invisible Man* by Ralph Ellison

6-C4   *Ceremony* by Leslie Marmon Silko

6-C5   *Their Eyes Were Watching God* by Zora Neale Hurston

Section D: Favorite Fictional Selections

6-D1   *The Joy Luck Club* by Amy Tan

6-D2   *The Shell Seekers* by Rosamunde Pilcher

6-D3   *The Sound of Waves* by Yukio Mishima

6-D4   *The Stories of John Cheever* by John Cheever

6-D5   *The Chosen* by Chaim Potok

Library #7: Health and Fitness

Section A: Caring for Mind and Body

7-A1   *Feed Yourself Right* by Lendon Smith

7-A2   *The Stress Solution: A Rational Approach to Increasing Corporate and Personal Effectiveness* by Samuel H. Klarreich

7-A3   *Sitting on the Job: How to Survive the Stresses of Sitting Down to Work* by Scott W. Donkin

7-A4   *Control Your Depression* by Peter Lewinsohn, et. al.

7-A5   **Headaches:** Their Causes and Cures

Section B: Nutrition and Dieting

7-B1   *Overcoming Overeating: Living Free in a World of Food* by Jane Hirschmann

7-B2   **Six Celebrated Diet Books**
The Popcorn-Plus Diet by Joel Herskowitz, *Beverly Hills Medical Diet* by Arnold Fox, *The Rice Diet Report* by Judy Moscovitz, *The Eight-Week Cholesterol Cure* by Robert E. Kowalski, *The Story of Weight Watchers* by Jean Nidetch and Joan Rattner Heilman, and *Fabulous Fructose Recipe Book* by J. T. Cooper and Jeanne Jones

7-B3   Twenty Food Tips for Lifetime Weight Control

7-B4   **Cholesterol, Fats and Sugars:** Three Most Talked-About Health Topics

▰▰▰ LIBRARY #8: Word Power ▰▰▰

Section A: Towards Effective Speech

8-A1   **500 Vocabulary-Building Words**

8-A2   **Foreign Words and Phrases**

8-A3   **Preparing and Presenting a Speech**

Section B: Wordsmith Guide

8-B1   **A Painless Grammar Guide**

8-B2   **Punctuation Primer**

8-B3   **Spelling Recommendations and Rules**

8-B4   **Spelling Help!** A Speller's Sound Guide

▰▰▰ LIBRARY #9: Expanding Knowledge ▰▰▰

Section A: Sports Shorts – "How the Games Are Played"

9-A1   **Facts of Football**

9-A2   **Beginning Basketball**

9-A3   **Baseball Basics**

9-A4   **Soccer Summary**

9-A5   **Ice Hockey Wrap-Up**

Section B: Trivia to Learn By

9-B1   **Geography**

9-B2   **History**

9-B3   **Science**

9-B4   **Literature**

9-B5   **Art and Architecture**

9-B6   **Music**

Section C: Trivia to Learn By

9-C1   **People Facts**

9-C2   **Quotes**

9-C3   **Sports**

9-C4   **Words and Phrases**

9-C5   **Miscellaneous Facts**

X

COMPACT

Classics™

LIBRARY #1: Business and Leadership

Section A

1-A1 *Entrepreneurial Megabucks: The 100 Greatest Entrepreneurs of the Last Twenty-Five Years* by A. David Silver

1-A2 *Megatrends* by John Naisbitt

1-A3 *Megatrends 2000: Ten New Directions For the 1990's* by John Naisbitt and Patricia Aburdene

1-A4 *What They Don't Teach You at Harvard Business School: Notes From a Street-Smart Executive* by Mark H. McCormack

1-A5 *The Managerial Mystique: Restoring Leadership in Business* by Abraham Zaleznik

Section B

1-B1 *A Passion for Excellence* by Tom Peters and Nancy Austin

1-B2 *Leadership Secrets of Attila the Hun* by Wess Roberts

1-B3 *Thriving on Chaos: Handbook for a Management Revolution* by Tom Peters

1-B4 *The Greatest Management Principle in the World* by Micheal LeBoeuf

1-B5 *The One-Minute Manager* by Kenneth Blanchard and Spencer Johnson

Section C

1-C1 *The Greatest Salesman in the World* by Og Mandino

1-C2 *Swim With the Sharks* (*Without Being Eaten Alive*) by Harvey Mackay

1-C3 *How to Talk So People Listen* by Sonya Hamlin

1-C4 *A Whack on the Side of the Head: How You Can Be More Creative* by Roger von Oech

1-C5 *Developing Critical Thinkers: Challenging Adults to Explore Alternative Ways of Thinking* by Stephen D. Brookfield

Section D

1-D1   Managing Conflict

1-D2   Maintaining Job Satisfaction

1-D3   Alleviating Worker Alienation

1-D4   Unlocking Your Workteam's Potential

1-D5   Attitudes at Work

1-D6   Dual-Career Couples

Section E

1-E1   Situational Leadership

1-E2   Leadership: A Behavioral View

1-E3   What Do Managers Do . . . Really?

1-E4   Understanding Managerial Communication

1-E5   Communication Skills for Managers

1-E6   Psychological Contracts: Forces That Bind Managers and Employees

Section F

1-F1   Employee Recruitment and Selection

1-F2   Employee and Management Rights

1-F3   Incentives for Productivity

1-F4   The Performance Appraisal Process

1-F5   The Art of Group Decision-Making

1-F6   On Organizational Culture

ENTREPRENEURIAL MEGABUCKS

The 100 Greatest Entrepreneurs of the Last 25 Years
by A. David Silver, John Wiley & Sons, Inc., New York, N.Y., 1985

Defining the entrepreneur as "America's new hero," Silver's book shows, by example, the process of entrepreneurship. As of 1985, the 92 men and 8 women biographically highlighted in *Entrepreneurial Megabucks* had aggregated approximately $100 billion, all on a combined $15 million of initial capital – and created or saved an estimated four million jobs.

Megabucks outlines an entrepreneurial "process" involving the birth, problems, solutions, team chemistry, and extraordinary growth of companies.

Silver selected his prototype entrepreneurs primarily on the basis of financial success. But he also weighed other factors – creativity, sustained entrepreneurship, absence of pride and arrogance, self-reliance, and charitable sensitivities. He feels that, despite the hectic schedules of many entrepreneurs, there is more to life than monetary success.

Only about one fourth of the entrepreneurial enterprises presented are in the "high tech" arena. Equally profitable and fast-growing firms dealing in leasing, manufacturing, transportation, medicine, education, publishing, advertising, real estate, entertainment, nutrition, clothing, safety, communications and information are included. Silver chronicles the rise of well-know corporations such as Atari, Shearson Lehman Brothers, McDonald's, MCI, U-Haul, Federal Express, Tandy, Sony, Wang, Apple, Honda, Intel, People Express, Pizza Hut, Mary Kay Cosmetics, NIKE, Toys 'R' Us, Lucasfilms, Turner Broadcasting, Hewlett-Packard, Charles Schwab & Co, as well as many modest, little-known companies.

Two shoe salesmen . . . find themselves in a rustic backward part of Africa. The first salesman wires back to his head office: "There is no prospect of sales. Natives do not wear shoes!" The other salesman wires: "No one wears shoes here. We can dominate the market. Send all possible stock."

This story by Akio Morita reveals Sony Corporation's philosophy "to create products for which no apparent demand exists, then create demand." The pocket radio, the tummy TV, the digital camera, the Walkman, and the Betamax all resulted from this philosophy.

The Entrepreneurial Process

The entrepreneur begins with an idea or insight, then becomes "transformed" into a "fanatical dreamchaser." Jack Tramiel, a stout survivor of Auschwitz, pushed Commodore Business Machines to the pinnacle of the home computer market. When he was forced to give up control of Commodore, he left, and, after a one-month vacation, resurfaced – as the owner of Atari . . .

At one time, Jack R. Simplot survived by buying "bum" lambs from sheep ranchers, raising them, then selling them back to the ranchers for a 1922 profit of 140 dollars. Simplot used this money to patent freeze-dried french-fried potatoes, which became a key to McDonald's success. A $20 million investment soon launched Micron Technology Corp., with $500 million in 1983 sales . . .

Generally beginning with nothing, entrepreneurs sacrifice their sleep, sweat, credit, time, and sometimes their families, to demonstrate that their dream can become reality. The equation of entrepreneurship is simple. "The goal of venture capital investing is the creation of wealth" or high valuation (V). This is reached by identifying a large problem (P), formulating an elegant solution to the problem (S), and matching these with a potentially successful entrepreneur and his or her team (E). Thus, a company is born. Looking at the formula $V = P \times S \times E$, the entrepreneur will naturally seek the highest values for P, S, and E, so that when they are multiplied together the result is a large V. Wealth is created!

A Six-Step Process:

1. *Identify the Problem (P):* First, point out the *need* for a solution; second, *show you have* a *bona fide solution;* and last, *convince others* that you have the credibility to make the solution work. The "concept of the big P" is crucial. . . . *It is necessary to adopt a problem, index its many features and parts, and begin arranging and rearranging the parts until you identify areas that appear to be receptive to solutions.*

   Texas Instruments failed to meet the demand for an inexpensive home computer; Topps' chocolate-flavored bubble gum fell flat; Xerox Corporation's hardware sales plummeted for lack of user-friendly oriented software. In these cases, the solution (or proper identification of the problem) was inadequate.

2. *Create the Solution (S):* Reformulate the problem until the most promising solution emerges. Objectively "see" the problem; try to be original; don't expect to be right the first time; make use of concrete representations (sketches, plans, etc.) to help you visualize and clarify the situation.

3. *Plan the Business:* Prepare a business plan to plot the potential users, how users will be located, and the all-important cash flow.

4. *Select the Entrepreneurial Team (E):* E is made up of the entrepreneur, the manager ("corporate achiever partner") and others,

often – and ideally – each with very different backgrounds and aptitudes. The unifying goal of all involved should be to make the company successful.

5. *Test the Prototype:* Producing and test-marketing the product is the most critical stage of development. At this stage, failure, if seen as a chance to alter the plan and emerge more prepared, can be a seasoning experience. By listening to client response, you can work again with pricing, appearance of advertising, the target consumer, etc.

6. *Raise Venture Capital:* Most entrepreneurial companies started from little or no capital. The marketing need (the problem) was so defined that firms were funded by either the stock market, the customer, or by vendor financing. The text offers scores of means by which an entrepreneur can unearth necessary start-up funds.

A Sampling of "The 100 Greatest Entrepreneurs of the Last 25 Years":

Martin Alpert, *Tecmar, Inc.,* 1974

The company designs, develops and manufactures software and peripheral products to expand the capabilities of the IBM and Apple personal computers. Tecmar produces on average one new product per week, from memory synthesizers to boards that permit two operators to share one printer.

Henry Wollman Block and **Richard A. Block,** *H&R Block, Inc.,* 1955

H&R Block excels in preparing individual federal tax returns. Recognizing the growing complexity of tax forms, the Blocks offered a trustworthy and accurate service, and quickly gained a high reputation. Rapid franchising made competition difficult.

Ronald E. Cape, *Cetus Corp.,* 1971

Cetus' "big P" is its convincing contention that company research in genetic engineering is on the way to finding solutions for world hunger and fatal diseases. Investors listened. In 1981 Cetus received America's largest initial public stock offering – some $115 million. By "artfully selling the problem" Cetus has elicited support and contracts from some very large corporations.

Richard Dotts, *Pedus International, Inc.,* 1979

Pedus provides maintenance, janitorial, and security services for office buildings. The company meets the demand for high-quality, reasonably priced work by eliminating bureaucracy, increasing autonomy, providing incentives, and by keeping the already strong management of the businesses it buys into.

William A. Fickling, Jr., *Charter Medical Corp.,* 1969

Fickling began Charter Medical after coming across the statistic that a large proportion of Americans will suffer a substance-abuse or psychiatric problem at some point in their lives. He converted hospitals into treatment facilities with the intent of dealing with these disorders.

Debbi Fields, *Mrs. Fields Cookies, Inc.,* 1977

The chocolate chip cookie is a reminder of home and the simple life. At malls, theaters and restaurants Americans consumed over $200 million worth of Fields' warm, fresh-baked cookies in 1984.

Roger Horchow, *Horchow Collection,* 1973

Demographic changes have led to increased catalog shopping. Horchow's descriptive, colorful catalogs provide a convenient way to shop. Combined with other service features (catering to luxury merchandise, and initialing items to lessen returns), a new segment of consumers was created.

Claude and Donna Jeanloz, *Renovator's Supply, Inc.,* 1978

The Jeanlozes correctly gauged that a lot of people, trying to restore or renovate their older homes, were frustrated by not being able to find vintage-looking hardware. Their hardware catalogs later split into other specialty markets – children's toys, left-hander's products, etc.

Lane Nemeth, *Discovery Toys,* 1977

High-quality educational toys and books are sold directly to the consumer on a home-party basis. Discovery's "sales consultants" purchase exclusive rights to territories and receive a portion of sales profits.

James W. Rouse, *Rouse Co.,* and *The Enterprise Development Co.,* 1939 and 1984

Enterprise Development is a not-for-profit company that renovates dilapidated buildings to create housing for the very poor. It also helps establish minority-owned-and-operated housing developments and shops to produce profitable and delightful urban centers.

James G. Treybig, *Tandem Computers, Inc.,* 1974

Computer systems break down. Tandem, Inc. makes fault-tolerant products that can help avoid breakdowns, or eliminate downtime by automatically shifting to another part of the system.

Charles Kemmons Wilson, *Holiday Inns of America, Inc.,* 1952

Wilson decided that "the public will like what I like," and came up with the world's largest motor-hotel chain by manipulating a formula of reasonable prices, standardized rooms and family accommodations, conveniently situated near major travel arteries. The Inn's many extras – besides swimming pools, ice machines, etc. – include on-call babysitters, clergymen, and dentists.

Megabucks' many entrepreneurial success stories may help generate interesting, original ideas in the minds of future entrepreneurs.

MEGATRENDS

by John Naisbitt, Warner Books, New York, N.Y., 1982

"Megatrends" are world trends with such great impact that they are already transforming our lives. These trends will continue evolving whether we are aware of them or not. Naisbitt's *Megatrends* seeks to "discover the ways in which America is restructuring, to understand how the pieces fit together, and try to see what the new society looks like."

Megatrends examines the "cutting edge" of events developing all around us. It contends that, in our changing world, information is power. And in order to succeed we must be able to use the extensive information at our disposal to take advantage of the prevailing flow. "Trends are like horses: they are easier to ride in the direction they are already going."

The book reads like a road map of where to be and what to do in the 1990's and beyond. Ten themes – ten "megatrends" – are discussed in ten separate chapters. Naisbitt emphasizes that each trend is important and closely related to the other nine; that each can be examined singly, but can only be totally appreciated in association with the others.

MEGATRENDS – Ten New Directions

(1) From an Industrial Society to an Information Society

"The most reliable way to anticipate the future is to understand the present." The birth of an information society, and the death of the old industrial society, is the most important "megatrend" – one that is still not universally recognized as a reality.

In the past, those who controlled capital controlled the world, but in an information society the "world-controller" will be those who control information. An example of this is the case of the founders of *Intel, Inc.* Starting with 2.5 million dollars in venture capital, they increased their sales to $900 million a year as of 1982. Having access to the facts is not the key; everyone receives more or less the same information. In fact, *we are drowning in information, but often starved for knowledge.* The trick is to filter out correct knowledge; to pull *useful* information from the endless sea of computerized data.

(2) From Forced Technology to High Tech/High Touch

In the past, technology has been forced upon us with little regard as to how we would interact with it. For this reason, some forms of technology have been sent back to the shop. Now, computers have become more "user friendly," and the ways in which we use any number of high-tech articles are increasingly being refined and simplified.

Whenever new technology is introduced, it must be coupled with human response. *"The more high technology around us, the more the need for human touch,"* though technology will never take the place of nor liberate us from personal discipline and responsibility.

(3) From a National Economy to a World Economy

Americans have for decades been the dominant industrial power in the world. But now, as the United States' share of goods on the world market has diminished, Asian nations and others have emerged as industrial powers. *Americans must play a new role if they are to continue to be a global economic power – a role of leadership, innovation and know-how.* We have already lost our industrial edge (it takes Japan eleven hours to build a car; American workers do it in thirty-one). Americans must lead out in exploring electronics, biotechnology, alternative energy sources, new mining techniques, robotics, etc.

As the world economy becomes more and more diverse, production sharing among nations will become the rule rather than the exception. And as countries become more dependent on each other for trade, the possibility of war over ideological differences will become more remote.

(4) From Short Term to Long Term

Rethinking our view of business success is essential to capitalize on this megatrend. We need to think more in terms of profits and planning over the long term. Management contracts have encouraged shortsightedness by rewarding short-term, quarterly profits rather than long-term, steady growth. Long-term planning requires insightful, futuristic vision without which strategic planning is worthless.

"Change," becoming *"alert"* to change, *"rethinking"* and *"reconceptualizing"* our roles, are the watchwords for the coming decade.

(5) From Centralization to Decentralization

With the failure of large centralized structures, Americans are beginning to look elsewhere for leadership. We are rebuilding from the bottom up. The idea of decentralization is not a new one, but is an idea whose time has come.

We are becoming ever more involved only with events that directly affect us. Local elections, for example, are drawing more voters, while national elections draw fewer than they have in the past. Regionalism, states' rights and special-interest lobbies continue to grow. Ethnic pride, separatism, and neighborhood-watch programs are on the upswing, while centralized labor unions struggle to stay alive.

(6) From Institutional Help to Self-Help

Recently we have become inundated with a barrage of self-help books and groups of all sorts. Where we formerly relied on government, the medical establishment and corporations, we now rely more on ourselves.

People are adopting new and better personal habits (exercise, proper diet, reduced smoking and alcohol consumption). "Self-care" is now considered smart, not selfish. Alternatives in life-styles and education have replaced the stodgy customs of the past. If you don't like the boss, start your own company; if your child's institution is failing her, start your own school. The self-help approach is exploding. Our society is shifting from one of managers to one of entrepreneurs.

(7) From Representative Democracy to Participatory Democracy

Representative democracy calls for strong unified leadership, while participatory democracy relies less on central leadership and more upon individuals or special-interest groups. *"The new leader is a facilitator not an order giver."*

Participatory democracy includes such notions as shareholders' rights, consumerism, and workers' rights. These groups don't control decisions, but their views are part of the process. With the increase in shared, instantaneous information, more people know what's going on and are more confident in their ability to make decisions. More and more, governments and corporations will operate with this in mind.

(8) From Hierarchies to Networking

Business hierarchies for years followed the old pyramidal top-to-bottom structure, where management's main purpose was to "keep track" of the workers. With the advent of the computer, however, "tracking" employees became much easier, leaving management free for more productive work.

"Networks" employ the horizontal system of management, where people interact and share ideas, information and resources. Hence, networks offer what bureaucracies never can deliver – precisely this direct, horizontal link with people. *In the network environment, "rewards come by empowering others, not climbing over them."*

(9) From North to South

The shift of American population – and job markets – from North to South has been well documented, but the reasons behind it have not. *The North represents the lagging industrial economy, while the Southwest and West represent the booming information economy.* The emerging "megastates" are California, Florida, and Texas. With industrial (northern) states losing thousands of workers each year during the '70's, the western states (plus Florida in the south) boomed: Nevada gained by 64% in population, Arizona, 53%; Florida, 43%; Wyoming, 42%; Utah, 38%; Idaho, 34%; Alaska, 32%; Colorado, 31%; New Mexico, 28%; and Texas 27%.

(10) From Either/Or to Multiple Option

We are becoming a multifaceted "Baskin Robbins Society," with thirty-one decisions at every turn. This is true even in television; where there were formerly three stations, there are now hundreds – "Something for everyone!"

A societal shift from the family towards the individual is taking place. Family life and decisions are increasingly complex. Single-parent households and homes with two working parents are now the rule, and it is projected that in the 1990's, only 14% of all two-parent households will be supported by one income. In an increasingly complicated world, understanding what options are available and acting on them is paramount.

To be financially successful in the decade of the '90's, most new companies must specialize in a product for a particular segment of people. Diversity – cultural, ethnic, religious – once decried as enemy to the "melting pot," is now celebrated.

Naisbitt alleges that we live in a "time of parenthesis, the time between eras." The information era is on the horizon, while the industrial age is ending. We will continue to use and value brainpower over physical power. These facts open up a wide range of realistic opportunities for those who are willing to take risks.

"But do we have the courage to abandon our traditional industries, industries that other countries can now do better?" Naisbitt asks. "Do we have the innovative ability to venture forward into the future?" The changing times ahead will be good to entrepreneurs. *Megatrends* urges you to take the initiative, accentuate the positive, and let the future trends work *for* you, not against you.

MEGATRENDS 2000

Ten New Directions For the 1990's
John Naisbitt and Patricia Aburdene, William Morrow and Co., New York, N.Y., 1990

John Naisbitt and Patricia Aburdene, the authors of *Megatrends 2000*, have been busy "uncovering the megatrends for a new millenium." They define "megatrends" as those large-scale social, economic, political, and technological influences that change the directions of our lives. The authors paint a fairly rosy picture for the people of the 90's, and predict ten new directions for the decade. These "millennial" trends are:

1. A Booming Global Economy
2. A Renaissance in the Arts
3. The Emergence of Free-Market Socialism
4. Global Lifestyles and Cultural Nationalism
5. The Privatization of the Welfare State
6. The Rise of the Pacific Rim
7. The Decade of Women in Leadership
8. The Age of Biology
9. The Religious Revival of the New Millennium
10. The Triumph of the Individual

Evidence for these ten trends was compiled by clipping newspaper articles, then analyzing their contents with a computer. Here are some predictions from Naisbitt and Aburdene based on the results:

The Global Economic Boom of the 1990's

Because of the increasing popularity of "doomsayers," *positive* economic indicators receive very little press right now, while any little in the economy receives blown-up coverage. But regardless of what gets covered, there is good economic news out there.

It is hard to talk about the U.S. economy today without considering the influence of Japan and the European countries. In fact, the economies of different countries are becoming more and more enmeshed all the time. For a multitude of reasons, a world economy will continue to emerge, as the European Common Market dissolves and the fall of the Iron Curtain opens the way for trade policies between more nations.

Free trade is mandatory for an effective global economy. Just as no one knows the trade imbalance between Denver and Dallas, in time the trade imbalance between the United States and Japan will be a non-issue. *As we turn to the next century, we will witness the linkup of North America, Europe, and Japan to form a golden triangle of free trade.*

Other factors that will influence the economic boom include:

• Advanced uses of telecommunications.

• No energy crisis to slow down or limit growth.

• Increased competition, which tends to lower taxes.

• A downsizing of economic output.

• Low inflation and interest rates.

• The emergence of an Asian consumer boom.

• The advancement of democracy and free enterprise.

Current media figures for trade and budget deficits are deceptive. The budget deficit, while large, represents a smaller percentage of income than in the past, and because no services are calculated into this deficit, its estimate is very inaccurate.

The fear of a Japanese takeover is media hype. Japan owns less than 5% of U.S. property, and U.S. investments in other countries far exceed foreign investments in the U.S.

Current global financial trends are swelling the ranks of the middle class and expanding the economic clout of minorities and women.

Renaissance in the Arts

In the final years before the millennium there will be a fundamental and revolutionary shift in leisure time and spending priorities. During the 1990's the arts will gradually replace sports as society's primary leisure activity.

This trend is already visible, as more and more people seek out the arts for a spiritual boost; and the future implications, both societal and economic, are staggering.

New and diversified art forms will emerge, and increased attendance at museums, symphonies, dance performances, etc. will open up many new jobs.

The Emergence of Free-Market Socialism

"Socialism, which at one time looked as if it might take over the world, is now faced with a challenge: Change or perish." There are several reasons for this:

• *The global economy.* Global economic interdependence will not allow a country with a closed, self-sufficient economy to survive. This has been the one driving force behind Mikhail Gorbachev's anti-socialist movement.

• *Technology.* Improved telecommunications have made a global economy possible in the first place, and further advances will only speed up the process.

• *The failure of centralization.* It is becoming clear that a command economy leads not to more efficient organization but to chaos.

• *The high cost of welfare-state socialist schemes.* "The cost of central-government supplied human services has caught up with almost all countries and overwhelmed many . . . ." *The ratio of working people to pensioners has declined dramatically since the end of World War II – in the United States, for example, from 32 to 1 to 3 to 1. People everywhere are blowing the whistle on growing public spending. Many of us will spend the last decade of this century asking the questions, What should government do for those who cannot help themselves and how can government meet such obligations without bankrupting the treasury?*

In addition to these factors, there is a marked decline in the number of blue-collar workers and in socialist union solidarity. These are the anchors of socialist economies. At the same time, the power of the individual is increasing.

In the post-industrial global economy, "small enterprise, not central planning, is the road to real prosperity."

Global Lifestyles and Cultural Nationalism

As technological and transportation advances make it easier to get products and services from anywhere, "the world is becoming more and more cosmopolitan, and we are all influencing each other." The Moscow McDonalds is a highly visible example of this global lifestyle.

But even as our lifestyles grow more similar, there are unmistakable signs of a powerful countertrend: a backlash against uniformity, a desire to assert the uniqueness of one's culture and language, a repudiation of foreign influence.

The Privatization of the Welfare State

Between 1980 and 1988, over 40 percent of the British government sector was transformed to private enterprise, resulting in the shift of more than 600,000 former government employees into the private sector. During the same 8-year period, over 1 million former tenants of public housing became homeowners.

In the United States, governmental controls are relaxing as private enterprise expands. The U.S. Postal Service is a prime example of privatization that will become more prevalent worldwide.

The Rise of the Pacific Rim

"The cities of the Pacific Rim – Los Angeles, Sydney, and Tokyo – are taking over from the old, established cities of the Atlantic – New York, Paris, and London. The population of Asia's Pacific Rim region is twice as large as that of Europe and the United States put together. "Any way you measure it, geographically, demographically, or economically, the Pacific Rim is a powerful global presence."

The Decade of Women in Leadership

For the last two decades U.S. women have

taken two thirds of the millions of new jobs created in the information era and will continue to do so well into the millennium.

Women now hold a large percentage of white-collar jobs (especially in business), and are starting up their own businesses at twice the rate of men. Realizing that they missed out on the past industrial era that began decades ago, women are positioning themselves in jobs that will blossom in the information era.

The Age of Biology

With the industrial age in the outmoded past, "we are shifting from the models and metaphors of physics to the models and metaphors of biology to help us understand today's dilemmas and opportunities."

Physics . . . suggests: energy-intensive, linear, macro, mechanistic, deterministic, outer directed . . . . Today, however, we are in the process of creating a society that is an elaborate array of information feedback systems, the very structure of the biological organism. Furthermore, we are poised on the threshold of a great era of biotechnology.

Biology as metaphor suggests: information-intensive, micro, inner-directed, adaptive, holistic.

Biology is the trend for the 1990's.

Religious Revival of the Third Millennium

The baby boomers, who rejected religion in the 1970's, are returning to church or joining churches at incredible rates, and taking their children with them. Mainline churches, however, which do well during stable times, will likely decline in popularity during this period of rapid change. Americans will increasingly value spirituality over organized religion.

Triumph of the Individual

"The great unifying theme at the conclusion of the 20th century is the triumph of the individual." It is individuals who seek religion, enjoy the arts, support political philosophies, become better educated, start new businesses, and do everything else that empowers the other nine "megatrends."

It remains to be seen whether these predictions will prove accurate. True, there will be many obstacles to overcome as we near the year 2000 – defeating AIDs and the various forms of cancer, Third World development, ending poverty and hunger, environmental "healing" . . . But today's megatrends, according to Naisbitt and Aburdene, will serve to strengthen our world society. Global collaboration and cooperation are on the rise; together we will confront and find answers to these social ills. "Get ready," *Megatrends 2000* heartily advocates. "You possess a front-row seat to the most challenging yet most exciting decade in the history of civilization."

WHAT THEY DON'T TEACH YOU AT HARVARD BUSINESS SCHOOL

Notes From a Street-Smart Executive
by Mark H. McCormack, Bantam Books, New York, N.Y., 1984

McCormack's best-seller has become the prototype manual for teaching executives the fine points of leadership.

I. PEOPLE

Reading People

"Business situations always come down to people situations."

The more you learn about the person you are dealing with, and the sooner you learn it, the more effective you are going to be. "Reading people" comes down to opening your senses to what is going on around you, the "whole level of personal dynamics operating just beneath the surface," and converting this knowledge to your advantage.

"Insight demands . . . talking less and listening more. I believe you can learn almost everything you need to know – and more than other people would like you to know – simply by watching and listening . . . "

The seven steps to build your people-reading skills are: *listen aggressively; observe aggressively; talk less; take a second look at first impressions; take time to use what you have learned; be discreet; and be detached* (emotional involvement blurs your vision of reality).

"Aggressive observation means going after the big picture, [weighing] conscious and unconscious signals . . . and converting them into usable perceptions." Observing aggressively does *not* mean jumping to conclusions.

Learn to read egos. "If you can read ego, understand its impact on business events, then control it by either stroking it, poking at it, or minimizing its damage, you can be the beneficiary . . . " But remember, nothing blocks your insight more than your own ego. Observe people wherever you happen to meet them, not just in business situations. You can learn a great deal about a person at a restaurant or on a golf course.

Creating Impressions

The right impression may be created simply by treating someone the way he or she wants to be treated. This applies to your correspondence, phone conversations and face to face meetings. Be your best self.

To impart a positive impression, do exactly what you say you will do exactly when you say you will do it. And don't be a time thief.

Common sense is the most important personal asset in business. Additionally, the ability to laugh at yourself is a plus that will create positive, lasting impressions.

Everyone has, or should have, *principles* that govern his business conduct. However, claiming too often that "this is a matter of principle" is usually a cover-up for a bruised ego.

Taking the Edge

"Taking the edge is the gamesmanship of business. It is taking everything you know about others and everything you have allowed them to know about yourself and using this information to load the deck – to tilt a business situation slightly to your advantage. It is winning through intuition."

To "take the edge" requires preparation. Know the facts of your deal, and know them well. Be familiar with the other parties; learn as much as you can about them and their company. The next step is backward: take a *step back and size up the situation. See what opportunities exist.*

A situation that might allow either one of the negotiators an edge is considered a "crisis." When a crisis – or what other people may perceive as a crisis – arises, take time to examine what's happening. Don't respond immediately. Look, listen – "observe aggressively" – and decide on a response that will sway things your way. Should you use discreet questions, a humorous rejoinder, or an honest reply? *Acting* rather than *reacting* to the situation will pay off.

Getting Ahead

Climbing the corporate ladder is a game. In order to move up you must learn the system and discover how to use it. Your peers are your best allies; "you get along by getting along."

In business there are three hard-to-say but extremely useful phrases: (1) *"I don't know."* If you don't know a thing, say so, then find out; (2) *"I need help."* The other side of this is knowing when and how to give help; (3) *"I was wrong."* "It is not the mistake itself but how a mistake is handled that forms the lasting impression."

Likewise, your "boss" (shareholders, voters or manager) will judge you by three criteria: (1) Your *commitment,* (2) Your *attention to detail,* and (3) Your *ability to follow up* on tasks. To make a positive and lasting impression you need to excel in all three areas.

Prevent boredom and burnout – keep the edge. One way to prevent burnout is to schedule time for exercise and relaxation. Boredom occurs when your learning curve goes flat. Never quit learning about your job and the ways you can do it better.

II. SALES AND NEGOTIATION

The Problems of Selling

Most people are born salesmen; even in early childhood we all learned and used sales tactics. The difficulty comes, however, when we enter the business world. Then we learn that our sales abilities are *judged,* and doubts creep in.

The biggest problem most people have in selling is *fear* – fear of rejection and fear of failure. But you can learn to accept rejection – without having to learn to like it. And you can put fear of failure in its place as a constructive motivator; after all, if you are afraid to fail, then you probably care enough to succeed.

Timing

Too many good ideas fail because the *timing is not right.* "A good general common sense rule of timing is: Don't blurt out anything. Take a moment to consider whether the situation demands a certain strategy or whether you can use timing to your advantage." Take your sales cues from the buyer, letting him dictate some of the timing.

You can also benefit from the bad timing of others. "Just as you should renew a contract when the client is the happiest, sell one when the prospective buyer is unhappiest with your competition."

Some other important "timing" advice: weigh present value against the future; plan years ahead on your calendar; don't give deadlines; use (prudently) phone calls during non-business hours; quickly get to the point of presentations; take less of a person's time than you asked for; and, if you have a good proposal but the customer balks, return to try again later. The toughest part of good timing is patience.

Silence

"Silence is what keeps you from saying more than you need to – and makes the other person want to say more than he means to." In sales, "once you get to the point . . . where you have asked for a commitment, *don't speak again* until the other person has replied . . . "

Marketability

Know your product or service well, including the reasons why someone might *not* want to buy or use it. *Believe* in what you're selling, and let others know you believe in it. Sell with enthusiasm, but sell smart, putting the bulk of your effort and focus on the "top 20 percent" customers. Figure out ways to keep their interest and business.

Negotiating

First, find out what it is a person or company wants to buy. Second, find out who does the buying. Third, use effective strategies: sell "defensively" (allow the client to say "no" to some proposals); expose rather than sell; present one-on-one, when possible; and use your positive reputation.

III. RUNNING A BUSINESS

Building a Business

"This may be one of the better ways to start a business: What are you really passionate about in life, and is there any way to make a living at it?" When you are *passionate* about what you are doing, going to "work" is like going to play.

Some good rules for building a business are: commit early to *quality; grow slowly; hire people who can teach you what you don't know; charge for your expertise.*

Staying in Business

Don't let structure slow you down; when it comes to your business' structure, think small. Refrain from doing things the same way every time just because they have worked in the past. *Look for ways to be creative* and still maintain consistency. Without creativity and flexibility, it is too easy to get locked into a rut.

"Manage unconventionally. Don't just look for opportunities to do the unexpected. Create them. Aggressively pursue change . . . " Spend the five hours now to train subordinates so you don't have to spend hundreds of hours in the future trying to retrain them. Hiring, training, managing and firing people takes consistency, planning, timing and sensitivity.

Getting Things Done

When you plan your time, don't look at a 40- or 50-hour work week. Examine all the available 168 hours. Plan time for sleep, exercise and relaxation, as well as for work.

Concoct some sort of *organizational system* where you can write down projects or ideas and then forget about them. Make them come back when they are needed.

Schedule your time. Decide what must be done for the day, week or month, and then establish a schedule and force yourself to stick to it. Honor appointments with yourself as you would appointments with others.

Rather than holding a formal meeting, meet in the hall for a few minutes, or else simply circulate a memo.

What They Don't Teach You . . . delves into many intricacies of business life. Sections on avoiding "telephone tag," conducting a meeting, making decisions, entrepreneurship, etc. may provide just the needed inside, "street-smart" tips and information that many business schools fail to explore.

THE MANAGERIAL MYSTIQUE

Restoring Leadership in Business
by Abraham Zaleznik, Harper & Row, New York, N.Y., 1989

Abraham Zaleznik's meaty book is a critical assessment of what he terms the "managerial mystique" – a false sense of how leaders should lead. The text is directed at today's managers, from the President of the United States to the plant foreman of a small Midwestern company, who blame subordinates for incompetence or ignorance, thus absolving themselves from accountability; managers "who can shift their stance, who adopt the coloration of their surroundings, and who understand how to play the game of control and compliance." Zaleznik claims that shoddy work, reduced productivity, and a growing sense of distrust, disloyalty, and "leaderlessness" among followers are direct results of the managerial mystique.

Watergate, a classic example of the "mystique" at work, "left a corrosive residue of apathy and skepticism that has eaten away at all major institutions." (*Time*, July 15, 1974). More recently, according to the official Tower Commission report, the Iran-Contra arms sales debacle was the result of a leader using an impersonal, "hands-off" style – a style that has gradually worn out over consistent, knowledgable, responsible leadership. *Business strategy has overcome business leadership, while concern for self has displaced the urge to make a difference in the lives and well-being of other people . . . . We are fabricating managers not educating leaders.*

Only when managers finally become aware of the potential impact of their power, both positive and negative, and are held accountable for their decisions – forced to "bring the human character back to center stage in the drama of business" – will trust, substance, morality, *leadership*, again reign. Through a blend of psychology, historical perspective, and business theory, Zaleznik argues for a mending of the "leadership gap."

"Management" and "leadership" are not necessarily synonomous. Typically, "leaders grow through mastering painful conflict during their developmental years [Lee Iacocca, for example], while managers confront few of the experiences that generally cause people to turn inward" for goals and direction. So, as managers have taken over many leadership positions, they have not evolved into leaders.

Current managerial technique encourages managers to dedicate themselves to process, politics, structures, roles, and inferential forms of communication and to ignore ideas, people, emotions and direct talk. Procedure, protocol and politics become ends in themselves, rather than the means to creating and marketing better products and services. Managers brought with them "what they learned from the business schools, namely, principles of bargaining, emotional control, human relations skills . . . . They left behind commitment, creativity, concern for others, and experimentation." The typical corporate executive distances himself from his organization, looking at company goals chiefly as a means to enhance self interest and requiring the same sort of "compliance without commitment" from his subordinates. He focuses on manipulative, impersonal control tactics: financial plans, budget allocations, monthly reviews.

True leaders, however, are not bound by the controls of protocol and "process"; they do not confuse means and ends. Unencumbered by "management theory," leaders focus on imaginative ideas; they take on risks; they're visionary, dramatic, trusting, hard-working and fair-minded. Their goals are entrepreneurial and active.

Analysis of the Mystique

It must be pointed out that managers possess many valuable assets. "Good" managers have "the ability to be dispassionate in the face of a problem, the skill to analyze facts, and the willingness to evaluate costs and benefits." But they also display typical weaknesses: fear of chaos, a need for distance in human relations, and separation of the thinking and feeling processes. Since managers "hate surprises" and "love to orchestrate events," they have the tendency to use inappropriate, sometimes unethical controls to force subordinates to meet expectations. Although in theory communication is democratic and decisions are autonomous at subordinate levels, "communication usually flows in one direction: from the top down. . . . More often than not the superior is trying to channel subordinates' thoughts and perceptions . . . " Zaleznik cites Lyndon Johnson, who often invoked Isaiah's words "Come let us reason together," while at the same time "using the power of position and personality to get his own way."

However, leaders ("wise, sensitive managers") understand that they don't have to manipulate every decision or personally instigate a "program" to rectify every problem that crops up. Somewhat weak on process but strong on substance, a leader often chooses to delegate to a trusted, personally-involved associate or subordinate the work of finding defects and implementing change in her organization.

This philosophy of "marrying" authority with competence, freeing up executives to solve problems at all levels, had a direct economic and organizational impact on the Cummins Engine Company. One Cummins executive reported that turning the company over to its best leaders simplified everyone's work: "Now we think in terms of work flow: how to reduce the handling of materials . . . We found, for example, that we were machining parts, moving them to a warehouse for storage, then bringing them back to complete the motor assembly. [Now], we've eliminated the warehousing . . . "

So, should a manager cease to wield control in his place of business? On the contrary, says Zaleznik. But control should be exercised openly and actively, rather than as a veiled, manipulative tool; it should be performance-enhancing and supportive. Professor Robert N. Anthony explains:

Action is a sure signal, probably the only effective signal, that management is interested in the control system. Basically, this involves praise or other reward for good performance, criticism of or removal of the causes for poor performance . . . .

For years managers have used flattery, acquiescence, confrontation, indirect threats, and position to manipulate subordinates. But this type of corrupt use of power became a kind of corporate "poison," a venomous monster that has since turned and bitten the business community. High moral standards frequently make the difference between the successful leader and the manipulative, scarecrow-type manager.

The Cure: Leadership

In order to override the "MBA mentality" that exists in many offices, leaders will strive to strike a more genuine emotional stance. They will work to create a balance between expressionism (the human touch, vital to purpose, cohesion and growth) and stoicism (the suppression or redirection of particularly sensitive feelings).

The substance of business is business: making products and going to market . . . . [And] the art of business leadership is imagination: The binding of leader and led in a cooperative relationship depends most on the respect the subordinate has for the leader's ability to originate ideas, suggest solutions to problems, and above all, translate visions into far-reaching goals . . . . Business needs talented people who apply their imagination to move an enterprise forward.

Substantive imagination includes the ability to:

- *Perceive opportunity* - "Opportunism," in its positive sense, means making the most of things; applying imagination to change situations or to create a new market; or, through delegation, formulating the elements necessary for success and then putting together the team to reach the goal. Back in the 1950's, Soichiro Honda recognized the need for a cleaner combustion engine. Though he did not invent the engine, through the use of "business imagination" he did perfect it.

- *Conceptualize* - New concepts – if not overworked before going to market – give industry its innovative drive.

- *Create* - Creativity is the rare ability to transcend imitation; to move toward a totally

new concept or product.

People, working with *information,* are the sources of imagination. A leader heightens her "financial imagination" (the faculty to make and use money) or her "marketing imagination" (the intuitive feel for consumer needs and desires) when she is close to the "pulse" of her company – in daily contact with managers and employees. Her understanding and skill are further honed when she keeps up her reading on the current literature in her field.

Along with imagination and skill, a leader exudes *personal influence,* approaching the ideal of a sort of "patriarchial amicitia" (an "extra-mile, the boss goes to bat for me, so I'll go to bat for him" mutual loyalty). Andrew Carnegie and John D. Rockefeller, for example, were early leaders who were able to inspire – not demand – the respect and loyalty of their followers. Today ". . . there is not just one type of personality that inspires loyalty . . . but the absence of loyalty and camaraderie, both in government and business . . . indicates a fatal weakness in America's leadership."

Artful leaders are *realistic:* they communicate clearly; they govern themselves ethically; they espouse practical philosophies; and most importantly, they breed success. . . . *People want to be successful at what they do. Show them how to be successful and they will feel indebted to you; set up roadblocks to their success and they will retaliate with hate if not revenge.*

Leaders are *skilled listeners.* They (1) take an active interest in the other person, (2) suspend judgment until all the facts are known, and (3) use a "third ear" to discover what the person wants to – but doesn't or can't – say.

Conclusion

Leaders must be critics rather than cheerleaders, yet their critical stance must avoid negativism. To be critical and positive is to be substantive. Therefore, leaders have to lead in the content and direction of change.

Zaleznik sums up his thoughts on true leadership by quoting from Machiavelli's *The Prince:*

Nothing makes a prince more esteemed than great enterprises and evidence of unusual abilities . . . Furthermore, a prince should show that he is an admirer of talent by giving recognition to talented men, and honoring those who excel in a particular art.

Indeed, talent in dealing with followers will carry a leader far. Charismatic leadership – not managerial manipulation – inspires others to perform beyond expectations. "Leadership in business is the fusion of work and human relations," concludes Zaleznik. *Good ideas and exciting directions for an enterprise generate enthusiasm, support, and cohesion. Self-esteem follows, not from submerging oneself in the team and following process, but from facing problems, assuming responsibility, and doing good work.*

A PASSION FOR EXCELLENCE

by Tom Peters and Nancy Austin, Random House, New York, N.Y., 1985

A Passion for Excellence offers stories, quotes, insights, questions and advice in an attempt to cultivate superb, personalized, "back-to-basics" leadership. Its authors recommend that you look for some "first steps" that fit in with your particular needs and style, and start with those. Here are some highlights:

PART I: COMMON SENSE

"The greatest problem American business faces is getting the boss back to work watching his customer and his product . . . . [Bosses] are too busy . . . to the point that they no longer know what the customer is saying, how he is being treated . . . "

- Stanley Marcus

Baltimore Mayor William Donald Schaefer regularly wanders his neighborhoods to get a feel for his city. Wandering is priority. He sees potholes, broken streetlights, dirty parks, abandoned cars, dead trees . . . and also manages to have his crews do something about them.

The Big Idea: MBWA (Management By Wandering Around) is a "leadership technology" that promises happy customers and co-workers. Its principles are obvious but usually ignored. MBWA is the crucial element of leadership, and the one element emphasized throughout the book.

Key MBWA Recommendations
• Recognize where the real-life action is. In any industry, corporation, sports team, club or educational facility the real action is not behind a desk.
• Give MBWA quality, calendar time (25 - 50% of an average day).
• Establish an open-door policy all through the organization.
• Randomly hold meetings in other people's offices or out in the field. Evaluate employees, in part, by how directly and frequently they are "in touch" with others.

PART II: CUSTOMERS

"Serve the customer . . . . The customer is the middle of the thrust of what we are trying to do . . . "

- Edson P. Williams, VP Ford Motor Co.

To eliminate the majority of hairs that stick to the average chicken wing, Frank Perdue, chairman of Perdue Farms, purchased a quarter-of-a-million dollar jet engine to blow them off – "the world's biggest blow dryer."

The Big Idea: Successful businesses put the customer first by providing slavish service, exceptional courtesy and responsive listening.

Key Recommendations for Satisfying Customers
• Offer superior service and quality.
• *Train* associates in "customer courtesy" – to apologize for delays or problems, to show an interest in people, to be friendly but businesslike, to answer the phone on the first ring, to do a little extra. Courtesy "buys" a lifetime of customer loyalty.
• Look out for *T.D.C.* (Thinly Disguised Contempt) that may be demonstrated in your people's language (sarcasm, blame . . .) or service ("sour" demeanor, tardiness . . .). Both complaints and compliments travel far. Your company's reputation is tested daily.
• *Trust* the customer. Questioning a product return or the validity of a complaint may appear as a lack of trust.
• Measure customer satisfaction by inviting frequent and honest *feedback* (phone calls, informal face-to-face polls, questionnaires). Ask simply, "How are we doing for you?" Then step back and "naively listen" to their response.
• Invite customers to visit your facilities.
• Use customer feedback as an opportunity to train, solve problems and adapt to the market. Share both good and bad news with employees.
• Emphasize *common sense*, rather than rules, when dealing with the public.
• Don't try to compete with the "30% OFF!" store down the street. In the long run, quality easily wins over low price.
• *Specialize* in a unique product or service. Be distinctive.
• Create a professional, modern, "clean" look. Fresh paint, flowers, shiny floors, comfortable, lighting and other details matter.
• If possible, provide an (800) call-in line, with a real live person answering the phone.

PART III: INNOVATION

Almost a dozen years elapsed between the "invention" of 3 M's Post-It Note Pads and their commercial debut. The developer, Art Fry, saw the need when the little bits of paper he used to mark hymns in a church choir kept falling out of the books. Despite the fact office supply distributors thought it was a silly idea and market surveys were negative, once 3 M secretaries started using the pads and were hooked, marketing went smoothly toward a $200 million success.

"A good plan violently executed right now is far better than a perfect plan executed next week."

- General George Patton

The Big Idea: Fostering innovative "champions" and workteams, who push their projects through to completion in a minimal amount of time, is better than setting up long-winded committees.

Key Recommendations for Fostering Innovation
• *Nurture experimentation* by celebrating "good failures," supporting persistence, eliminating "Mickey Mouse" rules, red tape, and procedures that stifle

initiative, and passing on stories (corporate myths) that suggest – for the project's good, of course – occasional "rule-breaking."
• Allow people to freely "own" ideas and to develop them in small unified teams. *Loosen control* so that success or failure devolves directly upon the teams.
• Encourage teams to put together prototypes of ideas, and to place them on the market within 60 to 120 days. This is usually possible when management is supportive.
• Urge your people to *make at least ten mistakes a day*. In skiing, for example, if you don't fall down, you're not learning.
• *Be tough on inaction*. Demand concrete action, without excuses.
• Ask: "Are we having fun? . . . " "Now, tell me something interesting that's going on . . . " By encouraging free thought and risk-taking, you openly declare your trust in your employees.
• Keep funding low, deadline pressure high.
• Focus on actual progress, not on paperwork.

PART IV: PEOPLE, PEOPLE, PEOPLE

A first-line supervisor – responsible for 25 to 30 people and up to $4 million worth of capital – doesn't have the authority to buy a nine-dollar can of paint to clean up her people's workspace. Do you think she feels in charge or trusted with making decisions?

The Big Idea: Employees need to be given solid responsibility, and to know that as an interested, wandering leader, you respect and support them. People produce; techniques don't.

Key Recommendations For Working With People
• Make people feel they're part of the company. Trust them to do their jobs. Recognize your employees' "bill of rights" – the rights to be *needed, involved, responsible* and *accountable*.
• Call your people "associates" or "colleagues" rather than "workers"; make each a "director" or a "manager," with control.
• *Decentralize.* Place dedicated leaders at all levels.
• Eliminate managerial "perks" – private parking spaces, executive dining areas or washrooms, and special privileges.
• Find fifty little marks that demonstrate *respect* (cleanliness, name plates, proper facilities . . .) and fifty that show *disrespect* (inappropriate language; discriminatory labels, facilities or rules).
• Lavishly reward good *and* exceptional performance. Make meetings and celebrations fun, imaginative, and memorable.
• Develop a five-minute informal questioning routine to get to know people and their jobs. What's working; what's not? The best source of ideas is the front-line, vendor-to-customer person. Spend one Saturday a month, or a week each quarter, on the sales floor, in the factory, or on the street crew. This front-line, hands-on, in the trenches experience is invaluable.
• *Rub shoulders*, fiddle with equipment, ask questions. *Practice MBWA.* Make PEOPLE your insistent theme and focus.

PART V: LEADERSHIP

"Make it fun to work in your agency. When people aren't having any fun, they don't produce good advertising . . . . Get rid of sad dogs who spread doom. What kind of paragons are the men and women who run successful advertising agencies? My observation has been that they are enthusiasts."

- David Ogilvy

A Domino's Pizza Store once faced the disaster of running out of pizza dough. What was President Don Vleek's immediate response? "Charter a plane. Get it there!"

"Love is loyalty. Love is teamwork. Love respects the dignity of the individual. Heartpower is the strength of your corporation."

- Coach Vince Lombardi,
speaking to corporate executives

During his 57 years as Marriott Corporation's CEO, founder J. Willard Marriott, Sr. read every customer complaint card.

The Big Idea: Leadership is "show business"; it is symbolic and often dramatic. The new leader is no longer a cop, referee, sole decision-maker or dispassionate analyst. The new leader is more of a cheerleader, coach, nurturer of heroes, builder, facilitator and historian.

Key Leadership Recommendations
• When touring your plant, school or corporation, visit the doing, *first-line people first;* then your visit with the upper manager will take on more meaning.
• Create a unique corporate culture for your business.
• *Love* your associates and what you do.
• *Listen* deeply.
• *Visit your competition* to find out what they're doing.
• Routinely gather together to train, gripe, change policies, nudge programs along, demand suggestions, celebrate . . .
• *Cut your meetings* from 24 to 17 per week to give time for real MBWA.

A Passion for Excellence carries two primary messages:
1. *Choose a priority* – and clearly, repeatedly, religiously, urgently, attentively, passionately focus all your discussion and energy on that priority. Do something – right now.
2. *Practice MBWA.* Whether your priority is product quality, customer service, innovation, courtesy, autonomy, customer input, or safety, it must revolve around committed people; and the art of MBWA is working with people. It is not socializing, it's finding out. It's talking last, not first. MBWA takes patient effort.

LEADERSHIP SECRETS OF ATTILA THE HUN

by Wess Roberts, Warner Books, New York, N.Y., 1987

Attila, King of the Huns, united Mongolia's "nomadic, multiracial and multilingual conglomeration of tribes" into a confederation with a common purpose – to plunder and pillage the eastern Roman Empire. Historically known as the "Scourge of God," Attila has been characterized as the incarnation of barbaric rule and ruthless terror. Thus, Attila is an unlikely subject on which to base a book on management. Yet the author of *Leadership Secrets*, Wess Roberts, formerly of the U.S. Army Combat Arms Training Board, has done just that. In this brief, witty, thought-provoking book, Roberts attempts to describe the essential qualities of leadership in terms of loyalty, courage, decisiveness, competitiveness, self-confidence, accountability, credibility, tenacity and stewardship – all by using a rich, story-telling style.

This book is not a unified thesis on leadership development. In fact, Roberts cautions that "there is no magical formula for [accelerating the development of] leadership abilities . . ." Rather, he uses the Hun chieftain as a symbolic mouthpiece to toss out – just as Attila himself might have done – various leadership principles. Themes are suggested by fictional storylines, and followed by maxims hypothetically spoken by Attila to his chosen chieftains and Hun warriors in campfire settings. Here is a sampling of proverbs, listed under assorted headings.

Lust for Leadership: "You've Got to Want to Be in Charge"

- Above all other traits, one who desires to lead must possess an intrinsic desire to achieve substantial personal recognition and be willing to earn it in all fairness.

- You must remember that success in your office will depend largely upon your sustained willingness to work hard. Sweat rules over inspiration!

- You must not be threatened by capable contemporaries or subordinates. Be wise in selecting capable captains to achieve those things a chieftain can attain only through strong subordinates.

Peace in the Camp: "Morale and Discipline"

- Huns seek discipline in their lives. They more willingly follow chieftains who are themselves disciplined.

- Wise chieftains realize that unduly harsh and unnecessarily lax discipline will undo the morale of their Huns.

The Fury of Internal Battles: "Cunning in the Tribes"

- Be wise and anticipate the "Brutus" of your

camp. . . . Beware of the treacherous Hun who pledges loyalty in public then spreads discontent in private. Make every effort to identify and remove these ignoble characters, be they chieftains or your best warriors.

- Be principled, not inflexible.

- Be approachable; listen to both good and bad news from your Huns . . .

The Tribute: "Paying and Receiving Deference"

- When deference is born of fear . . . it results in an unwillingness to serve and becomes manifested as passive resistance to authority and purpose . . .

- Real deference results in unyielding loyalty – a tribe full of spirit and willing to follow their chieftain into the mouth of hell . . .

- Always pay proper courtesy to your subordinate leaders. Should you fail to accord them respect, so will their subordinates.

Battle Dress and Armament: "Chieftains Are as they Appear to Their Huns"

- A chieftain should dress in fine skins and furs – not those draped by gold and silver adornments. Pompous appearance breeds hate and gives rise to contempt and laughter among the ranks.

- When on the hunt, be prepared to hunt. Take your best bow and lance, wear the clothing that will serve you well as you chase the wild beasts in the forest.

Leading the Charge: "Responsibilities of the Chieftain"

- By their own actions, not their words, do leaders establish the morale, integrity and sense of justice of their subordinate commanders. They cannot say one thing and do another.

- Leaders must attach value to high standards of performance and have no tolerance for the uncommitted.

- Chieftains must teach their Huns well that which is expected of them. Otherwise, Huns will probably do something not expected of them.

The Omen of Aquileia: "The Essentials of Decisiveness"

- Wise is the chieftain who never makes a decision when he doesn't understand the issue . . .

- A chieftain should allow his subordinates the privilege of making decisions appropriate to their level of responsibility. Weak is the chieftain who reserves every decision for himself out of fear that he might lose control.

- It takes less courage to criticize the decisions of others than to stand by your own.
- Self-confidence is critical to decisiveness, for without it, a chieftain loses his following in challenging situations.

Horse Holders: "The Art of Delegation"

- Chieftains should never delegate responsibilities necessitating their direct attention.
- Wise chieftains grant both authority and responsibility to those they have delegated assignments.

Booty: "Rewarding Your Huns"

- Be generous with small tokens of appreciation – they will multiply in returned loyalty and service.
- . . . Security is utmost for those who risk not. Give them, therefore, assurance – not great booty – lest they learn large value is given those who just get by.

Attila and the Pope: "The Art of Negotiation"

- It is never wise to gain by battle what may be gained through bloodless negotiations.
- Honor all commitments you make during negotiations lest your enemy fail to trust your word in the future.
- Never trust negotiation to luck. Enter every session armed with knowledge of the enemy's strengths and weaknesses; knowing his secrets makes you strong . . .

Surviving Defeat: "There is Another Day"

- . . . Sometimes you will lose, regardless of how prepared you are to win.
- . . . Lament, if necessary, but do not dwell too long on your bad moments lest they rise to rule your emotions forever.
- . . . As a Hun breathes, all is not lost.

The Bones of Caravans Past: "Lessons Learned"

- We must never fail to analyze the past. No bleached bone of a battle-lost Hun must go unnoticed as we prepare for the future by laying aside the ill-conceived and undisciplined strategies of our past . . .

The book ends with a selection of "Attilaisms." Consider these:

- A king with chieftains who always agree with him, reaps the counsel of mediocrity.
- The greatness of a Hun is measured by the sacrifices he is willing to make . . .
- Seldom are self-centered, conceited and self-admiring chieftains great leaders, but they are great idolizers of themselves.

- Great chieftains never take themselves too seriously.
- A Hun can achieve anything for which he is willing to pay the price. Competition thins out at the top of the ranks.
- Every decision involves some risk.
- It is unfortunate when final decisions are made by chieftains headquartered miles away from the front.
- The ability to make difficult decisions separates chieftains from Huns.
- Wise chieftains never place their Huns in situations where their weaknesses will prevail over their strengths.
- Delegation is not abdication. Abdication is a sign of weakness. Delegation is a sign of strength.
- Appropriate stress is essential in developing chieftains.
- Huns should engage only in wars they can win.
- For Huns, conflict is a natural state.
- Chieftains should remember that hospitality, warmth and courtesy will captivate even the most oppressive foe.
- Critical to a Hun's success is a clear understanding of what the King wants.
- Chieftains should always aim high, going after things that will make a difference rather than seeking the safe path of mediocrity.
- There is more nobility in being a good Hun than in being a poor chieftain.
- If an incompetent chieftain is removed, seldom do we appoint his highest-ranking subordinate to his place. For when a chieftain has failed, so likewise have his subordinate leaders.
- If you tell a Hun he is doing a good job when he isn't, he will not listen long and, worse, will not believe praise when it is justified.
- Suffer long for mediocre but loyal Huns. Suffer not for competent but disloyal Huns.
- Adequate training of Huns is essential to war and cannot be disregarded by chieftains in more peaceful times.

"Corporate Chieftains" – and others who are called on to lead – will find Roberts' *Attila* both helpful and highly entertaining.

THRIVING ON CHAOS

Handbook for a Management Revolution
by Tom Peters , Alfred A. Knopf, Inc., 1987

In 1982 Tom Peters co-authored a much heralded book titled, *In Search of Excellence*. A sequel, *A Passion for Excellence*, came out in 1985. Both best sellers extolled the principles of managerial excellence and cited examples of companies that employ these principles. But *Thriving on Chaos* opens with the radical thesis, "There are no excellent companies."

Unlike Peters' previous upbeat books, *Thriving on Chaos* begins with a foreboding view of the nation's business climate. Peters, the guru of managerial excellence, now argues that even the paradigm cases of well–managed companies – from Citicorp to IBM, from Intell to Hewlett Packard – are undergoing economic trauma. Decline in the national savings rate, drops in industrial productivity, a large trade deficit, the current "merger mania," and a trend towards exporting major segments of manufacturing to low labor-cost countries, all hint toward the fact that the emerging global economy does not favor America's large-scale, standardized, mass-production systems of manufacturing.

In order to promote a "competitive resurgence," Peters offers his step-by-step prescriptions as a "handbook for a management revolution."

Peters emphasizes a leadership that "loves change," embraces quality consciousness, perceives human resources (personnel) as assets, seeks market fragmentation (differentiation through market niche-orientation), and fosters short-run specialization manufacturing. Sections 2 through 6 of the book contain various prescriptive strategies titled "Capability Building Blocks," which promote the "guiding premise" of each section. Some of these strategies are summarized herein.

Section II:
Creating Total Customer Responsiveness

Guiding Premises:
Specialize/Create Niches/Differentiate

- "Constantly create new market niches via new products and continuous transformation of every product."

- "Ensure that quality is always defined in terms of customer perception."

- "Become a service fanatic. Emphasizing service in terms of the customer . . . consider every customer to be a potential lifelong customer."

- "Strive more valiantly than ever to achieve uniqueness, as an organization, in the customer's mind."

- "Give manufacturing/operations people respect and a lead role at the firm's top decision-making table . . . . Realize that manufacturing/operations is the source of superior quality."

Launch a customer revolution. Respond to customer needs and wants by specializing or expanding into a niche that may never even have been noticed before. Remember that if *customer responsiveness* is the superordinate objective of a firm, then both *awareness* of customer needs and *innovative response* to those needs should be central concerns. As consultant Mike Kami is prone to shout: "What's so *special* about your company? . . . How are you *different* from your competitors? . . . What is your *uniqueness* in the marketplace?"

Section III:
Pursuing Fast-Paced Innovation

Guiding Premise:
Invest in Applications-Oriented Small Starts

- "Develop an innovation strategy which is marked by an explosive number of lightning-fast small starts that match the environment's turbulence."

- "Mount completely independent teams that attack and make obsolete our most cherished (and profitable) product lines and services – before competitors do."

- "Maintain in most small starts an application (customer) focus rather than overemphasizing giant technological leaps."

- "Make word-of-mouth marketing systematic."

- "Put NIH (Not Invented Here) behind you – and learn to copy (with unique adaptation/enhancement) from the best." Practice "creative swiping."

- "Become a 'learning organization.' "

- "Get customers into the act, for they usually give more weight than insiders to minor innovation – and customer-oriented – advances."

- "Fail forward . . . . Support failure by actively and publicly rewarding mistakes – failed efforts that were well thought out, executed with alacrity, quickly adjusted, and thoroughly learned from."

Implement these strategies by practicing "purposeful impatience," working to turn adversaries into partners, and setting quantitative innovation goals. Yawn at even the good performance that doesn't carry with it a timely and innovative approach. Your firm's "new look" will soon include an innate, comfortable "corporate capacity for innovation."

Section IV:
"Achieving Flexibility by Empowering People"

Guiding Premises:

Involve Everyone in Everything and Use Self-Managing Teams

- "Involve all personnel at all levels in all functions in virtually everything: for example, quality improvement programs and 100 percent self-inspection; productivity improvement programs; measuring and monitoring results."

- "Organize as much as possible around teams, to achieve enhanced focus, task orientation, innovativeness, and individual commitment . . . . The modest-sized, task-oriented, semi-autonomous, mainly self-managing team should be the basic organization building block."

- "Wholesale worker involvement must become a national priority if we are to create the competitive strengths necessary just to maintain, let alone improve, our national economic well-being."

- "Invest in human capital as much as in hardware . . . . Use training as a vehicle for instilling a strategic trust."

- "Spend time lavishly on recruiting."

- "Provide bold financial incentives for everyone . . . . Above-average pay yields above-average work – or at least the converse is true."

- "Radically reduce layers of management . . . . Establish a radically increased ratio of non-supervisors to supervisors – a 'wide span of control' – at the organization's front line."

- "Get staffs out in the field, and encourage them to be "business team members" rather than narrow functional specialists."

- "De-bureaucratize: . . . Reduce and simplify paperwork and unnecessary procedures."

- "De-humiliate: Eliminate policies and practices . . . of the organization which demean and belittle human dignity."

" . . . Genuinely invite wholesale participation and commitment necessary for survival." Increase *flexibility* by empowering, celebrating, and listening to others. Ironically, greater employee participation will ultimately give a manager greater overall "control." Retrain all employees to enhance their own skills and to make your business a smoother, more well-rounded, upbeat entity.

Section V:
"Learning to Love Change: A New View of Leadership at All Levels"

Guiding Premise:
Master Paradox

- " . . . Challenge conventional wisdom, especially cause and effect relations that have been considered axiomatic."

- "Rip one front-line job apart: Listen to those who hold it. Learn their frustrations. Then act to clean up the mess and encourage them . . . "

- "Practice visible management."

- "Ensure that the front-line people – the implementers, the executors – know that they are the organization's heroes."

"Master paradox," counsels Peters. As defined by Webster's New World Dictionary, a paradox is "a statement that seems contradictory, unbelievable or absurd but that may actually be true in fact." Managers often carry around with them a fear of change – change is threatening; the status quo is the only safe road. But, paradoxically, if leaders attentively *seek change* and make *testing* and *improvement* part of the status quo by *delegating, deferring problems* to their front-line people, and *"bashing bureaucracy"* through "horizonal" management systems, they will be rewarded by greater progress and production.

Section VI:
"Building Systems for a World Turned Upside Down"

Guiding Premise:
Measure What's Important

- "Simple, visible measures of what's important should mark every square foot of every department in every operation."

- "Develop simple systems that encourage participation and understanding by everyone and that support initiative-taking on the front line."

- "Make . . . documents 'living' ones, subject to constant discussion . . . "

- "Decentralize control systems, and decentralize the accountants/systems people who oversee them."

- "Decentralize strategic planning."

- "The essential variables are these: (1) simplicity of presentation, (2) visibility of measurements, (3) everyone's involvement, (4) undistorted collection of primary information . . . , (5) the straightforward measurement of what's important, and (6) achievement of an overall feel of urgency and perpetual improvement."

Measuring only what's necessary will foster among employees a real *respect* for the organization; they will see it as a *thoughtful* and *professional* business that wants to make sense out of our frequently topsy-turvy world (an all too infrequent goal these days).

As a "true handbook to guide managers through the turbulent markets and economic climates of our times," *Thriving on Chaos* provocatively and systematically treats those problems that the author contends managers will have no choice but to face – or to flail away at – in the 90`s.

THE GREATEST MANAGEMENT PRINCIPLE IN THE WORLD

For Anyone Who Needs to Get Things Done
by Michael LeBoeuf, Ph.D., Berkley, Books, New York, N.Y., 1985

A weekend fisherman looked over the side of his boat and saw a snake with a frog in its mouth. Feeling sorry for the frog, he reached down, gently removed it from the snake's mouth and let it go free. But now he felt sorry for the hungry snake. Having no food, he took out a flask of bourbon and poured a few drops into the snake's mouth. The snake swam away happy, the frog was happy, and the fisherman was happy for having performed such good deeds. He thought all was well until a few minutes passed and he heard something knock against the side of his boat. The fisherman looked down and, with stunned disbelief, saw the snake was back – this time with two frogs!

This fable, told in LeBoeuf's first chapter of *The Greatest Management Principle (GMP)*, carries two important messages:

(1) *You get what you reward.*

(2) *We often reward inappropriate behaviors, while ignoring – or even punishing – correct ones.*

LeBoeuf insists that the single greatest management principle is this:

> *"THE THINGS THAT GET REWARDED, GET DONE."*

Is your company, organization, or family ignoring this principle?

The author uses "magic questions" in an attempt to simplify the process by which leaders go about "rewarding" behavior, desirable or undesirable. He proposes practical advice on how leaders can effectively reward their followers.

What's Commonly Being Rewarded?

In typical organizations, leaders reward busy work, long hours, massive reports, paper-shuffling, risk avoidance and "good" excuses. Short-term profits – and the requisite short-term reports, that "better be encouraging, or else!" – are emphasized over long-term, steady growth, and responsible action.

Quick fixes (doing things the quick, easy, cheap way) often override solid solutions, which focus on long-range investing, planning and commitment.

What Needs To Be Rewarded?

- *Problem-solving* (solid solutions, not "problem identification" or "analysis").

- *Risk taking* (instead of risk avoiding). " . . . The 'sure thing' boat never gets far from shore." – Dale Carnegie

- *Innovation* (applied creativity, even if it ultimately leads to failure). "In 1976 a young engineer got bored with laying out computer chips. On three different occasions he asked if he could work on designing a personal computer but his company said no each time. So he went home, built one and named it the Apple...'

- *Decisive, confident action* (results; productivity). "If Moses had been a committee, the Israelites would still be in Egypt." – Anon.

- *Smart work* (not busywork). "If you can't do your job in an eight-hour work day, then either you have too much work assigned or you're incompetent."

- *Simplification* (eliminating unnecessary reports, paper-work, procedures, etc.). " . . . Good organizations and managers work hard to keep things simple and prevent goals from getting lost in the shuffle of daily activities."

- *Quiet, effective behavior.* "Who is rarely . . . absent? . . . Who doesn't constantly pester others for advice and guidance? . . . Who can be trusted to work just as well in the boss's absence? . . . Who is so quiet and unassuming that you hardly know he's there except for his good work? . . . Who smoothes out conflicts, fosters cooperation and builds morale? . . . "

- *Quality work done on time* (rather than fast, haphazard work). " . . . During World War II the U.S. government discovered its parachutes failed to open 5 percent of the time. Clearly, nothing less than zero defects was an acceptable level of quality . . . The problem was solved by requiring parachute packers and inspectors to put on one of their products occasionally and jump out of a plane . . . "

- *Loyalty.* "You can buy a man's time; you can buy his physical presence . . . But you cannot buy enthusiasm . . . You cannot buy loyalty . . . You cannot buy the devotion of hearts, minds or souls. You must earn these." – Clarence Francis

- *Teamwork and cooperation* in reaching a common goal. "A man touring a mental institution was surprised to find only three guards watching over one hundred dangerous patients. 'Aren't you afraid they will overpower you and escape?' he asked. 'No,' replied one of the guards. 'Lunatics never unite.'"

Depending on the organization, magic questions might include: What behaviors do I want to see out of my staff (club members, salespeople, family members . . .)? How will I recognize hard and smart work (and other expected behaviors)? And how shall I reward those behaviors? Straightforward questions like these help a manager or leader gain a better "feel" for what behaviors he wants from his workers, and to determine possible ways of eliciting desired behaviors.

Rewards

Here are the ten best ways to reward good performance – in order of most powerful to least powerful motivator:

1. *Money* (raises, bonuses . . .)

2. *Recognition* (public citations, job title change, special praise . . .)

3. *Time off*

4. A *"piece of the action"* (ownership, stocks, ...)

5. The opportunity to do certain *favorite work*

6. *Advancement* (promotions – possibly within a variety of career ladder systems)

7. *Freedom* (autonomy in the workplace)

8. *Personal growth* (opportunity for additional training, to do interesting work, learn new skills, expand a field . . .)

9. *Fun* – in addition to an enjoyable workplace (sports or health facilities, parties, travel . . .)

10. *Prizes* (dinners, vacation trips, gift certificates . . .)

LeBoeuf asserts that people and ideas are an organization's most important capital "assets." Therefore, the successful company must hold on to these assets and foster their growth by rewarding productivity. The key is to identify, together with each employee, specific productivity goals, and then to provide rewards commensurate with (1) the merits of the behavior, (2) the nature of the organization, and (3) the particular worker involved.

The "fundamental task" of a successful leader or manager is to make people feel excited about the activity at hand. To make this happen, it is vital to establish some sort of Goals/Reward Contract (outlined in the book) with each group member. Clear and effective contracts share four ingredients:

1. *A meaningful goal* (including its level of achievement and when it will be realized)

2. *A way – formal or informal – to keep score* (People actually want to know where they are in relation to where they should be, and, the fact is, "People do what gets measured.")

3. *Responsibility and autonomy* for achieving the goal

4. *A meaningful reward*

While visiting with workers or team members, openly communicate these concepts. Confer responsibility, require results, allow freedom, and, finally, reward success.

A "Manager's Action Plan," outlined below, makes reward-giving the natural cul-

mination of a chain of behaviors elicited by four management actions:

(1) CHOOSE RESULTS THAT ARE:
- Specific
- Measurable
- Clear
- Challenging but attainable
- Compatible
- Written
- Mutually understood

(2) IDENTIFY THE BEHAVIOR NEEDED:
- Solid solutions
- Risk taking
- Applied creativity
- Decisive action
- Smart work
- Simplification
- Quietly effective behavior
- Quality work
- Loyalty
- Working together

(3) DECIDE ON THE PROPER REWARDS:
- Money
- Recognition
- Time off
- A piece of the action
- Favorite work
- Advancement
- Freedom
- Personal growth and development
- Fun
- Prizes

(4) USE THE POWER OF POSITIVE FEEDBACK:
- Frequently
- Specifically
- Sincerely
- Inconsistently
- On the spot
- Personally
- Proportionately

When the time comes for evaluation, the manager sits down with the worker and determines if the desired behaviors were shown. Were the desired results achieved? If not, you must both revaluate and clarify the goal, and try again, renewing the process. If the answer is yes, you dispense the promised rewards, bask in success for a few moments, and then set new goals; the cycle is set in motion once more.

GMP's many questions, charts and examples outline a process that can help you as a manager, parent, president – any kind of leader – to more operatively establish, advertise, review, reformulate, and achieve goals you wish your group members to achieve. And, most importantly, the book delineates practical, positive reward systems that can motivate your people to initiate suitable goals and to act consistently in order to attain them.

THE ONE MINUTE MANAGER

by Kenneth Blanchard, Ph.D, and Spencer Johnson, M.D.
Berkley Books, New York, N.Y., 1981

The One Minute Manager's purpose is to help people "produce valuable results, and feel good about themselves . . . " The book's concepts are developed within a storyline featuring the adventures of a bright young man *(you)* as he discovers and applies management principles. As the story opens, this young man has sought out his mentor, the One Minute Manager, for an interview. He is on a modern-day quest to find and implement management skills that will make him successful both in production and with people.

"Effective managers manage themselves and the people they work with so that both the organization and the people profit from their presence," the Manager instructs. He teaches his disciple some other basic principles, then ushers him into his organization, to watch and visit with others who model the same techniques of leadership.

The OMM Idea

Does it really take just a minute to do all the things managers do? No; "One Minute Management" represents a philosophy and a group of tools that demonstrate that being a manager "is not as complicated as people would have you believe. And . . managing people doesn't take as long as you think."

People who feel good about themselves, produce good results . . . . Productivity is both quantity and quality . . . . And frankly, the best way to achieve both of these results is through people.

A "One Minute Manager" can achieve big results from his people in very little time. You, as a manager, must learn to delegate authority and tasks. Then you must ensure that the people who accept these delegated responsibilities set goals, make decisions, and report to you on progress.

Three OMM Secrets

Secret #1 - *One Minute Goal Setting:* At the beginning of a new assignment, spend some time making it clear what each person will be accountable for. Have him describe what he would like to see happen. Then, write out the selected goals on a single sheet of paper using less than 250 words – so that anyone can read them in one minute. Retain a copy of the list so that you can help him check periodically on progress and identify actions that promote his goals.

The "80-20 rule" applies to goal-setting: "80% of your really important results will come from 20% of your goals." Concentrate with each worker on those goals that include the person's primary responsibilities – maybe 3 to 6 goals in all. With specific objectives established, everyone knows right from the beginning what he is trying to accomplish and what the standard is for performance.

The successful manager uses a direct approach in dealing with employees. If there is a problem, she first asks that it be described in *behavioral* terms.

. . . I do not want to hear about only attitudes or feelings. Tell me what is happening in observable, measurable terms . . . . Now tell me what you would like to see happening . . . . If you can't tell me what you'd like to see happening, you don't have a problem yet. You're just complaining.

After discussing the *actual* and *desired* situations, the manager responds:

Well, what are you going to do about it? . . . I just asked you questions – questions you are able to ask yourself. Now . . start solving your own problems on your own time, not mine.

Secret #2 - *One Minute Praisings:* Catch people "doing something right." Tell them up front that you are going to let them know how they are doing; that you'll provide them with frequent, crystal-clear feedback. This requires careful observation by you, the manager, plus frequent interviews and/or detailed progress reports with each employee. Progress reports provide fodder for frequent praisings; workers don't have to wait for an annual performance review to get a pat on the back.

Praise good performance immediately. You can see in a very short time the progress or mistakes a person is making. Tell people specifically what they did right. Speaking and responding in open, direct terms may be uncomfortable at first for some people. Encourage everyone to communicate in a close, direct, one-on-one way.

Secret #3 - *The One Minute Reprimand:* *If you have been doing a job for some time and you know how to do it well, and you make a [significant] mistake, the One Minute Manager is quick to respond.*

She can do this because she has already been quick to praise your good work and has explained beforehand that she will let you know when you are performing well and when you are not.

Give necessary reprimands immediately after seeing a problem. "Gunnysacking" negative feelings and letting them out only because the sack is full, is a "leave alone--zap!" form of discipline employed by many managers. Early intervention doesn't overwhelm people; it only helps them realize that "performance review" is an ongoing process of education.

First, confirm the facts. Then, get close to the employee, look him straight in the eye, and indicate exactly what the mistake was without any hint of personal attack. Tell him how it makes you feel (embarrassed, annoyed, frustrated . . .), then be silent for a moment "to let [him] feel how you feel."

The purpose of a One Minute Reprimand "is to eliminate the behavior and keep the person." . . . *You have to care enough to be tough . . . . I am very tough on the poor performance – but only on the performance. I am never tough on the person.*

A successful reprimand has three basic ingredients: (1) Telling the person what she did wrong; (2) Telling her how you feel about it; and (3) Reminding her that she is valuable and worthwhile.

Why not praise first and *then* reprimand? Because, says the manager, the most successful manager would be termed "Tough 'n' Nice" rather than "Nice 'n' Tough," as illustrated by an "ancient Chinese story":

. . . An emperor appointed a second in command. He called this prime minister in and, in effect, said to him, "Why don't we divide up the tasks? Why don't you do all the punishing and I'll do all the rewarding?" The prime minister said, "Fine. I'll do all the punishing and you do all the rewarding."

Now this emperor soon noticed that whenever he asked someone to do something, they might do it or they might not do it. However, when the prime minister spoke, people moved. So the emperor called the prime minister back in and said, "Why don't we divide the tasks again? You have been doing all the punishing here for quite a while. Now let me do the punishing and you do the rewarding." So the prime minister and the emperor switched roles again.

And, within a month the prime minister was emperor. The emperor had been a nice person, rewarding and being kind to everyone; then he started to punish people. People said, "What's wrong with that old codger?" and they threw him out on his ear. When they came to look for a replacement, they said, "You know who's really starting to come around now – the prime minister." So, they put him right into office.

If you are first tough on the behavior, and then supportive of the person, it works.

The second half of the reprimand begins with touching – shaking hands, a pat on the arm – to let the employee know you're on her side. Remind her of how valuable she is to the company. Leave her feeling that "the only reason he is angry with me is that he has so much respect for me." Then, exit; "When the reprimand is over, it's over."

Other Related OMM Concepts

On budgets and training: "It's ironic. Most companies spend 50% to 70% of their money on people's salaries. And yet they spend less than 1% of their budget to train their people . . . ."

On direct communication and goal-setting: "In most of the organizations I worked in before, I often didn't know what I was supposed to be doing. No one bothered to tell me. If you asked me whether I was doing a good job, I would say either 'I don't know' or 'I think so' . . . . My main motivation was to avoid punishment."

On motivation: "Feedback is the Breakfast of Champions. Feedback keeps us going . . . . Feedback on results is the number one motivator of people. [Many managers] don't tell their people what they expect of them; they just leave them alone and then 'zap' them when they don't perform at the desired level."

On winners and losers: "Everyone is a potential winner. Some are disguised as losers; don't let their appearances fool you."

On creating winners: A manager has three choices: either hire winners (hard to do, and costly), hire potential winners and systematically train them to win, or pray ("I hope this person works out").

On punishment: If a dog had an "accident" and we shoved his nose in it, beat him with a newspaper, then threw him out the window, we would be focusing not on the behavior we wanted, but on what we didn't want. "After about three days the dog would poop on the floor and jump out the window . . . " Rather than punish an employee, return to One Minute Goal Setting to clarify your expectations and help him see "what good performance looks like."

On One Minute Praising: "The key to training someone to do a new task is . . . to catch them doing something approximately right until they can eventually learn to do it exactly right." Training and goal setting, however, must be done with great amounts of respect and no trace of manipulation.

At the end of Blanchard and Johnson's book, the bright young protagonist – *you* – finally does become a One Minute Manager, "not because he thought like one, or talked like one, but because he behaved like one." He set goals, praised frequently, and used timely, informative reprimands.

He asked brief, important questions; spoke the simple truth; laughed, worked, and enjoyed. And, perhaps most important of all, he encouraged the people he worked with to do the same . . .

THE GREATEST SALESMAN IN THE WORLD

by Og Mandino, Bantam Books, New York, N.Y., 1968

Hafid is a master salesman and trader; a very wealthy man. He lives in an elegant palace equipped with every possible comfort. One day towards the end of his life, he requests a meeting with Erasmus, his trusted servant and friend. He asks Erasmus how much money is in the treasury and tells him to estimate the worth of his property. It is a large sum. Hafid then directs Erasmus to sell all his possessions in exchange for gold, and alludes to his long practice of distributing half his annual profit to the poor. Now, says the salesman, he wishes to divide all his riches with the most needy, keeping only enough to live out his remaining days in peace. He requests that Erasmus turn over each of his emporiums to the person who manages it, together with a reward of 5,000 talents. Hafid then gives Erasmus 50,000 talents and bequeathes upon him his palace and warehouse. Though Erasmus can hardly comprehend this, Hafid again orders him to do as he has asked, assuring the servant that on his return he will share with Erasmus a long-kept secret he has imparted to no one except his wife.

When Erasmus arrives back at the palace after distributing Hafid's property, he is led to a room kept bolted for as long as anyone can remember. The only object within the room is an old chest. Hafid unlocks the chest – empty, except for some tattered scrolls. Hafid then speaks: "All the success, happiness, love, peace of mind, and wealth that I have enjoyed is directly traceable to what is contained in these few scrolls. My debt to them, and to the wise one who entrusted them to my care, can never be repaid."

Hafid explains that each of the ten scrolls contains a principle, or law, that together will enable their possessor to accumulate all the wealth he desires. Long ago he was commissioned by the one who gave him the scrolls to share them only with one person, and was told he would be given a sign to know who that person was. He petitions Erasmus to stay with him until he receives this sign. The faithful servant agrees to do so.

The story then shifts back in time:

Young Hafid, a camel boy traveling with a caravan, beseeched the leader of the caravan, Pathros, to grant him the chance to be a merchant. After some argument, Pathros gave his approval and agreed to allow Hafid to sell a finely woven robe. However, he warned the boy that he would be confronted with temptations, and that his handling of these temptations would determine his success, both in life and as a salesman. Pathros then dispatched the would-be merchant to a poor settlement – Bethlehem – to sell the garment.

For three days Hafid worked to peddle the robe, but without success. On the night before he was to rejoin the caravan, Hafid sought out a stable to tend to his donkey. There he discovered a young couple with a shivering newborn baby. Both husband and wife had wrapped their own cloaks around the infant, trying to warm him, but to little avail. Hafid gave the worried parents back their cloaks and wrapped Pathros' fine robe around the beautiful child. The boy then commenced his trek back to the caravan, considering himself a failure and trying to find an excuse, some story to cover up what he had done.

When Hafid reached the caravan, Pathros was waiting outside his tent. He had observed a bright star that followed Hafid back to the camp. Something extraordinary had taken place. Hafid, in tears, blurted out the story of the robe; but instead of chiding the boy, Pathros assured Hafid that he had not failed. He would explain everything, said the merchant, once they returned to their headquarters.

There, the dying Pathros summoned the lad to him. He told how he once had rescued a traveler, and how this grateful traveler had insisted that Pathros come to live with him and his family. During this sojourn, the traveler conferred upon Pathros a chest containing ten scrolls, some money and a letter. For a year Pathros memorized the scrolls, incorporating their wisdom into his life. After leaving the traveler's home, he opened the letter, which instructed him to forever share with the poor half of his wealth, but never to divulge the information in the scrolls, except when he received a sign telling him of the person who would next guard the scrolls. As he watched the star following Hafid home that night, Pathros had come to realize that this was indeed the awaited sign.

Pathros' story ended, whereupon he instructed Hafid to go to Damascus and purchase a small supply of rugs. Hafid was to open the first scroll, study it until he fully understood its contents, and begin selling the rugs. He must proceed to study each scroll thoroughly in the same way, applying the principles one by one as he learned them. Finally, he was not to share with others the knowledge contained in the scrolls, nor show the scrolls to anyone, until he himself was given a sign.

Hafid set out to inquire of the scrolls as he sold the rugs, and was taught the keys to prosperous and triumphant living:

Scroll I: Everyday a person is reborn – he can *forget the failures of the past. Habits* are the difference between success and failure.

Therefore, in order to achieve success, it is necessary to form good habits and become their slave. This first scroll teaches the best way to learn the meaning of the others. Each successive scroll will contain a principle enabling the reader to *replace a bad habit with a good one.* Each scroll must be read three times a day – the last time out loud – for thirty consecutive days. This way, the scrolls' wisdom becomes both a part of the active and the subconscious mind.

Scroll II: *Love* can be the salesman's greatest weapon, for even if people reject many particulars concerning the salesman's wares, love will soften them. Love can be developed by always looking for the best in people. Each time we meet someone we should state silently, "I Love You." But in order to love others, we must love ourselves, treat ourselves with respect, and not be satisfied with anything but our finest efforts.

Scroll III: *"I will persist until I succeed."* People are born to succeed, not to fail. Defeat will not be considered, and words such as *quit, cannot, unable,* and *impossible* are not part of the growing disciple's vocabulary. Every failure moves a man closer to success. When the day ends and the salesman wants to quit, he must force himself to make one more sale; to end with success.

Scroll IV: *People are nature's greatest miracle.* Each person is different in appearance as well as ability, and we should capitalize on, rather than despise, these differences. We must concentrate on the task at hand, not allowing ourselves to be preoccupied with problems of home while in the marketplace, or of the marketplace while we are at home. We each have eyes to see, ears to hear, and a mind with which to think. This is everything we need to thrive.

Scroll V: *Live each day as if it were your last.* Dwelling on the failures or misfortunes of the past is useless, for we cannot change them. Nor should we think about tomorrow. The present hours and minutes, pass too quickly and are gone forever, and so, they must be traded only for things of value. We should always treat our family and our friends as if today were our last day together.

Scroll VI: *We are masters over our emotions.* Although we daily pass through different moods, each of us has the power to control them; to "create our own weather." If we bring *joy* and *enthusiasm* and *brightness* to all that we do, others will react in a similar manner. "Strong is he who forces his actions to control his thoughts." No matter how we feel when we arise in the morning, we can sing or laugh and *make ourselves feel better.* No matter what other people do or how they react, we can

decide to be positive and understanding.

Scroll VII: " . . . *Cultivate* the habit of *laughter.*" Man is the only creature who can laugh, and the best thing to laugh at is ourselves. Whenever things seem too serious or dismal, repeat the words, "This too shall pass," and all troublesome thoughts will seem lighter. Laughter puts events – successes as well as failures – into perspective. Only with laughter and gratitude can we *enjoy* the fruits of prosperity.

Scroll VIII: Seek out opportunities and experiences that will *multiply in value.* A grain of wheat has no choice as to what it will become – whether it will be ground into bread or planted in the earth to multiply – but each human being has a *choice* – to grow or to perish. In order to "multiply in value," we must set goals, short-term as well as long-term. We must not worry if we experience initial failure in reaching our goals; we compete only with ourselves. Upon reaching a goal, we multiply again by setting another, and by striving to constantly make the next hour better than the present one.

Scroll IX: Our dreams and plans are of no value without *action.* Procrastination comes from fear, and we overcome fear only through action. It is better to act now and risk failure, than to refrain from action and certainly flounder. Fireflies give light only when they fly. Through doing, we become like them, giving off light amid the darkness. Only action gives life significance. If success is *offered now,* we must *act now.*

Scroll X: Almost everyone, in a moment of terror or anguish, will *turn to God* for help. But a true believer will *pray for guidance,* not only for help. He calls on God not for material things, but for the knowledge to understand the way to acquire what is needed. Nevertheless, we must realize that sometimes we will not be given the sort of guidance we ask for – this, too, is an answer to prayer. Pray for ability equal to the opportunity, for good habits, for love, to use words well, to humbly forge through all obstacles, to reach worthwhile goals.

It is now three years since Hafid has sold all his goods. Together with his wife and Erasmus, he lives a simple life. One day an unkempt traveler comes to see him. It is Paul, follower of Jesus. Paul relates to Hafid his conversion to Christ, tells about Jesus' life, and declares that Jesus has sent him to find the greatest salesman in the world and ask him to share his miraculous secrets for converting others. At last the man to whom Hafid can confer the sacred instructive scrolls, has arrived.

SWIM WITH THE SHARKS

(Without Being Eaten Alive)
by Harvey Mackay, William Morrow and Co., Inc., New York, N.Y., 1988

Swim With the Sharks is a highly acclaimed and insightful look at what it takes to be successful in business. Harvey Mackay shares his ideas, secrets, and experiences on how to "outsell, outmanage, outmotivate, and outnegotiate your competition."

Mackay is a man known for making things happen. When the slumping Twins faced the possibility of being moved out of Minnesota, Mackay organized the campaign that kept them there, and later spearheaded the building of the Minneapolis Metrodome. At 26, Mackay bought a floundering envelope company for $200,000 and turned it into a 35-million-dollar-a-year business.

Most sales manuals emphasize selling yourself. This book does not, says Mackay, "because very often, my friend, you and I are lousy products."

Sharks is divided into 69 "lessons" and 19 "quickies." Here are samplings:

Short Course in Salesmanship

Marketing: If someone were to stand in front of a group, hold up a twenty-dollar bill, and try to sell it for one dollar, wouldn't most people be skeptical? We are programmed to think that there must be some kind of catch in such an offer. Good marketing doesn't depend on miracle deals; it aims at persuading others that they need your product.

Knowing the Customer: "*Knowing something about your customer is as important as knowing everything about your product.*" The Japanese use the phrase, "Ready? Fire! Aim" to describe common American marketing practices. Americans tend to ignore the importance of proper marketing and public relations. "In order to supply something you must first create a demand." And to create demand you must understand your customers; their needs and their complaints. Develop an effective scenario: "Ready? Aim. Fire!"

Mackay's key to learning about customers is a 66-point questionnaire (the "Mackay 66") that must be filled out on each customer. Mackay was fully aware that sales people hate filling out forms. Hence, his questionnaire is short and to the point, but includes such details on customers as personal and family background, education, business background, special interests, and lifestyle. It ends with a section called "The Customer and You," designed to profile the customer's loyalties and ethical positions.

Children learn at an early age to wait until their parents are in a good mood to hit them for "whatever the market will bear." The same is true of sales. *Timing is everything.*

When one of Mackay's customers has a birthday, she not only gets a card but is also taken to lunch. Mackay's salespeople make in commissions more than twice the average for their industry. He attributes this to his company's knowledge of customers.

The Salesman's Job: It's a customer's "job" to be suspicious and cynical about the product you are offering. "It's your job as a salesperson to neutralize these feelings so your product can get the fair hearing it deserves."

Soliciting Referrals: Most salespeople have heard of the 80/20 rule: Twenty percent of your customers provide eighty percent of your business. If suppliers depend on you for a substantial part of their business, then chances are they will feel a sense of loyalty towards you and your company. These suppliers can be a major source of referrals. They are the "second best place to look for business."

Hard, Smart Work: People in sales must be willing to work hard. Mackay quips: "I've known successful sales people who were drunks, gamblers, liars, and thieves . . . but I have never known a successful sales person who sat on his ass all day." Remember, it is the investment of your time in terms of availability and customer service that keeps accounts.

Preparing and Impressing for Success: While calling on tough prospects is never easy, some things can make it easier. First, find out all you can about your potential client. Second, be thorough. Send a letter stating your purpose for wanting to meet with him. Then phone to set up your meeting, referring to the earlier letter. Last, follow up with a note on the day of the meeting. Even if you don't immediately get the account, if you are in "second place" in the minds of several key decision makers, there will always be some "first place" people messing up – and you'll be there, ready to step in.

Mackay's "personalized" approach for contacting prospective clients begins with a conversation with the secretary:

Hello. Angela? I'm Harvey Mackay, President of Mackay Envelope Corporation. [Straight to her brain. Who is this guy? How does he know my name? Have I met him?] *I've written Mr. T.P. within the past two weeks, and now I'm calling him from Minneapolis. I would like to see Mr. T.P. for exactly three hundred seconds. I will go as far as . . . Sri Lanka just for the purpose of seeing him for those three hundred seconds. And if I take any longer, I'll donate five hundred dollars to T.P.'s favorite charity . . . which I believe is the Boy Scouts, isn't it?*

When you've done your homework, when you've looked up your prospect in

Who's Who and done some reconnaissance with his suppliers, then you know you're right. And what an impression it makes!

Getting the Sale: How does Mackay handle the meeting he has arranged? He speaks straightforwardly:

> *As you may know, we're bidding on your contract. I just came here to tell you, as president of Mackay Envelope, that . . . if we are fortunate enough to receive your business, I'll take a personal interest in seeing to it that you will receive the service and craftsmanship you have every right to expect.*

Setting Goals: If you don't have a destination you'll never get there. Set goals.

Short Course in Negotiation

• "Smile and say *no* until your tongue bleeds" is Mackay's most valuable negotiating advice. That saying is based on the premise that if you can *say no with a smile,* your deals will improve.

• One of the most forceful negotiating devices you have is walking away from the table without a deal. If the other party knows you have to settle a deal by a particular deadline, then all they have to do is set their terms and wait until the deadline arrives. Don't let them know your secrets.

• Make "heady" – not "heart-y" – decisions. "Make decisions with your heart and what you'll end up with is heart disease."

• One way to get a feel for a deal without "showing all your cards" is to "send in the clones." Hire someone – a ringer, if you will – to go in with a verbal offer to see how firm an asking price is. Such an arrangement can give you cheap information that you could get in no other way.

• "There is no such thing as a sold-out house." In negotiating for an "all booked up" hotel room, Mackay says to the reservations clerk:

> . . . *I know, and you know, somebody out of those five hundred people isn't going to show up . . . . So all I'm asking is . . . that you put my name on the top of the waiting list . . . . I'm sending the money in advance . . .*

• You can buy or sell anything "if you can get the other side of the table to see how the deal works to their advantage." Gaining customer information and giving confident perceptions sums up good negotiating technique.

Short Course in Management

• The biggest mistake a manager can make is not *knowing when to stay out of the way.* As a former chairman of Tenneco counseled: "Knowing when to get the hell out of the way [is] the hardest part, but that's the one that will make you rich."

• The speed with which you get bad news is a reliable gauge of what kind of manager you are. "Nobody wants to be the bearer of bad tidings, because that triggers the kill-the-messenger syndrome." So, it is the manager's responsibility to *encourage bad news,* because faulty concerns left unchecked get worse.

• "Efficiency, achieved at the cost of creativity, is counterproductive." We should encourage our people to *spend time thinking.* Time spent in creative pondering is more effectively used than time spent in most other activities.

• You can spot a winner by the quality of people surrounding him or her. Winners don't need "yes men." They are big enough to let other winners act *for* them.

• People make mistakes. "The best way to chew someone out is to have them do it themselves." Mackay is notorious for summoning a worker to his office, letting her stew in the waiting room for a while, then inviting her in, giving her his own chair, and asking her what she would feel and what she would say about her own performance if she were in Mackay's position. The employee is usually harder on herself than Mackay would have been.

• *Knowing the competition* is almost as important as knowing the customer. A "competitor questionnaire" (much like the one for customers) might be designed. Know, analyze and compare each competing firm, then decide what it will take to beat the competition and improve your own business.

• Knowing when to take it easy is as important as knowing when to work.

Some Final *Swim With the Sharks* "Quickies"

• *Utilize the public library.* It is the best and most convenient research facility.

• *Have confidence in yourself.* "Humility is the most overrated of human emotions."

• *Write things down.* Don't waste your energy remembering information you can just as easily look up.

• *Fly first class.* That's where you'll meet valuable contacts.

• *Maintain the illusion of demand.* On one occasion, hundreds of Twins season tickets were cancelled when the team was on a losing streak. Management didn't panic. Instead they ran a blind ad: "Leaving town. Four season tickets for sale." The response was overwhelming; the cancelled tickets were all resold.

• *Keep in touch with your mentors.* They are the ones that got you to where you are.

• There is always a place in the world for the person who says, *"I'll take care of it."*

HOW TO TALK SO PEOPLE LISTEN

the real key to job success
by Sonya Hamlin, Harper & Row, New York, N.Y., 1988

Communication is complex and dynamic; it is both a science and an art. No single prescription can bind it into a convenient, tractable bundle. However, Sonya Hamlin's book provides a few proven "handles" to the huge body of literature dealing with communication.

Hamlin's early experience as a television host, producer, lecturer and consultant provided the foundation from which she went on to work in the "real world" of trial lawyers, doctors, politicians and business-people. The ideas she presents and the strategies she offers have the solidity of being firmly grounded in scholarship, and also the flavor and nourishment of reality-testing. The purpose of *How to Talk So People Listen* is clear throughout: to help the reader get what he or she wants on the job through effective communication.

One basic approach to communication emphasizes the skills and abilities of the *sender*, the person actively "doing" the communicating. This approach places considerable weight on the communicator, who must somehow gauge the receptiveness, defenses, propensities, and background of his "audience," and then concoct just the right message in both form and content. Properly executed, the message hits its mark, and understanding or persuasion ensues.

Communication scholars have long since abandoned this approach, however. The current trend – of which Hamlin is a proponent – recognizes communication as a two-way, *interactive* process, where both sender and receiver continually influence each other and messages are cycled back and forth on non-verbal, barely perceptible levels. Most people do not process all these signals on a conscious, rational level; but they do process and respond to them on a semi-conscious, emotional level, and this subliminal processing leaves an indelible mark on the whole communications exchange.

The book first presents a brief outline of developmental psychology. Hamlin is concerned with looking at the *"whys"* behind the *"hows."* Her words attempt to imbue the reader with a base of *psychological* and *linguistic* data to show why one communication technique works where others fail.

Many of us became detached from our feelings in early life, and the impact of this disengagement on our communication has been immense.

Example: You're a kid and you tell your mother, "I don't like Aunt Agnes." What happened? You were told: "That's terrible. She's your aunt! Don't you let me hear you say that again!"

The result of such an exchange? Guilt, the need to put on a false front, stifled realtionships, doubt that others are being honest in their relations with you, etc. Because we have learned to deny or hide our feelings rather than accept and manage them, most of us carry hidden *"emotional agendas"* into communicative exchanges. The motivation underlying our words becomes an attempt to influence others and to win their "conditional acceptance" – conditional upon our doing and saying that which we think they expect of us. These "externalized motivations," established in early childhood when we first learn what is admired and rewarded – earning-power, compliancy, degrees, professional prestige – shape lifelong personal work styles and communication patterns.

Three basic "work personalities" are identified by the author, each distinguished by one of these "dominant motivators": "Achievers," "Affiliators," and "Influencers."

Achievers continually *strive to "win"* in the sense of reaching the next rung of the ladder. The business world has a preponderance of achievers. *Affiliators* are preoccupied with the quality of *social relations;* concerned with both their own and others' feelings. *Influencers* are largely interested in getting, holding, and *building a power base* within a given relationship. We must not only come to grips with the "hidden agenda" behind our own basic communications style, but also learn how to communicate with these three personality types when we encounter them in others.

Listening is treated by Hamlin in some depth. She poses an intriguing proposition about the visual orientation many of us have nowadays toward communication. Television has accustomed us to watching (not necessarily listening to) brief, yet complete, sequential, and intense stories that require little or no imagination. If in fact "the medium is the message," then television messages encourage passivity and breaks in attention. Just being aware of this can help a speaker (salesperson, presenter, parent, lawyer, teacher . . .) decide how best to get her message, demand or selling point across, using brief narratives and illustrations to support her main points, for example, and judiciously chosen "high-impact" visuals to help reinforce and explain. The overriding thesis here is that *the communicator needs to develop a thoughtful, listener-centered approach.*

A *"Fore-Thought Chart"* is offered as a tool to help clarify relationships between your goals and your listeners' goals, needs and expectations. *The chart's emphasis is on pre-planning.* It helps you analyze a situation before you say or do anything. What are your own objectives? What are those of the listener?

Fore-thought charts provide an explicit, deliberate occasion for thinking through how persuasive communication can best be achieved in a certain situation. Using empathy and observation, clearly state what your goals are and what you feel your audience will perceive as their own biggest needs. " . . .Hidden emotional needs are real and must be acknowledged and included in your communication strategy . . . even at the expense of your logical, well-thought-out plans." If you are speaking to an employee who happens to be an *Achiever*, he may respond more readily to how his behavior makes you feel personally; whereas, dealing with an *Affiliator* might require an approach that focuses on teamwork. By listening and applying forethought, you can uncover emotional needs, imagine outcomes, and be better prepared to respond intelligently to any circumstance.

The author goes on to describe preferred settings and times in which to discuss particular subjects. Inviting someone to a breakfast meeting who is a "night owl" instead of a "chirper," for instance, may not be at all wise.

Here are a few other communications skills that the book explores:

- Using vocal variety, eye contact, and body language.

- Structuring an interesting speech or presentation with smooth transitions, i.e. introduction, motivation, outline of agenda, main content, breaking the main topic into segments, presenting details, recapping key ideas, wrapping up, and conclusion.

- Designing high-impact visuals, i.e. deciding whether comparisons, facts, and data should be put in picture, graph, chart, slide, diagram, exhibit or video form.

- Selecting which areas to present vocally and which to present visually. Generally, feelings and narrative are best offered orally; new facts or data, numbers or trends, and direct comparisons are most effective and memorable when presented using visuals.

- Eliciting listener involvement and feedback through questions, discussion, effective listening, and appropriate monitoring of responses and idea exchange.

- Answering difficult questions and providing "creative criticism" while still maintaining a positive environment.

- Developing empathy and rapport with listeners.

- Handling disinterested or hostile listeners. Often, by pointing out to a listener that he seems angry or defensive, you put the ball in his court. Then he can deal with what is bothering him without blaming you or looking for some type of outside interference. Hostility can be lessened by allowing and understanding the anger, then getting out of the personal realm of the conflict and finding something in common.

- Getting group attention.

- Handling egos and conflict.

- Cultivating an air of confidence and preparedness when delivering a speech, answering questions, etc.

In each topical discussion the same theme emerges: *Effective communicators design their messages to grab listeners' attention, maintain their interest, allow for feedback, and enable them to visualize and retain information.* Hamlin frequently returns to the three basic listening personalities or styles, and shows how each is influenced by – or influences – various communication behaviors.

She examines, for example, what the distinct response might be of an *Affiliator* subordinate when directing comments to an *Achiever* boss versus an *Influencer* boss. When questioned about performance, an *Affiliator* usually takes criticism very personally; she dislikes any hostility. But her *Achiever* boss, who is trying to attack the problem from a rational, task-oriented viewpoint, cannot understand the *Affiliator's* hostile response. "How did this happen?" he will ask, scanning all the variables of success, including himself. On the other hand, an *Influencer* boss might ask, "Why didn't you do this?" to make sure that the subordinate's foul-up was not the result of defiance or negligence. For either of these responses it is important that the *Affiliator* employee not turn defensive or be tempted to counter-punch. Rather, she should work with the *Achiever* to help identify the problem; and from the *Influencer* she should seek suggestions or a clarification of duties, and admit fault when deserved.

An issue of ethics lies just below the surface in *How to Talk So People Listen:* Is it manipulative to use communication in a goal-oriented way? Should you communicate to serve your own ends? Hamlin's response is straightforward. Business communication is a process of gaining and attaining; of getting what you want; of using communication techniques to those ends. This is precisely what the other person you're dealing with is doing. Of course, honesty, candor and openness remain the underlying ingredients in any communication exchange.

Hamlin asserts that understanding your listeners' fears and motivations, being a good listener yourself, speaking in a smooth and personal manner, and making communication interactive (incorporating your audience's responses) are essential parts of your formal and informal speech. They are the ways to talk so people will listen.

A WHACK ON THE SIDE OF THE HEAD

How You Can Be More Creative
by Roger von Oech, Warner Books, New York, N.Y., 1990

Roger von Oech packs this book with creative examples and innovative exercises, together with incredible illustrations (by George Willett), all in a framework that is refreshing and imaginative. Though geared to the professional, the work is diverse enough to apply to anyone.

To von Oech, creativity is not only fun but necessary to success and survival in the nineties. But why? "Why be creative? Why challenge the rules? Why run the risk of failing and looking foolish?" For two good reasons: (1) *To discover new solutions to problems . . . ;* (2) *To generate new ideas when old ones become obsolete.*

The inventor-explorer plays with knowledge; he alters his perspective, making "the ordinary extraordinary and the unusual commonplace." Johann Gutenburg observed how grapes were crushed for wine in a wine press, and by combining two previously unconnected ideas invented the printing press and movable type.

An exercise: How can two people stand on the same piece of newspaper face to face, unrestrained, and still not be able to touch each other? If you couldn't come up with an answer (the book's answer is to put the newspaper in a doorway – door closed – with the people on opposite sides of the door), chances are, a "mental lock" impeded you from thinking out the solution. You may be imprisoned by a mandate to find "the right answer," for example, to "follow the rules," or to "avoid ambiguity."

So, how do you open your mental locks? One way is to "unlearn" them; temporarily forget that wine presses only squeeze grapes; go in a new direction with a less cluttered mind; "unimprison" yourself from routine and familiarity. *Sometimes, nothing short of a "whack on the side of the head" can dislodge the assumptions that keep us thinking "more of the same."*

"Whacks" come in many forms. Getting fired, having a teacher with a special talent, breaking your leg, or a business success or emergency might force you to "think something different," make you dislodge presuppositions that stifle thinking, and cause you to generate new questions.

Here are some of von Oech's "whacking" techniques to help you snap your mental locks:

"The Right Answer"

Educator Neil Postman said, "Children enter school as question marks and leave as periods." Our educational system channels us to seek "the right answer." We are taught to solve problems, not to recognize opportunities. But, in most arenas, " . . . if you think there is only one right answer, then you'll stop looking as soon as you find one."

"Look for the second right answer," von Oech recommends. He quotes Linus Pauling: "The best way to get a good idea is to get a lot of ideas." Professional photographers, for instance, take many pictures of a subject so that they can experiment with lighting, different filters, and changes in exposure, in order to find what they're looking for.

• *An idea:* Whack your thinking by changing the original question; play with the wording to approach it from a different angle. Instead of "What type of door can I use to connect these two rooms?" an architect might ask "What sort of passageway should I put here?"

"That's Not Logical"

Logical, analytical thinking is hard thinking. Soft thinking, on the other hand, is divergent, fantastical, visual and often poetic. There is a place for both, but true creativity usually begins with soft thinking, where similarities and connections between objects or situations are explored. Most people have developed a "creative rigor mortis due to excessive hard thinking." They don't give themselves license to use imagination or metaphors.

A metaphor is a "mental map"; a tool to compare something tangible to something abstract. Niels Bohr explained how an atom might look by comparing it to the structure of the solar system, with its central sun (nucleus) and revolving planets (electrons). By showing how dissimilar things are similar, good metaphors enable you "to gain a new perspective on both the unfamiliar and the quite familiar." Try some metaphors of your own: How is motivating a sales force like feeding zoo animals? How is a problem you're dealing with like building a house? . . .

"Follow the Rules"

Rules, routine, and patterns in life are important. But " . . . almost every advance in art, cooking, medicine, agriculture, engineering, marketing . . . has occurred when someone challenged the rules and tried another approach." In sports, if someone hadn't challenged the rules, football wouldn't be a passing game; and in basketball there would still be a jump ball after every field goal.

A rule sometimes outlives the purpose for which it was intended. The typewriter keyboard, for example, was originally positioned with letters in an illogical sequence in order to slow down typists and keep the keys' hammers from hitting each other. Now, although high-tech machines allow for much faster typing without jams, we continue to use this same configuration – only because it's "the rule."

Go after and slay your "sacred cows" –

rules that limit your thoughts and actions to one particular approach.

"Be Practical"

Try some exercises in *What-Iffing:* What would happen if gravity stopped functioning for one second every day? How would life be different? What would transportation be like? . . .

Seeding your imagination with questions like these can help you generate ideas, as well as help you cast off the constraints of the "real" (status-quo) world. Although "what-iffing"doesn't usually lead directly to practical answers, these questions can make excellent "stepping stones" to workable, creative solutions. Fortunately, an engineer's "silly" suggestion to put gunpowder in house paint so that it could be blown off the house when it started to peel, was not discarded as "mental trash," but was used by his team members to launch a search for additives that allowed paint to release when strippers were applied.

• *An idea:* Imagine how Winston Churchill, Mother Teresa, George Patton, the Three Stooges, a plumber, or a banker might solve your problem or perform your task. What expertise would each add? How would they see your situation differently?

"That's Not My Area"

Today we live in a world of specialization – relief pitchers in baseball, specialists in medicine. "So, we have a situation where people know more and more about less and less."

To avoid "tunnelvision," actively search for ideas outside your field; look for history in a hardware store, study fashion at a flea market. Football coach Knute Rockne came up with the concept for his "four horsemen" backfield while watching a burlesque chorus routine. The roll-on deodorant was an adaptation of the ballpoint pen. Nature inspired the Velcro fastener and new designs in windmill blades (the hook spine of the common burr and the spinning feature of falling elm seeds).

"Avoid Ambiguity"

On most occasions it helps to be clear and precise. At times, though, you can make ambiguity work for you:

• *Paradoxes.* "The ability to entertain two different, often contradictory notions at the same time" can stimulate thought. Niels Bohr stated this classic paradox: "The opposite of a great truth is another great truth."

• *Oracles.* Consult, not the oracle at Delphi, but the oracle of your own intuition. Take a random word or object and discover how it applies to your situation. Remember, ancient oracles were often deliberately ambiguous, forcing their petitioners to go beyond the literal, obvious answer and find hidden links to interpretations.

• *Dreams* are "naturals" as oracles. "Listening" to what your dream is really telling you, can provide insights into relationships, or even lead you to choosing the "right" pattern or design idea for your livingroom furniture.

"Don't Be Foolish"

We all tend to "go along with the crowd" to a certain extent; in fact, seeing how others do things is a good way to learn. But "when everyone thinks alike, no one is doing very much thinking."

In classical times, a king would hire a jester-fool to give him insight, which was frequently in direct contradiction to advice given by the "yes-men" of his court. Parody, irreverence, analogy, and offbeat observations were the fool's priceless wares. And today, "thinking like a fool" may be essential to breaking through and jolting your mind. After all, "some of the most foolish ideas from five years ago are now a reality."

• *Some ideas:* Reverse your point of view; disagree with yourself; sometimes do the opposite of what is expected.

Designer Christopher Williams instructed his landscape crew to wait to put sidewalks in around a new cluster of buildings. Over the subsequent months, as the buildings' occupants traversed the grounds, the new lawn became laced with pathways that followed the most efficient curves linking building to building. Only then, in response to user needs, did Williams have the sidewalks paved.

Especially in competetive situations such as sports, warfare, and business, doing the unexpected or seeing yourself from the other side's viewpoint are effective strategies to catch the opposition off-guard.

Some other common mental locks:

"Play is Frivolous." Is it really? Children do most of their learning through play. And "there is a close relationship between the 'haha' of humor and the 'aha' of discovery . . . . The next time you have a problem, play with it."

"To Err Is Wrong." Surely we all want to succeed; but the best stepping stone to real creative success can be failure. "Thomas Edison knew 1,800 ways not to build a light bulb." Keep your "risk muscles" in shape by regularly trying a new recipe or tackling a problem outside your area of expertise. You may fail – but you may also learn a whole new way of looking for answers.

Have fun using these strategic "whacks." Put yourself in a position to be creative: play with knowledge; find "the seventh right answer"; take some risks; open up a new idea.

Then, "don't wait for your idea to happen." Act on it. "If you want to be a singer, go sing. Sing in the shower. Sing for your friends. Join the choir . . . " And "after you implement your idea," says von Oech, "give yourself a pat on the back. And then go out and earn another one."

DEVELOPING CRITICAL THINKERS

Challenging Adults to Explore Alternative Ways of Thinking
by Stephen D. Brookfield, Jossey-Bass, San Francisco, California, 1987

Stephen Brookfield established his place as an author in the field of adult education with his award-winning book *Understanding and Facilitating Adult Learning* (Jossey-Bass, 1986). *Developing Critical Thinkers* continues his exploration of the fascinating phenomenon of thinking. Brookfield is one academic who is unafraid to dissolve theoretical abstractions into practical information; his book is both understandable and useful.

Developing Critical Thinkers covers some interesting ground, with chapters on decision-making, adult learning, creative problem-solving, values clarification, and change. The text is divided into three main sections. Part one focuses on the definition and description of critical thinking; part two deals with practical approaches to development; and the third section concentrates on urging adults to think critically in four major life contexts: the workplace, politics, television, and personal relationships. Throughout, the key issue remains "critical thinking," as defined by two simple principles or activities. People act as "critical thinkers" when they:

(1) Identify and challenge the *assumptions* underlying their own or another's beliefs and behavior.

(2) Explore and imagine *alternatives* to current ways of thinking and living.

The first step in critical thinking is to recognize and then scrutinize the assumptions that guide us through life. Philosophers, physicists, psychologists, and scientists in general acknowledge the foundational role that assumptions play in their work. Critical thinking is only possible when "people probe their habitual ways of thinking . . . for their underlying assumptions – those taken-for-granted values, commonsense ideas, and stereotypical notions about human nature . . . that underlie our actions."

Getting beneath the surface features of thought or behavior – to the thinking below the thinking – is tricky, but it is possible, and plainly in evidence when, for example, a management consultant asks an executive why she does something a certain way and gets the response, "That's just the way we do things around here." The consultant is *questioning the assumptions behind a practice.* In the same way, when a father has a heart-to-heart talk with his teenager and they both discover that they hold some erroneous preconceptions, the father and the son are *unearthing*

assumptions and *building new insights.* Critical thinking is the essence of such scenarios.

The second step involves becoming aware of *alternative perspectives* . . . perspectives that may be as valid as our own. Brookfield writes:

. . . Considering and imagining alternatives leads to the development of a particularly critical cast of mind, especially where any claims for the universal truth or validity of an idea or practice are concerned. We become suspicious of those who tell us that they have "the answer" to life or the solution to all our problems.

The message here is that critical thinkers don't automatically accept a particular idea, statement, lifestyle, or solution; rather, they examine the alternatives, make a conscious choice among them, and accept the consequences. The honest critical thinker recognizes that there are many paths to follow, not just his own.

In describing strategies for developing and nurturing critical thinking, Brookfield first outlines a *process* involving several phases:

(1) *A Triggering Event:* something that causes a sense of "inner discomfort and perplexity"

(2) *Exploration:* a search for ways of reducing this discomfort

(3) *Developing Alternative Perspectives:* the selection of "new roles we wish to play" and the development of "knowledge and skills for the action we wish to take"

(4) *Integration:* finding and integrating new ways of thinking and living

The author avers that the most important of these phases is the first. He describes two kinds of triggering events: positive and negative. *Positive triggers* are those that lead us to discover new ways of thinking in pleasant or fulfilling circumstances, as when we accomplish something we assumed we could not do. But far more common are the *negative triggers* of divorce, death, dislocation, and termination, which *force* us to confront and change dysfunctional assumptions. This explains why professional helpers – psychologists, counselors, therapists – have such a powerful impact on some lives; they intervene just as old assumptions are crumbling and help clients develop fresh assumptions to chart a new course through life.

How does one go about examining the basic assumptions that underlie thought and action? Brookfield lists a variety of tips and techniques, all revolving around a pivotal proposition:

"Challenge is central to helping people think critically."

Critical Questioning – This is questioning designed to bring to the surface basic assumptions and to prompt "reflective analysis" – to allow people to scrutinize the basis for their thinking or actions.

Critical Incident Exercises – Here, the individual identifies a specific incident or event that, for some reason, was of particular significance to her. This milestone is written down and then explored to reveal the assumptions that made it meaningful.

Criteria Analysis – By eliciting and then examining the criteria set for judging specific events, critical thinkers discover more about their unspoken assumptions of right and wrong, good or bad.

Crisis-Decision Simulations – For this exercise, people are asked to imagine themselves in a situation where they are forced to make a decision from among a number of uncomfortable choices. After making their choice, they are asked to justify and elaborate on their reasons for choosing one course of action over others. As they do so, their underlying assumptions become more evident.

Once assumptions have been identified, the next logical step is to develop alternative ways of thinking; to adopt (or become aware of) a different set of assumptions. Again, Brookfield suggests how critical thinking might be enhanced.

(1) Practice being a critical thinker:

(a)   *Reject standardized formats* for problem solving.

(b)   Cultivate interests in a *wide variety* of related and divergent fields.

(c)   Take *multiple perspectives* on a problem.

(d)   View the world as *relative* and *contextual* rather than universal and absolute.

(e)   Use *trial-and-error* – experimental and experiential – methods in daily living.

(f)   *Embrace change* as a valuable developmental opportunity.

(g)   *Build self-confidence and trust* in your own judgement.

(Brookfield stresses that these characteristics are developed over time, not overnight.)

(2) Make decisions by brainstorming, a respected technique for encouraging structured spontaneity among individuals or groups. Brainstorming follows three basic stages. After the problem is carefully specified:

(a)   Generate a free flow of ideas, with *no evaluation or criticism* allowed.

(b)   Encourage individuals to *propose outrageous solutions* or ideas.

(c)   Attempt to *build on these ideas.*

(3)   Heighten critical thinking by using a **futures invention** game. Participants are encouraged to imagine both individual and collective futures they desire (becoming an artist, getting the job of director of marketing, starting a family . . .). Through a process of revealing, comparing and negotiating visions of what people most desire in their personal and social worlds, a concrete, psychologically magnetic future scenario is generated revolving around four questions:

(a)   *Who am I?*

(b)   *What do I want to do?*

(c)   *How can I do it?*

(d)   *What are the grounds for inviting other persons to join me in making these decisions?*

Such a future vision can create, for some people, a "psychological magnetism" that can have great impact on their lives.

Brookfield's book goes on to discuss more ways of understanding and articulating our hidden assumptions and of positing new alternatives. Some methods are highly creative: writing an individual futures history and using "aesthetic triggers" (art, poetry, nature, fantasy or drama) to relax the mind.

In the final section of the book, Brookfield examines the value of critical thinking in different areas of life. In the workplace, critical thinking is a sorely needed commodity; but it can also be dangerous. For example, it is uncommon to see a subordinate publicly question his superior's underlying assumptions about a decision or course of action – although most of us do so privately. However, companies that reward and encourage critical thinking may be significantly more effective than traditional businesses.

This book may appeal to teachers, who might find that its games and techniques stimulate creative thinking in their students. Managers and executives interested in reducing pressures for conformity within their organizations can find new ways of "opening up" business cultures. Counselors and consultants involved in team building can discover valuable ideas for engaging their clients.

"Critical Thinking," is the highest and most human of human potentials.

MANAGING CONFLICT

He had been hand-picked by Steven Jobs, the company's founder, to become Apple Computer's president and CEO. But soon after his arrival, John Scully began to disagree sharply with Jobs about Apple's strategic direction. Jobs tried to outflank Scully by gaining board support for firing him; but, even though Jobs was Apple's largest stockholder, the board backed Scully, who, as president, removed Jobs' operating authority. Within six months Jobs cut all ties to Apple Computer.

Conflicts like this capture the headlines. But conflicts of lesser proportions are a daily reality for every man and woman who holds a job, and particularly for managers, who are expected to resolve the conflicts.

Two Approaches to Conflict

Tradition has it that conflict is bad; it's something to be avoided. Experts during the 1940's and 50's believed that conflict arose from interpersonal problems, and that the resolution of these problems would lead to improved work performance. Most of us still cling to the idea that good managers *resolve* conflicts.

Current thinking disputes this view. Contemporary perspective holds that conflict can actually be a positive force at work if it is managed skillfully. Experts now speak in terms of *Conflict Management*. Not only is conflict seen as a natural outgrowth of human interaction, but certain types of conflict are considered desirable.

In the absence of conflicting opinions, harmonious, tranquil work groups are prone to becoming static, apathetic and unresponsive to pressures for change and innovation. They also risk the danger of becoming so self-satisfied that dissenting views – which may offer important alternative information – are shut out. The world came the closest it has ever come to nuclear war for this very reason. President John F. Kennedy and his advisors had become very insular from the onset of the Cuban Missile Crisis. They had spurned outside information, heeding only those opinions consistent with their own. Historians subsequently discovered that these top decision makers operated with some wildly inaccurate information that needlessly inflamed the situation.

A Conflict Model

Ken Thomas, an influential conflict theorist and writer, has developed a useful model to assess conflict-handling styles. It starts by recognizing that any conflict situation is held in balance by two opposing factors:

(1) *The degree to which each participant wants to satisfy his own concerns (assertiveness).*

(2) *The degree to which each wants to satisfy the other's concerns (cooperativeness).*

When placed at right angles on a grid, these opposing forces can be used to structure five primary conflict-handling styles. (Each managerial style is charted by plotting independent trajectories from the horizontal and vertical axes.):

Choice of Conflict-Handling Styles

1. **Competition**

When one party struggles to achieve his or her goals regardless of the impact on other parties involved, the conflict is handled by competition and dominance. These familiar *"Win-Lose"* conditions occur when one party prevails only at the other's expense. Organizational gamesmen using Competition frequently call the formal authority system into play, seeking the support of organizational "power players" who will help them dominate their opposition. Notice that this style is high on the assertiveness scale and low with respect to cooperation.

2. **Collaboration**

When both conflicting parties work to satisfy each others' concerns, the style becomes one of Collaboration. Searching for a mutually beneficial outcome, both individuals or groups *emphasize solving the problem* by (1) sharpening the understanding of where differences lie, (2) generating as many alternatives as possible, and, only then (3) selecting a solution that fits both sets of concerns. Since the desired solution is advantageous to both parties, this is referred to as a *"Win-Win"* approach. Collaboration is a frequent tool of marriage counselors and labor mediators, who keep each side generating alternative solutions until an acceptable one is found.

3. **Avoidance**

By far the most frequent response, Avoidance occurs when one or both parties simply *withdraw from or suppress the conflict.* People avoid the problem either out of simple indifference to the outcome or because they feel inadequate to deal with it. If withdrawal is not possible, one or both parties may suppress the conflict, keeping it simmering just below the surface of everyday interaction, where it waits for the right (or wrong) moment to break through.

4. Accommodation

This style comes into play when one party is prepared to appease the other – to give them what they want – with little or no regard for personal concerns. This is generally done in the spirit of *self-sacrifice*, the Accommodator's sacrifice being made willingly because any perceived negative outcomes are deemed acceptable; he or she can live with them. Accommodation may take the form of a manipulated parent "giving in" to his whining and pouting child. In the very noblest situations, however, one party will – not only in a spirit of sincerity but also by way of well-grounded logic – place the other's welfare above his or her own, and suffer genuine change or genuine distress as a result.

5. Compromise

When each party in a conflict agrees to give something up in order to get something in return, Compromise, a *"give and take"* style, is in effect. There are no clear winners and losers with this approach; rather, there is (1) a rationing of the object of conflict (where the object is divisible, like sums of money), or (2) a reward yielded by one party to the other in return for concessions granted. Union-Management negotiations frequently take the Compromise approach, as concessions from one side of the table are mated with concessions from the other in order to reach an agreement.

Using the Model

The great usefulness of this model lies in its ability to define and describe a *variety* of ways to manage conflicts. No one style is appropriate in all business circumstances. Pity the Industrial Relations Manager, for example, who uses Avoidance at the bargaining table . . . or the Corporate Director of Purchasing who exclusively uses Competition to solve problems among his division executives.

But, while the freedom to choose among conflict-handling styles is attractive (and, indeed, always available to us), research indicates that most of us have a single *preferred style* of handling conflicts. We often fail to regard each conflict we come up against as separate; as requiring an individualized solution. This means that without conscious attention to the model and the options it offers, the likelihood is that we will use the same well-worn style across all situations – often inappropriately.

The following list, summarized from Ken Thomas' article entitled "Toward Multi-dimensional Values in Teaching: The Example of Conflict Behaviors" (*Academy of Management Review*, July 1977), indicates situations where each different conflict-handling style may be the best choice:

Competition
1. When quick, decisive action is vital.
2. On important issues where unpopular actions must be implemented.
3. Against people who take advantage of non-competitive behavior.

Collaboration
1. To find an integrative solution, when both sets of concerns are too important to be compromised.
2. To merge insights from people with different perspectives.
3. To gain commitment by incorporating the concerns of other parties.

Avoidance
1. When the issue is trivial, or when more important issues are pressing.
2. When the possible disruptions outweigh the benefits of resolution.
3. When other people or future scenarios may be able to resolve the conflict more effectively.

Accommodation
1. When issues are more important to others than to yourself; to satisfy others and maintain their cooperation.
2. To stockpile social credits for later use.
3. To minimize loss when you're outmatched and losing.

Compromise
1. When opponents of equal power are committed to mutually exclusive goals.
2. To achieve temporary settlements on complex issues.
3. To achieve expedient solutions under time pressures.

As leaders, spouses, parents, group members or friends, we encounter the challenge of conflict many times daily. Recognizing and practicing the various approaches to dealing with these conflicts is an essential skill for all of us to master.

For Further Reading:

Tjosvold, Dean. *Managing Conflict: the Key to Making Your Organization Work*. Minneapolis: Team Media. 1989.

Blake, R.R. and J.S. Mouton. *Solving Costly Organizational Conflicts*. San Francisco: Jossey-Bass. 1984.

Cliff, G. "Managing Organizational Conflict." *Management Review*. May, 1987: 51-53.

MAINTAINING JOB SATISFACTION

Are American workers satisfied with their jobs? According to Stephen Robbins, author of the popular management text *Organizational Behavior*, "The answer to this question . . . is a resounding 'Yes!'" Robbins writes that, based on employee surveys, about 8 out of 10 people say they're satisfied with their jobs. Older workers are most satisfied (92% for those age 65 and over), but figures are impressively high for young people as well (73% for those age 25 and younger). Still, says Robbins, other research demonstrates that only 41% of white-collar employees would again choose to enter their current occupation, and the statistic is only 24% for blue-collar workers. Satisfaction varies by profession: urban university professors (93%) and mathematicians (91%) rate high, while textile workers (31%), unskilled steelworkers (21%), and unskilled auto workers (16%) are at the low end of the spectrum.

So, how do we account for these disparities? What makes an employee resign from her job? Why is it that one, seemingly disgruntled employee will stay on with a company for decades, while another, apparently content worker will decide to "move on" after only a few months? What is considered the ideal work setting?

"Job satisfaction" is a very complex matter, comprised of many elements and dimensions that are not easily captured by a simple questionnaire. However, job satisfaction is an important issue to managers for at least three reasons: (1) There is unmistakable evidence linking job dissatisfaction to high absenteeism and turnover; (2) It has been demonstrated that satisfied employees are healthier and live longer lives; and (3) Satisfaction at work carries over to the employee's life away from work. Managers clearly need to understand the mechanics of job satisfaction and how best to encourage it among their employees.

Job Satisfaction: What Is It?

Job satisfaction is actually a bundle of concrete elements that coalesce into an *attitude* the employee holds about his or her job. Management writers speak of the "A-B" relationship – that is, "Attitudes affect Behavior." The professional manager is well advised to pay attention to the attitudes circulating among employees; auto executives who struggled through the crisis of low morale in their organizations during the 1970's will attest to this fact.

Jobs themselves are more than the actual tasks that define them. Jobs also require interaction with co-workers, are encircled by organizational policies and politics, demand adherance to company or work unit procedures, have performance standards to meet, exist in certain working conditions, and so on. The employee's overall sense of job satisfaction is a subjective tally of his or her reactions to many factors. Instruments designed to measure job satisfaction typically gauge the following core elements:

- *Nature of the work.* Do the requirements and benefits of the job fit the employee's personality, family and social lifestyle, financial needs, growth potential, etc.?

- *Nature of the supervision.* Does the job demand that the worker perform without constant supervision; or, on the other hand, is he suited to the pressures of close scrutiny? Are both supervisor and employee flexible enough to get along?

- *Present pay, and pay in relation to other jobs.* Does the employee feel that his salary is consistent with job difficulty, expected training and education, experience or expertise, and in line with other workers – inside or outside the company – who effectively perform the same task?

- *Promotion opportunities.* Within the company, is there a very real possibility of being promoted to a more prestigious, better paying level? Are the pay and perquisites that go along with advancement worth the hassles of increased responsibility?

- *Relationships with other employees.* Is the worker respected and valued by her peers, both as a fellow employee and as a person?

These seemingly straightforward elements actually comprise an intricate, ever-fluctuating, hard-to-decipher composite picture of job satisfaction.

What Affects a Worker's Job Satisfaction?

Research shows that job satisfaction is heightened or diminished according to how certain important contingencies are dealt with in the work environment. The following is a summary of the most significant variables.

Mentally Challenging Work

Most employees prefer work that allows them to *use and improve their skills and abilities.* They seek a job that offers a variety of tasks and that permits some *autonomy* in decision making. They also like to receive *feedback* on how well they're doing. The presence of these characteristics produces challenging work; their absence, a boring eight-hour day.

Equitable Rewards

Employees want pay systems they perceive as *fair, unambiguous,* and *in line with their expectations.* They form expectations by measuring their own work against other work in the company (or work unit, or community, or industry), comparing pay rates, and making a subjective assessment of fairness: "Compared to senior programmers and their compensation, I'm paid about right for what I do."

The key to linking pay systems with job satisfaction lies in understanding that only the employee's *perception* of fairness counts in attitude formation. Perceptions can be changed, of course, but managers should approach them as subjective "facts" at first.

Supportive Working Conditions

Working conditions make a difference – it's really that simple. Employees prefer working environments that are *safe* and *comfortable;* temperature, light, noise, smoke control and other environmental factors should be monitored and appropriate. In a larger sense, the working conditions established by a firm communicate a message to its employees: "Here's what we think of you . . . "

Most people prefer to work relatively close to home, in clean, modern facilities, and with adequate tools and equipment. Contrast, for example, the feelings of a claims clerk who works in hot, cramped surroundings with old typewriters, versus those of a clerk in a modern, air conditioned office that supplies state-of-the-art computers and color monitors.

Constructive Co-worker Relationships

People work for more than money – much more. For most of us the workplace is also an important source of *social interaction,* a place where we receive *validation* as worthwhile people and form long-lasting personal relationships. A work environment with friendly and supportive colleagues contributes to job satisfaction.

Not surprisingly, management behavior is the key determinant in how well employees work together. A manager's responsibility is two-fold: (1) The manager is a *leader* of his or her immediate work group, setting the *tone* for interaction and creating *expectations* regarding acceptable conduct;

and (2) The manager is also a *member* of this network of relationships, *interacting* with each employee in either a constructive or destructive way.

Managers can create high job satisfaction when they:

- Are understanding, friendly, and approachable.

- Set clear performance objectives.

- Praise good performance when it is demonstrated.

- Show personal interest.

- Genuinely listen to employee opinions.

What Will Having a Satisfied Employee Buy Me?

Many occupational studies have tried to assess the satisfaction-to-performance linkage. In general terms, findings indicate that satisfaction and productivity are positively related: *the higher the level of job satisfaction, the greater the productivity.* This finding, however, has a number of complex variables that moderate the connection. Upper level employees, for example, are free of the constraints imposed on the machine-paced assembly line worker; consequently, they are better able to demonstrate the effects of satisfaction on performance.

It has also been shown that higher job satisfaction is positively connected to *attendance at work;* but here, too, a number of intervening factors can skew the statistical picture.

In addition to performance and attendance, the third major benefit of job satisfaction involves *turnover.* And, just as common sense would suggest, satisfied employees do tend to stay with a company longer than dissatisfied ones. The connection of job satisfaction with turnover, in fact, is the strongest and most direct of these three.

What job satisfaction attitudes permeate your workplace? Are employees happy with what they do, the facilities, their associates and the rewards connected with their jobs? Knowing and acting on these determinants of satisfaction can lead to greater efforts and effectiveness in worker performance.

For Further Reading:

Greene, C.N. "The Satisfaction-Performance Controversy." *Business Horizons.* February, 1972: pp. 31-41.

Scarpello, V. and J.P. Campbell. "Job Satisfaction: Are All The Parts There?" *Personnel Psychology.* Autumn, 1983: pp. 577-600.

Staines, G.L and R.P Quinn. "American Workers Evaluate the Quality of Their Jobs." *Monthly Labor Review.* January, 1979: pp. 3-12.

ALLEVIATING WORKER ALIENATION

Citibank recently introduced various programs and systems designed to combat employee alienation and enhance productivity. Among the measures implemented were: (1) Refined communication programs to facilitate and enhance workflow between the operations, marketing, service, and functional departments; (2) Decentralization measures to make it possible for individual employees to handle an entire transaction from beginning to end; and (3) Job redesign efforts to put employees performing a consumer-contact job in direct contact with their customers.

Leaders who implement measures like these recognize that *employee commitment* is a powerful force for growth in organizations, and that *worker alienation* is a ruinous form of corporate cancer. There are many forces and issues that bear upon the alienation - commitment factor in a company; but one of the most telling is the way jobs are designed. *The Job Characteristics Model (JCM)* includes research on how jobs should be designed. This model identifies the job characteristics that are powerful determinants of commitment, and charts their relationship to personal and work-related outcomes. The model may help the professional manager draw implications to fit the right job to the right person.

Core Dimensions

According to the JCM, any job can be described in terms of five core dimensions. They are:

1. Skill Variety: This refers to the number of distinct skills and activities required by the job, allowing an employee to use and improve on a number of his abilities. The owner-operator of a garage that services radiators, repairs automotive air conditioners, services electrical systems, rebuilds engines, and interacts directly with customers, has a high degree of skill variety. A body shop technician who sprays paint eight hours a day has low skill variety.

2. Task Identity: We know that people enjoy tasks that lead to a whole or complete piece of work. The assembly line employee in an automobile factory, who tightens the three bolts of the front bumper, car after car, day after day, has relatively low task identity; while the cabinet maker who designs a piece of fine furniture, builds it, and finishes it to perfection, feels considerably more identity with the product.

3. Task Significance: This describes the degree to which the job has direct perceived impact on the lives or work of others. It involves the sense of "making a difference," by contributing to the company, for example, or by doing jobs that directly benefit others. Among healthcare workers, for instance, doctors, nurses, therapists and social workers usually feel a high degree of task significance. By contrast, employees in hospital housekeeping, who sweep floors, are likely to sense less significance in their work.

4. Autonomy: Most people prefer jobs that offer a substantial amount of discretion and independence. However, the opposite of this ideal is what we find in the typical bureaucracy: job functions that are tightly constrained by regulations and policies, and supervisors whose task it is to see that employees abide by these formalized strictures.

5. Feedback: Ideally, the individual carrying out a task will receive clear, direct and timely feedback on his or her performance, as well as on the results of his or her actions. Again, for contrast, consider the stereotypic bureaucrat who shuffles papers all day with no direct knowledge of the actual impact of her actions. This worker has little feedback; while the electronics worker who assembles a radio and then tests it to find out if it operates properly, sees the direct effects of his work and learns immediately what he has done right or wrong.

The Model

The JCM predicts that the higher a given job ranks in the dimensions of Skill Variety, Task Identity, Task Significance, Autonomy and Feedback, the greater the employee's commitment to his job. Conversely, jobs that offer few of these elements will generate more worker alienation.

The model shown on the next page uses the concepts of the JCM to define

the mechanisms of job commitment. This model introduces two ideas:
(1) The design of any job tends to induce certain *critical psychological states* among workers.
(2) Different people have different *growth-need strengths*.

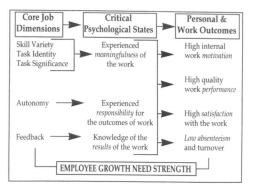

The notion of a "psychological state" is just what it sounds like: Experiences encountered in daily living are processed cognitively and lead to certain states of mind. Studies supporting the JCM indicate that doing *meaningful* work is satisfying to people, as is a sense of *responsibility*; and knowing the *results* of one's actions completes an emotional as well as a cognitive circuit.

The idea of a "growth need strength" relates to the concept of "self-actualization" – that is, to the business of continually becoming a more fully functioning person. Psychologists suggest that growth (or "actualization") – the acquisition of increasingly refined skills and competencies in all areas of life – is basic to human nature. We grow when we learn to handle difficult relationship situations, solve challenging technical problems or deal with troubling emotions. But it can also be the case that circumstances in a person's life can truncate her "need" for growth, so that she remains stuck at the lower stages of actualization.

The JCM deals with the realities of the workforce and recognizes that different people will enter the workplace with differing levels of growth need, i.e. some people will actively seek challenging assignments, while others will be content to put in their eight hours. An employee's growth need strength modifies the impact of adjustments made to the left side of the model. Thus, employ-

...ees who have a high growth need will respond to enriched tasks – those high in the core dimensions – more positively than those who have a comparatively low growth need.

Modeling human psychology and predicting behavior are tricky assignments at best. The JCM helps narrow down the immense range of variables that impinge on employee behavior, and in so doing, makes itself subject to criticism from many sectors. But serious analysis supports the thrust of the JCM and leaves us with two safely drawn conclusions:

(1) People who work on jobs with high core job dimensions are generally more motivated, satisfied, productive and committed than those who do not.

(2) Job dimensions operate through psychological states to influence personal and work-related outcomes rather than influencing them directly.

Perhaps equally compelling is the fact that most corporate job design efforts have been organized around the JCM's basic principles for two decades or more – *because they work*. Great power can be tapped from a committed and motivated workforce.

For Further Reading:

Hackman, J.R. and G.R. Oldham. "Work Design." In J.R. Hackman and J.L. Suttle (Eds.), *Improving Life at Work*. Santa Monica: Goodyear. 1977.

Kelly, J.E. *Scientific Management, Job Redesign and Work Performance*. New York: Academic Press. 1982.

Walton, R.E. "Quality of Working Life: What Is It?" *Sloan Management Review*. Fall, 1973: 11-21.

UNLOCKING YOUR WORKTEAM'S POTENTIAL

"It never fails," Bill muttered to the V.P. "Just when the crunch hits, the Division 3 sales team starts to pull in all directions at once. Nobody cooperates with anybody else, nothing gets done." Bill resigned himself to the fact that, once again, he would have to take time away from his own projects to march into another part of the office, spend two weeks or more laying down the law, and, in effect, do what he was already paying seven highly qualified people to do. And he knew that once they closed the quarter and the pressure was off, the team would function acceptably until the next busy part of their business cycle. "I wish I knew how to straighten things out once and for all," Bill thought to himself.

Scenarios like this one (drawn from an actual business situation) are played out regularly by businesses across the country – every day, every week, all year long. Why? Because organizing and then managing an effective, smooth, high-performing group is hard. It takes tremendous knowledge and skill. The initial organization of any group requires direct, hands-on management. Once organized, the group's leadership must still be vigilant in seeing that proper adjustments are made in response to internal change or external threats or opportunities.

Two areas of knowledge about groups and how they work have helped many managers become more effective. The first involves the stages of development that every group goes through, and the second addresses the individual roles that groups tend to divvy out in order to accomplish their work.

Stages of Group Development

Every group must pass through four distinct stages of development, resolving any number of important social and personal issues along the way, before it can function productively.

The Pre-Group Stage

Here, a number of independent, autonomous individuals exist within the corporate structure. They have no real ties to each other: no common goals, no common interests, no mutual dependencies. Six people who sit within ten feet of each other, day after day, without such ties, fail to constitute a group. A truly united group consists of two or more people who:

- Think of themselves as a unit, distinguishing members from outsiders.

- Share a common fate – that is, they're *interdependent*.

- Are identified by non-members as a group. In other words, they have a *group identity*.

- Have a *common goal*.

Stage 1: Forming

The first stage of group development is characterized by a great deal of *uncertainty* about the group's identity, purpose, structure and leadership. People literally "feel their way" and "test the waters" to determine what kinds of behaviors will be acceptable, what the norms are, what the personalities of those making up the group are like, and so on.

This stage is completed when people begin to think of themselves as part of a group.

Stage 2: Storming

This second stage involves inter-group conflict. People now know that they're included as members of a group, so the new key issue becomes "control": "Who's in charge here?" Groups must confront this issue of leadership. This can lead to either constructive outcomes or to a destructive spiral - a constant struggle for leadership positions.

Stage 2 ends when there is a relatively clear sense of hierarchy and leadership in the group.

Stage 3: Norming

During this stage, group members develop working relationships and a sense of cohesiveness. This cohesion is the result of *norms* that are explicitly or implicitly set by the members: "We work for an hour and then take a break." "Arguments are left out in the hall." "We'll follow an agenda in each meeting."

By this time there is a strong sense of group identity; and a set of expectations about who, what, where, when, why and how is shared by each member.

Stage 4: Performing

Now that each individual knows his or her place in the group, what to expect, what the rules are, and how problems are tackled, they are ready to function as one; they can go to work. Up to this point, their "work" has dealt more with group issues and solidifying the group's social infrastructure than with the assigned task.

In general, the closer a group comes to Stage 4, the more prepared it is to address work issues.

© 1991, Compact Classics, Inc.

The important thing for managers to recognize is that *all groups go through these stages*. In fact, a well established *Stage 4* group will cycle through the first three stages every time it meets (though very quickly and with few or no hitches); and this same group can be thrown back to *Stage 2* ("Storming") simply with the introduction of a new member or the promotion of an established one.

Managers can facilitate a group's more rapid development by (1) making authority patterns clear, (2) articulating norms and expectations, and (3) being sure the group has a clear sense of its objectives.

Group Membership Roles

Accompanying the stages of group development is another important phenomenon: a pattern of roles emerges. These roles are of three basic kinds: (1) *Task-Oriented*, (2) *Group Maintenance*, and (3) *Individual*. The interesting thing is that all groups develop this pattern of roles, and all members necessarily assume one or more functions in each new group interaction.

The following outline shows some of the more common roles and role behaviors observed in business groups. These come in three categories, depending on the particular personality and/or interest of the member:

Task-Oriented Roles
Initiator
Offers new ideas or suggests solutions to problems.

Information Seeker
Seeks pertinent facts or clarification of information.

Information Giver
Provides opinions, facts and information.

Group Maintenance Roles
Encourager
Promotes cohesiveness, warmth; praises and accepts others' ideas.

Harmonizer
Alleviates tensions; resolves intragroup disagreements.

Standard Setter
Raises questions about group goals; helps set and maintain group objectives and standards.

Follower
Agrees with others' ideas and emulates their actions.

Group Observer
Monitors group progress and operations; gives the group feedback on its performance.

Individual Roles
Blocker
Resists stubbornly; is negative; returns to issues already rejected by most group members.

Recognition Seeker
Calls attention to self by boasting; acts as if superior to others .

Dominator
Manipulates the group; interrupts others; looks for and gets attention .

Avoider
Remains apart from others; is passive and uninvolved.

Generally speaking, managers should try to create a balance between Task and Maintenance roles for their groups. A team composed solely of Initiators and Information Givers is a team in trouble: the focus is on the task at hand, but there will be no effort devoted to keeping the group alive and functioning. The converse is also true: exclusive concern with Maintenance roles will result in a happy and smoothly working team, but also a team without a task. In almost every case the Individual roles detract from group effectiveness, disturb the members, and lead to a downgrading of performance.

Working teams must be managed and molded to become effective. Wise management can facilitate a team's success by helping members through the stages of group development and working to strike a balance between Task and Maintenance roles.

For Further Reading:

Gist, M.E., E.A. Locke, and M.S. Taylor. "Organizational Behavior: Group Structure, Process, and Effectiveness." *Journal of Management*. Summer, 1987: 237-57.

Goodman, P.S. (Ed.). *Designing Effective Work Groups*. San Francisco: Jossey-Bass. 1986.

Seashore, S. *Group Cohesiveness in The Industrial Work Group*. Ann Arbor: Institute for Social Research, University of Michigan. 1954.

ATTITUDES AT WORK

"That was a lousy way for him to treat Darryl. I don't think you should insult a foreman in front of his crew."

"Did you hear that the president of this place made over a million dollars last year? That's ridiculous!"

"I'll put in a day's work and take the paycheck. But don't expect any miracles coming out of my office."

"To me, the best boss is an invisible boss. I don't like anyone breathing down my neck."

Negative statements like these are a regular feature of organizational life. At one level, they are only opinions, but all these opinions reflect deep-seated *attitudes* – attitudes that often shape *behavior*. Because there's no escaping the fact that employees *have* attitudes, and because attitudes and behavior are usually closely related, managers need insight into what influences attitudes and what their impact is at work.

Attitudes: What Are They?

Attitudes are *valuative stances* – favorable or unfavorable – towards specific objects, people, issues or events. They reflect feelings and basic values.

How Are Attitudes Molded?

Attitudes are acquired throughout life from significant others: parents, teachers, friends, leaders, co-workers, etc. In our early years we begin to model attitudes after those we admire, respect, or perhaps, fear. This same process continues in later life (people adopt the behavior and attitudes of popular figures, cult heroes, national figures), though most adults also form attitudes by reasoning through the details of issues or events and responding according to their own personal values, desires, or fears.

Attitudes are unstable entities that can be molded and changed almost day-to-day. Advertising, for example, aims squarely at our attitudes, trying to alter them with the kind of glitz and appeal we see on TV. If an automobile dealer can get you to form a favorable attitude towards her product and dealership, that attitude may lead you to the car lot.

Why Are Attitudes Important?

Attitudes in organizations are important because they can affect job behavior. An employee may possess thousands of attitudes about innumerable topics and objects,

but managers are concerned only with those that affect work performance. Three worker attitudes, in particular, have been scrutinized extensively: *job satisfaction, job involvement and organizational commitment.*

Job Satisfaction

An employee with high Job Satisfaction holds positive feelings about his work, while one with low Job Satisfaction is usually full of negative comments (attitudes) – and these are sure to show up on the job. Research reveals that Job Satisfaction is improved, generally, when workers have:

- Mentally *challenging* work
- Equitable *rewards* (as they *perceive* them)
- A *supportive* working environment
- Good working *relationships* with peers
- A good person-to-job *fit*

Studs Terkel, in his book *Working People Talk About What They Do All Day and How They Feel About What They Do* (Avon, New York, N.Y., 1975), graphically examines workers' attitudes:

. . . *The automated pace of our daily jobs wipes out name and face – and, in many instances, feelings* . . .
"*I'm a machine,*" *says the spot-welder.* "*I'm caged,*" *says the bank teller* . . .

Are these workers' feelings justified? Are corporate profits and governmental job security indeed more important than people? How can we get back in the habit of respecting men and women both for what they *do* and for what they *are,* bolstering their attitudes and that of the corporation as a whole?

Terkel concludes that, yes, there are "the happy few who find a savor in their daily job": *the Indiana stonemason, who looks upon his work and sees that it is good; the Chicago piano tuner, who seeks and finds the sound that delights; the bookbinder, who saves a piece of history; the Brooklyn fireman, who saves a piece of life* . . . *But don't these satisfactions . . . tell us more about the person than about his task? Perhaps. Nonetheless, there is a common attribute here: a meaning to their work well over and beyond the reward of the paycheck.*

Studies support the finding that high levels of Job Satisfaction lead to (1) increased productivity, (2) lower absenteeism, and (3) less turnover.

Job Involvement

This term is a recent addition to the

manager's vocabulary. It is a measure of the degree to which a person *identifies* psychologically with his job, *"owns"* it, and considers it *important* to his self worth. An employee with a high level of Job Involvement, is "wrapped up" in the work and really cares about what he accomplishes and how well the task is done. High levels of Job Involvement have been found to correlate with fewer absences and lower resignation rates.

Organizational Commitment

While Job Involvement involves a worker's identification with her job, Organizational Commitment reflects her sense of identity with the entire organization and its goals. "Membership" in the organization or "affiliation" with the company are important to her.

As is the case with Job Satisfaction and Job Involvement, high levels of Organizational Commitment lead to, among other things, lower absenteeism and turnover rates. In fact, this factor seems to be a stronger predictor of work performance than either Satisfaction or Involvement.

The A-B Relationship

Attitudes affect behavior. People naturally seek harmony and consistency between their attitudes and behaviors. When one contradicts the other, they try to change either the attitude or the behavior so that the two are in alignment.

Suppose, for example, your friend has always argued that Americans should own American-made cars, because they're superior to imports and they're built by U.S. workers. Then suppose he inherits a Ferrari. His attitudes about foreign cars may suddenly change, or, alternatively, he may sell the car. But the fact remains that he'll experience considerable discomfort – what psychologists call "cognitive dissonance" – while he maintains the original attitude but acts in a contradictory way.

The "A-B" relationship is subject to some moderating variables, however. Research has uncovered at least three reasons or situations where disharmony between attitude and behavior may be tolerated:

(1) When the issues underlying the dissonance are of minimal importance;

(2) When the individual perceives the source of the dissonance to be externally imposed and not under his control;

(3) When rewards are sufficient to make living with the dissonance acceptable.

When one of these three situations is present, a person may very well live with incompatible or mismatched attitudes and behaviors, and the organizational ramifications can be significant. To illustrate, many otherwise honest employees don't think twice about taking home company-owned pens or paper; the matter is perceived to be of minimal importance. But in the same way, a valued accountant may take excellent care of his company's funds for years on end, but jump at the chance to embezzle a million dollars; to him, the potential reward seems worth the risks.

Managers should realize that attitudes can be shaped through *persuasion* (the employee becomes convinced of the attitude's worth) and *modeling* (the employee admires an attitude exhibited by others, and adopts it). Moreover, employee dissonance can be managed: workers may be asked to engage in behaviors that are inconsistent with their attitudes. The dissonant pressure can be lessened, however, when they perceive that it is externally imposed, is beyond their control, or the rewards are significant enough to offset their discomfort.

Involved, committed employees generally have good attitudes – and correspondingly high productivity. In determining the factors that most affect the behaviors of individuals in your company or organization, you would do well to observe closely their work-related behavior and periodically ask them about their feelings concerning the various requirements of their work.

For Further Reading:

Calder, B.J. and P.H. Schurr. "Attitudinal Processes in Organizations." In L.L. Cummings and B.M. Staw (Eds.), *Research in Organizational Behavior*, Vol 3. Greenwich, CT.: JAI Press. 1981: 283-302.

Chaiken, S. and C. Stangor. "Attitudes and Attitude Change." In M.R. Rosenzweig and L.W. Porter (Eds.), *Annual Review of Psychology*, Vol. 38. Palo Alto: Annual reviews. 1987: 575-631.

Cooper, M.R., et al. "Changing Employee Values: Deepening Discontent?" *Harvard Business Review*. January-February, 1979: 117-125.

DUAL-CAREER COUPLES

A career is a curious thing. It's something most of us think we merely "have." Yet, we are largely defined – outwardly and in self-worth – by our careers.

Careers can give us a sense of direction in life. But, at the same time, to the extent that we rely on career counselors and organizationally-defined career paths for guidance, we may be giving up our autonomy and self-direction – the very things most of us are seeking in the first place. Thus, our "work career" clearly shares the stage of a balanced, happy life with two other important elements: family involvements and the opportunities for self development.

Today's family structure, however, is not always so simply defined. With increasing numbers of women in the workplace, modern society has seen, not only the emergence of *dual-career couples* (marriages or relationships where both partners pursue important independent work – frequently in separate organizations, and occasionally in separate cities or on both coasts) but now the *majority* of couples come under this heading. Some concept of this more complex relationship is shown below in the Model of the Dual-Career Couple.

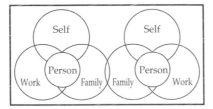

Such relationships, which consist of separate individuals who only overlap in their mutual relation in the family, and who have the added "detraction" of separate careers often pulling them in opposite directions, have the capacity of being potentially disruptive, or highly rewarding, depending on how the couples deal with them.

Dual-Career Relationships

The U.S. Bureau of Statistics reported in 1986 that 54% of all marriages were dual-career. Geographically, the leading areas of growth in this modern phenomenon are the West Coast, Denver, Chicago, New York and the Washington D.C.-Baltimore areas. Since 1970, the number of relationships where both partners are managers, professionals or technicians has doubled. The difficulties this poses for corporate transfers are obvious; these couples are far less mobile than their single-career counterparts.

Some companies, like Procter & Gamble and General Electric, require relatively few transfers for upward mobility. But in most organizations, a move is still the concomitant of advancement. IBM, for example, each year relocates three percent of its employees (some say the initials "IBM" stand for "I've Been Moved"). The Employee Relocation Council estimates that 600,000 annual moves involve dual-career relationships, and that one-half of all corporate transfers affect dual-career couples. The implications these figures have for companies lie primarily in the areas of succession planning and logistics, although scheduling and child care also pose challenges.

Absorption

Obviously, there is more than one model for dual-career relationships: different couples, like different individuals, integrate work into their lives in different ways. One of the main differences affecting dual-career relationships is the concept of *absorption*. A person is absorbed in his or her work to the degree that it takes the lion's share of time, energy and effort, leaving other areas of life correspondingly impoverished. A simple matrix helps to clarify the issues:

		Highly Absorbed	Not Absorbed
PERSON 1	Highly Absorbed	Quadrant 1	Quadrant 2
	Not Absorbed	Quadrant 3	Quadrant 4

PERSON 2

Q1: *Classic Dual-Career Dynamics* - In this quadrant fall relationships where both parties are pursuing their professions or work careers actively and aggressively. Both invest great time, effort and energy in their jobs. Everyday logistics – from coordinating child care and business travel, to simply putting a meal on the table – can result in major problems for these couples. Their mutual absorption in work can also cause headaches for their corporations; i.e. It may be impossible to recruit or transfer one without the other.

Q2 & Q3: *One Job, One Career* - The more traditional form of relationship predominates in these two quadrants: one partner's work is considered central and important, the other's is considered peripheral and supplementary. One of the partners, with little career investment in the company and with transportable skills (secretarial, construction, etc.), may be readily willing to leave an employer when a spouse is transferred. These relationships experience far less career-related stress than those in quadrant 1, and they are also easier to deal with from the corporate perspective; i.e. It's generally harder to recruit or transfer a comptroller with a lawyer spouse than it is a comptroller and a secretary.

Q4: *Two Jobs, Little Investment* - Here we find two individuals neither of whom has a serious investment in his work; rather, they both emphasize other areas of life. There are many couples who passionately seek to keep their careers in harmony with their recreation, family, community, church, and so on. A relationship founded on this basis is less likely to encounter work-related stress, and the organizations involved will probably have an easier time managing assignments and transfers as well.

Meeting the Challenge

How do couples and companies cope with the problems inherent in dual-career relationships? The following tried-and-true techniques have proven helpful to many successful dual-career couples:

• Develop a *joint commitment to both careers.* Each person agrees to his or her partner's need and right to pursue a career.

• Work at *becoming flexible* – at home and on the job. Each partner has to be willing to make adjustments and compromises in the interest of the other. This may mean that one of the partners may have to forego an advancement opportunity if it requires a move, which would disrupt the other's career plans. But it is also possible to opt into professions that have built-in

flexibility; university professors and medical specialists have more flexibility in their career options than branch-bank managers, for example.

• Develop a number of coping mechanisms to help *streamline and simplify* the logistics of the partnership. Shopping for food only once a week can save time and energy for more important things. There may be a need to change priorities attached to particular activities like eating a certain type of meal at a certain time of day. Favorite television programs may of necessity be sacrificed. Both family and individual social calendars might have to be "trimmed." And both partners may chose to forego certain volunteer responsibilities.

• Finally, in order to enhance their careers as well as their marriage, each partner strives to *develop career competencies,* such as self-assessment, collecting occupational information, goal setting, planning and problem-solving. This approach is necessary to facilitate their mutual career advancement.

For Further Reading:

Hall, D.T. *Careers in Organizations.* Santa Monica: Goodyear. 1976.

Hall, F.S. and D.T. Hall. "Dual Careers – How Do Couples and Companies Cope With The Problems?" *Organizational Dynamics.* Vol. 6, 1978: 57-77.

Webber, R.A. "Career Problems of Young Managers." *California Management Review.* Vol. 18, 1976: 19-33.

SITUATIONAL LEADERSHIP
Choosing the Best Pattern That Matches the Circumstances

"Iacocca Pulls Chrysler Into The Future." "Sculley Leads Apple Turnaround." "How Does Bush's Executive Ability Stack Up?" "Lakers Win Due To Magic's Command of the Court." Newspaper headlines highlight leadership roles; management magazines are rife with tips, tactics and techniques having to do with leadership. Strong leadership is obviously critical to an organization's success.

Consider the company as a coordination-and-control mechanism: managers use various rules, policies, job descriptions, authority hierarchies and other devices to ensure that collective effort becomes something more than individuals working as isolated molecules. Good leadership, however, contributes to coordination and control in ways that formal mechanisms cannot. Leadership is alive and flexible – a dynamic part of daily organizational life.

A Situational Perspective
While all of us acknowledge leadership's importance, there is some debate about how best to go about the job of leading. A leader's moods, attitudes, behaviors, and resources change. So do those of his subordinates and superiors. *Situational leadership* theories stress that leaders work in complex settings where rules, players, problems and objectives can change from hour to hour. It's unlikely that any one tactic or style will fit all these changing conditions; and so the credo for situational theories is: *"There is no one best way."* Rather, the "best" way is contingent on the situation.

A Continuum of Style
Leadership can be defined as *the exercise of influence.* Business leaders are concerned with moving various organizational stakeholders (subordinates, peers, superiors, stockholders, government officials, etc.) toward company goals. The *Leadership Continuum* diagram presented here illustrates a variety of ways to do this.

At the extreme left of the chart we

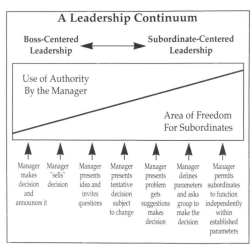

see that the leader can simply make decisions by fiat; at the extreme right, by delegating authority to subordinates; and toward the middle, by engaging in different forms of participative decision making. The diagonal line suggests the fact that leaders infuse their subordinates with the power to act only by relinquishing a portion of their own direct involvement. Note that it is only *direct* involvement that is given up; the leader's *total* influence on the situation may well be enhanced by inviting participation.

The Hersey-Blanchard Approach
Paul Hersey and Kenneth Blanchard have developed a leadership model that further depicts the spectrum of management styles. Their model has been used as a major training device by such *Fortune 500* firms as BankAmerica, Caterpillar, IBM, Mobil Oil and Xerox, and by all of the military services.

Leaders in this model can exhibit one of two basic types of behavior, depending on their objectives: *task-oriented* (emphasis on the technical or production aspects of the job, with goal accomplishment as the main concern), or *relationship-oriented* (emphasis on interpersonal relations).

The two critical situational variables identified in the Hershey-Blanchard Model are:

(1) The *willingness* of subordinates to do the work; a mixture of personal and

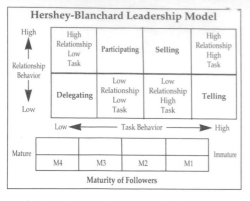

Hershey-Blanchard Leadership Model

High Relationship Low Task	Participating	Selling	High Relationship High Task	
Delegating	Low Relationship Low Task	Low Relationship High Task	Telling	

High ↑ Relationship Behavior ↓ Low

Low ◄──── Task Behavior ────► High

Mature					Immature
	M4	M3	M2	M1	

Maturity of Followers

professional commitment, motivation, drive, ego and fear of failure . . .

(2) The *ability* of subordinates to do the work; a mixture of individual knowledge, skills and aptitudes.

These variables, taken together, produce what the authors call the "Maturity Level" of subordinates.

Why this focus on followers? Because regardless of what the leader does, productivity depends on the actions and attitudes of her followers; it is they who accept or reject the leader and carry her strategies forward.

There are four stages of follower Maturity:

- **M1** people are both *unable and unwilling* to take responsibility for the work. They are neither competent nor confident.

- **M2** people are *unable but willing* to do the work. They are motivated, but currently lack the appropriate skills.

- **M3** people are *able but unwilling* to do what the leader wants.

- **M4** people are both *able and willing* to do what is asked of them.

As the Hersey-Blanchard curve indicates, *leaders should adjust their behavioral style according to the Maturity of their followers*. As subordinates reach higher levels of Maturity, the leader responds not only by decreasing direct control over activities but by decreasing relationship behavior as well. At stage *M1*, followers need clear and specific directions. Many managers lack the time or patience to handle these situations. At *M2*, both high-task and high-relationship behavior is needed. Followers require close supervision of

their work, together with trust and encouragement. An *M3* situation entails motivational challenges that are best solved by supportive, nondirective, participative leadership. Sometimes *M3* followers just need to know that the leader recognizes them, is interested in them and values them as individuals – then they *become* willing. And, finally arriving at this most effective *M4* stage, the leader's direct involvement is considerably reduced because subordinates are both able and willing to take on responsibility.

Leaders and Managers: Is There a Difference?

Obviously, not all leaders are managers; but, are all managers, by virtue of their authority positions, leaders? This question has real implications for both the way managers think of themselves and for their resulting behavior. The fact is that any time a manager makes decisions affecting the work lives of subordinates, he is acting as a leader.

Both the Situational (Hersey-Blanchard) Leadership Model and the Leadership Continuum offer useful guidelines. Truly professional managers are always mindful of the impact their behavior has on others. They know that their effectiveness is critically increased when they can define and manage each situation with the appropriate leadership style.

For Further Reading:

Filley, A.C. and R.J. House, and S. Kerr. *Managerial Process and Organizational Behavior*. Glenview: Scott, Foresman. 1976 (2/e).

Hersey, P. and K. Blanchard. *Management of Organizational Behavior: Utilizing Human Resources*. Englewood Cliffs: Prentice Hall. 1982 (4/e).

Tannenbaum, R. and W.H. Schmidt. "How to Choose a Leadership Pattern." *Harvard Business Review*. March-April, 1958.

LEADERSHIP: A BEHAVIORAL VIEW

Abraham Zaleznik, a respected management theorist from the Harvard Business School, believes that a manager and a leader are two very different people: different in their motivations, personal history, and in the ways they think and act. He suggests that:

• Managers tend to adopt an impersonal, almost passive attitude toward company goals. Leaders, on the other hand, actively embrace them and often inject a touch of personal passion.

• Managers view their work as an enabling process, one that molds people, resources and ideas into a forward-moving whole. Leaders are mostly concerned with ideas and seem predisposed to work from high-risk positions, especially when they sense extraordinary reward and opportunity.

• Managers prefer to work with people from an organizationally-conferred role position; as links in the decision making chain. Leaders relate to people and events in a more intuitive and empathic way, putting their personal stamp on actions. Leaders may be a part of a company, but they'll never be owned by the company.

Zaleznik's voice is one among thousands discussing some aspect of the leadership phenomenon. No area of management science has received more attention than has leadership (although motivation is a close second). Practicing managers recognize that good leadership is absolutely essential to the success of their businesses, as well as to the success of other institutions that shape our lives.

If leadership is so critical, the question is, "What makes a good leader?" It turns out, according to Zaleznik, that the answer is multifaceted. Most authorities currently recognize a number of factors involved, including: (1) The traits associated with leaders; (2) The behaviors they exhibit; (3) The situations in which they find themselves; (4) The attributions of others in close proximity to the leaders; and (5) The substitutes for leadership that exist in modern business organizations.

Leadership Behavior

"Leadership: The ability to influence a group toward the achievement of goals." This definition seems simple and straightforward. But notice that few of us are able to *consistently* and *effectively* move groups of individuals toward objectives that are only

ideas and ideals.

Some argue that the ability to lead stems from the position one holds in an organization. There are many people, however, who have held lofty positions, and yet failed the test of leadership. Conversely, there have been great leaders who have moved masses and mountains without the benefit of an organizational role (Gandhi, for example). Puzzles like this led early researchers to wonder if there was something unique in the way effective leaders behave. Are they more democratic or more autocratic in their interactions with others? What exactly do productive leaders do and say?

Zaleznik points to certain leadership fundamentals that have stood the test of time, both in theory and in practice.

The Early Studies

Beginning in the 1940's, behavioral scientists at Ohio State University and the University of Michigan addressed such questions concerning leadership. The Ohio State researchers studied hundreds of subjects and eventually segregated over a thousand dimensions of leadership behavior into two general categories:

(1) Initiating Structure: The extent to which a leader is likely to define and structure his or her role and those of subordinates.

(2) Consideration: The extent to which a leader is likely to build job relationships characterized by mutual trust, respect for subordinates' ideas, and regard for their feelings.

At about the same time, researchers at the University of Michigan, in their efforts to locate the behavioral characteristics – performance effectiveness – of leaders, came up with two primary "leader types":

(1) Production Oriented Leaders: These individuals tend to focus on the technical or task aspects of the job; their main concern is goal accomplishment, and people are seen as a means to that end.

(2) Employee Oriented Leaders: These emphasize interpersonal relations, take a personal interest in the needs of their subordinates, and accept individual differences among them.

While the Ohio State research indicated that, generally speaking, the most effective leaders were those who achieved "high" Initiating Structure *and* "high" Consideration, the Michigan studies held that higher group productivity was associated with Employee Oriented leadership behaviors. Notice, however, that the categories used by both groups are markedly similar: one emphasizes a "people" dimension, the other one relates to "production" or "task."

The Managerial Grid

Robert Blake and Jane Mouton developed their Managerial Grid on the heels of these early studies. Where before the two dimensions of leadership were conceptualized as being independent, Blake and Mouton placed them at right angles to one another:

9	**1,9**		**9,9**
8	Country Club		Team
	Management		Management
7			
6		**5,5**	
5		Organization-Man	
4		Management	
3			
2	**1,1**		**9,1**
	Impoverished		Authority-
1	Management		Obedience

Concern For People (vertical axis)

1 2 3 4 5 6 7 8 9

Concern For Production

1,9 - Country Club Management: Thoughtful attention is given to the needs of workers. Satisfying relationships lead to a comfortable, friendly environment and work tempo.

9,9 - Team Management: Work is accomplished by committed people. Interdependence, created by workers sharing a "common stake" in the organization, leads to relationships of trust and respect.

5,5 - Organization-Man Management: Adequate organization performance is made possible through balancing the necessity to get work out with the maintenance of employees.

1,1 - Impoverished Management: Exertion of minimum effort to get required work done is appropriate to sustain organization membership.

9,1 - Authority-Obedience Management: Efficiency in operation results from arranging conditions of work in such a way that human elements interfere to a minimal degree.

This grid has nine possible positions along each axis, creating eighty-one possible leadership "styles." The five major positions depicted do not show the actual results obtained, but rather the *dominant elements* in that "style" of leadership. Logically, Blake and Mouton found that the 9,9 style of leadership – *Team Management* – was the most effective.

People, Production, or People-Production

The accumulated evidence from these models is both enlightening and disturbing. On one hand, "Concern for People" and "Concern for Production" orientations seem valid in the steely, cold light of everyday experience; it's easy to look around and find leaders or managers who are skewed one way or the other, and then to catalog resulting achievements, problems and deficiencies in production or morale. It's harder – but possible, in most cases – to think of a manager who seems to exhibit both "people" *and* "production" qualities simultaneously. If you can point to such a person, chances are you'll consider him or her an effective leader: someone who gets the job done while caring about the people who do it.

Interestingly enough, this appealing idea doesn't hold up in all cases or at all times. It does make sense and is a useful general principle, but it fails to take into account the situational factors that complicate the leadership context. Accordingly, subsequent theorists have incorporated situational variables that tend to improve the predictive ability of the People-Production models. But, as always, there's something gained and something lost in such improvements. Increased complexity yields increased scientific precision, but the simple elegance of a potent idea is left by the wayside.

Ponder the People and Production aspects of leadership. If you aspire to a leadership position, what are your *own* predispositions?

For Further Reading:

Bennis, W. *The Unconscious Conspiracy: Why Leaders Can't Learn to Lead.* AMACOM. 1976.

Stogdill, R.M. *Handbook of Leadership.* New York: Free Press. 1974

Yukl, G.A. *Leadership in Organizations.* Englewood Cliffs: Prentice-Hall. 1988.

WHAT DO MANAGERS DO. . .REALLY?

Some Facts and Fallacies

Try this experiment. Walk into a business, find a typical manager, and ask him what he does. The answer will usually connect with what he learned in school: "I plan, organize, direct, coordinate, and control." Then spend a little time watching this manager. Don't be surprised if what you observe doesn't match with what he reported. In fact, a large body of research shows that most managerial jobs have very little to do with these five principles. This is somewhat surprising when you consider that the management vocabulary most of us know was built on the principles of planning, organizing, directing, coordinating and controlling . . . artifacts, really, of the early 1900's. It turns out that these principles are *prescriptive* . . . cloudy tactical objectives that managers have internalized and strive for from day to day. They are not, however, *descriptive* of what really happens on the firing line.

How Should a Manager Manage?

1. **Traditionalists** tell us that good managers are reflective, systematic, rational, and plan-oriented. In fact, study after study has shown that managers, in the real world, work at an *unrelenting pace,* that their work is characterized by *brevity, variety* and *discontinuity,* and that they are predisposed to *action* and disinclined to engage in mere reflective activity.

A study of CEOs found that half of managers' activities lasted less than nine minutes, and only ten percent exceeded one hour. Ninety-three percent of the verbal contacts were of an ad hoc nature, and only 1 out of 368 conversations was unrelated to a specific issue and could be called "general planning." Studies of foremen in the U.S. show that each averages 583 activities per eight-hour shift, or one every 48 seconds. Another study of 160 British middle and top managers found that they worked for more than one-half hour without interruption *only about once every two days.*

2. **Pragmatists** argue that managers should spend more time delegating and less time getting directly involved. Good managers are like good conductors: they orchestrate everything in advance and then monitor the results.

The truth is, however, that managers have a number of regular duties that only they can perform; the manager gets involved only because the work demands it. Presidents of small companies regularly do the type of work that staff specialists do for larger companies, and, when absences occur, they perform the duties of operating personnel as well. They have to – small companies are thinly staffed and require their presence and involvement.

Recent studies of successful field salesmen and CEOs suggest that it's a natural part of their jobs to see important customers (assuming they wish to keep those customers). Retirement parties, Christmas dinners, meetings with government officials, serving on the board of a trade association; these and other duties are a part of a manager's job that he neglects at great peril.

3. **Organizational technicians** inform us that managers need and want all the information the MIS can provide. The vaunted image is that of a manager perched atop a giant organizational pyramid that feeds her all the information needed to manage the enterprise.

But the fact is that, since their introduction in the 1960's, enthusiasm for "total information systems" has waned. They simply don't work. Why? Because they don't fit the way managers actually process information.

Managers have five media at their disposal: documents, the telephone, scheduled meetings, unscheduled meetings, and observational tours. Virtually every study conducted on the matter reports that managers strongly favor verbal media – namely, the telephone and meetings. Henry Mintzberg writes of observing a CEO go through the mail one Saturday morning: "[The CEO processed] 142 pieces of mail in just over three hours, to 'get rid of all the stuff.' This same manager looked at the first piece of 'hard' mail he had received all week, a standard cost report, and put it aside with the comment, 'I never look at this.'"

Information in hard copy – memos, letters, bulletins – simply fails to provide timely, vital information. It loses speed and relevance while traveling over the company's formal communication pathway. Seasoned managers, however, know that the "soft" information they get from gossip, hearsay and the grapevine can be invaluable. Why? Because, while it sometimes has its credibility problems, this type of information has its finger on the pulse of the company's direction.

What Do Managers Do?

Managerial work can be depicted by the following model. (In reality, the ten roles are combined to form a complete managerial job):

Interpersonal Roles
1. Figurehead
2. Leader
3. Liaison

Informational Roles
4. Monitor
5. Spokesman
6. Disseminator

Decisional Roles
7. Entrepreneur
8. Disturbance Handler
9. Resource Allocator
10. Negotiator

Interpersonal Roles

Managers spend a lot of time with people. Three roles under this heading capture most of their activities –

1. *Figurehead:* By virtue of position, every manager performs certain ceremonial duties: the foreman hands out paychecks, the president awards a gold watch, the sales manager dines with an important customer.

2. *Leader:* By virtue of formal authority, every manager is called on to make decisions, to motivate subordinates and to chart direction. Employees want and look for direction: "Is this OK?" "Should we do it this way or that?"

3. *Liaison:* Managers act as an interface between their unit and others on the same organizational level. They also cultivate contacts up and down the chain of command in an effort to create "cognitive buffers" that mitigate surprises and provide politically astute information to themselves and others.

Informational Roles

Information can be thought of as the lifeblood of an organization, and the manager as its heart. Three roles are identified under this heading –

4. *Monitor:* The manager continually scans the environment for information, questions liaison contacts, and obtains unsolicited information from the network of contacts he has built inside the organization. Recall that the manager prefers verbal media, and it is in connection with this role that that preference is most obvious.

5. *Disseminator:* Information does little good until it's properly placed in the organization, and in this role the manager passes his information along, when and where it will do the most good.

6. *Spokesman:* In this role, the manager sends information to people outside his or her unit. A foreman suggests a production line modification to an engineer, a president makes a speech to a community group, etc. The higher a person is in a business' formal chain of command, the more he acts as a spokesman.

Decisional Roles

Information is not an end in itself, but only an input to decision making. Managers encounter four decisional roles –

7. *Entrepreneur:* The entrepreneurial manager stays on the alert for opportunities to improve her work unit, seeks ways to adapt improvements to the company's environment, initiates developmental proposals, and sells her and her team's ideas to top management.

8. *Disturbance Handler:* While the entrepreneurial role is that of an initiator of change, this role depicts the manager as responding to pressures, changes, and shifts in the organization. Action is required to maintain the work unit, and only the manager has the position, information and perspective to act in handling problems as they crop up.

9. *Resource Allocator:* Managers typically have the responsibility of deciding who gets what in an organization, including money, time, privileges, chances at projects, and other benefits.

10. *Negotiator:* Managers spend considerable time in negotiations. These can be between employees, between the company and customers, between departments in the company, with outsiders for new stock issues, and so on. Negotiating becomes an integral part of the manager's job because only he has the authority necessary to commit organizational resources.

Managers have important jobs, ones that are poorly described by the traditional principles of planning, organizing, directing, controlling, and coordinating. The ten roles listed above more accurately describe the work most managers do. Recognizing the true nature of managerial work helps strip away stodgy conceptions to discover the realities of today's administration.

For Further Reading:

Mintzberg, Henry. *The Nature of Managerial Work.* New York: Harper & Row. 1973 (a classic in the field).

Mintzberg, Henry. "The Manager's Job: Folklore and Fact." *Harvard Business Review.* July-August, 1975: 49-61.

Copeman, G.H. *The Role of the Managing Director.* London: Business Publications. 1963.

UNDERSTANDING MANAGERIAL COMMUNICATION

Ask an exasperated employee what's wrong at work and 90 percent of the time the answer is, "Poor communication." But what is poor communication? For that matter, what is good communication? Most managers dismiss the issue as superficial; but, considering that we spend nearly 70 percent of our waking hours communicating, it is a key factor in the problems that confront us at work. Poor, distorted or filtered communication has a clear impact on business. No idea (not even a great one) is useful until it is transmitted and understood by others.

Consider the conceptual model below. Also examine some of the common barriers to effective communication and suggested ways to overcome them that follow.

A Communication Model

Communication is the *transfer of meaning:* the idea you have in mind has to somehow make it into the mind of your listener *with the original meaning relatively intact.* The way this occurs can be thought of as a process or flow of events with six key elements.

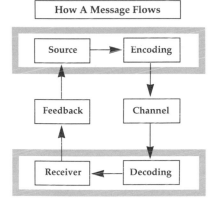

How A Message Flows

Source → Encoding

Feedback ← Channel

Receiver ← Decoding

When expressing a thought (initiating a communication) you act as the *source* and begin the communication cycle. The thought you have can be communicated in multiple ways: by speaking, in writing, through non-verbal signals, in English or Spanish . . . But in one way or another, the mental spark, an "idea," has to be *encoded* into some kind of symbolic form, or else it cannot be received by the world outside one's own mind.

The actual physical product of this encoding is the *message* itself. This message is then sent to the receiver via a *channel*, which in business offices can include such avenues as the formal authority system (memos, presentations, reports), the grapevine, the newsletter, or the after-hours watering hole.

Regardless of how it is transmitted, the message must also be *decoded* by the *receiver* for a transfer of meaning to occur. This means, for example, that in a memo the receiver must understand the language, words, nuances and any "techno-jargon." Note that both the encoding and decoding processes are dependent on the skills, attitudes, knowledge and cultural background of the sender and receiver.

The final link in communication is the feedback loop; a check on how successfully the intended meaning was transmitted and received. Feedback, however, is not always given, nor is it always solicited. So, while the feedback loop represents a type of fail-safe mechanism, it only operates if called into play by the sender or receiver.

In the best of all possible situations the source encodes a message that is sent to a receiver who is able to decode the message and extract all of the intended meaning. Unfortunately, this is rarely the case. Each element in this flow has potential communication barriers, which may lead to a complete break down. If the encoding is done carelessly, the message will leave in a distorted state; if the message contains strange and confusing symbols (a word like "obstreperous," for example), meaning may be lost by the receiver. A message can be distorted by a faulty channel (asking your secretary to tell a subordinate to tell the president that sales are off); or the receiver can infuse a message with values or attitudes that were never intended by the source.

Communication Barriers

There are, in fact, far more opportunities to generate problems than there are ways to send and receive a clear, effective message. Below are four of the most common communication barriers.

1. Filtering: Senders sometimes manipulate information to make it look good to a receiver. If a manager tells the vice president what he thinks she wants to hear about a project, he has filtered the information. This is common in organizational life. John DeLorean writes that while he was at GM he witnessed managers providing information "in such a way that they would get the answer they wanted. I know. I used to be down below and do it." In general, filtering proliferates as the number of organizational levels increases.

2. Selective Perception: Communication is an *interpretive* process. Receivers may selectively admit information based on their needs, motivations, experience, background and other personal characteristics. Receivers may also project their interests and expectations into communications as they decode them. The corporate recruiter who *expects* the female applicant to put family before job might interpret many of her communications in this light, when the reverse may actually be the case.

3. Emotions: Our emotional states and our cognitive systems are inseparable. They interact constantly. How a receiver *feels* at the time of a communication will influence how he or she *interprets* it. The same message, received during times of anger, euphoria, or amusement, will be interpreted distinctly – different emotions color the meaning of the message. Extreme shifts in feelings, one side or the other, produce the greatest distortions and make most of us prone to substitute emotional judgments for rational responses.

4. Language: Different words have different meanings for different people. As S.I. Hayakawa remarks, "The meanings of words are *not* in the words; they are in *us.*" For this reason, apprentice writers should stick to using simple, widely understood words, and refrain from the type of vocabulary associated with philosophers and nuclear physicists. A company's employees generally come from diverse backgrounds, generating shades of meaning for certain words. Large companies may also employ specialists who have their own jargon, some of which is unintelligible to the lay person.

Overcoming the Barriers

Happily, all is not lost. There are some simple ways to improve communication effectiveness. Three of the most useful methods are to:

- **Use Feedback -** Simply checking to see if the message sent was the message received can alleviate many communication problems. Asking, "Did you understand that?" is a good beginning but usually elicits a simple yes or no answer. It is better to ask a brief set of questions to confirm that the message was decoded in detail. If the sender hears back – and clarifies, if necessary – what he or she intended to send, then understanding and accuracy are enhanced.

  (Notice that the receiver can also initiate a feedback cycle: "Here's what I understand so far. . .")

- **Simplify Language -** In virtually every case, communication is enhanced when the sender uses clear, easily understood words and phrases. Avoid jargon, except when communicating with a specialized receiver or group. "Antecedent conditions," "beta weights," and "leverage" are examples of jargon; "ubiquitous," "magnanimous," and "avuncular" are examples of words that may be "scrambled." When in doubt, keep the language simple.

- **Listen Actively -** The most powerful tool at your disposal is to *work at listening. Listening is a skill. It is hard work.* Consider that most of us speak at a rate of about 150 words per minute, but have the capacity to listen at the rate of over 1,000 words per minute. The gap between these two creates "idle brain time" during which many people's minds wander; they think about a piece of unfinished business or impute meaning where none really exists. Active listening is the active search for meaning: the receiver reserves judgment, weighs the words, and places himself or herself in the sender's position. The goal is to receive as much of the original meaning as possible.

Any manager or employee would do well to avoid communication barriers by keeping messages simple and direct, by actively listening, and by inviting feedback from the receiver.

For Further Reading:

There are numerous books and articles on the topic of communication. Three that are especially helpful in the business context are:

Roberts, K. *Communication in Organizations*. Chicago: Science Research Associates. 1984.

Rogers, C. and F.J. Roethlisberger. "Barriers and Gateways to Communication." *Harvard Business Review*. August, 1952: 46-50.

Tompkins, P. "The Functions of Human Communication in Organizations." In C.C. Arnold and J.W. Bowers (Eds.), *Handbook of Rhetorical and Communication Theory*. Boston: Allyn & Bacon. 1984: 659-714.

COMMUNICATION SKILLS FOR MANAGERS

Communication is the common thread that runs through each of the challenges a manager faces every day. A manager is always communicating – sometimes verbally, other times through silence; sometimes through facial expressions or body language, other times with a written letter or memo. Whether a manager's communication is formal or informal, personal or business-like, it should convey and include four elements:

(1) A knowledge of the issues discussed

(2) An attitude of cooperation

(3) Positive and specific statements

(4) A definite purpose (share or seek information, show appreciation, congratulate, request or persuade, offer services, etc.)

Depending on the message sent and the person receiving it, communication can take any of various forms. Some common forms of managerial communication are ranked below, according to the richness of the information transferred. "Richness," in this context, denotes the degree to which the information being transmitted can change understanding within a given period of time.

Communication Media and Information Richness

Richness of Information Transfer

- Face-to-face discussion
- Telephone conversations
- Informal letters & memos (personally addressed)
- Formal written documents (impersonally addressed)
- Formal numeric documents (eg: computer printouts, balance sheets)

HIGH

LOW

According to this graphic, the poorest forms of communication include the statistical and formal written approaches; conversely, the closer a communicator can come to relating personally and informally to the other individual, the better the communication.

The richest communication method, as the chart points out, is a face-to-face discussion, where the entire range of verbal and non-verbal information is available, and where communicators can instantly check the accuracy of the information being transmitted and received. Roughly 75 percent of all managerial time is spent in verbal, one-on-one exchange.

Discussed below are the three major areas that contribute heavily to the quality of oral communication. They are: (1) *Quality of feedback*, (2) *Level of self-disclosure*, and (3) *Listening effectiveness*.

Feedback

Feedback falls into the categories of *supportive* (that which reinforces ongoing behavior) and *corrective* (that which indicates a need for change in behavior). Both types of feedback are beneficial when communicators observe these principles:

1) Ideally, feedback is given in an atmosphere of *mutual trust*. An organizational culture characterized by hostility – high competitiveness, emphasis on the use of power to punish and control subordinates, and rigid boss-employee relationships – lacks the level of trust necessary for effective feedback.

2) Feedback should be *specific* rather than general, using clear and, when possible, recent examples. "You are a dominating person," is not as effective as saying, "Just now, when you were talking to John, you didn't listen to what he said. You decided the matter yourself, with no input from him."

3) Feedback should be given when the receiver seems *ready* to accept it. When a person is angry, upset or defensive, it's probably a poor time to bring up new issues via feedback.

4) Feedback should be *audited* to determine if the receiver agrees with it and accepts its validity. The sender can ask the receiver to rephrase the information and see if it matches what the sender intended.

5) Feedback should be geared to the receiver's *capabilities;* that is, it should focus on issues the receiver can do something about.

6) Feedback should include an *appropriate level of information;* no greater detail or complexity should be offered than the receiver can handle at any one time. Anyone may become threatened and defensive after a shotgun blast of feedback about everything he or she does wrong on the job.

7) All employees, including managers, should be trained to understand the role of feedback. They should be shown that the feedback interchange is

an important psychological and social checking device. It allows us to see ourselves as others see us and adjust our behavior to match intentions and expectations.

Self-Disclosure

Self-disclosure can be defined as any information consciously offered by an individual about himself. It involves the ability to communicate *openly and non-defensively.*

The ability to express oneself to others is considered by most psychologists as the sine qua non of a healthy, growing personality. The reverse also holds: people who cloister their real feelings, who are secretive about their inner selves and motivations, generally feel threatened and stifled by the world. The connection between open communication and emotional well-being has been documented for over 40 years. Self-disclosure, appropriate to the situation, is among the most healthy and powerful of all communication skills.

There are two extremes of self-disclosure to recognize and avoid: the overly disclosing model, and the closed, non-disclosing model. The over-disclosing person is out of place and ineffective in a business organization because he shares feelings and thoughts that are inappropriate to the time and place. Offices are formal settings, and people who treat them otherwise (like a family or as a cause celebre, for example) can make others defensive and can actually curtail effective communication. On the other hand, people who never reach out or fail to share even small shards of their inner selves also prove to be ineffective in the workplace. The key is to offer the right amount of *appropriate* self-disclosure to bolster communication, morale and problem solving, and still maintain a professional attitude. This selective self-disclosure enhances teamwork because it improves camaraderie and stimulates deeper, more meaningful dialogue.

Listening

Possibly the most difficult communication skill to learn, productive listening requires hard work and participation. Active, attentive listening integrates all the physical, emotional and intellectual faculties.

As much as 40% of the workday among office employees is spent listening. Tests of listening comprehension, though, show that most of us only listen at 25% efficiency; 75% of the original message is lost.

There are seven keys to active listening:

1. Good listeners find a *reason or purpose* for listening in each new situation. They search for value and meaning in what is said. Good listeners are *interested.*

2. Good listeners *suspend judgement* on what is being said, at least initially. Listening requires concentration on the message being sent; attention devoted to forming impressions or developing a rebuttal only detracts from this.

3. Good listeners *resist distractions* such as noises, sights and other people, so that they can focus on the sender and the message.

4. *A pause* before responding to the sender often helps the good listener absorb the meaning of a message.

5. When the message is emotional or unclear, a good listener *restates* it in her own words. She paraphrases the meaning she received and directs it back to the sender for validation.

6. Good listeners search for *themes* in communication – the broad, important premise that the sender wishes to convey.

7. A good listener remembers that there is a time differential between his rate of thought (400-500 words per minute) and the sender's rate of speech (100-150 words per minute). He uses this "extra time" to search for meaning.

Most of these suggestions for improving listening skills are interrelated; it's hard to practice one without improving the others.

As always, it is easier to *understand* these principles of effective communication than it is to *develop* them on a skills level. But experience shows that the effort to communicate through giving and receiving feedback, through self-disclosure, and through active listening pays handsome dividends individually and corporately.

For Further Reading:

Baskin, O. and Aronoff, C. *Interpersonal Communication in Organizations.* Santa Monica, CA: Goodyear. 1980.

Huseman, R., Lahiff, J., and Penrose, J. *Business Communication: Strategies and Skills.* New York: Dryden. 1988.

Jablin, F., and Associates. *Handbook of Organizational Communication.* Newbury Park, CA: Sage. 1987.

PSYCHOLOGICAL CONTRACTS

Forces That Bind Managers And Employees

There is an unwritten "contract" existing between employers and employees called the *Psychological Contract* (see the reference to H.G. Baker's *Personnel Bulletin* article which follows). This term refers to the set of expectations found in all organizations; expectations that all managers have of their subordinates, that all employees have of their superiors, and that all co-workers have of their peers. These expectations focus on the behaviors that properly accompany a role, and they can be broad and general (civility in the workplace) or circumscribed and specific (the dress code for a bank teller). Psychological contracts and the impact they have on performance are crucial for the manager to understand.

Roles

When he or she sits down behind a desk at 8:00 A.M., a manager assumes numerous roles, largely defined by the specific organizational structure. A plant manager, for instance, may simultaneously fill the roles of (1) company employee, (2) member of senior management, (3) technical expert in some narrow domain, (4) chair of the executive committee, (5) spokesman to the community, and so on. Away from work, this plant manager again steps into multiple roles (Rotarian, Catholic, tennis player, parent, member of the country club, etc.).

The key that unlocks role behavior lies in understanding that *each of us enacts a given role in a given situation.* When presiding over a budget meeting, the plant manager *should* act in the role of a chairman. If he does not, the incongruities resulting from *expected* versus *actual* behavior usually cause considerable difficulty for others who rely on that role. This, then, begins to get at the meaning of a psychological contract: each member of a company expects other members of that company to act in a way that is *consistent* with their roles . . . or, rather, with the role they *should* be assuming at the moment.

Four important concepts, taken together, help clarify and convey the essence of psychological contracts: (1) Role Identity, (2) Role Perception, (3) Role Expectations, and (4) Role Conflict.

Role Identity

Certain attitudes and behaviors are considered consistent with a given role, and these create *role identity*. For example, one research study showed that when union stewards were promoted to supervisory positions, their attitudes changed from pro-union to pro-management within a few months; but when these promotions were rescinded due to economic problems and the new supervisors were demoted back to the union, they once again adopted pro-union attitudes. This shift from a managerial to a pro-union role identity demonstrates that each of us has the ability to shift our behaviors and attitudes to meet the perceived demands of a given function. We are, quite literally, different people in different contexts.

But what if the role is vague or unclear? How do we act when we have no clue how we should act? Another researcher found that former classmates attending high school reunions five, ten, even twenty years after graduation, unfamiliar with each other in their adult roles, assumed the roles they had held as students: football hero, cheerleader, recluse, scholar, etc. So the second important insight regarding role identity is that, when role requirements are ill-defined or clouded, individuals tend to revert to old and familiar patterns of behavior.

A manager's or a worker's role identity and personality, then, are hardly static. They are an ever-changing composite of past assumptions and experiences as well as present assumptions, relationships and circumstances.

Role Perceptions

Each of us has an idea of how we're supposed to act in a particular circumstance, and this is termed *role perception*. It's important for managers to know that their subordinates (and even their superiors) engage in certain kinds of behavior based on how they *believe* they are supposed to act in a given situation. Think of the first-line foreman who has recently returned from a supervisory training program after being taught that motivation is enhanced when clear, challenging and measurable goals are set. This foreman now has an idea of how she's supposed to deal with her employees, and is likely to behave as prescribed.

One of the primary reasons that apprenticeship programs exist in most trade occupations is to allow the novice to watch an "expert" at work, and thus learn new and better techniques; the same can be said for mentoring programs at higher levels.

Role perceptions, however, are not always accurate. Hence, to improve production and teach correct role perceptions, formal training, informal demonstrations, observation, goal-setting, etc. should be employed on a continual basis.

Role Expectations

While role perceptions are defined in terms of how one believes he or she should act in a given situation, *role expectations* are the converse; they are defined as how *others* believe one should act in a given situation.

The foreman, mentioned above, learned role expectations in the company training program – that is, "Set clear, challenging and measurable goals with your crew." But what happens when role expectations aren't met? The psychological contract is violated, and management is forced to take some sort of stance. If the violation has serious performance implications, the response may be counseling or disciplinary action; but if the violator maintains performance objectives, he or she will either be (1) tolerated and considered odd or unique, or (2) regarded as something of a prodigy who has defined a "new way."

Interestingly enough, employees often react in a similar way when a manager transgresses role expectations. But, because of the constraints put on employees, they usually levy a different, less formal kind of "discipline."

In any case, managers help to smooth out the work flow in their companies when they *communicate clearly* what the specific role expectations are for a job (a task the traditional job description only begins to address), and then consistently *reinforce and reward* proper execution.

Role Conflict

An individual experiences *role conflict* when he or she encounters divergent, incompatible, or inconsistent role expectations. Role conflict can result when compliance in one capacity makes it more difficult to comply with another, as when a team leader who is expected to act as a co-worker or mentor has to deliver a performance evaluation. He struggles to be buddy and boss both at the same time. Both roles may be expected as part of the job, yet one tends to conflict with the other.

An extreme case of conflict occurs when two or more role expectations are mutually exclusive, leaving the individual in a classic double-bind. Recall the plant manager described earlier; his role as a husband and father requires stability and time at home, while his position as an executive requires travel, late-night meetings and 80-hour work weeks. In such cases the manager is left with making a choice between one or the other expectation, or, in some cases, compromising both.

The issue of business ethics also illustrates this point. One study (see P.S. Goodman's book referred to below) uncovered the fact that 57 percent of Harvard Business Review readers had faced the dilemma of choosing between profits for their firm and following ethical business practices.

Managers should seek to develop a "feel" for the psychological contracts – both implied and formally stated – that exist in their organizations. They should also recognize that their employees, in genuine attempts to define their niches in the company, will actively search for and try to fill organizational roles.

Understanding the dynamics of Role Identity, Role Perception, Role Expectations and Role Conflicts enhances the manager's ability to develop lasting, effective and clearly defined expectations and working relationships.

For Further Reading:

Baker, H.G. "The Unwritten Contract: Job Perceptions." *Personnel Bulletin.* July, 1985, pp. 37-41.

Goodman, P.S. *Designing Effective Work Groups.* San Fransisco: Jossey-Bass. 1986.

Schein, E. *Organizational Psychology.* Englewood Cliffs: Prentice Hall. 1980.

EMPLOYEE RECRUITMENT AND SELECTION

I failed to get this job I wanted because I answered one of the questions on the application wrong. The question asked, "Do you advocate the overthrow of the United States Government by revolution or violence?" I chose violence!

-Dick Cavett

Dick Cavett here is poking fun at yet another one of his supposed shortcomings; but employee recruitment and selection is serious business, more important to organizational survival than many managers once realized. With the growing need for corporate competence to meet the pressures of competition, many companies are now taking a harder look at whom they recruit and how they make their selections.

The Recruiting Process

The steps in a typical recruiting approach are identified in the figure below. Ideally, the company already has an ongoing human-resource program that ties in with the company's overall business and strategic planning process.

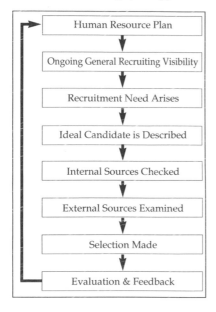

Waste and error in employee selection often result from scurrying around to fill "surprise" openings. Maintaining a company's visibility through a recruitment program – even during periods of reduced hiring – has definite benefits.

Line managers are often the triggers in the hiring process. Managers should work closely with knowledgeable human-resource personnel to list specific *desired qualifications* for the job. Next, it is usually advantageous to search inside the company for available candidates to transfer or promote into the position. If none are found,

talented individuals can be recruited from a number of external sources: college campuses, temporary agencies, search firms, trade and other media, and so on.

Ongoing recruitment and episodic hiring are each represented as varying by *time* and *place* in the following graphic, with examples given in each quadrant:

		PLACE	
		External	Internal
TIME	Episodic	Management, Development & Succession Programs	Campus Recruiting
	Continuous	Job Posting	Search Firms

Selection: The Attraction→Retention → Attrition Cycle

Think of recruitment and selection in terms of three concepts: attraction, retention and attrition. People are not randomly assigned by lottery to work for certain companies. In most cases they're attracted to a particular firm, apply for entry, are selected or rejected, and then either stay or leave. Also, different organizations select and retain different kinds of people. This attraction - selection / retention - attrition cycle leads to a natural but powerful tendency: over time, most companies become more and more homogenous; people who don't "fit in," leave, and those who do, remain and gain influence.

Recruiters and decision makers should keep this "homogeneity" in mind, because it has both positive and negative effects. On one hand, the company may become crippled by too much of the same kind of talent, the same kind of thinking, the same tired visions for the future. On the other hand, "dissidents" and "misfits" can sap a considerable amount of managerial energy as the company tries to cope with ideas and behaviors that are too atypical to be integrated. A balance has to be struck so that a "loyal and constructive cacophony" is heard around the conference table – both rebellion and similitude are avoided.

Tools Used in Hiring

Without a doubt, the most revered and frequently used employee-selection device is the personal interview or series of interviews. There is something about a face-to-face visit that appeals to our human nature. But as the following chart illustrates, research evidence points to better means for predicting job fit, tenure and productivity. (The higher the correlation number, the better the prediction.):

Predictor	Average Validity
Cognitive Ability Tests	.53
(What is the interviewee's	
learning ability and adaptability?)	
Job Tryout	.44
(What can he actually do?)	
Biographical Inventory	.37
(What is his experience?)	
Reference Checks	.26
GPA	.21
Experience	.18
Interview	.14
Ratings of Training & Experience	.13
Amount of Education	.10
Interest Level	.10

You may be surprised by this list. Notice that the amount of *Education* ties for last place, *Interviewing* is just .04 ahead, and a candidate's high school or college GPA doesn't fare much better in predicting a person's ability and job fit. *References* always have a built-in bias: who would ever think of listing their critics or enemies as references? *Resumes,* interestingly, are notoriously unreliable: one VP of a major corporation estimates that 20% of all resumes contain at least one "factual misstatement," and a firm that checks academic records for companies indicates that 30 to 40 percent of all people simply lie about themselves.

Interviewing

Even though the interviewing process may look inferior on paper, those who do the hiring wouldn't sleep at night without holding interviews. To help these talks be more valuable, here are a few well-documented cognitive biases that affect interviews and the decisions made from them.

1. The Illusion of Completeness: Decision-makers often perceive an information set to be complete, even in the absence of important facts. Short of time and energy, managers typically collect just enough information on candidates to make a decision – one often based on guesswork.

2. Arbitrary Standards: A manager will tend to fill in the gaps of his knowledge about a person by using information from his own past experience with people, places, events, etc. Subjective biases – factors that only "seem" to apply to the individual or issue, but are actually deep-rooted preferences found in the interviewer – creep in. Thus, a large, heavy woman may not be hired as a cosmetics salesperson because high fashion sales representatives are typically slim.

3. Overconfidence: Managers are often more confident in their own judgment than they should be. For example, research shows that a recruiter may make snap judgments about the quality of a candidate in the first four minutes of an interview! She may "triangulate" her considerable historical and current experience to arrive at

a "feel" or "sense" for the individual before her – and form a judgement that is incorrect.

4. Confirmatory Bias: All of us operate using our own distinct models and theories about the world. We tend to retain in memory information that supports our personal hypotheses and to criticize and cast away information with which we disagree.

Consider the previous example – the interview that is essentially over in the first four minutes. The remainder of such an interview is usually spent collecting only those facts that will confirm and support the interviewer's initial judgement; and, in her mind, her early views of the candidate are validated.

5. The Law of Small Numbers: Managers sometimes ignore the implications of sample size, attributing greater stability to results obtained from small samples than is warranted. In other words, most managers are poor statisticians.

Suppose a job-seeker is interviewed by you and by five other members of your staff. All the interviews go well except yours, which is a disaster for the candidate. What information will weigh most heavily in your decision? The experience in your own interview, or the favorable reports from the five others?

6. Either-Or Questions: Some types of questions produce more meaningful and revelatory answers than others. Open-ended questions – ones that can't be answered with a "yes" or a "no" – are helpful. Who, what, when, why, how, tell me, which . . . are all good ways to begin questions that will help draw out a candidate's true experience and knowledge. Also, queries that invite problem-solving and clarifications of job or craft descriptions can function as informal "tests" or "tryouts," which, according to the earlier research chart, are the two top job-performance predictors.

By carefully considering what type of on-the-job experience, education, abilities, and personality that you want in a new employee, and using selection devices that are most valuable in helping you to objectively "see" how he or she will fit in your job opening, a more accurate decision can be made.

For Further Reading:

Arvey, R. and J. Campion. "The Employment Interview: A Summary of Recent Research." *Personnel Psychology.* Vol. 35, 1982: 281-322.

Levesque, J. "Selecting and Managing Competent Managers." *Personnel Administrator.* March, 1985: 63-72.

Schuler, R., et al (EDs.), *Personnel and Human Resource Management.* New York: West. 1988: 193-205.

EMPLOYEE AND MANAGEMENT RIGHTS

Notes on Whistle-blowing, Drug Testing and Other Controversies

The Constitution and the Bill of Rights provide every American with what most of us consider the fundamental human rights: free speech, due process, and protection from "the tyranny of the majority." But such rights do not necessarily apply in the workplace. In fact, it is not the Constitution but a collection of federal, state and local statutes, along with specific labor-management contracts, that grant employees rights – such as due process – at work. Without such laws in place, the right of management to run its business as it sees fit has often overridden any employee rights.

New laws have changed so many traditional management prerogatives – in areas like safety, sexual harassment, and equal opportunity, for example – that considerable confusion now surrounds the issues. This article discusses some of the larger fields of concern in the unfolding and unresolved arena of employee and management rights.

Rights Defined

A "right" is a power which *belongs to a person by virtue of law, nature or tradition.* Some scholars separate moral and legal rights for clarity; a right in one category may or may not have the same standing in the other. Some employee rights apply both on and off the job; free speech and health and safety are two examples. Others apply only at work or only outside of the workplace, such as the right to smoke at home but not in the office. Additionally, there is a distinction between a "right" and a "privilege," the latter being implied or offered within the employment contract.

Following are some important rights affecting persons and companies:

1. *Employment at Will* (EAW) is a common-law doctrine giving employers the right to hire, fire, demote and promote whomever they wish, unless there is some covenant to the contrary. EAW is usually advanced by defenders of the free ownership of *private* enterprise. It is, however, an artifact of the industrial revolution. Although many states are enacting restraints on it, the doctrine still enjoys considerable exercise in daily commerce.

Our legal system has recognized three rationales for testing the principle of Employment at Will: (1) Actions against public policy (an employee is fired for refusing to conduct industrial espionage); (2) Actions rebutting the implied employment contract; and (3) Employer actions that fail to demonstrate good faith and fair dealing.

2. *Implied Contracts* can exist between employer and employee without any kind of written stipulation. An oral promise or agreement, sometimes even a history of actions, can qualify as an implied contract. The key elements are actions or words that establish employee *expectations*, which then become the basis for the employees' *actions*. Several courts have held, for example, that if an employer hires a person for an indefinite period or promises job security, the employer has lost the right to terminate at will.

Employee handbooks can also become the basis for an implied contract, and most Human Resource executives have their documents reviewed by legal experts to safeguard against unwarranted expectations.

3. *Due Process* is guaranteed by the Constitution and is generally spelled out in fine detail by collective bargaining agreements. But at-will employees have greater variability in the protections and procedures afforded them. They do have the right to due process; however, employees must be given the opportunity to present their side of the story during disciplinary hearings.

4. *Dismissal for Just Cause* is also specified in union contracts, but is often unclear in an at-will situation. Proving just cause depends on one or more of the following elements: (1) If warnings were given to the employee; (2) If the company's rule was reasonable; (3) If management investigated before applying discipline; (4) If the investigation was fair and reasonable; (5) If there was evidence of guilt; (6) If the rules and discipline were applied in an even-handed fashion; and (7) If the penalty was reasonable, given the offense.

There have also been cases where employers made the work situation so intolerable that the employee was "forced" to resign. Such cases are referred to as Constructive Discharge and can be treated as a dismissal by the courts.

5. Employees have *Rights to Records*, or,

the right of access to their personnel files. Specifically, they have: (1) The right of access to personal information; (2) The opportunity to respond to unfavorable information; (3) The right to correct erroneous information; (4) The right to be notified when information is given to a third party; (5) The right to know how information is being used internally; (6) The right to reasonable precautions by the employer so that personal information is safeguarded.

6. *Substance Abuse and Drug Testing* are two controversial areas of current employment law. An employer cannot discriminate against an employee because of alcohol or drug dependency if, after reasonable accommodations for this handicap, he or she can do the job. But blood tests, polygraph tests and urinalysis can and are being required of employees. Unless otherwise prohibited by state laws, employers have the right to require such tests of each and every employee.

The two main arguments against drug testing are that they violate employees' rights to privacy and that they are unreliable. To the first objection it must be noted that employers are not constrained by federal statutes regulating search and seizure (which apply only to governmental agents), and are not bound by the criminal standard of "beyond a reasonable doubt." Searches and testing *are* legal. However, research has shown that drug tests can be notoriously unreliable. The Center for Disease Control found in its ten-year study, that virtually every laboratory conducting drug tests had unacceptably high error rates. This and other complications raise the troubling prospect of a high rate of false accusations.

7. *Polygraph Tests* were dubbed "twentieth century witchcraft" by Senator Sam Ervin. But 20 percent of this country's major organizations and 50 percent of all retail establishments use polygraph tests even though studies show that such tests yield erroneous results about 33 percent of the time. The Office of Technology Assessment has determined that the validity of the polygraph can not be determined, and the American Psychological Association has confirmed that an unacceptable number of "false positives" occur. For these reasons there are few courts that will admit polygraph data as evidence.

Many objections to the polygraph test are aimed at its use in screening applicants for jobs. Because of the previously noted problems, 36 states have enacted laws regulating the use of these tests for employment purposes, and several bills have been introduced in Congress to eliminate them completely.

8. *Whistle-Blowers* are persons who report a real or perceived wrong done by an employer. The two key issues in the debate on whistle-blowing are:

(1) Do employees have the right to speak out with protection from retribution?

(2) When should employees violate the confidentiality of their jobs?

Many regard whistle-blowing as an important right in that it can shield fellow workers or the general public from employer misdeeds. But, because civil service systems have regulations protecting the whistle-blower, studies show that private sector whistle-blowers are more likely to lose their jobs than their public sector counterparts. The penalties levied against private sector employees by their employers, can be severe – especially if the whistle-blower goes outside of his organization with the information.

One of the few research studies on whistle-blowing gathered nearly 8,000 surveys from federal employees and concluded that parent organizations often lashed out at "stool pigeons," subjecting them to various formal and informal pressures to get back in line. If this represents the general situation, the idea that organizations should encourage valid whistle-blowing may be difficult to implement.

Worker rights may differ from state to state and company to company. Being informed of your rights can lead to greater security and personal confidence in your work.

For Further Reading:

Geldt, T. "Drug and Alcohol Abuse in the Workplace: Balancing Employer and Employee Rights." *Employee Relations Law Journal.* Vol. 11, 1986.

Gibson, M. *Workers' Rights.* New York: Rowman and Allenheld. 1983.

Werhane, P. Persons, *Rights and Corporations.* Englewood Cliffs: Prentice-Hall. 1985.

INCENTIVES FOR PRODUCTIVITY

Lincoln Electric is a ninety-year-old company that may be shedding some light on the future. In 1907, the company started using an incentive compensation program with its employees – most of them production line workers who turn out the company's mainstays, arc welding equipment and induction motors. The program's components are unique and effective:

1. Most workers are paid on a piece-rate basis, which means that there is no guaranteed base pay: if a worker is sick for a day, he or she takes home 4 days pay for the week.

2. Workers must repair defective machines on their own time.

3. Employees with over two years of service are guaranteed at least 30 hours of work each week.

4. Overtime is mandatory when orders are backed up.

5. Bonuses are given for teamwork, reliability, and productivity-enhancing suggestions.

At the heart of this management system is a framework that encourages *self-motivation*. Seniority carries little weight, and all employees compete on a merit basis for the few jobs that are not paid on a piece-rate basis. Interestingly, Lincoln's workers have averaged as much as $45,000 per capita earnings a year; further, they own over seventy percent of the company's stock. Turnover has averaged a low six percent per year, and the company hasn't had a layoff since 1951.

On the down-side, some Lincoln employees (and former employees) report that the working environment can be intensely competitive.

Incentives

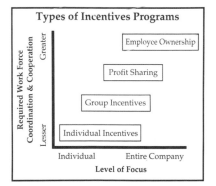

Types of Incentives Programs

Required Work Force Coordination & Cooperation
(Greater / Lesser)

- Employee Ownership
- Profit Sharing
- Group Incentives
- Individual Incentives

Individual — Entire Company
Level of Focus

The main purpose of incentives is to match pay with performance. While incentives can be complex and take many forms, the preceding chart presents four main classes of incentive programs: (1) Individual-based approaches; (2) Group-based approaches; (3) Profit sharing; and (4) Employee ownership. Most of these programs will be discussed here, but first consider some general principles that should be followed in establishing and maintaining any incentive system:

1. *A Linkage With Performance:* All incentive programs should tie pay as closely as possible to desired performance. Employees must see a direct relationship between their efforts and their rewards.

2. *Recognition of Individual Differences:* People are not all alike, and different people will value different rewards. A variety of appealing incentive programs may have to be developed.

3. *Recognition of Organizational Factors:* Incentives have to "fit" the structure, strategy, culture and financial resources of the organization. It is inconsistent, for example, to install a program that requires a high degree of employee participation into a tightly controlled bureaucracy.

4. *Continuous Monitoring:* Conditions in organizations change, and incentives need to be adjusted accordingly. New technology on the production line, for instance, may make a previously satisfactory system outmoded overnight. Programs should also be reviewed on a regular basis to ensure they are performing as planned.

Incentives For Individuals

The most basic individual-level incentive is the **piece-rate** system, in which wages are determined by multiplying the number of units produced by the piece-rate for a single unit. A variant of this, the **differential piece-rate** system, builds on the concept by paying employees one piece-rate wage if they produce less than a standard output, and a higher piece-rate wage if they produce more than the standard. The object in this latter case is to encourage workers to produce up to and beyond a pre-set output standard.

Despite their simplicity and incentive value, piece-rate systems are difficult to use in many cases, because the output standards for some jobs are difficult and costly to determine, or because the employee has no control over the number of units produced. For example, paying a bank teller for transactions processed would be inappropriate since the employee has little control over customer traffic.

Commissions are computed as a percentage of sales in units or dollars. There are two common computation methods: (1) *Straight commissions*, where the employee receives a percentage of the sales made; and (2) *Salary-plus-commissions*, which offer the employee both the stability of a salary and the incentive value of a commission (a common split being 80% salary, 20% commissions for the total compensation package). A national survey reports that about 21% of all sales representatives are paid through commissions only, while over 50% are on a salary-plus-commissions system.

Bonuses are frequently used as incentives at the executive level, although they can be used at lower levels too. Bonuses are organizationally attractive because they provide additional employee income when profits are up, and defer this expense when times are hard. Because of the broad nature of executive-level duties, most traditional bonus systems tie monetary or other rewards to overall corporate or divisional performance. But the same concept can easily apply to smaller groups – or to a total workforce.

Group Incentives

Incentives for groups are a direct result of the growing number of complex jobs requiring *interdependent* effort. Small-group incentive plans can encourage teamwork and enhance overall productivity where interdependence is required. The mechanics of group incentives are similar to those of individual-based plans – piece-rate, commission, and bonus systems. But when considering this approach, two conditions should be considered: (1) Do the tasks require significant *coordination?* and (2) Is the *group size* small?

If the answer to both questions is "yes," then a group incentive system may be appropriate; otherwise, use an individual or organization-based strategy. Most experts agree that group size should be kept under ten for best results from a group incentive plan. And, again, a pattern of interlocking, interdependent tasks is crucial.

Organizational Incentives

Organization-wide incentive systems compensate all employees based on how well the organization, as a whole, performs during a given period. One year at Kodak, for example, 93,000 employees shared $254.3 million in "wage dividends." Individual amounts were determined in part by seniority; the average check was $2,730.

Generally, such plans are most effective when all employees – exempt and non-exempt – are included. Some of the more significant organizational programs are described below.

Improshare (Improved Productivity Through Sharing) is similar to a piece-rate plan, except that it *rewards all company employees*. Input is measured in hours, output in physical units, and bonuses are distributed weekly when a discretionary standard is exceeded.

The Scanlon Plan rests on the premise that *efficiency depends on teamwork and plant-wide cooperation*. It offers two main features: (1) A setup of interdepartmental committees to hear and review cost-saving suggestions, and a separate screening committee which evaluates suggestions presented; (2) A direct incentive for all employees to improve efficiency. Incentive rewards are paid to employees based on pre-established ratios. Common ratios that are used include "labor costs to total sales," "total production," and "total hours to total production." Savings due to differences between *actual* and *expected* ratios are split between employees and the organization.

Profit sharing, as its name implies, distributes a *percentage* of the organization's profits *to employees*. Southland Corp., the holding company of 7-Eleven, shares 10% of its pre-tax profits with 50,000 employees at 7,000 store locations. Such programs foster within employees both cost- and profit-consciousness.

Linking an employee's earnings to his performance is paramount to improving that performance, and to cultivating overall productivity.

For Further Reading:

Dierks, W. and K. McNally. "Incentives You Can Bank On." *Personnel Administrator.* March, 1987.

Globerson, S. *Performance Criteria and Incentive Systems.* Amsterdam: Elsevier. 1985.

Robbins, Cheryl. "Designing Effective Incentive Systems." *Personnel Administrator.* May, 1983.

THE PERFORMANCE APPRAISAL PROCESS

A division of *Xerox* (the *Reprographic Business Group*, which makes copiers) had used performance appraisals for over 20 years. The system was typical of others around the country, using numbers to rate performance, but it had its problems: 95% of the ratings were 3's or 4's on a five-point scale, and merit increases were usually within one or two percent of each other. Xerox listened to its managers and did something. An employee task force designed a new program with:

(1) Six-month progress reviews
(2) Goal setting
(3) Year-end written appraisals
(4) No numerical ratings
(5) Merit increases separated from appraisal by two months
(6) Focus on coaching and development
(7) Extensive training.

The results were dramatic. Within a year, 81% of those surveyed felt they better understood what objectives their work was supposed to accomplish, 84% felt their appraisals were fair, 70% met their work objectives, and 72% said they understood how merit pay was determined.

A Look At Performance Appraisal

Performance appraisal is easy to define. It involves nothing more than *determining how well employees do their jobs* compared to a set of standards, and then *communicating that information* to employees.

Appraisal systems are in wide use today, for both white- and blue-collar employees (88% of white-collar and 63% of blue-collar organizations use some kind of performance appraisal system). The reasons are simple: effective performance appraisal systems contribute to a company's competitive position; they help to solve problems, improve morale, and ensure that important tasks get the main focus; and they contribute to the bottom line. Additionally, sophisticated appraisal systems help to groom the company's braintrust, ensuring a steady stream of the *right people* in the *right jobs* at the *right time*.

There are many ways to configure an appraisal system and many methods for structuring the form of the appraisal itself. This chart illustrates some of the options:

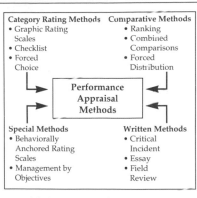

Category Rating Methods	Comparative Methods
• Graphic Rating Scales	• Ranking
• Checklist	• Combined Comparisons
• Forced Choice	• Forced Distribution

Performance Appraisal Methods

Special Methods	Written Methods
• Behaviorally Anchored Rating Scales	• Critical Incident
• Management by Objectives	• Essay
	• Field Review

(1) *Category* methods are the simplest; they usually require the manager only to mark an employee's level of performance on a specific form.

(2) *Comparative* methods demand that the manager directly compare the performance of one employee against another's.

(3) *Written* methods ask for documentary and descriptive information on each employee.

(4) Two *"special" systems* that have met with widespread acceptance are BARs, which examines specific employee behaviors, and MBO, which focuses on mutually set goals and objectives.

Common Problems and Errors

There are many sources of potential rating errors in any appraisal system. Some of the better documented ones are listed below:

1. Varying Standards: The manager should strive to keep standards and expectations consistent for all employees' appraisals. Consistency is always difficult, but especially so when ambiguous criteria or subjective weightings are used. And even when standards and criteria are held constant, an employee may not perceive this to be the case – *and it is the employee's perceptions that count*. To be most helpful, the rater must not only use the same standards and weights across employees, but be able to *defend and explain each appraisal* on the basis of fairness.

2. The Recency Problem: Remembering issues and performances that are six or nine months old is difficult; it's much easier to recall incidents that occurred in the last month. But some employees will take advantage of this human foible by "coasting" for months, then delivering exemplary work for a week or two before their appraisal dates. One way of minimizing this practice is through careful and consistent *documentation* of critical incidents and events on the job.

3. Rater Bias: It is not uncommon to see a rater's values, biases and prejudices creeping into an appraisal. This problem can be especially harmful if the appraiser *remains* blind to his own biases. Age, race, religion, personal habits, lifestyle, gender, appearance, and other attributes can easily cloud an otherwise objective assessment of job performance. Carefully designed appraisal methods can cut back on rater bias, as can a review of ratings by a management level person just above the rank of the actual appraiser.

4. Rater Patterns: Different raters will interpret even the best designed appraisal forms and methods differently. One appraiser may conscientiously rank employees on a curve, for example, with the majority rated "average," or somewhere in the 50% range; while another interviewer, accentuating the positive, may consistently rate her employees in the 75% range, or as "above average." Consequently, employee A may be rated as "excellent" by one manager, and only "average" by another. Making the rater aware of his or her response patterns is one way of dealing with this problem. Another involves the explicit definition of performance categories in the rating scale itself.

5. Halo Effect: Some managers will rate an employee high or low on all items because of one characteristic. If employee A is consistently tardy, this may become the *overriding image* carried in the manager's head, affecting all other dimensions of the appraisal. Enhancing managerial self-awareness and training in the effective use of an appraisal instrument are the two most valuable means of combating this obstacle to meaningful appraisals.

The Appraisal Interview

Appraisal sessions usually present both an opportunity and an obstacle: the manager has the chance to impart career-advancing and developmental feedback, but the interview itself is often highly charged with emotion. Below are some useful hints for conducting an interview:

- Prepare in advance.
- Focus on future performance and development.
- Don't do all the talking.
- Be specific about reasons for ratings.
- Decide on specific improvement measures.
- Consider your role in the subordinate's performance.
- Allow the employee to disagree on certain points.
- Reinforce and reward the behaviors you want.

Of major concern should be to emphasize the positive aspects of an employee's work performance, while still addressing those ways in which she can improve. This type of "constructive criticism" can be difficult for both parties to handle.

Like their employees, most managers are concerned about the fairness, consistency and usefulness of appraisals. Many managers conducting an appraisal feel as though they're being put in the unwanted position of playing *"God"* with the employee's career, but also see the need to coach, counsel and encourage professional development. This Catch-22 can lead to inconsistency or indecisiveness shown by the manager.

A common reaction to appraisals among employees is to view them as *"zero-sum" games*, where there must be winners and losers. ("In order for me to get high ratings, someone else has to get low ratings.") But, in fact, appraisals don't have to be zero-sum. If the manager frames each interview as a developmental and self-improvement exercise *conducted for the employee's benefit*, everyone can win.

There are a number of other technical and theoretical elements of effective performance appraisals. But by keeping squarely in mind the important objectives of any assessment system, and the tools and attitudes for conducting a helpful interview, managers will greatly multiply their chances of making such a review a successful experience for both themselves and their appraisees.

For Further Reading:

Bernarden, H. and R. Beatty. *Performance Appraisal*. Boston: Kent Publishing. 1984.

Henderson, R. *Practical Guide to Performance Appraisal*. Reston, VA: Reston Publishing. 1986.

Verespes, M. "Performance Appraisals." *Industry Week*. February 23, 1987.

THE ART OF GROUP DECISION-MAKING

A Guide For The Manager

Many organizations foster group decision-making, even at top levels, to meet varied challenges. *J.C. Penney*, for example, deliberately uses group decision-making at the upper reaches of its organization. A committee of fourteen top managers debates issues such as planning, managerial selection, merchandising, and public relations...and reaches effective decisions. *Penney's* management believes that this mechanism has successfully met some very tough, entrenched challenges, like allocating costs among divisions, determining merchandising mix and corporate staff compensation, expediting the use of computers, and improving overall profits.

Arguments For and Against Groups

The alluring thing about groups is that they can achieve *synergy*, to make 2 + 2 = 5. Unfortunately, if managed poorly, they can also make 2 + 2 = 3. Managers can help groups work synergistically through the applications of specific techniques. Over fifty years of research has been devoted to identifying and refining these techniques, and considerable knowledge now exists on how they work in group situations. Here, we will touch on three of the most celebrated methods for increasing the effectiveness of groups in making business decisions.

To begin with, there are both advantages and disadvantages in using groups for decision-making.

Advantages

(1) *Input.* Groups bring more complete information and knowledge to a decision-making situation than any of the individuals separately. Generally speaking, two heads *are* better than one – and three heads are better than two.

(2) *Diversity.* Groups usually guarantee a diversity of views. In addition to providing more raw input, this element of heterogeneity usually stimulates the formation of more approaches and alternatives among individual group members.

(3) *Acceptance.* A group decision is more likely to achieve acceptance than one made by an individual. A technically excellent decision may well fall flat when key players instrumental to its implementation are not involved in its development. Group decisions may take longer to make, but they are often carried through more effectively and enthusiastically than hand-me-down orders from "on high."

Disadvantages

(1) *Time.* It takes time to assemble a group, and the best-running groups are usually those that have spent months and years finding ways for the personalities to work most cogently together. But even the most seasoned groups can be very inefficient users of time when compared to a single executive. Quick, decisive action in the face of crisis is seldom the hallmark of group decision-makers.

(2) *Pressures toward conformity.* There are strong social pressures in groups. People have a desire to be accepted, to appear competent, to be seen as team players. Groups, working with the best of intentions, and with the purpose of eliminating conflict, can bring strong normative pressures to bear on dissenters. Most groups encourage conformity among viewpoints.

(3) *Domination.* Groups are composed of personalities who not only contribute different information and view points, but who take on different group roles. Frequently one or more of these personalities will assume leadership and dominate group discussion. If the dominant individual or cohort is of less than stellar ability, the group's overall effectiveness is likely to suffer.

These advantages and disadvantages will weigh differently against each other in different situations, but the fact remains that decisions made by groups tend to be more accurate and creative than those made by individuals. The trick lies in managing the group decision-making process to produce superior results and override potential hurdles.

Group Decision Techniques

The following techniques are time-tested, proven paths to coming up with creative and dynamic group decisions.

1- Brainstorming. Brainstorming is a technique designed to overcome the adverse pressures toward conformity or "group-think," to generate creative solutions. It does this by focusing on *ideation* (idea-generation) among group members, with the understanding that any evaluation or criticism of ideas will be initially withheld.

In a typical brainstorming meeting

the group members sit around a table and the leader states the problem or issue in clear, simple terms. The members then "free wheel" as many alternative solutions as they can for a given period of time. No criticism or evaluation is allowed – something that takes practice for most groups. The members are encouraged to let one idea feed another, and usually some truly ingenious proposals result. These are recorded in one form or another for later analysis and discussion. Many of the benefits of brainstorming can be transferred to more formal groups by simply asking people to refrain from criticizing ideas until later in the meeting.

The strength of brainstorming lies in the free generation of ideas it encourages. The refining process that leads to an actual decision, is the focus of the next two techniques.

2- Nominal Group Technique. The Nominal Group Technique restricts interpersonal communication during the decision-making process. Group members are all physically present, but they operate independently and fairly autonomously. First, the group convenes and the problem or issue is stated clearly and simply. Then:

a) Before discussion begins, each person writes down his or her ideas relating to the problem.

b) After this period of private ideation, each member in turn presents one of his ideas to the group until all original ideas are exhausted. All contributions are recorded in a master list (often on flip charts or a chalkboard).

c) The group discusses the list of ideas, with a focus on clarifying each contribution, and evaluates them. The list is trimmed of untenable ideas.

d) Each member, silently and independently, rank-orders the consolidated list.

e) The final decision can be determined by selecting the alternative with the highest aggregated ranking. Many groups also find that the top three or four solutions have attractive features which can be fitted or blended into the overall decision.

The main advantage of the Nominal Group Technique is that it allows the group to operate in a formal manner, but doesn't restrict independent thinking or force conformity.

3- Delphi Technique. This is similar to the Nominal Group Technique, but is more complex, more time-consuming, and does not require the physical presence of the participants. (In fact, it actually prohibits face-to-face interaction.) Again, the process starts with a clear and simple statement of the problem. Then:

a) Members are asked to provide potential solutions through a series of carefully designed questionnaires.

b) Each member anonymously and independently completes the first questionnaire, making sure it reflects her best thinking.

c) The results of this questionnaire are compiled by the administrator, and copies of the amassed results are sent back to each participant.

d) The members each review the results independently, and are then asked to generate fresh solutions or ideas based on their new knowledge. Changes from earlier positions are generally observed at this stage, since participants have the benefit of their colleagues' accumulated best thinking.

e) Steps (c) and (d) are repeated as many times as necessary until consensus – or its acceptable approximation – is achieved.

The Delphi Technique, though time-consuming, insulates group members from the undue influence of others and tries to build on the last, best ideas offered. Since it does not require the physical presence of the participants, it is often used to acquire best thinking of experts from outside the area, or to accumulate expertise and solve problems in a geographically dispersed company. In contrast to Brainstorming, it has a funneling effect on the alternatives generated.

Groups can serve as a varied, purposeful resource for better, more supportable ideas and decisions. The advantages of using groups usually outweigh the disadvantages when you are willing and able to take the time and effort to involve others in your work.

For Further Reading:

Guzzo, R.A. "Group Decision Making and Group Effectiveness in Organizations." In P.S. Goodman & Associates. *Designing Effective Work Groups.* San Francisco: Jossey-Bas, 1986: 34-71.

Roberts, K.H. *Communication in Organizations.* Chicago: Science Research Associates. 1984.

Schweiger, D.M., et al. "Group Approaches for Improving Strategic Decision Making: A Comparative Analysis of Dialectical Inquiry, Devil's Advocacy, and Consensus." *Academy of Management Journal.* March, 1986: 51-71.

ON ORGANIZATIONAL CULTURE

"In any organization, there are the ropes to skip and the ropes to know."
- R. Ritti & G. Funkhouser

There is a story about Thomas Watson, Jr., who, while chairman of IBM's board, was one day touring a plant with the usual entourage of managers and senior executives. The group made its way toward a security area of the plant but was stopped short by a twenty-two-year-old female supervisor whose job it was to admit only those wearing proper identification badges. Watson wore an orange badge; unfortunately, it was acceptable in every area of the facility except the one guarded by this young woman. Although she knew Watson by sight, the supervisor also knew her job: "You cannot enter. Your admittance is not recognized." The group gave a collective gasp and one of the senior officials barked, "Don't you know who this is?" But Watson quickly raised his hand for silence, had one of the executives fetch the proper identification, and entered only when the correct badge was clipped to his lapel.

Most IBM employees know this story and retell it with some delight to the company's newcomers. The tale does more than recount a simple incident, though; it imparts a "feeling" for or "sense" of and "knowledge" about – the fabled IBM culture; a culture that one has to live with to fully understand.

The concept of organizational culture is similarly ephemeral – hard to pin down concretely but nevertheless critical to performance. The following brief outline shows some important ways of thinking about organizational culture.

What is Organizational Culture?

Above all, organizational culture refers to a system of shared values held by members of a company. These values are known, communicated, and produce a corporate identity that distinguishes one firm from another.

Three Levels of Culture

Most cultures operate on several levels simultaneously. Edgar Schein has developed this model:

Level I:	Material, Symbolic, Behavioral Artifacts
Level II:	Values
Level III:	Basic Assumptions and Beliefs

The first level of corporate culture is easily observed but hard to interpret without access to deeper levels. Being admitted to the "Million Dollar Roundtable," for instance, is symbolic of high sales achievement in the insurance industry, but carries little meaning outside that group.

The second level stresses the way things *ought to be*, as contrasted with the way they *are*. Successful business people possess convictions about what constitutes proper and effective action in particular situations (that advertizing will increase sales, for example, or that a professional code of ethics should guide practice).

The third level – the cultural foundation – consists of basic beliefs and values that guide and construct social reality and the interpretation of "objective" environmental realities. Whether the business person is engaged in individualistic competition (often the case in Western business cultures) or as a member of a communitarian society (as in many Asian companies) is governed by the basic assumptions found at this ground level.

The Strength of a Culture

Business cultures are said to be either "strong" or "weak." Strong cultures characteristically have all three culture levels not only present, but *intensely held and widely shared*. The more the members of a group uniformly accept and use the beliefs, language and symbols of a culture, the stronger it is. Strong cultures (such as the one commonly ascribed to Procter & Gambel) forcefully influence the attitudes and actions of a workforce.

Weak cultures, by contrast, support competing beliefs, dissonant values, vague and multiple symbols of success, which dilute the culture's impact on employee behavior.

What Does A Culture Do?

First and foremost, a culture *yields identity*. "I'm an HP engineer," communicates corporate and professional membership to the incumbent, as well as to outsiders.

Second, the culture *sets boundaries* that distinguish the way things are done "here" as opposed to "everywhere else."

Cultures act as a "social glue" that holds employees together, conveying to them expected ways of behaving and working together, and creating a sense of community. Consequently, an organization's culture is often linked to the level of commitment among its employees.

Third, and perhaps most important, a culture *shapes the way its members think* about themselves, each other, and the "realities" that surround them. "Is leveraging a good thing?" "Is diversification feasible?" "If we buy that company, do we have the expertise to manage it?" An organization's culture can sway answers to questions like these.

Creating and Building Culture

Most organizational cultures have their roots in the beliefs and values held by the firm's founders. Think of Walt Disney's impact on Disney Productions, Ray Kroc's influence on McDonald's, Steve Wozniak's vision for Apple Computer. These founders infused their companies with a philosophical base that continues to influence corporate strategy decades later. Once in place, this bedrock of beliefs and values is perpetuated (and modified) by some very concrete choices that managers make.

One of the most useful actions in creating and building culture is the *culture audit* – a strategic assessment of what the company's culture is and what it should be. This is a non-trivial exercise carried out at the highest levels of corporate management and repeated on a regular basis. MBA's are taught the importance of examining the assumptions that underlie a course of action; in some ways this parallels the spirit of a culture audit.

Tactical mechanisms for creating and building culture include:

(1) **Recruitment practices,** where the "right" people are selected, based on their ability to support the cultural ideals.

(2) **Employee orientation programs,** which teach new employees about the company, and thus its cultural norms, values, and beliefs.

(3) **Attention to communication** and its various methods – verbal, written, gestural – all designed to impart meaning. Popular cultural texts tend to emphasize the importance of sto-

ries, myths, rituals and material symbols (the logo-adorned Cross pen, for instance), but these are only special cases of the communication imperative. The effective manager recognizes the broad range of communication phenomena. When trying to create a certain type of culture, he supports the effort with multiple forms of communication in harmony with the company's underlying values.

Culture: So What?

Can you afford to forget about the culture concept? Probably not, since every firm has one.

If it did nothing else, the book *In Search of Excellence* made clear the extensive impact culture can have in a company. Your business has a culture. The question is whether the culture contributes to overall productivity or lies unnoticed and untended, like a sea anchor that retards the progress of a ship.

For Further Reading:

There are many good books on organizational culture for the practicing manager; there are also some poor ones. The following are recommended for their even, scholarly-yet-practical treatment of this topic.

Harris, Paul & R.T. Morgan. *Managing Cultural Differences.* Houston: Gulf Publishing. 1987.

Peters, Thomas & R. H. Waterman. *In Search of Excellence.* New York: Harper & Row. 1982.

Schein, Edgar. *Organizational Culture and Leadership.* San Francisco: Jossey-Bass. 1985.

Sathe, Vijay. *Culture and Related Corporate Realities.* Homewood, Illinois: Irwin. 1985.

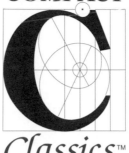

COMPACT

Classics™

LIBRARY #2: Personal Effectiveness

Section A: Personal Management

2-A1 *The Seven Habits of Highly Effective People* by Stephen R. Covey

2-A2 *Wishcraft: How to Get What You Really Want* by Barbara Sher

2-A3 *Peak Performance Principles for High Achievers* by John R. Noe

2-A4 *How to Get Control of Your Time and Your Life* by Alan Lakein

2-A5 *How to Put More Time in Your Life* by Dru Scott

2-A6 *Page-a-Minute Memory Book* by Harry Lorayne

Section B: Expanded Living

2-B1 *The Road Less Traveled* by M. Scott Peck

2-B2 *The Different Drum* by M. Scott Peck

2-B3 *Love is Letting Go of Fear* by Gerald G. Jampolsky

2-B4 *Psycho-cybernetics* by Maxwell Maltz

2-B5 *Understanding: Eliminating Stress and Finding Serenity in Life and Relationships* by Jane Nelsen

Section C: "Making It"

2-C1 *You Can Negotiate Anything: How To Get What You Want* by Herb Cohen

2-C2 *How to Prosper During the Coming Bad Years* by Howard J. Ruff

2-C3 *Wealth Without Risk: How to Develop a Personal Fortune Without Going Out On a Limb* by Charles J. Givens

2-C4 *The Richest Man in Babylon* by George S. Clason

2-C5 *Marshall Loeb's 1988 Money Guide* by Marshall Loeb

Section D: Tips and Techniques

2-D1 **Time-Saving Tips**

2-D2 **Business Gift-Giving Ideas**

2-D3 **Putting Spark in Your Relationships:** Activity Ideas

2-D4 **Dressing for Business**

2-D5 **Business and Executive Etiquette**

THE SEVEN HABITS OF HIGHLY EFFECTIVE PEOPLE

by Stephen R. Covey, Simon & Schuster, New York, 1989

"I've set and met my career goals and I'm having tremendous professional success. But it's cost me my personal and family life. I don't know my wife and children any more. I'm not even sure I know myself and what's really important to me. I've had to ask myself – is it worth it?"

"There's so much to do. And there's never enough time. I feel pressured and hassled all day, every day, seven days a week. I've attended time management seminars and I've tried half a dozen different planning systems. They've helped some, but I still don't feel I'm living the happy, productive, peaceful life I want to live."

In response to such sentiments, Covey's *Seven Habits of Highly Effective People* defines powerful principles for joyful, effective living. His book is saturated with advice on leadership, life management and relationships, all centered around the "inside-out" concept – behavior is *learned*, it is not instinctive. Old habits *can* be discarded and replaced by new and more effective habits.

Until 1930 or so, most success literature was based on the *Character Ethic* – the belief that there are basic principles of effective living and that people can only experience true success and enduring happiness as they integrate these principles into their lives. Then shortly after World War I, the central view of success shifted from the Character Ethic to the *Personality Ethic*. Success became a function of persona, of public image, of positive attitudes and behaviors, human-relations skills and techniques. The Personality Ethic is still in wide favor today. And adherents often do find temporary help by practicing these techniques, but sooner or later most realize that the underlying obstacles to happiness still persist.

Paradigms

A *paradigm* is a model or graph of the way we "see" the world – in terms of perceiving, understanding, and interpreting. A paradigm can be compared to a map. Improving behavior, doubling your effort, or thinking more positively would have no effect if you were given a map of Chicago and asked to find an address in Los Angeles. The frustrations you would face would have nothing to do with behavior or attitude: *they would arise out of having the wrong map.*

When *principles* – fundamental values, like fairness, integrity, human dignity and service – are *internalized into habits,* they empower people to formulate a wide variety of practices to deal with different situations. This involves developing an "inside-out" paradigm – maps and models generated of both the way things really *are* and the way we *want* them to be –

then *following* the maps and *living* the models.

We cannot change all situations, but we can change ourselves – inside-out.

Before detailing his seven habits, Covey quotes Ezra Taft Benson's words on the need for inner, spiritual training: "The Lord works from the inside-out. The world works from the outside-in. The world would take people out of the slums. Christ takes the slums out of people, and then they take themselves out of the slums . . . . The world would shape human behavior, but Christ can change human behavior."

HABIT 1: *Be Proactive (Initiative)*

Four main characteristics separate humans from animals: *imagination, conscience, independent will,* and *self-awareness.* In humans there is an interval between stimulus and response; we have the freedom to *choose,* not just to *react.* Being proactive means making this conscious "choice to choose"; being responsible for our own lives; taking the initiative; acting instead of being acted upon. Proactivity empowers us to *create* circumstances.

Effective people truly lead their lives. Instead of saying, "It's hopeless," they say, "Let's look at the alternatives." Instead of, "If only . . " they say, "I will."

Each of us possesses a *circle of concern,* which includes our state of health, our children, problems at work, the national debt, nuclear war . . . It is apparent that we have a great deal of control over some of these concerns and very little influence over others. The events we do have control over constitute our *circle of influence.* Proactive people focus their time and energy on their circle of influence – those things they can do something about.

HABIT 2: *Begin With the End in Mind (Creativity)*

All successful endeavors are created twice. There's a first, mental or spiritual creation, and a second, physical creation to all things. For example, if you were going to build a home, you wouldn't simply start hammering away. You would look at your budget, carefully plan what you wanted in the house, make a blueprint, and then develop construction plans. The same is true with parenting. If you want to raise responsible, self-disciplined children, you have to keep that end clearly in mind as you daily interact with your children.

Effective leaders *envision* what they want and how to get it. They habitually pick priorities stemming from their basic values.

In our personal lives, if we do not develop self-awareness and become responsible for our own "first creations," we empower other people and circumstances to shape our lives by default. Living "by default," we merely react to the scripts given to us by our family, associates, et al.

HABIT 3: *Put First Things First (Productivity)*

Habit 3 sparks the second, physical creation that fulfills habits 1 and 2. It entails the idea of management, or using our four human endowments (self-awareness, imagination, conscience and will) to accomplish *important* things.

In a time-management matrix, there are four "quadrants":

Quadrant I includes the affairs that are *urgent and important* – crises, pressing problems, deadline-driven projects. We react quickly to urgent matters. However, if we focus on Quadrant I, the "urgent" list tends to get bigger and bigger and we seem to go from one crisis to the next.

Quadrant III includes matters that are *urgent but not important* – some interruptions, phone calls and meetings. Many people spend much of their time reacting to things they deem urgent, assuming that they are also important.

Quadrant IV consists of activities that are *not urgent and not important* such as busy work and some recreation. These could be thought of as the "escape" portions of our lives.

Quadrant II is at the heart of effective personal management. It deals with concerns that are *important but not urgent* – building relationships, long-range planning, exercising . . . things we know we should do but seldom get around to actually doing. "Important matters that are not urgent require more initiative, more proactivity. We must *act* to seize opportunity, to make things happen." We become Quadrant II persons by learning to say no, by defining our roles in life, and by deciding what we want to accomplish in each of these roles.

HABIT 4: *Think Win/Win (Interdependence)*

Win/Win thinking is a frame of mind that constantly *seeks mutual benefit* in all human interactions – agreements or solutions that are satisfying to all involved. Most people are inclined to think in terms of competitive dichotomies: strong or weak, win or lose. But Win/Win thinking centers on the paradigm that there is plenty for everybody, and that one person's success is not achieved at the expense or exclusion of another person.

HABIT 5: *Seek First to Understand, Then to Be Understood (Empathy)*

Suppose you've been having trouble with your eyes and you go to an optometrist. After listening to your complaint, he takes off his glasses and hands them to you: "I've worn these glasses for years now and they've really helped me. I have an extra pair at home; you can wear these." Would you thank him for his generosity?

In the communications process, how often do we *prescribe* before we *diagnose*? We have a tendency to rush in, to fix things up with "good advice," but without deep understanding. Habit 5 involves fostering the habit of empathic listening – making deposits in the other person's "emotional bank account" by sincere validation and appreciation.

HABIT 6: *Synergize (Valuing Differences)*

"Synergy" implies that the whole is greater than the sum of its parts. Synergistic Communication begins with the assumption that cooperating individuals will *share* insights and open their minds and hearts. Then, if the opinions of all parties are valued, momentum will build and new alternatives will emerge where there were only roadblocks before.

HABIT 7: *Sharpen the Saw (Consistency)*

Habit 7 entails preserving, renewing and enhancing the greatest asset you have – *you*. It enables you to move on an upward spiral of growth.

Formulate a personal program to *keep in balance* the four dimensions of your nature – physical, spiritual, mental and social/emotional. To do this, again begin with habit 1 – be proactive. Taking the time to regularly "sharpen the saw" is a definite Quadrant II activity.

The *physical dimension* of saw-sharpening involves caring effectively for your body – eating the right foods, and getting sufficient rest, relaxation and exercise.

The *spiritual dimension* gives direction to your life. Find inner peace through daily prayer, meditation, reading from scripture, communing with nature, or habitually immersing yourself in great literature or music. Get up early ("mind over mattress") and live in harmony with the "still small voice" within you.

The *mental dimension* is central to life-long development. Education is a vital source of mental rejuvenation. Sometimes it requires the external discipline of the classroom or a systemized home study program; often it does not.

The *social/emotional dimension* embraces Habits 4, 5, and 6, which center on the principles of interpersonal leadership, empathic communications, and creative cooperation. This dimension is developed through service to others and self-discipline.

The *inside-out, upward spiral, self-renewal* concepts of *Seven Habits* revolve around becoming more *self-aware*. Only by knowing ourselves can we choose high purposes and principles to live by and find similar unity in our relationships with others. Developing the seven habits won't eliminate mistakes from our lives, Covey insists, but it will make us more able people. To quote Emerson: *"That which we persist in doing becomes easier – not that the nature of the task has changed, but our ability to do has increased."* And habits centered on correct principles can increase our ability to live peaceful, harmonized, loving, effective lives.

WISHCRAFT

by Barbara Sher, with Annie Gottlieb, Ballantine Books, New York, N.Y., 1979

I don't care how old you are, or what your past history has been, or what your present circumstances are: you can still do and have and be anything in the world you really want.

Barbara Sher's premise is that within every individual are unique – and unfulfilled – dreams and capabilities. Finding and defining your deepest wishes, then refining them through a "crafting" process, can be an exhilarating experience. And in her thinking, no dream is too far-fetched. Consider these *Wishcraft* precepts.

I. THE CARE AND FEEDING OF HUMAN GENIUS

We can all be winners and bring our dreams to life – from choral singing to writing children's books to selling blue-chip stocks. Winning – experiencing a joy-filled life-style – is a process, not a product. The search for the "lost treasure map of your talents [begins in the] first five precious and mysterious years of life – the greatest learning period you ever had . . . . All the people we call 'geniuses' are men and women who somehow escaped having to put that curious, wondering child in themselves to sleep . . . Einstein was able to make great discoveries precisely because he kept alive the originality and delight of a small child exploring its universe for the first time." In fact, all geniuses share three characteristics: great brilliance, original vision, and incredible determination.

Remembering what you loved to do as a child gives clues to the original genius within. Providing a nurturing environment, then, is the only challenge that remains in your unfolding. "All genuinely successful people – the ones who love their lives – have had that environment . . . or some parts of it . . . or they've figured out how to create it for themselves."

How well were your wishes nurtured as a child? Were you encouraged to build within yourself your own unique kind of genius? Were you given the freedom to explore your own talents and interests? Were you allowed to complain and make mistakes without feeling guilty?

Thinking about "what might have been" had the childhood conditions been right, is an exercise in cherishing and respecting yourself. Any discomfort you feel while pondering such dreams is a good sign; it shows that you recognize that there is more for you to accomplish. "Your capacity to *do* will depend on your capacity to *dream*, so prove that *that* capacity, at least, has survived intact."

II. WISHING

. . . Far from being "impractical" or "irresponsible," doing what's closest to your heart is like striking oil: you tap into a surge of energy that will propel you to the heights of success . . . . You will recognize your own path when you come upon it, because you will suddenly have all the energy and imagination you will ever need.

Three years ago Diane's secret dream was to become a city planner. However, she had no experience in planning, and besides, the city of New York was going broke – it was firing, not hiring, planners. As a 24-year-old secretary "with a B.A. in nothing special," a job she couldn't afford to quit for full-time study, and a pocketbook too drained to accommodate night classes, she felt her dream was impossible.

Still, Diane's favorite pastime was to stroll around the city, savoring the flavors and the architecture of the various neighborhoods. During these times she would brainstorm on what she could do. She began to attend local planning-board meetings and volunteered to help on projects; and her enthusiasm and deep understanding won the trust of city councilmen and other leaders. As a result of their high recommendations, Diane won a full-tuition scholarship to a nearby college and was able to secure part-time work . . . Today, despite her original staggering list of obstacles, this determined woman has a high-paying job in a field she loves.

Diane's story proves that with an open mind and the right encouragement, you can be doing at least some of what you're passionate about doing – right now. "If your goal is to make your living by doing what you love, start doing it just for love." If you've always wanted to paint landscapes, do it. Don't worry if your first attempts are disastrous; in fact, *plan* on them to be "bad" paintings. Just paint because you want to, for your own sense of fulfillment – and your work will improve.

A boy of 17 applying for college struck up a conversation with a white-haired seventy-four-year-old man, also in the admissions line. "I'm applying for college," said the old man, smiling. "But . . . you'll be seventy-eight by the time you graduate," the boy remarked.

"Son," said the old man, "I'll be seventy-eight anyway."

Stylesearch

"Remembering" and "taking note" assist you in finding your intuitive style. There are a thousand clues in your life to help you discover your style. The way you dress, the way you decorate your home, your favorite foods, colors, hobbies, etc. – these preferences declare your deepest self. "Your style is the place where you still exercise the creative power to shape your world and design yourself."

Make a list of twenty things you like to do – anything. Next, ask yourself questions about each activity: Did I do this yesterday, or has it been a long time since I did it? Why? What did it cost? Was it fast-paced, or slow and relaxed? Was it planned, or done spontaneously? Unearth patterns about the kind of life you live – and the kind you'd love to live. Unlock your true nature.

Goalsearch

Using this understanding of your personal style, begin to fantasize about what type of environment would allow your best self to emerge. Imagine what your ideal day would be like if you had no financial or time restraints. Prune that ideal by describing which elements of your day would be "indispensable," which would be "optional but desireable," and which you would consider "frill" activities. This exercise should help re-reveal your dreams, which you can now incorporate into your set of life *goals*.

Goals are the basic units of life design. They are targets, derived from your dream, and motivated by touchstones (insistent needs) and role models. Make your goals measurable and concrete – and make sure you really want the goals you chase.

If you had five lives, what would they be? Pull from each "life" the "something" you most value, and blend those vital parts into the design.

Hard Times, or the Power of Negative Thinking

Sher contends that there is a time and a need for negative thinking. Griping may be constructive, especially once it's out of the way; then you are ready for positive problem-solving, planning and action. Keep a "Problems List," a "Diary of Hard Times," and an "Action and Feelings Journal" to help propel you past negativity, and to remind you of "gained ground" – real progress you can see and savor.

III. CRAFTING: PLOTTING THE PATH TO YOUR GOAL

Here are the three "wishcrafting" strategies:

(1) *Brainstorming* (using human ingenuity) is a time-honored method of exploring all of the avenues leading toward your target. All ideas must be seriously considered, but only those that are workable and suit your style and ultimate destination need be pursued.

(2) *Barn-raising* (using human community), named after the pioneer practice, allows you to gain support, develop contacts, and gauge the strength of present resources that can help you in reaching your goal. In effect, throw a "barn-raising party," inviting all your trusted friends and acquaintances. Together, focus on your dreams and goals, and the steps necessary to turn them into reality. "The seeds of human genius happen to travel by a system of personal contacts."

(3) *Work with time.* The hard part is over; now the work begins. Devise a plan. "The only way to build a dream is brick by brick, action by action, day by day, in real time." Work with time by using six distinct but crucial tools:

a. A *planning wall* (any full-view wall space or bulletin board) helps you map out plans and chart progress across time. It also serves to motivate and remind. Your planning wall will include several of the other planning tools, as well as a picture of your personal *"saint"* who epitomizes your goal (businessman, movie star, singer, etc.) to help inspire and cheer you on.

b. A *flow chart* highlights your planned steps to achievement. Write out your goal, then list some first steps. Follow the steps one by one, day by day. Later, list some second steps and proceed to accomplish them . . .

c. A *goal calendar* consists of "a large sheet of paper divided into boxes, one box for each month between you and your target date." Appoint landmark *deadlines* (taken from your flow chart) to the months in which they can be realistically met. Setting personal, written deadlines "makes the difference between acting like you have all the time in the world and getting yourself in gear."

d. A *weekly calendar* is the principal tool for filling in the details of your plan. Assign each week's activities (appointments, phone calls, etc.) to specific days and times – and follow through. Also remember to put to good use the "free moments" in your day.

e. A *"tonight/tomorrow" sheet* is used to plan the all-important up-coming hours. Fill out a new sheet at the end of each day. "What do you have scheduled for tomorrow? What do you have to do tonight to prepare for it – lay out your clothes, lay out your paintbrushes and paints, make sure a phone number is in your pocket calendar, rehearse an interview in your mind? Now do it." Reward yourself often – a hot bath, a glass of brandy, a late movie. Self-congratulation is "food for your unfolding self."

f. A *five-year goal scheme* wraps up your plan into a real, year-by-year time frame. "Of course, you have no way of knowing what you'll really be doing – or wanting – in five years. But of all the forces that will be operating on your life over those years – chance and love and loss and luck, health and economics and history – your wish and will, your own unfolding, should be one of the strongest."

With a "head full of brains," "a room full of friends," and a solid plan, you can liberate your thinking and mobilize your efforts to allow you to attain what you want. *Wishing* is the starting point; *crafting* that wish becomes the continuum. There is no limit to your capabilities. There is no end to your potential. For it is the nature of the human animal to say "What next?" Once self confidence is attained in one thing, the search begins for something new – and you learn how to learn.

No matter how old you are, what your past history has been, or what your present circumstances are, know that "it is the journey, not the arrival, that matters."

PEAK PERFORMANCE PRINCIPLES FOR HIGH ACHIEVERS

by John R. Noe, Berkley Press, New York, N.Y., 1984

Peak Performance Principles, says its author, sets a new direction in the literature of self-improvement. The hype and cheerleading so often associated with motivational books is notably absent here; concise, inspirational stories take their place. Noe's book reflects his business opinions, his deeply religious views, and his experience as an expert mountain climber. "If a picture is worth a thousand words then reality is worth a thousand pictures," and the best life has to offer comes not only through "high achievement", but through "stopping and smelling the roses along the way."

Noe's first section begins with a warning: *"The ideas in this book are hazardous to your complacency."* To become a high achiever requires you to break out of personal or societal "comfort zones." High achievement means high adventure; climbing your own mountains; developing your personal potential.

Peak Performance Principles is designed to show the "achiever" how to become a "high achiever" – the difference being that while achievers may set and strive for goals, high achievers are only satisfied with reaching their full potential; they push themselves always just beyond the limits of their bodies and wills.

Ten Questions

In order to show what he means by "high achievers," Noe has devised "10 questions "that, if answered from the heart, can "change your life."

(1) *Do you really want to become a high achiever?* Self-discipline takes desire and personal investment. Most of us are constantly immersed in a world of noise; but creative self-discipline requires a degree of solitude. And since high achievement always involves creativity – breaking new ground – in the last decade of the 20th century high achievers must be willing to break away from their sometimes chaotic "comfort zones" to the silence and solitude of their own thoughts.

High achievers also typically reach out to embrace new situations; they are not afraid of change. The willingness to leave safe and comfortable surroundings in search of something better is their hallmark. Leaving a secure corporate position to start your own business may not be considered wise by statisticians, but it is a risk that high achievers often choose to take.

"To be great," Emerson wrote, "is to be misunderstood." Those who strive for great goals must risk rejection from their peers, and be confident enough to deal with the fact that not everyone will share their vision.

(2) *Do you have a strong inner urge to reach out?* High achievers reach out to new situations and people with enthusiasm, not fear.

(3) *What matters most to you?* "The key question for high achievers is never 'What have you done?' but 'What have you become?'" Material possessions have little meaning to the high achiever. Remember the "great secret" revealed by the fox in *The Little Prince?* "Only that which is invisible is essential." So, for high achievers, the intangible possessions – self-respect, pride of accomplishment, the capacity for love, and a positive outlook – are always paramount, and the primary goal is always to become a better, more able person.

(4) *What are you willing to invest?* High achievement requires an enormous amount of commitment and energy. Questions such as "How much longer will it take?" or "How much further do we have to go?" are self-defeating. The amount of time or effort required to obtain something worthwhile is secondary. The high achiever's answer to Question 4 is, "I am willing to invest whatever it takes."

(5) *What are you willing to endure?* "What a testing of character adversity is!" exclaims Harry Emerson Fosdick. And Noe concurs: "When the going gets tough . . . the high achiever shifts gears, and keeps going."

(6) *What are you willing to give up?* Society tends to define our comfort levels. But it can also desensitize us to our surroundings and distance us from other people – dangerous situations for even the high achiever. In high-performance driving, for instance, Noe points out that four small tire patches "are the only contact you have with the road. . . . You must be sensitive to the signals that are picked up by the tires and transferred to the wheels, suspension, car seat, and controls." Regular cars are designed to isolate and desensitize the driver from bumps; the goal is to make the car *comfortable.* High achievement, however, requires that we become, not comfortable and insulated from the bumps of living, but *sensitive* to the bumps of "high-performance living."

(7) *How much responsibility can you handle?* While others may complain when unexpected responsibilities are thrust upon them, the high achiever will simply do her best. "High achievement and responsiblity go hand in hand. You cannot have one without the other."

(8) *Are you willing to start where you are?* No one likes to start at the bottom, but high achievers first accept the circumstances in which they find themselves, and then go from there. Even the most accomplished entrepreneurs, artists and athletes had to begin at the beginning and then move toward their dreams. So, remember:

"you can always get to where you want to go, providing you are willing to start from where you are."

(9) *Are you willing to think for yourself?* Hard work is too frequently acclaimed as the whole answer for anyone striving toward a goal. True, there is no substitute for hard work; but the high achiever must develop a balance between hard work and hard, often solitary thought.

(10) *Are you willing to settle for nothing less than your full potential?* Benjamin Franklin wrote that "success has ruined many a man." Once you achieve your dream, don't allow yourself the luxury of becoming complacent – dream again. To be a genuine high achiever is to continue to forge ahead, regardless of what has already been accomplished.

The Six Attitudes of High Achievers

(1) *High achievers make no small plans* ("Big plans attract big people"). But high achievers also realize that small, everyday choices are the agents that ultimately shape the big decisions of our lives. So, seize control of your little choices – How will you spend today? What will you do first? Second? Next? . . . And, finally, what will you do when you don't have anything to do?

(2) *High achievers are willing to do what they fear.* "You don't conquer fears with cliches, but with actions." Fears and doubts waste time, energy, initiative and potential. Grieving over past decisions or actions is futile. Moreover, "fear is fraud"; only about 8% of our worries are real and legitimate concerns. And the sooner we challenge and act on those that are real, the sooner we resolve them. Noe suggests: "Sit down and make a list of all the things you are afraid to do, within legal, moral, and spiritual limits. Then go out and deliberately make yourself do every one of them. Each time you confront a fear, become sensitive to the atmosphere surrounding it . . . then fear will no longer control your life."

(3) *High achievers are willing to prepare.* "He profiteth, who hustles while he waits," said Thomas Edison. Organizing, planning, preparing for events is something we can all do. "High achievers get more excited about what they are becoming than what they have done." Preparation involves setting progressively higher intermediate goals, mastering technical skills, building endurance and, along the way, gaining much-needed confidence.

(4) *High achievers are willing to risk failure.* "Failure is not the enemy of success. It is a teacher – a harsh teacher, but the best . . . . If you are going to be a high achiever, you must learn to 'fail' your way to high achievement." Case in point: For three consecutive Olympic Games, beginning in 1952, each decathlon silver medalist went on to win the following Olympic's Gold Medal. We must not expect to win each time out, but let our losses teach and strengthen us. High achievers know the formula for success: "Double your failure rate."

(5) *High achievers are teachable.* The high achiever continually pursues new knowledge and insights. Staying teachable demands three activities – reading, observing, and listening. It also demands the recognition that "the higher you go the more help you need." Keep in mind that high-achievement goals can only be attained with the help of others. Take advantage of the many mentors along the way.

(6) *High achievers have heart.* Conflict is at the root of the plots of all great literature: the old man battling the sea and a great fish; the athlete working against almost impossible odds. However, "real life" struggles don't usually announce themselves as great adventures; they are much more likely to appear under the unglamorous guise of Murphy's-Law – "If anything can go wrong, it will." But the very weight of these burdensome challenges can impel us toward our highest goals. *Heart* – as in "courage," "persistence," "perspective," and "purpose" – will help you overcome the urge to quit the fight.

High Achievement: Putting It Into Action

Noe uses the rules of mountain climbing to illustrate his *Peak Performance* points. He talks of climbing "fully equipped" – prepared beforehand for any eventuality – and of setting your sights on ever higher heights. (A novice climber can't set out to conquer the Matterhorn, but must begin by ascending less rugged mountains or hills.) He also recommends using "goal-climbing momentum" – grabbing on to a goal you have already reached to launch you toward your next intermediate goal.

In mountain climbing it might seem appealing to be able to move from one peak to the next without descending. But this is not only impossible, *it is undesirable.* Without ever having to come down, at least part way, and begin the new adventure from the bottom of the next peak, we wouldn't be able to savor the difficult climb back up. Life is a series of new adventures, not endings. Changing careers, moving to a new city, or retiring, can be exciting, renewing experiences, depending on your outlook.

The straightforward concepts offered in *Peak Performance Principles* emphasize individual commitment and faith in God. Noe believes that if we dedicate ourselves over and over again to the goal of climbing from one peak to the next – resisting the urge to become discouraged by the heaviness of the task – every one of us can become a high achiever.

HOW TO GET CONTROL OF YOUR TIME AND YOUR LIFE

by Alan Lakein, Peter H. Wyden, Inc., New York, N.Y., 1973

How to Get Control of Your Time and Your Life teaches you how to determine what you want in life and how to get it. Alan Lakein, the long-standing guru of time management, has a simple plan for *setting goals* and *prioritizing* them – the heart and soul of time management.

"Time is life"; by wasting our time we waste our lives. Effective use of time means skillfully selecting the foremost tasks to accomplish and accomplishing them in the best way possible. *You* are the one who decides what is the best possible use of your time.

Getting Control

Lakein's key concept is *control*. Controlling time must be done with balance – neither too tight or too loose. Losing balance becomes a liability.

Three groups of people misuse time management principles, and lose control:

(1) *The over-organized* person is more interested in *feeling* organized than in accomplishing anything. He spends much of his time planning and little of it doing.

(2) *The over-doer* is always *busy* doing things, but seldom takes the time to assess the value of the tasks she is doing. As a result, she gets only a lot of low priority projects completed.

(3) *The "time nut"* is so preoccupied with time that he never wastes a second. He knows how to get everything done a couple of seconds quicker.

All three people drive those around them crazy. However, *scheduling* should mean "making time for what you want to do . . . . A too rigid or demanding schedule creates the feeling of being regimented by the clock." The purpose of controlling time is to instill into your life *greater freedom*, not to turn you into a compulsive organizer or clock watcher. In order to gain this freedom, some people work to follow all of the suggestions given in Lakein's book; others pick and choose only those which they believe will help them.

Life is a never-ending stream of possible activities, constantly being replenished by your family, your teachers, your boss, your subordinates, as well as by your own dreams, hopes, desires, and by the need to stay alive and functioning.

There are always more things that we need to do, or would like to do, than we have time to do. It is often difficult to decide what to do *first*, what can *wait*, and what *doesn't need to be done at all*.

Control Starts With Planning.

"Planning is bringing the future into the present so that you can do something about it now." In order to effectively plan your time you need to ask yourself:

(1) *What are my lifetime goals?*

(2) *What do I want to accomplish in the next three years?*

(3) *If I had six months to live, how would I live them?*

What are your lifetime goals? If you are not sure, take fifteen minutes and find out. First, write the question "What are my lifetime goals?" on a sheet of paper. Take two minutes and write down everything that comes into your mind that answers the question. Take another two minutes and make any changes you feel are necessary in the first list. It is not necessary to be completely satisfied with the list at this time. Now follow the same procedure for the other two questions.

Once you have spent four minutes on each list, take two additional minutes and review all three lists.

After compiling your list of lifetime goals, select the top three that are most important to you. Label them A-1, A-2 and A-3, in order of their importance. Then take a new sheet of paper and write "My three most important lifetime goals are . . ." Do the same thing with your "three-year" list and your "six-month" list. Repeat the process the next day and as often as needed to refine your goals. Once you are comfortable with the lists, it is time to get to work.

Accomplishing Your Goals

You cannot carry out goals; you can only carry out *activities*. To reach a goal you need to select activities that will get you there. To determine the best use of your time, brainstorm and be creative; think of as many possible strategies as you can. Go back over the brainstorming list to revaluate your ideas.

Now, *set priorities* for your tasks. Ask: "Am I willing to spend at least five minutes a day on this activity for the next seven days?" If the answer is no, you have just uncovered a low-priority task. Eliminate it. Perform this exercise for each goal. When you have eliminated all of the low-priority items for each goal, combine all of your lists into one list, and then set priorities for your activities.

The next step is to schedule *realistic deadlines* for completing each activity. Do the activities as scheduled by breaking them down into daily tasks pointed toward achieving your goals.

Daily Planning

Start by looking at your "A" activity list.

"The A's generally stand out clearly. They should be the attention-getters." Choose only those activities you can do *today*. Then, add to the list everything else you need, or would like, to get done today. Prioritize these tasks using A's (high value), B's (not quite so important), and C's (low value). Next, return to the list and select the highest priority A and label it A-1. Go through all the A's in this way, then do the same with the B's and C's. Don't let the number of items scare you. *You do not need to finish everything on the list.* Start with A-1 and go through the to-do list in the order of your selected priorities. *"People at the top use a to-do list every single day . . . . One of the real secrets of getting more done is to work on the list at the beginning and end of each day, keep it visible and use it as a guide as you go through the day."*

Look for opportunities to get started on activities. Take advantage of "open" minutes: commuting time, coffee breaks, lunch, and "waiting" occasions.

You will find that the 80/20 rule applies to your "to-do" list: Twenty percent of the items on the list will give you eighty percent of the positive results. For this reason, setting priorities is critical.

When planning your daily schedule, it is best to set aside a block of time to work exclusively on "A" activities. Start with fifteen minutes a day and increase it from there. Leave some "holes" in the day to allow for unexpected interruptions that pop up. Flexibility in your schedule will help you avoid frustration.

Be sure to schedule some quiet time for yourself. When you need time to work on projects, schedule appointments with yourself and then honor the appointments as you would any meeting. Lakein also suggests scheduling the times you will be available to others.

How can you deal with the demands other people put on your time? Two helpful suggestions: (1) Learn to say no, and (2) Learn to compromise without giving up control. The best technique for avoiding time thieves is to be honest with them. If someone asks, "Do you have a minute?" tell them you don't, or indicate exactly how many minutes you have available and ask if their discussion can be accomplished in that amount of time.

Possessions and paperwork also rob you of time. Again, A-B-C organizing is the key. Have a place for every item and put it back when you finish using it. Get rid of 20 percent of everything you own and "set a limit on how many things in each category are optimum – say, 20 ties. Then, before you buy a new one, get rid of an old one." With mail, "deal with each piece . . . only once and make a decision about it. Mail labeled A should always be handy, and the C's should be stashed away . . . . If you wait long enough, they will become obsolete."

A major stumbling block that everyone faces is *procrastination*. How can you overcome it? Lakein offers several ideas: Ask yourself the question "What is the best use of my time right now?" If you have properly planned your day, you can look at your "to-do" list and see how to best use that moment.

When overwhelmed, you might turn to the "Swiss Cheese" approach, which involves punching several holes into a large project. If you cannot force yourself to launch right into it, take five minutes and complete one of the project's small tasks. The purpose is to get you started on a hard-to-face, high-priority undertaking. Generally, once you begin such a task, you find that working on it is not as bad as you had thought.

Other suggestions to thwart procrastination include: giving yourself a pep talk; realizing that delay will only make the problem worse; making a commitment to someone else; and, slowing down the decision-making process and determining why you're avoiding the A-1 project. Recognize that you decided the A-1 task was the best use of your time; as a result, any other task you choose to do, although it may be valuable, is a comparative waste of time.

Lakein submits other little ideas on how to find time you didn't know you had, how to reduce stress, etc. Some tips:

- Perfection is a waste of time when completing lower priority tasks.

- Accept the fact that, at your choosing, some tasks are better left undone.

- Find "prime times" during the day when you characteristically do your best work. Plan your time blocks accordingly.

- Arrange for quiet times, breaks from extended activities, and times to simply do nothing. Balance work and play; you'll get more done in the long run.

- Experiment with reducing your sleep time.

- Train yourself to use your subconscious during sleep to help you solve difficult problems.

- Don't allow guilt or fear of failure to push you into an "escape" habit. Reading, socializing, daydreaming and indulging in over-scrupulous or menial tasks, while not wrong in and of themselves, are sometimes used as escapes from the A-1 activity.

- Wean yourself away from TV.

- Demonstrate willpower in little ways; it will develop your self-discipline and desire to make good use of time.

- "Do your best and consider it a success."

The real key to control – and the one most often ignored – is setting priorities in your life, both for long-term goals and daily planning. Once you get accustomed to setting priorities and schedules, and sticking to them, you will find that you have control of both your time and your life.

HOW TO PUT MORE TIME IN YOUR LIFE

by Dru Scott, Ph.D., Signet Books, New York, N.Y., 1981

How to Put More Time in Your Life is a "5-step program that puts you in charge of your clock, your calendar, and your life."

Dru Scott insists that while most time management systems are based on accomplishing tasks, the focus of her book is to help you *gain quality time* – time to do what's really important to you.

Scott feels that time management is not merely a matter of *knowing* what to do, but *getting yourself to do it.* At one period of her life, she was teaching and writing about time management, yet found herself always rushing from one appointment to another. Finally she admitted that she was failing to apply in her own work the principles she was teaching to others.

Briefly, these are some underlying themes behind the steps outlined in her book:

I. Clarify priorities: Concentrate on *quality* activities; fulfill your *wants* as well as your objectives; *define* and *do* what really counts.

II. Understand what motivates you: Face up to *mixed feelings* in yourself and others; *reward* and *reinforce* the best in yourself and others; *motivate* yourself, every day, to do what's important.

III. Do your best with this day: *Don't wait* to live fully; open yourself to the *joys* of the moment; go ahead, *do it* – the best time is now.

Step 1: Exploring the Psychology of Management (and Mismanagement)

Perhaps we feel out of control because – consciously or sub-consciously – we subscribe to some of the following myths concerning time management:

- "I'm waiting until I have more time."
- "I've already read the book (or taken the course)."
- "You just can't get organized around here."
- "People keep interrupting me."

Hiding behind such myths often allows us to shield ourselves from the real reasons behind our lack of time management. Some people actually mismanage time as a means of achieving unacknowledged "goals" – to get attention, blame others, gain control, escape unpleasant situations or risks, resist change, or to avoid close relationships.

Guilt

Guilt, "a feeling of deviation from a relevant standard" – a standard usually etched during our childhood – can become a major time-waster. *Inappropriate guilt* occurs when we assault ourselves for not doing everything perfectly. Three questions can help deal with guilt:

(1) "Specifically, what am I feeling guilty about?"

(2) "Is this something that is really an essential or central concern to me or someone else?"

(3) "Today, how can I best do what really counts?"

Elements of Time Design

Five elements of design make up your personal style of time management: *Order* (a direction of movement in life); *Balance* (regular, planned activities); *Contrast* (variety); *Unity* (total life "contributions"); and *Harmony* (connections that blend life experiences into a whole). The blend of these elements determines how we individually go about controlling our time.

Compulsive Controllers

Compulsive time control is typically seen in one of five basic personality styles:

1. **Hurry up:** This person puts things off until the last minute and then is forced to rush.

2. **Be perfect:** This person wastes time on trivial, peripheral matters.

3. **Please me:** This person yearns to satisfy everyone, and often over-commits.

4. **Try hard:** This person wants to be recognized for trying hard, even if failure is the end result.

5. **Be strong:** This person doesn't believe in asking anyone for help and must continually declare independence to prove self-worth.

Do you recognize yourself in one or more of these profiles?

Step 2: Choice Time – Getting Yourself Organized

Setting Priorities

Deciding on your broad objectives is essential. Create a list of what you want more of, and less of, in your life. Then do something towards making your "mores" more of a reality every day. Construct short-term objectives that will serve as daily "nudges" toward achieving your lifetime desires. Be *firm* about your *objectives,* but *flexible* about your *activities.*

Set priorities. Divide tasks into three categories: (1) *Marginal* (not important enough to worry about); (2) *Secondary* (worthwhile, but not the greatest time investment); (3) *Central* (areas that reflect your deepest values and desired direction). Decide what your objective is for any given activity, and plan accordingly.

Managing Time Decisions

Fast, effective decisions demand that you

first clarify your objective. Compare several alternatives; which will get you closer to where you want to go? *Decide,* and then *act* on your decision by listing the workable steps of your task, doing one thing at a time, and finishing each step fully.

Keep a *personal calendar* handy, combined with a *daily action* sheet. On your daily action ("to do") list, record objectives, listing urgent and central concerns first. Confine yourself to a realistic number of items so you won't feel overwhelmed.

Next, break your activities into "doable" tasks and prioritize them (1,2,3 or A,B,C . . .). You may then choose to group tasks, separating them into blocks of time.

Interruptions and demands from others are a part of life. For a week or so, track your interruptions on an "interruption sheet." This can help you detect hidden drains on your time, acting then to either curtail or deal with them.

Step 3: Staying Motivated

Each person has different "stimulation levels" – different needs. Some need to be with people; others require privacy. Some are motivated by another's authority; others work better when "self-inspired." We should seek to recognize what our unique stimulation levels are. What motivates and excites you?

Some people thrive on negative stimulation, often by procrastinating. To overcome this habit, analyze your procrastination patterns. When and how do you most often procrastinate? Why do these times or situations cause you discomfort? How do you feel after you've done an important task that you had previously put off? In some combination of the "Three R's" – *repetition* (making a "hard" task a habit), *reinforcement* (finding some type of satisfaction in performing the task), and *reward* (placing some sort of "carrot" at the end of the task) – you can keep yourself moving in the right direction.

When you are overwhelmed and time *refuses* to be managed, there are some emergency measures you can take. First, clear your mind by writing down everything you're feeling. Next, update your wants. Then add reinforcements and rewards. Last, compare your "feelings" list with your updated "wants" list, and decide what five items are most important to do right at that moment.

Step 4: Coping With Everyday Time Demands

Can you relate to any of these time issues?

* Is it hard to get going in the *morning?* To solve this problem requires planning. Determine the number of minutes you need to complete your morning routine, and add 15 minutes as a time cushion. Commit yourself to arising at the designated time. Don't

set your alarm for 5:00 if you don't intend to get up until 6:15.

* Decide if time spent *commuting* to work is worth it for you. Realize you do have a choice – about where you live, your job, car-pooling, etc. If you find that commuting is requisite, learn to make this time personally productive (listening to cassette tapes, planning . . .)

* If you find yourself consistently *running late,* start cultivating punctuality by picking one important daily commitment for which you will be on time. Reward yourself for being early or on time for an appointment. Mentally take note of your planned time of departure.

* Anticipate moments when you will be *waiting,* and be prepared to deal with them without fretting. Confirm your appointments the day before. If someone you have an appointment with is habitually late, call just before you leave to see if they're running on time. Make the most of your waiting time by carrying work or personal projects with you. "Cluster" appointments and errands whenever possible.

* *Shopping and housework* have to be done. Consider whether it's feasible to hire help. Use both a "standard" shopping list (for common weekly purchases) and a "special" list (for "one-time" purchases). For housework, systematically schedule recurring demands. This eliminates time wasted making decisions.

* Discover an *exercise* program that is enjoyable and practical. Add some reinforcements and rewards to keep you motivated.

Step 5: Putting Time to Work

* Realize that *paperwork* is a means, not an end. Separate "vital" papers from those that are "marginal." Set a time frame for keeping different types of documents.

* In a polite way, make *people* aware of the deadlines you need to meet.

* The *telephone* is a tool; it shouldn't control your life. Take hold of phone conversations from the start. State directly what you want. Develop tact and skill in closing a call – "Thanks for your help; I'll be back in touch . . . "

* Learn – and practice – to *say "no"* without apology. Say "yes" only if the obligation helps you accomplish one of your key objectives.

Remember: time is a gift. Habitual management of this gift can help you live a fuller life.

PAGE-A-MINUTE MEMORY BOOK

by Harry Lorayne, Holt, Rinehart & Winston, New York, N.Y., 1985

"There is no such thing as a poor memory! There are only trained and untrained memories."

Harry Lorayne wrote his book by compiling a lifetime of research, seminars, and radio and television demonstrations, and distilling them down to the basics. Lorayne's goal in teaching his techniques and applications is not only to improve your memory, but "to give you memory POWER you never imagined possible" – and to give it to you quickly. He claims that by following his simple systems you can train your memory to an unprecedented degree. "Trying the ideas is the key. Once you try, you'll be hooked, because you'll see immediate results . . . "

A chapter on "The Business Edge" emphasizes how indispensable memory is in business. An extraordinary memory stands out, gives you an extra edge. "Nothing sells better than facts . . . at your fingertips."

"All knowledge is but remembrance," said Plato. And to remember is to associate the past with some present stimulus. As Lorayne's "Reminder Principle" states, "We usually remember one thing because we are reminded of it by another thing." Training your memory, then, amounts to consciously controlling these associations.

Examples of association: remember the spelling of the word "piece" by imagining a PIEce of PIE; memorize the names of the five Great Lakes by visualizing many HOMES on the lake shores – Huron, Ontario, Michigan, Erie and Superior.

Thinking is seeing – visualizing pictures in your mind. "If it can be visualized it can be remembered."

You need a *unique* visual association to achieve a lasting memory. When Lorayne's son Robert was about five years old, he was frustrated because he could never remember to say "caterpillar" instead of "catterlipper." "I told him to picture a *cat* chasing that crawly, hairy thing up a *pillow*. It worked."

Learning New Words

Silly associations work. "Peduncle" means a flower stalk. If, by chance, you had to learn the word, you could visualize that you owe your uncle money and you pay him with flower stalks instead – you *paid uncle* with flower stalks. This simple association works both left to right and right to left. Needing to recall the biological word for flower stalk, you will be reminded that you paid your uncle with them – peduncle.

This "Substitute Word System" takes advantage of your ability to think of something that sounds like the unfamiliar word – enough to remind you of it. A silly image gives you a needed "slap in the face" – we easily forget commonplace occurrences, but tend to remember the rare, the unusual, or the violent. For example, an "endocarp" is a fruit pie. Picture: *ending* a *carp's* life by hitting it with fruit pies. A "litany" is a form of prayer. Picture: you have set fire to *(lit)* your *knee* and are saying a prayer over it.

You can make your own associations to learn other words. In word association you are using the OAR (Observe, Associate, Remember) method to force attention. This painless method can also be applied to learning foreign words or registering new concepts.

Names and Faces

Forgetting the name of a past business associate can be both embarrassing and a critical mistake. According to Lorayne: "I'm introduced to someone, and a few minutes later – no, seconds later – I've forgotten his or her name!" But this is a lie! You haven't forgotten the name; you simply didn't remember it in the first place.

Again using the Substitute Word System, you can easily recall names such as Wolfe, Rivers, and the like. But other names (Cohen, Betavagnia, Rafferty, Smith) must first be clearly heard and then actively associated with some forceful image. (Cameron = camera on; Carruthers = Car udders . . .)

Listening attentively and thinking up brief, pictorial "reminders" that will link names to faces, are fundamental to helping your memory do its work. Observe the detailed features of a face, then "lock in" on a particular feature for association. Examples: Mr. Betavagnia – his large nose will be a bent vane on his face; Mr. Brodsky – see the broad skis going down the deep lines in his forehead; Mrs. Smith – you're pounding in the prominent lines between her nostrils and her lips with a blacksmith's hammer.

You might practice this system using pictures in magazines: Look at the name, "christen" the face, apply the system, and after a few faces, see how you do on a self-test.

The Link System

This system is effective in memorizing lists of things or ideas by visually "linking" the items in order – the parts of a speech, shopping list items, school assignments, historical events, etc. Lorayne uses the "Three R's" – Register, Remember, and Recall – to connect items. For instance, to remember the words "book" and "airplane" in sequence, think of a giant book flying like an airplane.

Then you can link "airplane" to "eyeglasses" by picturing an airplane wearing glasses, and so on.

Fear of forgetting is the foremost fear in public speaking. By extracting key words from sections of a talk and linking them together visually, you can give a speech without using notes.

Numbers and the Phonic Alphabet

Lorayne teaches that number sequences can be memorized by breaking them down into smaller "units" (i.e. it's harder to remember "2-4-1-7-3" than "twenty-four, one seventy-three"). In a series of "Memory Breaks," he introduces the "Phonic Alphabet System," a technique based on associating the numbers 1 through 0 with sets of similarly grouped sounds and letters:

$$1 = T, D$$
$$2 = n$$
$$3 = m$$
$$4 = R$$
$$5 = L$$
$$6 = J, sh, ch, and soft g$$
$$7 = K, hard c, and hard g$$
$$8 = f, v, ph$$
$$9 = P, B$$
$$0 = z, s, and soft c$$

Full understanding and utilization of this complex system requires a careful reading of the related chapters; but the idea is basic: 5 = L, for example, because if you hold up your five fingers, the index finger and thumb form an "L". By creating sentences using the associated sounds and numbers, you can remember even long numerical sequences or multi-digit numbers.

Practical Memory Hints

Absentmindedness: Ever go somewhere and forget why you went, or put down an object and forget where you placed it? Doing things while your mind is "absent" can be time-wasting and aggravating.

To solve this problem, you can associate between item and place. If you put your eyeglasses on the TV in the spare bedroom, for example, envision the antenna penetrating and shattering the lens. It's like the Gracie Allen joke: When you put a large roast in the oven, put a small one in at the same time; when you smell the small one burning, you'll be reminded that the large one is ready.

It's true! Dropping a potholder in the middle of your floor or putting something conspicuously out of place – the old "string on the finger" trick – can remind you of a specific task you need to do at a specific time.

Poor spelling: As already mentioned, you can remember the spelling of a difficult word by connecting the "hard" word with an easier word in a brief sentence: It's neCESSary to clean a CESSpool. I take a BUS to my BUSiness. My PET learns by rePETition. DeSSert comes after diNNer. (Double nn reminds you of double ss.) Expen$e is not expen¢e . . .

School Memorization Tasks: By using imagery you can make learning a game instead of a boring task. Memorizing the names of state capitals is a good example: A *boy sees* an Idaho potato (*Boise*, Idaho); *Mary lands* on an apple (Annapolis, Maryland); you throw *little rocks* at an ark (Little Rock, Arkansas) . . .

"Substitute images" can also help you memorize items in sequence. For instance, to learn the U.S. presidents in order, link Washing machine to Adams apple to "d'ja have a son?" (Jefferson), and so forth.

Reading-Recall: Memory systems can also help you visualize and associate while you read. Picturing and connecting key words or thoughts may take some concentration, but soon it becomes a source of fun as well as super recall. " . . . Effective reading is . . . the art of boiling down dozens, hundreds, and thousands of words into a few vital thoughts." It's "a search for ideas, thoughts, answers." So when a thought is "located," try to "spear" it out of its surrounding pool of words. Then, "boil" the idea down into a few easily remembered words. This *locate, spear, and boil* concept starts you thinking about what or who is important in your reading. Separate ideas from their "padding" – words that can be eliminated from your mind. And remember, as Lorayne cautions: "How quickly you get through reading material is not as important as how much of the material gets through to you!"

Listening: Attentive listening requires a similar four-step approach: (1) Summarize in a short phrase or sentence what the speaker has said; (2) Anticipate the speaker's next points, and ask yourself questions about them; (3) Listen "between the lines" to grasp hidden meaning; and (4) Ask yourself if you agree with the speaker.

The systems and ideas outlined in the *Page-a-Minute Memory Book* are practical and flexible – "They can solve any memory problem with a slight (common sense) change here or there . . . " Alexander Smith said, "A man's real possession is his memory. In nothing else is he rich, in nothing else is he poor." Lorayne points out that a rich memory can also make learning and life more fun.

THE ROAD LESS TRAVELED

A New Psychology of Love, Traditional Values and Spiritual Growth
by M. Scott Peck, M.D., Simon and Schuster, New York, N.Y., 1978

Life is difficult. This is a great truth, one of the greatest truths. It is a great truth because once we indeed see this truth, we transcend it. Once we truly know that life is difficult – once we truly understand and accept it – then life is no longer difficult. Because once it is accepted, the fact that life is difficult no longer matters.

Confronting and solving problems is a painful, difficult process, one most people try to avoid. But complaints and avoidance actually contribute to our problems and hinder our mental and spiritual growth.

Drawing upon his years of experience as a psychiatrist, Dr. M. Scott Peck takes us along the rocky road – the one not often traveled – of confronting and solving our problems, to arrive at a greater understanding of ourselves and our place in the world.

Discipline

Discipline is the key theme throughout *The Road Less Traveled*. Discipline comprises the basic set of tools required to *constructively experience* the pain of problems. Four tools of discipline are: (1) *Delaying gratification.* The willingness to experience pain first, enabling us to go on to experience the pleasures of life; (2) *Accepting responsibility.* Not placing the blame for problems on our parents, friends, or society; being willing to solve our own problems; (3) *Dedication to truth (reality).* Seeing the world *as it is* in order to effectively deal with it. (We each have a "map" or view of the world which must be continually adjusted as new information is received.); (4) *Balancing.* The flexibility to give something up in order to gain something of transcendent importance.

Love

Love provides the *motivation* for discipline. Love is the will to *extend oneself* for the purpose of nurturing one's own or another's *spiritual growth.*

Love is not only a feeling; love entails *action.* Genuine love is shown by extending our own limits towards one whose growth we want to nurture.

A common fallacy about love is that dependency – wanting someone else to take care of our needs – is love. People who base their relationships on this concept lack self-discipline; they are "passively dependent" on others.

Neither is love self-sacrifice. Whenever we think of ourselves as doing something "for" someone else, we are in a sense denying her of taking responsibility herself. When we do something for someone that she could

just as easily do herself, we do it not out of love, but because it fulfills our own needs.

Love is work – and work involves *attention.* This can sometimes mean just being with someone, but usually it also means *listening.* There are different levels of listening. "Real" listening – the highest level – demands full, complete, and active attention.

When we extend ourselves in love we assume many risks:

- The risk of giving up our own "self." The self changes when we force ourselves (or are forced) to do things we are not accustomed to doing, and change usually includes some sense of loss, until we find a way to reintegrate the "old" self with the "new" self. But "Courage is not the absence of fear; it is the making of action in spite of fear . . . "

- The risk of standing alone – of facing our own independence. Independence means not relying on parents or other people for our "shoulds" and "wills" and "wants," but upon ourselves. "The highest forms of love are inevitably totally free choices and not acts of conformity."

- The risk of commitment. In Peck's clinical examples, he notes that many parents "failed to commit themselves to their children in any meaningful way . . . . [The children] grew up without experience of commitment." Commitment is necessary for love to develop and to resolve the issues surrounding a relationship.

Growth and Religion

The *understanding we have of the world is our religion.* Everyone has a religion, whether he formally belongs to a church or not. Often a person's world-view is only partially conscious; an expanded overview is lacking. The methods of science – stepping back skeptically to question our basic assumptions – can help us discover our personal religion. This, in turn, can lead us to new truths. It is not necessary to disregard everything we have believed in order to come to terms with our religious views; but we *do* need to *question the source* of these views and decide whether they still adequately and usefully serve our present values.

Grace and Miracles

As we become more spiritually aware, we must guard against "tunnel vision" in our seeking to reconcile science with seemingly unexplainable phenomena, such as the heal-ings and miracles that take place in religion.

If we look at life closely we see that frequent "miracles" do occur. It is not remarkable that we get sick; it is amazing that most of the time we get *healthy*. Think of the many examples of people who have overcome overwhelmingly negative factors in their lives and emerged with their physical and mental health intact. By analyzing such occurrences we can come to the understanding of a hidden truth, the answer to a problem, etc. To do this, however, we must remain *open* to the miraculous, and not dismiss our experiences merely because they don't appear to have a scientific basis.

In this realm lies the *miracle* of *the unconscious* – the part of our minds which lies beneath our awareness. Often our unconscious mind seizes on a word that suddenly pops into our thoughts, or yields a dream having no known origin. So-called "Freudian slips" (when we say or do something that doesn't make sense on the surface) are an attempt by our unconscious to let out a denied feeling.

Again, there are times when we feel we "re-know" or recognize something which was somehow "known" to us, but unacknowledged, before. Many psychologists feel that people have the innate relevant experiences to unlock this hidden knowledge.

And then there is the miracle of *serendipity*, when some fortunate revelation occurs that seems impossible according to the known laws of nature. This includes so-called "psychic phenomena," where, for example, a person is able to transmit images to the mind of someone sleeping several rooms away. People sometimes have a sense that they should or should not do a certain thing, which results in avoidance of a serious accident. Often we let these small miracles slip by because they do not fit our preconceived "slots" for sorting experience.

Evolution, both physical and spiritual, is clearly a miracle. According to laws of mechanics, evolution should not exist. However, human beings, as well as the whole plant and animal world around us, are living proof that it does exist. In the same vein, the force of entropy (natural disorder, chaos) would seem to preclude man's historical spiritual development. But despite the problems of society, *we do grow*. Our frequent contemporary sense of disillusionment with the human race arises in part from the fact that we expect more of ourselves than our ancestors did.

So, where do miracles and love and discipline come from? Evidence points to the existence of a supreme being who loves us – *God*. God apparently wants us to learn and grow, but what is his *ultimate* goal for us? It could only be for us *to become like him*. This is a frightening idea to many people, because of the tremendous effort involved. We don't want to have to work that hard.

The main impediment to love and spiritual growth is *laziness*. "Since love is work, the essence of nonlove is laziness." The author asserts that Adam and Eve's sin was not just the taking of the fruit; it was their unwillingness to find out why God had forbidden them to eat it in the first place. Thus, they took the fruit with an incomplete knowledge of the truth because they were unwilling to work to find that truth.

Peck believes that God is so closely associated with us that he must be *part* of us. God is a part of our unconscious mind. We can think of our unconscious as a rhizome, or hidden root system, which nourishes the small plant of consciousness – the part of us that can think, analyze, and make decisions. In order to become as God, we don't necessarily need to make the conscious and unconscious one entity. Rather, we may *become as God while preserving our consciousness*.

Power

There are two types of power: political and spiritual. Many people are afraid of power, afraid that they will misuse it. This fear can be so strong that it compels them to consciously or unconsciously *avoid* power – by shying away from job promotions, spousal responsibility, child-rearing, etc.

Most people make decisions without thinking very much. The secret to making *wise decisions* and using power as a path to enrichment is to become more *aware* of what we are doing and to enlarge our capacity for awareness. " . . . Godlike power is the power to make decisions with total awareness." This is a long, uphill process, requiring much work. But gradually, we can develop an inner God-like spiritual power.

What road does the author suggest we travel? The higher, steeper, more disciplined road – the Road Less Traveled – that brings *spiritual power*. Through this power we can receive grace. We cannot *seek* grace; it must come to us. What we *can* do is *prepare* ourselves by becoming wholly loving individuals. We can listen to our unconscious (God) speaking through us and follow those dictates. We can become spiritually evolved individuals of the highest order.

When we "nurture ourselves and others without a primary concern of finding reward, then we will have become loveable, and the reward of being loved, which we have not sought, will find us. So it is with human love and so it is with God's love."

THE DIFFERENT DRUM

by M. Scott Peck, M.D., Simon & Schuster, New York, N.Y., 1987

In and through community lies the salvation of the world. Nothing is more important. Yet it is virtually impossible to describe community meaningfully to someone who has never experienced it – and most of us have never had an experience of true community . . . . Still, the attempt must be made.

In this book, Dr. Peck attempts to describe the meaning of spiritual community, the stages of its development, and its importance to the individual and to the world.

Bases of Community

Dr. Peck tells us how he first stumbled into the experience of true community. As a boy he attended a prestigious boarding school where competition to belong to the "in" group was keen. For reasons he didn't fully understand, he felt unhappy there, even after finally becoming a member of this group. Peck then transferred to a small Quaker school, where he immediately felt accepted and loved. At this school, the boundaries between people were "soft." There were about two hundred students enrolled, all from different social and economic backgrounds, yet no one was excluded or made fun of for being different.

The disparity in his experiences at these two schools compelled Peck to seek out other "belonging" experiences. In the army, and later while training to become a psychiatrist, he finally found other groups where true community was achieved.

Peck defines community as "a group of individuals who have learned how to communicate honestly with each other, whose relationships go deeper than their masks of composure, and who have developed some significant commitment to rejoice together, mourn together, to delight in each other and make others' conditions their own."

Today we live in relative isolation from others, both physically and emotionally. Often we don't know the names of our next door neighbors. We give the impression of confidence, that we have it all together – because it is considered "weak" to express emotions like anxiety or depression. We feel we must be strong, rugged individualists. But true community helps us overcome these defensive barriers, freeing us to express our true selves.

There are two main characteristics of such a community:

(1) A community is inclusive. Groups that exclude anyone for any reason are not true communities but cliques. Genuine communities always reach out to extend themselves. Members of a community commit themselves to one another. Decisions that affect the group are arrived at by consensus.

(2) A community emulates the real world. It embraces members with many different points of view, who, as they work their challenges through together, come to share and appreciate the many different facets and dimensions of each situation.

True communities are bonded by an intense *vitality*. Anyone involved in a group crisis – a flood or an earthquake for example – has seen how this works. Suddenly everyone is vitally concerned for others and more than willing to help. However, problems usually crop up once the crisis is over; and the "crisis community" dissolves into one of four self-destructive responses: "flight" (from troublesome issues), "fight" (among group members for control), "pairing" (into alliances that set the community at odds), or "dependency" (choosing leaders). Sometimes all four responses emerge to feed on each other.

Dr. Peck has conducted hundreds of community-building workshops. Participants usually pass through a four-step process as they struggle towards community.

1. *PSEUDOCOMMUNITY.* Commonly the first response of a group trying to form a community is to *fake it.* In this superficial situation, everyone tries to be pleasant in order to avoid conflict, but people remain evasive, hiding their real feelings. A group of sophisticated professionals, for example, may seem to get along very well, forming an almost "instant community." However, different ideologies and unvoiced resentments are probably hidden under a layer of sophisticated social skills, and may surface rapidly. Without proceeding through the second and third steps, the process of reaching true community is only delayed.

2. *CHAOS.* "Chaos centers around well-intentioned but misguided attempts to *heal* and *convert.*" In this phase, each person seeks to advance his or her "cause." It is during this stage that individual differences are first brought out in the open. And, unfortunately, groups in chaos frequently seek to overcome personality or philosophical differences by attacking their leaders or by forming sub-committees to solve their problems, instead of facing them and working together. Still, open chaos in a church congregation or company workteam is preferrable to pseudocommunity; it's a painful stage, but only by way of this pain comes the understanding that differences must be acknowledged and dealt with at a new level of relationship.

3. *EMPTINESS.* There are only two ways to do away with chaos: by *organization* (which isn't community) or by *emptiness.* Emptying ourselves involves putting aside any personal feelings that are acting as barriers to communication. Expectations, assumptions, preconceptions, motives, prejudices, ideologies, prefabricated solutions, and the need to heal or convert, fix, solve, or control, are all "given away." When a friend is grieving, we can either be like Job's friends in the Bible, who gave him "curative" advice (which often makes us feel worse), or we can *share* his pain. Just being there to listen is often what really makes a difference.

4. *COMMUNITY.* When emptiness is finally achieved, the group enters community – a *peaceful* and *trusting* atmosphere of resolution. Individuals are now given the freedom to be vulnerable and genuine as they deal with the various social challenges that present themselves. In this stage, sadness and grief are readily expressed, as are laughter and joy. And finally, a comfortable consensus in decision-making ensues. Group members become individually more eloquent and expressive; as a group they become more gentle.

Communes and Communities

The driving concept behind most communes is that all members should adhere to the same schedules, rules, ideas and behaviors. But the key to creating true communities is to accept and welcome the fact that *we are all different.* It sounds nice to say, "Underneath their skins, Russians are really just like us," but that is simply not true. A Russian's idea of freedom and democracy has been shaped by a cultural hierarchy distinctly different from ours. What is considered *normal* in one culture is considered *abnormal* in another. Even conceptions of good and evil are, to a considerable extent, culturally determined.

But human beings have the unique capacity to change, to be transformed. By exercising this capacity, we can surpass our own individual backgrounds, to both experience and transcend the differences between cultures.

Both personal and collective change occurs through augmented spiritual development, which is cultivated in four stages:

Stage I: *Chaotic, antisocial.* A stage of undeveloped spirituality. The Stage I person is selfish, disordered, and generally incapable of loving others.

Stage II: *Formal, institutional.* The stage II person, typified by many churchgoers, is usually attached to the forms rather than the essence of her religion, and she may quickly take offense at anyone who attacks these forms. Personal stability and outward appearances are very important to her.

Stage III: *Skeptic, individual.* The stage III person is often referred to as a "nonbeliever" because he has given up being "conventional." He thinks independently and is often deeply involved in social causes. An advanced stage III individual is an active truth-seeker.

Stage IV: *Mystic, communal.* This is the stage of unity. A person arriving at stage 4 sees an underlying connectedness between herself, other creatures, and her surroundings. With little or no outside prodding, and as a confident yet humble,

self-governing human being, she reaches out to others in recognition of the whole world as part of her community.

"Mystics" comprehend the value of emptiness. Rather than being frightened by the enormity of the unknown, they acknowledge it and immerse themselves ever deeper into it, that they may understand more. Likewise, we can, despite our differences, unite to form communities of caring friends and associates; we can transcend bigotry, selfishness, "ownership," and learn to solve problems in empathy and love.

Many variations exist among individuals in these four phases of spiritual development. Some of us may bounce back and forth between stages; many may feel threatened or intimidated by those functioning in the upper stages (III or IV). Certainly, parents, teachers, ministers, friends, and neighbors – and that includes everyone in some capacity – should be aware of the threat they may represent to those in different stages of spiritual growth. But the paradox remains that it is hard to lift anyone else unless we are already in a more spiritually discerning position than the person we seek to lift.

These four personal spiritual stages are analogous to the development of community. The hardest stage of community formation is to achieve – and return to – emptiness. "Emptiness requires work. It is an exercise of discipline and is always the most difficult part of the process that a group must undergo if it is to become a community . . . . For emptiness always requires a negation of the self . . . a sacrifice." In order to make a significant change in our lives we must give something up, and consequently must go through a form of depression.

The Solution:
An Expanding Community

Inasmuch as small communities have been successfully established, why not extend the idea of community to entire neighborhoods and schools – even to countries and to the world? In fact, progress is being made towards forming a global community. Individuals are slowly becoming more aware that communication is the key to the effective functioning of any group enterprise – a marriage, a corporation, a unified world. Sadly, though, the institutions that can tip the balance between war and peace – the arms-race nations, many charitable organizations, unions, churches – have barely been touched by the concept of community.

Peck notes that in democracies "we the people" elect our leaders. Thus, it is up to us to begin peacemaking – or, community-making. Learn to communicate with peoples of other cultures by first learning to commune with your family and understand your neighbor, urges Peck. Establish peaceful communities where you are, and let your influence spread. "Sell the world on love."

LOVE IS LETTING GO OF FEAR

by Gerald G. Jampolsky, M.D. , Celestial Arts, Berkeley, Ca., 1979

"There must be another way to go through life besides being pulled through it kicking and screaming," says Hugh Prather. Gerald Jampolsky agrees. A former heavy drinker who denied responsibility for his own emotions and actions, Jampolsky overcame his bouts of depression, guilt and anger by finally recognizing the source of his feelings. He found, however, that to follow life's "better path" required of him a willingness to change his goal.

Most of us want to rid ourselves of pain and frustration and experience peace of mind, but, at the same time, we want to control and predict future events and maintain our old self-concept. Consequently, we resist any real change or human contact and continue to feel isolated and unloved.

Jampolsky's book is a compilation of therapeutic methods and practical applications for making a "personal transformation towards a life of giving and Love, and away from getting and fear." We can dissolve fear, it says, through consciously establishing peace as our goal and forgiveness as its vehicle.

Preparation for Personal Transformation

What is real? Too often we accept feedback from our physical senses as the only "reality." However, *love*, though intangible, is real; and so is the *fear (ego)* that frequently thwarts love.

Our minds constantly replay all our memories, like a videotape. Included are tons of distorted and obsolete guilts and fears, which squeeze out the joy of the present. But "Love is letting go of fear."

Even in the present, our priorities frequently become scattered and filled with conflict, as we try to juggle too much at once. But by choosing a single life goal – that of inner peace – we become better able to focus our energies. Peace of mind, however, demands mind control. Judging people comes naturally; it's more difficult to love them. Yet, if we start by *forgiving* them, it will become more and more apparent that "other people do not have to change for us to experience love and peace of mind."

Jampolsky offers several "themes to live by," centered around peace of mind, forgiveness, inner direction and active choice. He asks us to "retrain" our minds; to make active choice and "self-examination" a daily habit: *Do I choose to find love or find fault? Do I choose to be a love giver or a love seeker?*

Ingredients of Personal Transformation

We are what we believe.

We are always expressing either love or fear. Fear is really a call for help . . . a request for love.

Fear and love can never be experienced at the same time . . . . By choosing love more consistently than fear, we can change the nature and quality of our relationships.

Such "true concepts," if we are mindful of them, allow us to shake negative thoughts and feelings.

Lessons for Personal Transformation

Below, in brief, are some of Jampolsky's lessons and examples, designed to help us apply true principles of inner peace.

Lesson: All that I Give is Given to Myself. "I was mistaken in believing that I could give anyone anything other than what I want for myself. Since I want to experience peace, love and forgiveness, these are the only gifts I would offer others . . . "

After visiting with Mother Teresa, Jampolsky asked if he could fly with her on her way to Mexico City. With a gentle smile, she replied, " . . . I would have no objection about your joining me . . . . But you said you wanted to learn about inner peace. I think you would learn more about inner peace if you would find out how much it costs to fly to Mexico City and back, and give that money to the poor." Her's was a powerful lesson in giving and receiving.

Lesson: Forgiveness is the Key to Happiness. "I cannot forgive myself unless I am willing to forgive others . . . " Bitterness is a mixture of distorted perceptions. And holding grievances or speaking condemning words doesn't help anyone; it only brings more bitterness. But forgiveness opens new doors in both hearts. Neither "guilt" nor "innocence" should play a part in our forgiveness.

On one occasion, Jampolsky consciously determined to bury his long-kept anger over a client's unpaid bill, informing him that no more bills would be sent. Surprisingly, the man paid the money, and Jampolsky was able to give it to someone who was in real need. Thus, by the vehicle of forgiveness, many hearts were healed.

Lesson: I Am Never Upset for the Reason I Think. It's easy to presume that "the outside world is the cause and we are the effect." But this thinking is backwards. The world doesn't "cause" feelings. "Peace of mind begins with our own thoughts and extends outward."

All negative feelings (jealousy, anger, resentment, etc.) in reality represent some form of fear. And fear frequently triggers other problems. Back pain is sometimes a manifestation of harbored hatred or envy, for instance. So, " . . . whenever you are tempted to be fearful, remind yourself that you can experience Love instead."

Lesson: I Am Determined to See Things Differently. A "fearful past will extend into a fearful future," making us feel vulnerable and out of control. This cycle of fear holds the assumption "that anger occurs because we have been attacked. It also assumes that counterattack is justified . . . " But we are not robots; we are free to follow our inner guidance and respond with understanding and love.

Jampolsky once was put in the position of saving a tubercular woman's life by giving her mouth-to-mouth resuscitation. Where before he had felt "attacked" by his patients and lived in continual fear of catching the dreaded disease, now it suddenly dawned on him that he had just learned a valuable lesson: " . . . When I was totally absorbed in giving, I felt no fear."

Lesson: I Am Not the Victim of the World I See. "Attacks" originate in the mind. Replace thoughts that others are hurting you with love thoughts. "To be consistent in achieving inner peace, we must perceive a world where everyone is innocent . . . I can see the world differently by changing my mind about what I see."

Often, as we go through our maturing processes, we also tend to learn the art of distrust. We become paranoid of life itself, not to mention distrustful of others (work associates, sales clerks, car dealers, etc.). But when we let go of this sense of "victimization," then our relationships become based on genuine respect and love.

Joe, a fifteen-year-old boy whose head was run over twice by a tractor, was left blind and paralyzed. How does he maintain his optimism? "Oh, I just look at the positive things in everyone – and pay no attention to the negative things, and refuse to believe in the word, 'impossible'." Joe refuses to feel sorry for himself, and miracles have followed. "He could feel that the world had dealt him a horrible blow. However, he chooses peace instead of conflict."

Lesson: Today I Will Judge Nothing that Occurs. "Tunnel vision": it makes us prone to "pigeonhole" people upon first meeting them. "We just see a fragment of a person and our mind often interprets what we see as a fault." Faultfinding is a habit; but focusing on the strengths of others is also a habit. "See everyone you meet or think of as either extending love, or as being fearful and sending out a call for help, which is a request for love."

For example, in a restaurant we might feel inclined to correct (attack) a rude waitress. If, instead, some voice whispered the truth in our ear – that the waitress' husband had died two days before, or that she's worried about finances, or that her oldest child was recently arrested for dealing drugs – then we could see the waitress, not as rude, but as fearful and calling out for love. With any person, we have the innate capacity for unconditional love. The highest gift we might be capable of offering is to overlook his or her weaknesses and demonstrate total acceptance.

Lesson: This Instant is the Only Time There Is. As experienced adults, we may find ourselves continually recycling old judgments, vulnerability and guilt. To break this distorted cycle, we must look upon the past as "archeological garbage" with no recycling value. "The past is over . . . " Peace is found "only in this instant." But in order to concentrate on the present, we must release "others and ourselves from all the errors of past pain and suffering."

The exasperated parents of a chronic schizophrenic thirty-five-year-old son once asked Jampolsky how they could apply the principles of love. "Spend as much time as you can before tomorrow ridding yourself of all the past, painful, guilty, fearful thoughts and experiences you have had with your son," he responded. "Release yourselves from any guilt you have about your son's condition." He urged them to imagine themselves stuffing their built-up pain into a trash can attached to a yellow helium balloon, and letting it float away. "Pay attention to how much lighter you feel. . . . Look past what your eyes and ears report. Choose to see your son only through the window of Love . . . " Soon after, the parents wrote to say that that day they "experienced the most peaceful visit with their son they had ever had."

Lesson: I Could See Peace Instead of This. Is your happiness or unhappiness based on events or people or "luck"? It is a natural response to use blame as a defense, absolving ourselves of responsibility. But when we see the bits and pieces of a fragmented world, it is only a reflection of the chaos we see in ourselves. "Peace of mind is an internal . . . matter." Accordingly, "whenever you feel that your peace is threatened by anything or anyone," repeat in your mind, "I could see peace instead of this."

In sickness, for example, each of us has the tendency to focus only on our own discomfort – and we complain loudly to reinforce our hopelessness. Jampolsky suggests, rather, that we direct our minds away from our bodies and center all of our attention on serving others. By doing this, we cease to see our own suffering, finding meaning in the maxim, "To give is to receive."

Lesson: I Can Elect to Change All Thoughts that Hurt. One technique to leaving worries and problems behind is to retreat from them. Visualize yourself in a favorite hide-away. Imagination, selectively released, often brings about fresh solutions to problems. Still, remember: "We are never presented with lessons until we are ready to learn them."

Jampolsky perceived a club-wielding psychiatric patient, "gone berserk" one day, as a personal threat. The patient was scared; but when the doctor openly admitted that he too was frightened, a "common bond" was created between the two, and they were able to compose and help each other.

One final, brief *Lesson – "I Am Responsible for What I See"* – capsulizes *Love is Letting Go of Fear:*

> *I Am Responsible for What I See*
> *I choose the feelings I experience, and I decide*
> *upon the goal I would achieve.*
> *And everything that seems to happen to me,*
> *I ask for, and receive as I have asked.*

> **Teach only Love for that is what you are.**

PSYCHO-CYBERNETICS

by Maxwell Maltz, M.D., Simon and Schuster, Inc. New York, N.Y., 1960

Doctor Maxwell Maltz, a plastic surgeon, noticed that most of his patients who underwent surgery to correct a major defect experienced an accompanying rise in self-esteem. However, in some cases the patient continued to have feelings of inferiority. This phenomenon led Maltz to conclude that changed physical image was not the only key to the changes he saw in personality. He felt the need to treat the *whole* patient rather than just the defective part that required his surgical skills.

While struggling with these ideas, Dr. Maltz became interested in *cybernetics*. Cybernetics is based on "teleology" – the study of purpose or design – and deals with the goal-striving behavior of mechanical systems. Cybernetics attempts to explain the necessary steps of mechanical processes; to find mechanical analogies that can also be applied to humans. Scientific evidence shows that the brain and nervous system operate harmoniously in a purposeful manner, much like the components of a complex machine. Of course, man is not a machine – but he has and uses the ultimate machine: his brain.

Self-Image and Imagining

Dr. Maltz, ascribing the principles of cybernetics to the brain, created the term (and the success mechanism) *"psycho-cybernetics."* PC, as it is sometimes called, is based on "self-imaging" – imagining successful outcomes. Self-image is the key to human personality and human behavior; *change the self-image and you change the personality and the behavior.* But more than this, self-image sets the boundaries of individual accomplishment. It defines what you can and cannot do. *Expand the self-image and you expand your "area of the possible."*

The development of an adequate, realistic self-image actually does seem to imbue the individual with new capabilities, new talents, and the gifts to literally turn failure into success.

Self-image is altered by *experience.* It is remarkable, but experiences don't have to involve actual events – they may be *synthesized*, proxy experiences created by the mind. Since the nervous system and brain do not distinguish between real and imagined experience, you can exercise your imagination to discover a "success mechanism" within yourself.

We inevitably act in accordance with our self-image. For example, if a student feels he is "dumb" in math, he will live up to that image by avoiding math homework and freezing up on tests. He will be frustrated, feeling there is nothing he can do to improve

his ability, when what he really needs is to change the way he *thinks* about himself. *Our self-image prescribes the limits for the accomplishment of our goals.*

A Success Mechanism

A sense of success is a key ingredient of a positive self-image. We know that animals possess *instincts* that help them survive as "successful" predators, swimmers or nestmakers. In addition to our intellectual, emotional and spiritual endowments, humans also have instincts. We too are survival-oriented, but unlike other animals, whose "goals" are predetermined, we are left to select our own goals. Luckily, we are not left alone; our *creative imagination* allows us to consider many possibilities and goal paths.

In this creative process, the brain and nervous system act as a "servo-mechanism," which "learns" or programs itself as it makes mistakes and receives negative feedback. This can be compared to a guided missile, making its way to a prescribed target; it uses trial and error (mistakes) as guides to correct its course.

The process of arriving at a new mental picture of yourself involves six steps:
  (1) Relax.
  (2) Imagine success.
  (3) "Dehypothesize" yourself from false beliefs.
  (4) Visualize goals (targets) as if they were already in existence.
  (5) Resolve to be unafraid of making mistakes.
  (6) Trust your creative mechanism to do the work.

Hypnotism is an example of the power of imagination. A hypnotized person who is told she is at the North Pole will often start to shiver. If she imagines meeting a bear on her path, she will respond with a typical "fight or flight" syndrome – rapid heartbeat, dilated pupils, etc.

Imagination (really another form of hypnotism) allows us to *practice* new actions and attitudes. *Visualizing* a successful action – from a masterful golf swing to a favorable job interview – can dramatically improve performance in real life. *Role-playing* and *rehearsal* have also been employed for years to bolster confidence and competence among salespeople and actors. To make your imagination work for you, you must actually *see yourself in your new role.* Maltz suggests imagining yourself acting and reacting appropriately and consistently for thirty minutes each day, until your whole self-image is modified.

We all suffer from certain feelings of inferiority, and each of us is in fact inferior to others in some areas. It is not the *knowledge* that we are inferior, however, but the *feeling* of being somehow "inherently" inferior that increases our negative self-image. To counteract this feeling, remember that there is no one else exactly like you. You are not competing to be better than others; you are striving to develop – and become – *yourself.*

Physical and mental relaxation also may help you counteract the need to compete and conform. Imagine a beautiful and gentle scene in all its detail. Concentrate on it for a short while every day, letting your worries fade and each part of your body loosen up.

But imagination is not all there is to changing a negative complex. Actually, *most learning comes about through trial and error.* And we must also learn to forget our errors once they have taught us their lessons. Don't dwell on failure; remember instead the attempts that finally worked.

Solving Problems and Being Happy

When you doubt your ability to accomplish a task, simply ask yourself why you believe you can't do it. Then examine this belief to see if it is based on actual fact or on a false premise. Ask:

• Is there any rationale for such a belief?

• Could it be that I am mistaken in this belief?

• Would I come to the same conclusion about someone else in a similar situation?

Sometimes it is best to relax your mind in problem-soving; *solutions often come more freely when you are not concentrating on them.* Rational thought must be accompanied by *deep feeling and desire* – again engendered through imagining. Picture the outcome you would like to see, and go over it again and again in your mind. (We do this very thing the other way around when we worry.) *Focus* on a positive image. Decide what you *want* to happen, not what you don't want. Keep yourself focused on the goal.

Most of us are too hesitant; even after a decision has been made, we often sit and wonder whether we are doing the right thing. But the only way to know this for sure is to *act* – and find out.

We can be happy (most of the time) only if we *decide* to be happy. The basis of happiness is refusing to allow other people or outside events to control our responses, and dwelling instead on pleasant, joy-producing incidents. *Develop the habit of being happy.*

Mechanisms

Success-oriented personalities embrace the following qualities in their thought mechanisms:

S-ense of direction
U-nderstanding
C-ourage
C-harity
E-steem
S-elf-Confidence
S-elf-Acceptance

Most people, however, have formed emotional scars. They have reacted to harmful or embarrassing events in their lives by developing a thick, tough "skin," resolving to never let anything or anyone hurt them that way again. To rid yourself of emotional scars, cultivate and balance *self-reliance* and *forgiveness* of self and others. Become your *real self* (a frequently hidden entity); trust your true personality. Stop worrying about what others think of you. Shake inhibitions, worry, and self-criticism by ignoring feedback that is not instructive and realizing that in most situations there is no simple right or wrong way of acting.

More and more people are turning to artifical tranquilizers to help them cope with life. However, your mind can manufacture its own "tranquilizers"; it can be trained to ignore "bells" or "signals" that previously brought on an automatic alarm reflex. A ringing telephone, for example, is a signal that someone wishes to speak with you, but *you can choose* whether to respond (answer it) or to ignore it (let it ring). In the same way, you should consciously understand that you are in control of deciding whether to *react* to an event immediately, to *ignore* it completely, or to utilize your natural tranquilizer (your mind) to *delay* response until you have rationally, creatively, and peacefully analyzed the situation.

To control your mind, relaxation (again) is crucial. If your days are hectic, a quiet room in which to "escape" may be just what you need. Another healthy method for dealing with difficult circumstances is to practice responses during times when there is no pressure – like going through a fire drill. Visualize and rehearse confident behavior in order to overcome fear in social situations, business meetings, sports, or any other area. *"Non-crisis conditioning"* injects you with a winning feeling and assures that you will be well prepared when it comes to doing the real thing.

Our minds are like a stereo playing a record. We each have the power to choose what kind of music is played. *Psycho-cybernetics* urges you to "mechanize" your responses in life by *setting goals, letting your unconscious and conscious mind cultivate them, conquering negative beliefs and feelings of failure, visualizing your targets through positive experiencing,* and, finally, *achieving the ultimate life-goal – happiness.*

UNDERSTANDING

Eliminating Stress and Finding Serenity in Life and Relationships
by Jane Nelsen, Ed.D. , Prima Publishing and Communications, Rocklin, California, 1988

Though she was a successful marriage, family and child therapist, Jane Nelsen was dissatisfied with her life; something seemed to be missing. It was not until she applied the principles she later described in *Understanding* that she discovered peace and happiness. In her book, Nelsen confronts the many thoughts, moods and long-held myths that act as barriers to happiness in our personal lives and relationships.

Society defines success as fame, fortune and achievement. We will be happy, we believe, when we finally make our fortune, find the perfect spouse, graduate from college, or end up at the top in our business. But most people who define success in these terms are unhappy, and will likely remain in misery. Happiness really does come from within.

There are four principles that can serve as a treasure map, says Nelsen, which will lead us to true inner happiness. In life's journey, our natural feelings of peace, love and joy frequently become clouded over by negative feelings. These feelings are created by negative thoughts and beliefs implanted along the way. Negative thoughts easily enslave us, and our subsequent reactions to them usually cause a negative outcome (or loss of joy). Built-up stress and insecurity can be eliminated by rejecting the negative thoughts that engender them in the first place.

Principle No. 1: *Thinking as a Function*
Truly, thoughts determine attitudes. However, most people believe they are *victims* of their thoughts rather than *producers* of them. Nelsen counters: "We can think anything we choose to think, and our emotions are then a direct result of what we choose to think." For example, try feeling insecure without thinking thoughts dealing with insecurity. It can't be done.

"Melissa believes she is depressed because life is overwhelming. But life cannot be overwhelming; only what she thinks about life makes it feel overwhelming." The simple solution?: "If you don't like what you are thinking about, stop thinking about it." Don't let your thoughts take control of your life.

Principle No. 2: *Feelings as a Compass*
Try viewing feelings as an indicator or a compass. "Negative feelings tell us it is time to dismiss negative thoughts. Positive feelings tell us we are experiencing life through our natural state of mind, where we have access to our inherent good feelings." To know whether an emotion comes from your true, inner self or from a false thought system, Nelsen advises: "If the feeling comes first, it is from your natural state of mind; if the feeling comes second, it is from your thought system." Thus, "secondary" feelings become a good indicator of the negative or positive thought-systems we are involved with.

The author shares a personal illustration: Her thirteen-year-old son had been suspended from school because cigarettes were found in his locker. As he told it: "I don't know how they got there. I was just putting them in my pocket to take them to the principal when a teacher came by . . . " She writes:

My thoughts went crazy for a few minutes. "He is lying to us. I'm a failure as a mother. If he is smoking cigarettes, he is probably also using alcohol and drugs. He is going to ruin his life. What will people think?" I was feeling pretty upset, so my feeling compass let me know loud and clear that I was caught up in my thought system and was not seeing things clearly. I dismissed my compass instead of my thoughts for a minute and used more thoughts to argue with my inner wisdom. "Yes, but this is different. These are really terrible circumstances . . . . How could I possibly see them differently? I am going to have to scold him severely, 'ground' him for at least a month, take away all his privileges, and let him know he is ruining his life."

But rather than react immediately, Nelsen used the second principle of *Understanding*. She started to reason from her son's position:

I then saw the circumstances in a completely different way and felt understanding and compassion . . . . [My son] had just entered junior high school, where the pressure is enormous to follow the crowd rather than to follow common sense.

When I got home I listened to my inspiration and knew what to do. I sat down with my son, put my arm around him, and said, "I'll bet it's tough trying to figure out how to say no to your friends so you won't be called a nerd or a party pooper." He had been expecting my usual craziness and hardly knew how to respond to my sanity. He tentatively said, "Yeah." I went on, "And I'll bet the only reason you would ever lie to us is because you love us so much you don't want to disappoint us." Tears filled his eyes, and he gave me a hug. I responded with tears in my own eyes as we experienced those wonderful feelings of mutual love. I reassured him, "If you think you could ever disappoint us enough to diminish our love, then we are not doing a good enough job of letting you know how much we love you, unconditionally.

Principle No. 3: Separate Realities

Each of us interprets life differently. "The reason becomes obvious when we understand that everyone sees through the filters of his or her own unique thought system." But when we stop judging and start *appreciating* people's differences, we can learn from them. Any form of condemnatory judgment, hatred or self-righteousness only contaminates the common sense that could lead to positive action. Allowing negative feelings to persist makes you "become like the thing or person you judge or hate, spreading more negativity in the world." Conversely, "Higher levels of understanding will come naturally from the positive feelings that surface when judgmental thoughts about separate realities are dismissed."

Principle No.4: Mood Levels

"When you are in a high mood, you see things one way; when you are in a low mood, you see the same things differently." For example, your natural self might gladly let someone go in front of you at the grocery check-out stand: She's in a hurry and only has two items. But if your thought system takes over, you reason differently: I'm in a hurry; he'll just have to wait. According to the principle of Mood Levels, when you are in a pleasant mood you are living in your natural state of mind and when you are angry or sad you are too often living in your thought system.

Once these four related principles are understood, we can actively change our situational responses. "The secret is knowing that moods are not nearly as bad as the thoughts we have about them; it is our thoughts about low moods that can make them seem really awful. Patiently wait for the mood to pass. A quiet mind is the best cure for a low mood . . . . Quiet is listening without judgement. Sometimes the simple realization that it is just a mood, will be enough to immediately raise your level of consciousness."

Conscious gratitude can help in altering a bad mood. Just by appreciating your health, talents, children or simply a beautiful object, you begin to want to give rather than receive. "Expecting something back is manipulative, conditional giving."

Destructive Myths

We frequently hold false assumptions about relationships. Here are listed a few of these myths.

• *Love is Blind:* Love is not blind. When in love, we should notice differences and see them as interesting and endearing rather than ignore them.

• *It is important to be compatible:* The notion that people have to think about and enjoy doing the same things to be compatible is simply not true. By respecting differences, we all have the ability to be compatible.

• *We will be happy when circumstances change:* You cannot experience joy by focusing on circumstances and "what is not." Get rid of the "shoulds" and the "should nots" and start seeing what is. A letter to Dear Abby from a woman who complained about her husband's snoring was followed up by another woman's insight: "I used to complain about snoring. My husband is dead now. I would give anything . . . "

• *Jealousy* (imagined fear, insecurity and possessiveness caused by ego) and *assumptions* (imagined ideas about how another person thinks or feels, which leads to distrust or blame) are two other barriers that limit clear, real, happy thinking.

Another core component of Nelsen's book is a section entitled "Lack of Wisdom, from the Ages." One pearl of false wisdom which many of us have been subjected to growing up is the adage: "Anything worth doing, is worth doing well." Like many myths, this is just not so. If "doing well" simply meant "putting your heart in it" or "enjoying it," the saying would be a positive help to us. But most often we define doing a thing well as executing it perfectly – a judgement of what is ideal. The greatest treasures – joy and serenity in doing – should replace judgement.

"When happiness is more important to you than anything else, you will be happy," Nelsen says, "because there will be no thoughts you will be willing to give up your happiness for . . . . When understanding changes how we see things, everything and everyone in our world looks different. It may seem as though others have changed, but it is our thoughts, and thus our reality, and thus our feelings that have changed. Others often respond to our feeling level. When we give love, we get love – not necessarily because others give it back to us, but because love will emanate from within."

"AS A MAN THINKETH, SO IS HE."

YOU CAN NEGOTIATE ANYTHING

How To Get What You Want
by Herb Cohen, Citadel Press, Secaucus, N.J., 1980

All of us are participatants in negotiation, the theme of Herb Cohen's book. We constantly negotiate with others to get what we want out of life, and the most successful people often have developed the best negotiating skills. Three crucial variables need to be addressed in the art of negotiation: *power, time,* and *information.*

POWER

Power is the ability to get things done, to achieve goals. Whenever you can expand the options available to you, you have greater power. Below are some of Cohen's suggestions for using various types of power. (Keep in mind that an ethical stance and comportment need to be incorporated into each of these suggestions.)

- *The Power of Competition*
Whenever there is competition for a possession (money, time, or skills), that possession moves up in value. To make this power work for you, you can not let on that what you are seeking – a job, a bank loan, or whatever – means the world to you. For instance, if a prospective home-buyer's attitude is, "My wife and kids will leave home if we don't buy this dream house," he will be lucky not to pay more than the asking price! Presume that you can go elsewhere for your loan; you have other job offers you're considering. This instills within the other person greater eagerness to give you what you want.

- *The Power of Legitimacy*
In our society, people are conditioned to regard with awe anything that's in print. Most will not challenge documents and forms; they carry an assumed authority.

- *The Power of Risk-Taking*
Taking risks doesn't mean gambling all your savings. It simply means mixing courage with common sense. Intelligent risk-taking involves a knowledge of the odds as well as a willingness to walk away from a negotiation if things don't work out.

- *The Power of Expertise*
To establish your power base as an expert, subtly allude to your background and credentials early in the confrontation. That way your statements may not even be challenged. And when you are confronted by an "expert" on the other side of a negotiation, don't be over-impressed; if you didn't have something she really wanted, she wouldn't be there.

- *The Power of Knowing "Needs"*
"In all negotiations, two things are being bargained for: 1. The specific issues and demands, which are stated openly. 2. The real needs of the other side, which are rarely verbalized." Translation: When looking to buy a car, first gather specific data about the car itself (performance, costs, potential problems, etc.), and then find out about the various dealers you will visit. Do they have any cash-flow problems, larger than normal inventory, itemized costs? How are their salespeople compensated? After this preparation you can "adapt [your] purchasing style to satisfy the real needs of the seller."

- *The Power of Investment*
If you come to a sore spot in negotiating an issue, go on and talk about other aspects of the issue. Then come back to the unresolved question. Chances are the other party will be willing to negotiate on that aspect because he has already invested a large amount of time and energy.

- *The Power of Reward and Punishment*
The perception that someone else can either help or hurt you – physically, financially, or psychologically – gives him power in your relationship. "If I'm aware of your perceptions and needs, and if I know you think I have power over you, I can control your behavior."

- *The Power of Precedent*
Precedent limits our way of thinking to our own past experience and basic assumptions. To justify what you are asking for in a negotiation, refer to similar past situations where you or others did so-and-so with favorable results.

- *The Power of Persistence*
"Most people aren't persistent enough when negotiating." Stick to your goals and recognize that successful negotiaions generally take some time.

TIME

Most people envision negotiations as having a definite beginning and ending. Actually, there is usually no rigidly fixed time frame. However, since most concessions are made just before a perceived deadline, remaining calm and focused right to the "end" can help you feel less pressured to conclude a deal "on time." This was the North Vietnamese delegation's "ace in the hole" when dealing with U.S. negotiators, who wanted dearly to end the conflict. The Vietnamese did have a deadline, but their nonchalant posture and eagerness to question even the most trivial matters, made their deadline seem almost infinitely flexible – and they were very successful.

Remember, *"deadlines" are often more flexible than they may seem.* Granted, they should not be ignored, but they should be analyzed: "What will happen if I go beyond the deadline? What will be the extent of any penalty?" For example, if you owe taxes and file late, you will be penalized.

However, obtaining a loan to pay the tax on time would be unwise, since the interest on the loan would probably be greater than the penalty.

INFORMATION

Information-gathering – appraising the reality of the situation – can avert the "crisis" response that often mars our performance when we enter a negotiation unprepared. It gives you a huge advantage in a negotiation to anticipate what the other side *really* wants, along with her perceived limits and deadlines. Secretaries, technicians, customers or competitors – past or present – who deal with your opposition can provide invaluable information.

Approaching Negotiations

There are two primary methods of negotiating: *"win at all costs"* (sometimes called the "Soviet" style) and *"win-win."*

The "Soviet" negotiator sees every negotiation as a struggle between winning and losing – and he wants to win. Several clues can help you distinguish a negotiator using this style. Commonly, he will:

- Initially take positions that are extreme.

- Claim limited authority – so that you wind up bidding not against him, but against yourself.

- Employ emotional tactics.

- Treat you in an adversarial, competitive manner.

- Presume that any concessions you offer are a sign of weakness.

- Remain stingy in offering his own concessions.

- Ignore deadlines.

When confronted by someone using these tactics, you have several options:

(1) Walk away; don't play the game and get out of the negotiation.

(2) Try to use these same tactics yourself.

(3) Seek to switch the negotiation to a collaborative, win-win encounter.

By contrast, the person using a win-win approach tries to produce *acceptable gains for both parties.* She regards conflict as a problem to be solved, an opportunity to uncover creative, enhancing positions. And when both parties are committed to a win-win approach – a style marked by mutual "trust" and empathy – you can get down to hammering out an agreement.

"Have you not learned great lessons from those who braced themselves against you?" asked Walt Whitman. Certainly, fair competition and opposition is what growth is all about. In fact, you are likely skirting negotiation and conflict – and not getting even close to what you want – if you have no opponents.

"Opposition comes in two forms: A. Idea opponents, and B. Visceral opponents." Dealing with idea opponents requires pooling of information, experience and feelings. You must start from a perception of trust and agreement on something, and build from there. Maybe a "repackaging" of issues can be done to meet individual needs, i.e. moving an employment discussion away from salary itself and talk over other forms of compensation (company car, profit sharing . . .).

A visceral opponent is much more difficult to deal with, since he deals on an emotional level and "not only disagrees with your point of view, but disagrees with you as a human being." Often, he wants to save face publicly as well as preserve his private self-image. How do you deal with him when he attacks you personally by calling you a fraud, a clown, a liar? (1) Don't let yourself care too much, and (2) Never overtly judge your opponent's actions or motives. For example, a child arrives home and casually informs you that she's been offered a marijuana cigarette. Your judgmental and "caring too much" response? "You what!..." This will only turn any candid discussion sour. Your overall *bearing,* tone of *voice,* conveyed *attitude,* bartering *method,* and the *concern* exhibited for the other side's feelings and needs, all combine to help you succeed or fail.

The first few minutes of a negotiation are the most vital. Start off by stating your case *moderately,* nonjudgmentally, and with the attitude that you still harbor some questions about your own position. Instead of "This place looks like a pig sty . . . " (when shocked by your child's room), or "Your analysis of these data is all wrong . . . " (in a business meeting), try: "When this room is not tidy I feel frustrated and upset." and "I must be looking at the data differently than you. I feel that . . . "

The next step is to *harmonize* or *reconcile needs.* Needs must be brought out into the open so free interaction and sharing can take place. Conflicts regarding past experience, present information, or decision-making authority must also be resolved.

Finally, with no hint of intimidation or manipulation – for in collaborative negotiation there is no need for conniving or flimflamming – you can arrive at a *compromise solution;* a solution that meets both your needs.

Cohen examines other issues that can either make or break a negotiation. He treats how to personalize negotiation, how to be a "squeaky wheel," and the advantages and disadvantages of telephone negotiations. He is convinced that each of us has the inner strength to negotiate successfully – from everyday job and family matters to formal across-the-table corporate scale bargaining. The secret lies in detecting what the other side wants, and then showing him that you can help him obtain it, while still preserving your own goals and integrity. Power, Time and Information are the recognized keys to negotiating with authority.

HOW TO PROSPER DURING THE COMING BAD YEARS

by Howard J. Ruff, Times Books, New York, N.Y., 1979

"Invest in inflation, it's the only thing that's going up."

- Will Rogers

Howard Ruff does not believe that the United States is "going under." However, he does feel that the nation is in an increasingly fragile state, where collapses (national, local, or within families) are more and more likely to occur. Ruff's opinion is that we *will* survive the coming economic and social difficulties if we are prepared. *Personal preparation* is the focus of his book.

Part I: Problems

Odds are, your neighbor spends more than he makes. The same could be said of you, your county government, and most Washington offices. Debt and mortgages are the norm. But the result of spending money we don't have is inflation, and this is the monster creeping up to devour us. Nevertheless, you don't have to be eaten alive if you understand the dangers involved, and make some simple decisions to regulate your assets.

Economic trends indicate, says Ruff, that eventually, whether through inflation or national emergency, the nation's monetary system will forcibly be returned to the gold-backed standard. When that time comes, because our gold reserves have been greatly depleted, the price of metals will skyrocket. Investors in commodities such as precious metals, that either hold their values or go up in value, will not only survive, but prosper during this crisis. These financially shrewd individuals and families will remain "solvent, self-sufficient and panic-proof . . . "

What are the issues that will threaten your future prosperity? How will you react to these realities? Ruff suggests two possible problems, along with possible scenarios for each:

Inflation

Inflation is the decrease in value of your money. Both history and contemporary national and international crises have shown that inflation can weaken personal pocketbooks and shatter national economies. The world's economic future depends on the U.S. dollar, which is recurrently at risk of collapse.

In like manner, your individual retirement account robs you. The retirement annuity that looked so promising twenty years ago would now reduce you to living at the poverty level. Governmental inflation reduces your spending power, nibbles at your savings, your stocks . . . In short, most of your assets are diminishing in value.

Who loses money due to inflation?

- The lender (you, if you have a mortgage, a life insurance policy, or bonds)

- The saver (you again, if you put money into a bank or Savings and Loan)

- The pensioner (you, if you have set up an annuity or rely on Social Security, both of which feed on your interest and whose actual purchasing power will be close to nil by the time you cash in on them)

Who are the winners?

- Big borrowers (like the Government)

- Big business

- Mortgage companies

- Those who invest early to hedge potential financial chaos (possibly you!)

City Deterioration

The dearth of safety and services in our major cities, and their preponderance of poor and dissatisfied inhabitants, will make them the first victims of inflation and monetary disruption. The already dangerous climate of our cities is worsening. Crime *does* pay because so few criminals go to jail; welfare rolls swell because there is little economic incentive to work; slums expand; property values plummet; jobs are scarce. When the "crunch" hits, city families and property will be in danger.

Ruff further avows that, besides cities overcrowded with people "on the edge" of poverty, a combination of other factors puts us all at risk: decreasing birth rates and increasing longevity; general distrust, by most citizens, of governments and their economic future; and the reliance of American banks on foreign capital. These risk factors may cause many small breakdowns (materials shortages or a series of unsettled strikes, for instance), or they may lead to one major disaster. "Basically," says Ruff, "I am outlining a new way of helping people become financially secure at a time when the institutions they have come to depend on are clearly failing them."

Parts II and III:
Preservation and Strategy

Inflation can be good for you – *if you invest in it.* To make inflation work *for* you, you must own some of those things which are going up in value as fast or faster than inflation itself is rising.

If you have to periodically buy something on a regular basis, and prices rise, you are hurt by inflation. If you already bought a lot of it when it was cheap, you can watch your wealth increase and you are on good terms with the inflationary monster . . . [Then,] if you live in the right place and have a reasonable amount of self-sufficiency, and the distribution machine misses a few beats, you'll still be O.K.

Even if the odds favor good times in the coming few years, Ruff submits the following as sound advice. (For emphasis, he leaves his most important recommendation till last.):

- Keep, in a safe deposit box, a bag of "junk" silver (one per person), and, if feasible, an equivalent amount of gold to avoid the hazards of our paper-based economy. Metals hold steady in value even in the worst of times. (However, don't buy from a private mint or on margin.)

- Avoid unnecessary debt. Over-extension causes risks – and accompanying fear. Borrow only to purchase income-producing investments or those that inflate in overall value. Pay off your mortgage completely, if possible.

- Sell big-city or suburban real estate and purchase small-town property. Move there, if you are able. Small-town homes will be the safest in the event of a crisis – riot, disrupted services (water supply, electricity, etc.) or financial depression.

- When buying a home or investment property, either pay in immediate cash or invest as little cash as possible; "Nothing in between makes sense." By choosing one of these two paths, you either avoid the interest of a mortgage, or leave your funds available for other good investments.

- In less urban areas, small-scale residential units (up to a "four plex") are usually favorable investments. There will always be renters; everybody has to have a place to live. (Of course, remember that being a landlord also takes time and upkeep. Don't invest beyond your resources.)

- Spread your risks among as many inflation-beating investments as possible.

- Be highly self-sufficient. By all means, have some food stored and plant a garden. Keep chickens or rabbits; have a generator, a water well, a modern wood-burning stove and a supply of wood, an underground gas tank, a bicycle or moped. Know how to hunt and fish, and have the needed equipment. Learn practical skills such as home and auto repair.

- Plan your future as if Social Security didn't exist.

- Maintain some cash reserves for emergencies, but don't keep them in savings or checking accounts. Money-funds or Treasury Bills earn better rates and are liquid and safe.

- Have on hand a supply of those items that would likely be scarce in the event of a shortage: food, water, seeds, tools, ammunition, reading material, durable clothing, soap, toilet paper, motor oil, automobile replacement parts, light bulbs, etc. Buy these in quantity when they are at bargain prices. It will surely save you money; and the items you don't use yourself may serve as barter in times of need.

Top, Number One Recommendation:

- Store enough usable food to last one year (dehydrated food is top priority). In Europe during the early 1920's, diamonds, heirlooms, silver sets, and other luxury items were steadily transferred from their upper class owners to the peasants as barter for sacks of potatoes. Panic-proof yourself by having food on hand *before* the widespread hoarding that commonly accompanies a crisis. Many factors make food a vulnerable commodity – weather conditions, oil supply, transportation and worker demands, for example, not to mention your monetary ability to buy food if the economy goes sour.

Ruff stresses having a proper food supply; after all, "no one can raise prices on food you bought last year," and "food storage is the insurance you can eat." Stored food represents money well invested, and not only prepares you to meet a possible widespread disaster down the road, but hedges you up against personal hardship brought on by an accident or the loss of work.

■ ■ ■

How to Prosper in the Coming Bad Years provides details on many other subjects related to basic principles of preparedness: real estate; leveraging of money; metals-buying; negotiation techniques; securing a loan; steps and stages of survival; food production, planning, buying, and storage, etc.

The book's appendices list publications and newsletters that, in Ruff's view, offer good financial advice *(The Wall Street Journal, Business Week, Forbes)*. Also, Ruff endorses certain companies that can help make real progress toward your present goals of future prosperity and peace of mind.

WEALTH WITHOUT RISK

by Charles J. Givens, Simon and Schuster, New York, N.Y., 1988

Chuck Givens learned about money the hard way. At the youthful age of 25 he had already earned his first million in the music business; at 26 he lost his recording studio and office building in a fire – and he had no fire insurance.

Givens made his second fortune buying and selling stocks; but in 1968 the stock market collapsed, and so, again, did his wealth.

A third fortune was made – and subsequently lost – through the establishment of a luxurious yacht club. What he had not counted on was the Florida State Legislature passing an ecological bill that shut down his docks.

Thus, within a span of eight years, Givens had three times amassed and then lost multi-million dollar fortunes. Then in 1971, his success with real-estate investments and a leverage business enabled him to build and maintain his present wealth. Through the ups and downs of all these financial experiences, he feels that he has developed money strategies that can help anyone.

Wealth Without Risk was written to show anyone how to "build your wealth quickly and easily by making your financial decisions correctly and with confidence." Givens' philosophies are broken down into 268 financial strategies, under three major headings. Some "superstrategies" delve into the intricacies of mutual funds, annuities, IRA's and KEOGH's; others offer practical advice on cutting taxes, putting children through college and traveling on less money. Though some of these strategies are too complex to synopsize in a limited space, a few "select" strategies from each of the book's three sections are capsulized here.

I - PERSONAL FINANCES

First, figure out your goals in life and come up with a *dream list*. Ask: "If I had unlimited time, talent, money, ability, self-confidence and support from my family, what would I do?" Then, list the steps necessary to achieve these goals. This becomes the personal and financial road map to get you from where you are to where you want to be. "By clearly defining your directions and by adopting the correct money and attitude strategies for control, you will automatically establish the shortest possible route."

Insurance

Making big money does not take big money, only knowledge and a little time. However, "the more assets you acquire the more important your personal liability protection becomes," asserts Givens. He advises avoiding the two biggest insurance coverage mistakes: being either underinsured or overinsured.

Injury and Auto
Strategy #3: *Carry enough bodily injury liability insurance to cover your net assets plus all potential legal fees.*

Strategy #4: *Carry a minimum of $50,000 and a maximum of $100,000 in property damage liability.*

Strategy #5: *Buy $1,000,000 of umbrella liability coverage at a cost of under $150 per year.* This should protect all personal liabilities not covered under your existing policies.

Strategy #6: *When the value of your car drops below $1500, drop the collision and comprehensive coverage.* If your car is damaged you cannot collect more than the car is worth, and thieves and vandals are less likely to victimize older, less valuable vehicles.

Strategy #7: *Drop duplicate coverages – medical payments, no-fault (PIP) insurance, and uninsured motorists coverage (UMC).* You and your family members are already covered under your hospitalization policy, and others riding in your car are usually covered under either the liability portion of your insurance policy or by their own insurance. Since you cannot collect twice for the same medical expenses, drop the medical coverage under your existing automobile policy.

Don't buy any no-fault insurance unless it is required by state law.

Life
Strategy #38: *The purpose of life insurance is to take care of your family in the event of your death, not to serve as an investment or a savings plan.* Buy enough term insurance to provide 50% of current family income if invested at 15% per year. "Studies have shown that it will cost your spouse and children only 50% as much money if you are gone to maintain about the same lifestyle." This means that if you are making $100,000 per year you will need $350,000 of term coverage. Invested at 15%, this amount would provide your family with a $50,000 annual income.

Strategy #40: *Replace your existing whole life and universal life policies with term insurance.* Whole life cash value "is really the property of the insurance company and makes the insurance you are buying overpriced by 600%." Term coverage is pure insurance – the least expensive form of life insurance.

Credit and Mortgage
Strategy #59: *To rehabilitate credit, borrow the bank's money, and use it as security for the loan.* By borrowing money from the bank and immediately putting it into a savings account, you can establish a good credit rating by paying off the first two loan payments within 30 days and the remainder of the loan within 90 days.

Strategy #65: *When buying property, buy a 15-*

year mortgage instead of a 30-year mortgage. After ten years of making monthly payments on a 30-year loan, you have paid off only 5% of its principal. On the other hand, after ten years paying on a 15-year mortgage, you have paid off 45% of the original principal.

Strategy #66: *Cut your mortgage term in half with extra principal payments.* Since refinancing an existing mortgage could be costly, you can still pay off a 30-year mortgage in half the time by making extra principal payments.

II - REDUCING TAXES

Givens claims that the biggest expense you'll ever have in your lifetime is neither a home nor education, but income taxes. These strategies can help you reduce taxes up to 50% by "learning to turn the money you spend into legitimate tax deductions" and shelters. (Note: tax laws change from year to year and may be different from state to state.)

Strategy #94: *File your return later, not earlier.* Selection for possible audits come on a first come basis; when the chosen number of audits is filled, the computer stops spitting them out. So, the later you file, the less likely you are to be audited.

Strategy #119: *Borrow the money for your IRA – even if you have it.* The IRS has now ruled that the interest you pay on money borrowed for an IRA is tax deductible.

Strategy #123: *Contribute to your retirement plan now – don't wait until later.* "If you invest $2,000 in a tax-deferred retirement account each year between the ages of 20 and 26, and never invest another cent, you will have more money when you reach age 65 than if you wait until you are 26 and invest $2,000 every year for the next 40 years without retirement account tax protection."

Strategy #139: *Use job interviews to make vacations deductible.* Keep copies of job applications for your tax files along with airline, hotel, food, and rental car receipts.

Strategy #150: *Use employee business deductions to turn your job into a tax shelter.*

Strategy #159: *Get next year's tax refund this year.* By adding allowances to your W-4 form, you can get next year's refund in this year's paycheck. Then go ahead and invest the money to work for you, rather than for the government.

Strategy #161: *Turn home improvements into tax deductions.* Know the difference between home *repairs* – non-deductible upon resale of your home – and home *improvements*, which are deductible when you sell.

Strategy #167: *Use your boat, plane or motor home in your small business to create tax deductions.* You might use a motor home as an office, to display products or services, or as a traveling billboard.

III- POWERFUL INVESTMENTS

These strategies focus on three major investment objectives: (1) At least a 20% safe return; (2) No commissions payments; and (3) No tax payments.

Strategy #217: *Use the "10% solution" to go from paycheck to prosperity.* Take 10% off the top of each paycheck and send it to a mutual fund family. Pay yourself first, before you pay your monthly bills.

Strategy #224: *Choose an asset management account that offers a debit card.* With a debit card the amount you pay is directly deducted from your Asset Management Account; you do not have to write a check. Such an account usually pays interest on your money until you find a higher rate of interest in another investment vehicle.

Strategy #229: *Use only "no-load" mutual funds.* These funds charge no commissions on your money when you invest or withdraw. Though all mutual funds do charge a management fee of about 1% per year, the Net Asset Value (NAV), quoted in most newspapers, already reflects the deduction of this fee. When judging a loaded fund's performance, calculate the sales commission when you determine your overall return.

Strategy #231: *Invest in only one type of mutual fund at a time.* Many investment salespeople will urge you to overdiversify, dividing your capital into stocks, bonds, government securities, money market funds, etc. But Givens insists that since different market trends favor different mutual funds, if you overdiversify, then like a seesaw, one side goes down when the other goes up, leaving you with minimal profit.

Strategy #235: *Move your money into a bond fund when the prime rate is high – and just before it comes down.* When the prime rate drops 1%, bonds appreciate 10%; when the prime rate rises 1%, bonds depreciate 10%.

Strategy #248: *Use a self-directed annuity.* "A self-directed annuity is a tax-sheltered mutual fund family in which you have a choice of investments." All self-directed annuities offer three primary investment choices – stocks, bonds, and money-market mutual funds. Because the annuity is tax-sheltered, you may move your money from one fund to another with no tax liability, and, in most cases, it earns 20% interest and you can yearly withdraw 10% of your assets without penalty or commission, although you would be liable for any income taxes owed on this money.

This is just a sampler of the many money strategies and techniques found in *Wealth Without Risk* – today's ideas for creating wealth.

THE RICHEST MAN IN BABYLON

by George S. Clason, Hawthorn Books, New York, N.Y., 1955

The Richest Man in Babylon is a compilation of pamphlets dealing with personal finance, written as parables set in ancient Babylon. The book is based on the adage that "A lean purse is easier to cure than to endure."

Friends of Arkad approached him saying: "You, Arkad, are more fortunate than we. You have become the richest man in Babylon while we struggle for existence." Now these men had all been taught by the same teacher and had played the same games in their youth. They noted that Arkad had not outperformed them in either schooling or the games. So, how could his riches be explained?

Arkad answered his friends: "If you have not acquired more than a bare existence in the years since we were youths, it is because you either have failed to learn the laws that govern the building of wealth, or else you do not observe them." He then revealed how he had recognized early that if he was to achieve his youthful desire to accumulate wealth and put it to good use, two things – *time* and *study* – would be required.

"As for time, all men have it in abundance. You, each of you, have let slip by sufficient time to have made yourselves wealthy . . . " Arkad said. "As for study, did not our wise teacher teach us that learning was of two kinds: the one kind being the things we learned and knew, and the other being the training that taught us how to find out what we did not know?"

Arkad went on to share with his friends his story:

As a young man, he had found work inscribing clay tablets in the hall of records. One day Algamish, the money lender, ordered a copy of a law which must be ready within a very short time. "Algamish, you are a very rich man," said Arkad. "Tell me how I may also become rich, and all night I will carve upon the clay, and when the sun rises it shall be completed." Algamish smiled and replied, "We will call it a bargain." Arkad worked through the night and fulfilled the task.

Algamish told Arkad: "I found the road to wealth when I decided that *a part of all I earned was mine to keep*. And so will you." By faithfully following this principle, Arkad eventually became the richest man in all Babylon.

Seven Cures for a Lean Purse

After many years of prosperity, Babylon found itself in sore straits. Few people in the city had sufficient money to provide for their needs. The king called Arkad before him, questioned him about his secret of wealth and asked if it could be taught. Arkad responded, " . . . That which one man knows can be taught to others."

One hundred teachers assembled in the Temple of Learning, where Arkad instructed them in the seven cures for a lean purse.

The First Cure - *Start thy purse to fattening:* "For every ten coins thou placest within thy purse take out for use but nine. Thy purse will start to fatten . . . and bring satisfaction to thy soul." Arkad ended the first class by declaring: "Which desirest thou the most? Is it the gratification of thy desires of each day? Or is it for substantial belongings? The coins thou takest from thy purse bring the first. The coins thou leavest within it will bring the latter."

The Second Cure - *Control thy expenditures:* "That which each of us calls our 'necessary expenses' will always grow equal to our income unless we protest to the contrary." The key is to institute and observe a budget. "The purpose of a budget is to help thy purse to fatten."

The Third Cure - *Make thy gold multiply:* "Put each coin to laboring that it may reproduce its kind even as the flocks of the field and [bring] a stream of wealth that shall flow constantly into thy purse."

The Fourth Cure - *Guard thy treasures from loss:* The first rule for sound investing is "security for thy principal." Study investments wisely before parting with hard-earned money.

The Fifth Cure - *Make of thy dwelling a profitable investment:* By owning your home you can invest a portion of the nine-tenths of your money that you live on, and make your worth grow more rapidly.

The Sixth Cure - *Insure a future income:* Plan and save now for the time when you do not have the capacity to earn.

The Seventh Cure - *Increase thy ability to earn:* "The more . . . we know, the more we may earn. That man who seeks to learn more of his craft shall be richly rewarded."

Along with these cures, Arkad continually advised against "overstraining" (trying to save too much) and becoming "niggardly and afraid to spend." He suggested hard work, compassion toward those less fortunate, and making life "rich with things worthwhile and things to enjoy." He also counselled:

Desires must be simple and definite. They

defeat their own purpose should they be too many, too confusing, or beyond a man's training to accomplish.

Meet the Goddess of Good Luck

In ancient Babylon, those who sought greater understanding would meet in the Temple of Learning. There, rich and poor alike questioned one another and debated many issues.

On one evening, Arkad presided in the Temple of Learning over a discussion on how a person could attract the Goddess of Good Luck. The men mourned their lack of success – at finding unclaimed valuables, at the gaming tables, and at the race tracks – finding that none of these had made their fortune.

The group then observed those among them who had found good fortune in their professions, and concluded that "good luck can be enticed by accepting opportunity." "Luck" is created by taking action and overcoming procrastination.

The Laws of Gold

A bag heavy with gold or a clay tablet carved with words of wisdom: if thou hadst thy choice, which wouldst thou choose?

This question Kalabab asked of his servants. When they all responded that they would take the gold, Kalabab told them the story of Nomasir, Arkad's son . . .

The father called Nomasir to stand before him and stated that he would be required to prove himself in order to inherit Arkad's estate. He gave Nomasir a bag of gold and a tablet which had carved upon it five laws of gold.

Nomasir traveled to Ninevah to prove himself to his father. He had terrible experiences with the gold, spending it foolishly and without thought. Soon he had no money. At that point, he turned to the tablets and studied the Five Laws of Gold. Here he read his father's wisdom on reserving one tenth of all earnings and making gold multiply; and here he also found new wisdom:

Gold clingeth to the protection of the cautious owner who invests it under the advice of men wise in its handling . . . . Gold flees the man who would force it to impossible earnings or who followeth the alluring advice of tricksters and schemers or who trusts it to his own inexperience and romantic desires in investment.

When Nomasir discerned and applied the Five Laws of Gold, he was able to increase that which his father had given him many times over.

The Gold Lender of Babylon

Rodan had just received a tribute from the king – fifty pieces of gold. He retired to the gold lender to discuss the desires of family members to borrow the money. The gold lender advised Rodan that if his desire was to help his friends and family, he should do it in a way that would not bring their burdens upon himself, and illustrated this concept in a parable:

This farmer, who could understand what the animals said to each other, did linger in the farm yard each evening just to listen to their words. One evening he did hear the ox bemoaning to the ass the hardness of his lot: "I do labor pulling the plow from morning until night . . . . But you are a creature of leisure. You are trapped with a colorful blanket and do nothing more than carry our master about where he wishes to go. When he goes nowhere you do rest and eat the green grass all the day."

The ass replied,

My good friend, you do work very hard and I would ease your lot. Therefore . . . in the morning when the slave comes to fetch you to the plow, lie upon the ground and bellow much that he may say you are sick and cannot work.

The ox did as the ass had suggested, whereupon the farmer commanded, "Hitch the ass to the plow for the plowing must go on. All that day the ass, who had only intended to help his friend, found himself compelled to do the ox's task."

A man should not be "swayed by the fantastic plans of impractical men," but every time he allows a gold piece to leave his purse, he must be satisfied that at any time he can reclaim it with a profit.

The Camel Trader of Babylon

When a person is in debt he loses the soul of a free man and becomes a slave. But if he has the determination to regain his soul, the way can be found.

Five clay tablets, Babylonian in origin, were sent to Professor Caldwell to be translated. The tablets were records of a camel trader of Babylon, and contained this man's plan to get out of debt. He had resolved to put away ten percent of his income, live on seventy percent, and pay twenty percent to his creditors. Most of his creditors found this acceptable, because they were sure to ultimately be paid in full.

Professor Caldwell and his wife, who found themselves in financial difficulty, decided to try this approach. They found that the plan which had worked for a humble Babylonian camel trader long ago worked just as well for them today.

MARSHALL LOEB'S 1988 MONEY GUIDE

by Marshall Loeb, Little, Brown and Co., Boston, Massachusetts, 1987

"Greatly expanded and completely updated," reads the promotion for this edition of the *Money Guide*. Loeb, the managing editor of *Fortune Magazine*, took his 400-plus chapters from scripts of daily radio broadcasts on financial advice. In them, he details the many "sensible" ways your money can be handled to make it grow and provide you greater personal freedom. Here are some of his key recommendations:

10 Initial Steps
to Wise Financial Decisions

(1) Open an *Individual Retirement Account*, a "valuable device both for reducing your taxes and for increasing your capital."

(2) If you are eligible (self-employed), also open a *Keogh* account.

(3) Act now to further *reduce your taxes* by keeping records of deductible expenses, buying municipal bonds, depositing money into your company's profit-sharing or stock purchase programs . . .

(4) Build up a *cash cushion* to protect yourself against emergencies.

(5) *Start investing* regularly and faithfully by branching out from diversified mutual funds into stocks, bonds, limited partnerships and real estate.

(6) Be sure you have a sound, valid, hard-to-shake and up-to-date *will*.

(7) Save money on your *life insurance* by making sure you have the right kind of policies (term or universal life).

(8) Save money by *giving it away*; as a "gift," put it in the accounts of children or close relatives who are taxed at lower rates.

(9) Buy a *personal computer* and learn to use it to plan your strategy.

(10) Keep up with the *news* that affects your money.

In short, Loeb suggests ways to help you protect the assets you have now, and make them grow.

YOUR PERSONAL FINANCES

Become financially independent through shrewd, bold investing.

- Avoid money mistakes. Define your goals: What are you saving for? How much per month will it take? Maintain records of your transactions; seek advice from qualified people; diversify your investments; ask tough questions of yourself and others when deciding on an investment.

- Face up to your financial fears. We are sometimes afraid of wealth – of becoming victims, or of the risks involved . . .

- Make and stick to a budget. Trim excess spending to build savings and investments. Watch credit cards and debt payments, and their interest rates.

- Simplify. Take advantage of pay-roll deduction and dividend-reinvestment plans. Banks will sometimes pay utilities and other bills automatically. Open an asset management account offered through a broker or bank.

- Get help through financial books and tax guides, or from a highly-recommended, professional financial planner or investment advisor.

- Be wary of get-rich-quick seminars. Much of their advice is "simplistic, deceptive, wrong, or worthless."

YOUR INVESTMENTS

With your individual goals in mind, develop a financial strategy for regular investing. Start investing right away in low-risk bonds, stocks, mutual funds, or trust units that provide professional management and immediate diversification. Many institutions will accept as little as $100 initial investment.

- Do your homework; begin a stock portfolio to track up-and-coming, high-demand services and companies. Don't quickly dump a long-term growth stock when it levels off or sinks in value. "In fact, that is when smart investors consider buying even more shares – at bargain prices."

- Diversify your investments. Devote your money to inflationary products – a home, IRAs, or fairly aggressive stock mutual funds. Transfer wealth for a child's education through tax-exempt securities, life insurance, or series EE U.S. Savings Bonds. Retired couples might purchase bank-issued CDs. Put your money into investments that will yield the desired return to meet your goals.

- Take sensible risks determined by your age, short-term and long-term needs, family situation, current and prospective earning power, net worth, tax bracket – and temperament. (The book discusses "safest" investments in some detail.)

- Buy on margin – a less risky method of investing which allows your actual money outlay to work twice as hard for you. But "the key question to ask yourself is: Do you believe in the shares so wholeheartedly that you would be willing to borrow money . . . in order to own them? If not, a margin account is not for you."

- Buy stocks primarily when interest rates are low. Only natural resources – gas and oil, for example – stand to rise in value when interest rates are high.

- "Only four financial instruments offer a safe return at close to top interest rates: money-market funds; bank money-market deposit accounts; six-month money market certificates; and U.S. Treasury bills with maturities of 90 days to a year."

- Keep an eye on key economic indicators: interest rate on three-month Treasury bills, major labor contracts, strength of the dollar against foreign currency, the payroll employee figure, and the stock market.

- Beware of "boiler-room scams." Loeb presents a long list of investment companies that he considers reputable to help readers avoid being taken in by fraud.

Chapters are included on buying and selling strategies, bonds and mutual funds, choosing a broker, investing in precious metals and collectors' items, etc. The following sections include some of Loeb's advice on a few major topics.

Real Estate

The future of real estate as an investment is clouded because of tax reform; you can no longer assume that properties will automatically increase in value. Nevertheless, this "tangible" investment has many benefits.

Commercial properties require expert management. Residential properties are easier to handle and can be ideal investments depending on location, your skills and time, and potential for appreciation. "One sensible rule is to buy the worst house on the best block . . . "

Here, Loeb presents a number of chapters on buying, being a landlord, and renovation.

Your Home

Since 1980, home values have appreciated only about as fast as inflation (though this varies from city to city):

- "Now that inflation is moderate, real estate professionals advise you not to buy more house than you can handle."

- Look to buy a home in a superb neighborhood with superb schools and one that has been on the market for a while. Then "when it comes time to sell, try to make the sale before you buy and move into another house. Empty houses seldom command their asking prices."

- In buying or selling, count on a reliable real estate agent; ask up front about closing costs and other extra expenses. Shop around. Look for creative ways to come up with a down-payment or to finance your home.

Several chapters cover home improvement decisions and how to cope with contractors.

Your Taxes

Loeb describes a wide range of tax-cutting instruments and methods: company thrift plans, 401(k) plans, Keogh plans, employee pensions, sideline businesses, giving money away, investment deductions, capital gains, medical/dental deductions, home office deductions etc.:

- Avoid a tax audit by steering clear of debatable write-offs and tax-sheltering partnerships. Document times, places, purposes, and costs of all business events and travel.

- Engage a tax advisor best suited to your situation. A CPA might be needed if you are involved in any complex transactions.

- If you have any questions or complaints about a tax refund, get in touch with one of the IRS's "problem-resolution officers" (PROs), who can sweep through much bureaucratic frustration.

The last half of *Loeb's Money Guide* is taken up with specific advice on a wide variety of money-related topics: wedding costs; joint assets; the real costs of kids; teaching children to invest; the economics of divorce; how to get bargains and discounts; the costs of pets; guidelines to charitable giving; fundraising ideas; contracting for services; paying off debt; choosing a career; how to work smarter; negotiating to cut medical costs; health and dental plans; financial aids for education; vacation cost-cutting ideas; being an entrepreneur; publishing tips; getting the most from your car, life, disability, auto, and homeowners' insurance policies; consumer problems; retirement strategy planning; and estate and will planning.

Our financial world has changed greatly in the past 15 years. With alternating recessions and recoveries, gas prices exploding, inflation and interest rates fluctuating, nothing is certain. However, trends do exist, and Loeb predicts that in the next few years: consumer demand will rise as baby boomers increasingly seek goods and services; labor shortages will reflect fewer 18-year-olds entering the workforce; the tension between economic conservativism and social/environmental concerns will escalate; women will enter into greater positions of power; technological growth will continue to sky-rocket; superpower relations will improve, bringing greater economic cooperation; the international debt of developing nations will stretch the developed world; markets for quality goods will rise dramatically; new rules of tax reform will have a favorable impact on the economy and on stock and bond markets; energy-development interest will reemerge; and "the countries that possess the rare combination of human and material resources will prosper and inherit the future."

The book's postscript is an optimistic look ahead to the coming decade. Loeb believes that "revolutionary" trends and changes will persist: *If there is one certainty in our mercurial world, it is simply this: those of us who anticipate the changes and who sensibly act upon them not only will survive but also will prosper . . .*

TIME-SAVING TIPS

Seven ways to make the most of your time
(plus, some ideas for "doubling-up" activities to help you get more done)

Control or eliminate seven common time-wasters, and you can significantly improve your productivity and tranquility. Consider the ways you use your time; then take action against one or more of these robbers that may steal hours from a typical day:

• THINGS

"Do I compulsively collect or buy items that I don't need; things that have no particular value, bring no real joy, that I have no place for, or can't even find?" Things demand time: time to store, dust, move, sort, find, sell, replace and protect. What do you have *too much* of – clothes, garden tools, pencils, knickknacks, furniture? Simplify your life and unclutter your home or office by devising a plan to rid yourself of unnecessary articles. Limit the number of pairs of shoes, ties, sweaters, etc. that make their way into your closet; and when you buy a new piece of clothing, make sure one of the old pieces is eliminated from your wardrobe. Follow the same procedure with your kitchen, bathroom, garage and office collections. Handle mail, magazines, articles of clothing, paperwork, etc. only once. Don't stack things up, intending to get to them later. Put them away or throw them away – never pile them away.

• TELEVISION

"Is our television on too many hours in the day, inviting me or my family members to collapse at any time for a mindless hour or two?" Many of us waste thousands of hours each year in unplanned, indiscriminate viewing. If you complain of not having enough time to get important things done, *limit* your hours in front of the TV. Choose carefully those programs worth watching. Stick to a schedule, giving thought to how you might better spend your time.

• WAITING

"Are five or more minutes of my normal day spent waiting for someone or something: on the phone, in a line at the bank or grocery store, in a doctor's office, or for my friend to pick me up? Do feelings of resentment or nervousness sometimes well up in me due to these delays?" We can either develop the attitude that delays amount only to wasted time or we can welcome the waits as unexpected *gifts* – chances to get certain things done that we've been holding off doing. Establish the habit of carrying a book or magazine, planning book, craft, some postcards, thank-you notes, or other letter-writing materials – anything that can help you use spare time constructively. You never

know; today you might be given the opportunity to write that distant friend or to finish a *Sports Illustrated* or *Newsweek* article.

• SAYING "YES"

"Can I say ' no' gracefully, without excuse or embarrassment?" If not, you probably take on too many tasks – some tasks that you shouldn't have agreed to perform in the first place. One of the best ways to save time is to say no. The old adage "If you want a job done, give it to a busy person," is fine, but only to a point.

Most people feel some obligation to please others, and that's OK. But if your days are consumed by "doing for others," then you may be diluting the effectiveness of what you *are* doing. The cure? Take greater thought when you commit your time. When asked to serve on another committee or to "help out for a few minutes," take a few minutes of your own to ponder the priority of the task. Then get back to the "asker" with a rational reply. Practice not feeling guilty when you say no. You should feel flattered that you were deemed trustworthy and capable of carrying out an undertaking – but you need not accept it: "Sorry, not this year . . .", "Thanks for asking, but my time and commitments just won't allow me to do that right now."

• PEOPLE

"Do one-way conversations or unexpected drop-ins ever steal minutes from me or make me late for an appointment?" Too much politeness can bring about anxiety, hidden anger, and stressed relationships, in addition to lost time. Be more *honest* about your needs. Tell your friend you'll return his call in a few minutes. Tactfully yet firmly deal with the "talker": "I really don't want to take any more of your time, so I'd better say goodbye." Or inform the "drop-in": "Excuse me, but I really must get back to work." These remarks are not rude or ruthless. They simply and gently signify your needs. They also set a tone about how you use your time.

• WORRY

"Do minutes or even hours pass in a day with my mind centered on a problem? Do my small worries grow into larger concerns that cause me to waste both time and needed vitality?" Most worries are groundless; they are merely *perceived* as problems. It takes great insight and self-control to keep from agonizing over either past difficulties or future possibilities. Try to keep in mind that the *present*, this moment, is where you live, and that the only worthwhile thing you can do about your real problems is to make plans for their solution – and then carry out those plans. Also, try talking to others, working, serving, or laughing. Stay busy doing things that are rewarding and bring you joy. Positive activities are good medicine against worries.

• PROCRASTINATION

"Are some of my most meaningful, top priority to-do's ever 'put on the shelf' at the expense of busywork? Am I ignoring friends or family, talent-growth potential, more productive job tasks, or even needed car maintenance out of fear, ignorance or lack of time?" Separate the important ways you spend your time from the ways that aren't so important. Prioritize your goals and subsequent activities on a regular basis; then just get started (which is usually the hard part) and follow through. You will soon see real progress in reaching your goals. Be sure to include some time for leisure, exercise and hobbies, but build your days and weeks around your central, top-priority values. Set *deadlines* on the jobs you might tend to put off. Keep a list to remind you of appointments. Manage your tasks; pin down the minutes and use them efficiently. Do your most difficult tasks first, when you're sharp and alert; do the less crucial tasks when you don't need such a high energy level. To help keep decision-making time to a minimum, establish and stick to specific daily routines.

In addition, be realistic about minor problems and odd jobs that have a way, if left unchecked, of turning into major, horrendous "headaches." The spare tire that needs fixing, picking up the golf club left on the lawn, buying the birthday gift – don't put them off. "Do it now!" can be a lifesaving motto when you are confronted with such small but necessary chores.

■ ■ ■

Wouldn't it be nice if you could double the number of minutes available to you each day? Well, there are many odd jobs and small tasks that can be combined to save time – essentially doubling it. In fact, doing one chore together with another errand, good deed, or enterprise often lifts and stimulates you.

You'll probably be able to come up with many ideas besides the suggestions listed here. Depending on your interests and the assorted settings in which you find yourself, sometimes two things can be accomplished in the time it takes to do one.

• **While watching TV:** Soak your feet or body; do aerobics or lift weights; work on an art, craft or sewing project; polish your shoes or those of a family member; organize a storage box or drawer; during commercial breaks, read from a book or magazine, write a letter, plan, or brainstorm; snack; talk things over with a family member or friend; completely relax all parts of your body (a difficult but very beneficial activity); pay bills; mate socks; dust or straighten the family room . . .

• **While you're relaxing:** Check out a catalog or magazine; listen to music; watch TV; eat a healthy snack; look over or organize a favorite collection; gaze at your yard and do some mental planning/dreaming; soak in the tub; read a novel; phone a friend or relative . . .

• **While holding on the phone:** Arrange or dust a shelf or drawer; do hand, arm or leg isometrics, or stretch out and flex your neck and shoulders; open and read mail; cut, file, or polish your fingernails; plan an upcoming birthday or anniversary celebration; balance your checkbook; organize receipts for reimbursement or taxes; write part of a letter; clean out your wallet or purse; make up or add to a to-do list; put an address/phone list in order; read . . .

• **While brushing your teeth, shaving, applying makeup, or combing your hair:** Mentally repeat and memorize a quote or other selection posted on the mirror; plan in your mind the next few minutes or hours; check your clothing for lint and unbuttoned buttons; water a plant; use the toilet; pick up after yourself (or your children) . . .

• **While driving (staying alert to avoid an accident, of course):** Listen to motivational or instructional tapes; enjoy music or a talk show; mentally plan, visualizing your day or an upcoming event; snack; make a remote phone call; by observing, by combining the best elements of two distinct objects, or by asking "What if . . . " questions, come up with a new thought or idea; if possible, take someone else along to keep you company . . .

• **A Few Other Doubling Up Ideas:** Take out the trash on the same trip when you pick up the paper or feed the dog; get in the habit of always carrying something with you when you go up (or down) the stairs or down the hall; pick up and put away several different items at the same time; while doing yardwork or housework, listen to music on a walkman; make use of small amounts of free time that spring up unexpectedly to do those chores that take just a few minutes (clear out a tool box, clean one shelf of a closet) . . .

Now's a good time to take stock of your life and time. You're worth it!

BUSINESS GIFT-GIVING IDEAS
(plus, some notions on the art of giving)

For the proper reason, and at the timely moment, a gift is a token of sensitivity and refinement. A thoughtful gift might be presented: to say *thank you* (for a favor, the hosting of a party or for your stay in a home); to *congratulate* (on a promotion, an award, the birth of a baby, a good performance or impressive speech); to *encourage* (for someone experiencing a new career or job, an illness or accident, a death in the family); to *apologize* (for an offense, a missed appointment or forgotten promise, a troublesome incident); to wish *good luck* (on an important birthday or anniversary, a move to another city, a marriage, a retirement, a major change, a holiday); or to express *friendship* to an employee, boss or client, being careful, of course, to avoid any impropriety – suggestion of a bribe, a bid for influence or any other inappropriate motive.

The thought *does* count in gift-giving. While some situations may demand a more expensive present than others, your thoughtfulness in selection and presentation is much more important than the money spent.

Remembering when to give is vital. A daily calendar with important events noted, a tickler file system (3 x 5 cards or computerized), or a wall or desk calendar will all do the job. Jot down for the year, a week or so in front of each major occasion, all your personal gift-giving dates.

In giving, here are some pointers to keep in mind:

• Select an item with both the *occasion* and the recipient's *tastes* in mind. Give a cooking buff a book on seasonal recipes from around the world for Christmas; give a sports fan a videotape of great moments in football history for a September birthday.

• Buy something he or she can and will *use*. This can be determined by keen observation or by questioning acquaintances or family members.

• The *quality* of a gift is most important. Carefully chosen sale purchases, supermarket items and even some second-hand treasures (books, glass or porcelain pieces, old-fashioned jewelry, etc.) can make excellent gifts. But whatever you get or however much or little you spend, get something good of its kind.

• Demonstrate *high esteem* for the recipient; a "comical" gift may offend. Though a laugh-getting shirt slogan may be fine for a peer whose tastes you know well, joke gifts are, for the most part, taboo. Gifts that are too impersonal, on the other hand, may seem perfunctory.

• Photo albums, bookplates, stationery, and all kinds of leather accessories will mean and express many times more to a recipient when they are personalized with engraved or printed names, initials, designs, etc.

• Along with your gift, include an enclosure card with some brief (even one- or two-word) greeting or wish, hand-written on good note paper, and sealed or placed in an envelope.

• Use *attractive* gift-wrap.

• Use packaging that is reusable and handsome.

• Present the gift *in person* whenever possible.

Some Gift Ideas

Food

Cheeses, easily prepared gourmet dishes, jams and jellies, nuts, cookies, candy, fresh fruit, dried fruit, baked goods, exotic or regional foods, selected sauces, mustards or other condiments, selected teas, small squashes, smoked salmon, fresh lobster, caviar, frozen steaks, distinctive ice creams and toppings, coffees, liquors (wines or champagne).

For Travel

Luggage piece (matching existing pieces), tote bag or briefcase, folding umbrella, first-aid kit, sewing kit, toiletry or cosmetics kit, manicure kit, stationery and stamps, travel iron, magnified folding mirror, wallet, passport case, diary, alarm clock (wound or battery-operated), camera, rolls of film, hair dryer, best-selling novel, dictionary of foreign terms, regional guide or history book, travel game.

For the Office

Clock for desk or wall, desk-top organizer with matching wastebasket, letter opener, magazine subscription, briefcase, latest book on management, pocket calculator, desk calendar, pen-and-pencil set, dictionary/thesaurus set, magazine rack, ashtrays, thermos set with tray, bar accessories (if there's a bar), large standing plant, bookends, attractive jar filled with candies, wall mirror, leather telephone directory cover.

For the Home

Kitchen accessories (cooking equipment, cookbook, favorite recipes, house-hold hint book, knife set, cutting board, condiment set, specialty napkin rings, beverage or dessert set), bath or beach towels, serving tray, guest soaps, barbecue set, picnic basket, cooler, potpourri, bar implements (glasses, tray, pitcher, wine cooler, ice bucket, tongs, coasters), records or tapes, specialty gadgets, books relating to a hobby, games, food or drink, stationery, pieces to augment or complete an existing display or collection.

For a Special Occasion
(recognition, retirement . . .)
Tie clip or brooch, watch or bracelet, other jewelry, fine clock, photograph, plaque, embossed scrapbook (with pictures already mounted, if possible), tickets for an event, trip or cruise, personal presentation or "roasting," piece of antique furniture, work of art (a framed painting, drawing, lithograph, poster, or small statue), a hobby or sports item (painting, golf, tennis . . .), membership at a country club or health spa. (Many items can be embossed or engraved with the company logo and/or the recipient's name)

For Someone Who Is Ill

Amusing book, flowering plant, taped music or book, cologne, cosmetics or toiletries, room spray, bath soap, game, soft sculpture, robe or bed jacket, slippers, card, poster or cassette tape with individual good wishes from group members, memory book or filled photo album, recorded VCR tapes, hand-work set (needle point, knitting, etc.) if the person is bed bound but feeling quite well, blank note cards or stationery to make his or her time seem productive.

For a New Mother or Baby

Newborn diapers (disposable or cloth), plant or flower arrangement, card, baby quilt, baby mug or spoon, bibs, rattle, soft toy, baby book or journal, baby clothes sized between six and eighteen months, stroller, book on names, baby care booklet (for first babies), high-chair dining set, film, camera, individual or group collection of favorite lullabies, subscription to a parenting magazine offering baby-care or stay-sane mothering/fathering tips, baby travel kit.

For Sensitive Giving
(death, serious injury . . .)
Appropriate book for the time, fresh flowers, large plant, taped music, personal letter or card.

PUTTING SPARK IN YOUR RELATIONSHIPS
Activity Ideas

Dating and romancing, communicating and interacting, doing and sharing, all take time and effort. It is the price a couple, married or not, must pay in order to keep a relationship vibrant. The "classic" activities – movie, dancing, dinner – week after week, limit how close two people can become.

Likewise, family or friend get-togethers can become stale if little or no organizing is done.

But what more is there to do? Lots! At the price of some planning, you and your partner, or you and your group, can creatively grow, together.

Mix and match activity ideas from the different categories below. Make up your own variations. Check your local newspaper for those events taking place near where you live.

Some suggestions are more fit for groups; others are best accomplished as a couple. Some just may not appeal to you at this time – and maybe they never will. The key is to be intuitive and inventive, and to discover things that you enjoy doing together.

First, some planning.
* Remember, everything takes time. Don't plan too much. A simple activity savored is better than a larger agenda hurried or only half enjoyed.
* Understand clearly what your purpose is, i.e. simply being together, accomplishing a goal, getting to know one another, serving someone else, having fun, etc. Plan around one idea. Too many objectives leads to confusion.

IDEA CATEGORY INDEX
(1) Out on the Town
(2) Home for the Night
(3) Fun in the Sun
(4) Sports and Things
(5) Kids' Stuff
(6) Feeling Somewhat Strange?
(7) Holidays and Helping
(8) Food Thoughts

(1) *Out on the Town*
- Go window shopping. At each store window pick your favorite item. See how your tastes compare with your partner's.
- Take a moonlight walk.
- Attend a planetarium, museum, aquarium or art gallery.
- Play computer or video games at an arcade.
- See a local movie, play, concert, ballet, circus or sporting event.

- Have a quiet dinner at a favorite restaurant.
- Dance at a club or ballroom. Square dance for a change of pace.
- Take a drive to a place you've never been before.
- Attend an auction, bazaar or estate sale.
- Go midnight bowling; then have an early breakfast.
- Visit an old bookstore or a library. See who can find the strangest book.
- Go to an amusement park, state fair, festival, mall, or exhibit (car or boat show, food fair, antique show . . .)
- Attend a city council/legislature meeting.
- Tour a historic site in your area.
- See what can be done or purchased on a five- or ten-dollar limit.
- Attend a class at the library or university.
- View a competition: dog show, horse show, etc.
- Take a dance lesson – maybe two!
- Visit a relative or friend you haven't seen in a while.

(2) *Home for the Night*
- Rent a video, pop some popcorn, make a fire in the fireplace . . .
- Make a terrarium, holiday decoration, mobile, collage, flower arrangement or craft project.
- Learn a new craft, skill or hobby.
- Write a poem, short story or musical piece.
- Prepare a formal dinner.
- Have your own ping pong or miniature golf tournament.
- Decorate a dance floor and dance in your living room.
- Look for stars and constellations using a star book.
- Use a new recipe to make a food or candy.
- Sculpt using clay, or carve with soap.
- Play charades, TV games, card or board games.
- Go through your photographs; create captions for them and put together an album.

- Read and discuss a book, news article or the comics.
- Debate a world event or problem. Brainstorm for solutions.
- Watch TV – the late show, a cultural or sports event, the news, a favorite nature program, comedy series or movie.
- Find unusual words from a dictionary. Make up three definitions for each and see if others can pick the real meaning.
- Do a chore. Shine all the shoes in the house or go through a junk drawer together.
- Learn about a particular topic or famous person.
- Share and update your joint or individual goals.
- Get out your tape cassettes and record a home-made skit or commercial.
- Invent and write out a series of puns, jokes, "Mad Libs," or fortune-cookie tidbits for use at a future party.

(3) *Fun in the Sun*

- Take an early morning walk, watch the sun rise, then eat breakfast.
- Prepare a meal at an outdoor grill or fireplace.
- Visit a waterslide, canyon, park or zoo.
- Go for a hot-air balloon or airplane ride.
- Plant a tree or a garden.
- Make and fly kites.
- Gather pine cones, pinenuts, wild flowers, berries, fall leaves, butterflies, shells. etc.
- Hunt for rocks, toadstools or arrowheads.
- Pan for gold.
- Go horseback riding.
- Pick strawberries or other fruits and eat them with cream.
- Drive to a lake and rent a rowboat, skip stones, have an evening beach party, build sandcastles, fish . . .
- Hike or backpack on a nature trail.
- Visit an archeological or historical site.
- Visit a park and feed the ducks, dodge sprinklers, bicycle, picnic, play a game . . .
- Go bird-watching in a forest, park or bird refuge.
- Attend an outdoor arts, garden or international festival.
- Visit a cemetery and collect epitaphs, or do crayon rubbings of old headstones.

- Be an amateur photographer. Find artistic settings to take great pictures of nature, other people, or each other.
- Write messages in the sand, in the snow, or on the ground using rocks.
- Draw colored-chalk pictures on your patio, deck or entrywalk.
- Drive to a new location (mountains, beach, desert) for a picnic, clambake, bonfire (if allowed), or just to talk.
- Visit a local farm.

(4) *Sports and Things*

Indoor:
- Roller-skate, ice-skate, bowl, lift weights, have a ping pong tournament.
- Spend a day or evening at a gym or spa swimming, playing racket or "wallyball," practicing gymnastics, bouncing on the trampoline . . .
- Practice volleyball, soccer or basketball skills.
- Play broom hockey in a gym or large, tiled room. Use a tennis ball or chalkboard eraser as a puck.

Outdoor/Summer:
- Play tennis, golf, soccer, frisbee, badminton, volleyball, softball, miniature golf, croquet, horseshoes . . .
- Get some baseball mitts and a ball and play catch.
- Go ice-blocking (slide down a grassy hill on ice blocks).
- Play frisbee golf or frisbee football.
- Ride bikes.
- Rent dirtbikes or four wheelers.
- Swim, scuba dive, surf or body surf.
- Go moonlight sailing or canoeing.
- Do a river run in rafts or inflated tubes.
- Go mountain climbing, rappelling, hang gliding or parachuting.
- Fish, hunt, backpack or hike in a wilderness area.
- Practice your skills at a golf driving range, a go-cart track, or some batting cages.
- Go bird-watching, taking along a bird book from the library, or try the fascinating practice of bug-watching.
- Roller-skate or skateboard at a park.
- Ride horses.
- Target shoot, either with bow and arrows or a rifle.
- Go to the sand dunes for jumping or buggying.

- Jog or enter a road race.
- Fly a kite.
- Organize a complete sports day, in which you do a number of activities.

Outdoor/Winter:

- Snowshoe, ski (cross-country or down-hill), snowmobile, ice-skate, toboggan, or go sledding/tubing during the day or at night.
- Play snow football, hockey, or other snow games.
- Hike to a snowbound cabin.
- Sculpt using snow.
- Go ice fishing.
- Hunt for the perfect Christmas tree.

(5) Kids' Stuff

- Build a snow fort or snowman.
- Have a grass, pillow, or snow fight.
- Play marbles, jacks, hula hoop, hop-scotch, jump rope, tiddlywinks, hide and seek . . .
- Make a model car or plane.
- Create tin can stilts, a finger painting, or paper snowflakes.
- Do a jigsaw puzzle.
- Fly a kite.
- Make simple puppets and have a show.
- Have a water fight with balloons, hose and squirt guns.
- Tell ghost stories in the dark.
- Show a scary movie in a basement or garage.
- Devise a rope swing over a river.
- Invent a prank to play on someone, then play it. (Be nice!)
- Go to a playground or park and go on the slides, etc.
- Play foosball, air hockey or video games at an arcade.
- Attend a kids' matinee.
- Frost graham crackers, watch TV, color in a coloring book and eat ice cream.
- Run through the sprinklers or practice tumbling on the lawn.
- Design, decorate and fly paper airplanes.

(6) Feeling Somewhat Strange?

- Climb a tree and read together.
- Kidnap another person or couple and take him/them to dinner.
- Stage a bubble contest using chewing gum or soap.

- Hold a tape recording competition. With separate cassette recorders, create or find five or ten different sounds you don't think the other will recognize. Decide on a prize for the winner.
- Organize a treasure hunt, giving directions and number of steps in each direction to find some "treasure."
- Go on a date where no verbal communication is allowed.
- Make up a story from cut-out magazine pictures, or from your own photos.
- Paint a mural on a wall or on butcher paper.
- Cut an old inner tube to make a long tube. Tie off one end with wire, tie the other end to a hose and fill it with water. It makes a fun "bouncing log."
- Have a "mud bowl"; play soccer or tag in a muddy field.
- Blindfold and kidnap your partner. Drive around for a while and end up in one of your favorite spots.
- Tape record a "Mission Impossible" message. Mail or deliver it to him/her. Have the clues lead to a surprise gift or dinner.
- Paint the icicles on your house.
- Do familiar things blindfolded: decorate a cake, draw, or dance.
- Picnic in an unusual location.
- Play croquet or golf at night (use flash-lights or glow-in-the-dark balls).
- Ride a bus for the entire length of its route.
- Test-drive a sports car.
- Play "The Price is Right" at a store, with a candy bar or gum stick as prizes for each closest guess.
- Call a police station, fire station or industry for a tour.
- Sculpt with caramel corn.
- Eat at an odd site: in an empty swimming pool, under a waterfall or tree, in a tent or barn, on a raft, on the floor Japanese style . . .

(7) Holiday and Helping

General:

- Make and send a gift or some goodies to someone – known or unknown to you – far away.
- Color and decorate eggs for any holiday.
- Prepare baskets of fruit or candies to give away.
- Visit shut-ins or hospital patients.

New Years (Eve/Day):

- Make a piñata.
- Hold your own dance, or go to one already organized.
- Play snow football or another snow game.

Valentines:

- Take instant color photos of couples in love on the street and give them the pictures.
- Make Valentine cards from scrap material and paper.
- Have a "sing-in" of old love songs.
- Take Valentines to shut-ins at a hospital or rest home.

President's Day:

- Visit a museum.
- Read a historical biography.
- Make a cherry pie.
- Chop wood.
- Read by candle- or firelight.
- Give a political speech to one another.

St. Patrick's Day:

- Attend an Irish parade.
- Be a leprechaun – leave a pot of surprises on someone's doorstep.

Easter:

- Attend a different religious meeting.
- Color and decorate eggs.
- Set up an Easter egg hunt for neighbor children.
- Do an Easter brunch for someone.
- Set up and dance around a maypole.

Independence Day:

- Participate in a parade.
- Write a speech about what liberty means to you.
- Set off fireworks.
- Make homemade ice cream.
- Have a watermelon bust.

Halloween:

- Volunteer to help in a school classroom activity.
- Hold a Halloween spook alley or dance.
- Make a miniature paper haunted house and graveyard.
- Carve and decorate pumpkins to deliver to someone.
- Visit acquaintances or shut-ins in costume, as "treaters" rather than trick-or-treaters.

Thanksgiving:

- Invite a friend or stranger for the big meal.
- Send "Thanksgiving" cards to people you appreciate.
- Decorate a home with corn stalks, gourds, hay, etc.

Hanukkah:

- Visit a Jewish Center and participate in the celebration. (Call ahead to see if it's permitted.)
- Hold your own celebration, with dancing, candle-lighting, playing games, etc. all done in Jewish tradition.

Christmas:

- Go see Santa.
- Help with a Sub-for-Santa project.
- Carol to elderly neighbors or children in a hospital, giving out small gifts.
- Decorate a Christmas tree for a hospital or retirement home.

(8) *Food Thoughts*

- Cheese and chocolate fondue with cut vegetables and fruits.
- Chinese take-out with chopsticks and fortune cookies.
- Backyard barbecue with lawn games.
- Homemade ice cream, taffy, pie, bread, sandwiches, cookies, scones, chili, soup, pizza. . .
- Banana splits with many toppings.
- International or regional foods.
- Waffles or crepes with various toppings.
- A surprise breakfast or dinner.
- A progressive dinner, or a feast with friends where course items are mixed up (due to the odd descriptions of the items on the menu, choices may be made out of order).
- A "no utensils" meal.
- A tinfoil "hobo" dinner cooked by a campfire.
- Marshmallows roasted over a fire.
- A vegetarian or low-cal banquet.
- Selections from a Western, Renaissance or Pilgrim menu.
- A meal made from separate – and secret – food items, selections made by each group member.
- Create your own recipe for an omelet, soup, or other main dish.

DRESSING FOR BUSINESS

It's a fact of life: A businessperson dressed in simple fashion, well groomed, and in clean, quality, appropriate clothing, projects success.

Each company has its own dress code, usually unwritten, but unmistakably clear. The countless subtleties of dress can become apparent through close observation and daily experience. An executive can be creative with clothing, however, and still remain within the framework appropriate for his or her firm.

Select the advice that is helpful to you from the categories below:

Buying Sense

Ask yourself key questions when considering the purchase of a piece of business clothing:

- Is it suitable for my job and company?
- Does it fit properly now and will it fit in the future?
- Is the fabric and cut of top quality for long wear?
- Is it fashionable yet basic enough to stay in style?
- Is it right for my body and personal tastes?
- Are the colors neutral and the patterns and textures complimentary, to match other clothing in my ward-robe?

As you dress each day, combine and accessorize the clothing you've bought in order to feel confident and relaxed. Buying items with your age, body-build and professional position in mind will help keep your daily decision-making simple and anxious-free.

Image Decisions

Dress according to the image you want to project. This image will change somewhat depending on:

- The city you are in.
- The occasion.
- The people you are about to meet.
- The weather.
- The time of day.

Overall, however, your style will be fairly consistent. Aligning your dress with your desired image, may require some "editing." Sources of fashion advice include:

- A department or specialty store consultant.
- A friend with obvious fashion sense.
- A paid-by-the-hour, free-lance or company consultant.

Basic Don'ts

Avoid in business settings:

- Mismatched or clashing ensembles.
- Exaggerated future trends in grooming and apparel.
- Too much fragrance.
- Clothes that are too tight. (Snug clothing can magnify a weight gain – or give the appearance of one. It's best to either lose the weight, buy some new clothes, or have the clothes let out.)
- Wearing running shoes.
- Bragging about or displaying your designer-label clothing.
- Outfits that aren't fundamentally "you." Contrived fashions (for example, western duds on a city person) may look ridiculous.
- For men – socks that allow bare leg to show at the bottoms of slacks.
- For women – dressy fabrics more suitable for evening wear (satin, cut velvet, lame, brocade); also, stocking runs, or slip straps that show.

Jackets

- Select a jacket that is complimented by your shoes, slacks or skirt, shirt or blouse, tie, jewelry or other accessories. Check for color, texture, pattern and overall style compatibility.
- A jacket should either be part of a matching suit or not be too close in color to your pants or skirt. Generally, only one pattern, texture, or type of fabric should prevail.
- Keep a double-breasted jacket buttoned.
- If you normally work without your jacket on, a long-sleeved shirt or blouse looks much better than a short-sleeved one, even with sleeves rolled up to the elbow when it's hot.
- As a sign of deference, put on your jacket when – or before – an outside client or the "big boss" enters your office.

Grooming

You might want to post and consult (especially before important occasions) a *grooming checklist* to check yourself out before other people do:

Grooming Checklist

	General	For Men	For Women
HEAD	Clean face, ears and neck	Well shaven or trimmed facial hair	Make-up carefully applied
	Hair clean, cut and well combed	After-shave or cologne applied	Earrings and/or neck-lace shined
BODY	Clothing clean, pressed and checked for fraying	Shirt collar and cuffs adjusted	Slip not showing
	Deodorant applied	Tie neatly tied	No make-up on blouse collar
	Underwear fresh		Fragrance applied sparingly
	Clothing spot-free, buttoned and checked for lint and dandruff		
HANDS	Washed with nails clean and in good shape		Nail polish well done and in the proper color
	Watchband and rings free from soap film		Hand lotion applied
LEGS & FEET	Shoes in good condition, well polished and free of scuff marks; laces or tassels not broken or frayed	Clean socks pulled up high	Pantyhose run-free and, if seamed, with the seams straight
HAND-BAG / BRIEF-CASE	Polished and packed with all necessities for the day		

Since grooming is the cornerstone of good appearance, consider keeping a *grooming kit* in the office for "emergencies." The kit might include fragrance, comb or brush, hairspray, mouthwash, toothbrush, toothpaste, mirror, shoe polishing kit, spot-remover, (for men, a razor), (for women, make-up and extra hosiery).

Hair

- In some offices, a man's clean-shaven, beardless face, though not mandatory, may be expected.

- Keep hair combed or brushed at all times, but *don't* perform the ritual in public.

- Use a minimum of hairspray – especially if it's perfumed.

- Abstain from the habit of stroking or playing with your hair.

- Avoid wearing curlers in public.

- If a wig or hairpiece is worn, make sure it is conservative, fits properly, is of good quality, and that its color is consistent with your complexion.

Make-up

- Learn to apply make-up to *enhance* your appearance. A make-up specialist can offer hints to help you more deftly disguise your weaknesses and accentuate your attributes.

- "Subtract something" is a good rule before going out the door. Critique your face, then remove, lighten or blend as needed. Less is truly more.

- It's best to use less make-up in the office than you might use during off hours.

- Types and amounts of make-up needed for the office may include: a moisturizer, a colorless or skin-matching foundation, a light dusting powder, light blush to the cheeks, thin eyeliner (without noticeable color), and eyebrow pencil lightly applied to the contour of your natural brows.

- Thick mascara and eye shadow, beauty marks and false eyelashes are best left for socializing.

- Blot lipstick before a social or meeting where drinks are to be served to avoid getting lipstick on your glass.

Nails

- Well-shaped, clean – and unbitten – nails, along with healthy cuticles, are important to both men and women.

- Brightly colored or excessively long nails tend to be a distraction. A quiet-colored polish on shorter nails is attractive, and is preferred by most businesswomen.

Fragrance

- Buy only quality perfume, after-shave lotion or cologne.

- Apply fragrances lightly so that others are only slightly aware you are using them.

Remember: Good taste is mostly a matter of common sense, mixed with taking the time and thought necessary to constantly improve and refine your appearance.

BUSINESS AND EXECUTIVE ETIQUETTE

(guides to getting along and getting ahead)

OFFICE RELATIONSHIPS

Relating to others in a courteous, constructive manner is a valuable skill we can all refine. Continually violating the simple rules of civility conveys a lack of education and experience. Conversely, handling awkward moments with charm and grace shows you are in control.

You and Your Associates

*   Discover your office's unwritten code of behavior: formality of greetings and dress, expectations for lunch-time fraternizing, rules for maintaining office privacy, etc. Blend common sense with the atmosphere that prevails in your office.

*   To introduce two people, speak first to the "superior": "Mrs. Fox, this is Doug Weber, our new assistant editor. Doug, our accountant, Mrs. Fox." Use the titles each will use daily.

*   Acknowledging an introduction is done best with a simple, "How do you do."

*   Shake hands with any person you meet for the first time.

*   Stand to greet anyone who enters your office (excepting co-workers carrying out business matters) and invite them to be seated.

*   Escort a guest from your office, and to his or her car if it seems called for.

*   Office music should be appropriate and soft.

*   Unless you are in a designated smoking area, don't smoke without first asking others, "Would you mind very much if I smoked?"

*   If smoking is offensive or irritating to you, do speak up before a smoker lights up.

*   Romance and flirting have no place in the office. The smartest advice is: don't!

*   Don't snack in front of others unless you can fittingly offer to share.

*   Try to avoid bringing pets or children to the office for any extended periods of time. If exceptions are necessary, "guests" must be properly controlled.

*   In most offices, it is admissible to use first names between associates and subordinates.

*   Depending on office procedure, knock on a closed door and enter only after being invited. Ask if you're interrupting before initiating a conversation or question.

*   Speak fairly and politely. Abstain from gossip, threats, sarcasm or arrogance in speech.

*   Keep conversations honest and open. However, complaints or personal "fence-mending" should be done in private.

*   Choose office friendships wisely, while maintaining good relations with all peers. Too much socializing with co-workers outside of work can prove to be a detriment, as can excessive personal conversation. Disclosing all your opinions, personal hang-ups or plans could hurt you and interfere with work.

*   If you and a colleague just can't get along, formal politeness is still expected. It is totally unacceptable to complain openly or act spitefully. A "cease-fire" compromise must be reached, which later may lead to genuine respect.

*   Considerately and confidentially offer assistance to colleagues when it is perceived necessary, and only when they are not taking advantage of your good nature.

*   Give due credit to others when they have helped you.

*   "Talkers" can interfere with work. A response of, "I'm sorry, but I really must get back to work," will usually allow you to do so.

You and Your Boss

*   Understand your boss' expectations, time schedule, habits, plans and goals. What's important to him or her? Pay attention; try to sense a supervisor's needs without pandering to them.

*   Find out your manager's preferred method of communication (letter, memo, talking face-to-face . . .) and act accordingly.

*   An employer dismisses employees at the end of a meeting.

*   Be friendly with your boss, but remember: too much intimacy can backfire on you.

*   Keep your boss informed of what you're doing. Follow up on assignments without being reminded.

- Never embarrass an employer, particularly in public.

- Never threaten. Assertiveness often smacks of arrogance.

- Accept criticism graciously, not jokingly or defensively. The best reply: "Is there anything else I should know to help me in my work?"

- Vent disagreements privately. Pre-plan tactful discussions with your superior. Disagree without being disagreeable.

- If an office problem must be issued as a complaint, present it professionally rather than personally. Describe the problem using diplomacy, without placing blame. Have various possible solutions in mind.

- If you feel a raise in salary is in order, organize yourself. Write down your contributions to the company and your accepted responsibilities. Arrange a convenient time to meet your boss to present these facts. Calmly accept the initial response to your request. Ask that he or she "go to bat" for you as a valuable employee, and schedule a later time to discuss the matter further.

- Always be prompt for work, meetings and appointments.

- Being efficient and productive in your job show that you value your company, your colleagues and your employer. Such obvious caring will put you ahead.

When You're the Boss

- Constantly strive to improve relations with employees by being gracious and not too assertive, while still motivating each worker as part of the team. Try to be available and listen.

- Delegate clearly, defining expectations and objectives.

- Welcome opinions and feedback from your workers. Consider them experts at what they do, and refer to them as associates, colleagues, team members, managers or directors.

- Trust employees to work out personal and business problems on their own. At most, become involved only to the extent of listening, counseling and coaching, but leave ultimate solutions to them.

- Build confidence through sincere praise and enthusiasm.

■　■　■

COMMUNICATIONS

Effective communication is what much of business is all about. It is mostly a matter of common sense and courtesy; thinking how your method and manner will affect others. Passing out routine memos or unnecessary copying of forms and letters, passing on paperwork, and unthinking speech not only waste time, but may be viewed as breaches of etiquette.

Written Communication

- Letters should lean toward personal expression and away from stuffiness. They generally include the following parts: heading (your address and date of letter), inside address (person's name and title, company name and address), greeting (Dear Mr. Jones,), body (brief business, stated clearly), closing (Very truly yours, or Sincerely,) and signature (handwritten with typed name and title beneath).

- Personal letters of congratulation, appreciation or condolence are best if they are handwritten, concise, and contain no references to business.

- Business stationery and cards should be conservative.

- In-house, brief information can be written in a memo. A casual yet candid approach is best. Describe in plain language who, what, when, where, why and how.

- Don't waste the readers' time. Choice of words, spelling, grammar and simple sentence structure are vital.

- Convey a positive tone and sincere regard in all writing.

Telephone Etiquette

- Avoid machine-answering of incoming calls.

- Professional, simple courtesy needs to be evident upon answering a call. State your name and what company or department you represent.

- Speak softly and clearly.

- When receiving a call for another, screen it so that your associate may know how to respond: "May I say who is calling?"

- If a secretary places a call for you, be ready to get on the line immediately to avoid keeping that person waiting. Better yet, place your own calls when possible.

- When calling someone, identify yourself and with whom you would like to speak. "This is Mrs. Jones. May I speak to Dr. Waite, please?"

- If you are unavoidably interrupted during a conversation, say, "Excuse me a minute. I have to handle something." Take care of the problem with the mouthpiece covered, then apologize and resume your business.

- Normally, the call's initiator signs off. However, if you're busy and someone's call interrupts you, say so and indicate a time when you will call back.

- Graciously guard your business hours from "talkers": "I really don't want to take any more of your time, so I'll say goodbye."

Speaking Face-to-Face and in Public

- Recognize that choice of words, tone of voice, body language, gestures, and posture can be powerful tools – or frustrating obstacles – to effective speaking. If you don't speak well, do something about it: listen to and observe others; ask a friend to analyze your skills; take a class or read a book; join Toastmasters or other speaking group . . . Practice communicating aloud. Use a mirror and an audio or video recorder to diagnose yourself, if these seem helpful.

- Attentive listening is a compliment to any speaker, and can reap great benefits. Refrain from interrupting another or appearing only to be planning your next statement. Lean slightly forward, look at the speaker and focus your thoughts on what is being presented. Your facial expressions and slight nods indicate understanding.

- Verbal signals of agreement ("Yes, I agree completely...") or of disagreement ("I'm not sure about that point," or "You may be right, but...") can be "slipped in" as appropriate.

- Extend a genuine, brief compliment to someone who has impressed you. Avoid flattery or gushing praise.

- Cliches, slang or business jargon often seem insincerely spoken. Don't use "utilize" for "use"; or habitually insert the word "impact" when "affect" will do.

- Use jokes, wisecracks or anecdotes sparingly – or not at all – particularly in meetings. Perceived charlatans or jokers are often passed over on serious assignments.

- Avoid coarse or suggestive language.

- Public speaking will be less frightening and more comfortable if you overly prepare: know your topic; don't memorize your talk, but practice speaking about your subject in a natural way; add appropriate stories and humor; dress conservatively; the day of your speech, relax your mind; breath deeply several times before beginning your address.

- Be sure to stay well within your time limit. Make your point without exhausting either the topic or your audience.

- If you choose to use a specific word or phrase – especially a foreign word or phrase – be certain of pronunciation and meaning.

- Cultivate a well-modulated voice; not too high-pitched, too loud, or too soft. Enunciate properly. Vary, from time to time, your volume, intonation and speed.

- Practice discretion in all your speech. Consciously refrain from monopolizing meetings or conversations. Make your comments with respect and forethought. Remember Abigail Van Buren's observation: "The less you talk, the more you're listened to."

■ ■ ■

SOCIAL ETIQUETTE

The business lunch and company party have become common yet important affairs that require social poise and style. Even minor irritants or faux pas can terminate a relationship or a deal.

The Business Lunch

- If you would like to host someone for lunch for a particular purpose, extend the invitation within a phone conversation: "How about lunch next week?" Asking ahead of time will allow you both to calendar a mutually agreeable time.

- To further clarify that this person will be your guest, suggest a location and reconfirm the time.

- Call ahead for reservations, giving the number of guests and, if needed, the desired seating arrangement.

- Frequent one particular restaurant most often. Being recognized and getting quality, personal service make subtle impressions.

- Arrive before your guest. Wait in the lobby to check in coats and to be seated.

- It's best to sit in the nonsmoking section if any nonsmoker is included. If you are entertaining an important client who smokes, and you can tolerate it, it's polite to offer to sit in the smoking section.

- If the lunch involves a man and a woman, watch for cues on how the other person wants to be treated socially. Men usually open doors and offer assistance to remove coats.

- A woman is quite capable of ordering her own meal and drink. Either a man or a woman may order for the other, if requested.

- When asked if you wish to order drinks, put your guest at ease: "Yes, I would. What will you have, Frank?" The drink is a formality. Generally, only one drink (at most two) should be ordered, especially if it is alcoholic. No one, regardless of his drinking habits, wants to be perceived as a heavy drinker.

- Your guest orders his or her meal first.

- While ordering, do not comment about past or present diets.

- Show concern about your guest and his or her meal, without being overly dramatic.

- If you are the guest, remain low key and pleasant.

- During a "working" lunch, the host may be direct and ask, for instance, "Well, shall we discuss the Bailey account?" If you want to be more subtle, start with, "Well, what do you think about . . . ?" or "Tell me what's happening with you."

- When finished, or nearly finished, ask the waiter for the check. If the check is brought to your guest, simply reach over and take it (don't grab it). Look the bill over quickly and carefully and figure the tip. Place the check and your credit card(or money if you must) on the tray, with the check face down.

- The usual tip is 15 to 20 percent. Pennies, nickels or dimes are best not used unless they are from the change brought to you; then, leave all the coins.

- Both guest and host should thank the other for the pleasant time.

Entertaining at Home

- Good planning allows you, the host, to have as much fun as your guests.

- A formal dinner is no longer expected for successful gatherings in the home. Look to plan more personal, individual patio parties or simple buffet dinners.

- Plan the entertainment and meal or refreshments according to the occasion, your budget and the space available.

- Make up the guest list with care. Consider how many people you feel comfortable serving and can comfortably fit in your home. More people can be invited to a party where simple food and drinks are served than for a sit-down dinner. Invite persons who, for business or social reasons, will be compatible.

- Invitations to casual events are generally made by phone.

- For a formal dinner, on white or pastel stationery, hand-write a simple message: "We request the pleasure of your company . . . " and stating the occasion, date, time, place and appropriate dress. If necessary, request a response to your invitation by placing "RSVP" at the bottom.

- To reply to an invitation, "accept with pleasure . . . " or "regret that a previous engagement prevents our accepting . . . " on plain white stationery.

- A call made several days before the event to those who have not responded, is in order. You merely need ask if they are going to attend so that you may plan for them.

- For large parties, organize far in advance. The catering, bartending and serving staff must be sufficient to handle your group; for every 25 guests, one "helper" of each kind is about right. Providing these services frees you to be a more gracious host.

- Decide what you will need to borrow or rent: silverware, glasses, platters, dishes, tables, chairs, linens, bartending supplies, etc. These items may require time for cleaning or polishing.

- Be sure to have enough fresh soap, bathroom tissue, coasters, ash trays, matches, and guest towels on hand.

- Remember extras like candles, decorations, banners, and centerpieces. Dress up serving platters with simple garnishes: sprigs, herbs, cut fruits, baby vegetables, flowers or sauces.

4

- Food extras, such as nuts, olives, cut vegetables, and drinks, make marvelous "unstiffeners" to help guests feel welcome and comfortable when they first arrive. Stock your kitchen with quick-to-fix foods (deli meats, pre-cut or shredded cheese, frozen bread dough, etc.) and other munchies (nuts pretzels, cookies, candies, dried fruits, etc.).

- Arrange for food to be prepared in advance, as far as is possible. Choose recipes that can be frozen or refrigerated.

- Spend time greeting your guests. Take coats, or show where they may be taken, and usher new arrivals into the party. Make at least one introduction so newcomers will have an immediate acquaintance. If the gathering is small, they should be introduced to everyone.

- Along with the introduction, you might add something about each person or couple: "Rex, this is Mike and Jan Reid. They just returned from living in Maine. Mike, Jan, this is my business partner, Rex Dome."

- Tactfully guide conversations to include all guests in small visiting pockets. But don't forget to relax. If you enjoy the event, it's more likely your guests will too.

- Artful hints may be required to let guests know it's time to go. While visiting, state warmly, "Well, I hope you had a nice time." However, be prepared to take care of late-stayers, and even to provide an early morning round of food (coffee, eggs, donuts) to departing guests.

- Be a responsible host. If a visitor has had too many drinks, or if you at all question his ability to drive, don't argue. Discreetly arrange for a ride home with another guest, or else call a taxi. Then tell the guest you will bring his car over in the morning.

- If a guest is leaving and comes to thank you for the party (as she should), graciously inquire, "Why so soon?" (even if it's three in the morning). Then thank her for coming and escort her to the door.

- Elderly guests and single women should be escorted to their car or cab.

■ ■ ■

EATING AND DRINKING

Managing the task of putting food in your mouth can be as important as any other business skill. Dinner poise is one more indication of your education and caring. Modern rules are designed to help you show consideration for others and to make eating together an enjoyable, comfortable occasion. Excessive strictness is no longer the norm.

Eating Etiquette

- If you are unsure how to proceed with a dish or which spoon to use, wait a few moments. Someone else at the table will likely initiate the action and you may then nonchalantly follow suit.

- The rules governing the use of flatware are: start from the outside fork or spoon and work in as each course is served; keep used flatware on the plate, not on the tablecloth; place the knife and fork side by side on your plate to indicate to the waiter when you are finished.

- You may find a finger bowl on the table at very formal restaurants, which may appear before or after the meal. Dip only your fingers into the water and dry them with your napkin below table level.

- Place your napkin on your lap shortly after being seated. Unfold it to a comfortable size (usually so that it is still folded in half) and use it as needed to remove crumbs from your mouth before drinking. When finished, place it unfolded to the left of the plate.

- Bread or rolls should be broken in half before buttering, and may be supported in one hand to aid in picking up food. Rolls are not to be used to wipe a plate clean.

- Be seated and unseat yourself quietly, and always from the right of the chair.

- Excuse yourself if you leave the table for any reason.

- Maintain good posture. Don't support yourself with your elbows. An elbow on the table is permissible before and after the meal and between courses, but not while eating.

- A woman wearing lipstick might blot her lips in private before dinner to avoid getting lipstick on her water or wine glasses.

- Refrain from reaching across someone. If an item is not within reach, politely ask for it to be passed.

- To ask for something to be brought, or to request a change in improperly pre-pared food, firmly yet politely address the waiter or attendant without bring-ing your request to the attention of other diners.

- Don't slurp, smack your lips, or speak with food in your mouth. These errors are more common than you would think.

- Accidental slurping or spilling is easily handled with a quiet apology.

- Drink slowly and noiselessly after sweeping your lips with your napkin to remove particles that may stick to the glass.

- The soup spoon is moved away from the body during formal dinners. To extract the last bit of soup, tilt the bowl slightly away from you and spoon it out. Then rest the spoon in the bowl or on the plate under it.

- Eat the main course using the large fork and knife. The fork is placed in the left hand (for right handers) and the knife in the right for cutting. The fork should remain almost horizontal with the tines pointing down and the index finger on top of the handle. Transferring the fork to the right hand (American method) or leaving it in the left (Continental method) to bring food to the mouth are both acceptable. Cut food by moving mainly the wrists, with moderate or no movement of the elbows.

- To remove pits or bones from your mouth, cup your fingers to hide the food, bring the napkin to the mouth, and place particles discreetly on the side of your plate.

- Never spit out food that's too hot. Strategically and calmly take a drink.

- Drenching food with catsup or other bottled sauce can be viewed as an insult. A condiment may be applied directly to an open-faced sandwich or to the side of french fries.

- First transfer pats of butter (using a fork) or jams/jellies (using a spoon) to your plate, then spread them onto breads using the butter knife.

- Stirring or mashing food on your plate is offensive. A baked potato is general-ly eaten as it is forked from the shell.

- Steer your discussion to topics that won't cause others to feel uncomfort-able or squeamish. "Politics" and "reli-gion" might lead to an argument; and your recent surgery or illness might make someone ill.

- A waiter or waitress deserves your respect and an occasional thank you, especially for extra service. You need not thank them for every act.

- If you drop a fork or piece of food, it's best if you don't make even the slight-est scene. Casually scoot the article to an out-of-the-way spot, and, if conve-nient, quietly retrieve it after the meal.

- Never move your own dishes or stack them. This is left for the server to do.

- Toothpicks should not be used in pub-lic.

- After being served what to you might be a "tricky" food (lobster, specialty sandwich, etc.), either slow down and notice how others proceed, or speak up and say to a nearby acquaintence, "I've never eaten this. How do I go about doing it?" Most people are pleased to be able to provide instructions.

- Most foods are cut and eaten using the knife and fork. Unless your host decrees otherwise, only at drive-ins and picnics do chicken and french fries become fingerfoods. Strawberries, grapes, other fruits, and olives are most often eaten using the fingers.

- Spaghetti should be wound around the tines of the fork using one of several methods.

- The key is to leave no ends hanging that need to be sucked into the mouth. This may be difficult to master, but with some in-home practice you can become expert.

- Relax, and enjoy yourself.

COMPACT

Classics™

LIBRARY #3: Quotes and Anecdotes

Section A

3-A1   Work

3-A2   Adversity and Perseverance

3-A3   Achievement

3-A4   Leadership

Section B

3-B1   Business

3-B2   Money

3-B3   Learning

3-B4   Problem Solving

Section C

3-C1   Time and Life

3-C2   Relationships

3-C3   Communication

3-C4   Family Life

Section D

3-D1   Integrity

3-D2   Happiness

3-D3   Health

3-D4   Thought Gems

WORK

Quotes & Anecdotes
(doing, activity, effort)

O Lord,
Thou givest us everything,
At the price
Of an effort
- Leonardo da Vinci

Opportunity is missed by most people because it is dressed in overalls and looks like work.
- Thomas Edison

Work is doing what you now enjoy for the sake of a future which you clearly see and desire. Drudgery is doing under strain what you don't now enjoy and for no end that you can now appreciate.
- Richard C. Cabot

The heights by great men reached and kept
Were not attained by sudden flight,
But they, while their companions slept,
Were toiling upward in the night.
- Henry Wadsworth Longfellow

God gives every bird its food, but He does not throw it into the nest.
- J.G. Holland

Every man's work is a portrait of himself.

Effort is only effort when it begins to hurt.
- Jose Ortega Y Gasset

The beauty of work depends upon the way we meet it, whether we arm ourselves each morning to attack it as an enemy that must be vanquished before night comes – or whether we open our eyes with the sunrise to welcome it as an approaching friend who will keep us delightful company . . .
- Lucy Larcom

I wish to preach, not the doctrine of ignoble ease, but the doctrine of the strenuous life.
- Theodore Roosevelt

A widely prevalent notion today seems to demand instant achievement of goals, without any of the wearying, frustrating preparation that is indispensable to any task. As the exemplar of a way of life, the professional – that man or woman who injects every new task or duty, no matter how small, with discipline of mind and spirit – is a vanishing American, particularly among those who too often believe that dreams come true because they ought to and not because they are caused to materialize.
-Jack Valenti

The world cares very little about what a man or woman knows; it is what the man or woman is able to do that counts.
- Booker T. Washington

I have a kind of contempt for intelligence all by itself. Coupled with energy and willingness, it'll go. Alone, it winds up riding the rails.
- John Hersey

The real essence of work is concentrated energy – people who really have that in a superior degree by nature are independent of the forms and habits and artifices by which less able and less active people are kept up to their labors.
- Walter Bagehot

In order that people may be happy in their work, these three things are needed: They must be fit for it; They must not do too much of it; And they must have a sense of success in it.
- John Ruskin

Far and away the best prize that life offers is the chance to work hard at work worth doing.
- Theodore Roosevelt

I am a great believer in luck, and the harder I work the more I have of it.
- Stephen Leacock

For success: try aspiration, inspiration, and perspiration.

A man who works with his hands is a laborer; a man who works with his hands and his brain is a craftsman; but a man who works with his hands and his brain and his heart is an artist.
-Louis Nizer

Idle folks have the least leisure.
- John Ray

The first man gets the oyster, the second man gets the shell.
- Andrew Carnegie

I like to work half a day. I don't care if it's the first twelve hours or the second twelve hours. I just put in my half every day. It keeps me out of trouble.
- Kemmons Wilson, CEO, Holiday Inns

Genius is one percent inspiration and 99 percent perspiration.
- Thomas Alva Edison

God gave us a world unfinished, so that we might share in the joys and satisfaction of creation.
- Allen Stockdale

All this will not be finished in the first one hundred days, nor will it be finished in the first one thousand days, nor in the life of this administration, nor even perhaps in our lifetime on this planet. But let us begin.
- John F. Kennedy

St. Francis of Assisi was hoeing his garden when someone asked what he would do if he were suddenly to learn that he would die before sunset that very day. "I would finish hoeing my garden," he replied.
- Louis Fischer

1

The highest reward for a man's toil is not what he gets for it but what he becomes by it.
- *John Ruskin*

I never did anything worth doing by accident, nor did any of my inventions come by accident; they came by work.
- *Thomas Alva Edison*

He that would have fruit must climb the tree.
- *Thomas Fuller*

Of all the unhappy people in the world, the unhappiest are those who have not found something they want to do. True happiness comes to him who does his work well, followed by a relaxing and refreshing period of rest. True happiness comes from the right amount of work for the day.
- *Lin Yutang*

Men like to make the wheels go round, which is why so many men go around in circles.

If you have built castles in the air, your work need not be lost; that is where they should be. Now put foundations under them.
- *Henry David Thoreau*

When we do the best that we can, we never know what miracle is wrought in our life, or in the life of another.
- *Helen Keller*

When I was a young man I observed that nine out of ten things I did were failures. I didn't want to be a failure, so I did ten times more work.
- *George Bernard Shaw*

Nothing is really work unless you would rather be doing something else.
- *Sir James Barrie*

I can more easily see our Lord sweeping the streets of London, than issuing edicts from its cathedral.
- *Dick Sheppard*

Whatever is worth doing at all, is worth doing well.
- *Philip Dormer Stanhope, fourth Earl of Chesterfield, 1774*

The reward of a thing well done is to have done it.
- *Ralph Waldo Emerson*

The best way to appreciate leisure is to work hard for it.

Few things are of themselves impossible . . . we lack the application to make them a success rather than the means.
- *La Rochefoucauld*

Thank God every morning when you get up that you have something to do that day which must be done, whether you like it or not.
- *Charles Kingsley*

I Am Work
I am the foundation of all business.
I am the source of all prosperity.
I am the parent of genius.
I am the salt that gives life its savour . . .
Loved, I make life sweet, purposeful, and fruitful . . .
All progress springs from me.
- *Anonymous*

My father taught me to work; but he did not teach me to love it.
- *Abraham Lincoln*

There's nothing wrong with being a self-made man if you don't consider the job finished too soon.
- *John Mooney*

They that sow in tears shall reap in joy.
- *The Bible, Psalms 126:5*

Well done is better than well said.
- *Benjamin Franklin*

Shallow men believe in luck.
- *Ralph Waldo Emerson*

A Poet's Proverb
God's road is all uphill,
But do not tire,
Rejoice that we may still
Keep climbing higher.
- *Arthur Guiterman*

The battle is not to the strong alone; it is to the vigilant, the active, the brave.
- *Patrick Henry*

We cannot do everything at once, but we can do something at once.
- *Calvin Coolidge*

Be not simply good; be good for something.
-*Henry David Thoreau*

The greatest menace to freedom is an inert people.
- *Louis D. Brandeis*

Trouble is only opportunity in work clothes.
- *Henry J. Kaiser*

Opportunity doesn't necessarily knock on the door; it may be leaning against the wall waiting to be noticed.

The pessimist sees the difficulty in every opportunity; the optimist, the opportunity in every difficulty.
- *L.P. Jacks*

A generation ago there were a thousand men to every opportunity, while today there are a thousand opportunities to every man.
- *Henry Ford*

It is the feeling of exerting effort that exhilarates us, as a grasshopper is exhilarated by jumping. A hard job, full of impediments, is thus more satisfying than an easy job.
- *H.L. Mencken*

Geoffrey Fisher, ninety-ninth Archbishop of Canterbury, asked: "What does it take to be an Archbishop . . . ? The strength of a horse – and the ability to be a cart horse one day and a race horse the next."

Tenacita! Disciplina! Coraggio! And work!
Definition of Fascism by Benito Mussolini (The last two words were in English)

The dictionary is the only place where success comes before work.
- *Arthur Brisbane*

. . . Getting ready is the secret of success.
-Henry Ford

The haves and the have-nots can often be traced back to the dids and the did-nots.
- *D.O. Flynn*

When God wanted sponges and oysters, He made them, and put one on a rock, and the other in the mud. When He made men, He did not make him to be a sponge or an oyster; He made him with feet, and hands, and head, and heart, and vital blood, and a place to use them, and said to him, "Go, work!"
- *Henry Ward Beecher*

If people really liked to work, we'd still be plowing the ground with sticks and transporting goods on our backs.
- *William Feather*

No one ever got very far by working a 40-hour week. Most of the notable people I know are trying to manage a 40-hour day.
- *Channing Pollock*

Ambition often puts men upon doing the meanest offices: so climbing is performed in the same posture with creeping.
- *Jonathan Swift*

If my sister or I took one of those school examinations where you were required to answer only 10 questions out of 12, Mother's comment on hearing this would be, "I hope you chose the hardest ones."
- *Margaret Bourke-White*

I never practice; I always play.
- *Wanda Landowska, harpsichord master*

No one knows what he can do till he tries.
- *Publilius Syrus, 1st century B.C.*

Nothing can come of nothing.
- *Shakespeare, "King Lear"*

The best-kept secret in America today is that people would rather work hard for something they believe in than enjoy a pampered idleness.
- *John W. Gardner*

I've done my small part to stamp out boredom in certain quarters of this world where it threatened to become rampant. If I accomplish little else, I shall consider my life justified by that one fact. Down with boredom . . .
- *Elsa Maxwell*

Forty years ago people worked 12 hours a day, and it was called economic slavery. Now they work 14 hours a day, and it's called moonlighting.
- *Robert Orben*

Much of the good work of the world has been that of all the dull people who have done their best.
- *Senator George F. Hoar*

A great man leaves clean work behind him, and requires no sweeper up of the chips.
- *Elizabeth Barrett Browning*

The world stands aside to let anyone pass who knows where he is going.
- *David Starr Jordan*

Some people get the breaks; some people make their own.

Let us work without protest; it is the only way to make life endurable.
- *Voltair, Candide, 1759*

Man is the only creature that consumes without producing.
- *George Orwell, Animal Farm*

In life as in a football game, the principle to follow is: Hit the line hard.
- *Theodore Roosevelt*

The sleep of a laboring man is sweet.
- *The Bible, Ecclesiastes 5:12*

Blessed is he who has found his work; let him ask no other blessedness. He has . . . a life-purpose; he has found it, and will follow it.
- *Thomas Carlyle*

Where our work is, there let our joy be.
- *Tertullian, c. 220*

I don't believe one grows older. I think that what happens early on in life is that at a certain age one stands still and stagnates.
- *T. S. Eliot*

Growing old is no more than a bad habit which a busy man has no time to form.
- *Andre Maurois*

Work! God wills it. That, it seems to me, is clear.
- *Gustave Flaubert, 1845*

Behold the turtle: He only makes progress when he sticks his neck out.
- *James Bryant Conant*

Those who do good as opportunity offers are sowing seeds all the time, and they need not doubt the harvest.

A life spent making mistakes is not only more honorable but more useful than a life spent doing nothing.
- *George Bernard Shaw*

He that is busy is tempted by but one devil; he that is idle, by a legion.
- *Thomas Fuller, 1732*

Wisely, and slow. They stumble that run fast.
- Shakespeare, "Romeo and Juliet"

Make haste slowly.
- Latin proverb

The journey of a thousand miles begins with one step.
- Lao-Tse

If wishes were horses beggars might ride.
- John Ray, 1670

. . . Even for the neurotic executive – as for everyone else – work has great therapeutic value; it is generally his last refuge, and deterioration there marks the final collapse of the man . . .
- Richard Austin Smith

We have confused the free with the free and easy.
- Adlai Stevenson

The test of the artist does not lie in the will with which he goes to work, but in the excellence of the work he produces.
- Thomas Aquinas, c. 1265

Happiness consists in activity – it is a running stream, not a stagnant pool.
- John Mason Good

Our real problem is not our strength today; it is the vital necessity of action today to ensure our strength tomorrow.
- Dwight D. Eisenhower

Promise me, boy, if thou get a master, work for him as hard as thou canst. If he does not appreciate all thou do, never mind. Remember, work, well-done, does good to the man who does it. It makes him a better man.
- George S. Clason, The Richest Man in Babylon

The world is full of willing people; some willing to work, the rest willing to let them.
- Robert Frost

Give the best that you have to the highest you know – and do it now.
- Ralph W. Sockman

The first thing to do in life is to do with purpose what one proposes to do.
- Pablo Casals, cellist

A government official was discussing Prime Minister Ramsay MacDonald's point of view on peace. "The desire for peace," he said, "does not necessarily ensure peace."

MacDonald replied, "Quite true. Neither does the desire for food satisfy hunger. But at least it gets you started toward a restaurant."

Conviction is worthless unless it is converted into conduct.
- Thomas Carlyle

. . . I have always liked bird dogs better than kennel-fed dogs myself – you know, one that will get out and hunt for food rather than sit on his fanny and yell.
- Charles E. Wilson

When I've had a rough day, before I go to sleep I ask myself if there's anything more I can do right now. If there isn't, I sleep sound.
- L.L. Colbert

What counts is not the number of hours you put in, but how much you put in the hours.

I am only an average man, but, by George, I work harder at it than an average man . . . . I pity the creature who doesn't work, at whichever end of the social scale he may regard himself as being.
- Theodore Roosevelt

Work is the greatest thing in the world. So we should save some of it for tomorrow.
- Don Herold

The art of writing is the art of applying the seat of the pants to the seat of the chair.
- Mary Heaton Vorse

Nothing is particularly hard if you divide it into small jobs.
- Henry Ford

I long to accomplish a great and noble task, but it is my chief duty to accomplish humble tasks as though they were great and noble. The world is moved along, not only by the mighty shoves of its heroes, but also by the aggregate of the tiny pushes of each honest worker.
- Helen Keller

Passivity is fatal to us. Our goal is to make the enemy passive.
- Mao Tse-tung

I loathe drudgery as much as any man; but I have learned that the only way to conquer drudgery is to get through it as neatly, as efficiently, as one can. . . . A dull job slackly done becomes twice as dull; whereas a dull job which you try to do just as well as you can becomes half as dull.
- Sir Harold Nicolson

The way to Hell is plastered with good resolutions.
- German proverb

I feel that the greatest reward for doing is the opportunity to do more.
- Dr. Jonas Salk

I have tried my best to give the nation everything I had in me. There are probably a million people who could have done the job better than I did it, but I had the job and I always quote an epitaph on a tombstone in a cemetery in Tombstone, Arizona: "Here lies Jack Williams. He done his damndest."
- Harry S Truman

You can't build a reputation on what you are going to do.
- Henry Ford

What is the use of health, or of life, if not to do some work therewith?
- Thomas Carlyle, 1836

ADVERSITY AND PERSEVERANCE

Quotes & Anecdotes
(determination, courage, faith, understanding)

You gain strength, courage and confidence by every experience in which you really stop to look fear in the face. You are able to say to yourself, "I lived through this horror. I can take the next thing that comes along." . . . You must do the thing you think you cannot do.
- Eleanor Roosevelt

Aerodynamically speaking, the design of a bumblebee is a disaster. Too much body weight. Too little wing span. Just can't fly. But it does.
You will do foolish things, but do them with enthusiasm.
- Colette, French novelist, to her daughter

A man's errors are his portals of discovery.
- James Joyce

I'll die propped up in bed trying to do a poem about America.
- Carl Sandburg, on the eve of his 79th birthday

One doesn't discover new lands without consenting to lose sight of the shore for a very long time.
- Andre Gide

I expect to fight that proposition until hell freezes over. Then I propose to start fighting on the ice.
Senator Russell Long of Louisiana

. . . be thou faithful unto death, and I will give thee a crown of life.
- The Bible, Revelations 2:10

I have not yet begun to fight. (Sometimes quoted as "I have just begun to fight.")
- John Paul Jones aboard the Bonhomme Richard, when asked whether he was ready to surrender to the British warship Serapis, 1779.

Ambition should be made of sterner stuff.
- William Shakespeare, "Julius Caesar"

If at first you don't succeed, you're running about average.
- M. H. Alderson

A hero is one who knows how to hang on one minute longer.
- Norwegian proverb

Lincoln's Road To The White House
Failed in business in 1831.
Defeated for Legislature in 1832.
Second failure in business in 1833.
Suffered nervous breakdown in 1836.
Defeated for Speaker in 1838.
Defeated for Elector in 1840.
Defeated for Congress in 1843.
Defeated for Congress in 1848.
Defeated for Senate in 1855.

Defeated for Vice President in 1856.
Defeated for Senate in 1858.
Elected President in 1860.

Having chosen our course, without guile and with pure purpose, let us renew our trust in God, and go forward without fear and with manly hearts.
- Abraham Lincoln

We lay too much stress on stick-to-it-iveness. I once had a professor who wisely hung this sign over his desk: "Oh, Lord, teach me when to let go."
- W. G. Carleton

The only good luck many great men ever had was being born with the ability and determination to overcome bad luck.
- Channing Pollock

Keep on going and chances are you will stumble on something . . . . I have never heard of anyone stumbling on something sitting down.
- Charles F. Kettering

If your bayonet breaks, strike with the stock; if the stock gives way, hit with your fists; if your fists are hurt, bite with your teeth.
- M. I. Dragomiroff: Notes from Soldiers, c. 1890

Where The Determination Is, The Way Can Be Found.
- George S. Clason, The Richest Man in Babylon

Pennies do not come from heaven. They have to be earned here on earth.
- Margaret Thatcher

The race is not to the swift, nor the battle to the strong.
-The Bible, Ecclesiastes 9:11

Retreat, Hell! We're just advancing in another direction.
- General O. P. Smith, U.N. Forces Leader, Korean War

At first we hope too much, later on, not enough.
- Joseph Roux

The only thing that keeps a man going is energy. And what is energy but liking life?
- Louis Auchincloss

The big shots are only the little shots who keep shooting.
- Christopher Morley

Don't let life discourage you; everyone who got where he is had to begin where he was.
- Richard L. Evans

There is no failure except in no longer trying.

- Elbert Hubbard

Someone asked me . . . how I felt and I was reminded of a story that a fellow townsman of ours used to tell – Abraham Lincoln. They asked him how he felt once after an unsuccessful election. He said he felt like a little boy who had stubbed his toe in the dark. He said that he was too old to cry, but it hurt too much to laugh.

- Adlai Stevenson, commenting on his defeat by General Eisenhower in the presidential election of 1952

Grief drives men [to] serious reflection, sharpens the understanding and softens the heart.

- John Adams

I walked a mile with Pleasure,
She chatted all the way,
But left me none the wiser
For all she had to say.

I walked a mile with Sorrow,
And ne'er word said she'
But, oh, the things I learned from her
When Sorrow walked with me!

- Robert Browning Hamilton

Adversity comes with instruction in his hand.

- Welsh proverb

Good people are good because they've come to wisdom through failure. We get very little wisdom from success, you know . . . One who doesn't try cannot fail and become wise.

- William Saroyan

If we were logical, the future would be bleak indeed. But we are more than logical. We are human beings, and we have faith, and we have hope, and we can work.

- Jacques Cousteau

Hope is a risk that must be run.

- George Bernanos

I think and think for months and years. Ninety-nine times, the conclusion is false. The hundredth time I am right.

- Albert Einstein

Inventors and men of genius have almost always been regarded as fools at the beginning (and very often at the end) of their careers.

- Dostoevsky

I never have frustrations.
The reason is to wit:
If at first I don't succeed,
I quit!

Never bend your head. Always hold it high. Look the world straight in the face.

- Helen Keller, speaking to a five-year-old blind child

No man or woman is uniformly successful . . . we must all expect a rather high percentage of failure in the things we attempt.

- Barnaby Keeney

Happiness is beneficial for the body, but it is grief that develops the powers of the mind.

-Marcel Proust

If I had my whole life to live over again, I don't think I'd have the strength.

- Flip Wilson

A man is like a plank of wood – soft until seasoned.

Is life so wretched? Isn't it rather your hands which are too small, your vision which is muddled? You are the one who must grow up.

- Dag Hammerskjold

He banged the door on the way out, and out of that bang came eventually the Chrysler Corporation.

- Alfred P. Sloan, Jr., on Walter Chrysler's departure from General Motors

The art of living is more like wrestling than dancing.

- Marcus Aurelius, c. 160 A.D.

The Wright Brothers flew right through the smoke screen of impossibility.

- Charles F. Kettering

Men are failures, not because they are stupid, but because they are not sufficiently impassioned.

- Struthers Burt

Look around and you'll agree that the really happy people are those who have broken the chains of procrastination, those who find satisfaction in doing the job at hand. They're full of eagerness, zest, productivity. You can be, too.

- Norman Vincent Peale

Our belief at the beginning of a doubtful undertaking is the one thing that insures the successful outcome of our venture.

- William James

Damn the torpedoes, full speed ahead!

- Admiral David G. Farragut, 1864, at the Battle of Mobile Bay

The glory of the star, the glory of the sun – we must not lose either in the other. We must not be so full of the hope of heaven that we cannot do our work on the earth; we must not be so lost in the work of the earth that we shall not be inspired by the hope of heaven.

- Phillips Brooks

Is anything too hard for the Lord?
- The Bible, Genesis 18:14

Give the American people a good cause, and there's nothing they can't lick.
- John Wayne

You must pay the price if you wish to secure the blessings.
- Andrew Jackson

The hero is no braver than an ordinary man, but he is brave five minutes longer.
- Ralph Waldo Emerson

The world has no room for cowards. We must all be ready somehow to toil, to suffer, to die. And yours is not the less noble because no drum beats before you when you go out to your daily battlefields, and no crowds shout your coming when you return from your daily victory and defeat.
- Robert Louis Stevenson

Cannon to right of them,
Cannon to left of them,
Cannon in front of them
Volley'd and thunder'd;
Storm'd at with shot and shell,
Boldly they rode and well,
Into the jaws of Death,
Into the mouth of Hell,
Rode the six hundred
- Alfred Tennyson, "The Charge of the Light Brigade"

It is better to be a coward for a minute than dead for the rest of your life.
- Irish proverb

They conquer who believe they can. He has not learned the first lesson of life who does not every day surmount a fear.
- Ralph Waldo Emerson

"Cast Your Vote"
Never be afraid to stand with the minority when the minority is right, for the minority which is right will one day be the majority . . .
- William Jennings Bryan

Ah, great it is to believe the dream
As we stand in youth by the starry stream;
But a greater thing is to fight life through,
And say at the end, "The dream is true!"
- Edwin Markham

When the going gets tough, the tough get going.
- Maxim adopted by Joseph P. Kennedy

We must not hope to be mowers,
And to gather the ripe gold ears,
Unless we have first been sowers
And watered the furrows with tears.
It is not just as we take it,
This mystical world of ours,
Life's field will yield as we make it
A harvest of thorns or of flowers.
- Goethe

Rapture's self is three parts sorrow.
- Amy Lowell

Pain nourishes courage. You can't be brave if you've only had wonderful things happen to you.
- Mary Tyler Moore

There are some men whom a staggering emotional shock, so far from making them mental invalids for life, seems, on the other hand, to awaken, to galvanize, to arouse into an almost incredible activity of soul.
- William McFee

The only life worth living is the adventurous life. Of such a life the dominant characteristic is that it is unafraid. It is unafraid of what other people think . . . It does not adapt either its pace or its objectives to the pace and objectives of its neighbors. It thinks its own thoughts, it reads its own books, it develops its own hobbies, and it is governed by its own conscience. The herd may graze where it pleases or stampede where it pleases, but he who lives the adventurous life will remain unafraid when he finds himself alone.
- Raymond B. Fosdick

I shall grow old, but never lose life's zest,
Because the road's last turn will be the best.
- Henry Van Dyke

The world is round and the place which may seem like the end may also be only the beginning.
- Ivy Baker Priest

We do not stop playing because we are old. We grow old because we stop playing.

Diligence is the mother of good luck.
- Benjamin Franklin

'Tis sweet to think on what was hard t'endure.
-Robert Herrick, 17th century

. . . Let us remember that the times which future generations delight to recall are not those of ease and prosperity, but those of adversity bravely borne.
- Charles W. Eliot, Harvard President, 1877

Happy is the man whom God correcteth: therefore despise not the chastening of the Almighty.
- The Bible, Job 5:17

Every mile is two in Winter.
- George Herbert on perspective, 1640

The lowest ebb is the turn of the tide.
- Henry Wadsworth Longfellow

Perseverance is the most overrated of traits, if it is unaccompanied by talent; beating your head against a wall is more likely to produce a concussion in the head than a hole in the wall.

- Sydney J. Harris

Most people spend more time and energy in going around problems than in trying to solve them.

- Henry Ford

Writing is a difficult trade which must be learned slowly by reading great authors; by trying at the outset to imitate them; by daring then to be original; by destroying one's first productions; by comparing subsequent works to recognized masterpieces and, once more, by destroying them; by crossing out whole passages; by weeping from despair; by being more severe with oneself than even the critics will be. After ten years of such arduous activity, if one has talent, one may begin to write in an acceptable manner.

- Andre Maurois

Every new adjustment is a crisis in self-esteem . . .

- Eric Hoffer

Some griefs are medicinal.

- William Shakespeare

If I miss one day's practice, I notice it. If I miss two days, the critics notice it. If I miss three days, the audience notices it.

- Ignance Paderewski, Polish pianist-statesman

Perseverance is more prevailing than violence; and many things which cannot be overcome when they are together, yield themselves up when taken little by little.

- Plutarch, c. 100 A.D.

The difficult we do immediately; the impossible takes a little longer.

- Attributed variously to George Santayana, Fridtjof Nansen and the U.S. Army Corps of Engineers.

No great thing is created suddenly, any more than a bunch of grapes or a fig. If you tell me that you desire a fig, I answer that there must be time. Let it first blossom, then bear fruit, then ripen.

- Epictetus, c. 1st Century A.D.

A diamond is a piece of coal that stuck to the job.

If I set for myself a task, be it ever so trifling, I shall see it through. How else shall I have confidence in myself to do important things?

- George S. Clason, The Richest Man in Babylon

Thine was the prophet's vision, thine
The exaltation, the divine
Insanity of noble minds,
That never falters nor abates,
But labors and endures and waits,
Till all that it forsees it finds,
Or what it cannot find creates.

- Henry Wadsworth Longfellow

After he had finished a concert and had gone backstage, violinist Fritz Kreisler heard someone say, "I'd give my life to play as you do!" He turned and looked at the lady and said, "Madam, I did."

If one defines the term "dropout" to mean a person who has given up serious effort to meet his responsibilities, then every business office, government agency, golf club and university faculty would yield its quota.

- John W. Gardner

The true value of a human being is determined primarily by the measure and the sense in which he has attained liberation from the self.

- Albert Einstein

After you've done a thing for two years, you should look at it carefully. After five years, look at it with suspicion. After ten years, throw it away and start all over.

- Alfred E. Perlman

It is the character of a brave and resolute man not to be ruffled by adveristy and not to desert his post.

- Cicero, 78 BC

. . . What counts is not necessarily the size of the dog in the fight – it's the size of the fight in the dog.

- Dwight D. Eisenhower

Touch a thistle timidly, and it pricks you; grasp it boldly, and its spines crumble.

- William S. Halsey

Of all the traps and pitfalls in life, self-disesteem is the deadliest, and the hardest to overcome; for it is a pit designed and dug by our own hands, summed up in the phrase, "It's no use – I can't do it." . . . It is that good hard second look – taken not just for one's own sake but for everyone else's too – that very often reveals that the "impossible" task is quite possible after all.

- Dr. Maxwell Maltz

I am an optimist. It does not seem too much use being anything else.

- Winston Churchill

The man of character finds an especial attractiveness in difficulty since it is only by coming to grips with difficulty that he can realize his potentialities.

- Charles de Gaulle

Paul Galvin at the age of thirty-three had failed twice in business. He attended an auction of his failed storage-battery business and with his last $750 bought back the battery eliminator portion of it. That part became Motorola. When he retired in the 1960s he said, "Do not fear mistakes. You will know failure. Continue to reach out."

That is the light grief which can take counsel.
- Seneca, c. 60

Come unto me, all ye that labor and are heavy laden, and I will give you rest.
- The Bible, Matthew 11:28

Problems are the price of progress. Don't bring me anything but trouble. Good news weakens me.
- Charles F. Kettering

The worst bankrupt in the world is the man who has lost enthusiasm. Let him lose everything but enthusiasm and he will come through again to success.

Life is like playing a violin solo in public and learning the instrument as one goes on.
- Samuel Butler

Hardships, poverty and want are the best incentives and the best foundation for the success of a man.
- Bradford Merrill

They tried their best to find a place where I was isolated. But all the resources of a superpower cannot isolate a man who hears the voice of freedom, a voice I heard from the very chamber of my soul.
- Anatoly B. Shcharansky, Soviet dissident

Truly a little body often harbors a great soul.
- Nikita Khrushchev, on the U.S. Communist Party

If Winter comes, can Spring be far behind?
- Shelley

"Stubborn Ounces"
To one who doubts the worth of doing anything if you can't do everything.
You say the little efforts that I make
will do no good: they never will prevail
to tip the hovering scale
where Justice hangs in balance.
    I don't think
I ever thought they would.
But I am prejudiced beyond debate
in favor of my right to choose which side
shall feel the stubborn ounces of my weight.
- Bonaro W. Overstreet

The curtain is lifting. We can have triumph, or tragedy, for we are the play-wrights, the actors and the audience.
- John Macauley, Chairman, League of Red Cross Societies

Defeat isn't bitter, if you don't swallow it.

Self-pity is our worst enemy and if we yield to it, we can never do anything wise in the world.
- Helen Keller

Adversity introduces a man to himself.

That which is bitter to endure may be sweet to remember.
- Thomas Fuller, 1732.

A President has to expect those things. The only thing you have to worry about is bad luck. I never have bad luck.
- Harry S Truman, on his assassination attempt, 1950

Time and thinking tame the strongest grief.
- English proverb, borrowed from the Latin

Trouble is only opportunity in work clothes.
- Henry J. Kaiser

It is, of course, a trite observation to say that we live "in a period of transition." Many people have said this at many times. Adam may well have made the remark to Eve on leaving the Garden of Eden.
- Harold MacMillan, British Prime Minister

Act as if the whole election depended on your single vote . . .
- John Wesley

A battle sometimes decides everything; and sometimes the most trifling thing decides the fate of a battle.
- Napoleon Bonaparte

If thou faint in the day of adversity, thy strength is small.
- The Bible, Proverbs 24:10

Living is like licking honey off a thorn.

When I was 40, my doctor advised me that a man in his forties shouldn't play tennis. I heeded his advice carefully and could hardly wait until I reached 50 to start again.
- Hugo Black, Supreme Court Associate Justice

We're eye-ball to eye-ball and the other fellow just blinked.
- Dean Rusk, on the 1962 Cuban missile crisis

You've got to be a man to play baseball for a living, but you've got to have a lot of little boy in you, too.
- Roy Campanella

Any man who has had the job I've had and didn't have a sense of humor wouldn't still be here.

> *- Harry S Truman*

I have chosen thee in the furnace of affliction.

> *- The Bible, Isaiah 48:10*

Writing a book is an adventure; to begin with it is a toy and an amusement, then it becomes a master, and then it becomes a tyrant; and . . . just as you are about to be reconciled to your servitude – you kill the monster and fling him . . . to the public.

> *- Winston Churchill*

I have been driven to my knees many times because there was no place else to go.

> *- Abraham Lincoln*

Progress needs the brakeman, but the brakeman should not spend all his time putting on the brakes.

> *- Elbert Hubbard*

You're only young once. How long that once lasts is the question.

Most people say that as you get old, you have to give up things. I think you get old because you give up things.

> *- Senator Theodore Francis Green of Rhode Island, at 87*

Let every nation know, whether it wishes us well or ill, that we shall pay any price, bear any burden, meet any hardship, support any friend, oppose any foe to assure the survival and the success of liberty.

> *- John F. Kennedy*

A man can fail many times but he isn't a failure until he begins to blame somebody else.

Khrushchev reminds me of the tiger hunter who has picked a place on the wall to hang the tiger's skin long before he has caught the tiger. This tiger has other ideas.

> *- John F. Kennedy*

If you have an important point to make, don't try to be subtle or clever. Use a pile driver. Hit the point once. Then come back and hit it again. Then hit it a third time – a tremendous whack.

> *- Winston Churchill*

A ball player's got to be kept hungry to become a big-leaguer. That's why no boy from a rich family ever made the big leagues.

> *- Joe DiMaggio*

It circulated for five years, through the halls of 15 publishers, and finally ended up with Vanguard Press, which as you can see, is rather deep into the alphabet.

> *- Patrick Dennis (Edward Everett Tanner), on his novel, Auntie Mame*

What's gone and what's past help
Should be past grief.

> *- William Shakespeare, "The Winter's Tale"*

Every great discovery I ever made, I gambled that the truth was there, and then I acted on it in faith until I could prove its existence.

> *- Arthur H. Compton, Nobel Prize physicist*

What one approves, another scorns,
And thus his nature each discloses;
You find the rosebush full of thorns,
I find the thornbush full of roses.

> *- Arthur Guiterman*

Worry never robs tomorrow of its sorrow; it only saps today of its strength.

> *- A. J. Cronin*

I am an old man and have known a great many troubles, but most of them have never happened.

> *- Mark Twain*

Courage is armor
A blind man wears;
The calloused scars
Of outlived despairs:
Courage is fear
That has said its prayers.

> *- Karle Wilson Baker, "Courage"*

ACHIEVEMENT
Quotes & Anecdotes
(success, greatness, excellence)

It is no use saying, "We are doing our best." You have got to succeed in doing what is necessary.
- Winston Churchill

Getting something done is an accomplishment; getting something done right is an achievement.

Success is to be measured not so much by the position that one has reached in life as by the obstacles which he has overcome while trying to succeed.
- Booker T. Washington

Doubt is a thief that often makes us fear to tread where we might have won.
- William Shakespeare

I always turn to the sports pages first, which record people's accomplishments. The front page has nothing but man's failures.
- Chief Justice Earl Warren

He that will not sail until all dangers are over must never put to sea.
- Thomas Fuller

You can't steal second base and keep one foot on first.
- A 69-year-old junior executive

Ladder of Achievement
100% - I did. 90% - I will. 80% - I can. 70% I think I can. 60% - I might. 50% - I think I might. 40% - What is it? 30% - I wish I could. 20% - I don't know how. 10% - I can't. 0% - I won't.

They keep saying that what really matters is not whether you win or lose, but how you played the game. The trouble is that the best way to determine how you played the game is by whether you won or lost.

He who comes up to his own idea of greatness must always have had a very low standard of it in his mind.
- William Hazlitt

If at the end one can say, "This man used to the limit the powers that God granted him; he was worthy of love and respect and of the sacrifices of many people, made in order that he might achieve what he deemed to be his task," then that life has been lived well and there are no regrets.
- Eleanor Roosevelt

The best part of success is that, whether we know it or not, all of us have been successful at something, perhaps many times, during our lives. The most difficult part of success is knowing when it is really ours.

At a dinner for U.S. winners of the Nobel Prize in 1962, President John F. Kennedy remarked: "I think this is the most extraordinary collection of talent, of human knowledge, that has ever been gathered together at the White House – with the possible exception of when Thomas Jefferson dined alone."

Two roads diverged in a wood, and I
– I took the one less traveled by,
And that has made all the difference.
- Robert Frost, "The Road Not Taken"

Everyone is trying to accomplish something big, not realizing that life is made up of little things.
- Frank A. Clark

Desires must be simple and definite. They defeat their own purpose should they be too many, too confusing, or beyond a man's training to accomplish.
- George S. Clason

For success, try aspiration, inspiration, and perspiration.

There ain't no man can avoid being born average. But there ain't no man got to be common.
- Satchel Paige

God will not look you over for medals, degrees, or diplomas, but for scars.
- Elbert Hubbard

The door to the room of success swings on the hinges of opposition.

In this country, success is commonly regarded as an exclusively American product, and it is advertised on matchbook covers and in the back pages of adventure magazines, accessible by way of high-school education or a new truss. It is thought by some to have a distinctly bitter taste, not unlike a mouthful of dimes. But its smell is generally conceded to be sweet.
- Stephen Birmingham

We are more ready to try the untried when what we do is inconsequential. Hence the remarkable fact that many inventions had their birth as toys.
- Eric Hoffer

If A equals success, then the formula is A equals X plus Y plus Z. X is work. Y is play. Z is keep your mouth shut.
- Albert Einstein

I don't know the key to success, but the key to failure is to try to please everyone.
- Bill Cosby

. . . The average man who wins what we call success is not a genius. He is a man who has merely the ordinary qualities that he shares with his fellows, but who has developed those ordinary qualities to a more than ordinary degree.
- Theodore Roosevelt

Every great man is unique.
- Ralph Waldo Emerson

A man is rich according to what he is, not according to what he has.

Our business in life is not to get ahead of other people, but to get ahead of ourselves.
- Maltbie D. Babcock

Superior achievement, or making the most of one's capabilities, is to a very considerable degree a matter of habit. This was the reason why Joe used to say to the children, "We don't want any losers around here. In this family we want winners." They were encouraged to be winners, leaders, and victors in whatever they set their hand to . . . to develop the habit.
- Rose Fitzgerald Kennedy

Metaphors – Life is currently described in one of four ways: a journey, a battle, a pilgrimage, or a race. Select your own metaphors, but the necessity of finishing is all the same. For if life is a journey, it must be completed. If life is a battle, it must be finished. If life is a pilgrimage, it must be concluded. And if life is a race, it must be won.
- The War Cry

Hitch your wagon to a star.
- Ralph Waldo Emerson

Ideals are like stars. You will not succeed in touching them with your hands; but, like the seafaring man, you choose them as your guides, and, following them, you will reach your destiny.
- Charles Schurz

We succeed only as we identify in life, or in war, or in anything else, a single overriding objective, and make all other considerations bend to that one objective.
- Dwight D. Eisenhower

Nothing splendid has ever been achieved except by those who dared believe that something inside them was superior to circumstance.
- Bruce Barton

Glory gives herself only to those who always dreamed of her.
- Charles de Gaulle

As far back as I remember, long before I could write, I had played at making stories. But not until I was seven or more, did I begin to pray every night, "O God, let me write books! Please, God, let me write books!"
- Ellen Glasgow

The superior man makes the difficulty to be overcome his first interest; success comes only later.
- Confucius, c. 500 B.C.

I believe in the tragic element of history. I believe there is the tragedy of a man who works very hard and never gets what he wants. And then I believe there is the even more bitter tragedy of a man who finally gets what he wants and finds out that he doesn't want it.
- Henry Kissinger

I knew very well what I was undertaking, and very well how to do it, and have done it very well.
- Samuel Johnson, Speaking of his Dictionary, 1779

Success is not a harbor but a voyage with its own perils to the spirit. The game of life is to come up a winner, to be a success, or to achieve what we set out to do. Yet there is always the danger of failing as a human being. The lesson that most of us on this voyage never learn, but can never quite forget, is that to win is sometimes to lose.
- Richard M. Nixon

Some are born great, some achieve greatness, and some have greatness thrust upon them.
- William Shakespeare: Twelfth Night, c. 1601

That individuals have soared above the plane of their race is scarcely to be questioned; but, in looking back through history for traces of their existence we should pass over all biographies of "the good and the great," while we search carefully the slight records of wretches who died in prison, in Bedlam, or upon the gallows.
- Edgar Allen Poe

In America, anyone can become President. That's one of the risks you take.
- Adlai Stevenson

Meet success like a gentleman and disaster like a man.
- Lord Birkenhead

The two hardest things to handle in life are failure and success.

True success is overcoming the fear of being unsuccessful.
- Paul Seeney

The man of true greatness never loses his child's heart.
- Mencius, c. 300 B.C.

They don't sing about racing for the moon any more, because that boat has landed.

The gods favor the bold.
- Ovid

When a man's willing and eager, the gods join in.
- Aeschylus

On how she became an internationally famous aviatrix, Jacqueline Cochran explained: "I wanted to go higher than Rockefeller Center, which was going to cut off my view of the sky . . . . I might have been born in a hovel, but I determined to travel with the wind and the stars.

Dwight D. Eisenhower, when told that his birthday would make him the oldest President to serve in office, said: I believe it's a tradition in baseball that when a pitcher has a no-hitter going, no one reminds him of it.

Do not commit the error, common among the young, of assuming that if you cannot save the whole of mankind you have failed.

- Jan de Hartog

The riders in a race do not stop short when they reach the goal. There is a little finishing canter before coming to a standstill. There is time to hear the kind voices of friends and to say to one's self, "the work is done."

- Oliver Wendell Holmes, Jr.

I sincerely regret all my divorces because I don't like anything to be unsuccessful.

- John Paul Getty

Men may be divided almost any way we please, but I have found the most useful distinction to be made between those who devote their lives to conjugating the verb "to be," and those who spend their lives conjugating the verb "to have."

- Sydney J. Harris

A modest man often seems conceited because he is delighted with what he has done, thinking it better than anything of which he believed himself capable, whereas the conceited man is inclined to express dissatisfaction with his performances, thinking them unworthy of his genius.

- Hesketh Pearson

. . . I want it said of me by those who knew me best, that I always plucked a thistle and planted a flower where I thought a flower would grow.

Abraham Lincoln

A great man will not trample upon a worm, nor sneak to an emperor.

- Thomas Fuller, 1732

That man is a success who has lived well, laughed often and loved much; who has gained the respect of intelligent men and the love of children; who has filled his niche and accomplished his task; who leaves the world better than he found it, whether by an improved poppy, a perfect poem or a rescued soul; who never lacked appreciation of earth's beauty or failed to express it; who looked for the best in others and gave the best he had.

- Robert Louis Stevenson

The farmer's son said, "Good-bye, Dad, I'm off to the big city so my talents can flower."
"Same reason the corn stays here," said the farmer.

The lure of the distant and the difficult is deceptive. The great opportunity is where you are.

- John Burroughs

All you need in this life is ignorance and confidence, and then success is sure.

- Mark Twain

J. Paul Getty sent the following to a magazine requesting a short article explaining his success: "Some people find oil. Others don't."

- J. Paul Getty

The mere absence of war is not peace. The mere absence of recession is not growth.

- John F. Kennedy

Hell begins on the day when God grants us a clear vision of all that we might have achieved, of all the gifts which we might have wasted, of all that we might have done which we did not do.

- Gian-Carlo Menotti

Lord, I confess I am not what I ought to be, but I thank you, Lord, that I'm not what I used to be.

- Maxie Dunnan

A man who had been bypassed for promotion went to the president and complained, saying he had fifteen years of experience with the firm.
The president answered him, "Not so. You have had one year of experience fifteen times."

When you can, always advise people to do what you see they really want to do . . . . Doing what they want to do, they may succeed; doing what they don't want to do, they won't.

- James Gould Cozzens

A hundred times every day I remind myself that my inner and outer life depend on the labors of other men, living and dead, and that I must exert myself in order to give in the same measure as I have received and am still receiving.

- Albert Einstein

Skillful pilots gain their reputation from storms and tempests.

- Epicurus

Nothing succeeds like the appearance of success.

- Christopher Lasch

[The great society] is a place where men are more concerned with the quality of their goals than the quantity of their goods.

- Lyndon B. Johnson

When has lasting greatness ever been achieved by one who sought greatness for itself rather than allowing it to move quietly upon him as he worked for others . . . ? What did Dooley, or what did Rusk, or Kendall or Schweitzer set out to do but help his neighbor in the way he knew best?

- Dr. George Fister

Not often in the story of mankind does a man arrive on earth who is both steel and velvet, who is as hard as rock and soft as drifting fog, who holds in his heart and mind the paradox of terrible storm and peace unspeakable and perfect.

- Carl Sandburg, on 150th anniversary of
Abraham Lincoln's birth

If there is a single quality that is shared by all great men, it is vanity. But I mean by "vanity" only that they appreciate their own worth . . .

- Yussef Karsh, photographer

3

The lure of succeeding grandly before an audience is what keeps the performer alive. It was once aptly described by the late high-wire artist Karl Wallenda, who said: "Life is on the wire. All the rest is waiting around."

- Michael Fedo

. . . Applause. Enjoy it – but never quite believe it.

- Robert Montgomery

The bird of paradise alights only upon the hand that does not grasp.

- John Berry

I am proud but also, I must admit, awe-struck at your decision to include me. I do hope you are right. I feel we are both running a considerable risk and that I do not deserve it. But I shall have no misgivings if you have none.

- Winston Churchill, accepting Nobel Prize for Literature

I am very happy for any writer who deserves it to get the prize. I am sorry about any writer who deserves it and doesn't get it. This makes me very humble in accepting it.

- Ernest Hemingway, accepting Nobel Prize for Literature

Charles Lawrence, at a dinner honoring him for the development of the engine for Charles Lindbergh's historic non-stop flight to Paris, said: "This is nice and I appreciate it very much. But who ever heard of Paul Revere's horse?"

Recipe For Greatness – To bear up under loss; To fight the bitterness of defeat and the weakness of grief; To be victor over anger; To smile when tears are close; To resist disease and evil men and base instincts; To hate hate and to love love; To go on when it would seem good to die; To look up with unquenchable faith in something ever more about to be. That is what any man can do, and be great.

- Zane Grey

In his book, *Speaking of Bridge,* Marshall Smith describes the ideal player: "[He] has the conceit of a peacock, night habits of an owl, rapacity of a crocodile and the sly inscrutability of a snake. Along with these he needs the memory of an elephant, the boldness of a lion, endurance of a bulldog and killer instinct of a wolf. In such company, the average bridge player is nothing but a kibitzing monkey."

More worship the rising than the setting sun.

- Plutarch, c. 100

The toughest thing about success is that you've got to keep on being a success.

- Irving Berlin

Show me a thoroughly satisfied man, and I will show you a failure.

- Thomas Edison

To be successful is to achieve an objective, but to be a success is always to have yet another objective in mind . . .

Columbus set out to find a passage to the Indies and failed; he found America instead. Ponce de Leon looked for the fountain of youth and found Florida. The greatest explorers seem to find something other than what they are looking for.

The measure of success is not whether you have a tough problem to deal with, but whether it's the same problem you had last year.

- John Foster Dulles

Aviation is proof that, given the will, we have the capacity to achieve the impossible.

- Eddie Rickenbacker

Ah, but a man's reach should exceed his grasp, or what's heaven for?

- Robert Browning

There is nothing noble in being superior to some other man. The true nobility is in being superior to your previous self.

- Hindustani proverb

The graveyards are full of indispensable men.

- Charles de Gaulle

Philadelphia Phillies baseball star Mike Schmidt grew up in a sleepy, tree-lined, middle-class neighborhood in Dayton, Ohio. At the age of five he climbed a tree in his backyard and grabbed a 4000-volt power line. Knocked unconscious by the shock, he fell limp to the ground. The impact restarted his heart.

"I've never thought that I was given a second chance because I was supposed to do something great in my life," Schmidt says. "But I've looked back and wondered why that stupid little kid didn't die. Maybe that's the reason I've always worked so hard, because I don't want to think that I wasted that chance."

- Phil Axelrod, in Pittsburgh Post-Gazette

People are always blaming their circumstances for what they are. I don't believe in circumstances. The people who get on in this world are the people who look for the circumstances they want, and if they can't find them, make them.

- George Bernard Shaw

Being powerful is like being a lady. If you have to tell people you are, you aren't.

- Margaret Thatcher

LEADERSHIP

Quotes & Anecdotes
(management skills, delegation, government)

You done splendid.
> – *Casey Stengel, an accolade*
> *reserved for his best players*

If you want a track team to win the high jump, you find one person who can jump seven feet, not seven people who can jump one foot.
> – *Louis Terman*

A leader is best when people barely know he exists. Not so good when people obey and acclaim him. Worse when they despise him. But of a good leader who talks little when his work is done, his aim fulfilled, they will say "We did it ourselves."
> – *Lao-tzu, c. 550 B.C.*

A first-rate organizer is never in a hurry. He is never late. He always keeps up his sleeve a margin for the unexpected.
> – *Arnold Bennett*

I never give them hell. I just tell the truth, and they think it is hell.
> – *Harry S Truman*

The price of greatness is responsibility.
> – *Winston Churchill*

If we were all determined to play the first violin we should never have an ensemble. Therefore, respect every musician in his proper place.
> – *Robert Schumann, composer*

Certainly a leader needs a clear vision of the organization and where it is going, but a vision is of little value unless it is shared in a way so as to generate enthusiasm and commitment. Leadership and communication are inseparable.
> – *Claude I. Taylor, Chairman of*
> *the Board, Air Canada*

Judge a leader by the followers.

Confidence is contagious. So is lack of confidence.
> – *Michael O'Brien*

The American people want leadership which believes in them, not leadership which berates them.
> – *Lyndon B. Johnson*

A leader is a dealer in hope.
> – *Napoleon Bonaparte*

The spirited horse, which will try to win the race of its own accord, will run even faster if encouraged.
> – *Ovid, about 9 A.D.*

I consider my ability to arouse enthusiasm among people the greatest asset I possess.

I never use a score when conducting my orchestra . . . . Does a lion tamer enter a cage with a book on how to tame a lion?
> – *Dimitri Mitropolous*

The boss drives his men; the leader coaches them. The boss depends upon authority; the leader on good will. The boss inspires fear; the leader inspires enthusiasm. The boss says "I"; the leader "we." The boss fixes the blame for the breakdown; the leader fixes the breakdown. The boss says "go"; the leader says "let's go!"
> – *H. Gordon Selfridge, merchant*

The marksman hitteth the target partly by pulling, partly by letting go. The boatsman reacheth the landing partly by pulling, partly by letting go.
> – *Egyptian proverb*

Excellence is to do a common thing in an uncommon way.
> – *Booker T. Washington*

Message to corporate leaders: Bring your corporation out of the organizational swamp . . . ; spell out your twenty-to-twenty-five-year vision; get your organization structures right; and . . . create an environment in which everyone has the opportunity to do work which matches his potential capability and for which an equitable differential reward is provided.
> – *Elliott Jaques*

Big jobs usually go to the men who prove their ability to outgrow small ones.
> – *Ralph Waldo Emerson*

No man is fit to command another that cannot command himself.
> – *William Penn,*
> *"No Cross, No Crown," 1669.*

People ask the difference between a leader and a boss . . . The leader works in the open, and the boss in covert. The leader leads, and the boss drives.
> – *Theodore Roosevelt*

There is a singular quality about Abraham Lincoln which sets him apart from all our other Presidents . . . a dimension of brooding compassion, of love for humanity; a love which was, if anything, strengthened and deepened by the agony that drove lesser men to the protective shelter of callous indifference.
> – *Lyndon B. Johnson*

Not often in the story of mankind does a man arrive on earth who is both steel and velvet, who is as hard as a rock and soft as drifting fog, who holds in his heart and mind the paradox of terrible storm and peace unspeakable and perfect.
> – *Carl Sandburg, spoken on the 150th*
> *anniversary of Lincoln's birth*

During the Civil War, when someone complained to him that General Grant was a heavy drinker, President Lincoln is supposed to have said, "Find out what brand he drinks, so I can send some to my other generals."

I've met a few people in my time who were enthusiastic about hard work. And it was just my luck that all of them happened to be men I was working for at the time.
— *Bill Gold*

A good presentation has as many questions as answers.

By working faithfully eight hours a day, you may eventually get to be a boss and work 12 hours a day.
— *Robert Frost*

I am more afraid of an army of 100 sheep led by a lion than an army of 100 lions led by a sheep.
— *Talleyrand*

I make progress by having people around who are smarter than I am — and listening to them. And I assume that everyone is smarter about something than I am.
— *Henry J. Kaiser*

The chief executive who knows his strengths and weaknesses as a leader is likely to be far more effective than the one who remains blind to them. He also is on the road to humility — that priceless attitude of openness to life that can help a manager absorb mistakes, failures, or personal shortcomings.
— *John Adair*

Any man who has had the job I've have and didn't have a sense of humor, wouldn't still be here.
— *Harry S Truman*

Asked what his secret was for lasting so long and being so successful as the president of the University of Michigan, Dr. James R. Angell explained: "Grow antennae, not horns."

Preparation makes for leadership, and leadership is service to man.
— *Dr. Douglas Southall Freeman*

The best executive is the one who has sense enough to pick good men to do what he wants done, and the self-restraint to keep from meddling with them while they do it.
— *Theodore Roosevelt*

A matchmaker requested an experienced fighter for a match with the local boxing champion. On the day of the fight a middle-aged man with a much broken nose, a punch-drunk manner and two huge cauliflower ears arrived to enter the ring. The matchmaker was aghast. "I asked for an experienced fighter," he complained, "but not a damaged one."

A strong and secure man digests his experiences (deeds and misdeeds alike) just as he digests his meat, even when he has some bits to swallow.
— *Friedrich Nietsche*

Experience is largely non-transferable

There are two kinds of men who never amount to much — those who cannot do what they are told and those who can do nothing else.
— *Cyrus H.K. Curtis*

Respect a man, he will do the more.
— *James Howell, 1659*

Authority without wisdom is like a heavy ax without an edge, fitter to bruise than polish.
— *Anne Bradstreet, c. 1670*

Most people like hard work. Particularly when they are paying for it.
— *Franklin P. Jones*

Every great man is always being helped by everybody, for his gift is to get good out of all things and all persons.
— *John Ruskin, 1846*

Show me a man who cannot bother to do little things and I'll show you a man who cannot be trusted to do big things.
— *Lawrence D. Bell*

While I am not in favor of maladjustment, I view this cultivation of neutrality, this breeding of mental neuters, this hostility to eccentricity and controversy with grave misgiving. One looks back with dismay at the possibility of a Shakespeare perfectly adjusted to bourgeois life in Stratford, a Wesley contentedly administering a country parish, George Washington going to London to received a barony from George III, or Abraham Lincoln prospering in Springfield with nary a concern for the preservation of the crumbling Union.
— *Adlai Stevenson*

Every great advance in natural knowledge has involved the absolute rejection of authority.
— *Thomas Huxley, 1870*

There is no necessary connection between the desire to lead and the ability to lead, and even less the ability to lead somewhere that will be to the advantage of the led . . .
— *Bergen Evans*

. . . Government should do only those things the people cannot do for themselves.
— *Ronald Reagan*

That government is the strongest of which every man feels himself a part.
— *Thomas Jefferson*

Those who expect to reap the blessings of freedom must . . . undergo the fatigue of sup-

porting it.
— *Thomas Paine*

A man who wants to lead the orchestra must turn his back on the crowd.
— *James Crook*

Legislators who are of even average intelligence stand out among their colleagues . . . A cultured college president has become as much a rarity as a literate newspaper publisher. A financier interested in economics is as exceptional as a labor leader interested in the labor movement. For the most part our leaders are merely following out in front; they [only] marshal us in the way that we are going.
— *Bergen Evans*

There's plenty of room at the top, but there's no room to sit down.
— *Helen Downey*

The man whose authority is recent is always stern.
— *Aeschylus, Prometheus Bound, c 490 B.C.*

I am a man under authority, having soldiers under me: and I say to this man, Go, and he goeth; and to another, Come, and he cometh.
— *The Bible, Matthew 8:9*

The house shows the owner.
— *George Herbert, 1651*

A good government produces citizens distinguished for courage, love of justice, and every other good quality; a bad government makes them cowardly, rapacious, and the slaves of every foul desire.
— *Dionysius of Halicarnassus, 20 B.C.*

. . . I would rather have a first-class manager running a second-rate business than a second-class manager running a first-rate business.
— *Jack E. Reichert, President and CEO, Brunswick Corp.*

The same ambition can destroy or save, and makes a patriot as it makes a knave.
— *Alexander Pope, 1732*

Early in life, I had to choose between honest arrogance and hypocritical humility. I chose honest arrogance and have seen no occasion to change.
— *Frank Lloyd Wright, architect*

Nothing motivates a man more than to see his boss putting in an honest day's work.
— *Wain*

I offer neither pay, nor quarters, nor provisions; I offer hunger, thirst, forced marches, battles and death. Let him who loves his country in his heart and not with lips only, follow me.
— *Giuseppe Garibaldi, Italian patriot*

Follow me if I advance! Kill me if I retreat! Revenge me if I die!
— *Ngo Dinh Diem, battle cry on becoming President of Vietnam in 1954*

In enterprise of martial kind,
When there was any fighting,
He led his regiment from behind,
He found it less exciting.
— *W.S. Gilbert*

The lash may force men to physical labor; it cannot force them to spiritual creativity.
— *Sholem Asch*

It is not a government's obligation to provide services, but to see that they are provided.
— *Mario Cuomo, Governor of New York*

Walt Disney seldom surveyed his animators' work while they were creating. He understood the fragile nature of the creative process, and he wouldn't intrude. But there was nothing to stop him after the animator had left for the day. Walt's nighttime visits to the offices became legendary, and animators often left their best work on the drawing table overnight, anticipating that Walt would inspect it. But sometimes they arrived in the morning to find crumpled sheets of paper rescued from wastebaskets and pinned on a storyboard with the notation in the unmistakable Disney script: "Quit throwing the good stuff away."
— *Bob Thomas*

The day before my inauguration President Eisenhower told me, "You'll find that no easy problems ever come to the President of the United States. If they are easy to solve, somebody else has solved them."
— *John F. Kennedy*

A great leader molds public opinion; a wise leader listens to it.

When Leo Durocher was manager of the Dodgers he was booed for pulling a pitcher out in the eighth inning of a close game. A reporter later asked him how he felt about the crowd's reaction. He replied, "Baseball is like church. Many attend, few understand."

For every quarterback on the field, there are a thousand in the stands.

Trust men and they will be true to you; treat them greatly, and they will show themselves great.
— *Ralph Waldo Emerson*

Most of us can learn to live in perfect comfort on higher levels of power. Everyone knows that on any given day there are energies slumbering in him which the incitements of that day do not call forth. Compared with what we ought to be, we are only half awake. It is evident that our organism has stored-up reserves of energy that are ordinarily not called upon – deeper and deeper strata of explosible material, ready for use by anyone who probes so deep. The human individual usually lives far within his limits.

– William James

Gentleness is a divine trait: nothing is so strong as gentleness, and nothing is so gentle as real strength.

– Ralph W. Sockman

Upon what meat doth this our Caesar feed, That he is grown so great?

– William Shakespeare, Julius Caesar

No one is fit to be trusted with power . . . . No one . . . . Any man who has lived at all knows the follies and wickedness he's capable of. If he does not know it, he is not fit to govern others. And if he does know it, he knows also that neither he nor any man ought to be allowed to decide a single human fate.

– C.P. Snow

. . . I will not equivocate – I will not excuse – I will not retreat a single inch and – I will be heard.

– William Lloyd Garrison

All well-governed states and wise princes have taken care not to reduce the nobility to despair, nor the people to discontent.

– Machiavelli, The Prince, 1513

I have no ambition to govern men. It is a painful and thankless office.

– Thomas Jefferson

The world is ruled by a certain few, even as a little boy of twelve years old rules, governs, and keeps a hundred great and strong oxen upon a pasture.

– Martin Luther, 1569

A committee is a group that keeps minutes and loses hours.

– Milton Berle

You can delegate authority, but you can never delegate responsibility for delegating a task to someone else. If you picked the right man, fine, but if you picked the wrong man, the responsibility is yours – not his.

– Richard E. Krafve, President, Raytheon Company

For forms of government let fools contest: Whate'er is best administr'd is best.

– Alexander Pope, 1733

The leader must know, must know that he knows, and must be able to make it abundantly clear to those about him that he knows.

– Clarence B. Randall, retired chairman, Inland Steel Co.

In framing a government which is to be administered by men over men . . . you must first enable the government to control the governed, and in the next place, oblige it to control itself.

– Alexander Hamilton, 1788

The three great ends which a statesman ought to propose to himself in the government of a nation are: (1) security to possessors; (2) facility to acquirers; and (3) hope to all.

– Samuel Coleridge

P. J. Proudhon, in his Confessions of a Revolutionary (1849) stated: "To be governed is to be watched, inspected, spied upon, directed, law-ridden, regulated, penned up, indoctrinated, preached at, checked, appraised, seized, censured, commanded, by beings who have neither title, nor knowledge, nor virtue. To be governed is to have every operation, every transaction, every movement noted, registered, counted, rated, stamped, measured, numbered, assessed, licensed, refused, authorized, endorsed, admonished, prevented, reformed, redressed, corrected."

Every man who takes office in Washington either grows or swells, and when I give a man an office, I watch him carefully to see whether he is swelling or growing.

– Woodrow Wilson

It may be laid as an universal rule that a government which attempts more than it ought will perform less.

– T.B. Macaulay: 1841

It's a lot tougher to be a football coach than a President . . . A coach doesn't have anyone to protect him when things go wrong.

– Harry S Truman

With public sentiment, nothing can fail; without it, nothing can succeed.

– Abraham Lincoln

A static hero is a public liability. Progress grows out of motion.

– Admiral Richard E. Byrd, Arctic explorer

Government is merely an attempt to express the conscience of . . . the nation . . . . If the government is going faster than the public conscience, it will presently have to pull up; if it is not going as fast as the public conscience, it will presently have to be whipped up.

– Woodrow Wilson

To make laws that man cannot, and will not obey, serves to bring all law into contempt.

– Elizabeth Cady Stanton

Government has been a fossil; it should be a plant.

– Ralph Waldo Emerson

The best compliment to a child or a friend is the feeling you give him that he has been set free to make his own inquiries, to come to conclusions that are right for him, whether or not they coincide with your own.

– Alistair Cooke

Here I am at the end of the road and at the top of the heap.

– Pope John XXIII

What does it take to be an Archbishop of Canterbury? The strength of a horse – and the ability to be a cart horse one day and a race horse the next.

– Geoffrey Fisher

Psychology is the science of predicting how people behave – and explaining why they don't.

Until philosophers take to government, or those who now govern become philosophers, so that government and philosophy unite, there will be no end to the miseries of states.

– Plato, c. 370 B.C.

Too often our Washington reflex is to discover a problem and then throw money at it, hoping it will somehow go away.

– Senator Kenneth B. Keating

Those who do well, like criticism; those who do not do well, resent it.

The deterioration of every government begins with the decay of the principles on which it was founded.

– C.L. De Montesquieu

There are two ways of spreading light: to be the candle, or the mirror that reflects it.

– Edith Wharton

. . . Leadership is a word and a concept that has been more argued than almost any other I know . . . I would rather try to persuade a man to go along, because once I have persuaded him he will stick. If I scare him, he will stay just as long as he is scared, and then he is gone.

– Dwight D. Eisenhower

Why has government been instituted at all? Because the passions of men will not conform to the dictates of reason and justice without constraint.

– Alexander Hamilton, 1788

Nobody knows who devised the first flag, but there is a myth telling how it happened. Seems that one warrior got hurt in a fight between two tribes and held up his bloody garment to show that he needed help, and everybody followed him. That's why so many flags use the color red . . .

Great men are rarely isolated mountain peaks; they are the summits of ranges.

– T.W. Higginson, 1871

. . . What is a committee? A group of the unwilling, picked from the unfit, to do the unnecessary.

– Richard Harkness

The refreshing definition of a camel: a horse planned by a committee.

– Vogue Magazine, July 1958

Society in every state is a blessing, but government, even in its best state, is but a necessary evil; in its worst state an intolerable one.

– Thomas Paine, 1776

Laws too gentle are seldom obeyed; too severe, seldom executed.

– Benjamin Franklin

Only a man with the common touch would get his picture on the penny.

What sets American democracy apart is the abiding prejudice against party professionals. Wise candidates advertise themselves as ordinary citizens innocent of the dark arts. In this no one has been more successful than Ronald Reagan . . . the most artfully camouflaged politician in the business.

– Karl E. Meyer

It often happens that I wake at night and begin to think about a serious problem and decide I must tell the Pope about it. Then I wake up completely and remember that I am the Pope.

– Pope John XXIII

Government never shrinks.

Once upon a time my political opponents honored me as possessing the fabulous intellectual and economic power by which I created a world-wide depression all by myself.

– Herbert Hoover, on the depression days

Ideally, the umpire should combine the integrity of a Supreme Court justice, the physical agility of an acrobat, the endurance of Job and the imperturbability of Buddha.

– Time Magazine, August 25, 1961

A President's hardest task is not to do what is right, but to know what is right.

– Lyndon B. Johnson

No matter how humble a man's beginnings, he achieves the stature of the office to which he is elected.

– Nikita Khrushchev

The public demands that the [university] president be everywhere at all times. He is thought to be omniscient, omnipresent, and Mr. Chips all rolled into one.

– Whitney Griswold

It annoys me to see business people characterized as tight-lipped politicos who write memos that never express an opinion and who never say anything in meetings that deviates from the company line. It bothers me even more to think there are young people who believe that's the way to get ahead. In really good companies, you have to lead. You have to come up with . . . big ideas and express them forcefully.

I've always been encouraged – or sometimes forced – to confront the very natural fear of being wrong. I was constantly pushed to find out what I really thought and then to speak up. Over time, I came to see that waiting to discover which way the wind is blowing is an excellent way to learn how to be a follower.

– Roger Enrico, President and CEO of Pepsi-Cola, on corporate stereotypes

No government can be maintained without the principle of fear as well as of duty. Good men will obey the last, but bad ones the former only.

– Thomas Jefferson

It was the nation and the race dwelling all 'round the globe that had the lion's heart. I had the luck to be called upon to give the lion's roar. I also hope that I sometimes suggested to the lion the right place to use his claws.

– Winston Churchill, on the outcome of World War II

Whenever you are to do a thing, though it can never be known but to yourself, ask yourself how you would act were all the world looking at you, and act accordingly.

– Thomas Jefferson

When asked what kind of leader's hat he wears Lech Walesa answers: My hat will always be a worker's hat and it will always hang on a nail. It's a leader's hat but it shall always be a common hat, used by common people for common purposes.

A bore is a fellow who opens his mouth and puts his feats in it.

– Henry Ford

If everyone is thinking alike then somebody isn't thinking.

– George S. Patton

Leadership: the art of getting someone else to so something you want done because he wants to do it.

– Dwight D. Eisenhower

It's great to work with somebody who wants to do things differently.

– Keith Bellows

Leadership is the capacity to translate vision into reality.

– Warren G. Bennis

Where Example *keeps pace* with Authority, Power hardly fails to be obey'd.

– William Penn

The best leaders . . . almost without exception and at every level, are master users of stories and symbols.

– Tom Peters

Managers are people who do things right, and leaders are people who do the right things.

– Warren G. Bennis

My definition of a leader . . . is a man who can persuade people to do what they don't want to do, or do what they're too lazy to do, and like it.

– Harry S Truman

The Hall was the place where the great lord used to eat . . . . He ate not in private, except in time of sickness . . . Nay, the king himself used to eat in the Hall, and his lords sat with him, and he understood men.

– John Selden, about 1620

Character is power.

– Booker T. Washington

BUSINESS

Quotes & Anecdotes
(commerce, occupations, business success)

To business that we love we rise betime,
And go to't with delight.
- *William Shakespeare*

The brain is a wonderful organ; it starts the moment you get up in the morning and does not stop until you get to the office.
- *Robert Frost*

Businesses are successful because someone makes the sacrifices others are unwilling to.
- *Ki-Jung Kim, Korean businessman*

It takes twenty years to make an overnight success.

We're losing all across the board – steel, textiles, electrical machinery, paper, lumber – you name it. And . . . when you're losing a war, the first thing you do is to try for a truce before you bleed to death. Right now we're playing innocents abroad in a trade world that is definitely not innocent.
- *Lee A. Iacocca, Chairman of the board and CEO, Chrysler Corp.*

Never say no when a client asks for something – even if it is the moon. You can always try, and anyhow there is plenty of time afterward to explain that it was not possible.
- *Caesar Ritz, Swiss cowherder who later created hotels bearing his name*

Drive thy business; let it not drive thee.
- *Benjamin Franklin*

You have offered to trade us an apple for an orchard. We do not do that in this country.
- *John F. Kennedy*

Entrepreneurs are simply those who understand that there is little difference between obstacle and opportunity and are able to turn both to their advantage.
- *Victor Kiam, CEO, Remington*

The business executive is by profession a decision maker. Uncertainty is his opponent. Overcoming it is his mission. Whether the outcome is a consequence of luck or of wisdom, the moment of decision is without doubt the most creative and critical event in the life of the executive.
- *John McDonald*

Beware of little expenses: A small leak will sink a ship.
- *Benjamin Franklin*

Working people have a greatness. Given reasonable leadership they are all too willing to follow, do what is asked of them, and give their best to their employers. They are people. They are complex. They are not willing to be treated like indentured servants. Good business leadership can create and generate the work spirit, the wish to cooperate.
- *Arthur E. Imperatore, Chairman of the board, APA Transport Corp.*

A business was failing and a consultant was asked to make a survey . . . He recommended: "Start advertising, and use three media: radio, direct mail, and courtesy. The first two will cost money. The third is free, but it is the most important."

The secret of business is to know something that nobody else knows.
- *Aristotle Onassis*

And while I at length debate and beat the bush, there shall step in other men and catch the birds.
- *John Heywood*

If the profession you have chosen has some unexpected inconveniences, console yourself that no profession is without them, and that all of the perplexities of business are softness compared with the vacancy of idleness.
- *Samuel Johnson*

If you spend money on it, it's a hobby; if you make money on it, it's a business.

A message for businessmen: "Whatever happens, never happens by itself."
- *Sally Rand*

I don't meet competition. I crush it.
- *Charles Revson*

Excellent firms don't believe in excellence – only in constant improvement and constant change.
- *Tom Peters*

A friend said to a man who had a frankfurter stand by the side of the road, "If you put up a sign advertising your stand a mile up the road so people see it before they get here, they might be influenced to stop." The man put up the sign and it worked; so as time went on he put up more signs further and further away on the road, and more and more people bought the frankfurters and the owner was able to send his son to the finest university. When the son returned he said, "You're spending too much money on your advertising. You don't need all those signs." So the father took down some of the signs; the business went down a little, but so did the expense for advertising. With less business, they decided to cut down a little more on the advertising, and the business went down a little more, until finally they were back to a little frankfurter stand without any signs on the road at all.

. . . If you are quiet about your business, your business is apt to be quiet, too.

The smaller the role of marketing, the greater the possibility that the firm operates its marketing activities on a project, crisis, and fragmented basis.
- Joel R. Evans and Barry Berman

Doing business without advertising is like winking at a girl in the dark. You know what you are doing, but nobody else does.
- Stuart Henderson Britt

In some advertising, the selling message ends with a period. In other advertising, the selling message ends with a sale. In either, it costs the advertiser just as much to run a poor ad – as it does to run a good one.
- Young & Rubicam, Inc.

The faults of advertising are only those common to all human institutions. If advertising speaks to a thousand in order to influence one, so does the church. And if it encourages people to live beyond their means, so does matrimony. Good times, bad times, there will always be advertising. In good times, people want to advertise; in bad times, they have to.
- Bruce Barton, chairman, Batten, Barton, Durstine, & Osborne

A good manager is a man who isn't worried about his own career but rather the careers of those who work for him. . . . Don't worry about yourself. Take care of those who work for you and you'll float to greatness on their achievements.
- H.S.M. Burns, president, Shell Oil Co.

I want workers to go home at night and say, "I built that car."
- Pahr G. Gyllenhammar, Chairman, Volvo

Progress is a continuing effort to make the things we eat, drink and wear as good as they used to be.
- Bill Vaughan

A manpower policy should lead us to a society in which every person has full opportunity to develop his – or her – earning powers, where no willing worker lacks a job, and where no useful talent lacks an opportunity.
- Lyndon B. Johnson

A vice-president in an advertising agency is a "molehill man." A molehill man is a pseudo-busy executive who comes to work at 9 a.m. and finds a molehill on his desk. He has until 5 p.m. to make his molehill into a mountain. An accomplished molehill man will often have his mountain finished even before lunch.
- Fred Allen

A bad workman never gets a good tool.
- Thomas Fuller

Let a man practice the profession which he best knows.
- Cicero, c. 50 B.C.

I am rather like a mosquito in a nudist camp; I know what I ought to do, but I don't know where to begin.
- Stephen Bayne

People will buy anything that's one to a customer.
- Sinclair Lewis

Any woman who has a career and a family automatically develops something in the way of two personalities, like two sides of a dollar bill, each different in design. But one can complement the other to make a valuable whole. Her problem is to keep one from draining the life from the other.
- Ivy Baker Priest, U.S. Treasurer

Once upon a time there was a little girl who always said "Thank you" at birthday parties; who called friends of the family "Aunt" Helen and "Uncle" Jim; and who passed out free cookies the day her lemonade stand opened. When this little girl grew up she didn't go to heaven. She went into public relations. And learned that what to her had always been unconscious art is now classified as a science – "the engineering of consent" – worth a hundred a week to her and millions in good will to her clients.
- Mary Anne Guitar

[Ours is] a program whose basic thesis is not that the system of free private enterprise has failed . . . but that it has not yet been tried.
- Franklin D. Roosevelt

The business of America is business.
- Calvin Coolidge

Few people do business well who do nothing else.
- Lord Chesterfield

If I would be a young man again and had to decide how to make my living, I would not try to become a scientist or scholar or teacher. I would rather choose to be a plumber or a peddler, in the hope to find that modest degree of independence still available under present circumstances.
- *Albert Einstein*

If you have a job without aggravations, you don't have a job.
- *Malcom Forbes*

The worst crime against working people is a company which fails to operate at a profit.
- *Samuel Gompers*

Have the mental equipment to do your job, then take the job seriously, yourself not too seriously.
- *Francis Willis, U.S. ambassador to Switzerland*

A young man asked Bernard Baruch if there was a sure way to make a million dollars. Baruch told him that there was one. "All you need to do is purchase a million bags of flour at one dollar and sell them for two dollars each." Apparently the young man took him seriously. He was August Hecker, the founder of a flour mill company that became the largest of its kind.

Most men would feel insulted if it were proposed to employ them in throwing stones over a wall, and then in throwing them back, merely that they might earn their wages. But many are no more worthily employed now.
- *Henry David Thoreau*

Some who are not paid what they are worth ought to be glad.

Too many people quit looking for work when they find a job.

Without the element of uncertainty, the bringing off of even the greatest business triumph would be a dull, routine, and eminently unsatisfying affair.
- *J. Paul Getty*

Being in your own business is working 80 hours a week so that you can avoid working 40 hours a week for someone else.
- *Ramona E.F. Arnett*

Business is never so healthy as when, like a chicken, it must do a certain amount of scratching for what it gets.
- *Henry Ford*

When a child smiles, he gives pleasure. . . so relax. When a business man smiles, he intends to be pleased – so don't relax.

The harder I work, the luckier I get.
- *Samuel Goldwyn*

. . . Courtesy is as important within an organization as in dealing with outsiders.
- *Swift and Co.*

You can close more business in two months by becoming interested in other people than you can in two years by trying to get people interested in you.
- *Dale Carnegie*

There is one major reason why private companies make investments in the developing world: profit. Governments may make investments for political reasons. Companies do it for profit. So, a reasonable greed level is expected . . .
- *Frank G. Zarb*

I was made to work; if you are equally industrious, you will be equally successful.
- *Johann Sebastian Bach*

When you go to buy use your eyes, not your ears.
- *Czech proverb*

It is naught, it is naught, saith the buyer: but when he is gone his way, then he boasteth.
- *The Bible, Proverbs 20:14*

He who speaks ill of the mare, will buy her.
- *Benjamin Franklin*

The buyer buys for as little as possible; the seller sells for as much as possible. (Emptor emit quam minimo potest, venditor vendit quam maximo potest.)
- *Legal Maxim*

My sole inspiration is a telephone call from a producer.
- *Cole Porter*

It is necessary to relax your muscles when you can. Relaxing you brain is fatal.
- *Stirling Moss, British racing-car driver*

Winston Churchill, in reply to a post-war speech in the House of Commons, said, "The substance of the eminent Socialist gentleman's speech is that making a profit is a sin. It is my belief that the real sin is taking a loss."

The story is told of a multimillionaire who insisted on doing business in a genteel but very shabby office. His lawyer said to him, "A man of your position and resources should really have a better furnished office."

"Why?" asked the multimillionaire. "Everybody will charge me more for what I buy."

Keep thy shop and thy shop will keep thee.
- Benjamin Franklin

Business underlies everything in our national life, including our spiritual life. Witness the fact in the Lord's Prayer, the first petition is for daily bread. No one can worship God or love his neighbor on an empty stomach.
- Woodrow Wilson

You never get promoted when no one else knows your current job. The best basis for being advanced is to organize yourself out of every job you're put into. Most people are advanced because they're pushed up by the people underneath them rather than pulled up by the top.
- Donald David, former dean, Harvard Business School

The thing that really worries businesses today is the great number of people still on their payroll who are unemployed.

The trouble with the rat race is that even if you win you're still a rat.
- Lily Tomlin

Put all your eggs in the one basket and – WATCH THAT BASKET
- Mark Twain

The idea of public relations is that if you lead a horse to water, even if you can't make him drink, maybe you can make him swim.

We have witnessed in modern business the submergence of the individual within the organization, and yet the increase to an extraordinary degree of the power of the individual who happens to control the organization. Most men are individuals no longer so far as their business, its activities, or its moralities are concerned. They are not units but fractions.
- Woodrow Wilson

The workman is worthy of his meat.
- The Bible, Matthew 10:10

It is a great art to know how to sell wind.
- Baltasar Gracian, 1647

All business sagacity reduces itself in the last analysis to a judicious use of sabotage.
- Thorstein Veblen

Secrecy is the soul of business.
- Spanish proverb

Education is one of the keys to survival for large corporations in the remaining few years of the twentieth century. We are in transition from an industrial economy to a post-industrial economy where more people are involved in managing information than in producing goods.
- Gordon F. MacFarlane, Chairman and CEO, British Columbia Telephone Co.

Then there was the man whose life was so tied up in his business that his family organized a union so he'd have to meet them around the table.

Quite a few people are already working a four-day week. Trouble is, it takes 'em five or six days to do it.
- Earl Wilson

Call upon a man of business during hours of business only to transact your business. Then go about your business and give him time to attend to his business.

Country judge, chairman of a committee, President of the U.S.; they are all the same kind of jobs. It is the business of dealing with people.
- Harry S Truman

There is no such thing as "soft sell" and "hard sell." There is only "smart sell " and "stupid sell."
- Charles Brower

This is the great era of the goof-off, the age of the half-done job. The land from coast to coast has been enjoying a stampede away from responsibility. It is popularized with laundry men who won't iron shirts, with waiters who won't serve, with carpenters who will come around some day maybe, with executives whose mind is on the golf course, with teachers who demand a single salary scale so that achievement cannot be rewarded, with students who take cinch courses…
- Charles Brower

I encourage boldness because the danger of our seniority and pension plans tempt a young man to settle in a rut named security rather than find his own rainbow.
- Conrad Hilton

We have gone completely overboard on security. Everything has to be secured, jobs, wages, hours – although the ultimate in security is jail, the slave labor camp and the salt mine.
- Cola Parker, President, National Association of Manufacturers

In the tiny space of twenty years, we have bred a whole generation of working Americans who take it for granted that they will never be out of a job or go a single year without a salary increase.
- *K.K. DuVall, President, Chicago Merchandise National Bank*

[The way] a young man spends his evenings is a part of that thin area between success and failure.
- *Robert R. Young*

This is an industry of ideas and imagination, and what we are selling is hope.
- *Steve Mayham, fragrance executive*

There is nothing as universal in this world as human thirst . . . Our market is as big as the world and the people in it.
- *Lee Talley, on being elected president of Coca-Cola*

The phenomenon I refer to . . . is the tidal wave of craving for convenience that is sweeping over America. Today convenience is the success factor of just about every type of produce and service that is showing steady growth.
- *Charles Mortimer, President, General Foods Corporation*

One of the symptoms of an approaching nervous breakdown is the belief that one's work is terribly important.
- *Bertrand Russell*

Success is that old ABC – ability, breaks, and courage.
- *Charles Luckman, manufacturing executive and architect*

He who does not teach his son a trade teaches him to be a robber.
- *Hebrew proverb*

Creativity is our single product. And heaven help the agency management that does not recognize that fact of life. They may wind up as unemployed as Zeppelin pilots.
- *Ernest A. Jones*

The merchants will manage commerce the better, the more they are left free to manage for themselves.
- *Thomas Jefferson*

The good workman receives the bread of his labor with boldness; the lazy and careless cannot look his employer in the face.
- *St. Clement*

I have no complex about wealth. I have worked hard for my money, producing things people need. I believe that the able industrial leader who creates wealth and employment is more worthy of historical notice than politicians or soldiers.
- *John Paul Getty*

You will discover that while the patient wants the best and most modern treatment available, he is also badly in need of the old-fashioned friend that a doctor has always personified and which you must continue to be. In his mind's eye, the patient sees you as in the old paintings or in his real memories – rumpled and kindly, roused from your bed at 3 in the morning to come to his home and pull him through a crisis. But . . . you will treat him in the clinic or the hospital whenever possible because the care you can give is far better in those facilities. You will try to avoid night calls because you know you can diagnose better with your eyes open.
- *Dr. Gunnar Gundersen*

Their dedication is to competitive creativity – a deep desire within the consciousness of man to create something better today than yesterday's best.
- *John Orr Young, on what makes an advertising agency great*

The only thing that matters is caring, deep caring . . . The way to make your plans and your products and your themes and your campaigns and your shows and your letters and your programs more solid, more effective, is to go back to Main Street, your memory source of the things that are deepest and truest and greatest. Be the man or the woman you have it in you to be – and you won't be false to Main Street.
- *Jean Rindlaub, Vice President, Batten, Barton, Durstine & Osborn*

The growth of bigness has resulted in ruthless sacrifices of human values. The disappearance of free enterprise has submerged the individual in the impersonal corporation. When a nation of shopkeepers is transformed into a nation of clerks, enormous spiritual sacrifices are made.
- *William O. Douglas, Supreme Court Associate Justice*

The dinosaur's eloquent lesson is that if some bigness is good, an overabundance of bigness is not necessarily better.
- *Eric Johnson, President, U.S. Chamber of Commerce*

A skillful trade is better than an inherited fortune.
- *Welsh proverb*

Business more than any other occupation is a continual dealing with the future; it is a continual calculation, an instinctive exercise in foresight.

- Henry R. Luce

In many businesses, today will end at five o'clock. Those bent on success, however, make today last from yesterday right through tomorrow.

- Lawrence H. Martin, Boston banker

People who work sitting down get paid more than people who work standing up.

- Ogden Nash

A perfume manufacturer who ran out of superlatives and phrases to describe his product finally used this phrase in his advertising: "As we could not improve our product, we improved the box."

Those who scorn business never say it should not exist – rather that it should not exist for profit, but simply to do more for more people and be better and better at doing it. Being better is the eternal pursuit of the businessman. In fact, it might be easy to demonstrate that without the striving of business for an earned profit, there could be no "better."

- Anonymous

Your mental health will be better if you have lots of fun outside of that office.

- Dr. William Menninger

The marvels of modern technology include the development of a soda can which, when discarded, will last forever, and a $7,000 car which, when properly cared for, will rust out in two or three years.

- Paul Harwitz

The man who has a trade may go anywhere.

- Spanish proverb

Jack of all trades and master of none.

- Maria Edgeworth

We are all apprentices in a craft where no one ever becomes a master.

- Ernest Hemingway

The gambling known as business looks with austere disfavor on the business known as gambling.

- Ambrose Bierce

Polishing the client's apple is no way to improve his advertising. Polishing a good idea is. And polishing. And polishing. Until good becomes better. And becomes best.

- Young & Rubicam, Inc.

One's lifework, I have learned, grows with the working and the living. Serve others as if your life depended on it, and the first thing you know, you'll have made a life out of it. A good life, too.

In war, you win or lose, live or die – and the difference is just an eyelash.

- General Douglas MacArthur

Do not let what you cannot do interfere with what you can do.

- John Wooden, former UCLA basketball coach

Coming together is a beginning; keeping together is progress; working together is success.

- Henry Ford

Never tell people how to do things. Tell them what to do and they will surprise you with their ingenuity.

- George S. Patton

You're only as good as the people you hire.

- Ray Kroc

I believe that the true road to preeminent success in any line is to make yourself master of that line.

- Andrew Carnegie

MONEY

Quotes & Anecdotes
(wealth, prosperity, resourcefulness)

Thousands upon thousands are yearly brought into a state of real poverty by their great anxiety not to be thought poor.
- *William Cobbett*

We forget what gives money its value – that someone exchanged work for it.
- *Neal O'Hara*

Make all you can, save all you can, give all you can.
- *John Wesley*

Don't knock the rich. When did a poor person give you a job?
- *Dr. Laurence J. Peter*

The safe way to double your money is to fold it over once and put it in your pocket.
- *Frank "Kin" Hubbard*

Annual income twenty pounds, annual expenditure nineteen six, result happiness. Annual income twenty pounds, annual expenditure twenty pound ought and six, result misery.
- *Charles Dickens, David Copperfield*

One of the hardest things to teach our children about money matters is that it does.
- *William Randolph Hearst*

After the first million, it doesn't matter. You can only eat three meals a day – I tried eating four and I got sick. You can't sleep in more than one bed at night. Maybe I have twenty suits, but I can only wear one at a time, and I can't use more than two shirts a day.
- *Joseph Hirshhorn, multimillionaire*

We all have the means to become prosperous. We have to find the balance between our wealth and our needs.
- *Robert Bourassa*

The trick is to make sure you don't die waiting for prosperity to come.
- *Lee Iacocca*

Many enjoy a feeling of wealth no matter how little money they have. Wealth well used is a delight to observe; wealth unused is sad to see. Wealth . . . is not in the having, but in the using.

I was born into it and there was nothing I could do about it. It was there, like air or food or any other element . . . The only question with wealth is what you do with it.
- *John D. Rockefeller, Jr.*

Our child will not be raised in tissue paper! . . . We don't want her to even hear the word princess.
- *Juliana, Princess of the Netherlands, on engaging a nurse for her first child*

We should not be like misers, who never enjoy what they have but only bewail what they lose.
- *Plutarch*

The human race has had long experience and a fine tradition in surviving adversity. But we now face a task for which we have little experience, the task of surviving prosperity.
- *Alan Gregg*

Money is like muck, not good unless spread.
- *Francis Bacon, 1625*

Money is like manure. If you spread it around, it does a lot of good. But if you pile it up in one place, it stinks like hell.
- *Clint Murchison, Jr.*

Funny how a dollar can look so big when you take it to church, and so small when you take it to the store.
- *Frank Clark*

If ignorance paid dividends, most . . . could make a fortune out of what they don't know about economics.
- *Luther Hodges, Secretary of Commerce*

Alexander Woollcott went to visit Moss Hart at his estate in Pennsylvania. Hart had every inch of the grounds completely landscaped. He asked Woollcott what he thought of the place. His answer: "Well, it only shows what God could do if He had enough money."

If you want to know whether you are destined to be a success or a failure in life, you can easily find out. The test is simple and it is infallible. Are you able to save money? If not, drop out. You will lose. . . . You will lose, as sure as you live. The seed of success is not in you.
- *James J. Hill*

There is nothing in saving money. The thing to do with it is to put it back into yourself, into your work, into the thing that is important, into whatever you are so much interested in that it is more important than money.
- *Henry Ford*

Money can't buy happiness, but it certainly doesn't discourage it.

Necessity never made a good bargain.

There are more fools among buyers than among sellers.
- *French proverb*

True luck consists not in holding the best of the cards at the table: Luckiest is he who knows just when to rise and go home.
- *John Hay*

I don't think you can spend yourself rich.
- *George Humphrey*

Advice given by George S. Clason in *The Richest Man in Babylon:*
I found the road to wealth when I decided

that a part of all I earned was mine to keep. And so will you. Budget thy expenses that thou mayest have coins to pay for thy necessities, to pay for thy enjoyments and to gratify thy worthwhile desires without spending more than nine-tenths of thy earnings.

That what each of us calls our "necessary expenses" will always grow to equal our incomes unless we protest to the contrary. Confuse not . . . necessary expenses with . . . desires.

Study carefully, before parting with thy treasure . . . . Be not misled by thy own romantic desires to make wealth rapidly.

Consult with wise men. Secure the advice of those experienced in the profitable handling of gold. Let their wisdom protect thy treasure . . .

. . . Humans in the throes of great emotions are not safe risks for the gold lender.

In order to get a loan, you must first prove you don't need it.

If you think the world owes you a living – hustle out and collect it.

If a man runs after money, he's money-mad: if he keeps it he's a capitalist; if he spends it, he's a playboy; if he doesn't get it, he's a ne'er-do-well; if he doesn't try to get it, he lacks ambition. If he gets it without working for it, he's a parasite; and if he accumulates it after a lifetime of hard work, people call him a fool who never got anything out of life.

- Vic Oliver

Americans have an abiding belief in their ability to control reality by purely material means. Hence . . . airline insurance replaces the fear of death with the comforting prospect of cash.

- Cecil Beaton

Personally I do not feel that any amount can properly be called a surplus as long as the nation is in debt. I prefer to think of such an item as a reduction on our children's inherited mortgage.

- Dwight D. Eisenhower

Gertrude Berg of CBS Television, recalls: "I always remember the first script that I wrote [on The Goldbergs]. Jake came home for supper with a little ambitious bug in his brain. He wanted to go into business and he told this to Molly and Molly had some money she had put away anticipating just such a time and she gave it to him, and as they sat down to the dinner table he said to her, "Molly, darling, some day we will be eating out of golden plates," and Molly turned to him and said, "Jake, darling, will it taste any better?" I always remember that."

Great is he who uses earthenware as if it were silver; no less great is he who uses silver as if it were earthenware.

- Seneca, c. A.D. 63

When Benjamin Franklin was seven years old, a visitor gave him some small change. Later, seeing another boy playing with a whistle, young Benjamin gave the boy all his money for it. He played the whistle all over the house, enjoying it until he discovered that he'd given four times as much as the whistle was worth. Instantly, the whistle lost its charm. As he grew older, Franklin generalized this principle. When he saw a man neglecting his family or business for political popularity, or a miser giving up friendships for the sake of accumulating wealth, he'd say, "He pays too much for his whistle."

- Thomas Fleming

Asked when a wealthy man has enough money to be happy, J.P. Morgan replied, "When he has made the next million."

A billion here, a billion there – pretty soon it adds up to real money.
- Everett Dirksen, speaking to fellow Senators on government spending

Willful waste brings woeful want.
- Thomas Fuller

A status symbol is anything you can't afford, but did.
- Harold Coffin

Mention money and the whole world is silent.
- German proverb

A light purse is a heavy curse.
- Benjamin Franklin

Old men are always advising young men to save money. That is bad advice. Don't save every nickel. Invest in yourself. I never saved a dollar until I was 40 years old.
- Henry Ford

Always live within your income, even if you have to borrow money to do so.
- Josh Billings

Why is there so much month left at the end of the money?

There's no money in poetry, but then there's no poetry in money either.
- Robert Graves

Money itself isn't the primary factor in what one does. A person does things for the sake of accomplishing something. Money generally follows.
- Colonel Henry Crown

For every talent that poverty has stimulated it has blighted a hundred.
- John W. Gardner

Increased means and increased leisure are the two civilizers of man.
- Benjamin Disraeli, 1872

No men living are more worthy to be trusted than those who toil up from poverty . . .
- Abraham Lincoln

An elderly man said, "Thank God for my sons. My first is a doctor, the second a lawyer, the third a chemist, the fourth an artist, and the fifth a writer." He was asked, "What do you do?" He replied, "I have a dry goods store. Not a big one, but I manage to support them all."

- Gordon Dakins

I've never been poor, only broke. Being poor is a frame of mind. Being broke is only a temporary situation.

- Mike Todd, theatrical entrepreneur

Just about the time you think you can make both ends meet, somebody moves the ends.

- Pansy Penner

Sam Levenson often describes the funny and warm incidents of growing up in a family that was hard pressed for a decent income. He explains it by saying: "We didn't know we were poor."

There is inherited wealth in this country and also inherited poverty.

- John F. Kennedy

No one is ever hanged with money in his pocket.

- Russian proverb

A man who shows me his wealth is like the beggar who shows me his poverty; they are both looking for alms, the rich man for the alms of my envy, the poor man for the alms of my guilt.

- Ben Hecht

The share-the-wealth movement appeals the most to those with the least to share.

One man's wealth is another man's pocket money.

George Raft earned and disposed of about ten million dollars in the course of his career. "Part of the loot went for gambling," he explained, "part for horses, and part for women. The rest I spent foolishly."

There is no dignity quite so impressive, and no independence quite so important, as living within your means.

- Calvin Coolidge

Wealth is not his that has it, but his that enjoys it.

- Benjamin Franklin

Money and time are the heaviest burdens of life, and the unhappiest of all mortals are those who have more of either than they know how to use.

Our economy is the result of millions of decisions we all make every day about producing, earning, saving, investing, and spending.

- Dwight D. Eisenhower

So often we rob tomorrow's memories by today's economies.

- John Mason Brown

The chief value of money lies in the fact that one lives in a world in which it is overestimated.

- H.L. Mencken

In suggesting gifts: Money is appropriate, and one size fits all.

- William Randolph Hearst

There are a handful of people money won't spoil and we count ourselves among them.

- Mignon McLaughlin

Never steal more than you actually need, for the possession of surplus money leads to extravagance, foppish attire, frivolous thought.

- Dalton Trumbo, on stealing

The men who have earned five million dollars have been so busy earning it that they have not had time to collect it; and the men who have collected five million dollars have been so busy collecting it that they have not had time to earn it.

- William Jennings Bryan

It requires a great deal of boldness and a great deal of caution to make a great fortune, and when you have got it, it requires ten times as much wit to keep it.

- Ralph Waldo Emerson

In a country well governed, poverty is something to be ashamed of.
In a country badly governed, wealth is something to be ashamed of.

- Confucius, c. 500 B.C.

The rich who are unhappy are worse off than the poor who are unhappy; for the poor, at least, can cling to the hopeful delusion that more money would solve their problems . . .

- Sydney J. Harris

Fortune does not change men. It only unmasks them.

The reason the Yankees never lay an egg is because they don't operate on chicken feed.

- Dan Parker

Money has become the grand test of virtue.

- George Orwell

A man is never so on trial as in the moment of excessive good fortune.

- Lew Wallace, Ben-Hur

I have no complex about wealth. I have worked hard for my money, producing things people need. I believe that the able industrial leader who creates wealth and employment is more worthy of historical notice than politicians or soldiers.

- J. Paul Getty

There is none so poor as he who knows not the joy of what he has.

It's a terribly hard job to spend a billion dollars and get your money's worth.

- George Humphrey

I am not fond of money, or anxious about it. But, though every day makes me less and less eager for wealth, every day shows me more and more strongly how necessary a competence is to a man who desires to be either great or useful.
- *T.B. Macaulay: Letter to Hannah M. Macaulay, Aug. 17, 1833*

Whoso has sixpence is sovereign . . . over all men; commands cooks to feed him, philosophers to teach him, kings to mount guard over him – to the length of sixpence.
- *Thomas Carlyle, 1836*

The more you get, the more you got to take care of.
- *Alice K. Dormann*

Money, material though it be, does lie at the base of the most useful work you do. In itself nothing, it is the basis of much of the best effort which can be made for spiritual purposes.
- *Arthur J. Balfour*

Money begets money.
- *Giovanni Torriano, 1666*

. . . Money can beget money, and its offspring can beget more.
- *Benjamin Franklin*

When a feller says it ain't the money but the principle of the thing, it's the money.
- *Abe Martin*

Thanks a thousand.
- *Nelson Rockefeller*

After Clarence Darrow had solved a client's legal problem, the client asked, "How can I ever show my appreciation?" The lawyer replied, "My good friend, ever since the Phoenicians invented money, there has been only one answer to that question."

Money: a blessing that is of no advantage to us excepting when we part with it.
- *Ambrose Bierce*

There are people who have money and people who are rich.
- *Coco Chanel*

October. This is one of the peculiarly dangerous months to speculate in stocks. The others are July, January, September, April, November, May, March, June, December, August, and February.
- *Mark Twain*

Lack of money is the root of all evil.
- *George Bernard Shaw*

A gentleman . . . is one who has money enough to do what every fool would do if he could afford it: . . . consume without producing.
- *George Bernard Shaw*

Money-giving is a good criterion of a person's mental health. Generous people are rarely mentally ill people.
- *Dr. Karl Menninger*

Learn to give
Money to colleges while you live.
Don't be silly and think you'll try
To bother the colleges, when you die,
with codicil this, and codicil that,
That Knowledge may starve while Law grows fat . . .
- *Oliver Wendell Holmes*

One day a rich man of a miserly disposition visited a rabbi, who took him by the hand and led him to a window. "Look out there," he said. What do you see?" "I see men and women and little children," the man replied.

Again the rabbi took him to a mirror. "What do you see now?" "I see myself," was the answer.

"Behold, in the window there is glass and the mirror is glass also. But the glass of the mirror is covered with silver. No sooner is silver added than you cease to see others and see only yourself."

Let me tell you about the very rich. They are different from you and me. They possess and enjoy early, and it does something to them, makes them soft where we are hard, and cynical where we are trustful, in a way that, unless you were born rich, it is very difficult to understand.
- *F. Scott Fitzgerald*

A man builds a fine house; and now he has a master, and a task for life: he is to furnish, watch, show it, and keep it in repair the rest of his days.
- *Ralph Waldo Emerson*

The impoverished son of an impoverished family was asked how he could have managed to live so pennilessly for so long. "You must remember," he said, "I had a head start."

Costly thy habit as thy purse can buy,
But not express'd in fancy; rich, not gaudy;
For the apparel oft proclaims the man.
- *Shakespeare, "Hamlet"*

What a lot of people are saving for a rainy day is somebody else's umbrella.
- *Caroline Clark in the Saturday Evening Post*

When prosperity comes, do not use all of it.
- *Confucius*

How did a fool and his money get together in the first place?

LEARNING

Quotes & Anecdotes
(experience, education, discipline, training)

There is no lack of opportunity for learning among us. What is lacking is a respect for it . . . an honest respect such as we now have for technical competence or business success . . . We honor learning, but do not believe in it . . . Rather than submit to it ourselves, we hire substitutes; rather than cultivate our own brains, we pick theirs. We spend as much time and energy on short-cuts to learning and imitations of learning as we do on learning itself.
- *Whitney Griswold*

It wasn't until quite late in life that I discovered how easy it is to say, "I don't know."
- *Somerset Maugham*

The farther backward you can look, the farther forward you are likely to see.
- *Winston Churchill*

Men are wise in proportion not to their experience but to their capacity for experience.
- *James Boswell, 1791*

Every child is an artist. The problem is how to remain an artist after growing up.
- *Pablo Picasso*

A college education seldom hurts a man if he's willing to learn a little something after he graduates.

I am still learning. (*Ancora imparo.*)
- *Favorite saying of Michelangelo*

Experience is a good school. But the fees are high.
- *Heinrich Heine*

What you don't know can hurt you.

Learning is acquired by reading books; but the much more necessary learning, the knowledge of the world, is only to be acquired by reading men, and studying all the various editions of them.
- *Lord Chesterfield, 1752*

I cannot live without books.
- *Thomas Jefferson*

Books are good enough in their way, but they are a mighty bloodless substitute for life.
- *Robert Louis Stevenson*

What we learn after we know it all, is what counts.

We know so many things that aren't so.

A little learning is a dangerous thing;
Drink deep, or taste not the Pierian spring:
There shallow draughts intoxicate the brain,
And drinking largely sobers us again.
- *Alexander Pope: 1711*

Judith Swanson tells about how she learned a great lesson:

From the day we entered the ninth-grade health class, one blackboard was covered with the names and locations of the major bones and muscles of the human body. The diagram stayed on the board throughout the term, although the teacher never referred to it. The day of the final exam, we came to class to find the board wiped clean. The sole test question was: "Name and locate every major bone and muscle in the human body."

The class protested in unison: "We never studied that!"

"That's no excuse," said the teacher. "The information was there for months." After we struggled with the test for a while, he collected the papers and tore them up. "Always remember," he told us, "that education is more than just learning what you are told."

What school, college, or lecture bring to men depends on what men bring to carry it home in.
- *Ralph Waldo Emerson*

If you spend your time playing bridge, you will be a good bridge player; if you spend it in reading, discussing, and thinking of things that matter, you will be an educated person.
- *Sydney Smith, President, University of Toronto*

Men learn while they teach.
- *Seneca, c. A.D. 63*

Experience is the name everyone gives to their mistakes.
- *Oscar Wilde*

Asked what he thought should be taught to children first, Samuel Johnson replied that "it is no matter what you teach them first, any more than what leg you shall put into your breeches first. Sir, you may stand disputing which is best to put in first, but in the mean time your breech is bare. Sir, while you are considering which of two things you should teach your child first, another boy has learnt them both."

Knowledge and timber shouldn't be much used till they are seasoned.
- *Oliver Wendell Holmes*

A young man must let his ideas grow, not be continually rooting them up to see how they are getting on.
- *William McFee*

It is the province of knowledge to speak and it is the privilege of wisdom to listen.
- *Oliver Wendell Holmes*

A new graduate rushed out of his college on graduation day and shouted, "Here I am, world. I have my A.B.!" The world answered: "Sit down, young man, and I'll teach you the rest of the alphabet."

A man could retire nicely in his old age if he could dispose of his experience for what it cost him.

If I had my life to live again, I'd make the same mistakes, only sooner.
- *Tallulah Bankhead*

If you plan for a decade, plant trees. If you plan for a century, teach the children.

When you're through learning, you're through.
- *Vernon Law, pitcher, Pittsburgh Pirates*

Professionals built the Titanic – amateurs the ark.
- *Frank Pepper*

Every man is a damn fool for at least five minutes every day; wisdom consists in not exceeding the limit.
- *Elbert Hubbard*

We ought to hear at least one little song every day, read a good poem, see a first-rate painting, and if possible speak a few sensible words.
- *Johann Von Goethe*

History is the rear view mirror on the road of life.

When you reread a classic you do not see more in the book than you did before; you see more in you than there was before.
- *Clifton Fadiman*

The test and the use of man's education is that he finds pleasure in the exercise of his mind.
- *Jacques Barzun*

You can learn good manners from the bad manners of others.

It has been said that we have not had the three R's in America, we have had the six R's: remedial readin', remedial 'ritin', and remedial 'rithmetic.
- *Robert M. Hutchins*

The latter part of a wise man's life is taken up in curing the follies, prejudices, and false opinions he contracted in the former.
- *Jonathan Swift, 1706*

Every citizen of this country, whether he pounds nails, raises corn, designs rockets or writes poetry, should be taught to know and love his American heritage; to use the language well; to understand the physical universe, the arts, and to enjoy the arts. The dollars he gains in the absence of [this] enlightenment will be earned in drudgery and spent in ignorance.
- *Calvin Gross, superintendent, New York City public schools.*

None so deaf as those who will not hear.
- *English proverb*

For my confirmation, I didn't get a watch and my first pair of long pants, like most Lutheran boys. I got a telescope. My mother thought it would make the best gift.
- *Wernher Von Braun, rocket scientist*

A guidance counselor who has made a fetish of security, or who has unwittingly surrendered his thinking to economic determinism, may steer a youth away from his dream of becoming a poet, an artist, a musician, or any other of thousands of things, because it offers no security, it does not pay well, there are no vacancies, it has no "future." Among all the tragic consequences of depression and war, this suppression of personal self-expression through one's life work is among the most poignant.
- *Henry Wriston*

Teaching is not a lost art, but the regard for it is a lost tradition.
- *Jacques Barzun, dean, Columbia University*

I am quite sure that in the hereafter she will take me by the hand and lead me to my proper seat. I always have a great reverence for teachers . . . both lay and clerical . . .
- *Bernard Baruch, recalling one of his early teachers*

Modern cynics and skeptics . . . see no harm in paying those to whom they entrust the minds of their children a smaller wage than is paid to those to whom they entrust the care of their plumbing.
- *John F. Kennedy*

A Socrates in every classroom.
- *Whitney Griswold, President, Yale University, on his ambitious standard for building a faculty*

Learning makes the wise wiser and the fool more foolish.
- *John Ray, 1670*

Wisdom consists in knowing what to do with what you know.

We have two ears and only one tongue in order that we may hear more and speak less.
- *Diogenes Laertius, about 150 B.C.*

Learn to unlearn.
- *Benjamin Disraeli*

To be fond of learning is to be at the gate of knowledge.
- *Chinese proverb*

When you read, *read!* Too many students just half read . . . The art of memory is the art of understanding.
-*Roscoe Pound, dean emeritus, Harvard Law School*

The longer the island of knowledge, the longer the shore line of wonder.
- *Ralph W. Sockman*

The aims of pure basic science, unlike those of applied science, are neither fast flowing nor pragmatic. The quick harvest of applied science is the useable process, the medicine, the machine. The shy fruit of pure science is Understanding.
- *Lincoln Barnett, science writer, on Einstein's completion of the mathematical formula for the Unified Field Theory*

Each day I learn more
Than I teach;
I learn that half knowledge of another's life
Leads to false judgment;
I learn that there is a surprising kinship
In human nature;
I learn that it's a wise father who knows his own son;
I learn that what we expect we get;

I learn that there's more good than evil in this world;
That age is a question of spirit;
That youth is the best of life
No matter how numerous its years;
I learn how much there is to learn.
- Virginia Church

Old age is like climbing a mountain. You climb from ledge to ledge. The higher you get, the more tired and breathless you become, but your views become more intensive.
- Ingmar Bergman

Nothing ever becomes real till it is experienced.
- John Keats

Memory is the mother of all wisdom.
- Aeschylus, 5th Century B.C.

Knowledge is the food of the soul.
- Plato

Learning is a treasure which will follow its owner everywhere.
- Chinese proverb

It has been said that the only thing we learn from history is that we do not learn.
- Chief Justice Earl Warren, in eulogy of John F. Kennedy

We can draw lessons from the past, but we cannot live in it.
- Lyndon B. Johnson

The trouble with experience is that it sometimes teaches you too late.

Experience is the dividend you get from your mistakes.

One thorn of experience is worth a whole wilderness of warning.
- James Russell Lowell

. . . A page of history is worth a volume of logic.
- Oliver Wendell Holmes

I still find each day too short for all the thoughts I want to think, all the walks I want to take, all the books I want to read, and all the friends I want to see. The longer I live the more my mind dwells upon the beauty and the wonder of the world.
- John Burroughs

He is educated who knows how to find out what he doesn't know.
- George Simmel

A person who has had a bull by the tail once has learned 60 or 70 times as much as a person who hasn't.
- Mark Twain

A man of learning is never bored.
- Jean Paul Richter

The great difficulty in education is to get experience out of ideas.
- George Santayana

You don't set a fox to watching the chickens just because he has a lot of experience in the hen house.
- Harry S Truman, on Vice President Nixon's candidacy for the presidency in 1960

My definition of an educated man is the fellow who knows the right thing to do at the time it has to be done . . . You can be sincere and still be stupid.
- Charles F. Kettering

Education is a kind of continuing dialogue, and a dialogue assumes, in the nature of the case, different points of view . . .
- Robert M. Hutchins

A man is never too old to learn.
- Thomas Middleton, Mayor of Quinborough, 1651

Experience is not what happens to you; it is what you do with what happens to you.
- Aldous Huxley

A half century of living should put a good deal into a woman's face besides a few wrinkles and some unwelcome folds around the chin.
- Frances Parkinson Keyes

. . . There is a case for keeping wrinkles. They are the long-service stripes earned in the hard campaign of life . . . . Wrinkles are the dried-up riverbeds of a life-time's tears. Wrinkles are the nostalgic remnants of a million smiles. Wrinkles are . . . crannies and footholds on the smooth visage of life on which man can cling and gain some comfort and security.
- Daily Mail, London, Jan. 20, 1961

All a child's life depends on the ideal it has of its parents. Destroy that and everything goes – morals, behavior, everything. Absolute trust in someone else is the essence of education.
- E. M. Forster

You send your child to the schoolmaster, but 'tis the schoolboys who educate him.
- Ralph Waldo Emerson

The secret of education lies in respecting the pupil.
- Ralph Waldo Emerson

The ideas I stand for are not mine. I borrowed them from Socrates. I swiped them from Chesterfield. I stole them from Jesus. And I put them in a book.
- Dale Carnegie, on his book, How to Win Friends and Influence People

Work'em hard, play'em hard, feed'em up to the nines, and send'em to bed so tired that they are asleep before their heads are on the pillow.
- Frank Boyden of Deerfield Academy, on how to run a successful prep school.

A book is like a garden carried in the pocket.
- Arab proverb

All that mankind has done, thought, gained or been . . . is lying as in magic preservation in the pages of books.
- Thomas Carlyle

Age is only a number, a cipher for the records. A man can't retire his experience. He must use it . . .
- *Bernard Baruch*

To exclude from positions of trust and command all those below the age of 44 would have kept Jefferson from writing the Declaration of Independence, Washington from commanding the Continental Army, Madison from fathering the Constitution, Hamilton from serving as Secretary of the Treasury, Clay from being elected Speaker of the House, and Christopher Columbus from discovering America.
- *Senator John F. Kennedy, replying to ex-president Harry Truman's assertion that he might not be mature enough for the presidency*

The best cosmetic in the world is an active mind that is always finding something new.
- *Mary Meek Atkeson*

I do not know what I may appear to the world. But, to myself, I seem to have been only like a boy playing on the seashore, diverting myself in now and then finding a smoother pebble or a prettier shell than the ordinary, whilst the great ocean of truth lay all undiscovered before me.
- *Sir Isaac Newton, among his last words.*

The enormous multiplication of books in every branch of knowledge is one of the greatest evils of this age . . . it presents one of the most serious obstacles to the acquisition of correct information, by throwing in the reader's way piles of lumber in which he must painfully grope for . . . scraps of useful matter . . .
- *Edgar Allen Poe*

He that would govern others, first should be the master of himself.
- *Philip Massinger, 1624*

The close observer soon discovers that the teacher's task is not to implant facts but to place the subject to be learned in front of the learner and, through sympathy, emotion, imagination, and patience, to awaken in the learner the restless drive for answers and insights which enlarge the personal life and give it meaning.
- *Nathan Pusey*

Learning is ever young, even in old age.
- *Aeschylus, c. 490 B. C.*

A good scare is worth more to a man than good advice.
- *E.E. Howe*

A wise man will hear, and will increase in learning.
- *The Bible, Proverbs 1:5*

The growth of wisdom may be gauged accurately by the decline of ill-temper.
- *Freidrich Nietzche*

Samuel Taylor Coleridge was involved in a discussion about religion. The other person believed that children should not be given formal religious education of any kind. They would then be free to select their own religion when they were old enough to decide. Coleridge did not bother to debate the point, but invited the man to see his rather neglected garden.

"Do you call this a garden?" asked his visitor. "There are nothing but weeds here."

"Well, you see," said Coleridge, "I did not wish to infringe on the liberty of the garden in any way. I was just giving the garden a chance to express itself and choose its own production."

The clouds may drop down titles and estates; wealth may seek us; but wisdom must be sought.
- *Edward Young, 1744*

In proportion as the structure of a government gives force to public opinion, it is essential that public opinion should be enlightened.
- *George Washington*

Reading is one of our bad habits . . . We read, most of the time, not because we wish to instruct ourselves, not because we long to have our feelings touched and our imagination fired, but . . . because we have time to spare.
- *Aldous Huxley*

Where the press is free and every man able to read, all is safe.
- *Thomas Jefferson*

. . . Ever learning, and never able to come to the knowledge of the truth.
- *The Bible, II Timothy 3:7*

The differences in human life depend, for the most part, not on what men do, but upon the meaning and purpose of their acts. All are born, all die, all lose their loved ones, nearly all marry and nearly all work, but the significance of these acts may vary enormously. The same physical act may be in one situation vulgar and in another holy. The same work may be elevating or degrading. . . . Wisdom about life consists in taking the inevitable ventures which are the very stuff of common existence, and glorifying them.
- *Elton Trueblood*

We do not succeed in changing things according to our desire, but gradually our desire changes. The situation that we hoped to change because it was intolerable becomes unimportant. We have not managed to surmount the obstacle, as we were absolutely determined to do, but life has taken us round it, led us past it, and . . . if we turn round to gaze at the remote past, we can barely catch sight of it, so imperceptible has it become.
- *Marcel Proust*

Wise men don't need advice. Fools won't take it.
- *Benjamin Franklin*

To everyone, life in the first person is a mystery.

Recognizing what we have done in the past is a recognition of ourselves. By conducting a dialogue with our past, we are searching how to go forward.
- *Kiyoko Takeda*

The only fool bigger than the person who knows it all is the person who argues with him.

If you have knowledge, let others light their candles at it.
- Thomas Fuller

Wisdom is the reward you get for a lifetime of listening when you'd have preferred to talk.
- Doug Larson

An optimist is a person who sees a green light everywhere. The pessimist sees only the red light. But the truly wise person is color blind.
- Albert Schweitzer

I have walked with people whose eyes are full of light but who see nothing in sea or sky, nothing in city streets, nothing in books. It were far better to sail forever in the night of blindness with sense, and feeling, and mind, than to be content with the mere act of seeing. The only lightless dark is the night of darkness in ignorance and insensibility.
- Helen Keller

Learning by study must be won;
'Twas ne'er entail'd from son to son.
- John Gay, 1727

The heart has its reasons, which reason cannot know.
- Blaise Pascal

He who remembers from day to day what he has yet to learn, and from month to month what he has learned already, may be said to have a love of learning.
- Confucius, c. 500 B.C.

Pain makes man think. Thought makes man wise. Wisdom makes life endurable.
- John Patrick

Wear your learning, like your watch, in a private pocket; and do not pull it out and strike it, merely to show that you have one. If you are asked what o'clock it is, tell it; but do not proclaim it hourly and unasked, like the watchman.
-Lord Chesterfield: Letter to his son, 1748

Train up a child in the way he should go: and when he is old, he will not depart from it.
- The Bible, Proverbs, 22:6

Youth is . . . sure the rules have changed. Age is sure they haven't. Youth feels it knows how far it can go. Age is deeply aware of the danger. Youth feels it can always apply the brakes in time to save itself. Age knows it isn't always so.
- Richard L. Evans

Experience is a hard teacher because she gives the test first, the lesson afterwards.
- Vernon Law, pitcher, Pittsburgh Pirates

Learning without wisdom is a load of books on an ass's back.
- Japanese proverb

The greatest dangers to liberty lurk in insidious encroachment of men of zeal, well-meaning but without understanding.
- Louis D. Brandeis, Supreme Court Associate Justice, 1928

We do not remember days, we remember moments.
- Cesare Pavese

Education is the ability to listen to almost anything without losing your temper or your self-confidence.
- Robert Frost

My advice to young players is to see as much good tennis as possible and then attempt to copy the outstanding strokes of the former stars.
- William T. Tilden, player & coach

The simplest schoolboy is now aware of truths for which Archimedes would have given his life.
- Ernest Renan, 1883

That some good can be derived from every event is a better proposition than that everything happens for the best, which it assuredly does not.
- James K. Feibleman

The library is not a shrine for the worship of books. It is not a temple where literary incense must be burned or where one's devotion to the bound book is expressed in ritual. A library, to modify the famous metaphor of Socrates, should be the delivery room for the birth of ideas – a place where history comes to life.
- Norman Cousins

A handful of good life is better than a bushel of learning.
- George Herbert, 1640

Any piece of knowledge I acquire today has a value at this moment exactly proportioned to my skill to deal with it. Tomorrow, when I know more, I recall that piece of knowledge and use it better.
- Mark Van Doren

. . . I was still learning when I taught my last class.
- Claude Fuess, on retirement after 40 years as a teacher

One of the wisest things my daddy ever told me was that "so-and-so is a damned smart man, but the fool's got no sense."
- Lyndon B. Johnson

History not used is nothing, for all intellectual life is action, like practical life, and if you don't use the stuff – well, it might as well be dead.
- Arnold Toynbee

It would have been too bad to miss our mistakes that taught us so much about living. Just as we enjoyed the terror of the roller coaster when we were kids, we must enjoy the terror of life's errors and mistakes. The challenges we meet are the shapers . . . of our lives.

"Before you get to the three R's," said Grandpa, "you've got to master the three L's – look, listen and learn."

Never learn to do anything. If you don't learn, you will always find someone else to do it for you.
- Mark Twain

Some books are to be tasted, others to be swallowed, and some few to be chewed and digested.
- Francis Bacon, 1597

All books are divisible into two classes: the books of the hour, and the books of all time.
- John Ruskin

How many a man has dated a new era in his life from the reading of a book.
- Henry David Thoreau

Books give not wisdom where was none before,
But where some is, there reading makes it more.
- Sir John Harington, 1613

Go to school. I tell you to go to school. I'm well known and I made a lot of money and I lost a lot of money. I'd be better off if I had gone to school longer, and so will you.
- Joe Louis, Heavyweight boxing champion

What you bring away from the Bible depends to some extent on what you carry to it.
- Oliver Wendell Holmes

Knowledge begets knowledge. The more I see, the more impressed I am – not with what we know – but with how tremendous the areas are that are as yet unexplored.
- Lt. Col. John H. Glenn, Jr.

The Bible is like a telescope. If a man looks through his telescope, then he sees worlds beyond; but if he looks at his telescope, then he does not see anything but that. The Bible is a thing to be looked through, to see that which is beyond; but most people only look at it; and so they see only the dead letter.
- Phillips Brooks

Wisdom is ofttimes nearer when we stoop
Than when we soar.
- William Wordsworth

Training is everything. The peach was once a bitter almond; cauliflower is nothing but cabbage with a college education.
- Mark Twain

To be conscious that you are ignorant is a great step to knowledge.
- Benjamin Disraeli

School ends, but education doesn't.

Great minds are like eagles, and build their nest in some lofty solitude.
- Arthur Schopenhauer

Knowledge is power.
- Sir Francis Bacon, 1597

. . . It was in making education not only common to all, but in some sense compulsory on all, that the destiny of the free republics of America was practically settled.
- James Russell Lowell, 1870

'Tis education forms the common mind:
Just as the twig is bent the tree's inclined.
- Alexander Pope, 1731

Ignorance is the curse of God,
Knowledge the wing wherewith we fly to heaven.
- William Shakespeare, "Henry VI"

Knowledge is the antidote to fear.
- Ralph Waldo Emerson

To be proud of knowledge is to be blind with light.
- Benjamin Franklin

No man really becomes a fool until he stops asking questions.
- Charles P. Steinmetz

Knowledge is proud that it knows so much;
wisdom is humble that it knows no more.
- William Cowper

Knowledge is happiness, because to have knowledge – broad deep knowledge – is to know true ends from false, and lofty things from low. To know the thoughts and deeds that have marked man's progress is to feel the great heart-throbs of humanity through the centuries; and if one does not feel in these pulsations a heavenward striving, one must indeed be deaf to the harmonies of life.
- Helen Keller

Many books require no thought from those who read them, and for a very simple reason; they made no such demand upon those who wrote them.
- Charles Caleb Colton

College is a storehouse of learning because so little is taken away.

Only the educated are free.
- Epictetus, 1st century

Education: that which discloses to the wise and disguises from the foolish their lack of understanding.
- Ambrose Bierce

If you think education is expensive, try ignorance.
- Derek Bok, President, Harvard University

Aristotle was asked, "What is the difference between an educated and an uneducated man?" He replied, "The same difference as between being alive and being dead."

Books are the quietest and most constant of friends; they are the most accessible and wisest of counsellors, and the most patient of teachers.
- Charles W. Eliot

Books have to be read. It is the only way of discovering what they contain. A few savage tribes eat them, but reading is the only method of assimilation revealed to the West.
- E.M. Forster

. . . The love of learning, the sequestered nooks,
And all the sweet serenity books.
- Henry Wadsworth Longfellow

It is rare that one cannot learn from another or from life's experiences, if the effort is made. Perhaps that is the secret of achieving a peaceful society: searching for each other's unique and special knowledge.

PROBLEM SOLVING

Quotes & Anecdotes
(creativity, thought, teamwork)

Making up your mind is the hard part – the rest is just pure work.

The second assault on the same problem should come from a totally different direction.
- **Tom Hirshfield**

I am enthusiastic over humanity's extraordinary and sometimes very timely ingenuities. If you are in a shipwreck and all the boats are gone, a piano top buoyant enough to keep you afloat may come along and make a fortuitous life preserver. This is not to say, though, that the best way to design a life preserver is in the form of a piano top. I think that we are clinging to a great many piano tops in accepting yesterday's fortuitous contrivings as constituting the only means for solving a given problem.
- **R. Buckminster Fuller**

I have never seen a bad television program, because I refuse to. God gave me a mind, and a wrist that turns things off.
- **Jack Paar**

I have one yardstick by which I test every major problem – and that yardstick is: Is it good for America?
- **Dwight D. Eisenhower**

When nobody around you seems to measure up, it's time to check your yardstick.
- **Bill Lemley**

After you've done a thing the same way for two years, look it over carefully. After five years, look at it with suspicion. And after ten years, throw it away and start all over.
- **Alfred Edward Perlman**

You may have to fight a battle more than once to win it.
- **Margaret Thatcher**

Become a possibilitarian. No matter how dark things seem to be or actually are, raise your sights and see possibilities – always see them, for they're always there.
- **Norman Vincent Peale**

The invention of I.Q. did a great disservice to creativity in education . . . Individuality, personality, originality, are too precious to be meddled with by amateur psychiatrists whose patterns for a "wholesome personality" are inevitably their own.
- **Joel Hildebrand, professor of chemistry**

Many a man has fallen in love with a girl in a light so dim he would not have chosen a suit by it.
- **Maurice Chevalier**

Two brothers went to a judge to settle their dispute on the division of the estate left to them by their father. The judge ruled: "Let one brother divide the estate, and let the other brother have first choice."

Sometimes I think it sounds like I walked out of the room and left the typewriter running.
- *Gene Fowler, on his own written work*

Writers have two main problems. One is writer's block, when words won't come at all, and the other's logorrhea, when the words come so fast that they hardly get to the wastebasket in time.
- **Cecilia Bartholomew**

A new idea is delicate. It can be killed by a sneer or a yawn; it can be stabbed to death by a quip and worried to death by a frown on the right man's brow.
- **Charles Brower**

Whenever I think, I make a mistake.
- **Roger Stevens**

All the really good ideas I ever had came to me while I was milking a cow.
- **Grant Wood**

The time to repair the roof is when the sun is shining.
- **John F. Kennedy**

The best time for planning a book is while you're doing the dishes.
- **Agatha Christie**

Anyone can look for fashion in a boutique or history in a museum. The creative person looks for history in a hardware store and fashion in an airport.
- **Robert Wieder**

Mrs. Albert Einstein visited Mount Wilson Observatory in California and pointed to a complex piece of equipment and asked what it was used for. The guide said it was used to determine the shape of the universe. "Oh," she said, not impressed, "my husband uses the back of an old envelope to work that out."

We require from buildings, as from men, two kinds of goodness: first, doing their practical duty well; then that they be graceful and pleasing in doing it.
- **John Ruskin, 1851**

There is nothing more difficult for a truly creative painter than to paint a rose, because before he can do so he has first to forget all the roses that were ever painted.
- **Henri Matisse**

Nothing is particularly hard if you divide it into small jobs.
- **Henry Ford**

The best way to have a good idea is to have a lot of ideas.
- **Linus Pauling**

Concentration is my motto – first honesty, then industry, then concentration.
- **Andrew Carnegie**

Thinking well is wise: planning well, wiser: doing well, wisest and best of all.
- *Persian proverb*

If you are attempting the impossible, you will fail.

Morale is when your hands and feet keep on working when your head says it can't be done.
- *Admiral Ben Morrell*

Few men during their lifetime come anywhere near exhausting the resources dwelling within them. There are deep wells of strength that are never used.
- *Admiral Richard Byrd*

If you have built castles in the air, your work need not be lost; that is where they should be. Now put foundations under them.
- *Henry David Thoreau*

A committee is a cul-de-sac down which ideas are lured and then quietly strangled.
- *Sir Barnett Cocks*

The only reason some people get lost in thought is because it's unfamiliar territory.
- *Paul Fix*

My words fly up; my thoughts remain below. Words without thoughts never to heaven go.
- *William Shakespeare, "Hamlet"*

Too many decisions are measured with a micrometer, marked with chalk, and cut with an ax.

We ought to spend more time "wondering" than "doubting whether." Wondering is the key to progress.
- *Gerald Horton Bath*

When written in Chinese, the word "crisis" is composed of two characters. One represents danger, and the other represents opportunity.
- *John F. Kennedy*

The only angle from which to approach a problem is the try-angle.

The greatest discovery of my generation is that a human being can alter his life by altering his attitude.
- *William James*

You will never stub your toe standing still, but the faster you go, the more chance you have of getting somewhere.
- *Charles F. Kettering*

The doctor can bury his mistakes but an architect can only advise his client to plant vines.
- *Frank Lloyd Wright*

The person who has no imagination has no wings.
- *Muhammad*

When I examine myself and my methods of thought, I come to the conclusion that the gift of fantasy has meant more to me than my talent for absorbing positive knowledge.
- *Albert Einstein*

What good is a new-born baby?
- *Benjamin Franklin, when somebody asked what good was served by the first balloon ascension in Paris*

You can't see the good ideas behind you by looking twice as hard at what's in front of you.
- *Andrew Mercer*

Full bellies make empty skulls.
- *H.G. Bohn, 1855*

All rivers do what they can for the sea.
- *Thomas Fuller*

"Where is your story on the big game today?" the editor asked the new reporter. "I did not write it," said the reporter, "because the game was called off when the stadium collapsed." "Then where is the story on the collapse?" "That wasn't my assignment."

An idea is not worth much until a man is found who has the energy and the ability to make it work.

Every act of creation is first an act of destruction.
- *Pablo Picasso*

Creative thinking may simply mean the realization that there is no particular virtue in doing things the way they have always been done.
- *Rudolph Flesch*

Honest differences are often a healthy sign of progress.
- *Mahatma Gandhi*

Too many people think they are being creative when they are just being different.

Luck is what happens when preparation meets opportunity.
- *Elmer G. Leterman*

A man who works with his hands is a laborer; a man who works with his hands and his brain is a craftsman; but a man who works with his hands and his brain and his heart is an artist.
- *Louis Nizer*

A widely prevalent notion today seems to demand instant achievement of goals, without any of the wearying, frustrating preparation that is indispensable to any task. As the exemplar of a way of life, the professional – that man or woman who invests every new task or duty, no matter how small, with discipline of mind and spirit – is a vanishing American, particularly among those who too often believe that dreams come true because they ought to and not because they are caused to materialize.
- *Jack Valenti*

Before everything else, getting ready is the secret of success.
- *Henry Ford*

Why worry? 40% of my worries will never happen, for anxiety is the result of a tired mind;
30% concern old decisions which cannot be altered;
12% center in criticisms, mostly untrue, made by people who feel inferior;

10% are related to my health, which worsens while I worry;
and only 8% are "legitimate," showing that life does have real problems which may be met head-on when I have eliminated senseless worries.

When in danger or when in doubt,
Run in circles, scream and shout!
- Clint

One loss is good for the soul. Too many losses are not good for the coach.
- Knute Rockne

Those who dare, do: those who dare not, do not.

Writing isn't hard; no harder than ditch-digging.
- Patrick Dennis

Believe you are defeated, believe it long enough, and it is likely to become a fact.
- Norman Vincent Peale

It's not easy taking my problems one at a time when they refuse to get in line.
- Ashleigh Brilliant

Ah, good taste! What a dreadful thing! Taste is the enemy of creativeness.
- Pablo Picasso

Common sense is not so common.
- Voltaire

Facts, as such, never settled anything. They are working tools only. It is the implications that can be drawn from the facts that count, and to evaluate these requires wisdom and judgment that are unrelated to the computer approach to life.
- Clarence B. Randall

All you can do is try to use the best of your ability, and with all the input and knowledge you get, then hope that the decisions you make are based on what is morally right.
- Ronald Reagan

As regards intellectual work, it remains a fact, indeed, that great decisions in the realms of thought and momentous discoveries and solutions of problems are only possible to an individual, working in solitude.
- Sigmund Freud

When you try to formalize or socialize creative activity, the only sure result is commercial constipation . . . . The good ideas are all hammered out in agony by individuals, not spewed out by groups.
- Charles Brower

Between midnight and dawn, when sleep will not come and all the old wounds begin to ache, I often have a nightmare vision of a future world in which there are billions of people, all numbered and registered, with not a gleam of genius anywhere, not an original mind, a rich personality, on the whole packed globe. The twin ideals of our time, organization and quantity, will have won forever.
- J.B. Priestley

The function of genius is not to give new answers, but to pose new questions which time and mediocrity can resolve.
- H.R. Trevor-Roper

I wonder whether art has a higher function than to make me feel, appreciate, and enjoy natural objects for their art value? So, as I walk in the garden, I look at the flowers and shrubs and trees and discover in them an exquisiteness of contour, a vitality of edge or a vigor of spring as well as an infinite variety of color that no artifact I have seen in the last sixty years can rival . . . . Each day, as I look, I wonder where my eyes were yesterday.
- Bernard Berenson

Intuition – the supra-logic that cuts out all routine processes of thought and leaps straight from problem to answer.
- Robert Graves

In the power and splendor of the universe, inspiration waits for the millions to come. Man has only to strive for it. Poems greater than the *"Iliad,"* plays greater than *"Macbeth,"* stories more engaging than *Don Quixote* await their seeker and finder.
- John Masefield

Composers should write tunes that chauffeurs and errand boys can whistle . . . . That which penetrates the ear with facility and quits the memory with difficulty.
- Sir Thomas Beecham

We shall succeed only so far as we continue that most distasteful of all activity, the intolerable labor of thought.
- Judge Learned Hand

Thinking is the hardest work there is, which is probably the reason why so few engage in it.
- Henry Ford

If you keep on saying things are going to be bad, you have a good chance of being a prophet.
- Isaac Bashevis Singer

. . . Man is still the most extraordinary computer of all.
- John F. Kennedy

You can think about your problems or you can worry about them, and there is a vast difference between the two. Worry is thinking that has turned toxic. It is jarring music that goes round and round and never comes to either climax or conclusion. Thinking works its way through problems to conclusions and decisions; worry leaves you in a state of tensely suspended animation. When you worry, you go over the same ground endlessly and come out the same place you started. Thinking makes progress from one place to another; worry remains static. The problem of life is to change worry into thinking and anxiety into creative action.
- Harld B. Walker

Worry is a thin stream of fear trickling through the mind. If encouraged, it cuts a channel into which all other thoughts are drained.
- *Arthur Somers Roche*

First ask yourself: What is the worst that can happen? Then prepare to accept it. Then proceed to improve on the worst.
- *Dale Carnegie*

In relation to society and government it may be repeated that new ideas are rare; in regard to the latter, perhaps not more than two really large and new ideas have been developed in as many millenniums.
- *Henry Cabot Lodge*

There is no new thing under the sun.
- *Bible, Ecclesiastes*

Polishing the client's apple is no way to improve his advertising. Polishing a good idea is. And polishing. And polishing. Until good becomes better. And better becomes best.
- *Young & Rubicam, Inc.*

I had a monumental idea this morning, but I didn't like it.
- *Samuel Goldwyn*

You will find that at the times when life becomes most real, in the great times of life, almost every man or woman becomes a poet at heart, as when in love or in . . . moments of great loss or bereavement . . .
- *John Hall Wheelock*

Youth is the time for adventures of the body, but age for the triumphs of the mind.
- *Logan Pearsall Smith*

Inspiration starts with aspiration.

Trust in God – and do something.
- *Mary Lyon*

All good things which exist are the fruits of originality.
- *John Stuart Mill*

Every book is like a purge; at the end of it one is empty . . . like a dry shell on the beach, waiting for the tide to come in again.
- *Daphne du Maurier*

Did you ever think how much labor went into inventing a labor-saving device?

Don't find a fault. Find a remedy.
- *Henry Ford*

No man can think clearly when his fists are clenched
- *George Jean Nathan*

Let us never negotiate out of fear but let us never fear to negotiate.
- *John F. Kennedy*

The imagination is the very eye of faith.
- *Henry Ward Beecher*

I have often thought morality may perhaps consist solely in the courage of making a choice.
- *Leon Blum*

In composing, as a general rule, run your pen through every other word you have written; you have no idea what vigor it will give to your style.
- *Sydney Smith*

Brand-new ideas are rare; good new ideas are even rarer.

The most beautiful thing we can experience is the mysterious. It is the source of all true art and science. He to whom this emotion is a stranger, who can no longer pause to wonder and stand rapt in awe, is as good as dead: his eyes are closed.
- *Albert Einstein*

Any new formula which suddenly emerges in our consciousness has its roots in long trains of thought; it is virtually old when it first makes its appearance among the recognized growths of our intellect.
- *Oliver Wendell Holmes*

Inspiration is sometimes another name for desperation.

Every problem has in it the seeds of its own solution. If you don't have any problems, you don't get any seeds.
- *Norman Vincent Peale*

I don't know anything about art, but I know what I like.
- *American proverb*

. . . I meditate and put on a rubber tire with three bottles of beer. Most of the time I just sit picking my nose and thinking.
- *Writer James Gould Cozzens, on what he does in his study*

I can't write five words but that I change seven.
- *Dorothy Parker*

The successful man will profit from his mistakes and try again in a different way.
- *Dale Carnegie*

I write at high speed because boredom is bad for my health. It upsets my stomach more than anything else. I also avoid green vegetables. They're grossly overrated.
- *Noel Coward*

Mas Tiempo para el Amor. (Translation: "More Time For Love.")
- *Advertising slogan credited with swift sale of washing machines in Spain*

The banker asks, "how much?" The scientist asks, "how come?"

Less is more.
- *Mies Van Der Rohe, on restraint in architectural design*

You must treat a work of art like a great man: stand before it and wait patiently till it deigns to speak.
- *Arthur Schopenhauer*

Get a good idea and stay with it. Dog it, and work at it until it's done, and done right.
- *Walt Disney*

The best way out of a difficulty is through it.

TIME AND LIFE

Quotes & Anecdotes
(growth, goals, planning)

The older I get, the more wisdom I find in the ancient rule of taking first things first – a process which often reduces the most complex human problems to manageable proportions.
- *Dwight D. Eisenhower*

In the absence of clearly defined goals, we are forced to concentrate on activity and ultimately become enslaved by it.
- *Chuck Coonradt*

Never confuse motion with action.
- *Ernest Hemingway*

Along with being forever on the move, one is forever in a hurry, leaving things inadvertently behind – friend or fishing tackle, old raincoat or old allegiance.
- *Louis Kronenberger*

Time is really the only capital that any human being has, and the only thing he can't afford to lose.
- *Thomas Edison*

When Mrs. Smith was asked about her two children in elementary school, she answered: "The doctor is in the third grade and the lawyer is in the first!"

There are three ingredients in the good life: learning, earning, and yearning.
- *Christopher Morley*

Dreams are the stuff of progress.

Those who dare, do; those who dare not, do not.

Life is full of internal dramas, instantaneous and sensational, played to an audience of one.
- *Anthony Powell*

We are condemned to kill time: thus we die bit by bit.
- *Octavio Paz*

He who every morning plans the transaction of the day and follows out that plan carries a thread that will guide him through the labyrinth of the most busy life . . . But where no plan is laid, where the disposal of time is surrendered merely to the chance of incidents, chaos will soon reign.
- *Victor Hugo*

We should all be concerned about the future because we will have to spend the rest of our lives there.
- *Charles F. Kettering*

God asks no man whether he will accept life. That is not the choice. You must take it. The only choice is how.
- *Henry Ward Beecher*

When to the sessions of sweet silent thought
I summon up remembrance of things past,
I sigh the lack of many a thing I sought,
And with old woes new wail my dear time's waste.
- *William Shakespeare*

Take care of the minutes, for the hours will take care of themselves.
- *Lord Chesterfield*

The time which we have at our disposal every day is elastic; the passions that we feel expand it, those that we inspire contract it; and habit fills up what remains.
- *Marcel Proust*

Besides the noble art of getting things done, there is the noble art of leaving things undone. The wisdom of life consists in the elimination of nonessentials.
- *Lin Yutang*

Let the past drift away with the water.
- *Japanese saying*

To every thing there is a season, and a time to every purpose under the heaven:
A time to be born, and a time to die; a time to plant, and a time to pluck up that which is planted . . .
A time to get, and a time to lose; a time to keep, and a time to cast away . . .
A time to love, and a time to hate; a time of war, and a time of peace.
- *The Bible, Ecclesiastes 3:1-8*

We should take from the past its fires and not its ashes.
- *Jean Juares*

If spring came but once a century instead of once a year, or burst forth with the sound of an earthquake and not in silence, what wonder and expectation there would be in all hearts to behold the miraculous change.
- *Henry Wadsworth Longfellow*

God, give us grace to accept with serenity the things that cannot be changed, courage to change the things which should be changed, and the wisdom to distinguish one from the other.
- *Reinhold Niebuhr*

The greatest assassin of life is haste, the desire to reach things before the right time – which means overreaching them.
- *Juan Ramon Jimenez*

Does't thou love life? Then do not squander time, for that is the stuff life is made of.
- *Benjamin Franklin*

Time cannot be expanded, accumulated, mortgaged, hastened, or retarded.

Eternity is . . .
. . . keeping a smile on your face till the shutter clicks.
. . . waiting for the tow truck to show up.
. . . listening for the sound of a key in the lock at 2 a.m.
. . . trying to find a six-cent error in your bank balance.

. . . 20 minutes of aerobic exercises.

. . . not peeking till the popovers are done.

. . . awaiting the result of a pregnancy test.

. . . listening to a six-year-old relate the plot of this neat movie.

. . . looking for a freeway exit when you're headed in the wrong direction.

. . . housebreaking a new puppy.

. . . the second hour of Monopoly.

. . . waiting for the light to turn green when you've spotted an empty parking space across the intersection.

- Jane Goodsell

In one McGuffey's Reader there is a story about the clock that had been running for a long, long time on the mantelpiece. One day the clock began to think about how many times during the year ahead it would have to tick. It counted up the seconds – 31,536,000 in the year – and the old clock just got too tired and said, "I can't do it!" and stopped right there. When somebody reminded the clock that it did not have to tick the 31,536,000 seconds all at one time, but rather one by one, it began to run again and everything was all right.

- Nenien C. McPherson, Jr.

Time is dead as long as it is being clicked off by little wheels; only when the clock stops does time come to life.

- William Faulkner

Hell, by the time a man scratches his ass, clears his throat, and tells me how smart he is, we've already wasted fifteen minutes.

- Lyndon B. Johnson

The trouble with life in the fast lane is that you get to the other end in a awful hurry.

- John Jensen

Progress is a continuing effort to make the things we eat, drink and wear as good as they used to be.

- Bill Vaughn

Humanity . . . is like people packed in an automobile which is traveling down hill, without lights, on a dark night at terrific speed and driven by a four-year-oldchild. The signposts along the way are all marked "Progress."

- Lord Dunsany

Civilization is a stream with banks. The stream is sometimes filled with blood from people killing, shouting and doing things historians usually record, while on the banks, unnoticed, people build homes, make love, raise children, sing songs, write poetry and even whittle statues. The story of civilization is the story of what happened on the banks. Historians . . . ignore the banks of the river.

- Will Durant

You can save time, but you can't bank it.

This time, like all times, is a very good one, if we know what to do with it.

- Ralph Waldo Emerson

. . . Time is money

- Benjamin Franklin

The trouble with our age is all signposts and no destination.

- Louis Kronenberger

I am not young enough to know everything.

- J.M. Barrie

Young men think old men are fools, but old men know young men are fools.

- George Chapman, 1605

We think our fathers fools, so wise we grow;
Our wiser sons, no doubt, will think us so.

- Alexander Pope, 1711

We succeed only as we identify in life, or in war, or in anything else, a single overriding objective, and make all other considerations bend to that one objective.

- Dwight D. Eisenhower

. . . If one advances confidently in the direction of his dreams, and endeavors to live the life which he has imagined, he will meet with success unexpected in common hours.

- Henry David Thoreau

Perhaps it would be a good idea, fantastic as it sounds, to muffle every telephone, stop every motor, and halt all activity for an hour some day, to give people a chance to ponder for a few minutes on what it is all about, why they are living and what they really want.

- James Truslow Adams

Next to the dog, the wastebasket is a man's best friend.

Every step forward is made at the cost of mental and physical pain to someone.

- Frederick Nietzsche

Make no little plans; they have no magic to stir men's blood and probably themselves will not be realized. Make big plans; aim high in hope and work, remembering that a noble, logical diagram once recorded will never die, but long after we are gone will be a living thing, asserting itself with ever-growing insistency.

- Daniel H. Burnham

The art of progress is to preserve order amid change and to preserve change amid order.

- Alfred North Whitehead

The civilized man has built a [carriage], but has lost the use of his feet. He is supported on crutches, but lacks . . . support of his muscle. He has a fine Geneva watch, but he fails of the skill to tell the hour by the sun.

- Ralph Waldo Emerson

The tragedy of the world is that men have given first class loyalty to second class causes, and these causes have betrayed them.

- Lynn Harold Hough

No horse gets anywhere until he is harnessed. No steam or gas ever drives anything until it is confined. No Niagra is ever turned into light and power until it is tunneled. No life ever grows great until it is focused, dedicated, disciplined.

- Harry Emerson Fosdick

Change is one thing, progress is another. "Change" is scientific, "progress" is ethical; change is indubitable, whereas progress is a matter of controversy.

- Bertrand Russell

That some good can be derived from every event is a better proposition than that everything happens for the best, which it assuredly does not.

- James K. Feibleman

Growth for the sake of growth is the ideology of the cancer cell.

- Edward Abbey

The desire to be well thought of makes people reluctant to say no to anyone regarding anything. We should cultivate an ability to say no to activities for which we have no time, no talent, and in which we have no interest or real concern. If we learn to say no to many things, then we will be able to say yes to things that matter most.

Spontaneity is the quality of being able to do something just because you feel like it at the moment, of trusting your instincts, of taking yourself by surprise and snatching from the clutches of your well-organized routine a bit of unscheduled pleasure.

- Richard Iannelli

Great historical movements are never begun for the attainment of remote and imperfectly comprehended ends. They demand something concrete to work for; they need clearly defined, particular aims.

- J. L. JarÄs

I never think of the future. It comes soon enough.

- Albert Einstein

May you live all the days of your life.

- Jonathan Swift

I find the great thing in this world is not so much where we stand as in what direction we are moving.

- Oliver Wendell Holmes

Human nature craves a certain amount of variety. We plant several kinds of flowers in our gardens. We enjoy our meals most when the selection of food is varied from day to day. The same principle applies to our daily activities.

- Harold Shryock

Time rushes toward us with its hospital tray of infinitely varied narcotics, even while it is preparing us for its inevitably fatal operation.

- Tennessee Williams

Retirement is the time where there is plenty of it, or not enough.

If people start letting me know how old I am, and I listen, I might start playing like an old man. So, I don't listen.

- Pete Rose, near the end of his baseball career

The greatest use of life is to spend it for something that will outlast it.

- William James

They say such nice things about people at their funerals that it makes me sad to realize that I'm going to miss mine by just a few days.

- Garrison Keillor

I shall pass through this world but once; any good things, therefore, that I can do, or any kindness that I can show to any human being, or dumb animal, let me do it now. Let me not deter it or neglect it, for I shall not pass this way again.

- John Galsworthy

The years in your life are less important than the life in your years.

The years teach what the days never know.

- Ralph Waldo Emerson

Life should be measured by its breadth, not its length.

Three things return not, even for prayers and tears –
The arrow which the archer shoots at will;
The spoken word, keen-edged and sharp to sting;
The opportunity left unimproved.
If thou would'st speak a word of loving cheer,
Oh speak it now. This moment is thine own.

- Anonymous

Nothing is free. Even age. Age is the fee God charges for life.

Lost yesterday, somewhere between sunrise and sunset, two golden hours, each set with sixty diamond minutes. No reward is offered, for they are gone forever.

- Horace Mann

Winston Churchill once suggested that history would deal gently with him. "Because," he added, "I intend to write it."

Never before have we had so little time in which to do so much.

- Franklin D. Roosevelt

Time is both common and rare; we either have too much or too little. None of us believe we use it as well as we should. But unlike all the other ingredients in life, some time is for flavor and some time is just to give support to all the other ingredients we mix in. Time's importance is measured from where we sit when we do the measuring. Unfortunately, we frequently think to measure it after it is used rather than before. Then we realize that time is not a common luxury at all – but a rare and valuable gem.

No man is so methodical as a complete idler, and none so scrupulous in measuring out his time as he whose time is worth nothing.

- Washington Irving

One today is worth two tomorrows.

I always wake up in the morning a young man.

- Carlos Pena Romulo

"How do you explain the relativity of time?" the professor was asked. "Well," he said, "if I am rushing to catch a plane, and the check-in clerk is so slow that I miss it, the extra two minutes don't mean much to him but they sure make a difference to me. That's relativity."

I have no Yesterdays,
Time took them away;
Tomorrow may not be –
But I have today.

- Pearl Yeadon McGinnis

My mother was given to a typical question: "We have always done this. Why should we do anything else?" But my wife's typical question was "We have always done this. Why don't we do it another way or, better still, why not do something else?"

- John D. Rockefeller, Jr.

Perfection of planning is a symptom of decay. During a period of exciting discovery or progress, there is no time to plan the perfect headquarters.

- C. Northcote Parkinson

Those who cannot remember the past are condemned to repeat it.

- George Santayana

. . . Time is a circus – always packing up and moving away.

- Ben Hetch

Life's a pretty precious and wonderful thing. You can't sit down and let it lap around you... you have to plunge into it; you have to dive through it! And you can't save it, you can't store it up; you can't horde it in a vault. You've got to taste it; you've got to use it. The more you use, the more you have... that's the miracle of it!

- Kyle Chrichton

It is a mistake to look too far ahead. Only one link in the chain of destiny can be handled at a time.

- Winston Churchill

The history of free men is never really written by chance but by choice – their choice.

- Dwight D. Eisenhower

. . . Luddites were those frenzied traditionalists of the early 19th century who toured [England] wrecking new weaving machines on the theory that if they were destroyed . . . old jobs and old ways of life could be preserved . . .

At certain times in his life, each man is tempted to become a Luddite, for there is always something he would like to go back to. But to be against all change – against change in the abstract – is folly.

- James A. Michener

There are parts of a ship which taken by themselves would sink. The engine would sink. The propeller would sink. But when the parts of a ship are built together, they float. So with the events of my life. Some have been tragic. Some have been happy. But when they are built together, they form a craft that floats and is going someplace. And I am comforted.

- Ralph W. Sockman

Work expands so as to fill the time available for its completion . . .

- C. Northcote Parkinson

If a man constantly aspires, is he not elevated?

- Henry David Thoreau

Every day has been so short, every hour so fleeting, every minute so filled with the life I love, that time for me has fled on too swift a wing.

- Aga Khan

. . . Take time to absorb and enjoy the lovely world in which you live and come to know its inhabitants with affectionate amusement. You would do well to budget your time as follows: one-half in work, taking care of personal belongings, etc.; one-fourth in social pastimes with . . . both young and old; and one-fourth as an interested, pleased observer of life.

- William B. Terhune

Practical people would be a lot more practical if they were just a little more dreamy.

- J.P. McEvoy

In America half an hour is forty minutes

- German Proverb

Not so long ago, when I was a student in college, just flying an airplane seemed a dream. But that dream turned into a reality.

- Charles A. Lindbergh

Only in growth, reform and change, paradoxically enough, is true security to be found.

- Anne Morrow Lindberg

While all other sciences have advanced, that of government is at a standstill – little better understood, little better practised now than three or four thousand years ago.

- John Adams

The pace of events is moving so fast that unless we can find some way to keep our sights on tomorrow, we cannot expect to be in touch with today.

- Dean Rusk

Reach high, for stars lie hidden in your soul.
Dream deep, for every dream precedes the goal.

- Ralph Vaull Starr

Life is a fatal adventure. It can only have one end. So why not make it as far ranging and free as possible?

- Alexander Eliot

Time is a dressmaker specializing in alterations.

- Faith Baldwin

An elderly lady told me, "When I was younger I never went anywhere without a thermometer, a hot water bottle, a raincoat, and a parachute. Now that I'm older I wish I had walked more in my bare feet, had gone more places, and spent more time picking daisies."

- Roberta Figer

Life has a certain ending and uncertain timing.

RELATIONSHIPS

Quotes & Anecdotes
(companionship, equity, respect)

Treat people as if they were what they ought to be, and you help them to become what they are capable of being.
- *Goethe*

How much more grievous are the consequences of anger than the causes of it.
- *Marcus Aurelius, c. A.D. 170*

Offerings of food have been breaking down barriers for centuries.
- *Estee Lauder*

If a man does not make new acquaintances as he advances through life he will find himself alone. Man . . . should keep his acquaintances in constant repair.
- *Samuel Johnson*

He drew a circle that shut me out
Heretic, rebel, a thing to flout.

But Love and I had the wit to win;
We drew a circle that took him in!
- *Edwin Markham*

Peace is more precious than a piece of land.
- *Anwar al-Sadat*

When evil men plot, good men must plan. When evil men shout ugly words of hatred, good men must commit themselves to the glories of love.
- *Martin Luther King, Jr.*

I respect those who resist me, but I cannot tolerate them.
- *Charles de Gaulle*

There are only two ways to be quite unprejudiced and impartial. One is to be completely ignorant. The other is to be completely indifferent. Bias and prejudice are attitudes to be kept in hand, not attitudes to be avoided.
- *Charles P. Curtis*

The surest bond of friendship is having enemies in common.

Forgive your enemies, but never forget their names.
- *John F. Kennedy*

If you wish to be brothers, drop your weapons.
- *Pope John Paul II*

When a man points a finger at someone else, he should remember that four of his fingers are pointing at himself.
- *Louis Nizer*

Hold a true friend with both your hands.
- *Nigerian proverb*

Your own safety is at stake when your neighbor's house is burning.
- *Horace, about 10 B.C.*

Then there's the man who puts a sign on his front door when he goes off on vacation, reading: Attention thieves; do not bother to enter here; everything of value has already been borrowed by my neighbors.

The impersonal hand of government can never replace the helping hand of a neighbor.
- *Hubert H. Humphrey*

A true friend is someone who is there for you when he'd rather be anywhere else.
- *Len Wein*

You can make more friends in two months by becoming interested in other people than you can in two years by trying to get other people interested in you.
- *Dale Carnegie*

The best next-door neighbor is the one who overlooks things.

Be kind. Remember, everyone you meet is fighting a hard battle.
- *Thompson*

There is great comfort and inspiration in the feeling of close human relationships and its bearing on our mutual fortunes – a powerful force, to overcome the "tough breaks" which are certain to come to most of us from time to time.
- *Walt Disney*

I can't make people like me, but if I wasn't me, I would like me.
- *Third-grader*

You cannot be friends upon any other terms than upon the terms of equality.
- *Woodrow Wilson*

Commandment Number One of any truly civilized society is this: Let people be different.
- *David Grayson*

Some people can stay longer in an hour than others can in a week.
- *William Dean Howells*

Tale-bearers are as bad as tale-makers.
- *Sheridan*

A gossip was complaining about her neighbor to a visiting friend. Her neighbor was so dirty, it was a disgrace to the neighborhood. "Just look, those clothes she has on the line and sheets and pillowcases all have black streaks up and down them." Her guest said, "It appears, my dear, that the clothes are clean; the streaks you see are on your . . . windows."

Peace may cost as much as war, but it's a better buy.

If civilization is to survive, we must cultivate the science of human relationships – the ability of all peoples, of all kinds, to live together, in the same world at peace.
                            - Franklin D. Roosevelt

Friends are made by many acts – and lost by only one.

Eating words has never given me indigestion.
                            - Winston Churchill

I shall pass through life but once. Let me show kindness now, as I shall not pass this way again.
                            - William Penn

Forgiveness does not change the past, but it does enlarge the future.
                            - Paul Boese

It is easier to forgive an enemy than to forgive a friend.
                            - William Blake

He who cannot forgive breaks the bridge over which he himself must pass.
                            - George Herbert

Loneliness and the feeling of being unwanted is the most terrible poverty.
                            - Mother Teresa

Grief can take care of itself, but to get the full value out of a joy you must have somebody to divide it with.
                            - Mark Twain

If you want your friends to remember you, borrow something from them.

The most exhausting thing in life, I have discovered, is being insincere. That is why so much social life is exhausting; one is wearing a mask.
                            - Anne Morrow Lindbergh

Hatred is blind as well as love.
                            - Thomas Fuller, 1732

When you hear that someone has gossiped of you, kindly reply that he did not know the rest of your faults or he would not have mentioned only these.

The only gracious way to accept an insult is to ignore it; if you can't ignore it, top it; if you can't top it, laugh at it; if you can't laugh at it, it's probably deserved.
                            - Russell Lynes

A Washington lady explained how to be a successful hostess: When your guests arrive say, "At last!" And when they leave, "So soon!"

We like someone *because*. We love someone *although*.
                            - Henri De Montherlant

If a man does not keep pace with his companions, perhaps it is because he hears a different drummer. Let him step to the music which he hears, however measured or far away.
                            - Henry David Thoreau

I believe every person has a heart, and if you can reach it, you can make a difference.
                            - Uli Derickson

Robert Mueller shares this telling and tragically true human relations experience: "I asked a Burmese why women, after centuries of following their men, now walk ahead. He said there were many unexploded land mines since the war."

No one can be wrong with man and right with God.
                            - Harry Emerson Fosdick

You learn to speak by speaking, to study by studying, to run by running, to work by working; and just so you learn to love God and man by loving. Begin as a mere apprentice and the very power of love will lead you on to become a master of the art.
                            - St. Francis De Sales

Real friends are those who, when you've made a fool of yourself, don't feel you've done a permanent job.

When you see a worthy person, endeavor to emulate him. When you see an unworthy person, then examine your inner self.
                            - Confucius

Folks never understand the folks they hate.
                            - James Russell Lowell, 1862

Laugh at yourself first, before anybody else can.
                            - Elsa Maxwell, quoting death-bed advice of her father.

When I was a young man, I met Franklin Roosevelt and Harry Truman. I remarked to Mr. Truman that I thought Mr. Roosevelt was a wonderful man. Mr. Truman agreed. "Franklin likes me despite my shortcomings in my work, and I like him because he has none."
                            - Henry O. Dormann

Be generous with kindly words, especially about those who are absent.
                            - Goethe

Some people find fault as if it were buried treasure.
                            - Francis O'Walsh

Love your enemies, for they will tell you your faults.
                            - Benjamin Franklin

On a cold winter's day, a group of porcupines huddled together to stay warm and keep from freezing. But soon they felt one another's quills and moved apart. When the need for warmth brought them closer together again, their quills again forced them apart. They were driven back and forth at the mercy of their discomforts until they found the distance from one another that provided both a maximum of warmth and a minimum of pain.

In human beings, the emptiness and monotony of the isolated self produces a need for society. This brings people together, but their many offensive qualities and intolerable faults drive them apart again. The optimum distance that they finally find and that permits them to coexist is embodied in politeness and good manners. Because of this distance between us, we can only partially satisfy our need for warmth, but at the same time, we are spared the stab of one another's quills.
- Arthur Schopenhauer

If you hate a person, you hate something in him that is part of yourself. What isn't part of ourselves doesn't disturb us.
- Hermann Hesse, Demian

If you join little cliques, you will be self-satisfied; if you make friends widely, you will be interesting.
- Sydney Smith

To wrong those we hate is to add fuel to our hatred. Conversely, to treat an enemy with magnanimity is to blunt our hatred for him.
- Eric Hoffer

The best cure for anger is delay.
- Seneca, c. A.D. 63

Thank you all from the bottom of my heart for your hospitality and, as we say in Russia, for your bread and salt. Let us have more and more use for the short American word "O.K."
- Nikita Khrushchev, concluding his first visit to U.S.

I feel the necessity of deepening the stream of life; I must cultivate privacy. It is very dissipating to be with people too much.
- Henry David Thoreau

. . .The most important phase of living with a person: the respect for that person as an individual.
- Millicent Carey McIntosh

In expressing love we belong among the underdeveloped countries.
- Saul Bellow

The first duty of love is to LISTEN.
- Paul Tillich

To be humble to superiors is duty, to equals, courtesy, to inferiors, nobleness.
- Benjamin Franklin

I'd rather deal with a God-loving person than with a God-fearing one.

When the mouse laughs at the cat, there is a hole nearby.
- Nigerian proverb

Being taken for granted can be a compliment. It means that you've become a comfortable, trusted element in another person's life.
- Dr. Joyce Brothers

Each of us has his own little private conviction of rightness and almost by definition, the Utopian condition of which we all dream is that in which all people finally see the error of their ways and agree with us. And underlying practically all our attempts to bring agreement is the assumption that agreement is brought about by changing people's minds – other people's.
- S.I. Hayakawa

A gentleman saw a blind woman standing on a busy city corner waiting for someone to help her cross the intersection. He stepped up to her and asked, "May I go across with you?"

Practice smiling. Smile at lamp posts and mail boxes. Don't be modest – this isn't the time. Always eat a snack before going to a luncheon meeting so you can spend your time charming, not chewing.
- Jacque Mercer, former Miss America, on how to win a beauty contest

Some men still have their first dollar. The man who is really rich is the one who still has his first friend.

The acid test of hospitality is the uninvited guest.

Withdraw thy foot from thy neighbor's house; lest he be weary of thee, and so hate thee.
- The Bible, Proverbs 25:17

It is equally offensive to speed a guest who would like to stay and to detain one who is anxious to leave.
- Homer, The Odyssey

Fish and guests smell at three days old.
- Danish proverb

Friendship increases in visiting friends, but in visiting them seldom.
- Thomas Fuller

Go often to the house of thy friend, for weeds choke the unused path.
- Ralph Waldo Emerson

For any American who had the great and priceless privilege of being raised in a small town there always remains with him nostalgic memories . . . . And the older he grows the more he senses what he owed to the simple honesty and neighborliness, the integrity that he saw all around him in those days . . .
- *Dwight D. Eisenhower*

When there is room in the heart there is room in the house.

The time to win a fight is before it starts.
- *Frederick W. Lewis*

I have made a ceaseless effort not to ridicule, not to bewail, not to scorn human actions, but to understand them.
- *Spinoza*

In mixed doubles the mix is very important.

A man cannot be said to succeed in this life who does not satisfy one friend.
- *Henry David Thoreau*

He who forgives, ends the quarrel.

If I knew you and you knew me,
If both of us could clearly see,
And with an inner sight divine
The meaning of your heart and mine.

I'm sure that we would differ less,
and clasp our hands in friendliness,
Our thoughts would pleasantly agree
If I knew you and you knew me.
- *Nixon Waterman*

You punch me, I punch back. I do not believe it is good for one's self-respect to be a punching bag.
- *Edward Koch*

He that strives not to stem his anger's tide
Does a wild horse without a bridle ride.
- *Colley Cibber, 1696*

There are two statements about human beings that are true: that all human beings are alike, and that all are different. On those two facts all human wisdom is founded.
- *Mark Van Doren*

All is well with him who is beloved by his neighbors.
- *George Herbert*

Am I united with my friend in heart,
What matters if our place be wide apart?
- *Anwar-I-Suheili, Persian poet*

When you are down and out, something always turns up – and it is usually the noses of your friends.
- *Orson Welles*

Friendship makes prosperity more shining and lessens adversity by dividing and sharing it.
- *Cicero, 44 B.C.*

The only way to have a friend is to be one.
- *Ralph Waldo Emerson*

Check the neighbors before you buy the house.

. . . Six hundred men all thinking a great deal of themselves and very little of each other.
- *Sir James Cassels, on the House of Commons*

The love of humanity . . . is mitigated by violent dislike of the next-door neighbor.
- *Alfred North Whitehead*

Before borrowing money from a friend, decide which you need more.
- *Addison H. Hallock*

Let us endeavor so to live that when we come to die even the undertaker will be sorry.
- *Mark Twain*

The touch of human hands
Not vain, unthinking words,
Not that cold charity
Which shuns our misery;
We seek a loyal friend
Who understands,
And the warmth, the pulsing warmth
Of human hands.
- *Thomas Curtis Clark*

Can two walk together, except they be agreed?
- *The Bible, Amos 3:3*

Oh, the comfort, the inexpressible comfort of feeling safe with a person; having neither to weigh thoughts nor measure words, but to pour them all out, just as they are, chaff and grain together, knowing that a faithful hand will take and sift them, keep what is worth keeping, and then, with the breath of kindness, blow the rest away.
- *George Eliot*

A friend is someone who stimulates me and to whom I am stimulated to talk . . . When the stimulation no longer occurs, it is spent and exhausted friendship, and continues as a burden and a bore . . . Unfortunately in a long life one gets barnacled over with the mere shells of friendship and it is difficult without hurting one's self to scrape them off.
- *Bernard Berenson*

All the world's a stage,
And all the men and women merely players:
They have their exits and their entrances;

And one man in his time plays many parts . . .
- *William Shakespeare, As You Like It*

The first general rule for friendship is to be a friend, to be open, natural, interested; the second rule is to take time for friendship. Friendship, after all, is what life is finally about. Everything material and professional exists in the end for persons.
- *Nels F. S. Ferre*

I sought to hear the voice of God
And climbed the topmost steeple,
But God declared: "Go down again
– I dwell among the people."
- *John Henry Newman*

I cannot help believing that the world will be a better and a happier place when people are praised more and blamed less; when we utter in their hearing the good we think and also gently intimate the criticisms we hope may be of service. For the world grows smaller every day. It will be but a family circle after a while.
- *Francis E. Willard*

If a wife always laughs at her husband's jokes, is he funny or she smart?

Prejudice is the child of ignorance.
- *William Hazlitt*

True generosity requires more of us than kindly impulse. Above all it requires imagination – the capacity to see people in all their perplexities and needs, and to know how to expend ourselves effectively for them.
- *I.A.R. Wylie*

Politeness is the art of selecting among one's real thoughts.
- *Madame de Stael*

I don't really feel my poems are mine at all. I didn't create them out of nothing; I owe them to my relations with other people.
- *Robert Graves*

Who gossips to you will gossip of you.

We praise a man who is angry on the right grounds, against the right persons, in the right manner, at the right moment, and for the right length of time.
- *Aristotle, c.340 B.C.*

No man is an island, entire of itself; every man is a piece of the continent, a part of the main . . . . Any man's death diminishes me, because I am involved in mankind; and therefore never send to know for whom the bell tolls; it tolls for thee.
- *John Donne, 1624*

Thou canst not joke an enemy into a friend, but thou may'st a friend into an enemy.
- *Benjamin Franklin*

Great Spirit, help me never to judge another until I have walked in his moccasins.
- *Sioux Indian prayer*

No one can make you feel inferior without your consent.
- *Eleanor Roosevelt*

If the happiness of the mass of mankind can be secured at the expense of a little tempest now and then, or even of a little blood, it will be a precious purchase.
- *Thomas Jefferson in a letter to Ezra Stiles, 1786*

I wish she was smart enough to teach second grade, too, next year.
- *William Goumas, first-grade pupil, in his "favorite teacher" essay*

A friend is . . . a second self.
- *Cicero*

Always do what you say you are going to do. It is the glue and fiber that binds successful relationships.
- *Jeffry A. Timmons*

I always wanted to be somebody. If I made it, it's half because I was game enough to take a lot of punishment along the way and half because there were a lot of people who cared enough to help me.
- *Althea Gibson*

You can't hold a man down without staying down with him.
- *Booker T. Washington*

The longer we live, and the more we think, the higher value we learn to put on the friendship and tenderness of parents and of friends. Parents we can have but once; and he promises himself too much, who enters life with the expectation of finding many friends.
- *Samuel Johnson, 1766*

My own business always bores me to death; I prefer other people's.
- *Oscar Wilde*

Friendship, of itself a holy tie,
Is made more sacred by adversity.
- *John Dryden, 1687*

The average man is more interested in a woman who is interested in him than he is in a woman – any woman – with beautiful legs.
- *Marlene Dietrich*

Most of the trouble in the world is caused by people wanting to be important.
- *T.S. Eliot*

I've always believed in writing without a collaborator, because where two people are writing the same book, each believes he gets all the worries and only half the royalties.

- Agatha Christie

. . . Closer together than the hands of a clock at twenty minutes of eight.

- Robert Bedingfield, on the brothers John and Clint Murchison

The holy passion of friendship is of so sweet and steady and loyal and enduring a nature that it will last through a whole lifetime, if not asked to lend money.

- Mark Twain

We are all crazy when we are angry.

- Philemon, c. 300 B.C.

Am I not destroying my enemies when I make friends of them?

- Abraham Lincoln

Make no friendships with an angry man.

- The Bible, Proverbs 22:24

All government, indeed every human benefit and enjoyment, every virtue, and every prudent act, is founded on compromise and barter.

- Edmund Burke, on conciliation with America, 1775

You don't ever ask a barber whether you need a haircut.

- Greenberg

Blame-all and praise-all are two blockheads.

- Benjamin Franklin

God bears with imperfect beings . . . even when they resist His goodness. We ought to imitate this merciful patience and endurance. It is only imperfection that complains of what is imperfect. The more perfect we are, the more gentle and quiet we become toward the defects of other people.

- Francois de Fenelon

The only normal people are the ones you don't know very well.

- Joe Ancis

The first human being who hurled an insult instead of a stone was the founder of civilization.

- Attributed to Sigmund Freud

To put the world right in order, we must first put the nation in order; to put the nation in order, we must first put the family in order; to put the family in order, we must first cultivate our personal life; we must first set our hearts right.

- Confucius

COMMUNICATION

Quotes & Anecdotes
(speech, diplomacy, advice, public speaking)

Use soft words in hard arguments.
- H.G. Bohn, 1855

... It is always well to accept your own short-comings with candor but to regard those of your friends with polite incredulity.
- Russell Lynes

Only if we can restrain ourselves is conversation possible. Good talk rises upon much self-discipline.
- John Erskine

It is only the intellectually lost who ever argue.
- Oscar Wilde

We cannot learn from one another until we stop shouting at one another – until we speak quietly enough so that our words can be heard as well as our voices.
- Richard M. Nixon

A diplomat is a person who can tell you to go to hell in such a way that you actually look forward to the trip.
- Caskie Stinnett

A gossip is one who talks to you about others; a bore is one who talks to you about himself; and a brilliant conversationalist is one who talks to you about yourself.
- Lisa Kirk

Speak when you are angry and you will make the best speech you will ever regret.
- Ambrose Bierce

All the great speakers were bad speakers at first.
- Ralph Waldo Emerson

One of the best ways to persuade others is with your ears – by listening to them.
- Dean Rusk

Great public speakers listen to the audience with their eyes.

Exhaust neither the topic nor the audience.

O Lord, please fill my mouth with worthwhile stuff, and nudge me when I've said enough.

In order to speak short upon any subject, think long.
- H. H. Brackenridge

A wise man will not communicate his differing thoughts to unprepared minds, or in a disorderly manner.
- Benjamin Whichcote, 1753

People who know the very least seem to know the loudest.

A reporter, coming upon a big story, telegraphed his editor. The editor replied, "Send six hundred words." The reporter wired back, "Can't be told in less than twelve hundred words." The editor replied, "Story of creation of world told in six hundred. Try it."

President William Howard Taft was requested to attend a banquet and make a speech. The person inviting him said, "Just a brief one, Mr. President, since we can imagine how busy you must be – perhaps five minutes." The president declined. "Do you realize that to prepare even a five-minute speech would take several hours to plan, to draft, to rewrite, to pass through channels for clearance? I'm afraid that I just haven't got the time." The host persisted. "Well, as far as that goes, we'd be delighted to have you speak for an hour." President Taft replied, "Gentlemen, I am ready now!"

All propaganda has to be popular and has to accommodate itself to the comprehension of the least intelligent of those whom it seeks to reach.
- Adolf Hitler

We are fighting in the quarrel of civilization against barbarism, of liberty against tyranny. Germany has become a menace to the whole world. She is the most dangerous enemy of liberty now existing. She has shown herself utterly ruthless, treacherous, and brutal. When I use these words, I use them with scientific precision.
- Theodore Roosevelt

Better to remain silent and be thought a fool than to speak out and remove all doubt.
- Abraham Lincoln

A "no" uttered from the deepest conviction is better and greater than a "yes" merely uttered to please, or what is worse, to avoid trouble.
- Muhatma Gandhi

Silence is often misinterpreted, but never misquoted.

Baloney is the unvarnished lie laid on so thick you hate it. Blarney is flattery laid on so thin you love it.
- Fulton Sheen

Anyone who thinks the art of conversation is dead ought to tell a child to go to bed.
- Robert Gallagher

... Mass is the ceremony I most favor during my travels. Church is the only place where someone speaks to me ... and I do not have to answer back.
- Charles De Gaulle

True, lasting peace cannot be secured through the strength of arms alone. Among free peoples, the open exchange of ideas ultimately is our greatest security.
- Ronald Reagan

Some people mistake weakness for tact. If they are silent when they ought to speak and so feign an agreement they do not feel, they call it being tactful. Cowardice would be a much better name. Tact is an active quality that is not exercised by merely making a dash for cover. Be sure, when you think you are being extremely tactful, that you are not in reality running away from something you ought to face.

- Sir Frank Medlicott

Tact is the knack of making a point without making an enemy.

- Howard W. Newton

Let your discourse with men of business be short and comprehensive.

- George Washington

In the mid-1960's, FBI director J. Edgar Hoover was proofreading a letter he had just dictated to his secretary. He didn't like the way she had formatted it, so he wrote the words, "Watch the borders" at the bottom of the letter and asked her to retype it. The secretary did as she was told and sent it off to all top agents. For the next two weeks FBI agents were patrolling the Canadian and Mexican borders in droves as requested by their leader.

That which we are capable of feeling, we are capable of saying.

- Cervantes, 1613

The friend who can be silent with us in a moment of despair or confusion, who can stay with us in an hour of grief and bereavement, who can tolerate not knowing, not curing, not healing, and face us with the reality of our powerlessness, that is the friend who cares.

- Henri Nouwen

Do not the most moving moments of our lives find us all without words?

- Marcel Marceau, pantomimist

The late Sam Goldwyn is credited with devising the all-purpose answer when someone closely connected with a new film comes up to you after the preview to ask what you thought of it. Say "What a picture!" and leave fast.

The art of acceptance is the art of making someone who has just done you a small favor wish that he might have done you a greater one.

- Russell Lynes

Wit is a treacherous dart. It is perhaps the only weapon with which it is possible to stab oneself in one's own back.

- Geoffrey Bocca

I'm not capable of blathering pap. I'm not happy or comfortable engaging in mush statements. If I'm going to say something, it's going to be substantive and at least provocative. Hopefully, it will also have some humor. That's my style. It's me.

- Edward Koch

Flattery is from the teeth out. Sincere appreciation is from the heart out.

- Dale Carnegie

A good speech is like a pencil; it has to have a point.

A true sonnet goes eight lines and then takes a turn for better or worse and goes six or eight lines more.

- Robert Frost

New Englanders' lack of loquaciousness is legendary , as perhaps is this story of a New England President named Calvin Coolidge, who was asked what had been the subject of the pastor's sermon in church that Sunday and said, "Sin." "What did the preacher say?" "He's agin it," said Mr. Coolidge.

Talk low, talk slow, and don't say too much.

- John Wayne, on acting

A fool uttereth all his mind.

- The Bible, Proverbs 29:11

A man stopped in a small town on his journey through Vermont and decided to join a group of men sitting on the porch of the general store. They were quiet. After several tries at starting a conversation and not succeeding, he asked, "Is there a law against talking in this town?"

One of them replied, "There's no law against talking, but we have an understanding that one doesn't speak unless he is sure he can improve on the silence."

In the 5th century B.C., a barber asked King Archelaus how he would like his hair cut. "In silence," replied the king.

Let thy speech be better than silence, or be silent.

- Dionysius the Elder

First learn the meaning of what you say, and then speak.

- Epictetus

If you have an important point to make, don't try to be subtle or clever. Use a pile driver. Hit the point once. Then come back and hit it again. Then hit it a third time – a tremendous whack.

- Winston Churchill

Every time a controversial issue came up at the town meeting, the town dissenter said "We'll stage a demonstration." Finally one of the elders lost his temper. "You don't accomplish anything by your demonstrations," he said. "They always end up in a riot, and what good is that?" "Well," said the dissenter, "it gets a lot more attention than when I talk in the town meeting."

The opposite of talking isn't listening. The opposite of talking is waiting.

- Fran Lebowitz

Hear the other side.

- St. Augustine

Eating words has never given me indigestion.
- *Winston Churchill*

A good citizen is one who doesn't always keep his mouth shut.

. . . I have made this letter longer because I lack the time to make it shorter.
- *Blaise Pascal, 1656*

. . . I have found that the greatest help in meeting any problem with decency and self-respect and whatever courage is demanded, is to know where you yourself stand. That is, to have in words what you believe and are acting from.
- *William Faulkner, letter to a University of Alabama student during riots over enrollment of a black*

The right of every person "to be let alone" must be placed in the scales with the right of others to communicate.
- *Chief Justice Warren E. Burger*

The newly-arrived immigrant drove his host crazy by talking about how much better food was in the old country, and how much better the weather was and how much better everything was back where he came from. Finally his host said, "If everything was so much better there, why did you come here?" And the immigrant answered, "Because if I said over there that something was better elsewhere they would have shot me. The one thing that's better here is that now I can complain."

Let your speech be always with grace, seasoned with salt, that ye may know how ye ought to answer every man.
- *The Bible, Colossians 4:6*

During World War II, the Civil Defense authorities had posters printed which read: "Illumination must be extinguished when premises are vacated." When he saw these signs, President Franklin Roosevelt exclaimed, "Damn, why can't they say 'Put out the lights when you leave'?"
- *Franklin D. Roosevelt*

To say nothing often reflects a fine command of the English language.

Do not say things. What you are stands over you the while and thunders so that I cannot hear what you say to the contrary.
- *Ralph Waldo Emerson*

Channing Cox, who succeeded Calvin Coolidge as governor of Massachusetts, visited the vice-president. Cox asked him how he could see his visitors every day and manage to leave his office at five, while Cox could rarely leave before nine P.M. Coolidge replied, "You talk back."

Don't flatter yourself that friendship authorizes you to say disagreeable things to your intimates. The nearer you come into relation with a person, the more necessary do tact and courtesy become.
- *Oliver Wendell Holmes*

He who slings mud generally loses ground.
- *Adlai Stevenson*

Never answer a letter while you are angry.
- *Chinese proverb*

I was angry with my friend:
I told my wrath, my wrath did end.
I was angry with my foe:
I told it not, my wrath did grow.
- *William Blake, c. 1792*

When you are angry say nothing and do nothing until you have recited the alphabet.
- *Ascribed to Athenodorous Cananites, 1st century B.C.*

When angry, count ten before you speak; if very angry, a hundred.
- *Thomas Jefferson*

When angry, count four; when very angry, swear.
- *Mark Twain*

To speak ill of others is a dishonest way of praising ourselves . . . let us be above such transparent egotism.
- *Will Durant*

Having served on various committees, I have drawn up a list of rules: Never arrive on time; this stamps you as a beginner. Don't say anything until the meeting is half over; this stamps you as being wise. Be as vague as possible; this avoids irritating the others. When in doubt, suggest that a sub-committee be appointed. Be the first to move for adjournment; this will make you popular; it's what everyone is waiting for.
- *Harry Chapman*

Dentopedalogy is the science of opening your mouth and putting your foot in it. I've been practicing it for years.
- *Prince Philip*

A bishop was to make his first sermon at the court of Queen Victoria. He asked Disraeli for advice. "How long do you think my first sermon should last, Mr. Prime Minister?" Disraeli replied, "If you preach for forty minutes, Her Majesty will be satisfied; for thirty minutes, she will be delighted. If you preach for only fifteen minutes, Her Majesty will be enthusiastic!"

I can go on forever. To me, one thought becomes five hundred sentences.
- *Alice K. Dormann*

A scatterbrain is one who never has an unspoken thought.

A bore is a fellow who opens his mouth and puts his feats in it.
- *Henry Ford*

Blessed is he who, having nothing to say, refrains from giving wordy evidence of the fact.

The boor is of no use in conversation. He contributes nothing worth hearing, and takes offense at everything.

- Aristotle, c. 340 B.C.

Definition of a bore: A person who talks when you wish him to listen.

- Ambrose Bierce

Wisdom is divided into two parts: (a) having a great deal to say, and (b) not saying it.

The wise man, even when he holds his tongue, says more than the fool when he speaks.

- Thomas Fuller, 1642

There is no greater mistake than the hasty conclusion that opinions are worthless because they are badly argued.

- Thomas Huxley

Sometimes a fool makes a good suggestion.

- Nicolas Boileau, 1674

'Tis wisdom sometimes to seem a fool.

- Thomas Fuller, 1642

Nothing is often a good thing to say, and always a clever thing to say.

- Will Durant

To listen well is as powerful a means of communication and influence as to talk well.

- Chief Justice John Marshall

The less you talk, the more you're listened to.

- Abigail Van Buren

No one means all he says, and yet few say all they mean. For words are slippery and thought is vicious.

- Henry Brooks Adams

In the dark days and darker nights when England stood alone – and most men save Englishmen despaired of England's life – he mobilized the English language and sent it into battle. The incandescent quality of his words illuminated the courage of his countrymen.

- John F. Kennedy, conferring honorary citizenship on Winston Churchill, 1963

Civility costs nothing, and buys everything.

- Lady Mary Wortley Montagu, 1756

Only a brilliant man knows whether the applause for his words is politeness or appreciation.

To the press alone, checkered as it is with abuses, the world is indebted for all the triumphs which have been gained by reason and humanity over error and oppression.

- Thomas Jefferson

I know what I say at times is not very diplomatic.

- Nikita Khrushchev

Diplomacy is the language of international relations, which can say one thing that has two absolutely opposite meanings . . .

A diplomat is one who can tell a man he's open-minded when he means he has a hole in his head.

Let the lie be delivered full-face, eye to eye, and without scratching of the scalp, but let it, for all its simplicity, contain one fantastical element of creative ingenuity.

- Dalton Trumbo, on lying

In 1931, Charlie Chaplin and Albert Einstein drove down a street together. Pedestrians waved and cheered. Chaplin explained all of this: "The people are applauding you because none of them understands you, and applauding me, because everybody understands me."

I'm going to speak my mind because I have nothing to lose.

- S.I. Hayakawa

His enemies might have said before that he talked rather too much; but now he has occasional flashes of silence that make his conversation perfectly delightful.

- Syndey Smith writing on Thomas Macaulay, Scottish author and statesman

When Jimmy Carter of Georgia was elected President, a common comment in the South was that he was the first President in more than a hundred years who "spoke English without an accent."

If you can't get people to listen to you any other way, tell them it's confidential.

Cynicism is the intellectual cripple's substitute for intelligence. It is the dishonest businessman's substitute for conscience. It is the communicator's substitute, whether he is an advertising man or editor or writer, for self-respect.

- Russell Lynes

A man's judgment cannot be better than the information on which he has based it. Give him no news, or present him only with distorted and incomplete data, with ignorant, sloppy, or biased reporting, with propaganda and deliberate falsehoods, and you destroy his whole reasoning process and make him somewhat less than a man.

- Arthur Hays Sulzberger

The story is told of the way Secretary of State William M. Evarts began a Thanksgiving dinner speech. He said, "You have been giving your attention to a turkey stuffed with sage; you are now about to consider a sage stuffed with turkey."

It is better to advise than upbraid, for the one corrects the erring; the other only convicts them.

- Epictetus, 2nd century A.D.

Advice is less necessary to the wise than to fools, but the wise derive most advantage from it.

- Francesco Guicciardini, 1564

I was a code clerk in Washington . . . when we received an urgent message that twelve code clerks were needed by President Wilson at the Verailles Peace Conference. What they really wanted were twelve code books, but somebody got the message mixed up.
- *James Thurber, on his first trip to Paris*

He can compress the most words into the smallest idea of any man I ever met.
- *Abraham Lincoln*

Senator George H. Moses complained to President Calvin Coolidge that a man being considered for a Republican senatorial nomination was an "out-and-out S.O.B."
"That may be," agreed Coolidge, "but there's a lot of those in the country and I think they are entitled to representation in the Senate."

Be wiser than other people if you can; but do not tell them so.
- *Lord Chesterfield in a Letter to his son, 1745*

Never answer a question, other than an offer of marriage, by saying Yes or No.
- *Susan Chitty*

A powerful agent is the right word. Whenever we come upon one of those intensely right words in a book or newspaper the resulting effect is physical as well as spiritual, and electrically prompt.
- *Mark Twain*

It is not necessary to understand things in order to argue about them.
- *Caron De Beaumarchais, the Barber of Seville, 1775*

Never tell all that you know, or do all that you can, or believe all that you hear.
- *Portuguese proverb*

I narrow-mindedly outlawed the word "unique." Practically every press release contains it. Practically nothing ever is.
- *Fred Hechinger, editor*

Few sinners are saved after the first 20 minutes of a sermon.
- *Mark Twain*

If you haven't struck oil in five minutes, stop boring.
- *George Jessel, on after-dinner speakers*

Here comes the orator with his flood of words and his drop of reason
- *Benjamin Franklin*

When the main portion of the meal was finished, the presiding person whispered to the first speaker, "Shall we let the people enjoy themselves a little longer, or would you like to deliver your speech now?"

Be sure your brain is in gear before engaging your mouth.

Eloquence: saying the proper thing and stopping.
- *Francois de la Rochefoucauld*

The heart of a fool is in his mouth, but the mouth of a wise man is in his heart.
- *Benjamin Franklin*

Governor Claude A. Swanson of Virginia had made a long and rambling speech. Afterwards a woman came up to . . . shake his hand. "How did you like my speech?" he asked. She answered, "I liked it fine. But it seems to me you missed several excellent opportunities." Swanson was puzzled. "Several excellent opportunities to do what?" "To quit," she replied.

There is a story in Arabic which tells of a pupil asking a wise man how he could become a good conversationalist. The sage replied, "Listen, my son." After waiting a while, pupil said, "I am listening, Please continue your instruction." The sage smiled. "There is no more to tell."

Hearts may agree though heads differ.
- *Thomas Fuller, 1732*

A fanatic is one who can't change his mind and won't change the subject.
- *Winston Churchill*

A man of few words, Calvin Coolidge explained why: "I found out early in life that you never have to explain something you haven't said."

Scholarship is polite argument.
- *Philip Rieff, associate professor, University of California*

The grand aim of all science is to cover the greatest number of empirical facts by logical deduction from the smallest number of hypotheses or axioms.
- *Albert Einstein*

"For the first six months, you should listen and not become involved in debate," Disraeli advised a newly elected member of Parliament. "But," the man replied, "my colleagues will wonder why I do not speak." "Better they should wonder why you do not speak," explained Disraeli, "than why you do."

The best way I know of to win an argument is to start by being in the right.
- *Lord Hailsham*

Man does not live by words alone, despite the fact that sometimes he has to eat them.
- *Adlai Stevenson*

. . . Rhetoric that rolls like a freight train over a bridge.
- *David Brinkley, NBC commentator, on speechmaking of union czar John L. Lewis*

When dealing with people, remember you are not dealing with creatures of logic, but with creatures of emotion.
- *Dale Carnegie*

Writers have two main problems. One is writer's block, when the words won't come at all, and the other is logorrhea, when the words come so fast that they can hardly get to the wastebasket in time.

- Cecilia Bartholomew

I took a course in speed reading and was able to read *War and Peace* in twenty minutes. It's about Russia.

- Woody Allen

The most stringent protection of free speech would not protect a man in falsely shouting fire in a theatre and causing a panic.

- Associate Justice Oliver Wendell Holmes, Jr.

In every fat book there is a thin book trying to get out.

The covers of this book are too far apart.

- Ambrose Bierce

Thank you for sending me a copy of your book. I'll waste no time reading it.

- Moses Hadas, in a letter

It's a strange world of language in which skating on thin ice can get you into hot water.

- Franklin P. Jones

I don't care what is written about me so long as it isn't true.

- Katharine Hepburn, on gossip and publicity

The American arrives in Paris with a few French phrases he has culled from a conversational guide or picked up from a friend who owns a beret. He speaks the sort of French that is really understood only by another American who also has just arrived in Paris.

- Fred Allen

How often do we search in vain for a word to bring a thought properly to paper? . . . Admire words well used: They are living monuments to the power of the minds of men.

One day, while shaving, Mark Twain cut himself. He recited his entire vocabulary of swear words. His wife, hoping to stun him, repeated all the swear words. Then, Twain turned and said, "You have the words, my dear, but you don't know the tune."

If I had kept my mouth shut, I wouldn't be here.

- Sign under a mounted fish

Talk is cheap because supply exceeds demand.

A word, once let out of the cage, cannot be whistled back again.

- Horace

Nobody talks much who doesn't say unwise things – things he did not mean to say. Talk, to me, is only spading up the ground for crops of thought. I can't answer for what will turn up.

- Oliver Wendell Holmes

Anjelica Huston remembers what it was like growing up as John Huston's daughter. Because of his intellect, he didn't suffer fools gladly. Once, at the dinner table, the subject of van Gogh came up. I said somewhat flippantly that I didn't like van Gogh. "You don't like van Gogh?" he countered. "Then name six of his paintings and tell me why you don't like them." I couldn't, of course. And he said, "Leave the room, and until you know what you're talking about, don't come back with your opinions to the dinner table."

- Mark Morrison in the Los Angeles Times Magazine

"When you shout obscenities, you downgrade the game, the public – and the way you're going to be remembered," says Rod Laver, the two-time winner of tennis' Grand Slam. Asked the worst thing he ever said to an umpire, Laver replies, "It would have to have been, 'Are you sure?'"

The trouble with most of us is that we would rather be ruined by praise then saved by criticism.

- Norman Vincent Peale

FAMILY LIFE

Quotes & Anecdotes
(marriage, children, home)

Good family life is never an accident but always an achievement by those who share it.
— *James H. S. Bossard*

The great man is he who does not lose his child's heart.
— *Mencius*

He that would the daughter win
Must with the mother first begin.
— *Old English proverb*

Perhaps the greatest blessing in marriage is that it lasts so long. The years, like the varying interests of each year, combine to buttress and enrich each other. Out of many shared years, one life. In a series of temporary relationships, one misses the ripening, gathering, harvesting joys, the deep, hard-won truths of marriage.
— *Richard C. Cabot*

Youth fades, love droops, the leaves of friendship fall;
a mother's secret hope outlives them all.
— *Oliver Wendell Holmes*

How can I teach, how can I save,
This child whose features are my own,
Whose feet run down the ways where
I have walked?
— *Michael Roberts*

Respect the child. Be not too much his parent. Trespass not on his solitude.
— *Ralph Waldo Emerson*

How selfhood begins with a walking away,
And love is proved in the letting go.
— *C. Day-Lewis*

Fatherhood is pretending the present you love the most is soap-on-a-rope.
— *Bill Cosby*

God knows that a mother needs fortitude and courage and tolerance and flexibility and patience and firmness and nearly every other brave aspect of the human soul. But because I happen to be a parent of almost fiercely maternal nature, I praise casualness. It seems to me the rarest of virtues. It is useful enough when children are small. It is important to the point of necessity when they are adolescents.
— *Phyllis McGinley*

After his introduction at Baylor University, President Lyndon Johnson remarked: "This is a moment I deeply wish my parents could have lived to share. My father would have enjoyed what you have so generously said of me — and my mother would have believed it."

Home is the one place in all this world where hearts are sure of each other. It is the place of confidence. It is the place where we tear off that mask of guarded and suspicious coldness which the world forces us to wear in self-defense, and where we pour out the unreserved communications of full and confiding hearts. It is the spot where expressions of tenderness gush out without any sensation of awkwardness and without any dread of ridicule.
— *Frederick W. Robertson*

Heaven lies about us in our infancy!
— *William Wordsworth*

My most brilliant achievement was my ability to be able to persuade my wife to marry me.
— *Winston Churchill*

The most important thing a father can do for his children is to love their mother.
— *Reverend Theodore Hesburgh, president, Notre Dame University*

I would like to have engraved inside every wedding band, "Be kind to one another." This is the Golden Rule of marriage, and the secret of making love last through the years.
— *Randolph Ray*

It is better to advise than upbraid, for the one corrects the erring; the other only convicts them.
— *Epictetus*

We must combine the toughness of the serpent and the softness of the dove, a tough mind and a tender heart.
— *Martin Luther King, Jr.*

Before I got married I had six theories about bringing up children; now I have six children, and no theories.
— *John Wilmot, Earl of Rochester*

Train up a child in the way he should go: and when he is old, he will not depart from it.
— *The Bible, Proverbs 22:6*

To bring up a child in the way he should go, travel that way yourself once in a while.
— *Josh Billings*

Children need models more than they need critics.
— *Joseph Joubert*

What harsh judges fathers are to all young men!
— *Terence, c. 180 B.C.*

A daughter: The companion, the friend, and confidant of her mother, and the object of a pleasure something like the love between the angels to her father.
— *Richard Steele, 1710*

The suspicious parent makes an artful child.
— *Thomas G. Halliburton*

The hardest part of raising children is teaching them to ride bicycles. A father can run beside the bicycle or stand yelling directions while the child falls. A shaky child on a bicycle for the first time needs both support and freedom. The realization that this is what the child will always need can hit hard.

— Sloan Wilson

For there is no friend like a sister
In calm or stormy weather;
To cheer one on the tedious way,
To fetch one if one goes astray,
To lift one if one totters down,
To strengthen whilst one stands.

— Christina Rossetti

As a boy handed his father a poor report card, he asked, "Father, what do you think is my trouble – heredity or environment?"

I have found the best way to give advice to your children is to find out what they want and then advise them to do it.

— Harry S Truman

Never lend your car to anyone to whom you have given birth.

— Erma Bombeck

Keeping house is like stringing beads with no knot in the end of the thread.

Children sweeten labors, but they make misfortunes more bitter. They increase the cares of life, but they mitigate the remembrance of death.

— Francis Bacon, 1597

Children are certain cares and uncertain comforts.

— English proverb

After all, what is a pedestrian? He is a man who has two cars – one being driven by his wife, the other by one of his children.

— Robert Bradbury

. . . A family . . . is a little kingdom, torn with factions and exposed to revolutions.

— Samuel Johnson, 1759

You may give them your love but not your thoughts, For they have their own thoughts. You may house their bodies but not their souls, For their souls dwell in the house of tomorrow, which you cannot visit, not even in your dreams. You may strive to be like them, but seek not to make them like you. For life goes not backward nor tarries with yesterday. You are the bows from which your children as living arrows are sent forth.

— Kahlil Gibran

The greatest thing in family life is to take a hint when a hint is intended – and not to take a hint when a hint isn't intended.

— Robert Frost

If you want your children to keep their feet on the ground, put some responsibility on their shoulders.

— Abigail Van Buren

The best years of a man's life are when the kids are old enough to shovel the snow but too young to drive the car.

Give a little love to a child and you will get a great deal back.

— John Ruskin

Love your children with all your hearts, love them enough to discipline them before it is too late . . . . Praise them for important things, even if you have to stretch them a bit. Praise them a lot. They live on it like bread and butter and they need it more than bread and butter.

— Lavina Christensen Fugal

A teacher, noticing how courteous and polite one of her pupils was, wished to praise her and teach the class a lesson. She asked, "Who taught you to be so polite?" The girl laughed and answered, "Really, no one. It just runs in our family."

If you must hold yourself up to your children as an object lesson . . . hold yourself up as an example and not as a warning.

— George Bernard Shaw

We think our fathers fools, so wise we grow;
Our wiser sons, no doubt will think us so.

— Alexander Pope

When I was a boy of fourteen, my father was so ignorant I could hardly stand to have the old man around. But when I got to twenty-one, I was astonished at how much he had learned in seven years.

— Mark Twain

Mothers are the hardest to forgive;
Life is the gift they long to give us . . .

The commonest fallacy among women is that simply having children makes them a mother – which is as absurd as believing that having a piano makes one a musician.

— Sydney J. Harris

The most valuable gift you can give your family is a good example.

I think parents should forget the genius bit – what you want is a human being, a mensch, not a genius.

— Jerome Bruner

If you have never been hated by your child, you have never been a parent.

— Bette Davis

If you bungle raising your children, I don't think whatever else you do well matters very much.

— Jacqueline Kennedy Onassis

No success can compensate for failure in the home.

— David O. McKay

The happiest moments of my life have been the few which I have passed at home in the bosom of my family.

— Thomas Jefferson

A woman, speaking about her family's adjustment to having had to stay home more in order to take care of her dying father, said, " . . . You know what? It made us realize that we were hardly ever home together before."

Above all, I would teach him to tell the truth . . . Truth telling, I have found, is the key to responsible citizenship. The thousands of criminals I have seen in 40 years of law enforcement have had one thing in common: every single one was a liar.

> – *J. Edgar Hoover, "What I Would Tell A Son."*

Speaking of his ancestry, Lincoln once remarked, "I don't know who my grandfather was, but I am much more concerned to know what his grandson will be."

I can't help detesting my relations. I suppose it comes from the fact that none of us can stand other people having the same faults as ourselves.

> – *Oscar Wilde*

I never reprimand a boy in the evening – darkness and a troubled mind are a poor combination.

> – *Frank Boyden*

Perhaps host and guest is really the happiest relation for father and son.

> – *Evelyn Waugh*

Certainly the time when the young are to be seen and not heard is gone in America – and gone for good.

> – *Richard M. Nixon*

We cannot always build the future for our youth, but we can build our youth for the future.

> – *Franklin D. Roosevelt*

Children today are tyrants. They contradict their parents, gobble their food, and tyrannize their teachers.

> – *Socrates, c. 420 B.C.*

There are times when parenthood seems nothing but feeding the mouth that bites you.

> – *Peter de Vries*

Parenting is disruptive, with the possibility of harm, but also the possibility of growth.

> – *Frederick Grossman*

You never can tell about a marriage from the outside, said the old philosopher. Some couples hold hands because they're afraid that if they let go they'd kill each other.

Before marriage, a man will lie awake thinking about something you said; after marriage, he'll fall asleep before you finish saying it.

> – *Helen Rowland*

The most difficult year of marriage is the one you're in.

> – *Franklin P. Jones*

A successful marriage is an edifice that must be rebuilt every day.

> – *Andre Maurois*

Perhaps the greatest social service that can be rendered by anybody . . . to mankind is to bring up a family. But . . . because there is nothing to sell, there is a very general disposition to regard a married woman's work as no work at all, and to take it as a matter of course that she should not be paid for it.

> – *George Bernard Shaw*

What a father says to his children is not heard by the world, but it will be heard by posterity.

> – *Jean Paul Richter*

A child is fed with milk and praise.

> – *Mary Lamb*

Home is a place where, when you go there, They have to take you in.

> – *Robert Frost*

A man's home may seem to be his castle on the outside; inside, it is more often his nursery.

> – *Clare Boothe Luce*

Peace, like charity, begins at home.

> – *Franklin D. Roosevelt*

The father is always a Republican toward his son, and his mother's always a Democrat.

> – *Robert Frost*

Teenage means perpetual emotion.

He has quit the awkward stage; he is out of he teens.

> – *Terence, 166 B.C.*

Four is too big for his breeches,
Knows infinitely more than his mother,
Four is a matinee idol
To Two-and-a-Half, his brother.
Four is a lyric composer,
Raconteur extraordinaire,
Four gets away with murder,
Out of line, and into hair.
Where Four is, there dirt is also,
And nails and lengths of twine,
Four is Mr. Fix-it
And all of his tools are mine.
Four barges into everything
(Hearts, too) without a knock.
Four will be five on the twelfth of July,
And I wish I could stop the clock.

> – *Elsie Gibbs*

God sends children to enlarge our hearts, and to make us unselfish and full of kindly sympathies and affections.

> – *Mary Howitt*

Television is the third parent.

> – *Buckminster Fuller*

Television has proved that people will look at anything rather than each other.

> – *Ann Landers*

On Thanksgiving Day all over America, families sit down to dinner at the same moment – halftime.

There's always room for improvement, you know – it's the biggest room in the house.
— *Louise Heath Leber*

. . . Perhaps a child who is fussed over gets a feeling of destiny; he thinks he is in the world for something important and it gives him drive and confidence.
— *Dr. Benjamin Spock*

Could I climb to the highest place in Athens, I would lift my voice and proclaim, "Fellow citizens, why do you turn and scrape every stone to gather wealth and take so little care of your children to whom one day you must relinquish it all."
— *Socrates, about 420 B.C.*

It is a wise father that knows his own child.
— *William Shakespeare, The Merchant of Venice*

Men are what their mothers made them.
— *Ralph Waldo Emerson*

Parents who are afraid to put their foot down usually have children who step on their toes.
— *Fortune-cookie proverb*

The universal language of children is called "gimme," otherwise known as "I wanna."

As is the mother, so is her daughter.
— *The Bible, Ezekiel 16:44*

There is something frightful in the way in which not only characteristic qualities, but particular manifestations of them, are repeated from generation to generation.
— *Oliver Wendell Holmes*

If you know his father and grandfather you may trust his son.
— *Moroccan proverb*

"If . . . "
If a child lives with criticism,
  He learns to condemn.
If a child lives with hostility,
  He learns to fight.
If a child lives with ridicule,
  He learns to be shy.
If a child lives with shame,
  He learns to feel guilty.
If a child lives with tolerance,
  He learns to be patient.
If a child lives with encouragement,
  He learns confidence.
If a child lives with praise,
  He learns to appreciate.
If a child lives with fairness,
  He learns justice.
If a child lives with security,
  He learns to have faith.
If a child lives with approval,
  He learns to like himself.

If a child lives with acceptance and friendship,
  He learns to find love in the world.
— *Dorothy Law Nolte*

A child tells in the street what its father and mother say at home.
— *The Talmud*

I attribute my success in life to the moral, intellectual and physical education which I received from my mother.
— *George Washington*

The best way to keep children home is to make the home a pleasant atmosphere – and let the air out of the tires.
— *Dorothy Parker*

A parent's training starts when that future parent is still a child.

I wish I would have put as much emotion into my relationships with my mom and dad as I do now in my memories of them. We should pay more attention when we are making our memories. If we did, we wouldn't have so many regrets when all we have is memories.
— *Elderly woman*

"Cat's in the Cradle"
A child arrived just the other day,
He came to the world in the usual way.
But there were planes to catch and bills to pay.
He learned to walk while I was away.
He was talkin' before I knew
And as he grew he was saying:
"I'm gonna be like you, Dad.
You know I'm gonna be like you."

Well my son turned ten just the other day.
He said, "Thanks for the ball, Dad, let's play.
Can you teach me to throw?"
I said, "Not today; I got a lot to do – "
He said, "That's O.K." and he walked away.
He walked away, but his smile never dimmed.
It said, I'm gonna be like him, yeah.
You know, I'm gonna be like him.

Well, I've long since retired and my son's moved away.
I called him up just the other day.
I said, "I'd like to see you if you don't mind."
He said he'd love to if he could find the time.
"You see, my new job is a hassle and the kids have the flu,
But it's sure nice talking to you, Dad,
It's been sure nice talking to you."
And as he hung up the phone it occurred to me
He'd grown up just like me;
My boy was just like me.
— *Story Songs Ltd. (sung by Harry Chapin)*

There are three degrees of filial piety. The highest is being a credit to our parents, the second is not disgracing them; the lowest is being able simply to support them.
— *Confucius*

Parents should be their children's parents first, their children's friends later.

Most of all the other beautiful things in life come by twos and threes, by dozens and hundreds. Plenty of roses, stars, sunsets, rainbows, brothers and sisters, aunts and cousins, but only one mother in the whole world.
— *Kate Douglas Wiggin*

The family is one of nature's masterpieces.
— *George Santayana*

When I was young, my parents told me what to do; now that I am old, my children tell me what to do. I wonder when I will be able to do what I want to do.

One of the mysteries of life is how the boy who wasn't good enough to marry the daughter can be the father of the smartest grandchild in the world.

Keep your eyes wide open before marriage, half shut afterwards.
— *Benjamin Franklin*

A man in love is incomplete until he has married. Then he is finished.
— *Zsa Zsa Gabor*

We never know the love of our parents for us till we have become parents.
— *Henry Ward Beecher*

Nobody's family can hang out the sign, "Nothing the matter here."
— *Chinese proverb*

Science has established two facts meaningful for human welfare: first, the foundation of the structure of human personality is laid down in early childhood; and second, the chief engineer in charge of this construction is the family.
— *Meyer Francis Nimkoff*

Children can have no better inheritance than believing parents. Religion can become real in the midst of the family as in practically no other way. Many of us have inherited great riches from our parents — the bank account of their personal faith and family prayers.
— *Nels F.S. Ferre*

Love is an act of endless forgiveness, a tender look which becomes a habit.
— *Peter Ustinov*

A lady of 47 who has been married 27 years and has six children knows what love really is and once described it for me like this: "Love is what you've been through with somebody."
— *James Thurber*

A suburban mother's role is to deliver children obstetrically once, and by car for ever after.
— *Peter de Vries*

. . . If either side feels aggrieved, comfort rests in the knowledge that time will eventually even all scores. For yesterday's sittee is today's sitter. Today's employer of a sitter is tomorrow's parent of a sitter. And the sitter herself, incredibly soon, will have her own child to be sat for.
— *Jean Libman Block*

Security is when I'm very much in love with somebody extraordinary who loves me back.
— *Shelley Winters*

Some women work so hard to make good husbands that they never manage to make good wives.

My wife and I tried breakfast together, but we had to stop or our marriage would have been wrecked.
— *Winston Churchill*

There are two stages for parents — when your children ask all the questions and when they think they know all the answers.

In loco parentis — Latin for "Children can drive their parents crazy."

I never thought that you should be rewarded for the greatest privilege in life.
— *May Robert Coker, on being named Mother of the Year, 1958*

Marriage may be compared to a cage: the birds outside frantic to get in and those inside frantic to get out.
— *Montaigne, 1588*

One good turn gets most of the blanket.
— *Ellenberg*

The only thing worse that a husband who never notices what you cook or what you wear, is a husband who always notices what you cook and what you wear.
— *Sandra Litoff*

Marriage is not just spiritual communion and passionate embraces; marriage is also three meals a day, sharing the workload and remembering to carry out the trash.
— *Dr. Joyce Brothers*

A marriage without conflicts is almost as inconceivable as a nation without crises.
— *Andre Maurois*

A man travels the world over in search of what he needs, and returns home to find it.
— *George Moore*

The two things children wear out are clothes and parents.

Never grow a wishbone, daughter, where your backbone ought to be.
— *Clementine Paddleford, quoting advice from her mother*

Parents are wise to overlook seemingly disrespectful outbursts from time to time . . . The point must get across the idea that "I love you always, but sometimes I do not love your behavior."
— *Amy Vanderbilt, on teenagers*

The greatest aid to adult education is children.
— *Charlie T. Jones and Bob Phillips*

A boy is a magical creature – you can lock him out of your workshop, but you can't lock him out of your heart. You can get him out of your study, but you can't get him out of your mind. Might as well give up – he is your captor, your jailer, your boss, and your master – a freckled-faced, pint-sized, cat-chasing bundle of noise. But when you come home at night with only the shattered pieces of your hopes and dreams he can mend them like new with two magic words – "Hi, Dad!"

Little girls are the nicest things that happen to people. They are born with a little bit of angelshine about them and though it wears thin sometimes there is always enough left to lasso your heart – even when they are sitting in the mud, or crying temperamental tears, or parading up the street in mother's best clothes.

– Alan Beck

To know after absence the familiar street and road and village and house is to know again the satisfaction of home.

– Hal Borland

Children have never been good at listening to their elders, but they have never failed to imitate them.

– James Baldwin

Example is not the main thing in influencing others. It is the only thing.

– Albert Schweitzer

Teach your child to hold his tongue; he'll learn fast enough to speak.

– Benjamin Franklin

All our dreams can come true – if we have the courage to pursue them.

– Walt Disney

Let our children grow tall and some taller than others if they have it in them to do so.

– Margaret Thatcher

Honest differences are often a healthy sign of progress.

– Mahatma Gandhi

The time to repair the roof is when the sun is shining.

– John F. Kennedy

We can do no great things – only small things with great love.

– Mother Teresa

To maintain a joyful family requires much from both the parents and the children. Each member of the family has to become, in a special way, the servant of the others.

– Pope John Paul II

INTEGRITY

Quotes & Anecdotes
(character, service, loyalty)

We can't put our faults behind us until we face them.

Father taught us that opportunity and responsibility go hand in hand. I think we all act on that principle; on the basic human impulse that makes a man want to make the best of what's in him and what's been given him.
- Laurence Rockefeller

How many cares one loses when one decides not to be something, but to be someone.
- Gabrielle "Coco" Chanel

All that is essential for the triumph of evil is that good men do nothing.
- Edmund Burke

It's a matter of having principles. It's easy to have principles when you're rich. The important thing is to have principles when you're poor.
- Ray Kroc

The measure of a man's real character is what he would do if he knew he would never be found out.
- Thomas Macaulay

There's one way to find out if a man is honest — ask him. If he says "yes," you know he is crooked.
- Groucho Marx

They go forth [into the world] with well-developed bodies, fairly developed minds and undeveloped hearts. An undeveloped heart — not a cold one. The difference is important . . .
- E. M. Forster, novelist, on British public school boys

. . . Of those to whom much is given, much is required. And when at some future date the high court of history sits in judgment on each one of us — recording whether in our brief span of service we fulfilled our responsibilities to the state — our success or failure, in whatever office we may hold, will be measured by the answers to four questions — were we truly men of courage . . . were we truly men of judgment . . . were we truly men of integrity . . . were we truly men of dedication?
- John F. Kennedy

The herd may graze where it pleases or stampede where it pleases, but he who lives the adventurous life will remain unafraid when he finds himself alone.
- Raymond B. Fosdick

The world's best reformers are those who begin on themselves.

Think positively about yourself, keep your thoughts and your actions clean, ask God who made you to keep on remaking you.
- Norman Vincent Peale

The wicked flee when no man pursueth; but the righteous are bold as a lion.
- The Bible, Proverbs 28:1

This above all: to thine own self be true, And it must follow, as the night the day, Thou canst not then be false to any man.
- William Shakespeare

Let unswerving integrity ever be your watchword.
- Bernard Baruch, recalling his "most enduring lesson" from his father

Our scientific power has outrun our spiritual power. We have guided missiles and misguided men.
- Martin Luther King, Jr.

I do not pray for success. I ask for faithfulness.
- Mother Teresa

God frees our souls, not from service, not from duty, but into service and into duty, and he who mistakes the purpose of his freedom mistakes the character of his freedom. He who thinks that he is being released from the work, and not set free in order that he may accomplish that work, mistakes the condition into which his soul is invited to enter.
- Phillips Brooks

Beloved Pan, and all ye other gods who haunt this place, give me beauty in the inward soul; and may the outward and inward be at one.
- Socrates

Do something for somebody every day for which you do not get paid.
- Albert Schweitzer

Our humanity were a poor thing were it not for the divinity that stirs within us.
- Francis Bacon

Let then our first act every morning be to make the following resolve for the day: I shall not fear anyone on earth. I shall fear only God. I shall not bear ill will toward anyone. I shall not submit to injustice from anyone. I shall conquer untruth by truth. And in resisting untruth I shall put up with all suffering.
- Mahatma Gandhi

Men are valued, not for what they are, but for what they seem to be.
- E.G. Bulwer-Lytton, 1840

Ye are like whited sepulchers, which indeed appear beautiful outward, but are within full of dead men's bones.
- The Bible, Matthew 23:27

One man practicing sportsmanship is far better than a hundred teaching it.
- Knute Rockne

Nearly all men can stand adversity, but if you want to test a man's character, give him power.
- Abraham Lincoln

The more he talked of his honor the faster we counted our spoons.
- Ralph Waldo Emerson

The ability to think straight, some knowledge of the past, some vision of the future, some skill to do useful service, some urge to fit that service into the well-being of the community – these are the most vital things education must try to produce. If we can achieve them in the citizens of our land, then . . . we shall have brought to America the wisdom and the courage to match her destiny.
- Virginia Gildersleeve

A man has made at least a start on discovering the meaning of human life when he plants shade trees under which he knows full well he will never sit.
- Elton Trueblood

Abou Ben Adhem (may his tribe increase!)
Awoke one night from a deep dream of peace,
And saw within the moonlight in his room,
Making it rich and like a lily in bloom,
An angel writing in a book of gold;
Exceeding peace had made Ben Adhem bold,
And to the Presence in the room he said,
"What writest thou?" The vision raised its head,
And with a look made of all sweet accord,
Answered, "The names of those who love the Lord."
"And is mine one?" said Abou. "Nay, not so,"
Replied the angel. Abou spoke more low,
But cheerily still, and said, "I pray thee, then,
Write me as one that loves his fellow-men.
The angel wrote, and vanished. The next night
It came again with a great wakening light,
And showed the names whom love of God had blessed;
And, lo! Ben Adhem's name led all the rest!
- Leigh Hunt

Heaven will be inherited by every man who has heaven in his soul.
- Confucius

The farther a man knows himself to be from perfection, the nearer he is to it.
- Gerard Groote

Courage is the first of human qualities because it is the quality which guarantees all the others.
- Winston Churchill

The anger of a good man lasts an instant; that of a meddler two hours; that of a base man a day and a night; and that of a great sinner until death.
- Sanskrit proverb

The size of a man can be measured by the size of the thing that makes him angry.
- J. Kenfield Morley

Beautiful thoughts hardly bring us to God until they are acted upon. No one can have a true idea of right until he does it.
- William R. Inge

So long as a man is angry he can't be in the right.
- Chinese proverb

The best way to break a habit is to drop it.
- Bartig

Conviction is worthless unless it is converted into conduct.
- Thomas Carlyle

U-turn if you want to. This lady's not for turning.
- Margaret Thatcher

In a large sense we cannot dedicate, we cannot hallow this ground. The brave men, living and dead, who struggled here, have consecrated it far above our poor power to add or detract.
- Abraham Lincoln: Gettysburg Address, 1863

Good habits are not made on birthdays, nor Christian character at the new year. The workshop of character is everyday life. The uneventful and commonplace hour is where the battle is lost or won.
- Maltbie D. Babcock

Little white lies are for golfers.

Courage and cowardice are antithetical. Courage is an inner resolution to go forward in spite of obstacles and frightening situations; cowardice is a submissive surrender to circumstance. Courage breeds creative self-affirmation; cowardice produces destructive self-abnegation. Courage faces fear and thereby masters it; cowardice represses fear and is thereby mastered by it. Courageous men never lose the zest for living even though their life situation is zestless; cowardly men, overwhelmed by the uncertainties of life, lose the will to live. We must constantly build dykes of courage to hold back the flood of fear.
- Martin Luther King, Jr.

No man is free who is not master of himself.
- Epictetus

The ablest man I ever met is the man you think you are.

- Franklin D. Roosevelt

He who thinks he has no faults – has one.

When it come to giving, some people stop at nothing.

- Sheetz

Everyman has three friends – children, money, and his good deeds. When the time comes for him to leave the world he calls upon his children, who reply, "Don't you know that no one can conquer death?" Then he calls upon his money, saying, "Day and night I have worked for you, save me now." The money replies, "Wealth cannot deliver you from death." He next calls on his good deeds and they reply "Go in peace. By the time you arrive in the next world, we will be there before you to offer you help."

- The Talmud

After Benjamin Franklin had received a letter thanking him for having done a kindness, he replied: "As to the kindness you mention, I wish I could have been of more service to you than I have been, but if I had, the only thanks that I should desire are that you would always be ready to service any other person that may need your assistance, and so let good offices go around, for mankind are all of a family. As for my own part, when I am employed in serving others I do not look upon myself as conferring favors but paying debts "

I cannot tell you how much I love to play for people. Would you believe it – sometimes when I sit down to practice and there is no one else in the room, I have to stifle an impulse to ring for the elevator man and offer him money to come in and hear me.

- Arthur Rubenstein

A good example is the best sermon.

- Herbert J. Taylor

Anger is never without a reason, but seldom with a good one.

- Benjamin Franklin

Diplomats are useful only in fair weather. As soon as it rains they drown in every drop.

- Charles de Gaulle

'Tis better to suffer wrong than do it.

- Thomas Fuller

Character is something each one of us must build for himself, out of the laws of God and nature, the examples of others, and – most of all – out of the trials and errors of daily life. Character is the total of thousands of small daily strivings to live up to the best that is in us. Character is the final decision to reject whatever is demeaning to oneself or to others and with confidence and honesty to choose the right.

- General Arthur G. Trudeau

The question is not what man can scorn, or disparage, or find fault with, but what he can love, and value, and appreciate.

- John Ruskin

Youth is not entirely a time of life; it is a state of mind. Nobody grows old by merely living a number of years. People grow old by deserting their ideals. You are as young as your faith, as old as your doubt; as young as your self-confidence, as old as your fear; as young as your hope, as old as your despair.

- Douglas MacArthur

Always fall in with what you're asked to accept. Take what is given, and make it over your way. My aim in life has always been to hold my own with whatever's going. Not against: with.

- Robert Frost

We live in a society where the sin is getting caught.

I've helped some people.

- Anna Mary "Grandma" Moses' reply at 93 when asked what she was proudest of in her life

Loyalty is an animal instinct; we can take lessons in it from dogs.

In spite of everything, I still believe that people are really good at heart.

- Anne Frank, Dutch-Jewish teenage diarist, 1944

I've never signed a contract, so I never have a deadline. A deadline's an unnerving thing. I just finished a book, and if the publisher doesn't like it that's his privilege. There've been many, many rejections. If you want to write in your own way, that's the chance you take.

- Marchette Chute

During the Occupation, but before his imprisonment, King Christian X of Denmark noticed a Nazi flag flying over a Danish public building. He called the German commandant and demanded that the flag be immediately removed. The commandant refused. "Then a soldier will go and take it down," said the king. "He will be shot," replied the commandant. "I think not," retorted the king, "for I shall be the soldier." The flag was removed.

Blessed are those who can give without remembering and take without forgetting.

- Elizabeth Bibesco

Gratitude is not only the greatest of virtues, but the parent of all others.

- Cicero, 54 B.C.

Thanks is sometimes a mask for ingratitude. True gratitude is expressed in deeds rather than words.

Life is an exciting business and most exciting when it is lived for others.
- *Helen Keller*

There may be times when we are powerless to prevent injustice, but there must never be a time when we fail to protest.
- *Elie Wiesel*

The entire object of true education is to make people not merely to do the right things, but to enjoy them; not merely industrious, but to love industry; not merely learned, but to love knowledge; not merely pure, but to love purity; not merely just, but to hunger and thirst after justice.
- *John Ruskin*

We must have many Lincoln-hearted men.
- *Vachel Lindsay*

As for charity, it is a matter in which the immediate effect on the persons directly concerned, and the ultimate consequence to the general good, are apt to be at complete war with one another.
- *John Stuart Mill*

Civilization is just a slow process of learning to be kind.
- *Charles L. Lucas*

The weak can never forgive. Forgiveness is the attribute of the strong . . . Hatred can be overcome only by love.
- *Mahatma Gandhi*

When a man blames others for his failures, it's a good idea to credit others with his successes.
-*Howard W. Newton*

A gentleman is one who thinks more of other people's feelings than of his own rights; and more of other people's rights than of his own feelings.
- *Matthew Henry Buckham*

Men show their characters in nothing more clearly than in what they think laughable.
- *Goethe*

I have four things to learn in life: To think clearly without hurry or confusion; To love everybody sincerely; To act in everything with the highest motives; To trust in God unhesitatingly.
- *Albert Schweitzer*

It is a grand mistake to think of being great without goodness; and I pronounce it as certain that there was never yet a truly great man that was not at the same time truly virtuous.
- *Benjamin Franklin*

A man can stand a lot as long as he can stand himself. He can live without hope, without friends, without books, even without music, as long as he can listen to his own thoughts.
- *Axel Munthe*

A saint is one who makes goodness attractive.
- *Laurence Housman*

A test of any man's character is how he takes his praise.

Not that I would not, if I could, be both handsome and well-dressed and a great athlete, and make a million a year, be a wit, a bon vivant, and a lady killer, as well as a philosopher, a philanthropist, a statesman, warrior, and African explorer, as well as a "tone poet" and a saint. The thing is simply impossible. The millionaire's work would run counter to the saint's; the bon vivant and the philanthropist would trip each other up; the philosopher and the lady killer could not well keep house in the same tenement . . .
- *William James*

Right is more precious than peace.
- *Woodrow Wilson*

If all that Americans want is security they can go to prison. They'll have enough to eat, a bed and a roof over their heads. But if an American wants to preserve his dignity and his equality as a human being, he must not bow his neck to any dictorial government.
- *Dwight D. Eisenhower*

He errs as other men do, but errs with integrity.
- *Thomas Jefferson, speaking of George Washington*

A politician thinks of the next election – a statesman, of the next generation.
- *James Freeman Clarke*

"The worst thing that can happen to a youngster starting school," said the lawyer, "is to be caught cheating." "Not at all," said the clergyman, "the worst thing at the start of a person's life is to cheat and not get caught."

We will be remembered not for the power of our weapons but for the power of our compassion, our dedication to human welfare.
- *Hubert H. Humphrey*

Morality is a personal thing. Each of us, through the teachings of our childhood and our experience with others, has developed an unwritten list of criteria of behavior.

Too frequently I find that a person's morality is a code by which he believes others should perform toward him, rather than a code guiding his behavior toward others. It is our actual day-to-day behavior that determines and defines our morality.

We have grasped the mystery of the atom and rejected the Sermon on the Mount.

- General Omar Bradley

If a man be gracious, and courteous to strangers, it shows he is a citizen of the world . . .

- Sir Francis Bacon, 1597

An old grouch, about to enter a building, found that the door was being held open for him, with considerable effort, by a little boy. "Never mind that," said the old grouch, "I don't need your help." The little boy smiled up at him and said, "You're welcome."

The roots of responsibility run out to the ends of the earth and we can no more isolate our consciences from world issues than we can fence off our oyster beds from the tides of the ocean.

- Ralph W. Sockman

A people that values its privileges above its principles soon loses both.

- Dwight D. Eisenhower

Men make counterfeit money; in many more cases, money makes counterfeit men.

- Sydney J. Harris

Knowing what's right doesn't mean much unless you do what's right.

There are a large number of well-meaning ambassadors . . . what I call the pink-tea type, who merely reside in the service instead of working in the service.

- Theodore Roosevelt

You will never be sorry —
for thinking before acting,
for hearing before judging,
for forgiving your enemies,
for being candid and frank,
for helping a fallen brother,
for being honest in business,
for thinking before speaking,
for being loyal to your church,
for standing by your principles,
for stopping your ears to gossip,
for bridling a slanderous tongue,
for harboring only pure thoughts,
for sympathizing with the afflicted,
for being courteous and kind to all.

- Anonymous

The art of being yourself at your best is the art of unfolding your personality into the man you want to be . . . Be gentle with yourself, learn to love yourself, to forgive yourself, for only as we have the right attitude toward ourselves can we have the right attitude toward others.

- Wilfred Peterson

Non-violence and truth are inseparable and presuppose one another. There is no god higher than truth.

- Mahatma Gandhi

There are those who give little of the much they have – and they give it for recognition and their hidden desire makes their gifts unwholesome.
And there are those who have little and give it all.
These are the believers in life and the bounty of life, and their coffer is never empty.
There are those who give with joy, and that joy is their reward. And there are those who give with pain, and that pain is their baptism.
And there are those who give and know not pain in giving, nor do they seek joy, nor give with mindfulness of virtue; They give as in yonder valley the myrtle breathes its fragrance into space. Through the hands of such as these God speaks, and from behind their eyes He smiles upon the earth.

- Kahlil Gibran

Enlightened loyalty requires that each citizen take the trouble to learn about, to discuss, to think through, the crucial issues of our time.

- Lyndon B. Johnson

I don't want any yes-men around me. I want everybody to tell me the truth even if it costs them their jobs.

- Samuel Goldwyn

I decline to accept the end of man. It is easy enough to say that man is immortal simply because he will endure: that when the last ding-dong of doom has clanged and faded from the vast worthless rock hanging tideless in the last red and dying evening, that even then there will still be one more sound: that of his puny inexhaustible voice, still talking. I refuse to accept this, I believe that man will not merely endure: he will prevail. He is immortal, not because he alone among creatures has an inexhaustible voice, but because he has a soul, a spirit capable of compassion and sacrifice and endurance.

- William Faulkner, 1962 Nobel Prize
acceptance speech

My kind of loyalty was loyalty to one's country, not to its institutions or its office-holders.

- Mark Twain

. . . In about the same degree as you are helpful, you will be happy.

- Karl Reiland

We are a nation of many nationalities, many races, many religions – bound together by a single unity, the unity of freedom and equality.

- Franklin D. Roosevelt

One of the worst things that can happen in life is to win a bet on a horse at an early age.

- Danny McGoorty

Presidents learn – perhaps sooner than others – that our destiny is fashioned by what all of us do, by the deeds and desires of each citizen, as one tiny drop of water after another ultimately makes a big river.

- Lyndon B. Johnson

Liberty is not free; it is paid for with good citizenship.

And so, my fellow Americans: ask not what your country can do for you – ask what you can do for your country.

- John F. Kennedy

Ask not what your country can do for you, but rather what you can do for your country.

- Marcus Tullius Cicero, Roman orator and statesman, 63 B.C.

Self-respect cannot be hunted. It cannot be purchased. It is never for sale. It cannot be fabricated out of public relations. It comes to us when we are alone, in quiet moments, in quiet places, when we suddenly realize that, knowing the good, we have done it; knowing the beautiful, we have served it; knowing the truth, we have spoken it.

- Whitney Griswold, president, Yale University

My importance to the world is relatively small. On the other hand, my importance to myself is tremendous. I am all I have to work with, to play with, to suffer and to enjoy. It is not the eyes of others that I am wary of, but my own. I do not intend to let myself down more that I can possibly help, and I find that the fewer illusions I have about myself or the world around me, the better company I am for myself.

- Noel Coward

It takes good manners to put up with bad ones.

To let [yourself] be bound by a duty from the moment you see it approaching is a part of the integrity that alone justifies responsibility.

- Dag Hammarskjold, UN Secretary General

Thomas Jefferson's Decalogue
I. Never put off till tomorrow what you can do today.
II. Never trouble another for what you can do yourself.
III. Never spend your money before you have it.
IV. Never buy what you do not want . . . because it is cheap; it will be dear to you.
V. Pride costs us more than hunger, thirst, and cold.
VI. We never repent of having eaten too little.
VII. Nothing is troublesome that we do willingly.
VIII. How much pain have cost us the evils which have never happened.
IX. Take things always by their smooth handle.
X. When angry, count ten before you speak; if very angry, a hundred.

The foundation of morality is to have done, once and for all, with lying.

- T.H. Huxley

The tumult and the shouting dies;
the captains and the kings depart:
still stands thine ancient sacrifice,
an humble and a contrite heart.
Lord God of hosts, be with us yet,
Lest we forget – lest we forget!

- Rudyard Kipling

Not what we give, but what we share, –
For the gift without the giver is bare;
Who gives himself with his alms feeds three, –
Himself, his hungering neighbor, and Me.

- James Russell Lowell

Heroism is the brilliant triumph of the soul over the flesh: that is to say, over fear: fear of poverty, of suffering, of calumny, of sickness, of isolation, and of death.

- H. F. Amiel, 1849

The strongest man in the world is he who stands alone.

- Henrik Ibsen

Happy is he who has finished the labors of life.

- Euripides, 5th century B.C.

Rare is the person who can weigh the faults of others without his thumb on the scale.

- Byron Langfeld

The most difficult thing in the world is to know how to do a thing and to watch someone else doing it wrong, without commenting.

- T.H. White

Marie Antoinette's last words, reputedly spoken to her executioner on whose foot she had accidently stepped: "I beg your pardon. I did not do it on purpose."

Twelve Things To Remember
1. The value of time
2. The success of perseverance
3. The pleasure of working
4. The dignity of simplicity
5. The worth of character
6. The power of kindness
7. The influence of example
8. The obligation of duty
9. The wisdom of economy
10. The virtue of patience
11. The improvement of talent
12. The joy of originating.

- Anonymous

Life is what we are alive to. It is not length but breadth. To be alive only to appetite, pleasure, pride, money-making, and not to goodness, kindness, purity, love, history, poetry, music, flowers, stars, God, and eternal hope is to be all but dead.

- Maltbie D. Babcock

HAPPINESS

Quotes & Anecdotes
(satisfaction, contentment, confidence, life's joys)

Happiness is essentially a state of going somewhere, wholeheartedly, one-directionally, without regret or reservation.

- William H. Sheldon

If you can't change facts, try bending your attitude.

Wear a smile and have friends: wear a scowl and have wrinkles.

- George Eliot

Happiness comes of the capacity to feel deeply, to enjoy simply, to think freely, to risk life, to be needed.

- Storm Jameson

We cannot get grace from gadgets. In the bakelite house of the future, the dishes may not break, but the heart can. Even a man with ten shower baths may find life flat, stale and unprofitable.

- J.B. Priestley

Nobody can make you feel inferior without your consent.

- Eleanor Roosevelt

Laugh at yourself first, before anyone else can.

- Elsa Maxwell

Just think how happy you'd be if you lost everything you have right now – and then got it back again.

To be without some of the things you want is an indispensable part of happiness.

- Bertrand Russell

The happiest people are those who discover that what they should be doing and what they are doing are the same thing.

No one could be more unhappy than a man who has never known affliction.

- Ascribed to Demetrius Phalerens, c. 300 B.C.

It is a kind of happiness to know to what extent we may be unhappy.

- La Rochefoucauld, 1665

It is wrong to assume that men of immense wealth are always happy.

- John D. Rockefeller, Sr.

Walter Hagen, the highly successful golf professional, offered his secret of success: "You're here for only a short visit, so don't hurry, don't worry, and be sure to smell the flowers along the way."

Some cause happiness wherever they go; others whenever they go.

Laugh and the world laughs with you; Weep and you weep alone . . .

- Ella Wheeler Wilcox, 1883

This is the true joy in life, the being used for a purpose recognized by yourself as a mighty one; the being thoroughly worn out before you are thrown on the scrap heap; the being a force of Nature instead of a feverish selfish little clod of ailments and grievances complaining that the world will not devote itself to making you happy.

- George Bernard Shaw

Laughter is more contagious than tears.

You can't feel down in the mouth with the corners up.

If you are happy you can always learn to dance.

- Balinese Saying

Where ambition ends happiness begins.

- Hungarian proverb

A merry heart doeth good like a medicine . . .

- The Bible, Proverbs 17:22

Some people are happy remembering the past, and some happy forgetting it.

There is no duty we so much underrate, as the duty of being happy.

- Robert Louis Stevenson

The secret of happiness is this: let your interests be as wide as possible, and let your reactions to the things and persons that interest you be as far as possible friendly rather than hostile.

- Bertrand Russell

Success is getting what you want; happiness is wanting what you get.

- Dale Carnegie

The essentials for happiness are: Something to do, someone to love, and something to hope for.

What life means to us is determined not so much by what life brings to us as by the attitude we bring to life; not so much by what happens to us as by our reaction to what happens.

- Lewis L. Dunnington

People are constantly clamoring for the joy of life. As for me, I find the joy of life in the hard and cruel battle of life – to learn something is a joy to me.

- August Strindberg

It is not easy to find happiness in ourselves and it is not possible to find it elsewhere.

- Agnes Repplier

The hands of those I meet are dumbly eloquent to me. I have met people so empty of joy that when I clasped their frosty fingertips it seemed as if I were shaking hands with a northeast storm. Others there are whose hands have sunbeams in them, so that their grasp warms my heart. It may be only the clinging touch of a child's hand, but there is as much potential sunshine in it for me as there is in a loving glance for others.

- Helen Keller

If something is wrong, fix it if you can. But train yourself not to worry. Worry never fixes anything.

- Mrs. Ernest Hemingway

Happiness is possible only when one is busy. The body must toil, the mind must be occupied, and the heart must be satisfied.

Writing music is my one and only passion and joy.
- Mozart, 1777

Happiness consists in activity – it is a running stream, not a stagnant pool.
- John Mason Good

There must be more to life than having everything.
- Maurice Sendak, children's book author and illustrator

The Triple-A formula for experiencing happiness begins by accepting the moment, appreciating it, and adapting to its opportunities.

One of the most tragic things I know about human nature is that all of us tend to put off living. We are all dreaming of some magical rose garden over the horizon instead of enjoying the roses that are blooming outside our windows today.
- Dale Carnegie

Happiness is good health and a bad memory.
- Ingrid Bergman

There are as many nights as days, and the one is just as long as the other in the year's course. Even a happy life cannot be without a measure of darkness, and the word "happy" would lose its meaning if it were not balanced by sadness.
- Dr. Carl Jung

One would suffer a great deal to be happy.
- Mary Wortley Montagu, 1759

Labor, if it were not necessary for existence, would be indispensable for the happiness of man.
- Samuel Johnson, c. 1770

It is the inalienable right of all to be happy.
- Elizabeth Cady Stanton, 1861

Man is the artificer of his own happiness.
- Henry David Thoreau

One of the sanest, surest, and most generous joys of life comes from being happy over the good fortune of others.
- Archibald Rutledge

How to Live a Hundred Years Happily
1. Do not be on the lookout for ill health.
2. Keep usefully at work.
3. Have a hobby.
4. Learn to be satisfied.
5. Keep on liking people.
6. Meet adversity valiantly.
7. Meet the little problems of life with decision.
8. Above all, maintain a good sense of humor, best done by saying something pleasant every time you get a chance.
9. Live and make the present hour pleasant and cheerful. Keep your mind out of the past, and keep it out of the future.
- John A. Schindler

Happiness is the only good. The time to be happy is now. The place to be happy is here. The way to be happy is to make others so.
- Robert G. Ingersoll

Happiness, or misery, is in the mind. It is the mind that lives.
- William Cobbett, 1819

It gives me a deep comforting sense that "things seen are temporal and things unseen are eternal."
- Helen Keller

Gratitude is a fruit of great cultivation; you do not find it among gross people.
- Samuel Johnson on his journey to the Hebrides Islands, 1773

Wings
Be like the bird
That, pausing in her flight
Awhile on boughs too slight,
Feels them give way
Beneath her and yet sings,
Knowing that she hath wings.
- Victor Hugo

. . . There is only one way to achieve happiness on this terrestrial ball, and that is to have either a clear conscience or none at all.
- Ogden Nash

True happiness is of a retired nature, and an enemy to pomp and noise; it arises, in the first place, from the enjoyment of one's self, and in the next, from the friendship and conversation of a few select companions.
- Joseph Addison, 1711

Life's greatest happiness is to be convinced we are loved.
- Victor Hugo

Ten Spiritual Tonics
1. Stop worrying. Worry kills life.
2. Begin each day with a prayer. It will arm your soul.
3. Control appetite. Over-indulgence clogs body and mind.
4. Accept your limitations . . . .
5. Don't envy. It wastes time and energy.
6. Have faith in people. Cynicism sours the disposition.
7. Find a hobby. It will relax your nerves.
8. Read a book a week to stimulate imagination and broaden your view.
9. Spend some time alone for the peace of solitude and silence.
10. Try to want what you have, instead of spending your strength trying to get what you want.
- Abraham L. Feinberg

We need to find God, and he cannot be found in noise and restlessness. God is the friend of silence.
- Mother Teresa

Be unselfish. That is the first and final commandment for those who would be useful and happy
in their usefulness. If you think of yourself only,
you cannot develop because you are choking the
source of development, which is spiritual expansion through thought for others.
- Charles W. Eliot

Happiness doesn't come from doing what we
like to do but from liking what we have to do.
- Wilfred Peterson

All men have happiness as their object: there is
no exception. However different the means they
employ, they all aim at the same end.
- Blaise Pascal

If you observe a really happy man you will find
him building a boat, writing a symphony, educating his son, growing double dahlias in his garden, or looking for dinosaur eggs in the Gobi
desert. He will not be searching for happiness as
if it were a collar button that has rolled under the
radiator. He will not be striving for it as a goal in
itself. He will have become aware that he is
happy in the course of living life twenty-four
crowded hours of the day.
- W. Beran Wolfe

If one only wished to be happy, this could be easily accomplished; but we wish to be happier than
other people, and this is always difficult, for we
believe others to be happier than they are.
- Montesquieu

It is not easy to find happiness in ourselves, and
it is not possible to find it elsewhere.
- Agnes Repplier

Disdain for history is symptomatic of the malaise
of today's youth culture and of the larger society
which nurtured it. Resenting death, we murdered time. Almost too late we see that what we
have slain is not time but our sense of ourselves
as humans. To reject the past is to deprive today
of its meaning tomorrow. To evade the significance of time is to empty life of its significance. It
is that meaninglessness which pervades this age
of instant gratification and instant results and
permanent dissatisfaction.
- William V. Shannon

Real joy comes not from ease or riches or from
the praise of men, but from doing something
worthwhile.
- Wilfred T. Grenfell

Oh, how bitter a thing it is to look into happiness
through another man's eyes.
- William Shakespeare

Gratitude is the heart's memory.
- French proverb

Gratitude is not only the greatest of virtues, but
the parent of all the others.
- Cicero, 54 B.C.

The voluntary path to cheerfulness, if our sponta-
neous cheerfulness be lost, is to sit up cheerfully,
and act and speak as if cheerfulness were already

there. To feel brave, act as if we were brave, use
all our will to that end, and courage will very
likely replace fear. If we act as if from some better feeling, the bad feeling soon folds its tent like
an Arab and silently steals away.
- William James

Beauty is also to be found in a day's work.
- Mamie Sypert Burns

Happiness comes of the capacity to feel deeply,
to enjoy simply, to think freely, to risk life, to be
needed.
- Storm Jameson

The most certain sign of wisdom is a continual
cheerfulness; her state is like that of things in the
regions above the moon, always clear and serene.
- Michel de Montaigne, 1580

It is neither wealth nor splendor, but tranquility
and occupation, which give happiness.
- Thomas Jefferson

We never enjoy perfect happiness; our most fortunate successes are mingled with sadness; some
anxieties always perplex the reality of our satisfaction.
- Pierre Coneille, El Cid, 1636

Human felicity is produced not so much by great
pieces of good fortune that seldom happen, as by
little advantages that occur every day.
- Benjamin Franklin

One positive advantage to age for me is that I
have more time to smell the roses.
- Helen Hayes

One of the many things nobody ever tells you
about middle age is that it's such a nice change
from being young.
- Dorothy Canfield Fisher

In these times you have to be an optimist to open
your eyes when you awake in the morning.
- Carl Sandburg

I have now reigned about fifty years in victory or
peace, beloved by my subjects, dreaded by my
enemies, and respected by my allies. Riches and
honors, power and pleasure, have waited on my
call, nor does any earthly blessing appear to have
been wanting to my felicity. In this situation I
have diligently numbered the days of pure and
genuine happiness which have fallen to my lot:
they amount to fourteen.
- Ascribed to Abd-er-Rahman III
of Spain, c. A.D. 960

Start every day off with a smile and get it over
with.
- W. C. Fields

Everything has its beauty, but not everyone sees
it.
- Confucius

If, among the delights of the open world, I were
to choose the sights, the sounds and the fragrances I most want to see and hear and smell on
a final day on earth, I think I would choose these:

the clear, ethereal song of a white-throated
sparrow singing at dawn;
the smell of of pine trees in the room;
the lonely calling of Canadian geese;
the sight of a dragonfly glinting in the sunshine;
the voice of a hermit thrush far in a darkening
woods at evening;
and – most spirited and moving of sights – the
white cathedral of a cumulus cloud floating
serenely in the blue of the sky.

- Edwin Way Teale

He that keepeth the law, happy is he.

- The Bible, Proverbs 29:18

To fill the hour – that is happiness . . .

- Ralph Waldo Emerson

He is happy that knoweth not himself to be otherwise.

- Thomas Fuller, 1732

Happy is the man that findeth wisdom, and the
man that getteth understanding.

- The Bible, Proverbs 3:13

To business that we love we rise betime. And go
to't with delight.
- William Shakespeare, "Antony and Cleopatra,"
c. 1606

*Some people merely spend their leisure time; others
enjoy it.*

Humanly speaking, it is only when the hair is
white, when . . . life is almost over, that men
begin to realize how hopelessly elusive is the
happiness promised by wealth and fame.

- Joseph McSorley

Friends, books, cheerful heart, and conscience
clear
Are the most choice companions we have here.

- William Mather, 1681

Happiness in this world, when it comes, comes
incidentally. Make it the object of pursuit, and it
leads us a wild-goose chase, and is never
attained. Follow some other object, and very possibly we may find that we have caught happiness
without dreaming of it.

- Nathaniel Hawthorne

We do not remember days, we remember
moments.

- Cesare Pavese

We are more interested in making others believe
we are happy than in trying to be happy ourselves.

- La Rochefoucauld, 1665

It is something to be able to paint a particular
picture, or to carve a statue, and so to make a few
objects beautiful; but it is far more glorious to carve
and paint the very atmosphere and medi-
um through which we look. To affect the quality
of the day – that is the highest of arts.

- Henry David Thoreau

The happiness which brings enduring worth to
life is not the superficial happiness that is dependent on circumstances. It is the happiness and
contentment that fills the soul even in the midst
of the most distressing of circumstances and
most bitter environment. It is the kind of happiness that grins when things go wrong and smiles
through the tears. The happiness for which our
souls ache is one undisturbed by success or failure, one which will root deeply inside us and
give inward relaxation, peace, and contentment,
no matter what the surface problems may be.
That kind of happiness stands in need of no outward stimulus.

- Billy Graham

No gambler was ever yet a happy man.

- William Cobbett, 1829

The believer is happy; the doubter is wise.

- Hungarian proverb

When a man is happy, every effort to express his
happiness mars its completeness. I am not happy
at all unless I am happier than I know.

- Alexander Smith, 1863

Let us learn to be content with what we have.
Let us get rid of our false estimates, set up all the
higher ideals –
a quiet home,
vines our own planting,
a few books full of the inspiration of genius,
a few friends worthy of being loved and able to
love in return,
a hundred innocent pleasures that bring no pain
or remorse,
a devotion to the right that will never swerve,
a simple religion empty of all bigotry, full of trust
and hope and love
– and to such a philosophy this world will give
up all the joy it has.

- David Swing

If there were in the world today any large number of people who desired their own happiness
more than they desired the unhappiness of others, we could have a paradise in a few years.

- Bertrand Russell

All men have the same share of happiness.

- Napoleon Bonaparte

Our greatest happiness . . . does not depend on
the condition of life in which chance has placed
us, but is always the result of a good conscience,
good health, occupation, and freedom in all just
pursuits.

- Thomas Jefferson

HEALTH

Quotes & Anecdotes
(fitness, well-being, leisure, activity, aging)

Sometimes the most urgent and vital thing you can possibly do is take a complete rest.
- Ashleigh Brilliant

One of the symptoms of an approaching nervous breakdown is the belief that one's work is terribly important.
- Bertrand Russell

It is part of the cure to want to be cured.
- Seneca

Middle-aged rabbits don't have a paunch, do have their own teeth and haven't lost their romantic appeal.
- Dr. Aurelia Poter, endocrinologist, on why "rabbit food" may be good for executives

We sit at breakfast, we sit on the train on the way to work, we sit at work, we sit at lunch, we sit all afternoon . . . a hodgepodge of sagging livers, sinking gall bladders, drooping stomachs, compressed intestines, and squashed pelvic organs.
- Dr. John Button

To add life to years, not just years to life.
- Unofficial Motto of U.S. specialists in medicine for the aging and aged

On his eightieth birthday, John Quincy Adams responded to a query concerning his well-being: "John Quincy Adams is well. But the house in which he lives at present is becoming dilapidated. It is tottering upon its foundation. Time and the seasons have nearly destroyed it. Its roof is pretty well worn out. Its walls are much shattered and it trembles with every wind. I think John Quincy Adams will have to move out of it soon. But he himself is quite well, quite well."

Health is beauty, and the most perfect health is the most perfect beauty.
- William Shenstone, 1764

And the night shall be filled with music,
And the cares that infest the day,
Shall fold their tents, like the Arabs,
And as silently steal away.
- Henry Wadsworth Longfellow, "The Day is Done"

Take a music-bath once or twice a week for a few seasons, and you will find that it is to the soul what the water-bath is to the body.
- Oliver Wendell Holmes

Here is no sentiment, no contest, no grandeur, no economics. From the sanctity of this occupation, a man may emerge refreshed and in control of his own soul. He is not idle. He is fishing, alone with himself in dignity and peace. It seems a very precious thing to me.
- John Steinbeck

Giving is the secret of a healthy life. Not necessarily money, but whatever a man has of encouragement and sympathy and understanding.
- John D. Rockefeller, Jr.

If you would cure anger, do not feed it. Say to yourself: "I used to be angry every day; then every other day; now only every third or fourth day." When you reach thirty days offer a sacrifice of thanksgiving to the gods.
- Epictetus, c. A.D. 110

He who restrains his anger overcomes his greatest enemy.
- Latin proverb

Angry men make themselves beds of nettles.
- Samuel Richardson, 1748

If I had known I was going to live this long I would have taken better care of myself.
- Unknown

Striving to outdo one's companions on the golf course and tennis court or in the swimming pool constitutes several socially acceptable forms of suicide.
- Dr. George Griffith, professor of medicine, University of Southern California, on weekend athletics by men over forty

Adam and Eve ate the first vitamins, including the package.
- E.R. Squibb, in an advertisement advocating balanced diet rather than reliance on vitamin pills

The Autumn of the beautiful is beautiful.
- Latin proverb

You can take no credit for beauty at sixteen. But if you are beautiful at sixty, it will be your soul's own doing.
- Marie Stopes

What is beautiful is good, and who is good will soon be beautiful.
- Sappho, c. 610 B.C.

A thing of beauty is a joy forever;
Its loveliness increases; it will never
Pass into nothingness; but still will keep
A bower quiet for us, and a sleep
Full of sweet dreams, and health, and quiet breathing.
- John Keats

Zest is the secret of all beauty. There is no beauty that is attractive without zest.
- Christian Dior

Football today is far too much a sport for the few who can play it well; the rest of us, and too many of our children, get our exercise from climbing up the seats in stadiums, or from walking across the room to turn on our television sets.
- John F. Kennedy

Golf Definitions: "cow pasture pool"; a game in which the balls lie on the ground and the players lie in the clubhouse.

A golfer never feels better than when he's below par

O health, health! The blessing of the rich! the riches of the poor! who can buy thee at too dear a rate?

- Ben Jonson, 1605

The reason why worry kills more people than work is that more people worry than work.

- Robert Frost

Tell me what you eat, and I will tell you what you are.

- Anthelme Brillat-Savarin, 1825

Dieting is a losing battle.

- Anonymous

The waist is a terrible thing to mind.

- Ziggy (Tom Wilson)

What some people call health, if purchased by perpetual anxiety about diet isn't much better than tedious disease.

- George Dennison Prentice, 1860.

"I have the perfect diet," said Mr. Hopkins. "I eat my head off one day and starve the next." "And how do you feel?" he was asked. "Great," he said, "every other day."

To lengthen thy life, lessen thy meals.

- Benjamin Franklin

It is a boresome disease to try to keep health by following a too strict regimen.

- La Rochefoucauld, 1665

No diet will remove all the fat from your body because the brain is entirely fat. Without a brain you might look good, but all you could do is run for public office.

- Covert Bailey

A man takes a drink, the drink takes another, and the drink takes the man.

- Sinclair Lewis

We speak of alcohol and drugs as being addictive. So is work. Driving, ambitious people become slaves to work – and the resultant stress can cause serious problems. All work and no play doesn't make Jack a dull boy; it makes him a dead boy. This isn't to argue that hard work should be avoided, but to suggest that the hard driver allow some time for diverting recreation. It can be his best life-insurance policy.

- J.D. Ratcliff

Bacchus (Greek god of wine) hath drowned more men than Neptune.

- Thomas Fuller, 1732

Too much of here's mud in your eye can mean a face in the dirt.

Better a party-pooper than a pill-popper.

I've never been drunk, but often I've been over-served.

- George Gobel

If it keeps up, man will atrophy all his limbs but the push-button finger.

- Frank Lloyd Wright

The people who live long are those who long to live.

As for me, except for an occasional heart attack, I feel as young as I ever did.

- Robert Benchley

Perhaps one of the only positive pieces of advice that I was ever given was that supplied by an old courtier who observed: Only two rules really count. Never miss an opportunity to relieve yourself; never miss a chance to sit down and rest your feet.

- The Duke of Windsor

It's no longer a question of staying healthy. It's a question of finding a sickness you like.

- Jackie Mason

Fear less, hope more, eat less, chew more, whine less, breathe more, talk less, say more, hate less, love more, and all good things will be yours.

- Swedish proverb

Bitterness imprisons life; love releases it. Bitterness paralyzes life; love empowers it. Bitterness sours life; love sweetens it. Bitterness sickens life; love heals it. Bitterness blinds life; love anoints its eye.

- Harry Emerson Fosdick

Health is the vital principle of bliss.

- James Thomson, 1748

Health is not valued till sickness comes.

- Thomas Fuller, 1732

Better by far that you should forget and smile, Than you should remember and be sad.

- Christina Rossetti, 1862

Always do one thing less than you think you can do.

- Bernard Baruch, counseling businessmen on how to maintain good health.

Middle age is when your age starts to show around your middle.

- Bob Hope

People who enjoy good health should think of the doctor's bill as an amusement tax.

I keep myself in "puffect" shape. I get lots of exercise – in my own way – and I walk every day . . . . Knolls, you know, small knolls, they're very good for walking. Build up your muscles, going up and down the knolls.

- Mae West, at age 61

Health is not a condition of matter, but of Mind.

- Mary Baker Eddy

People who will try anything once may not get a second chance.

I am interested in physical medicine because my father was. I am interested in medical research because I believe in it. I am interested in arthritis because I have it.

- Bernard Baruch

I don't like the life here. There is no greenery. It would make a stone sick.

- Nikita Khrushchev, on a visit to New York City

Let me grow lovely, growing old
So many fine things do:
Laces, and ivory, and gold,
And silks need not be new;

And there is healing in old trees,
Old streets in glamour hold;
Why may not I, as well as these,
Grow lovely, growing old?

- Karle Wilson Baker

Always be on time. Do as little talking as humanly possible. Remember to lean back in the parade car so everybody can see the president. Be sure not to get too fat, because you'll have to sit three in the back seat.

- Eleanor Roosevelt, on campaign behavior for wives

Upon what meat doth this our Caesar feed,
That he is grown so great?

- William Shakespeare, Julius Caesar

Part of the secret of success in life is to eat what you like and let the food fight it out inside.

- Mark Twain

Athletics is America's favorite exercise – to sit and watch.

To go fishing is the chance to wash one's soul with pure air, with the rush of the brook, or with the shimmer of the sun on blue water. It brings meekness and inspiration from the decency of nature, charity toward tackle-makers, patience toward fish, a mockery of profits and egos, a quieting of hate, a rejoicing that you do not have to decide a darned thing until next week. And it is discipline in the equality of men – for all men are equal before fish.

- Herbert Hoover

We need time to dream, time to remember, and time to reach the infinite. Time to be.

- Gladys Taber

When it comes to your health, I recommend frequent doses of that rare commodity among Americans – common sense. We are rapidly becoming a land of hypochondriacs, from the ulcer-and-martini executives in the big city to the patent medicine patrons in the sulphur-and-molasses belt.

- Dr. Vincent Askey, former president of the AMA

The very success of medicine in a material way may now threaten the soul of medicine. Medicine is something more than the cold mechanical application of science to human disease. Medicine is a healing art. It must deal with individuals, their fears, their hopes and their sorrows. It must reach back further than a disease that the patient may have to those physical and emotional environmental factors which condition the individual for the reception of disease.

- Dr. Walter Martin, another former AMA president

The two biggest sellers in any bookstore are the cookbooks and the diet books. The cookbooks tell you how to prepare the food and the diet books tell you how not to eat any of it.

- Andy Rooney

Put a pot of chili on the stove to simmer. Let it simmer. Meanwhile, broil a good steak. Eat the steak. Let the chili simmer. Ignore it.

- Recipe for chili from Allan Shivers, former governor of Texas

Many a person has gone to their sarcophagus by what they put down their esophagus.

- Ponsy

There is no love sincerer than the love of food.

- George Bernard Shaw

An army marches on its stomach.

- Attributed to Napoleon Bonaparte

One must eat to live, not live to eat.

- Moliere, 1668

Eat, drink, and be merry, for tomorrow we diet.

Interest in hair today has grown to the proportion of a fetish. Think of the many loving ways in which advertisements refer to scalp hair- satiny, glowing, shimmering, breathing, living. Living indeed! It is as dead as a rope.

- Dr. William Montagna, dermatological researcher, Brown University

It's nature's way of telling you to slow down.

- Madison Avenue definition of death

Health nuts are going to feel stupid someday, lying in hospitals dying of nothing.

- Redd Foxx

If you see a snake coming toward you in a jungle, you have a right to be anxious. If you see it coming down Park Avenue, you're in trouble.

- Dr. Theodor Reik, psychoanalyst

We have to learn to be our own best friends because we fall too easily into the trap of being our worst enemies.

- Roderick Thorp

We too, the children of earth, have our moon phases all through any year; the darkness, the delivery from darkness, the waxing and waning. None lives, except the mindless, who does not in some degree experience this; hours of despair followed by hope or, perhaps, slow adjustment; times of fear, even panic, and then the light, however small. For in the normal human being it is impossible to live every day under emotional stress; there have to be, on this seesaw, periods of even balance.

- Faith Baldwin

At age fifty, every man has the face he deserves.

- George Orwell

Life, within doors, has few pleasanter prospects than a neatly arranged and well-provisioned breakfast table.

- Nathaniel Hawthorne

If one sets aside time for a business appointment, a trip to the hairdresser, a social engagement, or a shopping expedition, that time is accepted as inviolable. But if one says: I cannot come because that is my hour to be alone, one is considered rude, egotistical or strange. What a commentary on our civilization, when being alone is considered suspect; when one has to apologize for it, make excuses, hide the fact that one practices it – like a secret vice!

- Ann Morrow Lindbergh

Rest in bed will do more for diseases than any other single procedure.

- Logan Clendening, 1924

It's necessary to relax your muscles when you can. Relaxing your brain is fatal.

- Stirling Moss, race-car driver

On the seventh day God ended his work which he had made; and he rested on the seventh day.

- The Bible, Genesis 2:2

A time of quietude brings things into proportion and gives us strength. We all need to take time from the busyness of living, even if it be ten minutes to watch the sun go down or the city lights blossom against a canyoned sky.

We listen too much to the telephone and we listen too little to nature. The wind is one of my sounds. A lonely sound, perhaps, but soothing. Everybody should have his personal sounds to listen for – sounds that will make him exhilarated and alive, or quiet and calm . . . . As a matter of fact, one of the greatest sounds of them all – and to me it is a sound – is utter, complete silence.

- Andre Kostelanetz, conductor

Nature gives you the face you have at twenty; it is up to you to merit the face you have at fifty.

- Gabrielle "Coco" Chanel, designer

Look to your health; and if you have it, praise God, and value it next to a good conscience; for health is the second blessing that we mortals are capable of; a blessing that money cannot buy.

- Izaak Walton, 1653

He who has health has hope, and he who has hope has everything.

- Arab proverb

The poorest man would not part with health for money, but the richest would gladly part with all their money for health.

- C.C. Colton

Measure your health by your sympathy with morning and Spring.

- Henry David Thoreau

To lose one's health renders science null, art inglorious, strength unavailing, wealth useless, and eloquence powerless.

- Herophilus, c. 300 B.C.

If thou are sound in stomach, side, and feet, the riches of a king will add nothing to thy happiness.

- Horace, c. 5 B.C.

Among the innumerable follies by which we lay up in our youth repentance and remorse for the succeeding part of our lives, there is scarce any against which warnings are of less efficacy than the neglect of health.

- Samuel Johnson, 1750

A man too busy to take care of his health is like a mechanic too busy to take care of his tools.

- Spanish proverb

. . . The social climate must be changed so that smoking is looked upon as it used to be – a damned dirty habit and a vice.

- D.N. Golstein, M.D.

"Once a person is addicted," said Dr. Jones, "it is better to switch him to something like methadone than to try to cure him, because the odds against cure are so great." "That," said Dr. Smith, "is like saying if you can't lick them join them." "No," said Dr. Jones, "it's more like taking rat poison away from a baby and substituting a teething ring."

The graveyards are full of women whose houses were so spotless you could eat off the floor. Remember the second wife always has a maid.

- Heloise Cruse, column advice on housekeeping

Whether or not the world would be vastly benefitted by a total banishment from it of all intoxicating drinks seems not now an open question. Three-fourths of mankind confess the affirmative with their tongues, and I believe all the rest acknowledge it in their hearts.

- Abraham Lincoln

Cheerfulness and contentment are great beautifiers, and are famous preservers of youthful looks.

- Charles Dickens

A merry heart doeth good like a medicine . . .

- The Bible, Proverbs 17:22

He who laughs, lasts.

- Mary Pettibone Poole

Laughter crowds tension out of our lives, brings worry to a halt, and gives the personality a chance to stretch.

THOUGHT GEMS

Quotes & Anecdotes

(poignancies, truths, opinions, humor, and choice retorts on human perspective, human nature, politics and humanity)

Wisdom is the reward you get for a lifetime of listening when you'd have preferred to talk.
- *Doug Larson*

Tell a man there are 300 billion stars in the universe and he'll believe you. Tell him a bench has wet paint on it and he'll have to touch to be sure.
- *Jaeger*

I am a citizen not of Athens or Greece, but of the world.
- *Socrates*

He has the right to criticize who has the heart to help.
- *Abraham Lincoln*

It is a very melancholy reflection that men are usually so weak that it is absolutely necessary for them to know sorrow and pain to be in their right senses.
- *Richard Steele*

If I were given the opportunity to present a gift to the next generation, it would be the ability for each individual to learn to laugh at himself.
- *Charles Schulz*

Earnest people are often people who habitually look on the serious side of things that have no serious side.
- *Van Wyck Brooks*

Here I am at the end of the road and at the top of the heap.
- *Pope John XXII, after succeeding Pius XII*

John XII explained how he was kept on the straight and narrow as a youth: "Italians come to ruin most generally in three ways- women, gambling, and farming. My family chose the slowest one."

I am firm. You are obstinate. He is a pig-headed fool.
- *Katharine Whitehorn*

God has given us two hands – one to receive with and the other to give with. We are not cisterns made for hoarding; we are channels made for sharing.
- *Rev. Billy Graham*

What the public thinks depends on what the public hears.

Noise proves nothing; often a hen who has merely laid an egg cackles as if she had laid an asteroid.
- *Mark Twain*

Soldiers of the Western Front, your hour has come. The fight which begins today will determine Germany's destiny for a thousand years.
- *Adolf Hitler, order to the German Army, 1940*

After the First World War, President Warren G. Harding made the following declaration: "America's present need is not heroics but healing; not nostrums but normalcy; not revolution but restoration; not surgery but serenity; not the dramatic but the dispassionate..."

Politicians are the same all over. They promise to build a bridge even where there is no river.
- *Nikita Khrushchev*

...No matter how big a nation is, it is no stronger than its weakest people, and as long as you keep a person down, some part of you has to be down there to hold him down, so it means you cannot soar...
- *Marian Anderson, in a 1957 comment about Blacks in the U.S.*

The average person thinks he isn't.
- *Father Larry Lorenzoni*

Like all self-made men he worships his creator.

People used to go off to war, but modern science can now bring it to your doorstep.

Peace hath higher tests of manhood
Than battle ever knew.
- *John Greenleaf Whittier, 1853*

Better to keep peace than to have to make peace.

That's my private ant. You're liable to break its legs.
- *Albert Schweitzer, asking a 10-year-old boy not to brush an insect from his sleeve*

Think of our world as it looks from that rocket that's heading toward Mars. It is like a child's globe, hanging in space, the continents stuck to its side like colored maps. We are all fellow passengers on a dot of earth.
- *Lyndon B. Johnson*

And that's the world in a nutshell – an appropriate receptacle.
- *Stan Dunn*

Never go to bed mad. Stay up and fight.
- *Phyllis Diller*

Most of the trouble in the world is caused by people wanting to be important.
- *T.S. Eliot*

After twelve years of therapy my psychiatrist said something that brought tears to my eyes. He said, "No hablo ingles."
- *Ronnie Shakes*

As a rule, men worry more about what they can't see than about what they can.
- *Julius Caesar, during the Gallic Wars, 1st century B.C.*

...Violence is the sign of temporary weakness.
- *Jean Jaures*

What luck for rulers that men do not think.
- *Adolf Hitler*

Ninety-eight percent of the adults in this country are decent, hard-working, honest Americans. It's the other lousy two percent that get all the publicity. But then – we elected them.
- *Lily Tomlin*

It is better to light a candle than to curse the darkness.

Harry Chapman's advice: "Having served on various committees, I have drawn up a list of rules: Never arrive on time; this will stamp you as a beginner. Don't say anything until the meeting is half over; this stamps you as being wise. Be as vague as possible; this avoids irritating the others. When in doubt, suggest that a sub-committee be appointed. Be the first to move for adjournment; this will make you popular; it's what everyone is waiting for."

Television is a medium of entertainment which permits millions of people to listen to the same joke at the same time, and yet remain lonesome.
- *T.S. Eliot*

Television is a medium because anything well done is rare.
- *Fred Allen*

Television is the great democratizer; it gives everybody the same front row seat.

Is sloppiness in speech caused by ignorance or apathy? I don't know and I don't care.
- *William Safire*

The years teach what the days never know.
- *Ralph Waldo Emerson*

I am not young enough to know everything.
- *J.M. Barrie*

Young men think old men are fools, but old men know young men are fools.
- *George Chapman, 1605*

We think our fathers fools, so wise we grow;
Our wiser sons, no doubt, will think us so.
- *Alexander Pope, 1711*

I am a deeply superficial person.
- *Andy Warhol*

You will find that the truth is often unpopular and the contest between agreeable fancy and disagreeable fact is unequal. . . . In the vernacular, we Americans are suckers for good news.
- *Adlai E. Stevenson*

Too bad the only people who know how to run the country are busy driving cabs and cutting hair.
- *George Burns*

The age of social conscience, social justice and concern seems to have coincided with the age of crime, pornography, mugging and international terrorism. What started out as a liberalization of restrictive social conventions seems to have developed into a dictatorship of license.
- *Prince Philip of Great Britain*

An athiest is a guy who watches a Notre Dame-SMU football game and doesn't care who wins.
- *Dwight D. Eisenhower*

For a single woman, preparing for company means wiping the lipstick off the milk carton.
- *Elayne Boosler*

I can see . . . in what you call the dark, but which to me is golden. I can see a God-made world, not a man-made world.
- *Hellen Keller*

We are in bondage to the law so that we may be free.
- *Marcus Tullius Cicero, Roman orator, c. 60 B.C.*

In India, people have caught monkeys by setting out a small box with a tasty nut in it. There is an opening in the box large enough for the monkey to thrust in his hand, but too small for him to withdraw it once he's clutched the nut. When the monkey has grabbed the prize, he must either let go and regain his freedom or keep hold and stay trapped.
Most monkeys hold onto the nut, making it easy for hunters to pick them up.
People have been known to get caught in the same kind of trap. The person who puts the goodie in the box controls the person who grabs it, but if we are willing to let go of the goodies, we are free of control.
- *Elizabeth Brenner, Winning by Letting Go*

I submit that an individual who breaks a law that conscience tells him is unjust and willingly accepts the penalty by staying in jail to arouse the conscience of the community over its injustice, is in reality expressing the very highest respect for law.
- *Martin Luther King, Jr.*

I have a dream that one day on the red hills of Georgia, the sons of former slaves and the sons of former slave-owners will be able to sit together at the table of brotherhood . . . . That my four little children will one day live in a nation where they will not be judged by the color of their skin but by the content of their character.
- *ibid.*

The Negro says, "Now." Others say, "Never." The voice of responsible Americans . . . says, "Together." There is no other way. Until justice is blind to color, until education is unaware of race, until opportunity is unconcerned with the color of men's skins, emancipation will be a proclamation but not a fact.
- *Lyndon B. Johnson*

[This] is a good time to be a woman because your country, now more than at any time in its history, is utilizing your abilities and intelligence.
- *Ladybird Johnson*

Women's rights became a movement because of man's wrongs.

Too often the great decisions are originated and given form in bodies made up wholly of men, or so completely dominated by them that whatever of special value women have to offer is shunted aside without expression.
- *Eleanor Roosevelt*

Some of us are becoming the men we wanted to marry.
- *Gloria Steinem*

Illegal aliens have always been a problem in the United States. Ask any Indian.
- *Robert Orben*

Status quo: Latin for "the mess we're in."

How much money did you make last year?
Mail it in.
- *Simplified tax form suggested by Stanton Delaplane*

When you go into court you are putting your fate into the hands of twelve people who weren't smart enough to get out of jury duty.
- *Norm Crosby*

Weather forcast for tonight: dark.
- *George Carlin*

O Lord, thou knowest how busy I must be this day. If I forget thee, do not thou forget me.
- *Lord Ashley, before the Battle of Edge Hill*

An elderly cannibal sage and a missionary were comparing their philosophies. The cannibal reminisced about the tribal wars he had fought, and how he had eaten his foes. The missionary said, "We fight wars for higher reasons- for truth, for defense of democracy, for freedom." "You must eat many, many people," said the cannibal. "Oh, no," said the missionary, "we don't eat human beings." "Then," said the cannibal sage, "you have no reason to kill each other."

Remember, remember always that all of us . . . are descended from immigrants and revolutionists.
- *Franklin D. Roosevelt*

Ninety percent of the politicians give the other ten percent a bad reputation.
- *Henry Kissenger*

In America, anyone can become President. That's one of the risks you take.
- *Adlai Stevenson*

For every x on a ballot there is a why.

Everyone is a prisoner of his own experiences. No one can eliminate prejudices- just recognize them
- *Edward R. Murrow*

The difference of race is one of the reasons why I fear war may always exist; because race implies difference, difference implies superiority, and superiority leads to predominance.
- *Benjamin Disraeli, 1849*

It is one thing to be moved by events; it is another to be mastered by them.
- *Ralph W. Sockman*

Don't go around saying the world owes you a living. The world owes you nothing. It was here first.
- *Mark Twain*

Nobody roots for Goliath.
- *Wilt Chamberlain, seven-foot basketball giant*

I know a man who gave up smoking, drinking, sex, and rich food. He was healthy right up to the day he killed himself.
- *Johnny Carson*

When the going gets tough, the smart get lost.
- *Robert Byrne*

Nothing is impossible for the man who doesn't have to do it himself.
- *A.H. Weiler*

The best way to keep one's word is not to give it.
- *Napoleon Bonaparte*

It's a recession when your neighbor loses his job; it's a depression when you lose your own.
- *Harry S Truman*

To get back on your feet, miss two car payments.

I haven't been wrong since 1961, when I thought I made a mistake.
- *Bob Hudson*

As a madman is apt to think himself grown suddenly great, so he that grows suddenly great is apt to borrow a little from the madman.
- *Samuel Johnson, 1781*

It is not so important to be serious as it is to be serious about the important things. The monkey wears an expression of seriousness which would do credit to any college student, but the monkey is serious because he itches.
- *Robert M. Hutchins*

. . . I cut my own hair. I got sick of barbers because they talk too much. And too much of their talk was about my hair coming out.
- *Robert Frost*

Yesterday's fashion will probably be tomorrow's; but it isn't today's.

Who is the Forgotten Man? He is the clean, quiet, virtuous, domestic citizen who pays his debts and his taxes and is never heard out of his little circle.
- *William Graham Sumner, 1883*

Few great men could pass Personnel.
- *Paul Goodman*

The ancient Romans built their greatest masterpieces of architecture, the ampitheatres, for wild beasts to fight in.
- *Voltaire*

The length of a film should be directly related to the endurance of the human bladder.
- *Alfred Hitchcock*

In time we hate that which we often fear.
- *William Shakespeare, "Antony and Cleopatra"*

Two wrongs won't make a right, but three rights will make a left.

Roses are red, violets are blue,
I'm a schizophrenic, and so am I.
- *Frank Crow*

If adversity purifies men, why not nations?
- *Jean Paul Richter*

We can never make taxation popular, but we can make taxation fair.
- *Richard M. Nixon*

Justice often satisfies neither side.

Nothing is so soothing to our self-esteem as to find our bad traits in our forebears. It seems to absolve us.
- *Van Wyck Brooks*

The face which we [Americans] present to the world . . . is the face of the individual or the family as a high consumption unit with minimal social links or responsibilities – father happily drinking his beer, mother dreamily fondling soft garments newly rinsed in a wonderful new detergent, the children gaily calling from the barbeque pit for a famous sauce for their steak.

- Adlai Stevenson

For people who like peace and quiet: a phoneless cord.

The young man who has not wept is a savage, and the old man who will not laugh is a fool.

- George Santayana

If one man offers you democracy and another offers you a bag of grain, at what stage of starvation will you prefer the grain to the vote?

- Bertrand Russell

At the precise moment you take off your shoe in a shoestore, your big toe will pop out of your sock to see what is going on.

- Ginsburg

Personal Quips:
A team should be an extension of the coach's personality. My teams were arrogant and obnoxious.

- Al McGuire, former basketball coach

Another coach, Georgetown University's John Thompson, said, "I probably couldn't play for me. I wouldn't like my attitude."

If I ever needed a brain transplant, I'd choose a sportwriter because I'd want a brain that had never been used.

- Norm Van Brocklin, former Notre Dame football coach

The commedian Jim Samuels shouted back to a teenage heckler: "You're a good example of why some animals eat their young." Another comedian, Steven Pearl: "I can't believe that out of 100,000 sperm, you were the quickest."

Astrology is Taurus.

- F.W. Dedering

What gravestone epitaph was requested by Erma Bombeck? "Big deal! I'm used to dust."

Never accept a drink from a urologist.

- Erma Bombeck's father

If this is coffee, please bring me some tea; but if this is tea, please bring me some coffee.

- Abraham Lincoln

I don't know anything about music. In my line, you don't have to.

- Elvis Presley

I never forget a face, but in your case I'll be glad to make an exception.

- Groucho Marx

Nothing is wrong with Southern California that a rise in the ocean level wouldn't cure.

- Ross MacDonald

Motto for Cleveland suggested by Jimmy Brogan: "You gotta live somewhere."

When told it was 105° F in the shade, golfer Bobby Jones said, "I'm glad we don't have to play in the shade."

Toots Shor's restaurant is so crowded nobody goes there anymore.

- Yogi Berra

More Yogi: "If people don't want to come out to the ball park, nobody's going to stop them."

Most of our future lies ahead.

- Denny Crum, Louisville basketball coach

Patrick Dennis' standard reply to critical letters began: "Dear Sir: Thank you very much for your crank letter . . . "

My grandmother is over eighty and still doesn't need glasses. Drinks right out of the bottle.

- Henny Youngman

Political Personals:
Calvin Coolidge didn't say much, and when he did – he didn't say much.

- Will Rogers

Herbert Hoover said of his years in the White House: "The thing I enjoyed most were visits from children. They didn't want public office."

I don't make jokes. I just watch the government and report the facts.

- Will Rogers

You've got to be careful quoting Ronald Reagan, because when you quote him accurately it's called mudslinging.

- Walter Mondale

Walter Mondale has all the charisma of a speed bump.

- Will Durst

Reagan won [the Presidency] because he ran against Jimmy Carter. Had he run unopposed he would have lost.

- Mort Sahl

Ronald Reagan has held the two most demeaning jobs in the country – President of the United States and radio broadcaster for the Chicago Cubs.

- George Will

It's our fault. We should have given him better parts.

- Jack Warner, on hearing Reagan had been elected California's governor

Ronald Reagan, in 1973, publicly stated, "The thought of being President frightens me and I do not think I want the job."

John F. Kennedy, in 1960, quipped, "Do you realize the responsibility I carry? I'm the only person standing between Nixon and the White House."

Gerry Ford is a nice guy, but he played too much football with his helmet off.

- Lyndon B. Johnson

When asked what he thought of Western civilization, Mahatma Gandhi repiled, "I think it would be a good idea."

4

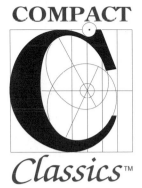

COMPACT

Classics™

LIBRARY #4: Biographies

Section A: Pioneers in Science

4-A1	Euclid
4-A2	Isaac Newton
4-A3	Galileo Galilei
4-A4	Nicolaus Copernicus
4-A5	Albert Einstein

Section B: Leaders in Crisis

4-B1	Winston Churchill
4-B2	Benjamin Franklin
4-B3	Abraham Lincoln
4-B4	George Washington
4-B5	Thomas Jefferson

Section C: Artists and Philosophers

4-C1	William Shakespeare
4-C2	Leonardo da Vinci
4-C3	Ludwig van Beethoven
4-C4	Michelangelo
4-C5	Aristotle

Section D: Inventors and Innovators

4-D1	Thomas Alva Edison
4-D2	Marie Curie
4-D3	Orville and Wilbur Wright
4-D4	Louis Pasteur
4-D5	Antoine Lavoisier

Section E: Leaders of the Spirit

4-E1   **Martin Luther King, Jr.**

4-E2   **Mahatma Gandhi**

4-E3   **Florence Nightingale**

4-E4   **Christopher Columbus**

4-E5   **Confucius**

Section F: A Medley of Books

4-F1   *My Life for the Poor: Mother Teresa of Calcutta*
         by Jose Luis Gonzalez-Balado and Janet N. Playfoot

4-F2   *Iacocca, An Autobiography* by Lee Iacocca, with William Novak

        The Last Lion: Winston Spencer Churchill

4-F3   Vol. I: *Visions of Glory (1874-1932)* by William Manchester

4-F4   Vol. II: *Alone (1932-1940)* by William Manchester

4-F5   *The Autobiography of Malcolm X* by Malcolm X, with Alex Haley

EUCLID

"Geometry's Genius"
(c. 300 B.C.)

Early Years

Almost none of the details of Euclid's life are known. His birth and death dates are uncertain, as are the city and even the continent of his birth. How ironic that a man of such enduring fame received such little attention while he was alive.

It is certain that Euclid was active as a teacher at the great library in Alexandria, Egypt, around the third century B.C. He was also a writer, devoted to explaining and expanding mathematical theories. His deductive mind led him to create a fascinating work that has been far more influential than any other treatise ever written on logical geometry. Though he wrote several books, this textbook of geometry titled *The Elements*, secured his place in history.

His Book: *The Elements*

The Elements has been used as a basis for teaching geometry for well over two thousand years. The first edition appeared in print about thirty years after Gutenburg invented his printing press in 1455. More than a thousand editions, many translated into other languages from the original Greek, have since been produced, making Euclid the most successful textbook writer of all time. So laudable was his work that all previous geometry texts were superseded and forgotten when Euclid's book appeared.

The majority of the principles contained in *The Elements* were already understood – and many were already proven – through the research of Hippocrates, Eudoxus and the Pythagoreans. Euclid's primary contribution consisted of a unique formulation of these theories and the arrangement of information into an overall plan based on a few select axioms. These axioms were then verified using mathematical precepts to develop a pattern of conclusions in succession. Along the way, the mathematician supplied the steps and proofs that had previously been missing.

The idea that everything within a discipline could be deduced from a few basic principles was new – and important to world history. Euclid's deductive examples, many centuries later, fueled the Western quest for scientific knowledge that was pioneered by thinkers like Newton, Galileo and Copernicus. It was substantially due to two factors, Greek rationalism and early Greek mathematical learning, that science arose and flourished in Europe. Other parts of the world (China, for instance), though technologically more advanced than Europe, never possessed the practical, theoretical pattern of spatial analysis that European intellectuals enjoyed. These thinkers had been conditioned to embrace Euclid's geometry as descriptive of the real world, not as merely an abstract system of postulates.

Sir Isaac Newton's elegant work, the *Principia*, written more than a millennium after Euclid's death, is a particularly obvious example of the Alexandrian's influence. It is organized in a classical geometric form similar to that of *The Elements*. Since Euclid's time, other mathematicians, as well as many scientists and philosophers, have attempted to show how all their conclusions could be logically derived from a small number of initial assumptions. Today, all branches of mathematics are organized into deductive systems.

Euclidean geometry does not always hold true in Einstein's "real" universe, but it does provide a very close map of reality in our everyday world.

While it primarily develops plane and solid geometry, *The Elements* also contains sections on algebra and number theory. The text was not intended as an encyclopedia of geometry. It had a more specialized purpose – to prepare students for philosophical studies, much in the abstract, "pure-ideas" spirit of Plato. King Ptolemy once asked if there was any shorter way through geometry than studying *The Elements*, to which Euclid replied, "There is no royal road to geometry." However true this may be, some points, as an overview of the work, are crudely summarized hereafter.

The work begins with a list of *assumptions* (axioms that are assumed to be true). It then draws *conclusions* from these assumptions by employing a *deductive reasoning* process (If . . . , then . . .).

Axioms are made up of "undefined" or "self-evident" terms – those having no need (or so Euclid thought) of being defined using other words. Euclid compares the axioms he uses in his reasoning system to the trunk of a tree; resultant *propositions*, deduced from the axioms, are like the branches supported by the trunk; additional propositions derived from these propositions are like the twigs that grow out of the branches, and so on. The line of propositions (if they don't circle back into themselves) must end somewhere; but at the same time a new, yet unfounded series of axioms is initiated, to prompt future thinking.

Five "postulates" and five "common notions" make up the ten axioms (or assumptions) of *The Elements*. As translated by Sir Thomas Heath in his famous annotated edition, these axioms are listed below:

Postulates

1. It is possible to draw a straight line from any point to any point.

2. It is possible to produce a finite straight line continuously in a straight line.

3. It is possible to describe a circle with any center and distance (diameter).

4. All right angles are equal to one another.

5. If a straight line falling on two straight lines makes the interior angles on the same side less than two right angles, the two straight lines, if produced indefinitely, meet on that side on which the angles are less than right angles.

Common notions

1. Things which are equal to the same thing are also equal to one another.

2. If equals be added to equals, the wholes are equal.

3. If equals be subtracted from equals, the remainders are equal.

4. Things which coincide with one another are equal to one another.

5. The whole is greater than the part.

Believe it or not, from these ten quite rudimentary concepts – in conjunction with a section on definitions – Euclid derived all of his geometric theorems. Again taking from Heath's edition, some of the most important of these theorums include:

• If in a triangle two angles be equal to one another, the sides which subtend

(are opposite) the equal angles will also be equal to one another.

• If two straight lines cut one another, they make the vertical (opposite) angles equal to one another.

• In any triangle, two angles taken together in any manner are less than two right angles.

• Straight lines parallel to the same straight line are also parallel to one another.

• In any triangle . . . the three interior angles (added together) are equal to two right angles (180 degrees).

• If a parallelogram (a four-sided figure) [has] the same base with a triangle and [is located] in the same parallels, the parallelogram is double the triangle (in area).

After stating each theorum, Euclid offers detailed, step-by-step drawings. Then he explains the significance of each of the lines, points, and numerals or letters he uses to arrive at his conclusions.

The Elements deals with abstract mathematical space rather than with physical space. The work was at times criticized for its lack of practical application for this very reason.

One anecdote illustrates Euclid's preferred emphasis on theory to the exclusion of practice. A student, after studying the first theorem contained in the book, asked the Teacher, "What shall I get by learning these things?" Euclid replied by calling one of his slaves and saying, "Give him a coin, since he must make gain out of what he learns."

■　■　■

As we have seen, Euclid's *Elements* was a crucial factor in the rise of science. Science is more than just an assembly of accurate ideas and observable facts; it is a mixture of thoughtful experimentation on the one hand and careful analysis and reasoning on the other. And Euclid's mastery of all three – logic, experimentation and analysis, along with rigorous, bold exercising of each – led to his elegant system; a system that has had a profound, "geometrically" increased influence on the world through the ages.

ISAAC NEWTON

"Solitary Scholar"
(1642 - 1727)

Early Years

Isaac Newton was born on Christmas morning 1642 to a humble family in Woolsthorpe, England. His uneducated father, Isaac, was described as a "wild, extravagant, and weak man." He died some three months before his son's premature birth. The sickly child hung between life and death, and it was doubted that he would live to manhood. But the baby did survive, to become a most celebrated scientist.

Isaac was raised by his elderly grandmother in a rural farmhouse. He grew up apart from other children, and even at school he preferred to play alone. Isaac studied little, until a certain turning point in his life: he got into a fight with a boy who ranked above him in class. When Isaac won the skirmish, he swore he would defeat his rival in scholarship as well. Now, as he rapidly rose to the top of his class, he began neglecting farm chores, opting instead to read and make mechanical tools and models. He built a miniature windmill for the top of his grandmother's house, and a water clock with a never-before-seen feature – a circular dial. He made paper kites with lanterns in them for night flying, carved sundials, drew birds and animals, and designed ships.

When Isaac was fifteen, his mother ruled that the sober, thoughtful youngster should become a farmer. She would send him to the local market to sell grain and vegetables. But each day Isaac left a servant to do the selling, then hurried to the attic apothecary of a Mr. Clark, where he threw himself into reading until it was time to return home. Soon he began using his spare time to run more intricate experiments and, fortunately, Hannah finally sent him back to school to prepare for studies at Cambridge University's Trinity College. Young Newton quickly absorbed the then known concepts of science and mathematics and moved on to his own, independent research. He also began studying comets and lunar phenomena. Though the college closed due to a plague the following year, Isaac returned to his home in Woolsthorpe, and, during the next eighteen months, made the major discoveries for which he is now famous. By the time Isaac Newton was twenty-seven years old, he had already laid the foundations that would revolutionize science.

Uncovering Nature's Laws

The mid-seventeenth century was a period of great scientific unrest. The invention of the refracting telescope by Lippershey and its development by Galileo had bolstered astronomical study, while philosophers like Bacon and Descartes were urging scientists to cease relying on Aristotle's authority and to experiment and observe on their own.

Intrigued with Galileo's mechanical experiments, and with the findings of William Harvey on the circulation of blood and Johannes Kepler on planetary motion, Newton set about to unify the discoveries of science into a cohesive theory, in an effort to help men better understand and predict their world.

In his twenty-first and twenty-second years, Newton formulated the binomial theorem of algebra (the expansion of a quantity to the nth power), the direct method of fluxions (the elements of differential calculus), the inverse method of fluxions (integral calculus), and his theory of gravitation.

Newton observed that the effects of "gravity" were not measurably less at the tops of trees or buildings or mountains; thus, he reasoned, the earth's attractive force might well extend to the moon, keeping it in its orbit. Could the same be said of the planets revolving around the sun?

During much of Newton's life he fancied chemistry and alchemy. One of the primary tests he applied to his chemicals was taste. And over the years of tasting heavy metals – including mercury – and vaporizing other chemicals to test for smell, the scientist very nearly poisoned himself.

In spite of his breadth of interest, Newton chose first to publish the results of his studies based on Cartesian theories of light and color. In a darkened room, he made a slit in his window shutter to admit a ray of light. Seeing the array of colors cast by a prism, he concluded that "Whiteness is the usual color of light; for light is a confused aggregate of rays imbued with all sorts of colors . . . " Descartes had regarded different colors as analogous to different musical tones, but Newton showed light's true properties. A leaf, for example, is green because it absorbs the red, blue, and violet rays of white light, and reflects the green.

Newton also discovered that red light is bent out of its course the least by a prism, and violet the most. He carefully analyzed the distinct refractions and reflections of colors, making the rare and undisputed claims that led to the science of spectroscopy.

Next, mathematically calculating the laws of light, he designed and built the first reflecting telescope in 1668. With a concave mirror, a secondary optical system, and an eyepiece, it is basically the same design as today's telescopes.

By age 30, Newton was an appointed professor of mathematics at Cambridge and a fellow of the British Royal Society. Still, although he was regarded as a man of "unparalleled genius," his theories of light were bitterly opposed, especially by the renowned scientist Christian Huygens. Growing tired of having to continually defend his ideas, Newton became quite caustic and reclusive, and threatened to cease publishing his works. "A man must either resolve to put out nothing new," he wrote, "or to become a slave to defend it."

Impoverished, the scientist resigned from membership in the Royal Society and contemplated studying law. However, he never abandoned his scientific career, though he "refreshed" himself with history when he tired and later even published a book on history, *Chronology of Ancient Kingdoms.*"

While serving as a Cambridge associate, Newton's peers report that only once did they see him laugh. He was a singleminded worker, "meek, sedate, and humble, never seeming angry," according to an associate. "I never knew him to take any recreation or pastime . . . thinking all hours lost that were not spent in his studies, to which he kept so close that he seldom left his chamber . . . he ate very sparingly, nay, ofttimes he has forgot to eat at all . . . He very rarely went to bed until two or three of the clock, sometimes not till five or six. [Later] he learned to go to bed at twelve, finding by experience that if he exceeded that hour by a little, it did him more harm in his health than a whole day's study."

Newton's work, up to that time, had been haphazard, largely unfinished, and disconnected. Had he died in 1886, it would only have been lamented that an unfulfilled genius had lived. But now, disciplining his brilliance and organizing his tenacity for excellence, Newton finally brought himself to unite his writings and publish his *Mathematical Principles of Natural Philosophy.*

More popularly known simply as *Principia*, this masterful work consists of three books: the first deals with the laws of force and motion, and their consequences; the second, with the oscillations of pendulums and the motion of distinct objects within various fluids; and the third, with gravity on the earth and in space. In the third volume, Newton states his principles of universal gravitation: "Any celestial body attracts every other body with a force directly proportional to the product of their masses and inversely proportional to the square of the distance between them." In addition, the works include the calculated masses of the sun and planets, their densities, the planets' predicted orbits, and the effects humans would experience if they lived on any one of them.

This "universal gravitation" theory was the last of Newton's *three laws of motion* that attempted to unify all physical systems, from the swinging of pendulums to planets swinging around the sun. The first law basically states that *an object will remain at rest unless moved by a force.* The second – the classical law of physics written mathematically as $F = ma$ – states that *an object's acceleration (movement) is equal to the net force on the object divided by its mass.* Newton's famous third law of motion combines the first two: *For every action (force) there is an equal and opposite reaction.* Through many elaborations, the *Principia* was able to explain how these three related principles could be used to solve a broad range of problems.

Both excitement and violent opposition to these ideas soon exploded throughout Europe. The notions were so confusing. How could an invisible force from the sun keep the planets in orderly orbit? After experiencing a similar response to the publication of his highly controversial discovery of calculus – made at the same time as, but independently of, Leibnitz's work – Newton once more withdrew into the solitude of his study. He turned to politics to augment his income, and was selected as a member of Parliament and as a representative in the House of Commons. Though he formed some friendships late in life, he never married.

In his eighties, his mind still accurate, Newton continued to write. In early March, 1727, after presiding at a Royal Society meeting, he was taken ill, and died later that month.

■ ■ ■

Isaac Newton became the first scientist to be buried at Westminster Abbey. His epitaph, written by Alexander Pope, reads, in part:

Nature and nature's laws lay his in night:
God said, Let Newton be! and all was light . . .
Let Mortals rejoice
That there has existed such and so great an
Ornament to the Human Race.

Newton would probably have dismissed such words as extravagant nonsense. Just before his illness, the modest old man spoke of how he personally viewed his achievements:

I do not know what I may appear to the world, but to myself I seem to have been only like a boy playing on the seashore, and diverting myself in now and then finding a smoother pebble or a prettier shell than ordinary, whilst the great ocean of truth lay all undiscovered before me.

GALILEO GALILEI

"Astronomer and Scientist"
(1564 - 1642)

Early Years

Galileo grew up in Florence, Italy. Taught by his poor yet titled and educated father Vincenzo, Galileo learned to play the lute and the organ. Originally, the young boy was slated to become a dealer in cloth. But as he continued to show great skill in poetry, drawing and mechanics, it became apparent that, for him, a merchant's life would be a mistake.

Galileo's innate gifts and his parents' sacrifice eventually allowed him to receive a formal education; he was accepted at the University of Pisa, the city of his birth. At the insistence of his father, Galileo enrolled to study the lucrative profession of medicine. But the young man instead became an ardent student of philosophy. He was known at school as "the wrangler," because he persistently dared to disagree with Aristotle's teachings. Though the story of Galileo experimenting by dropping weights from the Leaning Tower of Pisa is probably untrue, it was at this time that he first began to run tests using falling objects.

In Pisa, Galileo also became enamored with mathematics. With a background of little more than the rudiments of numbers, he would secretly stand outside the classroom door of a geometry professor, listening to Euclidean lectures.

One day, while nineteen-year-old Galileo was kneeling in the cathedral, he noticed a bronze lamp swinging from an archway. By feeling his pulse he verified that, though the oscillations grew shorter, each swing still took the same time to complete, regardless of the length of its arc. From this observation, Galileo invented a mechanism that instantly became popular with physicians, the "pulsilogium," a gadget using a pendulum to mark the rate and variation of the pulse. (Pendulumed clocks would not be introduced until a half-century later.)

Forced to drop out of school for financial reasons, Galileo left Pisa. Arriving back in Florence, he studied the works of "Master Archimedes," wrote his first essay on hydrostatic balance, and furthered his learning in geometry and mechanics.

Gravity, and More

Through the influence of the famed mathematician Marquis Guidubaldo, Galileo was appointed to a mathematical professorship at Pisa, supplementing his scanty salary by tutoring, lecturing on literary subjects, and practicing medicine.

As disciples of Aristotle, nearly every one of his fellow teachers opposed the new-comer. Even Galileo's logical, mathematical and experimental proofs could not convince his detractors. Aristotle's two-thousand-year-old laws were so revered that, after three years of persecution, Galileo resigned his post and was instated as a professor at the University of Padua. There, the now famous scientist attracted thousands at a time to his witty and enthusiastic lectures. And there, for the next eighteen years, the modest, unassuming professor performed the bulk of his scientific work, concentrated in two principal areas: mechanics and astronomy.

Mechanics

Aristotle had taught that heavy objects fall more rapidly than lighter ones, which generations of scholars had accepted as correct. But Galileo discovered that all bodies descend with an equal velocity, except when their fall is retarded by the friction of air (as happens with the descent of a feather). He further advanced the understanding of gravity by measuring the distances objects fall in given periods of time, then mathematically explaining the proportional relationships involved.

Galileo next probed the question of inertia. People had previously believed that an object would naturally tend to slow down and stop unless a force was exerted to keep it moving. But Galileo's formulae indicated that an object would keep moving indefinitely if forces such as friction and gravity could be eliminated. This principle was later inducted into Newton's system as the first law of motion, a vital tenet of physics.

During these years, Galileo also designed what he called a "thermoscope," a forerunner of the thermometer. He worked tirelessly, writing treatises on gnomonics (the science of using shadows to tell time), on the laws of motion, and on military strategy and fortifications. His students copied and distributed these papers throughout Europe.

Astronomy

In the 1600's, astronomical theory was in great ferment. Amid loud clerical and scientific disputes, Galileo announced his belief that Copernicus' theory was correct: the earth indeed revolved around the sun. Still, he had no way to prove this fact beyond mathematics, and was reluctant to publicize his conclusions. In a letter to the astronomer Johannes Kepler, he wrote: " . . . I have drawn up many arguments . . . which, however, I have not hitherto dared to publish, fearful of meeting the same fate as our master Copernicus . . . only worthy of hooting and derision; so great is the number of fools."

Then in 1609, after hearing about a simple spyglass magnifying device invented by the Dutchman Hans Lippershey, Galileo used his talented mind and hands to construct, in a matter of days, a vastly superior and practical apparatus (a modest lead tube with lenses at each end, one concave and the other convex) – the first complete astronomical telescope.

Galileo turned his observations to the heavens. In a single year, he made a series of spectacular discoveries:

* The moon is not a smooth sphere, but pitted with craters and covered with mountainous regions.

* Four moons revolve around Jupiter. (Twelve additional smaller satellites have since been discovered.) This was in clear contrast to the prevailing belief that all celestial bodies were made to circle about the earth.

* "Sunspots" darken portions of the solar surface.

* The Milky Way is made up of myriad single, far-away stars "planted together in clusters," and is not a milky nebula as was earlier assumed.

* A strange and beautiful ring encircles Saturn.

* Venus passes through phases similar to the cycles of our Moon.

To Galileo, these discoveries constituted undisputable evidence that the sun, rather than the earth, was the center of our planetary system. But he knew that they would also inevitably arouse public censure.

Since Galileo's strong support of Copernicus' ideas conflicted with Church dogma, Papal authorities began to forbid distribution of his teachings. Though he argued as ridiculous the contention that "the same God who has endowed us with senses, reason, and understanding does not permit us to use them," his pleas went unheeded. However, Galileo was allowed to publish his "non-Copernican" works: *Discourse on Floating Bodies, Spots Observed on the Body of the Sun,* and *Discourse on the Tides.* He led a secluded life, taking solace from his three children born to him of a working-class woman.

In 1616, the scientist was ordered to refrain from teaching his astronomical views; he continued for years to chafe under these restrictions. Finally, in 1623, the liberal-minded Pope Urban VIII, an admirer of Galileo, took office. With renewed hope, Galileo devoted the next six years to composing his great work *Dialogue on the Two Chief World Systems, the Ptolemaic and the Copernican,* a masterful expose of Copernican theory. Pope Urban did not object to its publishing, provided he be given the opportunity to write the closing argument.

Years passed, however, as various curates and papal authorities examined the manuscript. Galileo moved to his retreat at Arcetri, near Florence, to be near his daughter Polissena, who had taken the name Sister Maria Celeste when she entered the convent there. Eventually the *Dialogues* appeared, and copies were distributed all over Italy.

But enemies in the Church again began to prejudice the Pope's mind against the "damaging" effects of the scientist's teachings. Once more the now feeble man was summoned to appear before Rome's Holy Inquisition. Galileo had to be carried to the trial on a litter. " . . . I not only repent having given the world a portion of my writings," he wrote to a friend, "but feel inclined to suppress those still in hand, and to give them to the flames . . . "

Galileo endured several months in prison – sick and fearing torture – writing and presenting his defense. Nevertheless, he was convicted of heresy by the cardinals and prelates. The white-haired man of science knelt before the assembly and recanted his beliefs. Under house arrest, he lived out his remaining years at Arcetri.

However, Galileo never ceased to work and learn. He completed his *Dialogues on Motion* in 1636 and made his final discovery that same year – observing the librations (apparent rocking motions) of the moon. But Maria Celeste's death coupled with his own blindness sadly shrank Galileo's vast universe into the lonely confines of a dark room, until death overtook him in 1642. At the time, he was making secret arrangements to publish his last major work, *The New Sciences.*

■ ■ ■

Galileo's theories helped shape an adventurous, hopeful new world. His sixteen volumes full of countless theories and proofs – once derided and banned as heretical – replaced Aristotle's outmoded teachings and launched new discoveries that continue to this day.

Even more essential to scientific advancement was Galileo's reliance on experimentation coupled with mathematical coherence, and an eagerness to perfect his changing ideas to conform with his experience. His example was a guiding light to our age.

NICOLAUS COPERNICUS

"Religious Astronomer"
(1473 - 1543)

Early Years

Copernicus, the great Polish astronomer, was born Mikolaj Kopernik in 1473 in the city of Torun, the son of a successful tradesman. Little is known of his early life beyond the fact that he was a serious youth with particular interests in the Greek and Latin languages. He was educated at home until entering the University of Cracow to study medicine and law. But it was Nicolaus' "hobby" of astronomy (he never became a professional astronomer) along with his inherent aptitudes for mathematics, philosophy and draftsmanship (he was a talented painter), that made him into the famed founder of present-day astronomy. Copernicus revolutionized and radically expanded the western idea of the universe – all in his spare time.

After Nicolaus graduated from Cracow with degrees in art and medicine, he studied in Padua, Italy, where he received a doctorate in canon law from the University of Ferrara. With law classes finished, Copernicus began in earnest to study medicine. As a future Churchman, it was quite fitting that he should become a practitioner so as to be able to minister to the indigent sick.

Practical anatomy at the time was regarded with distrust and repugnance. Dissection was banned altogether; but now Copernicus and his associates utilized the bodies of executed criminals to expand this branch of science.

The practice of medicine was not an uncommon concomitant for an early astronomer; the gulf between the various sciences was not so great as it is today. In fact, it was supposed that there existed a mystic correspondence between the organs of the body and the divisions of the universe; a relationship between astronomy and medicine that grew from the common belief in astrology.

Copernicus was offered the canonry of the cathedral at Frauenburg by his uncle, the Bishop of Ermeland. Some months later, when his uncle died, the young monk found himself in sole control of the monastery. There, living a life of solitude, he conducted his daily routine according to a careful schedule – characteristic of this man of precision – intended to promote his development in all spheres of life. He divided his day into thirds, consigning one part to devotional performances and religious duties, another third to acts of charity (tending to the needs of the poor and sick), and the remaining third to the study of astronomy, combined with meditation. This disciplined adherence to a philosophy of balanced activity marked his entire life.

Unraveling Mysteries of the Planets

In the third century B.C., the Greek philosopher Pythagoras, using observations made by his disciple, Aristarchus of Samos, had correctly stated that the sun was the center of our solar system. The earth and other planets, he explained, rotated upon axes and revolved about the sun to create days, nights and changing seasons. Later, (about 170 B.C.), the astronomer Hipparchus catalogued the positions of the stars.

But these brilliant conclusions were superseded by the doctrines of Ptolemy, a hellenic Egyptian king. Guided by Aristotle's influential – but sometimes erroneous – teachings, Ptolemy believed that the earth was the immovable center of the universe, with all planets, stars and moons revolving about it. He argued that if the earth actually did rotate on an "axis" and revolve around another, central object, then the rush of atmosphere would sweep mankind off the face of the planet. This understanding had remained unchanged for fourteen hundred years.

Medieval European culture, in a careful, heroic, and paradoxical effort to save the remnants of classical western civilization in a continent that had been plundered and divided by its own barbarian peoples, had come to focus almost fanatically on the saving grace of preservation. Monks devoted whole lifetimes to copying and illuminating the words of Aristotle and his disciples, along with other Greek and Roman luminaries and Christian saints; but any attempt to continue in the questing spirit that had enlightened these early artisans and thinkers was considered the gravest sacrilege.

Copernicus, however, was convinced that nature tended to behave in the simplest and most economical of ways. He saw Ptolemy's ponderous, complicated scheme of circles within circles to describe planetary motion as confusing and illogical. He was satisfied that Pythagoras' earlier theory was correct, but was unable to empirically prove it. With no telescope (this wonderful machine would not come along to verify his theories for another hundred years), the cloistered monk was left to his own designs to observe and calculate data received from the heavens. And design he did. First, he cut slits into the walls of his observation room. Through these he plotted the stars that crossed a prescribed meridian. In a short time, he was able, by means of a home-fashioned quadrant, to measure the altitude of individual stars above the horizon.

At about forty years of age, Copernicus wrote a short manuscript setting forth his observations and conclusions. Though he only circulated his treatise among trusted friends, somehow word of his ideas leaked out. Soon, scientists flocked to Frauenburg in search of the truth about the planets and stars. However, Copernicus' loyalty to the Church was strong; he disliked argument, and he felt that if he wrote against the almost sacred decrees of Ptolemy, charges of heresy would be forthcoming. His theories went unpublished.

At this time Copernicus and others also sought to reform the calendar, which Julius Caesar had introduced 1500 years before. These skilled men minutely calculated the amount of time-adjustment that needed to be made in order to keep the calendar in line with nature's seasons, and inserted in their design (along with the Roman "leap-year" every four years) a one-day adjustment to be made every 128 years. They made these precise measurements of the earth's orbital rhythms with only the clumsey arithmetical methods available at the time, and without those invaluable aids to precision in astronomy, the telescope and the pendulum. However, their ideas were rejected – until they became the foundation for the calendrical reform carried out by Pope Gregory XIII some years after Copernicus' death.

The astronomer's next twenty years were devoted to careful observations and meticulous calculations. From these Copernicus composed a skillful masterpiece, *Concerning the Revolutions of the Celestial Spheres*, in which he cited evidence to help describe his detailed theories of planetary and lunar motion. This "Copernican" system of the universe expanded on the Pythagorean model, with the planets – respectively, Mercury, Venus, Earth (and its moon) Mars, Jupiter, and Saturn – revolving around a central sun. " . . . As if seated upon a royal throne, the Sun rules the family of the planets as they circle around him." These planets were ringed by what Copernicus termed the distant "Fixed Stars."

Copernicus proposed that the earth hurtles rapidly through space; we do not sense its motion simply because we travel with the planet. The apparent motions we see in the heavens are in reality products of the earth's rotation and revolution. These theories laid the groundwork for Galileo's invention of the telescope, the planetary laws of Kepler, and Newton's gravitation principle.

The astronomer was never compensated for his work, nor, as a Churchman, did he expect compensation. On the contrary, he feared that undue publicity of his ideas would result in their official condemnation. Notwithstanding, Copernicus remained relentless in recording and documenting his beliefs.

At age sixty, he finally delivered a series of lectures on his heliocentric universe in Rome, and was surprised when no papal censure followed. All the same, his findings were kept unpublished for nearly another decade, partly because he could never feel that they were quite ready to print – fresh observations were continually being added – and partly because he feared the storm of criticism which he was sure would be unleashed from all sides against these ideas. (And, in fact, a century later Galileo would receive, from both religious and philosophical movements that were at this time being instigated, persecution for teaching the very same concepts.)

When at length Copernicus was persuaded to publish his book, he dedicated the work to the reigning Pope Paul III, the first in a line of more liberal, humane, and scholarly pontiffs. The "dedicatory note" was a masterfully bold, yet humble, plea:

If there be some who, though ignorant of all mathematics, take [it] upon them to judge of these, and dare to reprove this work, because of some passage of Scripture, which they have miserably warped to their purpose, I regard them not, and even despise their rash judgement . . . . What I have done in this matter, I submit principally to your Holiness, and then to the judgement of all learned mathematicians. And that I may not seem to promise your Holiness more concerning the utility of this work than I am able to perform, I pass now to the work itself.

On May 24, 1543, just hours before the astronomer-priest died of a stroke, the first printer's copy of *Concerning the Revolutions of the Celestial Spheres* was placed into his frail hands.

His book instantly aroused great interest, and motivated other scientists to proceed with further exploration into the precise, mathematical laws of motion.

■ ■ ■

The significance of the contributions of Copernicus to science is immeasurable. Unaided by the tools of experimental verification, he produced the first detailed mathematical outline of the skies, showing that astronomical prediction was possible. He dared to differ radically from accepted religious and philosophical canon – all the while working within the conventions of Church authority – and to record his convictions. His work in delineating our solar system inaugurated the experiments and refinements of Galileo and Kepler, the predecessors of Newton, who would in turn eventually formulate and draft the more comprehensive general theory of motion and gravitation. Copernicus' dedicated life ushered in a new era of philosophical belief and, indeed, became the launching point of modern astronomy.

ALBERT EINSTEIN

"Scientist-Mathematician-Genius"
(1879 - 1955)

Early Years

Though he would someday by acclaimed as one of the supreme intellects of all time, young Albert Einstein was slow in learning to talk, he failed to play with friends, and he was a poor student. Shortly after his birth in Ulm, Germany, his parents moved to Munich.

At age five, Albert's father showed him a pocket compass, and watching its mysterious behavior brought the boy somewhat out of his shell. But his elementary and secondary teachers still thought him stupid: he could not grasp languages, and he was less than interested in rote memorization, which he deemed useless.

Then, at twelve, the shy lad picked up a geometry textbook and read it cover to cover. He later referred to it as a "holy booklet" which led him to believe he could "get certain knowledge . . . by means of pure thinking." After that, he read book after book on mathematics. He taught himself differential and integral calculus, and read a six-volume abridgement of all the scientific discoveries up to that period.

Around this time his father's business failed, and the rest of the family moved to Milan, Italy, leaving Albert behind to finish school. But Albert hated school, and now that he was alone, he schemed to get a doctor to certify him as "emotionally exhausted" and to prescribe a long vacation in Italy. However, instead the school itself solved his problem by asking him to leave; his indifference was setting a bad example for other students.

Now relaxed and unconstrained, Albert decided to become a teacher, not only to supplement his father's meager income, but because he felt that a teaching career would offer him time to devote to mathematics, his real love. He applied for admission to the Federal Institute of Technology in Zurich, Switzerland, but failed the examination, scoring low in botany, zoology and languages. After a year of remedial study at a secondary school, he passed the exam, and in 1900 he became a Swiss citizen. About this time he also met and married Mileva Marec, a Hungarian student. They had two sons before divorcing several years later.

Because Einstein devoted so much time, energy and attention to his own work, he did poorly at making a living. He finally found work in the Swiss patent office, where, between patents, he worked in secret on his theories.

Einstein's Contributions

In 1905, at only 26, Einstein submitted three papers to the German periodical *Annals of Physics*. Each paper became the basis for a new branch of physics:

QUANTUM THEORY

Einstein first suggested that the photoelectric effect (an observed electric current created when a bright beam of light forces metals to release electrons) could be thought of as a tiny stream of particles – known as "quanta." As quanta struck against the metals, electrons were jolted out of their orbits within the atoms. Freed from the older theory that light travels solely in waves, other thinkers, with an understanding of the *quantum theory* were now enabled to invent the photoelectric cell, or "electric eye," which in turn opened the way to other inventions, such as sound motion pictures and television. The quantum theory eventually earned Einstein the 1921 Nobel Prize in Physics.

SPECIAL THEORY OF RELATIVITY

In a 30-page paper entitled "The Electrodynamics of Moving Bodies," Einstein presented his theory of relativity, containing his most revolutionary and famous concepts. Here, previously unimaginable ideas about time, space, mass, motion and gravitation were presented, with few footnotes and no references to other authorities. Though written in a simple style, this radical theory was rumored to be understood by only a dozen people in the world. Einstein always denied this however. A terse description of relativity follows:

Subatomic particles, which must be treated statistically, and large-scale bodies in the universe, can be brought under one, unified set of determinate laws. In the case of bodies approaching the speed of light, puzzling phenomena occur such as objects becoming shorter and heavier. Thus, there is no fixed, absolute standard of comparison for judging the motion of the earth or planets. Most people believe that time and distance are absolutes – that they can be measured objectively. However, in truth, *movement can only be detected and measured as relative movement: the change of position of one body in respect to another.* An electron traveling at 99% the speed of light would weigh seven times more than what it weighed at rest. If it did reach the speed of light (186,000 miles per second) – an impossibility, according to Einstein – it would become infinitely heavy and have zero length! Light-speed is the one measure in the universe that *is* constant and absolute.

The idea that a body would increase in mass and decrease in length when it approached the speed of light, led Einstein to the conclusion that mass (m) and energy (E) were related; in a sense, equivalent. He expressed this relationship in the eminent equation $E = mc^2$; with c representing the speed of light. c x c is obviously an enormous number, so that even the partial conversion of a small amount of matter will release tremendous amounts of energy.

A mind-boggling corollary of relativity implies that gravity between stars and their planets is not due to physical forces, but rather to the curvature of space itself. (Observation of solar eclipses have since confirmed this idea.)

Einstein's third paper concerned Brownian motion (irregular movement of microscopic particles suspended in a liquid or gas), which he used to verify the atomic nature of matter.

GENERAL THEORY OF RELATIVITY, 1916

Working from the basis of his special relativity theory, Einstein next attempted to express all physical laws using equations. This highly complicated theory, sometimes called the law of gravitation, was not derived by experimentation, but on grounds of symmetry and mathematical elegance. Though its proofs derive events from principles running counter to the accepted empirical methods of science, even so, this beautiful, intellectually satisfying general theory has so far withstood every test to its validity. It remains the closest approximation to ultimate truth yet devised or discovered.

UNIFIED FIELD THEORY

The General Relativity theory failed to include a rational explanation for electromagnetism. Thus, Einstein sought to "unify" his theory to account for this. Though he ultimately failed, he spent the last twenty-five years of his life attempting to prove or disprove the Unified Field Theory.

Einstein's Personal Life

Einstein became the twentieth century's most famous and popular scientist. He accepted posts at universities in Germany, and for seventeen years was free to devote all his time to research. But trouble appeared with the rise of the Nazi Party. As a Jew, Einstein found his situation more and more precarious.

When the Nazis finally seized power, Einstein, in England at the time, refused to return. The Nazi government proceeded to confiscate his property. Princeton University had long been inviting him to join their Institute for Advanced Study, guaranteeing him a "position for life"; and now, without a home to go to, he immediately accepted. "As long as I have any choice," he declared, "I will stay only in a country where political liberty, toleration, and equality of all citizens before the law is the rule." While living in a simple frame house on Mercer Street near Princeton, he became a U. S. citizen and eventually married his first cousin, Elsa, who faithfully shared his life and guarded his ever-diminishing privacy.

Once in the United States, Einstein seldom deviated from a strict schedule. At eight he would awaken. Before nine he was on his mile-and-a-half walk through the Princeton campus, along a winding country road to the Institute. Rain, snow, cold – he was never seen wearing a hat or boots, or carrying an umbrella.

At his spacious office, he would retire to a small cubbyhole intended for an assistant. (His comfortably furnished professor's room was too cold and formal for his tastes.) There he would sit, with a pad of paper on his knees, filling out sheet after sheet of equations.

"I think and think for months, for years," he said. "Ninety-nine times the conclusion is false. The hundredth time I am right."

After noon, Einstein would leave his office, walk home, have lunch, then resume writing in his study. On his daily walks, he stood out from all others – the great physicist, his long, glistening, white hair, deep-set eyes, baggy pants, and turtleneck sweater. On close examination, he wore no socks. Why? He reasoned that by spending little time on unessential things (such as his appearance), he could spend more time in study.

When the day was over, Einstein played the violin; he occasionally performed in public. He was also a skilled pianist, but this he reserved for himself alone. To him, playing the piano was simply a "necessity of life."

Einstein enjoyed entertaining close friends, sailing, playing parlor games, and discussing politics, philosophy and science. He read passionately, but not for literary escape – though he admired the plays of Shakespeare and Sophocles, and the novels of Dostoevsky. The scientist believed in a God "who reveals himself in the harmony of all being." He practiced no set religion. Instead he worshipped knowledge: "The whole of science is nothing more than a refinement of everyday thinking . . . He who can no longer pause to wonder and stand rapt in awe is as good as dead; his eyes are closed."

To Einstein, war was the worst way to solve differences: "Anger dwells only in the bosom of fools." But, in 1939, feeling that an anti-Nazi war was justifiable, he wrote to President Franklin Roosevelt about a new source of energy which could be used to make "extremely powerful bombs," and warned that physicists in Germany were already working with nuclear fission. Roosevelt heeded the warning and launched the Manhattan Project, creating the first atomic bomb just months before the Germans were to have completed theirs.

Following the war, Einstein returned to his pacifist ways and spoke out for a unified world government that could control or ban nuclear weapons. The scientist also had a major impact on the formation of a Zionist nation.

■ ■ ■

Albert Einstein, the scientific genius of this century, died in 1955, and, as he had requested, his brain and vital organs were removed for scientific study.

WINSTON CHURCHILL

"Britain's Courageous Bulldog"
(1874 - 1965)

Early Years

As a stocky lad with a mop of red hair, the unhappy young Winston stuttered and lisped and did poorly in school. His stubbornness and high-spiritedness annoyed everyone, his parents included. As the oldest of two boys born to Lord Randolph and Lady Churchill (an American-born beauty named Jennie Jerome), Winston entered Harrow Secondary School at age twelve, the lowest boy in the lowest class. But about this time Winston began to experiment with the English language, and loved it. "I got into my bones the essential structure of the ordinary English sentence . . . " This newfound faculty with language was largely responsible for his becoming "the greatest Englishman" of his time, and indeed one of the great men of all time.

As a child, Winston had played with regiments of toy soldiers for entire days. Remembering this, his father decided that the military would be the best career for a boy of Winston's "limited intelligence," and at age 18, after failing the entrance exams twice, the young man finally was admitted into the Royal Military College at Sandhurst. In time, he led his class in tactics and fortifications and graduated eighth in a class of 150.

Winston soon ached for adventure. At 22 he served as an observer and reporter in the Cuban revolt against Spain (where he acquired his famous taste for Havana cigars). In India, while his fellow officers slept during the blistering hot afternoons, he doggedly read those books he had neglected in his earlier education and taught himself to write in a lucid, bold manner. Later, after taking part in bloody hand-to-hand fighting, Winston obtained a newspaper assignment and joined on the cavalry charge through Egypt in the invasion of Sudan. In each campaign his experiences led him to write many volumes of vivid recollections.

Next, Lieutenant Churchill was hired by a London newspaper to report on the Boer War in South Africa. During this assignment, the Boers (Dutch settlers) ambushed an armored train on which he was traveling, capturing and imprisoning him. One night he made a daring escape. Since he was the son of an English Lord, a huge reward was put on his head as he crossed 300 miles of enemy territory to safety – to become the most famous war correspondent in British history. Churchill not only reported the news, he made it.

A Persistent Career in Politics

Though Churchill had lost his initial bid for election into Parliament the year before, the 26-year-old hero won election into the House of Commons on his second try in 1900. But the policies of his Conservative Party became unacceptable to him, and he boldly crossed the floor of Commons to the Liberal side amid both cheers and jeers from his countrymen.

Churchill served in several government positions during the next five years. Then, in 1911, Prime Minister Asquith appointed him First Lord of the Admiralty.

Churchill was one of the few Englishmen who realized the dangers presented by the recent military build-up in Germany. As the German arsenal grew, he reorganized the navy, developed anti-submarine systems, and readied the British fleet for what he felt was inevitable action.

In 1914, Germany made its move. World War I had begun. A disastrous failure by the British in an attack urged by Churchill brought about his resignation and almost ruined his career. But the new Prime Minister, David Lloyd George, reinstated him in the government as munitions minister. In this capacity, he concentrated on the development of the tank (largely Churchill's own "brain-child") and produced thousands of new war machines in a massive armament effort.

Following the First World War, Churchill's career oscillated: At one moment it would be up and then it would come crashing down. Between stints as War Secretary and a member of Parliament he lost two elections, but he never gave up his courage or sense of humor. On one occasion, unable to campaign vigorously after his appendix was removed, he lost his seat in the House, thus finding himself "without office, without a seat, without a party, and without an appendix." In the interim, he took up painting, surprising many with his talented use of bold, brilliant colors; and he continued writing. In four volumes he movingly recorded the events of World War I, and in another six, he presented a study of his famous ancestor, England's great war commander the first Duke of Marlborough.

For six years, sensing the grave peril of Hitler's rise, Churchill cried out to warn his nation of another threat from Germany. He was received with scoffs and accusations of "war-mongering": Who was he to refute British military intelligence? These jabs continued – until Germany marched into Poland in 1939. Along with France, the tottering government of Neville Chamberlain declared war on Germany, and named Churchill to the admiralty. But when the Nazis attacked Denmark and Norway, Britain's government, ill-prepared for war, collapsed in chaos, and King George VI asked Churchill to head a new government. As Belgium, Luxembourg and the Netherlands were being invaded, the 66-year-old Prime Minister wrote, "I felt as if I were walking with destiny, and that all my past life had been but a preparation for this hour and for this trial."

Contributions to World Freedom

Churchill took charge of Britain's destiny in some of the most desperate days of world history. Still, his words reverberated with pugnacious courage:

[Though all Europe might fall] we shall not flag or fail. We shall go on to the end . . . we shall fight in the seas and oceans . . . we shall fight on the beaches . . . we shall fight in the fields and in the streets, we shall fight in the hills: we shall never surrender . . .

These words proved prophetic; all continental Europe did fall, and Britain stood alone. Nazi invasion seemed certain. But the great orator again spoke confidently:

Let us therefore brace ourselves to our duties, and so bear ourselves that, if the British Empire and its Commonwealth last for a thousand years, men will say, "this was their finest hour."

The Royal Air Force (RAF) was the last line of British defense, and the German Luftwaffe now began to bomb British airfields and ports. Badly outnumbered, the RAF still managed to defeat the Luftwaffe, and Churchill acknowledged the nation's gratitude: "Never in the field of human conflict was so much owed by so many to so few."

The Prime Minister always staunchly heeded his life-long motto: "Never run away from danger." He weathered assassination threats and thrilled in ill-advised, self-piloted flights over enemy territory.

Churchill cut an inspiring figure as he defied air-raid alarms to tour streets under bombardment. He turned up everywhere – visiting war victims, inspecting facilities – always flashing his patented two-fingered "V" (victory) salute and clenching a cigar in his mouth. His bold decisions and stirring faith led not only his nation, but Britain's American and Russian allies as well.

When the War was finally won, Churchill, Truman and Stalin met in Potsdam to discuss what to do with vanquished German territories. Churchill distrusted Stalin, fearing Russia might now seek hegemony in Eastern Europe; he wanted to ensure that this did not happen. But Churchill's authority was curtailed when he lost his post as prime minister – government officials were looking for Conservative scapegoats to blame for Britain's lack of war preparation. This dismissal hurt Churchill deeply.

Nevertheless, the "Bulldog" (an epithet coined by his grandmother) continued to lead the opposition in the House of Commons, warning the Western world against the dangers of Communism, arguing, "Beware . . . time may be short . . . . An Iron Curtain has descended across the continent." Again dismissed as a warmonger, he kept himself busy painting, lecturing and writing, eventually publishing six volumes of World War II memoirs.

When Churchill and the Conservatives regained Parliamentary control in 1951, he energetically concentrated on foreign affairs until his retirement at the age of 81 four years later. However, he retained his seat in Commons – where his voice had rung out for over 60 years in the cause of freedom – until 1965, when, at the age of ninety, he suffered a stroke and died nine days later. "I'm ready to meet my Maker," he had declared to the press some months before, "but whether He is ready for the ordeal of meeting me is another matter."

Personal Life

Winston married Clementine Hozier in 1908. He wrote, "My most brilliant achievement was my ability to persuade my wife to marry me." He was a devoted parent to three girls and a boy.

Though he suffered several severe strokes, Churchill always seemed to rebound promptly to renew his work. A true "character," he read for long hours in the tub and relished friendly debates in his home. He typically worked 14-hour days that kept six secretaries busy. He credited his drive and vitality to the fact that he relaxed while he worked and always rested before getting tired.

On his eightieth birthday, honored with well-wishes and gifts from all around the world, he tearfully denied being Britain's inspiration through World War II: "It was the nation and the race dwelling all round the globe that had the lion's heart. I had the luck to be called on to give the roar."

Churchill won the 1953 Nobel Prize for Literature for "his mastery of historical and biographical presentation and for his brilliant oratory . . . " His literary works include: *The Story of the Malakand Field Force* (1898); *The River War* (1899); *World Crisis* (four vol., 1923-1929); *Marlborough, His Life and Times* (six vol., 1933-1938); *Second World War* (six vol., 1948-1953); and *History of the English-Speaking Peoples* (four vol., 1956-1958).

■   ■   ■

Few men ever served their country for so long or so well. Blessed with limitless patriotism, a profound sense of history, an intense, vivid personality, and an ever-apparent imagination, passion and courage, Churchill was ultimately recognized as "the greatest living Englishman."

BENJAMIN FRANKLIN

"America's Renaissance Man"
(1706 - 1790)

Early Years

Benjamin Franklin loved the fun life. His birth in Boston in 1706 placed him in a world where his inherent qualities of insatiable curiosity, optimism and sense of humor would soon be much needed.

While new political doctrines, scientific discoveries, and musical innovations flourished in late-seventeeth-century Europe, political and educational movements were still quite dormant in the American colonies. About the year 1682, Josiah Franklin brought his young wife and three children to New England. In the years that followed, Franklin had fourteen more children by two different wives. Benjamin, the fifteenth child, later described his father as a man of "sound understanding and solid judgement . . . "

The home was plentiful in children, but in little else. Most of the family's meager candle- and soap-making income went to feed and clothe themselves. The few books in the house included Cotton Mather's "Essay upon the Good That Is Devised and Designed by Those Who Desire to Answer the Great End of Life and to Do Good While They Live." This booklet, advocating good works in everyday living, profoundly affected young Benjamin.

At age six, Benjamin learned a great lesson. Seeing a boy tooting a new kind of whistle, he used all his pennies to buy it and returned home, happily blowing on the toy. His brothers asked him how much he had paid for it. When Benjamin discovered, to the older boys' laughter, that he had laid out four times what the whistle was worth, he devised one of his first slogans: "Don't pay too much for the whistle."

Briefly enrolled in a ministerial school, Benjamin excelled at reading and writing but failed in arithmetic. Then the family's resources dried up, and the lad was taken out of school to help make candles. The drudgery of this daily work was tempered by Benjamin's waterfront activities – swimming and flying kites with his friends.

Even at this age, Benjamin was filled with drive, curiosity and raw skill. Fired by his love of books, he went to work at age twelve in his brother James' printing shop. He would often stay up all night to read books lent to him by the sellers; and setting aside half of his food money, he would purchase other books. While his fellow workers walked out for lunch, he would sit down to a baker's tart with a handful of raisins, and read. He studied poetry, navigation, philosophy, and worked at arithmetic. He taught himself written grammar. But, for all his determination and learning, Franklin maintained a sense of open diplomacy and common respect.

[I try to express] myself in terms of modest diffidence; never using, when I advance anything that may possibly be disputed, the words "certainly, undoubtedly . . . " but rather " . . . I should think it so or so, for such and such reasons," or "it is so, if I am not mistaken." This habit, I believe, has been of great advantage to me when I have had occasion to inculcate my opinions, and persuade men . . .

Day by day, Benjamin's writing improved. On one occasion, he penned an article under an assumed name and slipped it under "The New England Courant" editor's door. To his joy, it was printed. Soon he saw thirteen more of his articles published – with good reviews – and finally he confessed to writing them. Benjamin's brother, far from being pleased, chose to beat the boy for his impudence; so Ben quit James' employ to strike out on his own. He left Boston for a brief stay in the city of New York, then sailed south for Philadelphia. After a thirty-hour, storm-ridden journey in which he saved a drowning drunkard, Benjamin walked the remaining fifty miles to the city, half sick, in heavy rains. The penniless young pilgrim following a Quaker congregation down the street with three puffy rolls under his arm (two of which he gave to a needy woman) would someday be the city's most renowned resident, acclaimed as one of the most versatile geniuses in history.

Franklin found work in the shop of Samuel Keimer. Under the youth's management, the business – and Franklin's reputation – grew. Then one of Benjamin's acerbic letters fell into the hands of the governor of the Province of Pennsylvania, William Keith. Fearing Benjamin's talents, his growing fame, and perceiving him as a potentially hostile satirist, Keith promised to fund an enterprise in England to be managed by Franklin. But once the governor saw Franklin safely stowed in England, he abandoned the young upstart with no funding or support. Instead of jumping on the next ship to America, however, Benjamin decided to take up work in a London printing establishment. He was referred to there as the

"Water American," because he chose to drink water rather than the customary six daily pints of beer. His theory: there is "more nourishment in a pennyworth of bread than in a quart of beer."

A lucrative offer to open a new school tempted Benjamin to remain in England, but a Quaker merchant, Mr. Denham, stepped in and offered him a position in his Philadelphia store. Franklin's acceptance of Mr. Denham's offer changed the course of American history.

During the voyage home to America Benjamin developed a plan for his life. His aims: to live frugally until his debts were paid, to work industriously and patiently in his new business, to be sincere in word and action, and to speak ill of no man.

But some of his homecoming dreams were soon shattered. He found the girl he had hoped to marry, Deborah Read, already married to a "worthless character" who later deserted her. Then Mr. Denham suddenly died, leaving young Ben out of a job.

As usual, though, Franklin seized the new challenge of the day. With the backing of a friend's father, he set up the firm of *Franklin and Meredith.* Using the techniques for accuracy and attractiveness he had learned so well in England, he soon had a prospering business. Franklin paid off his debts, continued to write unique, humorous articles (a rarity in that day), and went on to buy both a small newspaper and a stationery shop.

Franklin's Remarkable Contributions

As his multifaceted interests continued to unfold, Franklin, together with a few close friends, organized a secret debating society (the *Junto*) to openly inquire about points of politics, morals and philosophy. For forty years the group met weekly to discuss the issues of the day. This twelve-member body later gave birth to the American Philosophical Society. The Junto profoundly influenced all of Franklin's many careers.

Regretting the results of some of his youthful "freethinking" ways (he had fathered an illegitimate son, and generally been somewhat of a "rascal"), Franklin resolved to elevate his life closer to his ideal. He wrote a little handbook, "Articles of Belief and Acts of Religion," to promulgate his refurbished beliefs in God and to formulate a method for attaining perfection in his personal life. "Contrary habits must be broken," he noted, "and good ones acquired and established, before we can have any dependence on a steady, uniform rectitude of conduct." Thirteen virtues comprised his method:

1. Temperance. Eat not to fullness; drink not to elevation.
2. Silence. Speak not but what may benefit others or yourself; avoid trifling conversation.
3. Order. Let all things have their places; let each part of your business have its time.
4. Resolution. Resolve to perform what you ought; perform without fail what you resolve.
5. Frugality. Make no expense but to do good to others or yourself – i.e., waste nothing.
6. Industry. Lose no time; be always employed in something useful; cut off all unnecessary action.
7. Sincerity. Use no hurtful deceit; think innocently and justly, and, if you speak, speak accordingly.
8. Justice. Wrong none by doing injuries, or omitting the benefits that are your duty.
9. Moderation. Avoid extremes; forbear resenting injuries so much as you think they deserve.
10. Cleanliness. Tolerate no uncleanliness in body, clothes, or habitation.
11. Tranquility. Be not disturbed at trifles, or at accidents common or unavoidable.
12. Chastity. Rarely use venery but for health and offspring, never to dullness, weakness, or the injury of your own or another's peace or reputation.
13. Humility. Imitate Jesus and Socrates. (Humility was added to the original list of 12 only after a friend of Franklin's "kindly informed" him that he was "generally thought proud.")

Franklin sought to cultivate one virtue at a time and made daily recordings of progress in his diary. At the beginning of each new week, he would move on to another virtue. Thus, he was able to focus on each of his virtues four times that first year, and found himself full of so many faults that he nearly gave up. He persisted, however, and this rigorous self-examination became a lifelong habit. Certainly he mastered "Industry" (virtue number six on his list); his spare time during these years was spent inventing stoves, bifocals and batteries, debating philosophy, and studying. He became fluent in four different languages.

Deborah Read, whose husband had died, entered again into Benjamin's life. He married her, and she proved to be a loving wife and a thrifty, affectionate mother to his son and her own two children.

Franklin enjoyed successful careers in at least five diverse fields of endeavor: business, journalism, citizenship, science, and statesmanship.

Writer and Businessman: Franklin's *Pennsylvania Gazette,* filled with humorous, insightful stories and articles, prospered. He pioneered the printing of advertisements, many for products he carried in his own store.

In 1732 he originated the celebrated *Poor Richard's Almanac,* in which he demonstrated his unique talent for turning a clever phrase. In the blank spaces between the usual agricultural and astronomical data, he inserted witty adages and bits of moral and practical advice. Examples: "Keep thy shop, and thy shop will keep thee," "Fish and visitors smell in three days," "Diligence is the mother of good luck." With profits from the *Almanac* (which he edited for 25 years), he trained apprentices in printing and expanded his distribution – along with his ideologies – into other towns. At the age of 42, he retired, a comparatively rich man.

His hundreds of well-remembered sayings are still quoted, and his Autobiography is one of the most widely read books of its kind.

Citizen of Philadelphia: As a prominent newspaperman, Franklin had the rare opportunity to sway public opinion. This he did by first identifying a need for public reform, then discussing it with his Junto colleagues, and, after receiving their criticisms and suggestions, publishing articles pro and con about the issue to elicit public debate. Through this process, Franklin garnered support to establish Philadelphia's first public library, a police force, the nation's first fire company, and its first scientific society. He stirred up citizens to demand a regiment of "home guards" for public self-defense, the building of the Philadelphia Academy (which would later become the University of Pennsylvania), and America's first hospital.

Franklin's public-spiritedness secured his election, and repeated re-election, to Pennsylvania's legislature.

Scientist: Light, heat, fire, air, stars, tides, wind, rainfall, waterspouts, ventilation, sound, magnetism, illnesses, prehistoric animals and navigation all fascinated Franklin, the born experimenter and self-trained observer. The man's "hobby" of inventing is well-documented. From bifocal lenses to treatments for paralysis, from the character of clouds to the cause of colds – all were studied earnestly in Franklin's few "extra" hours during each week.

The invention for which he became best known was the Franklin stove. He solved the problem of smoky, "cold" fireplaces by devising a stove placed inside the fireplace wherein heat was circulated before being expelled out the chimney. The result: shins were not roasted while the back was chilled; " . . . the whole room is equally warm, so that people need not crowd so close around the fire, but may sit near the window, and have the benefit of light for reading, writing, needlework, etc." Franklin philosophically refused to patent the design, preferring to make it a contribution to the public: " . . . As we enjoy great advantages from the inventions of others, we should be glad of an opportunity to serve others by any invention of ours . . . "

Franklin's most famous experiment, of course, was the kite and the key in the thunderstorm – a most successful demonstration that electricity and lightning are one and the same. Before this, he had developed the first electrical battery and explained the device as a collected "plus" charge that gravitates toward the "minus" charge, just as higher water seeks a lower area.

Absorbed in his projects, the scientist considered retiring from business to devote all his time to experimenting; but "the public, now considering me as a man of leisure, laid hold of me for their purposes," he wrote. His fellow citizens reached out for his aid in a desperate political struggle.

Statesman: At age forty-two, Franklin was enlisted as Postmaster General. Soon after, he was asked to furnish and transport supplies for the armed forces in the French and Indian War. And, while engaged in this effort, he met a young officer for the first time – George Washington. During the war, Franklin captained a force of five hundred men assigned to build forts, Philadelphia's first line of defense against encroaching Indian tribes.

When a quarrel involving taxes erupted between the Penn family (influential descendants of William Penn) and the colonies, Franklin was commissioned to go to England to represent Pennsylvania. There, Franklin again used news articles to his advantage in negotiating the issues. For five years, he held conferences with political leaders, carried on his scientific work with prominent English scientists, and invented and played musical instruments.

In his absence, Franklin's wife died. When he returned to America in 1762, he hoped to finally settle down full-time to his physics experiments. But again he was drafted and sent to England to work on America's taxation-representation problems. England was in the process of passing the famous Stamp Act to raise American money for the British war with France. Franklin's warnings about the long-term dangers of this policy for colonial ties and trade, went unheeded; his mission, it seemed, had failed. In Pennsylvania, the enraged colonists condemned their ambassador as a traitor, and his family was nearly mobbed. But Franklin eventually managed to secure a hearing before the British House of Commons, and, in a dramatic contest of wills, he won the Stamp Act's repeal.

But Britain's colonial policies remained shortsighted. Further duties and taxes were imposed; and when angry colonials rioted in protest, dumping a cargo of English tea into Boston Harbor, Franklin joined the cry: "No taxation without representation!"

"I have some little property in America," he wrote in his public statement. "I will freely spend nineteen shillings in the pound to defend my right of giving or refusing the other shilling . . . " Amid insults and accusations, he was dismissed by the English Government.

In 1775, Franklin came home to an America in conflict. Elected to the First Continental Congress, he served on as many as ten committees and was one of five representatives selected to draw up the Declaration of Independence (Jefferson, of course, was the primary author). After signing the document pledging "our lives, our fortunes, and our sacred honour," Franklin declared, "And now we must all hang together, or we shall all hang separately."

He was soon called by Congress as an envoy to enlist French support in the American struggle for independence. Franklin responded, "You may have me for what you please."

After loaning the Continental Congress much of his money and property, Franklin sailed to Paris, where he worked long and strenuous hours as ambassador. "His name was familiar . . . to such a degree that there was scarcely a peasant or a citizen . . . who was not familiar with it, and who did not consider him as a friend to human kind," reported John Adams.

For a patient six years, Franklin presented his cause to friends, statesmen, scientists, and philosophers, again using humorous speeches and articles as tools to rally support for the American cause. He ultimately received valuable assistance consisting of French troops and loans totaling nearly sixty million dollars.

Now, at age seventy-five, Franklin wanted to come home, but the newly formed United States beseeched him to perform one more task – to aid in forming a treaty of peace with Great Britain, which was signed in Paris in 1783. Then for yet two more years he composed and signed treaties with all the other European countries, except Denmark and Portugal. When finally replaced as ambassador by Thomas Jefferson, Jefferson remarked, "I succeed him; no one can replace him."

On the journey home, the eighty-year-old diplomat wrote three scientific essays, one suggesting the use of Chinese-style of water-tight compartments in the holds of ships. (Today, all sea vessels worldwide are built this way.) Back home in Philadelphia, he was hailed a hero. Against his protest, he was twice elected governor of Pennsylvania (he donated his salary to a German college in Lancaster); but still he continued with his inventing. Late in life, he designed an ironing machine, a combination chair-stepladder, a book extractor for high-shelved libraries, a new kind of bathtub, and many other gadgets.

Lastly, Franklin was called to help draft the Constitution of the United States. His still acute mind was responsible for the provision for the election of an equal number of senators from each state (while state population determined the number of representatives in the House), ensuring that smaller states would be fairly represented.

In his eighty-third year, Franklin was permitted to retire. He wrote to a friend: "Let us sit until the evening of life is spent. The last hours are always the most joyful. When we can stay no longer, it is time enough then to bid each other good-night, separate, and go quietly to bed." A few months later (1790) he peacefully passed away.

■ ■ ■

Benjamin Franklin was a happy man. He once said that he owed his happiness to the philosophy he had formulated half a century earlier, which he summarized: "The most acceptable service to God is doing good to man." And Franklin used his enormous energy, shrewd business judgment, common sense, patience, tact, native wit, and well-honed literary strength to do just that, in every conceivable way.

Franklin's long life was well spent. He served himself, his neighbors, his country and all humanity with generosity and genius.

ABRAHAM LINCOLN

"He saved the Union"
(1809 - 1865)

Early Years

More idealized legends have been written about this American than any other. However, the actual Lincoln – known through his friends, their recollections, conversations, and his personal writings – was more truly heroic, deeper, and far more interesting in deed and vision than his popular image as a saintly folk hero.

Born to Thomas Lincoln and Nancy Hanks in a cabin along Nolin Creek, south of Louisville, Abraham Lincoln knew grief at a young age. His younger brother Thomas died in infancy; at age nine, he lost his mother to "milk sickness." Even after his father remarried, the boy was given to long periods of despondency. Abe grew very attached to his sister, Sarah, and after she too passed away at age 21 during childbirth, the young man took on a sadness and sensitivity that lasted a lifetime. But later, even in conducting a terribly bitter war, the man himself never became bitter.

Young Abe attended a Baptist church that opposed slavery. He also made several trips with his father to New Orleans, where he saw slaves being sold at auction. Lincoln, like most people of the time, felt "Negroes" were indeed inferior to whites. However, he also grew to believe that they were entitled to the "inalienable rights" of "life, liberty, and the pursuit of happiness" vouchsafed by God, according to the Declaration of Independence, to all mankind.

Abraham reached his full height of 6 feet 4 inches in late boyhood. The family moved to Illinois in 1830. Here, after helping with the planting and cabin-building, he struck out on his own and was hired to manage a mill and operate a store in the tiny village of New Salem. Abraham quickly earned admiration for both his physical prowess and his educational pursuits. He had attended school for only a short time in Kentucky, and had obtained most of his learning by reading *The Bible, Life of Washington, Robinson Crusoe, Aesop's Fables, Pilgrim's Progress* and the few available school primers. But now he began to study in earnest and soon developed a lasting fondness for mathematics, debate, and the writings of Shakespeare and Robert Burns.

When the government moved the Fox and Sauk Indian tribes from Illinois, the tribes rebelled, and the governor called for volunteers. Lincoln, a skilled storyteller, and a strong, friendly and honest fellow, stepped forward, and was promptly elected group leader by his comrades. The regiment saw no fighting, but Lincoln recalled that he did suffer "a good many bloody struggles with the mosquitoes."

Like many ambitious young frontiersmen, Lincoln entered politics, finishing eighth out of thirteen in his first race for the state legislature. Yet, he was a man of great ambition and complex personality. Outwardly he appeared calm, simple, courteous, even slightly "countrified." But he suffered inwardly, through periods of deep despair and depression. And, as for his political aspirations, he once told a friend after his first election as President, "You know better than any man living that from my boyhood up my ambition was to be President."

An unreliable business partner dragged Lincoln into great debt. For three years he performed odd jobs and served as Postmaster and Deputy County Surveyor to earn a living and pay off the debt. At age 25, due to a split in partisan support, Lincoln was elected to the Illinois State Legislature, where he became the Whig floor leader. During this time, he was befriended by a respected lawyer and Whig leader, John T. Stuart. Lincoln began reading Stuart's law books and was admitted to the bar in 1837. He then moved to Springfield to set up practice with Stuart, and served four terms as a legislator.

Lincoln met, and – after a stormy courtship – proposed to a plump, vivacious, but emotionally immature girl, Mary Todd. She was the only woman he ever claimed to love. They had three children together.

Now a popular circuit lawyer traveling around the state, Lincoln became noted as an extremely capable, thorough and honest attorney. He could immediately get at the core of a controversy, and he presented his cases so that even uneducated jurors could not fail to understand the issues. He often persuaded clients to settle their differences out of court, if possible – which left him unpaid. Eventually, in 1846, he won election to Congress; and though he took a firm stand against President James Polk's Mexican War (to him it was an unjust cause), his term was generally unspectacular. Lincoln chose not to run for re-election, feeling he was too unpopular to win. In 1849 he took a five-year leave from politics, returning to his successful law practice.

Lincoln's reputation as a man of integrity and respect for others continued to grow. He revered the Founding Fathers and the Constitution that granted freedom of education and commerce.

Journey to the White House

Lincoln's political re-entry came about more by accident than by design. Stephen A. Douglas, the stout chairman of the federal Committee on Territories, was shepherding through Congress the "popular sovereignty" Kansas-Nebraska Bill, which would allow the settlers of each state to decide for themselves whether they wanted slavery. Lincoln, however, took the view that slavery was morally wrong and that it should be limited at least to those states already practicing it. This differing opinion caused him to withdraw from the Whigs to join the Republicans. In 1858 he was nominated to run against Douglas for the Senate. In his acceptance speech, Lincoln's words stirred up quite a controversy:

A house divided against itself cannot stand. I believe this government cannot endure, permanently half slave and half free . . . . I do not expect the house to fall – but I do expect it will cease to be divided. It will become all one thing, or all the other . . . North as well as South.

Lincoln now began to follow the more celebrated Senator Douglas from town to town, waiting for chances to speak to the large crowds attracted by his rival. Ridiculed for this maneuver, he changed his tactics and challenged Douglas to a series of debates. With nothing to gain, Douglas still accepted, and Lincoln found himself in a position to contest the moral issue of slavery to excited crowds of ten and fifteen thousand spectators. Douglas refused to take a position on the moral right or wrong of slavery, while Lincoln, in characteristic slow amiability, insisted that the nation stood for equality and freedom.

An outdated apportionment of votes gave Douglas the victory in this battle, but the experience allowed Lincoln to formulate his thoughts and his strategies. The many national news articles and political cartoons also served to popularize him as a wise and moderate figure, a man tolerated by slaveowners and abolitionists alike.

Recognized as a confident, yet humble country man of unusual persuasiveness and humor, Lincoln always was a modest sort. " . . . Nobody has ever expected me to be President," he said in an 1858 speech. "In my poor, lean, lank face nobody has ever seen that any cabbages were sprouting out."

Always a clever and powerful orator, Lincoln began to speak out even more decisively against slavery:

While Mr. Jefferson was the owner of slaves, as undoubtedly he was, in speaking upon this very subject, he used the strong language that "he trembled for his country when he remembered that God was just . . .

. . . You have succeeded in dehumanizing the Negro . . . you have put him down and made it forever impossible for him to be but as the beasts of the field . . .

. . . Two principles . . . have stood face to face from the beginning of time; and will ever continue to struggle. The one is the common right of humanity and the other is the divine right of kings . . . . It is the same spirit that says, "you toil and work and earn bread, and I'll eat it." No matter in what shape it comes, whether from the mouth of a king who seeks to bestride the people of his own nation and live by the fruit of their labor, or from one race of men as an apology for enslaving another race, it is the same tyrannical principle.

Let us . . . unite as one people throughout this land, until we shall once more stand up declaring that all men are created equal.

Though Lincoln's perceptions of the Negro were imperfect, they were far ahead of the popular thinking of his time. Blacks in America sensed in him a basic love and humanness possessed by few men. He, more than any, was responsible for giving them, as a minority group, a stake in the future of America.

Three years before the Civil War began, Lincoln, speaking of slavery, prophetically stated, "In my opinion, it will not cease until a crisis shall have been reached and passed." The distinct economies and philosophies of North and South did indeed cause them to engage in just such a crisis, propelling the lanky lawyer into a "Messianic" role as a new "American Moses."

During his bid for the Presidency, Lincoln's public expressions became much more conciliatory and closer to official party – and public – sentiment. Yet he foresaw the inherent difficulties that lay ahead if the slavery issue was ignored and merely masked; and if slavery was perpetuated throughout the nation, he feared it would be the decisive factor in the Union's undoing. While continuing to term slavery as America's greatest evil, he was forced by convention to insist, "I have no purpose, directly or indirectly to interfere with the institution of slavery in the states where it exists. I believe I have no lawful right to do so, and I have no inclination to do so." And after taking the oath of office, Lincoln declared that "the Union is unbroken," and urged a healing of differences between North and South.

Lincoln took over the Presidency at a most crucial period of American history. Nothing in his past experience had prepared him to meet the trials ahead and he was handicapped from the beginning. America's reigns of government had been weakened by three consecutive self-serving Presidents. He had also received a minority of the popular vote and, by the day of inauguration, eight states had already announced their secession from the Union. War was imminent.

After the South seceded, Lincoln was convinced that the fate of world democracy hung on the fate of the Union. If democracy failed in America, kings and dictators around the globe could justifiably claim that people were not capable of ruling themselves; that someone must rule them. He left Springfield for Washington with these words:

I now leave . . . with a task before me greater than that which rested upon Washington. Without the assistance of that Divine Being who ever attended him, I cannot succeed. With that assistance I cannot fail.

To suppress the "insurrection," he called for the blockade of Southern ports and expanded the size of the army. In 1863, Lincoln issued the Emancipation Proclamation: " . . . All persons held as slaves within any state . . . shall be then, henceforward, and forever free . . . " Even the loyal border states still balked at freeing those still enslaved, causing Lincoln to consider The Emancipation a disappointment and a failure, though it paved the way for passage of the Thirteenth Constitutional Amendment, passed shortly after Lincoln's death.

At first, Lincoln's lack of executive experience made his administration appear to be vacillating. But the admitted weak and inefficient administrator used his expert insight, speaking ability and iron will to push an issue, pull it, or "leave it be," depending on the situation at hand. Lincoln turned to the "Commander-in-Chief" clause of the Constitution that empowered him with any means necessary to preserve the peace: "These rebels are violating the Constitution to destroy the Union; I will violate the Constitution, if necessary, to save the Union . . . "

Necessarily dictatorial at times, President Lincoln generally acted with restraint throughout the War. Critics assailed his leadership. He promptly replied:

In God's name! If any one can do better in my place than I have done, or am endeavoring to do, let him try his hand at it, and no one will be better contented than myself . . . . I do the very best I know how – the very best I can; and I mean to keep doing so until the end. If the end brings me out all right, what is said against me won't amount to anything. If the end brings me out wrong, ten angels swearing I was right would make no difference.

Lincoln frequently grew despondent. Even so, his public sympathies were always directed outward: "[The difficulties of the Presidency] are scarcely so great as the difficulties of those who, upon the battlefield, are endeavoring to purchase with their blood and their lives the future happiness and prosperity of this country."

The Civil War

With the bombardment of Fort Sumter, civil war was a reality. The South was better prepared for war. Furthermore, its citizens possessed a greater unity of purpose: independence. But despite the deficiencies of the early Northern generals (who specialized in political, not military, tactics), the North was vastly superior in industry, transport capability, and population. The Confederacy, on the other hand, lacked a strong, organized central government; and once the Union Federal Government was put in order, the South's weaknesses became apparent.

Lincoln commissioned – and then relieved each in turn – a succession of four generals, all of them, in his opinion, too hesitant and ineffectual. Finally, in 1862, Lincoln found a general he felt could decisively lead the Union forces to victory: Ulysses S. Grant.

The President penned numerous words of encouragement, commendation, and indirect instruction to his generals. To General Hooker he warned: "Beware of rashness, but with energy and sleepless vigilance go forward and give us victories." Commending General Sherman, he said: "Many, many thanks for your Christmas gift, the capture of Savannah. When you were about leaving Atlanta for the Atlantic coast I was anxious if not fearful; but feeling that you were the better judge and remembering that 'nothing risked, nothing gained,' I did not interfere. Now, the undertaking being a success, the honor is all yours . . . " And to General Grant he wrote: " . . . I wish to express . . . my entire satisfaction with what you have done up to this time, so far as I understand it. The particulars of your plans I neither know or seek to know. You are vigilant and self-reliant; and, pleased with this, I wish not to obtrude any constraints or restraints upon you. While I am very anxious that any disaster or the capture of our men in great numbers shall be avoided, I know these points are less likely to escape your attention than they would be mine . . . If there is anything wanting which is within my power to give, do not fail to let me know it. And now with a brave Army, and a just cause, may God sustain you."

Lincoln and his small staff remained in the White House throughout the war years. He visited army hospitals as often as he could, each visit tearing at his gentle heart.

At times Lincoln was forced into sternness, but, for the most part, he was overwhelmingly moderate and sympathetic. He pardoned scores of soldiers and wrote numerous letters of condolence to grieving parents. To the mother of five sons killed in battle, he offered these "weak and fruitless words": "I pray that our Heavenly Father may assuage the anguish of your bereavement, and leave you only the cherished memory of the loved and lost, and the solemn pride that must be yours to have laid so costly a sacrifice upon the alter of freedom."

At the Cemetery at Gettysburg, after the great orator Edward Everett had spoken for two hours, Lincoln's immortal words, lasting but three minutes, were soft and inspiring: "Four score and seven years ago . . . " he began.

. . . We cannot dedicate – we cannot consecrate – we cannot hallow this ground. The brave men, living and dead, who struggled here, have consecrated it far above our poor power to add or detract. The world will little note nor long remember what we say here, but it can never forget what they did here. It is for us, the living, rather, to be dedicated here to the unfinished work which they who fought here have thus far so nobly advanced, [that] government of the people, by the people, for the people, shall not perish from the earth.

The war dragged on: victories at Gettysburg and Vicksburg, the army's march to Richmond, Sherman's famous march into Atlanta. Grant suffered thousands of casualties, and many condemned Lincoln for supporting "the butcher."

Just as Lincoln's popularity reached an all-time low, the war neared its end. A series of final Union victories allowed Lincoln to seal his reelection over the Democratic General George B. McClellan. In his second inaugural address, instead of demanding vengeance against the vanquished South, Lincoln asked for "malice toward none" and "charity for all." He challenged the people to bind up the nation's wounds; to care for him who shall have borne the battle, and for his widow, and his orphan – to do all which may achieve and cherish a just and lasting peace . . . "

The effects of the war, together with the deaths of two of his three children, had taken their toll. For four years Lincoln had slept little and eaten irregularly with almost no relaxation. His face was gaunt and deeply lined, and dark rings circled his eyes. But the war had brought out his best qualities of persuasion and humility, and his rustic, subtle humor never deserted him.

On a brilliant spring day, April 14, 1865, Lincoln received news of General Lee's surrender that had taken place five days earlier. Lincoln spoke kindly of Lee and expressed the hope that there would be leniency given. He urged reconstruction of the South and commanded that there be "no bloody work" or persecutions of any kind toward Confederate officers or soldiers.

After signing the pardon of a boy-deserter and revoking the death sentence of a Confederate spy, he escaped for an evening carriage ride with Mrs. Lincoln. "We must both be more cheerful in the future," he told her. "Between the war and the loss of our darling Willie, we have both been very miserable."

Later that evening, after seeing several visitors, the couple went to Ford's Theatre to see "Our American Cousin." Arriving late, the performance stopped, and everyone cheered as the Lincolns entered their box in the front balcony. Even the bodyguard assigned to watch the President found a seat and relaxed to enjoy the play. President and Mrs. Lincoln sat hand in hand. Then suddenly, a muffled shot and a scream were heard. The President's assassin, John Wilkes Booth, hurtled to the stage, shouted what sounded like "Sic semper tyrannis" ("Thus always to tyrants," the motto of Virginia), and limped away. President Lincoln died from a head wound at 7:22 the following morning in a modest home across from the theatre.

■ ■ ■

To put the great man's life into words seemed impossible at that time – as it has since. Accolades and expressions of saddness flowed in from all nations honoring "Father Abraham". Rev. Henry Ward Beecher proclaimed:

. . . Now his simple and weighty words will be gathered like those of Washington, and your children, and your children's children, shall be taught to ponder the simplicity and deep wisdom of utterances which, in their time, passed, in party heat, as idle words.

Perhaps the most poignant lamentations came from both those who loved him best and those who knew him least. From a former slave we read:

He is gone out of glory to glory,
A smile with a tear may be shed.
Oh, then let us tell the sweet story –
Triumphantly, Lincoln is dead.

And, in a plea to hear more about the man Lincoln, a tribal chief in Russia's Caucasus region wrote to Leo Tolstoy:

. . . You have not told us a syllable about the greatest general and greatest ruler of the world. We want to know something about him. He was a hero. He spoke with a voice of thunder, he laughed like the sunrise and his deeds were strong as the rock and as sweet as the fragrance of roses . . . . He was so great that he even forgave the crimes of his greatest enemies and shook brotherly hands with those who plotted against his life. His name was Lincoln and the country in which he lived is called America . . . . Tell us of that man.

GEORGE WASHINGTON

"American Patriot-Leader"
(1732 - 1799)

Early Years

Born in 1732 in Wakefield, Virginia, George Washington was an energetic, practical Virginia boy of eleven when his father, a wealthy planter, died. Responsible for much of his father's estate, George's sense of duty, as well as independence, grew rapidly. His disciplined nature was shaped by a strict mother. She proudly lived to see her son attain his prominent status as one of the world's greatest leaders.

George was well educated, a passionate reader and learner. He was active in many sports and occupations of his day aided by a large, strong, agile frame, and handsome countenance. He stood about six feet, three inches and had enormous hands.

At age sixteen, George became inspired with the greatness and future of America when he accompanied Lord Fairfax on a surveying trip into the western country. Within a few years, Washington's 21-year old enthusiasm, combined with the power and instinct of command generally reserved for a man much older, caused him to be Governor Dinwiddie's selection to take a small band of men to warn the French against encroaching too far into British claims. He was soon commissioned a Lieutenant Colonel in the British army, serving under the command of General Edward Braddock. Washington's regiment attacked and destroyed a French scouting party; but a later defeat humbled him, teaching him he still had more to learn about military strategy.

Washington kept a meticulous journal. Few men have written more, yet he was not one to waste words. Sports and recreation, horses, dogs and business all interested him. In social matters he was adept, though he never seemed at ease with ladies. However, he was an excellent dancer and had relationships with various women. He married Martha Custis, a wealthy widow with two children. No offspring resulted from this union, but Washington was a devoted father to his stepchildren.

Washington quickly established a reputation as an energetic, courageous commander. Early on, he wrote, "I heard the bullets whistle, and, believe me, there is something charming in the sound."

With the defeat of Braddock's troops (after the General had shunned his young Lieutenant Colonel's advice) Washington's feelings that the British could be beaten in battle were confirmed. But, for the most part, Washington remained out of public affairs until he was over forty. He managed his estates shrewdly and intelligently, keeping an endless diary of transactions.

Washington watched with interest the growing discontent of the colonies and soon joined in protesting the unjust dominance of the mother country. He was chosen as a delegate from Virginia to the First Continental Congress, never dreaming of the permanent separation from Britain that would occur in the critical years ahead.

Washington's Gifts to Liberty

George Washington's historical service can be categorized into three chronological leadership roles:

1. Commander of the Continental Army

The Second Continental Congress unanimously chose Washington to command the American army in June of 1775. He was by no means a military genius. Still, his spirit and energy, physical appearance, tactical experience, administrative talents and rare ability to inspire others, made him a logical choice. He served throughout the war without pay and with unusual dedication.

At this early stage, the Colonial Army was in disarray. Jealousies between colonies created massive shortages; weaponry, food, clothing, shoes, and other needed items were scarce. Men, loyal to their own colonies, were often reluctant to be controlled by a "federal" leadership. Repeatedly, just as a soldier was trained and became useful, he would pack up and leave for home. Most were undisciplined, and when Congress could not supply necessities for survival, the cold, hungry, barefoot fighters were quick to lose the morale and patriotism they had earlier shown. But, somehow, most of Washington's men stayed on; it gave them hope to see him suffering along with them, side by side.

Through the winter of 1775-1776, the Continental Army drew its circle around Boston, forcing the British General Lord Howe and his troops to retreat to New York. Washington's troops pursued, but the combination of poor skills and lack of supplies, together with more competent British officers, contributed to their defeat on Long Island. Washington sometimes lost patience with Congress' lack of understanding and with the cowardice of some of his followers – but he never lost faith in the cause. Finally, victories at Trenton and Princeton, with the daring crossing of the Delaware River, bolstered his soldiers' spirits.

Rival leaders and "back-stabbers" took their toll on General Washington. General

Charles Lee had a certain contempt and jealousy for his commander. Lieutenant Horatio Gates' triumph over the British Burgoyne at Saratoga, could likely have been perceived as a challenge to Washington's future leadership, but Washington showed great restraint, praising the Lieutenant's feat.

The most wrenching of American betrayals was that of the trusted and brilliant Benedict Arnold. Embittered by Congress' inattention, Arnold agreed to surrender the vital position of West Point to the British. Though the plot was exposed, he succeeded in escaping to the enemy side. Washington was hurt by this defection, both politically and personally.

With Lafayette's French troops moving against Cornwallis' position at Chesapeake Bay in 1781, joined by Washington's men, the British surrender was near at hand. The struggle begun at Lexington, Massachusetts in 1775, was finally over.

2. President of the Constitutional Convention

Washington's enormous leadership did not go unnoticed by his fellow countrymen. The task now was to rebuild and restructure a fragmented nation. He presided over the Constitutional Convention of 1787 held in Philadelphia. Though not one of the Constitution's designers, his effort, flexibility, management capacity and influence were immeasurable in getting it ratified by the state governments. Were it not for his support and prestige, it is quite conceivable that the Constitution would not have been adopted.

3. President of the United States of America

As the inevitable choice to be the new nation's first president, Washington needed all of his persuasiveness and tact, as well as fierce tenacity, to maintain the Union. The difficulties were huge and Washington's pessimism grew. Indian struggles, the defeat at St. Clair, efforts to suppress the Whiskey Rebellion, growing American "radicalism," and the strain of defending decisions concerning his handling of the myriad lingering disputes between the United States and Great Britain drove the great leader near despair. Though his persistent, peace-making disposition held steady through the turbulence, at the end of his two terms in office he strongly urged future U.S. leaders to avoid foreign entanglements.

Washington had a talent for bringing powerful, conflicting points of view into harmony. For example, such opposing characters as Jefferson and Hamilton could have split the nation into pieces, but realizing how badly the country needed both men, Washington labored successfully for cooperation and peace. Adopting Hamilton's fiscal policies, the President was able to place the federal government on a sound footing. And Jefferson's tremendous reasoning, writing and speaking talents were equally useful in helping to shape the infant government.

In 1797, after eight years in office – the last several filled with friction and controversy – President Washington stepped down. His humble exit from power set a fortunate precedent for the United States. As history has indicated, it is all too easy for a new republic, even a democratic one, to degenerate into a dictatorship. In fact, the majority of Americans in Washington's time wanted him to remain in office as king. But, though he was a firm, forceful leader, he held little ambition for power.

In the face of a new French threat to peace in the United States, Washington's readiness to again accept command of the Army at age sixty-seven (just months before his death) exemplified his supreme sense of duty and sacrifice. No wonder he was and has remained "Father of His Country" and "first in war, first in peace, and first in the hearts of his countrymen." A humble, almost self-abasing man, he received universal praise and commendation up until the time he died at his Mount Vernon home in December of 1799.

A gentleman of one of the first fortunes upon the continent . . . sacrificing his ease, and hazarding all in the cause of his country.

- John Adams

The character and service of this gentleman are sufficient to put all those men called kings to shame . . . He accepted no pay as commander-in-chief; he accepts none as President of the United States.

- Thomas Paine

He errs as other men do, but errs with integrity . . . No judgement was ever sounder. It was slow in operation, being little aided by invention or imagination, but sure in conclusion.

- Thomas Jefferson

His talents . . . were adapted to lead without dazzling mankind, and to draw forth and employ the talents of others without being misled by them.

- Fisher Ames

■   ■   ■

Washington acknowledged that he lacked the innate brilliance of many other U.S. political leaders of his day (Jefferson, Madison, Franklin, Hamilton . . .). Still, he stands apart as the vital key to America's birth. His executive leadership and patriotism were indispensable ingredients both to the nation's early and enduring success.

THOMAS JEFFERSON

"Quiet Author of Ideas"
(1743 - 1826)

Early Years

Thomas Jefferson's father, a surveyor and a successful planter, left a large Virginia estate to his son. The eager youth spent two years at the College of William and Mary and then studied law. For seven years Thomas practiced law and worked as a planter; during this time he also married and started a family of six children. He was elected as a member of the House of Burgess, the lower house of Virginia's legislature, where he joined the Revolutionary Party. The future president took a prominent part in calling the First Continental Congress in 1774, and from that time on sacrificed a huge portion of his life to his country.

Jefferson's Statesmanship

Though a man of many talents (he knew five or six foreign languages, was well versed in mathematics and sciences, and achieved success as a "scientific planter," a manufacturer, an inventor and an architect), Jefferson will always be remembered first, for his polished and persuasive intellectual writings, and second, for his deft political diplomacy.

Jefferson's first important essay, written in 1774, was entitled "A Summary View of the Rights of British America." Later he was chosen as a Virginia delegate to the Second Continental Congress, where his ease with words was soon recognized. As relations with Britain became more and more strained, Americans debated the critical decision: should the colonies demand outright independence – a frightening idea to many – or should they seek a compromise with the British government? In June 1776, Richard Henry Lee of Virginia stepped forward and formally proposed that the colonies declare their independence from England. Congress appointed Jefferson to head a five-man committee (Benjamin Franklin included) to weigh the decision and prepare a statement. He was given liberty to almost single-handedly draft the popular statement. This "Declaration of Independence," acclaimed by many as the most forceful political declaration ever written, was adopted by Congress (with some modifications) on the fourth day of July, 1776.

That same year Jefferson returned to the Virginia legislature, where he piloted the adoption of several major proposals. Two areas of reform in which Jefferson showed particular interest were public education and religious freedom. Jefferson's "Bill for the More General Diffusion of Knowledge" led to eventual advancements in the American educational system, including the availability of public elementary education for all, state universities for higher education, and a system of scholarships for worthy but needy students.

Jefferson sought a separation of church and state and complete religious freedom. In Virginia, the Anglican Church had been the officially dominant church. His proposal, the "Statute of Virginia for Religious Freedom," passed Congress in 1786 amid considerable opposition. The same ideas espoused in this statute were later incorporated into the U.S. Constitution and the bills of rights of other states.

After serving two years as Virginia's governor, Jefferson "retired" from politics and settled down to write his only book, *Notes on the State of Virginia*, in which he outlined his philosophies, including his opposition to slavery.

After ten years of marriage, Jefferson's wife died. Though still young, he never remarried, devoting his life instead to his country. Jefferson's first proposal as a member of Congress was for the adoption of a decimal system of coinage. He reasoned that it would make monetary figuring much simpler – and he was right. But this motion was not yet approved. Jefferson also introduced a bill that would prohibit slavery in all new states. However, the potential history-altering bill was defeated by a single vote.

In 1784 Jefferson went to France on a diplomatic mission. When Benjamin Franklin's distinguished term as French ambassador was over, Jefferson succeeded him. During his five-year absence, the United States Constitution was drafted and ratified. The principal author was James Madison, but this document was not written without Jefferson's input. Jefferson favored adopting the Constitution but strongly advocated adding a bill of citizens' rights. Thus he became, by mail, one of the intellectual drafters of our Federal Bill of Rights.

Jefferson came home in 1789 to become President Washington's first Secretary of State. A clash soon developed between Jefferson and the politically conservative Treasurer, Alexander Hamilton. Supporters lined up behind their leaders, creating two factions – the Federalist party, headed by Hamilton, and the Democratic-Republican party (later the Democratic party), led by Jefferson.

Jefferson's forceful ideas can best be summarized by a few of his words:

• *On America's fight for freedom:* "The God who gave us life gave us liberty . . . " "The tree of liberty must be refreshed from time to time with the blood of patriots and tyrants. It is the natural manure." "We are not to expect to be translated from despotism to liberty in a featherbed. "Eternal vigilance is the price of liberty."

• *On small government:* " . . . A wise and frugal government, which shall restrain men from injuring one another, which shall leave them otherwise free to regulate their own pursuits of industry and improvement [is desirable]."

- *On "government by the people":* "The natural progress of things is for liberty to yield and government to gain ground." "Governments derive their just powers from the consent of the governed." "I have no ambition to govern men. It is a painful and thankless job." "That government is the strongest of which every man feels himself a part."

- *On government's weakness:* "No government can be maintained without the principle of fear as well as of duty. Good men will obey the last, but bad ones the former only. If our government ever fails it will be from this weakness."

- *On public education:* "The tax which will be paid for the purpose of education is not more than the thousandth part of what will be paid to kings, priests and nobles who will rise up among us if we leave the people in ignorance."

- *On slavery:* "This abomination must have an end. And there is a superior bench reserved in Heaven for those who hasten it."

- *Other famous sayings:* "We confide in our strength, without boasting of it; we respect that of others, without fearing it." "It is the trade of lawyers to question everything, yield nothing, and talk by the hour." "A mind always employed is always happy . . . " "I'm a great believer in luck, and I find the harder I work the more I have of it."

In Jefferson's first candidacy for President, he came in second to John Adams, and under the legal provisions of the time he became Vice-President. The unfortunate result was a deep, bitter ideological and personal split between the two men.

Jefferson ran again for the presidency in 1800, and this time defeated Adams to become the third President of the United States. Like Washington, who also served two terms, President Jefferson maintained a moderate, cordial attitude toward his opponents that served as a valuable model of tolerance for citizens of the new nation.

Jefferson was a tremendously capable and active administrator. Most notable among his presidential accomplishments was the Louisiana Purchase, which doubled the area of the United States and gained U.S. control of the Mississippi River. This was the largest peaceful transfer of territory ever recorded and helped turn the nation into a world power. Formerly a Spanish territory, and of no consequence to the United States, under the French flag and Napoleon's aggressive expansionism, its strategic possibilities threatened American democracy. Jefferson and his delegates "stretched the Constitution till it cracked" to have the purchase ratified.

Landmarks of Jefferson's first term included a war with Tripoli's Barbary pirates, Ohio's admission into the Union, the Lewis and Clark Northwest expedition, and measures he implemented to improve education and governmental management.

His second term was marked by a number of trade agreements, skirmishes with the British navy, the ongoing U.S. struggle to remain neutral in the war between England and France, a peace treaty with the State of Tripoli, Aaron Burr's trial for treason (he was acquitted, to Jefferson's disgust) and the prohibition of the American slave trade.

At age 65, President Jefferson chose not to run for a third term. At last, he recorded, he felt free to cultivate the "tranquil pursuits of science. . . . Never did a prisoner released from his chains feel such relief as I shall on shaking off the shackles of power."

Jefferson's final eighteen years were peaceful, though far from dormant. He continued in the capacity of elder statesman and he turned to studying music, chemistry, architecture, farming techniques, philosophy, law and education. He worked tirelessly to establish the University of Virginia, seeing a portion of his educational reforms put into practice forty-three years after he had first proposed them. Jefferson organized the University's curriculum, hired the faculty, selected the texts, drew up plans for the buildings, and supervised construction. He cheerfully met with the guests that streamed to his Monticello home. He finally reconciled with his old nemesis, John Adams, and the two carried on a remarkable correspondence up to the day they both died – on the fiftieth anniversary of the Declaration of Independence, July 4, 1826.

Thomas Jefferson's self-written epitaph included the two achievements for which he wished to be remembered: the founding of the University of Virginia, and authorship of the "Statute of Virginia for Religious Freedom." He died almost destitute, having long since sold his library of over 6,400 volumes to Congress to replace those destroyed when the British burned the Capitol.

Jefferson's philosophies, as set forth in the Declaration of Independence, were not original to him – John Locke, Voltaire and others had earlier promulgated the ideals of basic human freedom. But Jefferson's recommendations went considerably further. He perceptibly held his finger on the pulse of the "average" American, and he used magnificent phrasing to forcefully and concisely state what he sensed were the people's demands.

■ ■ ■

It is generally agreed that the United States has been deeply affected by Jefferson's ideas and attitudes even more than by his official acts. He may well be history's preeminent spokesman for human liberty and individual rights. Along with George Washington, the man of action, Jefferson, the man of ideas, was an essential component in America's struggle for freedom.

WILLIAM SHAKESPEARE

"Master Poet and Dramatist"
(1564 - 1616)

Early Years

The life of England's foremost dramatic writer is dappled with mystery. In fact, very little is officially "known" about Shakespeare; but scholars have pieced together a reasonably comprehensive picture of his life and passions from traditions, contemporary memoirs, and a lengthy series of records – including his baptism at Stratford-on-Avon in 1564, his marriage to Anne Hathaway in 1582, the christenings of their three children, his patent applications and court testimonies, his lease agreements, tax records and purchase agreements. And most reputable critics irrefutably ascribe to him authorship of the major portion (he likely employed collaborators on some works) of thirty-eight of the world's most respected and ingenious plays, several excellent poems, and some 154 sonnets.

John Shakespeare was a tanner, a dealer in grain, and a Stratford town official. His wife, Mary, was born the daughter of a prosperous gentleman-farmer. When their son William was still a young man, it appears that his father suffered severe financial setbacks. Thus, William must have achieved success largely on his own. He apparently never attended college.

Successive purchases and sales of agricultural products and parcels of land near Stratford must have provided Shakespeare with greatly increased capital, which, when reinvested, paid him a steady income for many years. This gave him the freedom and time to concentrate on his first loves: acting and writing.

Shakespeare the Writer

When Shakespeare began his writing, he was attacked by his fellow playwrights as a "mere actor" presuming to write plays. Then, in 1594-95, he performed before Queen Elizabeth, and his name became widely recognized. Within a few years he was lionized by critics, notably Robert Greene, who compared his "honey-tongued" comedies, tragedies and histories with those of Plautus and Seneca.

In association with Richard Burbage's company of actors, Shakespeare grew in public stature to become one of the owners of London's Globe Theatre in 1599. A decade later, he and his colleagues purchased the enclosed Blackfriars Theatre as a "bad-weather" establishment.

Shakespeare developed a writing style which proved to be both dynamic and one-of-a-kind; a style that incorporated – and transcended – a number of literary elements. He was especially fascinated by the conflict and divergence between *individual feeling* and *public office*. In Shakespeare's plays, what the successful public man might do often seems to go against what the same admirable private man might do, evoking a sustained level of suspense and drama. Additionally, the eventual resolvers of conflict are usually men and women of deep principle, but without the trappings of conventional authority – another line of tension. These two elements can be seen in the character of Hamlet, for example: a private man placed in a public situation (to avenge his father's murder); asked to act on a matter for which, with his contemplative and peaceful nature, he feels profoundly unfitted.

In harmony with the demands of Elizabethan audiences, Shakespeare laced his plays with twisted plots, allegory, metaphor, puns (even the tragic lovers Romeo and Juliet have a conservative estimate of 175 "quibbles"), word-plays (dual-meanings), and a smooth-tongued, economical use of words.

Even up to the time of his death, on or about his fifty-second birthday in 1616, Shakespeare was still originating distinct, well-turned phrases. His last will and testament and the inscription carved above his tombstone, which lies before the altar of the Stratford church, exemplify this wry style:

> Good Friend, for Jesus' sake, forbear
> To dig the dust enclosed here;
> Blest be the man that spares these stones
> And curst be he who moves my bones.

For study, Shakespeare's works can be divided into six separate, somewhat chronological sections: *Early Works, Major Histories, The Problem Plays, Tragedies, The Roman Plays, and The Late Romances*. His comedies seem to be interspersed throughout these divisions.

Early Works

The historical play was the dominant and most popular form of drama in Shakespeare's day. With his first works, *Henry VI* and *Richard III*, he hammered out his writing methodologies.

In these early works, staging is undeveloped, verse-form is inflexible and sometimes monotonous, and dramatic construction is rather crude. A serious and philosophic tone dominates; imagery and intensity are used over inner conflict to generate drama; no Falstaffian characters arise to add breadth or comic relief. Soliloquies and pauses for self-explanation are common. For instance, *Richard III* begins with a chorus-like introduction ("Now is the winter of our discontent . . . ") and proceeds to describe the general scene before turning to the personal plight of the Machiavellian hero.

These two plays were followed by a prolific number of dramas, comedies and fantasies.

Titus Andronicus, Midsummer's Night Dream, The Merchant of Venice, The Comedy of Errors, Two Gentlemen of Verona, The Taming of the Shrew, and *Twelfth Night* all come from this period.

Major Histories

Though the popular *Romeo and Juliet* was written during this second period, Shakespeare occupied the majority of his time recording the epic lives of English history – *Richard II, Henry IV,* and the great classic, *Henry V.*

Now the playwright more fully develops his dramatic material to include in-depth examinations of men in high positions, and studies of different personalities reacting to and exercising power. Richard II is an ineffective king, unable to properly respond to crisis; Harry of Monmouth, on the other hand, is the prototypical leader of men. In this period, too, plump Falstaff (*Henry IV*) appears, bringing to the horrors of war and men's pretentiousness his ironic commentary and touch of humanness: " . . . If to be fat is to be hated, then Pharaoh's lean kine are to be loved . . . " "Hostess, my breakfast, come! O, I could wish this tavern were my drum." When the comic Falstaff just as suddenly disappears in *Henry V* (he is off-stage, conveniently ill), it evokes an even more horrible sense of villainy and inner fear in the spectators as the onstage portrayals are acted out.

The Problem Plays (Dark Comedies)

"Problem plays," a term coined by F.S. Boas in 1896, primarily refers to the three plays *Troilus and Cressida, All's Well That Ends Well,* and *Measure for Measure.* These are commonly considered too serious and analytic to be classified as comedies, yet they are clearly not tragedies. They deal with moral concerns, and, depending on the audience, have been received with both disgust and applause.

However, *Hamlet* (which was written about the same time and is usually classified as a tragedy), despite its many loose ends, has a coherence and dramatic effect that is missing from the other three. Here the focus is on Hamlet's predisposition towards reflection rather than action, which allows us to see man's dilemma – whether to abide by public codes of conduct or by personal ethics.

Most see these plays as "experiments" that prepare the way for the great moral questioning and self-discovery that typify the works which follow.

Tragedies

Othello, Macbeth, and *King Lear* highlight the Passionate Tragedies. In these, Shakespeare transforms melodrama into tragedy, to explore the forces that destroy men and empires. The character of Othello – the mirror image of Hamlet – is unreflective and impulsive; essentially a public man caught in a domestic situation. When jealousy grips him, his judgment and thinking are clouded, leading to the murder of his wife Desdemona.

The elegant and simple *Macbeth* is a concise and moving account of a man descending into evil. Out of ambition for power springs a masterful and tragic plot. In this play, minor characters, for the first time, take on roles of major moral significance.

In *Lear* we also see poor judgement and blindness to true character. The king ultimately must lose his authority – and his family – in order to capture the vision of how power should rightfully be exercised.

The Roman Plays

The three "Roman" plays all center around human passions and the fall of a great and powerful man. In *Coriolanus, Julius Caesar,* and *Antony and Cleopatra,* character relations are illuminated, wonderful speeches delivered, and divided loyalties examined. Note, for example, the contrast between Cassius' invective against Caesar and Brutus' reverence toward Caesar coupled with his undying loyalty to Rome. Here we see opposite values and distinct personalities combining in a common purpose. The plays plunge the audience into politics and treachery (again, both public and private), and, of course, love and death.

The Late Romances

In this last era, Shakespeare may have found himself in a state of world-weariness. Up to this point he had always presented as the center of his dramas a great soul in torment. But in *Cymbeline, The Winter's Tale, Pericles,* and *The Tempest,* a more magical, unrealistic quality and plot prevail. These plays depict royal or semi-divine children recovering their lost beauty or virtue; they celebrate renewal, forgiveness, beauty and reconciliation, retreating from politics, power and violence. Shakespeare now uses more visual and aural effects. This less moving, more artificial style – possibly designed to help his audiences see beyond reality to more eternal truths – is seen by some as be a fitting epilogue to the Bard's calculated retreat from the personal and public tensions of Renaissance life.

■ ■ ■

Shakespeare's works represent the height of genius. Many of his famous lines are so well known that they are even quoted by persons totally unfamiliar with his plays. His works have profoundly influenced the English language and its drama for nearly four centuries, and it is reasonable to assume that his plays – read or viewed – will continue to provide pleasure and wonderment for centuries to come.

LEONARDO DA VINCI

"Renaissance Man"
(1452 - 1519)

Early Years

The illegitimate son of Ser Piero da Vinci, a legal advisor, and an obscure peasant girl, Leonardo was born outside the village of Vinci, near Florence in central Italy. Not much is known of his childhood, his personal philosophies or his marital history.

In his teens, Leonardo was sent to Florence by his parents to begin his apprenticeship as a painter. Under the tutelage of a leading Florentine painter and sculptor, Andrea del Verrocchio, he became a full assistant, collaborating with his teacher on the celebrated work "The Baptism of Christ." However, Leonardo's delicate hues and soft shadings contrasted sharply with the defined, traditional figures of Verrocchio's Early Renaissance style. The youth's more refined technique marked the beginning of the High Renaissance period, though his distinctive works remained unpopular for another twenty-five years.

As a multi-talented, entrepreneurial "project man," Leonardo had a tendency to begin tasks only to find his "wanderlust" and high-minded ambitions carrying him elsewhere. This habit was illustrated early-on when he was commissioned to paint a prominent church altarpiece in representation of the three magi worshipping the Christ child. Known as "Adoration of the Three Kings," the painting unmistakably manifests da Vinci's lively, more unified style in that the figures are arranged in a semicircle around the Holy Family as opposed to the separated profiles of earlier classical portraits. But the artist never completed the work; it exists today only as a group of outlined figures, devoid of detail.

Leonardo's need for variety saw him moving from his own studio in Florence to become court artist for the duke of Milan, Lodovico Sforza. In Milan, he was given a number of duties. As civil engineer, he designed bridges and aqueducts, diverted rivers and devised revolving stages for pageants; as military planner, he invented weapons and artillery; as sculptor, he designed a massive monument portraying the duke's father mounted on a vaulting horse; and as chief painter, Leonardo executed a number of paintings, including his earliest surviving finished work, "Madonna of the Rocks."

Unprecedented Contributions to Art – and More

Leonardo was possibly the most talented man who ever lived. Long after his death, his surpassing genius in such fields as mechanical design and anatomical study was recognized. Still, it was da Vinci's painting that made him famous during his lifetime, and it is his painting for which he is now best-known. The wall of the dining hall in the monastery of Santa Maria delle Grazie formed a fitting stage for his most illustrious creation, "The Last Supper," completed around 1495.

Traditional Renaissance representations of the scene depict 13 figures sitting in a line. But Leonardo's depiction shows Jesus as the central figure, surrounded by several small groups of apostles, with each individual responding to Jesus' announcement of his imminent betrayal. Acclaimed for the clear and expressive faces of the apostles and for its motion-filled scheme, the painting demonstrates Leonardo's novel philosophy; a philosophy that extended even to his paint mixtures. Leonardo wanted to work slowly and carefully in order to defuse his shadows and make essential revisions. The fresco paints used at the time dried quickly, not allowing for this slower pace. So da Vinci concocted his own compound to coat the monastery wall. (In later years, his inferior resin began to flake off. Recent restorative work has uncovered previously unseen objects, colors, and expressions, and has brought the masterpiece up to near-original condition.)

Shortly, as da Vinci shifted his interest to the areas of anatomy, astronomy, botany, geology – fields usually considered to lie in the realm of science – his art output slowed. (Actually, it never was equal to the prolific production of other first-rate artists – Rembrandt, Raphael, Van Gogh, Picasso, and Michelangelo, for example.) Still, his creative and analytic mind, combined with his artist's touch, produced astonishingly futuristic drawings of flying machines, parachutes and submarines. He designed forerunner versions of leveling and surveying instruments, hydraulic lifts, swing bridges, pulley systems, canals, street-lighting systems, pumping mechanisms, a water turbine, dredging operations, a steam calorimeter, a water-well drill, cranes for canal construction, metal template rollers, a mechanical saw, a treadle-operated lathe, a variety of chain links, compasses, weapons, and even a convection roasting spit. He described – and illustrated on paper – highly ethereal concepts: friction, magnetism, planetary motion, sound, liquid and solid states, simple mechanics, flight, structural load-testing, and many other notions dealing with engineering and science.

But as brilliant and original as Leonardo's prophetic sketches of modern inventions were, he was still compelled to leave it for future inventors (Edison, Watts, the Wright brothers . . .) to supply patience, mechanical aptitude, advanced knowledge, working details, and necessary materials to construct functional models of his drawings, and to examine his ideas in greater depth.

Leonardo was an acute observer of his world. By dissecting human and animal corpses, he created the first "textbook" of anatomy. His sketches reflect an accurate understanding of the functions of muscles, tendons, bones and other parts of the human body. He examined and sketched plants and geological formations. Also, by watching the heavens, he became one of the first to reject the views of contemporary science and declare that the earth rotates andmoves around the sun. All these observations he recorded in a series of impressive notebooks (many written, incidentally, in mirror writing). But his restless mind and personality would not allow him to delve into highly abstract thought. He failed to formulate scientific principles or to develop a systematic approach to his studies.

Leonardo, nevertheless, forged ahead to study all those things his eyes could see and his hands could touch.

After da Vinci had spent seventeen years in Milan, Sforza, his patron, was overthrown by the French, and Leonardo fled, first to Mantua and then briefly to Venice, before returning to Florence. There he was welcomed as a hero. He found that his earlier paintings had served as a great influence on the younger Florentine painters (notably Botticelli and di Cosimo). And now that the High Renaissance master had come home, he began to inspire the next generation of art masters, including Michelangelo and Raphael.

Florence's officials were in the process of constructing a new city hall. They requested that Leonardo and Michelangelo, working together, should enhance its walls with scenes of military victories. Again, da Vinci rejected the quick-drying fresco paints, instead trying an experimental composite called "encaustic." The encaustic's colors ran, however, and the walls of the city hall were also left unfinished. The splendid projected painting (filled with calvary regiments on horseback in the midst of dust-filled battles) can only be seen in Leonardo's sketches and from copies painted by other artists.

But one final legendary masterpiece was completed at this time: the portrait of Lisa del Giocondo, the young bride of a local merchant. Mona Lisa's mysterious half-smile became renown throughout Europe. Unlike past portraits done by artists who cut off their subjects at the chest, which produced a stilted appearance, the "Mona Lisa" included the woman's hands, folded so as to form an overall pyramid effect. The work served to inspire other artists to paint their subjects in more natural poses.

In his final years, da Vinci did little art work, devoting his time instead to drawing mechanical devices. These drawings themselves rank as masterpieces in their delicacy, shading and sense of movement.

In 1517, Leonardo settled in France at the invitation of Francis I, as one of the few supreme representatives of Renaissance culture. He died two years later.

■   ■   ■

Though he was considered a great architect, Leonardo da Vinci probably never designed a building that was in fact constructed. Not one of his sculptures survives today, though he was acknowledged as an eminent sculptor. And he is not known or honored for an incredible quantity of paintings, nor as a man of intense drive or courage. What does remain as a legacy of Leonardo's prodigious talents are his numerous drawings, a few (nearly twenty) magnificent paintings, and a large set of filled notebooks. Granted, Leonardo's unique painting style initiated a more graceful approach to art, and, in a sense, transformed the history of painting. But his greatness doesn't lie in any one accomplishment; rather, it is a result of the amazing number of areas of human knowledge that he explored, and of the fact that his studies and thoughts were far ahead of their time. Twentieth-century students still marvel at his genius.

Though Leonardo had no particular interest in literature, history or religion, his high regard for so many other disciplines has, in the intervening centuries, brought to him a reputation as the paragon of the true "Renaissance Man," a most brilliant universal genius.

LUDWIG VAN BEETHOVEN

"Musical Genius"
(1770 - 1827)

Early Years

Born in Bonn, of Flemish ancestry, Ludwig's childhood was made miserable by a father determined to turn him into an infant prodigy, in the mold of the distinguished Mozart. In fact, the father's yearning to see his son succeed as a child was so intense that he had Ludwig's birth records post-dated to 1772. Preferring drink over work, the elder Beethoven saw the boy's four-year-old talent as a way to earn money to lift the family out of its impoverished conditions. Ludwig did his exercises frequently in tears, under the iron hand of his father and the beatings he imposed. One day, when Ludwig's mother protested this cruelty, she too was beaten, upsetting the boy so much that he resolved to become great in order to buy his mother a better life.

Beethoven began composing early on, publishing some compositions at age twelve. In 1787 he met and performed for Mozart in Vienna, who commented on the lad, "Keep your eyes on him. Someday, he will give the world something to talk about." Indeed, he was to become perhaps the greatest of all musical composers.

Returning to Bonn, Ludwig played viola in the city's orchestra, but composed without much promise. In 1792, with French troops marching on Bonn, he was again sent to Vienna, residing there the remainder of his life.

Young Ludwig studied under Haydn, Albrechtsberger and Salieri. These associations turned sour, however, due to Beethoven's radical ideas about his music. He felt confined by the rules of composition set forth by his teachers, and sought to write with a freer, more modern interpretation. Still, his talent and drive to succeed carried him even during the periods in which he felt shunned. And, over time, he became immensely popular both as a piano virtuoso and teacher. Soon, his compositions also became well-received.

Vienna's high society tolerated Beethoven despite his repulsive appearance (he was stocky, hairy, broad-handed, and his face was pock-marked) and his unruly manners (he laughed over-loudly, was arrogant and untidy). He frequently caused "unpleasant scenes" where he would excitedly call people cheats – or worse – in public. He was a stranger to rules of etiquette and never concerned himself about such things. As one of Beethoven's few students, Ferdinand Ries, explained:

Attempts were made to coerce Beethoven into behaving with the proper deference. This was, however, unbearable for him . . . One day, finally, when he was again, as he termed it, being "sermonized on court manners," he very angrily pushed his way up to the Archduke and said quite frankly that though he had the greatest possible reverence for his person, a strict observance of all the regulations to which his attention was called every day was beyond him. The Archduke laughed good-naturedly about the incident and gave orders to let Beethoven go his own way in peace; he must be taken as he was.

Ries went on to describe his mentor's personal habits, which were quite the opposite of what one would expect from a master musician:

Beethoven was most awkward and bungling in his behavior; his clumsy movements lacked all grace. He rarely picked up anything without dropping or breaking it . . . Everything was knocked over, soiled, or destroyed. How he ever managed to shave himself at all remains difficult to understand, even considering the frequent cuts on his cheeks . . . He never learned to dance in time with the music.

Growing Musical Brilliance

Beethoven's music, more than any composer, was characterized by his moods. Three periods seem to define his life, and thus his musical creations:

First Period (1792-1802): The composer's initial musical style didn't differ markedly from that of Haydn's or Mozart's. A traditional flavor dominated his first two symphonies, which included *Sonata in C Minor* and *"Pathetique"* and *"Moonlight"* Sonatas.

In his late-twenties, just as his reputation was climbing, Beethoven's first signs of deafness appeared. This crisis deeply disturbed the young man, who actually contemplated taking his life, though in a letter to his brother he bravely prescribed for himself "patience and determination."

Second Period (1802-1812): Beethoven's growing depression caused him to withdraw socially – and his musical style became dramatically altered as well. Though he never married, he had several romantic affairs with female pupils during these years, and the romantic, emotional notes harbored deep inside of him flowed out. He produced a prolific output of compositions within this ten-year time frame.

Despite the fact that he paid little attention to what was fashionable with the audiences of the day, Beethoven's music increased in popularity. His lengthy *Third Symphony*, the *"Eroica"* (originally dedicated to Napoleon, but recanted by an angry Beethoven when Napoleon crowned himself as France's sovereign), the dazzling *"Kreutzer" Sonata*, the celebrated *Fourth* and *Fifth Symphonies*, the *Violin Concerto*, the overture *"Lenore,"* followed by the quiet *Sixth Symphony*, all had an originality previously unseen. A number of songs, his first five quartets, and the brief, lilting *Seventh* and *Eighth Symphonies* closed out these impassioned years.

At this point, Beethoven was beset by health and business worries. Quarrels with some of his friends and contractual disappointments caused him much grief. Additionally, Beethoven was given custody of a nephew who brought the doting and eccentric uncle great sadness during the rest of his life.

Final Period (1817-1827): As the years passed, Beethoven became totally deaf. His compositions became both fewer and more difficult to understand, and critics often spoke unkindly of his works. Beethoven was said to have defended his latter masterpieces with the futurist's view. "They are not for you, but for a later age," he dictated in a letter.

Found within his last symphonies is Beethoven's masterpiece, the choral finale "Ode to Joy." Its last four quartets stand as Beethoven's supreme achievement.

"Ode to Joy's" final quartet was written in October of 1826, while the composer was housed at his cruel brother's farm. Prohibited from having a warming fire in his room, Beethoven developed a severe chill. Then, the journey back to Vienna in an open buggy dealt him his death-blow. But his final months were at last filled with confidence and contentment. As he himself proclaimed, he had "endured beyond grief"; he was now "above the battle."

Beethoven died of pneumonia in March of 1827. All of Vienna turned out to mourn his passing.

■ ■ ■

Beethoven was by far the premier musical innovator of his age. Mozart and Bach were traditional perfectionists of musical form and elegance, and truly great composers. But Beethoven was original, bending music to his own will. He made lasting changes in style: he enlarged the introduction and the coda; he extended the length and scope of the symphony; he introduced episodes; he multiplied key-relations within movements; he introduced the chorus for use in the symphony's finale; he invented "song-cycles" (sequences of songs connected in subject); he redefined the variation; he initiated modern "program-music"; and he was the driving force in achieving independence of musicians and composers from the control of either church or court. Two of his most important contributions included expanding the size of the orchestra and establishing the piano as the foremost symphony instrument.

Beethoven's works marked the transition from the classical to the romantic style of music and, more than any other musician before or since, inspired divergence from orthodox form among composers who followed after him. Among those who borrowed from his style and employed his freeing philosophies were Brahms, Wagner, Schubert, Tchaikovsky, Mahler and Strauss.

Beethoven's paradoxical loss of hearing drove him to frequent and deep melancholy. But unlike many afflicted persons, who might have given up, he continued to compose, and during his years of deafness produced his greatest masterpieces. Overall, he yielded nine symphonies, five piano concertos, thirty-two piano sonatas, sixteen magnificent string quartets, an opera, a mass, a ballet and some seventy songs and theatre arrangements. More important than his mere quantity of writings, Beethoven transformed instrumental music into a quality and sensitive art form. Though far from an ideal, dignified individual, Beethoven left us gifts of music and profound creativity in musical theory, plus an influence that will likely be felt for centuries to come.

Three years before his death, Beethoven conducted the first performance of his *Ninth Symphony*. When the "Ode to Joy" concluded, the soloist from the violin section took him by the arm and turned him around so he could see the wildly clapping audience. Clearly, his works were appreciated by his own generation, as well as by us in this later age.

MICHELANGELO

"Artist"
(1475 - 1564)

Early Years

Born into the Florentine Buonarroti family in the village of Caprese, Italy, Michelangelo was the second of five gifted, classically educated brothers. Unlike his brothers, the boy was a poor scholar. Nevertheless, Michelangelo outlived and easily outdistanced all of his brothers in his achievements. His genius drew him to the study of human forms rather than the study of words in books. His influence on the visual arts of the Renaissance would be profound, making him one of the most famous persons of his time and of history.

With the death of his mother at age six, the physically weak lad withdrew into imagination and art. Although his ill-tempered father considered art a lowly profession, unworthy of the family, young Michelangelo continued to demonstrate an unusual talent and satisfaction in drawing. Every chance he got, he stole away into surrounding galleries and churches to study works of admired artists. He was also drawn to poetry, especially the "vulgar" writings of his fellow Florentine, Dante.

At age 12, Michelangelo was apprenticed to the most famous painter in Florence, Domenico Ghirlandaio. However, discouraged and bored by his limited duties as an errand boy, he left Ghirlandaio's workshop before completing his apprenticeship. Influenced by Bertoldo, a disciple of the great sculptor Donatello, Michelangelo first followed, then quickly surpassed, his mentor's graceful style. Lorenzo the Magnificent, ruler of Florence, was impressed by the gifted fifteen-year-old and took him into the Medici palace to live with his own family. Lorenzo became the artist's patron and "second father." Michelangelo's earliest surviving sculpture, dating from that period, is a battle scene bearing the dynamic movement and force that became his stylistic mark.

Following Lorenzo's death in 1492, the Medici family lost power. After a period of mourning, the young artist purchased "an enormous block of marble" with the intent of carving a colossal mythological subject – Hercules. He was obsessed with creating objects of violence and power, some say as a result of his frail stature and inferior feelings as a youth. "Hercules" and other projects he began were often left unfinished.

Michelangelo described his own appearance as almost monstrous: his head was an "inverted pyramid," with a large-templed head tapering to a crooked, broken nose and a small chin and protruding lower lip. " . . . My face inspires fear," he wrote on one occasion. He had broad shoulders that quickly narrowed into a tangle of thin arms and legs.

Michelangelo began traveling between Rome and Florence, frequently commissioned by popes and dukes to design and produce works of art. The pay was meager, and Michelangelo's father warned him against the dangers of being overly "penurious." Though his genius was not as universal as that of his older contemporary, Leonardo da Vinci, Michelangelo showed amazing versatility. He studied every branch of learning related to his art: "It has always been my great delight to converse with learned persons, and if I recall correctly, there was not one literary man in Florence who was not my friend." He studied anatomy – by dissecting corpses – and was also interested in astronomy. However, his primary accomplishments were realized in three main creative areas: sculpture, painting, and architecture. Michelangelo is perhaps the only man in history to have reached the pinnacle of mastery in two of these fields.

Michelangelo as Sculptor

Most critics acclaim Michelangelo the greatest sculptor who ever lived. His first major work, commissioned by a prominent Roman banker, was a statue of the wine god Bacchus. At 23 he carved the "Pieta," a marble representation of the Virgin Mary cradling her crucified son. The statue projects a deep yet unsentimental emotional quality, great physical strength and power, and genuine heroism. This work established the sculptor's reputation as an exceptional artist.

Michelangelo fought for the commission to carve a badly damaged piece of marble that would become the enormous likeness of a "perfect" and vigorous young "David." This statue, and those that followed, demonstrate an unexcelled artistry. Somewhat more simplified than most sculpture of the day, all these works were characterized by a strong, solemn appearance.

During this time, Michelangelo accepted too many commissions. The large and numerous contracts frequently so distracted the artist that he became seriously depressed. Suffering from acute illnesses, frequent headaches and exhaustion all through his life, Michelangelo often simply chose to move on and begin another project, rather than fret over an unfinished one. In 1505 a tomb with 40 marble statues was ordered built by Pope Julius II. Forty years later, Michelangelo had completed only a few of the pieces – but fortunately these included his renowned "Moses" figure. "Moses," noble and deep in thought, was used as the centerpiece of the tomb. Other tombs, other "Pietas" (one designed for his own tomb), and many minor works were also begun – but only some were completed.

Michelangelo's difficulties continued. In a letter to his brother, Buonarroto, he described his state: "I am suffering greater hardships than any man endured, ill, and with overwhelming labor; still I have patience in order to reach the desired end . . . . I am practically barefoot and naked, I cannot collect any money until the work is finished; I am suffering the greatest discomforts and irritations."

During this time, while he was busy carving heroes and saints, his dominating thought was of his lost mother. His need for maternal caresses overshadowed all his other concerns. He completed at least four Madonnas with Child (three sculptures and one painting) in that four-year period.

Michelangelo loved freedom, and was one of Florence's foremost political reformers. Even so, for thirty years he lodged like a poor, imprisoned man in a small dark room full of spiders' webs – conditions which he facetiously described in verse:

I am shut up here like pith in the bark of a tree –
alone and miserable like a soul imprisoned in a vial,
and my dark tomb is a tiny wretched cave where
Arachne and her thousand workers spin their webs.

But even after he grew quite rich, the artist never wanted to move from these miserable quarters, which he called his "dark tomb."

My happiness is my melancholy
These discomforts my repose . . . .

The Painter Michelangelo

Florence's government petitioned Michelangelo and da Vinci to collaborate on painted battle scenes for the walls of the city hall. From Leonardo, Michelangelo picked up several techniques and even greater skill in interweaving his subjects. His figures became not only massive, but also filled with intense vitality and movement.

Julius II gave Michelangelo his next commission – the ceiling of the Sistine Chapel in the Vatican. The frescos show nine scenes from the Old Testament, including the creation, the story of Adam and Eve, and Noah and the flood. These are surrounded by twelve larger-than-life paintings of male and female prophets. For hours on end from the years 1508 to 1512 Michelangelo stood on the scaffolding with his hands raised above his head to brush the brilliant colors on the grand ceiling – a ceiling that would one day be his legacy. Solitude was a necessity for him to bring this project to conclusion. He wrote to Buonarroti: " . . . I have no friends, and I seek none . . . . "

As the work progressed, he gained confidence, characterized by more powerful and colorful strokes. But, later, his strokes depicted tension and violence, probably a reflection of the aging Pope Julius' impatience. The Pope would often reprove and goad the artist, once resorting to beating him. Nearing completion, Michelangelo turned to a more restrained, contemplative mood of composing his figures; and finally, in resolution, he "completed" the ceiling, leaving certain parts less detailed and unadorned with gold than others. When Julius complained, "It should be touched with gold . . . It will seem poor," Michelangelo replied, " . . . Those who are painted here were poor themselves." And so the masterpiece remained.

Michelangelo went home to Florence, but in 1534, disgruntled with the Medici's rule and the lowly commissions he was receiving, he again returned to Rome, where he spent the next ten years painting for Pope Paul III. His most notable project was "The Last Judgement," showing the souls of mankind rising on one side of the Sistine's altar wall and falling on the other.

Michelangelo – Architect and Poet

Michelangelo designed the Medici Chapel and the Medici family tombs in Florence. These, along with the majestic Laurentian library built at the same time, were his most complete and ornate works – magnificently intense, symbolic statements of his interpretations of human destiny. Four princely figures (Day, Night, Dawn and Evening) recline on the curved lids of the tombs. These, in concert with long, narrow arching walls, and hollow, elongated recesses, reveal how Michelangelo saw the soul rising from the body after death and the endless movement of time between this life and the eternities.

In his seventies, Michelangelo devoted most of his time to architecture, poetry, and some painting. These later creations emphasized emotional simplicity. He exchanged his earlier, more violent, popular style for one that was more subdued, classical. No longer was he concerned with complicated interlocking of bodies in his paintings, nor with intricately designed buildings or structured poems. Some 300 of his insightful sonnets still survive, though they were not published until long after his death.

In 1546, Pope Paul III appointed Michelangelo chief architect of St. Peter's Church. He also planned a plaza-type civic center for Rome. Built after his death, the square avoids ordinary shapes, and directs its focus to the Senate House.

Michelangelo suffered a cerebral hemorrhage in 1561. For several days his mind was confused and his speech disconnected; but once again his tireless spirit conquered the weakness of his body. Within days, he journeyed by horseback to work on his designs for the Porta Pia. " . . . Art and death are not good companions," he recorded.

■ ■ ■

Michelangelo kept up his rigorous routine to the end. In Rome, just before his eighty-ninth birthday, he died. He had never married: "I have too much of a wife in my art, and she has given me trouble enough; as to my children, they are the works which I shall leave behind me, and if they are not worth much at least they will live for a short time . . . " He left behind, indeed, an impressive "posterity" of masterpieces.

As a great leader of the Italian Renaissance, Michelangelo broke from tradition, brought artists greater respect throughout Europe, and used his creative energy to become a great artist, a paragon to those who follow after him.

ARISTOTLE

"Scientist and Prince of Philosophers"
(384 - 322 B.C.)

Early Years

If there existed a "Renaissance Man" before the advent of the Renaissance, it was Aristotle – the great universal thinker who lived and wrote over 2,000 years ago, and whose ideas are still discussed, applied and debated today. Born in the town of Stagira, Macedonia, 384 B.C., he gained his interest in biology and the "practical sciences" from his father, Nicomachus, a prominent physician. At age seventeen, Aristotle was sent to Athens to study in the Academy of Plato, where he cultivated his formal philosophical thinking. He went on to enrich almost every branch of philosophy and science.

The young man remained in the school until shortly after Plato died – a total of twenty years. He loved Plato, but often disagreed with him.

Little is known of Aristotle's personality. He loved fine clothes, jewelry, wore his hair fashionably short, and had a stinging wit. He was quite thin, suffering from poor digestion. He spoke in a lucid, persuasive, conversant, though, at times, arrogant and impersonal style.

Aristotle was driven throughout his life by one overpowering desire: to know the truth. Discovery of truth was his sole concern throughout his career.

In 342 B.C., the young scholar returned to Macedonia to become the private tutor of King Philip's thirteen-year-old son, later known as Alexander the Great. After seven years, when Alexander ascended to the throne, Aristotle returned again to Athens. There he opened his own gymnasium-school, called the Lyceum, funded by his Macedonian pupil-king. This was the first known state funding of research – and the last for many centuries to come. While Alexander furthered his military conquests, Aristotle spent twelve years teaching. He married a woman named Pythias, who became the mother of their two children, Pythias and Nicomachus.

Aristotle was no intellectual recluse; he loved his reputation as a public figure, enjoying the thrill of discourse. To him, knowledge and teaching were inseparable.

The philosopher's ethical beliefs and background often contrasted sharply with the dictatorial ruling style of his former pupil Alexander. When the conqueror executed Aristotle's nephew on suspicion of treason, the more democratic Aristotle naturally felt threatened as well. But, ironically, when Alexander died in 323 B.C., Aristotle found himself, due to his association with Alexander, scorned by the Athenian "anti-Macedonians" who came into power. Indicted for "impiety," and recalling the grisly fate of Socrates seventy-six years earlier, Aristotle fled the city. He would not allow the Athenians to commit their "second crime against philosophy."

Aristotle died in exile just a few months after his departure from Athens.

The Ideas of Aristotle

Aristotle is credited with writing some 170 books, 47 of which still survive. But it is his enormous range of subjects that has amazed his students for over 2300 years. Mention a field of research, and Aristotle labored in it; pick an area of human endeavor, and he spoke about it.

Aristotle created a veritable encyclopedia of the scientific knowledge of his day, including anatomy, physiology, zoology, geology, geography, physics, astronomy and almost every other Greek discipline. Most of these writings were never intended to be read by the public, but were kept for Aristotle's own use. Hence, his many separate treatises are rough reading compared to Plato's polished literature. His accumulated writings also encompass the discoveries of others, including his hired assistants – together with conclusions reached by his own observations.

As the acknowledged leading expert in all fields of Hellenistic science, Aristotle was the premier philosopher. He researched and wrote on ethics, metaphysics, psychology, theology, politics, history, sports, economics, rhetoric, and aesthetics. His studies delved into education, diverse cultures, poetry, and comparative government.

It was Aristotle's remarkable gift for defining terms and categorizing thoughts which enabled him to master so many fields. This capacity to organize within his mind led to perhaps his most important contribution – the theory of logic. The philosopher always used common sense, never relying on the mystical or undefinable. Aristotle made mistakes, of course, but, in the vastness of his encyclopedia of thought he made remarkably few foolish assertions.

It is impossible to list all the ancient and medieval scholars who were influenced by Aristotle. His translated works reached most civilizations of Europe, becoming a major thrust both in the Western scientific surge and in Islamic philosophy. Averroes, the Arab scholar, labored to synthesize Aristotelian rationalism with Islamic theology. The Jewish thinker Maimonides achieved a similar synthesis for Judaism. Aristotle's thought also deeply affected Christian theology. The *Summa Theologica*, written by St. Thomas Aquinas, is perhaps the clearest and broadest reflection of this influence.

Unfortunately, as the centuries unfolded, Aristotle's categories and concepts became so entrenched as unquestionable "fact" that further intellectual inquiry was suppressed. The ever-learning philosopher would certainly have disapproved of such blind and unyielding adherence.

Some of Aristotle's ideas seem reactionary by today's standards, though they merely reflected the popular beliefs of the time. He maintained that women were naturally inferior to men and that slavery, at least in its ideal state, was in accordance with natural law. But many other beliefs were strikingly modern in nature. He considered poverty, for instance, to be "the parent of revolution and crime." Speaking on education (though there was no public education in his time), Aristotle pronounced, "All who have meditated on the art of governing mankind are convinced that the fate of empires depends on the education of youth."

Some of his ideas can be vexing, cloaked in obscure and often "unscientific" language. Despite his great respect for observation and comparison, he was forced by the strict tenets of Greek rationalism to follow a more formal method: select a theme, expand and illustrate the argument, make clear transitions, then add some examples here and subtract a hypothesis there. Although slanted towards formal logic and idealism rather than the rigorous experimental proofs we expect today, his lectures must have been challenging and, at the same time, exciting and penetrating.

A smattering of Aristotle's studies follows:

Zoological Research - Primarily in two volumes (*History of Animals* and *Dissections*), Aristotle provides detailed descriptions and diagrams of the structures (internal and external) of many different mammals, fish, insects, birds and reptiles, including the anatomy of man. He describes mating rituals and means of locomotion and survival. He obtained much of his information from beekeepers, fishermen, and hunters. These gathered facts together with his own observations laid the foundations of today's biological sciences.

Logic - Aristotle's work became the basis of classical deductive logic. He perfected the *syllogism*, an argument "pattern" consisting of two premises, followed by a conclusion. The major premise states: "All X's are Y's," "No X's are Y's," or "Some X's are Y's." The minor premise identifies a more specific relationship, and the conclusion is predetermined by the form of these premises. One classic syllogism, for example, begins: "All men are mortal; Socrates is a man; therefore, Socrates is mortal." In any valid syllogism, it is only by consistently offering true premises that the truth of the conclusion is guaranteed.

Causes - Material objects change, and their changes are caused. Scientific knowledge requires explanations to state the causes of change. Aristotle sought a "Why . . . ? /Because . . . " unity (similar to logical reasoning) to all questions. He would ask: Because of what does one thing belong to another? "Because of what does noise (thunder) occur in the clouds?" and so on.

A "World Picture" - Aristotle was certain that he could unite science and philosophy into one form of empirical, systematic research, to arrive at reality. Earth, air, fire and water made up his basic earth constituents, each having "primary" qualities. Earth is governed by circular motion "of necessity," and is the center of the universe . . .

Practical Philosophy - Practical sciences are those whose purpose is not merely to spread truth, but also to affect action. "Ethika" (ethics; "matters of character"), "arete" (virtue; the qualities of a good human being), and "eudaimonia" (doing; flourishing and succeeding in life) are each discussed in terms of individual motives, society's responsibilities and the idealist point of view.

The Arts - One can judge or produce a work of art by "imitating" human existence. For example, dramatic tragedy has six elements – plot, character, language, thought, spectacle and song. Plot, as in real life, is the most important. And art is emotional and intellectual, as well as aesthetic.

■　■　■

If you wished to learn about biology or physics you would no longer consult Aristotle's writings, but this is not true of Aristotle's more philosophical works. Though some details of his thinking have been superseded, his rational approach to learning is still alive and useful in current debate. He was an extraordinary man, probing for relationships among even the most common things.

From a portion of *Parts of Animals*, he reveals his personal relationship with the world around him:

. . . About perishable substances – plants and animals – we are much better off with regard to knowledge, because we are brought up among them; for anyone willing to take enough trouble may learn much of the truth about each kind . . . In everything natural there is something marvelous.

THOMAS ALVA EDISON

"Blue-collar Inventor"
(1847 - 1931)

Early Years

The young Thomas Edison, with only three months of formal education (the schoolmaster had actually considered his pervasive inquisitiveness as a mark of inattention and retardation), could scarcely have been envisioned by his family and friends as the world's future foremost inventor.

Born in Milan, Ohio, the youngest of seven children, "Alva" constantly asked questions which his prosperous, shingle-making father and one-time schoolteacher mother could not answer. And so, his curious mind sought the answers through experimentation. His mother, far ahead of her time, made this learning fun, describing it as "exploring." At nine years old, his course of study consisted of setting up experiments from a chemistry book – and proving them wrong. Along with this amateur experimenting, at age twelve he began to sell newspapers on a railroad line. Purchasing some old type, he soon was publishing his own *Grand Truck Herald*, the first known newspaper to be printed on a train. This publication was terminated, however, when a stick of phosphorous reacted and set the box car on fire. Alva, along with all his equipment, was thrown from the train.

A station-master, grateful for Alva's earlier rescue of his son from a rolling freight car, taught him telegraphy. At 16 he obtained his first job in Ontario, Canada as a telegrapher.

Having to signal Toronto every hour was a waste of time, Alva thought on one occasion. Hence, his first invention became a gadget rigged up to issue the hourly signal automatically, even if the operator was asleep. (This "sleeping signaler" almost got him fired a second time, when a railroad official did indeed find Alva asleep on the job.)

At age twenty-one, Edison made his commercial debut as an inventor with an electric vote-recorder. It did not sell (Congress wanted the chance to change individual decisions as the votes were counted); so thereafter he decided to concentrate his efforts on inventions that he was sure would be in universal demand.

Inventions That Would Change the World

In 1869, arriving in Boston nearly penniless, Edison persuaded a broker to let him sleep in his office. When the broker's telegraph device (stock-ticker) broke down, Edison was able to fix it after many others had failed. The amazed manager immediately made him one of his supervisors. There at the Gold and Stock Telegraph Company, Edison invented the printing-telegraph. But before approaching the company president, General Lefferts, to sell the device, he paused to come up with what he thought was a fair selling price for his improved stock-ticker – $3,000. But hesitating, he instead asked General Lefferts to make him an offer. The offer turned out to be $40,000.00! Steadying himself, the young man slowly intoned, "Yes, I think that will be fair."

When the stock-ticker patents were sold, Edison had enough money to establish his own manufacturing workshop at Newark, New Jersey. The business later moved its plant to Menlo Park, New Jersey.

At Menlo Park some of Edison's most important inventions and refinements were dreamed up, drafted, refined and manufactured. These included:

- A modernized typewriter: The substitution of metal parts for wood, better aligned letters, and more even ink distribution, made for a drastically improved device.

- A practical telephone: With Edison's use of a much more efficient, carbon-built transmitter, the telephone's audibility was greatly enhanced.

- The first working model phonograph: This was Edison's favorite and most original invention. Using a diaphragm, or revolving disk, which respond to vibrations of sound, he put together a completely mechanical device, as opposed to his past chemical or electrical inventions. On only the second try, Edison surprised himself by making the contraption recite back the words, "Mary had a little lamb."

- An incandescent light: Edison was not the first to invent an electrical lighting system. The Russian engineer Paul Jablochkov had lit up the streets of Paris using arc lights for several years. But Edison wanted small lights to replace the gas lanterns commonly used in homes at the time.

For over two years the inventor struggled to develop and perfect a practical incandescent light bulb. Thousands of different filaments were tried as he searched for the one material that would give off a good light when energy passed through it. The search took Edison's teams of technicians to many parts of the world. Finally, after numerous failures, he succeeded in keeping a filament of carbonized thread glowing for a whole day. This was the start of advances that would soon bring electric power to homes and industries world-wide.

Edison soon discovered that an electric current could be made to flow between two wires that did not touch – if they were placed in a near-vacuum. The genesis of the vacuum tube in time became the foundation for the electronics industry.

Over the years Edison designed the first power station – a system of distributing electric power to millions of homes by way of a number of companies, one of which became the standard for companies to follow: General Electric. Together with Edison's invention and refinement of the light bulb, the advent of power stations fostered an enormous boom in home conveniences and industrial advances that still continues today.

By the late 1880's Edison had already made invaluable contributions leading to the invention of George Eastman's motion picture camera. Then, as early as 1914, Edison connected the camera to his phonograph to make talking pictures. He hoped this would benefit in the teaching of children.

His later inventions consisted of the storage battery, a cement mixer, the dictaphone, a duplicating machine, a mimeograph machine, and his last contribution, synthetic rubber made from goldenrod plants. All told, "The Wizard of Menlo Park" patented an incredible 1,093 inventions. His talent also included a knack for organizing research teams, the prototype of collaboration in contemporary large-scale research laboratories.

Due to several "explosively inventive" incidents that occurred in his boyhood, Edison became increasingly deaf throughout his life. But he claimed that he did not mind this affliction; it actually allowed him to concentrate more fully. He also compensated for his handicap in another important way – by an astonishing capacity for hard work. Edison defined genius as "one percent inspiration and ninety-nine percent perspiration," and he demonstrated this philosophy by working days at a stretch, stopping only for short naps. His energy and interest pushed him to experiment in areas of medicine and farming. He came close to inventing the radio, predicted the use of atomic energy, and upgraded many other people's inventions.

Edison tried everything when working on an experiment, often choosing to ignore previous research by others that could have saved him time. He never seemed to become discouraged or to give up. After approximately 10,000 failed experiments on the storage battery, Edison simply reasoned that, "I have not failed. I've just found 10,000 ways that won't work."

His commitment to hard work and dedication to his experiments hardly made him a family man, or a close friend to anyone. He married twice (his first wife dying young) and had three children by each marriage. However, only one day out of the year – July 4th – did he set aside to be with his children and grandchildren. On this special day he would assure himself and his family a wild celebration, but every other day was spent in the laboratory. His work was his greatest joy and his laboratory instruments were his most cherished company.

■ ■ ■

Thomas Edison integrated the knowledge previously stored up by Gilbert, Volta, Ampere, Oersted, Faraday, Maxwell and other great scientists. By determination and hard work, blended with his tremendous innate talents and simple brilliance, he harnessed this knowledge to the profit of both himself and the world. Our dependence on the inventions sparked by Edison are now so much taken for granted that life seems almost unimaginable without them.

The scientist was honored with awards and adulation up until the day of his death at age 84. And Edison is still esteemed as perhaps the greatest purely inventive genius who ever lived.

MARIE CURIE

"Lady of the Atomic Age"
(1867 - 1934)

Early Years

Little Marya Sklodovska was the youngest and most cherished of the five Sklodvoski children in the Polish city of Warsaw. A melancholy yet authentic love prevailed in the home, though Marya could never remember feeling her mother's kiss. Madame Sklodovska would not even embrace her children. Her family did not know it, but she had felt the first symptoms of tuberculosis about the time of Marya's birth. Now, though she carried on the illusion of good health, she was gravely ill. When her mother finally lost her battle to infection, Marya felt pained and abandoned. But faith and hard work carried her through her first years of mourning, as they would continue to carry her throughout life.

Even though she detested her school's severe director, the serious, erudite Marya excelled in her studies. Since her father was a secondary instructor in literature, the whole family spent entire evenings reading and chatting about poetry and masterpieces of the past. She matured in an intellectual climate known by few girls of the time. Laden with Russian prize books and gold medals, the young Sklodovska graduated with top honors.

As a young woman, Marya broke from "ladylike" tradition and embraced chemistry and biology above literature. Liberal "modern doctrine" politics also intrigued her. Although in Russian-ruled Poland any manifestation of independence of mind was at that time regarded suspiciously, she met secretly with a group of other student "intellectuals" at the home of a teacher, to study natural history and sociology. Their underlying vision of a free and independent Poland would have meant prison for all had the group been discovered.

Nowhere in Poland were women permitted to attend universities. Yet Marya's goal was to become a teacher in order to assist her countrymen, whom the Russian authorities had condemned to ignorance. To further her education, she would have to leave Poland, but first she chose work as a governess to support her sister Bronya at medical school in Paris. These proved to be decisive years in her life. Besides teaching and trading political information with her friends at night, Marya frequently visited a clandestine laboratory run by a cousin, where young Poles were taught in chemistry. There, Marya determined to make science her life.

Finally, with her father helping out from his meager pension, Marya journeyed to Paris and entered the Sorbonne. Frustrated by the rapid French lectures and sensing a sizeable deficiency in mathematics and physics skill, "Marie" threw herself feverishly into her studies. She sank into solitude, hardly speaking to anyone, living on very little money, boarding in a tiny attic room with no lights or heat, and working at odd jobs.

Absorbed in study, Marie often went for days without food.

After gaining a physics degree as the top-ranked graduate in her class, Marie went on to earn a degree in mathematics, finishing second in the school. Learning was her passion; the girl had very little interest in romance.

But one day Marie was introduced to the chief of the laboratory at the School of Physics and Chemistry, a man already known throughout Europe for his experiments with crystals and electronics. Pierre Curie had passed over many "suitable" girls. After all, what wife could tolerate his fervor for physics? But now he became smitten with this amazingly gifted young woman. However, finished with her schooling, Marie refused his initial proposal; it was time to return to Warsaw. But pursued by Pierre's letters, which stated that he would even move to Poland to be with her, Marie finally consented to marry the physicist. From then on, the couple could hardly stand to be apart.

Work in Radioactivity

Marie read about the work of the scientist Henri Becquerel with the rare metal uranium – and the strange radiation it emitted. She chose this phenomenon as the subject for her doctoral thesis.

Creating a laboratory out of the damp basement of the school where Pierre taught, the scientist methodically undertook to test the radiation level (if any) of each of the then-recognized 80 elements. Besides uranium, only one – thorium – was found to actively emit "radio" waves – or be "radioactive." Still not satisfied, Marie next began breaking down various ore specimens into their component parts. Mysteriously, time after time the radioactivity given off by these compounds was far greater than expected. Only one answer seemed plausible: an unknown radioactive element had to exist. Her discovery was widely reported. Pierre, intrigued by Marie's studies, abandoned his own research to help.

These "partners in science" set out together to isolate a new element from the common substance pitchblende, whose chemical composition was already thought to be known. First they broke the pitchblende down into its individual compounds; then continued breaking them down into simpler forms, each time discarding the samples that showed no radioactivity. One by one, all known elements were eliminated from the ore, and after many tedious, painstaking weeks, only two radioactive samples remained: one of bismuth, and one of barium. This could only mean that, in actuality, two new elements were present. In 1898, the Curies announced to the world one of these new elements, which Marie chose to call polonium, after her homeland.

After a brief holiday, the Curies, along with

their infant daughter, Irene, returned to the laboratory and spent the next three months extracting the second element – radium. But fellow scientists expressed skepticism. If what was claimed was true, it would upset some of science's most fundamental theories. But the Curies now faced greater obstacles than their colleagues' doubts. How would they obtain the tremendous amounts of the all-important ore necessary to extract useful quantities of their elements? Where was a place spacious enough to accommodate the necessary equipment? With some luck and a lot of work, these questions were soon answered. Securing the use of a leaky vacant shed, they found that certain nearby mines often dumped their uranium tailings after extracting the uranium salts. The Curies purchased hundreds of sacks of the dull brown residue that held the hidden elements.

Polonium was deemed too unstable for initial study. Its relative, radium, must come first. To avoid breathing poisonous fumes, Marie spent her days in the courtyard, stirring a huge iron kettle of the steaming ore, while Pierre, along with a few other volunteer scientists, studied the properties of radium. At one point, Pierre became discouraged with how little they had to show for their efforts. However, stubborn Marie would not hear of giving up.

At the end of four back-breaking years, the ore had yielded up one decigram of radium – enough to fill the tip of a teaspoon.

It was soon discovered to have remarkable effects. After Marie's fingers were permanently scarred from burns caused by the substance's rays, physicians began experimenting; perhaps the rays given off by radium could be used to destroy diseased cells in the body. Radiation therapy – "Curietherapy," as it was first called – became a reality.

The marvelous element was now in great demand, and large-scale industrial production began. The Curies freely donated the secret of radium isolation; they felt that to sell their knowledge would violate the spirit of science.

The year that Marie received her doctorate (1903), the couple was awarded the Davy Medal, (England's highest scientific honor), and the Academy of Science honored them with the Nobel Prize in physics. The next year brought both a second child, Eve, and Pierre's election to the Sorbonne Academy of Science. But only two years later, Pierre was killed when, deep in thought, he stepped into the path of a heavy wagon. Now Marie was left to direct the laboratory on her own.

Months passed. With assistance from the scientist Andre Debierne, Marie succeeded in isolating the highly unstable metal "licradium". For her further studies of polonium and the newly discovered "actinium", and the invention of a more accurate method to measure radium, she received a second Nobel Prize, this time in chemistry. But along with public acclaim came public threats and accusations; the idea of a strong woman working alone in a man's arena had its detractors. More

than once Marie was led to the brink of suicide and madness by the malicious rumors that flew.

Still, by 1914 Marie had carried out another of Pierre's dreams: The Sorbonne and the Pasteur Institute established the Institute of Radium, and a two-building laboratory was erected for the study of radioactivity and radiation treatment. But World War I blocked the Institute's opening. Now with a feeble body and gray, ashen eyes, Madame Curie put her work aside to help war victims. No longer a solitary scientist, she began installing X-ray units in European hospitals and training nurses and volunteers in their use. As usual, she neglected her own health in her single-minded effort. She realized, as few others did, that an X-ray picture could locate a bullet or shell fragment so a doctor could more easily operate to remove it. By the end of the war, over one million wounded had been examined by her mobile and hospital units.

With peace restored, Curie and her daughter Irene opened the Institute of Radium. With the many grants and awards that followed, she went on to spearhead the building of a second institute in Poland. But amid her fame, Curie perhaps took the greatest pleasure in serving in the League of Nations.

For years the scientific genius had surrounded herself with a rampart of projects and duties. She had been preoccupied with completing her monumental book outlining atomic structural theory. Dedicated to "lovers of physics," its title was made up of one severe and radiant word: *RADIOACTIVITY.*

However in 1934, an obscure illness overtook Marie. For months she worked on – like her mother before her – in sickness, dizziness, and fatigue. At last she was forced to her bed. But Madame Curie's still lucid mind would not accept the idea of death. Before being moved to a country cottage, she summoned a colleague, Mme. Cotelle, to her room: "You must carefully lock up the actinium until my return . . . . We shall resume this work after the holiday."

Poisoned by the very life-giving radium which had been so much a part of her career, Marie Curie died on the morning of July 4, 1934.

■   ■   ■

Madame Curie was responsible for the unfolding of a revolutionary medical treatment – radiation therapy. But more than this, she led scientists to accept shattering new truths about radioactive elements. Elements, before thought immutable, were now understood to be capable of change, and of decay into less complex elements.

Her discoveries led to further probes into the structure of the atom; to the identification of alpha, beta, and gamma rays – with their life-saving and life-destroying properties; to the now-familiar concept of atomic number; on to the laboratory creation of element "variants" – or "isotopes". The brilliant and tireless work of Marie Curie indeed opened the gates to a new scientific era: the atomic age.

WILBUR AND ORVILLE WRIGHT

"Fathers of Flight"
(1867 - 1912 and 1871 - 1948)

Early Years

Milton and Susan Wright's third and fourth sons, Wilbur and Orville, like their older brothers and younger sister, were very much influenced by their mother. Milton was a minister and traveled frequently. During his absences, Susan ran an experimentally inclined household. Her children thought she could fix or invent anything. Naturally, her charges became similarly creative and skilled in using their hands. The second boy, Loren, invented an improved hay-baling machine; Wilbur designed a paper-folding device; and Orville, at 12, built printing equipment.

The family's introduction to flight came when Milton fashioned a miniature cork-and-bamboo helicopter with paper wings and propelled by wound rubber bands. Teamwork soon meshed with a freethinking attitude and vigorous confidence. All the children felt at home with books, new ideas, and animated conversation.

Wilbur and Orville began cooperating on most of their ventures, first setting up a printing business, and then picking up on the fascinating new developments in cycling. The brothers opened their own sales and repair shop, and soon were manufacturing their improved, eighteen-dollar "Wright Special."

By this time, Germany's Otto Lilienthal had already designed and tested his flying machine, similar to today's hang glider. However, Lilienthal, whom Wilbur later termed "inspirational" and "the greatest of the precursors" to manned flight, was killed on one of his experimental glides.

Samuel Langley had also developed scale models of gliders, to which he attached single horsepower engines. His full-scale "Aerodrome" consisted of an unwieldy contraption, launched from a catapult.

Hearing the reports of these developments, Wilbur wrote to the Smithsonian Institute requesting information on aeronautics. But at this stage, the brothers hardly considered themselves capable of actually constructing a flying machine.

Toward Kitty Hawk

Wilbur and Orville poured over articles and books, plus, spent countless hours observing the natural flight of birds. They were immediately struck by the meager amount of practical knowledge available on the subject.

The Wrights first noticed that the "experts" were chiefly concerned with getting their machines off the ground; they gave little thought to the problem of controlling the crafts in flight. The brothers devised a "three-axis" means of maneuverability. Further experimentation with kites resulted in a "wing-warping system" that offered better balance.

After several months of work, Wilbur wrote to the noted engineer Octave Chanute, describing his ideas, the brothers' limitations, and asking Chanute's advice. From this request, a life-long friendship ensued.

Near Kitty Hawk, North Carolina, lay "a stretch of sandy land one mile by five with a bare hill in center 80 feet high, not a tree or bush anywhere to break the evenness of the wind current." It was the ideal site to conduct their tests. The brothers set up a large tent and assembled their 17-foot-wide test glider. Once, while they were controlling it, kite-like, from the ground, high winds slammed the glider to the earth. After a week's work, the brothers launched their patched glider again, loading it with various weights to get a feel for its balance. When the wind was right, the glider was shoved down the hill and launched, this time with one of the brothers lying prone in the hollow center section.

In time the young men headed home to advance their designs and build a second glider. A full-time employee was hired to run the bicycle shop: calculations had to be made, questions waited to be asked and answered, and material shaping and fitting was needed. A workshop over the store provided the space.

The brothers returned to Kill Devil Hills, a few miles south of Kitty Hawk, and constructed a spacious shed to replace the tent. But their new glider was a disappointment. Control of the craft was a dangerous problem, although, with adjustments of wing curvature and slant, the glider safely covered distances of up to 389 feet. With the addition of wing-warping controls, the machine could bank and turn. One difficulty persisted, however: on some turns the craft would shake and then stall. Wilbur once plummetted to the ground in a near-fatal crash. The only conclusion the two daredevil inventors could reach was that Lilienthal's calculations, which the machine was designed from, had to be wrong.

The Wrights assembled two wind tunnels out of wooden boxes and engines. Though the tunnels had been invented by Francis Wenham decades earlier, no one before had grasped their potential practical use. Over two hundred differently shaped wing surfaces were tested in the tunnels for lifting capacity, wind-cutting ability, etc.

1902 saw the Wrights with a more streamlined glider, featuring a 32-foot wingspan. Other changes were introduced, including the addition of a tail; and later, a maneuverable tail piece was constructed that could be linked to the wing assembly for simultaneous adjustment. The brothers made hundreds of glides, competing with each other for distance and time aloft. They now knew that they would return to attempt to fly a powered craft.

Meanwhile, Samuel Langley, using over $50,000 in Smithsonian funds, was determined to be the first man in flight. But his search for a light-weight yet powerful engine had been in vain. On the other hand, the Wrights' sleek, sturdy and well-designed plane would not require so much engine power. With the help of Charlie Taylor, a simple mechanic, they designed and cast their own parts, fabricating in only six weeks a four-cylinder, 12 horse-power, 140-pound motor.

Previous propeller design was also found to be "very badly mistaken!!!" and "with the machine moving forward, the air flying backward, the propellers turning sidewise, and nothing standing still, it seemed impossible to find a starting point from which to trace the various simultaneous reactions. Contemplation of it was confusing," Orville wrote. Arguments flared up. Taylor reported that one morning, "following the worst argument I ever heard, Orv came in and said he guessed he'd been wrong and they ought to do it Will's way. A few minutes later Will came in and said he'd been thinking it over and perhaps Orv was right. First thing I knew they were arguing the thing all over again, only this time they had switched ideas. When they were through, though, they knew where they were and could go ahead with the job."

Their first propellers were made to spin in opposite directions so the plane would not be pulled to one side. "Isn't it astonishing that all these secrets have been preserved for so many years just so that we could discover them!" Orville boyishly noted in his journal.

Back at Kitty Hawk in September of 1903, the brothers discovered that storms had destroyed their shed. Hampered by bad weather and mosquitoes, the Wrights constructed a new shed and, at the same time, made their glider airworthy. Reports circulated that Langley's Aerodrome would soon be flying, but after hearing of several embarrassing failures, Wilbur penned a letter to Chanute: "I see that Langley has had his fling, and failed. It seems to be our turn to throw now, and I wonder what our luck will be."

Since the craft weighed in at 605 pounds without the pilot, the Wrights built a skid with a track going down the hill to get it off the ground. Their first launches proved disastrous. The engine sputtered while the propellers spun irregularly and then finally jerked loose from their shafts. Repairs went slowly. Winter closed in. The men's hands grew numb as they worked.

Later, the sprockets that engaged the drive chains from the engine were found to be loose. The propellers wouldn't rotate. "Day closes in deep gloom," Orville inscribed that evening. But the next day, "Thanks to Arnstein's hard cement . . . we stuck those sprockets so tight I doubt whether they will ever come loose again."

Then a new problem cropped up: a crack was detected in one of the shafts. Orville returned to Dayton to purchase stronger ones. But the brothers remained optimistic: "There is now no question of final success."

On December 17, five observers from the nearby life-saving station arrived. The plane pointed silently down its track into the wind. Orville slipped into position behind the controls, released the restraining wires – and lifted into the air. One hundred twenty feet and 12 seconds later, the brothers could, at last, congratulate one another. That day Wilbur's final flight covered 852 feet and lasted 59 seconds. "They have done it! . . . Damned if they ain't flew!" a witness shouted as he reached the Kitty Hawk Post Office. An engine-powered plane costing less than a thousand dollars had defied gravity.

Newspaper reports on the "Flyer" turned out to be terribly inaccurate; Dayton papers ignored the feat completely. A more efficient "Flyer II" was tested in Dayton's cow pastures later that year, but no reporters or curiosity seekers came around to bother the brothers. "Knowing that longer flights had been made with air-ships, and not knowing any essential difference between air-ships and flying machines, [people] were but little interested."

In 1905, the "Flyer III" achieved almost daily records. The longest flight went 24 miles in 38 minutes, concluding only when the fuel ran out.

■ ■ ■

It took almost five years from the date of the Wright brothers' first gravity-defying success for the world at large to recognize that manned flight had actually taken place. Wilbur took the plane to Paris for public demonstrations. Contracts from the War Department allocated $30,000 to build Wright airplanes. In less than a decade, Wilbur and Orville Wright had unlocked the secrets of flight.

Wilbur died of typhoid fever in 1912. Orville sold his interests in the company and lived on quietly until 1948. Neither brother ever married.

The airplane and subsequent manned space travel have shrunk our universe. And it was the Wright brothers who first fulfilled mankind's ancient dream of flying, changing the course of the world forever.

LOUIS PASTEUR

"Chemist-Healer"
(1822 - 1895)

Early Years

Born at Dole, in eastern France, Louis Pasteur grew up a tanner's son. In his teens, Louis' father sent him to Paris to study, but the lad became so homesick that his father had to return by coach to retrieve the pining boy.

Enrolled in a nearby boarding-school, Louis flung himself into learning to draw, and became a distinguished draftsman. This was only because he was an unusually conscientious worker. His letter of advice to his sisters included:

An individual who gets used to hard work can thereafter never live without it . . . work is the foundation of everything in this world. Knowledge raises us high above our fellows. Work depends on determination; moreover, it nearly always leads to success . . . . Determination opens the door to a brilliant and prosperous career, hard work carries one over the threshold, and in the end comes the crown of success.

Despite his work ethic, as a college student in Paris Pasteur's science genius was not at first apparent; one of his professors once described him as "mediocre" in chemistry. After receiving his doctorate in 1847 and obtaining posts to study at Strasbourg, Lille and Paris, his later contributions would make him the single most important figure in medical history.

Pasteur always saw potential good in everything: "When I approach a child his presence inspires two feelings in me: affection for what he is now, and respect for what he may one day become." He always maintained that to become great, to have good fortune and "chance," one must be favored with two things: enthusiasm and a "prepared mind."

Pasteur's Medical Contributions

Pasteur first received renown in chemistry when, at twenty-six years of age, he revealed startling research on tartrate acid crystals, showing that there existed "right-handed" and "left-handed," mirror-image isomers in the acid. He went on to discover a "living ferment" (microorganism) comparable in power to the yeast-plant, which would select as food the right-handed tartrates, leaving the left-handed ones alone.

As dean of the Faculty of Science at Lille University, Pasteur demonstrated that during fermentation, certain microorganisms could produce deadly effects on animals and humans. He refuted the standing theory and standard "proofs" that germs could spontaneously generate. And by excluding certain microorganisms from foods and beverages, he found that fermentation (souring and decay) due to yeast could be prevented.

Advocating this "germ theory," the scientist logically stressed the importance of eating clean foods with clean hands, and urged antiseptic methods for physicians and surgeons to prevent germs from entering the bodies of their patients.

Pasteur next invented the heating process of "pasteurization" for destroying microorganisms in beverages — especially milk. This technique kills the tuberculosis bacteria without damaging the milk protein. Where it has since been applied, pasteurization has all but eradicated infection due to contaminated milk.

With a "never-rest-until-it's-done" mentality, Pasteur succeeded in discovering and fighting other maladies: silkworm disease, harmful growths in beer, splenic fever and fowl cholera. He not only prevented or reduced the suffering of thousands of people, but also preserved the commerce of many industries.

Pasteur became captivated by the phenomenon of "anaerobiosis," in which certain microorganisms become weakened but remain alive in the absence of air. This predominant interest resulted in future discoveries that changed the world.

In his mid-fifties, a partially paralyzed Pasteur directed his genius to the study of anthrax, an infectious disease which attacks several species of animals, but primarily cattle. He first was able to identify the particular bacterium responsible for the disease. He then showed that it was possible to weaken ("attenuate") the vitality of the harmful "anthrax bacillus" by exposing it to air, placing it in certain heated cultures, or by transmitting it through animals. When "vaccinated" with this weakened strain, experimental sheep and cows developed a mild, non-fatal, form of the disease, effectively "immunizing" them from any further potent effects of the virus.

Through five years of painstaking and emotion-packed research, Pasteur finally produced an effective rabies vaccine, probably his greatest offering to the world. The vaccine had worked on animals, but Pasteur was worried of using it on a human being. If he applied the painful injections on a bite victim that hadn't yet shown the symptoms of the disease, the vaccine itself might cause death by hydrophobia. However, if he waited until the symptoms were already apparent, it would be too late. His career, and someone's life, would be on the line.

Rather than endanger someone else, Pasteur determined that he would be his first patient; he would subject himself to the bite of a rabid dog and then inoculate himself in secret. The scheme was abandoned when, that very day, a man and a boy appeared in his office, the boy having been bitten fourteen times by a mad dog. Nine-year-old Joseph Meister's parents accepted the risk involved. After ascertaining the likelihood that the boy would indeed contract hydrophobia, the hesitant Pasteur began treatment, a series of fourteen injections, one per day, each gradually more potent than that of the day before until Joseph's resistance to the disease was built up. Each morning Pasteur expected to find Joseph stricken with dreaded sickness – craving water he could not drink and burning with fever – but it never came. The night before the final, most powerful injection, the scientist sleeplessly tossed in bed. But finally, after a month of watching the boy regain his health, Pasteur could write, "He is now safe. The vaccine is successful."

The news swept around the world. People everywhere rejoiced; the little Frenchman had done it again. Frightened people, bitten by rabid dogs or rats, flocked to the lab. Pasteur and his assistants worked an exhausting schedule, often day and night.

Pasteur's only failure was ten-year-old Louise Pelletier, brought in 37 days after being bitten. Knowing that the disease was too advanced, Pasteur still made the effort and hoped for a miracle. As the girl died, the scientist held her hand in comfort and announced to the parents, tears streaming from his eyes, "I did so wish I could have saved your little one." Out of 350 people treated in those first few weeks, only Louise met death.

In 1888, his admirers funded the Institut Pasteur, a center dedicated to rabies treatment and the battle against all disease. (The Institute has since become a world center for biological research.)

Pasteur did much in the way of ensuring future medical advances; many would eventuate long after his death. He fought for research funding. He argued that "Physicists and chemists without laboratories are like soldiers without arms on the battlefield." Napoleon III, impressed by the scientist's reasoning, donated 30,000 francs of his own money for research.

Though Pasteur's devoted wife, the former Marie Laurent whom he married in 1849, guarded his health zealously, time took its toll. "I should like to be younger, so as to devote myself with new ardor to the study of new diseases," he said before slipping into a coma and subsequent death. And the day previous to that, he had requested to be carried into the lab to gaze into the microscope a last time and impart his views.

■ ■ ■

Pasteur was not the first person to suggest the germ theory of disease. (Girolamo Fracastoro, Friedrich Henle, Robert Koch and others had advanced earlier hypotheses). Yet his tireless advocacy of the theory was unparalleled. What's more, his numerous and popular public demonstrations of his revolutionary techniques and experiments spawned widespread excitement that ultimately convinced the scientific community that his theories were correct.

For decades scientists have applied Pasteur's imaginative ideas and procedures. Frankland, Vallery-Radot, Emile Duclaux, Descours, Holmes, and many modern-day medical authorities have since developed vaccines against other communicable diseases such as typhus, poliomyelitis, diphtheria, tubercular disease, cholera, yellow fever and different strains of plague. With health being the principle ingredient for a happy life, Louis Pasteur must be recognized as a man who has improved life's lot for millions of human beings. Certainly, the dramatic increase in life expectancy – which began, not surprisingly, about the middle of the nineteeth century – is due in large measure to the efforts of this master chemist-physician.

ANTOINE LAVOISIER

"Founder of Modern Chemistry"
(1743 - 1794)

Early Years

At the time of Antoine Laurent Lavoisier's birth in the outskirts of Paris in 1743, the science of chemistry lagged far behind physics, mathematics and astronomy. Chemists had hypothesized on chemical composition and pinpointed individual facts, but a satisfactory unified theoretical framework remained to be born.

The Lavoisier family was aristocratic and well-to-do. When he was five years old, Antoine's mother died, and the boy turned to his father for companionship. The father-son friendship grew so close, however, that Antoine had few friends growing up; he was satisfied with associations in his own family circle. When his only sister Marie died, the intelligent and lively Antoine, then in his late teens, was called upon to provide consolation to the older members of the family, who now seemed to live only for him.

Antoine attended the prestigious College Mazarin. His first interests were of a literary nature. With dreams of becoming an author, the young student turned to writing plays and earned a number of awards for his Greek and Latin compositions. He also enthusiastically studied law and composed legal expositions in a clear, logical style. After receiving his degree, Lavoisier was admitted to the French bar. Though he never practiced law, he put his legal background to good use in public service and administrative duties.

Antoine now became extremely interested in mathematics, anatomy, weather, and the physical sciences; but his real love was chemistry, which he studied under the tutelage of some of the most outstanding French scientists.

According to the custom of the time, chemistry lectures were given jointly by a professor and a less-esteemed "demonstrator." The professors would not lower themselves to the drudgery of experiments, nor soil their hands with charcoal or lime, leaving these tasks to the demonstrators. Antoine's teachers would typically present a lengthy, detached lecture on chemical theory, and then, before exiting, announce: "Such, gentlemen, are the principles and the theory of this operation, as the demonstrator will now prove to you by his experiments." More often than not, the demonstration would contradict the professor's discourse. These contradictions caught the attention of Lavoisier and other students and thinkers in France, creating a surge of interest in "real," factual, hands-on chemistry, rather than commonly held mystical, ethereal theories.

Lavoisier was awarded a gold medal from the French Royal Academy of Sciences for the plan he submitted on lighting city streets. Two years later, at age 25, he became a member of the distinguished Academy. Lavoisier's mind worked at improving French farming methods; and in the true spirit of science he established agricultural experiment stations in several locations.

At 28, Lavoisier married a fourteen-year-old girl after an arrangement between their fathers. The marriage was a happy one; Marie was a brilliant woman who shared Antoine's enthusiasm for learning and assisted her husband in his research throughout his life. In addition, Marie had a talent for making sketches and diagrams, and she diligently kept notes on experiments – besides writing down, in later life, the chemist's memoirs.

Isolated bits of information – much of it false or unproved – were all that made up the chemical studies of the time. It was believed, for instance, that air and water were elementary substances. There also existed a complete misconception of the nature of fire, scientists taking the popular position that all combustible materials contained an abstract substance called "phlogiston." During combustion, these substances supposedly released their supply of phlogiston into the air. Even those gifted chemists (Priestly, Cavendish and others) who had already identified and isolated oxygen, nitrogen, hydrogen and carbon dioxide gases accepted the phlogiston theory, and, in so doing, cut themselves off from the possibility of investigating the true nature and significance of molecular activity. For example, oxygen, which was referred to as "dephlogistated air" (air from which all the phlogiston had been removed), was known to aid in the combustion of wood. But this phenomenon was simply presumed to result from the "fact" that the depleted and "hungry" oxygen could more readily pull phlogiston from the wood. Real advances in chemistry could not be made until the explicit fundamentals and structure of matter were understood.

The Nature of Matter Unfolds

Lavoisier boldly pronounced that there was no such substance as phlogiston; that the theory was totally incorrect. His careful experiments led him to insist that combustion consists of a chemical reaction between oxygen and the burning material.

Other studies convinced the chemist that water was not after all an elementary substance, but a chemical compound of oxygen and "inflammable air" (hydrogen). Lavoisier went on to show that air consists of a mixture of two main gases, oxygen and nitrogen. These ideas seem quite obvious today, but were considered major breakthroughs in the 1700's. Even after Lavoisier formulated his theories and presented supporting evidence for them, many leading chemists continued to disregard his discoveries.

Though principally known as a chemist, Lavoisier further applied his ideas to geology and physiology. Since the earth gave off heat, he inferred that combustion of some sort must be burning a yet-to-be-discovered source of energy. In a sense, he was right. The earth does act as a heat retainer, soaking up heat given off by the sun in the form of heat and light – energy radiated into space after being generated by nuclear fusion reactions at the sun's core. The source of this "borrowed" heat is indeed combustion.

Then, together with the astronomer Pierre Laplace, Lavoisier looked into "combustion" occurring within the human body. Here, too, he developed hypotheses as well as experiments to show that the physiological process of respiration is a sort of "slow burning" of inhaled oxygen, and that the body's source of energy must likewise be the burning of food.

In 1789, after many years of painstaking work and rework, Lavoisier published his prodigious textbook *Elements of Chemistry*. Instantly displacing all preceding chemistry texts, its clear, logical, convincing hypotheses and proofs were eagerly embraced by younger chemists.

Listed in his book were those substances Lavoisier believed to be *elements* (substances that cannot be broken down into simpler fragments by chemical means). Although the list contained some errors, our modern "Periodic Table of Elements" is basically an elaborated, expanded version of Lavoisier's table. Next, along with Berthollet, Fourcroi, and de Morveau, he organized the first system of elementary chemical nomenclature, foundational to today's labeling of elements and compounds. This uniformity in naming elements soon allowed scientists throughout the world to more easily communicate and share their discoveries.

Lavoisier insisted on meticulously weighing the components involved in a chemical reaction. With his careful, controlled experiments, he became the first person to conclusively state the principle of conservation of mass, which states that: though the distribution of elements within substances may be rearranged in a chemical reaction, no matter is destroyed, and the end products weigh the same as the original components. Lavoisier was also first to express this principle of the conservation of matter in the form of a chemical equation, wherein the mass of materials present before a chemical change must equal the mass of products after. His precise methods formed the basis of chemistry as an exact science.

As a distinguished member of the Academy of Sciences and part owner (along with his father-in-law) of the Ferme Generale, a financial company that collected taxes for the government, Lavoisier was a prime target for persecution and a leading suspect when the ten-year French Revolution broke out in 1789. The aristocracy, along with the more learned bourgeoisie citizens, were decried as part of an elitist faction treading on the rights and dignity of the proletariat poor.

Eventually, Lavoisier, Marie's father, and twenty-six others belonging to the Ferme Generale were arrested. In the swift, frenzied "justice" of the period, the men were tried – and convicted – in a single day. Each was sentenced to death at the guillotine that afternoon. Marie and Lavoisier's friends appealed for mercy, and cited his numerous services to country and science. Nevertheless, the judge rejected all pleas to spare the celebrated chemist, declaring bluntly, "The Republic has no need of geniuses."

■ ■ ■

Though Lavoisier and his achievements were rudely rebuffed by the sentencing judge, the esteemed mathematician Joseph Lagrange came closer to declaring the truth when he said, "It took but a moment to sever that head, though a hundred years perhaps will be unable to replace it."

Lavoisier's long overdue formulation of molecular theory finally guided the chaotic science of chemistry toward coherence and development. With the inestimable boost of his wife's expertise and knowledge (she carried on his work after his death), Lavoisier greatly furthered a field of knowledge from which we all benefit – medically, technologically, and in day-to-day ease of living.

MARTIN LUTHER KING, JR.

"Modern-day Author of American Civil Rights"
(1929 - 1968)

Early Years

Martin Luther King was born Michael Luther King in 1929 in Atlanta, Georgia. When he was six, his father, Michael, had both their names legally changed to Martin in honor of the German religious reformer Martin Luther. As the grandson of a sharecropper on his father's side and of a Baptist minister on his mother's, young Martin felt an early, almost religious connection to the difficult and tragic past of his people. This powerful sense of kinship led to his rise as one of the world's foremost social reformers, and as an unequalled American civil rights leader.

Watching his father, who served as a deacon in the Baptist ministry, Martin grew up longing to be a preacher and a teacher. He graduated from Morehouse College, completed advanced studies at Crozer Theological Seminary and Boston University, and was ordained a minister in 1947. Shortly following his marriage to Coretta Scott in 1953, he became pastor of the Dexter Avenue Baptist Church in Montgomery, Alabama, which would serve as his home church for the rest of his life.

King observed his people's plight. Blacks were discriminated against not only in private but also in systematic public ways, in obvious contradiction to the Constitution. The U.S. Government, as a whole, turned its head to most black-related situations. Many blacks had no jobs and lived in substandard housing; equality in education was neither a state or federal priority. These factors prodded some, especially younger blacks, to become involved in crime and drug abuse.

In addition to the doctrines of Christianity, Reverend King pored over the recent historical teachings of Mohandas Gandhi, who had earlier initiated India's nonviolent protests for social reform. Moreover, he seized upon the social ideals from Henry David Thoreau's *Civil Disobedience*, which espoused that "man should breathe after his own fashion" and should not obey those laws and customs of society which he perceived as wrong. From such sources King developed his philosophy: change could and would be wrought through quiet, nonviolent, yet determined and effective, means.

King's Civil Rights Contributions

With his congregation as a base, and together with other courageous blacks – like Rosa Parks, the first black to refuse to give up her seat to a white passenger while riding a bus – King led a boycott of Montgomery's city buses in objection to discrimination against black passengers, who, until that time, had been forced to sit in the rear. After much public outcry and press coverage, the boycott succeeded, spawning King's long crusade for civil rights.

Peaceful resistance became Reverend King's major tool in his battle to achieve equal economic, social, educational and political opportunities for Black Americans. To solidify the frequent conflicting efforts of several civil rights groups, King helped establish the Southern Christian Leadership Conference (SCLC), becoming its first president in 1957. His rise to prominence was furthered when he received the Spingarn Medal, the highest honor given by the National Association for the Advancement of Colored People (NAACP).

King's eloquent pleas for racial justice, his unfailingly courageous words and actions – broadcast nationwide via television, radio and newspaper – won the support of millions of Americans, black and white. He led demonstrations in various parts of the country, garnering support from local and national religious, equal rights and labor organizations.

In 1963 the dynamic leader mobilized a massive march in Birmingham, Alabama to protest citywide racial discrimination. That same year, as the nation looked on, more than 200,000 people took part in a symbolic march from the Washington Monument to the Lincoln Memorial in Washington, D.C. To Dr. King's surprise, a quarter of the marchers were white. The high point of the rally came when the minister told the throng:

. . . I have a dream that one day this nation will rise up and live out the true meaning of its creed: "We hold these truths to be self-evident; that all men are created equal." I have a dream . . . . I have a dream that my four little children will one day live in a nation where they will not be judged by the color of their skin but by the content of their character. I have a dream . . .

The crowd, carried by the soaring cadence of his voice and words, then heard a new phrase from their spokesman, his voice reverberating as a bell: "Let freedom ring . . . "

But just weeks after King's resounding message of brotherhood, a Birmingham church was bombed, killing four young girls. This senseless and tragic murder was followed by the assassination of President Kennedy, who represented, to many American blacks, an emancipator almost in the mold of Lincoln.

The despair and hostility that gripped the nation grew with the growing incidence of discrimination and violence. But Dr. King insisted that these trials were part of the "furnace of adversity" that had to be passed through before peace could be realized.

1964 saw King staging a sit-in protest in

St. Augustine, Florida. This effort was largely responsible for the enactment of the Civil Rights Act in Congress some months later. King was then honored as a Nobel Laureate for his devotion and leadership in his people's nonviolent struggle.

In 1965 a campaign was launched to gain guaranteed black voting rights. King headed the famed symbolic march from Selma, Alabama to the steps of the State Capitol in Montgomery. Most of the marchers were school children. Many arrests were made, but news coverage of police and anti-black brutality succeeded in carrying to the nation's conscience the need for political equality. Hundreds of frustrated citizens converged on Selma – including placard-bearing nuns – until President Johnson was forced to call in federal troops for the protection of all factions. The Voting Rights Act passed shortly thereafter; at the end of Johnson's televised message, he echoed King's words: " . . . It is not just Negroes, but really it is all of us who must overcome the crippling legacy of bigotry and injustice. And – we – shall – overcome!"

However, by 1965, a more militant attitude had surfaced in the black community. The Vietnam War (which King opposed, leading many to accuse him of Communist connections) drained away vast quantities of American resources and diverted public attention from Civil Rights reform. Additionally, many blacks themselves began to criticize the movement, citing little improvement in their employment, housing and living conditions, and insisting that legislation alone could not free them. These difficulties placed King's influence and leadership in jeopardy. His peaceful program was almost eclipsed by a "Black Power" movement, pushing for more immediate reforms. For King, this meant a step backward: it would now be more difficult to convince the white community in general that it had no reason to fear black equality.

In a bold move, Reverend King now turned his focus to uniting the poor. Hoping that a campaign against poverty might mitigate the growing "separatist" sentiments among many black and white Americans, he worked steadfastly to include Spanish-speaking Americans and American Indian groups in the effort; in early 1968 he organized a "Poor People's March" to be held in Washington later that year. But Reverend King would never live to lead it.

Soon the Watts riots mushroomed into nationwide urban unrest. As King pushed ahead to involve northern blacks in his cause and pled with city leaders to provide more public community services (swimming pools, educational programs, etc.) for ghetto youth, he was pained by the growing image of blacks fighting and looting in the streets.

But, ironically, the minister's emphasis on nonviolence was no deterrent to his opposition. He was stabbed in New York, stoned in Chicago, frequently spat upon, and jailed on a number of occasions. His home was bombed. And ultimately, a concealed sniper cut short his life in Memphis at age 39.

Shock and grief gave way to angry rioting throughout black neighborhoods. Ghettos exploded. Violence reigned, in paradoxical tribute to a firmly gentle man.

King was a masterful speaker. A few months before his murder, he prophetically chose as his sermon the subject of his own death: "I'd like somebody to mention that day that Martin Luther King, Jr. tried to give his life serving others. I'd like somebody to say that Martin Luther King, Jr. tried to love somebody." These words were followed by a plea to his adherents everywhere to forge ahead with the cause after his death.

On that last, fateful trip to Memphis, with his voice alternately rising and falling, he spoke again of life and death:

. . . Some began to talk about the threats that were out, of what would happen to me from some of our sick white brothers. Well, I don't know what will happen now. We've got some difficult days ahead. But it really doesn't matter to me now. Because I've been to the mountaintop! . . . Like anybody I would like to live . . . a long life . . . . But I'm not concerned about that now . . . I just want to do God's will! And He's allowed me to go up to the mountain, and I've seen the Promised Land. I may not get there with you, but I want you to know tonight, that we as a people will get to the Promised Land! So I'm happy tonight, I'm not worried about anything! I'm not fearing any man! Mine eyes have seen the glory of the coming of the Lord!

The next day, he was gone.

King's tenets are expounded in five books that he somehow found the time to write from 1958 to 1968: *Stride Toward Freedom, Strength to Love, Why We Can't Wait, Where Do We Go From Here:Chaos or Community?,* and *The Trumpet of Conscience.* The titles eloquently describe the struggle for which he gave his life.

■ ■ ■

Martin Luther King, Jr. did not create the Civil Rights Movement, but he rose up at a critical time to lead it; and his teachings and example still shine. King's assassination silenced his voice. But his life and death brought a rebirth of American hope for "freedom for all." Whatever its course, the fight for equality will continue.

King's tombstone near Atlanta's Ebenezer Baptist Church is fittingly inscribed both as a memorial and an impassioned call to hope: "Free at last, free at last, thank God Almighty, I'm free at last!"

MAHATMA GANDHI

"Peaceful, 'Great Soul'"
(1869 - 1948)

Early Years

"Mahatma" means "Great Soul"; and Mohandas Gandhi, born in 1869, was certainly one of history's most extraordinarily great men. As an undersized infant from a large household in the seaside town of Porbandar, India, the studious boy showed no early indication of leadership. School friends poked fun at his shyness and frailty, and laughed at the big ears that protruded from the sides of his thin face.

Mohandas learned piety from his mother, Putlibai, who rigorously followed Hindu customs and vows. Though she was illiterate, her character, common sense and vigorous speech impressed the boy.

The Gandhis belonged to the social caste of tradesmen; Gandhi means "grocer" in the Gujarati dialect. Mohandas' father, already an elderly man at the time of his last son's birth, arranged for the boy to marry the daughter of a merchant at age thirteen. Many years later, Mohandas criticized arranged marriage as a "preposterous" practice, though through his adult life it gave him the support and love of a wife and four children.

Mohandas had a profound experience in his mid-teens. He and his father attended a play called *Harischandra*, about an ancient king who sacrifices everything he owns in order to seek truth. Mohandas was troubled for months by the vivid drama. He finally asked himself why all men did not set the finding of truth as their supreme goal. He did not feel that final truth was to be found within the confines of any religion; rather, through mutal respect among people. Mohandas began to concentrate on the plight of his people, who were treated as inferior by their British sovereigns.

The spiritual youth, however, did have bouts of rebelliousness: eating meat with a Muslim friend, smoking cigarettes, and stealing. With each infraction his guilt increased – until after a painful confession to his dying father, he felt suddenly absolved. The calm tears of the dying man radiated love, forgiveness, and a new respect for the truthfulness of his son.

Chosen from among his brothers to fill his dead father's position as chief political aide to the tiny state government, Mohandas entered the nearest institute for higher learning, but returned in low spirits after only one term. Then a family friend suggested that he go to England to earn his degree in law. Pawning his wife's marriage jewels for money, and with his brothers' help, he left, after telling his friends quietly, "I hope that some of you will follow in my footsteps, and that after you return from England, you will work for big reforms in India."

The Indian youth worked hard to fit in with his British peers, though he felt some discrimination. His work with the non-sectarian Vegetarian Society gave Mohandas his first taste of organizing for group action. Then, when the Society asked him to help edit a translated version of the *Bhagavad Gita*, the Hindu holy book, he was reawakened through the epic poems and wisdom of his Hindu heritage, to his own religious nature.

A Christian *Bible*, purchased from a vendor, also became part of Mohandas' studies. One particular passage of Jesus' teachings went straight to his heart: "But I say unto you, that ye resist not evil: but whosoever shall smite thee on thy right cheek, turn to him the other also." Both Hinduism, with its emphasis on rising above bodily enjoyments, and Christianity, with its "Blessed are the meek" idealogies, thus came to profoundly influence Gandhi's life – even though he acknowledged excesses in both religious doctrines.

Completing his exams in 1891, Mohandas embarked for home with a deep, unified philosophy of selflessness.

Gandhi's Contributions to Peace

As a young lawyer with little opportunity for material success, Gandhi grew more and more resigned to an impoverished life spent writing legal documents. Then, in 1893, he was asked to work in British-controlled South Africa for one year. There, as an Indian claiming the rights of a British subject, he was immediately scorned. He also saw native blacks and South African Indians crippled by official discrimination.

Gandhi's one-year term in South Africa implanted him with a lifelong "magnificent obsession" for Indian rights. To test the effectiveness of his strategies for nonviolent protest, he initiated civil disobedience campaigns, organized numerous strikes and mass meetings, composed petitions, and spoke out for human rights. Enlarging upon this nonviolent philosophy of living the simple, humble life, which he called "satyagraha," Gandhi realized several reforms. He edited a weekly newspaper, the *Indian Opinion* and was arrested many times for subversion. But the humble, frail, yet courageous man also stood up for the British cause on those occasions when he thought it correct, and was decorated by the British for his efforts during both the Boer War and the Zulu Rebellion.

After a 21-year crusade for human rights in South Africa, in 1915 Gandhi returned to India and became the leader of the Indian Nationalist movement, which advocated Home Rule ("Swaraj"). Alarmed, the British government enacted bills to outlaw opposition movements. But "satyagraha" protests soon nullified the impact of these bills. "I had to disobey the British law because I was acting in obedience with a higher law, with the voice of my conscience," Gandhi declared. At one point, however, when rioting broke out, he halted the campaign and fasted to impress upon his people the need for civility: "Hatred can be overcome only by love."

Next, Gandhi recommended one- or two-day work stoppages ("hartal," or in English "shoplock"), to be spent in prayer and fasting. Hartal must be observed without even one brick being thrown, he cautioned; though the Indians could not physically defeat their oppressors, they could appeal to their higher human instincts. Though not always ideally peaceful, Hartal was an amazing success. The repeated city-wide shut-downs left the British in a complete quandary.

In 1919, almost four hundred Indians were massacred when a British general ordered his men to fire on an unarmed crowd of protesters. This only made Gandhi more determined to gain independence by cultivating satyagraha.

Satyagraha included the belief that personal discipline was far more important than achievements; that outward progress followed inner refinement. "To prepare for home-rule, individuals must cultivate the spirit of service, renunciation, truth, nonviolence, self-restraint, patience." Fear must also be overcome, as even violence was preferable to cowardice. He preached, however: "Let us fear God and we shall cease to fear man."

Gandhi engendered a nationwide program for hand spinning and weaving, which aided the cause of independence both by making Indians more economically self-sufficient and by preparing them for self-government, challenging the British-owned textiles industry.

In 1930, as a protest against the new "Salt Acts" stipulating that all salt must be purchased from the government, Gandhi led 200 followers on a march to the sea, where they made salt from seawater. Pictures of the little loin-clothed Indian wading into the water to extract the first crystal of salt, raised the consciousness of people all over the world.

Though Gandhi was arrested, twenty-five hundred "Satyagrahis" marched on, row by row, without him, to demonstrate at the Dharsana Salt Works – and four hundred police awaited them, armed with steel clubs. A United Press reporter described the horror to the Western world: "Not one of the marchers even raised an arm to fend off the blows . . . . From where I stood I heard the sickening whack of the clubs on unprotected skulls."

Jails overflowed. The country ground to a halt. The marches and boycotts were taking such an economic toll that the British government began to face the issue of Indian independence.

But, over the next several years, as new British viceroys instigated more controlling policies, Gandhi's civil disobedience protests reappeared, along with a crusade for dismantling the caste system: "Caste has nothing to do with reli-gion . . . . It is a sin to believe anyone else is inferior or superior to ourselves." Gandhi made it clear now that many of his fasts were not directed at the British, but rather at the hearts of his fellow Hindus. The fasts inspired the doors of Hindu temples to open to all worshippers – Brahman and outcast alike.

One six-day fast had as its objective the reform of the discriminatory British election system. Sensing bloodshed would be imminent, the British certainly feared the death of the sixty-two-year-old Gandhi. When he was finally read conciliatory provisions, the nation sighed in relief as the old man whispered, "Excellent." Gandhi's wife, also in prison at the time, was brought to his beside where she gently chided her husband: "Again the same story, eh?"

Altogether, Gandhi spent seven years in prison for his political beliefs; it was his honor to go to jail for a good cause. Nevertheless, he carried a private burden of guilt over the lack of attention he was able to give his children. Torn with sadness, he would proclaim, "All India is my family."

For years, Gandhi had been struggling to unite Hindus and Muslims. Despite their dissimilar beliefs and customs, Mahatma emphatically trusted that they could live in peace as one nation. When Great Britain granted India its freedom in 1947, Gandhi was heartbroken as India was partitioned into two nations: predominantly Hindu India and Moslem Pakistan. He spent Independence day alone, in prayer. Even Gandhi could not halt the fighting that soon broke out between Hindus and Moslems, and between the various Hindu sects.

At age 78, Gandhi entered into his last fast in hopes of ending the bloodshed. And five days later, the factious leaders did pledge to cease fighting. Then, just ten days later, on his way to a prayer service open to followers of any religion, the Mahatma was gunned down by a high-ranking Indian Brahman who feared Gandhi's tolerant teachings and programs. The entire country mourned, without any further violence, until the body had burned to ashes in its funeral pyre beside the holy river.

■   ■   ■

Mohandas Gandhi's life was guided by a search for truth, founded upon great respect and concern for one's fellow beings. His autobiography, *My Experiments with Truth*, outlines his principles of satyagraha. Though slight in build and humble in demeanor, Gandhi possessed limitless physical energy, moral wisdom and courage of conviction.

Before Gandhi's death, the Indian poet Tagore wrote of the "Great Soul": "Perhaps he will not succeed. Perhaps he will fail as Christ failed to wean men from their iniquities, but he will always be remembered as one who made his life a lesson for all ages to come."

FLORENCE NIGHTINGALE

"Nursing's Founder"
(1820 - 1910)

Early Years

Named for the Italian city in which she was born, Florence Nightingale was raised in affluence. Throughout her gentle, shy, yet playful childhood, she dreamed of someday becoming a nurse.

In her youth, Florence began restoring sick animals back to health at her family's summer estate, Lea Hurst. She used a corner of the estate greenhouse for her hospital.

Weekly, Florence was sent by her mother to deliver food to poor and ailing neighbors. During her visits she gave them advice on how to handle their colicky babies.

Back home in London, Florence unhappily tolerated the fashionable parties her parents gave. To her, books were more interesting than parties. Private tutors provided some of her education, but her most influential teacher was her father, William. His strict instruction in Greek, Latin, mathematics and philosophy further refined the already orderly young girl. Her mother taught her in the social graces of Victorian England and the management of a large household. But her parents worried about the solemn, sensitive Florence. When told that she could not change all of the sadness and poverty in the world, the girl challenged her father: " . . . I will change it. I will make the world better." To her mother's displeasure, she turned down parties and declined suitors, spending her time studying and planning reforms for the poor and suffering – unheard-of behavior for a wealthy sixteen-year-old girl.

Florence's parents shunned the idea of their daughter becoming a nurse. There were no schools in England to train nurses, and only disreputable women who could find no work elsewhere toiled in the dirty, crowded atmosphere of hospitals. Nevertheless, Florence would not give up her purpose in life.

By now Florence was a very attractive young woman, and one of the most eligible bachelors in England, Richard Milnes, begged her to marry him; but when she couldn't give up her "foolish ideas," he gave her an ultimatum: "Choose your work – or me." Florence tearfully replied: "I was not born to choose, I was born to do a special work."

Faced with such determination, Florence's parents finally relented and allowed their daughter to study in a Paris hospital and then to go to the Institute of Protestant Deaconesses in Kaiserswerth, Germany. There she happily accepted the long hours and primitive conditions heaped upon her. She exhibited extraordinary skill, intelligence, empathy and enthusiasm. "We learned to think of our work, not ourselves," she later wrote.

Health-Care Advancements

England and France soon went to war with Russia in the Crimea. Reports circulated of thousands of soldiers wounded in battle, dying under terrible conditions. Sir Sidney Herbert, a friend of the Nightingales and head of the War Department, petitioned Florence, who was by then supervising a London woman's hospital, to take charge of the nursing effort. "If this succeeds," his letter said, ". . . a prejudice will have been broken through, and a precedent established, which will multiply the good to all time." Florence accepted, and, with the help of her parents, purchased supplies and uniforms for a contingent of 40 nurses. A parade was planned to see them off, but Florence demured: "I am not afraid to go to war, but I am not brave enough to stand a fuss."

On the night of October 12, 1854, clad in ugly gray uniforms, the company, made up of rugged and experienced nurses and some Catholic sisters, slipped on board a ship. For over a month they braved cold, harsh storms – and seasickness. When the assemblage disembarked at the muddy harbor at Scutari, the ship's captain pointed to a hulking, shabby, wooden barracks on a steep hill. This was their hospital. Overrun by rats and cockroaches, it was the shelter for scores of wounded troops.

None of the women were prepared for the grisly sight they saw: soldiers lay on the icy ground, many with bloody bandages, most too sick and blue with cold to move. There were no beds or blankets, there was no fire for heat, and if a man's ration of half-cooked meat happened to consist of bone or gristle, that was his bad luck. If he was too weak to feed himself, he went hungry.

"The Army has never needed women. We do not need them now," muttered the officer in charge of the hospital when he saw them. "Perhaps they would like women cooks!" Florence persisted. The nurses set out scrubbing pots and pans, made soups and hot tea, and went through the hospital feeding the grateful soldiers: "Sometimes a few spoonfuls of hot food can save a man's life." The perseverance of the women and their dedication to the swelling tolls of wounded amassed into the grim quarters, finally won the officers over.

Word came that five hundred new troops would be shipped in the next day, casualties from the Light Brigade's famous and tragic Battle of Balaclava. The nurses worked all day and all night stuffing sackcloths with cut straw for matresses. All the following day the bleeding men were carried in. Many were already beyond help. Amputations and the removal of bullets were performed at the patients' beds, usually without anesthetics.

The next crisis came when the ship carrying the bulk of needed supplies to Scutari was destroyed in a hurricane. Winter winds froze many of the half-naked men. Not a stick of wood remained to be burned. And still, more filthy, gaunt skeleton-soldiers kept pouring in. Florence, with most of her personal funds depleted, requested emergency relief from a Mr. Macdonald of the *London Times*. She soon became "supply officer" for the hospital, dealing in socks, shirts, knives, forks, towels and soap. In time, Florence Nightingale herself was serving as the administrator for all the Crimean hospitals and their 12,500 wounded soldiers.

When Florence found men well enough, she set them to cleaning the barracks. Even then it was overrun by lice and fleas. And having been constructed over a vast cesspool, undrained for years, the unventilated building reeked with indescribable fumes. Her most difficult task was prodding the injured men into giving up their shirts and covers to be washed. (They said that they preferred to keep their own lice rather than swap with someone else.) She frequently wrote letters for soldiers until her fingers were cramped by cold. Sometimes she wrote to families with the painful news that sons or husbands had died. The British people, and Queen Victoria herself, read Florence's published petitions to the War Department for desperately needed supplies, and soon food, blankets, medicines and gifts poured into the hospital.

In mid-winter, more than five hundred new patients were on their way to Scutari. There was no room for five, let alone five hundred! Florence went against Turkish labor laws and hired two hundred workmen, who in a matter of weeks added a new wing onto the barracks. The wounded called this type of bold action "Nightingale Power."

Florence was seemingly everywhere at once. At night her lamp burned as she walked the four miles of corridors among the rows of feeble men, whispering words of courage. She became "The Lady of the Lamp." "What a comfort it was to see her . . . " one soldier wrote. "She would speak to one and nod and smile to as many more; but she could not do it to all, you know. We lay there by hundreds. But we could kiss her shadow as it fell, and lay our heads on the pillow again, content."

One night her oil was depleted and the lamp went out. Just then, hearing the sound of crying, Florence found a homesick lad who had lied about his age to join the Army. She promised the boy that when he was well he could stay there at the hospital and run errands. His proudest duty was to polish Florence's lamp and keep it filled with oil. It never went out again.

When spring's warmth arrived, Florence demanded action. A three-man Sanitary Commission arrived from England: The sewer under the hospital was drained, the floorboards disinfected, the rats driven out, the thawed water supply purified. The death rate in the hospital immediately dropped from 420 out of a thousand to 22. She fought – and won – a battle concerning wages for soldiers who were ill but not injured.

("A man half-frozen and half-starved to death in the line of duty," she reasoned, "deserved as much as a man who had actually stopped a bullet.") And when the hospital was running well, classes were organized to teach convalescent soldiers how to read and write.

At last the war was near an end. But as the exhausted "Nurse Nightingale" visited the Crimean battlefields, she collapsed with fever. When, after days near death her condition suddenly turned for the better, many claimed it was due to the countless prayers – that were offered on her behalf.

Florence resisted the doctors' urgings to return to England. "I can stand out the war with any man," she firmly replied, and she returned to nurse the remaining soldiers at Scutari hospital. Mother Bermondsey, a Catholic sister, remembered: " . . . Miss Nightingale never seemed tired. Her voice was always soft. Her smile was always beautiful. She kept us all working together."

When "the great heroine of the battlefields" finally sailed home in 1856, she used a $150,000 gift to open "The Nightingale Home for Nurses" at St. Thomas Hospital in London. "When I learned to be a nurse in Germany," she said, "I only learned to work. These girls must learn to study, too." As a result of her influence, almost over night new nursing schools opened in many countries of the world.

In 1859 Nightingale published her "Notes on Hospitals," and also found time to write "Notes on Nursing."

The strain and illness suffered during the war, however, finally left Florence a semi-invalid who seldom left her room. But she never considered giving up her work; she simply changed her methods. Dignitaries still came seeking her counsel; by correspondence she continued making studies of hospitals around the globe. Her 800-page report to the War Department brought about the formation of the Royal Commission on the Health of the British Army. The United States petitioned and received her recommendations for setting up military hospitals during the Civil War. And, many years later, the founding of the Red Cross was brought about by her basic common-sense advice: "Give the people better food, teach them to be clean, then they will be healthy."

■ ■ ■

Although Florence Nightingale's ninety-year-old mind remained clear, her frail body was tired. She died in her London apartment in 1910.

This "saintly woman" was unquestionably one of the most stalwart and able individuals of all time. Among countless other honors, she was the first woman to be awarded the British Order of Merit for her army and hospital reforms.

But likely her greatest pleasure was derived from the enduring cheer and care she gave thousands in the "trenches" of hospital work as "The Lady of the Lamp."

CHRISTOPHER COLUMBUS

"Master Sailor and Explorer"
(1451 - 1506)

Early Years

The eldest of five children of an Italian wool-weaving family, Cristobal Colon, as he was called, always longed to go to sea. Genoa's trade ships sailed to exotic ports, and the boy sharpened his wit and will as he convinced ship captains to take him along. On these voyages, Christopher avidly grasped the skills of a sailor.

Christopher received little schooling. However, clinging to dreams of travel and exploration, he readily came to understand Latin, in which most geography books were then written, and taught himself to speak and write in Spanish.

Not much is known of Columbus' youth, but he recorded that, once, aboard a galley, he was nearly killed when his ship was sunk by a hostile fleet. Wounded, he managed to cling to a long oar until he reached the Portuguese shore.

Exploring the World

Columbus was a true businessman. After procuring some newly designed, streamlined "caravel" ships, he set out to find a westward route to the Orient, in order to avoid the long, costly overland caravans that brought Italy's gold, gems, spices and drugs from China and India. Like all civilized people of his time, Columbus knew the world was round, and he put his trust in a learned Florencian friend who believed that Japan lay only about 3,000 miles west of Lisbon. It was there in Japan that he planned to establish a great trade center, transporting products between East and West.

But Columbus was overly optimistic in his estimates of the distance involved, and he had a difficult time "selling" warier souls on his plan. It was doubly hard to convince those in power to finance a voyage because he insisted on so many concessions. He had been raised in impoverished conditions, and wealth was one of his main concerns. Columbus asked for a share of whatever goods he transported, along with governorship of any lands he discovered, the title of Admiral (an admiral could serve as a judge on the open sea), a noble rank, and a minimum of three ships. No other explorer had dared even dream of demanding so much.

Refused by King John II of Portugal, who declared the enterprise impractical, Columbus spent the next three years on Portuguese ships. He rose to the rank of captain and married Felipa de Perestrello. Sadly, she died shortly after giving birth to their only child, Diego.

The impatient seaman next went to Spain to attempt to interest King Ferdinand and Queen Isabella in his enterprise. (Interestingly, Columbus' brother, Bartholomew, was at the same time trying to convince the royalty of England and France to back the voyage. If Bartholomew had achieved success, the history of the American continents – and of the world – would have been radically altered.) After months of failing to obtain even an audience with the Spanish court, Columbus became discouraged. The court advisors were against him; Spain, embroiled in conflict with the Moors, was too busy to focus its energies on the business of exploration. But through the persuasive efforts of intelligent Queen Isabella and her royal treasurer, Louis de Santangel, who countered that Columbus' plan was a great opportunity, the sailor was finally put on the royal payroll. In fact, though Spain invested a great deal in his first voyage (about 14,000 dollars at the time), Columbus would soon be able to repay it over and over again.

The *Nina* and the *Pinta*, along with the larger *Santa Maria*, set sail on August 3, 1492. Only about 90 men shared the three ships' even fewer bunks. Columbus had no way to measure distances and only a crude, inaccurate quadrant. He navigated using the North Star and an innate, skilled reckoning ability.

The ships stopped to take on provisions in the Canary Islands. Then they set out due west. Three weeks out, the crews began to fear the constant wind that drove them ahead. They had little dread of falling off the edge of the earth, but sailing directly away from all charted land and further out than any crew had ever gone before made the men anxious. "Adelante! Adelante!" (Sail on! Sail on!) they were exhorted by their Admiral. Columbus was resolute; "with the Lord's help," he would sail until he reached the Indies.

By October 10, however, murmuring and arguing among the crew members had become so unbearable that the ships' captain relented: if land were not found in three more days, they would turn back toward Spain. Then, at 2 A.M. on October 12, the sands of the Bahamas were sighted in the moonlight. After daybreak, the Europeans moored at a bay and came ashore, where gentle Arawak tribesmen offered these "men from heaven" all they had. Columbus pronounced these natives "Indians," believing himself to be on an Asian island near Japan.

Explorations began. The city of Holguin was visited in hopes that it was Peking. Columbus fully expected the emperor of China to come out to greet them. Dozens of harbors were charted among the islands, and Columbus named a north-coast island "Hispaniola" (Spanish Island) because it looked so much like Spain.

When the *Santa Maria* was tossed up on a reef, a local Indian chief and his braves kindly aided in salvaging the cargo. Columbus, impressed by the Indians' friendliness, decided to build a fort and leave 40 men there to search for gold. He – along with several captive Indians – then began the long voyage home on the *Nina* . The ship barely survived a series of storms; in fact, during one gale that almost toppled the ship, Columbus wrote a terse account of his journey, inserted it into a bottle, and threw it overboard, believing they would drown.

Finally the ship sailed back into the waters of the Mediterranean. There, another storm destroyed its sails, forcing the crew to take refuge in Lisbon, where , likely, Columbus used the occasion to exhibit the captured Indians and brag about his successful travels before King John.

Following their triumphant return to Spain, the band of sailors rode across the country to a hero's welcome in the court of Ferdinand and Isabella. Officially hailed as the "Admiral of the Ocean Sea," Columbus was commissioned to organize a second voyage in the name of Spain.

Seventeen ships and a thousand men soon headed toward the newly-discovered land. Columbus' remarkable navigational skills quickly led them back to their original fort. But there they found that the men had been killed by the badly-mistreated Indians.

The explorers turned eastward, where Columbus founded the first European colony in the Americas, "Isabela." They surveyed the southern coast of Cuba, discovered Jamaica, then returned to Isabela, where the men left there were found fighting amongst themselves.

On his return to Spain, Columbus was accused by his men of cruelty. They were, in truth, as it turned out, more disgruntled at not having returned enriched with Indian gold than by their captain's cruelty.

Another voyage was made. It was on this excursion that Columbus is believed to have set foot on what is now Venezuela. This brought on second thoughts concerning the land mass he had found. "I believe that this is a very great continent which until today has been unknown," he wrote in his journal; an "Other World."

Though Columbus searched for gold, his crew, suffering under tropical heat and the hardships of primitive living, were less than satisfied by their meager findings. Columbus tried to appease them by giving them land and by allowing them to take Indians as slaves. Still, most demanded to return to Europe. When the King and Queen came to realize that Columbus was a poor administrator, they sent a force to relieve him of his governorship and to bring him back in chains.

Nonetheless, Columbus' persistent pleadings led to their granting him a final voyage. This time, instead of the complaining old salts of earlier journeys, the aging Admiral sailed with a crew of high-spirited lads – including his thirteen-year-old illegitimate son Ferdinand, who kept a journal of the trip. This voyage proved to be the most adventurous of all: Columbus and his young seamen had a run-in with Ovando, the new governor of Isabela; obtained in trade vast numbers of native gold masks and pendants; participated in exciting but pathetic skirmishes with Indians; sailed along the Central American coast in search of a passage to the Indian Ocean; endured insufferable swarms of mosquitoes; and ran into violent storms. Young Ferdinand recorded: "What with the heat and the wet, our hardtack became so wormy that, God help me, I saw many sailors who waited till darkness to eat it so they would not see the maggots."

In time the sailors' explorations ended. The ships that were to return home, however, leaked so badly that the band was marooned on Jamaica for a year. Ovando, fearful that Columbus might seize his power, refused to send help, and the mutinous and hungry young men were about to kill their captain. But Columbus saved himself when he tricked the Indians into giving them food: Noting that his almanac predicted an eclipse of the Sun on Feb. 29, 1504, Columbus told the Indians he would intercede and restore the dying Sun to them – if they would provide him food.

At last, the 100 surviving castaways were picked up and returned to Spain.

At the age of 53, Columbus was confined to bed by arthritis and failing health. The last months of his life were filled with pain and sadness. Nevertheless, in a last hope that the King would restore him to his rightful share of American trade and power, he traveled by mule to be near the palace. Thus, Columbus, the "Admiral of the Ocean Sea" died in 1506 in a humble dwelling at Valladolid, Spain.

■ ■ ■

Columbus believed that God had intended him to spread Christianity by granting him access to far-away places. Previous world explorers almost certainly set foot on American soil before Columbus did. His voyages, however, truly unlocked the age of exploration and colonization of the New World. Regrettably, it also led to the later destruction of many Native American civilizations.

Though Columbus' character was not entirely admirable, he was perhaps the boldest seaman in history. In the end, this single-minded tenacity may have been his undoing in that many people found him tiresome, overly arrogant and too sure of himself. But it was just this arrogance and unyeilding persistence that allowed him to obtain his goal of finding his "Other World."

CONFUCIUS

"China's Wise Teacher"
(c. 551 - 479 B.C.)

Early Years

There was nothing auspicious about the year 551 B.C. when a male child was born to the K'ung family in the small dukedom of Lu. However, this child was to become the greatest sage of China, and would transform the whole of Chinese culture. We know him as Confucius.

K'ung Ch'iu ("Confucius" is the Latinized form of K'ung-fu-tzu, meaning "Great Master") grew up during the decline of the Chou dynasty. The idealistic glories of the past appealed to the lad, who loved its feudal system of order and peace. But as the Chou monarchs' authority weakened, tribal chieftains and lords took dominion. Chinese society soon consisted of scattered fiefs, with most of their subjects living in poverty. The "shih" class, into which Ch'iu was born, was the educated link between the few aristocrats ("mind-laborers") at the top of Chinese society and the mass of working peasants ("body-laborers") at the bottom.

The much-favored son of an elderly soldier-father who died when the boy was only three years old, Ch'iu was raised by his mother, and educated in the histories, ceremonies, poetry, music and etiquette of the ancient courts. This code of rituals, known as "Li," had long governed the moral and social activities of the aristocracy. But as the peasant class grew, it merged into a vast agrarian population, and the separate fiefdoms were drawn into a life-and-death struggle for supremacy. Ancient arts were put aside; feudal etiquette and morality were lost. Strife and bloodshed, corruption and filth, became the norm, and the royal dukes became mere puppets in the hands of three powerful clans.

Following his family tradition, Ch'iu became keeper of the granary and, later, supervisor of the flocks and herds, positions he fulfilled with exactness.

When his mother died, Ch'iu, in keeping with ancient ritual, observed a three-year period of seclusion and bereavement. This time of contemplation and serious thought launched the young man into the role of philosopher and instilled in him a longing for his society to return to the old ways.

Simple Life; Wise Teachings

Throughout Chinese history the title of scholar had been a hereditary rank attached to an office of the prince's court. Never before had a private individual engaged in public teaching. Now K'ung Ch'iu sought to enter this unexplored profession.

For four years Ch'iu instructed young men of all classes in the knowledge of Li – a combination of manners, ritual, custom and respect – and its accompanying arts. The only tuition he required was a bundle of dried meat. On one occasion, a dying nobleman, enthralled with the sage's teachings, made his final request for his sons to be taught in Li tradition: "A knowledge of Li is the stem of man, without which he cannot stand firm. I have heard that there is a rising man of great intelligence . . . " Soon, Ch'iu was the reputed master of Li ceremonials.

When the duke of Lu was ousted from the city by his ministers, Master K'ung also followed him into exile. He could not serve under tyrannical, unprincipled officials.

For over fourteen years K'ung traveled, attempting to perfect himself in the six ancient arts (charioteering, archery, history, numbers, music and ritual), inscribing poetry, studying history, and carefully instructing his small band of intimate students. The countless specific rites and maxims commended by Master K'ung were all considered elaborations of two ideals:

(1) The heart of all K'ung's teachings included the knitting of the words "chung" and "shu." Chung means "middle of the heart," faithfulness to oneself. Shu, meaning "as one's heart," follows chung "to do to others as your heart prompts or urges you." Basically, it encompasses Christianity's Golden Rule.

(2) Supreme virtue is "jen," a composite of "two" and "man." Jen – "human-heartedness," love, charity, genuine manhood, true benevolence – is the ideal of the superior man; an ideal which Master K'ung often admitted he fell short of achieving. Nevertheless, it is a goal within the grasp of all who will reach for it.

K'ung's beliefs harkened back to practical, of-this-world wisdom. He felt that the individual is the hub of the universe, and the "flowering of the individual" is the ultimate aim in life; for as a man cultivates harmony within himself, he brings peace everywhere. His sage teachings reflected his great regard for human growth:

- No ceremonies should be performed without regard for morality. "A man without virtue; what has he to do with rites? What has he to do with music?"

- The art of peace includes a knowledge of archery and war. These provide private contests and recreation to test nobility.

- Intellectual enlightenment consists of instruction in numbers (probably connected with divination), history, speech and government.

- " . . . What is knowledge? When you know a thing, to hold that you know it; and when you do not know a thing, to allow that you do not know it, – this is knowledge."

- Rituals, poetry, and meditation exalt and strengthen a man.

- Music consummates a man's life, giving his

rituals meaning. Music has a transforming effect on its listeners and should be the first principle of government.

- Nobility of character is preeminent over nobility of birth.

- A man should demand much from himself, but little from others. "When you meet a man of worth, think how you may attain to his excellence. When you meet an unworthy one, then look within and examine yourself."

- Man must be both proprietous and practical: one should be undeviating in the observance of feudal customs and respectfully refrain from singing or dancing on the day he attends a funeral; still, the humor and joy of everyday living must often be manifest.

- Li governs a well-ordered society; but Li must be transformed from a set of rites performed by the elite, to include a sense of piety and respect honored by all.

- "Behave in such a way that your father and mother will have no anxiety about you except for your health." A youth "should be earnest and sincere; he should be overflowing in love for all, while cultivating the friendship of the virtuous. If, when all that is done, he still has energy to spare, then let him study the polite arts."

K'ung's students loved and admired him: " . . . He is a man who forgets his food in his eager pursuit of knowledge, forgets his sorrows in its happy attainment, and does not perceive that old age is creeping up on him . . . "

Unlike many of the dogmatic sages, K'ung maintained a sense of fellowship with his students. He was optimistic: "Who knows, but that the future generation will surpass the present?" He regarded all men the same, though they were not necessarily equal in knowledge and morality. The Master jested with his students, questioned them on ideas, complimented and scolded them, and studied their characters with a view to shaping them into a perfect pattern. He wisely treated each student differently, trying to help the overconfident one to learn humility and the diffident one to be bold.

K'ung was finally goaded into public office. As chief administrator in Lu, he hoped to influence his employer, the Pi governor, to restore Li philosophy to prominence. His popularity rose dramatically as moral education replaced cruelty among the populace. Soon, the state government offered K'ung the office of Minister of Crime, the highest non-hereditary office attainable in China.

With the purpose of preparing China for a feudal restoration, K'ung demolished fortresses. The state prospered; but jealous enemies within the court eventually blocked K'ung's rise, and he departed Lu in sorrow.

Master K'ung wandered from city to city, his fame preceding him everywhere he went. He chided powerful, overly demanding ministers as well as common crowds.

On one occasion, the scholar's pragmatic attitude was clearly displayed. As they traveled to Wey, he and his disciples were set upon by the rebellious people of P'u, who made him swear that, if left in peace, he would not go on to Wey. But despite this oath, the party proceeded to Wey. "Can one break one's oath like that?" grumbled the P'u leader. The Master replied: "That was an extorted oath; such a one the deities do not hear!"

After fourteen years, the teacher grew weary and returned home. Seeing the series of failures and frustrations that his life-work had come to, he now took consolation only in the hope that his faithful students would hold aloft the torch of Chou culture. In his last years, he became the foremost author in China, putting his materials together in a collection of fundamental doctrines. Of the *Book of History*, the *Six Classics*, the *Book of Changes*, and others, only *Spring and Autumn*, a chronological record of the reigning dukes of Lu, survives.

Two years before Master K'ung's death, it was reported that a one-horned antelope had been wounded outside the city. When he saw the animal, K'ung burst into tears and explained that "the unicorn comes only when there is a sage-ruler. To see it appear untimely, and then get injured . . . " In halting manner, he then prophesied his own death and wrote his final entry on the bamboo tablets: "In the spring of the Duke's fourteenth year, during a hunt in the west, a unicorn was captured." And with these words, he threw away his stylus.

■ ■ ■

K'ung's disciples mourned his death for a period of three years, and his devoted student Tzu-kung stayed in the mud hut beside the burial mound for another three years.

Millions of followers – from about 200 B.C., when his philosophies took hold, to the mid-nineteenth century – are a witness to his magnetic personality and elevated wisdom.

Above all else, K'ung was an educator; a transmitter and lover of knowledge. "I was not born with knowledge," he would say. "I simply love the past and am earnest in its study." He worked no miracles, claimed no divine revelation. As a self-appointed "reformer," he owned a realistic interest in this present life, man's earthly ties and ethical relations, though he believed in the hope of another existence: "If we fail in our duty to the living, how can we serve the dead? Not knowing life, how can we know death?"

Confucius is still revered as the master of wise proverbs – insights that today, centuries later, still spark with brilliance. Most significant, Confucius' fight to return to traditional values gave root to a pattern that the Chinese community observed for the succeeding 2100 years – and may be continuing to observe, in some even deeper spirit, today.

MY LIFE FOR THE POOR: MOTHER TERESA OF CALCUTTA

by Jose Luis Gonzalez-Balado and Janet N. Playfoot
Ballantine Books, New York, N.Y., 1985

I am Albanian by birth. Now I am a citizen of India. I am also a Catholic nun. In my work, I belong to the whole world. But in my heart, I belong to Christ.

" . . . The nearest thing we shall probably ever have to an autobiography by Mother Teresa herself," is Brother Andrew's description of *My Life for the Poor*. "The best stories are not – cannot even be – written," he adds. Told in her own words as collected and recorded over the years by co-workers, the book summarizes select narratives and provides a sketch of her devoted, spiritual life.

From age twelve, Agnes Gonxha felt the desire to give herself completely to God. She prayed for six years about her feeling. Agnes received advice from her prayerful father and her compassionate mother: "When you accept a task, do it willingly. If not, don't accept it!" How would she know whether she was indeed called to become a nun? "You will know by your happiness," answered a local clergyman. Soon, in joy, she heard "the voice of God" calling her. *From then on, I have never had the least doubt of my decision. It was the will of God . . .*

Agnes left her home town of Skopje (now in Yugoslavia) to join the Loreto Sisters in Dublin, Ireland. Soon she was transferred to India, where she took the name Mother Teresa, after the humble Teresa of Lisieux. For twenty years she taught at St. Mary's High School overlooking the Calcutta slums. The teacher and her students did much to help the many diseased and destitute, who lived in the teaming neighborhoods surrounding the school.

Then came "a call," . . . *the inner command to renounce Loreto, where I was very happy, to go to serve the poor in the streets. [It was as though God] wanted me to be poor with the poor . . . . I had the blessing of obedience.*

During Mother Teresa's first day in the streets, she gave four of her five rupees to the poor. The remaining rupee she gave to a priest soliciting contributions to the Catholic press. She walked and walked; no food, no shelter, no promise. *Then, I understood better the exhaustion of the really poor, always in search of food, of medicines, of everything.* But that very afternoon, the same priest who had earlier accepted her donation, brought her an envelope from a man who had heard of her undertaking; it contained fifty rupees. *I was sure that the Lord wanted me to be where I was.*

Several former students expressed a desire to join Mother Teresa in helping the poor, the uncared for, the abandoned, the homeless. They came, one by one, often to trade in their expensive clothes for two simple, blue-bordered white cotton saris. "I took the vows of the new congregation," Mother Teresa said. " – poverty [complete freedom from possessions], chastity, obedience, and charity."

Her new order, the "Missionaries of Charity," grew in numbers. Each girl had to meet four conditions to join: she must be healthy, cheerful, able to learn, and possess common sense. Mother Teresa taught her followers to pray, to humbly accept praise, and to smile as they served (for smiling "helps one become holy"). The girls believed that whenever they touched a leper, a dirty, ragged man, or a maggot-covered woman, they indeed touched "the body of Christ in his distressing disguise."

The closer we are to them [the poor], the closer they are to Him. . . . It is a privilege . . . because in serving them we are really serving Christ himself who said, "I was hungry, I was naked, I was homeless, I was sick . . . . You did it to me."

At first, certain religious leaders were suspicious of the order. But as they saw how the sisters served, they learned that Mother Teresa's love extended across religious and political boundaries. The Mission soon branched into other countries, with thousands of members – men and women, Christian and non-Christian – scattered around the world, working with lepers, in schools, in the slums: "Our sisters [and brothers] walk and walk until their legs ache, to see which is the worst place, where the need is the greatest . . . " Mother Teresa explains.

We are first of all religious . . . . We serve Jesus . . . . We nurse him, feed him, clothe him, visit him, comfort him in the poor, the abandoned, the sick, the orphans, the dying . . . the people thrown away by society . . .

Through the generosity of individuals and corporations, separate foundations were gradually set up to care for people in need. But Mother Teresa's mission is much more than to merely provide material necessities: *Without our suffering, our work would just be social work: very good and helpful, but it would not be the work of Jesus Christ, not part of the redemption . . . bringing God into . . . lives . . .*

Mother Teresa's first contact with the dying destitute was a woman she picked up from the streets, her body chewed by rats. At first, the local hospital wouldn't admit her; only upon the nun's insistence did they finally take her in. Moved by many similar experiences, Mother Teresa founded the Kalighat Home for the Dying, two large rooms pegged onto a Hindu temple (which has since moved to a beautiful, gardened property). Its aim is "that we might help them think of God in their last moments . . . " Some of the 57,000-plus residents taken in up to 1985 have recovered from their illnesses to return home.

Even when dealing with death, Mother Teresa keeps her sense of humor. Once, she was taken very ill with fever. In her delirium, she went before Saint Peter, who ordered her to "Go back! There are no slums in heaven!" She relates: *So I got very angry with him and I said, "Very well! . . . I will fill heaven with slum people and you will have slums then!"*

In Calcutta, a leper rehabilitation center was opened, built with money raised from raffling a car given to Mother Teresa by Pope Paul VI. Her Nobel Laureate money went to construct homes and hospitals for 55,000 lepers in various parts of India. A Child's Home was built in Calcutta, where children of lepers can be taken for adoption; the children cannot even be kissed or fed by their natural parents for fear of spreading infection.

At the Home, two leper parents spent a few heartbreaking hours aching to touch and cuddle their newborn. Mother Teresa said, "It hurt them to give up the child, but because they loved the child more than they loved themselves, they gave it up."

When a Mission was opened in Australia in 1969, many objected, saying the sisters wouldn't have enough to do in that country. "What, no work for us?" Mother Teresa barely raised her voice. *And what about the habitual offenders when they come out of prison, what about their wives and children? What about the drug addicts, the alcoholics, are they not God's children . . . ?*

In Australia, while visiting a lonely aborigine man, she offered to clean his hut. In the hut was a beautiful lamp. When asked why he didn't light it, he replied, "For whom? Nobody comes here . . . " He was made to promise that, if visited regularly by the sisters, he would light it. Later, the man sent word to Mother Teresa: "Tell my friend, the light she lit in my life is still burning!"

As to money, Mother Teresa says, "I never think of it. It always comes. The Lord sends it."

When people ask what they can do, she suggests that they first help someone in their own family, then their next-door neighbor, and then find and influence the poor around them. She is adamant that the sisters and the foundations are not the sole answers to alleviating pain and suffering; governments must also better assist the needy. Though she avoids most political matters, when asked, Mother Teresa does have some words for politicians, who, for the most part, "don't spend enough time on their knees. I think they would be better politicians if they did . . . ."

Sharing is the key to providing real help: A Hindu woman was motivated to help the poor but could not give up her monthly purchases of expensive saris. ("Mine is only eight rupees; hers was 800 rupees.") Eventually, "the poor thing has come down to paying 100 for a sari," and the remaining 700 rupees go to the poor.

Two children who had not eaten for some time were given some bread. One, Mother Teresa noticed, did not eat. When prodded, she said, " . . . my father is sick and I think he would love to have this piece of bread."

Two kinds of poverty exist, Mother Teresa explains: the lack of material things, and the much deeper hunger for God, love and companionship. People everywhere are hungry for love. "Our poor are very great people, very lovable people," she says. *We don't know them, that's why we can't love them. And if we don't love them, we can't serve them . . . . I beg you . . . don't allow anybody to be lonely, to feel unwanted, unloved, but especially your own, especially your neighbor.* Loneliness is "today's biggest disease."

Each time I go to Europe and America . . . I am struck by the unhappiness of so many people living in those rich countries: so many broken homes; children not looked after by their parents. . . . They have material wealth; they lack spiritual values.

As an orthodox Catholic, Mother Teresa is deeply in favor of each child being born: "A child is a gift of God," she says. *We are fighting abortion by adoption . . . . I feel that the poorest country is the country that has to kill the unborn child to be able to have extra things and extra pleasures. They are afraid to have to feed one more child!*

So, they carry on – Mother Teresa and her dedicated co-workers. The fights have been many: saving "misused" Bangladeshi girls from abortion and life on the streets; sheltering the cold and homeless in London; listening to the elderly lonely; bathing and cleaning house for shut-ins; reassuring lepers that God has a special love for them; and sending the dying in India "to Saint Peter," bathed and clean, in a bed, forgiven, without fear, with a smile.

The miracle is not that we do this work, but that we are happy to do it.

God has not called me to be successful. He has called me to be faithful.

What we do is nothing but one drop in the ocean. But if we didn't do it, the ocean would be one drop less.

To all, Mother Teresa recommends kindness, charity, humility, activity, joy and the glory of God. And how do we find these? Quietly, she answers: *We need to find God, and he cannot be found in noise and restlessness. God is the friend of silence . . .*

IACOCCA, AN AUTOBIOGRAPHY

by Lee Iacocca with William Novak, Bantam Books, New York, N.Y., 1984

Lee Iacocca, the tough businessman who brought Chrysler back from the brink of collapse, offers his story here – along with his opinions on seat belts, Japanese self-interest, mandatory retirement, worker benefits, and how to make America great again.

Nicola Iacocca sailed into New York Harbor in 1902, a poor and solitary twelve-year-old. For him, America was a land where you were free "to become anything you wanted to be, if you wanted it bad enough and were willing to work for it." This philosophy he later infused into his daughter, Delma, and his son, Lido (Lee). The children were made to feel important and loved. "My father might have been busy with a dozen other things, but he always had time for us."

Nicola became the owner and promoter of several movie houses. He advertised "special offers" for Saturday matinees. ("People still talk about the day he announced that the ten kids with the dirtiest faces would be admitted free.") Then, the Depression hit. Lee was only six or seven at the time, but he still remembers the anxiety he felt about the future. The backbone of the family was his mother, Antoinette. She ensured they had enough to eat by sewing shirts for hire. His father's favorite theme during those years was that life has its ups and downs: "You've got to accept a little sorrow in life. You'll never really know what happiness is unless you have something to compare it to." Yet Nicola hated to see his children unhappy or disappointed. "The sun's gonna come out. It always does," he'd say.

Even in a restaurant, Lee's father demanded top performance. If the waitress was rude, he'd call her over and give her "a real tip": "Why are you unhappy in this job? Is anyone forcing you to be a waitress? . . . If you really want to be a waitress, then you should work at being the best damn waitress in the world. Otherwise, find yourself another line of work."

In predominantly Dutch Allentown, Pa., where the Iacoccas lived, being Italian was something you tried to hide. Bigotry left its mark. Years later, when Gerald Greenwald, named by Iacocca as vice-chairman of Chrysler, became the first Jew ever to reach the top ranks of the Big Three automakers, Iacocca commented briefly, "I find it a little hard to believe that none of them was qualified."

Meanwhile, in school young Lee discovered what was to become his most important lesson – "How to communicate." After earning engineering degrees at Lehigh University and Princeton, he began working for Ford Motor Company as a student engineer. On the assembly line he learned about every stage of car manufacturing. However, "I was eager to be where the action was – marketing or sales."

Though awkward and bashful, Lee was a willing learner and liked working with people.

Learning the skills of salesmanship takes time and effort. Not all young people understand that. They look at a successful businessman and they don't stop to think about all the mistakes he might have made . . . . Mistakes are a part of life; you can't avoid them. All you can hope is that they won't be too expensive and that you don't make the same mistake twice.

At Ford, Iacocca met Charlie Beacham, "a Southerner, a warm and brilliant man [and] the closest thing I ever had to a mentor." Charlie taught Lee to face up to his own failings and mistakes. He also advised Iacocca in matters of communication and public relations. Before Lee's first trip to the South, he said, " . . . You talk too fast for these guys – so slow it down. Second, they won't like your name. So here's what you do. Tell them you have a funny first name – Iacocca – and that your family name is Lee. They ought to like that in the South." And so it was that the newly appointed "Italian Yankee" found acceptance as a "good ole boy."

With sales slumping at Ford, Iacocca suggested offering a new 1956 Ford for a modest down payment, followed by three years of $56 monthly payments. The "56 for '56" idea "took off like a rocket" and "after ten years of preparation, I became an overnight success." Lee was promoted to become the Washington D.C. district manager. After an eight-year, off-and-on romance, he also finally married Mary McCleary, a former receptionist at the Ford assembly plant.

Twice more Iacocca was promoted – first to work as manager for Ford's national truck marketing, and then to head the company's car marketing. Robert McNamara, Iacocca's new boss, was a good businessman, and believed in producing a utilitarian car. He had come out with the extremely popular and inexpensive Falcon, but its profit margin was limited. So Iacocca set out to develop his own car – one "that would be popular and [also] make us a ton of money." He brought together a team of "creative young guys," with the goal of coming up with an auto that would appeal to the millions of teenaged postwar baby boomers who Iacocca knew would soon be screaming for the right car – a car with "great styling, strong performance and a low price." With time running out, and after 18 different clay models, none of which was quite right, the company staged a competition. An engineer named Dave Ash submitted a model that, to Iacocca, "looked like it was moving." From the names Bronco, Puma, Cheetah, Colt, Mustang and Cougar, they chose the name Mustang; it had "the excitement of wide-open spaces and was American as all hell."

At this time, Iacocca had his first confrontation with Henry Ford II. Ford complained, at a very late date, about the Mustang's dimensions: "It's a little tight in the back seat. Add another inch for leg room." "Henry's decisions were not open to debate," lamented Iacocca – even if styling and cost would suffer.

In March of 1964, the first Mustangs rolled off the assembly line. Ford dealerships were mobbed and a new yearly record was established.

Iacocca was in line to become the next president of Ford. Instead, Henry chose a highly regarded product man from GM, Bunkie Knudsen. Unfortunately, Knudsen began redesigning the new Mustangs and Thunderbirds to make them bigger. Still, it took more than creating lines of monstercars to get him fired: Knudsen started walking into Henry Ford's office without knocking! "He tried to get palsy-walsy with Henry, and that was a big mistake . . . . Give Henry a wide berth," as Beacham frequently advised. "Remember, he has blue blood. Yours is only red."

In 1970, Iacocca finally became president of Ford. He was officed next to Henry in the "Glass House," Ford's Headquarters, and given "royal class" service and accommodations.

The new president inaugurated a program to cut operating costs by $50 million in four areas: timing foul-ups (to limit machinery and worker "down-time"), product complexity, design costs, and outmoded business practices. He revised Ford's shipping procedures and rid the corporation of dozens of operations that either lost money or made minimal profits.

Now lacking the "stamina of the Mustang years," and with increased responsibilities, he hired a driver so he could use commuting time to read and answer his mail. He streamlined his workday schedule, and guarded his sanity by guarding his weekends.

I wouldn't open my briefcase until Sunday night. [And] by Monday morning I was ready to hit the ground running. I expected no less of the people who worked for me: I've always found that the speed of the boss is the speed of the team.

But even as business prospered, Iacocca worried about the company's future under Henry Ford.

He held the power of life and death over all of us. He could suddenly say 'off with his head' – and he often did. With out a fair hearing, one more promising career at Ford would bite the dust. It was the superficial things that counted for Henry. He was a sucker for appearances. If a guy wore the right clothes and used the right buzz words, Henry was impressed. "Keep your people anxious and off-balance," was his management philosophy. What made him so insecure? Perhaps the answer is that Henry Ford never had to work for anything in his life . . . . It seemed to me that Henry Ford II, grandson of the founder of the Ford Motor Company, had spent his whole life worrying that he would screw things up.

Once, when Iacocca forged a masterful bargain with Honda to have them put their engine in the Ford Fiesta, Henry promptly vetoed it: "No car with my name on the hood is going to have a Jap engine inside!"

Then, his health failing, "King Henry began to realize his mortality," and to worry about "that Italian interloper" taking over the family business. Ford "conducted a full-scale investigation of both my business and my personal life," interrogating executives and suppliers. When the witch hunt failed to turn up incriminating activities, he ordered some of Iacocca's most outstanding associates fired. Hal Sperlich was one of those "legendary Detroit types" with "gasoline in his veins." "Fire him now," said Henry. "If you don't can him right now, you'll go out the door with him." There was no reasoning with Henry. "It was salami-slicing time – one slice at a time."

Lee finally learned through a publishing friend that he himself had been fired. Henry would give no reason. "It's personal . . . . It's just one of those things," Henry muttered. He was unable to look his former president in the eye. "Look at me," Lee insisted. "I wanted him to know exactly what he was throwing away. 'We've made a billion eight for the second year in a row . . . . You may never see a billion eight again. And do you know why? Because you don't know how we made it in the first place!'"

Under his terms of "resignation," Iacocca was given use of an office until he found a job. "It turned out to be in an obscure warehouse – little more than a cubicle with a small desk and a telephone," and cracked linoleum on the floor. "For me, this was Siberia."

As you go through life, there are thousands of little forks in the road, and there are a few really big forks – moments of reckoning, moments of truth. This was mine . . . . I was financially secure. I could play golf for the rest of my life; but that just didn't feel right. I knew I had to pick up the pieces and carry on.

"As it turned out, I went from the frying pan into the fire" – the executive was offered the presidency of the troubled Chrysler Corporation. "Even its top management didn't have a very good idea of what was going on. They knew Chrysler was bleeding. What they didn't realize . . . was that it was hemorrhaging."

Though Mary had suffered tremendously in her husband's final pressure-packed months at Ford (her first heart attack came shortly after Lee's firing), she remained feisty: "You won't be happy doing anything except cars . . . . Let's give Henry a shot he'll always remember." The same day Chrysler announced the hiring of Lee Iacocca, they also announced their worst deficit in history.

In the end, all business operations can be reduced to three words: people, products, and profits. People come first. Unless you've got a good team, you can't do much with the other two." . . . Like Italy in the 1860s, the company consisted of a cluster of little duchies, each run by a prima donna. There were 31 vice presidents, each with his own turf. There was no real committee setup, no system of meetings to get people talking . . . . The guy running the engineering department wasn't in constant touch with his counterpart in manufacturing. People in engineering and manufacturing almost have to be sleeping together. These guys weren't even flirting.

Iacocca sensed that he must quickly bring cohesion to the company, rid it of incompetence, and install sound financial systems. He fired some workers and sought out others who had inner strength, who enjoyed adventure and risk, and who stuck with a task even when it wasn't fun. "Hal Sperlich was already at Chrysler when I arrived, having come over when Henry fired him in 1977. Having Hal at Chrysler was like finding a tall, cold beer in the middle of a desert. Thank you Henry!"

To create new images for Chrysler's Lincoln-Mercury division, Iacocca hired the same public relations firm who had come up with "Ford has a better idea," and "the sign of the cat," Kenyon & Eckhardt.

Their first decision was to bring back the symbol of the ram to impress the concept that "Dodge trucks are ram tough." Slowly people began perceiving that Dodge built "a durable, dependable, no-nonsense product . . . in the same league as Chevrolet and Ford." Kenyon & Eckhardt also launched the thirty-day, no-questions-asked, money-back guarantee.

Beset with letters from unhappy customers, Iacocca sent representatives to hold seminars with each dealership to underscore the need for courteous customer service. If salespeople couldn't provide that, then, as Lee's father had advised years earlier, "they should look for another line of work." Iacocca also jumped on quality control – building cars right the first time.

Things should have gotten better at Chrysler, but they didn't. In 1979 the world economy fell apart. The Shah was forced out of Iran, gas prices almost doubled, and the plentiful, fuel-efficient Japanese imports became high in demand, while Chrysler's full-sized-car plants were still working overtime. "Detroit got caught with its pants down . . . . Sure enough, as the weakest link in the chain, Chrysler got hit first." (Within six months, GM and Ford joined Chrysler in the loss column.)

There was only one course to take: Iacocca did his homework, and then went to ask the government for a loan. Though loan guarantees "were as American as apple pie," he was criticized for asking:

. . . Predictably, the greatest outcry came from the business community . . . . The old cliches got dusted off. Ours is a profit-and-loss system. Liquidations and close-downs are healthy . . . . A loan guarantee violates the spirit of free enterprise . . . . But they were wrong. . . . Free enterprise is really about competition. And competition was something the loan guarantees stood to provide a lot more of. Why? Because they would guarantee that Chrysler would still be around to compete with General Motors and Ford.

Saving Chrysler, argued Iacocca, would also preserve jobs – up to 600,000 of them. Chrysler's closing would only mean exporting more American jobs to Japan.

But Iacocca's biggest argument dealt with economics. "The Treasury Department had estimated that if Chrysler collapsed, it would cost the country $2.75 billion during the first year alone in unemployment insurance and welfare payments to all those laid off." It was a time for tough, straight talk: "You guys have a choice. Do you want to pay the $2.75 billion now, or do you want to guarantee loans of half that amount with a good chance of getting it all back? You can pay now or you can pay later."

Many members of Congress were ideologically against the loans, but when it was pointed out that their states risked job losses and lost revenues, "it was farewell, ideology."

In his fight for Chrysler's survival, Iacocca cut his own salary to a dollar a year. He cut pay at all but the lowest levels. "We left the secretaries alone. They deserved every cent they made." He caught the attention of the unions: "Hey, boys, I've got a shotgun at your head. I've got thousands of jobs available at seventeen bucks an hour. I've got none at twenty."

I discovered that people accepted a lot of pain if everybody's going through the chute together. I call this equality of sacrifice . . . . It wasn't the loans that saved us . . . . It was the hundreds of millions of dollars that were given up by everybody involved.

Chrysler cut back the layers of management and found that "running a large company with fewer people actually made things easier . . . . Chrysler had been top-heavy . . . . That's a lesson our competitors have yet to learn – and I hope they never do!"

The company began an all-American, "red, white and blue" ad campaign to promote the sturdy, comfortable, front-wheel drive K-car, pointing out that it was "roomy enough to hold 'six Americans' – a little shot at our Japanese competitors." Sales heated up. 1982's figures showed a modest profit, and in 1983 the company had its largest operating profit in history. Chrysler modernized its plants, converted to front-wheel drive technology, led out in fuel economy, and soon employed half-a-million workers. After paying off one-third of the guaranteed government loans, "we made a momentous decision--to pay back the entire loan right away, seven full years before it came due . . . " Iacocca announced the payback at a press conference: "This is the day that makes the last three miserable years all seem worthwhile," he said. "We at Chrysler borrow money the old-fashioned way. We pay it back."

"Now that we were out of danger it was time to think about having fun again." Iacocca had a custom LeBaron convertible made up and began driving it; the public's response was incredible. Skipping any preliminary studies, he ordered the cars onto the production line. "Before long, GM and Ford were making convertibles of their own. In other words, little old Chrysler was now leading the way . . . "

Though the minivan was actually conceived at Ford, it was first produced by Chrysler, where it became a hit. It was specifically designed with a low step, to accommodate a woman in a skirt; a low ceiling, to fit into a typical garage; and an engine up front to provide crush space in case of accident.

Chrysler's success also had a "dark side," however. Mary Iacocca, who now had diabetes, had carried on under an enormous load. She suffered a second coronary in 1980, and a stroke in 1982, each time following a period of stress at Chrysler. In 1983, Mary's heart finally gave out. "She was only 53 and still very beautiful." Even in all her pain she had stayed tough under tough conditions, even serving as a hospital volunteer. "You think you have it bad?" she would say to her husband. "You should have seen the people in the hospital."

Mary never got wrapped up in the corporate life. For both of us the family was supreme. As for the responsibilities of a corporate wife, she did what was necessary and she did it with a smile . . . . Yes, I've had a wonderful and successful career. But next to my family, it really hasn't mattered at all.

At one time Iacocca was brought up as a possible presidential candidate. Laughing the idea away, he added, "But I do think that our national leadership consists of too many lawyers and not enough people from business . . . . I'd like to see a system where we brought in twenty top managers to run the business side of the country and maybe even paid them $1 million a year, tax-free. That would be a real incentive, and then we'd see a lot more talented people interested in public life."

Asked by President Reagan to head the Statue of Liberty-Ellis Island Centennial Commission, Iacocca agreed to do the job as "a labor of love for my mother and father, who used to tell me about Ellis Island." To him, America is "roots," basic values, the dignity of labor and the fight for right.

People say to him, "You're a roaring success. How did you do it?"

"I go back to what my parents taught me," he answers.

Apply yourself. Get all the education you can, but then, by God, do something! Don't just stand there, make something happen. It isn't easy, but if you keep your nose to the grindstone and work at it, it's amazing how in a free society you can become as great as you want to be. And, of course, also be grateful for whatever blessings God bestows on you.

VISIONS OF GLORY

by William Manchester, Sphere Books Limited, London, 1984

The first in a projected three-volume biography of Winston Churchill entitled *The Last Lion, Visions of Glory* covers the period from Churchill's birth in 1874 to the year 1932.

"Sly allusions to the circumstances of his birth followed Winston all his life. He enjoyed them. He would reply: "Although present on the occasion, I have no recollection of the events leading up to it."

Churchill was born November 30, 1874 at Blenheim Palace, Oxfordshire, England. His mother was an American heiress, Jennie Jerome, and his father, Lord Randolph Henry Spencer Churchill.

The Churchills were members of the upper class during the height of the British Empire. The 7th Duke of Marlborough was Winston's grandfather. His father, twice elected to the British Parliament, also served as Chancellor of Exchequer. When the birth of this distinguisehd scion occurred less than nine months after his parent's marriage, it was understandably reported by The London Times as "premature."

Although he was born into privilege, Churchill's childhood was often lonely and sad. Neither of his parents had much time for him, and he was raised primarily by his nanny, Mrs. Everest. By the time he was in his teens, Winston's mother was well-known as a Victorian courtesan. Her affairs with various American and European public and royal figures of the time are well documented. As Manchester writes: "Jennie was one of those favored ladies, who, invited to dinner by his Royal Highness, found that she was the only guest." It is noted that one of Jennie's justifications for her sexual exploits was that her husband had contracted syphilis, probably before their marriage. (He died of the disease when his son was 20 years old.) Although Victorian England is renowned for its supposed sexual prudishness, *Visions* goes to considerable lengths to dispel this notion. Apparently, promiscuity was the rule rather than the exception for attractive, ambitious, upper-class British women.

Notwithstanding their genteel neglect, young Winston adored, even idolized his parents, and literally begged for their company. His letters from boarding schools are peppered with pathos: "Please do do do do do do come down to see me. . . . I have been disappointed so many times." In part, this longing could be attributed to the scorn of his schoolmates for his physical appearance. Winston appeared sickly, an "uncoordinated weakling with the pale fragile hands of a girl, speaking with a lisp and a slight stutter . . . hardly the stuff of which gladiators are made . . . "

The schoolboy was frequently beaten by his headmaster, and his "treatment at the hands of the other boys was, if anything, worse."

While Jennie loved Winston and on occasion wrote him letters, "his father would always be too busy . . . . Randolph actually disliked his son." This was due partly to the boy's poor showing as a student. He attended Harrow, a respected boarding school, where he was singled out as somewhat of a troublemaker who was always at or near the bottom of his class. Still, the boy worked hard to make his father proud of him. In spite of his stammering and guttural speech, he "modeled his tone and phrases after those of [Randolph], an embittered man who denounced 'a government which has boycotted and slandered me.'" The young Churchill early on began emulating his father's biting sarcasm and invective, which even further alienated his peers. Randolph's mother observantly described her grandson as "a naughty, sandy-haired little bulldog."

After Harrow, Winston opted for a career in the military and applied to the Royal Military College at Sandhurst. Although he failed to pass his first two entrance examinations, he was finally admitted on the third try, entering ninety-second in a class of 102. "His officers were dumbfounded to find that he wanted to argue about commands," but Churchill did well at Sandhurst. "His earlier status as public-school dolt was forgotten now that he was an admirable young soldier with a brilliant career ahead of him . . . . He was accepted here as a comrade, and he rejoiced."

Upon graduating, Churchill was commissioned into the British Cavalry. After spending a good portion of his preassignment leave covering the Cuban insurrection against Spain for a British newspaper, he left with his regiment for India. His experiences in that country were especially significant for two reasons. First, it was in India that Churchill "educated" himself by reading the non-fiction literature of the time, including the works of Gibbons, Macula, and Darwin, sowing the seeds for his own later achievements as a writer. Second, there Churchill had his long-awaited first taste of combat. His traditional Victorian colonialist background is clear from a later comment on British battle losses: "Whether it was worth it, I cannot tell. At any rate, at the end of a fortnight the valley was a desert, and honour was satisfied."

After serving for a time in Egypt under the commander in chief, Horatio Kitchener, Churchill returned to England and tried his hand at politics, which was destined to be his calling.

An anecdote offered by Manchester illustrates Churchill's leaning towards politics: After his father's death, a young man from the

Treasury had come to the Churchill estate to demand "the return of the robes Randolph had worn as chancellor of the Exchequer. His widow replied superbly – and prophetically – 'I am saving them for my son.'"

Churchill enjoyed a successful and satisfying marriage. He wed Clementine Hozier in 1908, and throughout his long life often declared, "My most brilliant achievement was my ability to be able to persuade my wife to marry me." The couple's affection for one another was evident from their letters and notes. " . . . My chief desire is to link myself to you week by week by bonds which shall ever become more intimate and profound," Winston wrote. "Beloved I kiss your memory – your sweetness and beauty have cast a glory upon my life . . . " When Clementine grew distraught with worry because of her husband's love of flying, he wrote to her that her complaints were justifiable: "So, I give it up decidedly for many months and perhaps forever. This is a gift . . . [I] lay it at your feet, because I know it will rejoice and relieve your heart."

Meanwhile, Churchill's political career flourished. In 1910 he was named Home Secretary and shortly thereafter was appointed First Lord of the Admiralty. Even at this early date, there was talk of Churchill as a future Prime Minister.

But World War I began in 1914. And by the end of 1915, Churchill had made, at least in the minds of most Englishmen, two major military mistakes: one at Antwerp, where he commanded the failed defense of the city, and the other at the Dardanelles. Although Churchill was widely criticized for Antwerp, Manchester points out that his holding off the Germans for one week was crucial to ultimate British victory. Churchill possibly could have survived Antwerp, however, if not for the tragedy of the Dardanelles. Churchill and others believed that if this narrow strip of water connecting the Aegean Sea to Constantinople could be captured from the Turks, along with Constantinople itself, the British could then strike at the German forces from the rear, substantially shortening the war. According to historians, the campaign would have succeeded had Churchill's strategy been pursued; but other advice was taken just as the British were unknowingly on the verge of victory. The campaign failed, at the cost of many lives. Churchill was dismissed from his Admiralty post. Though he was later cleared of wrong-doing, the resulting political damage scarred his career for years to come.

Churchill was next commissioned as a lieutenant colonel and sent to the front. There he performed admirably, leading a full battalion in the trenches of Europe.

Following Germany's surrender in 1918, Churchill was compelled to speak out against a new menace: Communism. While Leon Trotsky was executing hostages and spreading his dominion, the savage and ambitious Joseph Stalin was primed to seize control of Russia. "The Bolsheviks maintain themselves by bloody and wholesale butcheries . . . " Churchill warned. "[They] hop and caper like troops of ferocious baboons amid the ruins of cities and the corpses of their victims." He understood England's great yearning for peace, but fiercely argued, "We may abandon Russia: but Russia will not abandon us. We shall retire and she will follow. The bear is padding on bloody paws . . . "

By the early 1920's, Churchill had regained enough prestige to be elected to Parliament, where he was subsequently named as Secretary of War and Air, and later as Colonial Secretary. But soon after attaining this apex, his political fortunes again reversed. His controversial views on – and involvement in – the partitioning of Ireland; the collapse of Britain's postwar economic boom; the victory of the Bolsheviks; and continuing resentment over the Dardanelles tragedy, all led to Churchill's defeat in three succeeding elections. Lord Esher offered still another cause for these losses: "The women put Winston out. When he loses his temper, he looks so damned ugly."

During this time out of office, Churchill purchased his beloved Chartwell estate. He also wrote prolifically, completing, among other works, the historical five-volume *World Crisis*.

The year 1924 saw Churchill making another political rebound, and a second election to Parliament was soon followed by his appointment as Chancellor of the Exchequer.

But once more Churchill's reputation was damaged, this time over the question of home rule for India. As an ardent colonialist, Churchill felt strongly that India should remain part of the British Empire. In this he was out of step with England's prominent politicians of the day, his views eventually leading to his removal from office and to exile into the "wilderness." "He thought his world had come to an end – at least his political world."

Then, following a severe automobile accident, Churchill suffered "a great and sudden lack of power of concentration, and a strong sense of being unequal to the task which lay so soon ahead . . . " He brooded on his recent financial disasters, his loss of political position, and his terrible injury; Clementine, nursing him faithfully, reported that "he did not think he would ever recover completely from the three events." Noting these set-backs, Manchester concludes his first volume on the life of Churchill by quoting from a conversation between Lady Astor and Stalin in Russia. In response to a query from Stalin about Churchill, Lady Astor shook her head and laughed: "Churchill? Oh, he's finished."

ALONE

by William Manchester, Little, Brown & Company, Boston, Mass., 1988

Alone is the second volume in a projected three-volume biography of Winston Churchill entitled *The Last Lion*. The first volume, *Visions of Glory*, covers the period from Churchill's birth in 1874 to 1932. *Alone* comprises the years leading up to World War II, 1932 to 1940.

Beginning with a detailed look at a typical day for Churchill at his Chartwell home, the reader is allowed a fascinating glimpse into the statesman's eccentric personality. With his bedroom windows puttied shut to avoid chills caused by drafts, Churchill always arose late: "He, not the sun, determines when he will greet the new day." He seldom began working before noon.

Churchill would eat a late lunch and dinner, meals often spent discussing with friends his favorite topic: politics. His list of invited guests included Charlie Chaplin, Bernard Baruch and numerous contemporary British politicians.

His twice-daily ritual baths and a habit of roaming the Chartwell estate nude during bathtime, made Churchill a popular topic of gossip. On one occasion, a young housemaid, looking up the stairwell one morning, "beheld . . . Churchill in the buff – all 210 pounds of him . . . glaring down at her. The girl fled the house shrieking [and] sent for her belongings and her pay."

At 11:00 p.m. Churchill began the major part of his working day, reading, writing and pondering until between 2:00 and 4:00 a.m., when he would retire.

As a member of Parliament for 60-plus years, Churchill excelled in humor and debate – and especially in the mixing of the two: "It is wonderful how well men can keep secrets they have not been told," was one of his well publicized sardonic remarks. Concerning Britain's coalition government, he said, "Where there is a great deal of free speech there is always a certain amount of foolish speech." He admitted that he – like politics and the human experience itself – was unpredictable: "The element of the unexpected and the unforeseeable is what gives some of its relish to life . . . "

One of Churchill's chief political "baiters" was a feminist member of Parliament, Edith Summerskill, who insisted on interjecting the phrase "or woman" every time Churchill used the word "man" in an address. After several such interruptions, he once turned to her and said, "It is always the grammarian's answer that man embraces woman, unless otherwise stated in the text."

Such witicisms were common; his snide asides often broke up Parliamentary proceedings. Seemingly inattentive to the business at hand, he would close his eyes and breath heavily, waiting in ambush. "Must you fall asleep when I am speaking?" he was one time asked loudly. "No, it is purely voluntary," was Winston's rapid-fire comeback. On another occasion, a young – and boring – speaker was caught in Churchill's trap. He inquired if Churchill was asleep, to which came the immediate rejoinder, "I wish to God I were!"

The Minister also had a humble and serious side, though it seldom manifested itself as strongly as his wit. "I have always said to myself one thing," he prefaced his response to a colleague's criticism. "'Do not interrupt,' and I have never been able to keep to that resolution." He also confessed to never having succeeded in "curbing his savage tongue." He admitted, " . . . I wonder that a great many of my colleagues are on speaking terms with me."

But amid the ridicule and jibe – which, if not construed as personal insult, was permissible, according to British custom – a true patriot was cultivating himself for future use.

Churchill is portrayed as a prophet of his time. Very early he sensed the grave danger Hitler and the Third Reich posed to peaceful society. "Tell the truth to the British people," he begged the nation's leaders. "They are a tough people, a robust people. . . . If you have told them exactly what is going on you have ensured yourself against complaints and reproaches . . . " Unfortunately, few Britons took him seriously; they preferred civilized and optimistic interpretations of world events over an objective look at the harsh possibilities ahead.

Alone is a very appropriate title for this book, in that it covers an interval when Churchill was often a political outcast and a financial failure. He lost a fortune in the 1929 stockmarket crash. At best he was a poor money manager with extravagant tastes. But this financial weakness was the catalyst for some of Churchill's best and most prolific writing; he needed the money. For example, in 1938 alone he published two books and 59 articles, all the while doing research for two additional multi-volumed works, published later.

The beginning of the *"Alone"* era saw Churchill in a "political wilderness," because of his split with British governmental powers over the issue of India's independence. To him this signified the inception of the collapse of the British Empire. And, once again, his judgment proved prophetic.

Then in 1936, just as Churchill was recovering politically from his disparity over India, he misjudged public opinion and openly supported King Edward in his controversial marriage to an American divorcee, Wallis Simpson. Churchill was again ostracized.

Not until the early stages of World War II did it become obvious to Britons in general that Churchill had been correct in many of his "pessimistic" pronouncements, particularly in his brazen forewarnings with respect to Hitler. With Germany's strong-arm invasions into Poland and other European nations, Churchill quickly regained broad support of the people – and ultimately became British Prime Minister.

Notwithstanding his lack of early official political influence, Churchill had kept himself very much aware of Germany's massive military rearmament and Hitler's alliances and maneuverings throughout Europe. This was made possible, Manchester claims, because Churchill's informants were "of a much higher caliber than the government's."

Alone is laced with insights into the personalities of the chief European leaders of the day, including Hitler, Stalin and Mussolini. The book also contains a good deal of theorizing by Manchester as to how these leaders obtained their power and why they exercised it as they did.

Manchester repeatedly compares the personalities of Hitler and Churchill. Of Hitler he says: "He had never met Churchill, but he understood him, as Winston understood Hitler. Walter Lippman observed that the supreme qualification for high office is temperment not intellect, and on that level the two men had more in common than either would have acknowledged. The countless millions, spellbound by Winston's genius, would angrily reject any comparison of the two. Nevertheless they were mirror images of one another."

Churchill also understood Hitler's military mind; they shared an infatuation for tanks. The Briton postulated that Hitler would first invade Hungary and Rumania, before obstacles to tank invasion could be built. He reasoned that preceding an attack on the West, Hitler would collect "the easy spoils which await him in the East," thereby giving his people "the spectacle of repeated successes."

Long before Churchill became Prime Minister, Hitler seemed to sense that Britain – and Churchill specifically – was the primary barrier to his ambitions. On the eve of a 1936 meeting in Munich with then Prime Minister Neville Chamberlain, Manchester relates that Hitler said "he was 'fully aware' that one day Chamberlain might be replaced by Churchill, whose 'aim would be to unleash at once a new world war against Germany.' "

Alone concludes with descriptions of the successful German invasion and surrender of France and the lower countries, and Churchill's subsequent induction as Prime Minister. "He had come to power because he had seen through Hitler from the very beginning – but not, ironically, because his inner light, the source of that insight, was understood by Englishmen." Indeed, England's future appeared very grim. Churchill foresaw the bitter reality of war that lay ahead: "Death and sorrow will be the companions of our journey, hardship our garment, constancy and valour our only shield." However, he had an uncanny confidence in ultimate victory. In his nationwide BBC address, Churchill vividly and poetically called for all Britons, and all of Europe, to come together in purpose and resolve:

We have differed and quarreled in the past;
but now one bond unites us all –
to wage war until victory is won,
and never surrender ourselves to servitude
and shame,
whatever the cost and agony may be . . .
Upon all of whom a long night of barbarism will
descend
unbroken even by a star of hope,
unless we conquer, as conquer we must;
as conquer we shall.

Later, he went on the air again, vowing that if all Europe fell, "England would continue the battle alone."

Let us therefore brace ourselves to our duties,
and so bear ourselves
that if the British Empire and its
Commonwealth
last for a thousand years,
Men will still say:
"This was their finest hour."

Manchester closes this second volume with a breathless sentence that prepares his readers for the third, yet – untitled volume:

"And now, in the desperate spring of 1940, with the reins of power at last firm in his grasp, he resolved to lead Britain and her fading empire in one last great struggle worthy of all they had been and meant, to arm the nation, not only with weapons but also with the mace of honor, creating in every English breast a soul beneath the ribs of death."

THE AUTOBIOGRAPHY OF MALCOLM X

by Malcolm X, with the assistance of Alex Haley, Grove Press, New York, N.Y., 1965

Malcolm Little was born in Omaha, Nebraska on May 19, 1925. His family moved north, first to Milwaukee, Wisconsin, then to Lansing, Michigan. Malcolm's father, Earl Little, was both a Baptist preacher and a staunch supporter of Marcus Garvey, who believed that "freedom, independence, and self-respect could never be achieved by the Negro in America, and that therefore the Negro should leave America to the white man and return to his African homeland . . . " Because Earl held these views, rival blacks eventually burned the family's house down. Later, Malcolm's father was murdered by local "night riders."

Alone, Malcolm's mother was unable to feed her large family without state help. Constantly harassed by welfare workers and distraught over her husband's death, she gradually went insane, and her children were put into separate foster homes.

Malcolm was sent to a small town called Mason, where he was placed in a state detention home run by a white couple who Malcolm described as good people. He did well in school. But when Mr. Ostrowski, his English teacher, heard of the boy's desire to be an attorney, he was surprised: "Lawyer – that's no realistic goal for a nigger . . . . Why don't you plan on carpentry?" From that point forward, Malcolm's attitude toward school – and toward white people in general – soured. He no longer felt comfortable in Mason and decided to go to Boston to stay with his oldest sister, Ella.

His sister lived in the Roxbury area of Boston where "Negroes" acted and lived "differently from any black people I'd ever dreamed of in my life." Malcolm met a hustler named Shorty, who got him his first job – shining shoes. The young man quickly learned how to receive extra tips and how to work "sideline ventures." He began to gamble, drink, and smoke cigarettes and "reefers." He "conked" (straightened) his hair and wore a "zoot suit." Though just sixteen years old, he looked considerably older.

One night at a dance, Malcolm met Sophia, a white woman. From that night on they were lovers.

Soon, however, Malcolm's urge to move on resurfaced. He "left Boston and Roxbury forever," and moved to New York. There he went from working as a cook to being a bus boy. The street hustles and other illegal activities of Harlem became second nature to him. Now World War II was in full swing, and bars all over Harlem were filled with servicemen – and with military spies attempting to catch people "impairing the morals" of servicemen. One black soldier who accepted Malcolm's offer to find him "a woman for the night" turned out to be a spy, and he lost his bus boy job.

Malcolm descended further into Harlem's criminal world. He began peddling reefers, with the jazz musicians in and around Harlem as his biggest clients. But narcotics detectives learned that Malcolm was dealing and placed him under surveillance. Soon, things got too hot in Harlem. So, Malcolm boarded a train every day and sold "on the road." "I can't remember all the hustles I had during the next two years . . . " he admitted.

Before long, Malcolm was pulling "robberies and stick-ups" and had become addicted to cocaine. Things were getting sticky with the police, so Shorty drove down from Boston and took Malcolm back with him.

Though Sophia had married during Malcolm's stint in Harlem, they resumed their affair. After about a month of "laying dead," Malcolm decided he needed a new hustle to support himself: he and Shorty went in together to burglarize houses. Their system was simple. Shorty would case neighborhoods during the day; then, at night, they would return to empty the selected houses of their goods. With the help of Sophia and her little sister, this "perfect operation" went fine for a while – until Malcolm made a mistake: he sent a "hot" watch to a jeweler to be fixed. The jeweler recognized it as stolen and set Malcolm up for arrest.

" . . . The average burglary sentence for a first offender . . . was about two years. But we weren't going to get the average . . . " The "real crime," as Malcolm saw it, was "white women in league with Negroes." So, at age 21, he received ten years in the Charlestown State Prison, where he earned the nickname "Satan" because of his antireligious attitude.

It was in prison that Malcolm found the time to renew his education "more intensively than I would have if . . . I had attended some college."

One day Malcolm received a letter from his brother Reginald: "Malcolm, don't eat any more pork, and don't smoke any more cigarettes. I'll show you how to get out of prison." Malcolm followed his brother's advice. Perhaps Reginald had come up with a way to "work a hype on the penal authorities." But the "hype" turned out to be not quite what Malcolm expected. When Reginald came for a visit, he spoke to Malcolm about Allah, about Elijah Muhammad (Allah's American messenger), and about the Black Muslim Nation of Islam.

Though Malcolm's conversion to Islam was not instantaneous, he grew more receptive day by day. But as Malcolm reached out to accept, at the same time it appeared that Reginald was becoming an apostate. (He later went insane.)

When Malcolm was finally released, in 1952, he moved to Detroit, where relatives lived. Everyone in his family except Ella had converted to the Black Muslim faith. He moved in with another brother, Wilfred, and became increasingly involved in the affairs of Detroit's "Temple Number One."

Malcolm, possessing an animated personality and a persuasive gift brought in many converts. He was soon given the position of Assistant Minister. During this time he also adopted his new surname, "X", which "symbolized the true African name that he could never know." Malcolm X in time became the temple's minister, and eventually, after personal training by Elijah Muhammad, took over the ministry of the Nation of Islam's New York Temple. There he met Sister Betty. Their courtship was short and simple: "If you are thinking about doing a thing, you ought to make up your mind if you are going to do it, or not do it." In 1957 the two were married.

The Nation of Islam, and particularly Malcolm's temple, began to receive media attention, both positive and negative. Malcolm incessantly vocalized his opinions of and objections to both the white power structure and the less militant black civil rights movement.

Then, in 1963, a news story appeared: Elijah Muhammad faced two paternity suits, filed by former temple secretaries. Malcolm's mind "simply refused to accept anything so grotesque as adultery" associated with a man he "worshipped." However, the evidence was overwhelming. Malcolm X openly broke ties with the Nation of Islam and Black Muslims. Soon afterward, a death order was issued on him.

Fatigued by his years of working and traveling and lecturing, Malcolm made two spiritual pilgrimages to Saudi Arabia's Mecca, the holy city of Islam, a place where all races mixed on equal footing. Seeing whites and blacks treated as equals, he underwent "a radical alteration in my whole outlook about 'white' men." Following this visit, Malcolm toured parts of Africa and the U.S. giving speeches and holding press conferences. He had become a true international figure.

The last months of Malcolm X's life were turbulent ones, filled with death threats and bombings. Yet, in his interviews and speeches he sought to clarify those philosophies he felt were true.

The following quotes and incidents do not appear in Malcolm X's *Autobiography*. Extracted from letters, speeches and news articles, however, they more completely summarize his ideologies:

After a young Black had been killed in Harlem: " . . . As long as the police department doesn't use those methods in white neighborhoods, they shouldn't come to Harlem and use them in our neighborhood."

On Black Power: "I'm the man you think you are . . . . If you want to know what I'll do, figure out what you'll do. I'll do the same thing – only more of it."

On Black Political Support: " . . . 97 percent of the black American voters supported . . . the Democratic Party. Ninety-seven percent! . . . And what did Johnson say [when challenged with instances of discrimination]? Nothing! What did Humphrey say? Nothing! What did Robert Pretty-Boy Kennedy say? Nothing! Nothing! . . . "

On Racism: " . . . I am not a racist . . . . I don't believe in any form of racism . . . . In Asia or the Arab world or in Africa . . . if you find [a man] who says he's white, all he's doing is using an adjective to describe something that's incidental about him . . . he's just white. But when you get the white man over here in America and he says he's white, he means something else . . . he means he's boss . . . " And what is responsible for this? "Ignorance and greed . . . Miseducation . . . exploitation and oppression . . . "

On Violence: " . . . Let the government know that if they don't stop that Klan, we'll stop it ourselves . . . by any means necessary . . . . Now . . . the press calls us racist and people who are violent in reverse . . . . Well, if a criminal comes around your house with his gun, brother . . . it doesn't make you a robber because you grab your gun and run him out . . . "

On Being American: "Sitting at the table [with nothing to eat] doesn't make you a diner. . . . Being here in America doesn't make you an American."

■ ■ ■

Three days before his death, Malcolm X delivered his final speech:

It is incorrect to classify the revolt of the Negroes as simply a racial conflict of black against white . . . . Rather, we are today seeing a global rebellion of the oppressed against the oppressor, the exploited against the exploiter . . .

On February 21, 1965, while delivering a speech in New York City, Malcolm X was assassinated by rival Black Muslims. Most of Malcolm X's opinions were radical for his time – even to blacks. Nevertheless, he helped to shake and shape American culture and change American society forever.

COMPACT

Classics™

LIBRARY #5: Literary Classics

Section A: Reflective Realism

5-A1   *The Scarlet Letter* by Nathaniel Hawthorne
5-A2   *A Farewell to Arms* by Ernest Hemingway
5-A3   *For Whom the Bell Tolls* by Ernest Hemingway
5-A4   *Anna Karenina* by Leo Tolstoy
5-A5   *Of Mice and Men* by John Steinbeck

Section B: Heroic Epic and Allegory

5-B1   *Paradise Lost* by John Milton
5-B2   *Beowulf* author unknown
5-B3   *Prometheus Bound* by Aeschylus
5-B4   *The Divine Comedy* by Dante Alighieri
5-B5   *El Cid* author unknown

Section C: Historical Fiction

5-C1   *A Tale of Two Cities* by Charles Dickens
5-C2   *The Lady of the Lake* by Sir Walter Scott
5-C3   *Henry VIII* by William Shakespeare
5-C4   *The Travels of Marco Polo* by Marco Polo
5-C5   *The Last of the Mohicans* by James Fenimore Cooper

Section D: Symbolic Characterization and Thought

5-D1   *The Rime of the Ancient Mariner* by Samuel Taylor Coleridge
5-D2   *Moby Dick* by Herman Melville
5-D3   *The Old Man and the Sea* by Ernest Hemingway
5-D4   *Don Quixote de la Mancha* by Miguel de Cervantes
5-D5   *Peer Gynt* by Henrik Ibsen

Section E: Adventure and Intrigue

5-E1   *The Maltese Falcon* by Dashiell Hammett
5-E2   *Call of the Wild* by Jack London
5-E3   *The Great Gatsby* by F. Scott Fitzgerald
5-E4   *Ben-Hur: A Tale of the Christ* by Lew Wallace
5-E5   *Robinson Crusoe* by Daniel Defoe

Section F: Science Fiction

5-F1   *The Picture of Dorian Gray* by Oscar Wilde
5-F2   *Frankenstein* by Mary Shelly
5-F3   *The Time Machine* by H. G. Wells
5-F4   *The Turn of the Screw* by Henry James
5-F5   *The Fall of the House of Usher* by Edgar Allan Poe

Section G: Social/Political Commentary

5-G1   *The Grapes of Wrath* by John Steinbeck
5-G2   *Candide* by Voltaire
5-G3   *A Connecticut Yankee in King Arthur's Court* by Mark Twain
5-G4   *1984* by George Orwell
5-G5   *The Prince and the Pauper* by Mark Twain

Section H: Shakespearean Tragedies

5-H1   *Hamlet, Prince of Denmark*
5-H2   *King Lear*
5-H3   *Romeo and Juliet*
5-H4   *Macbeth*
5-H5   *Othello*

Section I: Shakespearean Comedies

5-I1   *The Taming of the Shrew*
5-I2   *The Tempest*
5-I3   *As You Like It*
5-I4   *The Merchant of Venice*
5-I5   *Much Ado About Nothing*

Section J: Human Drama

5-J1   *The Courtship of Miles Standish* by Henry Wadsworth Longfellow
5-J2   *Our Town* by Thornton Wilder
5-J3   *Silas Marner* by George Eliot
5-J4   *Little Women* by Louisa May Alcott
5-J5   *Jane Eyre* by Charlotte Bronte

Section K: Philosophy

5-K1   *The Origin of Species* by Charles Darwin
5-K2   *Walden* by Henry David Thoreau
5-K3   *The Prince* by Machiavelli
5-K4   *Das Kapital* by Karl Marx
5-K5   *The Republic* by Plato

Section L: Examining Relationships

5-L1   *The Importance of Being Earnest* by Oscar Wilde
5-L2   *Babbit* by Sinclair Lewis
5-L3   *Death of a Salesman* by Arthur Miller
5-L4   *Pride and Prejudice* by Jane Austen
5-L5   *Far From the Madding Crowd* by Thomas Hardy

Section M: A Composite of Classics

5-M1   *Julius Caesar* by William Shakespeare
5-M2   *To Kill a Mockingbird* by Harper Lee
5-M3   *Oedipus Rex* by Sophocles I
5-M4   *Utopia* by Sir Thomas More
5-M5   *Faust* by Goethe

THE SCARLET LETTER

by
Nathaniel Hawthorne
(1804 - 1864)

Type of work: Impressionistic fiction

Setting: Boston, Massachusetts;
seventeenth century

Principal characters:
Hester Prynne, a condemned adulteress
Pearl, her daughter
Arthur Dimmesdale, one of the
community's ministers
Roger Chillingsworth, Hester's estranged
husband (his assumed name)

Story Overview:

Condemned to wear a bright red "A" over her breast wherever she went, Hester Prynne had been convicted of adultery by Boston's Puritan leaders; a child had been born to her during her husband's long absence.

Emerging from the prisonhouse under the gaze of her neighbors, Hester surprised the townsfolk with her air of aloof and silent dignity. Led to the town square, she ascended a scaffold, her babe cradled in her arms. There on the scaffold she suffered scorn and public admonishment. One "good woman" loudly decried the elaborate letter Hester had embroidered into her frock: blazing scarlet, ornately fashioned and bordered with prominent gold stitching – the requisite token of her deed. A minister in the crowd denounced her crime and called on her to reveal the identity of her partner. Another minister, Arthur Dimmesdale, pled with her more gently. He, in compassion, also begged her to unmask her lover. Unknown to the multitude, however, Dimmesdale himself was that lover; his gentle prodding was in fact a distraught and convoluted effort to urge a confession from Hester which he knew she would never make – and which he could not find the courage to make for himself.

From her place on the pulpit, Hester's eyes met with those of a hunched, wrinkled man in the crowd, a stranger in the town but well known to her. He was Hester's husband, a scholar and a physician of sorts, who had spent years away, exploring the western wilderness. Now he had reappeared under the name of "Roger Chillingsworth."

Visiting Hester in her prison cell later that day, Chillingsworth expressed his rage that she should betray him and made her swear not to expose him as her husband. Furthermore, he vowed that he would discover the identity of his wife's lover.

Finally released, the adulteress took up residence in a lonely cottage by the sea. Her chief employment, for which she demonstrated a prodigious talent, was sewing. She managed to win the business of nearly everyone in the community. Still, despite the acceptance she won as a seamstress, Hester was forced to bear social ostracism: children jeered as she passed, other women avoided her, and clergymen pointed to her as a living example of the consequences of sin. Rumors circulated that she was a witch, and that the scarlet letter she bore on her clothing glowed a deep blood red in the dark. Still Hester withstood this abuse without complaint.

Hester felt much more concern for her daughter, Pearl, than for herself. She cringed when the illegitimate girl was pushed aside by other children. In contrast to Hester's remarkable dignity, Pearl displayed a wild, undisciplined character, seemingly incapable of natural affection. The governor of Boston and all the clergy publicly proclaimed their doubts that the sprite-like, curious child could develop the capacity to enter Christian society. Even more tragically, the townspeople looked on Pearl as a kind of evil spirit – the perverse offspring from a moment of unholy passion. Even Hester little understood her daughter, who served at once as both a comfort and a painful reminder of her past.

In the meantime, Roger Chillingsworth had taken lodgings with Minister Dimmesdale. Chillingsworth immediately suspected that the clergyman had been his wife's once-guilty partner in lust, and, posing as a true friend, he managed, over the course of months, to wring his roommate's conscience with subtle hints and comments about the dire strait of hypocrites in the eyes of God. Soon it became clear that Dimmesdale was indeed Hester's lover; but, rather than expose him then, Chillingsworth chose to continue torturing the preacher's moral sanity. Dimmesdale's sense of guilt grew, ultimately causing his health to wane. He took to holding his hand over his heart, as if he felt some deep pain. Yet he failed to recognize the treachery being perpetrated on him, blaming only himself for his growing infirmity.

To make matters worse, the weaker and more guilt-ridden Dimmesdale became, the holier he appeared to his congregation, whose members regarded him as unequaled in piety. Every sermon he preached seemed to be more inspired than the last. More than once the minister resolved to confess his hypocrisy and take his place beside Hester, but he was too afraid of the shame open confession would bring.

And so it was that the years passed: Hester, suffering in disgrace and isolation, devoting her life to charitable service and winning the hidden admiration of many of her peers; Pearl, maturing into a lovely girl but still showing no signs of outgrowing her eccentricities; Dimmesdale, weighed down by unbearable remorse even as his reputation for holiness increased; and Chillingsworth, daily tampering with Dimmesdale's fragile conscience. Frequently the four of them crossed paths. However, no momentous event transpired – until one day seven years after Hester's initial public censure. While Hester and Pearl were strolling in the woods, they came upon Dimmesdale, and he and Hester finally savored a long-awaited and emotional reunion. Speaking of their long-kept secret, Hester attempted to assure the minister that his good works and humility had gained him penance. But the priest cried, "Happy are you, Hester, that wear the scarlet letter openly upon your bosom! Mine burns in secret!" In sorrow and pity, Hester admitted that Chillingsworth, Dimmesdale's own valued friend, was in fact her estranged husband; and he the nurturing demon behind the minister's living hell. Then she convinced her dear Dimmesdale to escape with her to Europe, where they could enjoy a new, unfettered life together. Their plan was to depart after the minister had delivered his final sermon.

The day of departure came, and Hester waited anxiously outside the church. Nearby, the captain of the ship on which they would sail mentioned to her that Roger Chillingsworth was also booked as a passenger on his vessel. So, the evil man intended to follow them, she thought in horror. Their plans were dashed!

When the service ended, the townsfolk exited the chapel in a high state of emotion; Minister Dimmesdale had imparted an extraordinarily spiritual message. But to their surprise, Dimmesdale made his way out of the procession and feebly trod toward the scaffold in the marketplace. Then he turned and beckoned Hester and Pearl to come to him. Roger Chillingsworth thrust himself through the crowd and caught the minister by the arm. "Madman, hold! What is your purpose?" he whispered frantically. "Wave back that woman! Cast off this child! . . . Do not blacken your fame, and perish in dishonor! I can yet save you!"

"Ha, tempter!" Dimmesdale replied. "Me thinks thou art too late! Thy power is not what it was! With God's help, I shall escape thee now!" Then extending his hand to Hester, Dimmesdale admitted to his partnership in her sin, and berated himself for the years he had lived in deceit. Then he focused on Roger Chillingsworth and exposed the true identity and sinister nature of the man. This done, he turned and mounted the scaffold. His emotional anguish over the years, though, had devastated his body and his spirit: his confession proved to be fatal. As he collapsed on the wooden planks, supported on Hester's bosom, Dimmesdale bid farewell to his beloved, and then to little Pearl. Finally, in the triumph of a soul at last filled with peace, the minister breathed his last.

(Hawthorne, through his narrator, adds a final chapter, in which he speculates on the fate of the other characters. He proposes the following: Roger Chillingsworth, hatefully hunched over and shriveled, died within the year; but in sympathy he left his considerable estate to Pearl. Having come into such wealth, both Pearl and Hester sailed abroad. Hester eventually returned to Boston alone to occupy her old cottage, frequently receiving letters and gifts from her daughter. She became a trusted confidante to scores of local women, but never removed the scarlet letter from her breast. Her gravestone – it is suggested – can still be seen: a plain black headstone with no name engraved; only a blazing scarlet "A".)

Commentary:

The Scarlet Letter, as one of the first and finest "psychological gothics," may bewilder modern "T.V. readers," who keep waiting for something to happen. The book contains very little dramatic action. The bulk of the novel is occupied by the narrator's uniquely penetrating descriptions of his characters' thoughts, feelings and relationships. This narrator also breaks other literary ground: Not content to slip into the background and let the storyline flow, he constantly interrupts the plot, speculating on motives, offering his opinions, and suggesting alternative views. Sometimes he even takes part in the interactions, as when, in the first chapter, he plucks a rose from a bush outside the town prison and offers it to you, the reader. Furthermore, he claims to be guiding the story through its many macabre twists based on various sources (manuscripts, gossip, rumors and legends) that may or may not be reliable. The reader is often left to chose one or another version of the tale, or to reject them all.

Hester Prynne is one of the great heroines of literature. Though Hawthorne never condones her crime, he is, as described in Harry Levin's introduction, "concerned to show that fundamental morality is not so much a series of rigorous laws to be enforced by a meddling community as it is an insight to be attained through continuous exertion on the part of the individual conscience."

An ambiguous blend of sin and virtue, pride and humility, severity and gentleness, justice and mercy, the novel's true message may lie in what Hawthorne describes as its true genre: *The Scarlet Letter*, says its author, is not so much a novel as a "romance," filled with details that disclose the "truth of the human heart."

A FAREWELL TO ARMS

by
Ernest Hemingway
(1899 - 1961)

Type of work: Psychological realism

Setting: Italy and Switzerland;
World War I

Principal characters:
Frederic Henry, an American in the
Italian army
Catherine Barkley, a British nurse
Rinaldi, an Italian surgeon and
Frederic's friend
Miss Ferguson, a British nurse and
Catherine's friend

Story Overview:

Lieutenant Frederic Henry, a handsome young American, had returned from leave in southern Italy to the front, where he served in the Italian ambulance corps. The war was still leaning toward victory for the Italians. During dinner, Lieutenant Rinaldi, Frederic's jovial surgeon friend, needled Frederic about his youth and lack of experience with women, then sprang his surprise: A group of British nurses had arrived to set up a hospital unit nearby, and Rinaldi had become friends with a nurse, Catherine Barkley. He begged Frederic to come with him to meet Miss Barkley and help make a "good impression" on her.

Frederic was impressed by Catherine – so impressed that he, instead of Rinaldi, began romancing the nurse. Catherine and Frederic bantered back and forth to hide their mutual attraction, and the good-natured Rinaldi then couldn't help but tease Frederic about his new lady love.

Soon afterwards, while Frederic was on ambulance duty in the combat zone, an Austrian mortar shell exploded over his unit and scattered shrapnel through Frederic's legs, turning them into "hamburger." He was transported to Milan to heal and rehabilitate his wounded legs. Fortunately, Catherine was also soon transferred to Milan. During the day, Frederic worked diligently on the therapy machines to regain full use of his limbs, but the hot summer nights were spent by the reunited lovers on Frederic's hospital bed, with a hidden stash of wine. With Frederic improving in health, they managed to be together constantly – there were carriage rides in the park, horse races, dinners at street-side cafes. By summer's end Frederic's legs were completely healed and he was slated for return to his ambulance corps. But on their last night together, Catherine disclosed her news: she was pregnant.

Frederic returned to the front with orders to move hospital equipment south into the Po Valley – a familiar mission. By now, though, the war's complexion had changed. Italian forces had lost several key battles, and rumors circulated that the Austrians, along with German reinforcements, were about to mount a new attack. All of Frederic's friends were weary of war. Morale was sinking day by day. Surgeons, including Rinaldi, operated around the clock. "This war is killing me," Rinaldi told Frederic. "All summer and fall I've operated. I do everybody's work." Furthermore, Rinaldi admitted, he suspected that he had contracted syphilis. Rinaldi's condition confirmed to the despondent Frederic that one way or another this war was making everyone ill.

The fierce Austrian assault forced the demoralized Italians to begin their muddy retreat from Caporetto. Driving three ambulances cross-country to avoid the miles of stalled vehicles and guns lined up on the highways, Frederic and his comrades became lost on the back roads, where their vehicles mired in the thick, wet silt. Forced to travel on foot towards Udine, they ducked Austrian patrols and nervous Italian sentries who shot at anything that moved. After one of their group was killed by a sniper, they hid in barns and fields, part of a frantically retreating mob. Finally, the ragged group made their way to the Italian border. But as they crossed a check point, an Italian military policeman wrenched Frederic out of the line. A firing squad had been set up to execute accused spies and deserting Italian officers, who were cutting their insignias from their sleeves in order to flee. Spies and deserters were being put to death after the most cursory of trials. On that dark night, Frederic decided that the war was over for him; it was time to say his "farewell to arms." While the guards were busy dragging another poor victim to face death in front of the firing squad, Frederic scrambled away and plunged into an icy river. As the current swept him along, Frederic's frozen fingers clutched a timber which he used as a float until he floundered up onto a riverbank several miles downstream.

Frederic was now a defector. He stole onto a train bound for Milan, hiding beneath a tarp so the guards would not see him. He would find Catherine, he decided, and together, they would escape to Switzerland.

However, when he arrived in Milan Frederic discovered that Catherine had gone to Strega, a town on the border between Italy and Switzerland. He borrowed some civilian clothing from an American friend in Milan and caught a train to Strega, where he found Catherine on leave. Once he was united with Catherine, Frederic promised that they would never again part; war was a thing of the past for both of them.

But the police in Strega had been notified about Frederic and his desertion and were under orders to capture and execute him. At the last minute, a bartender-friend of Frederic's warned him of his impending arrest, which was planned for the following morning. This friend offered his row boat to aid them in their escape. All that night Frederic rowed doggedly across Lake Geneva. By morning, his hands were so raw that Catherine convinced him to let her row the rest of the way into neutral Switzerland. Their safety was assured when they were able to convince the Swiss authorities of their newly assumed identities.

The couple contentedly settled down for the winter in Montreux, a small town in the Alps. They played chess and cards and took long walks; sometimes Frederic went skiing. Long into the night they talked of what they would do at the end of the war.

A month before the baby was due, Frederic and Catherine moved to Lausanne to be close to the hospital, planning to return to Montreux in the spring.

Their anticipation and hope for happiness, however, proved to be futile. The long-awaited birth turned tragic. Catherine suffered in labor for many hours, and finally the doctors had to perform a Caesarean section. The baby was delivered dead; and a little later, Catherine hemorrhaged and died in Frederic's arms. Frederic had now lost everything he held dear. All his dreams for the future had disappeared in a matter of hours.

For Frederic, stunned by grief, there was no place to go, nothing to do, no one to talk to. He ambled aimlessly from the hospital through the rainy streets of Lausanne, a broken and lonely man.

Commentary:

Combining a depressing ending and austere realism with an idealistic, descriptive story is one of Hemingway's particulars of style. A subtle, emotional power permeates the story without the reader really being aware of Hemingway's hand in it. Gertrude Stein, the author's mentor, believed *A Farewell to Arms* was Hemingway's best novel. Certainly, it catapulted him into literary stardom.

Through the character of Frederic, Hemingway eloquently argues against war. Frederic accepts what life hands him without murmuring, but argues the fatalist's philosophy: whether you were good or bad, "they killed you in the end." Moreover, Hemingway shows how World War I, "the war to end all wars," transformed many of those who fought in it into a generation of cynics.

Hemingway himself served in the Italian army as an ambulance driver and, like Frederic, was wounded in the legs. Thus, much of *A Farewell to Arms'* emotional energy was taken from his own experiences.

The author portrays a sophisticated, intimate, caring relationship between Frederic and Catherine; a relationship entered into without the benefit of marriage. In the 1920's this was unheard of. The novel, in many other ways as well, helped break new social and literary frontiers, with its economical style and emotional understatement. And together with *A Sun Also Rises*, it established Hemingway as one of America's preeminent twentieth-century writers.

FOR WHOM THE BELL TOLLS

by
Ernest Hemingway
(1899 - 1961)

Type of work: Romantic war novel

Setting: Spain; 1937

Principal characters:
> *Robert Jordan,* an American fighting with Spanish Loyalists
> *Maria,* Jordan's lover
> *Anselmo,* Jordan's elderly guerilla guide
> *Pablo,* a drunken guerilla leader
> *Pilar,* Pablo's strong and commanding wife
> *El Sordo,* another guerilla leader
> *Rafael,* a gypsy member of Pablo's band

Story Overview:

Robert Jordan, the young American, could think of nothing but the bridge as he and his seasoned guide Anselmo hiked through the mountains behind Fascist lines. Golz, one of many Russians also working for the Loyalist forces in their civil war with the Fascists for control of Spain, explained the importance of Jordan's mission. Golz was organizing a major offensive against the enemy. To protect his troops from reinforcements sent up after the attack commenced, Golz needed the strategic bridge destroyed: "[Do it] as soon as the attack has started and not before. I must know that bridge is gone."

Jordan and Anselmo worked their way up the mountains where the bridge was located. The plan was for Jordan to make contact with a guerilla band led by Pablo and his devoted, fierce, and swarthy wife, Pilar. After taking a few days to examine the bridge and organize the attack, he would have to wait for the proper moment to blow it up.

Though he had destroyed other bridges, and trains as well, Jordan was apprehensive about this mission. He felt even worse when he made contact with Pablo's band. The guerilla leader was surly and insecure; he demanded to know what Jordan intended to do: "If it is in this territory, it is my business." Jordan quickly changed the subject.

That night Jordan stayed at the guerrilla's cave hideout with Pilar, Rafael the gypsy, six other guerrillas, and Maria, a young girl who had been rescued from the Fascists. Jordan asked Pilar if more guerrillas could be rounded up for the attack on the heavily guarded bridge. She said that she would enlist the help of a band of six or seven mountain men, led by the reclusive but proficient El Sordo. However, the attack would be very dangerous, and afterwards the entire band would have to abandon their mountain camps.

Pablo was drunk earlier than usual that evening. He criticized Jordan's plans and told everyone in the cave that the mission would fail. But Pilar stepped in and ushered Jordan outside for a breath of air. The gypsy, Rafael, quickly followed. "Three or four times we waited for you to kill him. Pablo has no friends," Rafael declared. Although the idea of killing Pablo had in fact flashed across Jordan's mind, he had restrained himself: "For a stranger to kill where he must work with the people afterwards is very bad."

For weeks all of Jordan's thoughts had centered on his mission. Now, however, all throughout the evening's tension-filled dinner, it was not Pablo or the bridge that occupied his mind, but Maria. The two flirted, sneaking glances and sly touches back and forth. Later, when Jordan bedded down outside beneath the stars – along with the dynamite, which no one wanted in the cave – Maria came to him, torn between hope and reluctance. Among the Fascists she had been subjected to starvation, torture and rape, and she believed that no one could love a defiled woman. But Jordan persuaded her to slide into his sleeping bag next to him, and they became lovers. And Jordan, who had lived until then mainly for the ceremony of risking his life, now knew that, though he would still fight for the cause, he no longer wished to court death; he wanted to live – for Maria.

The next day, Pilar, Jordan and Maria paid a visit to El Sordo's camp. Along the way Pilar spoke of how the war had begun in her native village. Pablo had led the attack on the local "civilia guardia," trapped in their barracks. After killing the soldiers, Pablo and his rebels gathered Fascist party members into the town hall. There, one by one, they were forced to run through a gauntlet formed by the townspeople, who beat them with shovels and rakes. To Robert Jordan, it was a horrible, disgusting story.

At the camp, El Sordo agreed to help with the mission to blow up the bridge, and assured that he could secure horses for the ensuing escape.

It was snowing heavily when they returned to their own camp. The snow was a bad omen. Jordan grimly acknowledged that it could ruin the entire mission. Pablo, on the other hand, was elated. He baited Jordan: "With this thy offensive goes, Ingles." But Jordan walked away from the guerilla's taunting. He couldn't risk muddling the mission with internal violence.

Earlier that day, Pablo had sent Anselmo

down near the bridge to watch the road and spy out the sentry positions. The storm was now in full force and Anselmo had not returned, so Jordan trekked to the bridge. There he found the old man at his post, still waiting and watching.

When Jordan and Anselmo returned to the cave, they found Pablo, "bleary-eyed drunk." While they ate, Pablo again tried to provoke Jordan into a fight. One of the other men punched Pablo in the face, but Pablo only laughed.

In the early light of morning, Jordan spied, and shot, an approaching Fascist cavalryman. Quickly he directed Pablo to lead the dead man's horse away from the camp while another man quickly hid the body. Next he ordered a large machine gun to be placed and camouflaged above the camp. Jordan figured the horseman must be part of a patrol searching for El Sordo, who had stolen horses the night before.

After a short time, four more cavalrymen passed – unmolested – below. "We could have killed all four," the gunner protested. "But with the firing who knows what might have come?" Jordan replied. And as he had surmised, twenty more soldiers soon followed in their wake. Later, when they heard the attack on El Sordo's camp, some of Pablo's men wanted to go to their aid. But Jordan said it would be useless. And no matter what the cost, the bridge had to come first.

Again, Jordan was right. For hours El Sordo's men fought valiantly. But when the Fascist bombers arrived, El Sordo and his band were slaughtered, and the Fascist officer ordered all the dead guerrillas beheaded to serve as a warning to other rebels.

Now, without El Sordo's men, Jordan knew the attack on the bridge would be almost impossible. Still, they watched the roads, as Fascist tanks, troops and trucks crossed over the bridge.

That night as Jordan slept, Pablo stole and destroyed the exploder, detonator and blasting caps from Jordan's pack, then disappeared. When Pilar woke Jordan to tell him this news, his stomach felt "hollow." They would now have to set off the dynamite using grenades – a much more dangerous method.

Before dawn Jordan and the others prepared for the operation. Most would divide and attack two Fascist flank posts, while Jordan and Anselmo killed the guards on the bridge and set the dynamite. Just as all was readied, Pablo appeared with five other men to join them. Jordan had mixed feelings about Pablo's return, but decided that any reinforcements were better than nothing.

Everything was set; everyone was in position. Now they must wait for the aerial bombardment to signal the beginning of the offensive. To Jordan it seemed that it would never come, "that nothing could happen on such a lovely late May morning." Suddenly they heard "clustered, thudding of the bombs," and Jordan and Anselmo opened fire on the two guards. As Jordan wired the bridge, the few minutes seemed like an eternity. Finally he was able to pull the pins and the bridge was blown high into the air. But in the explosion, Anselmo, a sensitive man who had always hated killing, was killed himself by a steel fragment. Jordan tearfully cursed Pablo; the old man might still be alive had Pablo not stolen the blasting caps.

Jordan raced to the designated meeting place to regroup. Crouched in the pines, he found only Pablo, Pilar, Maria and two other gypsy insurgents. Pablo was leading a dozen horses. Though Pablo claimed at first that the other guerrillas had been killed by Fascists, Jordan forced Pablo to admit that he himself had slaughtered them to get their horses.

The survivors were now hemmed in by Fascist troops and tanks. They needed to cross a road that led to safety, knowing full well that the Fascists would strafe the road with bullets once they were alerted. Jordan chose to cross last. As he made his move, a tank fired a shell, trapping him beneath his wounded horse. The others dragged him out of the line of fire, but Jordan knew his leg was hopelessly crushed. Maria knelt near him and sobbed. Jordan voiced his love for her, and though she begged to stay with him, he assured her that as long as she was alive, he would live too. Finally the others wrestled her away from him so they could leave.

Jordan gripped his submachine gun and waited. He pondered the events that had brought him there to die. He would not, however, die in vain. The fight of the common people was his fight; someday they would win, and hopefully struggle for peace as tenaciously as they strained for freedom. Jordan smiled, took aim at the leading Fascist officer who had come into view, and squeezed the trigger.

Commentary:

Hemingway once worked as a reporter covering the Spanish Civil War. *For Whom the Bell Tolls* was the most famous book to come out of that war, which served as a prelude to the devastation of World War II in which the free world united against Fascism. Perhaps overly romanticized, at the same time the novel illustrates humanity's great capacity for either hope or despair, as shown by the contrast between the devoted Anselmo and the brutish Pablo.

Written as though translated from formal Spanish, the novel evokes a realistic mood. The title was taken from a quote by John Donne: " . . . Any man's death diminishes me, because I am involved in Mankinde; And therefore never send to know for whom the bell tolls; It tolls for thee."

ANNA KARENINA

by
Leo Tolstoy
(1828 - 1910)

Type of work: Tragic love story

Setting: Moscow and St. Petersburg, Russia; nineteenth century

Principal characters:
Anna Karenina, a beautiful young woman
Alexey, her cold, vindictive husband
Count Vronsky, a young military officer who falls in love with Anna
Stepan Oblonsky, Anna's spendthrift brother
Dolly, Stepan's frustrated wife
Kitty, Dolly's sister
Levin, Stepan's rustic friend, and Kitty's suitor

Story Overview:

Stepan Oblonsky's wife Dolly had discovered that her husband was having an affair. With her beauty fading and her household a wreck, she had had enough. Stepan fretfully wrote to his sister, Anna Karenina, asking her to come to Moscow and convince Dolly not to leave him.

Later, while working at his job in the entrenched Moscow bureaucracy, Stepan received an unexpected visitor: Levin, an old friend from the university, came to discuss Dolly's sister Kitty, whom he wanted to marry. After being informed by Stepan that he had a rival for Kitty's affections, a certain Count Vronsky of St. Petersburg, Levin resolved that he would propose to Kitty that very night.

At that same moment, Anna and Count Vronsky were riding together in a train bound for Moscow. Vronsky noticed the charming woman as he made his way to the first-class compartment that he shared with his mother. He had time to take note of "the suppressed eagerness which played over her face" as their eyes met, and she remained in his mind. However, upon reaching their destination, the two went their separate ways – Anna to her brother's home, Vronsky and his mother to a hotel.

Approached by Anna, Dolly at first refused to discuss her husband's infidelity. "Everything's lost after what has happened, everything's over!" she raged. But finally she relented to Anna's pleas to keep the family together.

Meanwhile, Levin had arrived early at a dinner party hosted by the parents of Kitty and Dolly, determined to make his desires known to Kitty before the appearance of the rich and handsome Count. But "That cannot be . . . forgive me," Kitty replied upon hearing his stammering proposal. Crushed by the rejection, Levin escaped from the gathering at the first opportunity.

A few days later, at her coming-out ball, Kitty couldn't help but notice how Anna and Vronsky kept gazing at each other. Vronsky's face had a look that puzzled her . . . "like the expression of an intelligent dog when it had done wrong." It was clear to Kitty that the two were in love.

Nevertheless, with her task of seeing to Stepan and Dolly completed, Anna boarded the next train for St. Petersburg. She thought of her son, Seryozha, and her husband, Alexey. " . . . My life will go on in the old way, all nice and as usual," she thought. But she found that she could not easily dismiss Count Vronsky from her mind. And stopping along the way, as Anna stepped out for a breath of air, there he was. "You know that I have come to be where you are; I can't help it," confessed the officer. Anna was both delighted and flattered by this, but it was simply unthinkable that anything could come of his attraction to her. After all, she was a married woman.

Back in Moscow, Kitty was devastated. Not only had Count Vronsky spurned her, but Levin had also left the city to supervise work on his country estate. Humiliated and distraught, Kitty became so ill with despair that she was soon unable to eat or sleep. Her frantic parents, after finding no restorative medical treatment in Moscow, sent her to Europe to consult various doctors.

Meanwhile, life for Anna in St. Petersburg remained strangely unsettled. The happiness that in Moscow "had fairly flashed from her eyes, [now seemed] hidden somewhere far away." To her further disquiet, the love-struck Vronsky took every opportunity to see her. One night she knelt and begged him to leave her in peace; but still he persisted: "I can't think of you and myself apart. You and I are one to me." And at that moment Anna "let her eyes rest on him, full of love."

Soon afterward, Alexey Karenina walked into a party and found his wife with Vronsky; but Anna denied any impropriety. Still, she and Vronsky met night after night, with Alexey seemingly powerless or unwilling to stop them. Anna by now felt "so sinful, so guilty"; but still she could not curb her passion for the Count.

The following summer, while staying at her husband's villa outside the city, Anna confronted her lover with an announcement: she was pregnant. Though he understood the gravity of Anna's position, Vronsky smiled. This was the "turning point he had been longing for."

"Leave your husband and make our life one," he implored. But Anna shook her head. If she left, Alexey would take sole custody of Seryozha and she would not be allowed to see her son. But Anna did promise Vronsky that she would tell her husband the truth about the child she was carrying.

When Anna made her confession, Alexey, instead of showing jealousy or indignation, merely warned his wife against "public displays of flirtation." His sole concern was to preserve his social and business reputation; a duel or a divorce would only serve to disgrace him. "The family cannot be broken up by a whim, a caprice, or even by the sin of one of the partners in the marriage," he informed Anna. " . . . Our life must go on as it has done in the past."

Anna reacted to his words at first with guilt and shame, but this quickly turned to anger: "He knows that I can't repent that I breathe, that I love; he knows that it can lead to nothing but lying and deceit; but he wants to go on torturing me . . . " Vronsky also was increasingly anxious to begin a new life with Anna, who would not leave her son. And so, "the position was one of misery for all three . . . "

Kitty had by now returned to Moscow, feeling somewhat better. One morning, just after dawn, Levin caught sight of her in a carriage, as it skirted his estate destined for her family's summer home. The pangs of love, long since buried, welled up in him once more. Months later, taking advantage of a trip to the city, he called again upon Kitty. It was apparent to both that they cared deeply for each other, and, after a proper courtship, they were united as man and wife. Levin, for years caught up in trying to find out who he was and where he fit in God's universe, had finally and happily found his place.

But in St. Petersburg, relationships were breaking up. The nearer Anna came to the birth of her child, the more demanding and cold Alexey became. Then Anna survived a deadly fever to give birth to a baby girl. Oddly, the difficulty of the birth eased the tensions between herself and her husband. At the other extreme, Vronsky saw no end to the barriers separating him from his lover. Desperate at the prospect of living without Anna, he unsuccessfully tried shooting himself. Still torn, Anna finally did move in with him, and soon the couple left Russia to live in Italy for a time.

Meanwhile, Kitty and Levin were living on their estate outside of Moscow. Levin felt gratified to be spiritually sustained by a loving wife. Like Anna, Kitty went through a difficult pregnancy, but it culminated in the birth of a fine little boy. Theirs was an idyllic life.

Upon returning from Italy to St. Petersburg, Vronsky and Anna, found themselves ostracized. Gossip followed them everywhere. The couple argued frequently, and Anna, in a burst of depression, finally accused Vronsky of being unfaithful. Even after they moved into a newly-inherited estate, Anna felt alone in the world. She revived her habit of taking a little morphine to help her sleep, a legacy from her pregancy.

Summer turned to winter, and the family relocated again, this time to Moscow. There, the badly strained relationship fared no better. Though Anna pled for Vronsky to love her and give her security, at the same time she increasingly insisted on greater freedom. "This is becoming unbearable!" Vronsky screamed one day. "Why do you try my patience? It has limits." Anna could only gaze at him "with terror at the undisguised hatred in his whole face." Vronsky checked himself: "I mean to say . . . I must ask what it is you want of me?" "All I want," she replied, "is that you don't desert me, as you think of doing . . . . I want love, and there is none . . . " Vronsky vainly protested; he would never cease to love her.

Suddenly, Anna turned on Vronsky, cursing him for the sacrifices she had made to be with him – her marriage, her son, her social position . . .

Delirious with bitterness, Anna had no place to turn; Vronsky, she was convinced, had found another, and she could never return to Alexey. Ambling into the train station, she purchased a ticket. Then, standing on the platform, watching the trains, she said to herself, " . . . I will punish him and escape from everyone and from myself."

Measuring both the speed of the oncoming train and her resolve to end her suffering, she jumped. " . . . Something huge and merciless struck her on the head and rolled on her back . . . . 'Lord, forgive me all!'"

Anna Karenina was dead.

Commentary:

Leo Tolstoy is considered one of Russia's greatest nineteenth-century novelists, an honor he shares with Dostoievsky. Tolstoy, however, focuses his novels on the vicissitudes of the upper-classes rather than on Dostoievsky's underprivileged peasants or criminals.

Tolstoy foresaw the end of the aristocracy in Russian society. Serfs had already been set free; the working class was beginning to expand in power. Moreover, new mores and morals were being imported from the West, and society's upper crust was the first to feel the strain of these changes – a strain running an undercurrent throughout *Anna Karenina*.

The novel reads like a soap opera, with the exhaustive cast of characters continually creating their own problems. Contrast Anna's tragic quest for love and personal fulfillment with the spiritual odyssey of Levin. Through hard work and the support of an understanding family, his search is rewarded by happiness. Thus, Tolstoy's gripping masterpiece revolves around the dissimilar paths of these two characters, allowing a forum for the author's commentary on Russia's maze-like social system, fraught with unresolved incongruities.

OF MICE AND MEN

by
John Steinbeck
(1902 - 1968)

Type of work: Rustic, sentimental novel

Setting: Salinas Valley, California;
20th-century depression years

Principal characters:
Lennie Small, a clumsy, simple-
minded giant of a man
George Milton, Lennie's friend and
protector
Candy, a ranch swamper
Slim, a farm hand
Crooks, a Negro stable worker
Curley, the ranch owner's virulent son
Curley's wife

Story Overview:

George and his ponderous friend Lennie followed a dusty path leading to the banks of the Salinas River, toting their only possessions – bedrolls and a few articles of clothing. Slow-minded Lennie had cost them their previous jobs; his innocent fascination with a young girl's red dress and his awkward attempt to touch it had frightened the girl, forcing them to flee a lynch mob. Now they were heading for a nearby ranch to sign on as barley bucks.

George reminded Lennie once again to let him do all the talking when they met with the ranch owner. Lennie promised that he would, and then begged George to tell him again about the farm they hoped to own one day:

"Come on, George. Tell me. Please, George. Like you done before."
"You get a kick outta that, don't you?" George replied. "Awright, I'll tell you, and then we'll eat our supper . . . "

The dream farm will include all sorts of animals – and Lennie will be assigned to take care of the rabbits.

The two men neared the ranch. Using Lennie's love of animals as a means of control, George once more warned his friend that if he didn't keep quiet, or if he caused any trouble at the ranch, they wouldn't get the job they so badly needed; then they couldn't earn the money for their dream-farm.

As hiring negotiations began, the ranch boss questioned George about Lennie's quiet and slow manner. But George was ready with an excuse: "He's my . . . cousin. I told his old lady I'd take care of him. He got kicked in the head by a horse when he was a kid. He's alright. Just ain't bright."

Once they were hired, both George and Lennie went right to work. Later, as they waited for lunch to be served, in sauntered Curley, the ranch owner's son. He was there to look over the new men. After Curley had gone, Candy, the bunkhouse swamper, warned them about the young man. A former prizefighter, Curley took pleasure in boosting his ego by picking on others. He was also an insecure husband – he became insanely jealous of anyone who even got near his wife.

Seeming to sense that Curley would bring them trouble, Lennie now became agitated and nervous about the job; but with no money to fall back on, the pair was forced to continue working at the ranch.

Before nightfall, another ranch hand, a jerkline skinner named Slim, presented the childlike Lennie with a puppy from his dog's litter. Slim appeared to be a kind and sensitive man, so George confided in him about the troubles he and Lennie had had. As they finished their conversation, Lennie shuffled in, smiling, with his puppy hidden inside his coat. George told him to take it back to the barn to be with its mother.

That evening, in the deserted bunkhouse, George, Candy and Lennie – still cradling his puppy – quietly talked. Lennie prevailed on George to tell him still again about their future farm. When George had finished the story, Candy piped up: it seemed that he had three hundred and fifty dollars saved up and he would be retiring soon; could he join George and Lennie in their plan? George happily agreed to Candy's proposal. With the swamper's money added to their wages, the three of them would soon have enough to buy a decent farm.

Excited by this new development, Lennie was grinning with delight when Curley entered the bunkhouse in search of his wife. For days the ranch hands had been needling Curley about his wife's most recent wanderings. Now when the ill-humored husband spied Lennie's wide smile, and supposing that Lennie was taunting him, his temper boiled over.

Curley stepped over to Lennie like a terrier. "What the hell you laughin' at?"
Lennie looked blankly at him. "Huh?"

Then Curley's rage exploded. "Come on ya big bastard. Get up on your feet. No big son-of-a-bitch is gonna laugh at me. I'll show ya who's yella . . . "

The giant, confused over the violent pummeling, refused at first to defend himself; George had warned him against making trouble:

Lennie covered his face with his huge paws, and bleated in terror. He cried, "Make 'um stop, George." Then Curley attacked his stomach and cut off his wind . . .

George . . . cupped his hands around his mouth and yelled, "Get 'em, Lennie."

Lennie took his hands away from his face and looked about for George, and Curley slashed at his eyes. The big face was covered with blood. George yelled again, "I said get him!"

Curley's fist was swinging when Lennie reached for it. The next minute Curley was flopping like a fish on a line, and his closed fist was lost in Lennie's big hand. Every bone in Curley's hand was crushed.

Before Curley was taken to town for treatment, Slim advised him to say his hand had been caught in a machine, to avoid the embarrassment of the truth.

With the others on their way into town, Lennie went to visit Crooks, the black stable buck. Crooks liked talking to Lennie because of his innocent nature. Candy joined them. The shaken giant now voiced his intensified longings for escape to the tranquility and safety of the mythical farm, and he calmed himself by describing all the harmonious details of life on the glorified ranch-to-be. He would get to feed the rabbits; George had promised.

But abruptly this gentle vision was interrupted by the appearance of Curley's priggish wife, who had come looking for her husband. When Curley's "accident" was described to her, she wasn't fooled; she hinted, rather, at how pleased she was that Curley had been taught a lesson. Then, hearing the other men returning from town, she slipped out of the stable.

That evening, while the ranch hands entertained themselves with games of horseshoes, Lennie stayed alone in the barn holding his pup. He did not realize that, due to his incessant mauling, the puppy was dead. As he sat in the straw stroking the animal's fur, Curley's wife again wandered in. At first Lennie refused to speak to her – George might not let him feed the rabbits. But the girl was able to make him feel at ease; she even let Lennie stroke her long, soft hair. After a time she tried to pull away, but Lennie unexplainably held on, he was bewildered when the girl started to scream. He began to shake her to make her stop. However, in the process, the innocent but powerful Lennie broke the woman's neck.

Later that night, Candy entered the barn expecting to see Lennie; instead he found Curley's wife, in the shadows, half buried in straw, dead. Lennie had disappeared.

Hearing the disastrous news, George grabbed his gun to join the other men, who by now had been headed up by Curley into a revenge-seeking mob. Curley was determined to hunt down the hulking, simple-minded murderer and see justice done.

But fortunately, it was George who found Lennie, trembling with fear, hiding among the bushes by the stream. George too was fearful – of what Curley would do to Lennie when he found him. For the final time George solemnly recounted the story of the farm for Lennie. Yes, he could care for the rabbits.

Lennie then begged that they leave, right then, to seek out the farm. But George knew that they would never be capable of escaping Curley and his hatred. As Lennie gazed out over the river, George aimed the gun's muzzle at the back of his devoted friend's head, and pulled the trigger.

Commentary:

This touching story clearly illustrates Steinbeck's political and social philosophies. In frustration over what he perceived as the failed American dream, and perhaps with intentional Marxist overtones, Steinbeck populates Of Mice and Men with struggling and bewildered heroes – common souls caught up in tragic combats as they innocently pursue the raw and elusive promise of America. The novel's tragic irony serves to pique the conscience of the reader, as well as to spotlight Steinbeck's political concerns for the equality and happiness of all members of the human family.

Within the brief but dramatic three-day span covered by Of Mice and Men, the spectrum of human emotions is played out – physical pain, misunderstood intentions, jealous rage, longings for peaceful existence, tenderness, genuine friendship, heartrending pity, confusion, and finally, utter resignation. Steinbeck evokes the reader's most profound sympathy by the use of a simple plot, common language and an easy, natural setting.

PARADISE LOST

by
John Milton
(1608 - 1674)

Type of work: Narrative, epic poem

Setting: Hell, then Heaven, then newly-created Earth; all "in the beginning"

Principal characters:
Satan, earlier called Lucifer, a fallen angel
Adam, the first man
Eve, the first woman
God the Father
God the Son
Various angels and demons

Story Overview:

(Recounted here is the story of Man's fall,

Of Man's First Disobedience, and the Fruit
Of that Forbidden Tree, whose mortal taste
Brought Death into the World, and all our woe,
With loss of Eden, Till one greater Man
Restore us, and regain the blissful Seat . . .)

Satan, the once radiant Lucifer, and his angels, lay in a formless, sulphurous lake of fire having just been driven out of Heaven. Their fall had sent them plummeting through space from their heavenly home down to Hell, leaving them beaten senseless. Only now, after lying unconscious for nine days, did Satan and his demons begin to rouse themselves. Accustomed to living in heavenly glory, they found their new home horrifying, and convened a council to determine how they might escape Hell and recover at least some of their former glory.

Too proud to consider seeking re-admittance to Heaven through repentance, they agreed with Satan that it was "better to reign in Hell than serve in Heaven." One demon favored remaining in Hell, but transforming it into a kingdom as powerful and glorious as Heaven. But another, Beelzebub, second in command, proposed a different plan: He had heard that God had designs to create a new world, to be the home "of some new race called man . . . / To be created like to us, though less/ In power and excellence."

Beelzebub argued that, if they acted quickly, they could possess this new world and subdue as slaves the new race of men. His vengeful plot was eagerly approved by the hosts of Hell, and Satan himself volunteered to make the perilous journey past the Gates of Hell and through space to the new earth.

Satan, after a long trek, happened upon a heavenly angel, Uriel, custodian of the orb of the sun. Disguised as an angel, Satan managed to get the unsuspecting Uriel to point out where the new earth lay. The devil then flew off.

His earthly arrival, however, did not go unnoticed by God, who calmly explained to His Son that Satan's presence would, in time, lead to the fall of man, bringing upon him punishment and death. Moved by compassion, the Son offered to give his life in order to save men, which sacrifice the Father accepted. But for the time they left Satan to his wiles.

Satan was overwhelmed by the earth's beauty. But that very beauty, far from filling him with joy, stirred up memories of the Paradise he had lost. In a stormy speech full of self-doubt, fear, and envy, Satan lamented his fall and foretold a future filled with ever-worsening torments. He would never be able to escape Hell, he concluded, since "which way I fly is Hell; myself am Hell." But if he could not live in peace, at least he would divide Heaven's kingdom, and possibly rule over the greater part of God's creation.

Searching, Satan finally came upon Adam and Eve. Disguised in the forms of various beasts, he marvelled at the first man and woman, whose beauty and nobility inspired in him both admiration and jealousy. He watched them discharge their duties as caretakers of the Garden of Eden and eavesdropped on their long, affectionate conversations. He was astonished to find them endowed with full faculties of speech and reasoning, and yet they were so innocent as to enjoy sexual union without the slightest taint of lust. After performing their evening devotions, Adam and Eve retired to their bed. Satan, crouching as a toad beside the sleeping woman, whispered falsehoods and rumors into her ear. After a time, guardian angels arrived to interrupt his mischief, but allowed him to escape.

On the next morning Eve awoke complaining of a nightmare in which an angel had tempted her to eat the forbidden fruit of the Tree of Knowledge. God, seeing the peril his creation was in, sent the angel Raphael to explain to the couple that Satan had been the cause of the dream and to warn them against further temptation. Adam's curiosity was sparked; he asked Raphael about this "Satan" and how he had managed to come to the earth. The angel answered Adam with an account of Satan's fall. The problem, he related, began when God the Father announced to the assembled angels that He had anointed His Son, who stood at His right hand, as a Lord over them all. Lucifer, full of envy, managed to assemble a rival faction of angels to contest God's power. The ensuing battle lasted three days. On the first, the loyal angels routed the rebels. Satan retreated, but during the night manufactured a slew of weapons with which, on the second day's fighting, he surprised Heaven's angels. On the third day, God sent His Son to personally lead His forces. The Son drove Satan and his legions over the edge of Heaven into the waiting flames.

Raphael went on to describe the creation of the earth, the forming of man and woman, and advised Adam not to seek knowledge beyond his comprehension. Capping off his visit with a warning to beware of Satan, Raphael returned to Heaven.

But Satan was eager to succeed. Back in Eden, he assumed the form of a serpent and waited for his opportunity. Adam had reluctantly allowed his wife to work alone that day in another part of the garden. Satan accosted her, showering her with flattery, comparing her to a goddess. Astonished and a little pleased by the compliments, Eve demanded to know how the serpent managed to acquire speech. From eating a certain fruit, Satan explained; no sooner had he tasted it than he had found himself able to speak and reason. Though Eve was suspicious, she followed the snake to the tree bearing the fruit. Above the woman's protest that it was forbidden to her, Satan delivered a masterful, subtle argument that if the fruit of the tree could give a mere serpent human faculties, surely it would transform humans into gods! Furthermore, he asserted, the warning of certain death associated with eating the fruit could not be true, since he himself had eaten it and had not died. Swayed by these words, Eve took of the fruit and ate her fill. She returned to Adam, overcome with the sensation of knowledge and power. While horrified that she had partaken of the forbidden fruit, Adam chose to partake as well rather than be separated from her.

Their newfound knowledge, however, was already working changes in their nature. Once wholly innocent in their nakedness, the man and woman now looked on each other with licentiousness; lust overtook them. Afterwards, in guilt and remorse, the transgressors resorted to pleading with God for forgiveness of their sins. The Son, acting as intercessor on their behalf, carried their cries to the Father, who chose to forgive them on condition that they be expelled from Eden, in order to experience mortality. To the woman it would mean pain in childbearing. To Adam, their fall would bring a world of toil and sweat, and a curse of weeds, thorns and briars. God dispatched Michael, one of His chief angels, to carry out the expulsion.

In the meantime, Satan gleefully dashed back towards Hell with news of his victory. On the way he met Sin and Death, busily building a road to earth, and bargained with them to be his ambassadors on Earth.

In Hell, Satan haughtily told of his masterful seduction of Adam and Eve. But just at the very moment when he expected to receive their thunderous applause, he heard nothing but hisses – the host of them had been turned into serpents. Trees, exact in appearance to the Tree of Knowledge, appeared, laden with fruit. But when the mass of serpents struggled to bite into the fruit, it turned to bitter ashes. The Son had prevented Hell's hosts from becoming mortal; they would forever be the hated enemy of mankind.

On an earth filled with storms, floods, earthquakes, violent predators and the discomforts of changing seasons, Adam and Eve contemplated suicide. But Michael arrived, bringing hope – God would forgive their sin. Though in consequence of their sin they must be expelled from the Garden, Michael comforted them, manifesting to them a vision of mankind's future: their progeny; the rise and fall of kingdoms; Noah; Abraham; Moses; the coming of the Messiah, and His death, resurrection and expiration to redeem fallen man; the progress of God's church; and, in the end, the Lord's second coming. Cheered by the prospect of the ultimate redemption of their race, the man and woman followed the path leading from their paradisiacal garden to the barren and lonely world below.

The World was all before them, where to choose
Thir place of rest, and Providence thir guide:
They hand in hand with wand'ring steps and slow,
Through Eden took thir solitary way.

Commentary:

Few literary poems attempt to take on such a huge theme as *Paradise Lost*. Milton himself, in the *Argumentum* that begins the poem, claims to have produced the greatest poem ever written, "things unattempted yet in prose or rhyme." The poem's theme is nothing less than the origin of evil itself, which Milton sees as being embedded in man's nature as a result of the original transgression and subsequent sins of humanity's common ancestors. It recounts, in twelve expansive books, a story line that occupies only a few verses of the book of Genesis.

Aside from its sheer size, other elements might make the work somewhat difficult for a modern reader. It is told in the high formal style, filled with rhetorical speeches, invocations, elaborate similes, and long "catalogues" of names, places, and armies. Milton showers his poem with thousands of allusions to Hebraic, medieval, and renaissance culture, and his syntax may strike a modern reader as twisted. This striking and unusual word order is imitative of Vergil's *Aneid* and the structure of many other great classical epics.

But one need not be a classical scholar to enjoy *Paradise Lost*. The music of the language is often mesmerizing, and its imaginative retelling of the Genesis account is without equal.

The reader is immediately intrigued by Milton's portrait of Satan. In fact, it's not hard to sympathize with the fallen devil, or even side with him – his character is more fleshy and alluring than that of the somewhat bland God of the poem. But that is the very irony Milton wanted to achieve: Just as Satan makes evil appear good, so Satan's ways may appear, but only at first glance, attractive.

BEOWULF

author unknown

Type of work: Heroic epic poem

Setting: "Land of the Geats," southern Sweden and Denmark; c. sixth century

Principal characters:
Beowulf, a Geat hero
Hrothgar, King of the Danes
Unferth, a Danish warrior
Wiglaf, Beowulf's nephew and loyal court noble

Story Overview:

Long ago in Hrothgar's Danish kingdom lived a gruesome monster-giant named Grendel, who nightly roamed the countryside. Rising from his marshy home, he would stalk to the King's high hall, and there devour fifteen of Hrothgar's sleeping warriors. Then, before departing, the monster would seize fifteen more men with his huge arms and bear them back to his watery lair. For twelve years the slaughter continued.

Word of this terror spread across the sea to the land of the Geats, ruled by Hygelac. Beowulf, Hygelac's principal advisor and warrior and a man of great strength and courage, heard the tale of Grendel's murderous attacks. Straightway, he set sail to free the Danes from the demon's depredations.

In Denmark, a coast-watcher met the weary company of fifteen seafarers. Learning of Beowulf's intended mission, he permitted the Danes to pass.

> They started out then – the spacious ship
> remained behind, riding on its rope,
> . . . Figures of boars, bright
> and fire-hardened, gleamed gold-adorned
> above the cheek-guards; in war the boar
> helped guard those fierce men's lives . . .

To Hrothgar's high hall they marched. There the King spread a banquet feast in Beowulf's honor; the mead cup was passed around, and the boasting began. But the Danish warrior Unferth, "drunken with wine," taunted Beowulf, reminding him of a five-day swimming contest in which the Geat was said to have been bested. Beowulf answered boldly, however, that he had not only emerged victorious in the race, but had been forced to kill nine deadly sea-monsters during the course.

After the feast, Hrothgar and his warriors went to their rest, leaving Beowulf and his men in the hall.

Then came the fiendish Grendel, "with an unlovely light, like a hellish flame in his eyes." The ironbound door burst open at the touch of his fingers, and he rejoiced at the rich feast of human flesh awaiting him. He seized one sleeping warrior, tore him up furiously, bit through muscles and sinews, and drank the blood in streams. Then he quickly consumed the entire corpse "as a wolf might eat a rabbit." He reached toward another victim, but the beast was destined to dine no more that night. Without shield or spear, Beowulf took hold of the dreaded monster, wrenching off his right arm; and the maimed Grendel fled back to his home. " . . . The wise and brave warrior from afar/ had cleansed Hrothgar's hall, reclaiming it from woe." As a sign of victory, Beowulf hung his bloody trophy on the wall above the door inside the hall. The brave hero was honored once more with a sumptuous feast and magnificent priceless gifts.

But on the next night, Grendel's brooding and miserable mother made "a sorry journey to avenge her son." Rushing into the great hall, she seized Aeschere, Hrothgar's dearest counselor and a famed and heroic warrior, snatched Grendel's severed arm from the wall, and fled into the darkness. Asleep in a house at some distance from the hall, Beowulf did not learn of the she-monster's visit until the next morning. After vowing to rid the people of this second, even more wretched demon, Beowulf turned to comfort the King with his sage philosophy of life and death:

> Grieve not, wise warrior. It is better
> to avenge one's friend than mourn too much.
> Each of us must one day reach the end
> of worldly life; let him who can win
> glory before he dies: that lives on
> after him, when he lifeless lies.

With Hrothgar leading the way, the Danes cautiously approached the dreaded marsh-lair. Arriving at the moor's edge, the soldiers came upon the head of the ill-fated Aeschere and sighted a stain of blood on the water.

Beowulf prepared to descend to the home of the foe. Unferth nobly offered the Geat his own blood-hardened sword – the finest in the kingdom – thus forfeiting a chance to win for himself immortal glory and fame.

As Beowulf sank beneath the murky waters, he was immediately encircled by enormous and vicious creatures. After an immense struggle, he came to the cave of Grendel's mother and began to do battle. Beowulf, never lucky with weapons, failed in his first attempt to wound the she-monster with Unferth's sword and turned to his mighty handgrip, strong enough to "match the strength of thirty men." Though he was able to grasp the monster by the shoulder and throw her to the ground, still, in the grim hand-to-hand battle that ensued, Beowulf was almost overcome. But fate intervened. On the floor of the lair, in the midst of other weapons pried from the hands of fallen warriors, Beowulf spied a legendary sword that had once belonged to a race of ancient giants. Stretching with all his might, he managed to reach and take hold of the "invincible and strong-edged blade" and plunge it into the heart of Grendel's mother. She rose, then fell in a helpless heap of death. Beowulf turned and saw Grendel himself, lying crippled on the ground nearby. Swiftly, he swung the sword again, and smote Grendel's loathsome head from its body.

Then, as the hero swam to the surface of the marsh, the wondrous sword melted, leaving only the head and hilt intact.

Upon seeing Beowulf alive and undefeated, the Danes rejoiced and feasted him anew. The Geat warrior presented Hrothgar with the sword hilt and returned Unferth's weapon to him without revealing its failure.

Now the time had come for Beowulf to sail back to his Geat homeland. He left Denmark in great glory. Upon his return to the court of Lord Hygelac, he was revered and rewarded with riches and high position. And after several years, Beowulf himself became King among the Geats.

One day, after Beowulf had reigned wisely and courageously for some fifty years, a servant, troubled by his lack of prestige in Beowulf's court, stumbled upon an ancient treasure. While its guardian dragon slept, he stole away a golden goblet which he presented to his King, hoping to gain favor. But the dragon, discovering that the goblet was missing, rose up in fury and began to ravage the Geat villages with fire. Beowulf was now an old man. Nevertheless, he determined to rid his kingdom of this scourge and to win the dragon's rich hoard for his people. Sensing that this might be his final battle, he paused to gather strength, bid farewell to his faithful subjects, and to reflect on his long life of valiant deeds.

The moment of confrontation came. Beowulf advanced toward the dragon's cave, ordering his warriors to withdraw so that he alone might engage the beast in battle.

> . . . It is not your venture . . .
> to match [your] might with the fearful foe's,
> to do this heroic deed. By daring
> shall I gain the gold, or dire battle,
> ending life, will take your lord away!

Finding his shield less protection than he had hoped against the dragon's fiery breath, he still plunged on through the flames and struck the dragon's side with his famed and ancient sword – to no effect. His foil shattered on the creatures bony plate, and the infuriated dragon only belched forth more intense fire. Once again Beowulf was forced to rely on his mighty grip. In the savage exchange, of all the Geat-King's warrior companions, only Wiglaf, a younger kinsman, stood by to defend his ruler. All others had fled. The dragon rushed and sank its terrible teeth into Beowulf's neck. But Wiglaf fearlessly smote the beast on its underside with his sword, and, with his war-knife, Beowulf gave it the death blow.

Weak from loss of blood, the old hero was dying. As his last act, Beowulf gave loyal Wiglaf, the last of his family line, kingly jewels and armor. He rejoiced that he had succeeded in winning the treasure for his subjects, but mourned the fact that he must now leave them.

The Geat troops honored their fallen lord with magnificent funeral rites. The body of their hero was burned on a pyre, according to pagan custom; then the precious hoard was taken from the dragon's lair and buried in the great mound covering the King's ashes.

> Thus his hearth-companions in the host
> of the Geats mourned the going of their lord:
> they said that of worldly kings he was
> the mildest of men and the gentlest,
> most kind to his people, most eager for fame.

And so, with due ceremony, the Geats mourned the passing of the dauntless Beowulf, who had crowned a heroic life with an equally heroic death.

Commentary:

Beowulf, the great masterpiece of Anglo-Saxon literature, was orally passed from generation to generation by North European peoples. The highly artistic, action-filled narrative is replete with Christian theology mingled with pagan mythology, testifying to the great upheavals that occurred in northern civilizations as the poem took form during the early middle ages. Continuously, the principal narrative is interrupted by speeches, pronouncements, songs, chants, and remembrances of battles past – excellent mnemonic devices for transmitting oral history.

The poem contains a valuable record of customs and values from a harsh and heroic time. It embodies the message: "Do your utmost. A good name, a glorified example, and fame after death are all you can win in this world. It is the courage to strive – not success – which ultimately reveals and ennobles the true hero."

PROMETHEUS BOUND

by
Aeschylus
(525 - 456 B.C.)

Type of work: Classical tragic drama

Setting: A desolate Scythian cliff; remote antiquity

Principal characters:

Prometheus, the fire-bearing Titan demigod

Hephaestus, an Olympian fire god

Might (Kratos) and Force (Bia), beings representing Power and Violence

Oceanos, god of the sea, and brother to Prometheus

Io, a river princess

Hermes, Zeus the chief Olympian god's winged messenger

A Chorus composed of the daughters of Oceanos, who converse, comment, and sing throughout the play

Play Overview:

Prologue: Like other works of the Classical Age, Prometheus Bound doesn't begin at the beginning, but leaps *in medias res* ("into the middle of things"), just as Prometheus, a defiant demigod, is brought in chains to be fettered to a desolate mountain crag. For the modern reader – as opposed to an Aeschylian audience, who would have already been conversant with the plot – a bit of background is in order.

Prometheus was a god from the old order, the Titans, who had now all been overthrown by a group of young upstarts, the Olympians – all, that is, except for Prometheus. Rather than go down in honor, this half-god Prometheus, in order to avoid further violence, had chosen to desert over to the Olympian forces. In fact, he was instrumental in Zeus' usurpation of the throne from the old Titan king Chronus. In the new order, Zeus stood as chief god.

Now one of Zeus' first objectives was to destroy the race of men, who, until then, had been a primitive, unenlightened and miserable lot. Zeus' intent was to replace mankind with a new, more noble race, servile to the gods' every whim.

When the destructive proclamation went out, however, Prometheus alone objected to Zeus' heartless proposal. He saw in man a spark of divine promise that even the gods might envy, and in order to save the human race, he willingly and courageously committed a crime: he brought fire down from heaven and taught the mortals how to use it. Furthermore, he tutored them in practical arts, applied sciences and philosophy, that he might edify, ennoble and empower them.

But these saving acts were deemed highly treasonous; such knowledge in the hands of humans threatened to put them on an equal footing with the gods themselves. Furious, Zeus commanded the Olympian blacksmith god of fire, Hephaestus, and the gods of Might and Force, Kratos and Bia, to seize Prometheus and shackle

him to a barren mountainside. But Hephaestus approached his task halfheartedly. He had been taught to respect deity and he sympathized with Prometheus – after all, it didn't seem right that a divine being should suffer such scornful abuse. Pangs of sorrow overwhelmed him; to think that this god was doomed to remain in chains as the solitary guardian of a lonely Scythian cliff for all time to come! The exchange between Hephaestus and Might (Kratos) showed clearly their separate sentiments.

Even as the smithy was reasoning and pleading:

Compassion will not move the mind of Zeus:
All monarchs new to power show brutality . . . .
How bitterly I hate my craftsman's cunning now! . . .
Prometheus! I lament your pain . . .

Might stood by complaining of Hephaestus' delay, and demanding full punishment:

Now do your work – enough of useless pitying.
How can you fail to loathe this god whom all
　　gods hate,
Who has betrayed to man the prize that was
　　your right? . . .
The hammer! Strike, and rivet him against the rock! . . .
Teach this clever one he is less wise than Zeus.
Now take your wedge of steel and with its cruel point
Transfix him! Drive it through his breast with
　　all your strength!

The smithy had no choice but to comply with his orders; and tied with bonds "as strong as adamant," Prometheus was left alone on the jagged face of the cliff. Before departing, the mighty Kratos hurled one last taunt at the Titan god, asking how his human friends could help him now, and chuckling at the foolish Titans who had named him Prometheus, "the Forethinker." It seemed now, Kratos pointed out, that Prometheus required a higher intelligence to do his thinking for him.

The captive god called upon the wind, the waters, mother earth, and the sun to look on him and see how gods tortured a god. He bemoaned his invincible fate, puzzled that he should be punished simply for loving mankind.

Presently, a chorus of the daughters of Oceanos, Prometheus' brother, came on the scene. Seeing the tragic yet defiant figure on the crag, they felt both pity and admiration, and listened as their uncle described the events that had brought him to his exile. The chorus stayed to provide comforting music and cheer.

Next, Prometheus received separate visits from three characters – Oceanos himself, Io, and Hermes.

Oceanos came with a plan. He would go

before Zeus and convey his brother's sorrow and plead for forgiveness. He reasoned that if an apology were offered, and if the captive Titan subjected himself to Zeus' sovereignty, Prometheus might be granted a pardon. But Prometheus was outraged at this proposal; he was a god, and would not stoop to such an apology. Had not Zeus been the true traitor? Had he not betrayed and bound a fellow god?

Oceanos begged his brother to allow him at least a word with Zeus on his behalf, but Prometheus dismissed his offer, calling it a "useless effort" and claiming that if Oceanos tried to intervene, he too would be in danger of punishment for siding with a rebel.

Before his reluctant withdrawal, Oceanos chastised his brother for his arrogance and warned that he would someday be sorry for it. Prometheus responded that he would rather suffer forever than beg forgiveness of Zeus.

After he departed, Oceanos' daughters began to recite a lyrical passage, mourning Prometheus' predicament. As they sang, the Titan answered their lamentations, revealing a secret, an ancient prophecy, made known only to him, which stated that one day he would be freed from bondage and Zeus would be put under seige and defeated. Though he had no knowledge of how or when it would happen, this foreknowledge of Zeus' eventual downfall and Prometheus' satisfaction for having brought to man the arts of letters and numbers, and all manner of crafts, was what permitted him to endure his present punishment.

Io, the daughter of Inachus, a river god, was the next to pass. Zeus had once tried to seduce the lovely Io, but Hera, his jealous wife, had discovered her husband's intentions and turned poor Io into a cow, left to wander about the earth, constantly pursued and tormented by a pestilent gadfly. Io bewailed her unhappy fate. Prometheus only responded with fresh lamentations on his own misery. Finally, though, he offered Io some consolation: he revealed, again through prophetic knowledge, the time and day when she would be restored to her true form. Io pled for Prometheus to tell her more, but he would divulge only this: Zeus would one day give her back her beauty, and she would bear Zeus a son. After three generations had passed, one of this offspring's descendants (Hercules) would rise up and overpower Zeus, and finally free Prometheus from his mountain isolation.

No sooner did the Titan finish imparting this information, than the gadfly renewed his torment of poor Io, driving her off in a frenzy.

Now Prometheus had openly denounced Zeus and had predicted his downfall. This blasphemous invective did not go unheard by the chief god, who dispatched the messenger Hermes both to rebuke Prometheus and to inquire after the meaning of his prophecies.

This third visitor questioned Prometheus concerning the report that one of Zeus' own descendants would someday usurp him. Exactly who would bear the child? What would be the child's name? Prometheus, more bitter than ever, scornfully refused to answer any of these questions. Rather, in a brilliant and biting exchange, he belittled Hermes as nothing more than a puppet-slave to Zeus: "I'd rather suffer here in freedom than be a slave to Zeus as you are."

Hermes: Your words declare you mad.
Prometheus: Yes, if it's madness to detest my foes.
Hermes: No one could bear you in success.
Prometheus: Alas!
Hermes: Alas! Zeus does not know that word.
Prometheus: Time in its aging course teaches all things.
Hermes: But you have not yet learned a wise discretion.
Prometheus: True, or I would not speak so to a servant.

With this, Hermes made off in a huff, quicky retreating from the revenge he knew would arrive forthwith on the proud captive; and indeed Prometheus' fate was soon sealed. The enraged Zeus sent a thunderbolt hurtling down to shatter the cliff, and with blasts of wind, opened an abyss-dungeon deep within the trembling earth. Thus damned, the Titan fire-bearer was thrust down to this hellish punishment – until the time should come for his deliverance.

Commentary:

This simple yet compelling drama is almost devoid of action, but full of reflection and ideas. For this reason, it has enjoyed more success as a dramatic poem than as a play – a work to be read rather than staged.

It is quite natural for the reader to sympathize with Prometheus here, and to see Zeus as a pitiless, imperious young tyrant, more concerned with suppressing insubordination than with the general welfare of his subjects. We ought to remember, however, that *Prometheus Bound* is only the first in a trilogy. The Zeus depicted in the second play, *Prometheus Unbound*, is far less stern; he reconciles with Prometheus and frees him. (Incidentally, the third play, *Prometheus the Firebearer*, has been lost.)

The plots of these plays have frequently been used as figurative evidence by those who denounce governments and other institutions as oppressors of the individual. For instance, a scientist who uncovers a principle which appears to contradict established religious or scientific tenets can identify with Prometheus when his findings are ridiculed or suppressed.

Prometheus, a god made subject to suffering by the pettiness of gods, is symbolic of man's petty inhumanity to man. Even as the figure of Prometheus, with the daughters of Oceanos around him, sinks out of sight, the great Titan-god cries out:

Ocean and sky are one great chaos!
So mighty a gale comes only from Zeus:
He sends it to rouse wild fear in my heart . . . .
O glorious mother, O sky that sends
The racing sun to give all things light,
You see what injustice I suffer!

THE DIVINE COMEDY

by
Dante Alighieri
(1265 - 1321)

Type of work: Allegorical religious poem

Setting: Hell, Purgatory and Paradise; A.D. 1300

Principal characters:
Dante, the Pilgrim
Virgil, the Poet, and Dante's guide
Beatrice, Dante's womanly ideal and
religious inspiration

Story Overview:

Prologue:
Dante, realizing he has strayed from the "true way" into worldliness, tells of a vision where he travels through all the levels of Hell, up the mount of Purgatory, and finally through the realms of Paradise, where he is allowed a brief glimpse of God.

The traveler sets out on the night before Good Friday, and finds himself in the middle of a dark wood. There he encounters three beasts: a leopard (representing lust), a lion (pride) and a she-wolf (covetousness). Fortunately, his lady, Beatrice, along with the Virgin Mary herself, sends the spirit of Virgil, the classical Latin poet, to guide Dante through much of his journey. But as much as Dante admires and reveres Virgil, and though Dante considers him to have prophesied of the coming of Christ, Virgil is not a Christian. To Dante he represents human knowledge, or unholy reason, which cannot lead a person to God. This infidel may not pass into the highest realms. Thus, Dante is finally led to Heaven by Beatrice, his own personal and unattainable incarnation of the Virgin, who represents divine knowledge, or faith.

Pilgrimage:
Terrified, lost "midway in life's journey" in the worldly darkness of error, Dante met Virgil, who offered himself as a guide. Together they passed through the gates of Hell inscribed with the terrifying words: "Abandon every hope, Ye that Enter." Dante, however, as a living soul who had not yet tasted death, was exempt from such final despair. He found Hell to be a huge funnel-shaped pit divided into terraces, each a standing-place for those individuals who were guilty of a particular sin. After passing Limbo, reserved for the unbaptized, Dante observed and conversed with hundreds of Hell's souls, many of whom, guilty of carnal sins, were being whirled about in the air or forced to lie deep in mud or snow, under the decrees of eternal damnation. Ciacco, a fellow Florentine, implored of Dante, " . . . When thou shalt be in the sweet world, I pray thee bring me to men's memory."

In pity, Dante frequently offered to write about those he met when he returned to mortality. These gluttons, seducers, and robbers were, for the most part, either historical figures or Dante's personal acquaintances – and each one of them represented one of the apt and horrible possibilities of Hell. For example, Alexander the Great and Attila the Hun were found dwelling in Hell's seventh terrace, forced to grovel in boiling blood – a just end for those who in life loved violence.

In the very depths of Hell was Satan – with three heads, each grasping a sinner in its mouth, and with three pairs of wings that continuously beat over the waters around him, freezing them into perpetual currents of ice.

Dante and Virgil cautiously climbed down the body of Satan. About midway, they turned and scrambled out through an opening (earth's center of gravity) where all things were the opposite of Hell: The sun was shining; it was Easter morning. Now hiking on in silence, they finally arrived on the shores of the Mount of Purgatory, located exactly opposite Jerusalem on the globe.

First and lowest on the mountain was Ante-purgatory, a place reserved for those spirits who were penitent in life, who had died without achieving full repentance or without receiving the last sacrament of the church. They were required to spend time there before they could begin their arduous climb up the mountain. A group of those poor souls who had passed away suddenly, unable to receive extreme unction, pled with the mortal visitor to speak with their relatives and friends, urging them to pray that their stay in Ante-purgatory might be shortened.

As the pilgrims entered Purgatory, an angel inscribed the letter "P" on Dante's forehead seven times, to represent the seven deadly sins (pride, envy, anger, sloth, avarice, gluttony, and lust). As Dante made his way through the seven areas reserved for those who committed each of these sins, the letters were erased one by one, and the climb became less difficult.

Like Hell, Purgatory was arranged in terraces. However, the inhabitants here could, through confession, repentance, patience, and the prayers of the living, move on to higher realms after a time of proper purification. In the first terrace (pride), the occupants bowed down under huge stones which they carried on their backs, while reciting *The Lord's Prayer*, a fitting penance for haughty souls. Each terrace in turn was designed to purge its dead souls of one particular deadly sin.

The travelers finally moved beyond the seventh terrace. An angel directed them to pass through a huge wall of flames; on the other side they would find Beatrice. Dante did not hesitate. Emerging from the flames, he saw a mountain. At its summit, Virgil bade Dante farewell, for this was as far as Human Reason would allow a non-

Christian to go.

Dante noticed a beautiful garden nearby, and began to explore it. A young woman appeared to inform him that this was the Garden of Eden – and there, across a river, awaited Beatrice. But the woman called out to Dante, demanding that, before entering the stream, he stop to acknowledge remorse for his sins and confess them. Hearing her, Dante was so overcome with remorse that he fainted and had to be carried across Lethe, the river of forgetfulness of past sins.

On the other side of the river, accompanied now at last by the beautiful Beatrice, Dante discovered that Paradise was divided into various spheres orbiting the earth. Each of the first seven (the Moon, Mercury, Venus, the Sun, Mars, Jupiter, and Saturn) represented a particular virtue, and those who in life had exhibited this virtue became its inhabitants. Ascending through the spheres, Dante encountered various famous saints, martyrs, and crusaders, in addition to many of the just, the chaste and the meditative. One soul he greeted was Cacciaguida, his own great great grandfather, who had served as a crusader in the previous century. This ancestor addressed him: "O my own blood! O grace of God poured forth above measure! . . . " and then went on to reminisce on the earlier glory and splendor of Florence, and to lament its present fallen state.

Dante next followed Beatrice past the Fixed Stars, where many of the Apostles dwelt. These men, in turn, questioned the poet, examining his opinions. Dante offered complicated treatises on the duality of Christ (that he is both human and divine) and earthly versus godly love, and explained then-modern scientific theories to account, among other things, for moonspots.

At last Dante was conducted to the ninth heaven (outerspace), where he received grace, and was permitted to gaze upon divinity and hear the angels' chorus. Beatrice then departed the reverent admirer, who witnessed the entrance of the triumphal Christ, followed by Mary.

Then, in union with the divine, Dante was left alone to behold the glory of God on his throne. "O how scant is speech and how feeble to my conception," he gasped in a final, striking, poetic description of breathless awe.

Commentary:

"The Divine Comedy" is an epic poem brimming with information and eloquent literary devices. (The word "comedy" is used here in its classical sense – to denote a story which begins in suspense and ends well.) The lengthy work combines Dante's vast knowledge of classical Latin writers (Virgil, Ovid, Cicero, Seneca . . .) and Greek philosophers (Plato and Aristotle) with his readings from the religious and theological classics of Catholicism (Augustine, Thomas Acquinas . . .).

Some awareness of medieval symbolism and imagery can greatly enrich the modern reader's understanding and enjoyment of Dante's personal, visionary odyssey through the realms of the dead. For example, the significance of certain numbers figures importantly in both the structure of the work and the geography of the netherworld. The number three symbolizes the trinity; the "perfect" number, ten, was obtained by multiplying three times three, and adding one (which represented the unity of God). Furthermore, Dante's work is divided into three canticles (the Inferno, Purgatory and Paradise) and each canticle is then divided into thirty-three cantos. These, added to the book's general introductory canto, make for a grand total of one hundred, or, the square of ten. The poem's rhyme scheme, which Dante invented, is known as "terza rima" (third rhyme), where rhymed lines are grouped in interlocking sets of three (aba, bcb, cdc, etc.)

In addition to this obsession with numbers, the reader should also fathom the notion of ancient courtly love. Most poetry of Dante's age was written in praise of a woman whom the poet had chosen as an ideal, but with whom he was not intimate nor even necessarily personally acquainted; a pure love, an unattainable inspiration. Dante had met Beatrice Portinari at least twice, but had no intention of developing a relationship with her. She was married, as was he. "If it pleases God," Dante had written in the third person, "he will write of Beatrice, that which has never yet been said of mortal woman." This, in fact, Dante does in *The Divine Comedy*, placing his lady in the highest realms of Paradise.

Almost as much as he loved Beatrice, Dante loved Italy; and one of his greatest beliefs was the equal importance of the Church and the State. He became disgusted with the corruption of the Church by politics during his lifetime. In fact, it was while he was in political exile from Florence that he wrote this masterpiece, its complete title being "The Comedy of Dante Alighieri, Florentine by Citizenship, Not by Morals."

Dante also believed in matching writing style with the material being treated. Thus, in *Hell*, the language is laced with common, sometimes revolting phrasing. Then, in *Paradise* the speech turns much more ethereal and lofty. (Curiously, *Hell* was – and remains – the most popular of the three books.)

By using common expressions and the language of his native Tuscan dialect rather than the traditional Church Latin, Dante created a revolutionary work. His comedy, rich as it was in multilayered medieval allegory, set fire to the then radically modern idea that literature – works meant primarily to be read rather than retold or enacted – could be made both accessible and popular. So highly regarded was this comedy that it earned the eventual title of "Divine."

EL CID

author unknown
(written c. 12th century)

Type of work: Heroic epic poem

Setting: Spain; late eleventh century

Principal characters:

El Cid (Ruy Diaz), a spirited knight

King Alfonso, King of Leon and Castile
(Christian Spain)

Minaya Fanez, The Cid's chief lieutenant
and companion

Dona Ximena, The Cid's faithful wife

Dona Elvira and Dona Sol, The Cid's two
daughters

Diego and Fernando Gonzalez, villainous
princes of Carrion

Martin Antolinex, a nobleman of Burgos,
and ally of The Cid

Poem Overview:

Alfonso, the Christian King of Leon and Castile, sent his knight, El Cid, to collect the annual tribute owed to him by the Moorish King of Seville. In Seville, El Cid learned that soldiers governed by the King of Granada, along with certain Christian Leonese allies, were at that moment warring against the local King. Being a trustworthy and obedient knight, and inasmuch as Seville was a protectorate of King Alfonso, he led an expedition to meet this army. After emerging victorious, El Cid seized a traitorous Leonese count, Ordonez, and subjected him to the ultimate insult – he plucked the count's beard. But when this vengeful count returned home to Leon, he convinced King Alfonso that El Cid had become dangerously powerful and must be banished from the kingdom.

During the days before Cid was to be expelled, he gathered together a small band of troops loyal to him and traveled to Burgos. When the townfolk there, out of fear of punishment, refused to provide his rebels with any goods, his men pitched their camp outside of town and began devising plots to obtain the needed supplies. Finally they settled on the idea of sending an envoy, Martin Antolinez, to strike a deal with two pawnbrokers in the city. Antolinez would exchange two coffers – supposedly filled with gold and jewels but actually filled with sand – for the sum of six hundred marks, on the condition that the coffers would not be opened until El Cid had returned to buy them back. By this ploy, the group procured enough money to journey into the hostile lands of the Moors.

Before finally departing from his beloved Christian kingdom, Cid paid a visit to the abbey where his wife and daughters had sought sanctuary. He bade farewell to his wife, Dona Ximena: *I love you as I love my soul!*

We must part in life; I go and you remain. May it please God and St. Mary that I may yet give these daughters in marriage and that I have the good fortune to live yet a little while in which to serve you, my wife.

El Cid then paid the abbot for his family's keep and marched out of the city with his troops.

Along the way, the numbers in El Cid's band increased. He promised all who joined him that they would be rewarded twofold for their sacrifice. On their last night in Christendom, El Cid was visited in a dream by the Angel Gabriel. "Ride, O Cid," the angel exhorted, "for never did a knight ride so luckily! Things will go well with you so long as you shall live." The knight-captain took this message as an omen of good fortune, and entered the wilderness unafraid.

El Cid's knights met with early success. They easily conquered the city of Castejon, then marched deeper into the Moorish province, sacking villages and exacting tribute along the way. El Cid soon laid siege to the great metropolis of Alcocer. The city's citizens chose to pay tribute so they would not have to fight; but after accepting the tribute, Cid, stung by greed, moved in and took the city as well.

It was quickly noised throughout the land that My Cid has left Christendom and is now settled among the Moors, who hardly dare to work their fields.

One day word of El Cid's exploits reached the ear of King Mutamin of Moorish Valencia. Angered by the Christian's boldness, he dispatched a sizable army to retake Alcocer. These forces surrounded the city, cutting off the water supply, in hopes of driving El Cid out. Sure enough, sallying forth to do battle with Mutamin's waves of soldiers soon became the only choice. But, incited by their captain's courageous deeds and words, El Cid's men managed to drive the Moors away. Afterward, El Cid decided that some of the booty taken from the rout should go to King Alfonso as a peace offering. A nobleman, Minaya Fanez, was selected to deliver this gift – "thirty horses, all saddled and bridled, with swords hanging from their saddlebows."

King Alfonso was most pleased with Cid's generosity, and he opened the way for many of his men to go and serve in the rebel knight's army.

Bolstered by new recruits, El Cid next turned his attention to Valencia. Looting towns and defeating all forces gathered against them as they marched, El Cid's marauding troops at last surrounded the great city. The populace was given nine months to either hire mercenaries to fight for them or else surrender. " . . . At the tenth [month] they yielded," and El Cid settled down to enjoy his spoils. Again he presented King Alfonso with one hundred of the finest Moorish horses. But this time he also instructed Minaya to make a special plea to the king: " . . . kiss his hands for me, and beg him, if he will, to let me have my wife Dona Ximena and my dear daughters." The king not only gladly complied with this request, but also restored the property confiscated from El Cid when he was exiled.

When Cid beheld his wife and children approaching, he mounted his horse and rode out to embrace them, "weeping in his joy."

El Cid's power and influence continued to spread. Soon, many Moorish rulers felt "vexed" by him. One in particular, the King of Morocco, "gathered up all his forces, fifty thousand men," and set forth for Valencia to drive the Christian dog out. El Cid welcomed the attack: "My wife and daughters shall see me fight, and learn how we make our living in this foreign land." So, again shedding much blood, he and his troops met and defeated the Moroccans, who outnumbered them by more than twelvefold, and gathered together their riches, which were "beyond measure."

When this latest news reached Alfonso's court, two brother-princes of Carrion, Diego and Fernando Gonzalez, reasoned together: "My Cid's affairs go well! Let us beg of him his two daughters in marriage, and thus gain in honor and riches." The princes beseeched King Alfonso to act as their intermediary. He agreed and asked the visiting Minaya to convey the marriage proposals to El Cid back in Valencia.

El Cid hesitated to give his daughters in marriage, but because the request was from King Alfonso, he complied. A meeting to finalize the details for the weddings was arranged. When, after so many years, Cid finally once again saw Alfonso, he fell at his feet. Commanded to arise, he next received the Princes of Carrion. Then, after much gift-giving and celebrating, he and his future sons-in-law departed for Valencia.

"Rich was the wedding in the great palace." The feast alone lasted for two weeks; again, many gifts were exchanged. However, although the dual marriage was a joyous occasion, spousal relationships soon turned sour. Both Diego and Fernando proved to be immature and cowardly. A lion, escaped from its cage, caused one of the princes to hide beneath a bench while the other took cover behind the wine press, and he, in his terror, "quite defiled his tunic." But El Cid's flagging respect for his sons-in-law was revived when one day a Moroccan army was seen in the distance and the princes went forth to battle, later reporting their great valor in the skirmish. In reality,

they had hidden far from the action. After several weeks, the princes proposed to take their wives on a visit to Carrion. But, secretly, they intended to avenge themselves on the young women for their mocking after the episode with the lion. El Cid, sensing trouble, sent along his nephew, Munoz; but once outside of Moorish territory, the princes ordered Munoz back to Valencia. Then the wicked brothers whipped their wives "till they fall senseless, their garments soaked in blood. . . . They leave them there for dead." The faithful Munoz, however, returning to track the band through the wilderness, found the women's nearly lifeless bodies.

Diego and Fernando continued on their way, thinking their act still a secret. But "in all the land their deed was known, and good King Alfonso grieved in his heart." Likewise, El Cid was both saddened and angered. To preserve his own honor and that of his daughters, he ordered one of his knights to go to King Alfonso's court in demand of justice. The king complied and set up a trial date for the two brothers.

During this trial, the father demanded that the princes return his daughters' generous dowries. He also challenged them to combat, but they balked at this, claiming that "when we abandoned your daughters we did only what was our right, and did ourselves no dishonor thereby, but honor." The argument closed, King Alfonso made a ruling: El Cid was to select three of his knights to meet the Princes of Carrion in a duel to the death. Of course, the outcome of this jousting match was a grim one for the princes.

Vengeance satisfied, honor restored, El Cid gave his daughters in marriage to the Prince of Navarre and the Prince of Aragon; "the Kings of Spain were now among his kinsmen."

Commentary:

Perhaps the most famous poem to come out of southern Medevial Europe, *El Cid* contains descriptions of panoramic settings and colorful characters, which have since been adopted in the works of other writers.

The poem's rich storyline is largely based on fact. The knight El Cid in truth did live and accomplish many of the feats attributed to him. On the other hand, the poet telling the tale exaggerates a great deal. For instance, four thousand soldiers – even "Christian" soldiers – conquering fifty thousand Moors at Valencia is quite unbelievable. Nevertheless, the work is highly accurate in its depiction of the difficulties of ordinary life in a region of Spain split between the domination of two rival cultures. Moreover, "El Cid" portrays the struggles, challenges and potential for upward mobility that in reality did exist on the eleventh-century Spanish frontier.

A TALE OF TWO CITIES

by
Charles Dickens
(1812 - 1870)

Type of work: Historical fiction

Setting: London and Paris during the French Revolution (1789-1799)

Principal characters:
Dr. Manette, a French physician, wrongfully imprisoned for 18 years
Lucie Manette, his daughter
Charles Darnay, a former French aristocrat who has repudiated his title and left France to live in England
Jarvis Lorry, the able representative of Tellson & Co., a banking house
Sydney Carton, a law clerk
Madame Defarge, a French peasant and long-time revolutionary

Story Overview:

(In the year 1775, King George III sat on the throne of England, preoccupied with his rebellious colonies in America. Across a narrow neck of water to the east, Louis XVI reigned in France, not very much bothered by anything except seeing to his own comforts.)

On a cold and foggy night in late November, Mr. Jarvis Lorry was headed out of London bound for Paris, via Dover, on a matter of business. In the darkness of the coach, as he and the other passengers waked and drowsed by turns, Lorry was confronted by a gaunt and ghostly apparition, who engaged him in a silent and macabre conversation.

The figure haunting him through the night was Dr. Manette, a French physician and the father of Mr. Lorry's young ward. When the doctor had disappeared from his home eighteen years before, his young English wife had diligently and sorrowfully searched for him, until she died two years later, leaving her small daughter Lucie, who was placed in the care of Mr. Lorry. Lorry had brought the child to England, where she was turned over to Lorry's servant, Miss Pross, a wild-looking, wonderful woman who adored her.

At Dover, Lorry was joined by Lucie – now a young woman – and Miss Pross. Lorry informed Lucie that her father had been found alive after years as a political prisoner, and that he, Mr. Lorry, was making this trip to Paris in order to identify him. Lucie, it was hoped, could then help "restore him to life." The sudden reality of finally meeting her father was so great that Lucie could only mutter in an awestricken, doubting voice, "I am going to see his Ghost! It will be his Ghost – not him!"

In Paris, Mr. Lorry proceeded directly to the wine-shop of Monsieur Defarge, a former attendant to Dr. Manette, who was now looking after him. The company ascended to the attic. Lucie had been prophetic; indeed, Manette seemed but the ghost of a man, bending over his little shoe-maker's bench, unaware of anything around him. Still, together with the free and bewildered Manette, the little group journeyed back to England. Lucie already showed a love and understanding for her long-isolated father, and her companions felt sure she would accomplish the miracle of calling him back to his former self.

Five years later, Lucie and her father were called as witnesses in an English court, where a Frenchman, Charles Darnay, was on trial for treason. In the courtroom sat another young man, a lawyer's clerk named Sydney Carton. Carton was immediately struck by the resemblance he and Darnay bore to one another, and when a key witness identified the prisoner as the man he had seen gathering information at a dockyard, Carton managed to discredit the witness by calling attention to the fact that in that very courtroom sat another – himself – who could easily be mistaken for the prisoner. The jury was swayed, and Darnay was acquitted.

During the trial, both Carton and Darnay became acquainted with the Manettes. From that time on, they often visited the Manette's comfortable little house on Soho Square. Both men enjoyed the company of the good doctor, whose health of mind and body had been restored through Lucie's patient ministrations – and they also came to see Lucie. As suitors, their physical resemblance was never remarked upon because they were so different in attitude and demeanor. While Darnay, who had turned his back on his ancestral name and title, showed his refined upbringing in his confidence and courtliness, Carton seemed to be his own worst enemy. He was only confident of continued failure, and assured himself of it through drink, slovenliness and a morose character. Though Lucie welcomed them both, she was most drawn to Darnay. Being of a sympathetic and loving nature, she listened and wept one day as Carton, in uncharacteristic openness, confessed his love for her. He asked from her nothing in return because he believed even her love would not be enough to redeem him. The conversation ended with Carton's strange statement and promise:

It is useless to say it, I know, but . . . for you, and for any dear to you, I would do anything; think, now and then, that there is a man who would give his life, to keep a life you love beside you!

Lucie and Charles Darnay were eventually married and began their family. They were happy; but always in the background of their lives lurked a cloud, which seemed to draw menacingly closer year by year.

Finally, in 1789, the French Revolution exploded into being. Centuries of aristocrat indifference to the plight of the starving peasants, and the years of cruelty and selfishness, had at last brought on a bitter rebellion that turned Paris into a cauldron of chaos. Madame Defarge, the wife of Dr. Manette's former servant, became a leader in the Revolution. Through the long years from girlhood on, Madame Defarge had always kept her knitting in hand, recording with each stitch a death-list of the names of all those whose injustices she witnessed. Now her denunciations came forth as if they had been coiled inside the knitting; out came the hatred, vengeance and lust for blood that only a woman who had seen all her family killed by the aristocracy could feel. When Madame Defarge and her husband and cohorts, armed with knives and axes, stormed the Bastille, they opened a floodgate of mob violence that would inundate the country.

Three years of tumult elapsed. At last, both Mr. Lorry and Charles Darnay felt they must go to Paris. Lorry, true and loyal businessman that he was, looked after the affairs of the Paris branch of Tellson & Co., while Darnay visited a family retainer who had written, begging for his help and presence. But upon his arrival, Darnay was immediately taken into custody and imprisoned, along with many aristocrats and political victims.

When Lucie and her father discovered what had happened, Dr. Manette was convinced that, as a former prisoner of the Bastille, he alone could rescue his son-in-law. He hurried to Paris with his daughter and grandchild. There he was quickly accepted by the revolutionaries and allowed access to civil authorities who could perhaps help. But Charles, now identified under his true name as heir to the notorious house of Evremond, had become a certain target of Madame Defarge. She would not allow his release.

When, after fifteen months in prison, Charles was acquitted of his alleged crimes through the quiet, confident and moving defense of Dr. Manette, the family's rejoicing was short-lived. Four men came to arrest the young husband again that very afternoon, declaring that he had been denounced by three other accusers – the Defarges and one other. It was only at the second trial that the identity of the third accuser was discovered – Dr. Manette himself!

Now at last came the complete story of Manette's imprisonment. It was presented in the form of a letter written by the doctor after he had spent ten years in prison and was fearing for his sanity. He had hidden the letter behind a stone wall in his cell, where Defarge had encountered it the day the Bastille was stormed. The letter gave the names of those responsible for Manette's abduction and imprisonment – two brothers of the House of Evremond, Charles' father and his uncle – and ended with a condemnation of that house and its descendants. Thus, Dr. Manette, in a tragic and ironic turn of events, was named as his son-in-law's third accuser. And Charles, for his ancestor's crimes, was pronounced guilty and sentenced to death by guillotine.

Sydney Carton, who had by now come to Paris, appeared singly calm and purposeful in the face of such terrible news. With a disciplined courage quite foreign to himself, he gained entrance to Charles' cell as his final visitor. There he drugged Darnay, rendering him unconscious, exchanged clothes with him, and had him carried from the cell as "Sydney Carton," a friend of the prisoner totally overcome with grief. Carton remained in Darnay's stead.

Hours later, as the coach bearing the Manettes, Mr. Lorry and a still unconscious Darnay thundered toward the Channel and refuge in England, Sydney Carton was making his own escape – from his self-imposed prison of constant failure. Riding along at an unhurried pace in the third tumbrel of six bound that day for La Guillotine, Carton's face and demeanor were those of a man who had found his way. And he was unafraid of his destination. "It is a far, far better thing that I do, than I have ever done; it is a far better rest that I go to, than I have ever known," he whispered to himself. He was now about to offer up his life for his friends.

Commentary:

Dickens conceived the idea for this complicated plot while acting in a play. Every event penned in *A Tale of Two Cities* draws toward one great climax, set against the backdrop of the greater drama: history. Master of detailed settings and characterizations, Dickens gave himself the challenge of stripping details down to the bone and letting the many intertwining characters be swept along with the action and violence of the times.

Fortunately for the reader, the novelist couldn't resist the temptation of fleshing out his minor characters, who provide some relief in an otherwise grim account of the French Revolution. Dickens takes the least time with Lucie and Darnay, supposing, perhaps, that we would see them clearly enough; Sydney Carton's inner reform is more fully drawn; and Dr. Manette's brief lapses back into insanity are an early study of the psychological effects of extended inhumane treatment. Jarvis Lorry shows the most character development, evolving from a man of strict business and propriety to one of feeling and warmth. The vindictive Madame Defarge, at first glance, seems to be the main villain in the piece; but, on reflection, La Guillotine, a symbol of revenge run amok, seems to vie for the honor.

A Tale of Two Cities is a sad account of man's inhumanity to man, for even though Darnay escapes, the reader is left haunted by the many innocent who did not.

THE LADY OF THE LAKE

by
Sir Walter Scott
(1771 - 1832)

Type of work: Romantic metrical poem

Setting: Sixteenth-century Scotland

Principal characters:

James Douglas, outlawed uncle of the Earl of Angus

Ellen Douglas, his daughter (The Lady of the Lake)

Roderick Dhu, a rebel Highland chief of Clan Alpine, and protector of the Douglases

Allan-bane, the Douglas' minstrel and devoted servant

James Fitz-James, a Saxon Lowlander Knight

Malcolm Graeme, Ellen's young love

Commentary:

This absorbing tale, opening with an account of a stag hunt in the Highlands, is typical of Scott. He invented the historical fiction novel. But historicity for its own sake isn't as important to him as creating an accurate, vivid milieu from which the reader can emerge feeling he has lived the adventure himself.

Scott was fascinated with cultures in collision, and he always placed his heroes in the middle of the fray. In this poem, the opposing forces are two Scottish clans – the wild Celtic Highlanders, loyal only to their chieftain, and the peaceful, agrarian Saxon Lowlanders, devoted to following their King. Scott guides us through a maze of emotions, creating sympathy and understanding for both sides.

Story Overview:

James Fitz-James, a Saxon knight from Stirling Castle, became lost as he hunted in the Highlands. Sounding his horn, he was rescued – not by his comrades, but by Ellen Douglas, who, with her father, lived at Loch Katerine under the protection of her Highlander cousin, Roderick Dhu. Although the men were away, Fitz-James was taken in and extended Highland hospitality. It disturbed Fitz-James that this girl bore such a resemblance to members of the hunted Douglas clan. Nevertheless, he was smitten by Ellen's beauty and kindness and dreamed of her as he slept.

On the next morning Fitz-James left the island with a guide. Later, Roderick and Douglas returned home from their separate journeys, Douglas accompanied by young Malcolm Graeme. Roderick, a fierce, plundering, middle-aged warrior, hoped to marry Ellen, both because he loved her and because their marriage would unite Clan Douglas with Clan Alpine to create a powerful political force. Although Ellen appreciated Roderick's protection, she was frightened by his manner and had set her heart on Malcolm Graeme, her first suitor, whom Roderick despised.

When Roderick extended his marriage proposal to her in the company of all, Malcolm detected Ellen's deep disquiet; but before he could speak, her father interceded, explaining tactfully that such a union would be a political misalliance; Roderick was a sworn enemy of the King, while he, Douglas, in spite of his outlawed status, still loved his monarch.

The great chieftain hated the King and could not understand Douglas' loyalty. Now his disappointment at losing Ellen rose to intensify Roderick's anger. He sent out a terrible signal – a fiery cross summoning his Clan Alpine to war. As the cross was carried over the rocky highlands, all the clansmen rallied to support their chieftain. Roderick now petitioned Brian the Hermit to use his magic to give him an augury for the forthcoming battle. The oracle read: "Which spills the foremost foeman's life that party conquers in the strife." Roderick was reassured, for Clan Alpine had never fought but they were the first to kill a foe.

Meanwhile, before setting out for Stirling Castle to give himself up in hopes of averting war, Douglas had conducted his daughter, with the minstrel Allan-bane as her escort, to the safety of a wilderness cave. Ellen knew her father's intentions: "He goes to do what I had done,/ had Douglas' daughter been his son!" There the refugees were found by James Fitz-James, returning to see if he could persuade Ellen to accompany him to Stirling Castle. Ellen was dismayed. Hadn't Fitz-James seen the preparations for war, the hills alive with Roderick's men? No, the Saxon replied. The countryside had appeared quite serene. But this was the surest sign of danger, said Ellen; the wily Roderick's troops must already have him surrounded. She promised to help him escape, though she confessed that her heart belonged to Malcolm Graeme. The knight remained determined to help her save her father, however. He presented her with a ring from the Saxon royalty, saying that it would help her in her journey through Lowland territory and gain her an audience with King James.

Fitz-James departed, still following his guide, Red Murdoch. Soon they came upon Blanche, a poor, crazed woman living in the wilds. Long ago, on her wedding day, Clan Alpine had captured her and killed her bridegroom. From his green hunting attire, Blanche recognized Fitz-James as a fellow Lowlander. In a cryptic song she warned him to beware of Murdoch. The knight, acknowledging this warning, drew his sword just as the guide discharged an arrow in his bow. But the shaft missed its true target and felled the poor old woman. After chasing down and slaying the treacherous Murdoch, Fitz-James returned to dying Blanche, who gave him a broach made of a lock of her dead sweetheart's hair, with the charge to seek out Clan Alpine's Roderick Dhu and avenge her pitiful life.

The Saxon set out, stealthily picking his way through the undergrowth. Many hours later he stumbled upon a lone knight from Clan Alpine, bound by the same code of honor as he. The enemies shared food and a campfire, and the Highland knight promised to guide Fitz-James toward his own territory. As they traveled, the Highlander defended Roderick's belligerence, explaining that the Lowlands had been wrested long ago from the Scottish clan forefathers, forcing them into the inhospitable mountains. "Seek other cause 'gainst Roderick Dhu," he finished. Then, he whistled, and the woods sprang to life with warriors. The Highlander "Then fixed his eye and sable brow,/ full on Fitz-James – 'How say'st thou now?/ These are Clan Alpine's warriors true;/ and Saxon – I am Roderick Dhu!" Then Roderick waved his hand and all his men again vanished into the forest.

After leading his Saxon enemy into the Lowlands as promised, the Chieftain turned and challenged him to battle: "Now man to man and steel to steel,/ a Chieftain's vengeance thou shalt feel . . . " The Saxon, who wished no harm to his honorable foe, objected to the contest; still the Highlander cried that their battle must be fought, for the divination had stated, "Who spills the foremost foeman's life his party conquers in the strife." "Then by my word," the Saxon exclaimed, "The riddle is already read./ Seek yonder brake beneath the cliff,/ there lies Red Murdoch, stark and stiff."

But Roderick refused to admit that the guide's death had fulfilled the prophecy. He called Fitz-James a coward and taunted him for wearing a fair lady's hair braid. Thus reminded of the promise he had made to Blanche, the knight drew his sword. Roderick was large and powerful, but no match for Fitz-James' skill in swordsmanship, and eventually the chieftain fell unconscious from loss of blood. Fitz-James, now in his home territory, blew his bugle and crouched down to wash his own wounds. When his companions arrived, he bade them carry Roderick off to prison. Then he mounted a horse and headed for Stirling Castle.

In the meantime, Douglas, intending to offer his life to avert war – and to ransom the newly captured Malcolm Graeme and Roderick Dhu – entered the Castle grounds, to find himself in the midst of a royal holiday celebration, attended by King James himself. Unrecognized, Douglas decided to take part in the competitions. An agile giant of a fighter, he came out victorious in every event. Word soon spread through the crowd that this fierce competitor could only be "Douglas of the stalwart hand." Finally Douglas acknowledged his true identity to the circle of onlookers and turned himself over to the King, who immediately dispatched a messenger to halt the impending bat-

tle; with Roderick, Malcolm and now Douglas as prisoners, there was no need for the Saxons to go to war against Clan Alpine.

But the King's message went out too late. As the next morning dawned over Stirling Castle, hardened soldiers soberly spoke of yesterday's bloody battle.

Meanwhile, Ellen and Allan-bane arrived, seeking an audience with the King. When Ellen displayed the ring Fitz-James had given her, the two were treated with great respect. Ellen was taken to a room where she could rest until King James awakened, while Allan-bane was led to see the prisoner who he thought was his beloved master. However, the captive who turned to face Allan was not Douglas, but the wounded Roderick Dhu. Dhu asked the old minstrel to sing him the entire story of the preceding day's battle. As the song's tale progressed, Roderick grew weaker. When Allan sang of the messenger who had brought the flag of truce from the King, the smiling Chieftain, cheered by the melodious vision of his victorious clansmen, died.

Shortly thereafter, Fitz-James came to Ellen's room to take her to the King. She greeted him as a dear brother, and together they walked into the huge, crowded hall. Ellen nervously scanned the room for the monarch whose mercy she sought. However, all eyes rested on Fitz-James. Only when the multitude bowed down before him did Ellen understand: her Saxon Knight was in fact Scotland's King! She also fell at his feet, speechless. Fitz-James gently raised her to her feet and assured her that in fact his flag of truce had halted the battle. What's more, he and Ellen's father had reconciled their differences.

Ellen could hardly fathom such wonderful news – and wept joyfully at the loving embrace of her father. The monarch, enjoying her surprise, then referred to the ring on Ellen's clasped hand, and asked: "What seeks fair Ellen of the King?" Realizing that Malcolm Graeme now stood in little danger, Ellen asked for clemency towards Clan Alpine's, Roderick Dhu. But King James replied sadly, "Forbear thy suit – the King of Kings/ alone can stay life's parting wings . . . . my fairest earldom would I give/ to bid Clan Alpine's Chieftain live!"

"Hast thou no other boon to crave?" the King then asked; "No other captive friend to save?" Unable to resist teasing the blushing girl, he sternly pronounced: "Nay, then, my pledge has lost its force,/ and stubborn justice holds her course/ Malcolm come forth!"

As the young man knelt before his King, he was solemnly told that fetters and a jailer were what he deserved! Ellen was taken aback – but then the King's smile returned, as he removed the gold chain from his own neck, slipped it over the head of Malcolm, and layed its clasp in Ellen's hand.

HENRY VIII

by
William Shakespeare
(1564-1616)

Type of work: Historical, fictional play

Setting: London, England; 16th century

Principal characters:

Henry VIII, Tudor King of England

Katherine of Aragon, Queen of England

Anne Bullen, Henry's lover and subsequent queen

Wolsey, ambitious Cardinal of York

Duke Buckingham, Wolsey's adversary

Duke of Norfolk and Duke of Suffolk, also Wolsey's enemies

Cranmer, Archbishop of Canterbury

Story Overview:

Two noblemen, the Dukes Norfolk and Buckingham, met in the palace to converse. Norfolk was angered by the audacity of Henry VIII, who had signed a peace treaty with Francis I of France – a treaty financed by Cardinal Wolsey of York. Norfolk warned his friend of Wolsey's equal hatred for Buckingham: "Like it your grace, the state takes notice of the private difference betwixt you and the cardinal. I advise you . . . that you read the cardinal's malice and his potency together: to consider further, that, what his high hatred would effect wants not a minister in his power."

Just then Wolsey entered the palace and, after exchanging disdainful glances with Buckingham, headed towards the king's chamber. "I read in's looks matter against me," Buckingham whispered. "And his eye reviled me as his abject object . . . . He's gone to th' king!" Taking note of Buckingham's alarm and anger, Norfolk advised him to act prudently. Still, shortly thereafter, Buckingham was arrested for treason.

Meanwhile, in the throne room, Queen Katherine chided her husband about the heavy tax burden that Wolsey had ostensibly levied on the people. "Your subjects are in great grievance," she said, " and almost appear in loud rebellion." Unknown to King Henry, Norfolk had in actuality instituted a tax, in an effort to stir up Henry's subjects against the cardinal. The king demanded to know what she meant: "Taxation? Wherein? and what taxation? My lord Cardinal . . . know you of this taxation?" When Wolsey denied any knowledge of the affair, Henry immediately had the collections stopped.

Katherine later inquired about the Duke of Buckingham. Why had he been arrested? Henry and Wolsey brought forth their witness to Buckingham's treason. This man claimed to have heard Buckingham say, in effect, that if the king should die without male posterity then he would make the throne his own. Wolsey also stepped forward and further testified that Buckingham had suggested he would go so far as to kill the king in order to gain the scepter. Henry was convinced: "By day and night, he's traitor to the height."

That week, at a party given by Cardinal Wolsey, Henry met Anne Bullen. He was taken by her beauty and impulsively kissed her. And, on the following day, Henry sent Lord Chamberlain to bestow upon Anne the title of "Marchioness of Pembroke; to which . . . a thousand pounds a year, annual support, out of his grace he adds." Hours later, Buckingham was declared guilty of treason and condemned to die.

Now Henry, in the same way that he was accustomed to executing slanderous dukes, was prone also to divorcing his wives. With King Henry's infatuation with Anne, prompt separation from Queen Katherine was inevitable. A court of divorce was convened, in which Katherine, kneeling at Henry's feet, pled her case: "Alas, sir, in what have I offended you? . . . I have been to you a true and humble wife, at all times to your will conformable . . . When was the hour, I ever contradicted your desire, or made it not mine too?" Then Katherine directed her ire toward Wolsey: "I do believe . . . that you are mine enemy; and make my challenge, you shall not be my judge." But Wolsey refused to step down from the judge's seat, and Katherine, realizing that she had already lost her cause to Henry's whims, retired. "The queen of earthly queens," Henry lamented at her departure. Nevertheless, addressing the court, he stated his reasons for petitioning for divorce: Katherine had not produced a male heir, and "I weighed the danger which my realms stood in by this my issue's fail . . . " But one of his councillors cautioned him that Katherine had likely gone to appeal her case to the pope. To this potential challenge, the king replied, "I abhor this dilatory sloth and tricks of Rome."

Soon, Katherine was visited by Wolsey and another cardinal in an attitude of friendship and reconciliation, but she was not duped. " . . . Ye wish for my ruin," she charged, vowing to fight them and to restore herself to her former place of dignity, or die.

Back at the king's court, Norfolk, Suffolk, Surrey and Chamberlain all warily watched the cardinal's rapid rise to power. Chamberlain warned the others of Wolsey's influence over Henry: "I much fear. If you cannot bar his access to th' King, never attempt anything on him, for he hath a witchcraft over th' king's tongue." Suffolk, though, was unafraid. He knew that the letters the cardinal had sent to the pope had "miscarried and came to th' eye o' the king." These letters, intercepted by Henry, disclosed Wolsey's disloyalty. They urged the pope to stay the divorce because the King was "tangled in affection to . . . Lady Anne Bullen." King Henry hid his ire at this, Wolsey's devious act, and immediately married Anne, in defiance of the church.

Days later, at the castle, Henry sought out Wolsey. "What piles of wealth hath he accumulated to his own portion . . . " he stormed. "It may well be, there is a mutiny in's mind." Finally finding the cardinal, the king laid out the self-written evidence convicting him of disloyalty. As Wolsey looked over his own letters, filled with defamation toward his monarch, he cried, "I have touched the highest point of all my greatness, and from that full meridian of my glory I haste now to my setting."

The other nobles exulted in Wolsey's misfortune. Surrey gloated openly to Wolsey: "Thy ambition (thou scarlet sin) robbed this bewailing land . . . The king's further pleasure is . . . that therefore such a writ be sued against you, to forfeit all your goods, lands, tenements, chattels, and whatsoever." Then, their verbal barrage ended, the noblemen left Wolsey in his misery. As he bewailed his "fallen" state, Cromwell entered and informed him that Sir Thomas More had just been chosen Lord Chancellor in his place. "Farewell the hopes of court; my hopes in heaven do dwell," Wolsey cried.

That same day, the Coronation of Queen Anne Bullen was celebrated amid much pomp and splendor.

Now living in exile, Katherine discussed the recent news from London with her gentleman usher, Griffith. Griffith told her that Wolsey had taken ill as he was being transported to the tower of London after his arrest, and had died "full of repentance, continued meditations, tears and sorrows; he gave his honors to the world again . . . and slept in peace." Saddened, Katherine fell asleep herself, and as she slumbered, had a vision of six personages clad in white robes, who "promised me eternal happiness and brought me garlands," as she told Griffith when she awoke. Griffith noticed how weak and pale Katherine appeared; "She is going," he whispered.

Soon, a messenger arrived from King Henry expressing his grief over Katherine's illness. "That comfort comes too late," the former queen replied. "Tis like a pardon after execution." She then asked the messenger, "Remember me in all humility unto his highness: Say, his long trouble now is passing out of this world; tell him, in death, I blessed him . . . . I was a chaste wife to my grave . . . "

Some time later, it was whispered in court that Queen Anne was in labor with child and "that her suff'rance made almost pang a death." An old sorceress visited the king to report Anne's labors. Henry begged the woman to tell him that he had a son, but she brought other tidings. "'Tis a girl," she told him. Nevertheless, before she departed she promised him a future male heir.

While Henry went to see his wife and newborn child, his councillors held an assembly in secret. Their intent was to seize power by imprisoning the Archbishop of Canterbury, Cranmer, for "heresies." But just then the king unexpectedly entered the chamber and prevented the arrest. He reprimanded the nobles for their disrespect toward the Archbishop, and then turned to Cranmer and humbly asked, "Lord of Canterbury, I have a suit which you must not deny me; that is, a fair young maid that yet wants baptism, you must be godfather and answer for her."

Again royalty gathered in grandeur, with trumpets blaring, to witness the baptism of Henry's daughter, Elizabeth. Archbishop Cranmer pronounced that "this royal infant . . . though still in her cradle, yet now promises upon this land a thousand thousand blessings." He further prophesied that Elizabeth "shall be, to the happiness of England, an aged princess . . . but she must die . . . yet a virgin, a most unspotted lily she shall pass to the ground, and all the world shall mourn her."

King Henry smiled: "This oracle of comfort has so pleas'd me, that, when I am in heaven, I shall desire to see what this child does . . . "

Commentary:

From the start, this play seemed scourged. It closed after its debut because a fire burned down the theater where it was being performed. Critics have lambasted *Henry VIII* for its lack of action and rather anticlimactic ending. But the play was designed more as a display piece for its rich and elaborate staging and costumes than for its action or intrigue.

Another criticism leveled at the drama was its avoidance of the issues of the Protestant Reformation in England. Shakespeare was careful not to imply that the events of the play – Henry's divorce of Katherine and his subsequent marriage to Anne – had led in any way to England's still smoldering break with the Church in Rome. By limiting himself to a more subdued plot, Shakespeare tactfully avoided insulting the ruling House of Tudor. On the other hand, the drama does explore the type of political intrigue that may have actually taken place in the court of this flamboyant and controversial monarch.

THE TRAVELS OF MARCO POLO

by Marco Polo (approx. 1254 - 1324)
(as told to Rusticiano da Pisa and edited by Francis R. Gemma;
originally titled *A DESCRIPTION OF THE WORLD*)

Type of work: Autobiographical adventure

Setting: Venice, Italy and overland to Eastern China (Cathay)

Principal characters:
Marco Polo, a young nobleman, traveling merchant and adventurer
Niccolo Polo, Marco's father, also a merchant
Maffeo Polo, Niccolo's brother and business partner
Kublai Khan, Emperor of China, descendent of Ghenghis Khan

Commentary:

. . . Since . . . our first Father Adam . . . never hath there been Christian, or Pagan, or Tartar, or Indian or any man of any nation, who in his own person hath had so much knowledge and experience of the divers parts of the World and its Wonders as hath had this Messer Marco!

So begins *The Travels of Marco Polo.* Over the centuries numerous translations have appeared in many languages. The book has been popular since its publication and has served as a guide to various explorers and adventurers. Christopher Columbus, who wouldn't be sailing to the New World until almost two centuries later, was well acquainted with the text.

In Polo's day, the immensely popular and highly objective, descriptive tales were regarded as fiction. No one could accept that such fantastic places and people really existed. We must assume in reading the book that there are exaggerations, but the editor's notes indicate that some of the most fantastic elements are, indeed, based on fact.

The journal's literary style, in keeping with the times, is romanticized. In spite of this, on his deathbed, Marco, pressed to retract some of his stories, replied: "I have not told the half of it." And as travel to the East increased, more and more of Marco's claims were verified.

In some of the many renditions of the work, editors have chosen to omit repetitive information; therefore, each version varies somewhat in content. The excitement and adventure, however, do not vary, and the name Marco Polo still conjures up dreams of adventurous Oriental travel and fabulous discoveries.

Historical Overview:

Prologue: (The book contains the story of Marco Polo's life and his travels from his home in Venice, Italy across Eastern Europe, the Middle East, and Asia to the court of Khan, located in the area now known as Beijing, China. Marco was much liked by the Emperor, who made him his ambassador. The explorer describes his many adventures during his 26-year absence from home. An introduction outlines the biographical events (each that he himself personally witnessed or "heard tell by persons worthy of faith"), and sets us on our way with Marco en route to China.)

Two wealthy Venetian gentleman-merchants, Niccolo and Maffeo Polo, sailed eastward from Venice about 1254, leaving Niccolo's infant son, Marco, in the care of his aunt. The travelers journeyed as far as the court of the great emperor Kublai Khan, where they became highly favored. After learning a little about the exotic Catholic religion of his guests, the Khan dispatched envoys to return with them to Italy to meet with the Pope. His desire was that the Pope should lend the services of as many as a hundred scholars to come to his court and prove that the Law of Christ was "most agreeable." If they succeeded, he vowed that he and all his subjects would become Christians.

The Polos sailed into Acre, Italy in April of 1269, to the news that Pope Clement had died. Then the brothers journeyed on to Venice to await the anointing of a new pope. But after several years they tired of waiting and began to make their way again to Kublai's court, this time accompanied by young Marco.

Again in Acre, after some backtracking, the three finally met up with the newly-named Pope Gregory of Piacenza. He reluctantly agreed to cooperate with the Khan's commission, but sent only two ambassadors to accompany them. However, these priests soon became discouraged. Unwilling either to endure the privations the journey would require or to sacrifice their lives in the service of pagans, both eventually turned back.

The three explorers forged ahead.

Book-by-Book Summary:

Book I contains Marco's descriptions of his three-and-a-half year journey to Kublai's court. It is a fascinating narrative, with vivid renditions not only of geography, natural phenomena and traveling distances and conditions, but of histories, food preparation and production, trade, religious practices, and customs and oral traditions among the many tribes and civilizations they encountered.

Book II tells of life in the court of Kublai Khan. The person of the Khan is admiringly detailed: "He is of a good stature, neither tall nor short, but of a middle height. He has a becoming amount of flesh, and is very shapely in all his limbs. His complexion is white and red, the eyes black and fine, the nose well formed and well set on." The Khan's palaces, his vast court, his government and armies are depicted. An account is given of a battle led by great Khan himself. The narrative reports that "when all were in battle array [one could hear] a sound arise of many instruments of various music, and of the voices of the whole of the two hosts loudly singing. For this is the custom of the Tartars . . . "

Portrayals of court affairs such as the marking of the calendar, and the celebration of thousands of festivals and hunting trips, are eloquently recorded. Record-keeping was very important to the Chinese. Each household kept near the front door a list of the names of all the home's inhabitants, and the keepers of hostelries were required to record the names of all travelers and the dates of their visits.

Certain chapters relate some of the wondrous inventions Marco saw while serving the Khan. He writes of such marvels as paper money, a system of express messengers, fine highway systems (remnants of which are still in place), and a "black stone" (coal) used for fuel. For all of these wonders Marco gives full credit to the "Great Khan," whom he never tires of praising for his wisdom, power, wealth and skill.

Now fluent in four different languages, Marco became a valuable ambassador for the Emperor. **Book II** ends with brief descriptions of his separate missions.

Book III recounts in great detail the adventurous travels of the Polos on behalf of the Khan through Japan, Indochina, Southern India and "The Coast and Islands of the Indian Sea," including Ethiopia. The assemblage traveled as far north and west as Ormus (near the Strait of Hormuz).

After seventeen years at the Khan's court, the wealthy Polos, surrounded by envious princes, decided that if they ever wanted to return to Venice, they could most easily do so under the protection and safe conduct of their benefactor before he died. They asked his permission to return home, but were at first refused; the Great Emperor enjoyed their company. After a time, however, he reluctantly granted them leave.

Fourteen ships were prepared for the homeward voyage – during which six hundred crew members were lost in storms. En route, the news came of Kublai's death.

Marco writes of exotic regions visited: Armenia, where Noah's ark came to rest on Mount Ararat, and where camel caravans gathered by fountains of oil to haul off the black liquid as an amazing source of heat and light; Iraq's Saba, where the three Magi first saw the star that led them to Bethlehem; the hot, windy Ormus, filled with mounds of baked corpses from armies smitten by the foul water and intense sun; Karazan, with its huge serpents and crocodiles; the city of Mien, with its two great towers, one of silver, the other of pure gold; the paradisiacal Chinese city of Kin-sai, with twelve thousand bridges spanning its rivers and canals, its stone-paved streets, and its hundreds of beautiful carvings; the mountainous grave of Father Adam located in Ceylon; the magical Lac province, where people commonly lived to the age of 150.

Marco also describes strange characters and mystical tribes: a miserly ruler, unwilling to provide for his kingdom's protection, who was captured and locked in a tower where, surrounded by piles of gold, he starved to death; a robber band which had learned the diabolical art of calling down darkness upon caravans in order to rob them; nursing fathers; an ancient drug dealer who used his hallucinating followers as assassins to do his bidding; and various sorcerers and cannibals. The account includes stories of natives who made their living by selling pickled monkeys – passed off as pygmies – to naive sailors for souvenirs; men with tails; and brutal pirates.

On his way home to Venice, Marco also came across tribes who used gold, silver, pearls, diamonds and rubies as common barter and adornment, and who wore rich silks and embroidery for work and play. He saw asbestos, musk-scent and salt all used as money; he became acquainted with sumptuous spices, sugar, curious drugs, and flavorful incense; he came across fascinating animals – a raptor with talons large enough to seize an elephant, hair-covered chickens, and unicorns (actually rhinoceri) "which have hair like that of water buffalo and feet like those of an elephant . . . an ugly beast to behold."

When his foreign adventures were over and Marco finally settled again in his homeland, he took up arms in a war against Genoa, Venice's competitor in sea-going trade. He was captured, and as a prisoner of war, soon became an attraction, telling of his marvelous travels to distant lands. Finally he decided to save himself the trouble of retelling the same stories over and over, and wrote to his father, requesting his notes be sent. Using these – along with an exceptional memory and power of imagination – he dictated four books to a fellow prisoner and professional story-teller, Rusticiano da Pisa. Following Marco's release in 1298 and up to the time of his death 26 years later, these were published as one volume under the title *A Description of the World*, which remained almost the only source of information about the Far East until the late 19th century.

THE LAST OF THE MOHICANS

by
James Fenimore Cooper
(1789 - 1851)

Type of work: Historical romance

Setting: Upper New York region; 1757

Principal characters:

Hawkeye (Natty Bumppo), a skilled white scout and frontiersman

Chingachgook, Hawkeye's lifelong Mohican (Delaware) friend

Uncas, Chingachgook's son and last heir to the title of chief of the Mohican tribe

Major Duncan Heyward, Hawkeye's Scottish soldier-friend

David Gamut, a psalm singer, and comical, naive, self-proclaimed missionary

Magua (Le Renard Subtil---"The Sly Fox"), a displaced and bloodthirsty Canadian Huron Indian

Colonel Munro, defender of British Fort Henry

Alice Munro, fair and innocent daughter of Colonel Munro

Cora Munro, her darker, elder half-sister, and the story's real heroine

Story Overview:

War between England and France had spilled over into the North American continent. There, amid the various Indian tribal conflicts, a small party set out from the British Fort Edward toward Fort William Henry, defended by the Scottish veteran, Colonel Munro. Major Duncan Heyward, ordered to escort Colonel Munro's two daughters, Cora and Alice, to Fort William Henry, was followed by a tall, awkward, psalm singing missionary, David Gamut. Fort Edward's troops were in a weakened state. Now Major Heyward, in an attempt to reach Munro's fort before the French forces led by Montcalm could surround it, hired a renegade Huron Indian guide known as Magua, who claimed to know of a shorter route to their destination. But now, after traveling most of the day and finding themselves still only a few miles from Fort Edward, they at last decided the guide must be lost.

Late that same afternoon, a seasoned white scout bearing the fitting name of Hawkeye, sat by a stream, conversing with his Delaware Mohican friend Chingachgook. By their dress and weaponry it was obvious that they were not allied with the French or the Iriquois. The Indian lamented aloud the sad history of his people, who had dwindled after they foolishly parted with their land. He ended with a vision of his own death: "I am on the hill-top, and must go down into the valley; and when Uncas follows in my footsteps, there will no longer be any of the blood of the [Delaware], for my boy is the last of the Mohicans."

As if conjured up by his father's words, another voice announced, "Uncas is here! Who speaks to Uncas?" and stepping between the two, a young warrior seated himself.

Soon the three men heard "the horses of white men" approaching, and Hawkeye was appointed to speak to them in his native English tongue. He went out to meet Heyward's group. When told that the Indian guide, who was by this time lurking in the shadows, had lost his way, Hawkeye doubtingly asked what tribe he belonged to. He was Mohawk by birth, but an adopted Huron, came the reply. At this, both Chingachgook and Uncas sprang to their feet. "A Huron!" spat the scout. "They are a thievish race, nor do I care by whom they are adopted . . . . I should like to look at the creature." Now, Magua saw that his plan to betray Heyward and kidnap Munro's daughters had been foiled, and he fled into the forest.

Hawkeye and the Mohicans, sensing the danger the little party now faced, agreed to see them safely to Fort William Henry. But as Hawkeye had feared, Magua and his fellow Hurons gave chase. The woodsman guided his travelers to an island cave and hid them behind a waterfall; but they had been too closely followed, and the cave was soon under attack. With little ammunition, the capture of the little group was certain. In order to secure their only chance for rescue, Cora gallantly persuaded Hawkeye and the Mohicans to try an escape – which they managed to do by swimming underwater downriver.

Captured, Cora and Alice were taken by Magua on a path leading far away from the fort. As they walked, Magua spoke privately to Cora. Long ago, he divulged, after drinking the white man's firewater, he had lost control of himself, and Colonel Munro had ordered that he be publicly beaten. Magua's plan of revenge for this humiliation was to take Munro's daughter as his wife and slave.

Cora hid her fear and responded calmly: she would not go with him. In fury Magua was about to massacre the whole lot, when Hawkeye and his comrades rushed the camp, killing all the Hurons – except their villainous leader, who once again escaped. The group then journeyed on in the darkness toward Fort William Henry.

It was dawn when Hawkeye and his charges drew near the fort – only to find it already under siege by Montcalm and his French and Iriquois troops. Cora suggested that she go to Montcalm to beg that he grant them entry into the fort so they could be with their father. "You would scarce find the tent of the Frenchman with the hair on your head," Hawkeye told her bluntly. From that point, a quiet bond was formed between Uncas and the brunette Cora; while Heyward was taken by fair Alice.

Led by Hawkeye, the consummate frontiersman – a happy blend of the white man's "civilization" and the red man's noble "savagery" – the protagonists threaded their way through the thick morning mist to the gates of the fort. Happily united with his daughters, Munro exclaimed, "For this I thank thee, Lord! Let danger come as it will, thy servant is now prepared!"

After a few days of ominous quiet, Montcalm arranged a parley to reveal the text of a message he had intercepted, indicating that no troops could be dispatched from Fort Edward. Although Montcalm now held the upper hand, he offered the British honorable terms of surrender: He would ensure safe conduct for the entire garrison, if they would give up the fort peaceably. Dismayed by the cowardice of his allies, and with no other options open, Munro accepted the terms.

The next morning, as the evacuation of the women and children proceeded under the gaze of the victors – Magua included – one of the Indians tried to seize a brightly colored shawl worn by one of the women. In terror she wrapped her child in it and folded both close to her. Enraged, the Indian darted forward and grabbed the child from her arms and dashed its head against a rock. Excited by the sight of blood, he then turned on the mother and drove his tomahawk into her brain. Now Magua raised a bloodcurdling whoop of battle, and the Indians responded instantly, scalping and murdering with brutal abandon. Montcalm and his soldiers – perhaps surprised by the suddenness of the attack, perhaps out of fear for their own safety – did nothing to hold back their savage allies.

David Gamut stood in the midst of the killing to shield the two Munro girls, and burst forth singing hymns in an effort to calm the frenzied killers. Bemused by this eccentric display, the warriors left the sisters unmolested. But Gamut's singing finally attracted the attention of Magua, who quickly seized upon an opportunity to persuade Cora to accompany him. Reaching down and scooping up her sister Alice, Magua headed for the woods. Cora ran, shrieking, after him, and faithful Gamut followed, his voice still in song, his arm beating time. The astonished natives gazed on him as one who had been given the protecting spirit of madness.

Hawkeye and his companions searched in vain for the bodies of the girls, and were now certain that Magua had taken them captive. Heading north and then west, the scouts finally came across their trail. Heyward was particularly concerned for Alice's safety; and Uncas, admiring Cora's courage and depth of soul, hoped ardently for her rescue.

Paddling across lakes and hiking over mountain passes, the woodsmen traced Gamut and the girls to an Indian village. Wandering on its outskirts they found the psalmist, dressed as an Indian, who told them that Cora had been entrusted to the care of a tribe of peaceful Delawares, but that Alice was being held at the Huron camp. It was decided that Heyward would accompany Gamut into the village, disguised as a white medicine man

sent by Montcalm to heal the sick. But just as he was being led to the cave of a dying woman, Uncas was brought into camp, a captive. Inside the sick woman's cave, Heyward also found a large shaggy bear – whose head slipped back to reveal the face of Hawkeye; knowing that Huron conjurers often attired themselves in animal skins, he had used the bearskin to also gain entrance to the village. The two sought out Alice, wrapped her in a blanket, and carried her out of the camp under the pretense that she was Heyward's dying patient. Hawkeye, in his bear disguise, remained long enough to find and rescue Uncas.

As soon as Magua discovered Alice's disappearance, he hurried to the Delaware village to reclaim his wife-to-be. Uncas was already there before him, but had failed to negotiate Cora's release. Magua was allowed to pass unmolested into the forest with his prized prisoner, "protected by the inviolable laws of Indian hospitality."

A terrible battle ensued between the two tribes and their white allies. In the end, the Hurons were defeated, but Magua had kept Cora close, and, followed by a few braves, he now scrambled up a steep mountainside, with Uncas, Heyward and Hawkeye in hot pursuit. Cora refused to cooperate, and begged Magua to kill her; but just then a piercing cry diverted the villain's attention. It was Uncas, leaping down from a cliff above. At that moment one of the Huron braves sheathed his own knife in Cora's bosom. Infuriated, Magua turned to kill his companion, but Uncas leaped between them and became Magua's victim instead.

The Huron bounded off up the mountain. Shouting, he leaped a wide fissure and neared the summit. One more leap and escape would be ensured – but this time he fell short and clung to a shrub on the side of the cliff. Hawkeye, watching from below, sighted his long rifle. A loud crack pierced the air; then Magua gave a defiant shake of his fist and a menacing sneer, and fell headlong to his death.

Amid deep mourning, Uncas and Cora were laid side by side in their forest graves. Hawkeye returned to comfort his sorrowing friend Chingachgook. The Delaware patriarch Tamenund then lifted his voice to bewail the tragic death of "the last warrior of the wise race of the Mohicans."

Commentary:

Shortly after the birth of James Fenimore Cooper, his father came into possession of a vast tract of land around the headwaters of the Susquehanna River and built a mansion by Otsego Lake. A village grew up around the estate, eventually becoming Cooperstown, New York. Surrounded by primeval wilderness, alive with animals and still inhabited by a few Indians, and growing up on the frontier tales told by his father's guests, Cooper was able to bring to life a genuine and sympathetic view of both pioneer and Indian, and a first-hand knowledge of their lives, lore and surroundings, to become America's first significant novelist.

THE RIME OF THE ANCIENT MARINER

by
Samuel Taylor Coleridge
(1772 - 1834)

Type of work: Lyrical fantasy ballad

Setting: A sailing ship traveling the seas; late Medieval period

Principal characters:

The Ancient Mariner, a sailor-storyteller
The Wedding Guest, a listener
The Ship's Crew
The Albatross, a symbolic representation of God's creatures – and Man's guilt
The Hermit, a rescuer representing God

Story Overview:

(Coleridge introduces his tale by describing an old gray-headed sailor who approaches three young men headed for a wedding celebration and compels one of them, the groom's next-of-kin, to hear his story.

> O Wedding-Guest! this soul hath been
> Alone on a wide wide sea:
> So lonely 'twas, that God himself
> Scarce seemed there to be.

At first the intrusion is resented, but the story is remarkable indeed, and the listener – who, of course, represents you, the reader – soon falls captive to the building suspense, responding at first with fear and then with horror as the tale unfolds.)

There was little apprehension among the ship's crew as they sailed clear of the harbor, bound for the open sea. Several days out, however, a storm arose and the vessel was driven before the wind in a constant southerly direction, headed toward the South Pole. As it entered the "land of ice, and of fearful sounds, where no living thing was to be seen," a feeling of foreboding came over the helpless inmates; and so it was with great relief that the crew eventually greeted the sight of an albatross – a huge seabird – flying through the fog toward them.

("As if it had been a Christian soul," the Ancient Mariner tells his listener, "We hailed it in God's name.")

Everyone took this as a good omen, and the bird followed the ship faithfully as it returned northward. Then, one day, weary of the bird's incessant and now unnerving presence, the Mariner shot the albatross with his crossbow – and brought the curse down upon them all.

The south wind continued to propel them northward, but somehow the old sailor realized he had done "a hellish thing"; retribution would soon follow, in the form of loneliness and spiritual anguish, like that of Adam when he fell from God's grace.

The crew at first berated their mate for killing the bird that had brought the change in the breeze. But as the ship made its way out of the fog and mist and continued on, they decided it must be the bird that had brought the mist. Perhaps their shipmate had rightfully killed it after all.

The vessel sailed on northward until it reached the equator, where the breeze ceased and the craft became becalmed. After days without a breath of wind, it was decided by all that an avenging spirit had followed them from the land of mist and snow, leaving them surrounded only by foul water. With the unabsolved curse thus restored, the thirsting crew angrily hung the dead albatross around the Mariner's neck, as a symbol of his guilt. Time lost all meaning. The lips of the men baked and their eyes glazed over for want of water.

> I looked to heaven, and tried to pray;
> But or ever a prayer had gusht,
> A wicked whisper came, and made
> My heart as dry as dust.

Then the old sailor saw a speck on the horizon, which, as it watted towards them, became a sail. The men waited in silent dread. This could be no earthly ship – it moved along the water without the slightest breeze.

Wide-eyed and trembling, the crew looked on as this skeleton ship came alongside their own. On its deck the Mariner saw two spectres: a Woman, Life-in-Death; and her mate, Death himself. They were casting dice to see which of them would take control of the drifting ship. Death won the entire ship's crew – all but the Ancient Mariner, who was won by the Woman; he alone would live on, to expiate his sin against Nature.

There followed a ghastly scene as the sun dropped into the sea and night came over the silent waters. One by one the two hundred men on board turned toward the Mariner, denounced him with a soulful stare – for they could not speak – and dropped dead upon the deck. As their souls flew from their bodies and sped past the old seaman, the sound was "like the whizz of my crossbow" when he shot the albatross.

(The Wedding Guest by this time is terrified of the Ancient Mariner, who he thinks must be a ghost; but assuring him he is indeed mortal, the old man proceeds with his story.)

The Ancient Mariner was by now in agony, as he looked upon all those whom Death had taken:

> The many men, so beautiful!
> And they all dead did lie:
> And a thousand thousand slimy things
> Lived on; and so did I.

This, the Mariner's heartsick and acknowledged disgust for non-human life, showed that he had not yet learned his lesson nor completed the penance that Life-in-Death had prepared for him.

For seven days and seven nights the wretched survivor was forced to confront the open, accusing eyes of his dead shipmates.

The pang, the curse, with which they died,
Had never passed away:
I could not draw my eyes from theirs,
Nor turn them up to pray.

Finally, suspended in utter loneliness, the horrified sailor stood watching out over the moonlit water. Sea snakes darted and swam nearby. He was startled to behold their beauty, and at once felt a rush of love for these creatures, blessing them as the only other living things in his damnable world. *"O happy living things!"*, he cried. And with those few words, the spell was broken. The Ancient Mariner could pray at last, and the albatross fell from his neck and sank "like lead into the sea." With welcome release he fell into a deep sleep. When he awakened later, it was raining – and his body drank in the moisture.

Now gazing into the heavens, the seaman witnessed strange, never-before-seen sights. And stranger still, on the bloody deck of the ship, the bodies of his dead companions arose and went mutely about their mundane tasks of sailing, no longer transfixing him with their dead stares.

(Here the Mariner hastens to again reassure the Wedding Guest that the spirits animating the crew's bodies were not those souls which had fled them at death, but "a blessed troop of angelic spirits" called down by his guardian saint.)

At dawn the spirits left; but still the ship sailed on, with no help from any breeze. It was moved now by a spirit from the land of mist and snow – the Polar Spirit, still seeking cleansing repentence from the Mariner for having killed the albatross.

At noon the ship suddenly stood still, and then began moving back and forth in a bizarre, dancing tug-of-war. Was Death again trying to win the Ancient Mariner? Suddenly the ship leaped free of the unseen grapplers with such force that the sailor fell into a trance. He knew little of what transpired until he heard the voices of two spirits. Their conversation revealed that the ship was now being powered by angelic forces and traveling northward at such speed he could not have endured it in full consciousness.

When the dazed and astonished sailor again awoke, it was night, and the dead men stood together on the deck, the curse blazing anew in their eyes. What joy came to him when that spell finally broke and the ship sped homeward. At last he was among the dear and familar landmarks he had thought never to view again.

Soon the angelic spirits departed from the bodies of the Mariner's dead comrades, and standing on top of each lifeless form was a "man all light, a seraph man," shining as a rescue signal to the land. But just as a small rescue boat came alongside the ship, a terrible noise rumbled through the water, splitting and sinking the vessel and throwing the sailor overboard. He was quickly pulled into the boat – but his gruesome adventure had taken its toll; the sight of the ravaged Mariner terrified everyone aboard. Once ashore, the penitent old sailor begged the holy Hermit of the Wood to bless him and cast off his sin. "What manner of man art thou?" asked the man of God, crossing himself. At this question, an agony of spirit prompted the Ancient Mariner to recount his story, freeing himself for a brief hour from the curse of remembrance.

(And so the Mariner concludes his story once again. He tells the Wedding Guest that ever since the Hermit's blessing, he has been obliged to travel from land to land, never knowing when the agony of remembrance might return. But whenever the curse again darkens his soul, he recognizes the face of a man with whom he must share his message of love and reverence for God's creation:

He prayeth well, who loveth well
Both man and bird and beast.
He prayeth best, who loveth best
All things both great and small;
For the dear God who loveth us,
He made and loveth all.

The Wedding Guest, incidentally, never does go on to the wedding. So moved is he by the mood of the Mariner, that when the old man vanishes, he also departs, "a sadder and a wiser man.")

Commentary:

There are critics who contend that the *Rime of the Ancient Mariner* is autobiographical in its strange, imaginative theme and storyline. Coleridge, even this early in his writing, was haunted by remorse for his addiction to opium, which he had first taken to relieve pain as a patient at Christ's Hospital. But whether or not the poem actually served as a catharsis for its author's guilt, it stands on its own merits.

Coleridge's interests always lay with the exotic and the supernatural, which he hoped to make more real for his readers by employing simple, straightforward language in an archaic English ballad form. In this relatively brief poem, he succeeds in making the extraordinary believable; and his graphic word-pictures – some fraught with horror, others piercing us with brief visions of exquisite beauty – evoke images so clear and deep that they touch every one of our senses and emotions.

MOBY DICK

by
Herman Melville
(1819 - 1891)

Type of work: Allegorical novel

Setting: The high Seas; early nineteenth century

Principal characters:
Ishmael, a teacher-seaman (and narrator)
Queequeg, a hardened and savage
harpooner
Ahab, captain of the *Pequod*
Starbuck and Stubb, Ahab's first and
second mates
Fedallah, Captain Ahab's Parsee servant
and seer

Story Overview:

A schoolmaster, Ishmael chose to give up the comfort and security of his classroom and fulfill his romantic desire to go sea. Leaving Manhattan, he set out for New Bedford, near Cape Horn in the Pacific, in search of work on a whaler.

Ishmael's first night in New Bedford was spent in the crusty Spouter Inn near the waterfront. There he found the only bed available – which, by necessity, he consented to share with an unknown harpooner. His roommate turned out to be a bizarre fellow indeed, a hardened South-sea islander whose body was covered with tatoos. But after Ishmael's initial fear had subsided, he found this "strange bedfellow," Queequeg, to be quite friendly. The huge man offered to share his small fortune and an embalmed human head with Ishmael. "At first I knew not what to make of this," Ishmael said, "but soon an inkling of the truth occurred to me. I remembered a story of a white man – a whaleman too – who, falling among cannibals, had been tattooed by them. I concluded that this harpooner, in course of his distant voyages, must have met with a similar adventure. And what is it, thought I, after all! It's only his outside; a man can be honest in any sort of skin."

The two men became fast friends, both signing on as harpooners aboard the *Pequod*, a Quaker-owned whaler out of Nantucket. There had been some question around New Bedford as to the future fate of the *Pequod* because of its eccentric captain, Ahab. But both Ishmael and Queequeg had no intention of changing their plans.

They set sail. For the first few days the curious captain stayed out of sight in his cabin, and the *Pequod* was under the command of the first and second mates, Mr. Starbuck and Mr. Stubb. But as the ship continued to sail southward, a stern, relentless man suddenly strode out on deck: Captain Ahab himself. Ishmael was struck by the man's austere

expression, but even more by his spectacular artificial leg; instead of a wooden leg, Ahab wore an attachment carved from the jawbone of a whale. This was complemented by a gaping scar which ran down the side of his face into his collar, so that he appeared to be scarred from head to foot.

For several days the crew sailed on in search of whaling schools. Then one day Ahab appeared on deck and summoned all the men. He nailed a one-ounce gold piece to the mast and announced that the gold would become the property of the first man to sight the great white whale known as Moby Dick. All the men except Starbuck and Stubb were enthusiastic about the Captain's challenge. To the two top mates, Ahab's obsession with the white whale was far beyond reason. Starbuck contended that the Captain's madness over Moby Dick was a danger to those in his charge. Ahab had already lost his leg to the whale and his mates were afraid his reckless quest would end in the loss of all their lives at the next encounter. But none of this diminished the enthusiasm of the other crewmen; they drank an oath with Ahab to the destruction of the white whale.

Learning that the last sightings of the whale had been near the Cape of Good Hope, Ahab immediately plotted his course. Upon approaching the Cape, the ship came on a school of sperm whales, and the men busied themselves with harpooning and stripping the huge mammals, then melting down and storing the whale oil.

When they happened upon another whaling vessel, Captain Ahab inquired further about the white whale. The captain of the ship warned him not to pursue the whale, but Ahab could not be deterred.

Later, another ship stopped the *Pequod*, and the captain came aboard to buy some oil. He too was interrogated by Ahab about Moby Dick, but he replied that he had no news concerning the monster. Just after he had departed the *Pequod*, a school of whales surfaced, and both ships' crews set out after them. The rival crew had a commanding lead, but the men of the *Pequod*, spurred on by Starbuck and Stubb, soon outdistanced them, and Queequeg harpooned the school's largest whale. Now the work began. The carcass was dragged alongside and lashed to the ship by ropes so the men could begin to work on it. They quickly stripped off the meat and blubber before it was lost to the menacing sharks that inevitably tracked whaling vessels. The blubber was then melted down in huge try-pots, and stored below deck.

As the *Pequod* continued its voyage toward the Indian Ocean, the crew's sense of excitement was high. Before long they crossed paths with an English vessel, and Ahab once again demanded news of the white whale. In answer, the English captain held forth his right arm, which consisted of whale bone from the elbow down. Ahab quickly boarded the vessel to hear its captain's story. The old sailor gave Ahab still another grim warning that it was foolish to pursue Moby Dick; but, pressed, the Yankee captain finally revealed the coordinates of the whale's last sighting. Ahab then ordered the *Pequod* to change course for the latest haunts of Moby Dick.

Queequeg was taken ill, and it seemed sure that he would die. The ship's carpenter was summoned to fashion a coffin in the shape of a canoe, according to the customs of Queequeg's people. The coffin was then placed in the sick man's cabin. When Queequeg miraculously recovered, he carved exotic designs on his coffin and used it as a sea chest.

From the start of the voyage, the crew had been puzzled by the presence of the Persian, Fedallah, Captain Ahab's highly regarded servant and seer. Now Fedallah prophesied that Ahab would die, but only after he had seen two hearses for carrying the dead upon the sea, one not constructed by human hands and the other built of wood grown in America. Ironically, neither would be for Ahab's burial; the captain's death, said Fedallah, would come by hemp.

One night a terrible storm arose. Lightning struck the ship, and all three masts flamed against the black sky. The men took this as an omen – the hand of God was directing them to veer from their destructive course and return home. But still Ahab refused to abandon his quarry. He planted himself at the foot of the main mast and challenged the god of evil which blazed up before him in the fire. He was determined to find and destroy that evil-incarnate, Moby Dick.

Days passed as Ahab stalked the "odour" of the white whale. Then sounded "a gull-like cry in the air, 'there she blows! – there she blows! A hump like a snowhill! It is Moby Dick!'" The voice was that of Ahab himself, whose eyes were dim but whose passion was aflame. The boats were lowered – with Ahab, harpoon in hand, in the lead. Then, just as the captain was about to sink his harpoon into the majestic body of the whale, it dived under the boat, splitting it to pieces. Ahab and his men were rescued; only Fedallah had disappeared beneath the waves. The hunt continued. Harpoons were lost and boats were destroyed,

all for the annihilation of a beast by a mad-man.

On the third day, the wounded Moby Dick became listless, and the boats of the *Pequod* quickly overtook him. As the great whale surfaced for air, there, bound to its back by ropes from harpoons, was the body of Fedallah. The first part of the Persian's prophecy – a hearse not humanly constructed – had come to pass.

Wild with pain, Moby Dick abruptly turned on the boats, splintering them into pieces. From the deck of the *Pequod*, Starbuck watched the rage of the enormous beast and turned the ship towards it in hopes of saving the crew; but the infuriated animal swam directly into the *Pequod*, crushing the vessel's timbers. Ahab, seeing his ship founder, cried out that the second part of Fedallah's prophecy was fulfilled – the ship was constructed of American timber.

The final prophecy – that Ahab's death would come by hemp – was also shortly fulfilled. The rope from Ahab's harpoon coiled about his neck and wrenched him from his boat. All the crew was lost with the ship, except for Ishmael, who found safety by grasping onto Queequeg's floating coffin. He alone was rescued to tell the tale of Moby Dick, Ahab, and the *Pequod*, which, "like Satan, would not sink to hell till she had dragged a living part of heaven along with her . . . "

Commentary:

Moby Dick, or, *The White Whale* is a book of amazing depth. It can be read on several levels: for over a century it has captivated young readers, naturalists, historians and literary scholars alike. On the surface, it is both an adventure story set upon the high seas and a compendium of information about whales and the whaling industry. But the reader who searches more deeply discovers both a complex psychological study and a powerful allegory dealing with the archetypes of good and evil struggling together within the tenets of eighteenth-century Calvinism.

Melville wrestles in all his works with man's place in the cosmos, endeavoring to expose the unseen forces of the universe and the effects of these forces on man. In *Moby Dick*, he recognizes the power of both God and the Devil, and strains to comprehend their invisible source.

The great white whale symbolizes evil; however, Ahab's obsession to destroy the whale becomes an even darker manifestation of evil. Thus, Melville reveals, with unerring skill and passion, a dilemma that has plagued men and women since the garden of Eden.

THE OLD MAN & THE SEA

by
Ernest Hemingway
(1899 - 1961)

Type of work: Symbolic drama

Setting: North Coast of Cuba; early twentieth century

Principal characters:
  Santiago, an old, weathered fisherman
  Manolin, a boy, Santiago's young fishing companion
  The Marlin, a gigantic fish

Story Overview:

Eighty-four days had passed since Santiago, the old fisherman, had caught a fish, and he was forced to suffer not only the ridicule of younger fishermen, but near-starvation as well. Moreover, Santiago had lost his young companion, a boy named Manolin, whose father had ordered him to leave Santiago in order to work with more successful seamen. But the devoted child still loved Santiago, and each day brought food and bait to his shack, where they indulged in their favorite pastime: talking about the American baseball leagues. The old man's hero was the New York Yankees' Joe DiMaggio. Santiago identified with the ballplayer's skill and discipline, and declared he would like to take the great DiMaggio fishing some time.

After visiting one particular afternoon, the boy left Santiago, who fell asleep. Lions immediately filled his dreams. As a boy he had sailed to Africa and had seen lions on the beaches. Now, as an old man, he constantly dreamed of the great and noble beasts.

He no longer dreamed of storms, nor of women, nor of great occurrences, nor of great fish, nor fights, nor contests of strength, nor of his wife. He only dreamed of places now and of the lions on the beach. . . . He loved them as he loved the boy.

Before dawn of the next day, the fisherman, as usual, hauled his salt-encrusted skiff onto the beach and set out by himself. But today, in hopes of breaking his unlucky streak, he was determined to sail into deep waters, out much farther than the other anglers would go. He followed the sea birds and flying fish; they would tell him by their movements where the fish congregated.

He watched the turtles swimming near his boat. He loved the turtles, "with their elegance and speed . . . "

Most people are heartless about turtles because a turtle's heart will beat for hours after he has been cut up and butchered. . . . The old man thought, I have such a heart too . . .

Early on, Santiago managed to land a ten-pound tuna. Thinking this a good omen, he used the fresh meat to bait one of his lines. By now he was far away from land, and much far-ther out than all the other fishermen. Resisting the temptation to sleep or to let his mind wander, Santiago concentrated on his lines reaching deep into the dark green waters.

At noon he felt a bite. Testing his line, he guessed that it must be a marlin nibbling at the tuna bait. "He must be huge," the old man thought, and waited anxiously for a strike. Suddenly, the fish took the bait entirely and began to swim furiously out to sea, dragging the boat behind him. The fish was so powerful that Santiago was helpless to stop him; he could only brace himself against the weight placed on the taut line that cut across his shoulders and hold on until the fish exhausted its strength. Darkness fell, and still the fish swam steadily out to sea. The seaman spent a grueling night with the line looped painfully round his back. Though he was weak, old and all alone, Santiago knew many tricks, and possessed skills the young men yet lacked. Besides, he loved the sea with a passion and had faith that she would handle him with reverent, though bitter, kindness. Once, when the fish gave a sudden tug, the line slashed Santiago's cheek. "Fish," the old man vowed softly, "I'll stay with you until I am dead."

Then he began to pity the great fish that he had hooked. *He is wonderful and strange and who knows how old he is, he thought . . . Perhaps he is too wise to jump. He could ruin me by jumping or by a wild rush. But perhaps he has been hooked many times before and he knows that this is how he should make his fight. He cannot know that it is only one man against him, nor that it is an old man . . .*

His choice had been to stay in the deep dark water far out beyond all snares and traps and treacheries. My choice was to go there to find him beyond all people . . . . Now we are joined together and have been since noon. And no one to help either of us.

By morning of the second day the fish was still heading northward; vigorous, seemingly tireless strokes of its tail guided it forward. There was no land in sight. A stiffening cramp in Santiago's left hand, a wicked slice in his right, and his shivering from cold was hampering his work. "I wish I had the boy," he said aloud.

All at once the fish surfaced and leaped into the air. Santiago marvelled at the enormous, lavender marlin, two feet longer than the boat itself – the biggest fish the old man had ever seen.

Once again the fish set out, relentlessly towing the boat. Santiago could do nothing but hold on and wait.

Sitting in the hot afternoon sun, Santiago

cut strips from the tuna and chewed them slowly. He drank sparingly. Throughout his ordeal, he spoke to his only friends: the birds that came to rest on the side of the skiff. He spoke to his brother, the great fish. He also addressed his cramped hands and arms, as though they, like himself and the fish, were in their own, detatched struggles for survival. His mind constantly returned to baseball, the lions – and Manolin. Over and over he longed for the boy to be with him, to help him land the fish and to take his mind from his cut hand and aching back. He wondered how the Yankees were doing, envying the younger fishermen who could afford radios in their boats to listen to the games. He thought of DiMaggio, wondering if the "Yankee Clipper" would stay with a fish as long as Santiago had stayed with this one. "I am sure he would and more since he is young and strong," he thought. "Also his father was a fisherman."

At one point, Santiago fell into a daydream about an arm-wrestling match he'd had as a young man. The contest with "the great negro . . . who was the strongest man on the docks" had lasted twenty-four hours, but Santiago had held out – and won.

Amid these reveries, night fell again. Santiago allowed himself a moment's sleep, and dreamed of the lions. All night he instinctively played the line.

At sunrise on the third day, the marlin began to circle; and after hours of struggling, the drained and dizzy fisherman finally managed to bring the fish close to the surface. Then, on one of its many passes by the side of the boat, the old man took aim and drove the harpoon with all his strength into its side. The fish "came alive, with death in him"; it shook violently, rose high out of the water, hung in the air, then fell in a great mist of salt spray. Its struggle over, now it floated, motionless. " . . . I think the great DiMaggio would be proud of me today," said the old man.

After resting his sore muscles and sipping some water, Santiago examined his catch. Far too big to be brought into the boat, the fish had to be lashed alongside it. Santiago soaked his hands in the salt water and tried to keep his head clear. He mused on his great prize, which seemingly sailed next to his boat. "Is he bringing me in or am I bringing him in?" the old man thought. "Let him bring me in if it pleases him. I am only better than him through trickery and he meant me no harm." Still, the fish would bring him fame and fortune when he arrived in Havana Harbor.

But Santiago's problems were far from over; he was still a day's journey from land, and he knew that the fish's blood would attract sharks.

And after a short time, the swift, hungry makos and hammerheads did come. Without fear, they began tearing hunks of flesh from the marlin. Despite Santiago's all-day resolute efforts to kill and beat them off, sharks continued to close in, hitting the carcass again and again. His hands and arms bleeding and raw, the weary sailor was beaten – the sharks would leave him nothing but a huge skeleton. He bowed his head: "I'm sorry, fish."

Not until deep into the night did Santiago steer his skiff into the quiet village harbor. Dutifully, he beached his skiff, dragged his mast and sails into their shed, and finally crawled off to his shack, to welcome slumber.

The next morning, Manolin came to Santiago's shack and found his old friend. "The boy saw that the old man was breathing and then he saw the old man's hands and he started to cry." All the way down the road, as he retrieved some coffee for Santiago, he cried.

When Santiago woke, the boy told him that he'd been presumed lost at sea, and that search planes had been dispatched to find him. The other fishermen had seen the marlin's skeleton and were astonished at its size – eighteen feet from nose to tail. Manolin brought the old man food, nursed his wounds, and firmly told the fisherman, "Now we fish together again." Then he left Santiago, to sleep. And the old man dreamed about the lions.

Commentary:

Everything about *The Old Man & The Sea* is classically simple. The style is pure Hemingway: short, straightforward sentences with one-syllable words. The storyline is linear – easy enough for a child to follow – and the themes are clear and basic, touting manly courage, endurance, and noble suffering.

In fact, the novel would be little more than an adventure story were it not for Santiago's dialogues with himself – his repetitive and symbolic musings, daydreams and plottings.

Unlike other fishermen, who see the ocean merely in terms of economic gain, Santiago looks on the sea and its inhabitants with love and respect. Notably, he prefers to call the sea "la mar," its feminine form, rather than the harsher, masculine "el mar."

Some readers may see Christian symbolism in the story: Santiago means St. James in Spanish; the battle with the fish lasts three days; Santiago, arriving at the shore, carries his mast, like a cross, on his shoulders, and, like the biblical Christ, stumbles under its load. Later, the fisherman lies down exhausted on the floor of his hut with his arms stretched out stiffly and the palms of his hands up.

But the giant fish – representing the hopes and dreams of mankind – and the old man's relationship with it, is what creates the extraordinary pathos of the novel. And, in the end, even Santiago's (humankind's) modest expectations are snatched from his grasp.

DON QUIXOTE DE LA MANCHA

by
Miguel de Cervantes
(1547 - 1616)

Type of work: Symbolic Spanish novel

Setting: Spain; seventeenth century

Principal characters:
> *Don Quixote (Alonso Quejana)*, a retired country scholar turned knight-errant
> *Sancho Panza*, a rustic barber who becomes Don Quixote's squire
> *Dulcinea del Toboso (Aldonza Lorenzo)*, a village girl

Story Overview:

Alonso Quejana was an ordinary Spanish country gentlemen, except in one particular: he was addicted to books of chivalry. He spent every moment engrossed in thick, meandering tomes filled with tales of knights and squires, magicians and giants, and beautiful ladies.

At last, he began to sell parts of his estate in order to buy even more books. Devoting whole days to reading them, Quejana allowed the estate to fall into neglect. Still he paid no notice, and continued to immerse himself in his romantic stories "until, finally, from so little sleeping and so much reading, his brain dried up and he went completely out of his mind."

And so, the poor man who had read so much about great knights of the past now came upon the idea of becoming a knight himself. He poked around his house and found a moldering suit of armor left by his great-grandfather, polished it up, and put it on. Other odd knickknacks, including a helmet visor hastily made of cardboard, added just the "right" touches to his armor; and though his attire looked ridiculous, Quejana imaged it to be the finest in the world.

Since every good knight needed a horse, Quejana went to his stables, where he found only his dilapidated old nag, its hide blemished and its hooves full of cracks. But fancying it a healthy, noble steed, he renamed it "Rocinante," for "superlative Nag."

A knight, as well as his mount, ought to have a dignified, sonorous name. And so, Alonso Quejana determined henceforth to be known as Don Quixote de la Mancha, after his native village.

Finally, before roaming the world to right wrongs, Don Quixote chose his lady-love – a buxom country girl, Aldonza Lorenzo, famous for her skill at salting pork; and upon her he bestowed the title of Dulcinea del Toboso.

Decked out in his clattering armor and dreaming of fame, the Don wasted no time in mounting Rocinante and setting out in search of adventure. Early in his travels he happened upon an inn, which he imagined to be an enchanted castle. During his stay there, he persuaded the bewildered innkeeper to officially dub him a knight.

Meanwhile, back at Quixote's home, two of the townsmen had learned of their friend's strange departure. Blaming his foolishness on the books of chivalry, they conducted a rollicking inquisition, ordering dozens of the books to be burned. Then these men decided that they would pursue Quejana, bring him back to the village, and cure him of his madness.

Quixote, by this time, had already run into his first adventure: freeing a young boy from a flogging by his master. Later, he challenged a party of puzzled travelers, engaging them in battle; but Rocinante tripped, sending Don Quixote to the ground. The travelers seized him and promptly beat him senseless. Quixote then returned home long enough to cajole a rotund, unrefined barber, Sancho Panza, into accompanying him as his squire.

With Sancho in tow on Dapple, a small ass, the duo fell into outrageous undertakings, usually springing from Don Quixote's hallucinations. On the plains of La Mancha the pair spotted a cluster of huge windmills. Quixote instantly declared them to be giants, and, despite Sancho's protests, charged on them with lowered lance. The great arms of a windmill caught the knight and his steed and sent them both rolling. Quixote blamed the disaster on the work of a magician, who must have changed the giants into windmills "in order to deprive me of the glory of overcoming them."

Occasionally, though, the deluded Quixote came off the victor, as when he heroically broke up a band of innocent Biscayan travelers. He continually mistook the most common sights for exotic vistas. Once he insisted that a far-off herd of sheep was, in reality, an evil army, and launched an attack on the poor animals. This noble intervention only brought a volley of rocks from the angry shepherds whose sheep had been scattered. The knight also charged a funeral procession (claiming that the pallbearers were devils carrying away a princess), forced himself to undergo a solitary penance in the mountains, and mistook a common barber's basin for the magical Helmet of Mambrino. Knight and squire crossed paths with a variety of rural characters – goatherds, galley slaves, innkeepers, and others – all of whom had rambling stories to tell. Meeting such people, Don

Quixote inevitably embarked on long-winded, fantastic dissertations, which his listeners found either hilarious or annoying. Amid these blunders and misadventures, poor Sancho tried in vain to deal out a little common sense to his headstrong master.

But alas, Quixote's valiant exploits were soon to end. His two friends had located him and had enlisted the services of a young girl to pose as a damsel in distress to lure Don Quixote into their hands. The old knight, hungry and cold, was easily deceived; he was captured, placed in a cage, and hauled towards his village home. Along the way, his captors coaxed him to give up his preoccupation with chivalry, spelling out to him that the stories of knights were nothing but fanciful and vain fiction. "Do you mean to tell me they are but lies?" Quixote stormed in disbelief.

Arriving home, though welcomed by the villagers, Quejana could not be cured of his fantasies. He was, in fact, Don Quixote the knight. He remained tied up in bed most of the time, scheming his escape to resume his wanderings.

Sancho, for his part, found himself assailed by his enraged wife. How could he have spent so much time away and then come home not a penny richer than before? Following Don Quixote's example, Sancho calmed her by insisting that he would one day, as a reward for his brave exploits, be made governor of an island and become immensely rich.

Don Quixote and Sancho one day learned from a student that a best-selling book had already been written about their deeds. Thus encouraged, the knight and his squire set out again, and encountered scores of new adventures as violent and as absurd the first. Among the puppet-masters, apes, and other masquerading knights, they met a certain duke and duchess, who received the pair into their castle. Amused by this buffoon, they pretended to believe Quixote was a real knight, while at the same time eagerly dispatching the credulous knight on a series of wild escapades.

With Don Quixote away on one such errand, the duke and duchess fulfilled Sancho's dream of becoming a governor by granting him jurisdiction over a whole town. His governorship served the royalty with a good number of comic scenes.

Meanwhile, Don Quixote had suffered a humiliating defeat at the hands of a knight who had been so bold as to state that Dulcinea del Toboso was not the most beautiful of women. In consequence, the Don was forced to renounce his knighthood.

When he and faithful Sancho turned homeward a second time, the townspeople once more greeted them as returning heroes. But Don Quixote soon fell ill, and a physician's visit revealed that he was dying.

Neighbors waited at his death-bed as Don Quixote slept for long stretches of time. When he finally awoke, however, all were surprised to find that his mind had somehow cleared; his insanity had vanished. In stirring language, Don Quixote renounced his books of chivalry, confessing "how foolish I was and the danger I courted in reading them; but I am in my right sense now and I abominate them." Then, in a pathetic moment, he begged forgiveness of Sancho for the delusions he had inspired. Sancho beseeched his master not to die and encouraged him by reminding him of Dulcinea. But Don Quixote no longer believed in the fantasy, and insisted, "I was mad and now I am sane; I was Don Quixote de la Mancha, and now I am, as I have said, Alonso Quejana the Good." After dictating a will, he died.

The novel's closing lines sadly denounce the dreams of Don Quixote: " . . . Those false and nonsensical stories . . . are already tottering and without a doubt are doomed to fall."

Commentary:

It is surprising that *Don Quixote* should have come to be regarded as one of the greatest novels of all time, since Cervantes originally intended it to be little more than a hasty parody of the sort of popular romantic book of chivalry of his time – and a quick money-maker. The book did make money, too: it became a best-seller throughout Europe.

Over the years, the general interpretation of the novel has almost reversed. It is now regarded, not as crude, slapstick humor, but rather, as a warm, human tale, depicting the conflict between noble idealism and brute, unfeeling practicality. The foolish knight, once seen as the butt of all the other characters' jokes, is now perceived as a symbol of noble though impractical idealism, and has given the adjective "quixotic" to the English language.

In any case, it is hard not to sympathize with Don Quixote, despite his misconceptions. His devotion to high ideals in a world filled with scheming and base men is admirable. In fact, Quixote sometimes seems to be the only sane man in an insane society. Certainly he wins the reader over with his sincerity.

Sancho, too, despite his coarseness, is endearingly innocent. Bit by bit he becomes more and more like his master, until, by the end of the novel, he has become almost an heir to Don Quixote's purity and idealism.

The book is so full of events, meanderings, digressions, legends, conversations, and adventures, that a patient reader will never find his interest exhausted.

PEER GYNT

by
Henrik Ibsen
(1828 - 1906)

Type of work: Poetic drama

Setting: Norway, Morocco and Egypt; nineteenth century

Principal characters:
Peer Gynt, a non-heroic Norwegian farm boy
Aase, his mother
Solveig, his faithful love
The Troll King
The Button Molder, a "judge" of humanity

Story Overview:

"Peer, you're lying!" cried Aase to her son – and he was lying. He had been weaving a fantastic tale of a ride he'd taken on a runaway reindeer when Aase realized that the story was one she had heard as a young woman. She berated Peer and wept. Aase had hoped that her son would win the heart of pretty Ingrid Hegstad, a local farm girl. However, Peer hadn't shown much interest in Ingrid – until he discovered that her wedding was to take place that very evening; it was only then that he resolved to attend the marriage and talk the girl's father into letting him take the place of the intended bridegroom. When his mother protested, he seized her, placed her on the millhouse roof, and went merrily off, leaving her screaming. Rescued by neighbors, Aase, fearing trouble, followed after him.

At the wedding, Peer was shunned by all except a young girl named Solveig, with whom he danced during the festivities. Her innocence attracted him. But sadly, as the celebration wore on, Peer, now quite drunk, kidnapped the bride, shamed her, and then abandoned her. This brought down the wrath of the entire community on his head, but in characteristic fashion, Peer simply ran away into the forest.

Meanwhile, Aase managed to convince Solveig and her family that her son was in grave danger, and Christian duty dictated that they look for him. During the search, Aase spoke about her son:

The lout! Why the devil has to tease him?/ . . . Oh, we've had to stick close in misery/ Because, you know, my man – he drank/ . . . And we – well, we took to fairy tales/ Of princes and trolls and strange animals/ Stolen brides too. But who'd have thought/ Those infernal stories would be in him yet?

Hearing Aase's longings for Peer, Solveig began to both pity and love the scamp.

Peer continued to blunder and bluster about, spending one riotous night with three farm girls, and the next with the Troll King's daughter. While visiting there, Peer was delighted to find that if he married the troll-girl he could obtain quite a dowry. But his prospective father-in-law warned that there was quite a difference between a troll and a man:

Among men, under the shining sky/ They say: "Man, to yourself be true!" while here, under our mountain roof/ We say: "Troll, to yourself be – enough!"

Only when Peer found that if he stayed with the trolls he could "never die decently as a human" nor "go home the way the book says," did he give up the idea of becoming one of them. Indignantly, the King then turned the troll-children on him, and they would have killed him except, as he pleaded, "Help, Mother, I'll die!" immediately church bells rang, the children fled shrieking, and the troll hall collapsed and vanished.

After a frustrating encounter with The Great Boyg, an enigmatic troll monster, Peer fled into the high mountains and built a hut. It was winter when Solveig appeared, she having left her family to be with him. Peer was overjoyed. It seemed that now, with a princess at his side, his adventures might end as a genuine fairy tale. But after he hoisted his ax and started off to chop roots for a fire, Peer was accosted by an old woman and her "ugly brat" of a child. He soon discovered the woman to be the troll princess he had previously deserted – and the child was his own son! At last Peer's conscience roused itself enough to realize that his many sins were what stood between him and his love of faithful Solveig. "Be patient, my sweet . . . you must wait," Peer said to her as he entered the forest. "Yes, I'll wait!" Solveig called back to him.

Peer felt compelled to leave the country in order to avoid being punished for his crimes. Before departing, however, he stopped to say good-bye to his mother. He found that the troubles he had caused his mother had broken the poor woman – she was dying. The son tenderly tucked Aase into her bed, just as she had always done to him.

After journeying far from home, Peer made his fortune in the American slave-trade and by selling idols in China. In Morocco, now middle-aged, he lost most of his money to other unscrupulous businessmen, and found himself wandering alone in a desert, where he stumbled on an emperor's horse, clothing, jewels, and sword, all of which had been forsaken by frightened thieves. With these treasures, he pawned himself off as an Arab sheik-prophet and rounded up a company of dancing girls for his harem. One girl, the main dancer, Anitra, soon became his special protege. But she was not taken in by his charade and finally tricked him and galloped off with his mount and money alike.

Recognizing that he had been duped by the clever girl, Peer was at first solemn and thoughtful; but soon he burst out laughing at his foolishness. He had had his fun, he reasoned, but like a hen often does, he ended up "by getting plucked." Still, he was glad he'd kept a little money set aside – some in his pocket, some in America. "In short, I'm on top of the situation," he gloated. "Now what should I choose? . . . Choice marks the Master from the fool." He elected to become a scholar of history and travel the world as "the man, Peer Gynt,/ Known as the Emperor of Human Life."

Peer's planless plan next took him to Egypt, where he vainly sought to unravel the riddle and meaning of his wasted life. In time, he ended up in an insane asylum, and one might have assumed he would die there; but with amazing resilience he reappeared, this time as an old, hardened man on board a ship off the coast of Norway. The ship was caught in a storm and sank, but Peer surfaced, clinging to a small capsized boat. The ship's cook also emerged from the dark water on the other side of the boat. Peer ordered him to let go; the craft simply couldn't hold them both. "Spare me, please!" begged the cook. "Think of my children, what they'll lose!" But Peer, true to his baser nature, responded, "I'm more in need of life than you;/ I haven't had children up till now." With that, he grabbed the cook by the hair, jerked him from the boat and thrust him out to sea.

Peer managed to reach shore and make his way toward his boyhood village. There, he discovered that Ingrid, his kidnapped bride of long ago, had died. Hearing this, the old man finally decided to go home and settle down.

At a crossroads along the way, Peer met a Button Molder, whose office it was to melt down the souls ready for death; and more particularly, those whose sins hadn't been great enough to qualify them for Hell but who couldn't go to Heaven either. Peer was on the Button Molder's list. The very thing Peer had prided himself on all his life – being himself – was "just what you've never been," the Button Molder contended. He then began his preparations to melt Peer down. Frantically, Peer concluded that he'd rather go to Hell than become a non-entity boiling in a vat, and pleaded for time to find witnesses to testify how wicked his life had been. He would show he was worthy of Hell.

But Peer found that none of his former foes would testify against him. And, at the next crossroads Peer again tried desperately to convince the Button Molder that his kidnapping, his slave-trading, his cheating and lying, his drowning of another to save his own life – these surely had qualified him for Hell! "Mere trifles!" declared the Button Molder, waving his ladle.

At last Peer was sufficiently humbled to ask, "What is it 'to be yourself,' in truth?" The Button Molder seized Peer and condemned his actions. "Put your house in order!" he shouted. Peer managed to twist free and race from the woods. As he stepped out into a clearing, suddenly he spied his former hut. There before him was Solveig, stepping out of the doorway, on her way to church. Old Peer hobbled toward her in desperation, threw himself down at her feet, and called on her to save him by repeating his many sins to the Button Molder.

But instead Solveig praised God for Peer's return and told him he'd sinned in nothing. "So then I'm lost!" Peer cried. "Lost unless you can solve a riddle!" he said, again turning to his wife. "Where have I been myself, whole and true?/ Where have I been, with God's mark on my brow?" Solveig answered without hesitating: "In my faith, in my hope, and in my love." Stunned by her answer, Peer moaned, " . . . My wife! You innocent woman!/ O, hide me, hide me within!" He clung to her, his face in her lap; and a long, peaceful silence followed until the sun rose over them. Then the Button Molder's voice came again from behind the hut: "We'll meet at the final crossroads, Peer;/ And then we'll see I won't say more." Solveig sang softly as she cradled her sobbing husband:

 . . . The boy has lain so near to my heart/ His whole life's day. Now he's tired out. Sleep, my dear . . . I'll watch over thee!

Commentary:

For those whose only acquaintance with *Peer Gynt* is Edvard Grieg's hauntingly beautiful opera music, Ibsen's play may come as a shock, especially if one realizes it was written in 1867 and presented to a European audience steeped in Victorianism.

The drama is a satire on Man. Peer is one of modern drama's first anti-heroes, and Ibsen never tires of bringing out yet another flaw in his character. Starting out as a highly imaginative, irresponsible youth, Peer degenerates into a self-seeking opportunist. However, it is through his conversations – in which he often misquotes proverbs or scripture to justify his actions – that his hypocrisy begins to appear as uncomfortably symbolic of modern man. The underlying questions of the play are religious questions: What is man expected to do with his life? What sort of choices is he free to make?

Early on, Ibsen defines the two poles of choice: Either develop yourself as a true man or become a Troll. Even with this advice, Peer moves steadily away from humanity, and never does quite understand life's riddle. It is only near the end of the play, when Peer questions the Button Molder for the second time, that his riddle is answered:

To be yourself is to slay yourself./ But on you, that answer's sure to fail;/ So let's say: To make your life evolve/ From the Master's meaning to the last detail.

Peer Gynt's action, flavor, atmosphere, and characters are lifted from Norwegian folklore to function as shadows and types for Ibsen's satirical view of the human condition. The trolls typify all that is base and ugly in human nature, while Solveig represents an allegorical human figure of faith and loyalty. Even Peer, acting the scoundrel or fool, is not devoid of a certain charm, in part due to his eternal optimism and his often manipulative yet authentic congeniality. Perhaps in mirroring both the good and bad of modern man, Peer mirrors what we may all recognize in ourselves.

THE MALTESE FALCON

by
Dashiell Hammett
(1894 - 1961)

Type of work: Detective mystery novel

Setting: San Francisco; 1920's

Principal Characters:

> *Sam Spade*, a young hard-boiled detective
> *Miles Archer*, Spade's older partner
> *Brigid O'Shaughnessy*, a beautiful young
> woman (alias Miss Wonderly)
> *Joel Cairo*, an effeminate gangster-type
> *Casper Gutman*, a rotund, older man
> *Iva Archer*, Archer's wife and Spade's mistress

Story Overview:

Effie Perine, secretary to private detective Sam Spade, opened his door to announce that a client, Miss Wonderly, was there to see him. A stunning young woman entered and shyly took a seat. She stammered and bit her lip as she tried to relate her story. Finally the detective assured her it would be best to begin at the beginning. Miss Wonderly said that she was concerned for her seventeen-year-old sister, who had run off with an older man named Thursby. She had arranged a meeting with Thursby for that evening, and now wanted to hire a detective to follow him from the meeting – straight to her sister, she hoped.

Spade gave his partner, Miles Archer, the details of Miss Wonderly's case. She paid them two hundred dollars, and left with the agreement that Archer would tail Thursby that evening.

That night Spade was awakened by a phone call: Archer had been murdered. Spade rushed to the scene. According to the police, Archer was shot with a British-made Webley revolver. Spade phoned his secretary and asked her to call Iva, his partner's wife, to break the bad news. Then he returned to his apartment.

Sam had just "drunk his third glass of Bicardi and was lighting his fifth cigarette" when the doorbell rang. It was the police; Lieutenants Dundy and Polhaus wanted to question Sam about the death of yet another man. Thursby, it turned out, had been shot outside his hotel shortly after Spade left the Archer murder scene. Considering the circumstances of Archer's death, the police reasoned Spade must have shot Thursby out of revenge. However, Spade refused to give the cops any information about the case.

The next morning the detective had a visitor waiting for him at his office. Effie had tried to keep Iva Archer away, but she had come anyway. Sam was unhappy to see Iva, but still he kissed her. Then Iva asked him point-blank if he had shot her husband so he could marry her. Spade laughed and shook his head.

After Iva had left, Spade took a taxi to the hotel where Miss Wonderly was staying, only to find that she had mysteriously checked out, leaving no forwarding address. Back at the office, Effie informed her boss that Miss Wonderly had called to ask him to meet her at a new hotel.

Arriving at the hotel, "Miss Wonderly" confessed that her real name was Brigid O'Shaughnessy and that her story the day before was just that – "all a story." Spade also admitted that neither he nor Archer had bought her tale, but had indeed "believed the two hundred dollars." Brigid explained that she could not reveal the complete story of why Spade had been hired, but did say that she had earlier met Thursby in Hong Kong and feared that he would betray her. Then she announced that Thursby had been Archer's killer; he had shot Archer with the Webley he kept in his overcoat. Sam agreed to continue working on the case.

When Spade returned to his office, a gangster, Joel Cairo, was waiting to ask about the connection between the two murders. He confessed his interest was more than mere curiosity; it seemed that Cairo was searching for a missing black metallic bird – a falcon – and that, in some way, Thursby had been connected with the falcon's disappearance. Cairo was prepared to pay five thousand dollars for the statuette's return. Spade told him that when he could get his hands on the bird, Cairo would be contacted.

That evening, as Spade left his apartment to meet Brigid, he noticed a young punk following him. Spade quickly lost the tail and went to Brigid's hotel. Brigid became visibly upset on hearing of Cairo and the money he had offered for the "bird"; she believed that Spade intended to double-cross her, and before she would tell him anything more than what he already knew, she would have to speak with Cairo herself. They decided to meet with the two-bit thug later that night at Sam's apartment.

There, Brigid admitted that though she had no idea why the falcon was so important, she did know where it was hidden. But they would have to wait a week before she could get hold of it. Cairo and Brigid had become acquainted in Constantinople, where she and Thursby had stolen the bird ... At this point, the doorbell rang. It was Dundy and Polhaus again, this time to inform Spade that they knew he had been having an affair with Iva Archer and that this was his probable motive for killing his partner. As they were about to leave, they suddenly heard Cairo yell for help from Spade's apartment. When the cops rushed in and found Cairo holding a gun on Brigid, they naturally demanded to know what was going on. Spade offered them a contrived story about this all being a put-on to make them look foolish. The cops reluctantly left, obviously not falling for Spade's explanation.

Early the next morning, Spade received a visit from a Mr. Gutman. Gutman explained his position: He had hired Thursby and Brigid to procure the falcon's image for him, but instead they had fled with it to Hong Kong. The ornament, known as the "Maltese Falcon," had been fashioned by the Knights of Rhodes on Malta and sent as a tribute to King Charles of Spain. The "glorious golden falcon encrusted . . . with the finest jewels" had shifted hands for centuries and then disappeared – not to resurface until 1921, when a Greek dealer discovered it in an obscure shop. He had covered the falcon with black enamel to keep its value hidden. Unfortunately, the dealer was later murdered and the bird taken; but Gutman had traced the falcon to Constantinople and was on the verge of actually possessing it when Thursby and Brigid turned greedy. To retrieve the treasure, he now offered Spade fifty thousand dollars. The "bird" was obviously worth an enormous fortune.

Though Spade did not know where the falcon was, he did know that Brigid knew. But now Brigid turned up missing. Spade entered and searched her apartment for clues leading to the bird and found a newspaper, folded along the page announcing incoming ships. The falcon, he deduced, must be on the *La Paloma*, the one vessel sailing in from Hong Kong that day. Racing to the ship, Spade saw neither Brigid nor the ship's captain. They had departed – along with Cairo, Gutman, and Gutman's hired-gun, the one who had been tailing Sam for some time.

Later, as Detective Spade related these facts to Effie, a huge man barged into his office, held a package out to Sam, and keeled over, dead. Sam opened the package. The Maltese Falcon was inside. He guessed that the dead man was the *La Paloma's* captain; he also guessed that he would have some visitors soon. He quickly hid the statue away.

That night as Spade strolled up to his apartment, Brigid was there by the door to meet him. Inside waited Gutman, Cairo and the hired-gun. They demanded the falcon. Spade claimed, lying through his teeth, that they would have to wait until morning before he could get to the bird – and that the ever more valuable item would now cost them ten thousand dollars.

As the night wore on, Spade suggested that Gutman turn over the punk hired-gun to the cops: "Somebody had to take the fall for those murders." Gutman hesitated at first, but Spade warned he would not turn over the falcon unless they could produce a "fall guy." Gutman finally consented to make his sidekick the scapegoat, and before the lightweight could retaliate, Sam disarmed him and knocked him cold.

Morning came, and Spade, after a brief absence, finally brought out the prized falcon, collecting from Gutman ten one-thousand dollar bills. To make sure the falcon was genuine, Gutman scratched away some of the enamel; it proved to be a lead fake. He had been tricked! Gutman hurriedly reclaimed the money he had brought and, followed by the other men, scurried out of the apartment.

Spade picked up the phone and called the police, informing them that he had nabbed his partner's killer. This done, he turned to Brigid, who had stayed behind, and, breaking into a grin, told her that she was the one he was going to turn in for Archer's murder, not the punk still spread-eagle on the floor. Sam had figured out that Brigid, in a plan to frame Thursby, had drawn Archer into the alleyway and killed him with Thursby's weapon. What had tipped him off? Archer's trench coat was still buttoned when he was killed. It was clear to Sam that he had felt no danger before he was shot; he trusted the sensual woman and had taken no thought to ready his gun.

Brigid pleaded with Sam to let her go. She even tried to seduce him. But Sam sneered, "I won't play the sap for you." He had to clear himself from guilt, and no woman would stand in his way. His smile widened as he gazed at the ravishing woman. "If they hang you, I'll always remember you," he said.

Commentary:

The Maltese Falcon was written from experience – Dashiell Hammett spent several years as a Pinkerton detective. He was a superlative mystery writer. With this book, he ushered in a whole new genre of classical crime fiction. Colored with keen observations of the corruptions and violence permeating American life, Hammett's economical, suspenseful, hard-boiled style is still a model for today's typical detective novel.

Andre' Gide summarizes The Maltese Falcon's plot as one "in which every character is trying to deceive all the others and in which the truth slowly becomes visible through the haze of deception." Filled with slang, violence, sex, and misogyny, the novel is also touched with incredible pathos and with stark glimpses into the street's sleazier – and lonelier – side.

CALL OF THE WILD

by
Jack London
(1876 - 1916)

Type of work: Adventure novel

Setting: Northland (Alaska); the goldrush of the 1890's

Principal characters:
    Buck, a large, intelligent and well-bred dog
    Spitz, a cruel lead sled dog
    John Thornton, Buck's Northland master

Story Overview:

Buck, a huge four-year-old Scottish Shepherd-Saint Bernard cross-breed, lived a life of ease at Judge Miller's Santa Clara Valley estate. As the judge's loyal companion, working with his sons, and guarding his grandchildren, Buck ruled over all things – humans included. Combining his mother's intelligence with the size and strength of his father, Buck became the undisputed leader of all the dogs on the estate.

At this time, gold had been found in Alaska, and thousands of men were rushing to the Northland. They wanted dogs, dogs like Buck. One night, Manuel, the estate's gardener, who felt he was not earning enough to support both his family and his gambling habits, took Buck for a walk to the railroad station. There, money was exchanged, a rope was placed around Buck's neck, and his life in the civilized world had come to an end.

For two days and two nights Buck traveled northward in a baggage carrier. Caged, with no food or water, his placid disposition changed to that of a raging fiend. In Seattle, Buck was met by a man in a red sweater, holding a club. As Buck came charging out of the opened crate the man cruelly beat him into submission. Buck had learned his first lesson: he stood no chance against a man with a club.

Buck, along with other dogs, was purchased by Francois and Perrault, dispatchers for the Canadian government, and transported by ship to Alaska. Buck soon came to respect his French-Canadian masters. But life among the dogs was savage; no law existed but that of fang and force.

The first day, Buck looked on as one of his shipmates, downed in a fight, was savagely killed by the anxious pack of dogs. Thus he learned that in the event of a fight, he must always stay on his feet. Spitz, the sly-eyed and powerful lead dog of the sled team, took pleasure in these disputes. Dogs being slashed to ribbons seemed to amuse Spitz, making Buck hate him from the beginning.

Buck came to know his teammates: which dogs were approachable, and which to leave alone. He learned the necessary skills of a sled dog, which included digging under the snow at night for warmth, surviving on far less food than he was used to, stealing food from other dogs, and the knack for pulling a load. His body became hardened. And, over time, those instincts once possessed by his ancient ancestors sprang to life within him. The domesticated generations' softness fell from Buck, and the wilderness wolf emerged.

As time passed, Buck coveted the position of lead dog. He found that his size and cunning allowed him to come between Spitz and the shirkers, those that the cruel dog would have otherwise punished. With Buck protecting them, the pack lost its fear of Spitz, and discipline broke down. The dogs no longer worked as a team. Francois and Perrault became furious with the lack of order and the loss of time spent separating skirmishing animals.

One night Buck saw his chance, and a death-fight began. Spitz was a practiced fighter who felt a bitter rage toward Buck, but as the battle continued, Spitz slowly lost ground. With a final rush, Buck knocked his enemy to the snow and the eager pack moved in for the kill.

Though his masters beat him severely, Buck refused to be harnessed until he was given the lead position. He willingly accepted the demands of supremacy, and where judgement, quick-thinking and action were required, showed himself superior to all. With Buck in the lead, the team picked up and became as one, moving smoothly over the snow on a record run from Dawson to Skaguay. Buck's name soon became legendary.

In Skaguay, Francois and Perrault received orders to relinquish the team to a Scotch half-breed, and after only three days rest the team was back in the traces and headed for Dawson. It was a strenuous trip. The once-proud, confident dogs arrived short of weight, in poor condition and needing at least ten days to recuperate. Nonetheless, only two days later they were again out on the trail headed back to Skaguay. A heavier sled combined with bad weather made the going slow. At night, Buck would lie near the fire and dream of Judge Miller's big house, the great fight with Spitz, and his hunter ancestors. A wildness, long held in check, began to surface anew; he seemed to hear the far-away cries of a wolf.

The team arrived at Skaguay thirty days later, the dogs in wretched condition. In this sad, exhausted state, the team was sold to Hal, Charles and Mercedes. These two men and one woman were recent arrivals from the States, intent on getting rich in the Northland. As the team struck out, Buck could sense that the humans were undependable and knew nothing of wilderness travel. They journeyed at half speed, as if on an "extended social camping trip," and the food was quickly depleted. Dogs gradually died of starvation. Midway to Dawson only five of fourteen remained. What's more, the humans argued continually amongst themselves and Mercedes refused to walk, making the few dogs drag her extra 120-pound weight. The valiant animals often stumbled under the load; only the sting of the whip could bring them to their feet to strain for another mile.

. . . Through it all, Buck staggered along at the head of the team as in a nightmare. He pulled when he could; when he could no longer pull, he fell down and remained down till blows from whip or club drove him to his feet again. All the stiffness had gone out of his beautiful furry coat. The hair hung down, limp and draggled, or matted with dried blood where Hal's club had bruised him. His muscles had wasted away . . . each rib and every bone in his frame were outlined cleanly through the loose hide that was wrinkled in folds of emptiness. It was heartbreaking, only Buck's heart was unbreakable . . .

At last the team crept into John Thornton's camp at the mouth of White River. It was here that Buck refused to get up. He was dying, and sensed disaster close at hand. Despite the blows from Hal, Buck would not move. Suddenly, John Thornton jumped in and, after a brief scuffle, stopped Hal's brutality. He cut Buck from the traces and ordered the group to leave. Together, Buck and John watched as the team and sled crawled onto the ice-covered river. A quarter of a mile out the ice gave way, and the entire assembly disappeared into the frigid water. Thornton had saved Buck's life.

After traveling 3,000 miles, a rest was what Buck needed. As John waited for his partners by the White River, little by little Buck won back his strength. He romped through his convalescence and into a new existence. Not only respect, but a feeling of love grew between dog and master. One time, John was swept away by a river and Buck saved him, risking his own life. On another occasion, Buck won a bet of $1,600 dollars for John and his partners by breaking a sled carrying 1,000 pounds of flour out of the ice and pulling it a given distance. Offered great sums of money for his famous sled dog, John only replied, " . . . No sir. You can go to hell, sir . . . "

The group was finally able to pay off old debts and travel east into mining country. John and his friends were experienced trailmen. Months rolled by. Spring came, and they found a broad valley where the gold showed like yellow butter across the bottom of the washing pan. Here, John and his partners settled down and began piling up bags of gold.

In these warm, leisurely months, Buck's dreams turned more vivid. He began to feel ever more strongly the call of the wild. For days he would leave the camp, but his love for John always brought him back. But, over time, the blood-longing became stronger than ever.

He was a killer, a thing that preyed . . . unaided, alone, by virtue of his own strength and prowess, surviving triumphantly in a hostile environment where only the strong survived.

As the fall of the year arrived, Buck came across a herd of moose. The chief bull was well over six feet tall and as formidable a quarry as even Buck could desire. For five days he stalked the moose until he pulled the exhausted animal down. For another day and night Buck rested and feasted upon his kill; then he turned back to John and the camp.

Nearing camp, Buck paused, sensing danger. Arriving on the outskirts, he was stunned to find that the Yeehats had attacked the site; men and animals were dead and the tribe was performing a victory dance. The Yeehats heard a strange noise and suddenly a white monster raged amongst them, a "fiend incarnate," killing and destroying with a crazed fury and scattering the remaining braves.

Afterward, Buck returned to camp and mourned his loss. John Thornton was dead – and his passing left inside of Buck a huge, aching void.

The last vestige of civilization stripped from him, Buck was now a wild animal. He joined with his wild brothers in the wolf pack and became their leader. Even now, the Yeehats often speak of an evil Ghost-dog that inhabits the land, running at the head of the pack, killing any man it comes across. They tell the story of how the phantom selected a certain valley for an abiding place. All still bypass that valley.

Buck occasionally returns, alone, to the gold-speckled river, where he reflects on times past, howls long and mournfully, then steals back into the forest shadows.

Commentary:

Jack London led a life crammed with violence and adventure, both of which were transferred into his writing. He had virtually no childhood, starting work at age ten. At fifteen he became a hobo; at sixteen, an oyster pirate and longshoreman. Joining the Alaskan gold rush at nineteen, London hiked across the United States and Canada to the Klondike. He found no gold, but later used some of his Northland experiences to draft *The Call of the Wild.*

In Buck, London endows all of the cunning and savagery that he feels lurks not only in animals, but in human beings as well. Buck's tranformation into a ferocious animal is London's attempt to argue his "survival of the fittest" philosophy; the potential primitive beast he feels lies within each individual. However, London's great love for animals and nature inspired him to also write of the loyalty, affection, and excitement experienced by Buck. This adventuresome, emotion-packed novel seems to capture all of these qualities in a powerful way.

THE GREAT GATSBY

by
F. Scott Fitzgerald
(1896 - 1940)

Type of work: Human drama

Setting: New York City and Long Island; 1922

Principal characters:

> *Nick Carraway*, a young bond salesman from the midwest, and the story's narrator
>
> *Jay Gatsby*, a rich, young racketeer
>
> *Tom Buchanan*, a wealthy playboy
>
> *Daisy Buchanan*, his beautiful wife, and Nick's cousin
>
> *Jordan Baker*, an attractive pro golfer, and the Buchanan's friend
>
> *George Wilson*, a gas station owner
>
> *Myrtle Wilson*, his wife and Tom Buchanan's mistress

Story Overview:

After his return from the "Teutonic migration known as the Great War," Nick Carraway felt too restless to work selling hardware in his Midwestern home town. He moved east to New York and entered the "bond business." Settling on the low-budget side of Long Island in West Egg, Nick rented a bungalow next door to a mysterious, wealthy man-about-town known as Gatsby.

Shortly after arriving in New York, Nick was invited to dinner at the house of Tom and Daisy Buchanan on the more-fashionable side of Long Island. Nick did not know either Tom or Daisy very well, but he was Daisy's second cousin and had attended Yale with Tom. Tom led Nick into a back room of the Buchanan house, where they found Daisy talking with her friend Jordan Baker, a haughty yet beautiful young woman who appeared to be "balancing something on her chin." By the time dinner was served on the porch, some untold tension was obviously building between Tom and Daisy, which climaxed after Tom left to answer a phone call. When he did not return, Daisy stomped inside to see what was keeping her husband. Jordan hushed Nick before he could speak – she wanted to eavesdrop on the Buchanans' muffled argument. Apparently Tom had met "some woman in New York ..."

When Nick arrived at his apartment that evening, he saw the figure of the reclusive Mr. Gatsby himself, who had "come out to determine what share was his of [the] local heavens." Nick almost called out to introduce himself to his neighbor, but something in Gatsby's manner told Nick that he was content just then to be alone. From what Nick could see, Gatsby was staring towards the city at a "single green light, minute and far away."

A couple of days later, Tom invited Nick to meet his mistress. He led Nick off the commuter train into a sleazy, unkempt area filled with garbage heaps. From there, they made their way to a second-rate gas station owned by a "spiritless man" named Wilson. Under the pretext that he had a car he wanted to sell Wilson, Tom covertly arranged to meet Wilson's dowdy, plump wife, Myrtle, in New York. On the ride into the City, Myrtle, along with her sister and a few friends, sat judiciously in a train car separate from Tom's; then everyone took a taxi over to an apartment that Tom kept for his trysts with Myrtle. All that afternoon and evening the group drank whiskey and talked, while Nick tried unsuccessfully to find an excuse to leave. The party finally ended in a violent argument in which Tom broke Myrtle's nose.

One of the few things Nick knew about Gatsby was that he threw lavish parties, where hundreds of people "came and went like moths among the whisperings and the champagne and the stars." Finally, Nick was invited to one of the affairs, where he again ran into Jordan, and they mingled with others in conversations about who exactly the curious Gatsby was; it seemed none of the guests had even had a close view of their elusive host. Rumors placed him as the Kaiser's son, or as a German spy during the War, or maybe a fugitive killer.

As the party wore on, Nick and Jordan found themselves sitting at a table with a rowdy, drunken girl and a man about Nick's age. The two men began discussing their respective military service. Then Nick's new acquaintance introduced himself: he was Jay Gatsby.

Much further into the evening, Jordan and Gatsby met in private to discuss something that Jordan said she was pledged not to reveal to anyone, not even Nick, until the right time.

Weeks – and several parties – later, Gatsby arranged for Nick to have tea with Jordan, where she divulged the details of her conversation with Gatsby on the night of the party: It seemed that Gatsby and Daisy Buchanan had been well acquainted before the War. Gatsby at that time was a young lieutenant waiting to go to the front, and Daisy was "just eighteen . . . by far the most popular of all the young girls in Louisville." They had fallen in love. Unfortunately, Gatsby did not have the financial means to marry a girl of Daisy's class. When he was sent overseas, Daisy had decided that she could not wait, and married Tom Buchanan instead. Jordan then told Nick that Gatsby, still in love with Daisy, wanted him to invite Daisy to his place some afternoon and then let Gatsby "conveniently" drop in. Nick agreed to set things up.

And so, on a rainy afternoon, Gatsby and Daisy were reunited. After some nervous chitchat, Gatsby asked Daisy, along with Nick, to come next-door and see his place. As they moved from room to room and into the mansion's well-kept gardens and pool area, Gatsby's gaze was continually on Daisy. Finally, as dusk was settling, Gatsby pointed out to Daisy that "if it wasn't for the mist, we could see your home across the bay . . . . You always have a green light that burns all night."

The affair between Gatsby and Daisy went on for weeks, until one morning Gatsby unexpectedly asked Nick to lunch with him at Daisy's the following day.

The weather was broiling hot as Nick entered the Buchanan house. Gatsby, Jordan, Tom and Daisy were all there, and, after some tension-filled conversation, including several subtle challenges between Tom and Gatsby, they all decided to drive to New York to escape the heat in a hotel room. Tom insisted on trading cars with Gatsby for the drive into the city, so Gatsby and Daisy took Tom's car while Tom drove with Nick and Jordan in Gatsby's new yellow roadster.

As Tom sped towards New York, he decided to spin by Wilson's gas station to torment Mr. Wilson for a few minutes. At the station, Nick noticed Myrtle peering out her second-story window:

Her eyes, wide with jealous terror, were fixed not on Tom, but on Jordan Baker, whom she took to be his wife.

Meanwhile, Wilson was relating to Tom how he suspected that his wife was involved with another man, and how the two of them would soon be moving west. Feeling slandered and confused, Tom punched the gas pedal and raced off toward the city.

There is no confusion like the confusion of a simple mind, and as we drove away Tom was feeling the hot whips of panic. His wife and his mistress, until an hour ago secure and inviolate, were slipping precipitately from his control.

Arriving in New York, Tom's group met up with Gatsby and Daisy, and everyone retired to the Plaza Hotel to last out the heat sipping mint juleps. But soon Tom and Gatsby became embroiled in a heated argument. In anger, Gatsby roared that Daisy was in love with him now. What's more, he alleged that Daisy never did love Tom. Tom shouted that it was a lie, then turned to Daisy for acquittal. Although she wanted to side with Gatsby, she could not. "I can't say I never loved Tom . . . . It wouldn't be true," she stuttered; but then she tearfully turned to tell her husband that she was leaving him. Tom was devastated that Daisy would take up with a bootlegging, racketeering criminal.

Gatsby headed for home in his roadster with Daisy at his side; Tom, Nick and Jordan drove a few miles behind. Suddenly, Tom's group came upon the scene of an accident in front of Wilson's gas station. A woman, Myrtle Wilson, had been run over and killed; the "yellow car" that had hit her hadn't even stopped. Tom, convinced that Gatsby had struck Myrtle,

drove hurriedly on home. Tears streamed down his face. "The God damned coward!" he wimpered. "He didn't even stop his car."

After they came to the Buchanan house, Nick, deciding he'd had enough for one day, stepped out front to hail a taxi. There, concealed in the shadows, he found Gatsby, and learned about what had really happened: Daisy, angered and confused, had demanded to drive Gatsby's car home. When they had passed Wilson's gas station, Myrtle, thinking it was Tom in the car, ran into the path of the speeding roadster. Now Gatsby was there in the yard to make sure Tom didn't hurt Daisy. In time Nick convinced the shaken man to go home; Daisy would be alright.

All night George Wilson sat in a state of shock, weeping. By morning he had determined to punish the driver of the yellow car. He made his way to Tom's house. But Tom, fearing for his own life, lied, and told the distressed Wilson that Gatsby had been Myrtle's secret lover – and he was the owner of the yellow car. Crazed with grief, Wilson sped to Gatsby's estate. With the revolver he carried, he shot and killed the man as he swam in his pool. Wilson then turned the gun on himself.

Nick tried to make Gatsby's funeral a respectable affair. But nobody came; only Nick, the minister, and Mr. Gatz (Gatsby's father from Minnesota) were there – not one of Gatsby's party friends or racketeering buddies, not Daisy, not Jordan Baker. At the cemetery, an unknown man "with owl-eyed glasses" appeared. In a thick drizzle, the four of them laid the great Gatsby to rest.

. . . Owl-eyes spoke to me by the gate.
"I couldn't get to the house," he remarked.
"Neither could anybody else."
"Go on!" he started. "Why, my God! they used to go there by the hundreds."
He took off his glasses and wiped them . . . .
"The poor son-of-a-bitch," he said.

After that summer, Nick returned to his modest Midwest town, no longer in awe of the big-city lights.

Commentary:

The Great Gatsby is widely considered Fitzgerald's finest novel. In Tom and Daisy, he creates two "careless people [who] smash up things and then retreat back into their money . . . and let other people clean up the mess . . . "
Gatsby, on the other hand, is larger than life, a hopeless and hopeful "great romantic," who represents the worldly ambitions in all of us. He believes in seizing the "green light" and the dreams of youth, no matter what the cost.

Then there is Nick, who insightfully describes both the careless cruelty of the Buchanans and the high-reaching dreams of Gatsby. He chronicles the events in an honest, sometimes breathless fashion, then shovels them all into a pile – for the reader to sort out.

BEN-HUR: A TALE OF THE CHRIST

by
Lew Wallace
(1827 - 1905)

Type of work: Historical romantic fiction

Setting: Judea and Rome; during the time of Jesus Christ

Principal characters:

Judah Ben-Hur, a Jew
Ben-Hur's mother and sister, Tirzah
Messala, a Roman citizen; Judah's child
  hood friend, and later hated enemy
Arrius, a Roman commander
Simonides, an aged Hur servant
Mallach, Simonides' servant

Story Overview:

(The tale begins with an account of Jesus' humble birth, the adoration of the infant by three sages from the East, and the child's delivery from the hands of King Herod.)

Several years following Jesus' birth, Judah Ben-Hur was one day on the streets speaking to his childhood companion, Messala. Messala had grown up in Judea, but five years earlier had left to study in Rome. He had changed considerably in those years, and since his return Judah had found it difficult to speak with him. A wall had been cast up between them. Now, while Messala bragged, Judah grew more and more angry at his friend's new arrogance. Finally he erupted: "You have given me suffering today by convincing me that we can never be the friends we have been – never!" Thus they parted.

Alone in his room, Judah brooded. Although Messala's attitudes were insufferable, there was some justification to his pride. At least Messala now had a military profession; Judah had nothing. After much thought, Judah concluded that he himself would go to Rome, learn the arts of war, and return to drive the Romans out of his land. He would tell only Tirzah, his sister, of his plans.

Days later, Judah and Tirzah climbed to their rooftop to watch as the new – and much hated – Procurator of Judea, Valerius Gratus, passed with his legion on his way into the city. Jews lined the road to hurl insults at Gratus. As Judah leaned out to catch a glimpse of the Procurator, his hand accidentally displaced a loose tile, and he lunged out, trying to catch it. This act made it look as though Judah had pitched the tile like a missile – which unerringly flew to its mark. Gratus "fell from the seat as though dead."

In seconds, Roman soldiers had forced their way into the house and pinned the youth to the floor. Then Judah heard a familiar voice: "That is he!" Messala, dressed as an officer of the legion, pretended not to recognize Judah. "You have him," he sneered. "And that is his mother; yonder is his sister. You have his whole family." Judah watched as the Romans led his mother and sister away and confiscated their property.

As the soldiers moved on toward the coastal village of Nazareth, people wondered at their youthful, half-naked prisoner. When the Romans finally paused at the town well, "The prisoner sank down in the dust of the road." A young man stepped forward to offer the prisoner a drink. As the stranger laid his hand upon Judah's shoulder, Judah looked up – into "a face he never forgot." His vengeful spirit "melted under the stranger's look and became as a child's .... And so, for the first time, Judah and the son of Mary met and parted."

Three years later, Judah was an oarsman on a Roman galley commanded by the respected and able Arrius, who was leading an armada to rid the Mediterranean of pirates. As a "connoisseur of men physically," Arrius enjoyed descending below deck to watch the rowers. On this voyage, he was immensely impressed by one young man among the exhausted, emaciated slaves. The youth was tall, and "his limbs, upper and nether, were singularly perfect." Moreover, he rowed with a certain "harmony." When Arrius queried him about his background, Judah revealed that he was the son of a prince and merchant of Jerusalem, from the house of Hur. Arrius could not fathom that such a youth would attempt to assassinate a Roman official.

Presently the Roman ships overtook pirate vessels and the battle began. Ben-Hur could hear the clamor above deck and could smell the smoke of flaming arrows and "the scent of roasting human flesh." Pirates had boarded the battered ship and water was flooding the cabin. After finally escaping his chains, Ben-Hur made his way out to sea. As he swam desperately away from the turmoil of death and destruction, he paused to help a drowning Roman – Arrius.

As the two men – slave and master, Jew and Roman - awaited rescue, Arrius promised Judah, "If . . . we get well out of this peril, I will do thee such favor as becometh a Roman who hath power and opportunity to prove his gratitude." And, indeed, when the two returned from sea after being rescued by a Roman ship, Arrius adopted Ben-Hur as his own son.

Two years later, Ben-Hur returned to Judea in search of his mother and sister. Trained in the arts of combat, he now appeared as strong and as fierce as any Roman warrior. He began his inquiry at the house of Simonides, who had been a servant of his father. But Ben-Hur's new Roman dress and manner aroused Simonides' suspicions, and he revealed little. However, as Ben-Hur left, Simonides ordered his servant, Malluch, to follow him and judge his intentions.

Ben-Hur came upon a great coliseum. There he watched as chariot racers prepared for competition. He took particular notice of an Arab man who scolded a Roman driver for whipping his horses. Then, as the chariots lined up for the race, Judah turned to look at this same driver, now singled out in his resplendent chariot by the crowd's cheers – and he "stood transfixed . . . his instinct and memory had served him faithfully – the driver was Messala!"

After the race, won by Messala, the servant Malluch approached Ben-Hur. As they walked together, Ben-Hur quizzed Malluch about the chariot races and trustingly revealed his budding plan for revenge against Messala as well as his quest for his family. Malluch then returned to report to Simonides.

Upon learning that the Arab sheik, Ilderim, was interested in employing another driver, Ben-Hur offered his services. He proved to be so well trained in horsemanship, that any fears Ilderim may have had were satisfied.

The day of the race finally arrived. Ben-Hur "gave one searching look" at his "cruel, cunning, desperate" opponent. "At whatever cost, at all hazards, he would humble this enemy!" The trumpet sounded and the chariots strained forward behind their steeds. Ben-Hur kept abreast of Messala as they rounded the first turn, but suddenly, Messala gave Ben-Hur a savage glare and lashed Ilderim's horses, "a cut the like of which they had never known." Ben-Hur lost ground, but then regained it. Messala and Ben-Hur ran together at the front through the first six turns. Then, on the final lap, Ben-Hur, just inches behind, with a "cunning touch of the reins by which, turning a little to the left, he caught Messala's wheel with the iron-shod point of his axle, and crushed it." Messala's chariot splintered into the ground, sending its driver head over heels into the path of the onrushing chariots behind. Ben-Hur was declared the victor.

Remarkably, Messala lived, but he would never walk again. Shortly thereafter, he hired two brutes to murder Ben-Hur, but the Jewish rebel escaped and renewed his search for his mother and Tirzah.

It so happened that at this time the new Judean Procurator, Pontius Pilate, had ordered a review of all prisoners' penalties. Tirzah and Ben-Hur's mother were unearthed from deep in an underground cell and set free, both women leprous and near starvation. When they approached their house, the mother caught sight of someone asleep in the doorway. After a closer look, she cried, "As the Lord liveth, the man is my son." But as Tirzah ran to kiss her brother, her mother restrained her: they were "unclean" outcasts. The women left the city, eventually to enter a leper colony. It was better that Judah remember them as they had once been.

On the following day, Ben-Hur and other Jewish zealots made their way to Pilate to protest a recent tax edict. When the demonstration turned violent, Roman centurions pushed through the crowd swinging clubs. Challenged by a soldier, Ben-Hur found himself forced to fight. But his single sword thrust hit home and the Roman fell to the ground.

Ben-Hur became a hero in the village. Believing that his family was dead, he now turned his attention to another goal: the elimination of all Romans from Judea. Spurred on by Simonides' insistence that a "deliverer" would soon come to lead the Jews to victory against their oppressors, he secretly raised and trained three legions of Jewish soldiers.

Then one evening Ben-Hur received a letter from Malluch in Jerusalem. It told of the arrival in that city of a "King," a Savior, who was the one to lead the Jews out of bondage. Ben-Hur was stunned; he must go and discover for himself if this man was indeed the long-awaited "King of the Jews."

When Ben-Hur finally found this man, the Nazarene did not look at all like a king; his "calm, benignant countenance, the very idea of war and conquest, and lust of dominion, smote [Judah] like a profanation." He stared at the figure. "Faintly at first, at last a clear light, a burst of sunshine, the scene by the wall at Nazareth that time the Roman guard was dragging him to the galleys returned . . . " At once he fathomed the truth: "this is the SON of GOD!"

That same day, Ben-Hur's mother and sister were also seeking out this prophet, who was said to have the power to heal the afflicted. Amid a mob of admirers and curiosity seekers, they were finally able to approach him. All he asked them was if they believed. "Thou art he of whom the prophets spake. Thou art the Messiah!" they responded. Then Christ's "eyes grew radiant, his manner confident. 'Woman,' he said, 'great is thy faith; be it unto thee even as thou wilt.'" Immediately, each woman "felt the scourge going from her; their strength revived; they were returning to be themselves." Soon thereafter, these two were reunited with Ben-Hur and his bride Esther, Simonides' daughter. They were reunited in their love for one another – and for Christ.

Commentary:

Wallace's mixture of adventure, melodrama, period language, and accurately-depicted intercultural relations make *Ben-Hur* an amazing blend of history and intrigue. Wallace also revels in lengthy descriptions of ancient architecture and customs. At times these devices help pull the reader closer to the action, and, at other times, they produce fatigue.

Ben-Hur chronicles a man's triumphant rise not only out of the depths of slavery but also out of the depths of anger. Perhaps Ben-Hur's greatest victory came when he ultimately put off vengeance and chose instead to celebrate love, and to forgive his enemies as Jesus had taught.

ROBINSON CRUSOE

by
Daniel Defoe
(c. 1659-1731)

Type of work: Adventure novel

Setting: England, various ships at sea, and a small island near Trinidad; seventeenth century

Principal characters:
Robinson Crusoe, an Englishman
Friday, his island companion

Story Overview:

Young Robinson Crusoe told his parents that he wished more than anything else to go to sea. His father bitterly opposed the idea, and warned his son that "if I did take this foolish step, God would not bless me – and I would have leisure hereafter to reflect upon having neglected his counsel, when there might be none to assist in my recovery." These words proved prophetic.

The youthful Crusoe set out on his first voyage, with little knowledge about the perils of a sailor's life. In telling later about the tremendous storm in which his ship was caught, he remarked, "It was my advantage, in one respect, that I did not know what they meant by 'founder,' till I inquired." So ill and afraid was he during this first harrowing crisis, that he vowed never again to leave solid ground if he was blessed enough to escape drowning. But once safe on shore he found his old longing resurfacing, and Robinson took sail aboard another ship. Alas, the ill-fated vessel was captured by Turkish pirates. Crusoe managed to avoid capture and made off in a small craft. Together, he and a young companion navigated along the coast of Africa, where they were pursued by both wild beasts and natives. A Portuguese ship finally rescued them and they sailed for Brazil.

In the new land Crusoe established a prosperous sugar plantation. But again a feeling of lonely dissatisfaction overcame him: "I lived just like a man cast away upon some desolate island, that had nobody there but himself."

Then came an offer from some planters for Crusoe to act as a trader on a slave ship bound for Africa. But this voyage also met disaster: fierce hurricanes wrecked the ship, drowning everyone aboard except Robinson, who was finally tossed up on a desolate beach.

A subsequent storm washed the ship's wreckage close to shore and Crusoe constructed a raft to haul most of its supplies to land, where he stored them in a makeshift tent. After a few days, he climbed a hill and discovered that he was on what he assumed to be an uninhabited island. On his thirteenth day there, still another storm pushed the ship wreck back out to sea, where it sank, leaving him with no reminder of civilization.

Crusoe soon discovered that goats inhabited the island, and began domesticating some of them to provide himself with meat, milk, butter and cheese. Near the entrance of the cave where he stored his provisions taken from the ship, he painstakingly built a well-fortified home. After crafting a table, a chair and some shelves, Crusoe also began keeping a calendar and a journal.

Over the next few months, an earthquake and a hurricane damaged his supply cave, and though he still spent most of his time at his coastal home, in case a ship should happen by, he decided to erect an additional inland shelter.

Later, during a brief but raging fever, the adventurer was confronted by a terrifying apparition, who announced, "Seeing all these things have not brought thee to repentance, now thou shalt die!" Remembering the advice of his father, Crusoe commenced to pray and to read from the Bible. In a strangely inverted search, he began to seek deliverance from his sins rather than from his adverse situation.

In a small valley on the island, Crusoe found an abundance of wild grapes, lemons, limes and other fruits and vegetables. From the grapes he made raisins, which became a favorite staple food. In his wanderings he also caught a parrot, whom he taught to speak. With a few grains of rice and barley from the bottom of one of the ship's sacks, the sailor planted what would become large fields of grain. For several years he experimented with making bread and weaving baskets.

One of Crusoe's biggest frustrations was the lack of bottles or jars in which to cook or store food. Over time, he succeeded in making clay containers and even fired some pots that were solid enough to hold liquids. After four years on the island, he was a changed man: "I looked now upon the [civilized] world as a thing remote, which I had nothing to do with, no expectation from, and indeed no desires about. . ."

Crusoe dedicated his entire fifth year as a castaway to building and inventing. He constructed a "summer home" on the far side of the island; he fabricated for himself a suit made from skins, as well as an umbrella; he fashioned a small canoe in which he traveled around the island. And so the years passed in solitude.

One day, in his fifteenth year on the island, Crusoe spied a human footprint in the sand. When he finally summoned the courage to measure it against his own foot he found the strange print to be much larger. " . . . Fear of danger is ten thousand times more terrifying than danger itself," he declared. Still, for safety, he built a second wall around his home and fit it with six muskets.

Once, while exploring, Crusoe came upon a beach spread with human bones. He quickly abandoned the area, and for the next two years he stayed close to home, never fired a gun, and avoided making fires.

Twenty-four years had passed when one night Crusoe heard gun fire. And in the morning he spied a ship's hull impaled on the rocks. Then he saw something that sent shivers down his spine – about 30 cannibals on the beach, enjoying a gruesome feast. Robinson shot at them, killing some and driving the others away. He rescued one of their native prisoners and named his new companion Friday, for the day upon which he was delivered. Friday proved to be strong, loyal and intelligent, though Crusoe still had cause to worry – Friday was also a bit cannibalistic.

Crusoe began introducing Friday to his mode of living, especially hoping to turn him to Christianity. Friday managed to learn English quite well, and was pleased to answer his benefactor's questions concerning the surrounding islands and their inhabitants. Crusoe discovered that his island must be near Trinidad.

One day in the course of their conversation, Friday told Robinson about seventeen white men who were held prisoner on his home island, survivors of a shipwreck. If Crusoe rescued them, they might be the key to his return to the civilized world. But before the two men could finish constructing a canoe to reach the captives, another group of cannibals arrived. This time Crusoe and Friday were able to save two of their prisoners from the cooking pot; a Spaniard, and another islander – who turned out to be Friday's father.

After assuring Crusoe that the other Spanish and Portuguese prisoners would willingly follow the English castaway in an escape attempt, the Spaniard returned to the island with Friday's father to explain the plan and have the men sign an oath of allegiance.

While they were gone, an English ship anchored near the island and eleven men came ashore, three of them – the ship's captain, his mate, and a passenger – as prisoners of mutineers. Crusoe and Friday killed the most belligerent of them, and the others turned themselves over to Crusoe, swearing loyalty. With control of the ship, Crusoe prepared to return to England. Some of the mutineers, however, chose to remain on the island rather than return to England and hang.

Though Crusoe hated to leave the island before the return of the Spaniard and Friday's father, he sailed with the ship and arrived in England on June 11, 1687, thirty-five years after his earlier visit. Finding two sisters and two children of a brother still living, he decided to sail on to Lisbon to learn what had become of his Brazilian plantation. Friday, "in all these ramblings [proved] a most faithful servant on all occasions."

Surprisingly, Crusoe's holdings had been well-managed by his friends – in fact, they had earned him a small fortune. He generously gave portions of his profit to charity as well as to his family and others.

In Lisbon, Crusoe, apprehensive about traveling back to England by sea, organized a party of men to travel overland as far as the Channel. After many difficult adventures in the Pyrenees, and, as usual, with a great deal of luck, the company reached England.

Finally home, the wanderer married and had two sons and a daughter. But alas, Crusoe's wife died and he was compelled to join one of his nephews on a voyage to the East Indies. Miraculously, this ship sailed safely. Crusoe revisited his island, where he found that the Spaniards and the English mutineers had taken native wives. After hearing a full account of what had happened since his departure, he left supplies, furnished the islanders with a carpenter and a smith, and divided the island among them.

The ship then sailed around the Cape of Good Hope and on to China. On an overland trip through Siberia and on back to England, Crusoe had many more encounters. Ultimately, Robinson Crusoe, after a total of 54 years abroad, returned home, an old, weathered man, and lived out his remaining days in peace, never to take to the sea again.

Commentary:

An adventurous tale, *The Life and Strange Surprising Adventures of Robinson Crusoe,* as Defoe titled his novel, is especially loved by children, although there is certainly enough to keep an adult entertained as well. Since the story is told in the first person, it is easy to confuse the author with the character of Crusoe, and in fact the novel is based on the real-life adventures of a man named Alexander Selkirk, a Scottish sailor who was marooned for a little over four years on an island called Juan Fernandez. Defoe obviously added a great deal of imagination, adventure and romance to his tale. He also incorporates into his novel many of his own beliefs in divine providence and the importance of faith.

It is evidence of Defoe's talent and spirit that this book is still, after more than 250 years, popular reading.

THE PICTURE OF DORIAN GRAY

by
Oscar Wilde
(1856 - 1900)

Type of work: Fantasy novel

Setting: London, England; late nineteenth century

Principal characters:

Dorian Gray, an extremely handsome
young man

Basil Hallward, Dorian's older friend,
a portrait artist

Lord Henry Wotton, Dorian's vile tempter

Sibyl Vane, Dorian's actress-lover

James Vane, Sibyl's brother

Story Overview:

As Basil Hallward artfully put the finishing touches on his full-length portrait of an extraordinarily beautiful young man, Lord Henry Wotton paid him a call. Lord Henry much admired the painting and desired to meet the subject. The artist objected, knowing the poisonous influence of which Lord Henry was capable; young Dorian Gray was his ideal of purity and had inspired Basil to the most expressive art of his life.

Just then, in walked Dorian Gray. Against Hallward's wishes, the two met, and Dorian was immediately taken by Lord Henry's fascinating words, presence and wittiness. Henry flattered Dorian with his comments on the virtues of beauty, the charms of youth, and expressed his sadness at the thought that such youth should fade into the ugliness of age. This caused Dorian to plummet into melancholy.

Seeing his portrait for the first time, Dorian gasped at his own beauty. He lamented that the picture would mock him his entire life; age would indeed steal his color and grace: "I know, now, that when one loses one's good looks, whatever they may be, one loses everything ... Lord Henry Wotton is perfectly right. Youth is the only thing worth having. When I find that I am growing old, I shall kill myself." Then he wished instead that the picture might grow old while he remained forever young: "I would give everything. I would give my soul for that!" Alarmed by these passions in the young man, Hallward attempted to destroy the painting, but Dorian stopped him and had it taken home that very evening.

After that first meeting, Dorian and Lord Henry became fast friends and frequent partners at local theatres. Henry presented Dorian with a gift – a book about a young man's passions, sins and vileness. Dorian became captivated by its plot. For years he leafed through its pages – and the book became an entrenched, tragic guide in the life of Dorian Gray.

Dorian met and fell madly in love with Sibyl Vane, a beautiful and talented actress who was portraying Juliet in a cheap theatrical troupe. But the night Dorian invited Lord Henry and Basil Hallward to meet his new love, her performance was lifeless. She was hissed and booed by even the uneducated audience. Afterward, she joyfully explained to the disappointed Dorian that her love for her "Prince Charming," – as she knew him – had transformed her from a mere actress into a real woman. Dorian coldly shunned her, admitting that his love for her had been killed, and vowed that he would see her no more.

On returning home, he was surprised to notice that the face in his painting had changed. A touch of cruelty now lined the mouth. His wish that the painting might be seared with suffering and guilt while his own face was left untarnished, had been granted!

But now he pitied the portrait and resolved to live a pure life. He would return to Sibyl and marry her. He would see no more of the selfish Lord Henry. Dorian wrote Sibyl a passionate letter and fell asleep, confident that he would make amends to Sybil the following day.

However, that next morning Lord Henry brought bad news: in grief, Sibyl had killed herself during the night. Lord Henry charmed the devastated youth, urging him to imagine the tragedy as a drama, with Juliet or Ophelia the victims, not the flesh-and-blood Sibyl.

No, she will never come to life. She has played her last part ... To you at least she was always a dream, a phantom that flitted through Shakespeare's plays ... But don't waste your tears over Sibyl Vane. She was less real than they are.

Now Dorian forgot his good resolutions. If fate would deal unjustly with him, he, in turn, determined to give himself up to a life of pleasure and let the portrait bear the burden of his corrupting soul. Eternal youth, wild joys, infinite passion would be his.

Horrified at Dorian's lack of remorse and feeling, Basil Hallward tried to reason with him. But Dorian was unmoved. He continued to guard the secret of the portrait from Basil, first covering it with a sheet, and later moving it to an upstairs room, unopened since his grandfather had died there five years earlier. Separated by this chasm of secrecy and scorn that Dorian had created, the two could no longer be friends.

For years Dorian lived in cruel joy; yet he kept the look of one unspotted by the world. He derived pleasure from comparing his own virtuous face with the gruesome one appearing on the canvas. Dorian consorted both with the town's thieves and its social elite. He collected jewels, fine clothing and art. And when he would appear on the street, "men would whisper to each other in corners, or pass him with a sneer, or look at him with cold searching eyes, as though they were determined to discover his secret."

At age thirty-eight Dorian was again visited by his old friend Basil Hallward. It was on the eve of Hallward's departure for an extended stay in Paris. He came in hopes of persuading Dorian to finally change his ways, hardly believing the rumors concerning the young man's evil deeds.

By this time, Dorian had become totally corrupt, as vile and ugly as the figure in the portrait.

Through some strange quickening of inner life, the leprosies of sin were slowly eating the thing away. The rotting corpse in a watery grave was not so fearful.

One day, in spite, Dorian invited the elderly Hallward up to the room to see his filthy soul, face-to-face. As he drew back the curtain from the portrait, Hallward stood aghast at the hideous figure on the canvas; yes, there was his own signature, that onetime stood out beneath the portrait of a handsome young lad. Basil immediately begged Dorian to pray and repent. Instead, Dorian seized a knife and plunged it again and again into the painter's neck and back. Then, relocking the door, he left the slumping figure in the room, feeling sure that Basil would not be missed for months. After all, no one knew he had come to the house, and he was expected to be in Paris from that night forward.

A few days later, Dorian coerced a former acquaintance, a chemist, Alan Campbell, to destroy Basil's body using chemicals and fire. He threatened to expose a past crime Campbell had committed if he refused. That night red blood stained the hands of the loathsome image on the portrait.

Late one evening, as Dorian was leaving an opium den, a drunken woman called him "Prince Charming." A sailor standing nearby turned out to be Sibyl Vane's brother, James. Overhearing this familiar nickname, James siezed Dorian with the intent to kill him and avenge his sister's death. But Dorian's youthful appearance and smooth tongue saved him; when the crime had occurred Dorian could have been no more than a mere infant. When James returned to the den, however, the woman swore before God that Dorian was indeed the ruinous Prince Charming. After destroying her life too, he had once boasted that he had sold his soul to the Devil years earlier in exchange for a beautiful face; and he had not changed in appearance since then.

For months Dorian imagined himself being hunted – tracked down by a vengeful sailor. His mask of youth had saved his life, but not his conscience.

Then, during a hunt at Dorian's country home, an unknown man in sailor's garb was accidentally killed. Dorian rushed to where the body was taken and there discovered James Vane, dead. At last, they were all dead: Sibyl; Alan Campbell – a mysterious suicide victim; and Basil Hallward, though, lately, people were inquiring about his strange disappearance. Only Dorian knew the truth. But now he would welcome death for himself; his only terror lay in the waiting.

In his final, poignant visit with Lord Henry, Dorian admitted that, despite his unchanged features, he no longer thought himself handsome – his zest for life was shattered. "What does it profit a man if he gain the whole world and lose his own soul?" Lord Henry righteously quoted. Dorian begged Henry never to be the devil's advocate again, never again to poison another soul with his book or his evil thoughts.

Disheartened, alone, and longing to be at peace with himself, Dorian contemplated his situation. Should he confess and atone for his evils? No, the only evidence against him was that horrid, hidden pictorial record of his debauchery. "A new life! That is what he wanted."

Resolving to kill that "monstrous soul-life" in the portrait, Dorian hurried upstairs, seized the same knife he had used on poor Basil, and stabbed the picture. A horrible cry brought the house servants creeping up to the barred room. Finally gaining entrance, they found upon the wall the splendid portrait of their master, as fresh and beautiful as the day it was painted. On the floor was a dead man, "a withered, wrinkled, and loathsome man," with a knife in his heart. Only the rings on his fingers revealed his identity. It was Dorian Gray, who, in a miscarried struggle to kill his conscience, had killed himself.

Commentary:

In *The Picture of Dorian Gray*, Wilde produced a work very typical of the mood of the period as well as of his own personal love of paradox.

Himself an accomplished painter, Wilde took the theme of his book from a real-life event similar to the opening of the story. As Wilde finished the portrait of a "radiant lad," his close friend, Basil Hallward, wished aloud, "How delightful it would be if the youth could remain exactly as he is, while the portrait aged and withered in his stead." The Faustian motif of the novel – the willingness to sell one's soul to the Devil for worldly vanity – unfolded from this idle comment, together with the bizaare imagination of a brooding artist.

FRANKENSTEIN

by
Mary Shelley
(1797 - 1851)

Type of work: Conceptual horror novel

Setting: Switzerland; late 1700's

Principal characters:

Robert Walton, an explorer attempting
to sail to the North Pole

Victor Frankenstein, a young scientist
who creates a "monster"

Clerval, Frankenstein's friend

The Monster, Frankenstein's angry,
frustrated, and lonely creation

Story Overview:

His ship surrounded by ice, Robert Walton watched with his crew as a huge, misshapen "traveller" on a dog sled disappeared across the ice. The next morning, as the fog lifted and the ice broke up, they found another man, nearly frozen, on a slab of floating ice. By giving him hot soup and rubbing his body with brandy, the crew restored him to health. A few days later he was able to speak.

This stranger, Victor Frankenstein, seemed upset to hear that an earlier sled had been sighted. Then he began to tell his story:

Victor had been born the only child of a good Genevese family. During a journey with her husband abroad, his mother found a peasant and his wife with five hungry babies. All were dark-complected, save one, a very fair little girl. His mother decided at that moment to adopt the child.

Victor and his adopted sister, Elizabeth, came to love one another, though they were very diverse in character. Elizabeth "busied herself with following the aerial creations of poets," while, for Victor, "it was the secrets of heaven and earth that I desired to learn . . . the physical secrets of the world."

After the death of his mother when he was seventeen, Victor departed for the University of Inglostadt. There, young Frankenstein grew intensely interested in the phenomena of the human body: "Whence, I often asked myself, did the principle of life proceed?" He investigated the processes of death and decay, and soon became obsessed with the idea of creating life itself.

After days and nights of laboring, "I succeeded in discovering the cause of generation and life; nay, more, I became myself capable of bestowing animation upon lifeless matter." Frankenstein set out to create a superior living being, hoping to eventually uncover the formula for eternal life.

In his brilliant and terrible research, Frankenstein doggedly collected body parts from charnel-houses and cemeteries. Finally, "on a dreary night of November . . . I beheld the accomplishment of my toils": an eight-foot monster. Applying electricity to the "lifeless matter" before him, Victor saw "the dull yellow eye of the creature open; it breathed hard, and convulsive motion agitated its limbs." The scientist was appalled. "Breathless horror and disgust filled my heart." He had created a freak.

Exhausted, Frankenstein fell asleep, seeking a "few moments of forgetfulness." But, as he tossed in bed, a cold draft woke Victor, and "I beheld the wretch . . . his eyes . . . fixed on me." He shrieked in horror, scaring the monster away, then escaped downstairs.

A long depressive illness followed this episode. Victor slowly began to recover. But soon he received terrible news from his father: William, the youngest son, had been strangled, and his murderer remained at large. "Come dearest Victor; you alone can console Elizabeth," his father pled.

The scientist returned to Geneva during a terrible storm. As he plodded along, he "perceived in the gloom a figure," and knew instinctively that it was "the filthy demon to whom I had given life." Then a horrible thought struck him: this monster might be his brother's murderer.

But when Victor arrived at his mournful home, he was told that William's killer had already been unmasked. Justine, the family's long-time servant, had been found in possession of a locket which held a picture of their mother, taken from William during the murder. The poor girl seemed to confirm her own guilt "by her extreme confusion of manner"; and, though Victor believed Justine was innocent, he hesitated to come forward because he felt the story of his monster was too fantastic to be taken seriously. Justine was hanged, and Victor, "seized by remorse and a sense of guilt," took a solitary journey to Mont Blanc. During a hike up a mountain path he saw a strange, agile figure – his own monstrous creation – advancing towards him "with superhuman speed." "Begone, vile insect," he commanded. But the monster countered: " . . . You, my creator, detest and spurn me, thy creature . . . . How dare you sport thus with life?" Creature and creator argued back and forth until the monster convinced Victor to hear his account.

Life for the intelligent and sensitive being had been difficult. "I saw, felt, heard, and smelt at the same time . . . " he explained.

He wandered, surviving on berries and stream water, until he found a fire left by vagrants, and learned to keep warm. When food grew scarce he approached a village; but because of his hideous features, "some [of the villagers] fled, some attacked me, until grievously bruised by stones . . . I escaped to the open country."

He finally made his home in an abandoned hovel adjoining a cottage. In the cottage lived an old, impoverished, blind man, with his son and daughter. The creature learned the rudiments of verbal language by listening to their conversations. After some months, the monster gathered his courage and chatted with the blind man as he was alone, relating his situation. But just as the monster was about to ask his human friend for refuge, the son returned home and "with supernatural force tore me from his father." The disheartened, confused monster fled from the cottage.

Despised by all who saw him, he wandered the countryside until one day he came upon a young boy – Victor's brother – who " . . . loaded me with epithets which carried despair to my heart." In bitter rage, the monster killed the boy, then took the locket which hung around the child's neck and hid it on Justine's clothing as she slept.

After relating this tale, the monster made a frightful demand: "You must create a female for me . . . " "I do refuse it," Victor declared. Making a mate for this monster could give rise to a hostile superhuman race. However, promising that he and his mate would retreat in peace to the wilds of South America, the monster's pleas and threats finally moved Victor: "I consent to your demand . . . "

Still, back in his laboratory, Victor could not collect the courage for his work: "I feared the vengeance of the disappointed fiend, yet I was unable to overcome my repugnance to the task which was enjoined me."

Perplexed, Victor traveled to Britain with the intent of marrying his foster sister, Elizabeth. But first he retired to a remote area of Scotland, where he planned to finish his work in solitude. Even there he could sense the monster near, waiting for the "birth" of his mate. But shortly before the female's completion, Victor destroyed her in disgust. Watching at a window, the lonely, enraged brute forced his way into the house. But this time Victor was adamant; he would not again enter into such a work.

"Man, you shall repent of the injuries you inflict . . . . I shall be with you on your wedding night," the vengeful monster intoned. Despite these words, Victor determined that his marriage to Elizabeth would take place.

Following the wedding, Victor stood watch downstairs, waiting for the appearance of his rejected creature. Just as Victor began to believe that by some fortunate chance the monster would not come, a shrill and dreadful scream broke the stillness. Victor rushed to the nuptial chamber. But alas, he was too late. All he beheld was Elizabeth's "bloodless arms and relaxed form flung by the murderer on its bridal bier."

His story completed, the chilled and weakened Victor Frankenstein died there on the ice-bound ship, unavenged.

That night the monster visited Walton in the dead man's cabin. Standing over his creator's body, the beast first asked the dead scientist's pardon, but then blamed Frankenstein for his sorrow – and for destroying his unfinished mate:

My heart was fashioned to be susceptible of love and sympathy . . . . But when I discovered that he, the author at once of my existence and of its unspeakable torments, dared to hope for happiness . . . envy and bitter indignation filled me with an insatiable thirst for vengeance . . . I desired love and friendship . . . . Am I to be thought the only criminal, when all human kind sinned against me?

Then, predicting his own imminent death by fire, the monster bid Walton farewell, sprang from the window, and vanished across the Arctic ice fields.

Commentary:

Mary Shelley wrote this novel on a dare at the age of nineteen. While she and her husband (the renowned poet Percy Bysshe Shelley) were vacationing with Lord Byron and others in the Alps – where much of the story takes place – they started to exchange ghost stories. Intimidated at first by the fame of some of her companions, some of England's greatest writers, Mary finally offered up her contribution, *Frankenstein: the Modern Prometheus*. The work was a breakthrough, spawning the birth of two literary genres: science-fiction and horror fiction.

This novel – and resultant motion pictures, which have usually degenerated into simple horror plots – has had a recent resurgence in popularity due to the efforts of "feminist critics," who have penetrated its deeper themes. Along with her exposition of the dangers and ethical dilemmas involved in experimenting with life, and her homily against judging by appearances, perhaps one of Shelley's most important contributions in *Frankenstein* is her brilliant portrayal of the male desire – conscious or unconscious – to circumvent the role of woman in giving life. With a new focus on these deeper issues during the last half century, *Frankenstein* has achieved renewed status as a multi-dimensional literary classic.

THE TIME MACHINE

by
H. G. Wells
(1866 - 1946)

Type of work: Fantasy / science fiction novel

Setting: England; late nineteenth century, and
hundreds of thousands of years in
the future

Principal characters:
The Time Traveller, an inquisitive,
scientific man
Weena, a future woman

Story Overview:

One Thursday evening, four or five men
assembled for dinner at a friend's home near
London. But as the evening passed, their host
failed to appear. Finally, at half past seven the
guests agreed it was a pity to spoil a good
dinner and seated themselves to a delicious
meal. The main topic of their conversation
was time travel, a subject their host had seriously argued as a valid theory during an earlier dinner. He had gone so far as to show
them the model of a curious machine he had
built, which, he declared, could travel
through the fourth dimension – time.

While the guests conversed, the door
suddenly opened and in limped their host. He
was in a state of disarray His coat was dusty,
dirty and smeared with green; his hair was
markedly grayer than the last time they had
seen him, his face pale, and his expression
haggard and drawn as if by intense suffering.
As he stumbled back through the door in tattered, bloodstained socks, he promised his
guests that he would return shortly with an
explanation for his actions and appearance.

Soon after, the gentleman did reappear,
and commenced with his remarkable story.

That morning, his machine at last completed, he had begun his journey through
time. Increasing the angle of his levers, at first
he was able to maintain a sense of time and
place. His laboratory still looked the same,
but slowly its image dimmed. Then, faster
and faster, night followed day, until the palpi-
tation of night and day merged into one continuous grayness. New questions sprung up
in the Traveller's mind: What had happened
to civilization? How had humanity changed?

Now he saw great and splendid architecture rising about him, while the surrounding expanse became a richer green, with no
interruptions made by winter. The Time
Traveller decided to stop.

He fell from his machine to find himself
at the foot of a colossal, winged, sphinx-like
figure carved out of white stone on a bronze
pedestal. The huge image, outlined by early-
morning mist, made him somewhat ill at ease.
Then he noticed figures approaching; slight
creatures, perhaps four feet high, very beautiful and graceful, but indescribably frail. These
beings advanced toward the Time Traveller,
laughing without fear, and began touching
him all over. "So these are the citizens of the
future," he mused. They acted like five-year-
old children, and the Traveller was disappointed with their lack of intelligence and
refinement.

These gentle people, called Eloi, bore
their visitor to a towering building that
appeared ready to collapse. Their world in
general seemed in disrepair – a beautiful, tangled waste of bushes and flowers; a long-
neglected and yet weedless garden The Eloi
served their guest a meal that consisted
entirely of fruit. During this repast, they all
sat as close to the Time Traveller as they
could.

With much difficulty he began to learn
their language, but the Eloi, with their very
short attention spans, tired easily of teaching
him.

That evening, the Traveller began to
hypothesize how these people, who all looked
identical, dressed alike, and reacted to life in
the same way, had evolved. Perhaps, he
thought, mankind had overcome the numerous difficulties of life facing it in the late 19th
and early 20th centuries. Under new conditions of perfect comfort and security, perhaps
power and intellect – the very qualities he
most valued – had no longer been necessary.
He decided that he had emerged into the sunset of humanity; a vegetarian society – for he
had noticed no animals – where there was no
need for either reasoning or strength.

As night drew near, the Time Traveller
suddenly realized that his time machine had
vanished. Engulfed by the fear of losing contact with his own age and being left helpless
in this strange new world, he flew into a desperate rampage, a futile attempt to find his
machine.

Soon the voyager's panic faded as he
realized his machine was probably inside the
huge stone figure near the spot where he had
"landed." He pounded on the bronze doors
without effect, but he was certain he had
heard some voice from inside – a distinct little
chuckle. Calm, welcome sleep, finally overcame the adventurer, and he reasoned that in
time he would succeed in breaking into the

stone behemoth to regain his machine.

Another day passed. The Time Traveller came to realize that he had been wrong about the little beings. The Eloi had no machinery or appliances of any kind, yet they were clothed in pleasant fabric and their sandals were fairly complex specimens of metalwork. Perhaps this was a truly advanced society.

Later, the Time Traveller rescued an Eloi woman from drowning. Her name was Weena. Weena, unable to vocally express her gratitude and regard for the Time Traveller, slept by his side in the dark. This took great courage because the Eloi feared darkness and never ventured from their buildings after sunset. This point also puzzled the Time Traveller: If the Eloi lived in a perfect society, then why were they afraid of the dark?

On the fourth day of his adventure, the Traveller came across other earth creatures. These subterranean, ape-like vermin were called Morlocks. Summoning courage, the Time Traveller warily descended into their world to learn what he could about them. There he found the machines that he had not seen above ground. Morlocks were apparently another race of man's descendants, no longer able to tolerate the sun-lit surface of the planet. Here were the enemies who had taken his time machine. By their smell and appearance they were obviously carnivores.

Suddenly the Traveller understood why the Eloi feared darkness. They were like fatted calves, kept well and healthy, only to be seized and eaten when the Morlocks grew hungry. Eloi society wasn't perfect after all.

A few days later, Weena and the Time Traveller set out to search for a weapon they could use to break into the pedestal where the machine was hidden. Coming across an ancient museum, they collected matches, some camphor for a candle, and, most important of all, an iron mace. The sun was setting as they emerged from the museum. Though filled with a sense of doom, and having several miles of forest between them and safety, they nevertheless started for home in the shadowy darkness.

Morlocks proceeded to close in on them along the way. The beasts were temporarily driven off each time the Time Traveller lighted a match, but finally, in an effort to slow them down, he ignited a larger fire. In minutes the entire forest was in flames. The Traveller was able to escape – but Weena was lost in the flames. Standing on a knoll, he looked out over the burning wasteland, and mourned the loss of his devoted Eloi friend.

When morning came, the Time Traveller began retracing his steps to the place where he had originally landed. On the way he pondered how brief the reign of human intellect had been. Our priceless, heroic, human existence had been traded for a life of comfort and ease.

Now, as the voyager approached the stone relic, he found the door of the pedestal open. Inside was his time machine. It was an obvious trap, but the Morlocks had no idea how the device worked. The Traveller sprinted to his machine and adjusted the lever, while fighting off several Morlocks. Then he found himself enveloped by the same welcome grey light and tumult he had before observed. He had escaped that dismal future.

The visit to the Eloi took place in the year 802,701. The Time Traveller next journeyed through millions of years, seeing even more alien creatures than before. Finally halting thirty million years after he had departed, he found a distant age where the sun no longer shone brightly. In bitter cold and deathly stillness, the horrified Traveller started back toward the present.

The guests listened with mixed emotions to the last of this tale. Their host seemed sincere; but was such a feat possible? A few days later one of his friends came to hear more. Again, the Traveller excused himself, asking his guest to wait momentarily and he would be back with evidence of this excursion. Three years elapsed and the Time Traveller had not reappeared. He was considered by his friends as a lost wanderer, somewhere in time.

Commentary:

The Time Machine, H.G. Wells' first novel, is often referred to as "pseudo-scientific." Along with Jules Vernes, Wells was a pioneer in science-fiction writing, though he never liked having his novels compared to Vernes'. Wells claimed his novels always meant to depict political beliefs, and were never intended to be realistic.

Brought up in a lower-class section of Bromley, Kent, England, the author witnessed the conspicuous class distinctions of the late nineteenth century. In *The Time Machine* Wells portrays what he felt could happen to mankind as the divisive gulf between the indolent rich and hard-working poor became wider and wider. Though written in the late 1800's, Wells' descriptions of the weak Eloi and the predatory subterranean Morlocks are rooted in scientific hypotheses that are at once interesting, feasible and frightening possibilities for humanity's future.

THE TURN OF THE SCREW

by
Henry James
(1843 - 1916)

Type of work: Early psychological thriller

Setting: England; nineteenth century

Principal characters:
>The *"governess,"* an unnamed twenty-year-old woman
>*Mrs. Grose,* an older housekeeper
>*Flora,* an eight-year-old girl
>*Miles,* a ten-year-old boy

Story Overview:

At Christmas time, a group of people in an old country home swapped ghost stories. One story that particularly chilled the group involved the visitation of a ghost to a young boy. When it was finished, a man in the group, Douglas, asked: "If the child gives the effect, another turn of the screw, what do you say to two children – ?"

Weeks later, when Douglas was able to obtain the manuscript containing this second story, he read the narrative to his listeners, after prefacing it with a bit of background

The tale's author was a woman who had been his sister's governess, and Douglas was the only person to whom she had revealed her dreadful tale before her death . . .

On a pleasant June afternoon, a young lady of twenty, "the youngest of several daughters of a poor country parson," arrived in London to answer an advertisement for the position of governess. The advertiser was a bachelor who had been left guardian to his young nephew and niece. The uncle, a wealthy and charming gentleman, "beguiled" the young woman instantly. The terms of her employment were quite simple: she was to take charge of the two children on his country estate of Bly in Essex, and to "never trouble him . . . neither appear nor complain nor write about anything." She would be replacing the former governess, a young lady who had died under curious circumstances. While the mystery surrounding the prior governess's death did cause the woman to pause and consider, she nonetheless accepted the position and took the coach to Bly.

The new governess soon met stout Mrs. Grose, the Bly mansion's head housekeeper, and little Flora, the bachelor's niece. The girl was a "vision of angelic beauty," and the governess looked forward to "teaching" and "forming" the child.

Miles, the little boy, was due home in a few days for his school holiday, and according to Mrs. Grose, the governess would be equally "taken" with Miles. Both children seemed incapable of giving any trouble.

However, before Miles arrived, the governess received two letters. The first was from her employer, instructing her to handle the details of the second letter, sent from the headmaster of Miles' school. This second letter in effect stated that Miles was dismissed from school, permanently. This news worried the governess, but Mrs. Grose, upon hearing the report, could not believe it, and urged her to wait until she met Miles before forming a judgement.

A few days later Miles arrived, and the governess beheld his "positive fragrance of purity." In private she told Mrs. Grose that the headmaster's accusation was "grotesque." Together they decided not to bother Miles' uncle further about the matter.

The governess enjoyed the summer days in the country. It was the first time in her life that she "had known space and air and freedom."

Then, while strolling through the garden one day as the children napped, the governess allowed her imagination to wander. She imagined how charming it would be to meet a handsome young man around the turn of the path. Still deep in fantasy, she rounded the corner of the garden – and it was as though her "imagination had, in a flash turned real." On one of the towers of the old mansion stood a figure; not the man she had been dreaming of, but a strange fellow who stared at her menacingly for a minute, then disappeared.

The next Sunday evening as the governess entered the rain-shrouded dining room, she became aware of "a person on the other side of the window and looking straight in." It was the same man she had seen earlier, but at that instant she realized that "he had come for someone else." She rushed out of the house to the spot where he stood, but again he had vanished. She looked in through the window, as he had done, and there she saw Mrs. Grose, peering out just as she herself had stood a moment before. When the housekeeper asked for an explanation, the governess told her the whole story. As she described the elusive stranger, a flash of recognition crept into Mrs. Grose's face. The man the governess had seen, she said, was Peter Quint, their employer's former valet, who had died some time before.

The governess felt that Quint's hovering presence boded evil for the children; that he wanted "to appear to them." But the children never mentioned Quint, though, in life, he had been quite friendly with Miles.

Not too long after this episode, a second figure appeared to Flora and the governess as they walked near the estate's lake. Flora knew the woman as Miss Jessel, the children's former governess, but pretended that all was normal. The governess learned from Mrs. Grose that the two apparitions had been lovers while they were alive, the girl having been led by Quint down drunken and corrupt paths. Neither woman could guess what evil influences the ghosts might have on the seemingly oblivious children. What was particularly disturbing, however, was the children's secretiveness. Miles, they felt sure, was now meeting with the ghosts late at night, just as he had met with the lovers, concealing their illicit affair, in life.

Over the weeks, the children were several times found leaving their beds to wander the night. But when queried, the unflinching youngsters said nothing. They were in a world populated by the living-dead, and the governess could find no way to intercede.

Summer faded into autumn, and though the governess saw no more spirits, she sensed in the children's behavior that they were near. One day an animated Miles approached the governess to ask about returning to school. She side-stepped the question, fearing that the ghosts' influence might intensify if the boy went beyond her care; but she told him she would write the boy's uncle and ask him what was to be done.

That evening, before writing her letter, the governess entered Miles' room and gently asked him to let her help in his secret troubles. At that moment, a gush of cold air filled the closed room, blowing out the candle, leaving the two in silent, terrifying darkness.

The following day when Flora had disappeared for some time, both Mrs. Grose and the governess instinctively hurried to the estate's small lake, calling out the girl's name. They finally discovered her playing in a thicket; on the opposite bank of the lake stood Miss Jessel. The governess, badly shaken, demanded that Flora admit to seeing Miss Jessel, but Flora still would confess to seeing no one. And, when pressed, the once loveable angelic girl suddenly turned into a child demon, spouting filthy language and ordering the governess to leave.

It was decided that Flora, already dominated by evil, would be better off away from Bly. Mrs. Grose left with the child for London that very afternoon. The governess and Miles remained alone.

The governess knew by now that Miles had stolen the letter she had written to his uncle before it could be mailed. That evening she confronted Miles about the matter. Taking the boy and gazing into his face, she suddenly saw, behind Miles, the ghost of Peter Quint glaring at them through the dining room window. Swiftly she drew the boy close to her body, shielding him from Quint's "white face of damnation." Caught off guard by the woman's abrupt manner, Miles then solemnly confessed to stealing and burning the letter, fearing that the governess was sending a "bad report" to his uncle.

With rising courage, the governess now pressed Miles as to why he had been expelled from school. Miles reluctantly admitted that his lewd speech had caused problems, and the governess shook him in tender exasperation for the months of torment he had caused. In the boy's surrender, she thought she had won; the white-faced phantom outside the window vanished. She released her hold on the child and gave him a smile. But suddenly, there against the glass the hideous Quint reappeared. "No more, no more, no more!" the governess shrieked as she again tried to pull the boy close. Miles, his back still to the window, asked "It's he?"

"Whom do you mean by he?" she replied.

"Peter Quint – you devil!" Miles screamed.

"What will he ever matter?" cried out the governess. "I have you . . . " But the boy jerked from her grasp, turned, and glared at the once more empty window. With the loss of his dead companion, Miles uttered the cry of a hellish creature. He rolled back and fell into the protective arms of his governess, finally at peace.

After a minute, the governess found what she truly held. Death had won the child. "His little heart, dispossessed, had stopped."

Commentary:

In *The Turn of the Screw*, Henry James creates a masterful psychological thriller, with "the strange and sinister" occurring in the midst of the usual. He engenders a nightmare quality to his tales; an unspoken, ungruesome "sense of evil" that allows the reader to imagine the horror from within. Further, blending the innocence of children with ghostly evil creates a terrifying combination. The terror lies not in the apparitions themselves, but in what is happening to the children; they change from "sweet things" to open liars and mean-spirited little beings.

A particular "turn" is represented by James' young governess, who is frightened by the all-too-real daytime hauntings, but continually insists on telling the reader how calm she is. And the most haunting turn of all comes with the final questions left hovering before us: Was the deepening spell actually an emanation from forces beyond the dead? Or was it, in innocent and terrible fact, a manifestation of the young governess' own unconsciously possessive passion for the spirit of Miles – a passion first kindled by the uncle who had "charmed and beguiled" her, and then left abandoned in a lonely country household to spawn its own deadly ghosts within her soul and the souls of those around her? In essence asking, "What is the source of evil?" this tale, written in an eerily slow-moving, deliberate nineteenth-century style, has been called the greatest ghost story ever written.

THE FALL OF THE HOUSE OF USHER

by
Edgar Allan Poe
(1809 - 1849)

Type of work: Gothic horror story

Setting: An ancient English manor house; nineteenth century

Principal characters:
An unidentified Narrator
Roderick Usher, the Narrator's gravely ill friend
Lady Madeline, Roderick's even more infirm sister

Story Overview:

(Classical gothic imagery – drippingly dark surroundings and terrifying ghostly symbols – is used throughout this tale to evoke a sense of fear and forboding that present-day novels and films have made commonplace to modern lovers of horror. Thus, imagine yourself living in the relatively tranquil and circumscribed realm of rural England in the 1800's.)

The Narrator had received a letter from a boyhood acquaintance, Roderick Usher, begging that he come to him "posthaste." Usher had written to explain that he was suffering from a terrible mental and bodily illness, and longed for the companionship of "his only personal friend." The plea seemed so heartfelt that the Narrator immediately set out for the Usher ancestral home.

Approaching the ivy-covered, decaying old house, the Narrator was struck by an overwhelming sense of gloom which seemed to envelop the estate. The very sight of the manor caused within him "an illness, a sickening of the heart, an unredeemed dreariness." But even though the "eye-like" windows of the mansion seemed to be staring at him, he managed to swallow his fear and continue in his carriage up the path to the door. As he rode, he tried to recall Roderick Usher as he had once known him; years had passed since they had last met. He remembered his old friend as an extremely reserved fellow, quite handsome but possessing an eerie, morbid demeanor. Roderick's family was noted for its particular musical genius – and for the fact that no new branch of the family had ever been generated. For centuries, the title of the estate had passed directly from father to son, so that the term "House of Usher" had come to refer both to the family and to the mansion. Sadly, though, Roderick was the last surviving male issue of the Usher clan.

Finally, the carriage crossed over the creaking moat bridge to the door, and a servant admitted the Narrator. He was led through intricate passageways and past hung armored trophies to Roderick Usher's inner chamber, a sorrowful room where sunlight had never entered.

Usher himself looked equally shut in, almost terrifying: pallid skin like that of a corpse, lustrous eyes, and long hair that seemed to float about his head. Moreover, he was plagued by a kind of sullen, intense, nervous agitation, similar to that of a drug-addict experiencing withdrawl. The list of his complaints was dismaying:

He suffered much from a morbid accuteness of the senses; the most insipid food was alone endurable; he could wear only garments of a certain texture; the odors of all flowers were oppressive; his eyes were tortured even by faint light; and there were but peculiar sounds, and these from stringed instruments, which did not inspire him with horror.

But Usher wasn't alone in the house – the Narrator caught a fleeting glimpse of his friend's twin sister, Madeline, who bore an astonishing resemblance to Roderick. Additionally, it became evident that the brother and sister shared an eerie, almost supernatural, sympathetic bond. Roderick could sense just what Madeline was feeling, and she in turn could read his every thought. Pathetically, though, beloved Madeline was grievously ill, a "gradual wasting away of the person" that was beyond the powers of physicians to cure. On the very night of the Narrator's arrival, Madeline was confined to bed; he never again saw her alive.

For weeks the Narrator tried to distract his depressed friend. They talked, painted, and read together. Usher himself even played the guitar. Once he improvised a wildly horrible ballad about a noble castle invaded by demons – a song which finally convinced the Narrator that Usher had gone mad.

During this time, the two former schoolmates discussed their opinions on various matters. One discussion was especially intense: Usher believed that all matter, even inanimate objects, possessed some measure of intelligence; therefore the very stones of his house, he contended, were in essence alive. Indeed, he had long felt that the entire estate, with its dark atmosphere and personality, had "moulded the destinies of his family" and made him what he was.

Then one day Usher announced to his friend that Madeline was "no more," and that he intended to entomb her body in the house's dungeon rather than bury it. The two carried Madeline's encoffined corpse to the grim and moss-covered underground catacombs and laid it in a vault. There they unscrewed the coffin and lifted the lid. Again startled by the dead sister's resemblance to her brother, the Narrator was even more shocked to note a blush on her cheek. Nevertheless, they resealed the coffin and locked the vault's heavy iron door.

During the week that followed his beloved sister's death, a marked change came over Roderick Usher; he acted more agitated than ever and grew more and more pale. Often he would stare blankly into space, giving the appearance of "laboring with some oppressive secret, which, to divulge, he struggled for the necessary courage."

It happened late one night, when the Narrator found himself unable to sleep. An inexplicable terror took hold of him – a fright which was not at all soothed by the violent storm that raged outside. As he paced nervously about, suddenly Usher dashed into the room. "There was a species of mad hilarity in his eyes . . . hysteria in his whole demeanour."

In an attempt to calm Usher, his friend pulled from the bookcase a second-rate medieval romance and began to read aloud. But in the midst of a passage describing a knight who tears apart a wooden door, the Narrator thought he heard, somewhere in the house, the same cracking and ripping sound so vividly portrayed in the book. Undaunted, he read on – this time, a passage that described the knight's fatal blow to a dragon, which then cried out with a long, piercing wail. Again there immediately emanated from the dark recesses of the house a similar shriek.

Although shaken, the Narrator kept reading. Now the book told of "the clangorous sound of a knight's shield falling to the ground" – and once again, just as the words left his lips, the Narrator heard a distinct metallic ringing noise. At this, he became totally unnerved and turned to Usher, who made a chilling announcement: he had buried his sister alive! All week he had listened to her stirring in her coffin; heard her struggles; felt the beating of her heart. "I heard them – many, many days ago," he admitted. "Yet I dared not – I dared not speak!"

And now - tonight . . . the rending of her coffin, and the grating of the iron hinges of her prison, and her struggles within the copper archway of the vault! The heavy and horrible beating of her heart . . . . Madman! I tell you that she stands without the door!

At that, the antique doors flung open, and there stood the hideous, blood-stained apparition of Lady Madeline. With her last burst of energy, and with a bloodcurdling scream, she fell on her brother, and "in her violent and now final death-agonies, bore him to the floor, a corpse, a victim to the terrors he had anticipated."

Aghast, the Narrator fled down the shadowy halls and from the house. At some distance, he glanced back. There, in the light of the "full, setting and blood-red moon," he saw the massive House of Usher being rent into pieces by a whirlwind, and then swallowed up into the dark lake that surrounded it.

Commentary:

One of the earliest and most famous of all horror stories, *The Fall of the House of Usher* is filled with the elements that fans of the genre relish: a decaying manor house, dungeons, medieval trappings, suggestions of dementia . . . It's hard to say that Poe's plot is exceptional; it seems that he is attempting to create not so much a story as a *feeling* – a deep sense within the reader of mankind's "grim, phantasmic FEAR" (Roderick's words).

Some critics have suggested that the story is not meant to be taken seriously; that it is intended as a parody of traditional horror. Some may find tremendous symbolism in the tale: twins tied in life and in death as they had been in birth; a strong woman's struggle to free herself and survive being buried alive, then returning to punish a weak man. References to blood at the end suggest to some that Madeline perhaps was a vampiress. Still others simply enjoy Poe's unmatched style that conjures up remarkably horrid mental images and brings on a wonderfully grim suspense.

In all, the imaginative details and descriptions, the inventive drama, and the sheer popularity of the story, have made it a literary classic.

THE GRAPES OF WRATH

by
John Steinbeck
(1902 - 1968)

Type of work: Social/political criticism

Setting: Oklahoma and California; 1930's

Principal characters:

> *Tom Joad*, a recent parolee in his mid-twenties
>
> *Ma and Pa Joad*, a strong, middle-aged Oklahoma couple
>
> *Noah Joad*, their strange eldest son
>
> *Al*, their wild sixteen-year-old
>
> *Rose of Sharon*, eldest Joad daughter, married and pregnant
>
> *Gramma and Grampa Joad*, an earthy old couple
>
> *Jim Casy*, a preacher and, later, a labor agitator
>
> *Other Joad children*

Story Overview:

As Tom Joad hitchhiked his way home after a four-year stay in prison for killing a man in a fight, he met up with Jim Casy, a former preacher who was returning from a sojourn in the "wilderness," where he had been soul-searching. Tom invited Jim to walk with him on the dusty road to the Joad family farm, and to stay for dinner. Arriving there, he saw that "the small unpainted house was mashed at one corner, and it had been pushed off its foundations so that it slumped at an angle." The farm was deserted. Muley Graves, a near-by tenant farmer, told Tom that his family had moved to their Uncle John's house: " . . . They was going to stick it out when the bank come to tractorin' off the place." A long drought was making barren ground out of what had once been fertile farmland.

Early the following morning Tom and Casy walked the eight miles to Uncle John's farm. As they approached, Tom saw his Pa working on a truck in the yard. Pa's "eyes looked at Tom's face, and then gradually his brain became aware of what he saw." With Tom's homecoming, the Joad family unit was complete. Now Ma and Pa, the pregnant oldest daughter Rose of Sharon, and her husband Connie, Grampa, Gramma, and all the rest started packing: they were all "goin' to California" to start over as fruit pickers.

Like thousands of other displaced tenant farmers, the Joads, spurred on by the promise of good wages and sunshine, sold what they could, bought a used car and headed out on Highway 66, "a people in flight, refugees from dust and shrinking land, from the thunder of tractors and shrinking ownership."

After the supplies and tools were loaded into the old Hudson, which teen-aged Al Joad had converted into a truck, the Joad family and Casy (twelve people in all) squeezed into what little space was left and started west.

During the first overnight stop, Grampa suddenly was hit by a stroke and died. They buried him on the roadside.

Soon the Joads met up with the Wilsons, a married couple with a broken-down car. After Al had fixed the vehicle, Ma and Pa Joad invited the Wilsons to travel with them. "You won't be no burden. Each'll help each, an' we'll all git to California," Ma said.

The two groups "crawled westward as a unit", suffering along the way from too little money, not enough food, dilapidated vehicles, profiteering junk dealers and overpriced replacement parts. Eastward-bound migrants warned the travelers that working conditions in California were bad; but they still pressed on toward the "promised land."

Crossing the border into California, the family camped next to a river that ran parallel to the town of Needles. They'd wait until nightfall to cross the desert. As Tom, Noah and Pa sat down in the shallow river water to wash off the road grime, they were joined by an itinerant father and his son who apprised them of the treatment they could expect in California: "Okie use' ta mean you was from Oklahoma. Now it means you're a dirty son-of-a-bitch. Okie means you're scum."

Later that day, Tom's aloof and backward brother Noah notified him that he was staying to live by the river, and then wandered away. That evening, after saying good-bye to the Wilsons, the Joads began the last leg of their journey. Early during the desert crossing, Gramma quietly died, but Ma waited until they reached Bakersfield before she told anyone. After another roadside burial, the family drove on into a "Hooverville" – one of many designated migrant camps opened during the Depression. Like other Hoovervilles, it was a chaotic community; "little gray tents, shacks, and cars were scattered about at random." But the Joads elected to stay.

On their first evening in the camp, two men in a shiny sedan drove up, a labor contractor and a local sheriff. The contractor had come out to offer jobs to the migrants, but when he declined to reveal the actual wage he was prepared to pay, a fight ensued. Tom and Casy got in the middle of things and managed to knock the sheriff out cold. Since Tom was on parole and couldn't afford any more trouble, Casy ordered him to hide while he stayed behind to give himself up in Tom's place.

That night, before the family drove away, Rose of Sharon's husband sneaked off, abandoning his wife and soon-to-be-born child. From the Hooverville, sounds of shouts and screams could be heard as the clattering old Hudson crept away in the night.

The Joads headed south toward Weedpatch, where they had heard a government camp was located. Once there, they were immediately struck by how different this camp was from the Hooverville. Clean showers with hot water greeted them; indoor toilets, and the best Saturday night dances in the county. The camp's inhabitants had the right to make their own rules and elect their own leaders. Unfortunately, though, there was no work in any of the surrounding areas. The children began having dizzy spells from hunger, and with Rose of Sharon near to giving birth, they had to make a decision: they left the camp on their last tank of gas.

As the worn-out vehicle headed north, the Joads met a man who pointed them to possible work on the Hooper ranch near Pixley. When they finally reached the ranch, however, they found themselves in the middle of a heated dispute. A row of policemen held back picketing strikers, who shouted and cursed at the "scab" peach pickers crossing their lines. But the Joads didn't care – they were hungry. Everyone except Ma and Rose of Sharon, who stayed behind to clean their filthy new home, straightway went to work. Before nightfall, the men and children had earned one dollar among them, and Ma took their note of credit to the company store, where she was able to buy a little hamburger, bread, potatoes and coffee.

After eating his scanty dinner, Tom ambled down through the brush along the highway to investigate what all the commotion was about. He came upon a tent. To his surprise, he discovered that Casy the preacher was one of the main agitators. Casy gave Tom the lowdown: "We come to work there. They says it's gonna be fi' cents . . . . We got there an' they says they're payin' two an' a half cents . . . . Now they're payin' you five. When they bust this here strike – ya think they'll pay you five?"

Tom was about to return to the ranch when suddenly he heard "guys comin' from ever' which way." Everyone scattered for cover, but Tom and Casy were intercepted by two deputies. "You fellas don' know what you're doin'," protested Casy. "You're helpin' to starve kids." The nearest deputy snatched up a pick handle and cracked Casy's skull, killing him. In a fit of passion, Tom wrenched the club free and clubbed the deputy to the ground. As he bolted from the confusion, he received a deep gash on his face but managed to make it back to the ranch, where he hid out. As the family worked on, the strike was broken, and just as Casy had predicted, the pay for peaches dropped to two-and-a-half cents a box.

Soon, all the peaches were picked, and once again the Joads set out. Luckily, they happened on some work picking cotton. While they camped with other migrants in abandoned boxcars along a stream, Tom, still hunted by the law, stayed a few miles down the road in a clump of trees. At last the Joads were making enough money to eat properly.

Then the littlest girl, Ruthie, made a mistake: during a fight with another girl, she threatened to get her big brother, who had "already kil't two fellas . . . " That evening, Ma took Tom his dinner, told him about Ruthie's words, slipped him seven dollars that she had saved, and urged him to leave – for his own and the family's sake. Tom hugged Ma and promised he would carry on Casy's work of improving the worker's plight.

When the cotton picking ended, the Joads remained in the boxcar; winter was approaching, along with the birth of Rose of Sharon's baby. The money was nearly gone. Hunger and hopelessness grew.

Amid heavy rains, Rose finally gave birth – to a stillborn son. As the stream swelled into a thundering river, water began entering the boxcar. The soaked, frantic and fragmented family ran for higher ground. Finally sheltering in a rickety barn, they found inside a young boy tending his sickly father. "Got to have soup or milk," he told them. "You folks got money to git milk?"

Bereft of her baby, Rose of Sharon now went to the famished man, bared her breast, and nourished him with her milk. It was all she had.

Commentary:

Perhaps Steinbeck's most popular and true-to-life novel, *The Grapes of Wrath* exposes the grinding hardships of the "Okie" migrants. With brief yet descriptive passages moving quickly from one scene to another, he conveys a sustained air of urgency.

The novel is heavy with religious symbolism: Casy offers himself to suffer for Tom's crime, then later dies uttering, "Father forgive them . . . "; the family meets up with fathers and sons throughout; the stillborn baby is placed in a wooden box and set adrift, Moses-like, on the river; the name "Rose of Sharon" comes from the Song of Solomon . . . and the list goes on and on.

As a portrait of a family being destroyed by nature, mechanization, greed, and changing times, and as a sometimes sentimental yet powerful indictment of our capitalist economy, this book is a masterpiece.

However, it can be argued that even through all of the appallingly harsh events the Joad family endures, the book promotes optimism; a "milk-of-human-kindness" theme; a journey from "drought and despair" that ends in "water and hope." Though capricious nature – and human nature – can not always be depended upon to alleviate human misery, Rose's act of mercy symbolizes the need for all of us to develop within ourselves a genuine responsibility and compassion for each other.

CANDIDE

by
Voltaire
(1694 - 1778)

Type of work: Satirical novel

Setting: Europe and frontier South America; mid-eighteenth century

Principal characters:
  Candide, a naive young man
  Pangloss, Candide's tutor and philosopher friend
  Cunegonde, the beautiful daughter of a baron
  Cacambo, Candide's servant and companion
  Martin, a later traveling companion

Story Overview:

Candide, the illegitimate son of a Baron's sister, was sent to live with the Baron at his beautiful castle in Westphalia.

The Baroness weighed about three hundred and fifty pounds, was therefore greatly respected, and did the honors of the house with a dignity which rendered her still more respect. Her daughter Cunegonde, aged seventeen, was rosy-cheeked, fresh, plump and tempting. The Baron's son appeared in every respect worthy of his father. The tutor Pangloss was the oracle of the house, and little Candide followed his lessons with all the candor of his age and character.

Pangloss, "the greatest philosopher of the province and therefore of the whole world," taught Candide that he lived in "the best of all possible worlds." His theory was that "since everything is made for an end, everything is necessarily for the best end."

Observe that noses were made to wear spectacles; and so we have spectacles. Legs were visibly instituted to be breeched, and we have breeches ...

Over the years at the castle, Candide adopted dear Pangloss' optimism. However, his bliss was not to be. Candide soon became infatuated with the beauty of Cunegonde, and one day had an intimate encounter with her in the castle. The noble Baron witnessed this scene and drove his daughter's young suitor out of the house.

With no provisions and no money, Candide quickly found himself recruited into the Bulgar army. But, tiring of army routine, and following Pangloss' theory that all men were free, he simply walked away. He was caught, however, and forced to run the gauntlet. Collapsing after the second round, Candide begged to be killed, but was instead pardoned by the passing Bulgar king.

Later, after surviving a brutal battle and witnessing the repulsive treatment of innocent villagers, Candide once again walked away in disgust. As he wandered through the countryside, he was denied a piece of bread by a preacher who had just finished a sermon on charity. Near starvation, he was finally taken in by a kind Anabaptist.

The following day Candide met up with a wretched beggar who turned out to be his old tutor, Pangloss. Pangloss had shocking news for Candide: his beloved Cunegonde had been stolen away, raped, and disemboweled by Bulgar soldiers. The disheartened young man wept uncontrollably.

Months passed. Pangloss and Candide were appointed accountants to the generous Anabaptist and journeyed with him toward Lisbon. Nearing the city, their ship was caught in a storm and sank. All aboard were drowned except Candide, Pangloss, and a villainous sailor. Just as the three reached shore, a tremendous earthquake and volcanic eruption destroyed the city. The sailor went to work looting and plundering through the town's wreckage. Even though Candide and Pangloss tried to help the city's survivors, it was they who were arrested by a supersitious mob and slated to be human sacrifices to quell any further earthquakes.

The appointed day arrived. Pangloss was taken out to be hanged. But Candide, escaping a similar fate, was merely preached at, flogged – then absolved of his sin and blessed!

An old woman treated Candide's wounds and took him to a lonely house on the edge of town, where he was reunited with his beautiful Cunegonde. Cunegonde told her overjoyed lover that, since surviving the soldiers' obviously nonfatal mistreatment, she had served as a mistress to numerous men and currently worked for both a Jew and a Grand Inquisitor. Just then the Jew entered the room to find his mistress and Candide entwined on the couch. In self-defense, Candide killed him. As the lovers considered their plight, the Grand Inquisitor also entered, and Candide was forced to take his life as well. (The Jew's body was later thrown on a dungheap, while the remains of the Inquisitor were given a ceremonial burial at the local church.)

Candide, Cunegonde and the old woman fled on horseback. At last they reached Cadiz, where Candide was once again recruited into the army, this time as a captain. He was sent to Paraguay to purge the Jesuits. During the voyage, Candide frankly admitted that, contrary to Pangloss' idealistic theory, "regrettable things happen in this world of ours."

The ship reached Buenos Aires, and the governor sent the trusting Candide out to review the troops. Then, in Candide's absence, he proposed marriage to lovely Cunegonde.

As Candide was reviewing the troops, the old woman arrived to warn him that a Spanish ship had entered the harbor; officials had debarked to arrest the murderer of the Grand Inquisitor. Clearly unable to save Cunegonde from the governor's grasp, Candide and a servant, Cacambo, again fled for their lives. They joined with Paraguayan forces; and when Candide was taken to see the colonel, he was overwhelmed to recognize him as the son of the late Baron – Cunegonde's brother! The two hurriedly devised a plan for her rescue; but when Candide revealed his intentions to marry Cunegonde, the colonel flew into a rage. Candide was not of royal birth and had no claim to her. Candide stabbed him with his sword, then, once more, he and Cacambo excaped to the South American frontier.

In one of many strange encounters, Candide and Cacambo awoke one morning to find themselves in peril of being eaten by Oreillon natives. They were released, but only after convincing their captors that they were not Jesuits.

On another occasion, while wandering across the land the men discovered an underground river. They followed its course, which led to the hidden city of Eldorado. At last; here was the Utopian society which had built itself on Pangloss' "best of all possible worlds" philosophy. In Eldorado, there was only one religion, no civil or religious wars, no courts of law (for none were necessary), and the king was of high moral character. Diamonds and precious gems littered the ground like pebbles. But Candide could not be happy without Cunegonde, and he requested to leave that land of paradise in search of his beloved. The king graciously permitted the exit of Candide and Cacambo and supplied them with one hundred sheep loaded with jewels.

Only two sheep survived the perilous sea journey. With little remaining money, Candide ordered Cacambo return to Paraguay to buy Cunegonde from the governor. He would then rendezvous with them in Venice.

Candide continued alone on his journey. A dishonest ship's captain stole Candide's last sheep and jewels, leaving the traveler once again miserable and destitute. Nevertheless, together with a new traveling companion, Martin, who had a little money, Candide sailed for Venice. En route, they came upon a Dutch and a Spanish ship at battle. As the Dutch ship was sinking Candide learned it was the ship of the rogue who had stolen his sheep. Miraculously, he was able to recover one of the jewel-laden animals before the ship went down.

In France, Candide's last pocketful of jewels rapidly diminished, as he innocently satisfied the greed of deceiving strangers and corrupt officials. Surely even the idealist Pangloss would have viewed these predators as a most disgusting and wicked people.

Arriving in Venice, Candide searched in vain for Cunegonde and Cacambo. Martin, his new friend-turned-philosopher, added to Candide's despair by continually lamenting that all was not for the best; that all people were most miserable; that the world was "very mad and very abominable."

One evening Candide chanced to meet up with Cacambo, who was being held in bondage.

Cacambo informed his friend that Cunegonde had been forced to sail on to Constantinople. Immediately they set out to find her.

On the voyage, Candide recognized two of the galley slaves aboard the ship: one turned out to be his beloved Pangloss and the other Cunegonde's brother. Both were alive and well! The brother had survived the wound Candide had thought fatal, and the tutor-philosopher had escaped hanging in Lisbon due to the bungling hangman's ineptness in tying a proper knot. To Candide's dismay, Pangloss still clung to his optimistic views.

Candide purchased the two slaves and continued on with them toward Canstantinople. There they found Cunegonde and the old woman. However, Cunegonde was no longer beautiful, but shrewish and ugly. Yet once again Candide professed his love and desire to marry her. The brother again raged, so Candide returned him to the galley and back to slavery.

Pooling their money and talents, Candide, ugly Cunegonde, Pangloss, Martin, and a few others purchased a farm, and committed themselves to a life of duty and work. "Let us work without theorizing," said Martin; "'tis the only way to make life endurable."

Pangloss, though, still sometimes tried to persuade Candide otherwise:

All events are linked up in this best of all possible worlds; for, if you had not been expelled from the noble castle, by hard kicks in your backside for love of Mademoiselle Cunegonde, if you had not been clapped into the Inquisition, if you had not wandered about America on foot, if you had not stuck your sword in the Baron, if you had not lost all your sheep from the land of Eldorado, you would not be eating candied citrons and pistachios here.

"That's well said," replied Candide, "but we must cultivate our garden."

Commentary:

Candide is easily Voltaire's wittiest novel. In its time it was a powerful tool for political attack on Europe's degenerate and immoral society. The work vividly and satirically portrays the horrors of eitheenth-century life: civil and religious wars, sexual diseases, despotic rulers, the arbitrary punishment of innocent victims – the same enduring problems we witness today.

Through the constant misfortunes of Candide, Voltaire poses meaningful questions about the nature of suffering. Pangloss' philosophy is eagerly and enthusiastically accepted by Candide in the beginning of the novel. But toward the end of his life he refutes this Utopian theory, concluding that diligence in labor is the only answers to a life constantly riddled with bad luck. Indeed, Voltaire teaches that man is incapable of understanding the evil in the world, and concludes that the fundamental aim in life is not happiness, but survival.

A CONNECTICUT YANKEE IN KING ARTHUR'S COURT

by
Mark Twain
(1835 - 1910)

Type of work: Social satire

Setting: England; 6th-century, during the reign of King Arthur

Principal characters:
Hank Morgan, the Connecticut Yankee "Boss"; in reality a 19th-century mechanic
King Arthur, King of England
Merlin, Arthur's court magician
Sandy, Hank's sixth-century wife

Story Overview:

Hank Morgan, born in Hartford, Connecticut, was head superintendent at a vast arms factory. There he had the means to create anything – guns, revolvers, cannons, boilers, engines, and all sorts of labor-saving machinery. If there wasn't already a quick, newfangled way to do a thing, Hank could easily invent one. Supervising more than a thousand men had also taught Hank how to handle just about anybody – until he found himself involved with a bully named Hercules in a "misunderstanding conducted with crowbars," and was knocked out by a "crusher" to the side of his head. When he came to, Hank was sitting under an oak tree. A man decked out in polished armor appeared and thundered toward confused, groggy Hank. After confronting him rudely, the man claimed Hank as his prisoner and took him to his court in the land of Camelot.

Hank had been captured by Sir Kay of King Arthur's Roundtable. He was presented before a court led by Merlin, the braggart magician who had helped Arthur in his rise to the throne, and it was quickly decreed that Hank Morgan should die at mid-day on June twenty-first, the year of our Lord, 528. Certainly, King Arthur's England was not the gallant world depicted in Fairy Tales, but a cruel, feudalistic society; and it looked as though Morgan would be a casualty of this barbaric order. But, resourceful Yankee that he was, Hank remembered that on June 21, A.D. 528 a total eclipse of the sun had supposedly occurred. If indeed he was a nineteenth-century traveler lost in the days of chivalry, he could use this knowledge to his advantage.

The appointed day came and Hank was unshackled and taken out of his dungeon cell to be burned at the stake. While fagots were meticulously piled around him, Hank stood calmly, his hands pointing toward the sun. Then he solemnly warned the onlookers that he was about to smother the whole world in the dead blackness of midnight. At that moment, the eclipse began. As the earth was covered in shadows, the people turned in terror to Hank, who then extracted a promise from King Arthur: Hank demanded to be appointed the King's per-petual minister and chief executive. The clever Yankee supplanted Merlin as Arthur's advisor, and the magician was cast into prison.

Though he was now the second most powerful person in the kingdom, Hank missed the little conveniences he had left behind in modern life, such as soap, matches and candles. The castle walls were barren and cold; there was no looking glass and no glass in the windows; there were no books, pens, paper or ink. And worst of all, no sugar, coffee, tea or tobacco were anywhere to be found in the castle. If Hank's new life was going to be bearable, he would have to invent, contrive, create, and reorganize things – the very tasks he liked most.

Fearing interference from the church, Hank set out in secret to improve, not only his own living standards, but also the dreary lot of the commoners in Arthur's feudal kingdom. In a short time he had set up telegraph and telephone services. He scoured the land for bright young men to train as journalists and mechanics. Workmen in his newly built factories fabricated guns, cannons, soap, and almost any handy item imaginable. Known as "The Boss," Hank also established schools, but he was most proud of his "West Point" – a military and naval academy. Even though Hank was high in command, and feared as a powerful magician besides, he was not of noble birth, and the nobility looked down on him. This wasn't particularly bothersome to Hank, however, since he held them in the same low regard.

Three years passed. One day, Merlin, now released from prison and disguised as Sir Sagramor, challenged Hank to a duel. To prepare himself for the encounter, the Yankee decided to go on a quest. He donned a set of uncomfortable armor and off he went through the countryside. In the wake of his journey he encountered freemen, noblemen, and hermits. He spent many hours thinking about how to banish oppression from the land and restore rights to Camelot's citizens, without "disobliging anybody."

The Boss, however, also experienced numerous comical episodes. He once turned aside a half-dozen charging knights by blowing a column of pipe smoke from beneath his armored face shield. He later managed to rescue a talkative young maiden, Alisande, from some unknown danger. "Sandy" prattled endlessly as she rode with Hank through the countryside. All the while, he continued in his quest, educating spirited young men, pardoning those unjustly imprisoned, and altering the pitiable state of the commoner.

During his various wanderings, Hank

was once commissioned to restore water to a miraculous healing fount that had ceased to flow. Inspecting the well, he determined that it had merely sprung a leak. Much to the chagrin of the meddlesome Merlin, who had unsuccessfully attempted to bring back the water by magic, the Yankee "divinely" restored the water's flow. Merlin went home in shame, while Hank returned to Camelot a hero.

Still, Morgan was appalled by the lives the people led. They were trodden down by churchmen and nobility alike. Hank soon began to secretly work for the overthrow of the church and the end to royal privilege. To accomplish these ends, he donned common peasant garb and set out to travel the land. King Arthur, hearing of the idea, chose to accompany him. Arthur's eyes were quickly opened to the plight of his people. He beheld a pathetic family dying of smallpox. A young, broken-hearted girl with a baby was hanged because she had stolen some cloth. They met men confined to prison for thirty, forty, or fifty years, no one knowing why they were there in the first place.

Near the final stage of their quest, Hank and the King were forced into the horrors of slavery and taken, shackled, to London. King Arthur showed himself to be a stately man; never once did he lose his kingly demeanor or his virtuous approach to life. However, due to some slight misbehaviors, both he and his councilor were condemned to die by hanging. At this point, Hank made an ingenious escape, found a telephone, informed Camelot of what was happening, and received the reassurance that five hundred knights would hasten forthwith to London. But before he could rendezvous with the royal army, Hank found himself recaptured. Time was running out. The King was blindfolded and his head placed in the noose. Then, just at the last moment, Morgan spied Lancelot with his five hundred knights rushing toward the city square – on bicycles! By means of a modern invention, Hank and the King had been saved.

Back in Camelot, The Boss was still faced with a duel against Sir Sagramor. With no armor, Hank easily dodged the cumbersome knight until he was able to lasso him and pull him from his horse. But when the combatants returned for another round to the field of battle, the Yankee found that Merlin had stolen his lasso. He had no alternative except to shoot Sagramor with his gun.

King Arthur had seen enough of a decayed, immoral Camelot. Slavery was abolished. Knights gave up the deadly art of chivalry – though they still insisted on wearing their armor. Instead they became engineers or conductors on the railway between London and Camelot. They played baseball, sold sewing machines and soap, and played the stock market. Camelot had become a modern American town in the midst of ancient Great Britain.

In the meantime, Hank had married Sandy and they had a little girl. As the years passed and things continued to run smoothly, Hank took his family to tour in France. Four weeks later, when they returned to England, the land had been laid desolate by invading forces. Moreover, King Arthur had finally been forced to admit that Queen Guinevere and Lancelot were embroiled in an affair. In the resulting wars and battles, the King, Lancelot, and most of the major knights of the kingdom were killed. The church declared an Interdict against Hank Morgan and his work, and gathered all the remaining knights to uncover and execute the Yankee intruder.

Realizing the danger, The Boss gathered his few remaining supporters and retired to Merlin's former cave. There, they prepared for the upcoming battle by digging trenches and putting up electric fences. On the day of the attack, over 10,000 knights came forth to battle – and over 10,000 knights were either electrocuted or drowned. But in the midst of the action, Hank was stabbed. An old hag offered to nurse him to health; no one recognized her as Merlin.

Meanwhile, trapped inside the cave by piles of dead bodies of the knights who had earlier attacked, Hank's men were slowly dying, choked by a poisonous gas given off by the rotting corpses. The gas did, in fact, kill everyone – except Hank. The last spell Merlin cast before he himself perished, caused Hank Morgan to sleep for thirteen hundred years – until wakened safely once again in his own century.

Commentary:

Mark Twain was fascinated by Sir Thomas Malory's "Morte d'Arthur." According to his notebook, Twain dreamed one night of being a knight in Arthur's court and of the many inconveniences this presented. This dream inspired him with his story of a clever Yankee machinist who attempts to modernize and improve Camelot.

A Connecticut Yankee exposes the glorified knight errantry of legend as childish barbarism; a feudal system that abused and deprived the common people. Conversely, Twain's principles of good government lifted the commoners and the nobility alike into a new life of dignity and purpose.

From beginning to end, this book is a surprising and powerful combination of homiletics and humor. For instance, Twain vividly portrays the brutality of slavery, and immediately follows these scenes with a comical rescue of the King and Hank Morgan by knights on bicycles. The novel was originally envisioned as a pleasant burlesque of Camelot; but social conscience and outrage against man's inhumanity to man consistently found their way to the surface, producing a serious social satire layered with wit and wisdom. This constant shifting between social humor and social disgust makes this book one of Twain's most memorable.

1984

by
George Orwell
(1903 - 1949)

Type of work: Futuristic, cautionary novel

Setting: London, in the mythical country of Oceania; 1984 (in the future)

Principal characters:
Winston Smith, a rebel against society
Julia, his lover
Mr. Charrington, an elderly antique shop owner
O'Brien, the only member of the Inner Party Winston trusts

Story Overview:

As Winston Smith entered his apartment building, he passed a familiar poster. "It was one of those pictures which are so contrived that the eyes follow you about when you move. BIG BROTHER IS WATCHING YOU, the caption beneath it ran." Then Winston opened the door to his flat to be greeted by a voice on his "telescreen" – a device he could dim, but never shut off completely. Telescreens broadcasted government propaganda and served as the eyes and ears of the Thought Police, who scrutinized everyone for any possible deviation from acceptable thought or action.

In the flat was a tiny alcove just out of sight from the telescreen's vision. Winston sat down to write in his diary, an act that was not officially illegal "but if detected it was reasonably certain that it would be punished by death . . . " While he sat writing, a recent memory stirred in his mind; the "Two Minutes Hate," a government-sponsored work break in which every worker at the Ministry of Truth was required to participate, had consisted that day of an interlude when everyone raged and screamed as the telescreen alternately flashed images of enemy Eurasian soldiers and Golstein, an abhorred traitor. That morning, Winston had noticed a "bold-looking girl of about twenty-six" who worked in the Fiction Department. This particular girl – wearing the bright scarlet sash of the official anti-sex league – gave him "the impression of being more dangerous than most," and Winston had the unnerving feeling that she was watching him.

A few days later, Winston walked through the working-class "prole" neighborhood to the antique shop where he had bought his diary. Though class barriers stood tensely in place throughout Oceania, Mr. Charrington, the shop owner, welcomed him and invited him upstairs to see other items. There wasn't much there, but Winston liked the old-fashioned room; it didn't even have a telescreen.

When Winston again slipped out onto the street, he passed the dark-haired girl from the Fiction Department. Now he was sure she was an informant.

Back at work, as Winston walked toward the lavatory, the girl reappeared in the hall. Then, just a few feet in front of him, she stumbled and fell. When he offered his hand to help her up, she slipped him a scrap of paper. Shaken, Winston decided to open the paper later at the cubicle where he rewrote old newspaper articles, deleting any referrence to persons who had deviated from orthodoxy.

Back at his desk, Winston opened the message and read: "I love you." Now he was intrigued – and terrified. Like writing in a diary, an affair between party members was "legal", but punishable by death.

Winston and the girl were finally able to arrange a rendezvous in the country. But even there, there was always the possibility of concealed microphones. So, after meeting at the selected spot, the pair walked on in silence until they found a remote, heavily forested area. Winston didn't even yet know the girl's name: "I'm thirty-nine years old," he began. "I've got a wife that I can't get rid of. I've got varicose veins . . . " The girl replied, "I couldn't care less." She shared some blackmarket chocolate with him, and then they made love. Afterwards, while the girl slept, Winston thought about what they had done. "You could not have pure love or pure lust nowadays. No emotion was pure, because everything was mixed up with fear and hatred. Their embrace had been a battle, the climax a victory. It was a blow struck against the Party. It was a political act."

Winston now saw the girl – Julia – whenever he could. She explained her survival philosophy: "I always carry one end of a banner in the processions. I always look cheerful and I never shirk anything. Always yell with the crowd, that's what I say. It's the only way to be safe." For their clandestine meetings, Winston hit upon the idea of renting Mr. Charrington's room above the antique shop. However, although the room offered them privacy, "both of them knew it was lunacy"; in the end, they would be caught. Occasionally the lovers "talked of engaging in active rebellion against the Party, but with no notion of how to take the first step." They considered joining a mysterious subversive group called the "Brotherhood," but didn't know if this legendary underground cabal even existed.

Besides Julia, there was one person Winston felt he could trust. For months a "strange intimacy" had been ripening between himself and an Inner Party member named O'Brien, who worked at the Ministry of Truth. No words had passed between them; only glances that seemed to reflect the same brooding rebel spirit in both men. Then one day O'Brien spoke up and asked Winston his opinion of the revised "Newspeak" dictionary. Winston responded that he hadn't seen it yet. O'Brien invited him to pick up a copy at his house later that week.

When Winston and Julia arrived at O'Brien's spacious home, their host surprised them by instructing his servant to turn off the telescreen – one of many privileges extended to Inner Party members. Now that they could not be overheard, Winston admitted why they had really come: "We believe that there is some kind of conspiracy . . . working against the Party, and that you are involved in it. We want to join . . . . We are enemies of the Party." O'Brien nodded his head and lifted his glass. "To Emmanuel Goldstein," he intoned, referring to the reputed leader of the Brotherhood. The Brotherhood existed, then! But before they could join, O'Brien had to know the extent of their committment. When both Winston and Julia conceded that they would do anything to weaken the Party's power, he gave them a copy of Goldstein's book, the "Bible" of the Brotherhood.

The next week was "Hate Week" at the Ministry of Truth – seven hectic days devoted to stirring up hatred against the nation of Eurasia, Oceania's current enemy at arms. Unfortunately, on the sixth day of Hate Week, Oceania also declared war against Eastasia. This meant that Winston, already exhausted, had to go back and re-alter news articles to reflect the change in enemies. Finally though, he and Julia were able to sneak away to Charrington's shop to read Goldstein's treatise. It explained how the Party used the threat of outside aggression to control the people, diverting their frustrations away from pandemic governmental corruption and food shortages.

Suddenly an "iron voice" reverberated from behind a picture in the room. "Remain exactly where your are," the voice commanded. "Make no movement until you are ordered." Then Thought Police burst in, with Mr. Charrington behind them, shouting orders. The two were taken away in separate vehicles.

Standing alone in a tiny cell in the Ministry of Love, Winston observed as other prisoners were brought in, some badly beaten and pleading not to be exiled to "Room 101" – the room containing "the most horrible thing in the world." One man raved: " . . . I've got a wife and three children . . . . You can take the whole lot of them and cut their throats in front of my eyes, [but] not room 101!"

Winston had seen nothing of Julia, but after a while, O'Brien came to Winston's cell. "They got you too!" Winston cried. "They got me a long time ago," O'Brien answered back with "mild, almost regretful irony." As it turned out, O'Brien was to be Winston's interrogator; he was charged with the task of making Winston "love Big Brother."

For weeks Winston was beaten, starved, and deprived of sleep. He was hooked to a machine designed to teach him a new mode of thinking. O'Brien, acting as "teacher," would inflict greater and greater levels of pain on Winston, and then as "savior," would benevolently release the lever. When O'Brien held up four fingers and asked how many there were, Winston replied

four. The needle on the machine's dial shot up, as frightening shocks vibrated through his limbs and joints. Then Winston answered five fingers but O'Brien recognized the lie and delivered even greater pain. "You are a slow learner," said O'Brien gently. "How can I help it?" Winston blubbered. "How can I help seeing what is in front of my eyes? Two and two are four."

"Sometimes, Winston. Sometimes they are five. Sometimes they are three. Sometimes they are all of them at once. You must try harder. It is not easy to become sane," O'Brien shrieked. "You must love Big Brother. It is not enough to obey him . . . . Room 101!"

"Can you think of a single degradation that has not happened to you?" O'Brien asked as they reached Room 101. Winston could only answer, "I have not betrayed Julia . . . "

In Room 101 Winston was made to confront his personal "most horrible thing in the world" – a cage full of hungry rats. The moment that O'Brien reached to lift the gate of the cage, Winston's "bowels seemed to turn to water," and suddenly he knew that there was one and only one way to save himself; "he must interpose another human being . . . between himself and the rats."

"Do it to Julia!" he screamed frantically. "Not me! Julia! I don't care what you do to her . . . "

Released from the Ministry of Love, Winston spent his time in the Chestnut Tree Cafe, drinking an endless supply of "Victory Gin" and waiting for the day when "they" put a gun to the back of his head and pulled the trigger. He saw Julia on occasion, but there was really nothing left to say between them. A familiar and once sinister refrain from prison now echoed in them both: "Under the spreading chestnut tree, I sold you and you sold me."

And so, "everything was all right, the struggle was finished. [Winston] had won the victory over himself. He loved Big Brother."

Commentary:

Published in 1948, *1984* (the year-numbers were transposed) has provoked discussion and controversy ever since. Though a world war had just been fought to squelch the tyranny of a Totalitarian regime, Orwell warned that the world was yet heading towards just such a political system. He found it especially ironic that the champions of thought should become the chief instruments of its suppression.

Orwell's novel was intended as an urgent warning that political decisions in the near future could create a brutally stifled society of "Newspeak" (where words are so abstracted from events and actions that they take on their exact opposite meaning) and "Doublethink" (the power to hold two contradictory ideas simultaneously). "Big Brother" and "Room 101" – and many other graphic coinages from its pages – remain as standard references in our language, years after 1984 has come and gone, an indication of the book's profound social influence.

THE PRINCE AND THE PAUPER

by
Mark Twain
(1835 - 1910)

Type of work: Social and political satire

Setting: England; 1547

Principal characters:
Edward Tudor, young Prince of Wales
Tom Canty, a pauper boy
Miles Hendon, a kindhearted nobleman

Story Overview:

A boy was born on an autumn afternoon to the poverty-stricken Canty family. With the state of London's sixteenth-century economy staring them in the face, the family did not want the child.

On the same day another English lad was born into the rich and royal Tudor family. These parents savored their baby – in fact all of England had longed, hoped and prayed for this son. Now that he had arrived, the British subjects were overjoyed; young Edward Tudor, Prince of Wales, was revered by all – in stark contrast to Tom Canty's birth, of which no one took note excepting his family, who was only troubled by his arrival.

Tom Canty grew up in Offal Court. He lived a wretched life, and indeed, knew no other. Every morning Tom was sent off to beg. If he came home empty-handed, his father and his grandmother would soundly beat him. So, often, when the afternoon rolled around and the boy reckoned that he had begged enough to avoid a beating, he would race to Father Andrew's monastary for the remainder of the day. Over the months, the good Father taught Tom how to read, gave him some instruction in Latin, and recited wondrous tales of royalty. And because of his education, intelligence and grace, Tom seemed far wiser than others his age. People would frequently come seeking his advice, despite his low station.

But it was the beggar boy's greatest wish to witness a real prince all decked out in his royal attire; and one January morning Tom obtained his wish. He journeyed to Charing Village, the site of the King's majestic palace, and, to his amazement, inside the fence he beheld a young boy his age – a true prince. As he drew closer and closer to observe the little gentleman, suddenly he was rudely snatched up by a soldier. The prince, Edward Tudor, saw this action and came to Tom's rescue, and afterward he invited the young pauper into the palace. So, the Prince of Poverty passed the palace gates to join hands with the Prince of Limitless Plenty.

Safely within the castle, the prince gave Tom some food. Soon they were comfortably chatting back and forth about their different families and opposite lifestyles. On a whim, Tom and Edward changed into each others clothes. And when they stared into the mirror, a miracle seemed to have happened: they appeared to be twins – the same hair and eyes, face and countenance, voice and manner. Then, while still in the changed garments, Edward noticed Tom's bruised hand and went out to reprimand the guard who had caused it. The soldier laughed at the waif's pretense to royal wrath, and instantly tossed him out the gate. Tom Canty was now the new Prince of Wales and Edward became the prince of paupers.

Edward's life as a beggar was not as he had been accustomed. First, he was abused and ridiculed by a crowd as he professed to be England's rightful prince. Then, Tom's drunken father found him, and took him home to Offal Court, where Edward was beaten. That night, however, the father received word that he was wanted for murder. As he hurriedly rushed to escape, dragging the boy behind him, Edward managed to twist free from his grasp, and he disappeared into the crowded street.

Once a distance from the Canty house, Edward put himself in a precarious position by again trying to convince others that he was a prince. Of course, the commoners and merchants again mocked the young boy. But just at this moment a gentleman, Miles Hendon, stood up to defend Edward. While he did not believe Edward's wild claim to be the Prince of Wales, Hendon decided to be the boy's champion, take him on his journey back to his village, and minister to him until he came to his senses. It had been seven years since Miles Hendon had been home, and he was anxious to see his father, his older brother, Arthur, and Edith, his true love.

As Miles and Edward traveled together, they received word that King Henry VIII had died. Thus, Edward was now indeed King of all England – and most likely the only living soul who mourned the death of Henry.

Throughout his trek homeward, Miles treated Edward as though he were a real king. He helped him dress, waited on him, fed him, and took care of all his needs. In return, Edward dubbed Miles a knight.

When the twosome finally arrived at Hendon Hall, Miles was shocked to find that his older brother and his father had died;

even worse, his conniving younger brother Hugh had assumed control of his business and estate and had taken Edith for himself in marriage. No servants claimed to recognize Miles; even charming Edith failed to acknowledge him. In fact, Hugh had Miles and Edward thrown into prison, falsely accusing them of being beggars and vagabonds.

His stay in prison convinced Edward of the inhumanity of British justice. For example, after being comforted by two kind women prisoners, these were taken out and burned at the stake for being Baptists. He also came to know a half-witted spinster who, having stolen a yard or two of cloth from a weaver, was to be hanged for it. But the beggar-king was particularly distressed by the tale of a young imprisoned apprentice, who, having found an escaped hawk, took it home. The court convicted him of stealing the bird and sentenced him to death. Edward was taught a great lesson: "King's should go to school to try their own laws at times, and so learn mercy."

Miles finally was brought to trial and given a sentence of two hours in the stocks. Edward was furious with the humiliation of his friend. Then, after his release, Miles and Edward hurried toward London; a new king was about to be crowned.

While the true king wandered about the land "poorly clad, poorly fed, cuffed and derided, herded with thieves and murderers in a jail, and called idiot and imposter by all," the mock-King, Tom Canty, enjoyed his adventures. At first he felt as though he was imprisoned. Even the process of getting dressed took fourteen people! Eating was as difficult an undertaking. Moreover, he had to worry about all manner of dull work: petitions were read, proclamations heard, and patents and all manner of wordy, repetitious and wearisome papers had to be attended to. It was all very drab. But then Tom met Edward's former servant boy, a bright lad who told Tom all about the ways of the castle, its various degrees of rank and file, and how to deal with the palace intrigue. He proved to be a veritable gold mine for Tom. The unseasoned yet clever boy used the information he gained to become comfortable as a prince, and to reassure his "caretakers" that he hadn't gone mad.

Slowly, Tom grew to enjoy the privileges of a ruler. Early on, he often thought about the lost prince and sincerely longed for his return. But as time wore on, and Edward didn't appear, Tom thought less and less about him. When Tom's mind did call up the possible fate of the genuine prince, he felt even greater guilt and shame; and so he did his best to drive Edward from his mind. He

eventually succeeded so well at this that, after the death of King Henry, Tom actually looked forward to obtaining England's throne.

Now, all of England had come to Westminster Abbey to witness the coronation of King Edward. As the Archbishop of Canterbury lifted the crown to place it on Tom's head, a cry was heard: "I am the King!" Tom was delighted to see Edward and stepped down to allow the ragged youth to take his place on the throne. But the crowd was unconvinced; the real Edward must prove his claim to the crown: for weeks the Great Seal had been missing, and the true Prince of Wales would know where it was. After much fretting, Edward remembered where he had last placed it. This was evidence to all; Edward Tudor was immediately coronated King Edward VI.

Edward lived for only a few years, but during those years he reigned most mercifully. Miles was made Earl of Kent, while Miles' brother was stripped of his land and cast into prison. Tom Canty was commissioned as the King's Ward, and as Chief Governor over Christ's Hospital, a shelter that fed the minds, hearts, and stomachs of orphans and children of indigent people. Frequently reminiscing about his experience as a peasant, King Edward demonstrated great compassion during a harsh period of English history. Because he understood his people, and ruled them in love, they in turn loved him, and exceedingly mourned his passing.

Commentary:

In 1835, when Halley's comet streaked across the skies, Mark Twain was born in an obscure frontier town. Seventy five years later, when the comet reappeared, Twain died, a famous author. He is a well-loved American writer and the inventor of the mythical epitome of American boyhood, Tom Sawyer.

While his more famous *Adventures of Huckleberry Finn* was yet unfinished, Twain wrote *The Prince and the Pauper*. Here we have two people living one another's lives for a brief, instructive time. The reader wants to believe it could happen because he would secretly like to see the beggar boy rise in life, while the privileged princeling is brought down to have his nose rubbed in reality.

In this tale, Twain shares with us his outrage at the social injustice that existed in the 1500's, 1800's – and that even now exists in one form or another. By presenting a case of mistaken identity, Twain clearly and simply portrays these injustices. Such a situation seems impossible, but like Twain said, "It may have happened, it may not have happened; but it could have happened."

HAMLET, PRINCE OF DENMARK

by
William Shakespeare
(1564 - 1616)

Type of work: Tragic drama

Setting: Elsinore, Denmark; c. 1200

Principal characters:

Hamlet, Prince of Denmark and son of the former king

The Ghost, Hamlet's dead father

Gertrude, Hamlet's mother, and Queen of Denmark

Claudius, Hamlet's uncle and new stepfather, and now, King of Denmark

Polonius, Claudius' chief counselor

Laertes, Polonius' son

Ophelia, Polonius' obedient daughter

Horatio, Hamlet's faithful friend

Story Overview:

Prince Hamlet bitterly opposed the marriage of his mother, Gertrude, to Claudius, her own brother-in-law, so soon after her husband's death. Moreover, Hamlet had a strange suspicion that the new king – his stepfather and former uncle – had somehow plotted his father's mysterious demise, and he refused to cease mourning his natural father, now two months dead.

As Hamlet languished in resentfulness, he was approached by his close friend Horatio, who revealed that for three nights now castle guards had seen the former king stalking the parapets – as a ghost. He persuaded the prince that his father must have some message of importance to impart, and thus Hamlet should wait with him that night for the ghost to appear again.

The bloody apparition was indeed the image of Hamlet's father. In horror, the son listened with Horatio as the dead king described how his brother Claudius had seduced Gertrude, and how the two of them together had arranged for his murder, while claiming that a serpent had injected the fatal poison.

Hamlet was appalled – though not entirely surprised – at this revelation. But he was even more shaken when the ghost made a desperate plea: he ordered Hamlet to avenge his death by killing Claudius, but cautioned that Gertrude must be spared; heaven alone should punish her for her sins.

Now, Hamlet considered himself an intellectual, not a soldier or a man of action. This charge to exact revenge posed a real dilemma in the prince's mind. He swore Horatio to secrecy concerning the ghost and continued for the next few days to fret on what he must do.

Filled with suppressed anger toward both his mother and Claudius, and torn between doing his duty in honor and carrying out a most distasteful and bloody task, Hamlet began to act more and more erratic. Ophelia, his lady friend and the daughter of the new king's most trusted counselor, Polonius, reported Hamlet's eccentric behavior to her father. Polonius insisted that Hamlet had become demented, and cautioned Ophelia to keep her distance. He then reported Hamlet's bizarre turn to the king and queen.

Perceiving Hamlet as a possible threat to the throne, Claudius, Gertrude and Polonius hired two dull-witted courtiers, Rosencrantz and Guildenstern, to spy on the prince, to learn whether he in fact coveted their power or was merely mad. But Hamlet, within minutes, recognized the charade and the motives behind it, and caustically mocked them. And shortly, it seemed to Hamlet that everyone – including Ophelia – was a spy and an informant for King Claudius and Queen Gertrude.

By now the prince was dashed by doubts and worries. He began to wonder if his father's ghost had really appeared; maybe it had been a vision from the devil instead. After all, the thought of murdering Claudius, vile and hated though he was, still repelled Hamlet. But soon he struck upon an idea: a company of traveling actors visited Elsinore, and Hamlet persuaded them to perform a murder scene that was actually a reenactment of the death of the old king. He was sure that if Claudius and Gertrude had in fact killed his father, their guilt would play on their faces and show in their actions.

The play proceeded. Sure enough, Claudius became so unnerved both by the drama and by Hamlet's sly, taunting comments, that he stormed from the performance, with Gertrude close behind.

Gertrude immediately sent for her insolent son. When he visited her in her room to discuss the matter, Polonius was hidden behind a curtain, listening. Soon the exchange between mother and son grew more heated and violent. When Polonius cried out for the guards, Hamlet, thinking he was Claudius, stabbed through the curtain and killed him. Amid this confusion, the ghost of Hamlet's father once more appeared (invisible to Gertrude) and again reminded his son of his original commission: to kill Claudius.

With renewed determination, Hamlet gripped his dagger and made for Claudius' bedchamber. But when he entered the room, prepared at last to do the deed, he found Claudius praying. This undid the prince's resolve; he could not slay this man while in the posture of supplication to God – a prayerful soul, he reasoned, would be swept straight to heaven, and Claudius deserved nothing higher than hell. So, the prince once again delayed his revenge.

Now Claudius, seeing the danger he was in, ordered that Hamlet be hurried off to England on the next possible ship. Again, Rozencrantz and Guildenstern were commissioned to carry out this errand, which secretly included orders for the murder of the prince on his arrival.

Several days before Hamlet was taken aboard ship, he witnessed a conquering Norwegian army marching past enroute to a distant battle. Their leader-captain was young Fortinbras, whose father had once lost many skirmishes and much property to Hamlet's own father. In harmony with his threats to invade Denmark to avenge these losses, Fortinbras, "a delicate and tender prince," was now dutifully acting on his father's wishes. Hamlet felt ashamed that he lacked equal willpower and character in response to filial duty.

As Hamlet was departing for England, Laertes, Polonius' hot-tempered son, arrived from Paris, seeking his own revenge. Enraged that Ophelia, his own sister, would allow Hamlet to escape unpunished, he lashed into her. Ophelia, now rejected by her banished lover and driven to madness by feelings of guilt borrowed from an embittered brother, drowned herself.

Hamlet, sensing a plot against his life, had altered his guards' orders: Rosencrantz and Guildenstern, not he, were killed by assassins on touching English soil. The prince sent word back to Denmark that he had been captured by pirates and would soon be returning to his home.

Claudius was dismayed to learn that his plans to do away with his pesky stepson had gone awry. So, together with Laertes, he hatched a new plan: Laertes would challenge Hamlet to a duel and kill him with a poison-tipped foil. If the fencing match failed to do the trick, a poison-spiked drink would be in easy reach of the dueler. One way or another, meddling Prince Hamlet would be no more.

Upon Hamlet's return, he and Horatio stood in a churchyard, discussing the prince's perilous journey. In the distance they spied a funeral procession. The two concealed themselves and looked on at the passage of Ophelia's funeral train, led by Laertes, pompously bewailing his dead sister. Unable to endure such a false and pretentious display, Hamlet leapt out of hiding and lunged toward Laertes. Both men were restrained, but not until after the challenge to duel was made – and accepted.

To diminish suspicion that he was in any way involved with the plot, King Claudius bet heavily on the practiced swordsman Hamlet. Then, according to plan, poison was dripped onto Laertes' rapier and into the convenient cup.

But things soon began to miscarry. First the unsuspecting Gertrude raised and drank from the poison-laced cup in a toast to her son. In the contest that followed, Laertes wounded Hamlet, and Hamlet in turn fatally pierced Laertes. Then, as the queen fell to the ground crying, "The drink, the drink! I am poison'd!" Hamlet demanded that the treachery be revealed. At this, dying Laertes spoke up and exposed the plot – the poisoned wine and the venom-tipped foil, whose effects Hamlet would soon feel. Laertes further divulged that "the King's to blame": Claudius had authored the entire miserable scene.

Hesitating no longer, Hamlet rushed forward, stabbed Claudius, and cursed the "incestuous, murderous, damn'd Dane." Then Laertes and Hamlet turned and implored each other's forgiveness, that they might both die in peace. Within minutes, Fortinbras arrived, and, with Hamlet's dying approval, appropriated the throne of Denmark – a throne so tragically twice vacated in the previous few months.

Commentary:

What can be said about the most famous work of English drama? A lot, actually. In fact scholars have been pawing over this play for three hundred years, searching to explain the inner workings of its plot, and particularly debating why the intelligent young Hamlet had such a hard time mustering the courage to avenge his father's death. Often the only thing these scholars agree upon is that Hamlet's speeches and mannerisms are complex, allusive, and sometimes cryptic.

One thing is certain: *Hamlet* follows the conventions of a standard Elizabethan genre – the "revenge play" – of which there are many examples. But Shakespeare's poetic drama is by far more expansive and more ambiguous than any of these other works.

It has been suggested that the prince's delayed revenge, as opposed to Fortinbras' decisiveness, is meant to contrast two universal individuals – the man of contemplation and the man of action. The university-bred Hamlet analyzes everything too deeply and is thus prevented from taking any clear course:

. . . Thinking too precisely on the event
a thought which, quartered, hath but one part wisdom
and ever three parts coward, I do not know
why, yet I live to say "this thing's to do,"
sith I have cause and will and strength and means to do't.

But Hamlet's essential dilemma is one that has confronted men throughout the ages; and this confrontation – between duty and morality, courage and fear, right and wrong – will assuredly persist for all ages to come.

KING LEAR

by
William Shakespeare

Type of work: Tragic Drama

Setting: Medieval England

Principal characters:

Lear, King of Britain
Cordelia, his faithful daughter
Regan and Goneril, his two mean-spirited daughters
The Dukes of Cornwall and Albany, their husbands
The Earl of Gloucester
Edmund, the Earl's treacherous son
Edgar, the Earl's true son (later disguised as a madman)
The Duke of Kent, Cordelia's loyal helper
Lear's Fool, a comical character

Story Overview:

England's aged King Lear had chosen to renounce his throne and divide the kingdom among his three daughters. He promised the greatest portion of the empire to whichever daughter proved to love him most. Goneril lavished exaggerated praise on her father; Regan even outdid her sister with a wordy show of hollow affection. Cordelia, however, refused to stoop to flattery, and insisted that she loved her father no more and no less than was his due. Lear exploded at what seemed to him her untenderness and immediately disowned her. Moreover, Lear banished the Duke of Kent from the castle for defending Cordelia.

Two suitors had come to the British court to seek Cordelia's hand: the Duke of Burgundy and the King of France. After Lear had disinherited Cordelia, Burgundy suddenly lost interest in her – he aspired to a wealthy bride. The King of France, however, was delighted by Cordelia's honesty and immediately asked for her hand. They departed for France, without Lear's blessing, and Cordelia's part of the kingdom was divided between Goneril and Regan, who were all too happy at their sister's fall from grace. Furthermore, these two daughters decided that Lear had succumbed to a sort of senility, and they set upon a plan to exploit his weakness to their own advantage.

Meanwhile, in the Earl of Gloucester's castle, Edmund, Gloucester's bitter and cunning illegitimate son, was fretting over his father's preference toward the legitimate brother, Edgar. Edmund now forged a letter in which Edgar supposedly expressed his intent to murder their father. Gloucester immediately believed the letter and fled in distress from the palace. Then Edmund, in mock concern, went and warned his brother that someone had turned Gloucester against him. Edgar, too good at heart to suspect his brother's treachery, accepted the story and escaped to the forest. Thus, with two clever strokes, Edmund had managed to supplant his brother in his father's affections.

After dividing his kingdom, Lear decided to lodge for a time at Goneril's palace. Now that she had her half of his kingdom, however, she no longer feigned love for him. In fact, she so distained her father that she ordered her servants to mistreat and insult him. Accordingly, her servants began to deal with him as a senile old man rather than as a king.

In the meantime, the banished Duke of Kent disguised himself and presented himself to the king at Goneril's palace. Lear failed to recognize the disguise and hired Kent as a servant. Then, with the help of the King's Fool (whose biting jibes and puns provide some of the finest moments in all literature), Kent began hinting to Lear that he had acted unwisely in dealing with Cordelia, until the King began to perceive his folly. As Goneril continued to humiliate him, Lear, bemoaning his fate ("How sharper than a serpent's tooth it is / To have a thankless child!"), determined to move on to Regan's household. He did not know that Regan was at that moment on her way to visit Gloucester. (In fact, all of the characters were now converging on Gloucester's castle).

Near Gloucester, Edgar, still convinced that his life was in peril from his father, lingered in a local wood, disguised as a madman – Tom o' Bedlam.

Soon Regan and her husband, the Duke of Cornwall, arrived at Gloucester. They were followed by King Lear not long after. When Goneril and her household also appeared, the two sisters united to disgrace their father, ordering him to dismiss all his servants. But this humiliation proved too much for the old King, who, in a fit of anger and shame, rushed out of the castle into a furious storm, where he wandered about madly, screaming and cursing. Their plan having succeeded, the daughters locked the doors behind him.

Then follows a most famous and stirring scene: Lear raged and cursed in the midnight storm, with his frightened Fool cowering beside him, uttering the most biting and ironic jokes, while Kent watched in disbelief.

Fortunately, Gloucester found them and led them to a little hovel, where they encountered Edgar, still disguised as Tom o'Bedlam and pretending derangement. Lear, now half mad himself, set about conducting a bizarre mock trial of his daughters, with Kent, the Fool, and Edgar all serving in his "court." (The mixture of Lear's denunciations, Edgar's incoherent chatter, the Fool's punning and ironic commentary, and Kent's astonished silence, create a superb scene of absurdity and despair).

Meanwhile, Kent had heard that Cordelia, back in France, was preparing to ship a small army across the English Channel to rescue Lear. But Edmund, who had also got wind of this news, hinted to Regan's husband, the Duke of Cornwall, that Gloucester planned to side with Lear and the French army against Regan and Goneril. Cornwall was furious, and agreed to avenge himself on innocent Gloucester. (Very convenient for Edmund, of course, as he would inherit his father's earldom!)

It was now a race against time: could Gloucester, Edgar, Kent and Lear hold out against the treachery of Edmund, Regan, Goneril and Cornwall until help arrived from France? They devised a plan to flee to Dover, there to await the coming of Cordelia and the French troops. King Lear managed to make his escape in time, drawn by Kent in a litter, but Gloucester was not so lucky – Cornwall caught him, jabbed out both his eyes, then thrust him through the castle gates to "let him smell his way to Dover." Crawling about blindly, the earl bumped into none other than his own son, Edgar, still pretending to be insane. Edgar agreed to lead his father – who remained unapprised of his true identity – to Dover, though and Gloucester bitterly complained: "Tis the time's plague when madmen lead the blind."

While Kent with Lear and Edgar with Gloucester were making their separate ways to Dover, a love affair brewed among the villains. Goneril had become infatuated with the diabolical Edmund, who returned with her to her palace. There she fell into a bitter argument with her husband, the Duke of Albany, who vehemently chastised Goneril for her mistreatment of Lear. Albany also informed his wife that Cornwall had been killed – struck down by one of Gloucester's servants. Suddenly a frightening thought paralyzed Goneril: now that her sister was a widow, would she too pursue Edmund and his rising star? This fear was soon confirmed when Regan sent a message to the castle professing her love for Edmund, followed by an invitation to join forces with her. Since Albany's sympathies were now with Lear, Goneril was forced to watch in frustrated rage as her sister and Edmund set out together with their cohorts against the expected invasion.

In the mean time, at Dover, Kent met with the French officials while Cordelia sent doctors to treat her father, who, by that time, was mentally and physically spent. But Lear refused to meet with Cordelia; he had come to understand his injuries against his loyal daughter and now felt too ashamed to see her.

On his journey to Dover, the blind Gloucester had grown more and more distressed. At last he implored Edgar to guide him to the brink of a cliff so that he could throw himself off. But Edgar fooled him into thinking the level ground was actually the top of a ridge. And when Gloucester fell forward onto the ground, as if jumping from a cliff, Edgar changed his voice, pretending to be a passerby at the cliff's base. He assured his father that he had seen him fall from the dizzy height and survive – he'd seen a miracle! Gloucester believed the tale and accepted the "miracle" as a sign that he was meant to live.

Now Lear, who had been delirious before he was finally rescued by Cordelia, fell into a deep sleep. On awakening, he found himself purged of his madness and begged Cordelia's forgiveness. Their reconciliation complete, they were ready to join with Kent and the French army against Edmund and his forces.

But Cordelia's troops were defeated, and Edmund sent orders that Lear and his daughter be executed.

Meanwhile, Regan had collapsed in death, poisoned by her own jealous sister. (Goneril herself would later die by suicide.) Just at that moment Edgar burst in on the scene, engaged his brother Edmund in combat, and dealt him a mortal wound. He then cast off his disguise and revealed his true identity to his dying brother, also reporting that Gloucester, their father, had died a few hours before. Edmund, apparently touched by the news of his father's death, confessed that he had ordered the executions of Lear and Cordelia, and dispatched a messenger to stop them. It was, alas, too late – Lear entered, carrying the body of his beloved daughter, then he too fell and died, broken-hearted. Only Albany, Kent, and Edgar survived. It fell to these last two to jointly rule the shattered nation.

Commentary:

Since *King Lear's* setting is pre-Christian Britain, some readers chafe under the sort of nihilistic fatalism that colors the characters' thinking ("As flies to wanton boys we are to the gods . . . "). And truly, it's hard to think of any other play so vast, passionate and bitter as this. The work is unusually demanding on the reader or spectator, with so many prominent figures suffering so much for so long, only, in the end, to find so little redemption.

True, there is a good deal of humor throughout the play, especially in the lightning-fast wisecracks and puns of the Fool and in the cryptic babble of Edgar masquerading as a madman. But even the humor has a steady, grim undertone.

The main plot is marvelously conceived. Just as Lear mistakenly believes that Cordelia has wronged him and his other daughters have served him, so Gloucester jumps to the conclusion that Edgar opposes him and Edmund defends him – when in both cases precisely the opposite is true. The horrific consequences of these misjudgments intertwine and drive the action along.

ROMEO AND JULIET

by
William Shakespeare
(1567 - 1616)

Type of work: Romantic tragedy

Setting: Verona, Italy; Fifteenth century

Principal characters:
 Romeo, son of the house of Montague
 Juliet, daughter of the Capulet household
 Benvolio, Romeo's cousin
 Mercutio, Romeo's friend
 Tybalt, Juliet's cousin
 Lady Montague, the clan's matriarch
 Lady Capulet, Juliet's mother
 Juliet's ribald nurse
 Friar Lawrence, a Franciscan Monk

Story Overview:

For a very long time the Capulets and the Montagues had been feuding. Harsh words often led to violence between the two houses, who were sworn as deadly enemies. Prince Escalus of Verona happened upon one such bloody brawl and angrily pronounced, "If ever you disturb our streets again, your lives shall pay the forfeit of the peace."

Shortly after this, Romeo and his cousin Benvolio met on the street, and Romeo sadly confessed his unrequited love for an aloof and indifferent young woman. "[Give] liberty unto thine eyes; Examine other beauties," was Benvolio's curative. But Romeo was unmoved: "Thou canst not teach me to forget."

Meanwhile, as Lord Capulet arranged for the marriage of Juliet, his fourteen-year-old daughter, to Paris, a kinsman of the Prince, he advised Paris to woo the girl gently. That night Capulet was to give a party so Paris could meet Juliet. He called a servant to deliver the invitations.

Now the servant could not read, so as he walked along he petitioned Romeo and Benvolio to read the guest list to him. In thanks, he told Romeo, "If you be not of the house of Montagues, I pray come and crush a cup a wine." Since Romeo's unreceptive Rosaline was named among the guests, Benvolio urged Romeo to go and find out for himself that Rosaline was a "crow."

As Romeo and his friend Mercutio, both wearing masks, searched for Rosaline among the gathering, Romeo's eyes fell upon the exquisite Juliet – and Romeo remembered Rosaline no more: "O, she doth teach the torches to burn bright! . . . . Did my heart love till now?" he chimed. However, fiery Tybalt, Capulet's nephew, overheard Romeo pouring out his heart and reported to his uncle that a Montague had invaded their festivity. But Capulet was not alarmed and would have no bloodshed; besides Romeo seemed to be "a virtuous and well-governed youth."

Romeo approached Juliet offering "my lips, two blushing pilgrims," to which Juliet replied, "Ay, pilgrim, lips that thou must use in prayer." But Romeo at last convinced her to press her lips to his – just before Juliet's Capulet mother called her away. Romeo was stunned by this revelation that the girl was a daughter of his father's enemy, but vowed that not even death would keep him from his true love.

The party ended, leaving Romeo outside the Capulet house, gazing up in lovesick rapture at Juliet's window. Just then, to his joy, Juliet leaned from her balcony. Romeo whispered: "But soft! What light through yonder window breaks? It is the East, and Juliet is the sun!" As he debated within himself whether to speak to her, she, thinking herself alone, began to pour out her heart: "O Romeo, Romeo! wherefore art thou Romeo? Deny thy father and refuse thy name; or, if thou wilt not, be but sworn my love, and I'll no longer be a Capulet."

Unable to contain himself, Romeo stepped out of the shadows. Though ashamed at her overheard declaration, Juliet reconfirmed her passion, but warned him that if her family discovered him there, he would be killed. Romeo was not alarmed, "For stony limits cannot hold love out." As he swore of his love by the moon, and by his heart, Juliet begged him not to swear at all. Things were happening too fast; the world seemed suddenly brilliant and fragile "like the lightening which doth cease to be." So, the fragile lovers exchanged vows and agreed to meet the next morning.

On his way home, Romeo stopped by the monastery to visit Friar Lawrence. "Our Romeo hath not been in bed to-night," the Friar observed. "I have been feasting with mine enemy," replied the young man. " . . . Plainly know my heart's dear love is set on the fair daughter of rich Capulet . . . what thou must combine by holy marriage." The Friar teased Romeo for his fickle nature (only yesterday he had professed undying love for Rosaline), but agreed to perform the marriage, in the hope that "this alliance may so happy prove to turn your households' rancor to pure love."

The following morning, Mercutio and Benvolio were worriedly searching for Romeo; Tybalt had sent out a challenge for him to fight. But when the pair finally met up with their enamored young kinsman, he was in no mood for fighting. At this point Juliet's nurse came on the scene and took Romeo aside to demand his intentions. Romeo assured her that his love was in earnest and bade her bring Juliet to the Friar's cell, where they would be married that afternoon.

The wedding was performed; the lovers were to again meet later that evening. But that afternoon Benvolio and Mercutio ran into Tybalt and some of his men. Though Benvolio, remembering the Prince's edict, declined to duel, Mercutio and Tybalt began a joust of insults, with Mercutio's wit outdoing the other's words. Just then, the newly-married Romeo appeared, and Tybalt demanded that the "villain" fight. Romeo protested, "I never injured thee, but love thee better than thou canst devise." Mercutio, however, ached for a skirmish, and he and the equally hot-tempered Tybalt drew their sabers. Romeo stepped between the two, but Tybalt thrust forward and stabbed Mercutio, then bolted away. As the dying Mercutio was carried off, Romeo, torn with anger and mixed loyalties, confronted and killed Tybalt. Benvolio then implored his cousin to hide in order to avoid revenge or arrest.

The Prince and a group of citizens came upon the bloody scene and called for an explanation from Benvolio. Silencing arguments as to where the blame fell, the Prince declared, "I will be deaf to pleading and excuses. When Romeo is found he shall be put to death."

Juliet impatiently awaited the arrival of her husband, when her nurse came with the news: "Tybalt is gone, and . . . Romeo that killed him, he is banished." Distraught, Juliet sent the nurse off once again: "O, find him! give this ring to my true knight."

In the meantime, Romeo, hidden in the Friar's cell, had just been informed of a change of heart by the Prince – rather than death, Romeo should only be exiled from Verona. Then the nurse came with news from Juliet: "She weeps and weeps." The Friar advised Romeo to wait until nightfall and then go to his true love.

That night Romeo went to Juliet's room; as dawn broke, the lovers could barely let themselves part. Soon after, Lady Capulet entered Juliet's chamber, believing the girl had stayed secreted in mourning for Tybalt. She spoke of the murder and the vengeance it demanded. "But now," she announced at last, "I'll tell thee joyful tidings, girl"; and she apprised her daughter that she would soon be married to Paris. When Juliet balked at any such wedding, her father flared up in anger: "I tell thee what – get thee to church . . . or never after look me in the face."

Juliet now hurried to the Friar's cell, both to confess her filial disobedience and to see Romeo. There she met Paris, who was arranging for their forthcoming marriage. Though Juliet openly confessed to loving another, Paris mistook her words as a declaration towards him and promised that they would be married in bliss. After he left, Juliet turned to Friar Lawrence for help. The Friar had a plan: He gave her a vial with a potion inside that would make her appear to be dead, but in reality would only bring on a long sleep. When her family discovered her "lifeless" body, they would place it in the Capulets' tomb, and the Friar would then send for Romeo to rescue her and take her away from Verona.

The Capulets rejoiced when Juliet returned home and told her family that she would consent to marry Paris. But on the evening before the wedding, Juliet partook of the potion, and the next morning, when the Friar and Paris came to seek the bride, they found the parents filled with grief. They took Juliet's limp body, according to plan, to the family tomb.

Meanwhile, in Mantua, word of Juliet's death reached young Romeo ahead of the Friar's messenger. Rushing to Verona, the disheartened youth paused to purchase a vessel of poison: "Well, Juliet, I will lie with thee tonight," he pledged.

At the Capulet's vaulted tomb, there young Romeo found Paris, also in mourning. Recognizing Romeo, he drew his sword. The two fought and Paris was fatally wounded. In the throes of death, he pled with Romeo to lay him next to his love. Romeo hesitated, then dragged the other man inside the tomb so that he too could lie near Juliet. Then, looking down at his bride, Romeo cried out, " . . . Eyes, look your last! Arms, take your last embrace! and lips, O you . . . seal with a righteous kiss a dateless bargain to engrossing death." Leaving a kiss on the beauty's silent lips, Romeo drank the poison and lay motionless by her side.

Soon, Juliet awoke – to find her husband lying next to her, dead. Hearing footsteps approaching, she unsheathed Romeo's dagger and plunged it into her breast, bewailing, "O happy dagger! . . . Let me die!"

Just then the Friar entered, followed by the Montagues, the Capulets, and the Prince. Before them lay Paris, along with the limp bodies of the two lovers. At once each family began to cast blame upon the other for the tragedy. The Friar, however, stepped forward and explained the circumstances which had led to the deaths of their tender children, whose only sin was to have loved. When he heard the story, the Prince called out mournfully, "Where be these enemies? Capulet, Montague, see what a scourge is laid upon your hate, that heaven finds means to kill your joys with love . . . . All are punished."

At these words, the adversaries clasped hands in brotherhood. "A gloomy peace this morning with it brings . . . " intoned the Prince in a final note, "for never was a story of more woe than this of Juliet and her Romeo."

Commentary:

Perhaps Shakespeare's most famous play, *Romeo and Juliet* combines the contrasting elements of humor and sorrow, bawdiness and civil strife, and innocent love and ignorant hate to rouse an amazing depth of mixed tenderness and tension. Although a Chorus begins the play by notifying the audience that these near-perfect lovers will in the end take their own lives, an irrational sense of hope remains that somehow they might escape their destiny. But the pride-hardened hatred between the feuding families leads the play to its inevitable tragic end.

Moreover, though the drama is one of ultimate reconciliation, ironically, both families lose their only children – neither family line will be carried on. In a sense Shakespeare is suggesting that war and hate lead, not to victory for either side, but to spiritual annihilation.

MACBETH

by
William Shakespeare
(1564 - 1616)

Type of work: Tragic fatalistic drama

Setting: Eleventh-century Scotland

Principal characters:
  Macbeth, a noble Scottish chieftain
  Lady Macbeth, his wife
  Banquo, Macbeth's warrior-friend
  Fleance, Banquo's son
  Duncan, King of Scotland, a gentle and
      perfect ruler
  Macduff, a rebel lord
  Three Witches

Story Overview:

On a stormy night, Scottish armies managed to suppress a rebellion, largely through the valor of two noblemen, Macbeth and Banquo. They had also frustrated a Viking invasion that had received assistance from a prominent Scotsman, the Thane of Cawdor. When news of these two events reached Duncan, King of Scotland, he was delighted with Macbeth's performance, but insisted that Cawdor's treason warranted his death. Accordingly, the king declared that Cawdor be executed and that Macbeth be named in his stead, Thane of Cawdor.

Meanwhile, Macbeth and Banquo, on their way home from war, happened upon a trio of witches – hags stirring a blackened caldron and heralding Macbeth's arrival: "Double, Double, toil and trouble." The witches astonished the pair by prophesying that Macbeth would become first, the new Thane of Cawdor, and then, King of Scotland; and that Banquo would become the father of kings. Then the dark hags vanished, leaving Banquo and Macbeth to speculate over these strange prophecies.

No sooner had the witches departed than two of the king's messengers arrived with news that Macbeth had indeed been named to replace the deposed Thane of Cawdor. Macbeth was amazed to see the first of the witches' prophecies so quickly fulfilled, and began to believe in the ultimate fulfillment of the second. If he could be Thane of Cawdor, perhaps he could rule all of Scotland as well. This innocent belief quickly expanded into a deep-seated ambition, which began to taint Macbeth's mind with dark thoughts: Would the prophecy fulfill itself, or would he have to take action to usurp the throne? Since Duncan was king, would not one of his two sons follow him in ruling Scotland? All this time, Banquo resisted any thoughts of hastening the witches' prophecy that his children would be kings, but could sense the unrest stirring inside the soul of his fellow officer.

Banquo and Macbeth returned and reported to King Duncan, who warmly commended them both for their courage. But during the ensuing conversation he made two announcements which brought even more sinister ideas into Macbeth's mind: First, he declared his son, Malcolm, heir to the throne; and second, he expressed his intention to visit Macbeth for a night at Macbeth's castle. Macbeth felt he must somehow take advantage of Duncan's visit to advance his own ambitions – or, as he saw it, his own destiny.

Hearing of her returning husband's success and of the prophecies pronounced upon him, Macbeth's wife was filled with a consuming desire to see him ascend to the throne. Vowing to stop at nothing in this quest, Lady Macbeth urged her husband to help her murder the king as he slept. She would undertake to induce the king's guards to drink, giving Macbeth the opportunity to slip into Duncan's quarters, slay him, and plant the murder weapons on the drunken guards. Macbeth hesitated at first, but his shrewd and aspiring wife eventually prevailed.

As announced, Duncan did visit Macbeth, and after feasting there with Banquo and others, he prepared for bed. According to plan, Lady Macbeth arranged to intoxicate the guards, then sent her husband to do the deed. Presently, Macbeth returned to her, Duncan's murder accomplished. But now Macbeth was filled with guilt. Nonetheless, the conspiring spouses slipped, unseen, back to their chamber.

Two visiting nobles, Lennox and Macduff, finding the king's lifeless body the next morning, sounded the alarm. Everyone rushed to the site, where Macbeth and his wife pretended to be shocked and heartbroken. Duncan's two sons, suspecting a similar conspiracy would be attempted upon their lives, fled separately to England and Ireland.

After that, events moved swiftly. Everyone saw the flight of Duncan's sons as evidence that they had been the conspirators against their father. Macbeth was crowned as successor to the throne; he had fooled everyone – except Banquo, who was suspicious of Macbeth's sudden rise to power.

In fact, Banquo, remembering the promises made by the witches regarding his own progeny, feared jealous attempts on both his life and the life of his son Fleance. Immediately he informed Macbeth that the two of them would be leaving the country.

The tormented Macbeth, who also remembered the witches' ultimate prophecy, hired two assassins to kill Banquo and Fleance as they traveled. He could not allow Banquo's son to rule. Banquo was murdered, but Fleance managed to escape.

Many days later, Macbeth gave a feast for his compatriots. As he raised the glass, mourning that he would have liked his friend Banquo to be present, he was horrified at the appearance of Banquo's bloody ghost – seated on Macbeth's own throne. Now the terrified behavior of their new monarch virtually confirmed to the Scottish nobles that it was Macbeth who had contrived Duncan's assassination. One of the Lords – Macduff – immediately left for England to aid Duncan's avenging son, Malcolm, in assembling an army to usurp Macbeth.

When Macbeth and his wife learned of this counter plot, they found and consulted the witches for advice. The witches warned them to fear Lord Macduff, but added that no harm would come to Macbeth "until great Birnham Wood onto high Dunsinane hill shall come." Furthermore, "no man of woman born" should have power to harm him. Macbeth rejoiced: he was assured of ultimate victory. After all, how can a forest move itself? And what man is not born of a woman? But when the witches showed him a vision of eight Kings, Banquo among them, his enthusiasm melted away, and he ordered the prompt murder of Macduff's wife and children.

When Macduff, approaching with his armies, learned of these murders, his anguish only sharpened his resolve, and he swore to kill Macbeth with his own sword. When his armies reached Birnham Wood, Macduff instructed each soldier to cut tree boughs and hide behind them, in order to conceal their numbers. Like some kind of walking forest the men moved on Dunsinane, where Macbeth was poised to defend himself.

As Macbeth was preparing for war, his wife, chafing under her own guilty conscience, was walking in her sleep, attempting to wash from her hands invisible blood-stains. The horror of her crimes and the fear of death at the hands of her own untrusting subjects brought on her grim, agonizing dreams. Madness poisoned her spirit so bitterly that, on the eve of Macduff's attack, Lady Macbeth died.

The King's twisted mind too had been nearly destroyed. In his dementia, when word came that his wife had perished, he remained nearly unmoved. Moreover, as he dressed for battle, additional bad news arrived – Birnham Wood seemed to be moving toward them! Macbeth and his army rushed out to meet Macduff's approaching forest of men. Macbeth fought recklessly, only bolstered by the false courage instilled by the witches' pronouncement that "no man born of woman" could overthrow him.

Finally, the two warring leaders engaged in hand-to-hand combat. During the scuffle, Macbeth taunted Macduff; Macduff had not the capacity to kill him:

As easy mayst thou the intrenchant air
With thy keen sword impress as make me
bleed.
Let fall thy blade on vulnerable crests.
I bear a charmed life, which must not yield
To one of woman born.

But Macduff, still inflamed over the slaughter of his family, answered his enemy that he had never been, in a sense, "born of woman." "Macduff was from his mother's womb/ Untimely ripped," he replied.

Macbeth now fought in fear, with waning strength. The rebel at last gained the upper hand and plunged his sword into Macbeth's breast, then severed the head from the body of the bloody counterfeit King of Scotland.

Macduff returned to the castle and hailed Malcolm, good King Duncan's rightful heir, the new King of Scotland.

Commentary:

This popular, fast-moving and relatively uncomplicated play has become a standard of the effects of ambition. At the outset, Macbeth is perfectly honorable – and the object of special honor from his king. However, the witches' suggestion that he will attain the throne taps the well of ambition in him that (presumably) lies within us all. By the time he has slain Duncan, Macbeth is locked into a career of murder, and eventually becomes so desensitized as to remain unmoved even by his wife's death.

Granted, Macbeth likely would never have carried out his plans if not spurred on by his wife's stronger personality. In some ways, she is more of a man that he ("come you spirits," she prays, "unsex me here . . . "). But in the end she is overcome with guilt that manifests itself in crazed hallucinations.

Only Banquo, among those whose lives were "blessed" by the witches, escapes temptation: first, by refusing the seductions of ambition; and second, by refusing to conspire with Macbeth against Duncan. He is, as the witches prophesy, "lesser than Macbeth, and greater . . . not so happy, yet much happier." It is by no accident that Shakespeare's Banquo is a pure, upright fellow. The historical Banquo was the direct ancestor of James I, the King of England at the time of *Macbeth's* first performance.

OTHELLO

by
William Shakespeare
(1564 - 1616)

Type of work: Tragic, romantic drama

Setting: Venice and the island, Cyprus; early
sixteenth century

Principal characters:
Othello, the Moor of Venice, a black military
man acclaimed for his conquests
Desdemona, his wife, the beautiful
daughter of a government official
Iago, Othello's devious ensign
Emilia, Iago's wife, and attendant to
Desdemona
Cassio, Othello's devoted lieutenant

Story Overview:

Othello, Moorish commander of the
armed forces of Venice, had secretly married
Desdemona, the much younger daughter of
the respected Senator Brabantio. Capitalizing
on this news, Othello's ensign, Iago, who had
earlier professed his desires to Desdemona
without receiving her love in return, sought
revenge. Also passed over for promotion as
Othello's new lieutenant chief of staff, the
Moor having chosen instead a loyal Florentine,
Michael Cassio, Iago now devised a scheme to
rid himself of these sorry reminders of his own
failings. He dispatched his inexperienced fol
lower, Roderigo, to inform Brabantio of the
illicit marriage.

The thought of a beguiling Moor's marrying his beloved daughter without consent,
led the Senator with his guards to Othello's
house. However, violence was postponed by
the report of an imminent attack on Cyprus
from armed Turkish galleys. The Duke of
Venice summoned Othello to the senate cham-
bers. When Desdemona appeared and professed her love for Othello, the Duke cleared
him of wrongdoing, saying to Brabantio, "If
virtue no delighted beauty lack,/ Your son-in-
law is far more fair than black." Then the Duke
directed his courageous commander to lead
the Venetian forces to Cyprus in its defense.

With his honor intact, and through
Desdemona's pleas to remain with her love,
Othello gained permission to have her sail
with him. For the voyage, Othello entrusted
Desdemona to the care of Iago's wife, Emilia,
who did not suspect her husband's treachery.
Before the soldier band could reach its enemy,
a storm destroyed the Turkish fleet and dis-
persed the Venetian vessels. Fortunately, all of
Othello's ships returned safely to Cyprus and
Othello and his bride were reunited.

Iago's hateful plan turned now to lies
and innuendo. Seeing the infatuation his
pawn Roderigo had for Desdemona, Iago

engaged Roderigo in conversation, promising
that he could secure for him Desdemona's
love:

I hate the Moor. My cause is hearted: thine
hath no less reason. Let us be conjunctive in our
revenge against him. If thou canst cuckold him,
thou dost thyself a pleasure, me a sport.

But then evil Iago demanded a price for
Desdemona: Roderigo would have to engage
Cassio in a fight during the lieutenant's night
watch. Iago further fanned Roderigo's readi-
ness to kill Cassio by claiming that Cassio was
Desdemona's latest love.

That night Iago succeeded in getting
Cassio drunk, and the brawl turned to riot. By
way of reprimand, Othello was forced to
demote Cassio, a severe blow to the high-ranking officer. Desdemona nobly appealed to her
husband on Cassio's behalf, in an attempt to
revive their friendship. This innocent act provided Iago with yet another idea – a way to
convince the Moor of his wife's "natural attraction" to the handsome young Florentine.

Iago approached the despondent Cassio
and convinced him that a meeting could be
arranged between him and Desdemona; and
she could use her influence to have Cassio's
position restored. When the meeting took
place, Iago drew Othello aside to cause him to
see Cassio in the act of "soliciting" his wife. He
also began his line of subtle allusions to gossip
of a prior romance between the two. His
clever suggestions continued, daily planting
seeds of jealousy in Othello's heart.

Meanwhile, Desdemona could sense her
husband's growing despair. Othello's jealous
rages grieved not only her, his ill-starred wife,
but also all those under his command. Emilia,
Desdemona's loving caretaker, swore of her
mistress' fidelity, but the tormented Othello
would not listen.

Iago's plan was promoted even more
when he obtained a handkerchief Othello had
given to Desdemona as a love token. It had
been found by Emilia, who intended to return
it to her mistress. Instead, Iago secretly planted it in Cassio's bed.

Tortured over the weeks, and weary of
Iago's incessant insinuations, Othello finally
demanded proof from Iago of Desdemona's
unfaithfulness:

Villain, be sure thou prove my love a whore,
Or by the worth of man's eternal soul,
Thou hadst been better have been born a dog
Than answer my wak'd wrath . . .

Iago swore to have heard Cassio speak
words of love to Desdemona in his sleep. As

additional evidence he cited having seen Cassio wipe his beard with the missing scarf, which Cassio had since discovered in his quarters. Iago's cunning plan was working; Othello was finally convinced:

Othello: *Get me some poison, Iago, this night . . .*
Iago: *Do it not with poison. Strangle her in her bed, even the bed she hath contaminated.*
Othello: *Good, good. The justice of it pleases. Very good.*
Iago: *And for Cassio, let me be his undertaker . . .*

Overwhelmed with madness, Othello at once accepted Iago's words, making him his new lieutenant and charging him with his first order of business: Kill the deceitful Cassio.

In treacherous obedience to his commander, Iago enlisted Roderigo to ambush Cassio. With Iago hiding in the night's darkness, Roderigo confronted Cassio in a duel, but was wounded himself. Then, in the scuffle, Iago leaped out and wounded Cassio. In order to keep Roderigo from talking, Iago next turned on Roderigo, fatally stabbing the unfortunate lackey.

A crowd quickly gathered, including a harlot who claimed wounded Cassio as a friend. Iago, reasoning that a broken and a shunned Cassio would be an even sweeter revenge than a dead Cassio, decided this woman could be used to further defame his enemy. Pretending to have been a passer-by coming to Cassio's aid, Iago, along with some other Venetian gentlemen, assisted the wounded ensign toward Othello's home.

That same evening, Othello ordered Desdemona to excuse her servant early and retire to bed. In an anguished fit of passion, he then entered her chamber and kissed her:

Othello: *Have you pray'd to-night, Desdemon?*
Desdemona: *Ay, my lord.*
Othello: *If you bethink yourself of any crime Unreconcil'd as yet to heaven and grace, Solicit for it straight . . . . I would not kill thy unprepared spirit . . .*

Othello then spelled out the evidence which accused her of her crime, and demanded a confession. Desdemona denied any impropriety; Cassio must have found the handkerchief . . . But Othello spoke up, reporting that Cassio, her very lover, had already been justly assassinated. Desdemona burst into tears. "O strumpet! Weep'st thou for him in my face?" the husband cried. And then, despite her pleadings, he smothered her with a pillow.

The act completed, Othello was interrupted by Emilia at the door. She entered and told him that Roderigo had been killed, but Cassio yet lived. Distraught, and trying to justify his wife's murder, Othello disclosed to Emilia how he knew of his dead wife's infidelity – " . . . Thy husband knew it all . . . My

friend, thy husband, honest, honest Iago," he had made the accusation.

When Iago, Cassio and the nobles arrived, Emilia urged her husband to refute Othello's claim. Upon seeing the falseness reflected in Iago's eyes, however, and beholding his vain attempts to absolve himself, the general suddenly realized the tragic error he had made. His trusted ensign had orchestrated the entire affair. The missing scarf, the meeting between Cassio and Desdemona, the cause of his insane grief – all was Iago's doing.

Emilia became sickened at the reality of her husband's villainy. Amid sobs of grief, she began to rebuke him. Impulsively, Iago drew his dagger and stabbed his frenzied wife. Othello lunged at Iago, wounding him, but was restrained by the nobles from finishing the deed.

Faithful Emilia died, still calmly defending Desdemona's innocence and proclaiming her love for the virtuous woman. Othello, on the other hand, mad with guilt and sorrow, pleaded with his true friend, Cassio:

. . . When you shall these unlucky deeds relate, Speak of them as they are. Nothing extenuate, Nor set down in malice. Then must you speak Of one that lov'd not wisely but too well; Of one not easily jealous, but, being wrought, Perplex'd in the extreme; of one whose hand . . . threw a pearl away . . .

This said, Othello raised his dagger and thrust its blade into his own heart. As he lay dying, he could only be content with the promise that wicked, traitorous Iago would be tortured to death at the hands of the governor-general of Cyprus.

Commentary:

Shakespeare's *Othello* epitomizes the playwright's masterful ability to weave his characters' intricate motives and acts into one smooth plot. Of all his villains, Iago seems to be the most complete and sadistic, with no greater motive than wounded pride for his wickedness. Indeed, the drama might well be named "Iago," since he is the character most prominent throughout.

But the character most discussed by critics continues to be Othello. Is he an honorable, tragic hero who is ennobled by the unsuspecting confidence he places in his advisor, Iago? Or is he nothing more than a vulnerable, murderous and tragic fool? Othello himself recognizes this extraordinary paradox when, at the end of the play, he describes himself as "an honourable murderer"; as "one that loved not wisely but too well."

In contrast, we experience the authentic bond of love between two faithful women. And ultimately, love triumphs – even if only in death – over pride, envy, hate and evil.

THE TAMING OF THE SHREW

by
William Shakespeare
(1564 - 1616)

Type of work: Dramatic, farcical comedy

Setting: Warwickshire, England, and Padua, Italy; sixteenth century

Principal characters:
Christopher Sly, an indolent, fat tinker
Baptista Minola, a rich Italian gentleman
Bianca, his refined, youngest daughter
Katherine, his sharp-tongued, eldest daughter
Gremio, Bianca's rich and elderly suitor
Hortensio, Bianca's other suitor
Petruchio, Hortensio's friend
Lucentio, a rich and colorful gentleman
Tranio, Lucentio's servant

Story Overview:

The hostess of the inn bellowed at the drunken tinker, berating him for the glasses he had burst and threatening to call the constable. "Let him come," mumbled Christopher Sly as he slid under a stool and began to snore. The hostess shook her fist and ran out. At that moment, in strode a gallantly plumed lord with his servants.

The lord was a mischievous sort, and he, deciding that it would be an excellent joke to change this swinish drunkard slumped at his feet into a lord, ordered his servants to drag the man to his mansion, wash him, dress him in fine apparel, and lay him in the richest chamber. The company set off to do their lord's bidding.

Christopher Sly awoke. He blinked in the light of the magnificent room in which he found himself. He was sitting on a mountain of cushions; servants bowed to him in honor. Thinking this must all be the work of strong drink – as was often the case – he cried for more ale. When he was served all manner of rich food and drink, he objected, complaining that he was a simple tinker unaccustomed to such fare. As their lord had instructed them, the servants then informed him that Christopher Sly the tinker did not exist; that he was indeed a lord who had awakened from a bad dream.

Next, accompanied by sultry music, in danced the new lord's pageboy "wife," with bosoms as large as a pair of oranges (which in fact they were). Straightway, the tinker-lord wanted to carry her off to bed; but the servants insisted he must guard his strength, for he had been ill many weeks. So the ardent husband was forced to sit modestly by his bride and watch a play.

As he watched, he became transfixed by the dream-like drama that unfolded before his eyes:

In Padua, an old Italian town, lived rich old Baptista Minola and his two daughters. The younger girl, Bianca, was an angel from heaven; the elder, Katherine, was a scourge from the "other place," with a mustard-hot temper and a sizzling tongue to match. Katherine had no suitors, while Bianca had two, which posed a problem for their father. Baptista would not allow the younger Bianca to marry unless someone took Katherine off his hands first – but surely it would "snow in hell" before any man married such a shrew!

Baptista pled with Bianca's two suitors, elderly money-bag, Gremio and the younger Hortensio, to consider, instead, his eldest daughter. They vigorously shook their heads. The resigned father then charged them to find a tutor for his cherished young Bianca and hurried into the house, leaving the hapless pair to the mercies of Katherine. They soon conceded that if either wished to woo gentle Bianca, they must find a husband for her scolding sister.

Two strangers from Pisa had witnessed this family scene. One, Lucentio, had fallen in love with Bianca at first glimpse, and he caught upon the idea of becoming her tutor. When his servant Tranio reminded him that he had business errands in Padua for his father, Lucentio convinced Tranio to trade places with him. He would be two places at once – on business in the name of Lucentio, and as tutor-lover in the name of Tranio. The two exchanged clothes, and Lucentio stood transformed into a humble schoolteacher, while Tranio, in his master's wonderful raiment, became a wealthy merchant.

Meanwhile, Hortensio, still pondering possible ploys to marry off Katherine, encountered an old friend from Verona, Petruchio, who expressed a desire "to wive it wealthily in Padua." Hortensio impulsively alluded to Katherine, but then squelched the idea; he could not wish such a woman on his friend. But, amazingly, the thought of a spirited heiress was to Petruchio's liking, and Hortensio at last agreed to help him meet Katherine. In return, he asked Petruchio to recommend a schoolmaster for Bianca – who would, of course, be Hortensio himself, in disguise.

Then came Gremio, with a schoolmaster of his own to present to Baptista – the starry-eyed Lucentio. Behind them sauntered colorful Tranio, also on his devious way to woo Bianca – in his master's name.

As the beaus lined up to vie for Bianca's love, each agreed to pay an allotted amount to Petruchio for removing the impediment – Katherine – that blocked their contest for lovely Bianca. Petruchio, money in his pocket, beamed with joy.

Baptista had just reprimanded Katherine for her abusive manners, when visitors arrived. He was pleased that Gremio had found a suitable schoolmaster to teach Bianca in Latin and Greek, and even more pleased that a fine-looking, courteous gentleman, Petruchio of Verona, was inquiring after Katherine. "Pray have you not a daughter called Katherina, fair and virtuous?"

"I have a daughter called Katherina," Baptista responded, leaving it at that.

Petruchio, too, had brought a "learned" schoolmaster to teach Bianca in musical skills. And then still another suitor appeared to seek Bianca's hand – a colorful, richly dressed young "gentleman" from Pisa. What a glorious day! The father had secured, in a matter of minutes, a suitor for each of his daughters, and two schoolmasters. He turned quickly to Petruchio to settle on the amount of the dowry before the young fellow could change his mind.

When Petruchio finally did meet Katherine, he was genuinely taken with her, and began to court her amid a battle of wit and wills. She frowned; he smiled. She called him an ass; he called her a woman. Still, passion would not be deterred, for truly she was a beauty – though a sour one. When Katherine railed to her father about her hatred for her suitor, Petruchio, with utmost cheerfulness, assured Baptista that all was well; in fact, he would soon be off to Venice to purchase wedding clothes. "Kiss me, Kate!" he cried, seizing her around the waist. "We will be married o' Sunday!"

Baptista, meanwhile, decided to betrothe his popular Bianca to the highest bidder. Rich Gremio gleefully began to offer more and more of his properties, but each offer was bested by Tranio. Finally Gremio could offer nothing else and it appeared that Tranio had won Bianca.

All this time, Lucentio had been "tutoring" Bianca, not in Latin, but in love. He had confessed that he had disguised himself to make love to her, and that his servant Tranio was at that moment seeking, under Lucentio's name, to win her hand from her father.

Hortensio also sought a chance to teach Bianca in love, rather than music. But Bianca would have none of Hortensio, proclaiming the Latinist her choice.

The afternoon arrived for Kate's wedding to Petruchio. As part of a campaign to tame his wild bride, the groom showed up late, wearing rags and odd boots, and carrying a broken sword. In a drunken state, he cuffed the sexton and kissed Katherine with an "echoing smack" that could be heard throughout the church. At the wedding feast, he grabbed Katherine and, waving his battered sword, whisked her out of the hall to his shabby house. Baptista, more afraid *of* his daughter than *for* her, could only mutter, "Nay, let them go; a couple of quiet ones."

By now, Hortensio, tired of watching Bianca swoon so unaccountably over the pathetic Tranio, had decided to turn his attentions to a wealthy and eager Paduan widow. But first, he would see how his friend Petruchio had fared with the mean-spirited Kate.

Hortensio found Kate much changed – and miserable. Each time Petruchio's servants offered Kate food, her husband had contemptuously rejected it as unworthy of her. A tailor had brought her fine linen gowns, but Petruchio found fault in everything. Finally, he ordered the aching, weary woman onto a horse, and they both started back to Baptista's mansion. Petruchio had broken Katherine's will. This plain, rough fellow had weathered her storms and thrown them back in her face.

A wedding feast of huge proportions was soon held in old Baptista's house. A triple marriage was celebrated: Lucentio, at last as himself, had gained Baptista's blessing to wed Bianca; Hortensio had briskly courted his "ripe plum" of a widow; and Kate and Petruchio were now heart-to-heart in love.

At the wedding feast, Katherine's father drunkenly consoled Petruchio, saying, "I think thou hast the veriest shrew of all." But Petruchio disagreed, and wagered a hundred dollars that his Kate would obey his command to come to him more quickly than the other two brides would come at their husbands' calls; Kate by now surpassed the others in courtesy and attention to duty. When the three wives were summoned, only Kate appeared. In a seemingly demeaning gesture, she knelt and placed her hand beneath her husband's foot. But the act had not brought her down; it had raised her husband up, and showed to the silent guests how much she esteemed Petruchio. "Why, there's a wench! Come on, and kiss me, Kate!" he roared. He had courted her out of love of coins, but now he knew no greater riches than the coins of love.

Night fell. With Petruchio and Kate gone to bed, the empty chamber was silent – except for the soft snoring of a tinker, asleep on the floor.

Commentary:

This rough and bawdy play-within-a-play is unlike most of Shakespeare's works. Instead of lyrical poetry and delicate humor, *The Taming of the Shrew* is filled with coarse, vivid puns. In fact, some claim this disparity as evidence that Shakespeare was not the play's sole author.

Nonetheless, it is one of The Bard's most popular works. The lusty main characters have become models for the shrewish woman and the strong-willed woman-tamer.

THE TEMPEST

by
William Shakespeare
(1564 - 1616)

Type of work: Romantic fantasy

Setting: A remote island; fifteenth century

Principal characters:
Prospero, the rightful Duke of Milan, cast
away on an island in the sea
Miranda, his beautiful daughter
Alonso, King of Naples
Ferdinand, Alonso's son
Antonio, Prospero's wicked brother, and
false Duke of Milan
Sebastian, Alonso's brother
Gonzalo, a kind philosopher
Trinculo and Stephano, two drunken
courtiers
Ariel, Prospero's spirit servant
Caliban, Propero's grotesque slave-monster

Story Overview:

A great tempest arose that drove a certain
ship, bound to Naples from Tunis, off its course
and onto an uncharted island. The storm had
been magically called up by Prospero, one of
the two human inhabitants of the island, in
order to bring the vessel to shore.

Prospero had once been the mighty Duke
of Milan, and had reigned justly. But he had
grown so absorbed in his intellectual pursuits –
most of them relating to the supernatural – that
he turned over the tedious reins of government
to his "trusted" brother Antonio, freeing himself
to devote his time to the library and the studies
he loved. But, sadly, his ambitious brother, taking advantage of Prospero's naivete, usurped
his power – a plan he was only able to carry out
with the help of Alonso, the King of Naples and
sworn enemy of Milan. Antonio and Alonso
cruelly captured Prospero and his infant
daughter Miranda, and set them adrift at sea in
a small, rotting craft. They would have been
drowned – Antonio's wish – had not a counselor on the ship, Gonzalo, provided them with
food and drink, and with those volumes from
Prospero's collection that contained his magic
spells.

When Prospero and Miranda washed
ashore on their remote island, they found two
rather unusual inhabitants. The first was a fairy
spirit named Ariel, who had been imprisoned
within a tree by her former master, a witch
named Sycorax. Prospero freed Ariel from the
tree and thus became her new master.

The other creature, Caliban, son of
Sycorax, was a lumbering, deformed, half-sav-
age figure. He hated Prospero – and everyone
and everything else, for that matter – but was
also forced to acknowledge him as master. For
twelve years Prospero had kindly ruled over
the other three islanders, all the while practicing a form of benevolent sorcery.

Why, then, did Prospero incite the elements to cause this ship to be tossed aground
on his island? Because he knew, as it turned
out, that the ship bore the very people who had
usurped him of his power so many years before
– Antonio, Alonso, and their courtiers. The
kind, wise Gonzalo was also aboard, along with
Ferdinand, Alonso's honorable son. Prospero's
plan was to magically scatter the passengers
about the island in three groups, put them
through a series of trials and adventures by
which the bad would be chastised and the good
rewarded, and then bring them all together to
make peace once and for all.

Alonso, together with Antonio, Sebastian,
Gonzalo, and others, found themselves together
on the beach. They were astonished to discover
that not only had they survived the shipwreck,
but that their clothes were clean, dry and
pressed (one of Prospero's many bits of magic).
However, Alonso did not see Ferdinand among
the survivors, and supposing his son had
drowned, cried out in grief. Still the good-heart-
ed counselor, old Gonzalo tried to cheer the distraught Alonso, but Sebastian joined Antonio in
mocking his efforts at optimism.

At this time, the invisible Ariel came on
the scene. By playing her lilting music she
caused a deep sleep to come upon everyone
except Sebastian and Antonio. The situation
prompted Antonio to tempt Sebastian with a
proposition: "My strong imagination sees a
crown dropping upon thy head," he began. He
went on to say, in effect, "You remember how
simple it was for me to seize the entire rule of
Milan by overthrowing my brother? Well, by
killing your brother Alonso as he sleeps, you
could become King of Naples. No one would
ever know how you ascended to the throne."
Sebastian succumbed to the temptation, and
was just about to strike off his brother's head
when Ariel awakened the company. Antonio's
plot had been frustrated.

As the men tramped awkwardly around
the island in hopes of finding Ferdinand alive,
Sebastian and Antonio looked forward to a second opportunity to murder Alonso. But suddenly the group was beset by a miraculous
vision, sent by Prospero: a numerous troupe of
fairies and sprites, dancing about a table laden
with rich foods. The hungry company, invited
to eat, was just about to partake, when suddenly lightning struck and thunder rolled; Ariel
appeared in the form of a Harpy (a greedy
monster, part woman and part bird). As quickly as it had appeared, the banquet table vanished. Then Ariel rebuked Alonso, Antonio and

Sebastian for the crimes they had committed – or had intended to commit – and led them all, guilt-stricken and humbled, to Prospero.

Ferdinand had landed on another part of the island. As he mourned the father he believed to have drowned, he found himself helplessly guided by Ariel's music to Prospero and Miranda. No sooner had Ferdinand set eyes on Prospero's unspoiled, tender-hearted daughter, than he fell in love with her, and she with him. Prospero, however, concealed his pleasure in seeing these two youngsters so much enthralled by one another, and refused to allow Ferdinand to take Miranda as his queen until he had undergone an ordeal to prove his devotion. The wise magician then ordered the young prince to spend the day lugging and stacking a pile of huge logs, menial labor unbefitting royalty. But Ferdinand gladly accepted the task. He toiled, even through the pleadings of his beloved: " . . . Pray you, work not so hard! My father is hard at study. He's safe for these three hours."

Now Prospero was indeed at study; not the study of books, but of hearts. As he watched the two lovers, he smiled at his innocent daughter's conspiracy, and sighed with joy at Ferdinand's refusal to slacken his work.

When Prospero was satisfied with Ferdinand's probation, he gave him Miranda's hand and instructed the pair to wait with him until the other castaways should arrive.

Stephano and Trinculo, one a butler and the other a jester, had turned up on still another stretch of the island. They had managed to rescue several bottles of liquor from the ship and were lumbering about on the sand, blind drunk, when they had the misfortune of bumping into hideous Caliban, lying on the beach under a stinking cloak. After accepting a drink from the staggering courtiers, Caliban, now tipsy himself, promised to help them obtain sovereignty over the island – if they would help him murder the present ruler, Prospero. The drunkards agreed, and the three set off in a comical daze to seek out the magician. Ariel overheard their conspiracy and intervened to thwart their plan by placing diversions in their path – attacking hounds; rich, tempting raiment dangling on elusive clotheslines; and many other such conjurations.

Later, Ariel drove the pathetic trio through filthy ditches, swamps, and brier patches, until they finally reached Prospero's cave.

Now, with the entire ship's population reunited – minus Ferdinand, who was playing chess with Miranda inside the cave – Prospero gathered everyone into an enchanted circle and revealed his true identity. All were astonished, as they had thought the duke was long dead. Prospero mildly rebuked all the schemers of evil: First Alonso and Antonio, for overthrowing his dukedom and leaving him to perish; then Sebastian, for plotting to kill Alonso; and lastly Trinculo and Stephano, for conniving with Caliban to murder him. Then, assured that the company had repented of their evil deeds and intentions, he granted his full, sovereign forgiveness to all.

Prospero next warmly commended his benefactor Gonzalo for his "saintly" character and behavior. Finally, he beckoned penitent Alonso to enter the cave. There, the father tearfully embraced the son he had thought dead. When introduced to Miranda, Ferdinand's cherished bride-to-be, Alonso was equally captivated by her.

And now, with joy and reconciliation reigning, Ariel reported to Prospero that the beached vessel was repaired and ready for a return voyage to Milan. Before departing the island, however, the old magician, in a final act of kindness, freed Ariel from her servitude. He then took his books and staff and cast them into the sea, openly vowing to give up his long-held practice of sorcery.

Prospero sailed with the company back to Italy – to begin life anew, to reign once more in Milan, and to witness the marriage of his daughter to faithful Ferdinand.

Commentary:

This unusual play – full of music, sorcery, conspiracy, romance, comedy, and pathos – belongs to the last period of Shakespeare's career. The odd, bitter-sweet drama embodies qualities of both tragedy and comedy, though this and others of the final plays are usually classified as "romances."

In *The Tempest*, everybody, as Gonzalo notes, leaves the island in a changed state: Alonso finally suffers the pangs of guilt and begs forgiveness for his crimes against Prospero; Antonio eventually humbles himself. These two villains are mirrored in a kind of comic relief by Trinculo and Stephano, who are also led to repentance.

Since *The Tempest* is considered Shakespeare's final great play, many critics have suggested that Prospero represents Shakespeare himself at the end of his work; that the magician's final speech, in which he renounces magic, is meant to symbolize the Bard's farewell to the theater before retiring to his Stratford home. The entire allegorical plot, beginning with an ocean-going peril and subsequently spanning the breadth of human emotions, ending in a scene of serenity and joy, may indeed reflect and symbolize the writer's reflections on his life.

At any rate, the play stands as one of Shakespeare's greatest works, possessing a strange, undefinable, composite quality that sets it apart from all others.

AS YOU LIKE IT

by
William Shakespeare
(1564 - 1616)

Type of work: Romantic comedy

Setting: France; Duke Frederick's court and Forest of Arden; 1500's

Principal characters:

Duke Senior, exiled rightful ruler

Duke Frederick, usurper of his brother's dukedom

Oliver and Orlando, sons of Sir Rowland de Boys

Adam, long-time servant to Sir Rowland

Rosalind, Duke Senior's daughter

Celia, Duke Frederick's daughter

Phebe, a shepherdess

Silvius, a shepherd with unrequited love for Phebe

Touchstone, a "motley fool" jester who provides good-humor throughout the play

Story Overview:

Orlando was angry with his older brother Oliver for giving him nothing from their father's estate. He complained loudly to Adam, an old family servant. Just then, in walked Oliver, the object of Orlando's ire. They quarreled, and though Adam pled with them "for your father's remembrance" not to fight, Orlando continued to demand his share of the inheritance – which Oliver at last reluctantly granted in order to avoid violence. Then, as Orlando left, Oliver drove Adam out as well: "Get you with him, you old dog."

Left alone, Oliver summoned mighty Charles, the court wrestler. The next day Orlando was to wrestle Charles, and Oliver charged him, "I had as lief thou did'st break his neck as his finger."

Meanwhile, at the court of Duke Frederick, his daughter Celia consoled melancholy Rosalind, her cousin – and the daughter of the recently deposed duke Senior. But Celia's consolations were futile; Rosalind could not "forget a banished father." Only when Celia promised that she would turn over her whole future inheritance – the dukedom itself – to Rosalind, did Rosalind grow "merry" again. The cousins then decided to go watch the wrestling match. Meeting Orlando on the way, they tried to persuade him to "give over this attempt" at besting Charles, who had already crushed the ribs of three challengers. But Orlando would not be dissuaded.

The match ended quickly; to the astonishment of all, Charles was thrown and Orlando declared the victor. Duke Frederick called the champion forward to receive his reward, but upon learning that Orlando was the son of his enemy, Sir Rowland, he angrily sent the young man on his way. Rosalind, on the other hand, offered her hero a chain: "Wear this for me," she told him. Then she blushingly added, "Sir, you have wrestled well, and overthrown more than your enemies."

Just days later, Duke Frederick gruffly took Rosalind aside. "Within these ten days" he warned, "if that thou be'st found so near our public court as twenty miles, thou diest for it." When Rosalind protested that she was not a traitor, her uncle was unmoved. As the daughter of Duke Senior, Frederick's deposed brother, Rosalind was unwelcome in his realm. But unbeknownst to Frederick, his own daughter Celia offered to join her cousin in exile. That night the girls would depart for the forest of Arden, where Duke Senior now lived. Since the forest was a dangerous place for two women alone, the taller Rosalind dressed as a pageboy, calling herself "Ganymede," while Celia put on the rags of a shepherdess, and called herself "Aliena." They also invited the "clownish fool of [the] court," Touchstone, to accompany them. That evening, the three fugitives escaped, undetected.

Now that same night, Adam warned Orlando of Oliver's plan to burn Orlando's house, leaving him no safe refuge. Adam offered Orlando his life's savings and asked, "Let me be your servant." Orlando gladly accepted and together they, too, left for the forest of Arden.

As Celia, Touchstone, and Rosalind – she in boy's clothing – made their way through the woods, they overheard a shepherd, Silvius, pouring out his heart to his friend Corin: "O Corin, that thou knew'st how I do love her [Phebe]!" With this, the distraught shepherd ran away. Rosalind and company, "with travel much oppressed," then approached Corin, and he extended an invitation for them to eat and rest in his own humble cottage.

Meanwhile, in another part of the forest, Adam, faint after their long journey, complained to Orlando: "Dear master . . . I die for food." Orlando promised he would bring victuals to the faithful old servant, or die trying. As he searched for food, he came upon the exiled Duke Senior and his men, who were about to eat. Orlando strutted towards them and menacingly decreed, "Forebear, and eat no more! . . . He dies that touches any of this fruit till I and my affairs are answered." Duke Senior, unoffended, invited Orlando to sit down and join them. Then, embarrassed by his own behavior, Orlando begged their forgiveness and hurried to retrieve Adam. As everyone ate, Orlando revealed to Duke Senior that he was the son of Sir Rowland, whereupon the Duke exclaimed, "I am the Duke that loved your father."

Back at court, Duke Frederick, believing that Orlando had helped Celia and Rosalind escape, threatened Oliver with the seizure of his lands unless he brought his brother back to him in chains. With this, he sent the young man packing for the forest of Arden.

Now as Orlando made his way through the forest, he went about carving poems into trees declaring his love for Rosalind. Dressed as Ganymede, Rosalind found one of the verses: "Let no face be kept in mind but the fair of Rosalind." Celia also happened on one of the poems, good-naturedly teased Rosalind, and revealed that Rosalind's own Orlando was the author. Suddenly, up strode Orlando himself with one of Duke Senior's men. Rosalind – as Ganymede – decided to "play the knave with him" and addressed him "like a saucy lackey." Eventually, "Ganymede" posed a remedy for Orlando's love: Orlando was to woo Ganymede as though he were Rosalind. The "boy" would then run the gambit of emotions with his "suitor," thereby curing him of his passion.

The next morning "Ganymede" awaited Orlando, but he failed to come. As the disguised Rosalind confided her misery to Celia, Corin came to announce the approach of Phebe and Silvius. Sure enough, Silvius appeared, once more pleading with his shepherdess – "Sweet Phebe, do not scorn me" – which only made Phebe scorn him more. Then Rosalind stepped forward to berate them both. But even as "Ganymede" chided Phebe for her disdain and scolded Silvius for putting up with it, Phebe was enchanted by "his" beauty. "I had rather hear you chide," she simpered, "than this man woo."

Finally Orlando arrived. "Orlando, where have you been all this while? You a lover? . . . " Rosalind wailed, as if she were a boy mimicking a lady. Orlando begged her pardon, and, at last Rosalind forgave him: "Come, woo me, woo me; for now I am in a holiday humor and like enough to consent. What would you say to me now, and I were your very very Rosalind?" and they bantered back and forth until Rosalind manuevered Orlando into asking for her hand in marriage. Orlando later departed.

Soon after, Oliver came upon the boy Ganymede, whose name he recognized. Displaying Orlando's bloody handkerchief, Oliver explained his brother's earlier delay. It seems that while Oliver napped beneath a tree, Orlando, passing by on his way to woo Ganymede, had come upon his sleeping brother – in mortal danger from a lurking lioness – and turned back to the rescue. " . . . Kindness, nobler even than revenge, And nature, stronger than

his just occasion, made him give battle to the lioness." Orlando's intervention had converted his brother's hatred into love; the two were reconciled.

At the sight of Orlando's blood-stained handkerchief, however, Rosalind swooned, a most unmanly act. Though she quickly regained herself – "I pray you tell your brother how well I counterfeited" – Oliver was not fooled. "It was a passion of earnest," he was certain.

When Oliver returned to Orlando, he recounted all that had transpired. He also confessed his love for Aliena (Celia) and swore that Orlando could keep their father's entire estate; he, Oliver, would now prefer to stay in the forest to "live and die a shepherd."

Ganymede then advanced toward Orlando, offering once more to substitute for his beloved Rosalind. But Orlando could not play the part; his sadness was too deep. Filled with compassion, Ganymede promised him that on the morrow, by magical art, he would "set [Rosalind] before your eyes."

Then up walked Phebe, still in a huff, and still followed by the devoted Silvius. Ganymede once more chided her: " . . . You are followed by a faithful shepherd: Look upon him, love him; he worships you." Phebe, however, still proclaimed her love for Ganymede. So, Rosalind struck a bargain with Phebe: If on the following day Phebe still wanted to marry Ganymede, they would marry. But if Phebe refused, then she must wed the scorned Silvius. Phebe agreed.

The next day, as all the suitors waited in the forest, Hymen, the goddess of marriage, entered the clearing with Rosalind – dressed finally as herself. Orlando was thrilled; Phebe was shocked. "If sight and shape be true, why then, my love adieu!" she wailed.

Orlando and his Rosalind, Oliver and Celia, Phebe and Silvius – and even Touchstone with Aubrey, a "homely wench" from the forest – joined hands in marriage as Hymen chirped:

Whiles a wedlock hymn we sing,
Feed yourselves with questioning,
That reason wonder may diminish
how thus we met, and these things finish.

Commentary:

One of Shakespeare's most famous works, *As You Like It* possesses many classic elements of comedy. The personal divisions at the outset (two Duke-brothers at war, two other brothers filled with hate for one another, daughters separated from their fathers) all strike a discordant note central to the comedic form. Moreover, the device of Rosalind being mistaken for a man creates humorous tension throughout. As in most comedies, though, by the end of the play all wrongs are somehow righted; brothers come together and every Jack has his Jill.

THE MERCHANT OF VENICE

by
William Shakespeare
(1564 - 1616)

Type of work: Comedic drama

Setting: Renaissance Venice and Belmont

Principal characters:

Antonio, the merchant

Bassanio, his young friend, in love with Portia

Portia, a beautiful and wealthy young woman

Shylock, a rich Jew

Jessica, Shylock's lovely daughter

Story Overview:

Whenever Bassanio needed money he would go to his older friend Antonio, a wealthy Venetian merchant. Now Bassanio needed a sizable loan for a certain "enterprise." When questioned concerning this enterprise, Bassanio admitted he had fallen in love with Portia, a wealthy and famous lady. Unless Bassanio had money, he could never hope to compete with the myriad of rich noblemen and princes who vied for Portia's favor. Antonio would have gladly supplied his friend with the money, but he had no cash on hand; all of his capital was tied up in ships, not due to return from foreign ports for several weeks.

So Antonio and Bassanio found their way to Shylock, a rich Jewish moneylender who had made his fortune by charging exorbitant interest rates. Though they despised Shylock, the two managed to swallow their pride long enough to petition him to loan them three thousand ducats, to be paid back as soon as Antonio's ships returned to port. Shylock bitterly rebuked them for having the temerity to come crawling to him for a loan after publicly disdaining him:

You call me a misbeliever, cut-throat dog,
And spit upon my Jewish gaberdine . . .
Well then, it now appears you need help . . .
What should I say to you? Should I not say: . . .
"Fair sir, you spat on me on Wednesday last;
You spurned me such and such day; another
time
You call'd me dog; and for these courtesies
I'll lend you thus much moneys?"

Finally, though, glowing and rubbing his hands together as if he would "get to the bone" of his petitioners, Shylock agreed to lend the money, but on this condition: if the full sum were not repaid within three months, he could lawfully cut one pound of flesh from Antonio's body.

Bassanio was shocked at the proposal, but Antonio assured him there was no need to worry; his ships were expected home a full month before the debt would come due. Reluctantly, Bassanio accepted the terms of the loan.

Meanwhile, the lovely Portia had been receiving visits from prospective husbands – and she disliked them all. To make matters worse, she wasn't allowed to choose her husband for herself. Her late father had left a provision in his will that Portia's husband would be chosen by lottery. Three caskets – one of gold, one of silver, and one of lead – had been laid out, and only one of these contained a portrait of the lady. Any potential suitor must choose one of the caskets. If the casket he chose contained the portrait, he could marry Portia; if not, he would be compelled to leave and never woo another woman again. Fortunately for Portia, none of the suitors who had sought her had as yet guessed the right casket.

Elsewhere, Launcelot, Shylock's comical servant, decided he would finally escape from his master's employ; Shylock was simply too cruel to endure. Launcelot paused long enough to break the news to Jessica, Shylock's daughter, who was heartbroken to see him go. "Our house is a hell," she said, "and thou, a merry devil, Didst rob it of some taste of tediousness." Before he left, Jessica gave Launcelot a letter to deliver to Lorenzo, a friend of Bassanio's with whom she had fallen in love. The letter instructed Lorenzo to meet her at her house, where she would escape in disguise and elope with him. That night, Jessica and Lorenzo carried out their lovers' plan, fleeing the city in a gondola filled with Shylock's ducats. When Shylock learned that his daughter had run away to marry a Christian, he was at once crushed and furious, and grew all the more fervent in his hatred of Antonio and his Christian friends.

In the meantime, Bassanio had made his way to Portia, ready to hazard a try at the caskets. Portia immediately fell in love with him and feared lest he should choose the wrong box. But, guided by Portia's sea-blue eyes, Bassanio avoided the temptation to choose the gold or silver caskets, and, wisely declaring, "All that glitters is not gold," correctly selected the unassuming lead. Both Portia and Bassanio were elated. But no sooner were their wedding plans underway than they were interrupted by horrifying news from Venice: every one of Antonio's ships had been shipwrecked in a storm, leaving him penniless and unable to pay his debt to Shylock. Shylock would now obtain the revenge he sought. In a pathetic letter to Bassanio, Antonio resigned himself to his fate and bade farewell to his friend.

Bassanio and Portia postponed their marriage and rushed to Venice to aid their benefactor. But what could they do? Antonio had agreed to the contract of his own free will; and Shylock would surely insist on carrying out the penalty. The law was on his side.

It was Portia, after deep thought, who hatched a plot to save her husband's friend. Knowing that he would have to appear in court to either pay his debt or announce his default, Portia decided to masquerade herself as a young lawyer sent to act in Antonio's defense.

The day of the trial finally arrived. Antonio confessed to the Duke, acting as judge, that he could not pay his debt, and that he was prepared to allow the moneylender to exact his pound of flesh. The Duke and all those present at the court begged Shylock to spare Antonio, but he refused. Bassanio – now a rich man because of his betrothal to Portia – offered Shylock twice the amount of Antonio's debt, but still Shylock preferred that Antonio should die. The Duke, bound by law, sadly admitted that the penalty was valid.

At that moment, Portia, pretending to be "Balthasar," a lawyer sent by the respected but ill Doctor Bellario, entered the court to defend Antonio. In an elegant speech, she encouraged Shylock to lay aside the letter of the law in favor of mercy:

The quality of mercy is not strained, it droppeth as the gentle rain from heaven upon the place beneath; it is twice blessed, it blesseth him that gives, and him that takes . . .

But Shylock would have none of it. "I crave the law!" he raved. Next Portia asked if anyone would pay Antonio's bond, and this time Bassanio offered to pay ten times the debt. But once more Shylock refused, and insisted that justice be carried out.

Portia now changed her stance. She craftily pretended to agree with the Jew. If he insists on the letter of the law, it must be carried out, she said. Then she ordered a knife be brought. Shylock was ecstatic to find this defender in agreement with him, and raised his knife to inflict the fatal wound to his enemy's breast. But just then, Portia interjected to remind Shylock of one detail: the words in the contract stated that Shylock was to extract "a pound of flesh" – but mentioned nothing about blood. Therefore, if in cutting into Antonio's heart Shylock should shed even one drop of blood, he would violate the contract, and, by the laws of Venice, he must be executed and his lands confiscated.

Astonished and trembling, Shylock dropped the knife and scowled. The court rang with laughter.

Shylock offered to let Antonio go in peace, but Portia refused. After all, since he insisted on the letter of the law, he must have it. Now it was Shylock who pled for mercy. The court decided to spare his life, but to confiscate his lands (reserving half for his daughter after his death) and to force him to adopt Christianity. Shylock slumped from the courtroom, humiliated and bitter.

Jubilant, Antonio and his friends were soon made aware of Portia's cunning disguise. All returned to Belmont, where Bassanio and fair Portia established their new household.

Commentary:

As with many of Shakespeare's plays, the titular protagonist of *The Merchant of Venice* (Antonio) plays a relatively minor role in the action. Bassanio and Portia are more central characters, but even they are upstaged by the brilliant and perplexing character of Shylock.

How is the audience or reader meant to react to Shylock? He ought to strike us as thoroughly loathsome – he is a usurer, an abusive parent, violent, legalistic, bitter, unsociable and greedy. In spite of all these faults, though, one cannot help feeling some sympathy for him. After all, he is forced to live among neighbors who neither understand nor respect his religious beliefs; "Christians" who treat him with cruelty. Forced into his money-lending by legal restrictions on Jewish professions, he remains highly intelligent and capable of great eloquence, as in this passionate complaint against Antonio's abuses:

He hath . . . laughed at my losses, mocked at my gains, scorned my nation, thwarted my bargains, cooled my friends, heated mine enemies;
and what's his reason? I am a Jew.
Hath not a Jew eyes? hath not a Jew hands, organs, dimensions, sense, affections, passions? [Is not a Jew] fed with the same food, hurt with the same weapons, subject to the same diseases, healed by the same means, warmed and cooled by the same winter and summer, as a Christian is? If you prick us, do we not bleed? if you tickle us, do we not laugh? if you poison us, do we not die?

Marvelous lines, and in some respects a more compassionate speech than uttered by any of the Christian characters. So, Shylock is an ambiguous villain.

But the play is not Shylock's story; it is a comedy, and the triumph of mercy over unyielding justice is the theme that finally brings *The Merchant of Venice* to its happy resolution.

MUCH ADO ABOUT NOTHING

by
William Shakespeare
(1564 - 1616)

Type of work: Romantic comedy

Setting: Messina, Italy; sixteenth century

Principal characters:
Don Pedro, Prince of Arragon
Don John, his jealous brother
Claudio, a young Florentine lord loyal to
Don Pedro
Benedick, a witty bachelor and another
ally of Pedro
Leonato, governor of Messina
Hero, Leonato's daughter
Beatrice, Hero's cousin, also known for
her sharp wit
Borachio, aide to Don John

Story Overview:

After quashing the attempt of his bastard brother John to take control of Arragon, Don Pedro, bound for home with his two friends Claudio and Benedick, neared Messina. There, Governor Leonato, his daughter, Hero, and her cousin Beatrice, waited at the city gate to welcome both the victors and the defeated. Don John, as part of the truce, had agreed that Pedro would indeed rule Arragon; Pedro in turn agreed to permit John to return to his holdings there in peace. Leonato beamed to see Pedro on his way home with few casualties – and reconciled with his brother as well. Beatrice, on the other hand, felt mixed emotions on greeting Benedick, Pedro's ally and her own wordy rival. "There is a merry war betwixt Signior Benedick and her . . . " Leonato noted. "A skirmish of wits between them."

After formally greeting the victorious Pedro, the governor invited him and his entourage to stay in Messina with his family for a few days before pushing on to Arragon. On the way to Leonato's house, however, Benedick and Claudio lagged far behind; Claudio wished to solicit Benedick's opinion of Hero. To Claudio she was the sweetest lady he had ever laid eyes on. When Pedro, returning to hurry the two along, was told of Claudio's infatuation with Hero, he consented to help him gain favor with her; he would act as intermediary on Claudio's behalf.

Now, a passerby loyal to Don John happened to overhear this conversation, and promptly informed his master of Claudio's desires to marry Hero. "That young upstart hath all the glory of my overthrow," John sneered. "If I can cross him any way, I bless myself every way." And so, Don John launched his plot against Claudio – and his attack against his powerful brother.

That night at a masked celebration, it was agreed that Pedro would woo Hero for Claudio.

All went as planned – until Don John made insinuating remarks, well within Claudio's range of hearing, hinting that Pedro, even as he ostensibly courted Hero on Claudio's behalf, actually intended to keep her for himself. Claudio became distraught. By the time Pedro arrived to break the good news – Hero and Claudio were to be married – Claudio had fled, irate and humiliated, acting like "a schoolboy who, being overjoyed with finding a bird's nest, shows it his companion and he steals it." But at length Beatrice found the pouting Claudio, reasoned with him, and brought him back.

Later, in a gleeful, mischievous plan, Hero, Claudio, Pedro and Leonato decided to do some further matchmaking. They resolved that Benedick, a confirmed and contented bachelor, and Beatrice, a girl equally opposed to matrimony, would be impossible to match as husband and wife. So they undertook the devious challenge of bringing these two argumentative souls together before resuming their journey to Arragon.

That very afternoon, while Benedick strolled in the palace's garden, Claudio, Pedro and Leonato, pretending not to see him, sat lamenting poor Beatrice, so tortured by her love for Benedick. At the same time, Hero and her handmaiden walked through an orchard, and, knowing that Beatrice was hidden there, solemnly talked of how inwardly tormented Benedick was by his unrequited love for Beatrice. The plan worked perfectly. The next time the two "merry rivals" united, instead of trading the usual insults and quarrels, each determined to console the other's supposed passion.

Meanwhile, John, having learned of the forthcoming marriage of Claudio and Hero, conspired anew. He sent his aide, Borachio, to fool Claudio into believing that Hero had another lover.

That evening, John lured Claudio and Pedro to a place near the window of Hero's bedchamber. Borachio had persuaded one of Hero's servants to dress in her mistress' clothing. In pretense of wooing Hero, Borachio then went through the motions of seducing the maid, casting their embracing shadow on the window. Upon witnessing this, Claudio and Pedro grew livid, but decided to wait until the wedding to properly denounce the faithless Hero.

A nightwatchman later overheard Borachio bragging about his duplicity and arrested him. But in their stupidity, the town officials failed to reveal the plot in time to stay Hero's fall from grace. On the next morning, as the wedding vows were being taken, Claudio suddenly refused his bride. "There, Leonato," he told the governor, "take her back again. Give not this rotten orange to your friend . . . . She knows the heat of a luxurious bed." The wedding guests were stunned. Of course Hero denied everything, but to no avail. And then, flushed with disgrace, she swooned and fainted. Even Leonato accepted Claudio's eyewitness account of her betrayal. She has "fallen into a pit of ink, that the wide sea hath drops too few to wash her clean again," the father mourned. Nevertheless, before Leonato could disown his daughter, the friar performing the ceremony intervened. He believed in Hero's integrity, and counselled Leonato to have patience and trust. Then in a plan of his own, he convinced Leonato to give Hero a chance to "change slander to remorse." Leonato was to hide his daughter's slumped body away and let out word that she was dead. Meanwhile, the friar would seek evidence to prove her innocence. The two men then carried Hero out of the room, leaving only Benedick and Beatrice in the marriage hall. Though their talk was still filled with wit and jibes, now it was tempered with genuine affection. Benedick remarked: "I do love nothing in the world so well as you. Is not that strange?" But Beatrice held back her proclamations of love. She would not commit to him. First, to test his love, she made him promise to kill Claudio, the villain who had "slandered, scorned, dishonored [her] kinswoman."

In the meantime, the constable had arrested Borachio and brought him before the town sexton for questioning. After listening to the story, the sexton elected to take Borachio before Leonato so that he too could hear how Hero had been wronged. Unfortunately, Leonato and his older brother were already taking matters into their own hands. According to plan, they sought out Claudio and Pedro and challenged them to fight: "Thou hast killed my child. If thou kill'st me, boy, thou shall kill a man." But neither Pedro nor Claudio wanted any part of sending two elderly gentlemen to their deaths; they refused the challenge and went on their way.

Next, Benedick met Claudio and Pedro. He too dared the slanderous Claudio to duel. And still, Claudio refused the challenge.

Just then up marched the constable, leading Borachio toward Leonato's palace. Claudio and Pedro were told of what had actually happened the night before; they had been tricked – and Hero defamed – by the plot of wicked Don John. That very night these two sought to take revenge, but John had fled the city.

Also that night, Leonato, now informed about the truth behind his daughter's broken marriage ceremony, demanded that Claudio stand before him. He told Claudio that he could be forgiven of his offense against his dead daughter on two conditions: first, he must publicly confess Hero's innocence to all Messina and "hang an epitaph upon her tomb, and sing it to her bones"; secondly, he must marry Leonato's niece, who was "almost the copy" of Hero. Claudio gladly embraced Leonato's two requisites for penance.

The following morning, after Claudio had sung to an empty tomb, he and his unknown bride-to-be stood side by side in the marriage hall. Then, as the veil was lifted away from her face, Claudio discovered to his overwhelming joy his own beloved Hero – alive! The friar calmed the ecstatic groom and promised to explain the whole affair once the ceremony was finished.

Attending the wedding were Benedick and Beatrice – naturally matching wits again. In the course of their bantering, Benedick asked Beatrice why she did not show her love for him; after all, Leonato, Claudio and Pedro had indeed spoken of her feelings. In like manner, Beatrice insisted that Hero and her handmaiden must have been sorely deceived, for they had also sworn that Benedick loved her. Eventually, the pair of rivals did admit (reluctantly) that perhaps it was true – maybe they did love one another.

Before the procession could depart the chapel, Benedick called everyone together and announced that he and Beatrice were ready to wed.

That day, the double wedding, coupled with word that Don John had been captured, made Pedro's heart a merry one. And before leaving the chapel, the overjoyed Benedick gave Pedro, suddenly the sole bachelor among the three friends, some advice: "Get thee a wife, get thee a wife!"

Commentary:

Throughout *Much Ado About Nothing*, Shakespeare artfully combines comedy with near-tragedy. To complete his tapestry of interwoven plots, the resolution had to be brilliantly contrived. Some students of Shakespeare believe that, as one of the Bard's final comedies, this work inspired within him renewed moral consciousness. And indeed his tragic dramas from this point on focus on themes of ethical transgression and human weakness that had served only as fragmented bits of plots in previous plays.

Much Ado is fraught with allusions to the symbol of cuckoldry – the horns a husband (Claudio) must wear when his wife has had an adulterous affair. For Benedick as well, the fear of wearing "horns" on his head spawns many of his witticisms concerning marriage.

Often in Shakespeare's comedies, a strong woman such as Beatrice will at some point don men's clothing, as a sign of strength and equality in a man's world. However, Beatrice uses only her wit to protect her – a more than ample weapon. Men flee her cruel tongue as though it were a "drawn sword" or a "ferocious lion." The plot includes suggestions of violence, treachery and sorrow throughout; but, in the end, the schemes and threats amount merely to "much ado about nothing."

THE COURTSHIP OF MILES STANDISH

by
Henry Wadsworth Longfellow
(1807-1882)

Type of work: Romantic narrative poem

Setting: Plymouth, Massachusetts; 1621

Principal characters:

Miles Standish, a soldier and protector of the colony

John Alden, his younger, bookish friend

Priscilla, a young Puritan woman

Poem Overview:

On a spring afternoon in 1621, Captain Miles Standish, a short, powerfully-built man of middle age and a recent widower, stood in his house, surveying with pride his well-polished weapons of war. "If you wish a thing to be well done, you must do it yourself," he preached to his young friend John Alden, who sat writing letters to be sent back to England on the *May Flower* the next day. Since the death of his wife, Rose, the Captain had invited John to share his home. Captain Standish was a man of action. He treasured but three books: *Bariffe's Artillery Guide*, the *Commentaries of Caesar*, and *The Bible*, all full enough with rumblings of war to satisfy his soldier heart. Alden, on the other hand, was a gentle student; humble, pious – as a Puritan should be – and able in the art of words, not weapons.

The letters John wrote were full of the name "Priscilla." He had observed her quiet faith through the colony's harsh first winter, as well as her courage at the loss of her beloved parents and brother. All of John Alden's love and sympathy privately longed to envelop and protect her. But now the Captain broke the silence to divulge a secret that shocked his companion: He was much impressed with a girl who went by the name of "Priscilla"; he thought she would be the best choice to take the place of his Rose. Stunned by this disclosure, Alden's heart sank even more when Miles made a request: "I can march up to a fortress and summon the place to surrender, But march up to a woman with such a proposal, I dare not." Astonishingly, he was commissioning his young friend John, the man of well-turned phrases, to propose marriage in his behalf.

John Alden was left aghast – "Trying to smile and yet feeling his heart stand still in his bosom . . ." At last he recovered enough to remind the Good Captain of his maxim: "If you would have a thing well done . . ."

"Truly the maxim is good," Standish agreed, "but we must use it discreetly, and not waste powder for nothing. Surely you cannot refuse what I ask in the name of our friendship!"

Alas, "Friendship prevailed over love, and Alden went on his errand." His Puritan training had won out.

All is clear to me now;
This is the hand of the Lord; it is laid upon me in anger,
For I have followed too much the heart's desires and devices, This is the cross I must bear.

Perhaps it was the weight of that self-imposed cross that made Alden botch his errand. For as he approached her cabin door and heard Priscilla singing the Hundredth Psalm while she contentedly spun her cloth, he was filled with woe. Priscilla smiled upon seeing John, showing obvious delight in his visit. Then, as they spoke, she guiltily confessed how homesick she felt. But John blurted out:

Stouter hearts than a woman's have quailed in this terrible winter.
Yours is tender and trusting and needs a stronger to lean on;
So I have come to you now, with an offer and proffer of marriage
Made by a good man and true, Miles Standish, the Captain of Plymouth!

Priscilla's surprise at this offer was obvious; and Alden only made things worse as he warmed to his subject, extolling the virtues of his friend. Finally, Priscilla beamed impishly and asked, "Why don't you speak for yourself, John?" That question undid the poor scholar and he fled to the seashore to berate himself for his clumsiness. "Is it my fault that the maiden has chosen between us?" he cried to the sky. Immediately an answer thundered within him: "It hath displeased the Lord!" and John's sins now appeared as terrible to him as David's entanglement with Bathsheba. Seeing the *May Flower* still at anchor in the harbor, he resolved to return to England and take his guilty secret of love to the grave. "Better be dead and forgotten," he concluded dramatically, "than living in shame and dishonor!"

Having consigned himself to this course, John returned to Captain Standish and recounted Priscilla's reply. When he repeated her revealing question, "Up leaped the Captain of Plymouth, Wildly he shouted, and loud:

John Alden! you have betrayed me!
You, who have fed at my board, and drunk at my cup, to whose keeping
I have intrusted my honor, my thoughts the most sacred and secret –
Let there be nothing between us save war, and implacable hatred!

The captain might have continued this tirade, but just then a soldier arrived, bringing "rumors of danger and war and hostile incursions of Indians." Buckling on his sword and frowning fiercely, Standish stalked out of the cabin, leaving the chagrined Alden praying for forgiveness.

The choleric leader found the men of the colony debating on an answer to the symbolic message that had been brought by a defiant Indian brave: a rattlesnake skin filled with arrows. "Leave this matter to me," the angry captain exploded, "for to me by right it pertaineth." Then, jerking the arrows from the snakeskin, he filled it with powder and bullets and thrust it back at the Indian emissary, thundering, "Here, take it! This is your answer!"

Silently out of the room then glided the glistening savage,
Bearing the serpent's skin, and seeming himself like a serpent,
Winding his sinuous way in the dark to the depths of the forest.

Early the next morning, Standish and a few men marched northward "to quell the sudden revolt of the savage."

Giants they seemed in the mist, or the mighty men of King David;
Giants in heart they were, who believed in God and the Bible, – Ay, who believed in the smiting of Midianites and Philistines.

That same day the *May Flower* sailed home to England, and the little colony all assembled to bid her God-speed. In spite of the dreadful winter they had endured, none chose to return – not even John Alden. To carry out his impassioned decision of the day before seemed more cowardly than honorable, viewed against the prospect of Indian attack; and he found that renouncing the idea of having Priscilla for his wife did not prevent him from wanting to stay and protect her as a friend.

After the others had returned to their homes, Priscilla overtook John and they talked. Both had had time to think over their conversation of the previous day. Priscilla made a confession:

I have liked to be with you, to see you, to speak with you always.
So I was hurt at your words, and a little affronted to hear you
Urge me to marry your friend, though he were the Captain Miles Standish.
For I must tell you the truth: much more to me is your friendship
Than all the love he could give, were he twice the hero you think him.

Meanwhile, the brooding captain was showing himself to be indeed a soldier of skill and insight. After a three-day march, Standish's party entered an Indian village, where two young braves taunted and threatened him. He killed them both so quickly and effortlessly that the rest of the tribe was subdued. When word of this feat, accompanied by the head of one of the braves, was carried back to Plymouth, all rejoiced; but Priscilla wondered silently if such a hero might expect to claim her upon his return.

And so, "Month after month passed away . . . . All in the village was peace; but at times the rumor of warfare filled the air with alarm." Captain Standish was still out scouring the countryside, defeating all who came against him.

Anger was still in his heart, but at times that remorse and contrition
Which in all noble natures succeed the passionate outbreak,

Came like a rising tide . . . "

During these months John Alden often walked through the forest to see Priscilla, "Led by . . . pleasure disguised as duty, and love in the semblance of friendship." One afternoon as they visited, Priscilla teased John that he must not be so idle:

If I am a pattern for housewives (as he'd told her she was),
Show yourself equally worthy of being the model of husbands,
Hold this skein on your hands while I wind it, ready for knitting.

Onto this domestic scene burst a messenger with urgent news: Captain Standish had been killed in an ambush, and enemy Indians would likely try to burn the town and murder the people. Priscilla raised her hands in horror. At the same time, John felt all the turmoil of the mixed emotions thundering within him – the sorrow and pain at the loss of a friend, clashing with the joy of freedom from the bondage of that friendship. Out of that conflict he reached for Priscilla and, "Pressing her close to his heart, as forever his own," he exclaimed, "Those whom the Lord hath united, let no man put them asunder!"

The couple's wedding day dawned, and in spite of the imminent dangers, friends assembled in the village church to wish the young couple well. Just as the brief ceremony had ended, "A form appeared on the threshold, clad in armor of steel, a somber and sorrowful figure." The bridegroom stared; the bride turned pale. Was it a phantom? "A bodiless, spectral illusion?" But as the figure strode into the room, all realized with amazement that Miles Standish had survived; survived not only an Indian ambush, but the harder battle of his own pride. He went straight to John Alden, grasped his hand and begged his forgiveness: "I have been cruel and hard, but now, thank God, it is ended." Alden answered, "Let all be forgotten between us – All save the dear, old friendship, and that shall grow older and dearer!" Gallantly, then, the captain advanced and tenderly bowed to Priscilla, "wishing her joy of her wedding, and loudly lauding her husband."

Then he said with a smile: "I should have remembered the adage, – If you would be well served, you must serve yourself."

Commentary:

Henry Wadsworth Longfellow was brought up as a New England aristocrat steeped in European culture. His works, written in part as Americanized tributes to the works of Sir Walter Scott, were very popular during his lifetime, but an antagonistic attitude toward them later developed among critics with tastes of another age. Today they are enjoying a revival as early American epic myths.

The plot of this simple, gracefully written poem is reminiscent of *Cyrano de Bergerac*, but with twists of its own. Reunited friendship and requited young love told in the delicate detail of an old-English style, make Longfellow's poem a classic.

OUR TOWN

by
Thornton Wilder
(1897 - 1975)

Type of work: Presentational life drama

Setting: Grover's Corners, New Hampshire; 1901 to 1913

Principal characters:

Stage Manager, the play's all-wise narrator
Dr. and Mrs. Gibbs, an ordinary small-town physician and housewife
George Gibbs, their son
Mr. and Mrs. Webb, a news editor and his wife
Emily Webb, their daughter
Simon Stimson, the town drunkard and church choir organist
A conglomeration of other ordinary people living out ordinary lives

Commentary:

Thornton Wilder's *Our Town* provides the audience with an informal, intimate and compelling human drama. Wilder was dissatisfied with the unimaginative, stilted theatrical productions of his time: "[They] aimed to be soothing. The tragic had no heat; the comic had no bite; the social criticism failed to indict us with responsibility." *Our Town*, with its far-reaching theme and unmistakable symbolism, was a far cry from the typical bland depression era play (though, ironically, "the magic of the mundane" is the play's major theme).

Though set during the early Twentieth Century, Grover's Corner is anyplace and all places, anytime and all times. A constantly shifting verb tense throughout the play reveals that something strange is happening here with time. Pantomime and conversation simultaneously enact life's continuum of time and place.

The principal actor is the Stage Manager, who remains on stage the entire time explaining much of the action. He is aware of the present, and privy to both the past and the future. He knows the characters' feelings, and alternately takes on the roles of narrator, philosophical druggist, host, master of ceremonies, commentator and friend to the audience.

Wilder creates types rather than individuals in *Our Town*. Every audience member can say, "Yes, I know someone like that. He's just like so-and-so," or "I know what he is feeling. I've felt that way myself." This sense of "recollection" permeates the play to both thrill and haunt us with reminders of our common – and fragile – humanity.

By using the barest of scenery and props, Wilder reinforces that our hopes and despairs and loves begin and end not with things, but in the mind and the soul, as our lives unfold through one another. This focus on "absolute reality" allows us to see Emily's simplest pleasures and cares (algebra lessons, birthday presents, etc.) through child-like eyes. Her timelessness helps the audience understand, just as she herself comes to understand, the seamless relationship between past, present and future. Her commonplace experiences (marriage, family . . .) contrast sharply with her death experience, where she finally comes to appreciate the commonplace. The play motivates the audience to treasure everyday life just as it is.

Story Overview:

Act 1. *Daily Life:* The Stage Manager speaks while pointing to different parts of the stage: "Up here is Main Street . . . Here's the Town Hall and Post Office combined . . . First automobile's going to come along in about five years; belonged to Banker Cartwright, our richest citizen . . . lives in the big white house up on the hill." A train whistle is heard, and the early birds of the town start to appear. The newsboy and the milkman begin their rounds just as the doctor is finishing his. They stop for a brief exchange of gossip: the school teacher is getting married, the doctor just delivered twins, and the milkman's horse refuses to adjust to a change in route.

Now Mrs. Webb and Mrs. Gibbs are spotlighted in their respective kitchens, preparing breakfast. Mrs. Gibbs calls up to her children, George and Rebecca, and, as they appear, complains to her husband that George isn't helping with the chores. Mrs. Webb reminds her son Wally to wash thoroughly. The Gibbs daughter, Rebecca, doesn't want to wear her blue gingham dress. George negotiates for a raise in his allowance. Each child is reminded to eat slowly, finish his breakfast, stand up straight . . . The day has begun.

Later, coming home from school, Emily Webb promises to give George Gibbs some help with his algebra. At the Congregational Church, choir practice can be heard. In the Gibbs home, George and his father have a "serious" talk about growing up. Returning from choir practice, Mrs. Gibbs prattles on about the drunken choir organist, Simon Stimson. The town constable makes his rounds to ensure that all is well, and the Stage Manager calls an end to this typical day in Grover's Corners.

Act 2. *Love and Marriage:* "Three years have gone by," muses the Stage Manager. "Yes, the sun's come up over a thousand times . . . " The date is now July 7, 1904. It's been raining. As Mrs. Gibbs and Mrs. Webb reappear in their kitchens, he continues: "Both of those ladies cooked three meals a day – one of 'em for twenty years and the other for forty – and no summer vacation. They brought up two children a-piece, washed, cleaned the house . . . and never a nervous breakdown. It's like what one of those Middle West poets said: You've got to love life to have life, and you've got to have life to love life . . . It's what they call a vicious circle."

Howie, the milkman, makes his deliveries to Mrs. Webb and Mrs. Gibbs, and at each house you hear talk of the same two breakfast-table conversation topics: the weather and the upcoming wedding of Emily and George. The chit-chat is typical of things people say before weddings. Mrs. Gibbs worries out loud about the inexperience of the bride and groom; the doctor reminisces about being a groom himself. His fear was that he and his wife would run out of things to talk about – which, he chuckles, hasn't been the case at all.

When George comes downstairs and is about to leave for a visit with Emily, his mother reminds him to put on his overshoes. But Emily's mother, though she invites George into her kitchen, won't let him see her daughter. Traditionally, she says, a groom is not allowed to see his bride on the wedding day until the ceremony begins. Mr. Webb placates young George: "There is a lot of common sense in some superstitions." The nervous groom sits down to a cup of coffee with Mr. Webb, his equally nervous future father-in-law. Mr. Webb makes various attempts at small talk and reassures George that his nervousness about impending matrimony is typical. "A man looks pretty small at a wedding . . . all those women standing shoulder to shoulder making sure that the knot is tied in a might grand way." He then shares with George the advice his father gave him when he married; the stern counsel to keep his wife in line and show her who's in charge. George is puzzled until Mr. Webb goes on: "So I took the opposite of my father's advice and I've been happy ever since."

The Stage Manager interrupts this scene by dismissing the characters on stage and telling the audience that he wants to show them "how this all began – this wedding, this plan to spend a life-time together . . . I'm awfully interested in how big things like that begin." He takes two chairs from the Gibbs kitchen, arranges them back-to-back, with two planks across and two stools in front, to serve as Morgan's Main Street Drugstore Counter.

Emily and George again enter, now as high-school students. They call goodbye to their friends. Over an ice cream soda George asks Emily if she will write to him while he is away at college. She admits her concern that George will lose interest in Grover's Corners – and in her – once he is away. He unhappily contemplates this possibility for a moment, then decides that he shouldn't go: "I guess new people aren't any better than old ones." He tries to explain that he has decided to stay because

of the way he feels about her, and, in half-spoken sentences, the two manage to express their love. The act culminates in a moving wedding scene, containing all the elements of potential sorrow and abundant happiness.

Act 3. *Life and Death:* Nine years have passed, and we are looking down at a cemetery on a hill. We see that many of the townspeople we came to know in the first two acts have passed on. The Stage Manager slowly speaks: "Whenever you come near the human race, there's layers and layers of nonsense . . . . We all know that something is eternal. And it ain't houses and it ain't names . . . that something has to do with human beings." And so the dead stand, patient and smiling, awaiting not "judgement," but greater understanding of eternity.

Into the midst of the dead is led a young mother. Emily and her second baby have just died in childbirth. She timidly approaches the assemblage, glancing wistfully back toward the life she has just departed. Gradually recognizing the spirits before her, Emily suddenly realizes that none of these people truly understood or appreciated the greatness of being alive! There had been no appreciation of life's little, fleeting moments; no ability to stop and absorb life's essence; no comprehension of the deep human value of the moment.

Emily is given the choice to return to earth and relive a day in her life. The dead – including her mother-in-law, Mrs. Gibbs, try to discourage her, warning her that returning to earth will be too painful. Nonetheless, Emily elects to reexperience one of the happiest days of her life – her twelfth birthday.

As the day unfolds, however, Emily's excitement turns to disillusionment. She feels no joy in watching herself with her father and mother and her little brother Wally; the day is wasted with trivial preoccupations. She cries to her mother: "Just for a moment we're happy. Let's look at one another . . . " Then, pangs of remorse fill her – her life, just like the lives of her family members and Grover's Corners neighbors, was never fully savored either. It came, was lived in self-centeredness and petty preoccupations, then swiftly departed – all quite meaningless. The suicidal Simon Stimson appears and offers a poignant yet bitter comment: "Life is a time of supreme ignorance, folly and blindness."

Unable to endure this vision, Emily hurries back to her body's resting place. There she finds George, her husband, weeping by her grave. Too late, she now understands: Our time on earth is an irreplaceable gift, one to be treasured and relished every moment; life is a fragile gift that is delivered to us in pieces, and it only achieves meaning as we cherish and blend the pieces – even the seemingly insignificant pieces – into a full, universal whole.

SILAS MARNER

by
George Eliot (Mary Ann Evans)
(1819 - 1880)

Type of work: Symbolic, life drama

Setting: English village of Raveloe; early nineteenth century

Principal characters:

Silas Marner, a lonely and miserly linen-weaver

Godfrey Cass, an insensitive, yet charming, young man

Dunstan Cass, Godfrey's opportunistic brother

Squire Cass, Godfrey and Dunstan's lewd, dull-witted father

Eppie, an abandoned little girl

Story Overview:

Silas Marner, bent at his loom, was interrupted by some curious boys peering through his cabin window. Scaring them away with an icy stare, the shriveled linen-weaver returned to his work.

Fifteen years earlier Marner had come to Raveloe from a northern industrial town, where he had been a respected elder in a small fundamentalist sect. But one night as he watched over a deacon lying on his death-bed, Silas fell into a trance. While he slept, his best friend had stolen into the room and taken the deacon's money bag; then, in a move to win the affections of Silas' sweetheart, he had blamed the theft on Silas. The weaver was "convicted" in the case by the drawing of lots; and even God found him guilty. His faith shattered and "his trust in man . . . cruelly bruised," Silas had left his beloved home in Lantern Yard. The eccentric visionary now found himself a lone alien in the prosperous village of Raveloe.

Taking refuge in his work, Silas slowly began to accumulate gold. It became his one purpose in life, and every evening the near-sighted old man would count and caress his shiny coins.

Still, Silas' life grew more and more empty: "He hated the thought of the past; there was nothing that called out his love and fellowship toward the strangers he had come amongst; and the future was dark, for there was "no Unseen Love that cared for him."

Meanwhile, Squire Cass, the "greatest man in Raveloe," threw nightly parties and attended pubs by day. One of his sons, Dunstan, followed him in his drunken reveries. His other son, Godfrey, had a slightly better reputation, and it was presumed he would soon marry the lovely Nancy Lammeter. But Dunstan knew a secret about Godfrey, kept hidden from their harsh father: Godfrey was already married to Molly, a raucous tavern woman with whom he had shared a brief moment of passion. "Dunsey" continually manipulated his brother over this secret,

demanding money to pay gambling debts. In fact, Godfrey finally even handed over to his brother the Squire's rent money. Then, with no other way left to reimburse their father, Godfrey let his brother take his own prize horse to be sold at a nearby fair.

Dunstan was paid a good price for the horse, but while delivering it to its new owner he was diverted into joining a hunting party, where the animal was accidentally killed. Unfazed and drunken, Dunstan kept the payment. Then, taking a shortcut on his way home, he passed Silas Marner's cabin. Recalling rumors that the weaver kept a hoard of gold, Dunstan entered the empty cabin, uncovered the miser's money, and carted it off into the night.

Silas returned home that night in anticipation of sitting down to the roasted meat provided by the neighbor-lady. But, as was his ritual, when he lifted the bricks to gloat over his cache of gold, he found that it was gone. Hysterically, he rushed off to the nearby Rainbow Pub to alert the authorities.

For days the townsfolk debated the robbery. Some said that the Devil was the thief and that Silas' money was now in hell. Others blamed a ghost or a gypsy peddler.

When Dunstan didn't arrive home from selling his brother's horse, no one was concerned. Dunstan had a reputation for sporadic disappearances. The only notable reaction to his absence was Squire Cass' rage after Godfrey confessed to the reasons behind the missing rent money.

Over the weeks, village interest in Silas' problem died down, though the citizens still felt sorry for the withered and despondent recluse. A few neighbors – Dolly Winthrop and her little son, Aaron, in particular – invited Silas to church and sometimes prepared food for him.

As Christmas came and went Godfrey remained in frustration and turmoil. His father prodded him to propose to Nancy Lammeter. How Godfrey wished he could. Then, at Squire Cass' annual New Year's Eve party, Godfrey began to woo Nancy. Unbeknownst to him, however, his wife, Molly, was at that moment trudging through the snow towards the house, hand in hand with a ragged, golden-haired two-year-old girl. Seeking revenge, she intended to expose the marriage and force Godfrey to acknowledge their child. But fate intervened: before she arrived, the opium-crazed woman was overcome by weakness, and she collapsed. The child, seeing the light from Silas' cottage, toddled in through the doorway. Awakened from a trance and seeing the gleam of the sleeping child's hair by the fireplace, Silas at first imagined that his gold had been restored to him.

Regaining his senses, he fed and bundled the tot, then tracked her footprints out into the night where he found her mother, dead.

Silas wisked the little girl into his arms and rushed to where the party was being held. At the sight of the child, Godfrey raced through the snow to where the dead woman lay, his conscience seared by urgent questions: Should he acknowledge the truth and claim the child as his own, or marry Nancy and keep the identity of his daughter and estranged wife a secret? Godfrey chose the latter.

That night, Silas Marner made a startling announcement – he planned to keep the child. It was his right and blessing; she had come to replace his gold. The community rallied around the new guardian of Hephzibah – named after the weaver's mother and sister, and known as Eppie for short.

As spring approached, Silas' soul seemed to sprout and bloom like a flower. Lacy curtains graced his windows. Silas loved the delightful girl even more than he had loved his gold.

Unlike the gold which needed nothing, and must be worshipped in close-locked solitude . . . Eppie was a creature of endless claims and ever-growing desires, seeking and loving sunshine . . . The gold had asked that he should sit weaving longer and longer, deafened and blinded more and more to all things . . . but Eppie called him away from his weaving, and made him think all its pauses a holiday . . . warming him into joy because she had joy.

Godfrey, in contrast, grew more and more sullen. Though he had married Nancy, he could not forget little Eppie. He often stopped by Silas' cottage and left money to help support the growing girl.

Sixteen years passed. Silas was now a very old man; and though he was happy, he still clung to the past, searching for the meaning of his life. Eppie had grown into a beautiful, high-spirited, and well-bred young woman – with a beau, Aaron Winthrop, Dolly's industrious son. She spent her days gardening, caring for her pets, and fussing over her father.

Godfrey and Nancy Cass had been blessed over the years with wealth but with no living children, and Nancy would not hear of adoption. Godfrey felt disappointed, deprived, and punished.

Then, one day, pale and trembling, Godfrey entered and informed his wife that Dunstan's skeleton had been unearthed, along with Silas's stolen money, from the bottom of a recently drained quarry. Convinced that this was a sign that all truths would eventually come to light, Godfrey revealed his long-kept secret. To his joy, Nancy accepted what her husband had done and expressed the desire to adopt Eppie.

Meanwhile, Silas was delighted that his lost gold had returned to him. He now had two treasures; but Eppie remained by far the more precious of the two. Then a knock came at the door. Mr. and Mrs. Godfrey Cass appeared, congenially offering to take Eppie into their own home. Silas, astounded, rejected the idea. When the couple pressed the matter, Eppie instinctively cradled Silas' trembling body in her arms and again refused them. Godfrey then blurted out the truth – he was Eppie's father – and asserted his "claim" on her. But Silas chastised Godfrey for abandoning his daughter and reminded him of the long bonds of love between himself and Eppie. And once more Eppie begged to stay with Silas in his humble cottage.

Confused and angry, Godfrey stomped out of the house. But on the way home his mood mellowed. He expressed his love for his wife and told her in quiet irony, "I wanted to pass for childless once . . . I shall pass for childless now against my wish." The humbled couple determined to live out their lives in acceptance and love.

One day, Silas and Eppie made a journey to visit his old home, Lantern Yard. They found in the now dirty, noisy, joyless city that Lantern Yard had disappeared, torn down to make room for a factory. His mind now freed from his luckless past, Silas could go home in peace. The miracle of Eppie caused him to trust life, and "now she says she'll never leave me . . . I think I shall trusten till I die."

Godfrey supplied the funds to enlarge Silas' tiny cabin and hosted Eppie's marriage feast. Hand in hand with Aaron she stood, dressed in Nancy's wedding gown. And the guests gathered in the churchyard to retell the old story of Silas and Eppie. "O father, what a pretty home ours is!" Eppie exclaimed when they reached their flower-strewn cottage. "I think nobody could be happier than we are."

Commentary:

Eliot's *Silas Marner* is replete with religious overtones, class divisions, and interwoven human emotions. Life-mysteries such as luck and fate are examined. The contrast between Silas' urban home in Lantern Yard – pushed aside by the Industrial Revolution – and the bustling village of Raveloe, representing an unchanging, personable and rural society, shows Eliot's obvious preference.

George Eliot's real name was Mary Ann Evans. An intellectual, she lived in 19th-century scandal with a married man, who urged her to write fiction. Evans wrote under the pen name George Eliot out of fear of rejection.

Eliot's racy style and the fact that she chose to feature in her novels the complex psychological lives of ordinary laborers, made her, simultaneously, both an outcast and a beloved author. *Silas Marner* was written out of a floodgate of feelings she had acquired from her unhappy childhood. It teaches the values of honesty, kindness, and courage as it entertains, and is still quite a radical, intriguing vision of the world.

LITTLE WOMEN

by
Louisa May Alcott
(1832-1888)

Type of work: Sentimental, life drama

Setting: a small New England town; mid 1800's

Principal characters:
Mrs. March ("Marmee"), mother of four daughters
Mr. March, her husband, and army chaplain in the U.S. Civil War
Meg, their 16-year-old daughter
Jo, 15, wants to be an independent writer (and serves as the novel's narrator)
Beth, a frail girl of 13, the "heart" of her family
Amy, 12, the beautiful pampered youngest daughter
Theodore Lawrence ("Laurie"), the boy who moves in next door

Story Overview:

The upcoming Christmas looked like it would be a bleak affair to the four March girls. With their father at the Civil War battlefront, and their saintly mother, Marmee, as they called her, working to support her family, the holiday would be void of many of its traditional pleasures. With the dollar Marmee said they might spend, the girls each settled on buying simple gifts for their mother and for the Hummel family down the road; and receiving, in kind, surprise treats of ice cream and bonbons from rich old Mr. Lawrence next door.

The girls resolved to face life as Pilgrims, to overcome their weaknesses, and be "good little women" by the time their father returned. The oldest, Meg, determined to enjoy her work more and fret less about her looks. The tomboy, Jo, pledged to better control her temper, upgrade her writing abilities and develop feminine qualities. Amy desired to be less selfish and less vain concerning her beautiful golden hair. Everyone believed Beth, the home-body, to be perfect, but she earnestly prayed to overcome her fear of people. The girls labored for the next year to acquire these qualities, with much success and occasional failure.

At year's end, Meg confidently and excitedly attended a fashionable New Year's dance. She talked Jo into accompanying her, but Jo didn't care much for "girls or girlish gossip," and felt as much out of place as a "colt in a flower garden."

Running from a prospective dance-mate, Jo hid behind a curtain. But she wasn't the only bashful one. To her surprise, there she met little Theodore Lawrence, or "Laurie," as everyone referred to him, the new next-door-neighbor boy. Awkwardly, they introduced themselves, but as they peeped through the curtain together, gossiping and chatting, they soon felt like old acquaintances. A lifelong friendship was formed. Laurie had been orphaned as a baby and now lived with his crusty Grandfather Lawrence in his great mansion. In the March family, Laurie found a circle of sisters and a mother he never knew; and they found, in him, a brother and a son.

Through that year, the girls learned to be happy in their work. Meg, by spending two weeks at the estate of a wealthy girl friend, discovered how wonderful her own home life was, even if her family was poor. Jo detected that she was not the only one struggling with outbursts of anger. Much to her amazement, her mother also possessed a hidden temper. This knowledge helped Jo believe she could, with effort, control hers. After all, her great wish was to become a famous romance writer; reaching that goal would require discipline. Jo's romantic novels were soon published. Amy continued to grow more beautiful, but also came to understand the need for humility. After being embarrassingly reprimanded before the whole school, she began to understand that "conceit spoils the finest genius." And Beth remained extremely shy, but was still the heart and joy of her family. Everyone, especially Jo, came to gentle Beth for comfort.

One winter day, a telegram arrived from the war department: Mr. March was critically ill. Heartsick by this news, Marmee felt she needed to be with her husband. With no money to spare, Joe offered to sell her only vanity – her long, flowing chestnut hair. The sacrifice, though tearfully made, brought twenty-five dollars, and financed the trip. Mr. Lawrence sent along John Brooke, Laurie's tutor, to assist Mrs. March in her journey. Both Mr. and Mrs. March grew to be very fond of John – and he, in turn, became very fond of Meg.

Back at home, dark days were to visit the little women. Patterning herself after her mother, Beth continued to care for the large, impoverished Hummel family. One night she returned home depressed and crying. She had just held the Hummel baby in her arms as he died of Scarlet Fever. Beth also contracted the fever, becoming much more infirm than anyone expected. It was a somber time for all, as she hovered near death. Fearing the worst, the girls finally telegraphed their mother of Beth's deteriorating condition. But the very night Marmee returned, Beth's crisis passed and her health improved. It was a happy family that welcomed their mother home.

As the second Christmas arrived, the girls anticipated their father's homecoming. Their joy was complete when Laurie arrived and announced, "Here's another Christmas present for the March family," and in walked their father. During the jubilant family reunion, Mr. March admired his family, reflecting on how the girls had changed over the years. Meg had defeated much of her vanity, and had cultivated industry and the womanly skills to create a happy home. Jo had become a gentle young lady, who dressed properly and no longer used slang. He noticed that Amy now took the poorer cut of meat, waited on everyone with patience and humor, and seldom gazed at herself in the mirror. As for Beth, her father simply held her near, grateful she was still alive. They all agreed Mr. March's absence had been a productive period, and that the girls were becoming little women of great talent, beauty and grace.

Three years passed. Much to Jo's initial horror, she saw the family begin to split up when Meg became Mrs. John Brooke. Like all new wives, Meg learned the art of homemaking and how to organize and spend money frugally. Shortly, twins, Daisy and Demi, arrived. Meg discovered that John, too, could help take care of the children, as she began to include him even more in her life.

Jo also had matured, and her friend, Laurie, fell more deeply in love with her. Despite all her efforts to change his heart, Laurie proposed marriage. Jo, devoted to her writing and publishing, was dismayed because she could never love Laurie more than as a brother, and refused his proposal. Brokenhearted, Laurie left with his uncle on a tour of Europe. But Laurie was not the only one voyaging to Europe; Amy was traveling there, accompanying her rich aunt. She soon learned some of life's harsher lessons. To her initial disappointment, she first detected that she would never be a great artist. She also came to recognize that marrying for money rather than love would not lead to happiness. Inevitably, Amy's and Laurie's paths crossed and they each gradually grew in love for the other. To the delight of all, they too were wed.

But at home the family grieved a great loss. Beth, never fully recovered from the fever, had slowly faded away, no longer to sit contentedly by the fire knitting and smiling. Jo unearthed a great emptiness in her heart and life after her sister's death. Meg and John, and Amy and Laurie were happily married. Though Jo had resolved never to marry, still she felt an awful loneliness as she wondered what direction her life should take. While struggling with these feelings, a tutor entered her life, Professor Bhaer. He was an older, German gentleman, filled with a genteel love. People turned to him because of the compassion he so freely gave, akin to Beth's spirit. This love healed Jo. They married and opened a "school for lads, a good, happy homelike school." Jo looked after the boys while the professor taught them in the large, Plumfield home, willed to Jo by her aunt.

As the sisters gathered together to celebrate Marmee's birthday, they agreed that their lives were happy, rich and full. The little women had become cultured, confident young ladies. There at the table, surrounded by her children and grandchildren, along with one empty chair, symbolizing their love for Beth, sat the contented mother. She wished that such a moment could last forever.

Commentary:

Louisa May Alcott's most famous novel, *Little Women* is based on her own family life in Concord, Massachusetts. Like Jo, the book's heroine, Louisa hungered to gain independence and to improve her family's situation by writing successful novels.

Little Women is a cheerful, wholesome account of the daily life of a highly principled family. It is considered one of the earliest realistic novels suitable for older children; and, as a children's story, the language is often stilted. Alcott also tends to moralize. But the book also holds a personal charm for grownups, who may see their own carefree childhood – the simple joys of youth and deep love of family – mirrored in its pages.

JANE EYRE

by
Charlotte Bronte
(1816 - 1855)

Type of work: Psychological romance

Setting: Northern England; 1800's

Principal characters:

Jane Eyre, an orphan girl

Mrs. Reed, Jane's aunt, and mistress of Gateshead Hall

Edward Rochester, the handsome owner of Thornfield Manor

St. John Rivers, a young clergyman

Story Overview:

Orphaned at birth, Jane Eyre was left to live at Gateshead Hall Manor with her aunt-in-law, Mrs. Reed. Jane remained at the estate for ten years, subjected to hard work, mistreatment, and fixed hatred.

After a difficult childhood, the petite Jane was sent to Lowood School, a semi-charitable institution for girls. She excelled at Lowood and over the years advanced from pupil to teacher. Then she left Lowood to become the governess of a little girl, Adela, the ward of one Mr. Edward Rochester, master of Thornfield Manor.

At Thornfield, Jane was comfortable with life – what with the grand old house, its well-stocked and silent library, her private room, the garden with its many chestnut, oak and thorn trees, it was a veritable palace. Mr. Rochester was a princely and heroic master, but for some reason Jane always felt ill at ease in his somewhat somber, curiously insecure presence. Rochester confided that Adela was not his own child but the daughter of a Parisian dancer who had deserted her in his care. Still, even with this forthright confession, Jane sensed that there was something Rochester was hiding.

Off and on, Jane heard bizarre, mysterious sounds at Thornfield. She finally discovered that Rochester kept a strange tenant on the third floor of the mansion. This hermit-like woman, once employed by Rochester – or so he said – often laughed maniacally in the night. And other disturbances soon followed.

One evening, after the household had gone to sleep, Jane was aroused by the smell of smoke – to find Mr. Rochester's bed on fire. Only with a great deal of exertion did she manage to extinguish the flames and revive her employer.

Some time later, a Mr. Mason from Jamaica arrived for a house party. Shortly after retiring that evening, Jane and the house guests were awakened by the sound of a man screaming for help. Rochester reassured his guests that it was merely a servant's nightmare and persuaded them to return to their rooms. But Jane was obligated to spend the rest of the night caring for Mr. Mason, who had somehow received serious slashes to his arm and shoulder. After hinting that he had obtained these wounds from an attack by a madwoman, he quietly left the house on the next morning.

One day Jane was urgently summoned to Gateshead: Mrs. Reed was dying. Upon Jane's arrival, Mrs. Reed presented her with a letter from her childless uncle, John Eyre, requesting that Jane come to him in Madeira, as he wished to adopt her. The letter had been delivered three years before, but, because of her dislike for the girl, Mrs. Reed had written John Eyre to inform him that Jane had unfortunately died in an epidemic earlier that year. Adoption by her uncle would have given Jane not only a family but an inheritance – one she still might claim. However, she decided to return to Thornfield.

One night, in the garden at Thornfield, Mr. Rochester proposed marriage – and Jane accepted. She excitedly wrote to her Uncle John to tell him the news. But one month later, on the morning of her wedding day, Jane was startled from sleep by a repulsive, snarling old woman wearing Jane's wedding dress. Before bounding out the door, the wretch tore the dress off and shredded the veil. Jane's groom comforted her; and Jane calmed herself and prepared for the marriage.

The ceremony was near its end; the clergyman had just uttered the words, "Wilt thou have this woman for thy wedded wife?" when a voice suddenly broke in: "The marriage cannot go on. I declare the existence of an impediment." When asked for the facts, this man – a lawyer – produced a document proving that Rochester had married one Bertha Mason in Jamaica some fifteen years earlier. Mr. Mason, the mysteriously wounded house guest, stood as witness to the fact that

Bertha was still alive and living at Thornfield. At last Rochester stepped forward and acknowledged that the accusation was true, but that his wife had gone mad; in fact, she came from a family of idiots and maniacs for three generations back. Rochester further maintained that this early wedding had been arranged by his father and brother in hopes that he would marry into a fortune.

The groom-to-be next invited the lawyer, the clergyman, and Mr. Mason to accompany him to Thornfield and see for themselves the woman to whom he had been bridled. Only then could they judge if he didn't have the right to break this compact.

At the estate, Rochester led the company to the third-story room where his wife was kept. As he advanced toward a figure in the back corner of the room,"it grovelled, seemingly on all fours; it snatched and growled like some strange wild animal: but it was covered with clothing; and a quantity of dark, grizzled hair, wild as a mane, hid its head and face." When Rochester finally restrained the raging, bellowing beast, he turned to the spectators and declared, "That is my wife."

That night, Jane left Thornfield, bewildered and heartbroken. With the little money she had, she bought a ride on the first coach that happened by. After traveling for two days, she was dropped off at a remote crossroads and spent the night huddled in the heather. Her meager meals were made up of bilberries. Finally, the woman found her way to Marsh End, the home of St. John Rivers and his two sisters, Mary and Diana. They were very kind to the girl – who was introduced as Jane Elliot – and nursed her back to health.

Then one day St. John received word from Madeira that his cousin John Eyre had died, leaving twenty thousand pounds to his next of kin – Jane Eyre. The family lawyer was now trying to locate Jane through her uncle's cousin, St. John Rivers himself. Amazed and delighted to find that St. John and his sisters were in fact family, Jane insisted on apportioning them a share of the inheritance.

Jane remained in the home of St. John. One day, however, he came and expressed to Jane his long-felt desire to travel to India as a missionary, and asked Jane to accompany him – as his wife and assistant. Jane kindly declined his offer; by some intuition, she sensed that she was needed elsewhere.

Jane had a vivid dream one night, in which Edward Rochester called to her and beckoned her to come to him. In response to the dream she returned to Thornfield. But upon her arrival, she found only a blackened ruin where the mansion had stood. At a nearby inn Jane learned that during harvest time a fire had broken out in the night at Thornfield. Rochester had desperately attempted to rescue his lunatic wife, who was on the roof screaming wildly and waving her arms. But just as he approached her, she had leaped to her death.

Jane rushed to the farm where Mr. Rochester was now living, only to find her once strong and handsome master a lonely, helpless cripple. He had lost both his sight and his hand in the attempted rescue.

Jane's love for Rochester was still strong, and she gladly chose to marry him. Eventually, sight returned to one eye, so that her husband could witness the birth of a son – who had obviously inherited his father's once-fine features.

Commentary:

Because the publishing industry of the early and middle nineteenth century spurned female writers, Charlotte Bronte chose to work under the androgynous pseudonym Currier Bell.

Jane Eyre was written in the first-person, autobiographical form, allowing Bronte to draw the reader into her heroine's plight. This was a successful approach, for even though critics point out some structural flaws in the book, it has always remained a very popular work.

Jane Eyre is also an impassioned moral manifesto, as the *Preface to the Second Edition* makes clear:

Conventionality is not morality. Self-righteousness is not religion. To attack the first is not to assail the last . . . .

The world may not like to see these ideas dissevered, for it has been accustomed to blend them; finding it convenient to make external show pass for sterling worth – to let whitewashed walls vouch for clean shrines. It may hate him who dares to scrutinize and expose – to raise the gilding, and show base metal under it – to penetrate the sepulchre, and reveal charnel relics: but, hate as it will, it is indebted to him.

THE ORIGIN OF SPECIES

by
Charles Darwin
(1809 - 1882)

Type of work: Natural history text

First published: 1859

Complete title: *The Origin of Species by Means of Natural Selection, or the Preservation of Favored Races in the Struggle for Life*

Book Historical Commentary:

Charles Robert Darwin, the grandson of the English scientist Erasmus Darwin, studied medicine at the University of Edinburgh and prepared for the ministry at Cambridge. Following his abiding interest in natural history, however, he became a naturalist and sailed in this capacity on the *H.M.S. Beagle* from 1831 to 1838. The *Beagle's* expedition took Darwin to various Southern Pacific islands and to the coasts of South America and Australia.

Returning to England, Darwin became the secretary of the Geological Society and, in 1840, published a treatise, "Zoology of the Voyage of the Beagle." At this time he met Sir Charles Lyell, who encouraged him to write about his inbreeding experiments and to expound on his theory of evolution by natural selection.

Later, in 1844, Darwin received from a fellow naturalist, Alfred Wallace, notes outlining a theory – parallel to, but independent of, his own – on natural selection. Darwin carried on his research and, in 1858, published an essay delineating his own evolutionary theory along with Wallace's findings. The following year, *The Origin of Species* appeared. The book's first edition sold out in one day, stirring an immediate clamor of controversy. It is still recognized as one of the most disputed yet important works of biological study.

Darwin went on to publish *The Movements and Habits of Climbing Plants* (1865), *The Variation of Animals and Plants Under Domestication* (1868), *The Descent of Man* (1871), and *Selection in Relation to Sex* (1871).

The Origin of Species has powerfully influenced nearly every contemporary field of scientific and philosophical study: biology, literature, law, psychology, sociology, theology, and other fields of intellectual pursuit.

Despite the length and weighty content of Darwin's work, the text is remarkably easy reading. Unfortunately, through all the tempest and fanfare that have followed it for almost one and a half centuries, few have actually studied its pages.

Text Summary:

Early on in Darwin's first five-year voyage on the *Beagle,* he observed that, despite the distances between the remote areas he visited, the varieties of flora and fauna he found were similar in structure and function. This led him to develop his idea that species were not immutable, but were forced to adapt to their ever-changing environments. In his introduction to the first edition of *The Origin of Species,* Darwin noted: "I was much struck with certain facts in the distribution of the [plant and animal] inhabitants of South America, and in the geological relations of the present to the past inhabitants of that continent. These facts seemed to throw some light on the origin of the species – that mystery of mysteries, as it has been called by one of our greatest philosophers." After over twenty years of further research, Darwin published his findings.

Like all scientists, Darwin built his theory upon those of his predecessors. However, scientific opinion was always – and remains – somewhat divided as to what contribution the theory makes to the biological sciences. Throughout the book, Darwin openly admits to the possibility of error and the need for further investigation; he is careful to point out that the idea of evolution by natural selection is "one of long argument."

To comprehend the vast amount of information contained in the work, one must examine it in its entirety. Still, this sampling of chapter headings and brief content summaries may provide some general information.

Chapter II: Variation Under Nature

Variations within a species are indistinguishable at first, but gradually may develop into differences that can restrict one group's range or ability to obtain food or escape preditors . . . Thus, "varieties tend to become converted into new and distinct species . . . and throughout nature the forms of life which are now dominant tend to become still more dominant by leaving many modified and dominant descendants."

Chapter III: Struggle for Existence

" . . . When a plant or animal is placed in a new country amongst new competitors, the conditions of its life will generally be changed in an essential manner . . . . If its average numbers are to increase . . . we should have to give it some advantage over a different set of competitors or enemies." Each organic being is striving to multiply – to be vigorous, healthy, and to survive – *often at the expense of members of its own species or those of a competing species.*

Chapter IV: Natural Selection; or the Survival of the Fittest

The "fitness" of a species is modified by several different processes. For example, sexual selection may occur when males of a population must compete with other males to possess mates. Those possessing some *advantage* – better weapons, greater energy, or more beautiful song or plummage – are more apt to survive or attract a mate, likely to leave the most progeny. Over time, such gradual adaptation, along with changing conditions and outside competition, can cause "an infinite diversity in structure, constitution, and habits, advantageous to one set of offspring over another, or to one variety within a species over another. "This principle of preservation, or the survival of the fittest, I have called Natural Selection . . . "

As buds give rise by growth to fresh buds, and these, if vigorous, branch out and overtop on all sides many a feebler branch, so by generation I believe it has been with the great Tree of Life, which fills with its dead and broken branches the crust of the earth, and covers the surface with its ever-branching and beautiful ramifications.

Chapter V: Laws of Variation

Reproductive "chance" creates variations. When the conditions of a species alter, those individuals that survive to reproduce may have beneficial modifications – organs or limbs that either become stronger or more useful, or else, when not needed for survival, weakened and diminished. This is not to say, however, that the formation of organs serving little purpose does not occur; it most certainly does. The human appendix may exemplify just such a process phenomenon. But any variation within a species is, inevitably, a long, slow process.

Chapter VIII: Instinct

Habitual instincts are *inherited* within each species. Ants and bees build their nests and hives with no previous experience. Birds migrate and build homes according to their unique inner senses. But *instincts too may change over time* as "consequences of one general law leading to the advancement of all organic beings . . . multiply, vary, let the strongest live and the weakest die."

Other chapters deal with related topics: hybridism; living species compared to those of ancient geological periods; extinction; geographical distribution of organisms; relationships between species; and the classification of organisms. Objections to the general theory of evolution are presented in both Darwin's conclusion and glossary of terms.

Darwin's observations led him to believe that species *did* adapt to their changing surroundings. Furthermore, he was led to defend as a logical, observable – and even religious – corollary of this conclusion, a theory advancing the probability of common descent for *all* living creatures.

Authors of the highest eminence seem to be fully satisfied with the view that each species has been independently created. To my mind it accords better with what we know of the laws impressed on matter by the Creator, that the production and extinction of the past and present inhabitants of the world should have been due to secondary causes, like those determining the birth and death of an individual. When I view all beings not as special creations, but as lineal descendants of some few beings which have lived long before the first bed of the Cambrian system was deposited, they seem to me to become ennobled.

The Origin of Species represents Darwin's many years of personal and intellectual struggle. It is candidly argued and presented in a flowing, orderly manner, then left for each reader to weigh the evidence. As a text on natural history, its ideas are refreshingly comprehensible and insightful.

WALDEN

by
Henry David Thoreau
(1817 - 1862)

Type of work: Natural history essay

Setting: Walden Pond, Concord, Massachusetts; 1845 to 1847

Journal Overview:

(The summer of 1845 found Henry David Thoreau living in a rude shack on the banks of Walden Pond. The actual property was owned by Ralph Waldo Emerson, the great American philosopher. Emerson had earlier published the treatise entitled "Nature," and the young Thoreau was profoundly affected by its call for individuality and self-reliance. Thoreau planted a small garden, took pen and paper, and began to scribe the record of life at Walden.)

Thoreau's experiment in deliberate living began in March of 1845. By planting a two-and-a-half acre parcel borrowed from a neighbor who thought it useless, he harvested and sold enough peas, potatoes, corn, beans and turnips to build and to buy food. He purchased an old shanty from an Irish railroad worker and tore it down. He also cut timber from the woods surrounding Walden Pond. From the razed material, he was able to construct his cabin. He used the boards for siding and even salvaged the nails from the original shack.

By mid-summer, the house was ready to inhabit. Thoreau built a fireplace and chimney for heat and cooking. He plastered the inside walls and made sure he could comfortably survive the freezing New England winters. Doing all the work himself and using only native material, the house cost only about twenty-eight dollars to build, less than Thoreau had to pay for a year's lodging at Harvard.

But the main purpose for his experience was to allow time for writing, thinking, observing nature, and learning the "art of living."

I went to the woods because I wished to live deliberately, to front only the essential facts of life, and see if I could not learn what it had to teach, and not, when I came to die, discover that I had not lived . . . I wanted to live deep and suck out all the marrow of life . . .

Thoreau also went to Walden with the firm belief that man was too encumbered with material things – too much possessed by his belongings. He believed that a man is rich only "in proportion to the number of things he can afford to let alone."

One passage from Walden tells of an auction, held to dispose of a deacon neighbor's possessions. Thoreau scorned the affair, referring to the accumulations as "trumpetery" that had lain for "half a century in his garret and other dust holes":

[And now] . . . instead of a bonfire, or purifying destruction of them, there was an auction, of increasing of them. The neighbors eagerly collected to view them, bought them all, and carefully transported them to their garrets and dust holes, to lie there till their estates are settled, when they will start again. When a man dies he kicks the dust.

All aspects of life for Thoreau focused on simplicity. He ate simple meals, his diet consisting mostly of rye, Indian meal, potatoes, rice, a little pork, salt and molasses. He drank water. On such foods he was able to live for as little as a dollar a month. "The cost of a thing," he reasoned, "is the amount of what I will call life which is required to be exchanged for it, immediately or in the long run." The naturalist seldom ate meat and never hunted. He was far too interested in preserving the animals around the pond:

. . . Every man who has ever been earnest to preserve his higher poetic faculties in the best condition, has been particularly inclined to abstain from animal food, or from much food of any kind.

He did eat fish, but considered his time too valuable to spend merely fishing for food. And by following this Spartan ideology, Thoreau was left free to pursue to him were the important aspects of life; namely, observing, pondering, reading, and writing.

In warm evenings I frequently sat in the boat playing the flute, and saw perch, which I seem to have charmed, hovering around me, and the moon traveling over the ribbed bottom, which was strewn with the wrecks of the forest.

While at Walden, Thoreau lived quite independently of time. He used neither clock nor calendar – free to study the local plants, birds and animals: "Time is but the stream I go-a fishing in. I drink at it; but while I drink I see the sandy bottom and detect how shallow it is."

The only thing that reminded Thoreau of the hectic lives of others was the whistle of the Finchburg Railway train that passed a mile or so away. Though the "devilish Iron Horse, whose ear-rending neigh is heard throughout the town" held a fascination for him, he was glad he was not "chained to commerce," which the train – that "bloated pest" carrying a thousand men in its belly – represented.

The philosopher received some visitors; but they appear to be of little consequence to him, as he failed to even record their names.

I find it wholesome to be alone the greater part of the time. To be in company, even with the best, is soon wearisome and dissipating. I love to be alone . . .

On those occasions when people did come, it was normally one at a time. And when visitors numbered more than his three chairs could accommodate, Thoreau entertained them in his "drawing room" – the woods surrounding his home.

Living in quiet, joyous solitude, Thoreau spent his winter days at the pond, making surveys of its bottom, studying its ice conditions and observing the wild creatures that came daily to drink. At nights he would write down his expansive, whimsical, and thought-inspiring philosophies on life:

Why should we be in such desperate haste to succeed and in such desperate enterprises? If a man does not keep pace with his companions, perhaps it is because he hears a different drummer. Let him step to the music which he hears, however measured or far away . . .

Say what you have to say, not what you ought. Any truth is better than make-believe . . .

However mean your life is, meet it and live it; do not shun it and call it hard names. The fault finder will find faults even in paradise . . .

. . . The laboring man has not leisure for a true integrity day by day . . . . He has no time to be anything but a machine . . .

I called on the king, but he made me wait in his hall, and conducted like a man incapacitated for hospitality. There was a man in my neighborhood who lived in a hollow tree. His manners were truly regal. I should have done better had I called on him . . .

Let us spend one day as deliberately as nature, and not be thrown off the track by every nutshell and mosquito's wing that falls on the rails. Let us rise early and fast, or break fast, gently and without perturbation . . . determined to make a day of it . . .

While England endeavors to cure the potato-rot, will not any endeavor to cure the brain-rot, which prevails so much more widely and fatally? . . .

To the sick, the doctors wisely recommend a change of air and scenery. Thank Heaven, here is not all the world . . . . The universe is wider than our views of it . . .

If you have built castles in the air, your work need not be lost; that is where they should be. Now put foundations under them . . .

When Thoreau's two years at Walden had ended, he left with no regrets: "I left the woods for as good a reason as why I went there. Perhaps it seemed to me that I had several more lives to live, and could not spare any more time for that one . . . " His

experiment had been a success. He had learned many lessons, had taken time to examine his inner self and his world, and had proved he could live under the simplest conditions and still be fulfilled: "I learned this, at least, by my experiment; that as one advances confidently in the direction of his dreams, and endeavors to live the life which he has imagined, he will meet with a success unexpected in common hours."

What do we want most to dwell near to? Not to men surely . . . but to the perennial source of our life, whence in all our experience we have found that to issue, as the willow stands near the water and sends out its roots in that direction.

Upon returning to his cabin some six years after his experiment, Thoreau lamented that he could still distinguish the path he had worn from his door to the pond-side. He feared that others "may have fallen into it, and so helped keep it open . . . .

And so with the paths which the mind travels," he pondered. "How worn and dusty, then, must be the highways of the world, how deep the ruts of tradition and conformity!"

Commentary:

Walden, or, *Life in the Woods,* is a superbly written, imaginative and detailed account. The journal offers an introspective glimpse into two years of one of America's truly great philosophers and nonconformists. *Walden* is a classic piece of American literature which still serves as a blueprint for simple, frugal, ethereal living.

At first glance, the work may seem nothing more than a crude diary. But careful reading reveals a complex study comprising the human mind's attempt to discover both the obvious and obscure behind man's existence and his place in the natural world. Thoreau's collection of essays reflects the philosophy of American Transcendentalism in practice. To him, most men live lives of "quiet desperation," and have need to simplify, to cast off material encumbrances and achieve true freedom. The stages of spiritual evolution that a man passes through all prepare him for the more difficult inner development; and every man, he believed, possesses an inner spiritual instinct which, if nurtured and cared for, will reveal his divine nature.

Just before he died, Thoreau made what was considered his most pure yet subtly humorous religious utterance. When asked if he had made his peace with God, he replied, "I was not aware we had quarreled."

THE PRINCE

by
Niccolo Machiavelli
(1469-1532)

Type of work: Political and philosophical discourse

Book Overview:

"It is customary for those who wish to gain the favour of a prince to endeavour to do so by offering him gifts of those things which they hold most precious." To Machiavelli, his own most precious possession was the "knowledge of great men," which he acquired through experience and "constant study." He offered his guiding gift of knowledge to his prince, Lorenzo the Magnificent Di Medici.

"All states and dominions which hold or have held sway over mankind are either republics or monarchies." Thus begins his primer for princes, combining his detailed training, logic and imagination to teach how political power may be obtained and "how the various kinds of monarchies can be governed and maintained."

For the monarch who acquires a new state, there are many difficulties. According to Machiavelli, "Men change masters willingly [but a prince will] find enemies in all those whom you have injured by occupying that dominion." Moreover, those who have helped you in taking the new territory will stray from your camp because you cannot fulfill their expectations nor can you "use strong measures against them." Hence, "you will always need the favour of the inhabitants to take possession of a province." If a prince has the support of his new subjects, his position will be relatively secure.

When new provinces share the same nationality and language as the prince's main dominion, then "it is very easy to hold them." However, if great differences in language and customs exist, "the difficulties to be overcome are great." The best way to overcome such differences is for the new ruler to set up residence in the principality. This enables a prince to keep close watch on his state and to quickly resolve any troubles as they arise. The next best option is to "plant colonies in one or two key places." Colonies have several advantages: They are inexpensive and are far "more faithful, and give less offence," because those few landowners who are dispossessed are too weak and scattered to fight back. Maintaining a new state by posting armed guards is the least favorable method.

"The kingdoms known to history have been governed in two ways: either by a prince and his servants [ministers]; or by a prince and by barons." In the latter case, ruling is burdensome; barons have subjects of their own and are accustomed to exerting authority. In conquering a state, a prince can easily find barons who will join a movement to overthrow their king; but once the region is conquered it will be difficult to hold, since the barons may again band together to overthrow their new prince. On the other hand, "in those states which are governed by a prince and his servants, the prince possesses more authority."

Princes acquire power by a number of methods: by good fortune, ability, villainy, or by "the favour of his fellow-citizens, which may be called a civic principality." If a villain-prince conquers a state, he "must arrange to commit all his cruelties at once, so as not to have to recur to them every day, and so as to be able . . . to reassure people and win them over by benefitting them." In instances when a prince has been elevated to power by his fellow-citizens, authority is conferred either by the aristocracy or by the populace. However, " . . . he who becomes prince by help of the aristocracy has greater difficulty in maintaining his power than he who is raised by the populace," for the aristocracy rarely relinquishes complete power and often has the means to usurp a prince's authority.

The wise prince gains and maintains control of principalities both by "good laws and good arms." For these reasons an understanding of the various types of armies is essential. "The arms by which a prince defends his possessions are either his own, or else mercenaries, auxiliaries, or mixed." It is a mistake to employ mercenaries. They are "useless and dangerous" and cannot be trusted; "disunited, ambitious, without discipline, faithless . . . they have no fear of God and keep no faith with men." Likewise with the services of auxiliaries (powerful neighboring troops used for defense). Except in the most extreme case, it is wise to shy away from their aid. "If any one . . . wants to make sure of not winning he will avail himself of troops such as these." Both mercenary and auxiliary armies can turn on a prince: "If they lose, you are defeated, and if they conquer, you remain their prisoner."

His own subjects serve a prince much more effectively as soldiers, but this advantage also carries the responsibility of command. "A prince should therefore have no other aim or thought, nor take up any other thing for his study, but war and its organization and discipline, for that is the only art that is necessary to one who commands."

In times of peace, a prince should still practice the skills of war by action and study, and keep his troops well disciplined and exercised. "To exercise for the mind, the prince ought to read history and study the actions of eminent men."

As to the opinions of others toward the prince, "I say that it would be well to be considered liberal; nevertheless liberality such as the world understands it will injure you." Worldly liberality ("generosity, broad-mindedness") encourages luxurious "display," and a prince thereby "will consume by such means all his resources . . . . For these reasons a prince must [willingly accept] the reputation of being a miser, if he wishes to avoid robbing his subjects, if he wishes to be able to defend himself, and to avoid becoming poor and contemptible." There is one exception to this rule, however: In rewarding his army with plunder, the prince "may be very generous indeed" with what is not the property of himself or his subjects.

A ruler may wonder "whether it is better to be loved or feared." Machiavelli answers: "One ought to be both feared and loved, but as it is difficult for the two to go together, it is much safer to be feared than loved." It is also better to be bold than cautious. "Imitate the fox and the lion, for the lion cannot protect himself from traps and the fox cannot defend himself from wolves." Be both strong and clever.

Because men do not act in good faith, a wise prince is not "bound to keep faith with them." However, it is best for a prince to "appear" to possess the qualities of "mercy, faith, integrity, humanity, and religion." In short, "the ends justify the means." A prince may be ruthless when it is prudent, but wanton cruelty is foolish. He must avoid the hatred of his subjects by keeping them well armed and contented; and by refraining from "rapacious [acts], and usurping [their] property and women." In this way, he will convert potential enemies into partisans and keep his friends faithful.

"Great enterprises and giving proof of his prowess" bring a prince respect and esteem. "A prince is further esteemed when he is a true friend or a true enemy, when, that is, he declares himself without reserve in favour of some one or against another." Neutrality will bring him to ruin. By choosing to come to the aid of an ally, a prince wins in victory as well as in defeat. Either way, the ally "is under an obligation to you and friendship has been established."

Since it is better for a prince to rule by the counsel of ministers, these must be chosen carefully. The prince must select ministers who are completely devoted to him, and he, in return, must always reward his ministers with praise and wealth so that they remain devoted. "When a prince can discern what is good and bad in the words and deeds of another, he will be able to distinguish between his minister's good and bad performance, praising the one and correcting the other . . . . When you see a minister who thinks more about his own interests than about yours . . . then you will be sure that such a man will never be a good minister . . . " A

prince, at times, requires honest opinions. "A prudent prince [selects] for his council wise men, and [gives] these alone full liberty to speak the truth to him, but only of those things that he asks and of nothing else." Above all else, "flatterers must be shunned."

The conquering prince who follows these admonitions will do well for himself and will be "more secure and firmer in the state than if he had been established there of old." Men live in the present, not in the past, and when, by a prince's intelligent rule, "they find themselves well off in the present, they enjoy it and seek nothing more." They will defend their monarch when threatened in order to maintain their own security and high standard of living. But "those rulers of Italy who have lost their dominions" did not build up arms, and they alienated their subjects, "a common failing of men not to take account of tempests during fair weather."

Now, says Machiavelli, Italians everywhere have called on Lorenzo the Magnificent to act as their prince, "as a prudent and resourceful man to shape them . . . " Just as the Israelites waited to be led out of Egyptian bondage by mighty Moses, so Italy, left almost lifeless after years of foreign occupation and internal dissension, prays for someone "who may heal her wounds . . . who will rescue her from her barbarian insolence and cruelty . . . "

Commentary:

Machiavelli's prime motive in writing *The Prince* was to encourage Lorenzo the Magnificent to unite Italy. Like many writers during the Renaissance, Machiavelli was a student of history; this, tied to his fervent belief in an Italian nation-state, led him to hope that Lorenzo would use his advice to liberate Italy from its host of foreign invaders.

The modern usage of the term "Machiavellian" denotes ruthless opportunism and manipulative techniques. And, in fact, as a practical guide for leadership, the author's proffered advice lacks any semblance of morality. But in the Florentine theorist's world, morality was in short supply. His paradigm of princehood was Prince Cesare Borgia. Praising Borgia's killing and despoiling of as many lords and lands "as he could lay hands on," Machiavelli cites this Prince as an almost perfect archetype of bold rule: "I can find nothing with which to reproach him . . . "

The influence of *The Prince* has been felt deeply, even in the twentieth century, as evidenced by the actions of such men as Hitler, Stalin, Lenin, and many other international statesmen. Political leaders (Kennedy, Nixon, Reagan, Gordon Liddy, Oliver North, and countless other Presidential advisers), plus endless hordes of salesmen, advertisers and authors on managerial techniques all were ardent students of the book.

DAS KAPITAL

by Karl Marx
(1818 - 1883)

Commentary:

In the mid-nineteenth century, when Karl Marx wrote *Das Kapital* – an exhaustive work of more than one thousand pages – factory conditions were often intolerable, wages were at best barely adequate, and there were few groups or governments who advocated reform. Therefore, Marx took it upon himself to define "Capitalism," explain and condemn Capitalist methods, predict the inevitable doom of the system, and issue the rallying cry, "Workers of the world, unite!"

When Marx simply describes what he sees, his analyses and criticisms appear most lucid. In contrast, his theories become confusing as he attempts to prove even the vaguest point using mathematics. He felt that these elaborate equations and proofs were necessary because his book does not purport to be merely a *moral prescription* for society's ills, but a *scientific description* of the unavoidable course of history. It is, of course, actually not only a "prescription" but a passionate exhortation.

In any case, some of Marx's words still ring true; as a framework for analyzing the historical transformation of human society, *Das Kapital* succeeds quite well.

Marx's work draws heavily on the dialectical theories of Georg Hegel, an earlier 19th-century German idealist-philosopher. Hegel had posited that the world was in a constant process of transformation from lower to higher orders of existence. Each new order, he thought, emerged as an embodied idea, or "thesis"; and each thesis carried within itself the seeds of its own destruction – its own opposing force or "antithesis" (a "we-have-met-the-enemy-and-he-is-us" concept). But out of the inevitable clash between thesis and antithesis, a new and more perfect order – the synthesis – was destined to emerge (as Christianity, for example, had risen triumphant from the struggle between Greek and Hebrew thought). In its turn, then, this synthesis would now function as a new thesis, engendering another antithesis and advancing the conflict-resolution cycle, until finally history fought its way forward to the ultimate synthesis – the "total realization of the world spirit."

For religious disciples of Hegel, all this was tantamount to the coming of God's kingdom on earth; but for Marx (who admired Hegel's thought but despised religion as a tool of oppression and dismissed idealism as "unscientific") it was a challenge to ground Hegelian dialectic in the down-to-earth materialism of *economics* – which Marx saw as the engine of history.

The inherent tension between social classes under different economic orders has created both conflict and progress through the ages, he pronounces. Most recently, the emerging merchant-capitalist class that arose to service feudalism was broken down, as merchants overwhelmed their masters; it is this merchant class that rules today. But now, says Marx, is the hour for the "ultimate synthesis" – the Proletariat revolution and the final achievement of a classless and stateless society.

Book Overview:

To understand Marx, we must first establish some basic definitions:

* *commodities* - Things to be bought or sold.

* *use value* - Capacity to satisfy wants (to be "used" or "useful").

* *exchange value* - Price. (Distinguished from "use value" in that a society may value an article, yet not be accustomed to exchanging it.)

* *value* - The "socially necessary" time needed to produce a commodity.

* *surplus value* - Profit or land-rent; the sine qua non of Capitalism, created when the value of a day's labor exceeds the exchange value of "labour-power."

* *capital* - The surplus value that is invested in labor power and means of production (machines, plants, raw materials, etc.).

* *labor power* - The capacity or opportunity to work.

* *labor power (in Capitalism)* - A human commodity; work sold by a laborer to his "owner"-boss at less than the exchange value of labor produced.

* *money* - A valuable, produced commodity (gold, silver, etc.) employed as a universal equivalent for values of other commodities.

* *Proletariat* - Working class; propertyless wage-earners (who must remain propertyless for Capitalism to work, says Marx).

* *Bourgeoisie* - The Capitalist class, who – not acting with intentional evil, but as "capital personified" – serve as puppets of the system, exploiting the Proletariat.

Marx points out that "the circulation or exchange of commodities in itself creates no value." So, the trick the Capitalist must perform, in order to exact his profit, is "[to obtain] from his commodities a greater value than that invested by him in them . . . "

Capitalist-Laborer Relationship

Capitalistic society provides three main sources of "income": **(1)** *Capital* (which "profits" the Capitalist); **(2)** *Land* (which provides landowners with rent); and **(3)** *"Labour-power"* (which earns the worker his wage).

A laborer is, in a sense, a merchant, who sells his "labour-power" as a commodity. And "the value of labour-power is the value of the necessaries required to sustain its proprietor." Thus, the Capitalist purchases a laborer's work in exchange for a wage, which the worker then converts into food, shelter, and clothing – on the surface, a fair exchange. Because the Capitalist must make a profit, however, and the simple exchange of commodities does not produce any profit, Marx asserts that the Capitalist is forced to extract his profit from the labor of his workers; he must "lower . . . the wages of the labourer below the [true exchange] value of his labour power."

Profit can be increased by various means, the most common being "simply . . . prolonging the duration of the working day" – paying the same wage for more work. (Today, of course, this tactic would not be tolerated.) "More intense utilization of labour power" and the emergence of large-scale cooperative enterprises – with various hierarchies of merchants and managers – has subjected the Proletariat to a "serfdom" of wage-slavery, claims Marx.

Capitalist Methods

Manufacturing by machine gives the Capitalist an added advantage and further converts the worker into a "crippled monstrosity," cut off from the chance to cultivate "human" skills as an artisan or craftsman. (The garment worker in a factory doesn't make suits; he sews one hundred and twenty-seven shoulder seams every two hours.) What's more, technology tends to be self-generating – machinery begets more machinery. In the textile industry, for instance, the revolutionary spinning wheel prompted the demand for weaving machines in order to cope with the increased availability of threads and yarns. In turn, these spawned the "mechanical and chemical revolution that took place in bleaching, drying, and printing" of fabrics. While these innovations in themselves were good, under Capitalism they displaced many skilled textile workers and forced them into less skilled, lower-paying positions, vulnerable to be used and discarded as interchangeable cogs in the labor machine itself.

The use of machinery also undermined the wages of working-class males. The design of machines in Marx's time often demanded that workers be small and/or slim. "The labour of women and children was, therefore, the first thing sought for by Capitalists . . . " (An added bonus was "the docile character of women and children.") And with more members of a family working, subsistence wages for each worker could be gradually lowered. As labor-power became cheaper, the perceived value of individual workers was further diminished, fostering a cavalier disregard for their safety, health and comfort in the grim factories and workshops of the day.

A machine allows for round-the-clock use. "The longer a machine works, the greater is the mass of the products over which the value transmitted by the machine is spread, and the less is the portion of that value added to each commodity." The machine running at full capacity day and night will probably wear out sooner, but this is desireable because more profit can thus be extracted before it becomes obsolete. Thus, it is only the worker who wears out ahead of time – and he can be replaced at no extra cost from the ranks of idle and hungry workers who have been displaced by machines – the "reserve army of unemployed."

Capital and Surplus-Value

" . . . During the periods of stagnation and average prosperity," this group of excess workers "weighs down the active labour-army [i.e. acts as a brake against wage increases]; during the periods of over-production and paroxysm, it holds [the] claims [of the active labour-army] in check. Relative surplus-population is therefore the pivot upon which the law of supply and demand of labour works."

Improved manufacturing and farming methods, the proliferation of banks and loaning practices, increased ease of global transportation and travel . . . all have helped swell the Capitalist tide of expansionism and exploitation. The complex and selfish industrial society, declared Marx, was now ripe for revolt.

Summary

Throughout the last few centuries, according to Marx, it has been the common worker's fate to suffer the "maximum of working time and the minimum of wages" in order to supply Capitalists with profits. "Accumulation of wealth at one pole is, therefore, at the same time accumulation of misery, agony of toil, slavery, ignorance, brutality, moral degradation, at the opposite pole." This *must* and *shall* be ended.

Granted, says Marx, the Capitalist is in tight control. But the pendulum of power has swung many times in the past, and he promises that it will again shift. The Proletariat, under the banner of Communism, will ultimately be victorious. Revolution is the destined scenario – and the ultimate historical "synthesis" will be a perfectly just and egalitarian society, where everyone works "according to his ability" and receives "according to his needs"; where the state itself finally "withers away."

THE REPUBLIC

by Plato
(427 - 347 B.C.)

Book Overview:

(*The Republic* is an examination of the "Good Life"; the harmony reached by applying pure reason and justice. The ideas and arguments presented center on the social conditions of an ideal republic – those that lead each individual to the most perfect possible life for him. Socrates – Plato's early mentor in real life – moderates the discussion throughout, presumably as Plato's mouthpiece. Through Socrates' powerful and brilliant questions and summations on a series of topics, the reader comes to understand what Plato's model society would look like.)

Socrates was returning to Athens after attending a festival, when he met Polemarchos on the road. Upon Polemarchos' insistence, Socrates accompanied him to his home to meet his friends and family. As they entered the courtyard, Polemarchos' elderly father, Cephalus, greeted them and launched into a discussion of old age. Socrates seemed pleased to converse with the older man: "It seems right to enquire of them, as if they traversed a long journey which perhaps we will have to traverse."

The discussion then turned to the question of "justice," or "doing the right thing." Polemarchos suggested that "to give back what is owed to each is just." However, Socrates countered that to return a weapon to a friend who had gone mad was not just, but the opposite of justice. Still another man, Thrasymachos, offered his definition of justice: "I declare justice is nothing but the advantage of the stronger." But Socrates, again by logical argument, dismissed this definition: Since rulers are fallible, they often make decisions that are not in their best interest, thus requiring their subjects to do the wrong, unjust thing. But, according to Socrates, "right living," dutiful service to others, and doing that which is "appropriate" to the person and situation are the prerequisites to individual happiness – and prerequisites for avoiding chaos within a republic.

Still another in the group voiced his objections to Socrates' statement that justice is a virtue and injustice a vice; Glaucon was not entirely convinced that justice possessed any intrinsic value. Socrates began his examination of this concept by turning his focus from the individual to the city: people gathered together in cities in order that each individual might perform the task best suited to his or her nature. From this point, Socrates delineated the various classes of people in a city-state, from the peasant and beggar to the highest kings and rulers. He then posed a question: "Do you not think, that one who is to be guardian-like (a leader) needs

something more besides a spirited temper, and that is to be in his nature a lover of wisdom?" Socrates also wondered aloud how these traits could be instilled into potential leaders: "How shall our guardians be trained and educated?"

Socrates proceeded to weigh the numerous types of education and experience demanded of a good ruler, and divided education into two main areas: *music* (in this case, all the arts) and *gymnastics* (athletics). Fables, he observed, were the first "music" that children hear, and children are "easily molded" by these stories. Socrates recommended that "we must set up a censorship over the fable-makers, and approve any good fable they make, and disapprove the bad." Many classical fables and myths were to be censored as "false" because they portrayed the gods in an unfavorable light. Children "must never hear at all that the gods war against other gods and plot and fight," he said, for when they grow older, they will accept this behavior as virtuous. Instead, children should hear the "noblest things told in the best fables for encouraging virtue." He concluded: "God is simple and true in word and deed," and this must be held up as an example to children, especially to those who may grow up to become rulers.

Socrates extended his censorship argument to include craftsmen: artists and sculptors must be restrained from deformed, ignoble, morbid or "imaginary" creations, "to stop their implanting this spirit so evil and dissolute." Craftsmen "who by good natural powers can track out the nature of the beautiful and the graceful," should share their gifts so that young people would dwell in "wholesome country."

A delicate balance had to be maintained between gymnastic and "musical" education; an over-emphasis on gymnastics produced "savagery and hardness" in a person, while too much music spawned excessive "softness and gentleness." The two arts "may be fitted together in concord, by being strained and slackened to the proper point."

Now that the thrust of the future citizens' education was established, Socrates asked: "Which among these are to rule, and which to be ruled?" He then answered his own question, asserting that there were several ways of discovering those best suited to rule. He vaguely suggested that a true guardian would be diligent in keeping watch "on enemies without and friends within," and in seeing that no injury befell the city or its inhabitants. Of the three classes of citizens – the merchant class (the lowest of the low in that their primary purpose is greedy consumption), the high-spirited soldier class (quite like "animals"), and the high-minded, more human-minded philosopher – the philosopher would act most just and civil, and show the most ideal "harmony" in ruling over the passions and appetites of the other two classes.

To maintain harmony, true guardian-kings "must live in common" with their subjects, and must "dare not have any dealings with gold or silver." Rather, the city should supply all their needs.

Expanding these arguments to include the entire population of the city, Socrates preached that there should neither be great wealth nor great poverty; both extremes breed evil in men. Also, "as long as the growing city is willing to remain a unity, so big let it grow but no further." Each citizen must work in a profession fitted to his talents, and work with his neighbor in unity for the growth of his state.

Socrates next turned to the elements which make a city-state virtuous. In both the ruler and in the state, these principles are as follows: "Temperance and courage and intelligence, and here is a thing which makes it possible for [these] three to be there at all": justice. Socrates went on to compare a just city to a just person. Three elements combined make up the individual soul: reason, emotion, and desire. A person "must have all three parts in tune within him, highest [reason], and lowest [desire], and middle [emotion]."

Before the master philosopher could delve deeper into the two types of state – the just and the unjust – Glaucon interrupted to ask if Socrates truly believed that such a virtuous city was possible. "There is one change which I think would make the transformation," Socrates replied. As philosophers become "kings in our cities . . . political power and intellectual wisdom will be joined in one." But until this happened, Socrates saw no end to the troubles suffered worldwide.

Furthermore, for a man to be a genuine philosopher, he must pursue truth for an entire lifetime. This pursuit, Socrates affirmed, impels him from a state of darkness to a state of light. Just as objects in the shadows are more difficult to see while in sunlight they are easily discerned, so "truth" cannot be seen with eyes that are dark, but only through eyes of "understanding" (comprehending logical and mathematical concepts) and through "exercising reason" (dialectical thought). By experiencing "pure ideas," a man discovers the higher ideals such as "perfect beauty, justice and goodness." To escape the dark "shadows of the images" of reality, he must free himself from his fetters, turn to the "real light," and climb out of his cave of ignorance. Initially, the light of truth might hurt his eyes, but soon he will become accustomed to its brightness and multiple colors. Eventually, he will see everything – relationships, the soul, the human mind – through "new" eyes and use reason to understand all that he sees.

This difficult ascent and "view of the upper world is the rising of the soul into the world of mind." It is an arduous trek, but not an impossible one. By exploring abstractions, a person may reach the brilliant light. This trek, according to Socrates, requires the study of numbers, arithmetic, plane geometry, and astronomy. Though all these fields have their practical applications, their true value lies in the fact that they "compel the soul to use pure reason in order to find out the truth." Pure reason is expressed in the dialectical process – the very process they were all using in their exchange of views. Socrates urged everyone "to get a start towards the real thing"; for it is only "through reason and without any help from the senses [that the individual can arrive] at the very end of the world of thought."

A final question was raised: What of pleasure? Socrates boldly insisted that the highest pleasure was that enjoyed by the philosopher, "the lover of wisdom." A philosopher may or may not choose to experience the pleasures of gain and honor, but only he can "know how great is the pleasure of contemplating things as they are." The "greed-for-wealth" philosophy espoused by democracies, he argued, inevitably causes democratic societies to turn to tyranny. For this reason, he cautioned his listeners to guard their ideal city against the arts of "the imitators" – those who wrote poetry: "[Poets] do not lay hold of truth." The poetic artist projects images of "love-making and anger and all the desires and griefs and pleasures in the soul which we say go along with our every action." But this is not good in that "it nourishes [the passions] by watering what it ought to dry up, and makes them rulers in us . . . "

Socrates ended his involved analysis by exhorting his fellow philosophers to follow his advice. By employing all our faculties of reason and "believing the soul immortal and able to undergo all evil things and all good things, we will hold ever to the upper road, and we will practice in every way justice along with wisdom."

Commentary:

The Republic is one of the foundational writings of Western philosophy and civilization. We see Platonic thought and Socratic methodology still vitally evolving in today's world. Dialectic questioning is the basis of Marxism and many other schools of philosophy. Indeed, the question-and-answer method plays an expansive role in our legal, scientific and educational systems. Moreover, Plato's views concerning the nature of humankind – his notion of "mind over matter" in the individual soul – is a cornerstone of Christianity. The arguments and ideas of *The Republic* have had a profound influence on all the dialectic swings within our social, political, and religious quests and thinking since they were first written down in Athens twenty-five hundred years ago.

THE IMPORTANCE OF BEING EARNEST

by
Oscar Wilde
(1854 - 1900)

Type of work: Comic, farcical play

Setting: London, and a country house in Hertfordshire, England; the 1890's

Principal characters:

Jack Worthing, gentleman of the Manor House; also known as "Ernest"

Cecily Cardew, Worthing's pretty young ward

Miss Prism, Cecily's governess

Algernon Moncrieff, Worthing's friend

Lady Augusta Bracknell, Algernon's aunt

Gwendolen Fairfax, Lady Bracknell's daughter

The Reverend Canon Chasuble, Rector of Woolton

Play Overview:

While Algernon Moncrieff and his manservant prepared for a visit from his aunt, the formidable Lady Bracknell, their conversation turned to the question of marriage. Observing the servant's somewhat lax views on the subject, Algernon declared, "Really, if the lower orders don't set us a good example, what on earth is the use of them?"

This chat was interrupted by the unexpected arrival of Algernon's friend, Ernest Worthing. Worthing was pleased to hear that Lady Bracknell – and her beautiful daughter Gwendolen – would be appearing for tea. But Algernon warned, "I am afraid Aunt Augusta won't quite approve of your being here." Mildly insulted, Ernest demanded to know why. "My dear fellow," Algernon answered, "the way you flirt with Gwendolen is perfectly disgraceful. It is almost as bad as the way Gwendolen flirts with you." At this point Worthing announced that he intended to propose marriage to Gwendolen, but was taken aback by Algernon's response: "I don't give my consent." Worthing would first have to explain a certain "Cecily" in his life. As evidence of this relationship, he produced a cigarette case left behind by Worthing on an earlier visit – devotedly inscribed from "Cecily" to her loving "Uncle Jack."

"Well," admitted Worthing, "my name is Ernest in town and Jack in the country." It happened, he said, that Cecily was his ward, who lived in his country home under the watchful eyes of a stern governess, Miss Prism. But to escape the stuffy constraints of country living, Jack had invented an alter ego: " . . . In order to get up to town I have always pretended to have a younger brother of the name of Ernest, who lives in Albany, and gets into the most dreadful scrapes." Thus, Jack was often "called away" to the city to "rescue" irrepressible Ernest.

Smiling, Algernon now confessed that he too was a "Bunburyist," a friend of the equally fictitious "Bunbury," a "permanent invalid," whom he visited whenever he chose to get away.

When Lady Bracknell and Gwendolen arrived, Algernon took his aunt aside, leaving "Ernest" and Gwendolen alone. "Miss Fairfax," Worthing stammered, "ever since I met you I have admired you more than any girl – I have ever met since – I met you." Gwendolen admitted to returning these warm feelings, in part because "my ideal has always been to love someone of the name of Ernest." Would she still love him, asked Jack, if his name were, say, "Jack"? "There is very little music in the name Jack," observed Gwendolen. Before more could be said, Jack knelt and asked her to marry him. At that moment Lady Bracknell entered, and the couple announced their engagement. Highly displeased, Lady Bracknell requested a private conference with Mr. Worthing, in which she asked about his income, his politics, and, finally, his parentage. "I don't actually know who I am by birth," Jack explained; as a baby he had been found in a handbag in the coatroom of the train station. Lady Bracknell was shocked. Neither she nor her husband, she huffed, could allow Gwendolen to "marry into a cloak-room, and form an alliance with a parcel."

Now Jack considered his predicament. At least, he decided, he could deal with the complication of Ernest. His imaginary brother must soon "die" of a severe chill. Deep in these new intrigues, he left.

Meanwhile, Algernon, his curiosity piqued by Jack's mysterious young ward, decided he must meet this Cecily.

At the Manor in Hertfordshire, Miss Prism and Cecily were talking in the garden. Cecily expressed the hope that Jack would soon allow his reprobate brother Ernest to visit: "We might have a good influence over him." Miss Prism discouraged this idea, but just a few moments after she had left for a stroll with her own admirer, Dr. Chasuble, the local minister, the butler announced the arrival of Mr. Ernest Worthing, and in walked Algernon Moncrieff, posing as Jack's deliciously wicked – and non-existent – brother. After some chit-chat and over a bite to eat, "Ernest" (Algy) implored his "cousin" to "reform him".

Soon Miss Prism and the Reverend returned, just in time to be greeted by Jack Worthing, who arrived with tears of grief and the news that his brother Ernest was "quite dead." "What a lesson for him!" Miss Prism clucked. "I trust he will profit by it." Then Jack, overcome by sentiment, petitioned Chasuble to re-christen him with his poor brother's name. Chasuble agreed. Just then Cecily burst from the house to announce a surprise: "Your brother Ernest. He arrived about half an hour ago." This *was* a surprise – and was an even bigger surprise when Algernon appeared, addressed him as "Brother John," and announced: "I have come down from town to tell you that I am very sorry for all the trouble I have given you, and that I intend to lead a better life in the future." Jack glared at him, speechless.

When the conspirators were alone for a moment, Jack demanded that Algernon leave at once. But as he marched determinedly into the house, "Ernest" sought out Cecily to declare himself: "Cecily, ever since I first looked upon your wonderful and incomparable beauty, I have dared to love you wildly, passionately, devotedly, hopelessly . . . . You will marry me, won't you?" "You silly boy," she replied. "Of course . . . You see, it has always been a girlish dream of mine to love someone whose name was Ernest." Would she still love him, inquired Algernon, if his name were, but, say, "Algernon"? No; Cecily did not like the name Algernon.

Algernon too now resolved to be re-christened "Ernest," that very afternoon, and he rushed off to the rectory to find Reverend Chasuble.

Soon afterward, Gwendolen Fairfax also arrived at the estate. She eyed her lovely young hostess suspiciously, even after Cecily revealed that she was only Mr. Worthing's ward. "Strange," said Gwendolen, "he never mentioned to me that he had a ward. How secretive of him!" Speaking "with perfect candor," she added that it would be more to her liking if "Mr. Ernest Worthing's ward was forty-two and more than usually plain." Puzzled, Cecily explained that her guardian was not Ernest, but his brother Jack – Ernest, she clarified happily, was her new fiance.

At that moment the two "Ernests" entered the garden – and finally the two women learned that they had been the victims of "a gross deception." "I am afraid it is quite clear, Cecily," said Gwendolen, "that neither of us is engaged to be married to anyone." The dismissed suitors then marched off – to berate and console one another, and to eat muffins.

When the reprobates returned to beg forgiveness, Cecily pointedly asked Algernon why he had pretended to be Ernest. "In order that I might have the opportunity of meeting you," he replied humbly. Then Gwendolen asked Jack why he had misled her. "Was it in order that you might have an opportunity of coming up to town to see me as often as possible?" she prompted. "Can you doubt it, Miss Fairfax?" Jack answered innocently. Forgiveness was granted.

But the young couples were ill-prepared for the sudden appearance of Lady Bracknell, who was pained to discover that not only had Gwendolen pledged herself to Jack, but her nephew Algernon was engaged to marry Jack's lowly ward. When she found that Cecily was heiress to a considerable fortune, however, Lady Bracknell declared "Miss Cardew" to be a "most attractive young lady."

But Jack now stepped in – to refuse his consent. He questioned Algernon's "moral character"; had he not in fact come to Worthing's home under false pretenses, lied to Cecily – and eaten all the muffins? When Lady Bracknell tried to soften her stance, Jack announced that the matter lay in her hands: "The moment you consent to my marriage with Gwendolen, I will most gladly allow your nephew to form an alliance with my ward." But, to Lady Bracknell, this marraige remained out of the question.

At this point, Miss Prism entered the room – to be greeted by Lady Bracknell's instant glare of recognition. "Prism!" she exclaimed. "Twenty-eight years ago, Prism, you left Lord Bracknell's house in charge of a perambulator that contained a baby . . . . You never returned. Prism! Where is that baby?" Shame-faced, the governess admitted to having absent-mindedly stuffed the baby in a hand-bag which she left hanging in the cloak-room of a train station. When she had returned to the spot to retreive the child, he and the handbag were gone. Then, addressing the stunned Jack Worthing, she pointed to Lady Bracknell: "There is the lady who can tell you who you really are."

Lady Bracknell breathed a sigh. "You are the son of my poor sister, Mrs. Moncrieff," she muttered, "and consequently Algernon's elder brother." What's more, she revealed that Jack had indeed been christened after his late father, Ernest John.

As the two couples (along with Miss Prism and the Reverend Chasuble) joyfully embraced, Lady Bracknell chided Jack: "My nephew, you seem to be displaying signs of triviality." But Jack replied, "On the contrary, Aunt Augusta, I've now realized for the first time in my life the vital Importance of Being Earnest."

Commentary:

Oscar Wilde, the witty Edwardian poet, playwright, and author, was noted for his refined demeanor. The same mannersims and dress, however, that made him a popular guest at parties also labeled him as a homosexual; and although he was the married father of six, a sexual scandal which erupted just a few days after the opening of *The Importance of Being Earnest* eventually earned him two years of hard labor in prison, and effectively ended his career.

Perhaps his frequent use of the convolutions of deceit and misidentity as comic device was as much inspired by the rigid masks imposed in post-Victorian society as it was by the Shakespearean "Comedy of Errors" tradition he admired. Wilde's characters in *Earnest* are the "UN-earnest," idle rich, with abundant time and money at their disposal to make intricate messes out of their lives. It is only through the most amazing good fortune – often appearing in the writer's plays as obvious contrivances – that they are able to get past their own foolishness and flippancy (follies which typified Wilde's own tumultuous life) to achieve their desired ends.

BABBITT

by
Sinclair Lewis
(1885-1951)

Type of work: Social commentary

Setting: Zenith, a mythical Midwestern
American city; 1920's

Principal characters:
George F. Babbitt, a middle-aged real-
estate agent
Myra, his wife
Ted, their teenage son
Paul Reisling, George's buddy from college
Zilla, Paul's nagging wife
Tanis Judique, George's mistress
Seneca Doane, a radical lawyer and
George's former college friend

Story Overview:

As another day began in Zenith, sleeping
George Babbitt fought to ignore the morning
sounds – the milk truck, the furnace-man, a dog
barking – so that he could cling to the dream he
was having. He had the same dream often. It
involved a "fairy child" who discerned "gallant
youth" where "others saw but George Babbitt."

But now the day beckoned. George pulled
himself from bed, bathed, shaved, dressed, and
then trudged downstairs to eat. As usual,
Babbitt was a grumpy breakfast partner; a foul
mood was expected of a respectable businessman. He grumbled at his nearly adult children,
Verona and Ted, and argued with Myra, his
wife. No one in the house appreciated all he did
for them.

Babbitt gulped down his food, "laid
unmoving lips against [Myra's] unblushing
cheek," and left for work. Driving toward his
office in downtown Zenith, he admired the
"bigness" of the city. In fact, "Babbitt respected
bigness in anything: in mountains, jewels, muscles, wealth, or words . . . "

At the Reeves Building where the
Babbitt-Thompson Realty Company had its
offices, he wrote an advertisement designed to
entice buyers to purchase the company's cemetery plots, then phoned his old school friend
Paul Reisling and made arrangements for
lunch.

Babbitt always ate in the Zenith Athletic
Club, and today was no exception. He normally
sat with "the Roughnecks," an intimate group
of big businessmen, but today he and Paul sat
by themselves. Paul was more than a little
depressed with his shrewish wife Zilla, who
constantly badgered him, embarrassed him in
public, and treated him like a little boy.

While the two friends complained about
their colorless lives, they struck on the idea of
getting away to Maine by themselves that next
summer to "just loaf . . . and smoke and cuss
and be natural." Babbitt assured Paul that he

would arrange everything with their wives.

The day ended with Babbitt firing a salesman for being too honest. At home, as usual,
Babbitt ate dinner, the kids left the house, and
he plunked himself on the sofa for some lazy
reading. But a seed of dissatisfaction swelled
up in him; he vowed that the following year
would bring changes in his life.

The next year began well for Babbitt.
Money poured in as he secretly bought real
estate options in a Zenith suburb, Linton, in
anticipation of "the public announcement that
the Linton Avenue Car Line would be extended." Babbitt told Myra about his plan to run up
to Maine with Paul early that spring and bullied Zilla into letting Paul go, too.

Paul and Babbitt arrived in Maine's north
woods, and both found the climate, surroundings, fishing, hiking and camaraderie, soothing.
Paul started looking at his distant wife with a
more forgiving eye. He began to feel that his
marriage would somehow be different – better;
maybe he could "go back and start over again."
Babbitt, on the other hand, "sank into irritability," as though he had "uncovered layer upon
layer of hidden weariness." But he still
promised himself that his life would be, from
then on, less hurried and hectic.

After his return from Maine, Babbitt was
given the opportunity to address the State
Association of Real Estate Boards at their annual convention. He tried for days to come up
with a speech to express his new-found relaxation; to somehow convince businessmen that
they needed to see life from a deeper perspective. But just before the convention he trashed
his notes, and, instead, parroted the ideas he
knew his peers wanted to hear. Enthusiastically,
he proclaimed the real estate profession,
Zenith, and every good thing about the city, as
"God's gift to earth."

Babbitt's speech was a success. One of
Zenith's newspapers even printed his picture.

After that, things really took off. That
November, Harding won the Presidential election, but in Zenith the mayoral race was the
fight that really counted. Seneca Doane, a radical lawyer – and Babbitt's former college
acquaintance – was running on a liberal labor
ticket, while his opponent, Lucas Prout, had the
support of "the banks, the Chamber of
Commerce, all the decent newspapers, and
George F. Babbitt." "Prout represented honest
industry, Seneca Doane represented whining
laziness," Babbitt told campaign audiences. In
the end, Prout – and by extension, Babbitt –
won.

Soon thereafter, Babbitt was picked to

serve on a church committee formed to "build up the biggest darn Sunday School in the whole state." There Babbitt met a new business associate, William Washington Eathorne, president of the First State Bank. Eathorne symbolized old money, Victorian conservatism, and real power in the Zenith community. He liked Babbitt's ideas for increasing the size of the Sunday School by dividing it into four "armies," with military ranks to be awarded according to how many "souls" each member brought in. Babbit also authored the idea of hiring a Sunday School press agent.

Next, Babbitt was elected vice-president of the Zenith chapter of the International Organization of Booster's Clubs. He was riding high on success, when "all the charm in his life was smothered by a single event": Paul, his best friend, shot his wife. Babbitt was devastated. Because Zilla survived the shooting, Paul's sentence was light – only three years in the State penitentiary. But Babbitt now "faced a world which, without Paul, was meaningless."

That June, Myra went East to stay with relatives, and Babbitt was free to do as he pleased. He began to look on women with a cautious but desiring eye. Once or twice he even dated a manicurist he knew, but she quashed any thought of an affair, and eventually, Babbitt gave up the search for his "fairy child," choosing instead to return to Maine's wilderness. But this too proved disappointing: Babbitt was alone with no wife to coddle him, no friend to talk with, no children to visit him.

Returning by train, Babbitt bumped into Seneca Doane. As they reminisced about old college days, Doane told Babbitt that "in college you were an unusually liberal, sensitive chap. I can still recall your saying to me that you were going to be a lawyer, and take the cases of the poor for nothing, and fight the rich." Babbitt was impressed by this recollection. By the time he returned to Zenith, he had determined to be more open; "to give the other fellow a chance, and listen to his ideas."

One day, Tanis Judique, who rented one of Babbitt's properties, called on him about some repairs. Their relationship soon escalated, and Babbitt quickly became absorbed into Tanis' group of friends (called "the Bunch"), cavorting around town with them and drinking bootleg whiskey in roadside inns. Still feeling inexplicably unfulfilled, George secretly continued in these reveries even after Myra's return.

Babbitt's friends at the Athletic Club became aware of his changed attitudes. When, rather than flat-out condemning a group of city strikers Babbitt defended them, his colleagues met him with cold shoulders, glares and looks of disbelief.

One afternoon an associate approached Babbitt and invited him to join a new organization, the Good Citizen's League. When Babbitt refused, the man let it be known that he would regret his decision. Babbitt's business partner warned him, "One little rumor about you being a crank would do more to ruin this business than all the plots . . . these fool storywriters could think up in a month of Sundays." Sure enough, the real estate company began to lose lucrative opportunities. From all sides Babbitt was feeling pressure to return to his old, cynical self. His children were the only ones who approved of his new-found freedom.

Then Myra had a sudden attack of acute appendicitis. Babbitt felt guilty, then repentant. He decided to mend his ways. He cut off his affair with Tanis; he quit running with "the Bunch"; and he joined the G.C.L. Once again, George F. Babbitt became the model citizen – outwardly, at least. Inside, he still refused to conform.

Meanwhile, Ted, who had been away at college halfheartedly pursuing a career in law – Babbitt's dream for his son – eloped one night with a neighbor's daughter, Eunice Littlefield. The next morning, when Myra discovered the newlyweds in Ted's bedroom, she became hysterical. Later that day, the Littlefields demanded an annulment.

Babbitt took Ted aside to talk. But rather than condemn his son, Babbitt told Ted that he "got a sneaking pleasure out of the fact that you knew what you wanted to do and did it." As for himself, Babbitt lamented that he'd "never done a single thing I've wanted to in my whole life."

Commentary:

When Sinclair Lewis wrote *Babbitt*, he succeeded in creating a caricature of success typifying the mind-set of the twenties. The "big booster" filled with "vim and vigor," Babbitt is a character without a real soul. He gleans his opinions from newspapers or from business peers. Even Babbitt's extra-marital affair is a "standard deviation."

Lewis attempts to indict these "standard" symbols of American prosperity – popularity, hidden pleasures, money, shiny cars, and self-obsession – by citing the weaknesses of both radical and conservative viewpoints. George is truly discontent in both settings.

While *Babbitt* has been criticized for its lack of character depth, it seems that it would have been impossible to make Babbitt profound. The satirical essence of the novel requires that George be shallow and complacently mediocre. Lewis does provide some hope symbolized by Ted, who does exactly what his father would have liked to have done. However, perhaps Babbitt's reaction to his son's elopement suggests that there is still something more to him than a cardboard front. Ted's question to his father at novel's end divulges the true message of Babbitt: "Gosh, dad, are you really going to be human?"

DEATH OF A SALESMAN

by
Arthur Miller
(1915 -   )

Type of work: Dramatic play

Setting: New York and Boston; 1949

Principal characters:

Willy Loman, a disgruntled traveling salesman
Linda, his wife
Biff, Willy's favorite and most athletic son
Happy, another son

Play Overview:

(Like many plays, this one shifts back and forth in time and place. We view much of the Loman family's daily life through the eyes and mind of the father.)

Nobody believes more fervently in the American Dream than Willy, yet the dream has somehow eluded him. Now he is sixty years old, a beaten and discouraged traveling salesman, with nothing to show for a lifetime of hard work but a small house on a crowded street where grass doesn't grow anymore and apartment houses block his view.

Rustling about upstairs are Willy's grown sons, Happy and Biff, home for a visit. Their presence in the house causes Willy to reminisce on happier times; times when their growing strength and athletic feats – especially Biff's – were a source of pride and joy to him; times when it seemed certain that his kids would go out and conquer the world. In this heightened and reflective state, Willy speaks aloud to his boys as if the two youngsters he fondly remembers from the past had materialized in the room.

WILLY: That's just what I mean. Bernard [the son of Willy's friend] can get the best marks in school, y'understand, but when he gets out in the business world, y'understand, you are going to be five times ahead of him. That's why I thank Almighty God you're both built like Adonises. Because the man who makes an appearance in the business world, the man who creates personal interest, is the man who gets ahead. Be liked and you will never want.

Willy's philosophy is sound and foolproof, he feels, but, unaccountably, it hasn't worked for him, nor for his favorite son, Biff. Ever since graduation from high school when he inexplicably ignored a prestigious scholarship offer to play football for the University of Virginia, Biff had acted like a restless vagabond, moving from one place and one job to another, unable to get a hold on life. He had also had a run-in with the police – stealing, they said.

Willy paces the kitchen floor and strolls around the yard, trying to understand – how could a boy with such promise have gone so wrong? However, the father is never quite able to admit any responsibility for Biff's problems. "I never told him anything but decent things," he rationalizes.

During the boys' visit, Willy can not help but argue with Biff. His son's dreams are simply unacceptable. Biff's latest scheme is to own a ranch somewhere in the West. He figures that Bill Oliver, a man he used to work for, will loan him the ten thousand dollars to buy it.

Later that evening, Biff and Happy bound down the stairs to talk with their mother, Linda. Willy comes in from the garden just in time to hear Biff mention his plans to go see Oliver: "He always said he'd stake me. I'd like to go into business, so maybe I can take him up on it." Then, seeing Willy, and anxious to please his father, Biff stammers on, emphasizing that it is a "business" he wants, not necessarily a ranch.

Retiring to bed that night, Willy is convinced that Biff is off to a new start. "God Almighty, he'll be great yet," he says to Linda. "A star that magnificent can never really fade away!"

When Willy awakes the next morning, Biff and Happy are gone – Happy to his job, Biff to speak with Bill Oliver. Willy, still feeling the optimism of the night before, is now determined to also make his own life better. First thing he'll do is go to New York to tell his boss that he wants to be taken off the road; life's too short to be away from home all the time. He and his wife's future promises to be happy. "It's changing," she tells him excitedly. "Willy, I feel it changing!"

But, once again, things don't work out the way Willy plans. His boss, Howard – who had been named by young Willy himself after Will had just started to work for Howard's father – is not interested in the salesman's problems. When Willy asks that his traveling be cut down, Howard summarily fires him. Broken, Willy stops to see his old neighbor-buddy Charley in his office. But Willy has always been jealous of Charley; and his "friend" isn't much comfort to him now.

CHARLEY: Howard fired you?
WILLY: That snotnose. Imagine that. I named him. I named him Howard.
CHARLEY: Willy, when're you gonna' realize that them things don't mean anything? You named him Howard, but you can't sell that. The only thing you got in this world is what you can sell. And the funny things is is that you're a salesman, and you don't know that.

Near emotional collapse, Willy leaves and drives to Frank's Chop House, where Biff and Happy are to meet him.

Earlier, Biff, in trying to see Bill Oliver, had waited and waited in the reception area, but finally gave up late in the afternoon. However, before leaving, out of spite he had stolen Oliver's fountain pen. But through this experience Biff discovered something deep and previously hidden about himself, and he is anxious to communicate this new-found understanding to his father. But Willy isn't interested in hearing what Biff has learned: "I was fired, and I'm looking for a little good news to tell your mother, because the woman has waited and the woman has suffered." Biff starts, then stops, never really able to get the truth out.

Soon, Biff and Happy leave the restaurant, arm-in-arm with two girls Happy had managed to pick up. But Willy remains at the Chop House. There on the dirty floor of the men's room, he relives in his mind a sordid sexual affair from years ago. Biff had inadvertently stumbled onto the affair shortly after his graduation from high school – just before he was to begin college, and football . . .

When the young men arrive home that evening, they are greeted by their mother. She says that Willy has been puttering in the yard since he got home, talking to himself – and to Ben, his brother, who has been dead now for nine months. Biff informs his mom that he will be leaving the next day and probably won't be coming back, then walks outside to say goodbye to his father. By and by their father-and-son talk turns into an argument. Biff has already tried once to tell Willy what he had learned that day; now he is determined to make him hear.

WILLY: Then hang yourself! For spite, hang yourself!
BIFF: No! Nobody's hanging himself, Willy! I ran down eleven flights with a pen in my hand today. And suddenly I stopped . . . . I stopped in the middle of that building and I saw – the sky. I saw the things that I love in this world. The work and the food and time to sit and smoke. And I looked at the pen and said to myself, what the hell am I grabbing this for? Why am I trying to become what I don't want to be? What am I doing in an office, making a contemptuous, begging fool of myself, when all I want is out there, waiting for me the minute I say I know who I am! Why can't I say that, Willy?
WILLY: The door of your life is wide open!
BIFF: Pop! I'm a dime a dozen, and so are you!
WILLY: I am not a dime a dozen! I am Willy Loman, and you are Biff Loman!
BIFF: I am not a leader of men, Willy, and

neither are you. You were never anything but a hard-working drummer who landed in the ash can like all the rest of them! I'm one dollar an hour, Willy! I tried seven states and couldn't raise it. A buck an hour! Do you gather my meaning? I'm not bringing home any prizes any more, and you're going to stop waiting for me to bring them home!

Still, Willy can't – won't – grasp what Biff is saying. The argument escalates. But just as it looks as though Biff is ready to haul off and strike Willy, he falls into his arms, weeping. Deeply moved, as Biff stumbles up the stairs to his bedroom, Willy prophesies, "That boy – that boy is going to be magnificent!"

That night Willy remains alone in the kitchen. Everyone else has gone upstairs. He drifts in and out of the past, talking to himself and to his brother Ben, once a successful land developer, who once had gone into the "jungle" and come out rich. Linda is worried, and urges her exhausted husband to come to bed. But Willy puts her off. He's still speaking with Ben, his illusory ideal of complete success. Willy has a proposition to make. "Can you imagine that magnificence [Biff] with twenty-thousand dollars in his pocket?" he mutters across the table. Twenty-thousand dollars is the amount of the benefit in Willy's life insurance policy.

Suddenly, Linda hears the car motor turn over. Willy guns the engine, the car squeals off down the street – then comes the sound of grinding steal and shattering glass.

Commentary:

Death of a Salesman is perhaps the greatest and most significant American play of the 20th century. In many ways, it penetrates to the heart of the American experience, to the dark side of the capitalistic ideal. It is also a sensitive, heart-rending drama.

Miller's play is hard to classify. Some may label it a tragedy, and Willy Loman a tragic hero. But is he? Typically, heroes make the journey from darkness into light, from ignorance to understanding; but Willy never accepts the truth of what is going on in his or his family's life. He begins to catch a glimpse of the joy life can offer, and moves to take advantage of the time he has left, but his firing sends him into a tailspin. His delusions persist till the end, when he manages to misconstrue both his own motives and his son's aspirations, even in the act of suicide.

Early in the play, Willy reminisces on a fellow salesman who was highly successful and well-liked. When this man died, people from all over came to pay their respects. However, as the epitome of a shattered dream, Willy Loman dies a forgotten failure – and not one of his associates attends his funeral.

PRIDE AND PREJUDICE

by
Jane Austen
(1775 - 1817)

Type of work: Study of manners

Setting: Rural England; early nineteenth century

Principal characters:
Mr. Bennet, father of five daughters
Mrs. Bennet, his opinionated wife
Elizabeth, their intelligent middle daughter,
  and Mr. Bennet's favorite child
Jane, Elizabeth's beautiful older sister
Lydia, the Bennet's impetuous youngest
  daughter
Mr. Bingley, Jane's rich and amiable suitor
Mr. Darcy, Bingley's arrogant and wealthy
  friend
Reverend Collins, a conceited bore
Mr. Wickman, an army officer

Story Overview:

Mrs. Bennet felt delighted that Netherfield, a nearby estate, was again rented, and was especially pleased upon hearing that its new occupant, Mr. Bingley, was single and rich. "What a fine thing for our girls!" she beamed. She begged her husband to go make the acquaintance of their new neighbor, and, after some teasing, Mr. Bennet did pay Bingley a call. Mr. Bingley soon returned the visit but did not manage to meet any of the beautiful young women he had heard so much about. His interest piqued, he soon invited the entire Bennet family to dine.

Everyone at the dinner party was impressed with Bingley's fine appearance and gracious manners. However, his close friend, Mr. Darcy, though handsome and well-to-do, was not viewed so favorably. "His manners gave a disgust which turned the tide of his popularity." His pride ruled and ruined his conversation – particularly for Elizabeth. When Bingley suggested that Darcy ask Elizabeth to dance, Elizabeth indignantly overheard Mr. Darcy reply that she was "tolerable; but not handsome enough to tempt me." However, Bingley and Jane Bennet were soon drawn to one another, even though Mr. Bingley's two haughty sisters saw Jane as much beneath their brother. They pretended great fondness for Jane, but Elizabeth easily saw their hypocrisy.

The following day, as the Bennet women sat and discussed the prior evening's party, all were in agreement as to both Bingley's charm and Darcy's coarseness. "I could easily forgive his pride," Elizabeth huffed, "if he had not mortified mine."

In a matter of days, the ladies of Netherfield and those of the Bennet's Longbourne estate had exchanged visits. "By Jane this attention was received with great pleasure; but Elizabeth still saw superciliousness in their treatment of everybody . . . and could not like them." Bingley's sisters took an equal dislike to Elizabeth.

One morning Jane received an invitation from the Bingley girls to spend the day. Mrs. Bennet viewed this as an opportunity for Jane and Mr. Bingley to get better acquainted. "It seems likely to rain," she said hopefully, "and then you must spend the night."

Elizabeth, on the following day, received a note from Jane explaining that she had contracted a fever. When Elizabeth arrived at Netherfield after a muddy three-mile walk, she was quite a sight, "with weary ankles, dirty stockings, and a face glowing with the warmth of exercise." The Bingley sisters giggled, but Mr. Darcy seemed concerned to see her in that state. Privately, he found her charming, though, of course, still inferior due to her family connections.

Elizabeth immediately set about attending to her sister's needs. The two girls were compelled to remain a few days at Netherfield.

One evening Elizabeth sat quietly reading a book in the home's front room. She was quick to notice that one of Bingley's sisters seemed quite fond of Mr. Darcy. As Darcy sat writing a letter, this girl insisted on complimenting him "either on his handwriting, or on the evenness of his lines, or on the length of his letter." Mr. Darcy strained to ignore her comments, which greatly amused Elizabeth. Elizabeth and Mr. Darcy also bantered back and forth, with Elizabeth usually coming out on top.

With Jane recovered from her illness, the Bennet women returned home. And soon, the Bennets had a visitor of their own. The Reverend Collins had written his distant cousin at Longbourne to request the pleasure of a brief visit, and Mr. Bennet was inclined to honor the request. At first Mrs. Bennet was unhappy with the prospect of Collins' visit; since the Bennets had no male children, Collins stood next in line to inherit their estate, and she felt certain that he was coming to lord it over his cousins. But when the letter went on to explain that the Reverend's intent was to seek a suitable wife among the daughters, Mrs. Bennet's attitude quickly changed.

Mr. Collins arrived. However, his advances toward the Bennet girls lacked both grace and wit. When Collins saw that Jane, his first choice, had no interest in him, he turned his eye toward Elizabeth, who did not fail to detect the ease with which he changed his affections.

During this period the Bennets were invited to their uncle's estate for a party. One guest, a Mr. Wickman, a new officer from the nearby army post, was adored by all the girls. When he walked into the room, every female eye turned. Elizabeth felt fortunate that the officer chose to sit by her. As they chatted, Wickman divulged that the infamous Mr. Darcy had once cheated him out of an inheritance left by his godfather, Darcy's father. "This is quite shocking! . . . He deserves to be publicly disgraced," murmured Elizabeth. "Almost all his actions may be traced to pride" continued Wickman. "And pride has often been his best friend."

Now, while Elizabeth had set her eye on Mr. Wickman, Reverend Collins had set his eye on Elizabeth. One evening he made his desires known, listing his reasons for seeking marriage – the foremost being that his patroness, Lady Catherine, who employed him as the local pastor, had ordered him to find a wife. Elizabeth promptly rejected him, and although he did not quite believe her, still he hurriedly turned to ask the hand of a neighbor girl, Charlotte Lucas. They were soon married.

After this, the Bennets heard some distressing news – the Bingley family had returned to London. At first depressed, Jane welcomed an invitation to go to London to stay with an aunt and uncle – and to renew her acquaintance with Mr. Bingley. Elizabeth likewise was invited to visit the new bride and groom, Mr. and Mrs. Collins, and was amused to discover that Mr. Darcy would shortly be paying a visit.

Reunited with Darcy, Elizabeth observed that he "looked just as he had been used to look" – reserved, formal, and conceited. One morning Elizabeth was left alone in the Collins' house when Darcy knocked on the door. She coldly but politely invited him in, and, once again, they began to argue, their conversation punctuated by long periods of silence. Suddenly Mr. Darcy stated his purpose for calling: "In vain have I struggled. It will not do. My feelings will not be repressed. You must allow me to tell you how ardently I admire and love you." He explained that, in spite of her family's low social position, he wanted her to be his wife.

"Elizabeth's astonishment was beyond expression." She flatly refused him: Besides insulting her and her family, he had cheated Mr. Wickman from his inheritance. Darcy hastily exited. But before he left to return to his Pembury estate, he delivered a letter to Elizabeth, answering her charges. He assured her that Wickman had received more than his fair share from the will and that he personally had gone to great lengths to help the unprincipled wretch. But Wickman had become disgruntled when Darcy thwarted his intended elopement with Darcy's younger sister. Elizabeth's long-held prejudice toward her adversary began to melt.

Elizabeth returned home shortly thereafter. Jane was there to meet her, and Elizabeth was disappointed to hear that her sister had been unable to see Mr. Bingley while in London.

Soon it was springtime, and the youngest Bennet daughter, Lydia, was invited to visit the military home at Brighton. Elizabeth was asked once more to vacation with her aunt and uncle – near Pembury. "Elizabeth, as they drove along,

watched for the first appearance of Pembury Woods with some perturbation." She felt both relief and disappointment when she discovered that Darcy was away, indefinitely. But, as fate would have it, Darcy was called home early, and the two old antagonists once more confronted each other. This time, however, "their eyes instantly met, and the cheeks of each was overspread with the deepest blush."

Unfortunately, their day was cut short. Elizabeth received the distressing news that Lydia had run off to Scotland with one of the military officers – Wickman! This Elizabeth could not believe. Darcy, too, though not surprised, was concerned. Home again, Elizabeth learned that the couple had disappeared, apparently without the benefit of matrimony. Such a scandal could destroy Lydia's reputation. But Darcy, discovering their whereabouts, quietly convinced Wickman to marry the young girl and offered the man a vocation.

After Lydia's wedding, the inhabitants of Longbourne had further good news: Mr. Bingley and his friends were again at Netherfield. Elizabeth was sure that Bingley had returned at Darcy's request. Not long after, Mr. Bingley and Jane became engaged.

During one of their frequent walks, Darcy asked Elizabeth if his letter had lessened her dislike of him. When Elizabeth explained "how gradually all her former prejudices had been removed," he repeated his proposal of marriage – and this time Elizabeth was happy to accept.

Mr. Bennet was perturbed: "Lizzy, what are you doing? Have not you always hated this man?" He was mollified when Elizabeth revealed that it was the "arrogant" Darcy who had arranged Lydia's marriage and saved her reputation.

"Happy for all her maternal feelings was the day on which Mrs. Bennet got rid of her two most deserving daughters." With Elizabeth's engagement to Darcy, prejudice had dissolved, pride had been humbled. Love had prevailed.

Commentary:

Jane Austen's intricate novel exhibits dry, subtle humor. She paints her genteel and refined characters with a fine brush, allowing them to ennoble or lower themselves with their own actions and words. A symmetrical plot provides insight into both the foibles and the warmth of human nature.

Pride and Prejudice is a perceptive examination of the relationship between the classes in Britain – with middle class, upwardly mobile aspirations to progress rubbing against upper class efforts to keep them "in their place." Austen's adroit depiction of the plight of women in pre-Victorian Europe also shows her superlative insight into her own world. And this insight is skillfully mirrored through one of the most intriguing and admired heroines of English novels – Elizabeth Bennet.

FAR FROM THE MADDING CROWD

by
Thomas Hardy
(1840 - 1928)

Type of work: Characterization and
psychological novel

Setting: "Wessex," England; 1869 to 1873

Principal characters:
Bathsheba Everdene, a capricious young
lady
Gabriel Oak, a dependable shepherd
Mr. Boldwood, a staid, wealthy farmer
Sergeant Frank Troy, an unscrupulous
soldier
Fanny Robin, Troy's secret lover

Story Overview:

Gabriel Oak quietly scrutinized his new
neighbor from across the hedge. Bathsheba
Everdene appeared to be an overly-proud
woman, but he found himself attracted by her.
Oak's ability and initiative had taken him from
humble origins to become a respected shepherd
with sheep of his own. Now he prepared himself with care to meet Miss Everdene, then
made his way to the house of her aunt to propose marriage. Bathsheba, flattered by the
farmer's offer, flamed his hopes for a while, but
soon announced that she could not marry, nor
love, Gabriel.

Before long, Bathsheba unexplainably left
the area. Then fate dealt Gabriel another blow:
his dog ran his flock of sheep over a cliff, killing
them all. "Thank God I am not married," he
mused. "What would she have done in the
poverty now coming to me?"

Oak went to town to search for work.
Unsuccessful, at the end of the day he crawled
into a cart to sleep. That night the cart carried
him toward Weatherford, the very town to
which Bathsheba had moved. Near the town,
Oak spied a burning barn and bolted through
the fields to help. Putting out the fire, he discovered that the mistress he had served was his
own beloved Bathsheba, who had inherited her
uncle's Weatherbury Farm. Oak asked her to
hire him as the farm's new shepherd.
Hesitantly, Bathsheba agreed.

While searching for local lodgings, Oak
encountered a slim, poorly-clad girl heading
through the woods. Sensing her despair, he
pressed some money into her hand. This girl,
Fanny Robin, had once been a servant on the
Weatherbury Farm.

On that cold, snowy night, Fanny came
near a barracks looking for her secret lover,
Troy. They set a wedding date, but on the
appointed morning, Fanny mistakenly walked
to the wrong chapel. Troy, impatient and
embarrassed by her late arrival, derided her
and put her off indefinitely.

One day, a Mr. Boldwood, a true "gentleman," approached the farm to seek news of
Fanny, for whom he had long felt a fatherly
concern. Bathsheba, finding that Boldwood was
wealthy, unmarried, and seemingly indifferent
to women, set out to make him her challenge.

Bathsheba personally began overseeing
the farm in an attempt to impress Boldwood.
She skillfully took her place in the trading market; and soon she was admired by all – except
Boldwood.

Then one Sunday afternoon Bathsheba
prepared a valentine for Boldwood.
Impetuously, she used a seal on the envelope
which read "Marry Me." Even Bathsheba could
hardly imagine "that the dark and silent shape
upon which she had so carelessly thrown a
seed was a hotbed of tropic intensity"; and his
reaction was indeed intense. The elder gentleman now became a virtual slave to his new-
found feelings. When spring arrived, the
conservative Boldwood confronted Bathsheba
in the fields and proposed marriage. Though
she would not agree to anything, Gabriel and
the rest of the workers considered her as good
as married.

Later that season, the sheep broke their
fence and ate fresh clover. They would die if
not quickly treated, but only Gabriel knew how
to cure them. Bathsheba sent a note demanding
that he come. He replied that he would not
until he was addressed more courteously.
Desperately, she asked again. When he did
come, and the sheep were saved, Bathsheba
"smiled on him . . . "

At shearing time, Gabriel Oak was content to go about his work in the presence of
Bathsheba. But Boldwood once again interrupted his happiness, petitioning Bathsheba to be
his wife.

One evening, while she inspected the
farm, Bathsheba met Sergeant Troy, full of flattery and offering gifts. This soldier was "moderately truthful toward men, but to women lied
like a Cretin." Bathsheba fell for Troy "in the
way that only self-reliant women love when
they abandon their self-reliance." Gabriel, fearing for Bathsheba, tried to dissuade her, but she
would not listen. And Boldwood was almost
beside himself with jealousy and anger upon
hearing Bathsheba confess her love for Troy.

Soon the two suitors met. Boldwood at
first tried to bribe the soldier into leaving
Bathsheba for Fanny. But when Troy told him
that he had to marry Bathsheba in order to preserve her honor, Boldwood offered him money
to do so. With a mocking grin Troy accepted
the money, went into Bathsheba's house, then
returned and handed Boldwood a newspaper
account telling of the couple's marriage, weeks

© 1991, Compact Classics, Inc.

before. Roaring with laughter, he then flung the bag of coins out the door.

Troy proudly hosted the fall harvest supper, where all the men but Gabriel became drunk. Oak and Bathsheba spent that night together securing the grain from a sudden storm.

In contrast to Oak's devotion to her, Bathsheba quickly found that Troy was nothing more than an unreliable spendthrift and a gambler. One evening the couple came upon a terribly frail woman unknown to Bathsheba. It was Fanny. Troy spoke with her privately, gave her the little money he had, and agreed to meet her at a later time. Then he left her there; and Fanny, in terrible pain and exhaustion, trudged several miles to a poorhouse shelter.

That night the couple quarrelled. Troy spitefully revealed that he cared for another; his love for Bathsheba had faded. Then he stormed out of the house.

The next day, Bathsheba learned from some neighbors that the poor woman they had met on the road the night before had died at the poorhouse. And not knowing that she had been Troy's lover, she compassionately had the encoffined body brought to Weatherbury Farm for burial. Gabriel sensed the truth about Fanny and Troy's relationship, and, to spare Bathsheba from pain, he rubbed out a portion of the notation on the top of the coffin which read, "Fanny Robin and child."

But rumors, fear and loneliness got the better of Bathsheba. Suspecting that the coffin held some secret, she lifted its lid and discovered the certain identity of her husband's lover – and their baby. At that moment, in walked Troy, still unaware of Fanny's death. When he gazed into the coffin, he was shocked. He sank to his knees and reverently kissed the woman's lifeless lips. "Kiss me too, Frank – Kiss me!" cried Bathsheba. But the soldier pushed her away: "I will not kiss you!"

Troy carefully prepared Fanny's grave. He also made arrangements for a large tombstone to be carved, bearing the inscription "Erected by Francis Troy in Beloved Memory of Fanny Robin." The tragedy had almost managed to soften his heart; but when he returned to the cemetery the following morning to finish the task, he found a rainstorm had ravaged the grave site. "To find that Providence, far from helping him into a new course . . . actually jeered his first trembling and critical attempt in that kind, was more than nature could bear." Troy fled from the village in anguish. When he reached the seaboard, he disrobed to take a swim. The strong current nearly overwhelmed him, but fortunately a boat came to his rescue.

Meanwhile, a passerby found the Sergeant's clothes on the beach, and it was soon concluded by all that Troy had drowned. Taking advantage of this belief, he sailed to America, away from his troubles.

Bathsheba, though relieved by her husband's absence, was not convinced that he had drowned. Boldwood urged her to agree to marry him seven years hence, when Troy would be legally declared dead.

As Christmas approached, Boldwood prepared a lavish party for the neighborhood. At the gathering, Bathsheba gave in to her host's advances and formally announced that, if Troy failed to return, she would marry Boldwood. Just then there was a knock at the door and in burst Troy. When he caught Bathsheba by the arm to take her home, she fainted. Then a deafening noise filled the room: Boldwood had drawn a gun and discharged a bullet into Troy's chest. He then turned the gun on himself; but a farm-worker shoved it aside just in time. "There is another way for me to die," Boldwood declared calmly. He kissed Bathsheba's pale hand and marched out of the building toward the jailhouse, later to be confined for life in an institution.

Time passed. Bathsheba took ill and was nursed back to health by Oak, the caretaker of her farm. One day Oak told Bathsheba of his plans to go away to America. When she voiced her disappointment and her need for his help, he explained that it was precisely because of her vulnerability that he should go. "It broke upon her at length as a great pain that her last old disciple was about to forsake her . . ."

Bathsheba hurried to Oak's quarters. Finally admitting her love, she asked him to become the head master of Weatherbury Farm. And plans were soon made for "the most private, secret plainest wedding that it is possible to have."

Commentary:

Born and raised in rural Dorset, Thomas Hardy observed the disappearing lifestyles of his farmer, shepherd and artisan neighbors. Well-known as a naturalist, a musician and a poet, his novel is, at once, earthy, musical and poetic.

Hardy spent much of his life trying to reconcile his religious background with the discrepancies he felt were evident in nature. In an age of Victorian prudishness, he was often censored for being too descriptive – especially where sexual matters were concerned.

Far From the Madding Crowd (originally written in serial form for a newspaper) is not as fatalistic as Hardy's later works. Here he leans less towards the philosophy that all things eventually crumble into nothingness, offering up a more "happy ending" story. Though its outcome could be considered contrived, the plot is woven with skill, leaving us always anticipating when it will pick up and proceed with another thread. And the authenticity of Hardy's characters and plot leads us to the novel's logical conclusion.

JULIUS CAESAR

by
William Shakespeare
(1564 - 1616)

Type of work: Tragic drama

Setting: Rome; 44 B.C.

Principal characters:

Julius Caesar, popular Roman general and statesman

Brutus, a prominent and devout Roman, and close friend to Caesar

Cassius, a conspiring enemy of Caesar

Marcus Antonius, Caesar's supporter, a brilliant politician

Story Overview:

Rome was in an uproar. General Julius Caesar had just returned after having defeated his rival, Pompey. His many military triumphs had made him the most powerful man in Rome. The commoners – blindly cheering whoever was in power – flocked into the streets to hail him.

As Caesar passed through the city, a soothsayer caught his attention and called out. "Beware the Ides of March." But the general ignored the warning; he was too busy refusing the crown offered to him by his compatriot and fellow politician, Marcus Antonius. This humble denial of power fanned within the masses an even greater devotion to their beloved Caesar.

Meanwhile, among the throng stood Cassius, Caesar's avowed political opponent, and Brutus, the general's personal friend. Envious of Caesar's growing popularity, Cassius probed to discover where Brutus' deepest sympathies lay. He voiced a concern he had: Caesar was becoming overly "ambitious." Unless something was done to check his fame, he would soon seize all power for himself. This could, effectively, turn the Roman Republic into a dictatorship. Cassius then apprised Brutus of a plot he had hatched: He and a band of other prominent Romans were planning to assassinate Caesar. Was Brutus willing to join in the conspiracy?

Brutus admitted that he shared the same inner concern: "I do fear the people choose Caesar for their king." But still Brutus hesitated to involve himself in such a plot. After all, he dearly loved and admired Caesar. Even so, he couldn't deny that Caesar's rapid rise to power constituted a potential threat to the Republic. Brutus promised Cassius that he would consider the matter, but would withhold his decision until the following day.

The dilemma weighed upon Brutus throughout the night: should he aid in the killing of his beloved friend Caesar, or should he sit by and watch as Caesar destroyed the State?

The plotting band, hoping to gain the support of the highly respected Brutus, paid him an early morning visit. Referring to Caesar as an "immortal god," presenting false evidence of his intentions, and playing on Brutus' immense love for Rome, Cassius finally prevailed on him to help see to the man's death; Brutus agreed to take part in his friend's assassination, to "think of him as a serpent's egg, which, hatched, would as his kind, grow mischievous, and kill him in the shell." Assassination – a certain "righteous treason" – Brutus reluctantly decided, was justified under the circumstances.

Caesar had announced that he would appear before a vast crowd at the Capitol the next morning – the Ides of March. There the conspirators planned to attack and dagger him to death.

After an eery night, filled with reports of gaping graves and wandering ghosts throughout the city, Caesar set out early toward the Capitol, despite three separate warnings: an oracle, the self same soothsayer from before, and finally, his wife, Calpurnia, who experienced a violent and horrible dream, all prophesied that his life was in jeopardy.

As predicted, while Caesar stood addressing the multitude, his conspirators surrounded him and stabbed him, one by one. As Brutus finally stepped forward to thrust his dagger into his friend's side, Caesar whispered, "Et tu, Brute?" ("You too, Brutus?"). The great general then fell dead from twenty-three knife wounds.

The onlooking Romans were stunned and horrified, and Brutus immediately arranged for a public funeral where he could placate the masses by justifying the assassination. Then the conspirators bathed their hands in Caesar's blood and marched through the marketplace, brandishing their weapons over their heads, crying, "Peace, freedom, and liberty!"

At the funeral, Brutus sought to convince the angry mourners why it was requisite that Caesar die. Despite his love for Caesar, he frankly and honestly felt that he had been forced to kill him in order to save Rome from dictatorship. "Not that I loved Caesar less, but that I loved Rome more," he began.

As Caesar loved me, I weep for him; as he was fortunate, I rejoice at it; as he was valiant, I honour him; but, as he was ambitious, I slew

him. There are tears, for his love; joy, for his fortune; honour, for his valor; and death for his ambition . . . as I slew my best lover for the good of Rome, I have the same dagger for myself when it shall please my country to need my death.

His eloquence won over the heart of every Roman in the throng. They forgave Brutus and even cried, "Let him be Caesar!" But then, ill-advisedly, Brutus invited Marcus Antonius, Caesar's right-hand man, to address the crowd. Though Antonius had pretended at the time to tolerate the conspirators and accept their action, in fact, he regarded them as "butchers," and secretly vowed to avenge the murder. Antonius rose to deliver an even more brilliant and impassioned speech, in which he defended Caesar and forcefully, yet indirectly, condemned Brutus:

Friends, Romans, countrymen, lend me your ears; I come to bury Caesar, not to praise him. The evil that men do lives after them, the good is oft interred with their bones; so let it be with Caesar.
The noble Brutus hath told you Caesar was ambitious; If it were so, it was a grievous fault, and grievously hath Caesar answer'd it, here, under leave of Brutus and the rest . . . . For Brutus is an honourable man; so are they all, all honourable men.
Come I to speak in Caesar's funeral. He was my friend, faithful and just to me: But Brutus says he was ambitious: And Brutus is an honourable man. He [Caesar] hath brought many captives home to Rome, whose ransoms did the general coffers fill; Did this in Caesar seem ambitious? When that the poor have cried, Caesar hath wept; ambition should be made of sterner stuff: Yet Brutus says he was ambitious; And Brutus is an honourable man. You all did see that on the Lupercal I thrice presented him a kingly crown, which he did thrice refuse: was this ambition? Yet Brutus says he was ambitious; And, surely, he is an honourable man . . .

Antonius' listeners were so moved by his words that they now turned in rage against Brutus, driving him and his cohorts from the city. Then Antonius, with the help and encouragement of his friend, Octavian, an adopted relative of Caesar's, raised an army to hunt down the confederates.

But Brutus, having fled to Sardis, mustered his own army to counter this attack. Joined by Cassius and other insurgents, he determined to meet Antonius' troops at Phillipi.

The night before the battle, however, everything went askew for Brutus and his allies. Cassius and Brutus quarrelled constantly over military strategy; then, news came that Brutus' wife, ashamed by her hus-

band's actions, had killed herself at Rome; and, if this were not enough, Brutus received a visit to his tent from an alarming guest: none other than the Ghost of Caesar himself. The tide of fortune had long turned against the conspirators; they were soundly defeated the next day. In the heat of battle, Cassius, rather than be captured, took his life with his own sword, while calling up slain Caesar's spirit with the words: "Caesar, thou art revenged, even with the sword that killed thee." Brutus, seeing Cassius' body, likewise sensed the presence of Caesar's ghost, and cried, "O Julius Caesar, thou art mighty yet!"

When Brutus found his army surrounded, he begged that his men kill him. They refused. The commander then ordered a servant to hold his sword and to avert his face. Brutus ran onto the sword and died an agonizing death.

Before returning to Rome, Octavian, the future emperor, along with Caesar's loyal friend Antonius, paid tribute to Brutus; for here was a man, struggling in the midst of a tragic clash between two great loyalties, who, though deceived, had proved with his own blood and the blood of a friend he loved, his unconquerable devotion to his country. "This was the noblest Roman of them all . . ."

Commentary:

The reader cannot study Julius Caesar with an eye to learning Roman history. As usual, Shakespeare significantly alters actual sequences and events. For instance, the play is compressed into six days' time, while the events, as recorded in history, took place over the space of three years.

The play's central figure turns out to be not Julius Caesar at all, but Brutus, who (like Hamlet) feels compelled to commit a murder for the sake of a principle. All his life noble Brutus had been faithful; and through a labyrinthine tangle of plots, politics, and power bids, he had distinguished himself for his integrity, honor, and courage, so that, even after his defeat, his enemies recognize him as their moral superior.

Aside from the political intrigue of the plot, the play is filled with brilliant speeches, timeless both for their declamatory techniques and for the passions they reflect and evoke. Read from Cassius' speech as he fumes over Caesar's faults; or turn to the touching plea of Brutus' wife for her husband to surrender and return home to her. And certainly, the two speeches delivered by Brutus and Antonius at the funeral are classics in oratory.

TO KILL A MOCKINGBIRD

by
Harper Lee
(1926 -   )

Type of work: Symbolic drama

Setting: Southern Alabama; early 1930's.

Principal characters:

Atticus Finch, an attorney and single parent

Scout (Jean Louise Finch), his daughter, a young six-year old tomboy (and the story's narrator)

Jem (Jeremy Finch), Scout's older brother

Arthur "Boo" Radley, a mysterious, reclusive neighbor

Tom Robinson, Atticus' Negro client

Story Overview:

When Jem was nearly 13 years old his arm was badly broken at the elbow. After it healed and Jem was assured that he could still play football, his arm never bothered him – though it always remained shorter than the right, and hung at a funny angle. Years later, Jem and his sister, Scout, still talked about the accident and the events leading up to it. They finally agreed it had all started the summer when they tried to get Arthur "Boo" Radley to come out of his house.

Jem and Scout lived in Maycomb, Alabama, a drowsy, isolated town where everyone knew everyone. Their mother had died when Scout was two years old. Calpurnia, a Negro cook, took care of them and taught them tolerance that took them beyond the rigid prejudices of Maycomb society. Their wise father, an attorney, Atticus Finch, played with them and read them stories. In fact, Scout learned to read before going to school – which later caused trouble with her teacher, who didn't think early reading fit into proper educational theory.

During the summer when Scout was six and Jem was ten, the children became fascinated with the Radley place next door. Most of the community's young people believed the house was haunted. At night children would cross the street rather than walk in front of the Radley house. Nuts that fell from the Radley pecan tree into the school yard were never eaten; surely, Radley nuts would kill you. A baseball hit into the Radley yard was a lost ball. Scout and Jem raced past the property on their way to or from school. The only person seen going in and out of the dwelling was old Nathan Radley, "the meanest man ever God blew breath into," according to Calpurnia.

But inside the weathered home also lived "Boo," Nathan's younger brother. No one had seen Boo for the past twenty years. It was said that he had gotten "into trouble" all those years ago and had been imprisoned in the house ever since – first by his now dead father and then by Nathan.

All that summer Scout and Jem bravely assailed the Radley home, trying to get a glimpse of Boo. They never saw him; but they did see evidence of his existence. On one occasion, Jem's torn pants (lost on a wire fence while escaping from the Radley yard) were returned to him – mended. Another night, when a fire forced the Finches out of their house, Scout, shivering in the cold, found a blanket suddenly thrust around her shoulders. "We'd better keep . . . the blanket to ourselves," Atticus gently said. "Someday, maybe, Scout can thank him for covering her up." "Thank who?" Scout asked. "Boo Radley," replied her father. "You were so busy looking at the fire you didn't know it when he put the blanket around you."

Atticus finally ordered his two children to stop harassing Arthur: "What Mr. Radley did was his own business. If he wanted to come out, he would. If he wanted to stay inside his own house he had the right to stay inside free from the attention of inquisitive children."

Through the next fall and winter, objects began to mysteriously appear in the knot-hole of a tree on the corner of the Radley property: gum, then twine, a carved soap sculpture, Indian-head pennies, and other treasures – gifts clearly intended for Scout and Jem. Boo became even more of a puzzle.

The following summer, trouble cropped up over Atticus' recent appointment as defense counsel for Tom Robinson, a Negro accused of raping a white girl, Mayella Violet Ewell. The Ewells were the lowest family in Maycomb society. But Mayella was white and Tom was black: no matter how trashy the girl might be, her honor had to be upheld against a Negro. What angered many of the townspeople most was Atticus's attempt to truly defend Tom. Atticus and his children had several threats aimed at pressuring them to let things stay as they'd always been in the South. But Atticus felt Tom was innocent, and he would do all he could to prove it. "Every lawyer gets at least one case in his lifetime that affects him personally," he told Scout. Nevertheless, he had to be realistic. They would probably lose, he explained, because they had been "licked a hundred years before they had even started"; but that was no reason not to try. Atticus then extracted a promise from Scout not to fight her friends at school – a difficult promise to keep. She heard her father called "nigger-lover," and she herself, for the first time in her life, was labeled a coward. But Scout stayed true to her word; her father rarely asked for favors.

The day of Tom Robinson's trial dawned

hot and droopy, but it still seemed everyone in Maycomb was packed into the courthouse. Sheriff Heck Tate was the first witness. He testified that on answering a summons from her father, he had found Mayella at her home, her head bloodied, bruises on her arms and neck, and her right eye blackened. She claimed to have been beaten and raped by Tom Robinson. Sheriff Tate added that he personally felt Mayella had been battered by a left-handed person; her principal wounds were on her right side.

The next witness, Robert E. Lee Ewell, Mayella's ne'er-do-well father, described coming home to find Tom attacking his daughter. He had run Tom off, he said, and fetched the sheriff. Just before Mr. Ewell left the stand, Atticus demonstrated to the jury the fact that Bob Ewell was left-handed.

Then Mayella Ewell testified. Through careful questioning, Atticus was able to paint for the jury the type of life Mayella led. The welfare check never went far enough (her father drank most of it up); her many younger brothers and sisters were always dirty and sick; there was never enough food or clothes, and the family rummaged through the dump to find their belongings and food. Mayella was a lonely girl trying to make the most of a miserable situation.

The final witness was the defendant himself, Tom Robinson. As he took the oath, it became obvious to all that his left arm was totally useless. It had been mutilated in a farming accident. This gentle hired-hand could never have beaten up Mayella Ewell.

Atticus concluded his closing statement using Thomas Jefferson's words – "all men are created equal." All men aren't created equal, he argued. One individual may be faster than another; some people are gifted beyond the scope of most men. But in one arena this country presumes that all men are created equal: in their rights before a court of law.

Despite the many hours the jury spent deliberating, Tom Robinson was declared guilty. Though Atticus tried to describe that they would probably win when the case was appealed to a higher court, Tom was left without hope. Only a few weeks later, as he tried to escape from jail, he was shot and killed.

But the episode was not yet closed. Bob Ewell's anger still smoldered. Atticus Finch had made a fool of him, and he publicly vowed revenge.

School started that autumn, and life slipped back into the ordinary. For Halloween, the ladies of Maycomb decided to produce an original pageant at the elementary school, and Scout was assigned the role of a walking, talking ham, ingloriously costumed in chicken wire and brown paper. After the pageant, she waited, humiliated, backstage with Jem until everyone else had left. Then the two started for home.

It was dark, and Scout couldn't see much anyway because of her costume – but she could hear. Someone was following them! As they started running, suddenly someone seized Scout and she fell. After a brief, frenzied scuffle, the children dashed on toward the house. This time Scout felt Jem jerked backwards to the ground. More scuffling, then a dull, crunching sound – and Jem screamed.

"As Scout groped toward Jem, she was grabbed and her breath was slowly squeezed out of her. Suddenly the attacker lurched back, twitched and fell. Scout heard someone breathing heavily, and then a violent sobbing and coughing." This someone picked Jem up and staggered down the street to the Finch's home.

After Sheriff Tate had surveyed the scene of the fight, he reported to Atticus: "Bob Ewell's lyin' on the ground under that tree down yonder with a kitchen knife stuck up under his ribs. He's dead, Mr. Finch."

As the household calmed down that night and Scout was reassured that Jem would live, she suddenly realized that a stranger was standing behind the door – a man so white he looked as if he never saw the sun, his cheeks thin and hollow, his eyes colorless, and his hair disarranged and dead-looking. At last Scout had met Arthur Radley. "Hi Boo," she said, just as she always imagined greeting him.

According to Heck Tate, dragging shy Boo Radley into the limelight of a murder trial would be "as sinful as killing a mockingbird." There would be no trial. Heck Tate's report would read that Ewell had fallen on his knife.

Boo Radley hardly ever left his home. But one October night, when his friends, the children he had watched so frequently from his window, needed him, he came. "Thank you for my children, Arthur," said Atticus Finch as Scout turned to walk Boo home.

Commentary:

Upon receiving an air rifle for Christmas, Jem had been counseled by his father never to kill a mockingbird. It would be a sin because they "don't do one thing but make music for us to enjoy."

To Kill a Mockingbird tells of the gradual ethical awakening of Scout Finch and her brother Jem. Slowly they become aware of the difference between truth and gossip, and learn that people and things are often both more and less than what they seem; that kind, easy-going neighbors can be twisted by prejudice and convention. After the Halloween attempt on their lives, Jem and Scout finally see that the fear and ignorance behind their own harassment of gentle Boo Radley was not so different in essence from the suspicion and scapegoating that led to the killing of Tom. To tease Boo was "as shameful as killing a mockingbird."

OEDIPUS REX

by
Sophocles I
(c. 496 - 406 B.C.)

Type of work: Tragic, poetic Greek drama

Setting: Thebes, a city of ancient Greece

Principal characters:
Oedipus, King of Thebes
Jocasta, his mother . . . and finally his wife
Teiresias, a blind prophet
Creon, Oedipus' brother-in-law
A Chorus

Play Overview:

[The original 5th-century B.C. Greek audience was assumed to be familiar with the background of the play.] Laius and Jocasta were King and Queen of the Great City of Thebes. But it had been prophesied that their son would grow up to kill Laius, his own father, and then marry Jocasta, his own mother. Fearing the divination's fulfillment, Laius and Jocasta delivered Oedipus, their infant son, to a servant, with orders that he be killed. The servant bore the babe into the wilderness, but couldn't bring himself to carry out the command. Instead, he turned the child over to a Corinthian herdsman, who in turn passed the little boy on to Polybus, King of Corinth – who adopted him as his own. Oedipus was thus raised to believe that he was the natural son of Polybus.

But Oedipus' life began to unravel the day he overheard an oracle repeat to him the unthinkable prophecy: he would someday kill his father and marry his mother. Supposing that Polybus *was* his real father, Oedipus determined to leave Corinth so as not to remain anywhere near Polybus. In his travels, Oedipus came to a place where three roads converged. There he became caught up in a violent argument with a band of travelers. He managed to kill all but one of his attackers, but remained oblivious to the tragic irony of this triumph: among the men he had slain was Laius, his true father.

Later, the oracular prophecies completed their awful and ironic cycle of fulfillment when Oedipus undertook a mission to save Thebes, still acknowledged as his native city, from the predations of a dire female monster, the Sphinx. Of all the unlucky heroes to make the attempt, Oedipus alone was able to answer the riddle that was posed mockingly to all travelers along the Theban roadside by the winged lion-woman: "What goes first on four legs, then on two, and then on three?" The Sphynx had ravenously devoured all those brave and foolhardy souls who regaled her with exotic answers; but Oedipus, with the simple rejoinder "Man," gained the power to finally destroy her. The grateful populace of the city quickly acclaimed him as King, and in time, he met, fell in love with, and married his own mother, Jocasta. Of course Jocasta had no idea that her new young husband was the son she had sent off to be killed as an infant; nor did Oedipus realize that the loathsome prophecy had now at last been fulfilled.

[As the play begins, the story of how Oedipus discovers his "crimes" unfolds.]

In Thebes, a dreadful plague had struck. The citizens assembled to appeal to King Oedipus to curb the disease, and Oedipus reassured them that Creon, Jocasta's brother, had gone to Delphi to ask the great Apollo how the plague might be ended.

When Creon finally returned, he brought startling news: Apollo had declared that the scourge had come upon the city because the very man who had murdered King Laius years before was now a resident of Thebes. Apollo further swore that the plague would endure until the murderer was exposed and exiled from the city.

Oedipus, wholly unaware that he himself was the one who had struck down Laius, vowed to discover the identity of the murderer at all costs:

. . . Now I reign, holding the power which he had held before me, having the selfsame wife and marriage bed – and if his seed had not met barren fortune, we should be linked by offspring from one mother; but as it was, fate leapt upon his head, [and I shall search] to seize the hand which shed that blood.

Oedipus' first step was to call in Teiresias, a blind soothsayer of renowned wisdom. When the King questioned Teiresias as to the identity of Laius' murderer, the prophet first claimed that he did know the man's name, but then hesitated: "I shall never reveal . . . I will not hurt you or me." Still Oedipus pressed, and Teiresias finally relented. "You are the slayer whom you seek," he sadly disclosed; "And dreaded foot shall drive you from this land. You who now see straight shall then be blind." Oedipus, furious at the suggestion of his guilt, berated the prophet, who retorted by insisting that Oedipus was yet blind to the truth and would soon learn of his guilt. Oedipus angrily dismissed the sightless old man, accusing him of conspiring with Jocasta's brother, Creon, to overthrow him.

Afterwards, Jocasta unfolded to Oedipus the complete circumstances about the earlier prophecy, but maintained that it could not have come to pass – Laius had not been killed by his son, but by a band of robbers "at a place where three roads meet."

When Oedipus heard this he was stunned; quietly he told Jocasta how he himself had once killed a man at such a place. For the first time, both mother and son began to suspect that the words of Teiresias might be true.

Their suspicions were soon allayed, however, when a messenger arrived from Corinth with the news that Polybus had died. Oedipus and Jocasta were ecstatic; this meant that the whole chain of prophecy was false; since Oedipus had not killed his own father, there was no reason to believe the oracle's contention that he had also slain Jocasta's first husband. But when the king and queen explained their expressions of joy and relief to the messenger, this man imparted some disquieting news: "Oh, you did not know?" he said, in effect. "Polybus was not your natural father: you were adopted. It was said that a Theban herdsman found you as a baby on a hillside. He gave you to me, and I presented you to the childless King Polybus, who adopted you . "

Oedipus was horrified by this account, and immediately sent for the herdsman, who told him the full story of the servant and child he had dealt with years before. The now aged servant was then called forth. Naturally, he was reluctant to confess the truth; but urged on by Oedipus, he blurted out the tale of how Jocasta and Laius had ordered him to take their infant son into the country and slay him, and how he had not found the heart to do the deed.

At that moment, all the pieces of the puzzle fell into place: Oedipus was the infant of whom they spoke; Jocasta, his wife, was also his mother, who had long ago turned him over to be killed; and the man he had slain at the crossroads was none other than his true father.

At the awful realization that she had actually been an accomplice to the fulfillment of the holy and terrible prophecy she had so diligently sought to thwart, Jocasta rushed to her room. By the time Oedipus broke down the heavily bolted doors, it was too late: he saw his wife – his mother – "hung by her neck, from twisted cords, swinging to and fro." In agony, Oedipus cut down her body, tore the broaches from her clothes, and with them, put out his eyes, screaming,

> No more shall you
> behold the evils I have suffered and done.
> Be dark from now on, since you saw before,
> What you should not,
> and knew not what you should!

Miserable and repentant, Oedipus was led out of Corinth into exile by Creon, who became king in his stead. And the merciless Theban plague at last came to an end.

Commentary:

It would be hard to find a play that has been more universally praised than *Oedipus Rex* ("King Oedipus"). Aristotle considered it the model tragedy, and that opinion has been widely held to the present day. No drama before or since has managed to so successfully combine a rapid, compelling plot, superb characterization, and elegant poetry into such a tight bundle.

The tragedy of *Oedipus Rex* is not so much that Oedipus commits two horrible crimes; after all, he was fated to do so, and committed them unknowingly. It is, rather, that he, like his doomed parents before him, ran headlong into the destiny he was trying to defy, and then compounded his evils by his imperious refusal to believe the prophet's declaration of his guilt. Pride was his downfall. The Greeks had a distinct word for this: "Hubris," a heroically foolish defiance; the feeling that one is beyond the reaches of authority or convention.

Oedipus Rex is notable for its use of dramatic irony: everybody in the audience knows from the start that Oedipus himself is the guilty party he seeks out for punishment. The viewers' enjoyment comes as they see and hear the facts accumulate, bit by bit, until it suddenly dawns on Oedipus that he is his father's murderer. The irony is heightened by blind Teiresias' many tauntings and the chorus' musical references to "seeing the light." Oedipus, though his physical eyes can see, is blind to the truth; and when he finally does come to see the truth, ironically, he blinds himself.

The first and final – and most tragic and triumphant – irony, however, lies in the implicit acknowledgment that the very quality of Hubris (Oedipus' arrogance in defying cosmic and priestly authority, fate and prophecy) is the same quality that enabled him to earlier confront and defeat the Sphinx and to save an oppressed city. Oedipus, then, is a hero who pits his pride against both gods and fate in the mold of Prometheus (whose downfall was caused by his sharing the gift of fire with man) and another heroine, Cassandra, who was cursed with the blessing of prophecy. And indeed, most Greek dramas carry this theme of human paradox.

Perhaps the symbolism of the Sphinx, who haunts the background of *Oedipus Rex* with her simple yet terrible riddle, says all that is necessary: The true enigma of the universe lies not in any exotic intergalactic phenomenon; the greatest mystery begins and ends with man.

UTOPIA

by
Thomas More
(1478-1535)

Type of work: Social and philosophical commentary

Setting: Antwerp; early sixteenth century

Principal characters:
Sir Thomas More, emissary for Henry VIII
Peter Giles, More's friend
Raphael Hythloday, world traveler and witness to Utopia

Book Overview:

Thomas More toured Antwerp on a diplomatic mission for his king, Henry VIII. There, More's friend, Peter Giles, introduced the young ambassador to Raphael Hythloday, an educated sailor who had seen much of the world while voyaging with Amerigo Vespucci. The three of them convened in a garden so that More could question this learned and experienced man. More and Giles both wondered why a man of such wisdom and stature as Raphael had not entered into a king's service. Raphael scoffed at the idea: "The councillors of kings are so wise that they need no advice from others (or at least so it seems to themselves)." Moreover, Raphael opined that most councillors merely bowed to the king's inclinations and were more concerned with maintaining favor than with offering impartial and wise advice.

Raphael also believed that the average king possessed different goals than he himself had; that "most princes apply themselves to warlike pursuits," whereas he had no interest or skill in the acquisition of riches or territory. Raphael asked Giles and More to imagine him before a king, cautioning him that "wars would throw whole nations into chaos, would exhaust the King's treasury and destroy his own people, [and] that a prince should take more care of his people's happiness than of his own." How receptive would the king be to that kind of advice?

More asked Raphael if he had ever been to England; the traveler replied that he had, and then proceeded to relate a story about a discussion he had entered into there with a British lawyer. The lawyer commented that he approved of hanging thieves for their crimes. But Raphael struck up an argument against this form of "justice." The high incidence of theft in England, he claimed, was attributable to the increased sheepherding by wealthy landowners. This new industry had forced the poorer farmers off their land while at the same time boosting the price of goods and feed; and these combined factors had caused a rise in unemployment. Without work or land, many people had turned to a life of crime or to begging. This "policy [of hanging thieves] may have the appearance of justice, but it is really neither just nor expedient." In his view, English society was "first making [people] thieves and then punishing them for it."

Another of Raphael's complaints was that many English noblemen, along with their entourages of lazy friends, "live idly like drones and subsist on the labor of their tenants." Such "wanton luxury" only exacerbated the poverty of the common people.

While More and Giles could understand the justice in Raphael's social criticisms, they were still unable to understand why he would not help rescue society by offering his higher wisdom in the political arena. Raphael replied:

As long as there is private property and while money is the standard of all things, I do not think that a nation can be governed either justly or happily . . . . Unless private property is entirely done away with, there can be no fair distribution of goods, nor can the world be happily governed.

Neither More nor Giles believed that this prerequisite to peace would ever be possible to attain. Raphael was not surprised by their scoffs, but averred that had they traveled with him on the island haven of Utopia, there they would have seen a truly orderly, peaceful society. The two Englishmen then prevailed on Raphael to acquaint them, after their meal, with all the customs and institutions of the Utopians.

Dinner completed, Raphael began his descriptive tour:

First of all, Utopian society was uniform, with all cities sharing the "same language, customs, institutions and laws." Its economy was guided by one fundamental rule: "All the Utopians, men and women alike, work at agriculture." Additionally, everyone worked at a trade of his own choosing, provided the trade proved useful to society. Although every citizen was required to work, each labored only six hours out of twenty-four. While to many such liberal conditions might seem untenable, Raphael pointed out that "the actual number of workers who supply the needs of mankind is much smaller than imagined," considering the many noblemen, beggars and others in contemporary society who produced nothing. For Utopians, the chief aim was to allow everyone enough free time to develop his or her mind.

Food on the island was distributed equally, with the sick tended to first. The rest of the population ate together in vast communal halls. If the people harvested or produced any surplus goods, these were shared with neighboring nations who might be suffering from plague or famine, or else used in trade. The Utopians imported nothing themselves, but traded only for the wherewithal to hire mercenaries in times of war. Rather than store their precious metals in vaults, Utopians used gold and silver to make chamber pots and stools, and "for the chains and fetters of their bondsmen." In this way the citizenry held gold and silver "up to scorn in every way." Idling was despised and never tolerated. No gambling was allowed and there existed no brothels or taverns in which Utopians might while away their time. When Utopia's inhabitants were not working, they were expected to pursue worthwhile activities such as reading and learning, or, if they preferred, to practice their trades. Anyone who proved especially adept at learning was allowed to forego physical labor in order to pursue scholarly work.

Utopia's laws encompassed "no fixed . . . penalties, but the senate [persons elected by the citizenry] fixed the punishment according to the wickedness of the crime." Serious crimes were punished by bondage. If a bondsperson refused to work, he was put to death; if, on the other hand, the slave proved hardworking and repentant, he was freed. The islanders believed that bondage, as a form of punishment, was "more beneficial to the commonwealth," and that the sight of bondage "longer deters other men from similar crimes."

Nothing in Utopia was "so inglorious as the glory won in war." The community would "go to war cautiously and reluctantly," entering into combat for two reasons only: either "to protect their own territory or that of their friends . . . or to free some wretched people from tyrannous oppression." For the most part, when war was deemed necessary they hired mercenaries to do the fighting. If the mercenaries were defeated, then Utopians (men and women alike) would take up arms. In victory, they were "more ready to take prisoners than to make a great slaughter."

In all, Raphael was convinced that Utopian society was far superior to any other he had observed. He added particu-lars concerning Utopian marriage customs (prospective spouses were advised to see each other naked before they were wed, so that each would possess a full knowledge of what he or she was getting), fashion (all dressed in simple attire "fit both for winter and summer, to correspond to their gender and marital status), religious observances, foreign relations, health practices, and rules of the marketplace – each aspect of the island society having as its aim to make life better for everyone. In Raphael's opinion, Utopia was the only commonwealth which could accurately be called a "commonwealth"; all citizens there were treated equally and given equal opportunities and possessions: "When no one owns anything, all are rich."

Thus, Raphael ended his tale of Utopia, and even the practical, conventional Thomas More had to admit that "many things in the Utopian Commonwealth [he] wished . . . to see followed among [his] citizens."

Commentary:

The term "Utopia" has come to mean an idyllic, visionary Shang-ri-la type of community. However, when More derived the term from the Greek, it literally meant "nowhere." In essence, both are correct: Utopia can represent both a mythical, impossible retreat and a great guiding social ideal.

Much of More's book was extracted from and influenced by the *Bible*, especially from the "Christian Humanists" biblical interpretations that formed a vanguard of social criticism in his time. Along with Erasmus, another humanist philosopher, More yearned to change his world for the better. He saw that wanton greed and terrible poverty were often irrevocably bound to one another, and he argued vehemently for the closing of the separation between classes.

More's Utopia, of course, has never been achieved; perhaps it never will be achieved – nor should ever be sought. But this comment on European society in his own times reflects the great challenges that have faced societies throughout history. Tensions born of moral struggles – between power and equality; between work for survival and work to acquire luxury; between creative, joyful leisure and laziness; between the actual and the ideal – these are basic issues for our time and for all times. And More's Utopia embraces and attempts to clarify them all.

FAUST

by
Goethe
(1749 - 1832)

Type of work: Allegorical poetic drama

Setting: Germany; eighteenth century

Principal characters:

    Faust, a scholar who is offered knowledge
       by the Devil

    Mephistopheles (Mephisto, the Devil), the great
       Satanic tempter

    Gretchen (Margaret), a young woman who
       falls in love with Faust

    Martha, Gretchen's neighbor and friend

Play Overview:

In heaven, while angels sang praises to God and his grand creations, heaven and earth, Mephistopheles entered and began to complain about the lot of man on earth. The sinister Mephisto chided God for having given man just enough reason to make him "more brutish than any brute." God asked his adversary if there wasn't anything worthwhile about His creation. "No, Lord," answered Mephistopheles. "I find it still a sorry sight." They argued for some time, until they finally agreed to a wager: with God's permission, Mephisto would attempt to lure the soul of a certain scholar-alchemist named Faust ("who serves you most peculiarly") down with him to hell; God maintained that Faust would and could be saved, despite his proud reliance on reason and sorcery rather than faith.

Meanwhile, on earth, Faust sat at the desk in his dusky den and lamented all of his learning: "I have studied philosophy, jurisprudence and medicine, and worst of all theology, and here I am, for all my lore, the wretched fool I was before. Hence I have yielded to magic to see whether the spirit's mouth and might would bring some mysteries to light." Little by little his melancholy grew. How horribly idle his life had been; reading and thinking were all he had, never knowing the joy of doing.

One Easter morning, Wagner, one of Faust's students, convinced the professor to travel with him to the city to join in the festivities. As Faust and Wagner walked and talked, Faust expressed his indescribable discontent: "Two souls, alas, are dwelling in my breast, and one is striving to forsake his brother." Faust wept openly, begging in prayer that a spirit be sent to lead him to "distant lands." Then, even as Wagner cautioned his mentor not to call upon evil spirits, Faust noticed a black dog following them. He picked up the skinny stray poodle and carried it home.

Alone at his desk, Faust opened his Bible and began his studies. The dog, however, would not stop darting about the house, barking and growling. Eventually the poodle scurried behind the stove, and when he emerged, he had taken the form of Mephistopheles.

The sly Mephisto would answer the scholar's inquiries only through riddles, explaining that he was "part of that force which would do evil evermore, and yet creates the good; I am the spirit that negates." Faust, though, finally divined that he was speaking with the Devil. The two bantered back and forth until Faust could stay awake no longer. As he drifted into sleep, the Devil left, promising to return the following day.

The tempter arrived at dawn, dressed as a nobleman. He implored Faust to don the same attire so that he too could "feel released and free,/ and you would find what life could be." But Faust was too world-weary to even imagine happiness. "Death is desirable, and life I hate," he groaned.

In an attempt to release Faust from this melancholy, Mephisto now offered to be his slave. Faust was wary: "And for my part, what is it you require? . . . Not safely is such servant taken on." Mephisto then presented a proposition: " . . . You shall be the Master, and I Bond,/ and at your nod I'll work incessantly;/ but when we meet beyond,/ then you shall do the same for me." Faust, whose "two souls" had finally torn completely asunder, agreed to the bargain: "Beyond to me makes little matter . . . It is from out this earth my pleasures spring . . ."

Off they flew on the evil one's magic cloak. Their first stop was a tavern, where Mephisto intended to teach his new Master "how to live." He performed miracles for the drinking men (causing wine to flow from the barroom tables) – miracles that ultimately turned to torment them (the sweet wine turned to a fiery, "hellish brew.") But old Faust was unmoved: "Will this absurd swill-cookery/ Charm thirty winters off my back?"

Their next stop was a witch's kitchen, where Faust caught sight of the image of a comely woman in a mirror. "Is so much beauty found on earth?" he raved. Mephisto, pouncing on this first spark of energy and interest, promised Faust that the woman would soon become his wife. He ordered the mischievious hag of the house to mix up a potion; then, while she recited incantations, Faust downed the brew. From that moment, he knew he would never escape the love he felt for the woman in the mirror.

The next day, while wandering the streets, Faust encountered Gretchen, the very beauty whose mirror image had enslaved him. "Get me that girl!" he commanded Mephisto. And, as promised, the servant-Devil arranged for Faust to win Gretchen's virtuous heart with the gift of a luxurious necklace. Soon thereafter, the trusting girl found that she was pregnant with Faust's child.

Now, Gretchen's brother, a soldier named Valentine, vowed revenge against the lover who had dishonored his sister. Inside Gretchen's doorway he waited for the rogue to appear. When Faust arrived and began once again to woo Gretchen, Valentine stepped from the shadows and challeged him with a sword. Only with Mephisto's aid did Faust's sword hit home. Valentine dropped, mortally wounded. "Do not cry for me," were his last words to his anguished sister. "When you threw honor overboard,/ you pierced my heart more than the sword."

Months passed. While Faust and Mephisto partook of wild ribaldry and pleasurably summoned up wicked spirits with their sorcery, Gretchen was suffering scorn, ridicule, and imprisonment. But when Faust came to the knowledge that his beloved had been locked up in a dungeon, to be judged by mere mortals, he cursed his devilish companion: "Treacherous, despicable Spirit! Dog! Abominable monster! Save her! . . . Take me there! She shall be freed!"

The two easily gained entrance into Gretchen's cell, but she refused to leave with them. She confessed that the prison guards had taken her baby from her, "to give me pain." "My peace is gone,/ My heart is sore;/ Can find it never/ And never more," she cried, and threw herself on the mercy and justice of God.

Soon the prison authorities arrived. Mephisto and Faust were forced to flee to avoid capture. As they did, they heard a voice from heaven declare that Gretchen's enduring faith had saved her.

The years went by. Faust was now a great lord, with vast and rich land-holdings, which land he had himself "redeemed from the sea" by building a system of dikes. Nearing the end of his life, he gazed out from his huge palace at the gardens and orchards spreading far into the distance – only to find that he was yet discontent. Even when Mephisto returned from a voyage with much new wealth for Faust, he could not smile. "You spurn good fortune without joy . . . " the Devil observed. "The whole world is in your embrace." No, Faust told his servant; one cottage remained that he did not own – a small lot, within sight of the castle, that belonged to an elderly couple. "Go then, get them out of the way!" he ordered Mephisto.

That night, the Devil and his cohorts returned with the news that the deed was done. "Forgive," they told Faust, "but we had to use force. It burns, you see, a pretty pyre." Faust, now twisting against the pangs of his own guilt, angrily shifted the blame: "Did you not hear me that I bade not robbery but simple trade?" He retired to his garden. There he was seized upon by something hovering above him in the air. Then, out of the midnight blackness came four elderly women – Want, Debt, Care, and Need. Their brother, Death, was also nearby, they explained. Faust inquired of Care what it was she wanted. "Is Care a force you never faced?" she taunted. Haughtily, Faust replied, "Whatever I might crave, I laid my hands on . . . . I stormed through life." But still he had to admit that some inexplicable inner hunger had never been satisfied; and thus Care alone, of the four sister spirits, was able to gain entry into his soul. "The human being is, his life long, blind," she said. "Thus, Faustus, you shall meet your end."

But as precious sight was being drawn from his dying eyes, suddenly it was as though Faust could finally truly see. He called in excitement to his laborers to set forth and complete the work of draining the remaining tidal swamps, so that he might give all the reclaimed lands to his people. "This is the highest wisdom that I own,/ the best that mankind ever knew," he cried, as he raced about blindly.

> Yes – this I hold to with devout insistence,
> Wisdom's last verdict goes to say:
> He only earns both freedom and existence
> Who must reconquer them each day.

Then, in joy, Faust died.

Mephisto rose up, and gloated at his former master's ultimate, inevitable defeat – and at the wretched fate that awaited all men: "Why have eternal creation,/ when all is subject to annihilation?/ Now it is over. What meaning can one see?...'

But just as Mephisto reached to take the prize he had won, a host of angels descended and distracted him while Faust's soul escaped; it was the Devil who would taste defeat. Though Faust had sinned, even so he had struggled towards growth, knowledge, and transcendence. "Whoever strives in ceaseless toil/ Him we may grant redemption . . . " the seraphs sang.

Then, with the Devil still raging, the angelic chorus flew into heaven, "bearing off Faust's immortal part."

Commentary:

The legend of Faust is older than Goethe's version, dating back to the early years of Christianity. The English poet Christopher Marlowe wrote his own version of the play several centuries before Goethe's "Faust" appeared. Later, Wagner would use Goethe's lengthy yet brilliantly written poetic production as the text for an opera.

One idea animates Goethe's "Faust." All human souls are called to exist and struggle within a constant state of "becoming," a lifelong striving towards greater and greater realms of knowledge, action and feeling; and those who stay true to this call, even when they stumble into excesses and error will not go unrewarded by God. In fact, it is by right the Devil's place to blind man, to the end that man might come unto God:

> Man all too easily grows lax and mellow,
> He soon elects repose at any price;
> And so I like to pair him with a fellow
> To play the Deuce, to stir, and to entice.

And as "the Deuce" seducer causes man to fall away from innocence, ignorance and wavering bliss, toward a choice between righteousness and sin, man overcomes himself and achieves his true destiny.

COMPACT

Classics™

LIBRARY #6: Modern Literature

Section A: Popular Nonfiction

6-A1   *Life and Death in Shanghai* by Nien Cheng

6-A2   *The City of Joy* by Dominique Lapierre

6-A3   *Not Without My Daughter* by Betty Mahmoody, with William Hoffer

6-A4   *Blue Highways* by William Least Heat Moon

6-A5   *Hiroshima* by John Hersey

Section B: Worlds Away

6-B1   *One Hundred Years of Solitude* by Gabriel Garcia Marquez

6-B2   *The Painted Bird* by Jerzy Kosinski

6-B3   *Steppenwolf* by Hermann Hesse

6-B4   *The Handmaid's Tale* by Margaret Atwood

6-B5   *Lord of the Flies* by William Golding

Section C: Majorities of One

6-C1   *Henderson the Rain King* by Saul Bellow

6-C2   *My Name is Asher Lev* by Chaim Potok

6-C3   *Invisible Man* by Ralph Ellison

6-C4   *Ceremony* by Leslie Marmon Silko

6-C5   *Their Eyes Were Watching God* by Zora Neale Hurston

Section D: Favorite Fictional Selections

6-D1   *The Joy Luck Club* by Amy Tan

6-D2   *The Shell Seekers* by Rosamunde Pilcher

6-D3   *The Sound of Waves* by Yukio Mishima

6-D4   *The Stories of John Cheever* by John Cheever

6-D5   *The Chosen* by Chaim Potok

LIFE AND DEATH IN SHANGHAI

by Nien Cheng , Grove Press, New York, N.Y., 1986

Life and Death in Shanghai is a true, hauntingly human story based on one woman's experiences during China's Cultural Revolution. The author, Nien Cheng, met her husband while going to school in England. They returned home to China in 1939.

When the Communist Party defeated the Kuomintang government and infiltrated the nation ten years later, Nien Cheng and her husband, a Kuomintang diplomat, chose to remain in China and support the new Communist regime. With the approval of the newly appointed government, Mr. Cheng became general manager of Shell Oil International's Shanghai office. After he died of cancer in 1957, his wife went to work for Shell, where she acted as staff manager and as a liaison between the Shell labor union and the company's general manager. At that time, Nien Cheng was the only woman in Shanghai occupying a senior position with a large foreign company. Then, in 1966, Shell closed its Shanghai office and turned over the company's assets to a Chinese government agency, to provide Shell's non-senior staff with continued employment and pensions.

That same year, the Cultural Revolution was launched by Mao Ze Dong. Mao assembled the Red Guard and gave them the mandate to rid the country of the "Four Olds": old culture, old customs, old habits, and old ways of thinking. It was left up to the Red Guards to define just what "old" might mean; and define they did, with a vengeance. Street names were changed to reflect the revolutionary movement. Shops catering to the rich were destroyed. Sofas, innerspring mattresses, cosmetics, and clothes that reflected anything remotely capitalistic were burned. Names of stores were changed, and Mao's picture was hung in every store window. Mao's Red Guards ruled the streets. They would stop passersby who were not dressed and groomed in "laborer-drab" and ridicule them for their "western" ways: "Why do you wear shoes with pointed toes? Why do you wear slacks with narrow legs?" The Guards, young and idealistic, were leading a cause that would eventually set the country on a backward course.

Inevitably, the shouts arose: *Down with Tao Feng (Shell's chief accountant in China)! Down with the running dog of the Imperialists, Tao Feng! . . . Down with the capitalist class! Long live the Great Proletarian Cultural Revolution! Long live our Great Leader Chairman Mao!* "Reform" had taken the place of sanity.

Nien Cheng and her twenty-four-year-old daughter, Meiping, an actress at the Shanghai film studio, found themselves in the middle of this fevered chaos. Nien was an obvious target of persecution because of her foreign and capitalist connections.

One day, the fanatical Red Guards invaded and ransacked Nien's elegant Shanghai home. Shredding ancient Chinese paintings and smashing glass cabinets lined with antique porcelain pieces, inlaid ivory and jade figures, they shouted, "These things belong to the old culture . . . . Chairman Mao taught us, 'If we don't destroy, we cannot establish' . . . " Then they accused Nien of being an enemy of the People's Communist Government. The revolutionary "witch-hunt" had caught up with her.

Most "old" and foreign books were destroyed during these years by Mao's callous peasant armies of henchmen. Instead, everyone was given for study a copy of Mao's essays and sayings. During this Cultural Revolution, China closed its doors to the rest of the world and persecuted the educated and anyone who had dealt with foreigners. It was Mao's philosophy that the professional and intellectual classes must be humbled. The favored treatment they had traditionally been accorded now dictated that they be forcibly "equalized." So, learned, accomplished people were transported to remote provinces to labor in the fields. And because of Nien Cheng's senior position with Shell, her foreign education, and her affluent life-style, she, with others like her, was forced to spend long hours facing hostile accusations at the "struggle meetings" held to condemn the enemies of Communism.

"Are you going to confess?" asked Nien's interrogators.

"I have never done anything against the Chinese people and government," she rejoined. "The Shell office was here because the Chinese government wanted it to be here. The order to allow Shell to maintain its Shanghai office was issued by the State Council and signed by no less a person than Premier Zhou Enlai. Shell is full of goodwill for China and the Chinese people and always observed the laws and regulations scrupulously. It is not Shell's policy to meddle in politics . . . "

" . . . Even though I spoke in a loud voice, no one in the room could hear a complete sentence, for everything I said was drowned by angry shouts and screams of 'Confess! Confess!'"

Nien Cheng was thrown into prison because she would not falsely admit to being a "spy of the imperialists." During the Cultural Revolution, jailed inmates were coerced to denounce their relatives and break relations with them. Neighbors, friends and family members were pressured into giving false statements just so they themselves would not be imprisoned. At one time, even Nien's brother passed on lies about her to protect himself.

Still, Nien Cheng determined to tell the truth, notwithstanding the fact that a false confession could lighten her sentence. For six-and-a-half years she endured solitary confinement. "I've never committed a crime in my whole life," she protested.

"If you have not committed a crime, why are you locked up in prison? Your being here proves you have committed a crime," was the appalling logic used against her.

Because of her strong will and character, Nien survived. While in prison she was supplied only with Mao's books and Communist newspaper propaganda ("*Footpath News*") to read. But from the attitudes of the guards and from what she read between the lines, she gathered that political turmoil was growing within the party. (In fact, a struggle was building between senior party officials: Mao, Prime Minister Zhou Enlai, and Mao's wife, Jiang Qing, who was part of the Gang of Four which tried to gain power when Mao died.)

Nien Cheng's treatment during her imprisonment was modified by this left-to-right swing of the political pendulum. The authorities tried one sort of abuse and interrogation tactic after another to force a confession, but nothing could bend her. Kept in a tiny, cold, damp cell, she suffered bouts of pneumonia. Likewise weakening and disheartening were the lack of nutritious food, fresh air, and sunshine. But the "prospect of losing my ability to think clearly frightened me more than the fact that my hair was falling out by the handful, my gums bled, and I had lost a great deal of weight. The psychological effect of total isolation was also taking its toll. Often my mood was one of despair . . ."

Nien devised a regimen of discreet exercises to sustain her physical health. She could not afford to allow the guards to see her moving around with a purpose. For mental exercise, she turned to the dynasty poetry she had memorized as a girl – and learned Mao's essays by rote. Forced to stand for hours, day after day reading Mao's works aloud, Nien's legs wobbled and her dry throat reduced her voice to a hoarse whisper:

"Speak clearly! Are you going to surrender?" the well-dressed man asked.

I made a great effort. With all my strength I managed to say, "Not guilty!"

"You will surely be shot!" He left the room . . .

Unable to break Nien's will, the authorities finally released her in 1973. "It's high time isn't it? Six and a half years is a long time to lock up an innocent person," she scolded. Her spirit was still unbroken.

After obtaining a job as a teacher, Nien Cheng's next seven years were nearly as demanding as her years in prison. She learned that her daughter had died of mysterious causes in the interim. Corruption was everywhere, especially among government officials. China had become increasingly backward.

Nien was constantly shadowed by government agents. She became increasingly concerned that her maid, close friends, and even some of her students were government informants. Caution was her watchword for everything she said and did.

Over time, Nien conceded that she would have to leave her homeland. However, her exit, she deduced, must be timed to coincide with changes in political climate. The time was not right, until Den Xioaping was put back in power and his open-door policies were reinstated. In 1980, Nien Cheng sadly fled China and eventually moved to Washington D.C., where she wrote *Life and Death in Shanghai*. "God knows how hard I tried to remain true to my country," she concluded in anguished understatement. "But I failed utterly through no fault of my own."

THE CITY OF JOY

by Dominique Lapierre, Warner Books, Inc., New York, N.Y., 1985

After years of living on the Calcutta sidewalks as a rickshaw puller, Hasari Pal finally found a room for himself and his family in the slums, near the lodgings of Stephan Kovalski, a Polish priest. Racked with the "red fever" of tuberculosis, Hasari spent entire nights telling Kovalski about his life and his dreams. His whole tragic passage – from proud farmer to starving refugee to human horse – was chronicled. Then, knowing the sickness was about to kill him, Hasari "pre-sold" his bones to a medical research supplier in order to provide a dowry for his daughter. He celebrated at her wedding festival for only a few hours before slipping away to die. Before dawn of the next day, the bone collectors knocked on his door.

The City of Joy touches on life in one of the poorest slums of Calcutta. It highlights people facing almost unbelievable adversities day to day, who still find ways to be happy. Based on true stories as told by Dominique Lapierre, who lived in this Calcutta ghetto for two years, the book covers a wide range of experiences and emotions, mingled with graphic portrayals of both heartbreak and jubilation. Lapierre relates his own experience and reports on "man's capacity to . . . survive every possible tragedy":

During this long, difficult, and sometimes painful research, I had to adjust to all sorts of situations. I learned how to live with rats, scorpions, and insects; to survive on a few spoons of rice and two or three bananas a day; to queue up for hours for the latrines; to wash with less than a pint of water; to light a match in the monsoon; to share my living quarters with a group of eunuchs. Before being adopted by the inhabitants of the slum, I had to learn their customs, experience their fears and plights, share their struggles and hopes. This certainly was one of the most extraordinary experiences that a writer could live. It changed my life. Living with the heroic inhabitants of the City of Joy completely transformed my sense of priorities and my assessment of the true values of life. After this confrontation with the real issues of existence – hunger, disease, total absence of work . . . I no longer fight for things like a parking place when I return to Europe or America. Sharing for all these months the lives of a population who has less than ten cents each per day to survive on also taught me the real value of things . . . [and] the beauty of sharing with others. For two years nothing was asked of me but always given. The generosity of my friends in the City of Joy showed me that "everything that is not given is lost."

Lapierre shares his stories through two main characters. The first is Hasari Pal, the eldest son of a Hindu farming family struck down by drought with the charge to feed his wife and children, as well as his parents, brothers and sisters. Hasari abandons his rice farm in Bengal, hoping of locating work in Calcutta. The Pal family lives on the streets, without even enough money to feed themselves, let alone pay for shelter. To survive, Hasari's children are forced to search through rubbish for scraps of leftover food.

At first, the only income Hasari earns is from selling his blood; but the money he receives from each transaction is only enough to buy a bag of rice and some bananas – and, of course, he only has so much blood to sell.

With the help of a friend, Hasari finally finds employment pulling a rickshaw through the narrow streets of the city. However, because of "street politics," he is actually able to keep only a small portion of the receipts from his hard work. Even in these pathetic circumstances, Hasari still shows great love and compassion for his fellow men.

Stephan Kovalski, the book's second protagonist, is a Polish-Catholic priest who withdraws from mainstream society to live with Calcutta's lepers and other untouchables. He packs up his few belongings and migrates to the City of Joy, committed to "seek out the poorest of the poor and the disinherited in the places where they are, to share their life, and to die with them." Because Kovalski is so committed to sharing, his meager food rations are generally given away to the children who constantly follow him.

Once, a shoe-shine boy shyly approached the smiling priest. " . . . But a smile does not fill an empty stomach," Kovalski noted. He foraged in his knapsack and offered the boy the banana he had earlier promised himself. "At that rate I was condemned to die of starvation very rapidly," he observes wryly to LaPierre.

Kovalski considers his Listening Committee for Mutual Aid as his most "beneficial" gift to the City of Joy; a place where the poor can go to be heard: "The idea was so revolutionary . . . " The poor and outcasts now "take charge of themselves."

One day Kovalski paid a visit to a leper compound at the invitation of one of the residents, Anouar, a disfigured cripple with "a smile that was difficult to understand in the light of his suffering."

"Well, Stephan Daddah ("Big Brother"), are you well today?" Anouar asked in greeting.

"Coming from a human wreck groveling in the mud, the question seemed so incongruous . . . " recalls Kovalski. "I had formed the habit of stooping down to him and grasping the stump of his right hand with my hands. The first time I did it the gesture took him so much by surprise that he surveyed the people around him with an expression of triumph, as if to say, 'You see, I'm a man just like you. The Daddah is shaking my hand.' "

As Anouar guided Father Kovalski to administer aid to his friends in need, the priest was appalled by the utterly foul stench, by the "breathing corpses whose crackled skin oozed out a yellowish liquid," and by the children playing marbles among the rubbish and excreta. Eating with the lepers made him gag. "I thought I had come to terms with everything about poverty, yet I felt revolted by the idea of sharing food with the most bruised of all my brothers," he admitted. "What a failure! What lack of love! What a long way I still had to go!" That day he made a decision: he would set up a leprosy dispensary in the City of Joy, staffed by specialists who knew how to treat the disease.

One twelve-year-old Assamese girl, Bandona (which means "praise God"), has made "all suffering her suffering." As her family's only means of support, she had worked at a factory from 5:00 a.m. to sometimes as late as 10:00 p.m. But on Sundays and feast days, Bandona would prowl the slum, looking for distressed people. Donations now allow her to work full time with the Listening Committee. She knows "how to listen to the confessions of the dying, how to pray with the families of the dead, wash the corpses, accompany the deceased on the last journey to the cemetery . . . . No one . . . ever taught her, yet she [knows] through intuition, friendship, love." The selfless girl came to be known as "Anand Nagar ka Swarga Dug" – "Angel of the City of Joy."

Dedicated doctors, nurses, missionaries, and others have also given up or put on hold prestigious careers to come and serve in this squalid inner-city village. The stories of these many fascinating and devoted workers soon give LaPierre's readers to realize that Mother Teresa is not alone in her labors to help India's poor.

The City of Joy ("Anand Nagar" in Hindu) was named by a jute-factory owner at the turn of the century. Originally the community was set up as a lodging place for this man's factory workers; but after the factory closed down, the workers' tract expanded to become a veritable city within a city. "By now more than seventy thousand inhabi-

tants had congregated on an expanse of ground hardly three times the size of a football field."

Lapierre paints a graphic portrait of the slum.

[It is] a place where children did not even know what a bush, a forest, or a pond was; where the air was so bad with carbon dioxide and sulphur that pollution killed at least one member in every family; a place where men and beasts baked in a furnace for the eight months of summer until the monsoon transformed their alleyways and shacks into swamps of mud and excrement; a place where leprosy, tuberculosis, dysentery and all the malnutrition diseases . . . reduced the average life expectancy to one of the lowest in the world; a place where eighty-five hundred cows and buffalo, tied up to dung heaps, provided milk infected with germs. Above all, however, the City of Joy was a place where the most extreme economic poverty ran rife. Nine out of ten of its inhabitants did not have a single rupee per day with which to buy half a pound of rice. Furthermore, like all . . . slums, the City of Joy was generally ignored by other citizens of Calcutta, except in case of crime or strike. Considered a dangerous neighborhood with a terrible reputation, the haunt of untouchables, pariahs, social rejects, it was a world apart, living apart from the world.

But it is just through the existence of these appalling conditions that great gifts of love and sacrifice have been made possible. And now, thankfully, many inroads have been made to reduce the community's entrenched scourges – disease, unemployment, pollution, poverty, crime and filth. "Bless you, Calcutta," Kovalski says, "for in your wretchedness you have given birth to saints."

But the book's greatest message is that, despite the brutal squalor, despite the everyday human tragedies, the City of Joy is redeemed by the sublime desire among its inhabitants to share, to give something to the next person even when there isn't enough for oneself. In the midst of disease, hunger, and poverty, these uneducated citizens of Calcutta are indeed enlightened and ennobled. They give of themselves – even up to imparting their own bodies – when there is nothing else to give; and they still somehow manage to comply with their religious customs and beliefs. Their stoic, cheerful outlook remains constant. They truly know what it is to experience joy.

(Half of the royalties from Lapierre's book are donated to aid the people of the City of Joy.)

NOT WITHOUT MY DAUGHTER

by Betty Mahmoody with William Hoffer, St. Martin's Press, New York, N.Y., 1987

Book Overview:

It is difficult to convincingly encapsulate the tremendous heroism and devotion illustrated in Betty Mahmoody's true-life story, *Not Without My Daughter*. Betty Lover met and married Dr. Sayyed Bozorg Mahmoody, an American-trained anesthesiologist born in Iran, while they were both living in Michigan. When their little girl, Mahtob, was nearly five years old, Dr. Mahmoody (whose nickname was "Moody") decided that his family should visit his homeland. Moody assured his wife that the trip was just to introduce her and Mahtob to his relatives; but what started out as a two-week family reunion turned into a two-year nightmare.

Although his marriage to Betty seemed to be built on caring and love, the few years in America had been difficult ones for Moody. After he was hit with a malpractice suit which put him out of a job for a year, Betty recognized her husband's deep depression. Maybe it was these feelings of low self-worth that helped to ignite his sudden interest in the political affairs of his own country. At any rate, after the news that the Shah had been ousted from Iran, Moody's longing for his homeland intensified. Even his attitude toward America seemed to sour.

When Betty, Moody and Mahtob first arrived in Iran, they stayed with Moody's sister, Ameh Bozorg, and her family, whom Moody had not seen for years. The Bozorgs were strictly religious Muslims, getting up early in the morning to utter their Islamic prayers and to study the Koran.

Iran's hot summer enervated Betty. The heat was even more unbearable with the many pieces of clothing she was forced to wear. In male-dominated Iran a woman was expected to show modesty by wearing a chador – a large, half-moon shaped cloth entwined around the shoulders, forehead, and chin – designed to reveal only her eyes, nose and mouth. A large scarf tied in front completely covered the neck, and a montoe (a long coat with no waistline) was worn over everything else, covering her entire body. If a woman went out on the streets improperly dressed, the pasdar, a special police force stopped and harassed her. Betty writes: "It was difficult for me to comprehend this insistence upon propriety. Women nursed their babies in plain view, caring little how much they revealed of their bosoms, as long as their heads, chins, wrists, and ankles were covered."

Americans were looked upon with suspicion and disgust, as members of a corrupt society. Iranian news depicted America as the "Great Satan." Furthermore, Betty automatically lost her rights as an American citizen once she touched Iranian soil.

At times she was forced to cover up even inside her home. One evening, a religious leader came to the door and Betty was asked by her husband to cover herself: "There was . . . no opportunity to object to Moody's demand that I wear a chador, but as I donned the cumbersome robe I realized that it was filthy. The veil that covers the lower part of the face was caked with dried spittle. I had seen no handkerchiefs or tissues in the household. What I had seen was the women using these veils instead. The smell was repulsive."

Her sister-in-law, Ameh, thought it utterly wasteful to shower everyday; she rarely bathed and always seemed to wear the same clothes. There was also a lack of cleanliness in the kitchen which even upset Moody: "A pot of food stewed incessantly on the stove for the convenience of anyone who was hungry. Many times I saw people take a taste from a large ladle-like spoon, allowing the residue from their mouths to drip back into the pot or simply dribble onto the floor. Counter tops and floors were honeycombed with trains of sugar left by careless tea drinkers. The roaches flourished in the kitchen as well as in the bathroom." Betty would find quantities of bugs in every cupful of cooked rice.

Then, one day, hoping that the long-extended vacation had finally come to an end, Betty was informed that a mistake had been made: someone had forgotten to confirm their flight reservations, and they had been cancelled. Betty realized what she had not wanted to believe until then: her husband had planned this all along. "Moody held our American and Iranian passports as well as our birth certificates." Now all her fears were confirmed – Betty and her daughter could not leave Iran. Moody would never allow it.

Moody turned into a jail-keeper. He watched Betty's every move and whenever he went out, he had his sister's family stand watch over her. Finally, one afternoon when everyone in the house was napping, Betty took Mahtob into her arms and quietly walked out. She presumed she could seek asylum at the U.S. Interest Section of the Swiss Embassy (the U.S. Embassy having been closed since the Shah's departure). But when Betty arrived at the Swiss Embassy she met Helen, an Iranian woman dressed in Western style clothing:

"Give us refuge here," Betty pleaded. "Then find some way to get us home."

"What are you talking about?" Helen responded. "You cannot stay here! . . . You are an Iranian citizen."

"No, I'm an American citizen."

"You are Iranian," Helen repeated, "and you have to abide by Iranian law."

Betty wrote: . . . *From the moment I married an Iranian I became a citizen under Iranian law. Legally, both Mahtob and I were, indeed, Iranian. The simple, chilling fact was that Mahtob and I were totally subject to the laws of this fanatical patriarchy.*

Helen also informed her that even if there were any chance of Betty getting out, no one would risk smuggling a child. But Betty insisted, "I would not return to America alone, not without my daughter."

Throughout Betty's stay in Iran, many of the people who tried to help her exit told her the same thing: she would have to leave her child. And Betty always responded the same way: she would never leave Mahtob in Iran.

There were times when Betty hardly recognized the man she had married. Moody's attitudes altered almost hourly. His treatment of Mahtob pushed the child away from him. He would experience fits of anger, swearing at them both and sometimes beating them. Things gradually grew worse. Once, when Mahtob became very ill, Moody took her away and locked Betty up in a small room. Through jet attack air raid sirens and antiaircraft fire, Betty described her solitary, dark state:

I paced back and forth in anguish, not bothering to protect myself . . . . I cried for my daughter, the deepest darkest, most painful tears I had ever – would ever – could ever – shed.

After this incident, Betty often found herself praying that Moody would die. However, she reversed her wish upon examining Iran's constitution, which stated that if Moody died "Mahtob would not belong to me. Rather, she would become the custodial child of Moody's closest living relative, Ameh Bozorg!" With seemingly nowhere to turn "I [silently] renewed my vow. I would get us out. Both of us. Somehow, someday."

Betty now began to stroke Moody's ego and build up his trust in her. On one occasion, as he searched for a decent apartment for them, she said, "Things will work out. At least we have one another . . . " "Yes," Moody replied as he hugged and kissed his wife.

And during the few minutes of passion that followed I was able to disassociate myself from the present. At that moment my body was simply a tool that I would use, if I had to, to fashion freedom.

Betty commenced making friends and secret contacts, working around appointments, shopping trips or visits to the park. There was Hamid, the owner of a menswear store, who allowed her to use his phone. There was Mrs. Alavi, who, with her brother, also tried to help. And finally, there was Amahl, businessman and part-time smuggler, who laid his life and his money on the line to organize Betty's escape.

Others were more than willing to assist her, but for a terrible price. Several times people came to her with elaborate escape schemes, which Betty declined to attempt because of the dangers involved. Instead she waited patiently, calling Amahl every day to see what he had been able to arrange.

One day Moody told Betty that he had obtained an exit visa and wanted her to go back to liquidate their assets in America. She understood only too well that what he really wanted was for her to return alone, without Mahtob. Betty was frantic. The plans Amahl had made for her to flee through Pakistan had been put on hold because of bad weather; and she sensed that if she left, Moody would never let her back to see Mahtob again.

Only three days before she was to leave, Betty, with Mahtob, went into hiding. Amahl, still without all of his secondary contacts lined up, instructed Betty to phone Moody and tell him that she would only come home after the plane on which she was scheduled had left. This interlude bought Amahl and Betty enough time to fine-tune the details of her escape.

Since Moody had been practicing medicine in Iran without a license, Betty used his belief that she would turn him in to the authorities to keep him from going to the police. She also kept him hanging on to the hope that she would return with his daughter. Meanwhile, Amahl finalized the intricate chain of people and events that would take them from "hell" to "heaven."

So, putting all her trust in Amahl and his line of contacts, Betty and Mahtob, clinging to each other's courage, set out for their long, arduous journey: through villages, past menacing border guards, and over precarious snowy mountain passes; traveling on foot, by truck, car, bus, and horseback; in the company of men who could have, at any time, abandoned them, raped them, or slit their throats.

Finally, frozen, exhausted, and near starvation, they plodded and stumbled over the mountains into Turkey. From there they traveled on to freedom and family – to America.

BLUE HIGHWAYS

by William Least Heat Moon , Ballantine Books, New York, N.Y., 1982

Type of work: Nonfiction descriptive characterization

Setting: U.S.A.; contemporary

Journal Overview:

Beware of thoughts that come in the night. They aren't turned properly; they come in askew, free of sense and restriction . . . . Take the idea of Feb. 17, a day of canceled expectations, the day I learned my job teaching English was finished because of declining enrollment at the college, the day I called my wife from whom I'd been separated for nine months to give the news, the day she let slip about her "friend," – Rick or Dick or Chick. Something like that.

That night, William Least Heat Moon gave himself the task of traversing the United States, following the highways marked in blue on the map. These back-roads passed through towns long abandoned by the austere multi-lane interstates.

After converting his Ford van into a makeshift camper, Moon set out heading eastward. He passed through towns like Nameless, Tennessee, then turned south along the Atlantic coastline, driving through Fort Raleigh, North Carolina and Ninety-Six, South Carolina, striking up conversations with anyone willing to talk with him.

Outside of Conyers, Georgia, Moon happened upon the Monastery of the Holy Spirit. Though not a religious man, he stopped, in order to discover how a Trappist monastery was faring in the middle of Baptist country. Father Anthony welcomed him in and gave him lunch. Moon was intrigued by monastic life, the philosophy of silence and austerity, and expressed the desire to talk to one of the newer brothers about how he had come to embrace such an existence. The next day he was allowed to speak with former Patrolman Patrick Duffy, now known simply as Brother Patrick. Fed up with the "blindness, arrogance [and] selfishness" of society, Brother Patrick had quit his job as a cop in a tough section of Brooklyn: "For years I've been fascinated by intense spiritual experiences of one kind or another. When I was seventeen I thought of becoming a monk . . . . I felt an incompleteness in myself." The monastery was the one place where he had found an escape from the world's misery.

Days later, Moon found himself in Selma, Alabama. He drove down Martin Luther King, Jr. Drive to Brown's Chapel, where King's civil rights marches had originated. When he asked a passerby, James Walker, if things had progressed much since those days, Walker shook his head: "Been almost ten years to the day since King got shot and the movement's been

dead that long. Things slippin'. Black man's losin' ground again." Moon probed Walker's feelings further: "We got potential. First . . . brothers gotta see . . . where to go from here. I mean figurin' a new course. King said turn the other cheek. Malcolm X said fight fire with fire. I don't want that. But we gotta show the brothers they can do more than just hang cool like meat in a locker."

Just then a police undercover van passed. "Why are they watching you?" Moon asked. James grinned, "They ain't watchin' us, my man – they be watchin' you." Evidently, any non-black in the neighborhood *had* to be a dope dealer; Moon decided it was time to move on.

He drove west out of Alabama, through Mississippi and Louisiana, and on into Texas, observing that the "true West differs from the East in one great, pervasive, influential, and awesome way: space." Moon stopped in Dime Box, a town which "could have been an MGM backlot set for a Western," and got a dollar-fifty haircut. Claud Tyler, the patriarchal barber, reminisced about Dime Box's golden old railroad days. Model T's used to line up all along the road to the depot. Cars, trains, girls in big hats. "Dime Box made noise then," Tyler sighed.

Back on the road again, Moon wondered if he would ever find the end of Texas. Finally, he guided his van into Hachita, New Mexico's "Desert Den Bar and Filling Station" to get a bite to eat. The bar was a "genuine Western saloon primeval, a place where cattlemen once transacted affairs of commerce and of the passions." After some food and beer, William encountered a "real cowboy," who told him the 40-year-old story of the A-bomb test explosion at Los Alamos: It was daybreak and the cowboy was still asleep in his bedroll, "when comes a god-terrible flash. Couple of minutes later the ground starts rumblin'. Sound just kept roarin'." This cowboy went on to claim that the blast had "ruined his genetics."

The next morning, Moon continued north, passing through Holbrook, Arizona and other Indian reservation towns, and then into Utah. A seven-foot snow drift and a late-spring storm forced him to spend a night shivering on top of a mountain. He then turned back to take a different route into Cedar City, and had a welcome breakfast there at Southern Utah State College. During the meal, he struck up a conversation with a Hopi student, Kendrick Fritz, who's dream it was to become a doctor. Moon asked Fritz if he thought whites were prejudiced against Indians. "About fifty-fifty," Fritz answered. "Half show contempt . . . another half think we're noble savages. Who wants to be somebody's ideal myth?" Moon next inquired about Hopi religion and ethics. Fritz explained: "The Spider Grandmother did give two rules, to all men, not just Hopis. She said, 'Don't go around hurting each other,' and she said, 'Try to understand things.'" Moon agreed that these two rules covered most everything having to do with human relations.

At sunrise, Moon drove "into the middle of nowhere" to Frenchman, Nevada, population 4, a town on the edge of a U.S. Navy bombing range. From there he visited Reno, where the big news "was of a seventy-three-year-old Canadian who had been coming to the casinos three times a year for twenty years. She had met no success until last night when she won $183,000." Someone suggested that the whole thing was rigged by the casinos as a PR stunt. Moon left Nevada and drove on into California. "The day became a dim, sodden thing, damp without rain," and the traveler's mood swung accordingly. As he passed over Humbug Creek, he "could almost hear the laughter from on high."

Moon, by now a little weary, drove through Oregon into Vancouver, Washington, where, by virtue of a coin flip, he decided to take the "blue highway" that followed the Columbia River. He traversed the side of the river where towns were few. Barely avoiding running out of gas, Moon then crossed into Idaho and headed east to Montana, where he picked up a hitchhiker named Arthur O. Bakke, a self-described "International Missionary Volunteer," who shared with Moon the story of his sudden conversion to Jesus after his car had gone over a cliff. Later, Moon pondered what he had learned from the born-again preacher: *The word he carried to me wasn't the City of God; it was of simplicity, spareness, courage, directness, trust, and charity. Despite doctrinal differences, he reminded me of a Trappist monk or a Hopi shaman.* And, Moon decided, "I liked Arthur. I liked him very much."

After passing through the Blackfoot reservation, where little crosses on the highway marked the many traffic fatalities, Moon sped over the Continental Divide and on to the expansive plains. Rather than accept the luxury of driving on an interstate highway, he followed a road weaving through Southern Canada to upstate New York; there he helped build a rock retaining wall on the property of a friend, Sam Chisholm. As they worked, a "strange thing began to happen. We could feel an urging in the rocks. They fit one way and no other ways. It was as if the stones were, as Indians believed, alive." Later, as he lay in bed, Moon thought of how much the work and com-panionship of old friends had meant to him. "I wouldn't have been able to travel another mile if it had not been for these people."

The next morning, Moon started on the last leg of his journey, traveling north into Maine. A group of crusty fishermen invited him to join them for a day on their boat.

Soon, Moon found himself in Othello, New Jersey. Asking about the origin of the name "Othello," he was referred to Robert Roemer, the town's local historian. Their conversation ended on the topic of history and preservation. "The evidence of history is rare and worth preserving," Roemer pronounced. "Maybe I've been influenced by the old Quakers who believed it was a moral question always to consider what you're leaving behind. Why not?"

In Maryland, Moon was directed to another octogenarian who loved history. "Miz" Alice Venable Middleton lived on Smith Island, and was one of those women "who make age look like something you don't want to miss." As a retired schoolteacher, it was natural that she address the subject of education: "A teacher should carry a theme. Mine was what they call 'ecology' now. I taught children first the system of things." To Alice, education sprouted from inside the individual; learning "is thinking, and thinking is looking for yourself and seeing what's there, not what you got told was there." After touring the island, Moon asked Alice what was the hardest thing about living in isolation. Her answer became an echo of his own theme: The most difficult thing? "Having the gumption to live different and the sense to let everybody else live different."

A few days later, Moon once again neared Columbia, Missouri: home.

The circle almost complete, the truck ran the road like the old horse that knows the way. If the circle had come full turn, I hadn't. I did learn what I didn't know I wanted to know.

Commentary:

When *Blue Highways* was published it catapulted Moon into literary stardom. Part travelogue, part history book, and a mixture of comedy and tragedy, the book defies strict categorization.

One of Moon's central concerns is the grim reality of racial and ethnic tension in the United States; this issue is mingled with admiring homages to America as a dynamic multicultural patchwork. The book not only keys on "common folk" as being worthy of our interest and honor, but praises America's many other peripatetic writers, particularly Lewis and Clark, Walt Whitman and John Steinbeck, for their contributions to the travel genre and to the understanding and celebration of a continent.

HIROSHIMA

by John Hersey, Alfred A. Knopf, New York, N.Y., 1946 & 1985

Type of work: Nonfictional documentary

Setting: Hiroshima, Japan; 1946 to 1985

Principal characters:
> *Miss Sasaki*, a young clerk/secretary
> *Dr. Fujii*, a successful physician
> *Mrs. Nakamura*, a widow with three
> children
> *Father Kleinsorge*, a German-Catholic priest
> *Dr. Sasaki*, a young Red Cross Hospital
> doctor
> *Mr. Tanimoto*, a Protestant minister

Book Overview:

At 8:15 a.m. on August 6, 1945, the United States dropped an atomic bomb on Hiroshima that devastated the city. *Hiroshima* is an account of the lives of six survivors, who each reacted in a different way to the devastation. But all six share one thing in common: "They still wonder why they lived when so many others died."

Miss Sasaki was just settling into her job as a clerk for the East Asia Tin Works. As she turned her head away from the window to make a comment to a co-worker, "the room was filled with a blinding light." Her immediate terror was replaced by unconsciousness as loaded bookcases tumbled on top of her. "In the first moment of the atomic age, a human being was crushed by books." Three hours later someone dug her out. Her left leg, though not severed, "was badly broken and cut and it hung askew below the knee." Sasaki was taken outside into a downpour and left there on the ground, helpless and wet. Finally a man fashioned a lean-to out of some scraps to cover her, along with two other survivors. One "roommate" was a woman with one of her breasts blown off, and the other was a man whose face was completely burned. "Sasaki lay for two days and two nights under the piece of propped-up roofing with her crushed leg and two unpleasant comrades."

Dr. Fujii, a wealthy physician, had barely "sat down cross-legged in his underwear . . . and started reading the Osaka Asahi," when the bomb exploded, suddenly leaving him "squeezed tightly by two long timbers in a V across his chest, like a morsel suspended between two huge chopsticks," above the waters of the Kyo River. There he remained, until he realized that the tide was coming in – he would drown within minutes. With almost superhuman strength, Fujii extricated himself from his trap. By then fires were raging nearby. When the flames subsided, the doctor made his way to his family's home five miles outside of the city. Though his own shoulder was badly broken, he examined and treated many other wounded along the way.

Mrs. Nakamura was watching her neighbor at work on his house. Suddenly "everything flashed whiter than any white she had ever seen." She was thrown several feet, and timbers and tiles showered down upon her. Freeing herself from the rubble, Nakamura began a frantic search for her children. She found all three still alive, and after prying them loose from the wreckage of what had been their home, she led them to Asano Park, the neighborhood meeting place for bombing raids. There they joined others who, like themselves, were wounded, bewildered and in shock.

In the park was Father Kleinsorge. The blast had completely destroyed the mission where the Jesuit priest and other brothers lived, and they had sought refuge in the park's bamboos, pines, laurel and maples. Now Father Kleinsorge and the other priests were trying as best they could to provide aid and comfort. Near the faucet where the priests made trips to get water, were "about twenty men . . . all in the same nightmarish state: their faces were wholly burned, their eye-sockets were hollow, the fluid from their melted eyes had run down their cheeks." Offering them a drink, Father Kleinsorge found their mouths to be mere "swollen, pus-covered wounds" that could not draw the water in. He fashioned some straws from large stems of grass, an effort which saved a number of lives.

Like Father Kleinsorge, Mr. Tanimoto, a Protestant minister, gave spirited assistance in the bomb's aftermath. However, there was little he could do for those who were entangled in the ruins of toppled buildings. Fire swept through the city, preventing crews from reaching survivors. Tanimoto "was filled with compassion for those who were trapped, and . . . overwhelmed by the shame of being unhurt. As he ran, he prayed, 'God help them and take them out of the fire.'" Desperately he tried to extract the wounded; he transported water; and later, he piloted a boat to ferry survivors across the river to the sanctuary of Asano Park.

Dr. Sasaki was hurrying a blood sample down the hall of the Red Cross Hospital when his eyeglasses were blown off his face. The bottle he carried was broken, but he was unhurt. The hospital, though, flew into a state of chaos. Its staff was not prepared for the number of injured. "By nightfall, ten thousand victims of the explosion had invaded the Red Cross Hospital, and Dr. Sasaki, worn out, was moving aimlessly and dully up and down the stinking corridors with wads of bandage and bottles of Mercurochrome, still wearing the glasses he had taken from [a] wounded nurse, binding up the worse cuts as he came to them." After nineteen straight hours of work, when Sasaki tried to nap, wounded patients woke him up: "Doctor! Help us! How can you sleep?" There were so many dead that it was impossible to keep track of their names.

Rebuilding Hiroshima's devastated structures took many years. But rebuilding the shattered lives of its survivors took much longer. "The Japanese tended to shy away from the term 'survivors,' because in its focus on being alive it might suggest some slight to the sacred dead." Instead, those who came out alive, were "called by a more neutral name, 'hibakusha' – literally, 'explosion-affected persons.'" For years the "hibakusha" suffered – physically, emotionally and financially: The Japanese government refused to help them economically because they did not wish to take responsibility for "heinous acts of the victorious United States." Moreover, hibakusha were discriminated against by potential employers. This prejudice was not completely unfounded in that many survivors bore a lasting sickness that made victims weak, dizzy, and "aggravated by a feeling of oppression."

Following the war, Mrs. Nakamura lived in poverty. Widowed and sick, she was left with only an old sewing machine that she had hidden in a well. With this rusted machine, she was able to take in a little sewing, along with other odd jobs. She and her children were sustained by a short Japanese phrase: "Shikata ga-nai" ("It can't be helped"). In 1957, the Japanese government finally began paying some of her medical costs.

Economically, Dr. Sasaki suffered very little during the post-war years. However, he was "still racked by memories of the appalling days and nights right after the explosion." To distance himself from these memories, he quit the Red Cross and went into private practice. A bout with lung cancer nearly took his life in 1963. But as the years passed, "Sasaki came to think of that experience as the most important of his life." He sought closer relationships with family members and viewed medicine – the art of compassion – with a new eye. He devoted his medical attentions to serving the elderly. "Do your duty to your patients first," he would remind his staff each morning. "Let the money follow; our life is short, we don't live twice."

Father Kleinsorge was constantly vexed by "fever, diarrhea, wounds that would not heal, wildly fluctuating blood counts, and utter exhaustion." His was a classic example of radiation sickness. Nevertheless, he "lived this life of misery with the most extraordinarily selfless spirit," continuing his religious duties and visiting hibakushas. His colleagues thought that "he was a little too much concerned for others, and not enough for himself." Eventually he became a Japanese citizen; and died still doing what he could to relieve the suffering of others.

Among those introduced by Father Kleinsorge to Catholicism, Miss Sasaki, now crippled, was one of the most stubborn. How could she believe in a Christian God who would allow the suffering she had endured and witnessed? Still, Miss Sasaki was "warmed and healed by the priest's faithfulness to her, for it was obvious that he, too, was weak and in pain, yet he walked great distances to see her." In time, she was converted. Meanwhile, unable to support her siblings, she finally placed them in an orphanage. But fortunately, the orphanage gave her work so she could remain close to them. After a few years, nuns in the orphanage arranged for her to have orthopedic surgery, which partially straightened her leg. She developed the opinion "unconventional for a hibakusha: that too much attention was paid to the power of the A-bomb, and not enough to the evil of war." Devoted to the cause of peace and humanity, she later chose to enter a convent as a nun.

Dr. Fujii "suffered from none of the effects of radiation overdose, and he evidently felt that for any psychological damage the horrors of the bombing may have done him, the best therapy was to follow the pleasure principle." After constructing a new clinic in 1948, he ceased working long hours and increasingly sought the company of foreigners, spending his evenings drinking with U.S. soldiers and playing mah-jongg at his home. This life came to a sad end when a gas accident left him a brain-damaged vegetable until his death in 1973.

Finally, Mr. Tanimoto, unlike the others, grew intensely involved in the politics of the Hiroshima bombing. He devoted much time to helping women left with horrible keloid scars on their faces to travel to America for plastic surgery, while also actively fighting to secure financial aid for victims. He went on speaking tours of the United States and became so well-known in America, that he appeared as the main subject of the television program "This Is Your Life" and offered an invocation in the U.S. Senate. The reception he received when he arrived home, however, was not so warm. Some viewed him as a publicity monger. Furthermore, many U.S. agencies suspected his motives, or charged that his "naive" speeches were a boost to the leftist cause. Tanimoto finally retired from politics and refused to work in any of the local peace movements in Hiroshima.

Commentary:

John Hersey's *Hiroshima* became controversial with its initial publication right after the war. Some accused Hersey of being "un-American" for presenting a Japanese viewpoint. But the real impact of the book was made by its graphic, true to life portrayal of the horrors of atomic war.

Hiroshima, regardless of its ethical stance, is a valuable contribution to literature. We witness through Hersey's eyes the suffering and the triumph of many souls. The small kindnesses in the midst of horrible destruction are powerfully laid out in a style that is at once subtle and sensitive, vivid and hard-hitting.

ONE HUNDRED YEARS OF SOLITUDE

by Gabriel Garcia Marquez, Harper and Row, New York, N.Y., 1970

Type of work: Magical realism

Setting: Fictional town of Macondo; late nineteenth and twentieth centuries

Principal characters:

Jose Arcadio Buendia, the family's patriarch
Ursula Buendia, his wife
Melquiades, a gypsy magician, philosopher, and seer
A multitude of other characters: the Buendia children, grandchildren and great grandchildren; other gypsies; many different lovers, prostitutes and rapists; various revolutionaries and terrorists; a ballad singer, a charlatan, inventors, etc.

Commentary:

One Hundred Years of Solitude is like stepping into a trance, where past, present, and future seem to merge. A dream-like cadence of words combines with a wonderfully readable script to explore all the poles of life – births and deaths, marriages and executions, selflessness and suicide, solidarity and solitude, passion and pathos, love and bitter loneliness.

During a century of life in the village of Macondo, angels appear, a beautiful virgin ascends to heaven majestically veiled in bedlinen, gypsy ghosts stalk the Buendia's library, and a family corpse arrives in the mail, even while family liberals battle conservatives in civil wars and North American capitalists carve out a banana empire in the jungle. Flying carpets dodge under telegraph wires, the new-fangled ice box amazes Macondo's isolated citizenry, and countless legitimate and illegitimate Buendia offspring are christened after their aunts, uncles, parents and grandparents, intensifying the circular, surreal structure of the novel.

One Hundred Years of Solitude is not a book to be read casually – nor is it meant to be "studied." It is, more than anything, a pilgrimage into the mythic panorama of South American history, and into all the universal dimensions of human experience.

Story Overview:

Prologue: Though they were cousins, Ursula and Jose Arcadio Buendia courted and finally dared to marry. But Ursula, believing the whispers that such a union would result in the birth of offspring with pigs' tails, would not let Jose Arcadio consummate the marriage. Frustrated, and angered by the teasing he received concerning his wife's intransigence, he one day killed a townsman, Prudencio Aguilar, at a cockfight. Jose then returned to Ursula with the pronouncement that they would now commence normal marital relations. After a while, however, haunted by the ghost of Prudencio, he decided that they would

have to leave the area. Together with other settlers, Jose and Ursula "crossed the mountains in search of an outlet to the sea." After twenty-six months they gave up the expedition and founded the out-of-the-way hamlet of Macondo on the banks of a shallow tropical river embedded with "smooth, white, prehistoric stones." History was, once again, about to be born.

Every spring a band of gypsies visited the quiet village of Macondo, and Melquiades, their chief, became a valued friend to Jose Arcadio, the town leader. The gypsies always brought with them an assortment of telescopes and other "scientific toys," along with their flying carpets and magic spells, with which to entice and entertain the community – whose solitude was not only physical but cultural as well. Ice, a camera, and a pianola were followed many years later by automobiles and factories. But Jose Arcadio was even more captivated by Melquiades' beguiling Sanskrit writings. Nearly a century afterward, his great grandson would also be lured by the gypsy writings and would finally devote his whole life to their deciphering.

One year, the gypsy band returned to Macondo minus their clan leader – Melquiades had died. In honor of his departed friend, Jose Arcadio built a laboratory next to his house.

When the first Buendia son, Jose Arcadio II, was born without the curse of a pig's tail, Ursula was relieved. He grew to be an immense and strong young man, and his mother went on to bear a second son, Aureliano.

Much later, Jose Arcadio Buendia, now a weathered old man tormented by memories and ghosts, went insane, barking in a strange tongue and "giving off a green froth at the mouth." Aided by twenty men, Ursula had him dragged to a chestnut tree and securely bound. There he remained, month after month, fettered to the tree, until he joined Melquiades and Prudencio Aguilar in death.

(A few more exerpts are recapitulated here from the elaborately seductive chronicles of Macondo's appointed ten decades. Each highlights one of the main characters; and together with many other intertwining stories, they all blend in a slow arabesque that finally circles back to the book's beginning, as Macondo spirals towards its inevitable self-destruction.)

Pilar Ternera, a fortune teller, "fat, talkative, with airs of a matron in disgrace," became fond of the oversized Jose II, whom she lured into the granary night after night.

They were exuberant lovers . . . and they even came to suspect that love could be deeper and more vibrant than the wild but momentary passions displayed during their secret nights.

Then Pilar announced that Jose II was

going to be a father. She bore him a healthy son; but soon torn by the calls of the outside world, Jose II left his mistress. Pilar later gave birth to still another son, fathered by Aureliano, Jose II's brother.

After **Melquiades,** the gypsy, returned from death to rescue Macondo from a plague of amnesia (the townpeople had desperately compensated for their memory loss by making labels for every article in the village), he once again died – only to re-emerge as a ghost. He continued to use both magic and science as he helped guide Macondo out of its innocence toward "progress" – and at the same time to wrap it deeper in the isolation of parochial myth and sorcery.

Aureliano, the second Buendia son, seeing that civil war was imminent, proclaimed himself a colonel and formed a small militia. In the years that followed, he "organized thirty-two uprisings and he lost them all." Despite his ineptness, he somehow survived countless attempts at assassination and execution to achieve honor and fame as a great heroic liberator.

When Colonel Buendia's nephew, Aureliano Jose, was gunned down at a theatrical performance by a Captain Aquiles Ricardo, the vengeance of the colonel was swift and terrible. "Long live the Liberal party! Long live Colonel Aureliano Buendia!" shouted his loyal followers. Later that same night they filed past and mutilated the captain's freshly slain corpse. "A patrol had to use a wheelbarrow to carry the body, which was heavy with lead and fell apart like a watersoaked loaf of bread."

At last the legendary but aging Colonel Aureliano Buendia was forced to give up any further exploits, spending his remaining days in a stupor, fashioning little wooden fishes in his workshop. Along the way, he had fathered seventeen bastard sons – all bearing the name "Aureliano" – by seventeen different women. Each birth was duly recorded in a family ledger by his grandmother, Ursula.

"Meme" (Renata Remedios) spurned the warnings of her withered great-grandmother to break off her affair with Mauricio Babilonia, a local mechanic who was constantly surrounded by clouds of yellow butterflies. Fernanda, the girl's prudish mother, however, did more than issue warnings; she sensed the source of the insects she found hovering each morning throughout her home. Reporting that "hens were being stolen," Fernanda convinced the mayor to station an armed guard in the backyard.

That night the guard brought down Mauricio Babilonia as he was lifting up the tiles to get into the bathroom where Meme was waiting for him, naked and trembling with love among the scorpions and butterflies . . . . A bullet lodged in his spinal column reduced him to his bed for the rest of his life. He died of old age in solitude, without a moan, without a protest . . . tormented by memories and by the yellow butterflies . . . and ostracized as a chicken thief.

Meme was shuttled off to a convent and no one in Macondo heard from her again; but her son, Aureliano, was later sent to Macondo to be raised in the Buendia household. Fernanda, ashamed of the truth, always insisted that she had found the child "floating in a basket."

Jose Arcadio Segundo became involved in a strike against Macondo's Yankee-owned banana processing factory. An army, called in to break up the strike, fired on the crowd. When Jose Arcadio came to in the darkness, he realized that he was aboard a silent train in the midst of the riddled corpses of three thousand men, women and children. Managing to push himself off the train, he limped back to his village. No one would believe him when he tried to convince the people that the brutal massacre had indeed happened. "Always remember," he pronounced to his kin, "they were more than three thousand and that they were thrown into the sea."

Now it seemed as though a curse was brought upon the town. For five years straight, it rained, leaving Macondo in ruins. During the rains, Ursula, the founding mother, by now a centenarian, finally died.

After this, Jose Arcadio II shut himself up in the room in which Melquiades had once lived, in an effort to decipher the strange parchments the gypsy had left behind – the pages that contained the Buendia history and forewarnings of their ultimate end.

Epilogue: Though the Buendias were a robust, dynamic family, their fate had been spelled out from the day of the incestuous marriage a century earlier. Now Meme's Aureliano – ignoring his great-great grandmother's century-old superstition, in true, Buendia fashion – took his own Aunt Amaranta Ursula as his mistress. Alas, the prophecy proved to be more than simple myth when Amaranta Ursula gave birth to little Aureliano, a boy perfect in every way – except for the tiny curl of a tail that protruded from the base of his spine.

That night, "Melquiades' final keys were revealed" to the infant's father, "and he saw the epigraph of the parchments perfectly placed in the order of man's time and space." It said, "The first of the line is tied to a tree and the last is being eaten by the ants."

The accursed infant Aureliano was indeed at that moment being assaulted and carried off by a colony of ants, thus ending the Buendia's reign in Macondo. One hundred years of refusing to acknowledge the world outside of their village had destroyed them; and "races condemned to one hundred years of solitude did not have a second opportunity on earth."

THE PAINTED BIRD

by Jerzy Kosinski, Houghton Mifflin, Boston, Massachusetts, 1965

Type of work: Realistic Novel

Setting: Eastern Europe; World War II

Principal characters:

Narrator, an unnamed six-year-old boy of
Jewish or gypsy ancestry

Assorted peers and peasants who
alternately abuse, brutalize and use
the boy

Story Overview:

"In the first weeks of World War II, in the fall of 1939, a six-year-old boy from a large city in Eastern Europe was sent by his parents, like thousands of other children, to the shelter of a distant village." However, in the chaos of war, the parents lost track of their son. The boy was left in a rural village under the care of an old woman, Marta, who was "always bent over as though she wanted to break herself in half but could not."

The boy feared Marta, with her gnarled hands and foul smell. Marta also feared the boy, whose swarthy skin and dark eyes invoked her superstitious sentiments. She believed that one glance into his eyes could invoke an evil spell bringing disease, plague or death. And soon after the boy's arrival, Marta did become ill. One night, while she soaked her feet, she died; and the boy, thinking she was merely asleep, watched as the slumping corpse and the thatch house were engulfed in a fire he had accidentally caused.

Now the boy was on his own. Still, he had faith that his mother and father would somehow find him: " . . . Even far away, they must know all that had happened to me. Wasn't I their child?" So the boy crossed the fields into a nearby village in search of his parents. The villagers jeered at the dark child and soon were kicking him and poking him with farm tools. But a man worked his way through the crowd, grabbed the boy, and shoved him into a burlap sack. As he struggled, the peasant clubbed the lad into unconsciousness. Arriving home, the peasant presented his captive and began a practice of whipping the boy's legs to make him dance for the pleasure of his family and neighbors – until one day an old woman named Olga came to visit and decided to buy the boy.

In Olga's two-room hut, she kept "dried grasses, leaves . . . frogs, moles, and pots of wriggling lizards and worms." The boy became Olga's helper, tending her fire and feeding her animals. He accompanied her when she administered her "treatments" to local peasants. His job was to stare at her patients with his "bewitched eyes" to remove evil spirits which caused sickness.

But all this came to an end one day when a villager caught and cleaned a giant catfish, and, as a joke, the townsfolk flung the boy onto the huge discarded air bladder left floating in the river, and the boy was carried off by the current.

Again left to survive on his own, the boy stayed with a cruel miller for a time. He watched as the miller flogged his wife and blinded a plowboy suspected of sleeping with her: " . . . With a rapid movement such as women use to gouge out the rotten spots while peeling potatoes, he plunged the spoon into one of the boy's eyes and twisted it. The eye sprang out of his face like a yolk from a broken egg and rolled down the miller's hand onto the floor . . . " The boy wisely determined to flee the miller's company, and soon found himself with a new master, Lekh.

"My duty was to set snares for Lekh, who sold birds in several neighboring villages . . . . Lekh taught me that a man should always watch birds carefully and draw conclusions from their behavior." Some days Lekh would leave the boy in a clearing and go off to meet his lover, "Stupid Ludmila." "To Lekh she seemed to belong to that pagan, primitive kingdom of birds and forests where everything was infinitely abundant, wild, blooming." Ludmila often lured many of the townsmen into the bushes. Then one day the village wives captured Ludmila and kicked her to death. Afterwards, Lekh fell on her corpse and sobbed all night long. "Too afraid to return to the hut," the boy retreated into the woods.

The boy next lived with a carpenter and his wife, who feared that his coal black hair might attract lightning to their farm. When a storm raged, the carpenter would tie the boy onto a cart, and drive it to the middle of a field until the rain had ceased. However, one night when a ferocious storm suddenly struck the village, the boy ran into the barn for shelter. "In an instant the barn was jarred by an uncanny peal of thunder." It was quickly engulfed in flames. The boy barely made his escape into the forest, where he hid all night, convinced that his hair had brought the lightning down on the barn and knowing that the carpenter would punish him.

The next morning the boy wandered through the forest until he found an overgrown cobblestone road, which he followed to a deserted military bunker. Hearing a muffled squeaking from inside the bunker, he peered through an opening at a sea of rats "murdering and eating one another." As he hurried off in panic and disgust, the boy unwittingly circled back into the carpenter's village, where he was captured and returned to his master. The carpenter pummelled him, threatening a dire death. Just then an idea entered the boy's head: He promised his master that "if he would not drown me, I would show him a pillbox filled with old boots, uniforms, and military belts." The next morning the two headed for the bunker. As the carpenter leaned over the opening, squinting into the darkness for a glimpse of the treasure, the boy hurled against him, and he "dropped into the maw of the pillbox with a dull thud." Within minutes the rats had reduced the corpse to a pile of bones.

Continuing his journeys, the growing but still scrawny boy lived with a blacksmith for a time. But one day a group of Nazi-fighting partisans entered the village, accused the blacksmith of collaborating with Nazis, and butchered him on the spot. One soldier was assigned to take the boy into the forest and shoot him. However, the man merely feigned the execution and released the boy.

On one occasion, while the boy, his farmer-master, and other villagers were out gathering mushrooms, a new kind of train steamed up on the nearby rail line. "Living people were jammed in locked cattle cars . . . . In each car there were two hundred of them stacked like cornstalks, arms raised to take up less space." Sometimes these people threw out photographs, little remembrances of themselves. The village folk told the boy that "the Lord's punishment had finally reached the Jews. They had deserved it long ago, ever since they crucified Christ."

"German detachments began to search for partisans in the surrounding forests . . . " One night the farmer woke the boy and warned him that soldiers were coming. He scurried into the wheat fields, but was found and taken in a cart, along with another prisoner, who had been severely beaten, to a large town. From there they were dispatched to a military headquarters and presented to an SS officer. As the officer looked them over, the wounded man spat at him and called him a "pig." He was immediately shot. The boy was released and given over to a local priest, who, in turn, put him in custody of a man named Garbos. "There were three of us in the household. The farmer Garbos, who had a dead, unsmiling face and half-open mouth; the dog, Judas, with sly glowering eyes; and myself." Garbos, for no apparent reason, would nightly flog the boy, hang him by the arms from a ceiling beam, and incite the dog against him.

During a village-wide celebration, all gathered at the cathedral for mass, and the boy silently followed his master to watch. The priest's housekeeper found him hiding in a corner and decided that since one of the altar boys was ill, this "gypsy foundling" would serve as a replacement. During the service, it was the altar boy's duty to walk to the missal, lift it by its base, and take it before the altar. Weak from so many beatings, when the boy hoisted the holy object, he tipped backwards and "the missal and its tray tumbled down the steps." A group of peasants dragged the boy from the church and tossed him into a large manure pit. Retching and gasping for air, when he finally pulled himself out of the deep mire, he noticed that he had lost his voice: "I tried to cry out, but my tongue flapped hopelessly in my mouth."

The pathetic boy moved from village to village. Once, a group of ruffians pushed him into an ice-covered lake. Miraculously, he survived. Finally, after a brutal confrontation involving a group of villagers, a band of Russian deserters, and a brigade of Russian troops, some Russian soldiers took him in and gave him medical treatment and food. They taught the boy how to read and tutored him in Communism.

Eventually the war came to an end and the boy, still mute, was sent to an orphanage in the Polish city where he had lived with his parents before the war.

One morning, the principal ordered the boy to come to her office. There he saw a familiar-looking man and woman. Now twelve years old, the no-longer innocent boy was reunited with his stranger-parents. At their apartment an adopted four-year-old brother also awaited.

Over the weeks that followed, the boy remained thin and sickly. "The doctor advised mountain air and lots of exercise." He was sent to the mountains where an aged and kind ski instructor looked after him. One day the mountain where they skied was hit by a blizzard. "I lost sight of the instructor and started on my own down the steep slope," the boy recounted. "My skis bounced over hardened, icy snow and the speed took my breath away. When I suddenly saw a deep gully it was too late to make a turn."

When he woke up, the boy said, "I opened my mouth and strained. Sounds crawled up my throat . . . The voice lost in a faraway church had found me again and filled the room."

Commentary:

Kosinski's tale of a young boy left to survive a hostile, superstitious world, is partly autobiographical, partly fiction, but, as the author asserts, fiction is not that far from reality. *The Painted Bird* has been accused of being too brutal, too graphic, too sexually violent. These accusations appear weak, however, when compared to the stark reality of people in cattle cars being driven to their deaths.

Kosinski maintains that life – any life – even one that includes tremendous pain and injustice, is preferable to death. This story, as the book's jacket description indicates, is "about the proximity of terror and savagery to innocence and love . . . and exploration into the nature of evil and the totalitarian mind."

STEPPENWOLF

by Hermann Hesse, S. Fischer, Frankfurt, Germany, 1927 (English edition, 1947)

Type of work: Psychological and social
commentary

Setting: Small-town Germany, and Harry
Haller's wild imagination; the 1920's

Principal characters:
Harry Haller, the imaginative
Steppenwolf
Hermine, Harry's psychological female
double
Maria, Harry's lover
Pablo, a jazz musician and Harry's
guide through imagination

Story Overview:

When the bizarre and solitary Harry
Haller disappeared, his landlady's nephew,
who felt a kinship toward the lonely tenant,
found a manuscript in Harry's room.
Throughout its pages, Harry referred to himself as a "Steppenwolf": as two beings always
at odds: one, a learned, cultured, mild-man-
nered gentleman; the other, a fragmented animal, stunned by society and impatient with its
restraints, and continuously tempting Harry
into unacceptable behavior.

The manuscript, entitled "For Madmen
Only," recounted how one night Haller had
come upon a neon sign reading "Magic
Theater – Entrance Not For Everybody." On
the asphalt in front of the theater were the
words "For Madmen Only!"

Later that same night, at a comfortable
old tavern, the band began playing some
music that Harry detested: "It was the music
of decline. There must have been such music
in Rome under the later emperors . . . ."

Then a man gave Harry a tract: *Treatise
on the Steppenwolf*. It turned out to be a treatise
on himself – describing Harry Haller as if the
author knew things about him that even he
did not know. The tract explained that most
individuals have more than one "self" to deal
with:

*There are a good many people of the same
kind as Harry. Many artists are of his kind . . .
their lives are not their own.*

Now the powerful Steppenwolf began to
slowly suffocate him. " . . . Now it was his
wish no longer, nor his aim, to be alone and
independent, but rather his lot and his sentence."

Wandering, and feeling a strong resolve
to die, over a period of weeks Harry Haller
became freer in his use of opium and wine.
The Steppenwolf was overpowering.

One day Harry entered a bar and met a
strange girl, whose happiness and humor
appealed to him, though he had previously
avoided such women. She seemed to understand Harry's problem and convinced him that
he must open up, relax, and learn to dance.
"Fine views of life, you have," she added. "You
have always done the difficult and complicated things and the simple ones you haven't
even learned."

This fascinating girl, Hermine, reminded
Harry of his boyhood friend Herman. Harry
soon learned a new life under Hermine's tutelage. She appeared to speak to Harry from a
mirror, his alterego, another side of him.
Hermine made some prophecies: Harry would
fall in love with her, and, then, ultimately,
would kill her.

Hermine introduced Harry to Pablo, a
saxophone player at a dance club. Harry hated
Pablo at once – not only for his obvious friendship with Hermine, but because he was the
antithesis of Harry's great musical hero,
Mozart.

That same day Harry was also introduced to Maria. Her fleshiness was the
dichotomy of Hermine's spiritual mind. One
night when Harry returned to his room from a
church recital, he found Maria in his bed;
somehow he understood that she was a gift
from Hermine. The two became lovers, Maria
aiding Hermine in her quest to bring Harry
along his new path to self-acceptance and
pleasure.

Invited to a formal ball on another night,
Harry finally gathered enough courage to go.
Though he found the dance in full swing,
Harry could not shake an odd melancholy,
and at last he decided to get his coat and
leave. However, though he had put the cloak-
room number securely in his pocket in anticipation of just such an exit, the number was no
longer there. Then a small man standing
beside him handed him a number that had
writing on it: "Tonight At The Magic Theater –
For Madmen Only – Price Of Admittance,
Your Mind. Not For Everybody. Hermine Is In
Hell."

Harry quickly made his way to a basement theater, decorated to resemble Hell.
There at the bar he saw a handsome lad,
hauntingly familiar; but as he sat down to
greet who he believed was his old high-school
friend, Herman, the "boy" turned into
Hermine. As he danced and drank, Harry was
immediately caught up in "the intoxication of
a general festivity."

Soon, Pablo arrived with a looking glass
into which Harry gazed – and, for the first
time, he saw the Steppenwolf's image.

The theater's corridor was horseshoe-shaped, with many doors lining its walls. Pablo explained that behind the doors were assorted "entertainments". However, in order to enjoy them, Harry must leave his personality at the entrance. " . . . To teach you to laugh is the whole aim in getting up this entertainment," he said. And when Harry was at last made to laugh at the multifaceted reflection of himself produced by Paldo's mirror, he began his adventures in the Magic Theater.

Entering a room labeled "Jolly Hunting – Great Hunt in Automobiles," he found himself in the midst of a war between men and machines, and "joined the battle joyfully." He and a boyhood friend embarked on a "game" of killing people, then tossing them with their motorcars from a cliff. " . . . At bottom it's all the same," they joked.

After some time, Harry found himself again in the theater corridor. This time he chose a door marked "Guidance in the Building Up of the Personality. Success Guaranteed." Inside Harry met a man sitting before a chess board. He offered Harry some of the chess pieces – the pieces of himself that Harry had already seen reflected in Pablo's mirror. The man then launched into a discourse on schizophrenia, arguing that many who appear mad are completely sane, and vice versa. Harry soon discovered that by moving his chess pieces he could bring about friendships and enmities leading to varied outcomes; he was then told that only by opening up to the infinite possibilities within himself – and learning to laugh – could he reach out to govern his life. Harry pocketed the game pieces and found another door, "Marvelous Taming of the Steppenwolf." Within, he saw an animal tamer (resembling himself) who led on a leash "a large, beautiful but terribly emaciated wolf." After a time the roles were reversed and the wolf tamer became the tamed. Harry, horrified by the sight of the man on the leash, viciously tearing a lamb and a rabbit to pieces, dashed out of the room.

The next door he decided to try was labeled, "All Girls are Yours." Here he succeeded in inspiring love in every girl he had relished in his youth. After enjoying each of them, he finally felt ready to give himself over entirely to Hermine.

Once more Harry found himself in the theater passage. In front of him was a door which read, "How One Kills for Love." In despair he fumbled in his pocket for the game pieces, so that he might rearrange his fate and not turn into a killer; but instead, from his pocket he pulled a knife. To the lilting sounds of Mozart's *Don Giovanni*, Mozart himself approached, and laughed a hideous, mocking laugh. In anger, Harry caught hold of Mozart's pigtail. But instead of lifting and shaking Mozart, he found himself lifted into the sky and whirled around like a comet. "A bitter-sharp and steel-bright icy gaiety coursed through me and a desire to laugh as shrilly and wildly and unearthly as Mozart had done."

Suddenly, Harry was again in the corridor, looking at his pale image in the mirror. In desperation, he kicked the image to splinters, then went to find his true love. And there behind the last door lay Hermine, sleeping naked on a rug – in the arms of Pablo. Harry rushed forward and plunged his knife into her breast, then left, silently.

" . . . Learn what is to be taken seriously and laugh at the rest," preached Mozart, who appeared to scold Harry for his "crime." Then he flashed the words, "Harry's Execution." Instantly, Harry was standing before a guillotine. "Gentlemen, there stands before you Harry Haller," began a prosecutor, "accused and found guilty of the willful misuse of our Magic Theater: . . . he stabbed to death the reflection of a girl with the reflection of a knife; . . . displayed the intention of using our theater as a mechanism of suicide; and [has] shown himself devoid of humor." After Harry was laughed out of court, Mozart started in again: "You are willing to die, you coward, but not to live." Then Mozart transformed himself into Pablo, playing with the game pieces Harry had lost from his pocket. Now Harry understood: he could not continue to resist life. And now all the game pieces of his life were available to him. Only now could he achieve a measure of synthesis in his life. "One day I would be a better hand at the game," he vowed. "One day I would learn how to laugh."

Commentary:

Following a number of personal tragedies, Hermann Hesse (1877-1962) underwent psychoanalysis. Throughout his life he searched for a synthesis between various parts of himself, making the fragmented Harry Haller of *Steppenwolf* a highly autobiographical character.

Hesse describes *Steppenwolf* as his "most misunderstood novel," a long quest for identity in a world of kaleidoscopic values, where "mad hedonism [was] falling into degeneration." The storyline is often complex, and it is difficult to tell where reality ends and imagination begins. Indeed, the novel spawned many of the ideas behind the "60's" culture.

But behind all the mirrors, music, anti-establishment philosophy, and drug-induced hallucinations, is a man struggling – and failing – to find and cope with his soul. "You cannot be a vagabond and an artist and at the same time a bourgeoisie and a respectable, healthy person," Hesse offers in answer to life's conflicting paths. "You want the ecstacy so you have to take the hangover."

THE HANDMAID'S TALE

by Margaret Atwood, Houghton Mifflin, Boston, Mass., 1986

Type of work: Futuristic fiction

Setting: Mythical Republic of Gilead (USA); in the near future

Principal characters:

Offred, a "Rachel"; a woman kept for the purpose of producing a baby

Moira, Offred's best friend

The Commander (Fred), her "sixtyish" governmental master

Serena Joy, the Commander's wife

Nick, the Commander's chauffeur-body-guard

Ofglen, another "Rachel"

Story Overview:

The events that transformed the United States into the Republic of Gilead were quick and all-encompassing. Immediately after the catastrophe, "when they shot the president and machine-gunned the Congress and the army declared a state of emergency," the media blared, "Everything is under control." But shortly thereafter the Constitution was suspended, newspapers were censored or shut down, and roadblocks began to appear. And, eventually, even more radical changes took place. Women lost their jobs, their bank accounts were frozen, and they were assigned to the care of legal male "guardians," whose first names they generally assumed.

Fearing the worst if they stayed, "Offred" (named for "Fred," the man who later owned her) her husband, and their young daughter had passports forged for themselves and made a run for the Canadian border. They planned and prepared carefully: "When we get to the border we'll pretend we're just going over for a day trip." But when the border-guard checking their passports picked up a phone, they knew that the "Eyes of God" (the secret police) were waiting for them. Into the woods they raced on foot. Later, all that Offred could remember was her capture. She never knew what happened to her family.

In some ways Offred was fortunate. Since she was still young and fertile, she was not declared an "Unwoman" and sent to the "Colonies," where thousands of unfortunates were forced to work in agricultural camps or clean up toxic waste dumps. Life-expectancy was low in the Colonies. Instead, Offred was declared a "Rachel" (after the favored Biblical wife of Jacob) and sent to a center where women were "re-educated" and prepared for the duty of producing a baby in a "Commander's" house. In the center, Offred was overseen by an "Aunt" and shown movies depicting former society to make her see how "corrected" this new society was.

To her joy, Offred's old friend Moira arrived one day at the center. "This is a loony bin," Moira declared. The two women often talked secretly through a hole in the partition between stalls in the washroom, vowing covert rebellion.

During one of their bathroom conversations, Moira confided that she had to escape; she was "going batty." And, after recovering from the torture inflicted as punishment for her first, futile attempt, Moira finally did escape – by jumping one of the Aunts, putting on her clothes, and scurrying out of the building.

Soon Offred was sent to her first "post." Serena Joy, the Commander's hostile, blue-eyed wife, met her at the door. "So, you're the new one," she said. "I want to see as little of you as possible. If I get trouble, I'll give trouble. You understand?" Surprised by this warning, Offred quickly stammered that she understood. Serena Joy continued: "As for my husband, he's just that. My husband. I want that perfectly clear. Till death do us part. It's final."

Offred's duties were simple: Number one, get pregnant; and number two, go to town daily to buy food. On her excursions into town, of course, Offred had to be accompanied by another "Rachel." Widespread pollution and societal shake-up had made food scarce in Gilead. Thus, no one could trust any Rachel to shop alone; and informants were placed everywhere to ensure that any budding conspiracies were squelched.

Offred's shopping partner was Ofglen. Each day after the shopping was done, Ofglen suggested that they pass by The Wall, where Gilead executed its criminals. Abortionists, heretics, Quakers, Catholics, and Jews – they all hung suspended on hooks cemented into The Wall. Ofglen noted that the corpses looked "like scarecrows, which in a way is what they are, since they are meant to scare."

Books, pens, paper and television were all forbidden. Once, alone in her room, Offred recalled a film she had been shown at the Center. Meant to serve as an example of what not to be, the film had depicted women forced into a "rape march." Horribly, Offred had recognized her own mother in the movie; where she was now was anybody's guess.

Once each month, Offred, the Commander, and Serena Joy would retire to the bedroom for a ceremony of insemination. There, while the Commander read the Bible, his wife literally "offered" the handmaid to her husband, holding Offred by the arms throughout the proceeding, supposedly to signify that "we are one flesh, one being." All three remained fully clothed. There was "no passion or love or romance" involved.

Even in her confinement, Offred still indulged in certain small rebellions. She stole butter and other "cosmetics" with which to keep her skin soft. On one such escapade, she slipped into the sitting room to look around. Suddenly, she heard footsteps. Nick, the Commander's bodyguard and chauffeur, had brought news that the Commander wanted to see her in his office.

As Offred entered the Commander's office, he stuttered out his request: "I'd like you to play a game of *Scrabble* with me." Offred felt like laughing, but agreed. They played two games that night: " . . . I let him win the second." Before she left to return to her room, the Commander had one more wish: "I want you to kiss me." Offred complied.

After this, Offred would creep to the Commander's room two or three times a week and play *Scrabble*. Their "arrangement" required that they set up a signal involving Nick: if Nick's hat was on askew when Offred returned from shopping, that night they would meet.

On their second night together the Commander brought a gift for Offred – an old *Vogue* magazine. Offred hesitated, " . . . These were supposed to be burned."

By the third rendezvous she was bold enough to ask for some hand lotion, which she received. Obviously, the black market in Gilead was alive and thriving.

About halfway through the next "ceremony," the Commander, as though the act was done out of reflex, reached up and almost touched Offred's face. "You could get me transferred to the Colonies . . . " she said afterward. He promised to be more discreet.

Meanwhile, one afternoon Offred and Ofglen went to the Soul Scrolls store, where people solicited prayers from machines. As they stood watching the machine spin out prayers, Ofglen asked, "Do you think God listens to these machines?" Offred summoned her courage and said no. After this, the women began to open up to one another, eventually even devising a password for use in a crisis: "Mayday."

Later, Serena Joy asked Offred if she was pregnant yet. "No. Nothing," Offred answered with relief. Then Serena suggested that maybe the Commander was sterile, and perhaps she should try another man: Nick. Startled, Offred realized how much Serena wanted a baby. As incentive, if Offred slept with Nick and produced a child, then Serena promised to show her a picture of her daughter. In confusion, elation, hope and sadness, Offred walked away.

During one of Offred's visits to the Commander, he presented her with a pink, feather-adorned slip-on, the kind of thing – supposedly long-since burned – that women had once worn to look sexy for men. Then he led her outside, past roadblocks, to a building once used as a hotel. Inside were numerous men, along with women dressed like Offred. Each wore most laughable, dowdy lingerie or show-girl garb. "Well? What do you think of our little club?" he boasted. " . . . Nature demands variety, for men."

Then, Moira emerged from the crowd. Her eyes met Offred's, but neither woman flinched. Then Moira flashed the hidden signal they had used in the re-education center. Five minutes later the two were in the Ladies' Room, exchanging news – and barbs about one another's outfits – under the stall. Moira had almost escaped into Canada but was caught at the border. She thought they would kill her or send her back to the center, but instead they gave her two choices: The Colonies, where, eventually, "your nose falls off and your skin pulls away like rubber gloves"; or this – steady work as a prostitute for the government of Gilead.

While Offred spent that night with the Commander, Serena Joy was discreetly arranging with Nick to impregnate the "Rachel". At first this liaison with Nick was a duty, but soon Offred found herself freely in love with Nick – and she suspected he felt the same about her.

One morning, when Offred went to meet Ofglen for the day's shopping, a "new" Ofglen greeted her. For days Offred was gripped by fear. Had the "old" Ofglen "talked"? However, Offred's fears were finally allayed when she learned that Ofglen had committed suicide. Still, Offred remained unsure about who knew what.

Then one day Serena Joy confronted Offred, holding the lipstick-marked costume she had worn. "I trusted you. I tried to help you," she sobbed. "You could have left me something." Offred silently slipped back to her room – to await the black van that would surely come for her.

Offred heard the van pull up, and braced for the entrance of the military henchmen – "but it was Nick who pushed open the door."

"It's all right," he whispered. "It's Mayday. Go with them . . . . Trust me."

As the Guardians led the still wavering Offred away, the Commander and his wife protested. It was no use. As she was locked into the van, she wondered what would become of her: "And so I step up, into the darkness within; or else the light."

Commentary:

The Handmaid's Tale is meant as a warning shot. Atwood suggests that this type of rigid, joyless world is what we can expect when freedom is restricted by dogmatic fanatics – in this case, the Religious Right of the United States.

Though men, and patriarchal societies in particular, are the villains of the book, the male sex is redeemed somewhat by Nick's actions. This novel is Feminist at its core, and it may merit some criticism for the occasional preachy tone it takes. Atwood's writing, however, takes on an honest, hard-hitting tone, and is surprisingly humorous.

LORD OF THE FLIES

by William Golding, Coward-McCann, New York, N.Y., 1954

Type of work: Idealogical adventure novel

Setting: A deserted tropical island after a nuclear war

Principal characters:

Ralph, a likable, sensible boy of twelve

Jack, a cruel, power-hungry redheaded youth

Simon, a skinny, shy, thoughtful nine-year-old

Piggy, Ralph's intelligent friend – a fat boy with thick glasses

Story Overview:

Ralph wandered out of the tropical jungle paradise. "We are going to have fun on this island," he grinned. The blond boy turned cartwheels on the sand, while his friend Piggy, pudgy, thick-lensed, and asthmatic, looked on. "I can't move with all these creeper things," Piggy stammered, picking thorns from his plump bare legs. A whole load of school-boys had been jettisoned on the island before their plane crashed. Ralph was confident his father would rescue them; Piggy wasn't so certain.

Ralph found a large conch shell in the lagoon and Piggy urged him to blow it. Boys soon scampered out of the jungle toward the sound. One – tall, redheaded Jack Merridew – arrived, leading a procession of soldier-like followers.

Jack was disappointed when the others elected Ralph their leader. Still, he went off with Ralph and a thin boy named Simon to explore. From atop a mountain they recognized their isolation – but also a chance for adventure. On the way down, a wild pig crossed the path, but the boys were unable – and not quite willing – to kill it. Jack promised, though, that the next time he would stab the animal for meat.

Jack soon set about making good his "promise of meat." On all fours, smeared with clay to disguise his scent, he sniffed the warm, steamy pig droppings, and stalked his prey. Ralph, on the other hand, using a lens from Piggy's glasses, built a rescue fire on the mountain and started a project to erect shelters; but the other boys tended to enjoy Jack's fun and games more, and soon began following him on his hunts.

The conch became the symbol of order in the boys' meetings: holding the conch conferred the right to speak. Even Jack was convinced of the need for order: "We've got to have rules and obey them. After all, we're not savages. We're English . . ."

All the boys looked forward to a heroic, storybook island quest – until one little boy with a "mulberry-colored birthmark" on his face, began telling about a snake-like "beastie"

he'd seen in the woods. From then on, fear reigned, especially among the younger boys, the "littluns." Jack called them all batty; yet, using their terror to his advantage, he often alluded to the unmentionable thing that lurked in the forest.

Time passed. The heat of day and the cold dread of night began to overwhelm the "littluns," who often cried hysterically; the "biguns" began forgetting their childhoods altogether. Over the months, friction mounted between Jack and Ralph. Jack became more violent, breaking one of Piggy's lenses and leading hunting parties of ever more filthy and cruel boys.

Because it was a chore to keep the rescue fire lit, the boys abandoned it altogether – ironically, just weeks before a ship passed. Ralph scolded the hunters; they should have helped him instead of playing games all the time.

Meanwhile, Jack's words and deeds became primitive and savage. He would often reenact his hunts in a game. Making "pig-dying noises," the tribe, in swelling excitement, would pretend to kill a pig, represented by one of the "littluns." Ralph, with Piggy and Simon as his only friends, felt more and more isolated. He blew on the conch to call a meeting, still hoping to organize for survival and rescue. "Things are breaking up," Ralph explained. "I don't understand why . . . " His voice trailed off. Then Piggy took the conch and asked, "What are we? Humans? Or animals? Or savages?" When Jacked interrupted, Ralph shouted, "You're breaking the rules!"

"Who cares?" Jack responded.

Ralph answered, "The rules are the only thing we've got." But Jack no longer heard: "We're strong – we hunt! If there's a beast, we'll hunt it down! We'll close in and beat and beat and beat! . . . " and doing a deranged dance, he raced with his hunters into the night. "Blow the conch," whispered Piggy. "If you don't blow, we'll soon be animals . . . " But Ralph didn't blow. His command was finished.

The next morning, two boys urgently roused Ralph. They had seen the beast, they said, on the far side of the island. Led by Ralph, the group approached the "beast" – a dead pilot hanging from the entangled cords of his parachute. But even after showing them that there was no supernatural beast to fear, Ralph still found the filthy, tattered boys siding with Jack, the hunter. Finally, lonely and afraid, the chief allowed himself to give in and follow Jack too. He even made the decisive blow in a boar hunt. "I walloped him properly. That was the beast, I think," he gushed. Afterward, in a savage dance, they all reenacted the killing by striking at little Robert. The "game" quickly got out of hand, and Robert went down, sobbing. Even Ralph wanted "a handful of that brown, vulnerable flesh. The desire to squeeze and hurt was overpowering."

But Ralph soon regained his senses. Homesick and tired, he again competed with Jack for the role of leader. Sensing Jack's unstable nature, most of the boys again voted for Ralph, whereupon, Jack gathered his loyal hunters and struck out into the jungle to become his own tribal chieftain.

Jack's boys stalked and killed a sow and her piglets. In an orgy of killing, they smeared themselves with blood and impaled the sow's head on a stake as an offering to the revivified beast. But Simon, the loner who had never believed in the beast and who frequently wandered off in the forest by himself, witnessed the scene with disgust. Later, in a trance, he conversed with the devilish, fly-covered pig's head, calling it Lord of the Flies. The bloody head told him: "You knew, didn't you? I'm part of you? . . . I'm the reason why it's no go? Why things are what they are?" In an echo of Ralph's earlier cry, the skull finally gloated, "We are going to have fun on this island!"

Awakened from his vision, Simon understood. He needed to warn the others: The only evil on the island came from inside themselves. On his way back, Simon freed the rotting corpse of the parachutist from its cords. The beast would be no more.

In the mean time, Ralph and Piggy had painfully decided to rejoin the hunters. The boys had feasted, and then were gathered in a circle around the fire. "Kill the beast! Cut his throat! Spill his blood!" the ritualistic chant went up. Amidst the gusts and thunder claps of a storm, their bloodlust grew.

Just then, Simon arrived. The tribe closed in on the approaching "beast" with their sharpened sticks. Soon, Simon's silent body lay in a heap on the beach.

The next day, Ralph and Piggy moved to the opposite side of the island. In fear and nervous exhaustion, they dozed off. The fire – symbol of hope – flickered and went out.

But at the other end of the island Jack had incited his mob to believe the beast was somehow still alive, and the hunters prepared a massive lever-propelled rock for protection.

The following morning, Piggy discovered his glasses had been stolen. Ralph now decided that they must go and reason with the tribe. "I'll have to be led like a dog . . . " Piggy moaned, yet, carrying the conch, he rehearsed his address to Jack: "I don't ask for my glasses back, not as a favor . . . not because you're strong, but because what's right's right."

The pair arrived at Castle Rock, Jack's fort. Suddenly, Jack appeared with a gutted pig and goaded Ralph to fight. "You're a beast and a swine . . . " shouted Ralph as they came together. But Piggy, in a last, desperate attempt to make peace, held up the conch and demanded to speak. "Which is better – to be a pack of painted Indians . . . or to be sensible? . . ." Piggy's answer came quickly: "High overhead, Roger, with a sense of delerious abandonment, leaned all his weight on the lever." The giant boulder shattered down on Piggy, hurling him – and the conch – to the rocks below. "Piggy's arms and legs twitched a bit, like a pig's after it has been killed," and then went limp. Jack stepped forward and calmly announced, "The conch is gone . . . I'm chief."

Using "an instinct that he did not know he possessed," Ralph fled into the jungle. Now he was the beast.

Darkness fell. Ralph slept in a thicket. At dawn, the stick-wielding boys rushed, heaving stones and setting fire to the brush. The chase was on. "Think!" Ralph commanded himself. But he was past reason. He "shot forward . . . screaming, snarling, bloody . . . . He forgot his wounds, his hunger and thirst, and became fear; hopeless fear on flying feet."

Ralph sprinted for the beach, where he fell on the sand, crying for mercy. When he staggered to his feet, there stood a white-uniformed naval officer gazing down at him. Seeing the "little boys" in the distance, "bodies streaked with colored clay, sharp sticks in their hands," he spoke: "Fun and games. We saw the smoke. What have you been doing? Having a war or something? . . . Who's boss here?"

"I am," Ralph gasped.

Jack, now a little boy who carried the remains of a pair of spectacles, began to protest, but changed his mind.

The officer chided the children. Why had they not turned their predicament into an adventure? Ralph, unable to speak, could only weep for "the end of innocence, the darkness of man's heart, and the fall through the air of the true, wise friend called Piggy."

Commentary:

Everything about Lord of the Flies is thematic. The story revolves around a question: Is unshackled freedom a good thing? Golding's obvious answer is the need for civilization, its rules, laws, and expectations. (Ironically, the nearly blind Piggy was the one boy who could "see" this most clearly.) Yet, while Ralph personifies law, cooperation and democratic choice, it is Jack's reliance on charisma, brute force and authoritarian rule that wins out on the island.

Chilling words from Golding's Notes reveal the final irony of this book: "The officer, having interrupted a man-hunt, prepares to take the children off the island in a cruiser which will presently be hunting its [own] enemy in the same implacable way. And who will rescue the adult and his cruiser?"

HENDERSON THE RAIN KING

by Saul Bellow, Viking Press, New York, N.Y., 1959

Type of work: Contemporary comic novel

Setting: Present-day Africa

Principal characters:
> *Henderson,* a wealthy sixty-year-old American
> *Itelo,* King of the Arnewi
> *Dahfu,* King of the Wariri
> *Romilayu,* Henderson's African guide

Story Overview:

Henderson felt restless. Although he had inherited all the money he could possibly want, he still heard an inner voice saying, "I want, I want, I want." A large, hefty man, Henderson increasingly bullied his wife and children.

Soon Henderson's growing discontent led him to embark on a trip to Africa along with his recently married friend, Charlie Albert. However, sightseeing with Charlie and his new bride proved unsatisfactory; their photo safari was too "safe" for Henderson. So he hired a guide named Romilayu and struck out on his own, heading deep into the jungle. "Geographically speaking I didn't have the remotest idea where we were, and I didn't care too much."

One morning Henderson and Romilayu followed a dry river bed to the rustic village of Arnewi, where Henderson was surprised to find most of the villagers weeping – "mourning for cattle which had died in the drought."

Henderson and Romilayu were escorted to the Arnewi king, Itelo, and Henderson was impressed: "From his size alone I felt he must be an important person." He was a little disappointed, though, when the king addressed him in English, explaining that he had traveled to school with another young prince named Dahfu, from the Wariri tribe, and there they had learned English. Itelo then insisted that his new guest must go to meet Queen Willatale, Itelo's aunt.

As the procession made its way to the aunt's hut, Henderson caught a glimpse of a large cistern filled with water. At first he was bewildered. What about all the cattle dead of thirst? But on closer examination he discovered the water was alive with thousands of frogs. "The frogs? They kept you from watering the cattle?" he asked Itelo. Itelo nodded: "Mus' be no ahnimal in drink wattah." As they continued on to their appointment, Henderson muttered, "Just you wait, you little sons of bitches, you'll croak in hell before I'm done."

Before introducing Henderson to his aunt, Itelo explained that one matter of business had to first be taken care of: "When stranger guest comes we always make acquaintance by wrestle. Invariable."

Henderson demurred, but Itelo insisted. So they squared off, and, in spite of Henderson's age, he won the bout. Itelo, though the village champion, accepted defeat graciously. Now he could say to Henderson, "I know you."

Itelo's Aunt Willatale was wrapped in a regal-looking lion skin when the party arrived. With Itelo interpreting, Henderson explained to Willatale why he was in Africa; he was sick, not physically, but mentally. The queen nodded, telling Henderson that he had what the Arnewi called "grun-tu-molani, man want to live." Pleased, Henderson promised her majesty that he would rid the village of its frogs.

Henderson decided that it would be best to blow up the frogs. All night long he assembled his "bomb": an empty flashlight, gunpowder, and a fuse cut from a lighter's wick. The next morning he went to the cistern and, with all the tribesmen gathered around, lobbed the contraption into the water. Henderson shouted, "Hallelujah!" as frogs flew from the opening. But then, hearing "shrieks from the natives . . . I found that the dead frogs were pouring out of the cistern together with the water. The explosion had blasted out the retaining wall at the front end." Henderson was aghast. Itelo immediately suggested that it would be a good idea if Henderson left, so he hastily collected his belongings and, together with Romilayu, set out for the village of the Wariri.

Some ten days into their new journey, Henderson and Romilayu were ambushed by a group of tribesmen with guns and led conveniently to the very Wariri village they had been looking for. They were questioned, then placed in a guarded hut.

The next day, two strong, fierce-looking women conducted Henderson to King Dahfu, lounging on an old green sofa and fingering several ornamental skulls that sat before him. "Do not feel alarm," Dahfu said, "these are for employment in the ceremony of this afternoon."

Henderson became Dahfu's honored guest at the ceremony, the purpose of which was to bring desperately needed rain to the Wariri. Large wooden idols were carted in and placed in the middle of an arena. Then after several gun salutes to Dahfu and Henderson, Dahfu and a tall woman met in the arena. They began tossing two of the skulls back and forth, using tied ribbons as handholds and throwing them great heights. Afterwards, Henderson asked Dahfu what would have happened if one of the skulls had been dropped. "My own skull will get the air," was his candid reply.

Next, attention turned to the wooden gods in the center of the arena. Tribal members advanced one by one to pick up a heavy idol and move it away. Henderson cheered along with the others as each icon was muscled and hoisted. At length, only one remained – Mummah, goddess of the clouds. The strongest man in the village could not raise her. Excited, Henderson turned to the king and stammered, "Sir, sire, I mean . . . let me! I must." Dahfu gave him permission to try, but warned that there might be consequences, no matter the outcome. "Never hesitating, I encircled Mummah with my arms. I wasn't going to take no for an answer. The wood gave to my pressure and benevolent Mummah with her fixed smile yielded to me; I lifted her from the ground and carried her twenty feet to her new place among the other gods."

Almost on cue the sky filled with clouds and it began to rain. Dahfu declared that Henderson was now the respected "Sungo" of the Wariri tribe. The new Sungo was taken and forced to run naked through the town blessing the water; then he was returned to the arena where he beat the gods with whips. As the ceremony drew to a close, Henderson, overcome by exhaustion and fever, passed out.

The next morning Dahfu explained to Henderson his duties, which included wearing flimsy green shorts. Dahfu also clarified his own position in the tribe: he was not yet the king. After his father Gmilo died, the tribe's priest, following an age-old tribal myth, had pulled a maggot off the corpse and declared that the maggot was now mystically transformed into a lion cub. Before Dahfu could take his father's place as king, he must capture this full grown lion (named Gmilo, after his father). Instead of capturing Gmilo, however, Dahfu had, on an earlier attempt, captured a lioness, which he kept beneath the palace.

The friendship between Henderson and Dahfu grew. Henderson learned much from the prince; and Dahfu felt free to discuss important matters with Henderson that he could not discuss with the men of his tribe. Together they spent most afternoons beneath the palace with the lioness, Atti. At first Henderson kept his distance while Dahfu rubbed and stroked Atti; but soon Henderson was coaxed into moving closer. "Fear is the ruler of mankind," Dahfu theorized. Though Henderson did not like these sessions with the lioness, he endured them because he did not want to lose his friend's admiration.

One day Dahfu announced that Gmilo had been seen near the village. If he captured the lion, he would be able to claim kingship.

The Wariri fashioned a trap called a "hopo" and then sent out drum beaters to drive the lion into the hopo. Once he was inside, the entrance was blocked and the would-be king, standing on a cat-walk, tried to drop a net on the lion. However, as Dahfu lowered his net, something went wrong. Dahfu leaped from the platform to readjust the net, but fell onto the lion instead. "The claws tore. Instantly there came blood." Prince Dahfu rolled away, and with his dying breath pronounced Henderson the new Wariri king.

Only Henderson's grief for the loss of his friend could overshadow his distress at becoming king. Again, guards locked him up with the faithful Romilayu – this time in a hut next to Dahfu's sepulcher; but Henderson was determined to break out. As the tribal priest waited for the mystical maggot to appear on Dahfu's corpse, so that it could be plucked and transformed into a lion cub (a cub conveniently held by a tribesman near the tomb), Henderson planned his escape. When night came, Romilayu shouted, screaming that the Sungo had been bitten by a snake. As the guards rushed in, Henderson ran out, snatched the lion cub from the arms of the stunned tribesman, and dashed into the shadows.

Traveling at night to avoid being seen, and foraging for grubs and roots during the day, Henderson felt his fever worsening. He charged Romilayu to care for the cub while he recuperated: "This is Dahfu to me. Don't let anything happen, please, Romilayu. It would ruin me now."

Eventually reaching civilization, Henderson recovered his strength and prepared for his trek home. He gave many gifts to Romilayu and bid him a tearful goodbye. Arriving in Ethiopia, he boarded a plane bound for Europe; and from Europe, headed for America, where his wife and children were waiting.

When the plane landed to refuel in wintry Newfoundland, Henderson got off to stretch. The cold air "was like medicine applied, a remedy." At last, with the lion in tow, Henderson greeted his family. Once again he was safe and sound – and a little more sane.

Commentary:

For his fiction, Saul Bellow has received the Nobel Prize in Literature, the National Book Award, and the International Literary Prize (the first for an American). He received his college degree in Anthropology, a fact that is evident in *Henderson The Rain King*.

This novel is written in a bizarre, swift narrative. Its mixture of eccentric comedy, tribal superstition and imaginative detail, together with a hero who combines the qualities of both Don Quixote and Odysseus, make the novel a likely future classic.

MY NAME IS ASHER LEV

by Chaim Potok, Alfred A. Knopf, Inc., New York, N.Y., 1972

Type of work: Psychological realism

Setting: New York City; late 1940's through the early 60's

Principal characters:
Asher Lev, a young Hasidic Jew born with a gift of art
Rivkeh Lev, his mother
Aryeh Lev, his father
The Rebbe, spiritual leader of the Lev household
Jacob Kahn, an artist

Story Overview:

What is the mystery that forces a mother to watch her husband and son as they tear at each other's throats? Is the ability to be a great artist a gift from the Master of the Universe or from the Other Side? Is complete honesty with yourself worth the anguish that it may cause? Why would an observant Jew do a painting of a crucifixion scene?

Asher Lev was raised in Brooklyn. His first memories were of his mother, Rivkeh, before her illness changed their lives. Even at the age of four Asher drew pictures pictures of his mother playing with him in the snow, making angels and jumping into the drifts. Then in the spring they went rowing in Prospect Park – with Asher still faithfully recording events on his drawing pad.

During those early years, Asher also sketched pictures of his father, even though Aryeh Lev considered his son's art work a childish waste of time. Asher would outgrow the hobby, he thought, and turn to studying the Talmud.

Meanwhile, Asher depicted his father as he entered the synagogue on Yom Kippur, weeping and chanting the prayer describing the Roman slaughter of the ten great Jewish sages. His father would often explain to Asher how the murder of one man causes a whole world to perish. When one person is murdered his children and children's children are killed also.

The January that Asher turned six was filled with vague memories: darkness, fog, and his mother screaming as she learned about the death of her older brother, a Jewish diplomat. What followed were months of lethargy where Rivkeh wept easily and tired quickly, and cared nothing for her home, for food, or for her family. The boy was certain that she too was dying. He painted colorful flowers and birds for her in an attempt to brighten her mood, but his efforts were wasted; his mother's world was dark, and no pretty painting could change it. Over time, Asher's drawings began to reflect a like despair, both in color and content. "It's not a pretty world, Mama," he pronounced.

Asher's father worked for the Rebbe, head of the Ladover Jews and a wise man. Both Aryeh and the Rebbe were concerned with the fate of Russian Jews, who were not allowed to practice their religion nor to leave Russia.

That spring, Reb Yudel Krinsky, a Jew who had escaped Russia with Aryeh's help, arrived in America. After eleven years in Siberia, Krinsky was fascinated with his new freedom. Asher, too, was enthralled by Reb Krinsky. Over the months, the man and the boy became close friends.

As spring passed, Asher's mother slowly recuperated. One night Rivkeh made known her desires: she wanted to return to school, get her degree, and finish the work of liberation her dead brother had started. So, that September, with the support of the Rebbe, Asher entered the Ladover yeshiva while his mother studied at Brooklyn College. And, to his father's great satisfaction, Asher Lev stopped drawing.

The "great evil" at that time for practicing Jews was Stalin. It was Stalin who ordered the deaths of Jewish intellectuals and blocked Jewish migration from Russia. Aryeh's travels for the Rebbe, as Rivkeh's brother's had been, were an attempt to help these Jews through diplomatic channels.

One day Aryeh received word that he and his family were to be sent to Vienna. The thought of leaving his street, his school, and local synagogue, filled Asher with an overwhelming dread. But then, a miracle occurred: Stalin died. Jews throughout the city rejoiced. Asher stared at the newspaper pictures he saw of Stalin's funeral; the dark face surrounded by flowers. One day at school, as if on its own volition, Asher's hand began drawing Stalin as he had seen him in his coffin. He drew sketch after sketch. His gift had returned, strong and all-consuming.

As a result of many discussions between his parents and the Rebbe, it was finally decided that Asher and his mother would remain in Brooklyn while Aryeh journeyed to work alone in Vienna.

With his father gone, Asher spent more and more of his free time at the museum, where he copied many of the great artists. His school work soon suffered, and neighbors were shocked to see the son of Reb Aryeh Lev neglecting his study of the Torah while his father traveled through Europe to bring Jews back to Torah. But the neighbors' reaction paled to the anger expressed by Aryeh when he came home to celebrate Passover. Would his son never grow up? Would Asher always be driven by the "Other Side"?

The next year Aryeh returned for Asher's bar mitzvah. Still, the distance between Asher and his deeply traditional father continued to grow. "I had become alien to him. In some incomprehensible manner, a cosmic error had been made. The line of inheritance had been perverted. A demonic force had thrust itself into centuries of transmitted responsibility. He could not bear its presence. And he no longer knew how to engage it in battle." Throughout his son's bar mitzvah Aryeh walked in a shroud of pain and shame, a shroud that he carried with him when he returned to Europe.

In March, with the Rebbe's blessing but despite the fears of his father, Asher began studying art under Jacob Kahn, a celebrated Jewish artist. Soon it became evident that the youth possessed immense talent, an ability to see beyond the canvas. During Kahn's five-year tutelage Asher learned the intricacies of color, form, and shape. He also came to understand two things: the impact that Christianity had played on art, and the need to overcome some traditional Jewish restraints in order to paint the human form more precisely. Most important, Kahn taught Asher to be true to his own inner feelings, and never to leave a work uncompleted, even when it might cause pain. As an artist, Asher could not take responsibility for the reactions or the anguish of another – even a Jew. His highest loyalty must be to his art.

When his father returned home to visit, he denounced Asher's painting of nude women and expressed shock over the Christian themes in his son's work. He wouldn't even pronounce the name "Jesus."

Did I know how much Jewish blood had been spilled because of that man? . . . Did I know that the reason Hitler had been able to slaughter six million Jews without too much complaint from the world was that for two thousand years the world had been taught that Jews, not Romans, had killed that man? Did I know that his father, Olov Hasholom, my grandfather, had been murdered by a Russian peasant who was celebrating a holiday having to do with that man?

Finally, at age 18, Asher Lev had his first show – a great success. About this time, Aryeh's work in Europe came to an end. His mission had brought about the release of many Jews, and this had mellowed him. He now displayed a distant tolerance toward Asher's art, which relieved a great burden for Asher's mother: she was no longer torn between the anger of her husband and the defiance of her son.

Asher decided the time had come to study in Europe. There he created his own masterpieces. One notable painting depicted his mother peering out her front room window, stretched – crucified – between her husband and her son.

Standing between two different ways of giving meaning to the world, and at the same time possessed by her own fears and memories, she had moved now toward me, now toward my father, keeping both worlds of meaning alive . . . and she had kept herself alive by picking up her dead brother's work . . .

Asher had painted this dark work "in a strange nerveless frenzy of energy . . . . For the unspeakable mystery that brings good fathers and sons into the world and lets a mother watch them tear at each other's throats." He had chosen a crucifixion motif because there was no aesthetic mold in his own religious tradition into which he could pour a painting of ultimate pain and torment.

Asher's next show was received with impressive reviews; but, as Jacob Kahn had foreseen, the crucifixion painting left Asher's parents devastated. Aryeh, whose dark eyes had glistened with pride as he entered the museum only moments before, now turned to gaze at his son in "awe and rage and bewilderment and sadness, all at the same time." He and his wife slowly made their way through the silent crowd and went home. "But why didn't you draw the pretty birds, Asher? And the flowers?" his mother mourned. What else could she say? To them, the crucifix symbolized the cause of all the anguish Jews had suffered for centuries.

Unlike Asher's father, the Rebbe could not believe Asher's gift was from the "Other Side"; but neither could he understand or explain Asher's Crucifix. He petitioned Asher to leave home; his staying could only hurt the people he loved: "You have crossed a boundary. I cannot help you. You are alone now. I give you my blessings."

As Asher Lev departed for Europe, he could not rid his mind of one final picture: that of his parents standing framed in their living room window, betrayed and still watching him, unable and unwilling to understand.

Commentary:

Rather than creating a work of suspense or action, Potok develops his plot and characters in *Asher Lev* on a psychological level. Detailed descriptions and deep introspection are the vehicles he uses to give his reader a sense of drama and compassion.

His story of a deep-seated clash between father and son is a classic modern family tragedy. Parents try to inculcate their deepest beliefs and values in their children; but children, following their own dreams, may not choose to become what their parents want them to become. Asher is finally able to resolve his own inner conflict between his art and his Jewish beliefs, but he is never able either to please or to comfort the father he loves and admires. And, in an ironic and poignant climax, he wrenchingly betrays his parents – with a work inspired by his love both for them and for truth.

INVISIBLE MAN

by Ralph Ellison, Random House, New York, N.Y., 1947

Type of work: Realistic, psychological fiction

Setting: The deep South and New York City; 1930's

Principal characters:

The Invisible Man, an unnamed black in search of his identity

Dr. Bledsoe, President of a Negro college

Mr. Norton, a white philanthropic contributor to the college

Brother Jack, leader of the Brotherhood, a white group preaching nonviolence to blacks

Ras the Exhortor, a West Indian Black Nationalist

Story Overview:

I am an invisible man. I am invisible, understand, simply because people refuse to see me . . . . All my life I had been looking . . . for myself and asking everyone except myself questions which I, and only I, could answer.

The Invisible Man was the intelligent and soft-spoken grandson of black slaves. At his high-school graduation, he explained, "I delivered an oration in which I showed that humility was the secret, indeed, the very essence of progress." He was asked to repeat the speech at a gathering of the town's leading white citizens. Upon arriving, "I was told that since I was to be there anyway, I might as well take part in the 'battle royal'" slated for the night's entertainment. He and his black companions were blindfolded, placed in a ring, and goaded to fight by men in the audience. "Kill him! Kill him! Slug him, black boy!" they called. Before he realized it, only himself and one other boy, Tatlock, the biggest of the gang, were left in the ring. Tatlock pummeled his rival until he hit the mat. The fight was over; the face and the dignity of the young man were shattered.

When the bloody, sweaty, humiliated youth finally did give his speech, no one really listened; the onlookers returned to their talking and drinking. Frustrated, the Invisible Man spoke two words that silenced the crowd – *social equality*. " . . . Laughter hung smoke-like in the sudden stillness." The men turned on him, forcing him to recant. "You sure that about 'equality' was a mistake?" the M.C. asked. "Oh yes sir, I was swallowing blood."

But the young man was allowed to finish his speech, and was afterwards handed a calfskin briefcase: "Boy, take this prize and keep it well . . . . Some day it will be filled with important papers that will help shape the destiny of your people." Inside the briefcase was a scholarship to a nearby Negro college.

The Invisible Man did well in school. Success was just within his reach; a success that depended on humility and conformity – on invisibility. Then in his junior year the eager young man was asked to serve as chauffeur for visiting dignitaries. One day, while driving off campus with a Mr. Norton, one of the school's white benefactors, they passed some log cabins. Mr. Norton could not quite believe it when the Negro student explained that these cabins dated back to the times of slavery. He demanded that they stop at one particular cabin, but the boy hesitated; Jim Trueblood, who had scandalized the black community by having a child with his own daughter, lived in that cabin. But Norton insisted that they stop and talk. After hearing Trueblood's story, the white man appeared ready to faint. "I might have a stimulant, young man. A little whiskey," he groaned as they drove on.

Now the only place nearby to get whiskey was the Golden Day, a combination tavern and brothel. When the bartender there would not let the black student buy whiskey, he returned to the car, only to find his passenger barely breathing, lying "like a figure of chalk." Frantically, the Invisible Man rushed back in the tavern for help. After being carried inside, the old man finally came around. As he sipped some brandy, drunkards, prostitutes and "lunatics" crowded around him, nearly breaking into a riot with their shoving and gutter-talk.

When Dr. Bledsoe, president of the college, found out about the incident, he exploded. "Boy! Are you serious? . . . Why that Trueblood shack? You're black and living in the South – did you forget how to lie?" The Invisible Man tried to defend his actions, but Bledsoe pronounced his sentence: "Boy . . . I want you to go to New York for the summer and save your pride – and your money. You go there and earn your next year's fees." The following day, Bledsoe handed him some letters of recommendation and a list of job contacts.

On his way north, the Invisible Man resolved to "work hard and serve my employer so well that he would shower Dr. Bledsoe with favorable reports. And I would save my money and return in the fall full of New York culture. I'd be indisputably the leading campus figure."

However, in New York the young man's job search proved curiously fruitless. Secretaries would take his letters, disappear into an office, and then come out and tell the young man that they would let him know "if anything came up." Finally after a number of interviews, the young man was asked if he had read Bledsoe's introductory letter. No, he hadn't; the letters had been sealed. Now he found that they all began: "The bearer . . . is a former student of ours (I say former because he shall never be enrolled as a student again) . . . . It is to the best interests of the great work which we are dedicated to perform that he continue undisturbed in [his] vain hopes while remaining as far as possible from our midst." As the young man sat dumbfounded, the embarrassed interviewer recommended a paint factory where he might apply for a job.

Liberty Paints hired the Invisible Man. "The wise guys firing the regular guys and putting on you colored college boys. Pretty smart," was the first comment he heard. "That way they don't have to pay union wages."

Sent to the basement as a "janitorial assistant," the young man was given the job of watching the paint gauges. He got along reasonably well with his crusty boss, Brockway, until lunchtime, when he was detained at a union meeting he had accidentally walked in on. As he faced his supervisor and tried to explain the delay, Brockway smacked him. Suddenly the boy's mind snapped in anger and frustration and he knocked Brockway's dentures across the floor. Just then they heard a shrill whistling sound. The Invisible Man grabbed at the gauge valves, but too late. "I seemed to run swiftly up an incline and shot forward with sudden acceleration into a wet . . . bath of whiteness."

When he awoke, he was in a hospital room, hooked up to a menagerie of electrical devices. He couldn't even remember his name. Later, he was released and given some compensation checks to tide him over. But as he emerged from the darkness of the subway, he passed out. A woman named Mary helped him up and took him to her home to rest.

The "rest" turned into a stay of several months. Mary was a kind and generous woman. But, when his compensation checks ran out, the Invisible Man began to feel guilty. Gradually he lost faith in himself. Then one day while he was wandering around Harlem, he saw an old couple being evicted from their apartment. A crowd had gathered at the scene and some of them were attacking the white man directing the eviction. But the Invisible Man stepped in and began to speak: "We're a law-abiding people and a slow-to-anger people . . . " Soon he had the crowd under control. His words had attracted some other whites, and when the police showed up looking for black suspects, these whites and scattered blacks, members of an organization called the "Brotherhood," helped him escape.

Brother Jack, their spokesman, complimented the Invisible Man on his eloquence. Because of this exceptional gift with words, Brother Jack hired him on the spot as the movement's new "black" spokesman.

The first speech the Invisible Man gave for the Brotherhood was an electrifying masterpiece. Many members of the group, however, complained that this black man was appealing essentially to the crowd's emotions, while their organization believed in rational persuasion. "The audience isn't thinking, it's yelling its head off." So Brother Jack decided that the Brotherhood's newest brother would "undergo a period of intense study and indoctrination."

For the next few months, white brothers – some filled with guilt, some looking for a social cause, and still others dedicated to "freeing" blacks – smothered the Invisible Man with ideology. They spoke of the black repossessing their heritage and banding together in brotherhood to unite the races.

The training period over, Brother Jack appointed his new charismatic speaker as leader of the group's Harlem district. "The Brotherhood was a world within a world," the Invisible Man said, "and I was determined to discover all its secrets and to advance as far as I could." With a new identity and confidence he went into the ghettos to preach peace. But confrontations with a rival group, the Black Nationalist gang, soon flared up. Both sides claimed Harlem as their territory. The Nationalists were led by a man named Ras the Exhortor, a West Indian committed to the extermination of whites and "Uncle Toms." "You're BLACK! . . . AFRICAN!" he constantly reminded his fellow ghetto dwellers in a bid to win them over as "his" people.

Then one day, Brother Clifton, an important and influential Brotherhood supporter, disappeared. With Clifton gone, Ras and his gang gained a stronghold in Harlem. The Invisible Man was called in to repair the damage. While walking through Harlem, he spotted Brother Clifton – selling dancing black "Sambo" dolls. Clifton could not even look him in the eye. Later, Brother Clifton was killed in an arrest attempt. When the Invisible Man used his funeral as a forum against police violence, Brother Jack scolded him for celebrating a man who sold racist dolls. "You were not hired to think. You were hired to talk," he chided in an ironic about-face.

Finally, Harlem erupted. Clifton's death and other similar incidents, combined with the inflammatory words of Ras the Exhortor, pushed the black community over the edge. Now Ras the Exhorter became Ras the Destroyer, taking to the streets with his followers in an all-out offensive against the white man. The Brotherhood abandoned the Invisible Man; they had no more use for him. However, even as the Invisible Man saw how he had been used and betrayed, he also saw himself more clearly. He had lived his life up to that point under an assumed identity; he had never known who he was. Now, finally, he understood the source of his invisibility: he saw Bledsoe, Norton, Brother Jack, and Ras as all the same man – all destroyers, bent on hatred instead of understanding; focused on color, blind to character.

Commentary:

Blacks have experienced exceptional prejudice, which has united them under a strong sense of purpose. However, most people experience some sort of "invisibility" – some deep lack of acknowledgment in the world – which can help them relate to this book and to the extreme situations encountered by the Invisible Man.

With its plethora of insights, Ellison's *Invisible Man* is perhaps the most important black novel of the twentieth century.

CEREMONY

by Leslie Marmon Silko, Viking Press, New York, N.Y., 1977

Type of work: Spiritual, cultural novel

Setting: New Mexico; 1940's

Principal characters:

Tayo, a troubled half-breed war veteran

Rocky, Tayo's Navajo cousin, who died during World War II

Auntie, Tayo's aunt and Rocky's mother

Josiah, Tayo's dead uncle

Betonie, a medicine man

Harley, Tayo's alcoholic war buddy

Emo, Tayo's Indian enemy, also a veteran

Story Overview:

Ceremony. I will tell you something about stories . . . They aren't just entertainment. Don't be fooled. They are all we have, you see, all we have to fight off illness and death.

When the United States entered World War II, Tayo and his cousin Rocky instantly enlisted; it was their way of escaping the reservation. Stationed in the Philippines, both were among the troops captured during the Japanese invasion, and for the two Navajo soldiers, along with other P.O.W.'s, the Bataan Death March followed. Rain poured down as Tayo and a captured corporal trudged through the mud, carrying the wounded Rocky on a blanket stretcher. "When Tayo prayed on the long muddy road to the prison camp, it was for dry air . . . air to dry out the oozing wounds of Rocky's leg." The oppression of the jungle also induced hallucinations; only a few days earlier Tayo had seen his uncle Josiah's face on a dead Japanese soldier. These visions continued as he marched.

Then came the day when the corporal slipped and a Japanese guard raised his rifle butt and crushed Rocky's skull; Tayo's sanity was rent.

At War's end, Tayo was ushered into Los Angeles' Veteran's Hospital. His mind had become dense, "white smoke . . . where there was no pain, only pale, pale gray of the north wall by his bed." Finally, a young doctor managed to invade Tayo's smoky world, and he became well enough to return home. But he was not completely cured; after making his way to his Auntie's reservation home, he lay in bed vomiting for a solid month. Night and day he was bombarded by dreams of soldiers . . . the Death March . . . Rocky.

When he eventually recovered enough to help with work around the ranch, he sometimes met with other war veterans in nearby bars and reminisced about the days before they were shipped overseas; they had felt so important and respected in their army uniforms. It was on one such night that Tayo stabbed Emo. "Emo had hated him since . . . grade school . . . and the only reason for this hate was that Tayo was part white." Now, while Emo bragged about all the "Japs" he had killed, Tayo, bursting with rage, charged at his "fat, laughing belly" with a broken bottle . . .

After that, people kept their distance. "They all had their explanations" about Tayo's deteriorating condition; "they blamed liquor and they blamed the war."

Left alone, Tayo reflected on his uncle Josiah. Tayo and Rocky were supposed to tend Josiah's cattle for him, but instead, they had joined the army. In their absence, Josiah had died, and Tayo blamed himself; he should have stayed . . .

One afternoon, Harley, a war-buddy-turned-alcoholic, arrived riding on a burro and persuaded Tayo to go with him for a beer. As they set off, Tayo's mind wandered: "He was four years old the night his mother left him" with his Auntie – and Auntie never let him forget that he didn't belong there. He was the shame of the family, the symbol of his mother's wild and drunken ways . . .

Time passed. "I've been doing okay. I can start helping you now," Tayo told Auntie's husband, Robert. But Robert wasn't so sure: "The old men of the tribe, they think you better get help pretty soon." And Tayo knew it was true, not only of him, but of the other veterans who wasted themselves on liquor. Betonie, the medicine man, had performed an ancient ceremony to give them power, but "that ceremony didn't help them," thought Tayo. Yet, just the same, he decided to give Betonie's ceremony a chance.

Robert drove Tayo into Gallup, where many Indians, seeking jobs, had ended up living in cardboard shanties on the outskirts of town. Tayo recalled his earliest years with his mother in one of those shacks. Light-skinned Tayo was one of the children the women were "ashamed to send home for their families to raise." The little boy "learned to listen in the darkness . . . to voices and sounds of wine; to know when the mother was returning with a man." He foraged for food, "watching for someone to drop a potato chip bag or a wad of gum." Then Tayo remembered how he and Rocky had dropped coins from a bridge into a little pond in San Diego the night before they shipped out. What had Rocky's wish been? "A safe return."

Betonie did not behave like most medicine men. His hogan was filled with boxes of old clothing, dried roots, newspapers and telephone books. Betonie explained that in the olden days they had not needed these things, but the ceremonies had been changed as times changed. Tayo thought the old man was crazy. Betonie read his mind: "If you don't trust me, you better get going before dark. I couldn't help anyone who was afraid of me." But Tayo stayed.

As Betonie listened patiently, Tayo's life story spilled out. Then, evening fell and it was time for the ceremony. "They will try to stop you from completing the ceremony," Betonie warned. The medicine man knelt and drew "stories" in the sand and chanted. "I will bring you back," he prophesied, "[but] one night or nine nights won't do it . . . . Remember these stars [he pointed to a drawing in the sand]. I've seen them and I've seen the spotted cattle; I've seen a mountain and I've seen a woman." Next, Betonie cautioned against the "evil ones" and "witches," who were bent on destroying the earth and its native people. Among these evil ones were those white men who fenced off and bulldozed the land and who sold Indians liquor; and among them also were those Indians who numbed themselves with this liquor. "Old Betonie shook his head. 'This has been going on for a long long time now. It's up to you. Don't let them stop you. Don't let them finish off this world.'"

The ceremony came to an end. Tayo hitched a ride partway home, then started walking. Soon Harley and Leroy drove by on a drunken spree and picked him up. The group cruised to a bar, where Harley and Leroy fought drunkenly with some Mexicans. But Tayo didn't notice; he was lost inside his own head – summoning up the songs Betonie had given him. Finally, he wandered away. He did not know why he was led to follow a certain path, but shortly he found himself in a yard, where a woman called out. Tayo explained that he was looking for some spotted cattle. "Somebody sent you," she said, welcoming him into her home. All night Tayo watched Betonie's stars, and when the sun appeared he saddled his horse and resumed his journey.

Instinctively he rode northward to a mountain, and soon he saw the spotted cattle in the distance. He set out to retrieve them. After a run-in with a group of ranch guards, he followed the animals' tracks back to the same house where he had stayed earlier.

The following summer was a happy one. Tayo helped the "spotted-cattle woman," Ts'eh, care for her animals, while she taught him old Indian secrets. "Their days together had a gravity emanating from the mesas and arroyos, and it replaced the rhythm that had been replaced long ago."

One day Ts'eh told Tayo that she had to leave, but warned him that in a vision she had seen his friends coming with white doctors and policemen: "They'll call to you. Friendly voices. If you come . . . they will take you and lock you in the white walls of the hospital."

Tayo traipsed far into the mountains, but still he worried. Emo would not stop hunting Tayo until his blood revenge was satisfied.

The next morning, as Tayo was hitching a ride, Leroy and Harley pulled over, drunk, as usual. Tayo could sense "something terrible inside" as he heard their casual story about driving over from Gallup – but still he went with them.

The next thing Tayo knew, he was in a car with its windows rolled up, sweating. The sun was high in the sky and beating through the windshield. Harley and Leroy had vanished. Tayo, searching for them, was "halfway to the top of the hill before he stopped; suddenly it hit him, in the belly . . . he knew that they weren't his friends but had turned against him, and the knowledge left him dry and hollow inside." He tried in futility to hot-wire the truck; in the attempt, a screwdriver found its way into his back pocket. Then he sprinted off, ending up at the site of an old uranium mine, where he lay down to rest. He woke up to the sound of a car – Emo's car. Hiding in the shadows of the moonlight, he watched as Emo, Leroy and Pinkie stopped and got out to build a fire. Harley was not with them. Then Tayo looked on in horror as they pulled Harley out of the trunk and stripped off his clothes. "We told you to watch him [Tayo]. We told you, and now you know what you got for yourself," they growled as they hung his body between strands of a barbed wire fence. Then they began to torture the drunkard by cutting away the skin from his toes.

Tayo's hand fumbled for the screwdriver. Clenching it tightly he started in a frenzy towards Emo – but something stopped him: He "had almost jammed the screwdriver into Emo's skull the way the witchery had wanted . . . " But, by holding back, he had defeated the witches' forces of evil. Tayo's ceremonial refusal had frustrated their plan to transform him into another victim – into one of them.

Commentary:

This is a brilliant novel written by a Native American (Silko is of Mexican, Pueblo, and white extraction) about Native Americans. But *Ceremony* also offers much to people of all cultures. Its structure is as intricate as a spider web, which happens to be a recurring image throughout the book. Shifts in time and place are intersected by prayers and chants, which pull a reader otherwise unacquainted with Indian ways much closer to the traditional thinking of the Navajo.

Silko, though a woman, writes hauntingly in the male voice. She directs her message not only toward whites, who continue to keep Native Americans on the fringes of society, but also towards Indians too easily accepting a numbing, brutal way of life.

A powerful story of redemption and love and perseverance, *Ceremony* has the essence of a spiritual journey, not only for one man, but for all humankind, to rediscover an ancient heritage of wholeness.

THEIR EYES WERE WATCHING GOD

by
Zora Neale Hurston
(190? - 1960)

Type of work: Rural, Black literature

Setting: Eatonsville, Florida; early 1900's

Principal characters:
Janie Woods/Starks, the novel's beautiful heroine
Tea Cake Woods, Janie's third and most loving husband
Joe Starks, her powerful and selfish second husband
Logan Killicks, her first husband
Phoeby, Janie's only friend in Eatonsville
Grandma, a former slave who raised Janie

Story Overview:

When Janie eventually returned to Eatonsville the townsfolk could barely conceal their envy. As she walked home from the fields in her overalls, her neighbors, sitting on their porches, lowered their voices: "What she doin' coming back here in dem overalls? Where all dat money her husband took and died and left her? What dat ole forty year ole 'oman doin wid her hair swingin' down her back lak some young gal?" Most of all they wanted to know what had become of Tea Cake, the man she had left town with two years earlier. Janie's old friend Phoeby tried to soften the town's "mass cruelty." She brought Janie a plate of food, and their friendship was instantly renewed.

"Ah don't mean to bother wid tellin' 'em nothin', Phoeby," Janie scoffed. "You can tell 'em what Ah say if you wants to." And Janie began her story:

Janie looked back on her childhood "like a great tree in leaf." She had been raised by her grandma, who worked as a nanny for a white family named Washburn. Janie was raised with the Washburn children and was totally unaware of the color of her skin until she was six years old, when she saw a photograph of herself with the other children.

When Janie was about sixteen, she was sitting beneath a pear tree dreaming away an afternoon. Something about the blossoms on the tree "stirred her tremendously." She felt as though she was on the threshold of something – perhaps life. Just then, "shiftless" Johnny Taylor came up the road; but, for some reason, that afternoon Janie saw him as "glorious." Her grandma awoke just in time to see the two kissing, and straightway called Janie into the house. "Janie, youse got yo' womanhood on yuh. Ah wants to see you married right away."

Despite Janie's protests, Grandma decided that she should marry an older man named Logan Killicks. "He looks like some ole skullhead in de ole grave yard," whined Janie. But she married Logan anyway.

Not long afterward, Janie returned to Grandma's kitchen and revealed that she didn't love Logan at all. Grandma countered bluntly that Logan had sixty acres and a house bought and paid for; Janie should be grateful for her security.

In some ways, Logan was a good husband. He never laid a hand on Janie in anger. But he soon left Janie with all the chores, and one day he announced that he was going to buy another mule so she could help him in the fields.

While Logan was out, down the road came Joe Starks, a new man in town. Joe had big plans and plenty of money. When he heard about Logan's intention to put Janie behind a plow, he could scarcely believe his ears. "You behind a plow? You ain't got no mo' business wid uh plow than uh hog is wid uh holiday!"

So Janie left with Joe Starks. Joe had a dream of moving to a town he had heard of called Eatonsville founded and inhabited entirely by "colored folks"; but when the couple arrived there, Joe was dumbfounded: "God, they call this a town? Why, 'tain't nothing but a raw place in de woods." Joe demanded to see the mayor. "Us ain't got none yit," he was told.

Over the next few months, Joe bought some land and started to build a store. After he and Janie were settled, Joe called for a town meeting and convinced the people that they needed a road. Later, he invited the town to a celebration for the opening of his store, where he declared his intentions to run for mayor: "Ah means tuh put mah hands tuh de plow heah, and strain every nerve tuh make dis our town de metropolis uh de state." Joe Starks, man of dreams, was elected. He enticed more settlers to Eatonsville, and even bought a streetlamp – impressing the entire town.

Now Janie was the mayor's wife. This separated her from the rest of the town. Not only did her husband rule the town with "a bow-down command in his face," his two-story house made the other houses look like servants' quarters. Joe made Janie keep her hair wrapped in a cloth because he had seen some of the men in the store admiring it too much. He would not allow her to visit with the townsfolk: "You'se Mrs. Mayor Starks, Janie."

"The years took all the fight out of Janie's face." She learned to keep her thoughts and emotions hidden, receiving "nothing from Joe except what money could buy."

Then one day Joe scolded his wife in front of a crowd of people on the porch. "Don't stand dere rollin' yo' pop eyes at me wid yo' rump hangin' nearly to yo' knees!" he taunted, seeing his wife's embarrassed reaction. Angered, Janie made a cutting remark about Joe's manhood – irreversibly demolishing his "illusion of irresistible maleness." After that, things could never be the same between husband and wife. When Joe took sick, he imagined that Janie was trying to poison him and refused to eat at home. He went to a root-doctor, who promised a miracle cure. And soon he confined himself to bed and would not allow Janie near him.

Joe's funeral was "the finest ever seen with Negro eyes." Afterward, Janie went home and burned all the headrags that had covered her hair.

Janie was half-heartedly working in the family store when one day a young man came in. "Tea Cake" Woods flirted with Janie. Soon, after a few other visits, he took her to the church picnic. That really got people talking.

But Janie harbored suspicions about Tea Cake's advances. She wondered what a young man wanted with a woman thirteen years his senior. Was it her money? Was he playing her for a fool? He tried to reassure her: "Janie, Ah hope God may kill me, if Ah'm lyin'. Nobody else on earth kin hold a candle tuh you. You got de keys to de kingdom."

Following the couple's wedding, they left Eatonsville and all its rumormongers. Tea Cake taught Janie how to have fun. They played checkers, went fishing, and he even showed her how to hunt. They often stayed up talking long into the night. But Janie was still worried about her husband's motives. She thought it best not to tell him about the money that she had hidden away. Then one morning Tea Cake left for a trip to the store – and he didn't come back. Janie became frantic when she discovered that her money was missing. Late that night, when Tea Cake finally returned to their hotel room, he could see that Janie had feared the worst. "You doubted me 'bout de money. Thought Ah had done took it and gone [to waste it on] some woman." Instead, he had thrown a party for his friends at the railroad station where he had once worked. Janie made him promise not to leave like that again; afterall, she enjoyed fun too, and did not want to miss out on any of Tea Cake's adventures. Tea Cake advised her to keep the rest of her money in the bank. He would support her, he promised.

Tea Cake and Janie moved south to the "muck" which the white folk called the Everglades, where he went to work as a picker. At first Janie stayed home, cooking and keeping house. But after Tea Cake complained of lonliness, Janie decided to go out to pick alongside her husband.

When the picking ended, they decided to stay on in the muck, alternately working, hunting, chatting and laughing on their porch with other black workers, and occasionally heading to Palm Beach for a movie. They both had their problems with jealousy, but each time they managed to work things through.

Then one afternoon groups of people hurried by, heading for high ground and reporting that a hurricane was on the way. Tea Cake said it was nothing to worry about – just a storm. But that night a hard rain fell and the wind howled mercilessly. When Tea Cake ventured outside, he immediately realized that the bulging dike was about to rupture; they would have to run.

The road to Palm Beach was filled with refugees trying to escape the raging waters. Exhausted, Tea Cake lay down to snatch a little sleep. As Janie picked up a piece of tar-paper roofing to cover him with, the wind caught it and sent her plunging into the waters alongside the road. Tea Cake came running. A cow floated by with a dog on its back and Tea Cake told Janie to grab the cow's tail. As she did, the dog turned on her "like a lion." Tea Cake dove into the water, opening his knife as he swam. In the rescue, the dog bit Tea Cake high on his cheek-bone.

As the storm subsided, the refugees were told that Palm Beach too had been devastated. Tea Cake and Janie decided to return to the muck.

Then came the day when Tea Cake returned home early from work, complaining of sickness. That night "he woke Janie up in his nightmarish struggle with an enemy that was at his throat," and the next day he would ask for a drink of water and then, each time, fling it to the ground.

After a doctor had examined Tea Cake, he took Janie aside and told her that her husband had contracted rabies.

For days Janie tried to comfort her hallucinating husband. Then one night he pulled a gun on her. Instinctively, Janie grabbed a rifle. She tried to calm the delirious man, "but the fiend in him must kill and Janie was the only thing living he saw." Before Tea Cake could shoot her, Janie pulled the trigger.

Her story ended, Janie said to her friend, "Ah know all dem sitters-and-talkers goin' tuh worry they guts into fiddle strings till dey find out whut we been talkin' 'bout. Dat's all right, Phoeby, tell 'em." And Phoeby vowed that she would.

Commentary:

Zora Neale Hurston and her masterful novel, *Their Eyes Were Watching God,* are both recent discoveries. Written in the twenties and published in 1937, this work is partly autobiographical. The novel reveals Hurston's own childhood in a black Florida town and is rich in folklore.

In many of the novel's porch-side conversations Hurston's characters tell stories, both to entertain and to relieve the frustrations of being black in a white man's world. Janie may be viewed as a modern woman, striking out for equality, nevermore to be a "mule" on Logan's farm or a showpiece for Stark's store. She finally finds her identity in Tea Cake, a man to whom she can relate to as an equal.

THE JOY LUCK CLUB

by Amy Tan, Ballantine Books, New York, N.Y., 1989

Commentary:

This is a book about mothers and daughters, facing each other through all the veils that separate their cultures and their generations. In twenty intricately interwoven vignettes, Amy Tan probes the love, the passion, the humor, and the deep exasperation that mold their relationships – and celebrates the unpredictable tenacity of the mother-daughter bond.

Dedication:

To my mother
and the memory of her mother.
You asked me once
what I would remember.
This, and much more.

Story Overview and Excerpts:

Suyuan Woo was suddenly dead. Many years earlier she had brought to America a swan that was said to have once been a duck. At that time she promised herself that she would have a daughter who would grow up just like herself. And like that duck, transformed into a swan by stretching its neck, her American daughter would unfold into "someone unexpected."

Now, Suyuan's daughter, Jing-Mei, was invited to take her mother's place at the East corner of the mahjong table in the meeting of the Joy Luck Club, where four friends from four different corners of China for years had come together every month, hoping, like the four winds, to breathe success and happiness into the trajectories of their bright game tiles.

Suyuan had told her daughter many times about the origins of the Joy Luck Club. As a young military wife in China, she had been left, along with her twin baby daughters, to stay for safety in the enchanted, mountain city of Kweilin. Though the Japanese army had not as yet penetrated there, refugees flooded in from every pocket of the country until Kweilin lost its enchantment.

Finally, on a summer night "so hot that even the moths fainted to the ground," Suyuan turned away from the unbearable smells floating up through the sewers and decided to hold a gathering of four women, "one for each corner of my mahjong table."

. . . Each week one of us would host a party to raise money and to raise our spirits. The hostess had to serve special foods . . . dumplings shaped like silver money ingots . . . boiled peanuts for conceiving sons . . . People in the city . . . thought we were possessed by demons to celebrate . . . . But [was it worse to] sit and wait for our own deaths . . . [or] . . . to choose our own happiness? . . . Each week we could hope to be lucky. That hope was our only joy. And that's how we came to call our little parties the Joy Luck Club.

Suyuan had finally fled Kweilin just ahead of the Japanese slaughter. "I lost everything," she told Jing-Mei as the girl grew older. "Everything?" gasped Jing-Mei. "What happened to the babies?" But her mother's story always ended there.

Tonight, however, just weeks after Suyuan's death, the story was continued. The three remaining ladies from the Joy Luck Club – Jing-Mei's unofficial "aunties" – addressed her by her Chinese name and handed her a check for twelve hundred dollars. Through her mother's untiring queries over the years, they told her, the missing twin babies had at last been found. And now the aunties had taken up a collection to send Suyuan's American daughter for a visit with her older Chinese sisters.

"Tell them about your mother," said Auntie Ying, the south-wind at the mahjong table. "What will I say?" asked Jing-Mei. "I don't know anything." (A friend had once told her she was very like her mother: "the same wispy hand gestures, the same . . . sideways look." And Suyuan had seemed insulted. "You don't know little percent of me," she had said.)

"Not know your mother!" cried Auntie An-Mei. "How can you say that? Your mother is in your bones!" And at that moment Jing-Mei saw that all the aunties were seeing their own daughters in her face, " . . . daughters who think they are stupid when they explain things in broken English. They see that joy and luck do not mean the same thing to their daughters, that to these closed American minds, 'joy luck' is not a word. It does not exist."

The Prodigy

Of all the Joy Luck Club daughters, Waverly Jong was Jing-Mei's closest friend. At age nine, Waverly had become intrigued with a second-hand chess set and emerged as a local prodigy – "Chinatown's Littlest Chess Champion."

"Of course you can be a prodigy, too," Suyuan assured her daughter. But after many anguished months at the library, on the piano bench, and in the museum, it was finally determined that Jing-Mei was not to become a prodigy after all. "You just aren't a genius like me," Waverly announced, smiling.

The Red Candle

"Blow like the wind," instructed Waverly's mother, Lindo, standing over her daughter's chessboard. "Blow from the North, South, East and West." Lindo was not really sure which chessmen moved in which direction; but she knew about the wind.

Many years earlier in China, she had been joined in an arranged marriage to the teenage son of a prosperous family. When months passed, however, and she did not conceive, her mother-in-law, Hwang Taitai, was advised that the girl had too much metal; a girl with too much metal would find it difficult to conceive sons, who grew best in a belly where their own strong metal balanced a deficiency. So Hwang Taitai removed all the metal wedding bracelets from Lindo's thin arms and consigned the girl to bed, to ensure that the seeds planted by her son did not fall out.

But the fact was, her son was planting no seeds. Dismayed and shamed by his aversion to women, he lived in sullen silence, while Lindo obediently awaited whatever destiny might decree for her as his "true spiritual wife," in a marriage sealed forever by a red candle which – or so the matchmaker had triumphantly declared the next morning – had "burned continuously from both ends" throughout their wedding night.

But now, relieved of her heavy gold bracelets, Lindo grew light with an unexpected surge of freedom, and once again pondered on what had truly occurred at the time of her wedding. On that gray, windy afternoon she had waited, weeping, at a neighbor's house to ride the red bridal Palanquin. Uneasy rumors swirled in the stiff breeze, blowing from a hundred nearby Japanese assaults. "And then I realized . . . I could see the power of the wind. I couldn't see the wind itself, but I could see it carried the water that filled the rivers and shaped the countryside . . . "

That night, banished from her unconsummated bridal bed, Lindo had sat again by herself. Across the courtyard, under the dozing gaze of the matchmaker's servant, burned the red candle. Then, suddenly, as a thunderclap echoed through the rain, the servant woman started from her half-sleep, and fled into the storm, crying out unheard warnings of a Japanese attack. By the time she made her embarrassed return, Lindo had crossed the courtyard "like the breath of the south wind itself," and blown out the candle.

In careful tears, Lindo now told Hwang Taitai of a "dream" which had warned her that she was cursed with barrenness and decay because she had entered into a forbidden marriage. But what about the good binding omen – the wedding candle? "In my dream," she told her mother-in-law, "the servant left the room and a big wind came and blew the candle out." And so, the matchmaker's servant was questioned; and Lindo left with a little money and a ticket to Peking – the first passage on her long journey to America.

One day, Waverly the prodigy turned on her mother. "Why do you have to use me to show off? . . . Why don't you learn to play chess?" Running off into the Chinatown alleyways, she hid in silence for the rest of the afternoon.

Days passed. Lindo wisely said nothing to Waverly about the missed practice sessions, the unused chessboard. But "I knew the strategy," remembered Waverly. "The sneaky way to get someone to . . . fall into a trap." Not until weeks later did Waverly announce, "I am ready to play chess again."

"No," responded the mother who had put her whole soul into her daughter's chess games. "It is not so easy now." And it was not.

Waverly was free to return to her practice and her tournaments, but without her mother standing behind her, admiring, uninitiated, and breathing "useless instructions" into her soul. She never regained her early victories. "I had lost my magic armor . . . I had lost the gift and turned into someone quite ordinary."

Years later, on the eve of her own second wedding, Waverly, now a successful tax lawyer, brought Lindo into the city for a style and set. "It's uncanny how much you two look alike!" exclaimed the hairdresser, patting down Lindo's wet hair. Waverly's eyes grew narrow, as her mother squinted at her through the mirror. "Ai-yaa!" said Lindo. "What happened to your nose?" But her daughter's slightly crooked nose, as she discovered when Waverly bent closer, was the replica of her own.

"Our nose isn't so bad." Waverly sounded pleased: "It makes us look devious." "Devious?" "It means we're looking one way, while following another . . . . We mean what we say, but our intentions are different."

"This is good?" asked Lindo.

"This is good," said Waverly, "If you get what you want."

Independently, mother and daughter had each learned to think for herself and to "blow like the wind" in order to attain her ends.

Ticket to China

Auntie An-Mei's words from the Joy Luck Club still haunted Jing-Mei: "Your mother is in your bones!" An-Mei had stories to tell of a long-ago China where she had lived in a fine house with her mother, her merchant father, and his three concubines. What part of Auntie An-Mei lived in the bones of her American daughter Rose, who sat in a psychiatrist's office twice a week to "work out" her upcoming divorce?

And Auntie Ying – dreamy, detached Auntie Ying-Ying – who had lost her own concubine-mother to suicide? "Chunwang Chihan," Auntie Ying frequently repeated, whispering into the air. "If the lips are gone, the teeth will be cold." Her daughter Lena was an architect, dedicated to the "open and independent" marriage contract which she shared with her caucasian husband Harold. Did the meaning of her mother's cryptic chant live anywhere at all inside Lena?

On the plane to Shanghai, Jing Mei still wondered how she would know her sisters. And what would she say? But at the airport, all questions ended. There before her stood the answer:

Her short hair. Her small body. And that same look on her face . . . . She is crying . . . . And I know it's not my mother, yet it is the same look she had when I was five . . .

And now I see her again, two of her . . . . We run toward each other . . . embracing . . . . "Mama, Mama," we all murmur, as if she is among us.

– And so, in fact, she was.

THE SHELL SEEKERS

by Rosamunde Pilcher, St. Martin's Press, New York, N.Y., 1988

Type of work: Contemporary humanistic novel

Setting: London and Southern England; pre-World War II era to the present

Principal characters:

Penelope Keeling, a refined woman
Nancy, her oldest daughter
Olivia, her second daughter
Noel, her son
Cosmo, Olivia's lover
Antonia, Cosmo's sensitive, friendly daughter
Danus, Penelope's loyal gardener
Richard, Penelope's true love
Ambrose, Penelope's fickle husband

Story Overview:

Penelope Keeling, recovering from a heart attack, in characteristic fashion discharged herself from the hospital and went home to her country cottage in Gloucester, southwest of London.

She was alone. The relief of it. Home. Her own house, her own possessions, her own kitchen . . . . The thought of her precious plants, possibly dying of cold or thirst, had bothered her . . . Seeing that the care of her beloved garden was too big a job for her, Penelope hired a gardener, Danus. She also received a most welcome house guest when Antonia came to stay. Antonia and Danus were now her most beloved friends, but Penelope could remember better times . . .

Her parents, Lawrence and Sophie Stern, had been popular among a group of artists who lived and worked in Cornwall just before World War II. Sophie was French by birth, and Penelope's memories of childhood were fond ones: happy, sunny days spent at Carn Cottage in Cornwall or in the South of France; cozy winters in the London family home. As an only child, she had received much love and attention both from her parents and from the large "family" of friends who always seemed to be around.

Then the War struck. The London house was large, and the Sterns generously took in those in need. One night as the family listened to their current guests – a young Jewish couple – describe the horrors they had endured, Penelope resolved to do her part in the fight. The next day she joined the *WRENS* as a female military aid.

But before long, the young woman regretted her decision. Extreme loneliness weighed her down. It didn't appear that her work, which consisted mostly of clerical duties and transporting officers, was doing much real good. In this depressed state, Penelope met a young officer, Ambrose Keeling. He seemed interesting – and interested in her. When Penelope became pregnant, she was quite glad; pregnancy gave her an excuse to leave the *WRENS* and return

home. She and her parents were excited with the prospect of a baby. None of them felt inclined to force Ambrose into marriage. He soon proposed, however, and the couple was married in London.

But it soon became evident that Ambrose was far from an ideal husband. He was in fact quite egotistical, and a womanizer and spendthrift as well. When he left for combat duty, Penelope hoped he would write and ask her for a divorce.

Meanwhile, the Stern home became even more crowded when Doris, a homeless woman, moved in, along with her two children. After working out some initial differences, the two families came to care a great deal for each other. But Lawrence Stern now began to sense a restlessness in his wife. "For two years . . . his Sophie who had never lived more than three months in any place during the whole of their married life," had been confined in Cornwall, a town that in wartime was "grey and dull and empty." Lawrence insisted that Sophie take a holiday in London. But during the visit, she and some of her close friends were killed in a bombing raid. Lawrence and his daughter were heartbroken. Then Doris also received word that her husband had been killed in the fighting. While struggling with lonliness, and sharing the responsibilities of caring for Penelope's new daughter Nancy along with Doris' two boys, Penelope and Doris grew very close.

Some time later, Penelope met Richard, a British officer. Almost from the start he seemed a part of the family.

Over the next few weeks he came and went and his random appearances, unexpected and unannounced, soon became totally taken for granted by the occupants of Carn Cottage . . . . Even Nancy finally thawed . . .

Richard and Penelope fell deeply in love; he would forever be the only great love in her life. However, as Penelope prepared to ask Ambrose to grant a divorce, she received bad news: Richard had been killed during the invasion of France. "She felt . . . cold as ice." She looked at Richard's photograph; saw his smile; remembered his voice reading aloud, " . . . There will be sunshine later, And the equation will come out at last."

"There will be sunlight later," she thought. "I must tell Papa that." And it seemed as good a way to start out on the left-over life that lay ahead.

After the war, Penelope left Cornwall and stoically braced herself to live out the rest of her days with Ambrose. Two more children were soon added to the family, Olivia and then Noel. But her husband became increasingly irresponsible and pessimistic. Eventually he abandoned

Penelope, and died a few years after that. For the first time, Penelope felt free to do with her life as she chose; and she chose a life devoted to her friends, her neighbors, her home and her garden. She was content.

As Penelope's children matured they were not exactly a comfort to her. Nancy's greatest ambition had always been to have a large home, a professional husband and the life of a well-bred woman. Her marriage to George brought her all of this.

The Old Vicarage, Bamworth. It was a good address, and . . . she had it embossed, at Harrods, at the head of her expensive blue writing paper. Little things like writing paper mattered to Nancy. They made a good impression.

It appeared that Nancy had achieved her childhood wish; but it was obvious to her mother and her friends that her life was empty, her children ill-mannered, and her husband a bore.

The second child, Olivia, single by choice, became a determined career woman. As the editor of a large womens' magazine, she was caught up in a hectic London lifestyle. Then a long vacation to Ibiza resulted in her affair with a handsome lover, Cosmo. Soon she decided that Ibiza "was exactly her mother's environment," and invited Penelope to join her, Cosmo, and Antonia, Cosmo's daughter by a past lover, to spend the summer. Antonia and Penelope became instant friends; but the idyllic Ibizan life couldn't hold Olivia forever. She returned to London. Later, she was grieved to learn that Cosmo had suddenly died of a heart attack, leaving his daughter alone.

Penelope's Noel seemed the epitome of a spoiled youngest child. He dabbled in business, but was mostly interested in women and in spending weekends with a wealthy and lazy crowd that could provide him with a good time. In fact, he was very like his father, Ambrose.

Noel was quite hurt when his mother turned him out of the house to live on his own. One day, on the pretense of fire danger, he cleaned out his mother's attic. In truth, he was searching for his Grandfather Lawrence's sketches, which he hoped would turn a sizable profit. Nancy was as insistent as Noel that Penelope should have her father's works appraised and sold while the market was good. But though Penelope loved her children, she knew them too well. They needed to finally take some responsibility for their own lives. Long before, she had removed the sketches and hidden them in back of her wardrobe. Now, during her convalescence, Penelope rewrote her will to give Cosmos' daughter Antonia and Danus the gardener the proceeds from the art. She donated one painting, "The Shell Seekers," to the nearby museum her father had helped establish, and divided her remaining estate between the three children.

After her heart attack Penelope felt a deep longing to return to Cornwall. She had been away for forty years. Perhaps it would be her final visit. She asked her children to accompany her, but each gave some excuse. Finally she invited Antonia and Danus to go with her. They were delighted.

The trip was a wonderful success on most counts: Penelope called on Doris at old Carn Cottage, revisited old sites, and toured the museum. But Danus and Antonia quarrelled. Penelope took them aside and offered them some sage motherly advice – and before long the young couple was engaged, with dreams of developing a garden center in the country. However, with little money, their dreams would have to remain on hold.

On a morning shortly after her holiday, Penelope unexpectedly died while working in her garden. In a family meeting held after the funeral, all were surprised by the large sum bequeathed from the sale of the paintings. Danus and Antonia were stunned with joy, and grateful for the gift. Naturally, Nancy and Noel felt slighted by Penelope's generosity to her young friends. But Olivia, always the most like her mother, went to clean out the house and reminisce on bygone days. There she discovered a love-letter Penelope had long kept secret. With tears streaking down her cheeks, Olivia finally saw how Penelope must have seen a flicker of her beloved Richard in the eyes of Danus, and had tried to ensure a happy start in marriage for Danus and Antonia. Right then she determined to become more like her mother and to make a trip to Cornwall in the spring.

Downstairs in the kitchen, Olivia lifted the lid from the boiler and "dropped Mumma's secret into the heart of the glowing coals . . . It took only seconds, and then was gone forever."

Commentary:

The Shell Seekers is a work dealing with relationships and remembrances. Each chapter is named for a different character, who becomes the main focus of that chapter. We experience in a very personal way the bonds Penelope shares with her parents and their friends during the war years, and later with her three children and her own friends. The plot is simple, but the splendid, human fabric into which it is woven rightfully supersedes the story.

Penelope's full life was nearly Bohemian in nature primarily because of her own immense enthusiasm. The work skips back and forth in time, which helps to hold our interest as the events that have shaped Penelope slowly become clear to us. In fact, at the end of the book we realize that we know her better than do her children. There are many ironic twists in Penelope's life, and the ultimate irony is that, only in her final years and only through the fondness and care offered by two "strangers," is she allowed to unlock and integrate all the rich and intimate secrets of her past.

THE SOUND OF WAVES

by Yukio Mishima, Charles E. Tuttle Co., Inc., Tokyo, Japan, 1956

Type of work: Lyrical love novel

Setting: Uta-Jima ("Song Island"), Japan; 1950's

Principal characters:

Shinji, a strong, eighteen-year-old fisherman

Tomi Kubo, Shinji's widowed mother

Hatsue, a beautiful girl loved by Shinji

Uncle Teru Miyata, Hatsue's wealthy, influential father

Yasuo Kawamoto, son of a leading family on the island and Shinji's rival

The master and mistress of the lighthouse

Chiyoko, the homely daughter of the lighthouse couple

Story Overview:

The young fisherman hurried up the mountain carrying his gift to the couple who operated the Uta-Jima Island lighthouse. Shinji often brought them gifts of fish for the help they had given him during his high school years. His graduation had been both an honor and a necessity for his family; since the boy's father had died during World War I, his mother and brother needed his income.

As Shinji climbed, his thoughts turned to a new girl he had seen earlier. "There was something refreshing about the cast of her eyes, something serene about her eyebrows." Shinji blushed, remembering how he had stared at her like a child.

At home, Shinji waited for his mother to mention the girl, but she was not "given to idle gossip." Later, with his brother Hiroshi at the public bath, Shinji again hoped to hear something about the girl, but no one even mentioned her name.

After a sleepless night, Shinji was still afflicted with a "strange unrest." He poured his energy into his fishing. Then at lunch, his boss, Jukichi, finally brought up the subject of the girl: "Say, what do you think about old Uncle Teru Miyata bringing his girl back?" No one had even been aware that Teru had a young daughter; years before he had sent her to grow up on another island claiming that he had "more than enough of girls." However, since his son's death Teru had grown lonely and called the girl home. Her name was Hatsue.

That night when Shinji attended the regular meeting of the Young Men's Association, their leader, Yasuo, rushed through the Association's business and left. Shinji asked a friend why Yasuo was in such a hurry. "Don't you know? He's invited to the party Uncle Teru is giving to celebrate his daughter's homecoming," he was told. Later, as Shinji walked to Yashiro Shrine, he imagined the celebration; "how the sensitive flame of the lamps . . . must be throwing flickering shadows from the girl's tranquil eyebrows and long lashes down onto her cheeks." At the Shrine, he prayed for God to give the island good fishing – and for a "good-natured, beautiful bride . . . like Teru Miyata's returned daughter."

Days later, Shinji was exploring an old military observation tower. He thought he was alone – until he heard a girl crying. It was Hatsue. When Shinji asked her why she cried, Hatsue explained that she had lost her way to the lighthouse, where she was going for lessons in etiquette and homemaking. Shinji led the girl to her destination, but made Hatsue promise not to mention their meeting; he "well knew how sharp the villagers' tongues could be."

On payday, Shinji found another opportunity to talk with Hatsue when he saw her with a group struggling to pull a boat onto the beach. He hurried to help, and "in an instant the boat was sliding up over the sand." But when Shinji got home and reached inside his pocket for his pay envelope, the money was gone. Shinji raced back to the beach. Meanwhile, Hatsue, who had already found his money, brought it to his house, and hearing that Shinji was at the beach searching, she hurried to tell him it was safe. Afterward, they stayed, talking. "I hear you're going to marry Yasuo. Is it true?" Shinji asked. Hatsue laughed. "It's a big lie." The two were standing close, very close, and at that moment they kissed. Tomorrow they would meet again at the lighthouse.

With their own daughter Chiyoko away at school, the lighthouse couple all but adopted Hatsue. When she came the next day, they persuaded her to stay for supper, and as Hatsue helped in the kitchen, Shinji appeared with his usual gift of fish. The mistress of the lighthouse invited him. She could not help but "intercept" the shy smiles Hatsue and Shinji exchanged. Then she mentioned to Shinji that Chiyoko had written to ask about him. But Chiyoko's name sent the boy retreating "back into the dusk."

There Shinji waited for Hatsue. He heard her coming, but as she passed "her footsteps never paused." Shinji ran after her. "What made you so mad?" "All that talk about you and Chiyoko-san," Hatsue sobbed. Shinji assured her that there was nothing between Chiyoko and him, and they agreed to meet again the next time the fishing fleet encountered bad weather.

Soon Chiyoko came home for vacation, sailing on the same boat as Yasuo. As they greeted each other, Chiyoko sadly wished "that she could have a man look at her at least once with eyes saying 'I love you' instead of 'You love me.'"

A stormy day eventually came and the fishing boats could not go out to sea. Elated, Shinji sloshed through the rain toward the tower to await Hatsue. There he made a fire to dry off his clothing, and fell asleep. When Shinji awoke, "a strange, indistinct shadow was standing across the fire from him." It was Hatsue, naked, drying her clothing before the fire. On seeing that Shinji was awake, she cried out, "Keep your eyes shut!" But the young lovers could not be held apart; they came together and embraced. Before they could consummate their love, however, Hatsue stopped them. She could not dishonor herself nor her father.

As the couple left the tower and passed the lighthouse, Chiyoko spied them, Hatsue snuggled close to Shinji. Filled with jealousy, she related what she had seen to a vengeful and equally jealous Yasuo.

Before dawn of the next day, Yasuo waited for Hatsue on the path he knew she would take to fetch water. But as he hid himself to spy on her, a hornet stung him, and his sudden yell drew Hatsue's instant notice. Yasuo grabbed the girl and forced her to the ground, but as they wrestled the hornet returned to sting him again, and Hatsue gained her feet. Seeing Yasuo's fearful and embarrassed expression, she promised she would not tell her father about the incident if he would draw and carry her water all the way to her house.

Yasuo soon avenged his humiliation by slandering Hatsue's reputation; rumors about Shinji and Hatsue soon spread through the village.

One day Jukichi handed Shinji a note from Hatsue: " . . . Last night at the bath Father heard some very bad gossip about us and became terribly angry . . . " After that, it was impossible for Shinji and Hatsue to meet, but as Shinji one night "prowled about the neighborhood of Hatsue's house," he could see her through an upstairs window, "her eyes wet with tears."

Shinji's unhappiness caused his mother to worry. One afternoon she finally paid a courageous visit to the Miyata household, where Hatsue reluctantly told her, " . . . Father says he won't see you . . . " Humiliated, Shinji's mother shouted: " . . . Never in my life will I ever cross his damned threshold again!"

Summer brought the diving season, and one day an old peddler proposed a contest among the women: whoever brought up the most abalone in one hour would win a handbag. Eight women dived to exhaustion for the prize. After an hour when the buckets were counted, Hatsue-san had won. But Hatsue pressed her prize into the hands of Shinji's mother. "I've always wanted to apologize," she said, "ever since my father spoke so rudely."

Shortly after this, Teru declared that anyone seeking betrothal to his daughter must serve an apprenticeship as seaman on the *Utajima-mura*, a freighter he owned. Both Shinji and Yasuo signed on, but they turned out to be very different seamen. Yasuo often hid from his tasks, while Shinji, spurred on by his love for Hatsue, applied himself with vigor.

Then one frightening night, a typhoon raged so hard that the *Utajima-mura* was forced to take refuge in a harbor, tied to a buoy. Yasuo and Shinji, on the midnight watch, suddenly saw one of the lines give way. Now the other lines were surely in danger of snapping, leaving the untethered ship to be dashed against the rocks. "Which one of you fellows is going to take this life line over there and tie it to the buoy?" shouted the captain. "I'll do it!" Shinji volunteered. Quickly he stripped down to his T-shirt and dove into the rough waters. Fighting the waves and the weight of the rope, he finally reached the buoy and cinched up the lifeline. Then he faced the storm, "inhaled his fill of air and . . . dived in the sea for the return trip." Back on board, the captain clapped Shinji on the shoulder for a job well done.

Young love triumphed. In time, Shinji and Hatsue announced their engagement. And now they walked together to express their thanks at Yashiro Shrine.

Commentary:

The lyricism of *The Sound of Waves*, one of Mishima's earliest novels, is markedly different from the sharper, less poetic edge of his later works, which focus on death, suicide and war. This novel, with its intimate portrayal of island life, a people's connection with the sea, and the triumph of good over evil, is Mishima's most musical, most simple, and most translated work. It is also his kindest.

The Sound of Waves was largely responsible for Mishima's rise to Nobel Laureate status. Then, in 1970, the Japanese author shocked the world by committing hara-kiri as a personal protest against what he perceived as his country's post-war weakness.

THE STORIES OF JOHN CHEEVER

Random House, New York, N.Y., Fourth Printing, Dec. 1978

Cheever's 61-story collection was written over a 29-year period. Most of these dramatic psychological tales were composed aloud, then transcribed from tape and published in various magazines. Their settings seem to be in some "long-lost world," where, as Cheever explains, "almost everybody wore a hat" and listened to Benny Goodman.

Here are four of those stories:

"The Country Husband"
(a 1950's and 60's community setting)

"To begin at the beginning, the airplane from Minneapolis in which Francis Weed was traveling East ran into heavy weather," and was forced to make a belly-landing in a cornfield near Philadelphia. The passengers scrambled out of the plane happy to still be among the living. Weed and the others were transported by taxi to Philadelphia, and from there by train to New York. On the train from New York to Shady Hill, the suburb where he lived, Francis tried to tell an acquaintance seated next to him what had happened: "You know, I was on that plane that just crashed outside Philadelphia. We came down in a field." The man replied with a comment on the dryness of the weather. "Francis had no powers that would let him recreate a brush with death."

(The action turns to present tense as Weed finally arrives home.)

"Nine times out of ten, Francis would be greeted with affection, but tonight the children are absorbed in their own antagonisms." As Francis tries to describe his harrowing experience, the children start quarreling. He has just separated the combatants when Julia, his wife, walks into the room to announce that dinner is ready. "Francis says loudly that he has been in a plane crash and that he is tired." Julia's only response is to ask her husband to go upstairs and get Helen for dinner.

Perhaps Helen, his eldest daughter, will hear him out. "But Helen is lying on her bed reading a True Romance Magazine," the sort that Francis detests. Once more he is ignored.

At the dinner table, the children renew their bickering and whining, and soon Francis and Julia are fighting too. Julia begins to cry.

(Now the author takes over to tell what happens next.)

By the next evening the Weeds had reconciled and were going to a party. Afterwards, Francis waited in the car to give the babysitter a ride home. But instead of their regular babysitter, middle-aged Mrs. Henlien, a beautiful young girl named Anne Murchison came out of the door. She had been crying; her alcoholic father had called her "immoral," and as she told Francis her story she fell into his arms. "Francis lost his head and pulled her roughly against him." At her house, Francis walked her to the door, and they kissed before she went in.

"Francis was overcome with emotions. The girl promised to bring back into his life something like the sound of music." He bought her a bracelet the next morning, not knowing when he would see her again. But that evening as Francis opened the door to his home, there she stood. "He seized her and covered her lips with his" – and as he did, in walked a little neighbor girl, Gertrude. Francis gave Gertrude a quarter and made her promise not to tell on him. Then Julia called down to him to hurry and dress for the party.

Francis spent the whole night dreaming of driving the babysitter home. But when he and Julia returned, she informed him he did not have to wait for Anne – she had arranged to be picked up by someone else. Francis sat in the dark feeling like a fool.

On the following evening the Weeds were paid a visit; young Clayton Thomas had come on an errand for his mother. As they talked, Clayton related to them how badly he needed a job, because, it turned out, he was getting married – to Anne Murchison. "Francis recoiled at the mention of the girl's name."

After Clayton had left, he grumbled that the boy was "lazy, irresponsible, affected and smelly." But Julia defended Clayton, accusing Francis of intolerance. Again they fought, and this time Julia threatened to leave him. She relented only when her husband begged her to stay.

What should Francis do now? Go to church and confess his lusts; or visit a Danish massage parlor recommended by a salesman?

At work, Francis received a phone call from a friend of Clayton's, asking him to help the kid find a job. He refused. After lunch, he called up his secretary's psychiatrist and demanded an appointment. At

1

five that evening Francis entered the doctor's office, tears in his eyes, and confessed hoarsely, "I'm in love, Dr. Herzog."

Weeks later "the village hangs, morally and economically, from a thread; but it hangs from its thread in the evening light." In the basement of his house, Francis Weed is constructing a coffee table while Julia works in the garden. Outwardly, at least, all is peaceful.

"The Five-Forty-Eight"
(a contemporary New York setting)

Blake noticed the woman, and immediately, instinctively, he realized she was waiting for him. "He wondered what she had hoped to gain by a glimpse of him coming out of the office building at the end of the day." As Blake walked down Madison Avenue, he paused in front of a store window, thinking that he might see her following him in the reflection from the glass. At first he saw nothing, but just when he had begun to feel at ease, he caught her image a foot or two behind him. Maybe she intended to harm him, Blake thought; he walked faster. He ducked into a bakery, bought a donut then came back onto the street. Again she was there, waiting.

Walking on, Blake saw his chance to shake the strangely familiar woman – "the door of a men's bar. Oh, it was so simple!" He crowded in and ordered a drink, trying to relax. "He tried to remember her name – Miss Dent, Miss Bent, Miss Lent – " Only six months ago she had been employed as his secretary. She had been in a lonely hospital for a time and seemed grateful for the job. Then one night after working late he had suggested they go for a drink. "If you really want a drink, I have some whiskey at my place," she had said.

Their affair both began and ended that night. At the time, he really did not worry. "Most of the women he had known had been picked for their lack of self-esteem," and to Blake, this woman was no different. The next day, while she was out for lunch, he had her fired.

By the time Blake had finished his second drink at the bar, he realized that he would have to take the later 5:48 train home. Boarding the train, he searched the rows of faces. Although he spied a few neighbors that he knew, he was not on good terms with any of them. Then, as Blake sat there musing, he heard a voice: "'Mr. Blake' . . . It was she." For some reason, "he remembered her name then –

Miss Dent." She sat down next to him. Blake attempted some small talk, but the stern woman would have none of it; she had been sick in bed for two weeks and was not in the mood for his babbling. Blake inquired about where she was working. "'Oh, don't make me laugh,' she said softly."

At that moment, Blake knew she meant trouble. He tried to stand. "Oh, no," she warned. "No, no, no . . . . Don't do that. Don't try and escape me. I have a pistol and I'll have to kill you . . . " Blake was struck dumb; his tongue seemed swollen and he felt immobile. When his mouth finally functioned again, he tried to persuade her to visit him later in his office, but Miss Dent said that would not do. She handed him a letter she had written to him, and Blake began to read: "Dear Husband, they say that human love leads us to divine love, but is this true? I dream about you every night. When I was in the hospital they said they wanted to cure me but they only wanted to take away my self-respect . . . "

As Blake finished reading, Miss Dent suddenly pressed her face against his. "I've been thinking about devils," she whispered. "I mean, if there are devils in the world . . . is it our duty to exterminate them? I know that you always prey on weak people. I can tell."

When the conductor called out Blake's stop, Miss Dent hissed for him to walk ahead of her off the train. After all the commuters had left the platform, she directed Blake to a coal yard north of the station where she ordered him to stop. She ranted on about her angry life and her unfulfilled dreams, ending her diatribe with the observation, " . . . after all I know more about love than you."

"Kneel down! Kneel down!" commanded Miss Dent, in near hysteria. "Do what I say. Kneel down!" Blake did as he was told. Then the madwoman's demeanor suddenly changed. "I want to help you," she explained gently, "but when I see your face it sometimes seems to me that I can't help you." Finally she demanded that he put his face in the dirt and "he fell forward in the filth." The coal skinned his face. He stretched out on the ground, weeping. "Now I feel better" she sneered. "Now I can wash my hands of you . . . " and with that, she straightened up and walked away.

Blake, still trembling, trudged home in the evening gloom.

"The Enormous Radio"
(a 1940's apartment building setting)

Jim and Irene Westcott were average people. Jim earned a middle-class income. Irene was "a pleasant, rather plain girl." In fact, "the Westcotts differed from their friends, their classmates, and their neighbors only in an interest they shared in serious music." They frequented concerts and spent most of their time at home listening to the radio. Their radio, though, was old, "unpredictable, and beyond repair." Finally it stopped working altogether.

The following day Jim bought his wife a new radio, and that afternoon it was delivered to the Westcott's apartment. Irene "was struck at once with the physical ugliness of the large gumwood cabinet." However, after the children were put to bed, she turned it on and admired its pure tone. For a moment Irene was happy; then the "interference" began. Irene tried to adjust the radio, but could not eliminate the static. She soon discovered that the radio, besides playing her Mozart, was picking up sounds from the elevator, the apartment building's doorbells, and from Waring blenders.

When Jim arrived home, Irene complained that the radio was reproducing sounds from all over the building. Jim tested the radio with the same result and promised that the people had who sold it to him would fix it.

The next day when Irene came home from a luncheon date, the cleaning woman informed her that a man had been there to repair the radio. But as she listened, the instrument once again picked up background noises, this time from a phonograph, rattling jewelry, ringing bells, and a confusion of voices.

After dinner, Jim turned on the radio and listened in on an argument taking place in another apartment. He fiddled with the knobs, next tuning in on a couple getting dressed for a party. Again and again he adjusted the tuner, invading the private transactions of their neighbors: a marriage proposal to the Sweeney nurse, quarrels of all kinds, the Fullers' cocktail party. Finally the Westcotts "turned off the radio at midnight and went to bed, weak with laughter."

From then on Irene spent her days listening in on lives throughout the building. She reveled in the romantic interludes she was privileged to take in; nevertheless, she became more and more troubled by her neighbors' cries of despair and their sometimes brutal language.

When Jim returned from work one evening, Irene told him to hurry up to Apartment 16C: Mr. Osborn was beating his wife. But Jim had had enough. He turned off the radio. "It's like looking in people's windows . . . " he told Irene. Irene sobbed and admitted that she had daily become more depressed by her eavesdropping. "Life is too terrible, too sordid and awful." Then she turned to her husband: "Our lives aren't sordid, are they darling? . . . We are happy aren't we?"

The very next day the repairman came again and fixed the radio. Irene listened, and this time it played music; just music.

"The Swimmer"
(Suburbia, USA)

One clear midsummer afternoon, Neddy Merrill was resting by the side of a friend's pool, drinking gin. Ned gave the impression "of youth, sport, and clement weather." As he gazed out over the endless expanse of pools and patios running through Westchester county, "it occurred to him that by taking a dogleg to the southwest he could reach his home by water." The more Ned thought about it, the more plausible it seemed. Besides, Ned thought of himself as something of a "legendary figure" – and the day was beautiful; "a long swim might enlarge and celebrate its beauty."

Ned began his odyssey feeling like a pilgrim or an explorer. He would swim the length of each swimming pool and then walk to the next pool and repeat the exercise. He knew that along the way he would encounter friends, hospitality and adventure. However, Ned ran into an unexpected obstacle: The Welcher's pool was dry, and "this breach in his chain of water disappointed him absurdly."

Next came the problem of crossing the highway. Although Ned had foreseen this momentary delay, he was unprepared for what happened: "He was laughed at, jeered at, a beer can was thrown at him, and he had no dignity or humor to bring to the situation." Finally, an old, slow-driving man gave Ned time to cross to the other side.

The next pool in Ned's imaginary river belonged to the Hallorans, an elderly couple who "did not wear bathing suits." Ned, not wishing to offend, stripped out of his trunks and dove into the pool. When he came out at the other end, he stopped to chat with the Hallorans for a moment, announcing that he was swimming across-the county, which elicited little surprise from the couple. Before Ned continued his journey, Mrs. Halloran said, "We've been terribly sorry to hear about all your misfortunes, Neddy." But Ned had no idea what he was referring to, even after she shook her head and mumbled something about Ned's "poor children."

A few pools later, Ned came upon the Biswangers, who were throwing a pool-party. Though he did not belong to their "set," still he was caught off-guard when Grace Biswanger approached him with rancor. "Why this party has everything including a gate crasher," she hooted. When Ned went to get a drink, even the bartender treated him rudely. It then dawned on him that perhaps he had "suffered some loss of social esteem." As the swimmer got up to leave, he heard Grace telling loudly about how "he showed up drunk one Sunday and asked us to loan him five thousand dollars."

The next pool belonged to his former mistress, Shirley Adams, who demanded to know what he wanted. When Ned explained that he only wanted to swim across her pool, all Shirley bothered to say was, "Good Christ. Will you every grow up?" Then she added under her breath that under no circumstances would she lend him any money. Ned swam across the pool, but as he tried to pull himself out, he felt weak, especially in the shoulders.

Walking away, Ned looked into the sky, where the first stars were just coming out. He began to sob. "It was probably the first time in his adult life that he had ever cried, certainly the first time in his life that he had ever felt so miserable, cold, tired, and bewildered."

Ned was almost home. As he stumbled up his driveway "he was so stupefied with exhaustion that his triumph seemed vague." The house was uncommonly dark. "Was it so late that they had all gone to bed? . . . " The doors were locked.

Then, as Ned peered through the window, he "saw that the place was empty."

Commentary:

The majority of Cheever's narratives concern ordinary people in extraordinary circumstances. Cheever's characters are fairly average types, living out their existences in the suburbs. Yet, beneath these well-groomed facades are the traits which lie waiting to reveal them as unique, and at the same time, human. Ned, in "The Swimmer," is blind to his own social, spiritual and financial bankruptcy; only his strange, quixotic journey reveals just how far he has fallen. Likewise, in "The Five-Forty-Eight," Blake does not realize how cruel he actually is until Miss Dent hunts him down and confronts him.

Cheever's stories rarely end like fables, with morals directing the reader how to feel. Rather, he leaves us both free enough and unsettled enough to reexamine our own minds, relationships, feelings and self-images – and to ask ourselves once again just what our lives should mean.

THE CHOSEN

by Chaim Potok, Ballentine Books, New York, N.Y. 1967

Type of work: Introspective, "coming of age" novel

Setting: New York; 1944 - 1947, near the end of World War II

Principal characters:
Reuven Malter, fifteen-year-old Jewish narrator
Mr. Malter, Reuven's father, a liberal Jewish teacher and writer
Danny Saunders, Reuven's Hasidic Jewish friend
Reb Saunders, Danny's strict rabbi father

Story Overview:

A baseball game was about to change the lives of two Jewish parochial school rivals. As the opposing team began to warm up on the field, Reuven Malter could not help but laugh. The team, made up of orthodox Hasidic boys, dropped fly balls and bobbled grounders. Reuven could not help but notice, however, how one of the boys, Danny Saunders, totally ignored his laughter. "I told myself that I did not like his Hasidic-bred sense of superiority and that it would be a great pleasure to defeat him and his team in this afternoon's game."

During the game, Danny had only one thing to say to Reuven: "I told my team we're going to kill you Apikorsim this afternoon." Reuven felt the sting of that insult. "[Apikorsim] had meant, originally, a Jew educated in Judaism who denied basic tenets of his faith, like the existence of God, the revelation, the resurrection of the dead. To people like Reb Saunders [Danny's father], the term also meant any educated Jew who might be reading, say, Darwin."

The game soon turned into a tightly fought religious civil war. Toward the end, Reuven was called upon to pitch. He struck out the first batter with his mean curve ball. Next up was Danny, his team's best hitter. After Reuven threw two wicked curves in a row, Danny sneered as he took his stance for the third pitch. It was another curve, but this time Danny was ready: he dropped the end of his bat and hammered the ball straight back at Reuven, smashing into the left lens of his glasses and knocking him to the ground.

Reuven awoke the next day, lying in the hospital's eye ward. When Mr. Malter, Reuven's father, arrived, he explained that the doctors had removed a piece of glass from his eye. "I stared at him. 'The scar tissue,' I said slowly. 'The scar tissue can grow over the pupil.' And I felt myself go sick with fear."

Since Reuven was not allowed to read until his eye healed, Mr. Malter brought him a radio to help pass the time. He and his hospital friends listened to news reports of the D-Day invasion. Reuven also had a visit from Danny Saunders, who attempted to apologize; but Reuven only snapped at him: "How does it feel to know you've made someone blind in one eye?"

That evening when Reuven told his father

about Danny's visit, Mr. Malter felt that he was being unfair. The following day Danny came again, and the two boys finally discussed the game. "Do you know what I don't understand about that ball game?" said Danny. "I don't understand why I wanted to kill you." Reuven confessed that he, too, had felt like beating Danny's team into the turf.

Later, Danny told Reuven of his all-too-certain future: someday he would become the rabbi of his father's Hasidic sect; he had no choice. Reuven then revealed his own lifelong desire to become a rabbi, explaining that his father was pressing him to be a mathematician instead. Now Danny divulged his own dark secret: he often read on the sly at the public library, even studying Darwin and Freud – books forbidden by his father – under the guidance of an unnamed mentor he had met there. Just then, Mr. Malter arrived for a visit; to Reuven's surprise, his father greeted Danny as though they had already met. "I suddenly realized it was my father who all along had been suggesting books for Danny to read. My father was the man Danny had been meeting in the library."

Mr. Malter later explained that he had only the day before made the connection himself. He also admitted that he felt a little guilty betraying Danny's rabbi father by recommending forbidden books, but he reasoned that Danny would find them for himself anyway.

On Friday afternoon the bandage was removed from Reuven's eye, and he was allowed to go home. That night, he questioned his father about why Danny felt he must become a rabbi. Mr. Malter expounded on the origins of Hasidism and gave his son some advice: "Now Reuven, listen carefully . . . . Reb Saunders' son is a terribly torn and lonely boy. There is literally no one in the world he can talk to. He needs a friend. The accident with the baseball has bound him to you."

The next day, Danny came to Reuven's home and asked if he would go to see the rabbi: "He wants to meet you. He always has to approve of my friends. Especially if they're outside the fold." So Reuven attended evening services with Danny – feeling very conspicuous, as the only one there without Hasidic garb or long earlocks. After the service, Reuven joined Reb Saunders, Danny, and others around a table, where the rabbi offered a lecture about doing God's will. Then he launched into a heated dialogue with Danny on the Talmud. "As I sat there listening to . . . Danny and his father, I slowly realized . . . I was witnessing a kind of public quiz – more a contest than a quiz." The father was preparing his son to become a rabbi. Then Reb Saunders turned to Reuven and asked if he had spotted any errors in their math-laced religious discussion. When Reuven admitted that he had, and corrected the rabbi's intentional mistake, Reb Saunders was won over. The boys were permitted to be friends. They met at the library the next day, where Danny announced that he wanted to become, of all things, a psychologist.

One day Reuven accepted an invitation to dine at the Saunders' home. After the meal, father and son again entered into an intense debate of Talmudic principles – and before long, Reuven was also a participant. When Danny left the room to get some tea, Reb Saunders admitted to Reuven that he knew about Danny's library visits. "Master of the Universe," he chanted, "you gave me a brilliant son, and I thanked you for him a million times. But you had to make him so brilliant?" After making Reuven covenant not to make a Gentile of his son, the father divulged that he could not discuss any of this with Danny. Reuven could not understand why, except for religious discussion, there existed only silence between the rabbi and his son.

World War II came to an end, and American Jewry learned of the brutal Holocaust. Mr. Malter was deeply shocked. Only a few days after Reuven's final examinations, his father had a heart attack. After his recovery, Mr. Malter constantly warned of the need for building a Jewish homeland and began to spearhead various committees geared to that end.

Then one evening, while dining with the Saunders, Reuven also expounded on the need for a Jewish state. The rabbi exploded: "When the Messiah comes, we will have a Holy Land, not a land contaminated by Jewish goyim (non-believers)."

By the time Danny and Reuven had graduated from high school and begun attending the yeshiva college, the Zionist movement was gaining momentum. Mr. Malter, despite ill health, was heavily involved in speaking, organizing and fund-raising for the future state of Israel.

One night, after heading a particularly important pro-Zionist rally, Mr. Malter returned home flushed with excitement. The rally had been a wild success. But as Malter's viewpoints became more and more accepted throughout the Jewish community, Danny and Reuven found themselves compelled to meet secretly in the bathroom for talks. Reb Saunders had decreed that "Danny was not to see me, talk to me, listen to me or be found within four feet of me. My father and I had been excommunicated from the Saunders family."

Shortly thereafter, Mr. Malter had another heart attack. The double burden of his father's condition and the loss of Danny's companionship nearly broke Reuven. He threw himself into his studies with renewed vigor – especially the Talmud class, which he attended with Danny.

A Jewish state was now close to reality, but Mr. Malter's health prevented him from attending a key conference in Palestine. "He had worked so hard for a Jewish state, and that very work now kept him from seeing it." He gently told Reuven,

You have become a small giant since the day Danny's ball struck your eye. You do not see it. But I

see it. And it's a beautiful thing to see . . . . A man must fill his life with meaning, meaning is not automatically given . . . . That I do not think you understand yet. A life filled with meaning is worthy of rest. I want to be worthy of rest when I am no longer here. Do you understand what I am saying?

For two years Danny and Reuven painfully endured Reb Saunders' ban. However, with the formation of an Israeli state, the issue died, and the young men were allowed to renew their friendship. Danny had still not told his father of his "heretical" designs to become a psychologist, though Danny had shown him his letters of acceptance to non-Jewish universities. Reb Saunders now frequently insisted that Reuven come to dinner, but Reuven did not wish to see the rabbi. "I hated him as much now as I had when he had forced his silence between me and Danny."

But Mr. Malter urged his son to accept Reb Saunders' invitation for Passover. " . . . When someone asks to speak to you, you must let him speak to you. You still have not learned that?" So, Reuven sat again in the Saunders' study. This time, however, he heard Reb Saunders finally admit that he was aware of Danny's reluctance to become a rabbi. Though Danny began to weep, "Reb Saunders did not look at him. He was talking to Danny through me." He finally divulged the reason for his long-running silence with Danny. Reb had once had a brother with a brilliant mind like Danny's, but his brother's "was a cold mind, almost cruel, untouched by his soul." The brother had left home early, refusing to become a rabbi. When Reb Saunders had recognized his son's intellectual gift, he had decided to use silence to create a soul for Danny; to teach Danny how to suffer, how to care for others. "Compassion I want for my son, not a mind without a soul!"

Now Reb Saunders finally turned to Danny and tenderly endorsed his career plans. He made Danny promise to observe the Commandments, and asked his forgiveness for not having been a wiser father. Although he would be disheartened to see Danny shorn of his earlocks – being both Hasidic and a psychologist was certainly contradictory – the rabbi gave his son his blessing.

Commentary:

Potok's *The Chosen* is a poignant look at tensions between the two poles of tradition and progress that almost inevitably develop within any culture – and that, ironically, give it both its life and its identity, even while pulling its members, sometimes tragically, in opposite directions. The novel considers in particular, the disharmony that may exist between traditional religious values and modern scholarship.

A recurring theme revolves around *seeing*: When Reuven is threatened with blindness he begins to see things more deeply. The strange and fanatical ways of Reb Saunders bewilder him at first, but as time passes, he begins to see both the great depth and sorrowful shallowness of human relationships.

COMPACT
Classics™

LIBRARY #7: Health and Fitness

Section A: Caring for Mind and Body

7-A1   *Feed Yourself Right* by Lendon Smith

7-A2   *The Stress Solution: A Rational Approach to Increasing Corporate and Personal Effectiveness* by Samuel H. Klarreich

7-A3   *Sitting on the Job: How to Survive the Stresses of Sitting Down to Work* by Scott W. Donkin

7-A4   *Control Your Depression* by Peter Lewinsohn, et. al.

7-A5   **Headaches:** Their Causes and Cures

Section B: Nutrition and Dieting

7-B1   *Overcoming Overeating: Living Free in a World of Food* by Jane Hirschmann

7-B2   **Six Celebrated Diet Books**
The Popcorn-Plus Diet by Joel Herskowitz, **Beverly Hills Medical Diet** by Arnold Fox, **The Rice Diet Report** by Judy Moscovitz, **The Eight-Week Cholesterol Cure** by Robert E. Kowalski, **The Story of Weight Watchers** by Jean Nidetch and Joan Rattner Heilman, and **Fabulous Fructose Recipe Book** by J. T. Cooper and Jeanne Jones

7-B3   **Twenty Food Tips for Lifetime Weight Control**

7-B4   **Cholesterol, Fats and Sugars:** Three Most Talked-About Health Topics

FEED YOURSELF RIGHT

by Lendon Smith, M.D., McGraw-Hill Book Co., New York, N.Y., 1983

Dr. Smith is a highly respected authority on pediatrics and a well-known author of several best-selling books in the field of child nutrition, including the celebrated *Feed Your Kids Right*. While attending to children's maladies, Dr. Smith began to successfully treat adults complaining of "headaches, allergies, hypertension, infections, depression, and undesirable behavior." By "changing their eating habits and lifestyles," he succeeded. *Feed Yourself Right* was written only after a 32-year career of observing how chemicals, vitamins, minerals and nutrients affect the body.

The book confronts the common cycles of ill-health: " . . . The unhealthy person (because of stress or prolonged poor diet) cannot absorb the vitamins to help the enzymes absorb the vitamins . . . . The key organs . . . need vitamins and minerals to do their work. They are all stressed when the blood sugar bounces around as a result of eating the wrong foods . . . "

Smith teaches how to "read" your body; to understand its dietary pleas and the warning signs indicating that your nutritional plan needs bolstering:

- There's no such thing as *a little bit sick:* "You have to be healthy to be healthy . . . "

- " . . . You can't have good health with bad nutrition – and by health I mean the capacity to live a long and zestful life free of illnesses and untimely degeneration of body tissue."

- "You are a tossed salad" – an accumulation of genetic makeup, biochemical influences during your mother's pregnancy, possible birth trauma, and the collection of emotional, physical, chemical and nutritional forces during your life.

- Your body "speaks" to you by its reactions. People suffering from cold hands and feet, nausea, menopause, depression, insomnia, tics or twitches . . . *can* come to determine and deal with their problems.

- Distinct health patterns emerge as we go from adolescence into the stages of adulthood. Eating habits and dietary requirements may need altering. For example, in the "Thirties" section of the chapter entitled "Making it to 120," Smith recommends that if you notice any new and persistent indications setting in (fatigue, headaches, hay fever, muscle cramps, irritability, skin rashes, forgetfulness, etc.), ingestion of certain minimum nutrients will help keep your body machinery running adequately. He recommends

- **Vitamin C:** 1000 to 5000 mg per day, and more if allergies or sickness occur.

- **B complex vitamins:** B1, B2, B6 (25 to 50 mg), B3 and pantothenic acid (50 to 100 mg), folic acid (0.4 mg), B12 (100 mcg), inositol and choline (1 gram each).

- **Calcium:** 1000 mg a day. Calcium deficiency is common because many people *avoid dairy products* for their potentially harmful salt and fat content.

- **Magnesium:** 500 mg a day. Magnesium controls irritability, helps muscles function, cuts down on body odor, and may prevent heart attack.

- **Iron:** 10 to 20 mg. daily are recommended, and higher amounts are needed by many women.

- **Vitamins E** (400-1200 units), **A** (10,000-20,000 units), and **D** (400-1000 units) need to be supplemented for most individuals, since diet and sunshine are unreliable sources.

In Chapter 6, "Find Yourself (Or Skip This If You Are In Perfect Health)," Smith analyzes a host of symptoms. "Find your symptom, find your disease, find yourself." This is followed by a "dictionary of nutritional deficiencies." The reader is invited to "find his or her own unique complaints and try to remedy them before they increase in severity . . , "

Smith documents his preventative approach. "Most chest pains are not due to heart attacks but may be the body's way of saying it needs calcium and magnesium. A runny nose and sneeze should be an indication that an allergy is nearby, but it may or may not mean that asthma is down the road. One can become tired before the laboratory shows anemia."

The book covers all the plagues of maturity from A through Z – from abdominal disorders, obesity, allergies, and high blood pressure, to moodiness, fatigue, sinusitis and night blindness – all of which can be alleviated through improved nutrition. Some of the listings are definitely not diseases in themselves, but possible symptoms of illness. "We must be more aware of what our bodies are telling us. Every symptom is urging us to take some remedial action."

Below are listed some common nutritional problems along with sampled advice offered in *Feed Yourself Right*.

ADDICTION – People can become addicted to any food or drug. The body produces its own "endorphins," natural chemical narcotics. When we take drugs to reduce pain (or foods or drinks to wake up in the morning or to feel good), the body reduces its production of endorphins, and we become "hooked" on these outside chemicals. Acupuncture and massive vitamin supplements have been found to be accepted techniques for the addict to "perhaps stimulate the production of the person's own narcotic."

ALLERGIES – "Allergy cannot cause everything, but may be the cause of anything," says Dr. James Breneman. Milk intolerance, for instance, can cause a host of problems from rashes, bed-wetting, and constipation to anemia, runny nose, and body aches. "We have a rule: if you don't understand a symptom or a sign, it is probably an allergy . . . "

Allergic symptoms manifest themselves in the body when it is repeatedly exposed to "sensitive" environments or foods. Relief is a matter of identifying and removing or immunizing against the "allergen" that triggers the reaction.

Often, a "tingling or burning sensation" when a food is placed in the mouth is an indication of sensitivity to that food. Skin testing can be quite unreliable. A four-day water-only fast is suggested, ending with the gradual introduction of different foods to observe their reactions. Remember: "The foods we love and eat frequently are the ones to which we are usually allergic and addicted." To wean yourself from foods harmful to you, and to ease withdrawal, Smith recommends vitamins C and B6, calcium, Niacin, Vitamin A, and zinc.

ANXIETY, CONCENTRATION DIFFICULTY, IRRITABILITY, and STRESS are common "professional" ailments, which could lead to neurosis. " . . . If you are alive you will have some stress. Getting married may be as stressful as getting a divorce . . . . You can help restore homeostasis with nutrition, but try climbing out of the ice water too." Increase your intake of those vitamins and minerals that have a calming effect and that are most easily depleted by stress – calcium, niacin or vitamin B3, magnesium, and vitamins B12, B6 and B1. Extra zinc can make a difference, as can folic acid and added protein. Avoid sugar and junk foods, especially before bedtime. While Valium may treat your symptoms, a better diet will go much further toward balancing your world.

Chemical "helpers" (lecithin and L-glutamine) have been found to help construct the chemicals that aid in concentration.

DEPRESSION and FATIGUE may generate a nutrient deficiency cycle, where not enough vitamins and minerals are present to help the brain produce enough necessary chemicals to "keep us sane and cheerful." Often we crave a food that will give us a quick lift, but eating such foods will likely lead to an equally rapid "downer."

Again, the whole range of B vitamins – sometimes administered by injection at first – is vital. B1, in particular, fights the fatigue accompanying depression. Folic acid and B12 in combination, tend to produce a lift. Pantothenic acid, vitamins C and A, magnesium, zinc and iron (in the right proportions for you), and certain prescribed drugs may also improve your outlook.

HEADACHES – Stress (anger, guilt . . .), har-

bored over time and then released, can cause a multitude of problems – including headaches. But so can improper diet.

Dilated blood vessels induce the throbbing feeling in the head. "Two things can be done: reduce the stresses, and nourish the vascular system . . . " Look for food sensitivities and steer clear of suspect foods. Intramuscular shots of B complex vitamins have been known to help. Avoid ingesting allergens or sweets at night, which trigger falling blood sugar during sleep. "Seeds, nuts, and protein at bedtime along with calcium (1000 mg) and magnesium (500 mg) might prevent the blood sugar drop," and the headache that follows.

MENSTRUAL DISORDERS – Any marked change from a woman's "normal" cycle is a clue leading to either disease, stress or nutritional imbalance. Good diet, besides relieving menstrual discomfort, helps the body form and metabolize needed hormones at the right time. Extra B vitamins, calcium, magnesium, zinc and vitamin E, taken over time, can help relieve pain.

SPOILED BRATS or SURLY ADULTS – "Crabby people may simply not feel well," so "put together the following potion: 1 drop of Lugol's solution (potassium iodide) and 1 teaspoon of apple cider vinegar in a glass of fruit juice; taken twice daily, it could change someone nasty into a sweet, compliant human being."

Smith acknowledges that, apparently, the extra acid from the fruit juice allows for better absorption of calcium, magnesium and zinc, and helps nutrients enter the body's cells more easily.

ULCERS: STOMACH and DUODENAL – Ulcers appear when digestive acid and pepsin from the stomach lining slowly eat away at the stomach and duodenum. Aging, protein deprivation, aspirin ingestion, smoking and stress worsen the condition. But, strangely, highly "stressed-out" German soldiers on the World War II Russian front were found to have a very low incidence of ulcers. Their diet made a difference. They ate little sugar or white flour, and no processed foods. Raw, natural foods such as fruits, vegetables, and a little meat had a buffering effect on their stomachs. A sensible, nutritional diet (possibly supplemented by vitamins) can aid in healing an existing ulcer.

Dr. Smith insists that indeed "You are what you eat." He emphasizes in *Feed Yourself Right* that *YOU are the expert for your body. You* get the messages, and as you become more adept at reading your body's little slips from the norm, and compensate with nutrition before the condition worsens, you'll be that much healthier.

A doctor's tests, diagnosis and recommendations should not go unheeded, but doctors and patients alike need to recognize that "Medicine is an art [that] works a lot better if each cell of the body and brain has the correct amount of energy, amino acids, vitamins, and minerals."

THE STRESS SOLUTION

A Rational Approach to Increasing Corporate and Personal Effectiveness
by Samuel H. Klarreich, Key Porter Books, Toronto, Canada, 1988.

What is "counterthinking"? Klarreich's *The Stress Solution* defines it as *"thinking which is in opposition to previous thinking,"* and applauds it as the key to "managing stress and burnout, the two ills of the corporate world." By citing personal examples, experiments, and suggestions for realistic approaches to the stress/burnout syndromes, the book offers its "stress solution."

Part I: STRESS

The warning signals of stress include rapid breathing, increased heart rate, withdrawal, headaches, chain smoking, chest pains, insomnia, ulcers, and reduced sex drive, symptons often accompanied by thoughts and feelings of despair or panic ("I'm doomed"; "I'll never succeed . . . "). Stress means dollars lost, projects delayed, poor morale, poor health and prophetic failure.

Behavior: Type A and Type B Personalities

Type A personalities are impatient, hurried, fidgety, driven to be successful, performance oriented, competitive . . . If that's you, you've trained yourself to be that way over many years. But these types of stress behaviors aren't necessarily bad – *if they are managed positively.*

Type B personalities seem to know their limitations; they are low-key and can relax and enjoy themselves without feeling guilty. Often they're described as having little drive or ambition to succeed.

Of course all people exhibit varying degrees of these two opposite personality types; Klarreich believes most of us do some things in a type A way and others in a type B way.

Stressors

Most "significant" life situations or events, either positive or negative, function as natural "stresses." On one hand, a constant barrage of noise, being fired, competition, the death of someone close, separation or divorce; and on the other hand, moving, starting a new job, making a large purchase, vacations, marriage . . . any of these circumstances can evoke emotions like worry, grief, or depression. However, such feelings need not result in long-term, chronic dis function.

You may be able to relate to Klarreich's list of *"Sixteen Irrational Thoughts"* that commonly heighten feelings of dread:

1. Something terrible will happen to me if I make a mistake.

2. There is a right and a wrong way to do things.

3. It is awful and horrible to be criticized.

4. I must be approved of, all the time.

5. I must be competent, and I must be viewed as competent.

6. People in authority should never be challenged.

7. Life in the workplace must be fair and just.

8. I must be in control all of the time.

9. I must anticipate everything.

10. I must have things the way I want them.

11. Employees who are wrong should be punished.

12. I must have somebody's shoulder to cry on.

13. I must feel perfect all the time.

14. My worth as a person is exactly equated to my job performance.

15. I was promised a corporate rose garden.

16. It is too late for me to change, and if you expect it, I won't be able to handle it.

The consequences of irrational thoughts can be: "dumb behavior" ("fight or flight" when the occasion calls for something much less drastic), a vicious cycle of psychological stress symptoms, or the use of false strategies for dealing with anxiety (excessive dieting, jogging or exercising, taking "avoidance"-type vacations, sleeping excessively, using tranquilizers, or turning to alcohol). Such strategies can only work counterproductively in relieving long-term stress.

Two more effective strategies might include:

(1) Relaxation. Klarreich urges anxious people to find a friend, a book, or a course to help them master some procedure that will relax them. This could take the form of a breathing exercise, a gradual relaxation of your body, or an "imaging" process. At first the mind technique you choose may take a half-hour to "bring you down," but once you become adept at it, all you may need is ten seconds.

(2) Time Management. Managing phone calls and interruptions, and making at least a tentative daily plan, helps you accomplish critical or urgent jobs – those that create the most stress. The simpler the management plan, the better.

Counterthinking

The thrust of counterthinking is found in sixteen "Rational Thoughts" to oppose and rid you of the "stinking thinking" which produces stress. These "counter" the *"Sixteen Irrational Thoughts"*:

1. Mistakes happen and nothing terrible results.

2. There is usually no one clear right and wrong way to do things.

3. I will accept criticism and see how I can benefit from it.

4. I will not demand approval.

5. I will not demand of myself that I always be competent, though I will certainly strive for competence.

6. I will not be fearful in the presence of authority.

7. I accept the fact that life in the workplace is not always fair and just.

8. I give myself the right to be out of control once in a while.

9. I can neither anticipate nor be certain of everything.

10. I accept the fact that I will not always get what I want, though I will continue to strive for it.

11. I will give others the right to be wrong, and will not be angry or hostile toward them.

12. If I do not receive full support and enjoy a caring attitude from people around me, it will not be the end of the world.

13. I accept the fact that I will not feel superb all of the time.

14. I will not judge myself only according to what I do or don't do in the workplace.

15. I was not promised a corporate rose garden.

16. It is not too late for me to change.

Though "self-talk" (internal dialogue) and imagining (visualization) are OK, Klarreich warns against too much "positive thinking." This, too, can lead to excessively high, unrealistic expectations.

Certain *actions* reduce stress:

Asserting: Not in a critical, aggressive fashion, but with a tactful, flexible approach, make your wants and needs known. Begin statements with "I believe . . . " or "I would like to try . . . " rather than "You . . . "

Negotiating: Cooperate toward a "win-win" alternative – a solution where both sides "score."

Communicating: "People skills" are invaluable investments.

Problem Solving: Evaluate many possible solutions, then decide and implement the one that seems best.

Risk Taking: Be willing to be embarrassed and non-traditional. Have fun. The discomfort of opening yourself up will gradually fade as you experiment by taking risks.

What do you do when your body tells you you're stressed? Take 90 seconds for stress management.

(1) STOP. Abandon what you're doing.

(2) RELAX. Free your mind of distractions.

(3) THINK. Identify your irrational thoughts.

(4) COUNTERTHINK. Replace these thoughts with more rational ones.

(5) RISK. Break the routine; try something new.

This simple sequence will improve your job performance.

Part II: Burnout

What if you're already "over the edge," completely "stressed out" – burned out? Burnout can manifest itself in: irresponsibility, exhaustion, lack of concern for others, anger, cynicism, lack of motivation, poor appetite, disruption of sleep, withdrawal, frequent quarreling, depression . . . Your emotional reserves are depleted! The stressed-out person is anxious and aggressive; the burnt-out person has progressed to despair.

Burnout can originate from a combination of *un-managed stresses:* work overload or not enough work; too much supervision or lack of supervision; job insecurity or the feeling of being "tied down" to a job. Mid-life crises and their accompanying emotional/hormonal effects also play a part.

Burnout Strategies

(1) Cool Off. Step back from the problem at hand (take a "time out"); consider the situation, and then return and deal with it.

(2) Inventory Yourself. Rate your thoughts and feelings about the various obstacles in your life. Such an inventory can help you reason through problems.

Strategic counterthinking also applies to burnout. "Distorted beliefs and exaggerated expectations are the most critical ingredients in burnout. Changing those beliefs is fundamental if burnout is to be avoided . . . " *Transform your expectations* to something more reasonable. You can do this by:

• **Open Admission:** Concede to yourself (and significant others) that you have a problem.

• **Taking Responsibility:** Accept your problems as your own.

• **Accepting yourself:** Do not condemn yourself. Self-criticism only exacerbates problems.

• **Giving yourself credit:** Your progress may be slow, especially since you're confronting a low frustration tolerance built up over many years.

• **Viewing A New Philosophy:** Change your approach from demanding certainty, to accepting uncertainty.

• **Reducing Your Needs:** Let go of some of your conditions for the "good life." You may not need two cars, the biggest office, etc.

• **Rejecting Perfectionism:** " . . . If you dedicate yourself to perfection, you will achieve the exact opposite." That "perfect" presentation – or perfect family or ideal job – can seldom be reached, or even defined.

• **Withholding Judgment:** Your harsh evaluation of yourself is subjectively biased. Degrading your performance won't bring success – or self-love.

• **Not Waiting For "Inspiration":** You don't need to be motivated or inspired or overjoyed by something in order to go ahead and do it. You can complete even unpleasant tasks under less-than-ideal conditions.

• **Taking Risks:** "Burnout victims tend to specialize in one area and one area alone: work." Most "workaholics" are only comfortable and safe in what they know they can do successfully. Step beyond this safety zone – take risks.

The Stress Solution also suggests regularly turning to one of many social support systems, taking daily diversions from routine, enlisting a "happiness training" program, frequently practicing humor, and generating a hardy commitment to more productive, less stress-producing thinking, feeling and doing. *It's your choice.* The key to the way out of your stress or burnout cycle is in your hands.

SITTING ON THE JOB

by Scott W. Donkin, DC, Houghton Mifflin Co., Boston, Mass., 1989

Millions of people earn their living sitting down; and many of these sitters suffer pain and distress. In *Sitting on the Job*, Scott Donkin examines body mechanics, office environment and job stresses, to come up with practical techniques and exercises that can help repair ailing body parts, relieve tension, induce energy, and generally make you a healthier, more productive person.

Our bodies are made up of an amazing array of shock absorbers, hinges, electrical impulses, and rope-like bands, all designed for ease in movement. Improper habits can put strain on this intricate web of machinery. Cultivating proper habits, however, can help executives, secretaries, telemarketers and countless others be more content and effective in their work.

Here are some of the tips Donkin offers:

Check Out Your Chair

Good sitting posture is a must for good health. Slumping forward or backward in an ill-fitted chair compresses your spine and forces your body to work harder.

Your chair may need to be adjusted to your body's unique size and shape. It should be lightly padded to cushion and distribute your weight. The backrest should fit into the small of your back, allowing you to sit erect. The seat should not be either too low for comfort or so high that it pulls your feet off the floor, putting undue stress on your knee joints and hips. It may be tilted forward or back to relieve pressure on the spine. Armrests can provide support and take strain off your shoulders and neck.

Use your chair's backrest – which should curve forward into the center of the natural curve of the spine – to divert pressure from your lower back and to keep your shoulders upright.

Inventory Your Work Space

• Your desktop should be low enough so that your arms bend at between 70 and 90 degrees at the elbow, allowing your forearms to rest comfortably on the work surface. Repeatedly reaching too far out or cramping your arms too close to the body can result in spinal and joint fatigue.

• Read or view material at an optimum angle so that your head doesn't thrust forward. (Handwriting demands closer focusing than typing, and thus requires a higher work surface.)

• To avoid unnecessary and awkward twists and bends, take advantage of your chair's ability to swivel and roll.

• Make sure the items you use most frequently are in easy reach. Prioritize materials to "reduce repetitious or prolonged one-sided movements." Avoid clutter.

• Place the center of your computer at about chin level. The ideal "eye-to-screen" distance varies from 14 to 30 inches.

• Position your desk telephone near enough so that you can work and hold it at the same time. However, use a shoulder-rest attachment, headphone system, or speaker attachment; tilting your head to brace the phone between your shoulder and cheek forces pressure on the muscles and nerves of the neck and spine.

• In general, adjust your work station to fit your body, not your body to fit the work station.

Stressproof Your Office Environment

"Many factors in your work environment directly affect your body and your ability to focus on your tasks."

• Obviously, lighting should be adequate. Some types of bright lighting, however, can be detrimental to your performance. Direct light from a window in front of you can almost imperceptibly reflect from your desk and into your eyes. Therefore, light should be directed from the back or side.

• Give special consideration to the reflective quality of your computer screen. Low-level or overhead lighting are best for cutting down on glare.

• Be aware of room temperature and air flow. Too much heat or air conditioning directed towards you can not only distract you but also cause muscles on one side of your body to contract, pulling vertebrae out of proper alignment and irritating the nerves that contribute to headache and other discomforts.

• Noise (equipment, music, voices, etc.) can interfere with concentration and cause anxiety. Special filters, proper maintenance of equipment, and padded room dividers can cut down on noise.

Some Common Physical Complaints

Donkin suggests ways to help you deal with – or prevent – many of the physical problems related to sitting. (He hastens to warn that these ideas should not be construed as substitutes for appropriate medical care.)

• *Eye Strain:* Frequently divert your eyes to objects farther away; exercise eye muscles by rolling your eyes up and down, right and left; adjust the brightness level on your computer screen; to cut glare, tilt or rotate the screen, or purchase a glare-reduction filter; change your eye-glass prescription; schedule breaks between periods of intense concentration.

• *Back Pain:* When seated, ensure that your chair fits your body structure. Make it a habit to maintain good seating posture and keep your spine straight (not curved or twisted to one side or to the back); take the time to relax and gently stretch your back, or rotate it in a controlled, slow manner from one side to the other; lift heavy objects by bending your knees, keeping your back straight; avoid sitting or standing for too long at a time.

- *Neck Pain:* Keep your head erect, with the small neck vertebrae curved slightly forward; routinely exercise your neck, shoulders, and arms during the day; adjust your chair and the items in your work station to avoid prolonged or repetitious tilting or craning of your head.

- *Shoulder, Arm, and Hand Symptoms (aching or numbness):* Add some comfortable support to your hands, forearms and elbows while typing, writing, reading, etc.; keep your hands in the "neutral" position as much as possible (wrists straight, fingers relaxed and slightly bent); look for off-the-job activities (cycling, weightlifting, etc.) to strengthen your arms, hands and wrists; shake out and flex these body parts from time to time.

- *Leg and Foot Symptoms (fatigue, cramping or tingling):* Take a brisk walk; adjust your chair's seat height; sit in a balanced (not side-saddle), upright position; see if a back-pocket billfold is pinching your upper leg or causing your pelvis to tilt; wear well-fitted shoes with cushiony supports; keep legs at a comfortable temperature.

- *Headache:* Maintain good posture; keep your head in a "neutral" position; avoid eye strain; keep blood pressure in check; seek professional counsel for any abnormally persistent or painful symptoms.

- *Fatigue:* Get adequate rest and relaxation; maintain a regular exercise routine (your body was "meant to move" – it wants exercise); eat nutritious foods; reduce or learn to handle mental and emotional stress.

Donkin advises that you follow good sleep habits to maximize your time at rest. Proper sleep positions – just like sitting and exercising effectively – require that you employ a neutral posture (head and neck supported and kept in line with your body – not allowed to slump down or to be jammed upward – and, for side-sleeping, knees together to avoid twisting your pelvis and spine).

Break the Stress Cycle

During the work day we often gear up for an activity, and then try to relax once it's accomplished. However, the effects of worries about performance and deadlines can imprison you in a state of tension for hours after the "show" itself is over – sometimes even into the next day.

Dr. Donkin gives a step-by-step technique to help you wind down:

- Sit or lie down and close your eyes.
- Tense successive parts of your body (hands, feet, neck, mouth, etc.), and then relax them, allowing tension to flow out.
- Breathe in, hold the breath, then exhale.
- Daydream about a peaceful setting.

The following two bits of advice can also help you *manage* stress:

1. Try to perceive change as a *welcome* challenge.
2. Exhibit a sense of *optimism,* finding *meaning* in even mundane tasks; actively *control* your life ("turn lemons into lemonade").

Give Exercise a Chance

Exercise keeps your body healthy and flexible, eliminates joint misalignment and instability, and prevents muscle degeneration and organ malfunction.

Take a "personal inventory" of your body's range of motion. Can your head rotate at least 80 degrees both ways? Does it tilt side to side at least 45 degrees? Can your back bend forward about 90 degrees, and backward and sideways to about 30 degrees? Do your abdominal, buttock, and front- and inner-thigh muscles (the most vulnerable for sedentary workers) feel fit? Are your neck, shoulder, and spinal movements painless and unrestricted?

If your inventory looks bad, you can probably benefit from some simple "job-break" exercises. Repeat each sequence five or more times, depending on individual need:

- Stretch backward on your chair, arms reaching above your head, with feet stretching alternately up and out.

- Shrug your shoulders and rotate them forward and back, until muscles relax.

- Sit upright and bring your head and shoulders down to your knees.

- Seated, and with head erect, take hold of one knee at a time and lift it up to your chest.

- While standing, lean over and place your hands on a desk. With your head down, slowly arch your back upward, like a cat, then arch it downward, at the same time raising your head toward the ceiling.

- Lie on your back. Alternately raise your legs to your chest.

- To add strength and flexibility, do a series of leg extensions and lifts, first from a crawling position, then standing, and finally from a prone position.

- Look out the window . . . lean your head back and stare at the ceiling . . . exercise and relax your mind as well as your body. Stretch your hands, forearms, and wrists . . . Relax by lying flat on the floor, with your neck and lower back supported by cushions.

"Take the aching back out of your work." Now that you know the basics for maintaining healthy body posture, the rest is up to you. Sustain and protect good mental, sitting, standing, and exercise habits; consciously change undesirable habits. Then, be consistent in your efforts to not only "exist and survive," but to *"thrive and enjoy."*

CONTROL YOUR DEPRESSION

by Peter M. Lewinsohn, Ricardo F. Munoz, Mary Ann Youngren, and Antonette M. Zeiss,
Prentice Hall, New York, N.Y., 1986

Most people have felt the pangs of depression – mourning, melancholia, "the blues." Nearly all of us experience at least some mild forms of distress at certain periods in our lives. In fact, depression is so much a part of the human condition that it has been called "the common cold of mental health."

The self-help book *Control Your Depression*, written, in conjunction with other clinical colleagues, by Peter Lewinsohn, professor of psychology at the University of Oregon, is designed primarily for persons with mild or moderate (non-clinical) depression who choose NOT to seek professional help. Its personalized therapeutic techniques are not considered complete treatment for severe depression – which may require medical intervention – or for depression associated with strong suicidal responses. The authors suggest that individuals suffering from severe depression solicit help from a local community mental health center or from a certified and licensed psychologist or psychiatrist. However, many persons plagued by depression will find this book both informative and helpful.

Depression is defined as an intense and prolonged period of dysphoria associated with feelings of worthlessness and inadequacy, sleep disturbances, loss of appetite, and a low activity level. Depression often accompanies significant life events such as divorce or marital separation, major changes in the health of oneself or a family member, and burdensome debt or financial setbacks. It is usually triggered by one of two situations: when "too few of our interactions [have] positive outcomes" or "too many of them [have] negative outcomes . . . " "These states of affairs lead to a vicious cycle," Lewinsohn explains. "When we feel depressed we also feel discouraged, and are thus less likely to approach situations that might lead to satisfactory outcomes." This cycle of continual perceived failure can lead to deep depression.

Controlling depression through self-help requires a program that draws heavily on social-learning theory. The program must include:

(1) *Self-change,* based on slow, deliberate, step-by-step *modification* and *modeling;* and

(2) *Detailed self-monitoring and observation.*

The book's first recommendation in devising a personal plan to overcome depression, is to monitor daily mood swings and the specific interactions that relate to attitude changes. Charting your mood swings helps you become aware of the specific circumstances associated with these responses. Such self-monitoring and assessment will usually reveal an obstacle in one or more of the following areas:

1. *An inability to relax*

2. *A lack of pleasant activities*

3. *Difficulties in social behavior* ("problems with people")

4. *Troublesome thoughts*

Lewinsohn outlines a process for rehabilitation in each depression-producing area.

1. If your problem is primarily an *inability to relax:*

(a) Track your average relaxation capability to determine a base level against which to compare progress. A two-week diary or chart correlating your relaxation with daily situations should serve this purpose.

(b) Learn to relax through a process of control.

- Sit quietly in a comfortable room.
- Close your eyes.
- Relax your muscles.
- Breathe slowly and easily.
- Perform this sequential relaxation technique for ten to twenty minutes once or twice each day.

(c) Apply this relaxation technique to tension-producing situations. In time, your proficiency to relax will increase and enable you to use your mind and body to quickly bring you in control.

2. If the problem is primarily a *lack of pleasant activities:*

(a) Recognize that your depression may stem partly from too few gratifying, enjoyable experiences that could otherwise brighten your daily outlook.

(b) Gather base-line data by determining the frequency of pleasant events in your life, and your accompanying moods, during a two-week period. (A "Pleasant Events Scale," in which you rate many mood-related activities, is included.)

(c) Using your base-line data, construct a personal-activities schedule ("Pleasant Event Schedule") to multiply your joy-producing activities. Follow through on your plan to make finding joy a habit.

3. If your problem is primarily a *lack of social skills:*

(a) Realize that non-depressed persons are rated as more socially assertive and skillful than depressed persons. Make assertion a part of your social-skills training.

(b) Monitor your social interactions, fears and feelings for two weeks. Note those events that produce the greatest anxiety for you.

(c) Practice assertive imagery "in the privacy of your mind." Create vivid images of concrete social situations; then rehearse numerous responses in order to refine your social skills and increase your level of comfort.

(d) Gradually transfer these experiences from imagery to real life. Initially, select situations that will most likely have successful outcomes.

(e) List the social activities that you would like – or need – to increase (dating, expressing yourself in groups, attending social gatherings, smiling and confidently addressing others . . .) and set a goal to systematically work towards boosting the occurrence of these activities.

4. If you are depressed as a result of *negative thinking:*

(a) Monitor your troublesome thinking patterns by compiling a personal list of "negative thoughts." For two weeks, whenever you feel depressed, write down your reflections. As in the other three "problem areas," a check-list-type questionnaire (or comprehensive rating list, or some other systematic method to help you specifically identify, your sources of discomfort and how to monitor progress) is included to help you monitor your negative patterns of thought.

(b) With this inventory of negative thinking, consciously decrease negative thoughts.

 • Actively dispute negative, non-constructive self-talk by challenging exaggerated or valuative statements ("I should . . . " "I never . . . " "I ought to . . . ").

 • Minimize the effects of negative-thinking by blowing up such thinking beyond all reasonable proportions. Make it exaggerated, ridiculous. ("I'll bet everyone noticed the mustard stain on my sweater at the party. I'll bet they're still talking about it. I'll bet they'll be shaking their heads for months about that stain. I'll bet they tell everyone in the office. I'll never get invited to another party again. I'm ruined socially . . . ")

 • Perhaps establishing a scheduled "worry time" for particularly troublesome "obsessive thoughts" would alleviate their hour after hour, day after day impact.

 • Another method is to program in your brain a cue to remind yourself to think a positive thought. For example, each time you brush your teeth, get in your car or eat a meal, try thinking or reading something positive.

 • The book's most recommended technique for managing thoughts, however, is to yell, within your mind, "STOP!" when a negative thought appears; then take a minute to interrupt the thought, allowing your mind to flow back to a non-negative idea.

The authors close their book with chapters devoted to several depression-related topics such as fostering constructive thinking, using appropriate rewards for improvement, evaluating your efforts, maintaining your gains, and preventing further occurrences of depression by preparing and planning for stressful life events. Among the suggestions given, are:

 • Realistically acknowledge that negative feelings are common to many people. You are not alone in grief or boredom or self-devaluation. Strengthen your psychological base by knowing that "junk happens," to you and to others.

 • Set tangible goals that you truly plan to achieve.

 • Continually build your social skills/friendship network. Friends and confidants provide needed support. Having a sturdy social base will help you offset failures in other areas – areas that without this support could have the effect of tearing your life apart.

Control Your Depression submits that *you* are the one who needs to plan *your* personal "mental health," and you do this by determining the *source* of your depression. You then can deal in a knowledgeable manner with your feelings – and the events that spawn those feelings. In exchange for diligent efforts at self-monitoring, self-assertion and self-instruction, the book proposes techniques for meaningfully controlling your moods by controlling your thoughts and behaviors.

HEADACHES: THEIR CAUSES AND CURES

Headaches remain the most common and confusing physical malady in America. Sadly, they are often casually dismissed by the medical community and even by sufferers themselves. Yet, the time lost, monetary cost, and human pain – not only physical but emotional – incurred from headaches is incalculable.

The good news is that there are now many home measures that can be taken to tame most headaches; and, nowadays, most chronic, recurring, and even debilitating headaches can be eased if not cured by drugs or other treatments.

The first step is to determine the primary cause of your headaches – a cause that may be obscure. Is your head pain a result of anxiety or depression having to do with school or work, eyestrain, high blood pressure, sensitivity to a certain chemical (for some victims, one bite of ice cream can bring on a sudden, sharp pain), fasting, menstruation, or some other cause? Are you vulnerable to one of the mysterious triggers of migraine? Did you inherit "headache genes" that make you susceptible? Or are your headaches a result of multiple, overlapping causes?

Take a look at the various types of headaches, their symptoms and triggers listed below, along with tips for treatment and prevention. Also, seek the care of a physician for chronically severe or disabling headaches.

Tension Headaches (the most common type of head pain): Dull non-throbbing pain, usually on both sides of the head; tight scalp and achy neck.
Triggers: Long- or short-term stress or anxiety; emotional pain such as guilt, grief, or anger; a stuffy room; noise; prolonged muscle tension; mis-aligned teeth or jaw.
Treatment: Rest; aspirin, ibuprofen, or acetaminophen; ice packs, muscle relaxants; antidepressants, if appropriate.
Prevention: Lessen stress-producing activities; use a relaxation technique: 1. Shut your eyes and tighten every muscle in your face and neck. Then, slowly relax all those muscles. 2. With your fingertips, gently massage around your eyes, temples, neck, forehead, and the bridge of your nose. 3. Stretch your neck and move your head from side to side and front to back.

Eyestrain Headaches: Eye fatigue and head pain.
Triggers: Too much close, concentrated work by the muscles that control the eyes.
Treatment: Aspirin or ibuprofen; cold packs; eye rest.
Prevention: Use a stronger reading lamp and a good overhead light; keep reading materials propped at a 45-degree angle to the desk; take rest periods during long study sessions – every two hours or so; regularly have your eyeglasses prescription re-checked.

Common Migraines: Severe, violently throbbing, frequently one-sided head pain, which may subside into a steady ache. Often accompanied by nausea, cold hands, tremor, dizziness, extreme light and sound sensitivity, and feelings of anxiety or disgust. Triggers, location, longevity, and intensity may vary; sometimes run in cycles.
Triggers: Certain foods (chocolate, nuts, cheese) and chemicals (nitrites, MSG, and others); taking birth-control pills; smoking; alcohol (especially red wine); emotional stress (usually strikes once the immediate causes of stress have ended); stimulation of senses (particular smells or sights . . .); changes in weather or climate; onset of menstruation; pregnancy; an inherited chemical imbalance. (Possibly result from a blood vessel suddenly constricting and then dilating.)
Treatment: Ice packs; a dark and quiet environment; pain relievers (Darvon or codeine) or a vasoconstrictor (blood vessel constricting medication); steroids (for prolonged attacks); using coping techniques and "mind-power": 1. Lie down. Breathe deeply. 2. Imagine your hands stretched on the warm sand of a favorite beach. Visualize the blood vessels of your hands opening up to allow greater flow. 3. As your hands warm up, the blood supply to your brain will increase, diverting your headache.
Prevention: Avoid triggering factors; take a prescribed beta-blocker such as propranolol, use blood regulating biofeedback. (Also, take heart; most migraine sufferers' pain lessens or vanishes as they get older.)

Classical Migraines: Migraines accompanied by nervous-system disorders and other warning signs – sudden and strange mood swings, cravings and other changes in appetite, vertigo (disabling dizziness), blurred or "shimmering" vision, the temporary appearance of blind-spots, numbness in an arm or leg, hallucinatory odors, or colorful and transluscent visual hallucinations.
Triggers, Treatment, and Prevention: Same as for a common migraine.

Cluster Headaches: Severe aching around or behind one eye, often occurring in several brief episodes during the day; tearing of eye, blurred vision, a single bloodshot eye, nasal congestion, flushed face, etc. May develop during sleep, and attacks may occur over a period of weeks or months, then disappear for a time.
Triggers: Alcohol, heavy smoking.
Treatment: Vasoconstrictors; oxygen inhalation.
Prevention: Cutting down on smoking and drinking; short-term use of prescription steroids or other drugs.

Hangover Headaches: Migraine-like symptoms such as throbbing pain and nausea.
Triggers: Alcohol, which even in small amounts can cause body dehydration and irritation and dilation of the blood vessels in the brain.
Treatment: Liquids (especially broth or tomato juice); honey.
Prevention: Drink in moderation or not at all; when drinking, stick to a single type of drink;

especially avoid rum, red wine, brandy, and port liquors.

Caffeine or Nicotine Headaches: "Rebound" aches, often dull and pounding, caused by blood vessel constriction.
Triggers: Too much caffeine (a stimulant found in coffee, tea, colas, and some over-the-counter drugs) or nicotine (found in tobacco) taken on a regular basis.
Treatment: Rest; aspirin or ibuprofen; ice packs.
Prevention: Gradually decrease caffeine intake; 250 milligrams of caffeine or more per day – roughly the amount in four cups of coffee – is thought to be too much (but stopping "cold turkey" will probably bring on a dreadful headache, due to the rebounding of vessels to a dilated state); cut down or abstain from tobacco.

Other Chemically Induced (Vascular) Headaches: Pounding pain caused by swelling of blood vessels in the head; may include a burning sensation around the neck and shoulders.
Triggers: Nitrites (preservatives found in hot dogs, lunch meats, bacon, ham, and other artificial foods); monosodium glutamate (MSG) – a taste-enhancer found particularly in Chinese food – especially when ingested on an empty stomach; other chemical compounds.
Treatment: Same as for caffeine headaches.
Prevention: Avoid triggering foods.

Exertion Headaches: Head pain during or following rigorous – or sometimes mild – physical exercise.
Triggers: Tumors or blood vessel abnormalities account for approximately 10% of these headaches. The rest are usually related to cluster or migraine headaches already in progress.
Treatment: Aspirin, propranolol; surgery to correct an abnormality.
Prevention: Prescribed drugs taken before exercise that prevent excessive vessel dilation; participation only in low-level exertion.

Menstrual or Menopausal Headaches:
Migraine-type pain that occurs shortly before, during or after menstruation, or at mid-cycle; can also occur during menopause.
Triggers: Changes in estrogen levels; highly salty foods can intensify pain.
Treatment: For menstrual headaches, same as for migraines; for menopausal headaches, same as for tension headaches; hormone-replacement therapy and relaxation may also provide relief.
Prevention: Small doses of vasoconstrictors before and during a menstrual period; anti-inflammatory drugs (aspirin) may help. Avoid overly-salty foods.

Allergy Headaches: Head pain accompanied by nasal congestion and watery eyes.
Triggers: Seasonal allergens such as pollen.
Treatment and Prevention: Medications (antihistamines or desensitization injections).

Sinus Headaches: Gnawing, tight pain over nasal area, which often increases in intensity as the day progresses; tenderness and/or swelling over a portion of the face.
Triggers: Infections or a deviated or swollen septum in the nose that blocks the sinus ducts (often occurs after a cold when the sinuses are inflamed).
Treatment: Antibiotics or decongestants to relieve pressure; steam breathed in from a bowl of hot water; surgical drainage.
Prevention: None.

Secondary Headaches: Flu symptoms – along with headache – usually after an injury or illness.
Triggers: Whiplash or other injury (especially one affecting the nerves); "referred" or "traveling" pain caused by an infected tooth or arthritis.
Treatment: Antibiotics.
Prevention: None.

Sexual Headaches: Sharp, one-sided pain before, during or after intercourse.
Triggers: Performance anxiety, nervousness or guilt; believed to be caused by a rise in blood pressure or pulse rate, or by changed breathing patterns.
Treatment: Pause and take some slow, deep breaths; use other common headache treatments.
Prevention: Therapy; deep breathing and/or medication before sex.

Fasting Headaches: Dull, throbbing pain inside the forehead and around the eyes.
Triggers: Not enough food (low blood sugar results in an overabundance of fatty acids in the bloodstream, which leads to vascular expansion); irregular eating patterns.
Treatment: Food; common headache treatments.
Prevention: Eat four to six small low-sugar meals per day; have a light snack before bedtime.

Hypertention Headaches: Dull, pounding, or "hatband"-type pain in the morning that diminishes as the day goes by.
Triggers: High blood pressure (more than 200/110); sudden rise in blood pressure.
Treatment: Doctor-prescribed blood pressure medication.
Prevention: Keep blood pressure under control; mild exercise; avoid animal fats, cut down on salt, and increase potassium intake (bananas, apples, potatoes, etc.).

Glaucoma Headaches: Serious headaches often accompanied by a visual "halo" effect and other vision problems; frequent pressure around the eyes.
Triggers: Extreme fluid pressure build-up inside the eye.
Treatment and Prevention: See a doctor. Untreated glaucoma may lead to blindness.

■ ■ ■

Overall, eating a balanced, more natural diet, scheduling yearly eye, dental, and medical examinations, exercising on a regular basis, keeping uniform sleep times and habits, and maintaining good posture will keep you fit and less vulnerable to headaches.

OVERCOMING OVEREATING

by Jane Hirschmann and Carol Munter, Addison-Wesley Publishing, New York, N.Y., 1988

Overcoming Overeating offers an interesting approach to weight-loss and control. According to the authors, Hirschmann and Munter, if you follow the book's principles, you will never again have to submit yourself to the rigors of another diet: no formulas, no more calorie counting, no more weigh-ins, no more scanty meals. Instead of this, you can *eat whatever you want, whenever you want.*

The book focuses on a program that teaches *sensitivity* to your body's *needs.* Your body will tell you when you are full; then you can choose to stop eating at that time. *The more aware you are of when and why you overeat, the more likely you will be to abstain from overeating and recognize when real hunger is satisfied.*

In addition to helping you know when you are really full, Hirschmann and Munter seek to present a new perspective on food. They believe that each of us needs to get back in touch with our natural hunger. As children, we intuitively knew when we were full, and we also knew what foods we wanted to eat. When we became bold enough to tell our parents that we were full or that we wanted another serving of such-and-such a food, they did not believe us. As a result, over the years we were "trained" in when, what, and how much to eat – even though our bodies may have not necessarily agreed. The "eat-everything-on-your-plate – or else!" mentality created within us a *distrust of our own physical hunger,* engendering deep-seated conflict between our brains and our bodies.

The basic premise of *Overcoming Overeating* is that *fat is not the main issue,* but merely a consequence of the true problem: overeating. If we come to understand why we overeat, we can deal effectively with this dilemma.

What is Overeating?

The book defines overeating as "eating in excess of your body's natural requirements."

There are three necessary phases in learning to overcome overeating:

Phase I: This first step consists of *freeing yourself from diets and the diet mentality.* Dieting may indeed lead to weight reduction, but since it does very little for the mental side of weight control, it is often little more than a temporary solution. If your body image is still "I'm fat," then after a diet you will probably grow right back into your fat body.

Let's say, for example, that you have just completed a strict four-week diet in which you lost fifteen pounds. Your fellow workers and your friends all comment on how great you look, but inside you still perceive that you have to lose another ten pounds to look your best. The image you had of your body before you went on the diet hasn't changed along with your new body weight, and so you at some point start eating your way back to your original weight – often even to a heavier weight. "Rapid weight loss is a health hazard, but so is rapid weight gain," the authors warn; and both extremes are caused or influenced by dieting. Conventional diets, by forcefully restricting intake, often end up stimulating a whole new overeating cycle.

The book's plan allows its adherents to eat any foods they want – but *only those they truly want.* Before eating, ask yourself: "What do I really want to eat? Do I want something chewy, hard, smooth, crunchy, cold, wet, or hot?" Is this food readily available? If not, go out and buy it. Don't substitute something else for the food you really want. There is no such thing as a bad food or a good food. All foods serve the purpose of fueling the body.

Relax in the knowledge that you can eat as much as you want. There is no need to be afraid of a food for which you once thought you had a "weakness." In fact, the book suggests keeping extra quantities of your favorite foods on hand.

Another important question to ask yourself is, "Am I full?" If the answer is "yes," then ask, "Why am I eating?" Helpful hints are offered throughout the book to help you stop feasting when actual hunger is no longer prompting it.

Phase II: Now you can start *retraining yourself to eat on physical demand.* We don't eat just to keep our bodies healthy; we eat for psychological and emotional reasons as well. In fact, we tend to overeat when we are anxious, upset, frustrated, angry, lonely or bored – using food as a reward, a comforter or a tranquilizer.

Suppose someone phones to share some news that upsets you. You may suddenly find yourself in the kitchen though you are not especially hungry, and using food as a pacifier. Or maybe you begin to eat in order to forget or avoid dealing with uncomfortable feelings.

Phase II teaches how to *distinguish between physical (stomach) hunger and psychological (mouth) hunger.* This is the big Phase-II question to ask yourself over and over again: "Am I eating out of stomach hunger or mouth hunger?" If mouth hunger is the honest answer, then investigate further: "What has driven me to eat when I am not physically hungry?"

Below are some other techniques to use when tempted to eat out of psychological hunger:

- Recognize that "normal" eating is "eating when you're hungry, what you're hungry for, and stopping when you've had enough."

- Work to become a noncompulsive eater. Use phrases such as: "Thanks, but I'm not hungry right now"; or "I've eaten, but I'll be happy to sit with you while you eat something"; or "Gee, it was delicious and I'd love to have more, but I'm really too full." These phrases draw you away from "diet type" responses when turning down food.

- Plan, in order to eat on your own schedule of hunger rather than that of your family. Sharing mealtimes, without necessarily sharing meals, will gradually become easier on you and them – and your eating experience when you *are* truly hungry will be more rewarding.

- Do not count calories (a common dieting practice). This only throws off your real biological responses to food.

- At a restaurant, remember that you don't have to finish everything on your plate; when you are full, simply ask for a carry-out container, and eat the remainder later.

Phase III: The emphasis in this final phase is *learning how to love yourself as you are*. This means accepting yourself as you are *right now*, not when you are thirty – or even five – pounds lighter. Self-contempt, any one of various obsessions, and an inability to say no have probably sapped your energies for many years. These need to be dealt with. "Unlike your compulsion to eat, which will fade as you feed yourself differently and treat yourself with compassion, your compulsion to yell at yourself requires direct intervention." The circuit between compulsive eating and obsessive thinking has to be severed.

One fantasy from the book illustrates this point: Imagine that some strange gas has just been injected into the earth's atmosphere. The moment you inhale this gas it becomes impossible for you to ever gain or lose weight again – not a pound, not an ounce. Your body will remain in its present shape for the rest of your life. Would you continue to berate yourself for your shape once you accept the fantasy that your body will never change? Would you continue to wear uncomfortable clothing if you knew that your weight was not going anywhere? Would you run five miles today? Would you stay away from the beach forever? Would you continue to "feast" on celery and carrot sticks, or would you relax and eat what you want?

This exercise leaves the reader with much to think about. Why do we fear being fat? Conversely, why are we afraid to be thin? The authors suggest a crucial answer for both sides of this dilemma: "Accept the fat in order to give it up."

Overcoming Overeating warns against "set-ups" – negative thoughts that lead to overeating. While passing a bakery, for instance, you smell the wonderful aroma of fresh bread and donuts. Peering in the store window, you notice your reflection in the glass and immediately commence criticizng yourself: "You're too fat," "You can't even think of eating these types of goodies," "You're no good . . . " Then you make a declaration: "I'll show you!" and you turn and march right into the bakery, order a two-pound bag of cookies, and shove them down as fast as you can before anyone sees you. Later, guilty and angry with yourself for having so little self-control, you decide to punish yourself by promising, "Tomorrow I'll diet." Hirschmann and Munter theorize that had you not beaten yourself up with negative thoughts and tried to deprive yourself of your wishes, you probably would have never gorged on the cookies in the first place. Rather, if you had announced, "I can eat all the cookies I want," most likely your desire for them would have diminished; your craving would have been detected as a sign of false, psychological hunger.

The concept of "body image" is explored further here. *Self-acceptance is necessary to change body image*, especially if you view yourself as overweight. Look at yourself in the mirror. Picture your body as a piece of art; something that is valued, that can be admired instead of criticized. Only by accepting extra pounds as part of your *whole body* can you begin to let those pounds go. With self-acceptance comes self-love and positive thoughts. Now you can respect yourself enough to change those habits you feel need to be changed. It is *impossible to change that which you are not willing to accept.*

Every person seeks greater harmony, within himself and within his relationships. The pursuit of *harmony* is at the heart of *Overcoming Overeating*. As you alter the way you think about yourself and redesign your perceptions about food, over time you stop seeing food as your enemy. You start living in a diet-free world; a world that is a whole lot more fun, and where your mind, emotions, spirit, and body co-exist in harmonic peace and love.

SIX CELEBRATED DIET BOOKS

**Summarized below are six diet books
that you might find interesting and informative.**

The Popcorn-Plus Diet
by Joel Herskowitz, M.D.
Pharos Books
New York, N.Y., 1987

As a former fifty-pound-overweight medical student, Dr. Herskowitz developed the *Popcorn Plus Diet* based both on his medical training and his personal experience with weight-loss and maintenance. Dr. Herskowitz claims that if you can recognize your pattern of eating, construct a specific personal goal statement to read out loud twice daily, and then follow a sensible diet, you can lose weight.

Dr. Herskowitz provides a 21-day meal plan in his book, allowing for 1,000 to 1,400 calories of nutritional food per day, with popcorn used as the "filler." This lightly regarded snack is actually a highly nutritious food, rich in complex carbohydrates and fiber. Popcorn is about 80% carbohydrate and 16% protein, with only trace amounts of fat and virtually no salt. (However, some popcorn brands are loaded with chemical additives, so read labels.)

Popcorn is chewy, taking longer to consume than other fillers, and has far fewer calories than most foods. Herskowitz reports that carrying popcorn with you during the day allows you to respond promptly to hunger and prevents you from impulsively eating higher calorie snacks. The high carbohydrate content of popcorn also appears to play an important role in shutting off hunger signals. Since popcorn is high in fiber, it has been cited as a food that may help prevent cancer of the gastrointestinal tract. And again, since fiber requires more chewing and provides added bulk, you are more satisfied with fewer calories.

Popcorn can also be used as an after-dinner reward instead of dessert. Cooked in an air popper, it contains 40 to 50 calories per cup.

During the weight-loss phase of your diet, a pinch of salt or a sprinkling of grated cheese may be added. No margarine or butter is permitted until you enter the maintenance phase.

By sticking to the diet plan and eating the required amount of butterless popcorn every day, your weight-loss goals can be reached. Then you can move to the maintenance phase.

The book provides graphs and checklists to help monitor your weight and waist measurements. It also contains guidelines for treating and preventing obesity in children.

■ ■ ■

Beverly Hills Medical Diet
by Arnold Fox, M.D.
Chain-Pinkham Books
St. Louis Park, Minnesota, 1981

Dr. Fox has named his diet in honor of the City of Beverly Hills, where he based his practice. He saw numerous patients there who were wealthy, successful and active, but who were also usually stressed out, overweight, and victims of poor eating habits. Dr. Fox wanted to develop a program that would change these negative conditions. He knew that diets high in protein often create more water loss than fat loss. Fat eventually clogs arteries, which slows down the flow of blood to the heart.

With these facts in mind, Fox devised a diet that is high in complex carbohydrates, moderate to low in protein, and very low in fat. It recommends foods containing starch and fiber, like grains, vegetables and fruits. No refined sugars, salt or diet colas are allowed. These are considered stress-related foods.

Dr. Fox suggests exercise be incorporated into most diets to combat stress. To provide "helpful" exercise, he introduces an exercise called "wogging" – a mixture of walking and jogging. The minimum 30-minute daily "wog" will also help relieve depression: "Improved circulation of blood to the brain chases the blues away," and wogging, like jogging and walking, does improve circulation and oxygen volume to the lungs.

There are three phases to the Beverly Hills diet: *The Plunge Phase* which, if followed properly, should yield a loss of 10 pounds or more in two weeks; the *Everyday Phase,* in which a loss of about 3 pounds a week will occur; and the *Maintenance Phase,* which will help you maintain your loss and keep you feeling fit.

The Plunge Phase follows a specific menu plan for 14 days, during which time you may not mix or combine recipes. The "Plunge" can be repeated until you either arrive at your ideal weight or become bored with the menus.

The Everyday Phase involves calorie counting, with total intake not to exceed 1200 calories a day. Diet plans and recipes are offered for this stage.

The Maintenance Phase still confines you to certain foods, but leaves you more on your own to plan meals as long as intake is no more than 1500 to 2000 calories per day. A detailed calorie chart is included.

Dr. Fox extends helpful tips for eating out, traveling, and going to parties. He even has advice on what to eat when visiting restaurants that serve different cuisines.

The Beverly Hills Medical Diet details a specific, step-by-step method to lose weight. According to the author, it is a very effective and safe program. Coupled with exercise, it can help you relieve stress and live longer. Dr. Fox says, "Since the [diet] teaches you a new way to eat by incorporating a proper nutrition program, it reduces the stress which leads to heart disease and cancer. But I don't tell people to diet. I tell them to EAT FOR THE REST OF THEIR LIVES."

■ ■ ■

The Rice Diet Report
by Judy Moscovitz
G.P. Putnam & Sons
New York, NY, 1986

The *Rice Diet* is a low-salt, low-protein, low-fat, low-cholesterol, and high-fiber program originally designed by a Doctor Walter Kempner after years of research in heart disease, circulatory difficulties and kidney problems. He introduced the diet to his patients at Duke University in Durham, North Carolina in 1939. It wasn't until later that he realized weight reduction was an added benefit.

Judy Moscovitz, the author of this report, weighed 275 pounds before beginning the diet; nine months later she had lost 140 pounds.

North Americans tend to ingest too much salt, fat and protein. In contrast, the diets of almost half the rest of the world's population consists of 80% to 90% rice. Our bodies need three times more carbohydrates than protein or fat, according to Moscovitz. "Rice offers a form of protein that is easily assimilated by the body, and the protein content of rice surpasses the others in its amino-acid structure in the grain group."

The diet is broken into six phases. Throughout, absolutely "no spices, herbs or condiments of any sort are permitted, with the exceptions of fresh lemon juice and sodium-free sweeteners." All fruits are permitted except dates, avocados and tomatoes.

Most kinds of rice are allowed on the diet, as long as they contain no added salt and are thoroughly rinsed before cooking. A serving consists of 3/4 cup of cooked rice per meal. Of course portion sizes vary for equivalents, which include puffed rice, puffed wheat, shredded wheat and cream-of-rice.

Phase I: During Phase I the typical daily menu looks like this.

Breakfast: 1 fruit; any non-caloric, sodium-free beverage
Lunch: 2 fruits; 1 portion cooked rice or its equivalent; any non-caloric beverage
Dinner: 2 fruits; 1 portion cooked rice or its equivalent; any non-caloric beverage

This first phase is the most difficult, allowing only the consumption of rice and fruit. Yet, it is during this phase that the bulk of weight-loss occurs, with an average expected two-week loss of 15 to 25 pounds. You may remain with this phase for as long as you can stand it. The diet is certainly monotonous and bland, yet it promises the reward of rapid weight-loss.

Phases II through V offer a new selection of food with every phase.

In Phase II, tomatoes and tomato sauce are introduced.

Phase III includes vegetables – except for celery, spinach and watercress, which have high sodium content. Frozen and canned foods are fine as long as they are sodium-free. Plain white vinegar may also be added, along with fresh lemon juice and sodium-free sweeteners.

In Phase IV, chicken, fish, and turkey are gradually included. If you are a vegetarian, dried peas, dried beans, legumes and tofu can now be eaten.

Phase V is not for everyone. People with high-blood pressure, diabetes or kidney problems should not move on to this stage, which incorporates pasta, salt-free breads and eggs.

Recipes are provided with each successive phase. It is recommended that you stick to each phase for as long as possible. Maintenance (Phase VI) delineates strict guidelines to follow, even though you are now allowed all the natural foods you want. Up to this point the diet has averaged an intake of 700 calories a day. On Maintenance you can increase food intake up to 100 calories per week until you are eating enough to feel comfortable. But no snacking is allowed; only three meals a day.

The author stresses the importance of an exercise program while on this diet for healthier results. Aerobic exercises are recommended, with walking as the favored activity. In addition, the book offers many helpful tips for staying on the diet.

■ ■ ■

The 8-Week Cholesterol Cure
by Robert E. Kowalski
Harper & Row
New York, N.Y., 1987

Medical writer Robert Kowalski's cholesterol level was 284 milligrams – almost 100 points too high. He tried various cholesterol diets, which brought this level down by only 13 points. As he reports in his book, "The National Institutes of Health in January 1985, stated that 'one-half of the U.S. population is at risk of coronary heart disease, with blood cholesterol levels above 200 mg.'"

After suffering a heart attack due to clogged coronary arteries and undergoing a quadruple coronary bypass, Kowalski decided something had to be done. With ready access to medical literature, he started his research. "People have elevated, high-risk cholesterol levels for three reasons," he discovered. "First, their diets contain too much fat and cholesterol, which [their bodies] are unable to properly handle. Second, they do not excrete sufficient amounts of cholesterol through bile acids in the colon. Third, they produce a large amount of cholesterol in their livers. Put the three together, and the cholesterol count soars." According to Kowalski, The 8-Week Cholesterol Cure considers all three aspects of elevated cholesterol, and suggests a three-step approach for lowering your level to below 200 mg – and keeping it there. By (1) changing and tracking your diet, (2) eating oat bran, and (3) supplementing your food with niacin, you can lower your cholesterol level. The author writes: "My hypothesis was that if I put the three together, they would work synergistically to achieve the total effect I was hoping for. Bingo!" His cholesterol level dropped from 284 to 169 milligrams within eight weeks. In the process he also lost 12 pounds.

The first step of the Kowalski's approach is to keep track of your fat and cholesterol intake by maintaining a diet diary of the foods you eat. A diary allows you to more objectively review your diet –

and then reduce the amount of fat and cholesterol consumed. The book offers equations to calculate the amount of fat and calories right for your body.

The second step is increasing your oat bran intake. "Oat bran has more soluble fiber than any other food; it is an ultimate natural laxative." Because bran is a soluble fiber, it readily absorbs bile acids, and "when oat bran is included in the diet, the excretion of bile acids increases. Bile acids are formed by the liver from cholesterol. The more bile acids are excreted, the more the liver has to make. The more acids are made, the more cholesterol is drawn out of the blood, and eventually, out of other parts of the body . . . . Thus there is less chance of cholesterol being deposited in the arteries." An additional benefit of high-fiber oat bran is that it can lower insulin requirements for diabetic patients.

Also, as oat bran soaks up water in the digestive tract it expands, giving you a satisfied feeling. The author recommends you eat 1/2 cup of oat bran a day, the equivalent of three oat bran muffins along with a glass of water before each meal, which will decrease your appetite and supply your daily amount of oat bran.

Step three proposes supplementing your diet with niacin. "Niacin" is an interchangeable term for water-soluble vitamin B. Since cholesterol is manufactured by the liver, niacin can reduce cholesterol right at its source – by decreasing the liver's production of cholesterol.

The 8-Week Cholesterol Cure contains weight charts, a large selection of recipes to choose from and a chart listing fat, cholesterol and caloric contents for a variety of foods. Also included are clinical studies on high-cholesterol patients.

■ ■ ■

The Story of Weight Watchers
by Jean Nidetch and Joan Rattner Heilman
The American Library
New York, N.Y., 1972

Weight Watchers was conceived 25 years ago by Jean Nidetch. At age 38 Nidetch weighed 214 pounds and was a size 44. One day she was walking down the street when an acquaintance passed and told her how great she looked – then asked when her baby was due. When she realized that she really did look nine months pregnant, she decided to visit an obesity clinic. "I'll never forget that day if I live to be 1000," she writes. "I wore a big flaring coat – they were in style fortunately

– and I thought I was hiding my fat. I stood as tall as I could and wore high heels. . . . I took hours with my hair and my face, hoping that the people there would never look below my neck." At the clinic, she was told her weight should be 142 pounds and that she needed to stay on a strict diet with no substitutions. To her surprise, she lost two pounds every week for several months, but could have lost more if she hadn't been cheating. (She was too embarrassed to tell the lady at the clinic that she was eating cookies by the box.) She called six friends and asked them to come over. When they arrived, she announced that she had lost 20 pounds, and then showed the diet to her friends, who showed interest. Nidetch suggested that they take the diet plan to their doctors for approval. After that, they met to compare notes. To Nidetch's surprise, they returned with three more friends also wanting to discuss their problems with dieting and food. Within two months there were 40 women meeting weekly in the author's home. They bought a scale and started recording each other's weight. In May of 1963 *Weight Watchers* was born as a business – with the first official *Weight Watchers* group opening in Little Neck, New York.

Weight Watchers charges a registration fee and a weekly fee whether you attend or not. Each meeting is structured, starting with a weigh-in, followed by a brief lecture, a question-and-answer session, and socializing. In sharing the triumph of others' accomplishments, the members are encouraged to lose weight.

Dr. William H. Sebrell, one-time Assistant Surgeon General of the United States, began to revise the diet when he joined *Weight Watchers* in 1971. There are now three basic diet programs, one each for men, women, and youth. Programs are broken down into a reducing diet, a leveling plan, and a maintenance outline.

The reducing diet plan is geared for an average weight loss of 2 to 2-1/2 pounds per week.

Weight Watchers identifies "legal" foods heavy in pita bread, low-fat meats, fruits and vegetables, and other natural – and surprisingly tasty – items. It allows no diet pills, no alcohol, no substitutions, and no meal-skipping. Artificial sweeteners and sugarless sodas are recommended. Recipes are constantly being revised and added to *Weight Watchers Magazine* and *The Program Cookbook*.

■ ■ ■

Fabulous Fructose Recipe Book
by J. T. Cooper, M.D. and Jeanne Jones
M. Evans and Co., Inc.
New York, N.Y., 1979

Dr. Cooper's fructose diet is low in carbohydrates, low in fat, and high in protein. Fructose is a natural sugar, found in most fruits; it is also available in tablet form or in packets of powder to be mixed with drinks. The author recommends 30 to 40 grams of fructose per day, along with plenty of salads and protein foods – fish, poultry, meat – plus concentrated potassium and other minerals and vitamins, and lots of liquids. "That's all there is to the diet," writes Dr. Cooper. "The protein keeps you healthy; the fructose gives you energy; and the potassium and other minerals and vitamins keep the wheels oiled." Three meals must be eaten every day, with no substitutions. Ideally, one-third to one-half pound of fat will be shed per day; about 2-1/2 to 3-1/2 pounds per week. The high-protein diet consists of about 1500 daily calories.

Dr. Cooper explains in his book how fructose works: "Almost every carbohydrate is converted in the body into a simple sugar, glucose. Glucose enters the blood stream and travels throughout the body. While it does so, signals are set off that the glucose levels are rising. This sets off the release of insulin. Insulin is the hormone that assists the glucose in leaving the blood stream and entering most of the body's cells, where it is either stored as fat or used for energy." In many overweight individuals, an excess of insulin is secreted. Erratic insulin levels lead to a see-saw effect of high glucose levels followed by low levels – low blood sugar. But fructose, unlike glucose, is absorbed slowly in the small intestine, bypassing the channels that signal insulin flow. For these reasons, claims Dr. Cooper, not only will your craving for sugar be satisfied by fructose, but you will feel little hunger while on the diet. "Fructose trickles into the blood stream and is absorbed into certain cells of the body without the need for insulin, so dieting is easier."

The book features five different diet plans to choose from, including one especially designed for vegetarians.

Dr. Cooper recommends you see your doctor before starting his diet to determine whether you have an abnormal glucose tolerance.

TWENTY FOOD TIPS FOR LIFETIME WEIGHT CONTROL

(plus, some bits of advice on selecting a weight-loss program that's right for you)

Permanent weight control consists of a lifelong commitment to a set of proven concepts. As these concepts are learned, remembered and followed, you not only come closer to achieving your weight-loss or maintenance goal, but, as a natural consequence, you enhance your overall health as well. Here are twenty tips that may help:

Mind-wise tips:

1. Be *positive* in your everyday comments concerning your diet. Replace "I'll try . . . " with "I will . . . " Avoid any phrases that imply failure or dissatisfaction with the restraints you've chosen to comply with. Look for mottos, phrases or sayings that will encourage and support your resolve. Post them and refer to them often. Be your own cheerleader. "You can do it!"

2. Select a *short term weight goal.* Write it down and post it where you'll see it every day. Revise this number goal before you reach it on your scales so that you always have something to work for.

3. Weigh yourself each day at approximately the same time. The best time might be the hours when you must work extra hard to avoid falling into old – or new – eating patterns.

4. Create a simple chart or graph to daily *monitor* your success.

5. Never grocery shop when you're hungry. Today's marketplace is laced with smells, visuals and convenience pitches, all luring you to buy or eat – right now.

6. Never use food as a reward. Find other ways to reinforce your victories.

7. Whenever you feel a stress-related urge to eat, break the stress-response cycle: alter what you are doing at the moment, exercise, relax, take a hot bath, or talk to a friend. Listen to what your body really is craving – liquid, rest, chewing, diversion, sympathy, love, laughter, nourishment, stimulation. Then do something to fill that specific need, something that you know will change your thoughts, mood and attitude.

8. *Love yourself as you are.* Be patient with yourself. Remember: it will take time to lose weight, just as it took time to gain it.

Food-wise tips:

9. *Eat slowly.* Take *20 minutes or longer* to finish each meal. Read, converse, or just sit back and relax as you eat. Pay attention to your body. At some mealtimes you don't need as much food. When you've had enough, believe your body . . . Quit eating! There is always another meal ahead.

10. Maintain control by observing a *regular schedule* for meals. Knowing that "food time" is only an hour – or several minutes – away can give you the strength to resist.

11. Drink *6 to 8 glasses of water* each day. Good for digestion, calorie-free, and inexpensive, water is the ideal drink.

12. Carefully read *nutrition labels.* Become more aware of the number of calories in the foods you eat. Especially avoid too many sugary or fatty calories.

13. Choose foods low in fat. Reduce total fat intake from 35% (the daily average for Americans) to 25% or less. Substitute sauces, cheeses, ice cream, pastries, red meats, sausage, bacon or deep-fried items with salads, beans, whole grains, fish, fowl, lean meat and low-fat yogurt.

14. Use more herbs and spices in your cooking. If foods low in fat and sugar still taste bland to you, add flavor and aroma with a shot of cooking spray. The taste and texture of soups and salads are greatly enhanced by just a small amount of this oil. Be creative in the variety of good foods you eat and in your methods of preparation.

15. In order to get the benefit of odor and the sense of eating a "real" meal, eat foods hot rather than cold when given a choice.

16. Stay away from most *fast foods.* Most fast food chains have an array of salads in their selection, and some are even offering a sort of "lean burger." Many of these foods, however, may

not be as low-calorie/low fat as advertising makes them out to be.

17. Go easy on *salt*. Munching on salty foods usually will induce you to snack even more.

18. Drink only moderate amounts of sodas containing caffeine. Besides causing a rise in blood pressure, "caffeine jitters" can lead to overeating. Learn to distinguish your "physical cues" – the ways that you react to chemicals, relationships, events and food products.

19. Eat foods that are *high in fiber,* that can be prepared in a *variety of ways,* and that promote a *feeling of fullness.* Oatmeal, rice, potatoes and popcorn are highly touted fare of several diet plans.

20. Strive to eat *balanced meals.* Load your menus with raw fruits, vegetables and whole-grain cereals.

■ ■ ■

Many of the "mass-market" or "fad" diet plans and programs are designed and marketed with only one purpose in mind: to make money for the corporation that puts it out, not to help you lose weight. Some programs promote worthwhile and healthy principles; some don't. Many work only temporarily by creating an imbalance in your diet to one extreme or another (high protein or high carbohydrate diets, for example). Often, these diets can be both unhealthy and completely unbearable if followed over a long period of time.

In choosing a diet program, look for one that:

• Promises (or advocates) no more than *one to two pounds of weight-loss per week.*

• Offers *continued support* for maintenance.

• Encourages exercise, which burns calories, tones muscles, improves your psychological outlook, and reduces appetite.

• Allows for some *flexibility* in food variety and rate of loss.

• Provides (or recommends) food that you will enjoy eating – or at least tolerate without complaint – for the prescribed period of time.

• Includes a good amount of fiber in your diet, and all the vitamins and minerals recommended by federal health agencies (approximately 60% carbohydrates – only 5 to 10% of which are in the form of sweets – 25% fat and 15% protein).

• Doesn't push pills or other "artificial" means of weight control.

• Is *step-by-step* in nature so you can see gradual progress and be encouraged by it.

• Seems *fair in price* for the amount of food, counseling and facilities offered.

• States all promises and contractual obligations clearly and in writing, with *no additional charges* for food, facilities or counseling that are not stipulated in the contract.

• Doesn't "tie you in" to a program for an excessive period of time.

• Makes you *feel good about yourself* regardless of your weight.

• Comes with good *references,* obtained either from a friend, doctor, business bureau, or other trusted source.

In essence, insist on a program – whether it's company-produced, personally designed, or from a book – that gives you not only a healthier body, but a livelier, more positive outlook on life.

CHOLESTEROL, FATS AND SUGARS

Three Most Talked-About Health Topics

"I'm off to the delicatessen for some fried cholesterol. But what a way to go." Here, a nightclub comedian pokes fun at a well-publicized health issue. Sadly, though, this is the attitude many of us take when deciding what we put into our mouths. Cholesterol, in reality, can be a deadly substance; fats are "necessary evils"; and sugars, however filled with energy they might be, tell a bitter-sweet story.

Hopefully, by learning more about the foods we choose to eat and understanding the potential results of our decisions, we can improve both our diets and our health.

CHOLESTEROL

Facts

- In the last two decades, heart disease has dropped nearly 30 percent – mostly because of increased health consciousness.

- There is an irrefutable link between cholesterol levels in the blood and the risk of heart disease.

- According to the American Heart Association, over 50 percent of middle-aged Americans have blood-count cholesterol levels above 200 milligrams per deciliter. The ideal is between 130 and 190 milligrams.

- The average American ingests about double the desirable daily amount of cholesterol.

- Blood cholesterol levels can usually be controlled through dietary reform.

- Red meat – not eggs or dairy products – constitutes the largest food-derived source of cholesterol.

Helpful Definitions

Cholesterol - A complex compound produced in the liver. Known as a "sterol" or "solid alcohol," it is a distinct, white, waxy substance present in cell membranes.

Lipoprotein - A combination of fat, cholesterol and protein packaged together in "sacs" to travel through the bloodstream.

High Density Lipoprotein (HDL, a kind of "healthful" cholesterol) - Small, tightly packed lipoprotein bundles of fat that have the ability to pick up cholesterol and carry it away from arterial walls.

Low Density Lipoprotein (LDL, the "lethal" variety) - Packages whose job it is to transport cholesterol to body cells. LDL consists of large, loosely packed protein bundles that, if found in surplus, are abandoned as "dump deposits" along the artery walls, causing cholesterol build-up.

Total Blood Cholesterol Level - The amount of all types of cholesterol in the bloodstream, as measured by testing parts per deciliter.

What Cholesterol Does FOR You

Cholesterol and fat are two different substances necessary for good health. Fat is converted by the body into sugars and used for energy, while cholesterol performs other jobs. It.

- Helps manufacture the outer tissues of cells, digestive bile, hormones, and vitamin D.

- Is a key ingredient in the fatty insulation of nerves, a vital part of sex hormones, and an enzyme that helps digest fat.

What Cholesterol Can Do TO You

Although cholesterol is found in every organ of the body, our bodies don't need the extra amounts we commonly take in from foods. On its own, the liver produces the small amounts necessary to good health.

If too much LDL cholesterol runs in your blood, each day a little more sticks to the walls of your arteries. Over the years, "sacs" of the substance can bunch up, narrowing the arteries and slowing circulation of the blood (arteriosclerosis).

This situation may lead to:

- Heart attack - Acute distress of the heart muscle, brought on by sudden lack of oxygen.

- Stroke - The cutting off of oxygen to the brain due to a blocked artery.

- Arterial hemorrhage.

- Muscle cramps due to poor circulation.

- Tiredness.

So, What Can You Do?

Visit your doctor and have your total blood cholesterol level checked. If your level is below 200 mg/dl (200 milligrams per deciliter of blood) you're considered "safe." If your level falls within the 240 or 250 range, however, your risk of heart attack jumps twofold. And at 300 or above, you could be in severe danger.

If your score is borderline or in the high-risk realm (or if you smoke, have heart disease, high blood pressure, diabetes, are more than 30% overweight, suffer from extreme stress, or have a family history of heart attack) you'd be advised to take action to reduce your cholesterol intake and to yearly monitor your cholesterol level.

The amount of LCL in your blood-stream is pivotal to calculating your overall risks. A healthy diet will usually reward you with an LDL level of 130 mg/dl or less. A level of 160 or more reveals that LDL bundles are clinging to your arteries faster than they can be removed by the HDL's, and you may need to combat this condition by committing to a diet/exercise program.

As you try to reduce your LDL's, at the same time you should try to maintain a high HDL level. HDL's scavenge the blood and remove cholesterol from the body, possibly even extracting the substance from existing "hard" arteries, reversing the effects of arterioscleosis. A low total cholesterol level combined with an equally low ratio of HDL (less than 1 part HDL to 4.5 parts total cholesterol) may still lead to the formation of arterial deposits. Conversely, someone with a high total cholesterol level offset by an equally high HDL level may not be at risk.

In general, studies show that by taking three steps, you can lessen your cholesterol-related health risks:

(1) *Modify your lifestyle,* replacing bad habits (like smoking) with good habits (like regular aerobic exercise).

(2) *Lower your blood pressure* through exercise, weight-loss, dietary changes and, when necessary, medication.

(3) *Reduce your total blood cholesterol level* to 200 or less, and your LDL to 130 or less.

Here's how to accomplish this third essential step.

- Eat foods yielding little or no cholesterol: replace red (even lean) meats, eggs, baked goods, butter, whole milk, ice cream or other dairy products, with fish (6 ounces or less per day), skinless chicken or turkey, oat bran, low-fat yogurt . . .

- Acquire vital calories by eating complex carbohydrates (starches) and fibrous foods such as breads, oat and wheat bran, butterless popcorn, fruits, vegetables, rice, cereals, pastas, dried beans and peas. Some experts claim that fiber-rich foods bind with cholesterol in the digestive tract, eliminating it before it can enter the bloodstream.

- Limit portion sizes of foods that contain or produce cholesterol.

- Lessen your consumption of saturated fats, which stimulate your liver to manufacture more cholesterol than is needed.

Avoid or limit chocolate, eggs (at most, 3-4 per week), lard, butter, cheese, fatty meats, and coconut or palm oils.

- When cooking, use vegetable oils (corn, olive, safflower) containing unsaturated fats. Bake using egg whites. Substitute oil and cocoa for chocolate. Recipes and menu plans abound that can assist in your low-cholesterol kitchen.

- Read food labels. Remember, though, that labels can be deceiving. "Cholesterol-free" does not necessarily mean the food contains no saturated fats – the chief culprits in raising blood cholesterol levels.

- Refrain from smoking and lose or guard against gaining excess weight. Tobacco and obesity are two factors which seem to reduce healthful HDL levels and thus increase the ratio of lethal LDL levels in the bloodstream.

- Engage in an exercise program. Greater activity – especially aerobic activity – increases HDL levels in the blood.

- Follow a doctor's advice on frequency of cholesterol blood-level testing, exercise, and diet.

- If cholesterol levels remain very high, your doctor, while continuing to recommend good eating habits, may also prescribe drugs that reprocess or remove cholesterol from the blood, or that slow production of LDL. Some of these may produce side effects.

- Surgery might be needed as a last resort in treating diseased arteries.

Most adults already have enough to worry about without fretting constantly over their health. But cholesterol control is vital, and is relatively simple to monitor – and it also usually pays a bonus of easier weight loss.

To optimize your chances for a healthy life – to reduce the risks of heart attack, arterial conditions or stroke – you may have to make some minor sacrifices. Have your cholesterol level checked yearly, especially if you're in the high-risk category, and watch your weight and your diet to avoid cholesterol build-up.

■ ■ ■

FATS

Facts

- The average American consumes far more fats than needed and would do well to decrease his total fat intake by 25 percent.

- Some fats are visible: well-marbled meats, poultry skins, butter, margarine, and the oil in salad dressing are easy to identify. But many fats are hidden in our diets. Deep-fried dishes, cheeses, seeds, nuts, avocados, creams, ice cream, chocolate, whole milk and some bakery products are all laden with fat.

Helpful Definitions

Triglycerides - Chemically made up of glycerol (an alcohol) and the three fatty acids.

Fatty acids - Basic chemical units in fats; chains of carbon atoms with hydrogen atoms attached.

Saturated fatty acids (Avoid these) - Long chemical chains found mostly in fats of animal origin (meat, fish, poultry, cream, cheese, milk, eggs and butter) and also in coconut oil, palm oil and cocoa butter (chocolate).

Monounsaturated fatty acids (Restrict these) - Shorter chemical chains found in both animal and plant sources (olive and peanut oil, margarine, and hydrogenated vegetable shortenings).

Polyunsaturated fatty acids (Most wholesome of the fatty acids) - The shortest and most easily broken down chemical chains; found primarily in plant fats (sunflower, olive, corn, safflower, soybean and other plant oils) and in some fish.

What Fats Do FOR You

- Essential for daily energy, fats provide the most concentrated source of calories available. (They contain 9 calories per gram compared to about 4 calories per gram of protein or carbohydrate.)
- Aid in the absorption of vitamins.
- Insulate the body against cold.
- Protect vital organs.
- Form part of the body's cellular membrane.
- Provide needed fatty acids.
- Make foods taste good.

What Fats Do TO You

- Increase the risk of heart attack.
- Contribute to obesity.
- May contribute to sluggishness and rapid tiring.
- May precipitate some types of cancer.

So, What Can You Do?

Important ways to cut down on fats, specifically saturated fats, are to trim excess fat off meats and limit foods such as butter, creams, hydrogenated shortenings, eggs and organ meats. Eat instead, as protein substitutes, lean meat, fish, poultry (without the skin), dry beans and peas.

Watch out for fast-foods! Select the lesser of the two evils: Rather than a hot dog, fried chicken, a quarter-pound hamburger, a cheeseburger, fries, onion rings or a shake, consider thin-crust pizza, broiled fish or chicken, a taco, coleslaw, yogurt, or a fruit juice. According to the USDA, three ounces of roast beef contain 16 grams of total fat and 8 grams of the saturated variety, while lean roast beef contains 6 grams total fat and only 3 grams saturated fat. Examine these other comparisons: one cup whole milk (8 total, 5 saturated), one cup skim (1 total, trace saturated); two ounces butter (11 and 7), margarine (11 and 2); roasted chicken, with skin (12 and 3), broiled halibut, with margarine (6 and 1).

Making sensible trade-offs and maintaining a diet rich in fresh fruit, green and yellow vegetables, whole grains and beans (foods brimming with vitamins A, C, B complex and iron), should keep your fat consumption to a healthy minimum.

■ ■ ■

SUGARS

Facts

- On the average, each American eats 140 pounds of sugar annually.
- Most of us would prefer that sugar be a less prominent part of our diets, yet it accounts for more than 24% of our daily caloric intake.
- Sugars show up in products we normally wouldn't think contained any sugar: canned vegetables, peanut butter, salt, sugarless gums, breath mints and medicines.
- A 12-ounce serving of Canada Dry Tonic Water contains over 18 teaspoons of sugar; a slice of apple pie contains 12 teaspoons.
- All sugars are not the same. Few have any nutritional value, and all have potentially hazardous effects. Dieticians and physicians agree almost unanimously that sugar ingestion should be reduced.

What Sugar Does FOR You

- Provides temporary energy.
- Makes food tastier.

What Sugar Does TO You

- Contributes to obesity and high blood pressure.
- Causes tooth decay.
- May produce personality changes and mood swings.
- Leads to the loss of essential nutrients.
- Upsets the body's natural, balanced calcium-to-phosphorous ratio.
- Aggravates asthma, mental illness and nervous disorders.
- Increases the possibility of yeast infections, diabetes, heart disease, arthritis, back problems, gallstones, and other afflictions.

Helpful Definitions and Comparisons

Sucrose - Refined table sugar from sugar-cane or -beets; lacks any food value; must be assimilated by B vitamins, causing vitamin B deficiencies.

Glucose - The body's blood sugar; found in fruits. As a monosaccharide, can be rapidly assimilated into the body, but may disturb the sugar-balance the same as sucrose.

Dextrose - Made from cornstarch; chemically like glucose.

Fructose - Natural, extremely sweet sugar found in fruits. Devoid in nutrients, but better than most sugars because it's assimilated by the body more slowly; can cause diarrhea and stomach pain if eaten in large amounts.

Maltose - A disaccharide made from whole grains, but still lacking any nutrition; not as sweet as sucrose, but less likely to cause cavities.

Lactose - Derived from milk; non-nutritive, least sweet combination of glucose and galactose.

Brown sugar - Simply refined sugar with molasses added.

Molasses - The liquid remaining after sugar has been processed; approximately 65% sucrose. Certain brands have minor amounts of useful vitamins (B,B6), calcium and iron.

Raw sugar - About 96% sucrose; often professed to be nutritious, but actually has nothing but empty calories.

Honey - Highest sugar content of all; most of the original, natural nutrients are destroyed in heating and processing. Usually rots teeth faster than other sugars and can contain carcinogens from pesticides.

Maple syrup - Very sweet sugar tapped from Maple Sugar trees; still 65% sucrose. May contain formaldehyde and/or lead which can cause stomach cramps, nausea or even death.

Malt syrups - Made from cereal grains containing mostly maltose and glucose; not as sweet, but generally considered more wholesome than most sugars.

Xylitol - Found in berries, fruits and mushrooms; produced commercially from birch cellulose (wood sugar). Metabolized in such a way that it can be used in diabetic or hypoglycemic products. Used in sugar-free gums in that it doesn't produce cavity-causing acids; however, its long term effects are still under scrutiny.

Sorbitol - Extracted from corn sugar; its properties are similar to Xylitol, but considered safer.

Mannitol - Comparable to Xylitol and Sorbitol; used on breakfast cereals and chewing gums; still under study after 30 years of use.

Artificial sweeteners - Many Americans, including diabetics, consume sugar substitutes. They aid slightly in weight control, but all pose potential health risks. Saccharin, Cyclamate, Aspartame and Nutra-sweet are some of the many products marketed over the past several years.

So, What Can You Do?

Most candy-type sugars give you a big lift that's really a downer in disguise. The sucrose quickly enters the bloodstream, but the pancreas, whose job it is to regulate insulin flow to process carbohydrates, is caught off guard. The pancreas releases too much insulin, pulling your energy and vitality down within the hour. You become less alert, more lethargic, and more hungry and irritable than before.

To avoid this scenario, don't snack on sodas and colas, sweet teas and coffee, candies, chocolate, chewing gum, pies, pastries, or creamy desserts. Instead, drink mixed fruit juices, club sodas, unsweetened tea or coffee; eat more fresh fruits, raw vegetables, nuts, and plain yogurt. Better yet, don't snack at all, but eat any sweets along with meals to neutralize the cavity-causing acid and to assimilate the sugars more slowly.

Sweets are not in and of themselves bad. Indeed, taken in moderation, they can be an integral part of your daily eating habits. Most healthcare experts recommend, however, that the most people's sugar intake be reduced. Sugars precipitate so many problems and give back so little of value, that cutting back on their use will make a difference in your attitude, long term energy level, and overall health.

COMPACT

Classics™

LIBRARY #8: Word Power

Section A: Towards Effective Speech

8-A1   **500 Vocabulary-Building Words**

8-A2   **Foreign Words and Phrases**

8-A3   **Preparing and Presenting a Speech**

Section B: Wordsmith Guide

8-B1   **A Painless Grammar Guide**

8-B2   **Punctuation Primer**

8-B3   **Spelling Recommendations and Rules**

8-B4   **Spelling Help! A Speller's Sound Guide**

VOCABULARY-BUILDING

The following words are quite commonly used, and can add flavor and precision to your vocabulary. This list should enhance your reading experiences and provide you with a treasury of expressive words for writing and conversation. Only one pronunciation is provided for each word though others may be used.

Pronunciation Key

Vowels

a	**a** as in ash
ah	**a** as in father
ai	**y** as in why
au	**ow** as in how
ay	**ay** as in play
e	**e** as in let
ee	**ee** as in see
i	**i** as in bit
o	**o** as in go
oo	**oo** as in food
ooh	**oo** as in foot
oy	**oy** as in toy
u	**u** as in but
uh	the schwa sound of a non-accented syllable – **(ə)**
a	**a** as in aloud
e	**e** as in item
i	**i** as in edible
o	**o** as in gallop
u	**u** as in circus
y	**y** as in you

Consonants

Consonants are usually pronounced as in English. Where confusion is possible, the following symbols are used:

ch	**ch** as in church
g	**g** as in gap
j	**j** as in jar
k	**k** as in kayak
s	**s** as in soft
sh	**sh** as in shirt
th	**th** as in thin
Th	**th** as in there
z	**s** as in wise
zh	**si** as in vision

The accented syllable (or syllables) in each listing is capitalized---for example, "impunity (im PYOO nuh tee)."

1- **pretext** (PREE tekst) *n.* An excuse to hide the real reason for something. *He entered under the pretext of being a policeman.*
2- **mundane** (mun DAYN) *adj.* Worldly or ordinary. *Without training, she had to accept a mundane job.*
3- **fiasco** (fee AS ko) *n.* A complete failure; a mess. *The performance of "Hamlet" turned into a fiasco!*
4- **pernicious** (per NISH uhs) *adj.* Harmful, destructive. *Cancer is one of the most pernicious of diseases.*
5- **impunity** (im PYOO nuh tee) *n.* Freedom from punishment. *The little boy hurt other children with impunity.*
6- **reticent** (RET i suhnt) *adj.* Quiet, hesitant, reserved in style. *You can't be reticent and be a good salesman.*
7- **quash** (kwahsh) *v.* To put down forcibly or verbally. *The government will immediately quash any violent demonstrations.*
8- **entourage** (AHN tooh rahzh) *n.* A group of attendants for an important person. *Her entourage included two public relations agents, three secretaries and a maid.*
9- **spew** (spyoo) *v.* Eject, force out or vomit. *Water spewed from the hydrant, drenching the*

screaming crowd.

10- **reverberate** (ree VUR buh rayt) *v.* To echo, resound. *The old anthems still reverberate through the halls.*

11- **extenuate** (eks TEN yoo ait) *v.* To make less serious; diminsh. *Ignorance of the law does not extenuate the seriousness of your crime.*

12- **latent** (LAY tuhnt) *adj.* Lying hidden; potential but not evident. *Her latent desires for power finally revealed themselves.*

13- **deem** (deem) *v.* To think or judge; believe. *We did not deem it a serious enough injury to require surgery.*

14- **epithet** (EP uh thet) *n.* A descriptive, often insulting term or name. *The mob fired epithets at the accused killer.*

15- **intrinsic** (in TRIN sik) *adj.* From within; inherent; belonging to. *He posessed an intrinsic, magnetic charm.*

16- **jettison** (JET uh suhn) *v.* Discard, throw overboard. *We must jettison some employees, or sink!*

17- **myriad** (MIR ee uhd) *adj.* A very large number; countless. *For myriad reasons, I can't marry you.*

18- **fetter** (FET uhr) *v.* To hamper, shackle or restrain. *Her refusal to comply will fetter our progress.*

19- **paragon** (PER uh gahn) *n.* A model of perfection or excellence. *He was a paragon of strength and integrity.*

20- **premise** (PREM is) *n.* The grounds upon which an argument or conclusion is based. *We acted on the premise that he had money to invest.*

21- **impious** (IM pee uhs) *adj.* Not pious, irreverent, disrespectful. *I was dismayed by the impious attitude of my guest.*

22- **bogus** (BO guhs) *adj.* Fake, counterfeit. *He made a bogus claim about his credentials.*

23- **taciturn** (TAS i tuhrn) *adj.* Habitually silent; uncommunicative. *The taciturn youth could never express his love for the girl.*

24- **covert** (KO vuhrt) *adj.* Concealed, hidden or sheltered. *If you keep your information covert, we will be safe.*

25- **juxtapose** (juk stuh POZ) *v.* To place side by side. *Let's juxtapose the two concepts for comparison.*

26- **liaison** (lee ay ZAHN) *n.* Communication between groups; a channel or means of communication. *Our liaison with them has been horrible.*

27- **corroborate** (kuh RAHB uh rayt) *v.* To support or confirm with evidence. *Can you corroborate his findings?*

28- **dregs** (dregz) pl. *n.* The least desirable or worthless part of something. *I decided I must stop associating with the dregs of society.*

29- **legion** (LEE juhn) *n.* A large number, multitude. *They joined a legion of volunteers.* adj. Multitudinous, many. *His war stories are legion.*

30- **subterfuge** (SUB tuhr fyooj) *n.* A plan, trickery. *The general used subterfuge in dealing with the enemy.*

31- **incubus** (IN kyoo buhs) *n.* A nightmare; a depressing burden. *An incubus of fear of failure haunted him continually.*

32- **integral** (IN tuh gruhl) *adj.* Essential, necessary to the whole. *That point is integral to the argument.*

33- **ilk** (ilk) *n.* Type or kind; sort. *A remark of that ilk doesn't deserve a response.*

34- **remuneration** (ree MYOO nuh RAY shuhn) *n.* Payment for services performed or losses incurred. *Remuneration was insufficient for all the work performed.*

35- **oblique** (o BLEEK) *adj.* Not straightforward, indirect. *I sensed by her oblique mannerisms that she was hiding something.*

36- **rue** (roo) *v.* To feel remorse or sorrow for; regret. *He will someday rue his decision to resign.*

37- **urbane** (uhr BAYN) *adj.* Refined or polished; polite or witty. *The contestant from New York had such an urbane personality.*

38- **manifold** (MAN uh fold) *adj.* Many and complex; having diverse features. *The family's problems are manifold.*

39- **coerce** (ko URS) *v.* To control or force. *They had to coerce the boys into cleaning their room.*

40- **didactic** (dai DAK tik) *adj.* Morally instructive; "teacherlike," often in an unfavorable sense. *The class quickly grew tired of the didactic poetry.*

41- **fraught** (fraht) *adj.* Filled or accompanied (usually derogatory). *The city government was fraught with waste and corruption.*

42- **conflagration** (KAHN fluh GRAY shuhn) *n.* A large, destructive fire. *All was lost in the conflagration.*

43- **dissent** (di SENT) *v.* To differ or disagree markedly. *If you dissent from our policy, you could be terminated.* n. a disagreement.

44- **attenuate** (uh TEN yoo ayt) *v*. To weaken or decrease. *Your ability to act will attenuate as you delay your decision.*

45- **emulate** (EM yoo layt) *v*. To strive to equal; to imitate. *The youngster emulated his hero, Henry Ford.*

46- **impasse** (im PAS) *n*. A deadlock; a situation from which there is no escape. *We reached an impasse on the negotiations.*

47- **profligate** (PRAHF li guht) *adj*. Wasteful or extravagant; given to self-indulgence. *His profligate vacation budget is ridiculous.*

48- **repugnant** (ri PUG nuhnt) *adj*. Offensive, distasteful. *That's the most repugnant looking animal I ever saw.*

49- **copious** (KO pee uhs) *adj*. Plentiful, abundant. *She kept copious minutes for each meeting.*

50- **belated** (bi LAY tuhd) *adj*. Tardy or delayed. *Her mother received a belated birthday gift in the mail.*

51- **Machiavellian** (MAK ee uh VEL ee uhn) *adj*. Governed by principles of manipulative deceit and cunning. *His Machiavellian ploys fooled us all.*

52- **ignoble** (ig NO buhl) *adj*. Dishonorable; not having a noble character or purpose. *How ignoble of them to treat her that way.*

53- **perfunctory** (puhr FUNGK tuh ree) *adj*. Done with little care or interest; performed routinely. *Please give her message more than perfunctory attention.*

54- **stipulate** (STIP yoo layt) *v*. To specify a condition; demand. *Stipulate in the contract that the purchase is subject to the sale of our home.*

55- **cessation** (se SAY shuhn) *n*. A complete halt; stoppage. *Cessation of construction will cost taxpayers many dollars.*

56- **prognosticate** (prahg NAHS tuh kayt) *v*. To predict the future from present indications. *Erin prognosticates growth in software sales using economic trends.*

57- **usurp** (yoo SURP) *v*. To seize control without authority; grab. He usurped the presidency by stealth and collusion.

58- **idyllic** (ai DIL ik) *adj*. Simple, romanticized, peaceful. *In those idyllic days we had time to talk and walk.*

59- **encumbrance** (en KUM bruhns) *n*. A burden, load; a hindrance. *Every encumbrance imaginable was encountered in their search.*

60- **garrulous** (GAR yuh luhs) *adj*. Talkative, chatty; wordy. *All evening the garrulous guest dominated the conversation.*

61- **demur** (di MUR) *v*. To take exception to; object. *I demur at the implication that I lied.*

62- **appellation** (ap uh LAY shuhn) *n*. A name or title. *She bristled at the appellation, "communist."*

63- **pluck** (pluk) *n*. Resourceful courage; spirit. *Though hurt badly, she has so much pluck that I'm sure she'll be OK.*

64- **augment** (ahg MENT) *v*. To make larger; increase. *Can you augment my allowance during this time of emergency?*

65- **malign** (muh LAIN) *v*. To speak evil of; slander. *Do not malign the team or the management.*

66- **doldrums** (DOL druhmz) *n*. A period of listlessness or depression; a period of inactivity. *We're just now climbing out of the doldrums.*

67- **respite** (RES pit) *n*. A short interval of rest; relief. *After only a brief respite, he again began his journey.*

68- **homage** (HAHM ij) *n*. Respect, reverence. *Today we wish to pay homage to a woman who, for fifty years now, has served our community.*

69- **frenetic** (fruh NET ik) *adj*. Frantic, frenzied. *As the seasonal rush began, we suddenly had a frenetic boost in activity.*

70- **vindicate** (VIN duh kayt) *v*. To clear of blame; absolve. *The jury will vindicate him of all wrongdoing.*

71- **voluble** (VAHL yuh buhl) *adj*. Glib and fluent in speech. *Because she was so voluble and vivacious, they made her their representative.*

72- **arbiter** (AHR bi tuhr) *n*. Judge, umpire (arbitrator). *The labor dispute must be settled by an arbiter.*

73- **succinct** (suhk SINGKT) *adj*. Clear and brief. *A succinct rebuttal will be appreciated.*

74- **impresario** (im pruh SAHR ee o) *n*. Manager of a cultural event; organizer. *She did a wonderful job as the civic opera impresario.*

75- **exacerbate** (eg ZAS uhr bayt) *v*. To aggravate or irritate. *Your anger will only exacerbate the already tense situation.*

76- **labyrinth** (LAB uh rinth) *n*. A maze; a confusing, winding passage or course. *The book is a labyrinth of interconnected events.*

77- **salubrious** (suh LOO bree uhs) *adj*. Healthful, wholesome. *Most salubrious meals include* *plenty of complex carbohydrates.*

78- **promulgate** (PRAHM uhl gayt) *v.* To make widespread; to make known officially. *We'll promulgate our product by launching an aggressive ad campaign.*

79- **fray** (fray) *n.* A quarrel or fight (*v.* To make worn). *"Jump into the fray and go to work!" he advised me.*

80- **fastidious** (fa STID ee uhs) *adj.* Meticulous, careful; choosy and difficult to please. *He's such a fastidious dresser.*

81- **indict** (in DAIT) *v.* To accuse of an offense; formally charge with a crime. *Officials indicted him on two counts of larceny.*

82- **flout** (flaut) *v.* To scoff or show contempt for. *After a time, the gang began to openly flout police authority.*

83- **cognizant** (KAHG nuh zuhnt) *adj.* Conscious, aware; knowledgeable. *Are they cognizant of their constitutional rights?*

84- **eminent** (EM uh nuhnt) *adj.* Outstanding, of high reputation, distinguished. *Many eminent actors attended the dinner.*

85- **abrogate** (AB ruh gayt) *v.* To annul, abolish. *King Olaf abrogated his successor's right to the throne.*

86- **recant** (ri KANT) *v.* To disavaow, deny; to withdraw previous words. *Recant your testimony, or die!*

87- **cavil** (KAV il) *v.* To quibble or find fault unnecessarily. *It seemed that she could always find something new to cavil about.*

88- **fledgling** (FLEJ ling) *n.* A young or inexperienced person; a young bird. *The foreman railed at the fledgling carpenter for his mistakes.*

89- **orotund** (AHR uh tund) *adj.* Pompous, bombastic; full in sound. *The orotund gentleman went from town to town, peddling his wares.*

90- **calumny** (KAHL uhm nee) *n.* A maliciously false and injurious statement; slander. *Certainly, our store's reputation was damaged by this patron's calumny.*

91- **complicity** (kuhm PLIS uh tee) *n.* Involvement as a partner in wrong-doing. *He confessed to complicity in the caper.*

92- **sumptuous** (SUMP choo uhs) *adj.* Lavish; of a size indicating great expense. *A sumptuous meal awaited the royal guests.*

93- **exonerate** (eg ZAHN uh rayt) *v.* To free from blame or guilt. *The prisoners have finally been exonerated and set free.*

94- **permeate** (PUR mee ayt) *v.* To spread throughout. *Joy and thanksgiving permeate our community today.*

95- **cryptic** (KRIP tik) *adj.* Having a hidden meaning; puzzling. *Archeologists could not translate the cryptic cave drawings.*

96- **surmise** (suhr MAIZ) *v.* To guess, to infer with only scant evidence. *What do you surmise is the real reason for his trip?*

97- **replete** (ri PLEET) *adj.* Completely filled, abounding. *Swedish folklore is replete with strange and wonderful characters.*

98- **finagle** (fi NAY guhl) *v.* To get or achieve by dubious or crafty methods. *I'm confident that you can finagle some type of a deal.*

99- **besiege** (bi SEEJ) *v.* To surround; to make requests, harass. *Angry callers often besiege his talk show.*

100- **sally** (SAL ee) *v.* To suddenly rush forth. (*n.* a quick assault) *The troops will sally forth today and take the bridge.*

101- **reiterate** (ree IT uh rayt) *v.* Repeat, to say or do again. *Will you please reiterate that point once more?*

102- **egregious** (i GREE juhs) *adj.* Outrageously bad; flagrant. *Her egregious and repeated errors cost her a job.*

103- **itinerant** (ai TIN uhr uhnt) *adj.* Traveling, wandering. *Itinerant farmers have no permanent homes.*

104- **postulate** (PAHS chuh layt) *v.* To assume to be true or real. *Astronomers postulate that the earth is between four and five billion years old.*

105- **debilitate** (di BIL uh tayt) *v.* To make weak. *An illness of this sort can quickly debilitate you.*

106- **furbish** (FUR bish) *v.* To polish; renovate. *While furbishing the apartment, they discovered a hidden closet.*

107- **insouciant** (in SOO see uhnt) *adj.* Blithely indifferent; carefree. *Do you regret your insouciant and thoughtless words?*

108- **aversion** (uh VUR zhuhn) *n.* Strong dislike, opposition. *She once had an intense aversion to marriage.*

109- **remiss** (ri MIS) *adj.* Careless, negligent. *Don't be remiss in your duty to visit the shop each day.*

110- **viable** (VAI uh buhl) *adj.* Workable, possible. *Quitting the program is just not a viable option.*

111- **sanctum** (SAYNGK tuhm) *n.* A private room or place of refuge; haven. *My personal sanctum is a back porch overlooking the lake.*

112- **pacific** (puh SIF ik) *adj.* Peaceable, peace-promoting; tranquil. *You two can find a pacific solution to your differences.*

113- **balk** (bahk) *v.* To hesitate; refuse to act. *Most people balk when they are threatened.*

114- **levity** (LEV uh tee) *n.* Frivolity; lightness of disposition. *The Seahawks' boisterous levity surprised the media.*

115- **affable** (AF uh buhl) *adj.* Amiable or sociable; mild, gentle. *He is one of the most affable young men I know.*

116- **wanton** (WAHN tuhn) *adj.* Uncontrolled, unprovoked or malicious. *Her wanton disregard for privacy has got to stop.*

117- **veiled** (vayld) *adj.* Disguised, obscured. *A thinly veiled sarcasm manifested itself in her voice.*

118- **duress** (doo RES) *n.* Force, coercion; imprisonment. *Our employees seem to be under extreme duress to perform.*

119- **duplicity** (doo PLIS uh tee) *n.* Cunning, trickery, deception. *Hal's duplicity on the job did not go unnoticed.*

120- **thespian** (THES pee uhn) *n.* An actor or actress (often used in mild contempt or humor). *So, you've become a great thespian, have you?*

121- **impede** (im PEED) *v.* To hinder or obstruct. *Certain drugs impede the user's ability to think and act.*

122- **morass** (muh RAS) *n.* A bog; a perplexing or difficult situation. *We've created a morass that we may never recover from.*

123- **ostensible** (ah STEN suh buhl) *adj.* Outwardly apparent; seeming, professed. *The ostensible reason is not always the true reason.*

124- **nullify** (NUL uh fai) *v.* To cancel out; make null or valueless. *Your reckless actions could nullify your hunting privileges.*

125- **unconscionable** (un KAHN shuh nuh buhl) *adj.* Beyond reason, excessive; not guided by conscience. *That offer is totally unconscionable.*

126- **vouchsafe** (vauch SAYF) *v.* To grant or give (as in a favor). *I vouchsafe you my undivided attention for five minutes.*

127- **inane** (i NAYN) *adj.* Pointless, lacking sense, silly. *How can you be so inane as to believe their story?*

128- **attache** (at uh SHAY) *n.* An advisor assigned to a diplomatic mission. *Can we safely dispatch an attache to the region?*

129- **dour** (daur) *adj.* Stern, strict; gloomy or grim. *His dour expression told me he was displeased.*

130- **portend** (por TEND) *v.* To indicate or suggest; predict, serve as a warning. *His lack of understanding portends marital tragedy.*

131- **analogous** (uh NAL uh guhs) *adj.* Similar, comparable. *The two sets of test scores are roughly analogous.*

132- **exult** (eg ZULT) *v.* To rejoice greatly; glory. *Her graduation is cause to exult.*

133- **motley** (MAHT lee) *adj.* Varied in elements, color, or kinds; heterogeneous. *A motley crowd flocked into the store in a frenzied rush to buy.*

134- **elapse** (i LAPS) *v.* To slip by, pass. *Only after six tense minutes had elapsed did she finally swim to the surface.*

135- **servile** (SUR vuhl) *adj.* Slavish; submissive or humble. *The Incas bowed in servile reverence to their king.*

136- **ignominious** (IG nuh MIN ee uhs) *adj.* Shameful, humiliating. *Finally, their ignominious affair came to an end.*

137- **cull** (kul) *v.* To select or gather; to pick out from others. *She culled through the selection until she found the right size.*

138- **enigma** (i NIG muh) *n.* A riddle; a baffling matter or person. *How a fragile moth can travel that far is a biological enigma.*

139- **forthwith** (forth WITH) *adv.* Without delay, immediately. *You may receive your check forthwith, if you like.*

140- **ingenuous** (in JEN yoo uhs) *adj.* Straightforward, candid; artless, without sophistication. *The ingenuous reply took me by surprise.*

141- **assay** (a SAY) *v.* To analyze, assess, or evaluate. *Assay the situation and come back to me with three possible solutions.*

142- **intrepid** (in TREP id) *adj.* fearless, dauntless. *The World War II aviator had to develop an intrepid attitude.*

143- **adverse** (ad VURS) *adj.* Unfavorable, hostile, opposed. *I'm adverse to building the dam so close to town.*

144- **harbinger** (HAHR bin juhr) *n.* A forerunner; advance notice. *Her huge vocabulary was a harbinger of her prolific medical skill.*

145- **epitome** (i PIT uh mee) *n.* A person or thing that perfectly represents a whole class; a summary. *He's the epitome of what a student should be.*

146- **choleric** (kuh LER ik) *adj.* Bad-tempered, irritable. *She was pleasant, but her choleric husband made for a difficult evening.*

147- **dupe** (doop) *v.* To deceive, trick. *You won't be able to dupe me like you did before.* n. a person easily tricked.

148- **kibosh** (KAI bahsh) *n.* Something that checks or stops. *She put the kibosh on the rumor that she would leave the firm.*

149- **deluge** (DEL yooj) *v.* To flood; overwhelm. *We plan to deluge the governor's office with letters of protest.* n. a great flood or rainfall.

150- **hyperbole** (hai PUR buh lee) *n.* Extravagant exaggeration for effect. *He described the adventure with comic hyperbole.*

151- **comely** (KUM lee) *adj.* Attractive, beautiful or handsome. *I've never seen a more comely face.*

152- **feint** (faynt) *v.* To pretend to attack. *Rocky feinted with the left jab and then led with the right.*

153- **propriety** (pruh PRAI uh tee) *n.* Quality of being proper; correctness. *Please observe propriety when meeting with Father O'Malley.*

154- **spate** (spayt) *n.* A massive outpouring; a rush or flood. *A spate of invective rushed from the prisoner's lips.*

155- **raucous** (RAH kuhs) *adj.* Loud, rowdy, shrill. *This peaceful protest could turn into a raucous riot.*

156- **inadvertent** (in uhd VUR tuhnt) *adj.* Not attentive; heedless. *Such an inadvertent remark was inexcusable.*

157- **sedulous** (SEJ uh luhs) *adj.* Diligent, industrious. *Did you find the natives sedulous, or were they lazy?*

158- **substantiate** (suhb STAN shee ayt) *v.* To prove true using evidence; confirm. *It won't be difficult to substantiate the experiment.*

159- **sultry** (SUL tree) *adj.* Oppressively hot and moist; torrid, inflamed. *The first-ever football game was played on a sultry day in August.*

160- **volition** (vo LISH uhn) *n.* Will-power; choice. *You will leave of your own volition or you will be removed by force.*

161- **glib** (glib) *adj.* Smooth of speech. *Salesmen surrounded him offering up their glib pitches.*

162- **germane** (juhr MAYN) *adj.* Helpful, relevant, pertinent. *That evidence is germane to solving the case.*

163- **envisage** (en VIZ ij) *v.* To imagine; picture in the mind. *I envisage a corporation composed of three separate divisions.*

164- **mortify** (MOR tuh fai) *v.* To embarrass, humiliate. *My own fears of swimming have mortified me for years.*

165- **gaunt** (gahnt) *adj.* Haggard; thin or bony. *The old woman's gaunt, hungry appearance saddened me.*

166- **riposte** (ri POST) *n.* A retaliatory maneuver; a retort. *Taken aback by his scathing riposte, I stood there, speechless.*

167- **imperious** (im PIR ee uhs) *adj.* Urgent, pressing; domineering. *I could tell by her imperious manner that something was wrong.*

168- **perpetuate** (puhr PECH yoo ayt) *v.* To cause to continue. *They want to perpetuate the myth that only big businesses have high profits.*

169- **iota** (ai O tuh) *n.* A very small amount. *Don't give an inch, not one iota!*

170- **synergy** (SIN uhr jee) *n.* The action of a group achieving a greater effect than that of which each individual is capable. *Our relationship was built on synergy.*

171- **droll** (drol) *adj.* Oddly comical or amusing. *We all enjoyed the pet chicken's droll antics.*

172- **vestige** (VES tij) *n.* A trace; evidence of past existence. *He's merely a vestige of his former talented self.*

173- **sophistry** (SAHF uh stree) *n.* False reasoning, clever but misleading argument. *Their sophistry convinced me to go along with them.*

174- **penchant** (PEN chuhnt) *n.* A strong liking, fetish; an inclination. *He had a penchant for fast cars.*

175- **guise** (gaiz) *n.* Manner, appearance; a false appearance. *Under the guise of romance, she* *was able to obtain the top-secret information.*

176- **quandary** (KWAHN dree) *n.* A state of doubt; a dilemma. *I was in a quandary over the marriage proposal.*

177- **pragmatic** (prag MAT ik) *adj.* Practical, workable, based on experience. *That might be the most pragmatic solution.*

178- **blase** (blah ZAY) *adj.* Bored, indifferent. *This blase young student leads an empty life.*

179- **wreak** (reek) *v.* To inflict; vent, express or gratify. *"Wreak destruction on the aliens!" shouted Captain Kirk.*

180- **solicitous** (suh LIS i tuhs) *adj.* Concerned; attentive; eager. *Solicitous youths are the most likely to be hired.*

181- **blunt** (blunt) *v.* To deter, disincline; desensitize; dull. *I hate to blunt your enthusiasm, but your plan simply will not work.*

182- **pugnacious** (puhg NAY shuhs) *adj.* Quarrelsome, eager to fight. *Fido is an extremely pugnacious poodle.*

183- **regale** (ruh GAYL) *v.* To entertain, delight. *For three hours she regaled us with her adventurous life.*

184- **tantamount** (TAN tuh maunt) *adj.* Equal in effect; identical. *The hateful glare was tantamount to an open challenge.*

185- **impugn** (im PYOON) *v.* To reproach or attack as false; cast doubt on. *When you impugn my ideas, you make me depressed.*

186- **abate** (uh BAYT) *v.* To lessen in amount or intensity. *The rock band abated the volume of their music after I asked for their help.*

187- **preclude** (pree KLOOD) *v.* To prevent, make impossible from the start. *Insufficient funds may preclude holding a festival at all.*

188- **glean** (gleen) *v.* To collect, gather (facts, grain, etc.). *Gleaning signatures on this petition will not be easy.*

189- **alacrity** (uh LAK ruh tee) *n.* Eagerness; briskness, lively action. *Go to the task with alacrity, and don't give up.*

190- **desuetude** (DES wi tood) *n.* The condition of disuse. *The machine had fallen into obsolescence and desuetude.*

191- **foment** (fo MENT) *v.* To stir up, instigate. *They are trying to foment the carpetlayers to go on strike.*

192- **aesthetic** (es THET ik) *adj.* Relating to beauty or to the arts. *Your home has a very aesthetic quality.*

193- **lucid** (LOO sid) *adj.* Clear, easily understood; transparent. *Her lucid arguments convinced me to contribute to the charity.*

194- **sanctimonious** (SAYNGK tuh MO nee uhs) *adj.* Pretending to be holy or pious. *Surely that sanctimonious bum will not be elected.*

195- **culpable** (KUL puh buhl) *adj.* Deserving blame. *The plane's mechanics are clearly the culpable party in the accident.*

196- **slovenly** (SLUV uhn lee) *adj.* Careless; untidy, slipshod. *Slovenly architectural drawings need not be submitted.*

197- **facetious** (fuh SEE shuhs) *adj.* Joking, comical. *Are you being serious or facetious?*

198- **stymie** (STAI mee) *v.* To block, impede. *Her current reputation will stymie her television comeback.*

199- **brazen** (BRAY zuhn) *adj.* Insolent; rudely bold. *In a brazen act, he pounded his fist on the desk and demanded a raise.*

200- **nondescript** (nahn di SKRIPT) *adj.* Not belonging to any certain class; undistinguished. *The earthenware bowl is of nondescript workmanship.*

201- **avarice** (AV uhr is) *n.* Greed for money. *The investors' avarice eventually brought them to poverty.*

202- **equanimity** (ek wuh NIM uh tee) *n.* Evenness, calmness of mind, composure. *Mr. Reynold's equanimity under pressure is amazing.*

203- **synthesize** (SIN thuh saiz) *v.* To combine separate elements to form a coherent whole. *Let's try to synthesize the best ideas from each proposal.*

204- **gist** (jist) *n.* Main point, essence. *Just give me the gist of the story, without any details.*

205- **fecund** (FEE kuhnd) *adj.* Productive, fruitful; fertile. *Her fecund mind will take the task and map out a way to accomplish it.*

206- **ardent** (AHR duhnt) *adj.* Passionate, zealous. *I'm an ardent fan of bluegrass music.*

207- **temporize** (TEM puh raiz) *v.* To postpone an action or decision; to compromise. *Please allow me to temporize my decision until next week.*

208- **mandate** (MAN dayt) *n.* An order or command (*v.* To order). *The coach issued a man-*

date to each running back to keep both hands on the ball.

209- **bedlam** (BED luhm) *n.* Confusion, noise, uproar. *Bedlam broke out as the cars screeched onto the track.*

210- **indolent** (IN duh luhnt) *adj.* Idle, lazy. *There's not one indolent artist among the bunch.*

211- **cumulative** (KYOOM yuh luh tiv) *adj.* Successively increasing. *The cumulative effects of alcohol are harmful.*

212- **mire** (mair) *v.* To get stuck. *He wants to mire you in irrelevant details.* *n.* deep mud or a soggy area.

213- **supplicate** (SUP luh kayt) *v.* Humbly request; pray. *They came to supplicate our urgently needed help.*

214- **nebulous** (NEB yoo luhs) *adj.* Unclear, hazy, vague. *Your experiment is well thought-out, but your written descriptions are nebulous.*

215- **agitant** (AJ i tuhnt) *n.* One who is active in a course of action; an exciter. *She became an agitant for animal rights.*

216- **metamorphosis** (met uh MOR phuh suhs) *n.* A marked change; transformation. *She's gone through a metamorphosis since we last saw her.*

217- **scrutable** (SKROOT uh buhl) *adj.* Comprehensible, easy to be seen or understood. *This book made each of Einstein's theories somewhat scrutable.*

218- **extempore** (ik STEM puh ree) *adj.* Impromptu, unrehearsed. *The group did an extempore rendition of "Heartbreak Hotel."*

219- **vacuous** (VAK yoo uhs) *adj.* Empty; stupid. *With a vacuous smile, he walked on down the road.*

220- **fealty** (FEE uhl tee) *n.* Loyalty, fidelity. *Your fealty to the team is inspiring.*

221- **callosity** (ka LAHS i tee) *n.* Lack of feeling; hardheartedness. *Callosity and bitterness poisoned her.*

222- **spiel** (speel) *n.* A talk (as in selling). *The bunco telephone spiel is nothing more than a persuasive plea for money.*

223- **inalienable** (in AY lee uhn uh buhl) *adj.* Incapable of being taken away. *Our organization would ensure the inalienable rights of all minorities.*

224- **dispassionate** (dis PASH uh nit) *adj.* Not influenced by emotion; impartial. *A dispassionate judge, he always rendered an evenhanded verdict.*

225- **wont** (wahnt) *adj.* Customary, habitual; apt. *It was wont in those pioneer times to discuss the day before eating the evening meal.*

226- **reprehensible** (rep ri HEN suh buhl) *adj.* Deserving of blame or censure. *Laughing at his misfortune was a reprehensible thing to do.*

227- **dubious** (DOO bee uhs) *adj.* Causing doubt, questionable. *It is dubious whether the Ram quarterback can get his passes off in time.*

228- **renege** (ree NIG) *v.* To go back on a promise. *If you renege on our deal, it could mean a lawsuit.*

229- **grapple** (GRAP uhl) *v.* To grip and hold; wrestle. *We grappled with the idea all day long and into the night.*

230- **decorum** (di KOR uhm) *n.* What is polite; correct behavior. *The choir's decorum was excellent; their singing, mediocre.*

231- **platitude** (PLAT uh tood) *n.* A commonplace or trite remark. *The newscaster rattled off one platitude after another.*

232- **adherent** (ad HIR uhnt) *n.* A supporter or follower. *She is an adherent of an organization favoring peaceful reform.*

233- **repose** (ree POZ) *n.* The act of resting; a rest. *The painting showed a girl in repose on a sofa.* *v.* to rest, relax; to place – faith, trust, etc.

234- **veneer** (vuh NEER) *n.* A thin surface layer; outside appearance. *He hid his insecurities behind a veneer of confidence.*

235- **embellish** (em BEL ish) *v.* To decorate; to improve (fictitiously) on a story. *Fishermen tend to embellish their fishing adventures.*

236- **proliferate** (pruh LIF uh rayt) *v.* To rapidly produce new growth; teem. *Rabbits will likely proliferate until they take over an area.*

237- **repulse** (ree PULS) *v.* To drive back; refuse. *Our forces fought valiantly to repulse the enemy.*

238- **wane** (wayn) *v.* To lessen, decrease; decline in power. *Though her strength steadily waned, her sense of humor remained vital.*

239- **salutary** (SAL yuh ter ee) *adj.* Beneficial; wholesome. *His jogging routine definitely had its salutary effects.*

240- **kilter** (KIL tuhr) *n.* Proper condition. *These files are all out of kilter.*

241- **insatiable** (in SAY shuh buhl) *adj.* That cannot be statisfied. *Scouts are notorious for hav-*

ing insatiable appetites.

242- overt (o VURT) *adj.* Open, not hidden. *Do you always have to be so overt and forward with your feelings?*

243- recidivism (ri SID uh viz uhm) *n.* A tendency to relapse into former behavior patterns. *Recidivism among juvenile offenders is quite high.*

244- invective (in VEK tiv) *n.* An abusive verbal attack; insulting speech. *The assistant coach lit into him with invective.*

245- bona fide (BO nuh faid) *adj.* Genuine, without fraud. *Are the bolts made of bona fide hardened steel?*

246- impeccable (im PEK uh buhl) *adj.* Flawless, without defect. *She has an impeccable memory.*

247- altruistic (ahl troo IS tik) *adj.* Unselfish; concerned about others. *A beehive exemplifies an altruistic society.*

248- lithe (laith) *adj.* Graceful; bending easily, soft. *The lithe dancer smilingly skipped off stage.*

249- disgruntle (dis GRUN tuhl) *v.* To make discontented; upset. *Disgruntled at not being picked up on time, he got in and slammed the door.*

250- connote (kuh NOT) *v.* To suggest or convey meaning. *Do raised eyebrows always connote surprise?*

251- quiescent (kwee ES uhnt) *adj.* Inactive, sedentary; dormant. *Ever since the death of Grandma, Ruth has been quiescent and withdrawn.*

252- interloper (IN tuhr lo puhr) *n.* A meddler; unauthorized person. *These interlopers want to divide the club in two.*

253- temerity (tuh MER uh tee) *n.* Fearlessness, foolish boldness. *No knight would have the temerity to challenge him.*

254- acute (uh KYOOT) *adj.* Sharp-pointed; keen; sensitive. *For very acute psychological problems, he's the one to see.*

255- obtuse (ahb TOOS) *adj.* Dull; slow, dense. *Woody Allen always had an obtuse look on his face.*

256- consummate (kahn SOOM uht) *adj.* Complete, perfect. *He can act the part of the consummate villain.*

257- virtuosity (vuhr choo WAHS uh tee) *n.* Great technical skill. *Her virtuosity with the cello and viola is remarkable.*

258- raze (rayz) *v.* To tear down; destroy. *The entire block has been razed to make room for a basketball arena.*

259- retrospect (RET ruh spekt) *n.* Hindsight, looking back on the past. *In retrospect, buying the home was the right thing to do.*

260- culminate (KUL muh nayt) *v.* To reach the top or summit; climax. *The performance will culminate in a rousing finale.*

261- relegate (REL uh gayt) *v.* To assign an inferior position; banish. *I was relegated to washing dishes day and night.*

262- nominal (NAHM uh nuhl) *adj.* Slight; very small amount. *I would do the job for a nominal sum.*

263- eventuate (i VEN choo wayt) *v.* To result, to happen in the end. *Only hard work will eventuate in your graduation.*

264- backslide (BAK slaid) *v.* To revert to wrongdoing; relapse. *Now that we've progressed beyond name-calling, let us not backslide.*

265- adamant (AD uh muhnt) *adj.* Inflexible, unyielding. *Our neighborhood is adamant about having a crosswalk at that intersection.*

266- evince (i VINS) *v.* To show plainly, make clear. *You evince a lack of interest in the trade.*

267- schism (SKIZ uhm) *n.* A split. *A great schism occurred between the bourgeoisie and the proletariat.*

268- assiduous (uh SIJ oo uhs) *adj.* Diligent, persevering; careful. *She conducted an assiduous campaign for the mayoral post.*

269- apposite (AP uh zit) *adj.* Suitable; appropriate. *Where is the most apposite spot to display the collection?*

270- proffer (PRAHF uhr) *v.* To present for acceptance; tender, offer. *The umpire proffered her the right to serve or receive at the onset of the match.*

271- cataclysmic (kat uh KLIZ mik) *adj.* Violent and sudden. *Such a cataclysmic act of aggression will not be tolerated.*

272- curtail (kur TAYL) *v.* To cut short, reduce. *In an effort to curtail crime, the police posted a curfew.*

273- conjecture (kuhn JEK choohr) *n.* A guess, theory. *Though it was only conjecture, I felt I was on the right track.*

274- poignant (POYN yuhnt) *adj.* Affecting the feelings; moving, emotional. *It is a poignant time for the recent widow.*

275- **inert** (in URT) *adj.* Slow, inactive; without power. *That particular gas is completely inert and harmless.*

276- **wan** (wahn) *adj.* Sickly, pale; weak. *Our baby's wan appearance worried us.*

277- **amicable** (AM i kuh buhl) *adj.* Peaceful, friendly. *An amicable cease-fire is the only way to live with your differences.*

278- **excruciating** (ek SKROO shee ay ting) *adj.* Agonizing, intense. *Excruciating cramps kept the runner from crossing the finish line.*

279- **junta** (HOON tah) *n.* A group of persons who govern a country after a takeover.*The junta declined to release any political prisoners.*

280- **umbrage** (UM brij) *n.* Offense, resentment. *He took umbrage at the remarks of his wife during the party.*

281- **abet** (uh BET) *v.* To encourage; incite. *Please don't abet our employees to attempt a buyout of the company.*

282- **inexorable** (in EK suhr uh buhl) *adj.* Unrelenting; not to be influenced. *His inexorable refusal made further reasoning useless.*

283- **monolithic** (mahn uh LITH ik) *adj.* Unyielding; massively solid. *Our educational system is a monolithic giant.*

284- **inclement** (in KLEM uhnt) *adj.* Rough, stormy; harsh. *We couldn't have predicted such inclement weather so early in the season.*

285- **salient** (SAYL yuhnt) *adj.* Prominent, outstanding; conspicuous. *Only the most salient arguments will be presented.*

286- **demure** (di MYOOHR) *adj.* Modest in manner; reserved, sedate. *A young woman glanced my way and flashed a demure smile.*

287- **precocious** (pri KO shuhs) *adj.* Reaching early maturity (especially mentally). *Gazing down at my precocious child, I wept with joy.*

288- **inclusive** (in KLOO siv) *adj.* Taking everything into account. *It lengthened into an inclusive survey.*

289- **misconstrue** (mis kuhn STROO) *v.* To incorrectly interpret. *You misconstrue nearly everything I say.*

290- **laudable** (LAHD uh buhl) *adj.* Praiseworthy, commendable. *The actors gave a laudable performance of "Bolero."*

291- **magnific** (mag NIF ik) *adj.* Magnificent; made great. *Donned in magnific apparel, the princess took the throne.*

292- **factitious** (fak TISH uhs) *adj.* Artificial; forced. *He manifested a factitious concern for the life-or-death issue.*

293- **rampant** (RAM puhnt) *adj.* Growing; widespread. *We must check the rampant illiteracy in our schools.*

294- **corpulent** (KOR pyoo luhnt) *adj.* Obese, fleshy, fat. *The corpulent guest confessed his fondness for pastry.*

295- **raiment** (RAY muhnt) *n.* Clothing, dress. *The groom's kingly raiment became soaked by rain.*

296- **descry** (di SKRAI) *v.* To catch sight of; to discover by observation. *I descried the algebraic solution after much pondering.*

297- **quell** (kwel) *v.* To put an end to; subdue. *His voice will ring out eternally; time shall not quell it!*

298- **purview** (PUR vyoo) *n.* Scope, range of vision; outlook. *Profits from one quarter don't reveal a complete purview of the possibilities.*

299- **yen** (yen) *v.* A strong longing; desire. *I have a yen for pizza and rootbeer.*

300- **defamatory** (di FAM uh tor ee) *adj.* Damaging character by false reports. *Defamatory articles ruined his career.*

301- **consternation** (kahn stuhr NAY shuhn) *n.* Great fear or worry. *Growing consternation creased the parents' haggard faces.*

302- **proclivity** (pro KLIV i tee) *n.* A natural inclination; propensity. *Puppies have a proclivity to seek warmth and protection.*

303- **manifest** (MAN uh fest) *adj.* Obvious, clearly apparent. *It's manifest that at this time parole should not be granted.*

304- **qualm** (kwahm) *n.* Doubt, uneasiness. *They haven't the slightest qualm about leaving him home alone.*

305- **lassitude** (LAS uh tood) *n.* Weakness, weariness. *Extreme lassitude overcame us after the hike.*

306- **diminutive** (di MIN yoo tiv) *adj.* Small, tiny. *The diminutive horse stood no more than three feet tall.*

307- **cloistered** (KLOY stuhrd) *adj.* Secluded or confined. *To be cloistered safely away in a monastery would feel good right now.*

308- **transcend** (tran SEND) *v.* To rise above, surpass; exist independently. *Your gambling luck transcends the odds.*

309- **feckless** (FEK lis) *adj.* Lacking purpose or vitality; ineffective, weak, irresponsible. *He became a feckless wanderer, having no aspirations.*

310- **capricious** (kuh PREE shuhs) *adj.* Whimsical, inclined to change one's mind. *Sports fans are capricious, booing one minute, cheering the next.*

311- **synchronous** (SING kruh nuhs) *adj.* Occurring at the same time or rate. *Our synchronous arrivals were ironic.*

312- **discomfit** (dis KUM fit) *v.* To disconcert; defeat; make uneasy or confused. *Her constant stare discomfits me.*

313- **atrophy** (AT ruh fee) *v.* To waste away, wither. *Muscles often atrophy while a patient is bedridden.*

314- **doctrinaire** (dahk truh NER) *n.* One who holds to a theory or practice without regard to its practicality. *"You inflexible doctrinaire!" he said accusingly.*

315- **maunder** (MAHN duhr) *v.* To mutter; talk incoherently or aimlessly. *His maundering could be heard all the way down the hall.*

316- **banal** (buh NAHL or BAY nuhl) *adj.* Ordinary; trite; meaningless from overuse. *The speech seemed banal; there was nothing special about it.*

317- **picayune** (pik ee YOON) *adj.* Of little value; paltry. *I can't accept such a picayune sum for the car.*

318- **skud** (skud) *v.* To move along swiftly and easily. *Thin clouds scudded across the sky.*

319- **guffaw** (guh FAH) *n.* Hearty, bursting laughter. *He let out a guffaw at the silly punchline.*

320- **fatuous** (FACH oo uhs) *adj.* Foolish, inane; futile. *In fatuous desperation, the antelope turned and charged the lion.*

321- **precipitate** (pri SIP uh tayt) *v.* To hasten; to cause to happen. *A brush-back pitch precipitated a brawl between the teams.*

322 **staid** (stayd) *adj.* Reserved, dignified, serious. *Her grandmother always seemed so staid and pensive.*

323- **harlequin** (HAHR luh kwin) *n.* A clown, buffoon. *The plant manager is a pistol, a real harlequin.*

324- **inviolate** (in VAI uh lit) *adj.* Intact, unscathed; not violated. *Wearing an apron on the job is an inviolate rule.*

325- **extrusion** (ik STROO zhuhn) *n.* A jutting, pushed-out shape or object. *Its extrusions give the building a gothic affect.*

326- **transient** (TRAN shuhnt) *adj.* Passing through with only brief stops; passing away over time. *Happiness is only a transient illusion.*

327- **bagatelle** (bag uh TEL) *n.* A trifle; unimportant. *Money is a bagatelle to him.*

328- **allude** (uh LOOD) *v.* To hint or suggest. *She alluded to having family, though we never met them.*

329- **omnibus** (AHM ni buhs) *adj.* All-inclusive; covering many things or classes. *The omnibus budget law was a thousand pages long.*

330- **causal** (KAH zuhl) *adj.* Indicating or constituting a cause. *Acid rain is a causal factor in global deforestation.*

331- **expedite** (EK spi dait) *v.* To speed the progress of; make easier. *Expedite the delivery of that valve; we needed it yesterday!*

332- **marked** (mahrkt) *adj.* Noticeable, distinctive. *A marked increase in civil rights reforms became his legacy.*

333- **stultify** (STUL tuh fai) *v.* To stifle; cause to appear stupid. *A dictator can no longer stultify the free thought of his followers.*

334- **caveat** (KAV ee aht) *n.* A warning. *His caveat against buying the watch went unheeded.*

335- **suppliant** (SUP lee uhnt) *adj.* Asking humbly and earnestly; beseeching. *How could she refuse the explorer's suppliant words?*

336- **palliate** (PAL ee ayt) *v.* To excuse; to relieve without curing. *It disappoints me that you seek to palliate your mistakes rather than own up to them.*

337- **dissipate** (DIS uh payt) *v.* To vanish; to drive away; waste. *His entire inheritance will soon dissipate.*

338- **ennui** (AHN wee) *n.* Boredom; world weariness. *Such ennui set in that even engaging in conversation became an effort.*

339- **profuse** (pro FYOOS) *adj.* Overflowing, abundant. *Her writing is colorful and profuse.*

340- **expurgate** (EK spuhr gayt) *v.* To remove objectionable parts or passages from written material. *Resubmit your manuscript after expurgating chapter seven.*

341- **mercenary** (MUR suh ne ree) *adj.* Motivated by greed. *I don't care if it appears to be a mercenary act; I'm just looking out for myself.*

342- **requisite** (REK wuh zit) *adj.* Required, necessary (n. a requirement). *It's requisite that you register at least an hour before the event is to begin.*

343- **potpourri** (po pooh REE) *n.* A combination, mixture. *What potpourri of fruits is in this salad?*

344- **niggling** (NIG ling) *adj.* Fussy; petty; requiring attention to detail. *Quit your niggling quarrel and get back to work.*

345- **facsimile** (fak SIM uh lee) *n.* An exact copy; an electronic transmission. *No, this is not a facsimile of what I typed.*

346- **libel** (LAI buhl) *n.* Ruining a reputation by unjust publicity. *There are laws to protect you against libel.*

347- **circumspect** (SUR kuhm spekt) *adj.* Heedful, watchful; careful. *Her circumspect investigations make her a superior detective.*

348- **flaccid** (FLAS id) *adj.* Soft and limp; baggy, loose. *When we returned after two weeks away, all the vegetables were flaccid.*

349- **acclimate** (AK luh mayt) *v.* To make or become accustomed. *Will it take long to acclimate myself to his working style?*

350- **grovel** (GRAHV uhl) *v.* To humble oneself; cringe. *Don't grovel before her, but do apologize.*

351- **capacious** (kuh PAY shuhs) *adj.* Voluminous, spacious, roomy. *Three capacious video tapes have so far been filled with data.*

352- **indefatigable** (in di FAT i guh buhl) *adj.* Tireless. *It will take an indefatigable effort to be ready by Christmas time.*

353- **precipice** (PRES uh pis) *n.* A dangerous edge; cliff. *When you're on the precipice of disaster, hang on.*

354- **anomaly** (uh NAHM uh lee) *n.* An irregularity; deviation from the normal. *His taking a day off from work is an anomaly.*

355- **chaff** (chaf) *n.* Worthless or trivial matter. *To him, fishing is serious business; it's far from being chaff.*

356- **utilitarian** (yoo TIL uh TER ee uhn) *adj.* Stressing usefulness over beauty. *The inexpensive home is modest and utilitarian.*

357- **preferment** (pri FUR muhnt) *n.* The condition of being favored; singled out. *It's blatant perferment when he is promoted and I am not.*

358- **sundry** (SUN dree) *adj.* Miscellaneous, various. *For many and sundry reasons, I can't divulge the secret.*

359- **lade** (layd) *v.* To load or be loaded (as with cargo). *After the ship was laded (laden) with spices, the crew voyaged back to Spain.*

360- **assimilate** (uh SIM uh layt) *v.* To take in (as in food or knowledge); understand. *It was difficult to assimilate all that information at once.*

361- **coincident** (co IN si duhnt) *adj.* The condition of coinciding (seemingly arranged). *How coincident that they should both show up simultaneously.*

362- **apropos** (ap ruh PO) *adj.* Appropriate, pertinent. *One's language should be apropos to the circumstances.*

363- **stentorian** (sten TOR ee uhn) *adj.* Extremely loud (as a voice). *The stentorian tones of the orator stirred the congregation's emotions.*

364- **abstract** (AB strakt) *adj.* Theoretical; removed from material content. *Some art is too abstract for me to enjoy.*

365- **hale** (hayl) *adj.* Sound, healthy. *Dr. George says I'm hale and hearty.* v. To compel to go.

366- **deride** (di RAID) *v.* To scoff at; treat with scorn. *To deride a child for an accident constitutes emotional abuse.*

367- **prolixity** (pro LIKS uh tee) *n.* Wordiness, overly verbose; tediousness. *Due to her prolixity, it's hard to participate in conversation with her.*

368- **equivocal** (i KWIV uh kuhl) *adj.* Ambiguous; questionable, inconclusive. *To avoid an equivocal discussion, let's get right to the point.*

369- **impromptu** (im PRAHMP too) *adj.* Without rehearsal; spur of the moment. *Impromptu skits helped us act out our aggression.*

370- **expedient** (ek SPEE dee uhnt) *adj.* Convenient, useful for achieving desired ends. *He found that the truth was not always expedient.*

371- **reputed** (ri PYOO tuhd) *adj.* Generally supposed; believed. *Columbian coffee is reputed to be the best in the world.*

372- **discreet** (di SKREET) *adj.* Prudent, showing good judgment and restraint. *Be discreet* *when you exit the lobby; don't attract attention.*

373- **Freudian** (FROY dee uhn) *adj.* Inwardly revealing, subconscious; pertaining to Freud's theories. *Your Freudian slip-of-the-tongue told how you really feel.*

374- **verve** (vurv) *n.* Energy, enthusiasm; animation. *I was thrilled by the verve running throughout the composition.*

375- **vapid** (VAP id) *adj.* Boring, dull, lackluster, without zest. *Half of the audience slept through his vapid anatomy lecture.*

376- **curry** (KOOH ree) *v.* To seek (favor) by flattery. *She wants to curry support by her lavish gift-giving.*

377- **ancillary** (AN suh ler ee) *adj.* Subordinate; auxiliary, supplementary. *Those details and facts are ancillary to the real issue.*

378- **abridge** (uh BRIJ) *v.* To shorten, cut back. *We must abridge the time the seminar takes by one-third.*

379- **fluster** (FLUS tuhr) *v.* To make or become confused or upset. *The piano teacher was easily flustered by his students' conduct.*

380- **celerity** (suh LER i tee) *n.* Speed, swiftness. *He acted with celerity to quiet the spreading rumors.*

381- **rhetoric** (RET uh rik) *n.* Effective use of language (often artificial or eggagerated). *The rhetoric-filled meeting finally ended.*

382- **proximity** (prahk SIM uh tee) *n.* Nearness, closeness. *Get in the ticket line early to ensure our proximity to the stage.*

383- **delve** (delv) *v.* To search deeply, dig, research. *Let's delve into the real reason why Hawkeye drinks.*

384- **affable** (AF uh buhl) *adj.* Amiable; mild, gentle. *Her affable personality impressed him the moment they met.*

385- **criterion** (krai TIR ee ahn) *n.* A standard or model for judgment. *On what single criterion is your decision based?*

386- **domineer** (dahm uh NIR) *v.* To rule arrogantly. *Usually, she domineers her timid younger sisters.*

387- **precis** (pray SEE) *n.* A concise summary of essential facts, an abstract. *Include a list of books on the topic in the precis.*

388- **excoriate** (ek SKOR ee ayt) *v.* To criticize severely, denounce. *His book excoriates the government's monopolizing practices.*

389- **dulcet** (DUL sit) *adj.* Soothing; melodious to the ear. *The dulcet tones of an oboe floated out over the desert.*

390- **cogent** (KO juhnt) *adj.* To the point; forcefully convincing. *The second part of his cogent speech was most incisive.*

391- **propinquity** (pruh PING kwuh tee) *n.* Nearness in time or place; kinship. *After nine months, the propinquity of the birth became frightening.*

392- **impolitic** (im PAHL i tik) *adj.* Not wise or expedient, injudicious. *An impolitic action such as that could ruin you.*

393- **recondite** (REK uhn dait) *adj.* Beyond ordinary understanding, obscure. *That theory, recondite as it is, may be correct.*

394- **doddering** (DAHD uhr ing) *adj.* Shaky, tremulous. *Grandpa is no doddering, helpless old man; he still runs a mile every morning.*

395- **disparate** (DIS puhr uht) *adj.* Unequal; distinct. *For fun, we wore clothes of many disparate styles and tastes.*

396- **fiat** (FEE uht) *n.* An arbitrary order or decree; official sanction. *The fiat on trade is restrictive and unfair.*

397- **pecuniary** (pi KYOO nee er ee) *adj.* Financial; involving money. *The auditor examined the condition of our pecuniary system.*

398- **coterie** (KO tuh ree) *n.* A clique; close circle of friends. *One small coterie of inmates considered themselves elite.*

399- **irrelevant** (i REL uh vuhnt) *adj.* Not pertinent; unrelated to the subject. *Why bring up details that are irrelevant to the case?*

400- **nirvana** (nir VAH nuh) *n.* State of supreme bliss; happiness (Buddist heaven). *When he looked my way, I floated for days in nirvana.*

401- **glower** (GLAU uhr) *v.* To scowl; look or stare angrily. *Our secretary glowered back at us in dismay.*

402- **aegis** (EE jis) *n.* Protection; sponsorship. *Two ships entered the race under the aegis of New Zealand.*

403- **moribund** (MOR uh buhnd) *adj.* Dying; at the point of death. *Sales are moribund right now, but business will bounce back.*

404- **perspicacious** (puhr spuh KAY shuhs) *adj.* Discerning, shrewd, having keen judgment. *The perspicacious judge dismissed the plea.*

405- **voluble** (VAHL yoo buhl) *adj.* Talkative. *The master of ceremonies was irritatingly voluble.*

406- **inveterate** (in VET uhr uht) *adj.* Firmly established, habitual. *The annual bizarre was an inveterate tradition.*

407- **obsequious** (ahb SEE kwee uhs) *adj.* Currying favor; fawning. *The obsequious waiter obviously hoped for a generous tip.*

408- **virulent** (VIR yoo luhnt) *adj.* Poisonous, deadly; antagonistic, bitterly hostile. *A virulent letter, with no return address, arrived at his desk.*

409- **protract** (pro TRAKT) *v.* To draw out, prolong. *Don't try to protract the Senate debate by using filibustering tactics.*

410- **fillip** (FIL uhp) *n.* An incentive or stimulus; a snap of the fingers. *With those kind of lucrative fillips, I think we'll reach our goal.*

411- **zenith** (ZEE nuhth) *n.* The highest point in the sky; summit, top. *He is now at the zenith of the legal profession.*

412- **nadir** (NAY duhr) *n.* The lowest point (opposite the zenith). *The economy reached its nadir in 1932.*

413- **fulsome** (FUL suhm) *adj.* Insincere; disgustingly excessive. *The ambassador's welcoming speech amounted to a hollow, fulsome tribute.*

414- **pique** (peek) *v.* To excite, arouse; offend. *My interest was piqued by her question.*

415- **wheedle** (HWEE duhl) *v.* To obtain by flattery; coax, persuade. *The little girl wheedled five dollars out of me.*

416- **exiduous** (ig ZIG yoo uhs) *adj.* Scanty, meager. *The exiduous report consisted of nothing but two pages of drivel.*

417- **besmirch** (bee SMURCH) *v.* To soil, stain; tarnish. *I will not allow your lies to besmirch this foundation's reputation.*

418- **eschew** (es CHOO) *v.* To avoid; to shun. *"Encourage peace and love; eschew war and hate," she admonished.*

419- **juggernaut** (JUG uhr naht) *n.* A massive advancing force; irresistible fetish. *The juggernaut of larceny overtook him, and he returned to prison.*

420- **antithesis** (an TITH uh sis) *n.* The exact opposite. *He's the antithesis of the typically quiet scientist.*

421- **incisive** (in SAI siv) *adj.* Sharp, penetrating, acute. *Their analysis was incisive and to the point.*

422- **anathema** (uh NA thuh muh) *n.* A curse; a person or thing that is greatly detested; a formal ban. *After failing miserably that year, math became anathema to him.*

423- **sanguine** (SANG gwin) *adj.* Confident, cheerful. *Rick has such a sanguine, relaxed outlook on life.*

424- **truncate** (TRUNG kayt) *v.* To cut short; abbreviate. *Reading a truncated version of the status report provides all the information I need.*

425- **sinecure** (SIN i kyoor) *n.* A soft job that requires little or no work. *This job is no sinecure, I'll tell you that!*

426- **nuance** (NOO ahns) *n.* A subtle or slight degree of difference. *The peaceful nuances of the inn give it an air of safeness.*

427- **inept** (in EPT) *adj.* Unfit; foolishly awkward. *Inept mistakes can be avoided by heightening your concentration.*

428- **peruse** (puh ROOZ) *v.* To read or study carefully. *Give them time to peruse the printed instructions before offering your help.*

429- **importune** (im por TOON) *v.* To ask urgently. *Importune your boss to permit us use of his office.*

430- **supine** (soo PAIN) *adj.* Lying on the back. *From a supine position, he rose to his full seven-foot height.*

431- **esplanade** (es pluh NAHD) *n.* a public stretch of ground, walkway. *Lovers strolled hand-in-hand down the esplanade.*

432- **obviate** (AHB vee ayt) *v.* To make unnecessary; eliminate. *A simple tablet can obviate the previous painful treatments.*

433- **devoid** (di VOID) *adj.* Completely lacking; destitute. *Our home is devoid of anger and hatred, but it also is lacking in love.*

434- **mutable** (MYOO tuh buhl) *adj.* Subject to change; prone to change, fickle. *The laws of physics are only slightly mutable.*

435- **disparage** (dis PER ij) *v.* To discredit; belittle. *No one can disparage their mammoth achievement.*

436- **emissary** (EM uh ser ee) *n.* An agent, one sent on a mission. *Tillson, Inc.'s official emissary should arrive shortly.*

437- **fortuitous** (for TOO uh tuhs) *adj.* Happening by chance; lucky. *A fortuitous chain of events saved his life.*

438- **expunge** (ek SPUNJ) *v.* To blot out, erase. *Please expunge my name from your list of subscribers.*

439- **retrograde** (RET ruh grayd) *v.* To move backward; to decline, deteriorate. *Overall, the organization's strength has retrograded under his leadership.*

440- **prevaricate** (pri VER i kayt) *v.* To equivocate; to stray from or evade the truth. *Don't prevaricate in stating what you know.*

441- **ubiquitous** (yoo BIK wuh tuhs) *adj.* Seemingly universal; everywhere at the same time. *A ubiquitous Santa character appears in December.*

442- **ruminate** (ROO muh nayt) *v.* To meditate, ponder. *While you sit ruminating on the meaning of events, others are out creating events.*

443- **encomium** (en KO mee uhm) *n.* High praise; a eulogy. *It's sad that the best encomium is spoken only after you die.*

444- **phlegmatic** (fleg MAT ik) *adj.* Unexcited, calm; sluggish. *Our normally phlegamtic cat is acting terribly upset.*

445- **implacable** (im PLAK uh buhl) *adj.* Relentless; not easily halted. *The implacable Mr. Davis took the issue all the way to the school board.*

446- **erudite** (ER yoo dait) *adj.* Very scholarly, learned. *Her erudite book convinced me to delve deeper into the subject.*

447- **mien** (meen) *n.* Bearing; appearence or manner. *The actor could change his mien at will.*

448- **whet** (hwet) *v.* To stimulate; sharpen. *Doesn't the prospect of discovering who killed her whet your appetite to continue reading?*

449- **peremptory** (puh REM tuh ree) *adj.* Absolute; that can not be denied; compulsory. *Ten peremptory laws are binding on all.*

450- **ascetic** (uh SET ik) *adj.* Self-denying, austere (as for religious reasons). *Could you adapt to the ascetic lifesyle of this commune?*

451- **inordinate** (in OR dn it) *adj.* Excessive. *Most breakfast cereals contain an inordinate amount of sugar.*

452- **pedantic** (pi DAN tik) *adj.* Narrow-minded, book-learned; emphasizing trivial points. *A pedantic approach will drive clients away.*

453- **gamut** (GAM uht) *n.* The entire range. *Give me the gamut of tests, from A to Z.*

454- **delude** (di LOOD) *v.* To fool, mislead. *I won't delude you into thinking yours is not a serious illness.*

455- **fallacious** (fuh LAY shuhs) *adj.* Misleading, erroneous. *Those fallacious and forged documents ought to be burned.*

456- **antipathy** (an TIP uh thee) *n.* A strong dislike, aversion. *The mutual antipathy of the players ended any possibility for teamwork.*

457- **halcyon** (HAL see yuhn) *adj.* Peaceful, calm; idyllic. *Oh, to return to the halcyon days of childhood!*

458- **chimerical** (ki MER i kuhl) *adj.* Imaginary, unreal; visionary. *Your fears are all chimerical worries.*

459- **irascible** (i RAS uh buhl) *adj.* Easily angered; prone to irritability. *Your irascible mood has hindered finalizing the deal.*

460- **tyro** (TAI ro) *n.* A beginner, novice. *Being a tyro in bridge, she lost the first tournaments she entered to more experienced players.*

461- **mollify** (MAHL uh fai) *v.* To soothe, appease; make less severe. *His words were calculated to mollify any pangs of conscience.*

462- **termagant** (TUR muh guhnt) *n.* A quarrelsome, scolding woman. *Her landlady is an unbearable termagant.*

463- **pariah** (puh RAI uh) *n.* An outcast, a social untouchable. *His political opinions had turned him into a pariah in the neighborhood.*

464- **callow** (KAL o) *adj.* Immature, inexperienced, unripe. *The class' flippant replies to my questions betrayed a callow understanding.*

465- **propensity** (pruh PEN suh tee) *n.* A natural inclination, disposition. *The propensity of that particular horse is to buck and spin.*

466- **largess** (lahr JES) *n.* Generous giving. *My neighbor's largess made that year's Christmas season a wonderful memory.*

467- **allay** (uh LAY) *v.* To lessen or relieve; calm or pacify. *I called an ambulance while Marge tried to allay the fears of the injured child.*

468- **tacit** (TAS it) *adj.* Unspoken but implied; silent, reserved. *Their lack of response was interpreted as tacit approval.*

469- **extant** (ik STANT) *adj.* Still in existence, not destroyed or lost. *Next, we traveled through the city's mostly extant historical district.*

470- **abjure** (ab JOOHR) *v.* Renounce, abstain from; give up rights. *Will you abjure your commitments in order to run for office?*

471- **lugubrious** (loo GOO bree uhs) *adj.* Sad, mournful (usually exaggerated). *I had to laugh* *at his lugubrious complaints.*

472- **nascent** (NAY suhnt) *adj.* At conception, beginning to form; developing. *The youth's nascent philosophy was still full of contradictions.*

473- **malleable** (MAL ee uh buhl) *adj.* Flexible, adaptable; capable of being shaped. *The wood was not malleable enough to be carved.*

474- **fulminate** (FUL muh nayt) *v.* To speak out against or explode (always followed by "against"). *He fulminated against any such discriminatory policies.*

475- **ameliorate** (uh MEEL yuh rayt) *v.* To improve a deplorable condition. *Ameliorate, if you can, our nation's refugee situation.*

476- **desultory** (DES uhl tor ee) *adj.* Aimless, proceeding without a goal or purpose. *Her desultory life-style worries me.*

477- **mendacious** (men DAY shuhs) *adj.* Deceptive, lying. *Congressman, that insinuation is both mendacious and laughable.*

478- **paucity** (PAH suh tee) *n.* Scarcity. *The paucity of deer in the area is deplorable.*

479- **ossify** (AHS uh fai) *v.* To make into a rigid custom; to harden into bone. *Let's stay flexible and not let our attitudes ossify.*

480- **spurious** (SPYOOHR ee uhs) *adj.* Not genuine, false. *A totally spurious injury reportedly earned him a sizeable insurance payment.*

481- **pontificate** (pahn TIF i kayt) *v.* To speak or officiate as a pontiff (pope or bishop). *He, least of all, is qualified to pontificate on the virtues of discipline.*

482- **lambaste** (lam BAYST) *v.* To thrash, beat; to find fault with sharply. *Supervisors, motivate employees rather than lambaste them.*

483- **tractable** (TRAK tuh buhl) *adj.* Easily managed, docile. *Our sewing club seems to be a tractable bunch.*

484- **propitious** (pruh PISH uhs) *adj.* Favorable, promising; auspicious. *The store has gotten off to a propitious start this year.*

485- **stupefy** (STOO puh fai) *v.* To stun or produce stupor; amaze. *The clown's stunt never failed to stupefy audiences.*

486- **prodigality** (prahd uh GAL uh tee) *adj.* Wastefulness, extravagance. *America's prodigality with its resources is well-documented.*

487- **asperity** (a SPER i tee) *n.* Roughness, harshness; sharpness of temper. *Sergeant White's asperity caused many new recruits to drop out.*

488- **surreptitious** (soohr uhp TISH uhs) *adj.* Stealthy; obtained or done secretly. *He warned her with a surreptitious touch to say no more.*

489- **panacea** (pan uh SEE uh) *n.* An ideal remedy, cure-all. *Money is not a panacea for all social ills.*

490- **cacophony** (kuh KAHF uh nee) *n.* A harsh or dissonant sound; discord. *Elementary school bands can produce quite a cacophony.*

491- **subjegate** (SUB jooh gayt) *v.* To conquer; make subservient. *In order to subjugate the lower classes, they placed taxes on food and tools.*

492- **vicissitudes** (vi SIS i toodz) pl. *n.* The shifting ups and downs of life; difficulties. *To obtain the glory, we must endure life's vicissitudes.*

493- **puissant** (PWIS uhnt) *adj.* Powerful, effective. *At this point, we resorted to puissant measures to curb the drug trade.*

494- **rife** (raif) *adj.* Widespread, abounding. *Washington is rife with political intrigue and rumors.*

495- **cursory** (KUR suh ree) *adj.* Hastily done, not thorough. *She gave the apartment a cursory inspection and returned my deposit.*

496- **bulwark** (BUL wuhrk) *n.* Protection; a defensive wall. *You have served as a bulwark, warding off potential tragedy.*

497- **trenchant** (TREN shuhnt) *adj.* Keen, sharp, incisive; vigorous. *She made a trenchant analysis of the European market.*

498- **inchoate** (in KO it) *adj.* At an early stage; not yet formed. *Our ideas were enthusiastic but inchoate.*

499- **maudlin** (MAHD luhn) *adj.* Overly or foolishly sentimental. *My folks became increasingly maudlin about their keepsakes.*

500- **nefarious** (ni FER ee uhs) *adj.* Very wicked, evil; vicious. *He hatched a nefarious scheme to control the election.*

FOREIGN WORDS AND PHRASES TO ENHANCE YOUR ENGLISH

Over the centuries, foreign words and phrases have been directly assimilated into the English language. Here are some words and phrases that have not yet been formally adopted into English, but are used often to add flavor, nuance, and precision to the language.

Pronunciation Guide

Sound equivalents and letter symbols that are already familiar to English speakers are used in this guide. A few foreign sounds that have no English equivalents are also listed. Where the common English pronunciation does not approximate the "true" native pronunciation, both alternatives are usually listed, with the native approximation shown first.

Vowels

a	**a** as in ash
ah	**a** as in father
ai	**y** as in why
au	**ow** as in how
ay	**ay** as in play
e	**e** as in bet
ee	**ee** as in see
eu	**eu** as in French peut (Make a "closed" sound somewhere between English **e**, as in bet, and English **ooh**, as in foot.)
i	**i** as in bill
ing	**ing** as in sing
o	**o** as in go
oe	**o** as in German volkische (Round the lips for English **o**, as in born, and try to say English **ee**, as in see.)
oh	**o** as in born
oo	**oo** as in food
ooh	**oo** as in foot
oy	**oy** as in toy
ue	**u** as in German **uber** or French **vu** (Round lips for English **oo**, as in food and try to say English **ee**, as in see.)
uh	**uh** as in but
y	**y** as in your

French Nasal Vowels

French vowels followed by **n** or **m** are usually pronounced with an indeterminate nasal-hum ending. (Pronounce the French word **mo**n, for example, as if you were saying the English **mow** with a head cold.)

To ensure that these nasalized vowels are pronounced as vowels, **n** or **m** endings are omitted from the pronunciation key, and a tilde (~) is placed over the nasalized letter [(**mon** (mõ)]. Sometimes a French nasal vowel "slides" into a "genuine" nasal consonant. In these cases, both sounds are shown [**beau monde** (bo MÕND)].

Consonants

Most foreign consonant sounds have approximate English equivalents. To avoid confusion, note the special key symbols given below.

ch	**ch** as in church
sh	**sh** as in shop
g	**g** as in gone
k	**k** as in kayak
kh	**kh** as in German ach (Prepare the mouth to say k, then say h instead.)
s	**s** as in soft
th	**th** as in thin
Th	**th** as in there
z	**s** as in wise
zh	**si** as in vision

a bon marché (ah BÕ mahr shay) **Fr.** "At a bargain price."

ad infinitum (ad in fi NEE tuhm or in fi NAI tuhm) **Lat.** "To infinity"; without end.

ad valorem (ad vah LOHR em) **Lat.** According to something's value.

al dente (ahl DEN tay) **It.** "To the tooth"; slightly undercooked; chewy ("spaghetti al dente").

aloha oe (uh LO hah oy) **Hawaiian.** "Love, warm wishes"; greeting or farewell.

ante bellum (AN tay or AN tee BEL uhm) **Lat.** "Before the war." (In the U.S., specifically before the Civil War.)

arivederci (ah REE ve DER chee) **It.** "Until we meet again"; goodbye.

au contraire (oh cõ TRER) **Fr.** "On the contrary"; just the opposite.

au courant (oh koo RÃH) **Fr.** "Up-to-date" ("The manuscript is au courant").

au fait (oh FAY) **Fr.** Well-informed, skilled or knowledgeable; sophisticated.

au naturel (oh na tyue REL) **Fr.** In the natural state; nude.

au revoir (oh ruh VWAHR) **Fr.** "Until the next seeing"; goodbye.

auf Wiedersehen (auf VEE duhr zain) **Ger.** "Until we meet again"; goodbye.

Autobahn (AU to bahn) **Ger.**, autoroute (OH toh root) **Fr.**, autostrada (AU to STRAH dah) **It.** Superhighway.

a votre sante (ah VOH trũh SÃH TAY) **Fr.** "To your health"; a toast.

beau geste (bo ZHEST) **Fr.** A "beautiful gesture"; a futile but gracious act.

beau monde (bo MÕND) **Fr.** Fashionable society.

bien venu (byē vuh NUE) **Fr.** Welcome.

bon appetit´ (bõ na puh TEE) **Fr.** "Good appetite"; eat well.

bon jour (bõ ZHOOR) **Fr.** "Good day."

bon mot (bõ MO) **Fr.** "Good word"; a clever or witty remark.

bon vivant (bõ vee VAH) **Fr.** A refined person with an appetite for the "good life."

bon voyage (bõ vwah YAHZH) **Fr.** "Have a good trip"; farewell.

bona fide (BO nah FEE day **or** BO nuh FAI dee) **Lat.** "In good faith"; genuine.

caballero (kahb ahl YER o) **Sp.** A gentleman, cavalier; gallant horseman.

carpe diem (KAHR puh DEE yem) **Lat.** "Sieze the day"; enjoy or make the most of right now.

carte blanche (kahrt BLÃHSH) **Fr.** Unlimited authority; total freedom to act.

causa sine qua non (KAU sah SEE nay kwah NON) **Lat.** "The thing without which" (often shortened to "sine qua non"). An indispensable condition. ("Fresh eggs are the sine qua non of a good omlet.")

caveat emptor (KAH vay at EMP tohr) **Lat.** Let the buyer beware.

c'est la vie (SAY lah VEE) **Fr.** "Such is life"; so let it be.

che será será (kay se RAH se RAH) **It.** "What will be, will be."

circa (KIR ke or SIR kuh) **Lat.** "Near"; approximately, around. (Often used with dates and abbreviated as **c.** or **ca.**)

comme si comme sa (kuhm SEE kuhm SAH) **Fr.** So-so; "neither here nor there."

cordon bleu (KOHR do BLEU) **Fr.** "Blue ribbon"; a prize winner.

corpus delicti (KOHR puhs di LIK tee) **Lat.** The facts connected with a crime.

coup de grace (koo duh GRAHS) **Fr.** "Blow of mercy"; the finishing blow.

de facto (day **or** dee FAK to) **Lat.** "From the fact"; in reality.

deja vu (DAY zhah VUE) **Fr.** "Already seen"; the feeling that one has previously experienced an event.

de jure (day JOOR ay) **Lat.** According to law; by right.

Deo volente (DAY o vo LEN te) **Lat.** "God willing."

en fin (āh FEH **or** en FEEN) **Fr.** "In the end"; finally; in brief.

en garde (āh GAHRD) **Fr.** "On guard"; watch out.

en masse (āh MAHS or en MAS) **Fr.** All together; as a group; collectively.

en passant (āh pa SAH) **Fr.** "In passing"; by the way.

en rapport (āh ra POHR) **Fr.** "With rapport"; in sympathy or harmony.

entre nous (ÃH truh NOO) **Fr.** "Between us"; confidentially.

e pluribus unum (ay PLOOR ee boohs OO nuhm **or** ee PLOOHR uh buhs U nuhm) **Lat.** "Out of many, one"; many united (motto of the United States).

ex more (eks MO ray) **Lat.** According to custom or mores.

ex parte (eks PAHR tay) **Lat.** "From one side only"; from a partisan viewpoint.

ex post facto (eks post FAK to) **Lat.** "After the fact"; after the deed is done.

faux pas (FO PAH) **Fr.** "False step"; a social blunder.

femme fatale (fahm fa TAHL) **Fr.** A dangerous woman; a seductress.

Gesundheit (ge ZOOHNT hait) **Ger.** "Good health." (Usually pronounced after someone sneezes.)

grand prix (grah pree) **Fr.** "First prize."

haut monde (o MOND) **Fr.** "High world"; high society.

idee fixe (ee day FEEKS) **Fr.** "Fixed idea"; an obsession.

in loco parentis (in LO co pah REN tees) **Lat.** "In the place of a parent." ("Should the colleges act in loco parentis and set dorm rules?")

in medias res (in MAY dee uhs RAYS) **Lat.** In the middle of a sequence of events; thrust into the middle.

in situ (in SEE too) **Lat.** "In its place."

in statu quo (in STAH too KWO) **Lat.** "In the same condition."

in toto (in TO to) **Lat.** "Totally"; altogether, entirely.

inter nos (IN tuhr NOS) **Lat.** "Between us"; privately.

ipso facto (IP so FAK to) **Lat.** "From the fact itself"; by definition; as a logical extension.

je ne sais quoi (zhuh nuh say KWAH) **Fr.** "I don't know what"; a certain (usually fascinating) something.

laissez faire (les ay FER) **Fr.** "Let things go"; let it be, don't meddle or interfere ("a laissez faire attitude"; used especially in economics).

lapsus linguae (LAP soohs LING gwai) **Lat.** "A slip of the tongue."

me'a culpa (MAY ah KOOHL pah) **Lat.** "My fault"; I am to blame. (Often used to beg someone's pardon.)

modus operandi (MO duhs o per AHN dee **or** ah pur AN dai) **Lat.** "Method of operating"; the working system.

modus vivendi (MO duhs vee VEN dee) **Lat.** "Way of living"; how one manages to get along.

mon ami (mo nah MEE) **Fr.** "My friend"; my dear.

n'est-ce pas? (nes PAH) **Fr.** "Is it not so?"; right?

no lens vo lens (NO luhnz VOH luhnz) **Lat.** Willy-nilly; whether willing or not; with no order.

peccadillo (pek uh DEE yo **or** pek uh DIL o) **Sp.-Lat.** A minor sin; an offense.

per annum (per **or** puhr AN uhm) **Lat.** "By the year"; yearly.

per capita (per **or** puhr KAP i tuh) **Lat.** "By the head"; per person.

per diem (per DEE em **or** puhr DEE uhm) **Lat.** "By the day"; per day.

per se (per **or** puhr SAY) **Lat.** "As such"; by itself. ("The plan per se is fine; but the cost is too high.")

persona grata (per **or** puhr SO nah GRAH tah) **Lat.** Fully accepted person.

persona non grata (per **or** puhr SO nah nahn GRAH tah) **Lat.** Unwelcome, unacceptable person.

piece de resistance (PYES duh ray zees TÃHNS) **Fr.** The main dish or event; the most distinctive of things; outstanding accomplishment.

prima facie (PREE mah FAH kee ay **or** FAY shuh) **Lat.** "At first sight"; on the outside.

pro bono publico (pro BO no POO blee ko) **Lat.** "For the public good."

pro forma (pro FOHR mah) **Lat.** "As a matter of form"; done according to form; performed in a perfunctory way.

pro tempore (pro TEM poh re **or** ruh) **Lat.** "For the time [being]"; temporarily; (often shortened to "protem").

provocateur (pro voh kah TEUR **or** pro vah kah TEUR) **Fr.** "A provoker"; an agitator.

quien sabe? (kyen SAH bay) **Sp.** "Who knows?"

quid pro quo (KWID pro KWO) **Lat.** "This for that"; something in return for work; a reward; a substitute.

reductio ad absurdum (reh DOOK tee o ad ahb ZOOHR duhm) **Lat.** "Reduction to the absurd"; the process of demolishing an argument by showing how its premises lead to bizarre or impossible conclusions.

salaam (suh LAHM) **Arabic. Shahlom** (shah LOHM) **Hebrew.** Peace.

salaam aleikum (suh LAHM a LAY kuhm or kem) **Arabic** or **Hebrew.** Peace be with you.

salud (sah LOOTh) **Sp.** "Health"; to your health.

sans (sãh[z] or sãnz) **Fr.** "Without."

sans pareil (sãh pah RAY or sãnz pah REEL) **Fr.** "Without equal."

sans souci (sãnz sue CEE) **Fr.** "Without care"; carefree.

savoir faire (sav wahr FER) **Fr.** Tact; the ability to say and do the correct thing.

semper fidelis (SEM per or SEM puhr fi DE lis) **Lat.** "Ever faithful" (U.S. Marine Corps motto).

schlemiel (shluh MEEL) **Yiddish.** A dolt.

schlep (shlep) **Yiddish.** "Lug or drag." To carry clumsily or with difficulty.

schmaltz (shmahlts) **Yiddish.** Overly sentimental music or art.

sic (sik) **Lat.** so; thus it is.

s'il vous plait (seel voo PLAY) **Fr.** "If it pleases you"; please.

sine qua non (SEE nay or SEE nuh quah NOHN) **Lat.** See "causa sine qua non"

status quo (STAY tuhs or STA tuhs KWO) **Lat.** The existing condition; as it now is.

summum bonum (SOO muhm BO nuhm) **Lat.** "The greatest good."

tête à tété (TET ah TET) **Fr.** "Head to head"; one-on-one chat.

veni, vidi, vici (VAY nee VEE dee VEE kee or VEE chee) **Lat.** "I came, I saw, I conquered."

vis-a-vis (VEE zah VEE) **Fr.** "Face-to-face"; opposite to; in relation to.

vive le or **vive la** (VEE vuh luh or lah) **Fr.** "Long live . . . " ("Vive l'amour!"; "Long live love.")

voila (vwah LAH) **Fr.** "Look there!"; see!; there (it is)!

Weltschmerz (VELT shmayrts) **Ger.** "World pain"; world weariness.

Zeitgeist (ZAIT gaist) **Ger.** "Spirit of the times."

PREPARING AND PRESENTING A SPEECH

An edited summary (written by the author) of chapter 7 of *Change Your Voice, Change Your Image*, by Shirley Shields, Ph. D., Alliance Publishing, San Francisco, Ca., 1989

No one can learn to speak well without study and practice. Confidence, skill, poise, and effectiveness ("the arts of public speaking") will emerge as you make the effort.

Preparing and Outlining a Speech

Consider these ten key steps when preparing a talk:

1. *Choose your subject with care:* Be sure the topic is appropriate to the audience, the occasion, the environment and your expertise. Be certain there is enough material available to present an adequate discussion of the subject in the time alloted.

2. *Analyze the audience:* Ask: What is the average age of my listeners? In what range of occupations and social standing are they? What are their customs, prejudices and principal beliefs? Why are they here?

3. *Ascertain your purpose:* Are you speaking chiefly to persuade, entertain, or inform?

4. *Gather materials:* Visit the public library, or use books, objects, examples, etc. from your own collections or experience. Locate sources and/or conduct interviews, and take notes on what you read, hear and think. (Don't be afraid to use some original thoughts and concepts. Add your own color!)

5. *Organize the material:* Take several index cards or 3-by-5 pieces of paper, and write on each one a central phrase or sentence, which conveys an important fact, quote, comparison, statistic, or illustration relative to the subject. Lay the cards on a table and study them. Find the basic theme of the talk. Choose a statement, story, question . . . that might make for an interesting opening, then further arrange the cards to form a sequence of facts and examples that support your main idea.

Now, expand and formalize your outline. To avoid a cascade of cards during your delivery, write or type your notes on paper.

Divide your speech into an introduction, body, and conclusion.

a. The introduction should immediately engage attention, good will and respect, as well as lead into the subject matter. Do not promise more in the introduction than you have time to discuss in the body of the speech. An introduction might take any of the following forms:

- An initial, impacting statement. ("The best-kept secret of the fashion industry is that for fifteen years there has been no fundamental change in fashion.")
- A pointed question. ("How have your basic convictions been altered since you were seventeen years old?")
- A brief statement about global events. ("Just what does it mean to the future of the United States that we have become the world's largest debtor nation?")
- A reasonable challenge. ("Give me three good reasons why learning a foreign language can be important for business.")
- An evaluation of a local happening. ("Our community's response to the zoning initiative shows that we value our residential lifestyle more than profits.")

b. The body of your talk will reflect your topical knowledge – and your hours of preparation. Use appropriate examples, short stories and quotations to highlight pivotal points. Use your own words to sum up vital information you've gleaned from your research.

c. The conclusion may take many forms – an emotional appeal, a short summary, a challenge, a suggested action to be taken, or a provocative question. You may choose to harken back to the essential point made in your introduction to tie the speech together. Most important, remember that a conclusion is best when it is brief, crisp, and unannounced; and when it leaves a "sweet aftertaste" and fosters a positive attitude.

6. *Select words carefully:* Avoid these lines when wording your speech–

- "I'll be brief . . . " Don't lengthen your message (or arouse audience suspicions) by voicing a promise to be brief. It's best to get on with your subject.
- "I don't know why I was chosen to give this speech . . . " Such a statement reduces your credibility and also may embarrass the person who invited you to talk.
- "I don't want to offend anyone, but . . . " If you must use a disclaimer like this, yes, your remarks may offend somebody (or everybody).

In addition, avoid these pitfalls–

- Apologies for being an ineffective speaker.

- Difficult, trite or tiresome words or phrases.
- Overly abstract or confusing phrases or analogies. (A good story or example is better than a complex, analytical explanation.)
- Redundancies in descriptions ("a component part," "an icy blizzard," "a terrible disaster . . . ").
- Unnecessary descriptiveness. (Is a very big dept larger than a big dept? "Very" is a word that is rarely needed, as are "major," "absolutely," and "completely.")

7. *Use quotations correctly:* Back up your own opinions and ideas with those of experts; but be sure to give proper credit ("In his book *Talking Straight,* Lee Iacocca urges . . . ").

8. *Employ* (on a limited basis) *personal references:* Pertinent personal stories, used in an unassuming manner, serve to embellish a talk. Rather than use the expression, "Pardon the personal reference . . . " to try to "soften" your words: "It has been my experience . . . " or "My daughter went through a similar turn of events when she . . . "

9. *Make your speech your own:* Prepare and deliver your own message in your own words – and let others' stories and examples serve as support and filler material.

10. *Time your speech:* Nothing kills a good speech faster than going overtime.

Practicing For Better Delivery

1. Use a recorder to practice your delivery; or, if possible, videotape your rehearsal. Most people don't know how they look or sound when they speak. Identify areas where you can improve. Ask a trusted friend to give you feedback, if you don't mind a critique. Try to pick out nervous habits and poor posture. Examine your eye contact with the audience, voice inflection, energy of delivery, and the speech content itself.

2. Practice so that your speech seems alive and real, rather than "perfect." Rehearse until you are comfortable. Just thinking about your talk is different than rehearsing, and makes your actual speech, as delivered, your only "trial run" – a "first try" address that may prove quite uninspiring. Remember: your rehearsals will almost always be "worse" than the real thing. Work at creating a sincere, relaxed image.

3. Practice speaking on a "full breath." The primary source of speech projection is in the solar plexus – the upper abdominal region just beneath the rib cage. Powering (and controlling) the voice from this all-important center provides projection, a pleasant pitch, and a sense of authority, that a "throaty" voice can't offer.

4. Place more emphasis on key words and phrases. Slow down on, or repeat, sentences that capture the essence of your message.

5. Use gestures only to "suggest" action rather than to imitate it. Let the motivation for your gestures flow from the emotion and meaning of your talk.

Presenting Your Speech

Add to your confidence by walking calmly to the podium, breathing slowly and deeply, pausing to establish initial eye contact with three or four friendly faces, then pausing or slowing down again whenever necessary to maintain calm rapport. Above all, remind yourself "I'm glad to be here; I've prepared well and I have something interesting and important to share."

DO:
- Dress to enhance attention and self-confidence.
- Smile.
- Make the audience a partner by referring to them and their interests.
- Try to sense the "vibrations" that emanate from the audience.
- Use a minimim of notes.
- Speak loudly enough so that those on the back row can hear.
- Balance yourself on two feet, maintaining good posture.
- Make your closing sentences as loud and vibrant as the rest of your speech. (Many speakers have a tendency to "drop" their last few words.)

DON'T:
- Look at the clock. (Your speech should already be timed.)
- Let distracting mannerisms creep in (clearing your throat, shuffling your feet, fidgeting with the microphone, fumbling with notes, sniffling, nose twitching, lip biting, grimacing . . .).
- Speak to the person next to you immediately after taking your seat.

By engaging in thoughtful preparation and practice, you can't help but be a success.

A PAINLESS GRAMMAR GUIDE

Grammar Secrets Your Teacher Never Told You

Grammar – an alliance with the way words, phrases and sentences function together in our language – is a vital tool for helping you think, speak and write with precision and panache.

The tips, definitions, discussions and "games" that follow are dedicated to your re-initiation into the power, pitfalls, joys and glory of English grammar.

Parts of Speech Revisited

The Liberated Noun

Nouns – from the Latin word for "name" – are, not surprisingly, names. And names – with some help from *articles* ("the," "a" and "an"), along with other modifiers – obviously answer the question "What's that?" (or, in the plural, "What are those?") by pointing to literal or figurative "objects" and giving them a label: "What's that?"

- That's a *goldfish*.
- That's a *shame*.
- That's *democracy* at work.
- That's *green* for envy you see in my eyes.
- That's real *living*!

Any surprises? Be reassured, in case you're wondering, that *green* (usually an adjective, as in "That's a big, green, hairy thing) is legitimately functioning here as a true-blue noun – it answers "What's that?" (In fact, it can also be used as a verb: "'I green the leaves every spring`/ said the bright sprite of April . . . ")

Living, here, is also a noun. In fact, the whole function of the *-ing* suffix is to transform verbs into either slightly verbish nouns (*gerunds*, as in "*Singing* makes me nervous,") or slightly verbish adjectives (*present participles*, as in "The *singing* waters" or "The sailors were *singing*.") Such "verboid" forms – gerunds, past and present participles, and infinitives – are related to real, red-blooded conjugated verbs in the same way that androids (robots, like R-2 D-2) are related to real, red-blooded humans: they serve, support, and resemble, but still function as different parts of speech.

Actually, it is not very helpful to make up lists of "nouns," "verbs," "conjunctions," etc. *In English, any word can function as almost any part of speech, depending on how and where it is used in the sentence.* For example, what part of speech is the word *but* in Shakespeare's "But me no buts"? And what about these?:

"He *tight-fisted* his way to wealth." (an "adjective" used as a verb)

"The *wellness* clinic has just opened." ("noun" as adjective)

"Our company is in a *Catch-22* predicament." ("compound noun" as adjective)

"We deliver the *sizzle* for the meat." ("verb" as noun)

Moral: If a word or word group answers the question "What's that?" it's functioning as a noun. In formal situations you may want to set off your "games" with quotation marks to show that you are playing: "Reach for that candlestick and I'll `candle-stick` you!" (Notice, though, that too many "quote marks" in any "wordplay" can make your "write-outs" seem laborious, contrived and "arch.") But quotes or no quotes, pushing and squeezing parts of speech is legal, refreshing, and often genuinely inventive.

Moral: Don't be afraid to play with parts of speech.

Nouns and Proper Etiquette

Proper nouns (from the Latin for "one's own name") are conveniently capitalized to denote their function as specific titles. Notice the difference between "The President is a staunch Democrat," where *President* is used as a sort of formal nickname referring to a specific individual holding a specifically understood title (President of the United States) and *Democrat* is the official title of a political party, and "The club president was a true democrat," where *president* refers to a general office, and *democrat* connotes a general adherent of democracy.

As this serves to illustrate, what "properly" constitutes a proper noun is often debatable. The pronouncements of style guides vary. So, for consistency in formal writing, choose one style guide and stick to it. In your personal writing, you may capitalize (and thus "properize") any noun you like for emphasis or irony: "She had, she announced, found the Final Answer to Life." Of course, here again, one rule of propriety applies: Don't overdo. Too much Capitalization, just like too many quotation marks for "Irony" or "New-Noun" coinages, becomes tiresome and ineffective.

Pronouns: In Search of Antecedents

Many people manage to write beautiful, coherent, correct English sentences without ever suspecting that "cases" might occur outside the offices of lawyers or that "gender" is anything more than a sexist plot. But despite their humble status as noun "stand-ins," *pronouns* lie close to the heart of countless grammatical whirlpools – and their mysteries are worth penetrating.

The first and final thing to remember about pronouns is that they are, literally, *noun substitutes*: They are "stand-ins" for more specific words, phrases, or clauses that aren't there. These "missing specifics" are officially known as *antecedents*.

Coherent writing demands that every time we use any pronoun – a "personal" pronoun (first person – *I, my, mine, our* . . . ; second person – *you, yours, its* . . . ; or third person – *it, he, she, him, her, they* . . .); a "relative" pronoun (a sentence connector or stand-in – *who, whom, whose, that,* which . . .); a "demonstrative" pronoun (a word that points out items under discussion – *this, these, those, that* . . .); an "interrogative" pronoun (a stand-in for an unknown antecedent – *who, what, which, whom* . . .); or an "indefinite" pronoun (*anyone, somebody, nothing, everything* . . .) – we must anchor that pronoun either to an exact, *specific* antecedent or else (as in questions) to an acknowledged *unspecified* antecedent. (When you're talking about a girl *who* is happy, then "girl" is the antecedent of "who"; for the indefinite "Nobody knows *his* own name around here," you must *know* that "his" harks back to "nobody.")

Anchor your pronouns to their antecedents on two levels: the "spiritual-heights" level, where you know in your own soul just what or whom you are talking about; and the "down-to-earth" level, where you let your audience know too. In the sentence, "If her daughter didn't see the show she said that she would never forgive her," the speaker is probably clear about her antecedent, but the rest of us are left in the dark. Who said who would never forgive whom? Better: "My friend said she would never forgive her daughter for missing the show," or "My friend said that if she missed the show she would never forgive her daughter."

Another true-life sentence: "Guilt, bitterness, and envy can destroy your children; get rid of them." Here, we can probably guess the speaker's true intentions, but the ambiguity remains intriguing. Better: "Get rid of guilt, bitterness and envy; they can destroy your children."

And finally: "He said that Keynes' ideas were flawed, *which* will be discussed at the meeting." In this example, the writer himself may be unclear about his antecedent. Exactly *what* will be discussed at the meeting – Keynes' ideas, the contention that Keynes' ideas are flawed, or the heresy of the upstart executive who pronounced Keynes' ideas flawed?
Moral: When using pronouns, make sure that both you and your audience know exactly what or whom you're talking about, then anchor your pronouns in antecedents.

All You Ever Wanted to Know About Agreement – and Maybe More: Personal pronouns must also agree with their antecedents both in number (singular or plural) and in gender (masculine, feminine, or neuter). This sounds straightforward enough, but sometimes the problem of number can become sticky. Do we say, for instance, "The group *have* reached *their* consensus," "The group *has* reached *its* consensus," or "The group is tearing *its* hair out because *they* can't reach a consensus"?

Obviously number three is out; the two pronominal adjectives (singular *its* and plural *their*), both referring to the same antecedent (*group*), do not even agree with each other. To decide between the two remaining choices, look into your heart. Words like *group, family, class,*

army, etc. – known collectively as "collectives" – can be construed as either singular *or* plural nouns, depending on whether you wish to consider them as united entities or as unruly bands of individuals.

Thus, if the *group* has reached a consensus, *it* has probably reached *its* consensus. If *they* are still tearing *their* hair out, or if *they* reached *their* consensus after long and bitter infighting, we emphasize their disunity by announcing, "The *group* (or, even better, the group *members*) *have* not (or finally *have*) reached *their* consensus."

Defining Indefinites: What about agreement and indefinite pronouns? Which is correct?: "Does everyone have *his* (his or her) answer (or is it *their* answer? *their answers*?) ready?" Does anyone, in fact, have any definite answers at all to the quandary of indefinites?

Well, maybe. Notice that the noun-ending *-one* in words like *everyone, someone,* and *anyone* is obviously singular – as is its fleshier counterpart *-body* in the more informal *anybody, somebody,* and *nobody.* It isn't hard to choose a singular verb to agree with indefinite pronouns: "*Does* something tell you [not the singular "Do something tell you"] the answer may lie here?" One helpful hint is to check by using the pronoun in a question: "*Is* everyone [not *are* everyone] in agreement?"

We can therefore concede that replacement pronouns for indefinites must also be written in the singular. (Although in informal usage this rule is frequently overruled, and "Everyone has *their* own ideas about the subject," "their" remains technically incorrect, and can cause confusion in written English.)
Moral: For posh and easily understood sentences, everyone should anchor his indefinites to singular pronoun stand-ins.

The Gender Gap: Now on to the next question: Do we say "*his* indefinites," "*her* indefinites," or "*his or her* stand-ins"? Third-person singular personal pronouns (*it, he, she, him, her* . . .) are all classed by gender – as either masculine, feminine or neuter. Traditionally, the masculine pronouns and possessives *he, him,* and *his,* were, unless otherwise specified, supposed to "embrace" their feminine counterparts *she, her,* and *hers* – so that, for example, "To each *his* own" was tacitly interpreted as "To each *his (or her)* own." In current usage, however, the feminine grammatical gender has followed the lead of culture and declared its (her?) independence. "He" and "she" are now granted equal and separate billing. But this development presents some grammatical challenges: "To each *his or her* own" sounds only slightly less dampened than "*Anyone* coming through that door will get *his or her* neck broken." And compromising with a nice, neutral neuter ("To each *its* own") doesn't work well either.

The beleaguered writer is left with three choices:

1. *She* can plunge straight through the gender

jungle, wielding genders right and left to clear the brush – just as we are doing here. This preserves (and sometimes even enhances) the lively individuality of the third-person singular: "Anyone coming through that door will get *her* neck broken."

2. Instead of remaining lonely and beleaguered, the writer can detour around the trees by *generalizing* himself into "beleaguered writers" – exchanging the vigorous singular for the more formal plural. These new pluralized writers can then re-render "To each *his* own" as something like "Tastes differ." Notice how these "generalized plurals" tend to create a more detatched, objective tone: "All persons coming through that door will get *their* necks broken." For official pronouncements, scholarly papers and managerial memos, some writers prefer this style to distance themselves from their audiences.

3. As a final remedy, you – the writer or speaker – may stage an all-out rebellion against the formal constraints of the third person and burst out into the wilds of the second-person singular. If you feel the urge to do this, and if the occasion is not too formal, then you can evoke a powerful response by engaging your audience face-to-face and one-to-one: "Come through that door and *you'll* get *your* neck broken."

Sentences: Attacking the Jigsaw

Verbs and Pronouns : The Case for Cases

One impulsive first response to the foregoing might be: "Yeah? I'm gonna get my neck broken? Who by?" The sensitive grammarian, however, will think twice and change this to "By whom?" At issue is the use of *whom* as an interrogative pronoun in the *objective* case.

Here we graduate from isolated parts of speech into the grammatical big leagues: *sentences.* And sentences draw their life's blood from "action" or "mirror" words – "to *do*" and "to *be*" *verbs.*

Active verbs (*swims, gave, wonder, cares, realized . . .*) act; they tell us what's going on in sentences. What happened? "He fell," "She jumped," "The goldfish disappeared."

"Magic Mirror" verbs (*"copulas"* or *"linking"* verbs – *am, is, were, appears, looked, seems . . .*) function like mirrors, held up in front of nouns in order to reveal more about them: "I *am* the fairest in the land"; "That man standing behind you *looks* frightened"; "His goldfish *is* a fantail comet." In these sentences, a noun subject (*I, that man, his goldfish*) is further revealed or defined through another noun or adjective (*fairest, frightened, fantail comet*), and connected to it by a linking verb (*am, look, is*).

Because these *copulas* (from the Latin for "couplers") act as mirrors rather than as swashbuckling deed-doers like the active verbs, many grammarians insist that pronoun subject complements must also always take the subjective case: "This is *she.*" "It was you who lied, not *we.*" "The real heroes were *they.*" Sometimes these locutions sound eloquent and appropriate. Often, however, they only sound unbearably stiff and formal.

In livelier situations, it's fine to be yourself and to proudly proclaim, "It's *me!*"

Subjective Viewpoints – Who's Talking?:

Just as all deeds need doers, all verbs must have *subjects.* And, of course each verb must agree with its subject in *person* and *number.*

Subjects come in all sizes and shapes. They may consist of one noun (*"Goldfish* make good pets.") or of long phrases or clauses with verbs and subjects of their own (*"The goldfish that I brought home yesterday in my briefcase* still isn't eating."); they may also be *compounds* – made up of two or more separate subjects joined by a conjunction: "The goldfish I brought home *and* the tarantula you brought home both need more space."

So what exactly does the verb need to agree with?

First, in complex subjects, find the pivotal noun or pronoun. In the second goldfish sentence, "that I brought home . . . in my briefcase" all functions as an *adjective clause,* answering which or what goldfish. *Goldfish* is the *simple subject.* In the case of the goldfish and the tarantula, there are *two* simple subjects for the same verb, and they take the plural form – they *need,* not *needs.* (Notice, though, that when you want to "marry" two subjects with a conjunction – making them a separate entity – a singular verb is fine: "Ham and eggs *makes* a good breakfast.")

There are only two places where modern English verbs still change endings to show "person" and number. But these "places" are basic grammatical intersections:
• The copula "be" changes throughout the present tense ("I *am* a sparkling conversationalist; you *are* very talkative; she *is* a non-stop chatterbox"), and distinguishes between singular and plural throughout the past tense ("I, he, she, or it *was;* we, you or they *were*).
• All verbs (except the "incomplete" verbs *can, may* and *will*) either add or substitute an "s" ending in the third-person singular. ("I, you, we or they *have* three goldfish; he or she *has* an African parrot.")

Moral: When a verb has a long, tortuous subject, make sure it agrees with the "simple subject" – the one noun or pronoun at the heart of things: "Each of the representatives from the six southern districts *was* (not plural *were*) awarded a fantail goldfish," or "All of the representatives *were* (not the singular *was*) awarded . . ."

An Objective Viewpoint: Gifts, Givers and Giftees

Transitive verbs are "givers" as well as "doers." They come attached to **direct objects** (which specify what "gifts" they are giving – "He gave *his prize-winning goldfish . . .* ") and to **indirect objects** (which tell who or what received the gift – "He gave his prize-winning goldfish *to our charity*.")

Direct and indirect object pronouns are, naturally, always in the objective case: "He gave them to *us*." – not the subjective "they" or "we."

Prepositions (which are not necessarily literally pre-positions at all, but "direction" words – *to, in, above, up*) also have objects ("up the *down staircase*," "over *the hill*," etc.). In fact, indirect verbal objects are actually a specialized brand of prepositional phrase: "Send the goldfish *to your boss*." And pronoun objects of prepostions also naturally take the objective case: "Get that goldfish away from *me*. Give it to *her* and *them* instead."

Moral: When you encounter pronouns a long way from their "home" verbs or prepositions, and whenever you find pronouns in clumps of two or three, be sure to trace them to their rightful owners: "He said he would give three goldfish to *whoever* (subjective case) beat the quota first." (*Whoever* is the subject of the verb "beat.") But notice also: "He said he would give the goldfish to *whomever* it loved best." Here, the objective "whom" is fine; *whomever* is the direct object of the verb "loved."

Adverbs: Circumstantial Evidence

Verbs can also be completed by adverbial or "circumstantial" *complements* that answer *how, when, where* or *why*. Like direct and indirect objects, these complements may consist of single words, or of complex phrases or clauses:

"He gave the goldfish *freely*."
"*Outside of what we have already discussed*, there is nothing new to tell."

Adding to Adjectives

The trademark of the typical English adverb is the suffix *-ly* added to a typical adjective: *Free-ly, tru-ly, erratic(al)ly*, etc. And such converted adjectives may then turn around and modify not only verbs but also their old grammatical sister adjectives or adjective clauses:

"Was he *truly* free?" "Was she *freely* true to him?" "A *beautifully* bound book . . . "
"She is *high* strung . . . " (Not *highly*, since *high* is already a half-breed adverb – "Way up high," for instance.)
"You look *well*." (This phrase, by the way, is not more elegant than "You look *good*" – which, as an adjective, is, in fact, theoretically more correct. Though both looking *well* and looking *good* are fine ways to look, they do, by convention, mean different things: "well" usually connotes "healthy"; "good" connotes "attractive.")

Of course, adjectives, in turn, modify or complete nouns:"The *reddest* roses . . . " "The woman *I saw you talking with* . . . " Like adverbs and nouns, they may be composed of single words or complex word groups: "The *sole* survivor *of the storm* . . . " (A simple adjective and adjective phrase both modifying the same noun.)

*A Recap – First and Final Moral: In English, parts of speech are dynamic and often interchangeable. Enjoy them; play with them. Just make sure that both you and your readers or listeners know **what** you are relating to in your sentences.*

A Few "Missing Pieces"

Bypassing the Passive

The passive voice, in English, is more a stylistic than a grammatical convention. It turns active verbs into *past participles* (verboid adjectives, remember?), using copulas as verbs (often as crutches), and consequently muffling the impact of both the deed and the doer: "He slashed and ransacked the briefcase," thus becomes "The briefcase *was* slashed and ransacked by him."

Certainly, the passive voice does have legitimate uses. But, like the generalized third person, it can become an addictive cop-out from personal engagement and action.

The Misunderstood Subjunctive: Was he or were she?

The subjunctive *were* is probably the most misunderstood convention in the English language. But the rule here is both easy and intriguing:

"If I *were* you . . . " (Obviously, I'm not you. I'm merely asserting a contrary-to-fact condition with the "if" clause.)
"If he *was* there, then that explains everything." (He may have been there; the "if" asserts a possible condition in the past.)
"If he *were* only here . . . " (Another contrary-to-fact statement in the present.)
"If he only *had been* here . . . " (A contrary-to-fact assertion in the past.)

May we or might we?

"He *said* that I *might* be able to take the goldfish home." (Past possibility or permission.)
"They *say* we *may* take the goldfish now." (Present possibility or permission.)
"She *says* we *might* [or *may*] pick up the goldfish tomorrow." (Future possibility.)
"They *said* they *may* [or *might*] take the the goldfish home tomorrow." (Past assertion of future possibility.)
But not "They *told* them that they *may* take the goldfish home." (A mixed "past-present" message, when the intent is to say that he gave them permission in the past.)

We hope these grammatical tidbits have been enlightening and liberating. By experimenting with parts of speech, word order, word usage, etc., and by expanding on these ideas, you can confidently adventure towards the horizons of communication with precise, elegant, flexible grammar.

PUNCTUATION PRIMER

In spoken language, we automatically use pauses and inflections – along with gestures and facial expressions – to help show how our words, phrases and sentences are related to each other and in what way we intend them to be understood.

In written language, however, punctuation takes on this role. Each punctuation mark serves one of four general aims: to terminate, to introduce, to separate, or to enclose.

The following individual marks are arranged alphabetically for easy reference. Examples serve to show the various ways each mark can be used.

As you rely on a blend of proper punctuation habits and your own intuition, your writing will be precise and understandable.

APOSTROPHE '

• *Indicates where letters or numbers have been omitted in contracted words –*
aren't I'll o'clock (short for "of the clock") it's (when used as a contraction for "it is")
gold rush of '49 class of '89
national = nat'l (or natl.)   secretary = sec'y (or sec.)

• *Denotes possession –*
the man's jacket it's anybody's game our children's school an hour's delay Julie's favorite niece the doctor's prescription Three doctors' offices were affected (plural) the ladies' department Mr. Jones' home Marx's theories hers is lost its cover is torn
(**Note:** For either singular or plural possessives ending in s, only an apostrophe is added; no additional s is required. Also, possessive pronouns ending in s such as *its, hers, theirs, ours* . . . require no apostrophe.)

• *Often forms plurals where some punctuation is needed to avoid confusion –*
Dot your *i*'s. We only have size *9*'s. Receive all C.O.D.'s.
You use too many "*I*'s" when you speak.

• *Indicates omissions in dialectal speech –*
It's 'bout time you started tryin'.

BAR (or VIRGULE) /

• *Divides lines of poetry when written in a prose sentence –*
Weariness/ Can snore upon the flint, when resty sloth/ Finds the down pillow hard. (Shakespeare)

• *Separates numbers on some occasions –*
The date was 11/24/87   The fraction 4/5 is larger than 3/4

BRACES { }

• *Groups items –*

Calif. } Pacific   set   { daily
Ore.   } Coast   goals { weekly
Wash. } States   { monthly
                           { yearly

BRACKETS [ ]

• *Primarily used to denote inserts in a quotation –*
"[The rock] is obviously from the precambrian era," she determined.

• *Can be used to make corrections in spelling or to add clarifying material, when needed –*
He wrote: "Kingsbery [Kingsbury] is her home town."
They [the vice presidents] felt they should resign.

CAPITAL LETTERS

• *Used to begin sentences and direct quotes; for proper (individual) names of people, places, times (weeks, days, months, centuries, eras) or things; for holidays; for titles –*
I live in the East, near Atlanta. On Wednesday, March 17th of our vacation (St. Patrick's Day) we'll stop to visit Uncle Matt in Shreveport, Louisiana. His home on Lincoln Street is alive with flowers in the spring. I know he'll say, "My how you've grown!" Then, we'll continue heading west.
(**Note:** In the first sentence, *East* is a region of the country; in the last sentence, *west* is merely a direction.)

CARET ^   or amended
• *To insert words in a handwritten ^ page (usually the page will be retyped) –*
                    and value
We appreciate ^ your assistance in this matter.

COLON :

• *Signals "watch what's coming next"; precedes added details or explanations –*
I have a single goal: success.
In summary: save your money, invest it wisely, and be bold.
We have offices in the following cities: New York, San Francisco and Denver.
Here is the last line of "The Star Spangled Banner": "O'er the land of the free, and the home of the brave."
(**Note:** The colon is placed outside the quotation mark.)

• *Separates two independent clauses when the second helps to clarify the first –*
Yoda's hair was matted and wet: he'd been trudging through the rain all night.

• *Introduces formal quotations (especially lengthy quotes, that are often italicized)* –
In her inaugural address, she stated: "I have only one qualification for this job . . . "
Slowly, deliberately, Lincoln began:
Four score and seven years ago . . .

• *Marks some types of separations* –
Dear Gentlemen: 1:40 p.m.   Luke 4:9 (chapter and verse)   I Can: A Book of Faith   see History, IV:25 (volume and page)

COMMA *,*

• *Generally signals a pause in a long sentence (particularly before conjunctions such as but, and, or, etc.)* –
I have not yet received his reply, nor do I expect one.
Your firm is a good one, but not quite what we're looking for.
Realizing that this is a large and lucrative account, we should also realize that we can't afford to treat it with any degree of carelessness.

• *Divides members of a series or list (words, phrases, or clauses)* –
She smiled, accepted, then placed her arms around his neck.
Buy the following: potato chips, flour, sugar and shortening.

• *Separates "equal" adjectives (to test, just make sure the adjectives can be reversed without interrupting sentence flow)* –
Down the narrow, winding, and dark corridor we made our way.
Her tender, gracious manners appealed to me.

• *Splits parenthetical phrases; adds information* –
We believe, and the evidence shows, that he acted illegally.
Sometime, at your convenience, we can get together for lunch.
When can you meet with our foreman, James Bond?
(**Note:** When in doubt here, ask yourself whether your sentence would make sense, as spoken, to pause and "set off" the material [if so, add commas] or whether a pause would change the intended meaning [omit commas].)

• *Used to separate direct quotations from informational material* –
Donna asked, "Why do you always stay in your office?"
"If you do," the letter read, "I will never see you again."

• *Separates words in direct address* –
Listen, gentlemen, to what I have to say.
Well, which way should we go now, Pete?

• *Sets off certain phrases and clauses (especially transitional words, parenthetical phrases, noun clauses and introductory clauses) for emphasis* –
There is great doubt, however, about the book's authenticity.
That it was the right thing to do, I had no question.
The examination, in short, was not worth taking.
By hard work, Peter soon rose to store manager.
If you finish before I return, start unloading the truck.
Let's begin with line b, not a.
Note, for example, the paragraph below.

• *Sets off an adverbial clause of concession (although . . .) or reason (because . . .)* –
The judge examined the evidence carefully, although there wasn't much to examine.

• *Used to avoid confusion (particularly in sentences which contain a grammatical construction – the non-restrictive phrase or clause – that is common in written English but rare in speech). Notice the difference in meaning between these examples* –
"He bought the package, which was already discounted." (Non-restrictive) and "He bought the package which was already discounted." (Restrictive)
"The children, who were napping, felt nothing." and "The children who were napping felt nothing."

• *Indicates an omission of words* –
Here we have six volumes; there, twenty.
I handle finances; Bennett, customers; Jones, operations.

• *In some cases, separates titles from each other or titles from word or number groups* –
Sarah Barnes, Ph.D., and her son, Bill Barnes, Jr.
Allen Street, San Antonio, TX   July 8, 1984
four thousand, eight hundred, and sixty-nine dollars ($4,869.00)

Remember, commas are meant to clarify, *not to confound.* Don't overuse them. If a spoken sentence does not require a definite pause, the written version probably doesn't require a comma. For example, in the sentence "Certainly, the most rewarding action, after returning home, would be to get counseling," each comma could be justified; but unless some special emphasis is intended, they could all be omitted to create a cleaner, clearer sentence.

DASH –

• *Denotes a sudden interruption or shift in thought, especially when an emotional comment is made* –
We demand the right to assemble, the right to speak our minds, the right to a fair wage – we demand respect!
A free ride, money, sex – that's all they wanted.

• *May terminate, interrupt, introduce, or enclose other phrases (especially those contain-*

ing internal punctuation) –
"May I ask you – " "No you may not!" she inter-
jected.
It's beautiful here – but soon the ground will be
covered with snow.
Finding a buyer – that is the biggest problem.
Only three new players – the catcher, Gomez,
Adams, a reserve shortstop, and Baker of the
pitching staff – were on the team last year.
The manual – the one on purchasing proce-
dures, I believe – should give that information.
(**Note:** Avoid using a dash along with a period
or comma. The dash is plenty strong enough to
stand on its own.)

• *Shows omission* –
They're in one h – of a mess!
The actor, a Mr. A – , spoke on behalf of the
union.

DITTO MARKS "
• *May substitute for repeated words or phrases;
infrequently used* –
They can not lend a hand.
   "   "   " do something extra.
   "   "   " offer any support at all.
They should be fired!

ELLIPSES ...
• *Indicate omission from a sentence or quote* –
"My love is like a red, red rose . . . " he droned.
" . . . our forefathers brought forth . . . a new
country, conceived in liberty   "

• *Show that other listed items are not named* –
Jeff, Marti . . . bring them all, if you can.

• *Suggest hesitation, a temporary break in dialogue, or a passage or continuation of time* –
"You think you can . . . . Why, I don't believe it!"
And then . . . a scream tore through the quiet
air . . .
The cool morning passed . . . slow, sweltering
afternoon . . . and then the freezing night.

Note: Three or four periods may be used in an
ellipsis. Generally, four are used only at the end
of a sentence to indicate that the speaker continues on with that particular sentence.

EXCLAMATION POINT !
• *Expresses surprise, emphasis, sarcasm, or
strong emotion* –
You were rude to him!
"It must be my lucky day!" she gushed.
Derisively, he replied, "So shoot me, why don't
you!"

• *Follows forceful commands* –
"Leave me be!" he shot back.
Let's get going – now! – before it's too late.

• *Sets off interjections* –
Ouch!   That hurts!   "Bravo!" they cried.

HYPHEN -

• *Sometimes used in compound words (consult
a dictionary when in doubt)* –
ne'er-do-well   brother-in-law   well-known
Anglo-Saxon first-rate   best-known trademark anti-American X-ray U-turn ex-
spouse self-service plant-like re-cover
(**Note:** Many compounds are hyphenated or left
unhyphenated depending on their function or
position in the sentence: "She was a first-rate
dancer." "Her dancing was truly first rate." "Did
they take off in spite of the storm?" "Yes, but
the take-off was rough.")

• *Forms prefixes, suffixes and prepositions; clarifies words not yet assimilated into English* –
anti-American passers-by semi-interested

• *Substitutes for the word "to" between two
figures or numbers* –
the years 1941-1945   pages 216-305   the New
York-Hartford train

• *Separates the parts of cardinal and ordinal
numbers from twenty to one hundred; also separates the numbers in fractions, when written
out* –
one hundred and twenty-five   forty-first two-
fifths sixty-one ninty-ninths

• *Often joins numbers and their units when
used together as adjectives preceding a noun* –
6-foot board   50-hour week 26-yard gain
a nine-year-old girl

• *Denotes spelled-out words* –
E-n-o-u-g-h is pronounced "i-nuf'."

• *Suggests stuttering* –
It's c-c-certainly c-c-cold!

ITALICS *italics*
• *Used to show unusual emphasis; for reference*–
Never say that word again.
The key to living a long life: *keep breathing.*

• *Designate words, letters or figures spoken of
as such* –
The word *zipper* should have read *dipper.*
The *i* and the *e* should have been transposed.
6's and 8's are sometimes mistaken for each
other.

• *Set off titles of books, book-length plays and
poems, movies, magazines, newspapers, musical scores, etc.* –
*Love Story   Washington Post   Tell-Tale Heart
Time* Magazine   Beethoven's *Fifth Symphony*

• *Set apart the names of ships, trains, legal
cases, scentific names, foreign phrases etc.* –
Titanic The *Queen Mary*   The *Enola Gay   Roe
vs. Wade   Homo sapiens   annuit coeptis* ("He hath
smiled on our undertakings")

PARENTHESES ( )

• *Clarify or add information related to a sentence's context* –
Glaucoma (a disease of the eyes) is one of the most serious problems of the elderly.
Mammals appeared long after the large dinosaurs had died out. (See "Mammals," chapter 17.)
The issue on civil rights (June, 1988) is recommended reading.
Iguanodon was 16 feet tall (about 5 meters).
The total amount due is sixty dollars ($60).

• *Often enclose numbers in a list* –
(1) Write letters to your senator. (2) Organize a march. (3) Begin a newsletter.

PERIOD .

• *Used for terminating sentences (declaratives, some interrogatives, requests, fragments . . .)* –
"I'll be home soon." Then he hung up.
"Where have you been?" she asked. "Over at Bob's."
She asked if I had ever been arrested.
Take your time when you shoot a free throw.

• *Ends standard abbreviations* –
Mo. (Missouri)   U.S.A. (or USA)   Dr.   Ave.
(**Note:** In most abbreviations consisting of three or more capital letters, periods are omitted, as in NRA, NAACP . . .)

• *Delineates decimal fractions* –
You owe $1.75.   .098 is the answer.   10.00 is a perfect score.

QUESTION MARK ?

• *Completes direct questions* –
May the other children come with us too?
"How many?" she questioned.
Which one of them asked "When will we get there?" (**Note:** Only one question mark is used.)
Will he bite? or chew up things? or just sit there?

• *Enclosed within parentheses, expresses doubt as to the content of a statement* –
Lincoln was born May 8 (?), 1809.
She gave me a gentle (could it be called that?) pat on the rear end.

QUOTATION MARKS " " and ' '

• *Surround direct quotes* –
"So, what will it be?" he sneered.
"Well surely," I replied, "you already know my answer."
"It's true!" she gasped. "I know it is."
(**Note:** A comma comes after the "I replied" above, since the sentence was continued afterward. A period is used after "she gasped," since she had begun a new sentence.)
He indicated how "stupid" it was to play tennis in my condition.
"We'll take your application," she told me; "but

we have no openings at this time."
(**Note:** For quotes of more than one paragraph, place marks at the beginning of each paragraph but at the end of only the last, or choose to indent or italicize the entire passage in lieu of quotation marks.)

• *Set apart words having a different level of usage* –
You are a real "stuffed shirt."
I'm not necessarily "old" you know.
He's so new at golf; he doesn't even know what a "birdie" is yet.

• *Enclose titles of articles and short stories, and some chapter headings* –
John Updike's "The Witches of Eastwick" is my favorite.
The article, "Good Advice for Teens," didn't impress me.

• *Draw special attention* –
The phrase "Not on your life!" has several interpretations.

• *Used singly, they allow you to set off a quote within a quote* –
"If you tell me, 'Be there on time,' I expect you will be on time, too," my father warned.

Note: Periods and commas *always* appear inside quotation marks; but, unless exclamation points or question marks are part of a quote, these appear outside the marks. And semicolons and colons always appear outside of quotation marks, as in the following examples:
One judge rated the pie "excellent," but the other only ranked it as "good."
What did you mean by "Maybe I will"?
You would enjoy "boogie-boarding"; it's a lot of fun.
Three points are emphasized in "Filing to Find": habit, accuracy, and speed.

SEMICOLON ;

• *Stronger than a comma, weaker than a period; separates two related sentences, or divides a sentence without the need for a conjunction* –
We washed; we mopped; we broke our backs cleaning.
You have done enough today; go home and rest.
Family life is great; however, it has its up's and down's.
Go to school for six more months; then come and see me.

• *Sets apart clauses, phrases or members of a series that are equal in rank within a sentence, especially when the elements to be set off already contain commas or other internal punctuation* –
Our president is Mel Taylor; our vice-president, Cindy Cap; and our secretary, Dan Stokes.
See *Genesis* chapter 3, verse 9; *Romans* 2:14; and *I Cor.* 6:7.

SPELLING RECOMMENDATIONS AND RULES

For every spelling rule, inevitably there are "exceptions." By applying the basic spelling rules and recognizing some of the exceptions explained here, your spelling will improve.

Some immediate recommendations:

1. When you speak, pronounce words carefully. The word "probably" will likely be mis-spelled if pronounced "probly".

2. List your spelling "enemies" and attack them. Look at your past letters and papers. Then write or type out in sentences and read back those words that have given you trouble. Soon the correct spelling will become second nature.

3. Make it a habit to look at words carefully. Practice seeing each letter in a word. Repeat it aloud if possible. It might help to pronounce difficult words the way they are spelled, for spelling purposes. A memory device ("Eeee! I am seized!" for example, to remember the e-before-i reversal in seizure) may be used with some words.

4. Take time to proofread what you write. Experienced writers habitually reexamine their work for misspellings and punctuation errors.

5. Consult the dictionary for words you question, with the understanding that some words have multiple spellings or distinct foreign spellings.

6. Review the following spelling rules as necessary. Take a few minutes to put each rule in your own words for easier recall.

First Rule: **Adding suffixes to one-syllable words**

The word "pat" is a one-syllable word that ends in a single consonant preceded by a single vowel. In such words, double the last consonant when adding a suffix:

patted, hottest, shopper, mapping, bigger

If the word ends in two consonants, or if two vowels precede the final consonant, this rule does not apply:

sharper, pulled, climbed; meeting, loaned, screamer

Second Rule: **Adding suffixes to words of two or more syllables**

If the word is accented on the last syllable (prefer), you may treat it as a one-syllable word:

preferring, combatting, rebelling

Again, if the word ends in two consonants, or if two vowels precede the consonant, the rule does not apply:

alarmed, reflection; ballooning, retained

If the last syllable is not accented, generally just add the suffix:

showering, profitable, rancorous

Third Rule: **Adding suffixes beginning with vowels to words ending in silent e**

A silent e is usually dropped from a word to add a suffix, if the suffix begins with a vowel:

sliding, advisor, believable, finest, expensive

Exceptions:

If the suffix -able or -ous is added to a word with a soft g or c sound, keep the e:

outrageous, traceable, changeable

Keep the e if the new word could be misunderstood or mistaken for another:

dyeing (from the verb to dye), *mileage, acreage*

If the word ends in ie (die), drop the e and change the i to y before adding the suffix:

dying, lying,

Fourth Rule: Adding a suffix beginning with a consonant to a word ending in silent e
Keep the silent e on the end of words where the suffix begins with a consonant:

engagement, fateful, extremely, sameness, shoeless

Exceptions:

truly, argument, awful, acknowledgment (or acknowledgement) judgment (or judgement)

Fifth Rule: Using ie and ei

Use the well-known "i before e, except after c," unless the word makes the long a sound as in neighbor or weigh:

receive, conceited, ceiling; believe, pier, piece, chief, fierce; sleigh, reign, feign

Exceptions:

ancient; sleight, foreign, height, weird, neither,seize, forfeit, sovereign, either, leisure

Sixth Rule: Adding suffixes to words ending in y

If a y is preceded by a vowel, leave it alone and add the suffix:

honeys, stayed, playful, displaying, boyish, preys

If the y follows a consonant, change it to an i and add the suffix:

pitiful, penniless, happily, funniest, tried

Exceptions:

To use the suffix -ing, keep the y:

partying, worrying, denying

Other exceptions:

babyhood, ladylike, beauteous, wryly.

Seventh Rule: Making singular words plural

Add an s to most words:

computers, books, files

If a word ends in s, ss, sh, ch or x, always add es:

taxes, businesses, gases, matches, dishes

If a word ends in a y preceded by a consonant, change the y to ies:

armies, booties, ladies, parties, libraries

If the y follows a vowel, just add s:

says, joys, days

Some words can be used as plurals with no changes:

deer, fish, antelope

Other words change their root spelling to form plurals:

goose becomes *geese, tooth/teeth, leaf/leaves, wolf/wolves*

Changed word-endings can also indicate a plural:

compendium/compendia, octopus/octopi, cactus/cacti, synopsis/synopses

English words, with their multiple root languages, are often difficult to spell, and many have variant spellings (theater, theatre). Consulting a dictionary can even be frustrating. The following article, "SPELLING HELP! A Speller's Sound Guide," might help in locating a hard-to-spell word.

SPELLING HELP!

A Speller's Sound Guide

Even with only twenty-six letters to represent the forty or more sounds of standard American English pronunciation, it can be difficult to find a word in the dictionary because of the myriad possibilities for combining these letters. Regional pronunciations complicate things even more.

The following guide is designed to help you translate sounds into some of their more common spellings. An asterisk (*) indicates the most common spelling used for a particular sound; try these spellings first.

VOWEL SOUNDS	SPELLING	SAMPLE WORD
a (name,	ai *	main, claim, aid
blade, shape)	au	gauge
	ay *	display, pay, clay
	ea	steak
	eig	feign, reign
	eigh *	freight, neighbor, sleigh
	ey	they
a, (gather, fad)	ai	plaid
	al	calf, half
	au	laugh
a, (part, star)	e	sergeant
	ea	heart
a or e, (share,	ae	aerial, aerobics
care);(there,	ai	said, air
get)	ay	prayer
	ea *	thread, tear
	ei	heir
	eo	leopard
	ie	friend
	u	bury
e, (she, we)	ea *	reach, weak, please
	ee *	meet, week, flee
	ei *	either, receive, ceiling
	eo	people
	ey *	money, key, donkey
	i	ski, piano, Figi
	ie *	believe, chief, yield
i, (crime, I)	ai	aisle
	ay	aye
	ei	height
	ey	eye
	ie	tie
	ig	sign
	igh *	light, sigh, frighten
	is	island
	uy	buy
	y *	try, byte, gyroscope
	ye	goodbye
i, (win, fill)	e	here
	ea *	dear, ear,
	ee	been
	ei	forfeit
	ie	pier

i – continued	o	women
	u	busy
	ui	build, guild
	y *	symphony, gym, symbol
o, (go, rope)	eau	beau, trousseau
	ew	sew
	oa *	goal, moan, oats
	oe	foe
	oh	oh
	ou	boulder, shoulder
	ough	though
	ow *	owner, showed, flow
	owe	owe
o or a,	al	talk, chalk
(bomb, hobby;	ah	shah
water, palm)	au *	taught, automobile
	aw *	flaw, shawl, awning
	ho	honor
	oa	broad
	ou	cough
	ough	brought, thought
o, (for, torn)	a	warm
	oa	oar
oi, (noise, oil)	oy *	ploy, loyal
ou, (shout, our)	hou	hourly
	ough	plough
	ow *	brow, owl, crowd
oo, (book, took)	o	woman
	ou *	could, would, tour
	u *	cushion, pudding
oo, (fool, room)	eu	maneuver
	ew *	grew, ewe, lewd
	ieu	lieutenant
	o	do
	oe	canoe
	ou	group, route
	ough	through
	u *	rude, costume
	ue	clue, true
	ui	suit, fruitful
	wo	two
u, (unit, unite)	eau	beauty
	eu	feud
	ew *	few, grew
	ieu	adieu
	iew	review
	ue	cue, fuel
	you	youth
	yu	yulelog, Yuma
u, (punt, sun)	o *	income, son, wonder
	oe	does
	oo	flood
	ou	trouble

u, (turn, lurk)	e	term,
	ear	heard, earn, earliest
	i *	first, sir, bird
	o	worker
	our	journal

ə (definite, absent) The "schwa" sound has an indeterminate vowel sound in an unstressed syllable.

	a *	about, ago
	e	item, agent
	i	edible, insanity
	io	nation, mission
	o *	gallop, comply
	u *	circus. focus

CONSONANT SOUNDS	SPELLING	SAMPLE WORD
b, (baby, bib)	bb *	robber, cabby, rubble
	pb	cupboard
ch, (chin, champ)	c	cello
	tch	match, itch
	ti	question
	tu *	future, legislature
d, (dad, didn't)	dd *	middle, addition
	ed *	sailed, died
f, (five, after)	ff *	cliff, different, buff
	gh	tough, enough, cough
	lf	half
	ph *	graph, phony, pharmacy
g, (gas, gone)	gg *	baggage, bigger, egg
	gh	ghetto, ghost
	gu	guess, guest
	gue	monologue, rogue
h, (high, hum)	wh	whole, who
	j or g	(some Spanish words: gila monster, Jose)
j, (jewel, join)	du	graduate, education
	dg *	ridge, ledger, smudge
	di	soldier
	dj	adjust, adjacent
	g *	gym, register
	ge *	vengeful, aging, sage
	gg	exaggerate
k, (cake, kill)	c *	captain, cook, cart
	cc	accomplish
	ch *	chemical, schedule
	che	ache
	ck *	track, chicken, lock
	cqu	lacquer
	cu	circuit
	lk	walk
	que *	plaque, antique
kw, (quit, quote)	ch	choir

3

kw – continued	cqu	acquired
l, (lose, lilly)	ll *	wall, tally, pill, ally
m, (mad, mom)	mb	climb, lamb
	mm *	common, ammunition
	mn	hymn, damn
n, (nine, no)	gn	feign, gnaw, foreign
	kn *	knight, know, knit
	mn	mnemonic
	nn *	inner, announce, funny
	pn	pneumatic
ng, (ring, fang)	n *	ink, uncle, ankle, thank
	ngue	tongue
p, (pipe, pad)	pp *	happen, nippy, apparent
r, (risk, roar)	rh	rhyme, rheumatism
	rr *	worry, irrational, array
	wr *	wrench, wrong, write
s, (sigh, send)	c *	city, cell, cylinder
	ce *	race, mice, deface
	ps	psychology, pseudonym
	sc	scent, fluorescent
	ss *	miss, essence, glass
	st	fasten
sh, (ship, slush)	ce	ocean
	ch *	champagne, cache, chandelier
	ci *	ancient, facial, vicious
	s	sugary
	sc	conscious
	si	pension, mansion
	ss	issue, mission
	ti *	vacation, patient, facetious
t, (test, tin)	bt	subtle, debt
	ed *	mapped, whipped
	ght *	might, bought, bright
	pt	pterodactyl
	tt *	better, attitude, mitt
	tw	two
v, (vest, live)	f	of
w, (we, away)	o	one
	wh	whistle, why
y, (yam, yell)	i	onion
	j	hallelujah
z, (zip, zoo)	cz	czar
	s *	his, as, frisbee
	se	wise, tease,
	ss	dessert
	x	Xerox
	zz	buzz
zh	ge	garage
	s *	measure, fusion, vision
	z	azure

COMPACT
C
Classics™

LIBRARY # 9: Expanding Knowledge

Section A: Sports Shorts – "How the Games Are Played"

9-A1   **Facts of Football**
9-A2   **Beginning Basketball**
9-A3   **Baseball Basics**
9-A4   **Soccer Summary**
9-A5   **Ice Hockey Wrap-Up**

Section B: Trivia to Learn By

9-B1   **Geography**
9-B2   **History**
9-B3   **Science**
9-B4   **Literature**
9-B5   **Art and Architecture**
9-B6   **Music**

Section C: Trivia to Learn By

9-C1   **People Facts**
9-C2   **Quotes**
9-C3   **Sports**
9-C4   **Words and Phrases**
9-C5   **Miscellaneous Facts**

FACTS OF FOOTBALL

THE GAME

Football is an exciting and rugged sport. Millions gather each year to cheer for their favorite teams in organized contests between little league, high school, college, and professional squads.

Football players wear spiked *cleats*, padding such as *thigh, hip,* and *shoulder pads,* and *helmets* with *face masks (bars)* to protect their heads and faces. In American football, eleven players from each team are on the field at any one time, but most teams have many more players waiting on the side lines. Each team tries to score points, mainly by using *plays* (maneuvers) to move the oval-shaped ball across the opposing team's goal line (a touchdown). *Possession* of the ball shifts back and forth, with each team's offensive unit trying to score and the other team's defensive unit trying to stop their progress and make them give up the ball.

We will concentrate here on the professional rules of the *National Football League (NFL)*. College and high school rules may vary slightly.

A game is played over a 60-minute period divided into four 15-minute quarters. The game clock stops for times out, for "incomplete" passes, after scores, and whenever a ball carrier goes out of bounds. Thus, the actual game may last three to four hours.

THE FIELD

Football is played on grass or on a synthetic turf surface. The field is 120 yards long – 100 yards for play, with two ten-yard-long *end zones* at each end. Often called a "gridiron," it is marked with white chalk lines. *Sidelines* border the long sides of the field. Any player who touches or steps on or over a sideline is ruled *out of bounds*. Near each end of the field is a *goal line*, which a ball carrier must cross to enter the end zone and score a touchdown. *Yard lines* cross the field at five-yard intervals and are numbered every ten yards; the fifty-yard line is exactly halfway between the goal lines, at *mid-field*. Two rows of short lines, called *hash marks*, run down the center of the field. All plays begin between the hash marks. Even if a play ends out of bounds – or between one row of hash marks and a sideline – the ball is brought back to the nearest hash mark for the next play. Two *goal posts* with a connecting horizontal crossbar stand at the back of each end zone.

THE PARTICIPANTS

Before each play, both the offensive and defensive teams *huddle* to decide their strategies. Then they line up facing each other on opposite sides of the ball. The *line of scrimmage,* (actually, two imaginary lines running along both ends of the ball), and a

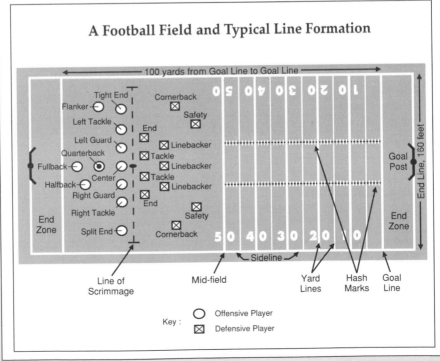

A Football Field and Typical Line Formation

100 yards from Goal Line to Goal Line

Tight End
Flanker
Left Tackle
Left Guard
Quarterback
Fullback
Center
Halfback
Right Guard
Right Tackle
Split End
End Zone

Cornerback
Safety
End
Linebacker
Tackle
Linebacker
Tackle
Linebacker
End
Safety
Cornerback

End Line, 150 feet

Goal Post

Goal Post

End Zone

Line of Scrimmage

Mid-field

Sideline

Yard Lines

Hash Marks

Goal Line

Key : ◯ Offensive Player
       ⊠ Defensive Player

neutral zone (the length of the ball) separate them. At the end of each play, a new line of scrimmage is established, crossing the field at the point of the ball's new position on the field.

Coaches assign team members to particular positions on the field based on their skills, size, strength, speed, quickness, and agility.

The Offense

A typical offense is made up of seven **linemen** and four **backs**. The linemen are normally divided into a group of five *interior linemen* and flanked by two *ends*. The interior line includes a *center*, (who *snaps* – hands or tosses – the ball through his legs to the quarterback to begin each play), two *guards*, and two *tackles*. The linemen *block* for the passer or ball carrier. Depending on what formation is used, the ends – one usually acting as a *tight end*, who lines up on the line of scrimmage near one of the tackles, and the other as a *split end*, or *wide receiver*, who lines up nearer a sideline – can either block or run designed *patterns* (routes) into defensive territory, trying to get into an open area where they can more easily catch a pass. The backfield includes the *quarterback*, two *halfbacks* (one is termed a *flanker* if he lines up near the outside of the line) and a *fullback* (often called the *blocking* back).

The quarterback, after receiving the snap from the center, may hand off or pitch the ball backward to a halfback or fullback, run the football himself, or pass it forward – from behind the line of scrimmage – to a wide receiver, a tight end, or one of the backs. The other offensive team members then serve as blockers for the teammate with the ball.

The Defense

On the defensive side of the ball, three units attempt to stop the offensive team's progress. These are the **line**, the **linebackers**, and the **secondary**. Two *tackles* and two *ends* (and sometimes a *nose tackle* who lines up in front of the center) make up the defensive line who try to use their size, speed, and strength to *rush* the passer or ball carrier.

The linebacking unit is composed of a *middle linebacker* and two *outside linebackers*, who position themselves behind the line. They combine their speed and power to rush the passer (this extra pressure is termed a *blitz*), or else move back or sideways to tackle ball carriers or knock down or "intercept" passes.

The defensive secondary (or *defensive backs*) includes two *cornerbacks*, who defend against shorter passes, and two *safeties*, who cover longer passes. Secondary players must be fast in order cover speedy receivers and sure tacklers to deal with ball carriers who break through the defensive line and the linebackers. Additional "deep" safeties may be used in a *prevent defense,* designed in anticipation of a long pass.

A defensive unit may favor either *man-to-man coverage* (where each defensive back is assigned to cover a particular player) or a *zone defense* (where each player is responsible for a certain area).

The *head coach* and his assistants prepare a *game plan* for each game, listing the offensive plays and defensive formations they believe will be effective against their opponent. They also run practices, see to players' physical conditioning, cultivate teamwork within the different units, and scout opposing teams.

Various officials oversee the game and enforce the rules. The *referee* has general charge of the contest, and other *linesmen* and *judges* are positioned on the field to ensure fair play. A *replay official* examines televised replays to determine whether certain calls made by officials are correct. (In college, no call can be *overturned* and there are no replay officials.) Three people move *yard markers* up and down the field: one marker marks the line of scrimmage; two others, attached by a ten-yard-long chain, help the officials measure to see if "first downs" are made.

SCORING

A team can score in one of four ways:

*   A *touchdown* - A player running or catching a ball across an opponent's goal line scores six points. A touchdown may be scored by the offensive unit running its plays and moving the ball over the goal line. The defensive player at times may also score for his team by recovering a *fumble* (dropped ball), *intercepting* a pass meant for a receiver, or picking up a blocked kick and running it over the offensive team's goal line.

*   A *conversion (extra point attempt)* - Following a touchdown, the team can score *one extra point* by *place-kicking* the ball through the goal posts. The center snaps the ball from the 3-yard line to a *place-holder*, who balances it, point down, on the ground. The kicker then tries to boot it over the crossbar and through the uprights. (In college and high school, a team can score a two-point conversion by running or passing the ball into the end zone.)

*   A *field goal* - Place-kicking the ball through the opposing team's goal post

scores *three points* for the kicking team.

- A *safety* - When a defensive player tackles a ball carrier in his own end zone or blocks a punt out of the offensive end zone, he scores *two points* for his team. The defensive team also earns possession of the ball on the ensuing kickoff.

PLAYING THE GAME

A coin-toss determines which team will *kick off* and which will receive the kickoff. A *special-teams* (or *kicking*) *unit*, comprised of a kicker and tacklers, undertakes to drive the ball from its own 35-yard line deep into opposition territory so that the receiving special-teams unit can not advance the ball too far up the field. The player receiving the kickoff lines up near his own goal line and runs the ball back while teammates block opposing players who try to *tackle* him. A tackle is made when the ball carrier goes out of bounds or when any part of his body (except feet or hands) touches the ground. At times (specifically when the team kicking off needs to get the ball back late in a game in order to score) a kicker will boot the ball only a short distance; this is an *onside kick.* Once the ball travels ten yards or more, it is a *free ball,* and may be recovered by a member of either team. If the ball goes out of bounds on a kickoff, it is a penalty; the offensive team can either take the ball at that spot, or require that it be re-kicked from five yards further back. If the ball goes out of the end zone, or is *downed* in the end zone (the receiver catches the ball and touches his knee down in the end zone), it is a *touchback,* and the ball is put in play from the twenty-yard line.

The respective offensive and defensive units then come on the field. After they line up, the quarterback steps behind the center and calls out *signals* to tell his team when the ball will be snapped. When he receives the ball, he can run, hand off or pitch to a back, or pass to a receiver. If a ball carrier fumbles the ball, it becomes a free ball, and any player – offensive or defensive – can recover it and run until tackled. A fumbled ball that is knocked out of bounds goes to the last team having possession. If the quarterback throws a forward pass and a defender intercepts it, the defender may also advance the ball until he is tackled. After a ball carrier is tackled, play stops and the teams line up again to run another play. A forward pass that hits the ground is *incomplete,* and the ball is returned to the original line of scrimmage for the next offensive try.

The offense has four tries, called *downs,* to advance the ball *at least ten yards* beyond the initial line of scrimmage. When the team is successful, they earn four more downs to try to gain ten more yards. By consistently achieving *first downs* the team gains yardage, moving the ball down field. For example, the first play of a series of downs is called *first and ten.* (It is the first down and the team has ten yards to go in order to reach another first down.) If the team loses 3 yards on the first play, the situation becomes *second down* and 13 yards to go (second and 13). On second down, if the team moves the ball 8 yards, the situation becomes third and 5. If on *third down* the team moves the ball five or more yards, it gets a new set of four downs (again, first and ten).

If a team fails to make a new first down after four downs, the other team takes possession of the ball at its current position on the field. On *fourth down* a team often chooses to *punt* the ball. A *punter* comes into the game and stands some ten yards behind the line of scrimmage. When the center snaps him the ball, he tries to kick it high and deep to the opposite side of the field before the defensive team can rush and block his kick. A *punt returner* can catch the punt and run the ball back the other way. He may choose to let the ball drop without catching it, allowing the kicking team to *down* (touch) it where it comes to rest; or he can wave his hand to call a *fair catch,* which tells the defensive players that he will not run with the ball upon catching it. If the punt-return man drops the ball, any player on the field can recover it for his own team.

A team will usually select to punt on fourth down rather than try for a first down: (1) When the ball is too close to the offensive team's goal line (If the team should fail in its attempt to gain first down yardage, it would give the opponents the ball in *good field position* and give them an easier chance to score – see Other Terms; (2) when the offense is too far away from the opponent's goal post to try for a field goal; or (3) when the offensive team wants to "pin" the opposition far back in their own side of the field, giving them *"bad" field position.*

On any down (and particularly on fourth down), if the ball is close enough to the opposing end zone, a coach may elect to try a field goal. If the attempt is made (scoring three points) the scoring team then kicks off to the other team; if it is missed, the opposing team takes possession at the line of scrimmage (or else the ball is moved up to the twenty yard line if the line of scrimmage was inside of that area). If a defensive player breaks through the kicking team's offensive line and blocks a field goal attempt (or a punt), either team may recover the free ball and advance it until a tackle is made. A team may *fake* a punt or field goal and run or pass instead to try to reach first down yardage and keep the ball. Of course, if the attempt fails on fourth down, the defensive team takes possession of the ball at that point.

RULES VIOLATIONS

A *penalty* may be assessed when a player breaks the rules. This usually results in the offending team losing yardage or forfeiting a down (sometimes both). An official throws a yellow cloth *flag* into the air to signal a violation. The captain of the fouled team can normally elect whether to *accept* the penalty or *refuse* it and accept the completed play, if it is to his team's advantage.

The most common violations include:

- *Clipping* - Blocking or pushing a defensive player from behind (15-yard loss).

- *Holding (illegal use of hands)* - Grabbing an opposing player while blocking (a 10-yard loss for offensive holding; 5, for defensive holding).

- *Offside* - When a player crosses the line of scrimmage into the neutral zone before the ball is snapped (5-yard penalty). If no contact is made, a player who jumps back on his own side of the ball before it's snapped, is not offside.

- *Illegal procedure* - When the offense moves before the ball is snapped, or when a team has more than eleven players on the field (5-yard penalty).

- *Interference* - When a pass receiver (or a defender) is shoved or tackled while the ball is in the air. (The ball is moved to the point of infraction when a defensive player interferes; a 15-yard loss is assessed for offensive interference.)

- *Delay of game* - When the 25-second clock expires before the ball is snapped (5-yard loss).

- *Roughing* - When the quarterback, punter, or place kicker is hit after passing or kicking the ball (15-yard penalty and an automatic first down). If a rusher blocks or tips the ball and then hits the quarterback or kicker, it is not considered roughing.

- *Grounding* - When the quarterback intentionally throws the ball to the ground to avoid being sacked (tackled behind the line of scrimmage).

- *Unnecessary roughness* or *unsportsmanlike behavior* - (15-yard penalty).

- *Grabbing the face mask* - (15-yard penalty for a flagrant, dangerous foul; a 5-yard penalty otherwise.)

OTHER TERMS

Draw - A play in which the quarterback steps back as if he is going to pass, but instead hands off to a running back.

Field position - Refers to where the ball is on the field. (If it is out near mid-field or close to your opponent's goal line, you have good field position; if the ball is near your own goal line, you have bad field position.)

Option play - A play where the quarterback runs along the line of scrimmage to give him time to choose whether to keep the ball, toss it back to a running back, or throw a forward pass.

Pocket - Refers to the protected area (supplied by his blockers) that a quarterback stands in as he tries to pass to a teammate.

Reverse - A running play that appears to be going to one side of the field in order to fool the defense. The ball is then handed off to a wide receiver coming from the opposite direction, who streaks the other way.

Roll-out - When the passer retreats and runs sideways behind the line of scrimmage to avoid tacklers and provide more time to find an open down-field receiver.

Rush - Refers either to the defensive line's attack of the quarterback or to the ball-carrying by a fullback or halfback.

Sack - To tackle the quarterback behind the line of scrimmage before he can pass the ball.

Screen pass - A short pass where the offensive blockers let the defensive linemen through the line to rush the quarterback, and then form a wall of blockers to block for the halfback or fullback receiving the ball.

Shotgun - When the quarterback lines up four or five yards behind the center to receive the snap. This passing formation allows him more time to "see" receivers down-field.

Sweep - A running play around either end of the offensive line.

Trap - A running play in which an offensive blocker allows a defender to move into the backfield, then blocks him from the side, creating a hole through which a running back can carry the ball.

BEGINNING BASKETBALL

THE GAME

The object in basketball is to score more points than the opposing team before a set time expires. The *offensive team* (the team with the ball) scores points by advancing the inflated leather or rubber ball as near as possible to their own goal, and shooting it through a basket-like metal hoop. These same players then become *defensive* players, to try to stop the opposing team from scoring at their end of the court.

Basketball can be enjoyed in the backyard or on the playground, and is played on an organized basis by high school, college, and professional men's and women's teams. The *National Basketball Association (NBA)* is the premier men's pro league. (All rules discussed here, unless otherwise stated, will follow the official NBA format.)

To play or practice basketball, only a ball, a basket, and a level surface are needed. In an organized game, two teams, each composed of five players, are on the court at one time. A coach may substitute players during the competition when play is stopped.

THE COURT

Most courts feature a level wooden floor with painted lines demarcating an area 94 feet long by 50 feet wide.

Sidelines and *end lines* mark court boundaries, and a *half-court (division) line* separates the court into two halves. A *free-throw line* 19 feet from each end line is inside of a *free-throw circle*. A *free-throw lane* is set off by two lines, 16 feet apart, extending from the free-throw line down to each end line. There are two circles in the middle of the court: the *restraining circle* (with a 16-foot diameter) and the inner *center circle* (with a 4-foot diameter).

A circular *hoop*, 18 inches in diameter, is set at a height of ten feet, and attached to a glass backboard that hangs out four feet inside each end line at the center of the free-throw lane. Attached

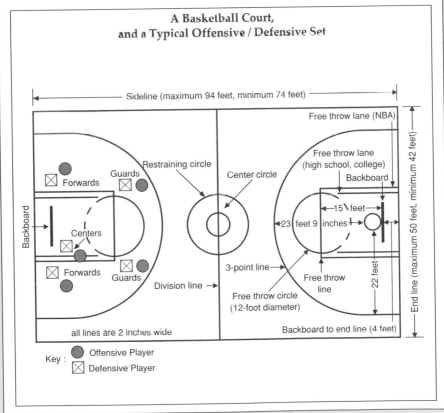

**A Basketball Court,
and a Typical Offensive / Defensive Set**

Sideline (maximum 94 feet, minimum 74 feet)

Free throw lane (NBA)

Free throw lane (high school, college)

Backboard

Restraining circle

Center circle

Guards

Forwards

Backboard

Centers

Forwards

Guards

15 feet

23 feet 9 inches

3-point line

Division line

Free throw circle (12-foot diameter)

Free throw line

22 feet

End line (maximum 50 feet, minimum 42 feet)

all lines are 2 inches wide

Backboard to end line (4 feet)

Key :   ● Offensive Player
        ☒ Defensive Player

to the hoop is a white twine net, open at the bottom, to slow the ball as it passes through the *"basket."*

THE PARTICIPANTS

Teams are made up of five players who work on both offense and defense. Though players may move anywhere on the court, most teams designate certain players to perform in specific "positions," according to their height, strength, quickness and special skills.

Two **guards** – a *point guard* and a *shooting,* or *"off" guard* – are generally shorter, quicker players who handle the ball further from the basket. They attempt to work the ball inside (by dribbling or passing) to the bigger players for shorter shots, penetrate to the basket past the defense where they can shoot or pass off, or, sometimes, they themselves shoot from outside.

The **forwards** – the *power forward* and the *small forward* – are generally taller than the guards. They usually play on each side of, and closer to, the basket.

A **center** normally plays nearest the basket and is often the strongest and tallest player. He tries to position himself to receive passes where he can "muscle up" inside shots. Along with the forwards, a center also wants to be in position to rebound (jump and grab) missed shots.

For all players, jumping, dribbling (bouncing the ball) with either hand, passing, catching, shooting, agile footwork, quickness, intelligence and court savvy, are important skills to develop.

Also on the court are two (sometimes three) officials called *referees.* A referee blows a whistle to stop play, signals if a violation of rules or a foul is committed, and then enforces the prescribed penalty. Other scorers and time-keepers assist.

SCORING

Teams score points either by making a *field goal* or a *free-throw (foul shot).* A player scores a *two-point field goal* by shooting the ball through the basket from anywhere on the court, except from beyond an arc lying 22 feet to 23 feet 9 inches from the basket (20 feet in college). A successful shot from outside this arc counts as a *3-point field goal* (some-

times called a "home run").

A successful free-throw counts one point. When a player is fouled, he may receive two free-throws from behind the free-throw line.

PLAYING THE GAME

The contest begins with the opposing centers standing inside the restraining circle, and the other players stationed outside the circle. The referee tosses the ball into the air, and each center jumps and tries to tap it to a teammate. This is called the *center jump,* or *jump ball.*

When one team gains possession of the ball, its players move toward their basket and try to score. A player can advance the ball either by *dribbling* it with one hand, passing it to a teammate, or shooting it at the basket. If a player stops dribbling, one foot (the *pivot foot*) must stay on the floor. As he holds the ball, looking to pass or shoot, he can swing the other foot right or left, but may not drag his pivot foot as he rotates; moving his pivot foot would result in a "traveling" violation.

When a shot is missed, both teams try to *rebound* the ball as it bounces off the backboard or the rim of the basket. After a team scores, an opposing player takes the ball out behind the end line. He then has five seconds to *inbound* the ball to a teammate, and his team has ten more seconds to move the ball across the center line to score at their own basket. If a *foul* is called (if someone is hit or bumped; see **Fouls**), the ball is either taken out of bounds by the fouled team, or the players line up outside of the free-throw lane in alternate order (with two defensive players closest to the basket) to rebound the ball in case the ensuing foul shot is missed.

Professional games have four 12-minute quarters, with violations, fouls, a half-time, and called time-outs interrupting play. If the score is tied after regulation time has expired, the teams play as many 5-minute *overtime* periods as are needed to determine a winner.

TEAMWORK

Teamwork is the combining of individual skills so that the team works as a successful unit. Coaches design sophisticated *offensive systems* with the aim of creating good, high-percentage shots for their teams. These systems can be grouped under two basic styles:

(1) *Fast-break system* - A style where the offensive team hurries the ball up the floor, in hopes of getting an easy shot before the defense can "set up" to stop them.

(2) *Set (pattern) offense* - A slower, more deliberate system where players work to elude the defenders for a chance at an open shot. Preplanned *plays* (maneuvers) are frequently called by a designated player using hand signals. These plays determine where the players will move, where the ball should be passed or dribbled, etc. A *pick* is a tactic in which an offensive player remains in place to shield a teammate from defenders thus freeing him to shoot, to drive for the basket or to receive a pass. A *screen* consists of a group formation that works the same way as a pick.

Defensive systems are basically of three types:

(1) *Man-to-man defense* - Each defender is assigned a specified opponent, trying to stay between him and the basket anywhere on the court. This defense requires sharp communication between players; a defensive teammate must be ready to "switch" to another player's assigned man, for instance, if a pick is applied.

(2) *Zone defense* - Each defender is responsible for a certain area on the court, and shifts to guard any player who enters his zone. Though it is used extensively in college ball, the zone defense is illegal in professional basketball, generating a more wide-open, fast-paced game. After one warning, each time a team is called for an "illegal" (zone) defense, the opposition is awarded one free-throw.

(3) *Combination defenses* - These use various elements of both man-to-man and zone defenses to interfere with the opposing team's offense. Often, "mixed" systems involve a type of *trapping* defense, where two players *double-team* (they both guard) the

ballhandler, and their teammates switch into a kind of zone formation to intercept passes.

A defensive player guarding a ballhandler wants to stay close to him to keep him from taking an uncontested shot or from passing or dribbling too near the basket. Meanwhile, the offensive player wants to *fake* the defender up in the air or to one side so he can more easily shoot, dribble, or pass to a teammate.

FOULS

Both offensive and defensive players may commit *fouls* by holding, pushing, or charging into another player, or by hitting the arm or body of a player in the act of shooting. These are whistled and then announced ("called") by the referee. A *loose ball foul* is a personal foul called when neither team has possession of the ball. When a *personal* or *common* foul (one not committed in the act of shooting or committed unintentionally) is called and there are fewer than 5 *team fouls* in the quarter (accumulated personal fouls of a team) the other team merely takes possession of the ball. However, if the offending team has accumulated more than five fouls in the quarter (seven fouls in a half for college ball), it is in the *penalty situation*, and each time its players commit a foul, the fouled player is awarded two free-throws. (In college, he is given "one-and-one" – that is, if he makes the first free throw, a second shot is awarded.) *Shooting fouls* (fouls committed against a player who is in the act of shooting the ball) and *flagrant fouls* always result in two free throws awarded to the player; and, for grossly intentional or flagrant fouls (those that endanger another player's safety) the referee may eject the player from the game. Free-throws are not shot if an offensive foul is called; the team simply loses possession of the ball.

A *technical foul* may be called for unsportsmanlike conduct by a player or coach. In the NBA, a "technical" specifies that a free throw is given a member of the other team, while the team with possession retains the ball. In college games, a team loses the ball and gives up a free-throw to the other team, unless the technical foul is called on a coach. In this case two foul shots are awarded to the opposition, plus possession of the ball.

A player *fouls out* (is disqualified) from a game after committing six fouls (five, for college players).

BALLHANDLING VIOLATIONS

A team commits a *turnover* when it loses possession of the ball without being able to take a shot. Ball possession is lost for any of the following infractions.

• *Traveling:* A player who is holding the ball taking more than two steps or moving his pivot foot without dribbling the ball.

• *Losing the ball out of bounds:* Being the last to touch the ball before it goes out of bounds.

• *Double dribble:* Dribbling with both hands at the same time, or stopping the dribble and then starting again.

• *A called 5 seconds:* Taking more than five seconds to inbound the ball from out of bounds. In college ball, a five-second call may be made against a player who is holding or dribbling the ball while being closely guarded (within 5 feet) for more than 5 seconds.

• *The ten-second rule:* When the offensive team cannot advance the ball beyond half-court before a ten second count.

• *The three-second rule:* When an offensive player stands in the free-throw lane for more than three seconds at a time. (This rule prevents a tall, strong player from simply "camping" under the basket to receive a pass for an easy shot.)

• *Shot-clock violation:* When the offensive team is unable to shoot the ball – hitting the rim or backboard – within a 24-second period from time of possession (45 seconds in college).

• *Charging:* An offensive foul where a player crashes into a stationary defensive player.

• *Kicking the ball:* If an offensive player kicks the ball, he commits a turnover. When a defender kicks the ball, the offensive team retains possession and the shot-clock is re-set.

OTHER TERMS AND INFORMATION

Air ball - A shot that fails to hit the basket.

Assist - A pass to a teammate who then scores a basket.

Block - When a defender stops a player's shot without fouling him.

Boxing out - Positioning the body so as to come between the basket and an opponent to prevent him from rebounding a missed shot.

Dunk - A basket scored when a player jumps with the ball, reaches above the rim, and slams it through the hoop.

Goal-tending, or *basket interference* - When a defensive or offensive player touches either the ball or the basket while the ball is on its way down into the basket. For defensive interference, the basket counts; for offensive interference, the field goal is not scored.

Hand check - When the defensive player puts his hand on the ballhandler to keep him from moving toward him. (This is illegal for college players.)

Jump ball (held ball) - Called when two opposing players have a hold on the ball at the same time. In the NBA, an actual jump ball is enacted between the two players holding the ball inside the nearest free-throw circle. College teams take turns, alternately gaining possession of the ball after each held ball situation.

Jump shot - The most used and useful shot in basketball. Performed by jumping and releasing the ball from over the head, it often prevents the defending player from blocking the attempt.

Lay-up - An easy shot taken when the offensive player is able to escape defenders under the basket.

Pass - To accurately throw or bounce the ball to a teammate. Varieties of passes include the chest pass, bounce pass, lob pass, baseball pass and touch pass.

Press - When defensive players closely guard the offensive team in backcourt (a full-court press) or at mid-court (a half-court press) to steal the ball or cause turnovers. (Frequently used when the defensive team is behind late in a game.)

Tip-in - A basket made by an offensive player leaping for a missed shot and tipping it into the hoop.

BASEBALL BASICS

THE GAME

Baseball is the "national pastime" of the United States and is also immensely popular throughout Latin America and the Orient. The sport is played on many levels, from peewee teams on up to the professional leagues. In the *Major Leagues* of the U.S. (*American* and *National*), two teams consisting of nine players each (plus substitute players) compete against one another. The teams take turns "at bat" (on offense) and playing "in the field" (on defense). A pitcher on the defensive squad throws a ball to a catcher while a batter on the other team tries to hit the ball with a bat and drive it out of the reach of defensive players, thus advancing himself and his teammates around four bases. A player who touches all the bases scores a *run* for his team; and the team with the most runs after nine *innings* wins.

THE FIELD

A baseball field is bounded by two chalked-in *foul lines* that extend from *home plate* at a 90 degree angle to each other. These lines separate the field into two sections: *fair territory* (the area between and on the lines where the ball must be hit to remain "in play"), and *foul territory* (the area outside the lines).

Fair territory encompasses two sections: the *infield* and the *outfield*. The infield is made up of four bases, each marking one corner of a "diamond" plotted counterclockwise from *first* to *second* to *third* and finally to "home plate." The *pitcher's mound* is in the center of the diamond, a *catcher's box* behind home plate, and a *batter's box* on each side of the plate. *Home plate* is a 17-inch-wide slab of hard rubber sunk into the ground so as to be level with the dirt. First, second and third bases are filled canvas bags attached to the ground. In the middle of the slightly raised pitcher's mound is the *pitcher's plate* (or *rubber*), a rectangular slab from which the pitcher throws the ball.

The outfield lies between the infield and the fences farthest from home plate. Field dimensions differ, with most outfield fences or walls erected at least 325 feet from home plate as sighted down the first and third base lines (foul lines), and at least 400 feet from home plate to the fence in center field.

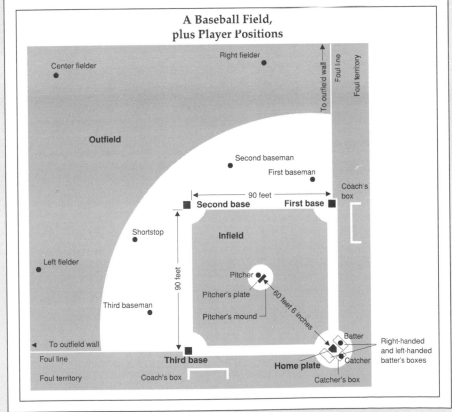

A Baseball Field, plus Player Positions

Center fielder

Right fielder

To outfield wall

Foul line

Foul territory

Outfield

Second baseman

First baseman

Coach's box

90 feet

Second base

First base

Shortstop

Infield

90 feet

Left fielder

Pitcher

Pitcher's plate

60 feet 6 inches

Third baseman

Pitcher's mound

Batter

Right-handed and left-handed batter's boxes

To outfield wall

Third base

Home plate

Catcher

Foul line

Foul territory

Coach's box

Catcher's box

Foul ground may be a sizable area in some parks and quite limited in others. It includes the area behind home plate and any territory outside of the first and third base lines. In foul territory (near first and third bases) are two *coach's boxes*, where a coach may stand to tell runners or batters what to do in a given situation; and two *dugouts*, where managers and players not required on the field may sit during the game.

Also in foul territory are two *on-deck circles*, located near each team's dugout. There, the next batter may warm up (practice) before he bats. A bull pen is provided for each team's *pitching staff* to warm up before and during the game. Bull pens may be located either beyond the outfield fences or out of bounds near the foul lines.

THE PARTICIPANTS

The defending team's *manager* (or an assistant) positions his players depending on where he thinks a particular batter will hit the ball. The *pitcher*, on the mound, and the *catcher*, crouching behind home plate, form the defensive team's *battery*. Using flashing signals, the catcher communicates with the pitcher to decide what kind of pitches to throw (see **The Art of Pitching**). Other *infielders* try to catch balls hit short distances. The *first baseman* and the *second baseman* play between first and second base; while the *third baseman* and the *shortstop* position themselves in the gap between second and third base.

Three *outfielders* – a *left fielder*, a *center fielder*, and a *right fielder* – try to catch or retrieve balls hit past or over the heads of the infielders.

When three outs are declared against the offensive team, all fielders come in to take their turn at bat, while the other team takes the field.

In the American League, a tenth player, the *designated hitter*, does not play the field, but specializes in batting (usually in place of the pitcher, often the weakest batter). In the National League, the pitcher must hit in his turn as long as he is in the game.

Coaches may substitute players at any time, but once a player leaves a game, he may not return.

Four *umpires*, one on each base, officiate the game. They decide whether players are "out" or "safe" and whether a ball struck by a batter is "fair" or "foul." The *home plate umpire* has an additional and all-important responsibility: Every time a pitch is thrown, he must determine whether it's a "strike" or a "ball" (see **Playing the Game**).

EQUIPMENT

Equipment is designed for ease in competing and for protection. *Mitts*, or *gloves*, used to catch the ball, can be no more than twelve inches long. A first baseman's glove is generally larger than a fielder's glove in order to scoop up balls thrown to one side of him or into the dirt. A catcher's glove often has a deep pocket and extra padding.

Bats are made of wood (in college, metal bats are used), and may be no more than 42 inches long. The ball is cork-centered and covered by two strips of white cowhide stitched with red thread. Metal or rubber *spikes (cleats)* are worn on the feet, and a cap with a visor on the head. A shirt and "knickerbocker" pants that extend to just below the knees, round out the uniform.

Batters are required to wear *helmets* to protect them if they get hit by the ball when up to bat or while running the bases.

The catcher requires the most protection. He wears, at the minimum, a catcher's *mask*, a *chest protector*, and *shin guards*.

BASEBALL SKILLS
The Art of Pitching

Pitchers work to master a variety of pitches in order to fool the different batters they face. A *fast ball* may travel close to 100 miles per hour. *Breaking balls* (the *curve* ball and the *screwball*) curl to the left or the right depending on how the ball is spinning. A *slider* resembles a curve ball at first, but suddenly seems to "slide" past the batter rather than curve. A *sinker* drops sharply as it approaches the batter; and a *knuckleball*, which does not spin, may break in any direction.

The Art of Hitting

Batters undertake to swing only at "good" pitches (see **Playing the Game**). To execute a solid hit, a player brings the bat around from behind his back shoulder, and, while shifting his weight forward, makes a smooth, level swing. As he swings, he keeps his head down and his eyes on the ball, and then follows through completely. *Power hitters* drive the ball with a full swing, sometimes hitting *home runs* (balls hit over the fence in fair territory) or *line drives* (hard hits that go on a line through the air). *Place hitters* may "cut down" on their swings to try to skillfully poke the ball between fielders. A batter may square around to face the pitcher and let the ball hit his bat, "bunting" the ball into fair territory, then race to first base. This is called *laying down a bunt*.

Fielding

Fielders must chase after a ball when

it's hit. If they catch the "fly ball" before it hits the ground, an out is called against their opponents. If they stop a "ground ball," they may be able to throw it to a teammate to try for an out or to stop base runners from advancing to the next base.

Base Running

Skillful base runners may *steal* a base (run to the next base before a defensive player with the ball can tag (touch) them, or they can try to *take an extra base* on a batted ball if they judge that they can reach the base without being tagged.

PLAYING THE GAME

Before the game, each manager gives his *starting lineup* and *batting order* to the head umpire to tell him which players will start on defense and the order in which the players will bat.

The "home" team takes the field first. The "visiting" players take turns at bat until they make three outs. Every time a batter safely advances around the bases to home plate, the team is awarded a run. When three outs are made by the team, the home team comes to bat while the visiting team positions itself in the field. If the game is tied after nine innings, the teams play *extra innings* until one team breaks the tie and wins.

Strikes, Balls, and Outs

An *out* (or *put out*) is made when a batter either **strikes out, grounds out**, or **flies out:**

A *strike-out* occurs when three *strikes* are called against a batter. A strike may be a *swinging strike* (where he swings and misses the ball), a *foul strike* (where he hits the ball onto foul ground), a *foul tip* (where he tips the ball back into the catcher's glove), or a *called strike*. A pitch which the batter *takes* (that is, doesn't swing at) will be called a strike by the umpire if he decides that the ball passed over home plate and between the batter's knees and armpits – the *strike zone*. A pitch thrown outside the strike zone and "taken" by the batter is a *ball*. When a batter has two strikes against him, a foul ball does not count as a strike, unless he tries to bunt the ball; then the foul counts as the third strike, and the batter is out.

A *ground out* is called when a player hits a fair ball that touches ground in the infield and an infielder throws or runs the ball to first base before the batter can reach the base.

A *fly out* results whenever a ball – fair or foul – is caught in the air before touching the ground.

A base runner may also either be *tagged out* or *forced out.*

In a tag out, a runner who is off base is touched by a defensive player who has the ball.

A force out may occur when a base runner is forced to run to the next base. He must advance while between bases if a runner behind him is entitled to the base he is on. For example, runners on first and second bases must both advance to the succeeding base on a ground ball. But if a defender with the ball touches either base first, the runner heading for that base is forced out.

More About Base Running

Runners may not advance to a base on a fly out unless they first touch the base they are on *(tag up)* after the ball is caught. If a base runner fails to tag up, and a fielder throws the caught ball to the base he was on, the runner is out.

A runner sometimes *runs with the pitch;* that is, he runs as soon as the pitcher throws the ball. If the ball is not hit, he can *steal* the base by touching it before he is tagged. He is *caught stealing* if he is tagged out before getting to the base. If the pitch is fouled off (it is struck and then hits the ground in foul territory) the base runner must return to his original base.

A *hit-and-run play* is usually intended to move a runner from first to third base. The first-base runner runs with the pitch, which forces either the second baseman or the shortstop to *cover* second base trying to tag the runner out. This creates a "hole" in the defense. The batter then hits the ball into the gap, and, with a good head start, the base runner should be able to reach third base. However, if the base runner is hit by a batted ball while he is off base in fair ground, he is called out.

Walks, Hits, Runs, Plays, and Errors

To score a run, a batter must move, base-by-base, to home plate. A player can get safely on base in three ways without ever hitting the ball:

• A *walk (base on balls)* - When four pitches are thrown outside the strike zone during a player's turn at bat, a batter is walked, or awarded first base. (Other runners forced to advance by the walk are also awarded their bases.)

• *Hit by the pitch* - A batter may also go to first base if a pitch hits him.

• *Catcher interference* - If the catcher touches the bat as a player swings, the batter is awarded first base.

A *hit* is when a batter hits a fair ball

that is not caught in the air, and, running, he is able to touch first base before an opposing player with the ball can reach the base or tag the runner. This is called a *single*, or *base hit*. The batter may overrun first base, turn into foul ground, and return safely without the threat of being tagged out. If, however, he turns toward second base in fair territory, he can be tagged out.

A *double* and a *triple* are hits that allow a batter to safely reach, respectively, second and third bases. If he overruns either of these bases, however, he can be tagged out before he returns to the base.

A *home run* allows the batter to touch all the bases and score a run. (A home run ball is usually hit over the outfield fence.)

A batter may hit a fair ball and reach base without getting credited for a hit. A fielder may commit an **error**, for example, a mistake that permits the batter (and/or other runners) to get on base; or the fielder may make a choice between getting the batter out or a base runner out (a *fielder's choice*). He will usually try to put out the "lead" runner (the one closest to reaching home) rather than throw to first base, often allowing the hitter to reach first base.

If a team is able to force, tag or throw out two players in a single play, it is called a *double play*. A *triple play* is rare but can occur when a fielder catches a line drive and then throws the ball to teammates, who either tag the runners off base or step on the bases before the runners can return to them.

OTHER TERMS

There is a rich lexicon of baseball expressions. Below are some of the most frequently heard terms.

Bad hop - A ground ball making a tricky bounce.

Balk - One of 13 illegal moves that a pitcher can make, such as feigning a throw to first or third while his foot is on the rubber, or starting his delivery to the catcher and then stopping. When a balk is called by an umpire, all base runners move up one base.

Batting Average - The number of hits a player would be estimated to get out of a thousand official at-bats. To calculate, divide a player's number of hits by his official number of times at bat. Any average over .300 (30 hits out of 100 at-bats) is considered excellent.

Called game - A game stopped by the umpires (usually for bad weather). Such an interruption before the fifth inning discounts that game as official, and it is replayed from the start at a later date. For a contest called after five innings, the team ahead in runs is declared the winner.

Checked swing - A half-swing where the bat does not go around past the front of the plate. A checked swing doesn't count as a strike unless the pitch is in the strike zone.

The count - The number of balls and strikes against a batter. The number of balls is always given first; a count of "2 and 1" means there are two balls and one strike.

Cut-off man - A fielder who may take a throw from a teammate and relay the ball to another fielder on base.

Earned-Run Average (ERA) - The average number of runs scored against a pitcher in nine innings pitched. The lower a pitcher's ERA, the better he is doing.

Grand slam - A home run with the bases loaded, scoring four runs.

Infield fly rule - Designed to keep infielders from purposely dropping fly balls in order to get force-outs or double plays. The umpire may call an automatic out when the team at bat has fewer than two outs, with runners on first or second (or bases loaded), and a batter hits a pop-up into the infield.

Lead - The distance that a base runner gets from his base in an attempt to steal or to advance on a hit ball.

Passed ball - A "catchable" pitch that gets by the catcher, allowing runners to advance.

Pick-off - A throw from a pitcher to a baseman, who then tries to tag a runner who is off his base.

Pinch hitter or pinch runner - A substitute for a hitter or base runner.

Runs Batted In (RBI) - The number of runs scored as a result of a player getting hits or "sacrificing" runners home.

Run-down - When a runner is trapped between bases the fielders try to "run him down" and tag him out.

Sacrifice - A player executing a sacrifice bunt allows himself to be put out at first in order to move a teammate up a base into scoring position. A sacrifice fly occurs when a batter slaps a long fly ball, permitting a runner at third base to tag up and score on the caught ball.

Save - Earned when a relief pitcher preserves another pitcher's lead to win the game.

Squeeze play - A play that calls for the batter to bunt the ball so a runner can score from third base.

Wild pitch - Just what it sounds like; a pitch the catcher cannot catch or stop, which allows base runners to advance or to score.

SOCCER SUMMARY

THE GAME

By far the world's most popular sport, soccer (known world-wide as *football* or *association football*) is one of the fastest-growing sports in the United States. Its rapid pace and subtle team maneuvers please millions of players and fans alike. The idea of the game is simple: Two teams each try to kick, bump, or hit the round leather ball into the opposition's goal, and to win the game by scoring the most goals. With the exception of the goalie, team members may not touch the ball with their hands or arms.

The *Federation Internationale de Football Association (FIFA)* governs over 140 countries' national soccer associations around the world, including the *United States Soccer Federation (USSF)*. Two major leagues – the *North American Soccer League (NASL)* and the *Major Indoor Soccer League (MISL)* – are made up of professional teams in the U.S. The numerous junior league, high school and college teams play by the same integral set of rules. Players dream about playing in the *World Cup*, a tournament held every four years, where the best 24 teams in the world compete.

THE FIELD

The large, rectangular, grassy field has a flag placed at each corner to help the officials see when a ball goes "out of bounds." Chalk boundaries on the sides of the field are called *touch lines;* they may be from 100 to 130 yards long and spaced from 50 to 100 yards apart. The lines at each end of the field are called *endlines* (or *goal lines*). A ball passing over – not merely touching – any of these lines, is ruled *out of bounds.*

Goals stand at the middle of each end line. Each goal is made up of two posts and a crossbar with a net attached, forming an opening 24 feet across and 8 feet high. A shot in which the ball passes beyond the goal line through the posts is scored as a "goal" (one point).

A large rectanglar area extending in front of the goal defines the *penalty area.* Defending players are penalized if they commit certain infractions within this area. The *goal area* is a smaller rectangle inside of the penalty area. Players on the attack cannot come into contact

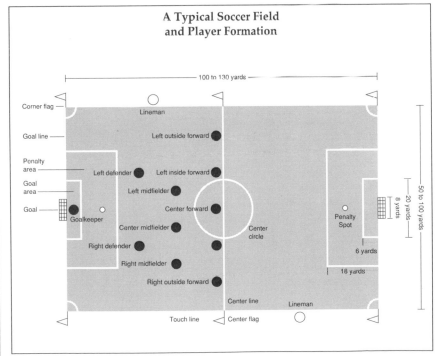

A Typical Soccer Field and Player Formation

- 100 to 130 yards
- Corner flag
- Lineman
- Goal line
- Left outside forward
- Penalty area
- Left defender
- Left inside forward
- Goal area
- Left midfielder
- Goal
- Goalkeeper
- Center forward
- Center midfielder
- Penalty Spot
- Right defender
- Center circle
- 8 yards
- 20 yards
- 50 to 100 yards
- Right midfielder
- 6 yards
- Right outside forward
- 18 yards
- Center line
- Touch line
- Center flag
- Lineman

with the goalkeeper in this area unless the goalie has the ball and both of his feet on the ground.

A *center line* divides the field in half and intersects the *center spot* inside the large *center circle* in the middle of the field.

THE PARTICIPANTS

The eleven players on a soccer team wear colorfully designed shirts and trunks, and knee-length socks, that in some way distinguish and designate their team. Shoes with hard rubber cleats complete the simple uniform. Since a lot of kicking goes on, most players place shin guards under their socks for protection.

A team goes on *offense* when it gains possession of the ball. It uses various *formations*, determined by the *coach* according to the situation. For example, when a team is ahead, its coach may insert extra defenders and employ a defensive formation. If his team is behind, he will frequently send in more offensive players, going with a formation that emphasizes attack. Coaches also scout other teams and design some formations to take advantage of the weaknesses they see. Still other formations may center on a star player, with plays conceived to allow him to use his exceptional talents.

Three *lines* define a team's formation. The big scorers on a team are the *forwards,* who form the *first* (offensive) *line.* A forward line usually starts with five players: a *center forward*, *left* and *right inside forwards,* (these three are often known as *strikers*) and *left* and *right outside forwards* (also called *wings* or *wingers*). These players must be fast and shifty, and accurate at shooting and passing. They exchange passes and *dribble* (move the ball along the ground with their feet) in crisscrossing patterns; they fake shots to draw defenders out of position; and they shoot when open. Forwards also drop back to break up the opposing team's attacks.

Three **midfielders** (also called *halfbacks* or *linkmen*) form the *second line.* A *left,* a *center,* and a *right midfielder* race up and down the field to unite their team's offense and defense. Pushing down-field, they sometimes score goals.

Two defenders, labelled *fullbacks,* seldom score but remain back in front of their team's goalkeeper as the last line of defense. The fullbacks' job is to take the ball from the opposition and pass it to a midfielder to initiate an attack. One fullback generally plays near the goal while his teammate (the *sweeper*) roams out to intercept passes.

This *5-3-2 formation* (5 forwards, 3 midfielders, 2 fullbacks) may shift to another configuration based on the need for either an offensive or defensive surge. For example, a *4-2-4 formation* stresses a tight defense by using four defenders and a first line of only two strikers flanked by two wings. For greater offense, additional wings or inside forwards – or forward-moving midfielders – may promote more and better shots.

The **goalkeeper** (*goalie* or *goal tender*) generally remains near the goal he is defending. He must move quickly to steal crossing passes or to stop or tip away shots taken by the opposition. By rushing nearby ballhandlers, he tries to *cut down the angle* at which they may shoot; moving closer to an opponent before he shoots the ball, a good goalie can either block the shot, or, more often than not, make the player shoot wide of the goal posts. The goalkeeper is the only player who may grasp or touch the ball with his hands and arms. When he controls the ball in this manner, he may elect to kick it far down-field or throw it to a teammate in order to start an attack the other way.

International rules allow for only two substitutions per game, and a player who is pulled out cannot re-enter the match. (College coaches may substitute five players per game; high school rules allow unlimited replacement of players.)

One *referee* and two *linesmen* normally officiate the game. The referee keeps time and enforces the rules. Linesmen help watch for fouls, determine which team gets the ball when it goes out of bounds, and call "offside" infractions.

PLAYING THE GAME

Pro soccer matches are divided into two 45-minute *halves* (termed "periods" in college). Depending on the abilities of the players, leagues are allowed to adjust the length of the halves. Only the referee may call time out to stop the clock (in most cases, only for an injury). The team winning a coin-toss chooses to either *kick off* or to defend a particular goal. A *kickoff* from the center spot begins play. With each team on its own side of the field, and with the defensive team outside the center circle, one offensive player softly kicks the ball forward to be retrieved by a teammate. All players are then free to move the ball with their feet as they advance it past the defense. Hard bodily contact is permitted only when attempting to kick the ball or hit it with the head. Near the opposing goal, the offensive players undertake to pull the defense out of position by faking and moving the ball quickly. By keeping players in motion, using crossing patterns, booting "centering" kicks, etc., the attackers hope to get a good shot on goal. If a shot bounces off the goal post or crossbar, or off another player, the ball is still considered in play and a goal may be scored on the rebound.

A ball that goes out of bounds is "out of play." Play is restarted by one of four methods:

1. A *throw-in* is required when the ball is knocked over a touch line (on the side of the field). An opposing player steps out of bounds and grasps the ball with both hands. Keeping both feet on the ground, he throws it in bounds to a teammate using an over-the-head motion.

2. A *corner kick* is awarded when a defensive player is last to touch a ball that crosses out of bounds over his own goal line. An offensive player boots the ball off of the ground from the nearest corner, and the other forwards and midfielders, positioned around the mouth of the goal, try to jump or race to kick or *head* the ball (strike it with the forehead) into the net.

3. A *goal kick* is given to the defense when an offensive player hits the ball out of bounds over the opponent's goal line. A formerly defensive player kicks the ball from the goal area out of the penalty area down-field or to a member of his team.

4. A *drop ball*, where the ball is dropped by the referee between two opposite

players, may also resume play when it is stopped for any reason.

When regulation game time expires, tied games go into an *overtime* period. (The NASL uses a *sudden death* overtime, in which the first team to score wins the game.) After the specified overtime, if teams are still tied they each take a series of tie-breaking "penalty shots" to decide the outcome.

INFRACTIONS

A *penalty kick* (*penalty shot*), a *direct free kick*, or an *indirect free kick* is awarded to the opposing team for most fouls.

A player who kicks a *penalty kick* is quite likely to score a goal, since he shoots from the *penalty spot* (12 yards in front of the goal) with only the goalkeeper defending. A player is given a penalty kick when an opposing team member commits one of eight deliberate *fouls against a player within his own penalty area:*

- Kicking (or attempting to kick) an opponent
- Obstructing (blocking an opponent's path)
- Tripping
- Rough pushing
- Bumping from behind
- Hitting
- Holding
- Touching the ball with the hands or arms

A *direct free kick* is awarded, from the point of the infraction when one of these eight fouls occurs *outside the penalty area.* Defenders may elect to line up shoulder-to-shoulder, no closer than ten yards away, to form a wall to block the free kick shot at their goal. After the kick, if no score was made, play resumes uninterrupted.

An *indirect free kick* must touch at least one other player before entering the goal. It is granted when an opposing player employs dangerous play (kicks the ball out of the goalie's hands, pushes a player without the ball, or strikes an opponent), exhibits ungentlemanly conduct, or is *offside*. Offside is called when an attacker without the ball enters the opponent's half of the field before the ball does. There are, however, four exceptions to this rule: (1) When two or more defenders are nearer their goal line than the offensive player; (2) When the offensive player moves between the ball and the goal line *after* a teammate kicks the ball; (3) When the ball was last touched by a defensive player; and (4) When the offensive player receives the ball from a throw-in, corner kick, goal kick, or drop ball.

For excessive or dangerous fouling, the referee may take out and flash a yellow card as a warning to the player. For subsequent fouls by the same player, the referee may choose to bring out a red card, meaning the player is ejected from the game with no substitution allowed.

SOCCER SKILLS

Seven fundamental soccer skills, in addition to basic training skills gained by running, conditioning, and quickness drills, all emphasize ball control. They make up a player's repertoire of abilities.

- *Kicking* is the essential method of moving the ball around the field and attempting goals. A player must be able to kick with precision using either foot. An *instep* kick is the most accurate and widely used technique. Placing the plant foot next to the ball, and keeping the eyes on the ball, the playerswings his other leg through, driving the ball forward with the instep of his foot. Depending on how it is struck, the ball will sail in the air, scoot along the grass, or skim just above the ground. Other less accurate kicks use the outer side of the foot or the heel. In one spectacular kick, the *overhead* kick, the player's feet extend over his head, booting the ball backward. (This is most often employed by a defensive player to *clear* a ball that is dangerously close to his own goal.)

- *Passing* with precision enables a team to move the ball into scoring position by kicking or bumping it beyond the reach of defenders. Short, decisive passes are more effective – and less likely to be intercepted – than longer ones. A *center* (or *crossing*) pass is directed through the air toward a teammate close to the opposing team's goal. *Square* passes are simple, back-and-forth exchanges between teammates, with the open player advancing the ball up the field. A *give-and-go (wall)* pass begins with a player bumping the ball to a teammate; the passer then races past or around defenders into an open area to receive a return pass.

- *Heading* the ball as it flies through the air requires a player to time his jump and snap his head forward, punching the ball with his forehead as it arrives. Using their heads, highly skilled players can pass or shoot with great accuracy.

- *Dribbling* (running with the ball) involves tapping the ball forward with the feet and maintaining control. Players use foot or body fakes, or stop-and-go fakes, to feint passes or shots and get the ball past defenders.

- *Trapping* the ball with the feet, knees, thighs, or chest helps a player control the ball so he can dribble with it or position it for a pass or a shot.

- *Marking* is a defensive skill that consists of sighting and following the ball, guarding against shots or passes. If a player is too easily faked out and allows the ball to be advanced past him, he needs practice in marking and footwork.

- *Tackling,* another defensive maneuver, involves using the feet to hook or poke the ball from a dribbling player without hitting or otherwise fouling him. A player trying a sliding tackle slides his body along the ground and extends one leg to pull or push the ball away from his opponent.

SOME OTHER TERMS

Centering - Passing the ball from near a touch line into the penalty area where teammates can shoot at the goal.

Half-volley - A kick made on a ball just as it bounces off the ground.

Save - Refers to a goalkeeper preventing a shot from entering his goal.

Screening - Keeping the ball from an opponent by shielding it with the body.

Volleying - Kicking the ball while it is still in the air.

ICE HOCKEY WRAP-UP

THE GAME

Ice hockey is a fast, aggressive game played on an ice-covered *rink*. Six players on a team skate up and down the ice trying to score more *goals* than the opposition by passing and hitting a *puck* (a one-inch thick hard rubber disk with a three-inch diameter) using long wooden sticks. Meanwhile, the defending squad works to steal the puck and skate with it to the other end of the rink to shoot at the opposite goal. Because of the fierce competition and bodily contact, at times fights break out between players, though fighting is against the rules.

Both the United States and Canada have national hockey teams, as do many European countries. Amateur teams vie to compete in the *Winter Olympic Games* held every four years. Youth hockey, emphasizing individual skills and teamwork, flourishes in the U.S. High school and college teams play under essentially the same set of rules as the professional teams of the *NHL (National Hockey League)*.

THE RINK

A standard indoor rink measures 200 feet by 85 feet. It has rounded corners and is surrounded by a wooden or clear-plastic fence, 40 or more inches tall, called the *boards*. The rink itself consists of one layer of artificial ice with lines, spots and circles painted on it, and another ice layer covering the first.

Near each end of the rink are *goal lines* that extend across the rink. A *goal cage* (usually referred to as the *net* or *goal*) stands at the center of each goal line. Goal cages are made up of two vertical posts 6 feet apart, connected by a four-foot high crossbar with a net at the back. A small, outlined area in front of each net is known as the *goal crease*. Players may not skate into this area unless they are going for the puck.

Two *blue lines* divide the rink into three sections – two *end zones* and a *center zone*. The end zone into which a team attacks is that team's *attacking zone*, and the defenders' *defending* zone. The center zone is also known as the *neutral zone*. A *red (or center) line* splits the neutral zone (and the rink) in half. Five *face-off circles*, one in the middle of the rink and two on each side of the goal cages, surround *face-off spots*. Only one player from each team may enter a circle during a *face-off*. In a face-off, an official drops the puck between the sticks of two opposing players, who attempt to slap it with their sticks to a teammate or towards the opposing goal. Four other face-off spots, with no sur-

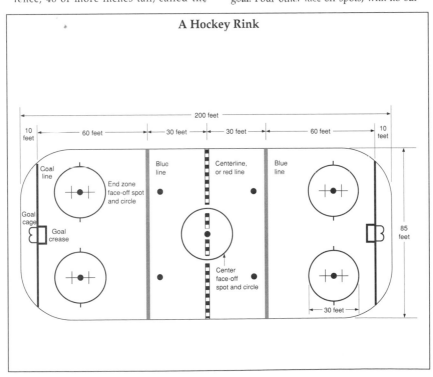

A Hockey Rink

200 feet

10 feet | 60 feet | 30 feet | 30 feet | 60 feet | 10 feet

Blue line — Centerline, or red line — Blue line

Goal line

End zone face-off spot and circle

Goal cage

Goal crease

Center face-off spot and circle

85 feet

30 feet

rounding circles, are located inside the neutral zone near the blue lines.

Outside the rink are two sets of *benches*. On one side are the players' benches, where the teams sit. On the opposite side are smaller benches called *penalty boxes*, where players must temporarily sit if they break the rules.

THE PARTICIPANTS

A team's *starting line* includes one **goalkeeper** (*goalie* or *goal tender*), two **defensemen**, and three **forwards.** These players wear protective padding, shin guards, thick gloves and helmets. The blades of their skates are rounded to provide greater maneuverability. Each player carries an L-shaped *stick* which consists of a long *shaft* (no more than 55 inches) and a *blade* about a foot long by 3 inches high.

The goalkeeper usually remains near his net to knock away or catch the puck before it can cross the line into the goal cage. A goalie must be extremely flexible in order to spread his legs or arms as he blocks shots or to launch his body in front of shots on his goal. Since a speeding puck may travel at more than 100 miles an hour, the goalie is well-protected by a face mask, massive arm, shoulder and body pads, and thick leg guards. He may catch the puck in his *catching glove,* designed like a long baseball mitt, or bat it away with the sturdy back of his *stick-hand glove.* His stick is wider and more blunt than those of other team members.

A *left defenseman* and a *right defenseman* guard their team's defending zone. Their job is to *intercept* passes, *check* (bump) attackers away from the puck, *clear* the puck away from the net and, generally, keep the offensive team from scoring. When defensemen are able to obtain possession of the puck for their team, they sometimes streak down the ice to push an attack at the other team's goal. However, they must be careful not to leave their own zone vulnerable.

Forwards are often called on to defend their own goal, but their main role is to run the team's offensive attack. A *center*, a *left wing*, and a *right wing* position themselves so that when they get the puck they can pass or skate with it to create a shot at the opposing net. The center exchanges passes with his *"wing-men"* and tries to steer his team's *rush* toward the opponent's goal. He takes part in most face-offs and, basically, follows the puck wherever it goes. The two wings cover both sides of the rink, staying abreast of the center to receive passes and shoot at the net.

Hockey is one of the few sports in which a coach may substitute players into the game at any time during the action.

Ordinarily, a *coach* will change *lines* (offensive and defensive units) about every two minutes, and other players may enter as the situation dictates. In most cases, however, barring injury or a *blow-out* (when one team is far ahead of the other in points), a goalie plays the entire game.

The officials inside the rink consist of a *referee* and two *linesmen*. The referee supervises the contest and determines all penalties. The linesmen call "offside" and "icing" violations and conduct face-offs. Off the ice, a *goal judge* sits behind each goal cage to note when shots pass beyond the goal line into the net. He turns on a red signal light if a score is made. One *timekeeper* stops the game clock when an official blows his whistle for a penalty or face-off. Another timekeeper tracks the time players spend in the penalty box. Other scorers and statisticians record each player's goals and *assists* (passes or plays that contribute to goals made by a teammate).

HOCKEY SKILLS

Using very few preplanned *plays* (team maneuvers), together, skaters must function using their experience and intuition. Over time, defensive units develop strategies to steal the puck; offensive units find tactics for putting the puck in the opposition's net with greater frequency.

Individual players depend on their varying personal strengths – quickness, speed, power, endurance, toughness, and intelligence – along with the specific hockey skills covered below, to help their teams win:

- *Skating* is the most important hockey skill. Hockey's fast action requires players to stop, move laterally and turn sharply, all at top speed. They must be able to skate backwards, especially the defensemen, who often need to retreat quickly while keeping their eyes on the attackers flashing toward them with the puck. Their skating reflexes need to be automatic, instantaneous, and purposeful.

- *Stickhandling* is the use of the stick to *carry* (move), control, and protect the puck. It involves *sweeping* the puck first with one side of the blade and then with the other (shifting it from side to side or front to back) and moving the stick to *fake* pass-offs and shots. In this way defenders are put off balance guessing which direction a skater may move next.

- *Passing* the puck to a teammate first requires controlling it. Then the puck can be propelled with the blade of the stick toward an open receiver. A *flat* (or *sweep*) *pass* skims along the surface of the ice. A *flip pass* comes off the ice and is used to avoid interception by an opponent. When a player leaves the puck behind him for a teammate to pick up, the maneuver is termed a *drop pass*.

- *Shooting* refers to wielding the stick in order to drive the puck towards the opposition's goal. In general, there are four types of shots. For a *wrist shot*, the blade does not leave the ice until after the puck is shot. The shooter uses strong and quick wrist action to fire the puck at the goal. In the more powerful but less accurate *slap shot*, the player raises his stick in a backswing and brings it down, slapping the puck forward with great force. A player executes a *flip shot* by scooping the puck up on his blade when he needs to toss it into the net – over sticks, skates, or a sprawling goalie. A *tip shot* is basically a deflected pass that is angled into the goal.

  Shots may be struck either forehand (using the curved side of the blade) or backhand (with the back of the blade). Most shots on goal are made from the forehand position.

- *Checking* is the chief means of getting the puck from an opponent. A player applies a *stick check* to poke, hook or sweep the puck away from his rival. He administers a *body check* by bumping the man with his hip or shoulder. Both methods of checking are allowed only for use against a player who either is controlling the puck or was last to control the puck. (High school and college players may only check in the defending or neutral zones.)

PLAYING THE GAME

Three 20-minute *periods*, separated by 10- or 15-minute intermissions, make up a game. The clock stops only after an official's whistle or during the one 30-second timeout allowed each team per game. Tied games result in a 5-minute *overtime* with the first team to score emerging as the victor. Some ties are broken by assigning each team a specified number of penalty shots to determine a winner. (See **Penalty Shots.**)

Each game period begins with a face-off. Whenever play stops, another face-off (performed at a face-off spot designated according to the reason play was stopped) commences play once more. The team gaining possession of the puck at the face-off then tries to carry or pass it into scoring posi-

tion. The puck must be kept moving at all times; if it is held or pinned to the ice, "frozen" between two players, trapped up against the boards, or hit out of the rink, a new face-off results.

As players attempt to advance the puck, each is careful not to cross into the attacking zone (beyond the opponent's blue line) ahead of the puck. The puck must be carried or shot across the blue line *before* any team member enters the attacking zone. A violation of this rule results in the team being declared *off side*, and a face-off follows in the neutral zone.

Likewise, offside is called when the puck is passed across two lines. For example, a team member may legally pass from his defending zone to his own side of the neutral zone, but he may not pass from his zone to a receiver in the opposing team's half of the neutral zone; if this happens, a face-off is effected at the face-off spot nearest to where the play began. These offside rules force teams to employ more controlled passing attacks.

Offensive Play

Once a team on defense gains control of the puck, it moves on offense by *rushing* to gain an advantage with more offensive players on fewer defensive players on the attack – three-on-two or two-on-one, for instance. But if the opposing team drops back quickly, the team with the puck will usually set up (position themselves) in their own attack zone and pass the puck around looking for a good shot. The attacking team's defensemen will station themselves as point men on opposite ends of the blue line. They try to keep the puck inside the attacking zone. (If the puck is slapped out beyond the blue line, all attacking players must come out of the zone before the team can again rush; if they didn't, the attack would be called offside.) The point men may attempt long slap shots or they may feed the puck to the center or wings, who, in turn, may choose either to shoot or to pass off to a teammate in better scoring position.

Following a missed shot, offensive players try to score on the *rebound*. If an opponent obtains possession of the puck, attackers quickly move to regain control by *fore-checking* (checking in the attacking zone).

If one squad is *short-handed*, meaning that it has temporarily lost one or two players due to penalties, the team with the advantage of more players can more easily move the puck. An opposing coach often takes advantage of this situation by sending all his players on a *power play* – a spectacular, all-out rushing effort to score. Frequently, the coach with a power play initiative will replace one of his defenders with a forward to pick up the attack, while the short-handed coach will insert additional defensive specialists.

Defensive Play

On defense, a player's job is to break up attacks and recover the puck for his team. At the start of an attack, both defensemen begin retreating to guard their goal. They skate backwards in order to anticipate and pick off passes and shots. The wings and center also race back to harass the puck carrier and defend their goal. Players use their checking skills to block (check) men away from the puck. A defender's check in the defending zone is called a *back-check*.

A common defensive rule violation is *icing*, or *icing the puck*. The purpose of the rule is to assure an even, fast-moving contest. Simply stated, icing occurs when a defender shoots the puck from his half of the ice across the opposing team's goal line, and an opponent touches the puck. This results in a face-off in the offending team's end zone. However, in a power-play situation the team with the manpower shortage may legally ice the puck until both teams are returned to equal force. Hence, a *clearing* shot (one made from a defender's own goal the length of the rink) is good strategy when trying to "kill" a penalty. A short-handed team may call on *penalty killers* – substitutes expert at backchecking and puck control – until the team is restored to equal strength.

PENALTIES

Most rules violations involve either icing or offside. For these infractions, teams merely risk losing the puck in the ensuing face-off. However, more serious violations, termed *penalties*, call for offending players being removed from the game for a stretch of two minutes or more. Still, a team must have at least four players on the ice; if two of its players are already in the penalty box and another is assessed a penalty, a substitute may come into the game until the penalty time is served. (In most cases, a teammate can serve penalty time for a goalie.)

There are five penalty classifications:

1. **Minors** - Called for violations such as *holding, tripping, elbowing, highsticking* (aggressive play with the stick held above shoulder level), *hooking* (using the blade as a weapon), *cross-checking* (jamming the stick across an opponent's body), *slashing* (otherwise hitting with the stick), and *interference* (pushing or bumping someone not involved with the play). Any of these bring the perpetrator 2 minutes in the penalty box. His team plays a man short until the two minutes expire, or until the opposition scores a goal.

2. **Majors** - Imposed for more aggressive violations – *fighting, spearing* (jabbing a player with the stick), or other actions the referee deems as severe. Major penalties earn an offender *5 minutes* in "the box." If a player on each team is given a major penalty at the same time, substitutes may replace them. Second major violations sentence a player to fifteen minutes in the box; a third infraction means expulsion from the game.

3. **Misconduct penalties** - Assessed for unsportsmanlike behavior toward an official. A misconduct violation results in a *10-minute penalty*, but a substitute may replace the offender. A player receiving a *game misconduct penalty* (primarily given to the first man to enter a fight between two others) is ejected and a teammate is called to take his place in the game.

4. **Match penalties** - Assigned to a player for deliberate *attempts to injure. 5-minutes in the penalty box is called* – with no substitution. Deliberately *harming* a player draws a 10-minute match penalty. Depending on the severity of the offense, the player may be replaced after the 5 or 10 minutes have elapsed.

5. **Penalty Shots** - Awarded when a skater in control of the puck, with a clear, unopposed path to the goal, is pulled down from behind by a defender, thus preventing him from taking the shot. The wronged player is given a chance to score with only the opposing goalie defending. Taking the puck in the neutral zone, he attacks the net and shoots. Play ends after the first shot; that is, the player can not score on a rebound.

SOME OTHER TERMS

Breakaway - A shot attempt where an attacker has no other defensive player between him and the goaltender.

Hat trick - When a player scores three goals in a single game.

Power-skating - Skating techniques using long, thrusting strides with the edges of the skate blades to accelerate forward, backward, or sideways across the ice.

GEOGRAPHY

Trivia to Learn By

• What country now owns the Galapagos Islands, famous for the studies made there by Charles Darwin?	Ecuador
• Name the capital city in the Americas that has the smallest population – only about 3,000 inhabitants.	Belmapan, Belize
• What modern country is home to the ancient city of Babylon?	Iraq
• The famous London Bridge is now located where?	Lake Havasu City, Arizona, U.S.A.
• Excluding Alaska, which U.S. state has had below-zero weather for the longest period?	North Dakota
• The Turkish city Constantinople is now known by what name?	Istanbul
• What is the name of the French airport where Lindbergh landed in his 1927 flight over the Atlantic?	Le Bourget
• In Mohammedan tradition, Adam and Eve settled on what island after being expelled from paradise?	Sri Lanka
• What is China's most populous city?	Shanghai
• What river flows through Rome?	The Tiber River
• The now – extinct dodo bird once lived on what two Indian Ocean islands?	Mauritius and La Reunion
• What is the tallest mountain in Africa – and the world's largest volcano?	Mt. Kilimanjaro
• The native people of New Zealand are called what?	Maoris

• Identify the new nations (or new names of countries) by the descriptions given below:

– A small Central American country that gained independence from Britain in 1981; formerly called British Honduras.	Belize
– Once called Formosa ("beautiful"), this island country broke politically from mainland China in 1949.	Taiwan
– Formerly the French Territory of Afars and Issas, it lies on the "horn" of eastern Africa near the Red Sea; gained independence in 1977.	Djibouti
– A large southern African nation that obtained its independence from Portugal after a long civil war that ended in 1975.	Mozambique
– A tiny Caribbean West Indies island that gained independence from Britain in 1974.	Grenada
– The country bordering Thailand and Vietnam; formerly known as Cambodia.	Kampuchea
– Previously East Pakistan, it borders Pakistan and India; seceded from Pakistan in 1971.	Bangladesh
– Presently comprising the eastern half of the island of New Guinea and some adjacent islands, it broke from Australia and New Guinea in 1975 under a mandate by the United Nations.	Papua New Guinea
– Formerly called the Malagasy Republic, this large island off the east coast of Africa took its new name in 1975.	Madagascar
• What country produces most of the world's diamonds?	South Africa

• What are the capital cities for the following U.S. states?

– Wyoming	Cheyenne
– Maine	Augusta
– North Carolina	Raleigh
– Minnesota	St. Paul

1

– Idaho	Boise
– New Mexico	Santa Fe
– Alabama	Montgomery
– Tennessee	Nashville
– Pennsylvania	Harrisburg
• What California valley is best known for its quality grapes and wines?	Napa Valley
• The river Danube flows through what six countries?	Germany, Austria, Czechoslovakia, Hungary, Yugoslavia, Romania
• In what U.S. state was the Girl Scouts founded?	Georgia (1912)
• The Gobi Desert extends through what two countries?	China and Mongolia
• The source of the Nile River is found in what country?	Uganda
• The world's largest obelisk, the Egyptian obelisk, is located where?	The Hippodrome in Istanbul, Turkey
• What is the name of the cliff-like fortress battlefield where Jewish nationalist zealots committed suicide rather than surrender to the Romans?	Masada
• Name Belgium's busiest and largest harbor.	Antwerp
• What country, lying mostly in the Sahara Desert, finally abolished slavery in 1980?	Mauritania
• Name the city that was declared the temporary capital of France during World War II, and has since been converted into a health resort.	Vichy
• Macau, an island at the mouth of the Canton River in China, is a dependency of what European country?	Portugal
• What is the most populous city in these geographic regions?	
– Africa	Cairo, Egypt
– Canada	Montreal
– Asia	Tokyo, Japan
– Eastern Europe	Moscow, U.S.S.R.
– Western Europe	London, England
– United States of America	New York City
– South America	Sao Paulo, Brazil
• What island country has: a Spanish name, a French-named capital, and English as its official language?	Grenada
• In which South American country can you visit the shores of both the Atlantic and Pacific Oceans?	Colombia
• In what country is "goulash" the specialty dish?	Hungary
• Identify the island made famous by Gauguin's paintings.	Tahiti
• What is the former name of New York's J.F. Kennedy Airport?	Idlewild
• What two Western Hemisphere countries are named after famous explorers?	Columbia and the Cook Islands
• Gin, the drink, derives its name from what European city?	Geneva, Switzerland
• The mysterious city of Timbuktu is found in what country?	Mali
• What country contains 60,000 lakes and has at least 30,000 islands off its shores?	Finland
• What mountain is the most celebrated and sacred in all Japan?	Mt. Fuji
• Lebanon is famous for what trees?	Cedar
• The "Emerald Isle" is the nickname of what country?	Ireland
• What is the deepest fresh-water lake in the world, and where is it situated?	Lake Baikal, Siberia, Russia
• What country borders both the Caspian Sea and the Persian Gulf?	Iran

2

- Name the only walled city in North America.

  Quebec, Canada

- N'Djamena is what African nation's capital?

  Chad

- Ownership of the Caribbean island Hispaniola is shared by what two countries?

  Haiti and the Dominican Republic

- Venice is crisscrossed by canals that create some ninety islands. What other European city has been constructed to form more than 100 islands?

  Amsterdam, Netherlands

- Tikal, the oldest of the Mayan ruins, is located in what country?

  Guatemala

- White-ruled South Africa established ten black (Bantu) "homelands" within its borders as part of its apartheid policy. Four of the ten have since been declared by South Africa as separate countries, though most nations of the world refuse to acknowledge them as such. Name these four "new nations."

  Bophuthatswana, Ciskei, Transkei, and Venda

- The Suez Canal connects what two bodies of water?

  The Red Sea and the Mediterranean Sea

- In what country do Paguan tribal girls wear tight metal necklaces in order to lengthen their necks as a beautifying process?

  Burma

- What city is known as "Fragant Harbor"?

  Hong Kong

- The snowcapped Tatra Mountains separate what two countries?

  Poland and Czechoslovakia

- "Fjords," long, narrow inlets of the sea between steep cliffs and slopes, are most commonly found where?

  Norway

- What is the more common name of the Chinese Imperial Palace of Beijing?

  The Forbidden City

- In what city can you visit Peace Memorial Park?

  Hiroshima, Japan

- What two countries, by far the richest in the world, boasted respective 1985 GNP per capita incomes of $30,000 and $25,850?

  The United Arab Emirates and Kuwait

- The world's tallest full-figure statue, "Motherland," can be seen where?

  Volgograd, U.S.S.R.

- A popular casino and spa is located in Germany's Black Forest. What is it called?

  Baden-Baden

- "Philadelphia" is the original name of what city in the Middle East?

  Amman, Jordan

- On Temple Street, all the stores stay open 24 hours a day. In what city is this street?

  Hong Kong

- The Statue of Liberty stands rising out of what body of water?

  New York Harbor

- Napolean spent his first exile on what Italian island?

  Elba

- Name both the most populous and most *densely* populated nations of each continent or world sector (figures are from are 1985 approximations):

  - Africa

    Nigeria (85 million); Mauritius (1,297 per sq. mile)

  - North America

    United States (235 million); Barbados (1506 per sq. mile)

  - South America

    Brazil (134 million); Ecuador (84 per sq. mile)

  - Asia

    China (1.08 billion); Singapore (11,361 per sq. mile)

  - Europe

    U.S.S.R. (276 million); Monaco (46,667 per sq. mile)

  - Oceania

    Australia (16 million); Tuvalu (820 per sq. mile)

- What is the name of the largest resort on Mexico's Pacific Coast?

  Acapulco

- Name the three Caribbean islands known as the "ABC" islands.

  Aruba, Bonaire and Curacao

- What is the official language of the Philippines?

  English

- Andorra is a tiny country lying in what mountain range?

  The Pyrenees

• Identify the only Southeast Asian country that was never colonized by non-native peoples.	Thailand
• Name the third-largest English-speaking republic. (The U.S. and England are numbers 1 and 2.)	The Philippines
• To what African country did Alex Haley trace his roots?	Gambia
• How many republics make up the Soviet Union?	15
• The Watusi tribe (with an average height of 6 feet) and the Pygmies (less than 5 feet) both reside in what African country?	Rwanda
• Identify the country that presently lays claim to each of the following geographical locations:	
– Galapagos Archipelago	Ecuador
– The island of Tasmania	Australia
– The Aral Sea	Soviet Union
– Corsica	France
– Casablanca	Morocco
– The largest stretch of the Congo River	Zaire
– The Falkland Islands	Great Britain
– Mindanau	Philippines
– Plateau of Tibet	China
– Cape Horn	Chile
– Ho Chi Minh City	Vietnam
• What city is known as the "Eternal City"?	Rome
• What is the town – containing a legendary edifice landmark – where Galileo made the majority of his discoveries?	Pisa, Italy
• Which is the saltiest natural lake on earth – and also the earth's lowest inland elevation point?	The Dead Sea
• The first tank battle took place in what country?	France
• Descendants of the Bounty's mutineers still comprise the major populations of what two Pacific islands?	Norfolk and Pitcairn
• South Africa recognizes two official languages. What are they?	Afrikaans and English
• The once-great coffee port city Mocha is located in what country?	Yeman
• Name the five world oceans.	Atlantic, Pacific, Indian, Arctic and Antarctic
• Strong and fierce women warriors once lived in what is now Benin, Africa. What name were they known by?	Amazons
• Zaire, Africa formerly went by what name?	The Belgian Congo
• What is the only man-made structure visible to the naked eye from the moon?	The Great Wall of China
• In what country is the world's highest commercial airport, El Alto?	Bolivia (La Paz)
• Over half the world's cork is exported by what country?	Portugal
• What is India's best-known shrine – originally built in honor of a princess?	The Taj Mahal
• Identify the highest waterfalls in South America.	Angel Falls, Venezuela
• Five of the seven ancient wonders of the world have been destroyed without a trace. Only two still exist. Name them.	The Pyramids of Giza, Eqypt; The Temple of Artemis of the Ephesians, Ephesus, Turkey
• American University is located in what Middle East capital city?	Beirut, Lebanon
• Identify the famous fountain in Rome that is traditionally strewn with tourists' coins.	Trevi
• The Alps are shared within the borders of seven countries. Name them.	France, Switzerland, Austria, Germany, Yugoslavia, Italy and Albania

• The ruins of the Palace of Knossos lie on what island?	Crete, Greece
• Kronenbourg beer is brewed in what country?	France
• The ancient "City of Temples" near Cairo, Egypt is best known by what name?	Karnak
• What American beach is famous for its auto races?	Daytona Beach, Florida
• What mountain chain divides Europe from Asia?	The Urals
• What is Israel's largest city?	Tel Aviv
• Which is the only South American country to have English as its official language? Also, name its capital.	Guyana; Georgetown
• What sea separates Italy and Yugoslavia?	The Adriatic
• What two countries are separated by the Khyber pass?	Pakistan and Afghanistan
• What U.S. state receives the highest number of government defense contracts?	California
• Name the largest of Australia's southern cities.	Melbourne
• In Switzerland, four languages are commonly spoken. Name them.	German, Italian, French and Romansch
• Hyde Park is found in what city?	London
• In what city is "Simon the Just Gate" located?	Jerusalem
• Link the correct country to each of these capital cities:	
– Montevideo	Uruguay
– Damascus	Syria
– Tegucigalpa	Honduras
– Budapest	Hungary
– Lagos	Nigeria
– Riyadh	Saudi Arabia
– Nairobi	Kenya
– Port-au-Prince	Dominican Republic
– Caracas	Venezuela
– Ulan Bator	Mongolia
– Pyongyang	North Korea
– Wellington	New Zealand
– Islambad	Pakistan
– Viangchan	Laos
– Monrovia	Liberia
– Nuku'alofa	Tonga
– Helsinki	Finland
– Kampala	Uganda
• The nearly inaccessible Rainbow Bridge, a natural sandstone formation, is found in what U.S. state?	Utah
• What British colony sits at the entrance to the Mediterranean Sea?	Gibralter
• Which U.S. state name is derived from the Spanish for "big eared men"?	Oregon ("orejon")
• What American city was once the capital of a Russian territory?	Sitka, Alaska
• Germans call their turnpikes by what term?	"Autobahnen"
• Name the three Baltic republics of the Soviet Union?	Lithuania, Latvia and Estonia
• What castle stands in the heart of Moscow?	The Kremlin
• What city has over 20,000 windmills – more than any other city worldwide?	Merida, Mexico
• Basques reside primarily in what two countries?	Spain and France

• What three African countries have names beginning with the letter Z?	Zambia, Zimbabwe, Zaire
• List other countries beginning with the letter named that are located on the following continents:	
– South America - P (2)	Paraguay, Peru
– Asia - I (5)	India, Indonesia, Iran, Iraq, Israel
– North America - H (2)	Haiti, Honduras
– Africa - T (3)	Tanzania, Togo, Tunisia
– Europe - L (2)	Liechtenstein, Luxembourg
– North America - B (3)	Bahamas, Barbados, Belize
– Asia - S (4)	Saudi Arabia, Singapore, Sri Lanka, Syria
• In what country is Byblos – the city from which the word "Bible" was extracted – located?	Lebanon
• What country is home to the ruins and caves of Cappadocia?	Turkey
• Name the six smallest European countries that are not islands.	Vatican City, San Marino, Lichtenstein, Luxembourg, Monaco, Andorra
• What volcano buried the Italian city of Pompeii in ash in A.D. 79, preserving it until it was rediscovered in 1789?	Mt. Vesuvius
• What do the Argentines call the Falkland Islands over which, in 1982, they fought a war with England?	Islas Malvinas
• What country is home to the polka?	Czechoslovakia
• Name the world's greatest waterfalls – twice as high and twice as wide as Niagra Falls.	Victoria Falls, Zimbabwe
• A European country derives most of its income from an activity which is prohibited to its citizens. What is the activity and the country?	Gambling; Monaco
• Name the country that is spread over 7,100 islands?	The Philippines
• The famous night-time entertainment spot "Crazy Horse" is located in what city?	Paris, France
• Identify the largest noncontinental island in the world.	Greenland

HISTORY
Trivia to Learn By

• Hannibal crossed the Alps using elephants. How did World War I General Galliani move his troops for the 1914 Battle of the Marne?	In taxi cabs
• What state was first to abolish slavery, using a 1780 law stating that no child could be born a slave, thus gradually eliminating slavery in the state?	Pennsylvania
• What British Admiral is known as "The Hero of Trafalgar"?	Horatio Nelson
• Today, income taxes make up most of the federal revenue. A century ago, what was the government's principal source of income?	Tariffs (or duties/customs)
• Who the first woman to be killed in World War II?	Carole Lombard, wife of Clark Gable
• Name the *Mayflower's* last port of call before setting sail to establish the New World's Plymouth Plantation.	Plymouth, England
• What hated Austrian archduke, installed by the French as Emperor of Mexico, was executed by Benito Juarez's firing squad after being captured in 1867 in Mexico City?	Ferdinand Maximilian
• Martin Luther King, Jr. was assassinated in what city?	Memphis, Tennessee
• In what year was the Berlin Wall erected? In what year did its dismantling begin?	1961; 1989
• Who was the U.S. President tried for "High Crimes and Misdemeanors in office"? Who was the vice-president tried for treason?	Andrew Johnson; Aaron Burr
• The Central Pacific and Union Pacific railroads met in 1869 to complete America's first transcontinental rail route at what location?	Promontory Point, Utah
• Name the last three U.S. states to join the Union.	Arizona, Alaska, and Hawaii
• What French diplomat authored the 1834 treaty uniting France, Britain, Spain, and Portugal?	Talleyrand
• Spain recognized free navigation by U.S. ships on the Mississippi in a 1795 treaty named for what American? (At the time, his brother Charles made the declaration, "Millions for defense, but not one cent for tribute.")	Thomas Pinckney
• Name the Iriquois Indian tribes comprising the "six nations" of the 1700's.	Mohawk, Onondaga, Tuscarora, Oneida, Seneca, and Cayuga
• Henry VIII was from the House of Tudor and Queen Victoria from the House of Hanover. To what house does twentieth-century British royalty belong, and who was its first monarch?	The House of Windsor; George V
• What two countries suffered the most combat deaths – a combined total of almost 10 million – in World War II?	Russia and Germany
• Name the Norwegian explorer who was first to reach the South Pole. (He also directed the first successful navigation of the Northwest Passage.)	Roald Amundsen
• What woman, born in Holland, married a Scotsman, billed herself as an Oriental dancer, was known to the Germans as H-21, and was executed by the French at Vincennes in 1917?	Mata Hari (Margaretha Geertruida Zelle McLeod)
• Name the founder of the Democratic Party in the United States.	Andrew Jackson

• Ethan Allen led what Vermont revolutionary group?	The Green Mountain Boys
• In 753 B.C. what general founded the city of Rome – which later annexed surrounding Latin and other Italic tribes to form Italy?	Romulus
• Now a British Museum treasure, what "document" of routine business performed by Ptolemy V in about 196 B.C. was written in two languages and three different scripts, later becoming the key to deciphering Egyptian hieroglyphics?	The Rosetta Stone
• During the 13th-century Crusades, they wore white robes with large red crosses. Due to their secret initiation rites and the great wealth and power they gained over the years, France's King Philip had many of them arrested, tortured, and burned at the stake. The order officially ceased to exist in 1313. What were these men called.	The Knights Templars
• Name the primary occupations of the following ancient Greeks:	
– Epicurus	Philosopher
– Homer	Poet
– Sophocles	Dramatist
– Herodotus	Historian
– Pythagoras	Mathematician and philosopher
– Aesop	Fablist
– Galen	Physician
– Euclid	Mathematician
– Plutarch	Biographer
• Who killed his brother, then led his conquering tribe across central Europe around A.D. 443? How did Rome avoid destruction by his marauders?	Attila the Hun; the pope paid him to spare the city
• In what war did Florence Nightingale serve as the first woman nurse?	The Crimean War
• The civilization preceding the Aztec and Mayan peoples in what is now Mexico, is now known by what name?	The Olmec
• What was the sentimental nickname for the Confederate flag?	The Stars and Bars
• What woman from which state was first to serve in both the U.S. Senate and House of Representatives, and first to campaign for the presidency?	Margaret Chase Smith from Maine
• George Washington, before the calendar was changed to reflect leap years, was actually born on what day of 1732?	Feb. 11, not Feb. 22
• Once an army scout, pony express rider, and meat supplier to Union Pacific Railroad workers, who went on to become the Wild West Show's showman-founder?	"Buffalo" Bill (William) Cody
• What two countries did Daniel O'Connell and Bernardo O'Higgins help liberate from domination? Against what other two countries did they fight?	Ireland and Chile (from England and Spain, respectively)
• Located along the coast of the Dead Sea, identify the Roman fortress, built on a steep hill about 100 B.C., that was later seized by Jewish zealot revolutionists. Also, about how many Jews took their own lives by throwing themselves from the cliff rather than surrender to the Roman tenth legion after it laid siege to the fort?	Masada; 960 people
• Which philosopher wrote down and passed on the thoughts of Socrates?	Plato

• Who defeated Abraham Lincoln in his first U.S. Senatorial race in 1858?	Stephen Douglas
• In 1956, what Jewish patriot did Israel's president David Ben-Gurion refer to as "the only man in my cabinet"?	Golda Meir
• What 3-day American Civil War battle left 5655 killed and 37,783 wounded or missing?	Gettysburg
• What leader's fifth-century defeat near Chalons has been called one of the 15 decisive battles of world history?	Attila the Hun's
• What three Baltic states were annexed by Russia in 1940?	Lithuania, Latvia, and Estonia
• Who dug a canal from the Nile to the port of Suez and the Red Sea, and invaded Russia, India, and Greece?	Darius the Great
• Name the tribe of exceedingly tall, proud warrior-aristocrats who formerly ruled Ruanda-Urundi.	The Watusis
• What conqueror seized Gaul (the area which now includes Belgium, France and Germany west of the Rhine) in 51 B.C.?	Julius Caesar
• In 1652, the Dutch founded what important city in Africa?	Cape Town
• Ponce de Leon explored most of Florida while searching for what?	The Fountain of Youth
• Imre Nagy led what country in a 1950 revolt?	Hungary
• What Chinese Communist leader drove the Nationalists out of mainland China? Who was the Nationalist leader?	Mao Zedong; Chaing Kai-shek
• In which war did each of the following men fight?	
– Sir George Otto Trevelyan	American Revolution
– Herodotus	Persian Wars
– Bruce Catton	American Civil War
– Thomas Carlyle	French Revolution
• Hernando Cortez defeated what Mexican Aztec Emperor, and Francisco Pizarro murdered what Peruvian Incan Emperor?	Montezuma; Atahualpa
• What woman was the first to be awarded a second Nobel Prize?	Marie Curie
• Name the man who served as both the 22nd and 24th President of the United States.	Grover Cleveland
• Before they were purchased by the United States in 1917, what country controlled the Virgin Islands?	Denmark
• In the 1430's and 1440's, what history-altering invention did Johann Gutenberg come up with?	Printing using movable metal type
• Name Israel's first elected president and the prime minister he appointed in 1949.	Chaim Weizmann and David Ben-Gurion
• During Thomas Jefferson's administration, Napoleon sold some real estate to the U.S. (for $15 million) that nearly doubled its domain. What was the name of this transaction?	The Louisiana Purchase
• From the administration of John Adams in 1800 up until 1913, no U.S. President appeared to speak before Congress. Which President reestablished the custom of delivering an Annual Message; and who renamed it the State of the Union Address?	Woodrow Wilson; Harry Truman
• Who and what was overthrown in Russia's 1917 October Revolution? (The Czar had been deposed several months earlier.)	Kernsky; the Second Provisional Government

- Name the dictator who led his army out of Morocco in 1936 and deposed Spain's President Azana? (He later named Prince Juan Carlos to succeed him as King after his death.) — General Francisco Franco

- What historical and apocryphal documents – the first of which were discovered in a cave by a shepherd boy in 1947 – contain the library of a Jewish community inhabiting the area from about 125 B.C. to A.D. 70? — The Dead Sea Scrolls

- What event supposedly caused the great Chicago fire of 1871? — Mrs. O'Leary's cow kicked over a kerosene lantern

- In the Crimean War (1853-56), what four countries opposed Russia? — England, France, Turkey (Sardinia), and Ichnousa (Piedmont-Sardinia)

- Identify the following pre-Columbian civilizations:
  - The empire centered in Peru; destroyed in the 1500's. — Incan
  - A culture scattered throughout the Yucatan in Mexico and parts of Central America primarily from A.D. 300 to 900. — Mayan
  - The dominant group living in Central Mexico before the Spanish Conquests of the 1600's. — Aztec

- What B-29 airplane dropped the atomic bomb on Hiroshima in 1945? Who was the plane named after? — The *Enola Gay*; the pilot's mother

- In what war was the first aerial bomb used? From what was it dropped? — The Mexican-American War (1846-48); from a hot-air balloon

- What two European countries sided with the United States against the British in the Revolutionary War? — France and Spain

- Who was Argentina's president from 1946 to 1955, and again from 1973 to 74? — Juan Domingo Peron

- What dictator seized control of the government when the 10-year French Revolution's political and class struggles ended? — Napoleon Bonaparte

- What scourge swept Egypt in A.D. 542, Italy in 1348, London in 1666, and Hong Kong in 1894? — The Black (or Pneumonic) Plague

- China's first dynasty, the Shang, began about 1766 B.C. What was its last dynasty, ending in A.D. 1912? — Ch'ing (or Manchu)

- The Rough Rider Regiment, led by Teddy Roosevelt, participated in what war for the independence of Cuba? — The Spanish-American War

- Hitler ruled the Third Reich. What tenth-century Emperor was crowned to inaugurate the First Reich, and who established the second? — Otto I (The Great); Bismark (or some say William I of Prussia)

- Who located New York City's deep water harbor for the Dutch East India Company around 1610, introduced liquor into the Mohawk Indian Tribe, and was last seen by his mutinying men as they cast him adrift on the sea? — Henry Hudson

- Before World War I, who were the British Prime Minister and French Premier? After the War, who held these posts? — Herbert Asquith and Rene Viviana; Lloyd George and Clemenceau

- What Prussian-born U.S. soldier was appointed George Washington's inspector general and played a key role in training the raw American troops? — Baron von Steuben

- In the American Civil War, which was the first state to secede from the Union? — South Carolina

- Name the girls of the 1920's known for their flashy dressing and "free thinking." — "Flappers"

4

• What country's leader, Houari Boumedienne, proclaimed Arabic, not French, its official language in 1965?	Algeria
• The Boxer Rebellion of 1900 began and ended in what city?	Beijing, China
• What was Al Capone's nickname?	"Scarface"
• In which Crusade did the Crusaders get carried away and conquer the Christian city of Constantinople?	The Fourth
• Christopher Columbus sailed from what port city on his famous expedition? And who financed the voyage?	Palos, Spain; Queen Isabella
• Name the four men who served in George Washington's first cabinet as, respectively, secretaries of state, treasury and war, and Attorney general.	Thomas Jefferson, Alexander Hamilton, Henry Knox, and Edmund Randolph
• What national organization did Clara Barton found in 1881? Who established its international counterpart 22 years earlier?	The American Red Cross; Jean Henri Dunant
• Only one U.S. president has received a patent for a device he invented. Who was this man who came up with a way to lift ships over shoals?	Abraham Lincoln
• What African tribe was led by Shaka, until he and his warriors were defeated by the Boers in 1838?	The Zulus
• What event in 1980 took 60 lives and destroyed more than 150 square miles of U.S. timberland?	The eruption of Mount St. Helens
• What Chilean leader, the first Marxist to be elected into power, was overthrown and killed by a 1973 military coup?	Salvadore Allende
• The *Koran* was said to have been revealed to Muhammad by what angel? In what language was it written?	Gabriel; Arabic
• What password was used for World War II's D-Day invasion?	"Mickey Mouse"
• What city was created for the purpose of making an atomic bomb, and what was the name of the project?	Los Alamos, New Mexico; the Manhattan Project
• Name the Italian secret society ("charcoal burners") that organized to free Italy from foreign domination in the early 19th century.	Carbonari
• In 1969, the U.S. waged a "secret war" in what country, supporting Lon Nol against what Communist guerrilla regime force and leader?	Cambodia (Kampuchea); the Khmer Rouge, led by Pol Pot
• What U.S. Revolutionary War hero wrote, "These are the times that try men's souls"?	Thomas Paine
• In 1923, the republic of Turkey was founded. Who was its first president?	Kemal Ataturk
• The lyrics "From the Halls of Montezuma . . . " refer to U.S. Marine action in what war?	The Mexican War
• From what country did exiled Ayatollah Khomeini return when he overthrew the Shah of Iran? In what country did the Shah finally find refuge?	France; Egypt
• After World War II, what African colony was first to gain independence? What name did it adopt?	The Gold Coast when it broke away from England; Ghana
• The brutal Russian Czar, Ivan (1530-84), is historically known by what title?	Ivan the Terrible
• Which pope called for the opening of the Crusades, in order to "rescue the Holy Land from the Turkish (Ottoman) Empire"?	Pope Urban II
• What island, captured by Italy in World War II, was retaken and now headquarters the French Foreign Legion?	Corsica

• What hatchet-wielding Kansas woman, whose first husband had died from alcoholism, took upon herself a crusade against liquor (and for women's rights) by destroying illegal saloons in the 1890's and early 1900's?	Carrie Nation
• Where did the 1916 Easter Rebellion take place?	Dublin, Ireland
• What well-known Siberian youth was influenced by the "Flagellant" sect?	Rasputan
• In 1956, what country was granted a place in the United Nations, after years of opposition from the U.S.S.R.?	Japan
• As perhaps the first Roman cultural historian, who described the daily lives of the 1st century Teutonic Tribes?	Tacitus
• At which two battles did American forces fire an estimated 75,000 bullets to kill only 273 enemy forces?	Lexington and Concord
• During the Vietnam War, peace talks were delayed for weeks on account of an argument over what insignificant matter?	The shape of the bargaining table
• At what cost did the U.S. purchase Florida from Spain in 1819? What did the U.S. pay France's Napoleon for the vast Louisiana Territory in 1803? And what was the price paid to the Indians by Peter Minuit for Manhattan Island in 1626?	$5 million; $15 million (an average of 2 cents per acre); beads and trinkets estimated to be worth about $24
• From 1931 to 1941, all graduating cadets of Japan's Naval Academy were asked what one question?	"How would you carry out a surprise attack on Pearl Harbor?"
• In 323 B.C., who established an empire extending throughout the Middle East, into India and the present-day Soviet Union, Northern Africa, and much of Southern and Eastern Europe?	Alexander the Great (III)
• Name the explorer who is credited with first discovering or exploring (in chronological order):	
– Newfoundland or Nova Scotia	Leif Erickson (about A.D. 1000) and later John Cabot (1497)
– Cuba	Christopher Columbus (1492)
– The Pacific Ocean (on the coast of the New World)	Vasco Nunez de Balboa (1513)
– Florida	Juan Ponce de Leon (1513)
– Mexico	Hernando Cortes (1519)
– The Mississippi River	Hernando de Soto (1539)
– The California coast	Francis Drake, (c. 1579)
• What commander surrendered to George Washington in 1781 at Yorktown?	Lord Charles Cornwallis
• Martin Luther was excommunicated by what ecclesiastical council?	The Diet at Worms
• Who shot the Federalist Alexander Hamilton in a duel?	The Republican Aaron Burr
• What "Big Three" leaders met at the Yalta Conference in 1945, near the end of World War II? What three leaders met at the Potsdam Conference later that year?	Roosevelt, Churchill, Stalin; Truman, Attlee, Stalin
• At what "parallel" was Korea divided during and after the Korean War?	38th
• Name the Icelandic (Norwegian) explorer and first European to set foot on the coast of Canada.	Leif Erickson
• What world organization was chartered in San Francisco following the Yalta Conference in 1945?	The United Nations

• Who was known as the "Man Without a Country"?	Edward Everett Hale
• What modern-day monarch, with more than 40 sons as royal princes, created the present kingdom of Saudi Arabia?	Ibn Saud
• What term did the U.S. use to justify its expansion during the 19th century?	Manifest Destiny
• England's "Bankers of Kings" bore what family name?	Rothschild
• Who, descended from the first Duke of Marlborough, offered his "blood, toil, tears, and sweat" during World War II?	Winston Churchill
• What "3 R's" defined the goals of Roosevelt's New Deal program?	Relief, Recovery, Reform
• Who was the last U.S. President to be born in a log cabin?	James A. Garfield
• Bound for the Flemish coast, the Spanish ("Invincible") Armada was defeated by the navy of what country?	France
• A World War II "airlift" brought needed supplies to what blockaded city?	Berlin
• In 1974, Northern Rhodesia's name was changed to what?	Zambia
• What organization received the only Nobel Peace Prize awarded during World War I?	The International Red Cross
• "Gallows Hill," known for events occurring around 1692, is a coastal point located outside of what U.S. city?	Salem, Massachusetts
• Following World War II, what memorable two-word phrase did Churchill coin when he declared: "A shadow has fallen upon the scenes so lately lighted by the Allied victory . . . . From Stetting in the Baltic to Trieste in the Adriatic, an _____ _____ has descended across the continent"?	"Iron curtain"
• What small Pyrenees principality has been jointly ruled by France and Spain for over 750 years?	Andorra
• How many people were executed for the 1865 assassination of President Abraham Lincoln?	Five (John Wilkes Booth and 4 accomplices)
• During the French Revolution, what church was converted into the "Temple of Reason"?	Notre Dame
• Ethiopia's long-standing ruler, Haile Selassie I, originally went by what name?	Ras Tafari
• What "King of the Franks" was preceded by Pepin the Short and followed by Louis the Pious?	Charlemagne (Charles I)
• Who was Japan's World War II voice to American G.I.'s in the Pacific?	Tokyo Rose
• What did George M. Pullman invent?	Railway sleeping and dining cars
• Which U.S. President went by the nickname "Old Rough and Ready"?	Zachary Taylor
• Iceland was populated in the year 870 by what nation and what fleeing leader?	Norway; Ingolfur Arnason
• What civilization flourished during Mexico's "Classical Period" (A.D. 300 to 900), preceding the Toltec and Aztec cultures?	The Mayan
• Who led the "Free French" from London during World War II?	Charles de Gaulle
• What German government was in power before the Third Reich took control of the country?	The Weimar Republic
• Who was Pocahontas' father, and for whom did she serve as guide?	Chief Powhattan; John Fremont

• What name was given the North Vietnamese attack of February, 1968?	The Tet Offensive
• Name the man known as "Genius of the Renaissance"?	Leonardo da Vinci
• The Alamo is located in what Texas city?	San Antonio
• From about the time of Christ, a great 1000-year migration of blacks across Africa spread what language type?	Bantu
• Which two white explorers were the first to sail up the Mississippi River to the Great Lakes region?	Louis Jolliet and Jacques Marquette
• What "Magnificent" Ottoman sultan successfully invaded Hungary, Persia, North Africa, and Southern Europe through the mid-1500's?	Suleiman I
• What Emperor rescheduled the A.D. 76 "Olympic" games so he could compete?	Nero
• Israel's 1967 "Six-Day War" pitted Israel against what three neighboring countries?	Egypt, Jordan, and Syria
• What German president installed Adolph Hitler as Chancellor of Germany?	Paul von Hindenburg
• Who was British Prime Minister for the six years following World War II?	Clement R. Attlee
• Traditionally, Pheidippides ran 26-plus miles to announce what victory?	The Greek victory at Marathon
• What distinction does Valentina Tereshkova hold?	She was the first woman space traveler
• Which Russian czar – after being forced to abdicate his rule as a result of Russia's losses to Germany in World War I – was executed along with his family by the revolutionary Bolsheviks in 1918?	Nicholas II
• Who is considered the American "father" of Quakerism?	William Penn
• In what harbor was the battleship Maine sunk?	Havana Harbor
• Who made the first successful round-the-world solo flight?	Wiley Post
• In what year did the U.S. Congress first exercise its power to declare war?	1812
• What last Apache chief carried on his campaign against restrictions on his people until 1896, long after Cochise had ended his attacks in 1872?	Geronimo

SCIENCE

Trivia to Learn By

• Some animals live only on land, some live only in the water, and others can live or operate both on land and in the water. Name these three groups of animals.

Terrestrial, aquatic and amphibious

• What is the name of the substance that changes the rate of a chemical reaction but is not itself altered in the process?

A catalyst

• Driving at 60 MPH, how many years would it take to travel the 93 million miles to the Sun?

A little more than 176 years

• How does temperature affect the speed of sound?

As the temperature rises one degree, the speed of sound increases by about one foot per second

• What is the scientific name for the "Northern Lights"?

Aurora Borealis

• Identify, respectively, both the swift Australian bird and the South American bird resembling Africa's ostrich. What ostrich-like bird, now extinct, once inhabited New Zealand?

The emu and the rhea; the moa

• What is the point in temperature at which condensation of a vapor begins?

The dew point

• What human body function can generate speeds up to 100 miles per hour?

Sneezing

• An organism that lives on or in another organism, taking nourishment from it and doing it more or less harm, is called what? What is the organism being harmed called?

A parasite; the host

• What is the name for molten rock inside the earth? What is it called once it reaches the earth's surface?

Magma; lava

• What are the largest and the smallest cells found in the human body?

The female ovum and the male sperm

• What rock class was formed from molten rock? Which rocks formed from sediments? What is the name for rocks that have been changed by great heat, pressure, or chemical reactions in the Earth's crust?

Igneous; sedimentary; metamorphic

• From the definitions listed, identify each word having to do with the planet Earth:

    – The theory that the continents have moved and are still moving.

Continental drift

    – Rises and falls in sea level – occuring about twice a day – caused by the pull of the sun and moon on the Earth's waters.

Tides

    – Eroded grains of quartz and other rock, which are coarser than silt but finer than gravel.

Sand

    – An isolated, flat-topped and steep-sided hill; a remnant of a former plateau.

Butte

    – Name for the gently-sloping sea bed around continents which forms the real boundary between the continents and the deep oceans.

Continental shelf

    – The wearing down of the land by natural forces (wind, rivers, rain, ice sheets, etc.).

Erosion

    – Broken fragments of rock ejected from volcanoes during eruptions.

Pyroclasts

    – An icicle-like growth of calcium carbonate, hanging from the the roof of a limestone cave.

Stalactite

    – A column of calcium carbonate growing up from a cave floor.

Stalacmite

– A great waterfall or a series of lesser waterfalls.	Cataract (or rapids)
• Name the simple machine composed of a rigid beam that pivots at a fixed point (fulcrum).	A lever
• What is the element that constitutes about 78% of the air we breathe? What element is next in abundance?	Nitrogen; oxygen
• A giant wave – caused by an earthquake or a volcanic explosion – that can reach coastal heights of 130 feet, is known by what Japanese name?	Tsunami
• In Einstein's theory of the universe, what is the forth dimension?	Time
• What plant can grow up to 35 inches in a single day?	Bamboo
• After oxygen, what is the most abundant element in the crust of the Earth?	Silicon (sand)
• What is the most ancient form of vertebrate?	The fish
• Certain solid substances, such as dry ice, pass directly into the gas state without first melting to a liquid. What is this called? What is it called when a liquid turns to a gas? A gas into a liquid?	Sublimation; evaporation; condensation
• What is a line called that runs outside of a circle and touches the circle at only one point?	The tangent
• What is the oldest and most numerous class of animal?	Insectia
• Identify the astronomical term for each of these general definitions:	
– The general force of attraction between bodies in the universe.	Gravity
– A stellar outburst caused by the transfer and ignition of gas between binary (double) stars.	Nova
– The nuclear explosion of a giant star at the end of its life.	Supernova
– A tiny, hot star that's left when a star runs out of fuel at the end of its life.	White dwarf
– The thin gaseous atmosphere of the Sun.	Corona
– The path in space of one body around another.	Orbit
– The name given to a giant explosion occurring 20,000 million years ago, which is believed to have marked the origin of the universe.	Big Bang
– The theory that the universe never had a single beginning, but that matter is continually being created in space.	Steady-state theory
– An area in space in which the pull of gravity is so strong that not even light can escape.	Black hole
– The time taken for an object to complete one axial rotation around the Sun.	Solar day
– The faint band of starlight seen crossing the sky on clear, dark evenings.	Milky Way (our galaxy)
– The time it takes for an object to complete one orbit relative to the stars.	Sidereal period
– A scaled measurement of the brightness of stars (the faintest stars visible to the naked eye equal a "6").	Magnitude
– A collection of stars bound together by gravity.	Galaxy
– An alignment in space of celestial bodies.	Conjunction
– The slight wobbling of the Earth on its axis caused by the gravitational pulls of the Sun and Moon.	Precession

– Consisting of powdery rock and ice, a small body – only a few miles in diameter – that orbits the Sun.	Comet
– A dust particle from space that can be seen as it burns up in Earth's atmosphere.	Meteor
– A lump of rock or metal that penetrates the atmosphere to fall to the Earth's surface.	Meteorite
• As a pendulum's end weight gets lighter, how does the period (the time it takes to swing from one side to the other) change?	It doesn't change
• To make about one pound of honeycomb, bees must collect nectar from about how many flowers?	2 million
• Who performed the first successful heart transplant in the U.S.?	Dr. Denton Cooley
• Birds have accounted for what percent of the one million species of animals that have become extinct?	90%
• Taken from "light amplification by stimulated emission of radiation," what is the name for a monochromatic (single color), coherent (all waves in step) intense beam of light called?	A laser
• About 99% of all the ice on the earth is found on and surrounding what two land masses? The level of the earth's oceans would rise about how many feet if this ice melted?	Antarctica and Greenland; 200 feet
• The sites at which nerve cells communicate with each other are called what?	Synapses
• The Asteroid Belt, consisting of many orbiting fragments of rock and dust, is found between what two planets?	Mars and Jupiter
• A landslide, carrying millions of tons of rock and soil down a slope, can move at speeds of up to 100 mph. How does it approach such a speed; and how is it that grass and pebbles it passes over can remain undisturbed?	Air, trapped and compressed, acts as a cushion, keeping the moving debris a few inches above the ground. (As the air escapes, it rushes out from under the slide at velocities of 50 or 60 mph.)
• What is the phenomenon called when a Plutonium nucleus separates into two or more smaller nuclei?	Fission
• Give the biological term for each of the following descriptions:	
– A sudden change in the DNA of a gene or genes.	Mutation
– An organism that can infect plants or animals and can only reproduce within a living cell.	Virus
– Vessels that carry blood toward the heart.	Veins
– Vessels that carry blood away from the heart.	Arteries
– The end product of succession in a region; a stable group of plants and animals.	Climax community
– The community of organisms and the habitat in which they live.	Ecosystem
– A plant or animal (usually sterile) produced as the result of the mating of genetically unalike parents (different species or varieties).	Hybrid
– A functional, multi-celled, structural unit of a plant or animal.	Organ
– Spores of a seed plant that contain the male reproductive cells.	Pollen
– Wood; tissue in a plant that provides support and transports water and nutrients.	Xylem

– Survival of the organisms that are best suited to the habitat in which they live.	Natural selection
– Any characteristic that improves an organism's chances of survival (i.e. flying allows an organism to more easily escape enemies).	Adaptation
– Any young animal developing from a fertilized ovum.	Embryo
– The transformation an insect makes from a less developed larval form to its adult form.	Metamorphosis
– The series of stages between fertilization and the death of an organism.	Life cycle
– The substance used by organisms to store energy-rich food.	Fat
– The chemical processes that occur within an organism.	Metabolism
– Process by which certain organisms obtain energy from their food, using oxygen from their surroundings.	Respiration
– Loss of water by evaporation from the undersides of a plant's leaves.	Transpiration
– Minute, thread-like structures consisting largely of DNA and protein, that are present in a cell nucleus.	Chromosomes
– The animal population of a particular area; the plant population of the area.	Fauna; flora
• What is the device that converts chemical energy into electrical energy?	A battery
• Which two planets' days last longer than their years?	Mercury and Venus
• It was once thought that frogs could originate from a mud puddle, and maggots, from a rotten fruit. What was this theoretical belief called?	Spontaneous generation
• What type of doctor specializes in diseases of the bones and joints?	An orthopedist
• What type of vision is achieved when both eyes focus on an object at the same time, each eye seeing the object from a slightly different angle?	Binocular vision
• Name the most common metabolic hormones, which control a number of bodily functions.	Steroids
• What articles of ladies' clothing were named after the chemical polymer from which they were made?	Nylons
• Which two planets' orbits are closest to earth?	Mars and Venus
• A total eclipse of the moon can occur only during which of its phases?	Full
• In proportion to its size, what animal has the largest brain of any creature?	The ant
• Hepatitis is a disease of what body organ?	The liver
• One type of light (e.g. fluorescent and phosphorescent) is emitted at low temperatures; another type is emitted at high temperatures. Identify these two kinds of emission.	Luminescence and incandescence
• What is believed to be the oldest man-made material?	Glass
• Combustion (burning) is a chemical reaction that changes the substance that burns. What element is required for combustion to occur, and what two things are given off by the reaction?	Oxygen; heat and light

• One force acts outward on an object moving in a circular path, the other acts inward in response to this outward force (i.e. to keep water in a bucket as it's spun around). What are these two forces called?	Centrifugal and centripetal
• What is the weight of one cubic centimeter of water?	1 gram
• A heliologist studies what?	The sun
• Oxygen was first discovered by whom?	Joseph Priestly
• Which river carries as much water in one day as the Thames, largest river in England, carries in a whole year?	Amazon
• What part of the human body is the "oxter"?	The armpit
• In 700 B.C. Greece it was 18 years. In 1980 in the United States it was 73 years. What is it?	Average life expectancy
• It takes 4 years for light to reach us from what object?	Alpha Centauri, the closest star to our solar system
• Who invented the self-contained underwater breathing apparatus?	Jacques Cousteau
• About a fourth of your bones are located in what part of your body?	Your foot
• What are the two main causes of acid rain?	Factories and automobiles
• What are the metals called (for example, gold, silver and platinum) that are chemically unreactive?	Noble metals
• What are the four primary tastes distinguished by the tongue?	Sweet, sour, bitter and salty
• Fibrous proteins provide an animal's structural framework. What substance does the same for plants?	Cellulose
• At what temperature is water the densest?	4° Celsius/about 39° Fahrenheit (close to freezing)
• Name the largest of the asteroids orbiting between Mars and Jupiter.	Ceres (about 500 miles in diameter)
• What is the animal for which the word "vaccine" is named?	The cow (from the Latin "vaca")
• What do doctors call a medication or treatment that contains no real medicinal value?	A placebo
• What weather forecasting device was invented by Terricelli?	The barometer
• The binary system of numbers uses only what two numbers?	1 and 0
• A substance that is a poor conductor of heat, sound, or electricity is called what?	An insulator
• What are the two most abundant metals in the Earth's crust?	Aluminum and iron
• "Equinox" ("equal night") is the name for two occasions that occur every year, when the Sun is directly overhead at the equator and the entire earth has 12 hours each of day and night. One equinox takes place about March 21 and the the other about Sept. 23. Name these two equinoxes.	Vernal (spring) and autumnal
• A housefly detects sugar in food using what part of its anatomy?	Its feet
• If all the oceans in the world were drained, where would you find the tallest mountain on earth, measured bottom to top?	On the island of Hawaii
• A "sphygmomanometer" measures what?	Blood pressure
• What constellation is named for rainy, wintery weather?	Aquarius
• Fortunately for all life on earth, what liquid, unlike nearly all other substances, expands instead of contracts when frozen?	Water

5

• By age 60, most people have lost what percent of their taste buds?	50%
• A typical caterpillar has how many legs?	16
• Name the four general chronological eras of Earth's history corresponding to the simplified descriptions below:	
– Earth formed; first primitive plants and animals appear.	Precambrian
– Abundant invertebrates; fish and other vertebrates introduced; first forests and land animals appear; onset of reptiles.	Paleozoic
– Introduction of the first small dinosaurs, followed by a few types of mammals; great dinosaurs and first birds introduced; end of the great dinosaurs.	Mesozoic
– Domination of mammals; ice age begins, over takes much of the earth, and then comes to an end.	Cenozoic
• The Vitamin C in your orange juice is composed of what type of acid?	Ascorbic
• Identify the most popular American beverage.	Milk
• Certain measurements are considered "constants," in that they do not change. Identify the following numbers or symbols with their constants:	
– c	Speed of light (186,000 miles/second)
– 331.7 meters per second (approx. 1130 feet/sec.)	Speed of sound (at sea level at $0°C$)
– π	Circumference of a circle divided by the diameter
– $0°C$	Melting point of ice
– g	Acceleration due to gravity
• As of 1990, how many manned spacecraft have landed on the moon, and how many people have set foot on its surface?	6 crafts, 12 people
• Name the three main zones that make up the Earth's biosphere (the part that is occupied by living things).	Atmosphere, hydrosphere and lithosphere
• When a base reacts with an acid, what chemical compound is formed?	Salt
• On Moh's hardness scale, which two gemstones rank just below a diamond (which is a number "10") in hardness?	A ruby and a sapphire (both "9's")
• Name the three African antelopes with, respectively, horns curving down, spiral horns, and straight horns.	Gnu, eland and onyx
• What common element can be found among both the softest and hardest known substances?	Carbon
• The man known as the father of modern astronomy was a Polish scientist. What is his name?	Nicolas Copernicus
• What is the one-celled animal whose name means "first animal"?	Protozoa
• A kilometer equals how many millimeters?	One million
• In an average day on earth, what natural phenomenon kills 20 people and injures 80?	Lightning
• All organic chemical substances contain one common element. What is it?	Carbon
• A normal human has twenty-three what?	Pairs of chromosomes
• What is the world's slowest-growing plant? (It takes about 30 years for just one branch to form.)	The saguaro cactus

• What do REM's stand for, and in what area of study are they used?	Rapid eye movements; the study of sleep
• What substances are formed by combining quartz, feldspar and clay at high temperatures?	Ceramics
• What planet – due to an overlapping orbit lasting from 1979 to 1999 – is now closer to earth than the planet that normally precedes it in order from the Sun?	Pluto (now closer to Earth than Neptune)
• According to Boyle's Law, if you double the pressure on a gas, what happens to its volume?	It is halved
• A bee has how many wings? How many does a flea have?	Four; none, it can only jump
• What geometric shape contains the greatest area in proportion to the length of its perimeter?	A circle
• Who invented the vaccine for Polio – and when did he do it?	Jonas Salk in 1954
• The technique of purifying or separating liquids by boiling them and condensing the vapour, is known as what?	Distillation
• What is the technology that enables a few glass fibers to carry as much information as hundreds of copper wire circuits?	Fiber-optics (opto-electronics)
• What birds, in essence, "hibernate" every night?	Hummingbirds (their metabolic rate is reduced dramatically at night to compensate for their tremendous activity output during the day)
• Metabolism, explained simplistically, can be divided into two components: one involves the building up of the tissues and organs of the body; the other involves the breaking down of substances to produce waste products. What are these two opposite processes called?	Anabolism and catabolism
• What particle has only one-1800th of the mass but an identical amount of charge as a proton?	An electron
• The muscle of what organ of the body continually contracts, causing it to quiver 30 to 60 times per second?	The eye
• Four is the cube root of what number?	64 (4 x 4 x 4)
• RAM's and ROM's make up what functional part of a computer?	Memory (core storage)
• Give the correct definition for these other common computer terms:	
– Complete sequence of instructions or steps for a job to be performed by a computer.	Program
– Translated, encoded information.	Input
– General term for basic elements of information for processing.	Data
– Beginners All-purpose Symbolic Instruction Code; a simplified computing language.	BASIC
– What a computer does – receiving, analyzing, and producing a result from data.	Data processing
– Any form of instruction from the computer, whether printed or on TV display.	Output
– Physical working units of a computer system.	Hardware
– To locate and correct errors in a computer program.	Debug
• Diffusion of fluids through a semipermeable membrane is called what?	Osmosis

• What is the most widely eaten tuberous root?	The potato
• Who or what is "Roy G. Biv"? Hint: It is a common mnemonic device used to remember a certain physics phenomenon.	It contains the first letters of each of the colors of the spectrum, red through violet.
• What fish lives and feeds in salt water, but spawns in fresh water?	The salmon
• Which of all the metals is the best conductor of electricity?	Silver
• If an electronic circuit operates once in 10 nanoseconds, how many operations does it perform in a second?	100 million
• Give the name for each wind defined below:	
– Used by aircraft pilots to increase speed, a powerful wind which blows around the "tropopause" in the atmosphere and which can reach speeds of up to 300 mph.	The jet stream
– Prevailing winds which blow toward the low-air-pressure "doldrums."	Trade winds
– A wind system in which the directions of the prevailing winds are reversed from one season to the other.	Monsoon
– A dry wind, having lost most of its moisture to the Rocky Mountains, which blows down the central region of North America usually in winter and spring.	Chinook
– A hot, dry wind that blows across northern Africa and on over the Mediterranean Sea.	Sirocco
• Name the object that, on average, weighs about three pounds, uses twenty watts of power in an hour, and stores one hundred trillion bits of information.	The human brain
• The body's anti-viral agent, known for its link in the study of cancer, is called what?	Interferon
• A temperature of -273.15 degrees Celsius is theoretically the lowest temperature possible. It best known by what name?	Absolute zero
• How many total bones are in the human body?	206
• There are approximately 4,250 species of mammals. What specific type of animal makes up nearly one-forth of all the mammal species?	The bat (over 900 different species)
• The alloy of steel and chromium (sometimes combined with other elements) is commonly known as what?	Stainless steel
• If you took graphite (pencil lead) and applied 100,000 atmospheres of pressure at 2500 degrees Celsius, you would end up with what?	A diamond
• What would you call the study of:	
– Paths taken by projectiles (bullets, rockets . . .)?	Ballistics
– Animals?	Zoology
– Plants?	Botany
– The chemical makeup of the many compounds of carbon?	Organic chemistry
• How many degrees from vertical is the earth in relation to the sun?	23-and-a-half

LITERATURE

Trivia to Learn By

• Who wrote about Meg, Jo, Beth, and Amy in her popular 1868 novel? Name the book.	Louisa May Alcott; *Little Women*
• The Mystery Writers of America give an annual award to the writer of the year's best mystery. What is it called?	The "Edgar" (after Edgar Allan Poe)
• In *The Divine Comedy*, Dante places Plato and other "pagan" philosophers in what circle? Where does he place St. Thomas Aquinas?	In Limbo (the first circle of Hell); in Paradise
• Sara Josepha Hale (1788-1879) wrote a poem – one of the few of its kind with a documented author – celebrating an actual happening from her school days. It has since been put to song. What is the poem?	"Mary Had a Little Lamb"
• Anne Frank's diary covers a span of how many years? In what city was the Frank family hiding?	Two years; Amsterdam
• In Samuel Taylor Coleridge's poem, "Rime of the Ancient Mariner," what animal does the Mariner kill which is later tied around his neck?	An albatross
• What character in what famous novel survives a shipwreck by clinging to his fellow shipmate's coffin?	Ishmael, in *Moby Dick* by Melville
• *Time* magazine was originally going to be known by what name?	*Facts*
• Who wrote a play based on the life of Savinien Cyrano de Bergerac, a real-life large-nosed seventeenth-century swordsman, lover, and author?	Edmond Rostand
• Rip Van Winkle slept for how many years?	Twenty
• "For now we see through a glass darkly" was written by who?	St. Paul (I Cor. 13:12)
• John F. Kennedy won a Pulitzer Prize for what 1957 biographical work?	*Profiles in Courage*
• From 1850 to 1892, Lord Tennyson, following in a position vacated due to the death of William Wordsworth, was officially known as England's premier poet. What is this distinction called?	Poet Laureate
• Who killed the following "monstrous" beings or beasts:	
– Grendel	Beowulf
– Cormoran	Jack the Giant Killer
– Goliath	David
– The Nemean Lion	Hercules
• "Love is blind." What two famed writers expressed this sentiment?	Chaucer ("The Merchant's Tale") and Shakespeare ("The Merchant of Venice")
• When Sherlock Holmes retired, what vocation did he follow?	Beekeeping
• "It is a far, far better thing that I do, than I have ever done; it is a far, far better rest that I go to, than I have ever known," was spoken by whom, in what Charles Dickens novel?	Sidney Carton; *A Tale of Two Cities*
• Sancho Panza followed what character around on his escapades?	Don Quixote
• What was the original title of Joseph Heller's *Catch-22*? Whose book caused him to change the title?	*Catch-18*; Leon Uris' *Mila 18*
• How many fans watched Casey strike out in the poem "Casey At the Bat"?	5000 ("10,000 eyes were on him . . . ")
• The Apocalyptic *Four Horsemen* are on mounts of different colors symbolizing war, famine, death, and one unknown evil (or perhaps good). What are, respectively, their four colors?	Red, black, "pale," and white
• What five books – known as the "Pentateuch" – constitute the five rolls or scrolls of the Jewish Torah (law)?	Genesis, Exodus, Leviticus, Numbers, and Deuteronomy

- The titles of all of Erle Stanley Gardner's "Perry Mason" novels begin with what four words?

The Case of the . . .

- How is Gardner's "Perry Mason" story "The Case of the Terrified Typist" distinct from any of his others? In addition to being a writer, what was Gardner's other profession?

It is the only case that Perry Mason lost; Lawyer

- Name the black author of each of the following works on freedom and equality:
  - *Soul on Ice*

Eldridge Cleaver

  - *Why We Can't Wait*

Martin Luther King Jr.

  - *Black Power*

Stokeley Carmichael

  - *Black Man's America*

Simeon Booker

- What author won a Pulitzer Prize for writing *The Caine Mutiny?*

Herman Wouk

- Between 1933 and 1938, a literary rodent was banned from Germany by Hitler, from the Soviet Union by Stalin, and from Italy by Mussolini. Who was this rodent?

Mickey Mouse

- *Happiness is a Warm Puppy* is the title of a book by what modern-day author?

Charles Schulz

- *Zorba the Greek* was written in 1946 by what author?

Nikos Kazantzakis

- What writer of over 450 works, including many books, histories, biographies and essays, in 1675 entered Harvard at age 12 as the youngest student ever admitted?

Cotton Mather

- Who wrote *East of Eden?*

John Steinbeck

- What actual king, the captain of the Greek army against Troy, obeyed a prophet and offered his own daughter as a human sacrifice in order to change the sailing winds?

Agamemnon (sacrificed Iphigenia)

- Name the gourmet who wrote the 1935 restaurant guide *Adventures in Good Eating.*

Duncan Hines

- In Greek myth, what one thing remained in Pandora's box after she opened it?

Hope

- The *Bible's* Jacob labored for how many years before being granted permission to marry Rachel?

Fourteen

- What do the critics and commentators Roger Ebert, George F. Will and Art Buchwald have in common?

They all received Pulitzer Prizes

- What are the surnames of the feuding families in Shakespeare's *Romeo and Juliet?*

Montague and Capulet

- Who is the reputed "Father of Poetry"?

Homer (he wrote *The Iliad* in the 8th century B.C.)

- Of whom was Abraham Lincoln speaking when he referred to "the little lady who made this big war"?

Harriet Beecher Stowe, author of *Uncle Tom's Cabin*

- "Water, water, everywhere, nor any drop to drink," is a famous lamentation found where?

Samuel Coleridge's *The Rime of the Ancient Mariner*

- In A.A. Milne's *Winnie the Pooh,* what name is over the door of Pooh's house?

Mr. Sanders

- In Beatrix Potter's *Peter Rabbit* (1902) what are the names of Peter's two sisters and his brother?

Flopsy, Mopsy, and Cotton-tail

- What are the occupations of the two principal characters in Ernest Hemingway's *A Farewell To Arms?*

Soldier and nurse

- "Two roads diverged in a wood, and I – I took the one less traveled by, and that has made all the difference," are the well-known lines that climax what poem, written by whom?

"The Road Not Taken"; Robert Frost

- What doctors wrote these books?
  - *Horton Hears a Who*

Dr. Seuss (Theodore Seuss Geisel)

  - *Civilization and Its Discontents*

Sigmund Freud

- *The Chambered Nautilus* — Oliver Wendell Holmes
- *The Citadel* — A.J. Cronin

• What former dentist wrote 54 western romances, including *Riders of the Purple Sage* and *Wildfire*? — Zane Gray

• Daniel Defoe used the four-year island experience of Alexander Selkirk to write a classic novel. What is the name of the novel, and how many years did its character spend on his island? — Robinson Crusoe; 24 years

• Who said, "I've had such a curious dream"? — Alice, of *Alice in Wonderland*

• What fictional Frenchman was acclaimed "Pope of Fools" because of his extraordinary ugliness? Who wrote this novel? — Quasimodo in *The Hunchback of Notre Dame;* Victor Hugo

• Sixteenth-century Japan is the setting for what James Clavell novel? Who is the novel's principal character? — *Shogun;* John Blackthorne

• What character crossed a partially frozen river to escape from Haley, a slave-trader? — Eliza in *Uncle Tom's Cabin* by Harriet Stowe

• What generalization was made about men's tastes in the title of Anita Loos' 1925 novel? — *Gentlemen Prefer Blondes*

• Name the two Shakespearean tragedies in which the victims receive a kiss from their murderers just before being killed. Also, who are the "kissers" and "kissees"? — *Julius Caesar* (Brutus kisses Caesar) and *Othello* (Othello kisses Desdemona, his wife)

• Who died before finishing *The Last Tycoon*, based on the life of Metro-Goldwyn-Mayer production executive Irving Thalberg? — F. Scott Fitzgerald

• Certain descriptive words have been derived from literary characters who demonstrated certain traits. What adjectives came from:

   – A Shakespeare character – to mean "grossly fat" or "witty"? — Falstaffian

   – An Eleanor Porter character – to mean "perennially optimistic"? — Pollyanna or Pollyannish

   – A Cervantes character – to mean "idealistic but impractical"? — Quixotic

• Ian Fleming first introduced his character James Bond in what work? — *Casino Royale*

• Who narrates all of the Sherlock Holmes stories? — Dr. Watson

• What hero lifted the unbeaten giant wrestler Antaeus from his mother, Earth, thus weakening and conquering the giant? — Hercules

• Though he never had any direct experience in war, Stephen Crane was made a war correspondent after writing what novel? — *The Red Badge of Courage*

• What celebrated writer's handwriting was so poor that even now it isn't certain how his name should be spelled? — William Shakespeare (only 7 known specimens of his signature still exist)

• What is Alexandre Dumas Peres' most acclaimed novel, written in 1844? — *The Three Musketeers*

• Name the two wars Ernest Hemingway covered as a correspondent. — The Spanish Civil War and World War II

• Edgar Allan Poe is credited with writing the first detective story. What is its name? — "The Murders in the Rue Morgue"

• Sir Thomas More invented and wrote about what imaginary island in 1516? — *Utopia*

• *For Whom the Bell Tolls'* action takes place during what war? — Spanish Civil War

• In what work, by what author, do you find detailed descriptions of the seven deadly sins: gluttony, pride, covetousness, lust, anger, envy, sloth? — *The Divine Comedy,* by Dante Alighieri

• What novelist was, at the last minute, reprieved from being executed before a firing squad, and instead was sentenced to four years of hard labor in Siberia for printing socialist propaganda? — Fedor Mikhailovich Dostoievski

- Name the character who:
  - Was dipped in the River Styx
  - Discovered the land of Lilliput
  - Was king of Camelot
  - Was swallowed by a large fish or whale
  - Turned his daughter to gold
  - Could eat no lean
  - Was a talking, politicized pig
  - Killed Cock Robin
  - Was, secretly, the Godfather
  - Was despised by Anastasia and Drizella

Achilles
Gulliver
Arthur
Jonah and/or Pinocchio
Midas
Jack Sprat's wife
Napoleon
Sparrow
Don Vito Corleone
Cinderella

- Who is James Fenimore Cooper's hero in his novels *The Deerslayer, The Last of the Mohicans, The Pathfinder, The Pioneers,* and *The Prairie?*

Natty Bumppo (also known as Deerslayer, Hawkeye, Trapper, and Pathfinder)

- The two bungling spy-friends, Rosencrantz and Guildenstern, appear in what Shakespearean play?

Hamlet

- *Uncle Tom's Cabin,* by Harriet Beecher Stowe, was based on the life of what real-life slave who escaped from Maryland to Canada, and then helped over 100 other slaves to escape as well?

Josiah Henson

- Who instituted the first newspaper, a single page which was posted daily in public places?

Julius Caesar (the "Acta Diurna")

- Name the fictional stories featuring these anthropomorphic characters – (animals or objects endowed with human traits):
  - A cobra and a mongoose
  - Watty Piper, a persistent locomotive
  - Rat, Mole, and Mr. Toad
  - A pig and a spider

Rikki-tikki-tavi
The Little Engine that Could
The Wind in the Willows
Charlotte's Web

- Known universally by a nickname meaning "broad-shouldered," what father of Western philosophy wrote a series of *Dialogues?* What was his actual name?

Plato; Aristocles

- Whose brother, Fred, was a drunkard in "Old Curiosity Shop"?

Little Nell's

- In what play do you find the "nice" Jim O'Connor, the poet/warehouseman, Tom Wingfield, Tom's crippled sister, Laura, and his mother, Anna?

The Glass Menagerie, by Tennessee Williams

- Who created the character of Mike Hammer, detective?

Mickey Spillane

- "Go placidly amid the noise and haste, and remember what peace there may be in silence," are the opening lines of what anonymous verse found on the wall of Baltimore's Old St. Paul's Church in 1692?

"Desiderata"

- What Apostle is lionized in Taylor Caldwell's "Great Lion of God"?

Paul

- "Pshaw! I can write a better novel than that," was spoken by what gentleman farmer to his wife, who challenged him to do just that?

James Fenimore Cooper (*The Last of the Mohicans . . .*)

- What novel, published in 1867, includes the famed yet fictional recreation of the Battle of Borodino?

War and Peace, by Leo Tolstoy

- Name Tom Sawyer's girlfriend, aunt, and black river companion. On what island does Tom first meet up with the runaway slave?

Beckie Thatcher, Polly, and Jim; Jackson Island

- The character of "The Mad Hatter" in Lewis Carroll's *Alice in Wonderland,* was derived from the fact that, at the time, a poisonous substance was used in the production of felt hats. What was this substance that made the hatters go "mad"?

Mercury

- Name the ghosts that appeared to each of the following characters:
  - Scrooge (his first ghost) in *The Christmas Carol*
  - Macbeth, in *Macbeth*

Marley, his former partner
Banquo

    – Brutus, in *Julius Caesar*   Caesar

    – The governess in James' *The Turn of the Screw*   Miss Jessel and Peter Quint

• Who wrote: "O Captain! my Captain! our fearful trip is done,/ the ship has weathered every rack,/ the prize we sought is won!"?   Walt Whitman

• With the exception of the *Bible*, which book has been reprinted more often than any other volume?   Cervantes' *Don Quixote de la Mancha*

• After Shakespeare, what British writer is translated most?   Agatha Christie

• In the *Bible*, who baked bread for the two angels who visited Sodom, on a mission to find righteous men so that the city could be spared?   Lot

• What playwright, known as the "Father of Spanish Drama," wrote his first play at age 12, and wrote some plays in twenty-four-hour sittings?   Lope de Vega

• What author wrote under the pen names "Geoffrey Crayon" and "Jonathan Oldstyle" (among others), and chronicled a *History of New York* under the pseudonym "Diedrich Knickerbocker"?   Washington Irving

• Name the fastidious author who, among his final statements before dying, said, "This wallpaper is killing me; one of us has got to go."   Oscar Wilde

• What poem by what poet includes the lines, " . . . I have promises to keep, and miles to go before I sleep . . . "?   "Stopping By Woods On A Snowy Evening," by Robert Frost

• e.e. cummings was noted for his peculiar typography, punctuation, and aversion to capital letters. This eccentric use of language got him tossed into a French prison for using codelike grammar. What book did he write while incarcerated?   *The Enormous Room*

• Who, after selling over 20 million copies of his rags-to-riches tales, gave away nearly all his money and died in poverty?   Horatio Alger (1832-1899)

• What is the most famous work of the writer of *The Eclogues* and *The Georgics*?   *The Aeneid*, by Virgil

• Shakespeare died on April 23, 1616. What other great writer died on the same day?   Cervantes

• What Jules Verne character boasted that he could fly around the world in 80 days? In the novel, who, thinking he is a bank robber, tracks this character on his journey?   Phileas T. Fogg; Scotland Yard's Inspector Fix

• Who wrote *Dr. Jekyll and Mr. Hyde*?   Robert Louis Stevenson

• Name the character of Greek mythology:

    – Whose wax wings melted as he neared the sun.   Icarus

    – Who was the first mortal woman.   Pandora

    – Who rules over Hades.   Pluto

    – Who is part god and part goat.   Pan

    – Who is the god of love.   Eros

• What was the name of Ali Baba's woman slave? How many thieves did she discover and then kill, as they hid in oil jars?   Morgiana; 40 thieves

• Whose complete name (in the book named for his shorter title) is Oscar Zoroaster Phadrig Isaac Norman Henkle Emmanuel Ambroise Diggs?   *The Wizard of Oz*, by L. Frank Baum

• What rhyme is based on the old English belief that fortunes could be told by leaping over a particular object? What was this object?   "Jack Be Nimble"; a lighted candle (If it stayed lit, it was a bright omen for the future; if it went out, dark days lay ahead)

• Name the type of novel – Spanish in origin – that presents society as seen through the eyes of a rogue or a rascal.   Picaresque

• What writing technique is illustrated by the following samples?

    – "With slow, sweet sensuality . . . "   Alliteration

- "Silent night . . . " — Assonance
- He was built like a brick wall. — Simile
- Pow, sock, chop, poof! — Onomatopoeia
- "How is my cute little buttercup?" he asked his daughter. — Metaphor
- Only the moon looked down on the deed. — Personification

• John Steinbeck took the title for *The Grapes of Wrath* from what hymn? — "The Battle Hymn of the Republic"

• The Greek "Odysseus" was called by what name by the Romans? — Ulysses

• Besides being authors, what did Ernest Hemingway, e.e. cummings, John Dos Passos, Robert Service, Dashiell Hammett and Malcolm Cowley have in common? — They all served as volunteer ambulance drivers during World War I

• What verse form:
   - Has 14 lines and is associated with Spenser? — Sonnet
   - Has a rhyming, two-line form, each line with the same meter? — Couplet
   - Is a well-known Oriental structure containing 17 syllables? — Haiku
   - Is a four-line stanza or poem? — Quatrain
   - Has no meter or rhyme? — Free verse
   - Has five lines and is usually humorous? — Limerick

• Among U.S. presidents, who was the most prolific writer, authoring 37 books? — Theodore Roosevelt

• What U.S. dramatist left as his last words, "I knew it, I knew it! Born in a hotel room – goddamn it! – and dying in a hotel room!" — Eugene O'Neill

• Give the common names of Dumas' *Three Musketeers*, and name the fourth member who later joined them. Also, what was their motto or rallying cry? — Athos, Porthos, Aramis, and D'Artagnan; "All for One and One for All!"

• Complete this line from Lewis Carroll's poem "Jabberwocky": "And hast thou slain the Jabberwock? Come to my arms, my beamish boy! O frabjous day! 'Callooh! Callay' He _____ " — "chortled in his joy."

• At age 7, Orson Welles could recite what entire Shakespeare play from memory? — *King Lear*

• What kind of creature is each of the following characters?
   - *Treasure Island's* Captain Flint — A parrot
   - Tolkien's Bilbo Baggins — A Hobbit
   - Mopsy, in the Beatrix Potter story — A Rabbit
   - *Jungle Book's* Kaa — A python

• To whom is Longfellow referring when he relates: "His brow is wet with honest sweat, And looks the whole world in the face, For he owes not any man"? — "The Village Blacksmith"

• In Voltaire's *Candide,* who was saved from hanging because the hangman was unable to tie the proper knot? — Dr. Pangloss

• According to the *Bible,* what "turneth away wrath"? — "A soft answer"

• What heroic character tried to dodge the draft by planting salt and plowing the sea shore with a horse and an ox yoked together? — Ulysses (Odysseus)

• It was well known that Louisa May Alcott detested little girls. Why then did she write *Little Women*? — For money

• Who wrote the lines: "Half a league, half a league, half a league onward,/ All in the valley of Death rode the six hundred"; and, later sought to delete the line: "Not tho' the soldier knew someone had blundered" to hide the facts of military incompetence in which most of the 607 British were killed"? — Alfred Tennyson

• What classic, like a true-confession romance, is the story of a beautiful woman who marries a pompous man, soon runs off with a dashing young Russian officer, and ultimately ends up committing suicide? — Tolstoy's *Anna Karenina*

- Edward Stratemeyer wrote *Tom Swift* based on his personal idol. Who was this successful man?

  Henry Ford

- Who wrote a play featuring John, Michael and Wendy, and a ship named the *Jolly Roger;* and what is the play called?

  J. M. Barrie; "Peter Pan"

- Herman Melville dedicated *Moby Dick* to what good friend and neighbor of his?

  Nathaniel Hawthorne

- Who wrote the French fairy tales, Cinderella and Sleeping Beauty?

  Charles Perrault

- Who was known as "the good, gray poet"?

  Walt Whitman

- What was the given name of the author who wrote under each of these pen names?

  - Boz — Charles Dickens
  - George Elliot — Mary Challans
  - Mark Twain — Samuel Langhorne Clemens
  - George Orwell — Eric Blair
  - Voltaire — Francois Marie Arouet
  - Richard Saunders — Ben Franklin
  - William Sydney Porter — O. Henry
  - The Bell Brothers (Currer, Ellis, & Acton) — The Bronte sisters (Charlotte, Emily and Anne)
  - Nancy Boyd — Edna St. Vincent Millay
  - Lewis Carroll — Charles Ludwidge Dodgson

- The "ideal" Renaissance prince, Cesare Borgia, was described as intelligent, cruel, and treacherous. What book by what Florentine philosopher was based on Borgia's example?

  The Prince, by Niccolo Machiavelli

- "As there cannot be good laws where the state is not well armed, it follows that where they are well-armed they have good laws." What 15th- to 16th-century writer offered this illogical advice?

  Machiavelli

- What black author wrote *Nobody Knows My Name* and *Another Country?*

  James Baldwin

- Arthur Conan Doyle wrote what series of books after being taught by the eminent surgeon Dr. Joseph Bell, who could deduce the livelihood, personal habits, nationality and general history of a man just by looking at him?

  Sherlock Holmes

- A London rhyme refers to rashlike sores of a deadly plague that appeared in 1665. Since it was thought to be spread by a victim's putrid breath, sweet-smelling herbs were thrown, but the victims still sneezed, and a large portion of the population died. What is the rhyme?

  "Ring a ring of roses,/ A pocket full of posies./ A-tishoo! a-tishoo!/ We all fall down!

- What young girl wrote: "Think of all the beauty still left around you and be happy"?

  Anne Frank, in her *Diary of A Young Girl*

- George Orwell nearly titled his last novel, *The Last Man in Europe.* What was his ultimate choice for a title? What three superpowers does the book forsee?

  1984; "Oceania," "Eurasia" and "Eastasia"

- Who wrote the following mysteries?

  - *The Murder of Roger Ackroyd* — Agatha Christie
  - "Murder in the Cathedral" — T.S. Elliot
  - *The Mystery of Edwin Drood* — Charles Dickens
  - "The Mystery of Marie Roget" — Edgar Allan Poe
  - *The Mysteries of Udolpho* — Ann Radcliffe

- In what adventure tale do you read, "Yo-ho-ho, and a bottle of rum!"? What is the name of this book's peg-legged pirate character?

  Treasure Island; Long John Silver

- Part of a four-million dollar estate was given to Dashiell Hammett's Fund for Marxist Writers by his lover. Who was the donor?

Lillian Hellman

- *The Love Machine* was what author's second novel?

Jacqueline Susanne's

- What is Al Capp's most famous creation?

"L'il Abner"

- In what English classic do you find the wife of Bath, who took firemen as husbands and found them all good?

Chaucer's *Canterbury Tales*

- What contemporary writer wrote: "In The Fall Alas, after a certain age, every man is responsible for his own face"?

Albert Camus

- *Pride and Prejudice, Northanger Abbey,* and *Emma* were included among what writer's novels?

Jane Austen

- "What animal goes on four legs in the morning, on two at noon and on three in the evening?" (The answer: man. He crawls as a baby, walks as a man, and uses a cane in old age.) Who posed this riddle? Who solved it?

The Sphinx; Oedipus

- What poet exclaimed: "To have great poets, there must be great audiences, too"?

Walt Whitman

- Who penned the social protest *Civil Disobedience* in 1849? For what nature-study is he best known?

Henry David Thoreau; *Walden*

- Name the characters who spoke these familiar Shakespearean lines, and the plays in which they are found:

  – "A horse! A horse! My kingdom for a horse!"

King Richard; *Richard III*

  – "The quality of mercy is not strained . . . "

Portia; *The Merchant of Venice*

  – "All the world's a stage . . . "

Jacques; *As You Like It*

  – "Our revels now are ended."

Prospero; *The Tempest*

  – "Good Night, sweet prince . . . "

Horatio; *Hamlet*

  – "Goodnight! goodnight! Parting is such sweet sorrow . . . "

Romeo; *Romeo and Juliet*

  – "Nothing will come of nothing."

King Lear; *King Lear*

- Who wrote: "I was a child and she was a child, In this kingdom by the sea; But we loved with a love that was more than love – I and my Annabel Lee"?

Edgar Allan Poe

- What famous George Orwell novel was rejected by 23 publishing houses – even by Faber and Faber's chief editor, T.S. Eliot – before being published?

Animal Farm

- In Edgar Rice Burrough's novels, what is Tarzan's son's name?

Korak

- Match the author to the work:

  – *Dr. Zhivago*

Boris Pasternak

  – *The Defense Never Rests* (an autobiography)

F. Lee Bailey

  – *Death on the Nile*

Agatha Christie

  – *The Pilgrim's Progress*

John Bunyan

  – *Man and Superman*

George Bernard Shaw

  – *The Maltese Falcon*

Dashiell Hammett

  – *The Wealth of Nations*

Adam Smith

  – *Jungle Book*

Rudyard Kipling

  – *Peyton Place*

Grace Metalious

  – *The Fellowship of the Ring* (first of a trilogy)

J. R. R. Tolkein

  – *Sex and the Single Girl*

Helen Gurley Brown

  – *The Prophet*

Kahlil Gibran

  – *The Secret Life of Walter Mitty*

James Thurber

- In the first line of the *Bible,* what does God create?

The heavens and the earth

8

ART AND ARCHITECTURE

Trivia to Learn By

• Following the classical 13th-century Romanesque revival, what new architectural style – named after a barbarian tribe because it was first considered base and unsophisticated – was characterized by pointed arches, vaulted ceilings, slender pillars, and flying buttresses?	Gothic
• Norman Rockwell painted 318 covers for what magazine? He also painted the greater majority of the calendars for what organization?	*The Saturday Evening Post*; The Boy Scouts of America
• The portrait masterpiece "La Giaconda" is best known by what name?	"Mona Lisa"
• Who, in painting the famous work that depicts Washington crossing the Delaware, employed American tourists to pose as his soldiers and used the Rhine to represent the Delaware?	The German painter Emanuel Leutze
• What post-impressionist French painter was strongly affected by primitive art and Japanese prints?	Paul Gauguin
• Give the art terms used to denote:	
– A 20th-century movement aimed at expressing the subconscious	Surrealism
– An exact copy of a work by the artist	Replica
– The greenish coating on bronze-cast sculptures	Patina
– A mixture of plaster and glue used to coat a surface before painting it	Gesso
– A sculpture of the upper part of the human body	Bust
– A layered painting	Montage
– A sculpture extending from the background of a flat work	Relief
– An old religious painting (usually on wood or ivory)	Icon
– A work made up of small tiles	Mosaic
• What is the sculptor Gutzon Borglum's most celebrated work of art?	Mount Rushmore
• Where would one visit the decoratively tiled Dome of the Rock, built by Islamic craftsmen around A.D. 684? What two events were said to have occurred at the Dome's site?	Jerusalem; Abraham's near-sacrifice and Muhammed's ascent into heaven
• What famed first-name artists had these surnames?	
– Buonarroti	Michelangelo
– Van Rijn	Rembrandt
– Sanzio (or Santi) de Urbino	Raphael
• There are two stylistically identical paintings entitled "Madonna of the Rocks" by Leonardo da Vinci. In which two galleries do the works hang?	The Louvre in Paris and Britain's National Gallery in London
• As the forerunner of Cubist painters, what French artist wrote: "You must see in nature the cylinder, the sphere, the cone, all put into perspective, so that every side of an object . . . recedes to a central point"?	Paul Cezanne
• The Verrazano-Narrows suspension bridge spans a breadth 60 feet longer than the Golden Gate Bridge, making it the longest bridge in North America. Where is it?	New York City
• Name the painting in which a stolid farmer holding a pitchfork stands next to his equally solemn, sturdy wife.	"American Gothic" by Grant Wood

- What frequently visited Roman Amphitheater, with outer walls approximately 150 feet high, was constructed between A.D. 72 and 80?

The Colosseum

- What Gothic art-form added "living color" to the French cathedrals?

Stained-glass windows

- Fra Filippo Lippi (1406-69) was a famed Renaissance painter with the curious inability to paint what body part correctly?

Hands (he tended to conceal them in clothing or behind objects)

- What American artist specialized in drawing birds?

John James Audubon

- What famous domed cathedral, jointly designed by Michelangelo and Giacomo della Porta, sits on Vatican Hill?

St. Peter's Basilica

- What error did New York's Museum of Modern Art commit in displaying Matisse's "Le Bateau"?

It hung on the wall, upside-down, for 47 years

- The seven ancient wonders of the world are (or were) all art or architectural works. Name them from their descriptions below:

   – Three structures constructed of approximately 2,300,000 blocks weighing about 2.5 tons each.

Pyramids of Giza, Egypt

   – Built in 600 B.C. by Nebuchadnezzar, on terraces laid out atop a vaulted building, with provisions to raise water to its roof.

Hanging Gardens of Babylon

   – Fifth-century B.C. giant gold and ivory figure, since lost or destroyed; reputedly 40 feet high.

Statue of Zeus at Olympia

   – A beautiful, 60-foot-high structure, later named in honor of a Greek Goddess. Destroyed by Goths in A.D. 262.

Temple of Artemis (Diana) at Ephesus

   – A monument erected in remembrance of King Mausolus of Asia Minor by his wife in 353 B.C. Parts still remain.

Mausoleum at Halicarnassus

   – An approximately 105-foot-high bronze statue of Apollo; fashioned over a 12-year period and completed in 280 B.C. Destroyed by earthquake in 224 B.C.

Colossus at Rhodes

   – A lighthouse built on the island of Pharos off the coast of Egypt by Sostratus during the 3rd century B.C. Demolished in an earthquake in the 13th century.

Pharos at Alexandria

- Besides being the premier Florentine artists of their time, what else did Michelangelo and Leonardo da Vinci have in common?

They were both left-handed

- "Two Laundresses," "Women on the Terrace of a Cafe," and "Woman with a Glass of Absinthe" are the masterful works of what celebrated French painter?

Edgar Degas

- Certain artists are noted for the distinct subject matter they dealt with. Name the well-known painters whose passions were:

   – Pop art; soup cans and the like

Andy Warhol

   – French peasants

Jean-Francois Millet

   – Analytical, cubical portrayals of "anatomically different" women

Pablo Picasso

   – Ballet dancers and race-track scenes

Edgar Degas

   – Lithographs of 19th-century American rural, historical and folk scenes

Nathaniel Currier and James Ives

   – Tahiti

Pierre-Auguste Renoir and Paul Gaugin

– Nudes cavorting in pastoral settings	Edouard Manet
– Haystacks and garden scenes	Claude Monet
– Abstract, active paint spattering	Jackson Pollock
– Parisian night-life – cafes, music halls . . .	Henry de Toulouse-Loutrec
– Naive yet lively rural winter scenes	Grandma Moses
– Geometrically distorted hills and trees	Paul Cezanne
– Biblical stories and other subjects, plus, over 100 self-portraits	Rembrandt van Rijn
• Name the colossal sculpture that guards the pyramids at Giza. What is the name of the most famous of the pyramids there?	The Sphinx; Cheops
• What richly embellished 17th- to 18th-century architectural age followed the more simple and classical Renaissance era (its name meant "irregular" or "misshapen")?	Baroque
• Over 1400 of Camille Pissaro's paintings vanished during the 1871 Franco-Prussian War. Some were taken as souvenirs, but most were ruined in what way?	Soldiers used the finished canvasses to construct walkways through the spring mud
• Around 2780 B.C., the mastaba, a common ancient, flat-topped tomb with sloping walls, was the forerunner of what colossal structures?	The Egyptian Pyramids
• What color, often made from cheap ammoniated copper, was known to quickly fade in paintings using this pigment?	Blue
• Vincent Van Gogh sold how many of his works during his lifetime?	Only one
• What inventor supported himself by painting portraits while working on his inventions?	Samuel B. Morse
• Who designed the oldest known uniforms in the world, those worn by the Vatican's Swiss Guards – a style which is still in use today?	Michelangelo
• At Montreal's Expo '67, Buckminster Fuller introduced what experimental prefabricated building?	The geodesic dome
• Salvador Dali and Max Ernst's paintings characterized the school of art known by what name?	Surrealism
• *Time* magazine dubbed what abstract painter, "Jack the Dripper"?	Jackson Pollock
• Which of all the sculptures by Michelangelo was the only one actually signed by the sculptor?	"Pieta"
• Frank Lloyd Wright regarded what architect as his predessessor and mentor in designing free-flowing, open, and functional buildings?	Louis Sullivan
• In order to keep Francesco del Giocondo's wife smiling while sitting for the portrait "Mona Lisa," what did Leonardo da Vinci do?	He hired jesters, singers and musicians to perform for her
• What is the better-known designation for the Greek Temple of Athena, located on the Acropolis at Athens and built around 440 B.C.?	The Parthenon
• What English portrait artist was in such demand that, in the year 1757 alone, 677 clients sat for him?	Joshua Reynolds
• Identify the architectural term by its definition:	
– An abutting wall, inside or outside a building, that adds additional strength	Buttress

– Fired but unglazed clay	Terracotta
– A plaster mixture to cover walls	Stucco
– The vertical grooves in a column	Fluting (or channels)
– A church's semicircular niche, which usually contains an altar	Apse
– An upright round support	Column
– An upright square or polygon-shaped support	Pillar
– A small court in the middle of a Roman house	Atrium

• The great architectural masterpiece "Santa Sophia, the Great Church of the Holy Wisdom," in Istanbul, and another church by the same name in Kiev, Russia, are splendid examples of what Greek building age? — Byzantine

• Following Japan's disastrous earthquake in 1923, who received a cablegram stating, "Hotel Imperial Stands Undamaged, Monument to Your Genius In Japan?" — Frank Lloyd Wright

• Who created the portrait of George Washington that appears on the one-dollar bill? — Gilbert Stuart

• Whenever painting a crucifixion scene, what did the artist Fra Angelico (1387-1455) do? — He wept uncontrollably

• "Arch" and "cantilever" are two types of what? — Bridges

• Leonardo da Vinci recommended staring at what object and studying its random textural irregularities, when no subject matter or inspiration presented itself? — A bare stucco wall

• Who produced the following art works?

– The impressionistic "Water Lilies"	Claude Monet
– "The Last Supper"	Leonardo da Vinci
– The colorfully splattered "Winding Paths"	Jackson Pollock
– "The Bar"	Henri de Toulouse-Lautrec
– The statue "David"	Michelangelo
– The painting "Man with a Golden Helmet"	Rembrandt
– The eerie and surrealistic "The Burning Giraffe"	Salvador Dali

• What is the name for ancient Japanese Buddhist temples usually characterized by five roofs, one atop the other? — Pagodas

• What famed Florentine medallion artist was christened by his parents with the Italian word for "Welcome," because he was their first child after 18 years of marriage? — Benvenuto Cellini

MUSIC
Trivia to Learn By

• Name the composer of the music for "West Side Story."	Leonard Bernstein
• Who was the first white band leader to employ black musicians in his band; and who was the first black band leader to employ white musicians (he called them "colorless")?	Benny Goodman; Charlie Mingus
• We associate the name Rodgers with Hammerstein. With what musician would you associate Lorenzo da Ponte?	Mozart (Ponte was co-writer of "The Marriage of Figaro," "Don Giovanni," and others)
• Who composed the Tonight Show theme song entitled, "Here's Johnny"?	Paul Anka
• What was the name of Puff the Magic Dragon's human friend?	Jackie Paper
• On the night he died, what rock musician was working on a song called "The Story of Life"?	Jimi Hendrix
• Tschaikovsky created two symphonies on Shakespearean themes, the "Romeo and Juliet" and "Hamlet" overtures. For what three great ballets did he also compose the music?	"The Nutcracker," "Swan Lake," and "Sleeping Beauty"
• Who sang these crazy-sounding 1950's songs?	
– "Mamma Look A Boo Boo"	Harry Belafonte
– "Ob La Di Ob La Da"	The Beatles
– "Doo Wah Diddy"	Manfred Mann
"My Ding A Ling"	Chuck Berry
• Who composed "An American in Paris"?	George Gershwin
• In the 1950's what rock performer and what rock group – enormously successful in their later careers – failed their auditions for Arthur Godfrey's Talent Scouts, a feature designed to showcase promising talent?	Elvis Presley (in 1955) and Buddy Holly and the Crickets (in 1957)
• Name the favorite song sung by the forty-niners bound for the California gold rush?	"O, Susanna"
• The spread of jazz began in 1918 when an all-white band traveled from New Orleans to New York City to become an international sensation. What was the band's name?	The Dixieland Jazz Band
• What famous Tchaikovsky ballet features appearances by Red Riding Hood and Cinderella?	"Sleeping Beauty"
• A musical instrument, the Portugese "machete" was popularized by Edward Putvis, a Britisher. Its name was changed to commemorate the jumping antics of the diminutive Putvis during performances. What is this "flea-jumping" instrument?	The ukulele
• What term describes a Renaissance musical group consisting of one type or family of instrument – e.g., all viols?	Consort
• Name the parts of the body found in these song titles:	
– "I Want to Hold Your _____"	Hand
– "Put Your ____ on My ____"	Head; Shoulder
– "These ____"	Eyes
– "Back in My ____ Again"	Arms
– "Put Your ____ in the ____"	Hand; Hand.
– "I Only Have ____ for You"	Eyes
• What group asked the question: "Do you Believe in Magic?"?	The Lovin' Spoonful
• The ailing Franz Joseph Haydn was carried to the piano each day in May, 1809 to play what piece, in symbolic protest of the French bombardment of Vienna?	"The Austrian Imperial Anthem"
• What four musicians, playing 3 different instruments, make up a standard string quartet?	First and Second Violinists, Violist, and Cellist

- Big Band leader Paul Whiteman was responsible for introducing symphonic jazz to the concert hall in 1924 when his band played a composition by young George Gershwin. What was the name of the piece? What famed crooner was in Whiteman's band? — "Rhapsody in Blue"; Bing Crosby

- Bob Dylan's "Like a Rolling Stone" shattered what assumption about which songs could become Number One Hits? — That hits are no more than 2 to 3 minutes long (Dylan's song ran for a full 6 minutes)

- Besides being country-western stars, what else did Gene Autry, Roy Rogers, Tex Ritter, Jimmy Wakely, and T. Tex Tyler have in common? — They were all Hollywood singing cowboys

- What "March King" and one-time leader of the U.S. Marine Corps Band wrote, among numerous other marches, "The Stars and Stripes Forever" and "Semper Fidelis"? — John Philip Sousa

- Name the U.S. armed forces' hymns:
    - Navy — "Anchors Aweigh"
    - Army — "The Caisons Go Rolling Along"
    - Marines — "The Marine Hymn" ("From the Halls of Montezuma")
    - Air Force — "The U.S. Air Force" ("The Wild Blue Yonder")

- The same man who wrote "Surprise Symphony" also organized "Lark," "Joke" and "Quinten" string quartet pieces. Who was he? — Franz Joseph Haydn

- What composers wrote the following operatic pieces?
    - "Carmen" — Georges Bizet
    - "The Marriage of Figaro" and "Don Giovanni" — Wolfgang Amadeus Mozart
    - "La Boheme," "Madame Butterfly" and "Tosca" — Giacomo Puccini
    - "Faust" — Charles Gounod
    - "The Tales of Hoffman" — Jacques Offenbach
    - "Rigoletto," "La Traviata" and "Aida" — Giuseppe Verdi
    - "Der Rosenkavalier" and "Salome" — Richard Strauss
    - "The Barber of Seville" — Gioacchino Rossini
    - "Siegfried," "Tristan and Isolde" and "Lohengrin" — Richard Wagner

- What group popularized "Mrs. Brown You've Got A Lovely Daughter," and "Henry the VIII"? — Herman's Hermits

- After the opening of his opera "Hansel and Gretel" in 1893, what German composer suddenly became famous throughout Europe? — Englebert Humperdinck

- Name the four classes of instruments in an orchestra. — Strings, brass, woodwinds and percussion

- What two singers were the first female country artists to receive platinum records for their "Here You Come Again" and "Don't It Make My Brown Eyes Blue"? — Dolly Parton and Crystal Gayle

- What prominent black composer died in 1912 propped up by pillows with a smile on his lips, and leading an imagined symphony of one of his violin concertos? — Samuel Coleridge-Taylor

- "Old Folks At Home," "Away Down South," "O, Susanna," and "My Old Kentucky Home," were all written by whom? — Stephen Foster

- "The Stammering Song" was the subtitle for what World War I hit? — "K-K-K-Katy"

- Neil Sedaka's "The Immigrant" was dedicated to what singer-musician who at the time was fighting deportation from the U.S.? — John Lennon

- The Bohemian composer, Antonin Dvorák, wrote what celebrated work with an American theme? — The "New World Symphony"

- What male duet's members both graduated from high school at age 15? — Paul Simon and Art Garfunkel

- What was the theme song for Roy Rogers and Dale Evans? — "Happy Trails"
- Ray Charles sings and plays an emotional blues-gospel-jazz combination of music called what? — Soul
- What Aaron Copeland composition has a decidedly Western flavor? — "Rodeo"
- By what common name do we know the following Beethoven symphonies?
    - Symphony No. 6 in F Major — "Pastoral"
    - Symphony No. 9 in D Minor — "Choral"
    - Symphony No. 3 in E-flat Major — "Eroica"
- What Beatles' song did Frank Sinatra call "the greatest love song of the past 50 years"? — "Something"
- Who said, "Rock 'n' roll is phony and false, and sung, written and played for the most part by cretinous goons"? — Frank Sinatra
- Who wrote about 500 dance works, primarily waltzes, including the famed "Blue Danube"? — Johann Strauss II
- The song "Danny Boy" is sung to what old tune? — "Londonderry Air"
- Crosby, Stills, Nash and Young made their debut performance where? — At Woodstock
- Name the singer who sang backup for The Drifters and The Shirelles, and lead for The Gospelaires. — Dionne Warwick
- What famous TV series' theme song did Alexander Courage write? — "Star Trek"
- Name the three Andrews Sisters. — Patricia, LaVerne (the eldest) and Maxine

- What great composer of comic opera used satirical music equal in feeling to the lyrics of his companion and collaborator, W.S. Gilbert? Also what was the most famous hymn he wrote? — Sir Arthur Sullivan; "Onward Christian Soldiers"
- Who sang the '68 hit "This Guy's in Love With You"? — Herb Alpert
- Stephen Foster wrote a song about the Yazoo River. After being scolded by his brother, he changed the name and published what well-known song? — "Swanee River"
- The following songs celebrate states of the United States. Name the artists who performed them.
    - "The Night the Lights Went Out in Georgia" — Vickie Lawrence
    - "California Dreamin'" — The Mamas and the Papas
    - "Hawaii Five-O" — The Ventures
    - "The Yellow Rose of Texas" — Mitch Miller
    - "Kentucky Rain" — Elvis Presley
- When The Temptations signed with Motown Records they called themselves The Miracles, but another Motown group already went by that name. Who led this second group? Who was the future-star drummer for these original Miracles? — Smokey Robinson (and The Miracles); Marvin Gaye
- Name the classical music term that describes:
    - A night piece; tuneful but sad — Nocturne
    - Increasing in loudness — Crescendo
    - Very soft (pp) — Pianissimo
    - A musician of outstanding technical skill — Virtuoso
    - A lively, jesting, unsentimental piece — Scherzo
    - A second, added melody to be sung or played above the first melody — Descant
    - At a fast pace — Presto
    - Musical notes played in a short, detatched fashion — Staccato

3

– At a slow pace	Adagio
– At a lively pace	Allegro
– A composition where one or a few instruments stand out against the orchestra	Concerto

• What rock legend was voted "Ugliest Man on Campus" at the University of Texas, precipitating her escape to San Francisco's more hospitable climate? — **Janis Joplin**

• "Over There" and "It's a Long Way to Tipperary" were hit songs from what war? — **World War I**

• What performers recorded these "tough guy" songs?

– "Big Bad John"	Jimmy Dean
– "Bad, Bad Leroy Brown"	Jim Croce
– "The Devil Went Down to Georgia"	Charlie Daniels Band
– Theme from "Shaft"	Isaac Hayes

• Name the composer of "Leaving on a Jet Plane," made famous by the group Peter, Paul, and Mary. — **John Denver**

• What kind of music is "a composition in duple rhythm (as 4/4 time) or triple compound rhythm (as 6/8 time) with a strongly accentuated beat suitable for the guidance of a steady, measured stride"? — **A march**

• "Kiss Me Kate," and "The Gay Divorcee" were among his musicals, and "Night and Day" was one of his most popular songs. Who was he, and what was his real first name? — **Cole (Albert) Porter**

• What black rock 'n' roll innovator studied classical violin for seven years and later played rhythm guitar for Chuck Berry? — **Bo Diddley**

• What contemporary British composer wrote the operas "Billy Budd" and "Peter Grimes"? — **Benjamin Britten**

• Katharine Lee Bates, an American professor of English, wrote the words to what patriotic song, inspired by a climb to the top of Pikes Peak in 1893? — **"America the Beautiful"**

• Who wrote the 1966 song "Woman" for Peter and Gordon under the pseudonym "Bernard Webb," in order to see if it would sell without the use of his famous name? — **Paul McCartney**

• Who originally replaced Brian Wilson when he ceased performing concerts with The Beach Boys in 1964? — **Glen Campbell**

• Napoleon banned the playing of what song because of its revolutionary tone? — **"La Marseillaise," (The French national anthem)**

• "Sweet Adeline" and "Meet Me In St. Louis" are early 1900's examples of what kind of song? — **Barbershop**

• Michael Jackson was nominated for how many Grammys – and won what unprecedented number – in 1983? — **Twelve; he won 8**

• What has been called "The Carnegie Hall of Hillbillies"? Where is it located? — **The Grand Ole Opry; Nashville**

• Dick Clark's wife inspired one singer's stage name when she remarked, "He's cute. He looks like a little Fats Domino." Who is this musician, and what is his best-known song? — **Chubby Checker; "Let's Twist Again"**

• In what familiar opera does a jealous husband kill his wife outside a sports arena? — **"Carmen" by Bizet**

• The "swing" and "jazz" music of Benny Goodman, Paul Whiteman, Guy Lombardi, the Dorsey brothers, and others were most popular in what golden era of American music? — **The Big Band Era**

• When Cat Stevens converted to Islam, he stopped doing what and changed his name to what? — **Singing; Yusef Islam**

4

- What gospel-singing great proclaimed: "The first gospels may have been the source from which the first jazz caught its beat . . . . For me, there is a fundamental joy in everything I sing, 'cause I sing for the Lord."

Mahalia Jackson

- "I'm a Yankee Doodle Dandy" was written by whom? On what day of the year 1878 was he born?

George M. Cohen; July 3rd (his father changed the date to the 4th out of patriotic fervor)

- Complete the following song titles bearing boy's names:
    - The Kingston Trio's "Tom _____"

    . . . Dooley
    - Dionne Warwick's "_____ Michael"

    Message to . . .
    - The Beatles' "Rocky _____"

    . . . Racoon
    - Gene Autry's "Rudolph _____"

    . . . the Red-Nosed Reindeer
    - Chuck Berry's "_____ B. Goode"

    Johnny . . .
    - Paul Simon's "_____ Julio _____"

    Me and . . . Down By the Schoolyard
    - Fess Parker's "_____ Davy _____"

    The Ballad of . . . Crockett
- What are the last names of Peter, Paul and Mary? What is Paul's real first name?

Yarrow, Stookey, and Travers; Noel

- Norway's most celebrated composer, Edvard Grieg, composed the hauntingly beautiful music for what Henrik Ibsen verse-drama?

Peer Gynt

- Name the artists whose last recorded tunes before their deaths were the following:
    - "I'll Never Get Out Of This World Alive"

    Hank Williams
    - "My Way"

    Elvis Presley
    - "(Just Like) Starting Over"

    John Lennon
    - "It Doesn't Matter Anymore"

    Buddy Holly
- After being turned down by Bob Dylan and Bobby Vinton, who was hired to record Burt Bacharach's hit, "Raindrops Keep Falling On My Head" for the movie "Butch Cassidy and the Sundance Kid"?

B. J. Thomas

- In opera and ballet, the principal female singer and dancer are called by what respective titles?

Prima Donna and Prima Ballerina

- Who wrote "I'm a Believer," made famous by The Monkees?

Neil Diamond

- The Beatles produced the song "Strawberry Fields." What and where is the actual Strawberry Fields?

An orphanage in Liverpool

- What composers wrote, respectively, the "Italian Symphony" and the "French Suites"?

Felix Mendelssohn and Johann Sebastian Bach

- What famed rock guitarist was a paratrooper in the 101st Airborne Division of the U.S. Air Force?

Jimi Hendrix

- What individuals or groups recorded the following popular fifties songs?
    - "Poor Little Fool"

    Ricky Nelson
    - "Venus"

    Frankie Avalon
    - "Mack the Knife"

    Bobby Darin
    - "Mona Lisa"

    Nat "King" Cole
    - "Chances Are"

    Johnny Mathis
    - "Whatever Will Be, Will Be"

    Doris Day
    - "Lonely Boy"

    Paul Anka
    - "Doggie in the Window"

    Patti Page
    - "Don't Be Cruel" and "All Shook Up"

    Elvis Presley
    - "Sincerely"

    The McGuire Sisters

– "Rock Around the Clock"	Bill Haley and the Comets
• What was the major difference between the 1920's-40's swing and ballroom dancing, and the rock 'n' roll dancing of the 1950's (to the horror of many adults)?	The female partner was not restricted to following the male's lead
• What Bob Dylan song did Jimmy Carter quote in his 1976 Democratic Convention acceptance speech, saying "he who is not busy being born is busy dying"?	"It's All Right Ma (I'm Only Bleeding)"
• What was the section of New York City called where the tinkling music of the "Gay Nineties" (1880 to 1910) originated?	"Tin Pan Alley"
• "Blues" music wasn't recognized as such until W.C. Handy published what song in 1912?	"Memphis Blues"
• Marilyn McCoo was a one-time member of what group?	The Fifth Dimension
• What 1961 international hit record was based on a traditional South African folk song called "Wimoweh"?	"The Lion Sleeps Tonight" by The Tokens
• The modern "do, re, mi . . . "scaled phrase was taken from the Latin Hymn "St. John's Day." What was the original syllable for "do," the first in the scale?	"Ut," (as in running the gamut)
• Identify the person associated with each of these big-band theme songs:	
– "Bubbles in the Wine"	Lawrence Welk
– "Babalu"	Desi Arnaz
– "Auld Lang Syne"	Guy Lombardo
– "Melancholy Serenade"	Jackie Gleason
– "My Shawl"	Xavier Cugat
• What was Elvis Presley's first number-one hit, released in 1956?	"Heartbreak Hotel"
• What does BB King claim his initials stand for? He became the first R & B artist to tour what country?	"Blues Boy"; The Soviet Union
• Who wrote the following classical pieces?	
– "The Messiah" oratorio	George Frederick Handel
– "Symphony from the New World"	Antonin Dvorák
– "William Tell" overture	Gioacchino Rossini
– "Hungarian Fantasy"	Franz Liszt
– "Don Quixote"	Anton Rubinstein
– "The Moldau"	Bedrich Smetana
• What is C.W. McCall's "handle" in his 1976 tune "Convoy"?	Rubber Duck
• What Guess Who 1970 single was banned in several southern states for being "Communistic"?	"Share the Land"
• Name Hoagy Carmichael's biggest hit, released in 1930.	"Stardust"
• What two inventions are most responsible for the spread and diversity of music around the globe? Who invented them?	The phonograph (Thomas Edison who also built the first juke box) and the radio (Gulielmo Marconi)
• What rock singer-pianist's name was Reginald Dwight before he changed it to add some "zing"?	Elton John's
• What soloist-guitarist, who spent time in two mental institutions after the breakup of his band (The Original Flying Machine), was moved to write, "sweet dreams and flying machines in pieces on the ground . . . "?	James Taylor
• Country music has many individual stars: Johnny Cash, Jimmie Rodgers, Loretta Lynn, Kenny Rogers, etc. But what family was clearly the leader in making country/bluegrass flourish?	The Carters

- Who sang these popular songs?
    - "I Can't Stop Loving You" and "Unchain My Heart"
    - "Don't Sleep in the Subway, Darling" and "I Know a Place"
    - "The Boxer" and "My Little Town"
    - "Lay Lady Lay" and "Like a Rolling Stone"
    - "I Hear You Knockin'" and "Ain't That a Shame"
    - "Cathy's Clown" and "All I Have to Do Is Dream"
    - "Crystal Blue Persuasion" and "I Think We're Alone Now"

Ray Charles
Petula Clark
Simon and Garfunkel
Bob Dylan
Fats Domino
The Everly Brothers
Tommy James and the Shondells

- Who performed:
    - "The Ballad of Jed Clampett" on the *Beverly Hillbillies* TV show?
    - The theme song from *My Three Sons*?
    - The *Rawhide* theme?
    - The *Ironside* theme song?

Lester Flatt and Earl Scruggs
Lawrence Welk Orchestra
Frankie Laine
Quincy Jones

- After his "The Times They Are A-Changin'," what two singers joined Bob Dylan to record his protest song "Blowin' in the Wind" at the Newport Folk Festival?

Joan Baez and Pete Seeger

- What "crying" singer came along to wean Americans away from the "dozing," relaxing songs of the crooners (Perry Como, et. al.) to the sweaty, soul-baring emotionalism of 1950's music?

Johnnie Ray

- Who, in the scores he wrote for many musicals and films, introduced such renowned songs as "White Christmas," "God Bless America," and "Blue Skies"?

Irving Berlin

- Give the performer associated with the following country songs:
    - "Stand By Your Man"
    - "I Walk the Line"
    - "With Loving on Your Mind"
    - "This Land is Your Land"
    - "Back in the Saddle Again"

Tammy Wynette
Johnny Cash
Loretta Lynn
Woodie Guthrie
Gene Autry

- What group produced "Midnight Train to Georgia"; and what was the song's original title?

Gladys Knight and the Pips; "Midnight Plane to Houston"

- Which of all the symphonic musical instruments (besides piano) has the largest range of notes? Which has the smallest range?

The harp; the timpani (kettle drums)

- In the midst of a difficult and tragic life, what composer's principal works included the "Faust" and "Dante" symphonies?

Franz Liszt

- Who spouted: "We're more popular than Jesus now"?

John Lennon (speaking of The Beatles)

- In the Big Band Era, what instrument did these men play?
    - Duke Ellington
    - Benny Goodman
    - Tommy Dorsey
    - Glen Miller
    - Harry James
    - Gene Krupa
    - Count Basie
    - Lionel Hampton

Piano
Clarinet
Trombone
Clarinet
Trumpet
Drums
Piano
Vibraphone

- Country-western and "Nashville Sound" were derived from what type of music?

Hillbilly mountain music (or Bluegrass)

- What song is traditionally played when the President of the United States enters a gathering?

"Hail to the Chief"

- What simplistic yet successful Beach Boy hit was released against the wishes of the group, which was looking for greater credibility as a "progressive" entity? — "Barbara Ann"

- Often called the "Black Stephen Foster," what song-writer used the plantation-slave theme to write songs such as "Oh, Dem Golden Slippers" and "Carry Me Back to Old Virginny"? — James A. Bland

- Give the "and the" or "and" rock groups that backed up these lead singers:
  - Freddy — and the Dreamers
  - Paul McCartney — and Wings
  - Sam the Sham — and the Pharoahs
  - Diana Ross — and the Supremes
  - Sly — and the Family Stone
  - Bill Haley — and the Comets
  - Tommy James — and the Shondells
  - Buddy Holly — and the Crickets
  - Linda Ronstadt — and the Stone Poneys
  - Gary Lewis — and the Playboys
  - James Brown — and the Famous Flames
  - Paul Revere — and the Raiders
  - Gary Puckett — and the Union Gapp
  - Gladys Knight — and the Pips

- Which of Bach's compositions – "Passion According to St. Matthew," "Christmas Oratorio," and "Mass in B-minor" – is considered his greatest masterpiece of all? — "Mass in B-minor"

- Musicians Jim Morrison, Jim Croce, Ritchie Valens, Janis Joplin, Jimi Hendrix, Hank Williams, Elvis Presley, Bix Beiderbecke, John Lennon, Marvin Gaye and Buddy Holly all had what in common? — They all died "young"

- What great composer was also Mozart's mentor, and, until the day he died sought recognition for young Mozart? — Joseph Haydn

- Taken from the nickname for beer joints of the late 1930's, what musical form was played with a strong dance rhythm, by a pianist who had to deftly dodge beer bottles? — Honky Tonk

- What opera – Gioacchino Rossini's most famous work – at first failed to appeal to audiences, causing him to put down his pen for the last forty years of his life? — "William Tell"

- To whom were the following songs dedicated?
  - Elton John's "Candle in the Wind" — Marilyn Monroe
  - Joan Baez's "Diamonds and Rust" — Bob Dylan
  - George Harrison's "All Those Years Ago" — John Lennon
  - Carly Simon's LP Album "Anticipation" — Cat Stevens
  - Stevie Wonder's "Sir Duke" — Duke Ellington

- In the '40's and 50's, while Billie Holiday, The Ink Spots, and the Mills Brothers sang, what two male vocalists – both introduced by the Tommy Dorsey Band – caused near riots among fainting mobs of "bobby soxers"? — Frank Sinatra and Elvis Presley

- The scores for "Jonathan Livingston Seagull," "The Jazz Singer," "I'm a Believer," – who wrote them? — Neil Diamond

PEOPLE FACTS
Trivia to Learn By

• The aqualung (underwater breathing device) was developed during World War II by what two French Resistance fighters? — Jacques Cousteau and Emil Gagnan

• At Henry VIII's deathbed, his physicians, though competent, wisely reported that the King was not seriously ill. Why? — It was considered high treason to predict a king's death

• Whose mother accompanied him to West Point and rented an apartment overlooking the dormitory, to ensure that he studied? (He did, graduating first in his class.) — Douglas MacArthur's

• Who was the U.S. President voted "most likely to succeed," though he graduated sixty-fourth out of his high school class of 112? — John F. Kennedy

• Cleopatra, Queen of Egypt, hearing reports (which turned out to be false) that her husband Mark Antony had committed suicide after his defeat by Octavian, took her own life by what sacred method? Also, she was not Egyptian. Of what nationality was she? — She chose to die by snake bite; Greek, with some Iranian blood

• Babe Ruth wore what item beneath his baseball cap to keep his head cool on hot days? — A cabbage leaf (he changed it every two innings)

• What movie actress in the 1940's was known as "The Sweater Girl"? — Lana Turner

• Who sang "The Battle Hymn of the Republic" at Lyndon B Johnson's 1973 funeral? — Anita Bryant

• Karl Marx is buried in what European city? — London

• What 19th-century emperor adopted the bumblebee as his official emblem? — Napoleon

• Who wrote a multitude of notebooks on diverse subjects (such as how to make webbed gloves for swimming) and scribbled many of his ideas in a kind of mirror writing that went right to left? — Leonardo da Vinci

• Melville Louis Kossuth Dewey became a staunch proponent of simplification. He changed his name to Melvil Dui, fought against time-wasting, campaigned for a simplified English spelling system, and came up with what system of organization? — The Dewey Decimal System (until then, library books were sorted according to title, color, size . . .)

• The route on which Jesus carried his cross is known by what name? — Via Dolorosa, "The Way of Sorrows"

• Menachem Begin (Israel) and Anwar Sadat (Egypt) in 1978; Mother Teresa (Calcutta, India) in 1979; Lech Walesa (Poland) in 1983; and Bishop Desmond Tutu (So. Africa) in 1984: What happened to all of these people in these years? — They received Nobel Peace Prizes

• Asked how he calms himself while on the mound facing a tough batter, the pitcher Tug McGraw used what slugger as an example, saying, " . . . I remind myself that in a few billion years the sun is going to burn out and the earth will become a frozen snowball hurtling through space. And when that happens, nobody's going to care what _____ did with the bases loaded"? — Willie Stargell

• Marie Taglioni was the first prima ballerina to do what two things? — Dance on her toes and wear a tutu

• What mass murderer recorded "Lie," an album designed to spread his philosophies? — Charles Manson

• Historically, what are the names of the two thieves crucified with Jesus? How were their crucifixions distinct from Jesus'? — Dismas and Gestas; they were tied to the cross, Jesus was nailed

• What singer's twin brother, Jessie Garon, died at birth in 1935?	Elvis Aaron Presley's
• Mark Twain introduced Winston Churchill as he lectured in New York, not as "British," but as what?	"Half-American" (since Churchill's mother was American-born)
• Who was the only person to be sworn into the office of the U.S. Presidency by his father?	Calvin Coolidge
• What was John L. Jones (of Casey Jones fame) trying to do when he died in 1900?	Trying to brake his Illinois Central Cannonball train
• The first cover of *TV Guide* was graced by the baby of what comedienne-actress?	Lucille Ball
• Who, worried about his grades at Duke University Law School, broke into the dean's office to find records indicating he was at the top of his class?	Richard Nixon
• Louis XIV of France smelled terrible. Why?	He never took a bath in his life
• Florence Nightingale always traveled with what object in her pocket?	Her pet owl
• Juanita, a Miami drugstore owner and ardent anti-Communist, is the sister of what national leader?	Fidel Castro
• What happened to the Archbishop of Krakow in 1978?	He became Pope John Paul II
• What author was wife to aviator Charles Lindbergh?	Anne Morrow (Lindbergh)
• Stonewall Jackson, the Confederate general, always had what three books with him in the field?	*The Bible, Webster's Dictionary,* and *Napoleon's Maxims of War*
• What two black leaders won Nobel Peace Prizes, one in 1950 and the other in 1964?	Ralph Bunche and Martin Luther King, Jr.
• In 1962, what two famous spies were exchanged – a U.S. pilot held by the Soviets for a top Soviet agent?	Francis Gary Powers for Rudolf Abel
• Identify the person:	
– Who was nicknamed "The Legs."	Betty Grable
– Whose kidnapping was termed "The Crime of the Century."	Charles Lindbergh, Jr.
– Who, as a former Olympic hero, played the movies' first talking Tarzan.	Johnny Weissmuller
– Who owned a Louisville Slugger named Black Betsy.	George (Babe) Ruth
– Who killed Lee Harvey Oswald.	Jack Ruby
– Who was the voice of Porky Pig and Bugs Bunny.	Mel Blanc
– Whose 1926 death at age 31 prompted over 100,000 people to attend his funeral.	Rudolph Valentino
– Who was Napoleon's first wife (and whose name was the last word he spoke before dying).	Josephine
– Who was the original MC of the TV game Jeopardy.	Art Fleming
• Who first introduced Europeans to ice cream made with milk (before this time ice cream was merely flavored ice)? From where did this man obtain the idea?	Marco Polo; from the Chinese court of Kublai Khan
• Who sang "The Star-Spangled Banner" at the game in 1974 when Hank Aaron broke Babe Ruth's homerun record, hitting his 715th?	Pearl Bailey
• Who was the first statesman to be popularly known as "father of his country"?	Cicero

- Who created, among others, the Snickers, Mars, and Milky Way chocolate bars?

Frank Mars

- The youngest person to serve as U.S. President was not John F. Kennedy at Age 43 (though he was the youngest ever elected). Who was the youngster that took over the Presidency at age 42, after McKinley's assassination?

Theodore Roosevelt

- Identify Poland's Solidarity leader, and his occupation before being elected president.

Lech Walesa; electrician

- Napoleon Bonaparte was born on an island, exiled to an island, and died on an island. Name these three islands.

Corsica, Elba, St. Helena

- Restored to power after being ousted by a brother, who was the final ruler of the Ptolemies dynasty in Egypt? Who were this person's two most famous lovers?

Cleopatra VII; Julius Caesar and Mark Anthony

- What does the "S" stand for in the name Harry S Truman?

Nothing (therefore no period appears after the S)

- What relationship did Wilbur Wright have with Charles W. Furnas, the first airplane passenger (on a 1908, 29-second flight)?

Furnas was the Wright brother's mechanic

- Who was known as the "Swedish Nightingale"?

Jenny Lind

- What well-known pirate-leader demanded written agreements with his buccaneers that strictly prohibited them from gambling, quarreling, deserting, or smuggling women aboard ship (and who left them marooned if they broke the contract) but who also contracted to give them equal division of spoils and to compensate them for loss of a limb?

Bartholomew Roberts

- Who in history was known as "The Mad Monk"?

Rasputin

- John Dillinger was once stationed on what Navy ship, which was later sunk in Japan's Pearl Harbor attack?

The U.S.S. Utah

- Eddie Rickenbacker once owned a race car, "The Rickenbacker" (slogan: " A Car Worthy of His Name"). He also owned what famous sports complex?

The Indianapolis Speedway

- Isabella, daughter of 16th-century King Phillip II of Spain, swore not to do what until the rebellious seaport of Ostend was retaken.

Change her underwear (the resulting seige lasted 3 years)

- What actress' mother made sure her daughter's hair was set each day with exactly 56 curls?

Shirley Temple's

- Match the people listed here with their better-known pseudonyms:
    - John Chapman
    - Stanley R. Soog
    - Frederick Austerlitz
    - Ehrich Weiss
    - Israel Baline
    - Joseph Levitch
    - Walker Smith
    - Norma Jean Baker
    - Frances Gumm
    - Vladimir Ilyich Ulyanov
    - Nathan Burnbaum
    - Doroteo Arango
    - Marion Michael Morrison

Johnny Appleseed

Jackie Gleason

Fred Astaire

Harry Houdini

Irving Berlin

Jerry Lewis

Sugar Ray Robinson

Marilyn Monroe

Judy Garland

Nikolai Lenin

George Burns

Francisco (Pancho) Villa

John Wayne

Linus Pauling

- An American chemist is the only person to have received Nobel Prizes in two different areas – Chemistry (1954) and Peace (1962). Who was this chemist?

• One of Lyndon B. Johnson's favorite quotes was, "Come now, and let us reason together." What Biblical prophet first said these words?	Isaiah (chapter 1, verse 18)
• Who was the longest-playing, most famous "Dolly" in "Hello, Dolly"?	Carol Channing
• Salome demanded whose head?	John the Baptist's
• Who is TV's Captain Kangaroo?	Bob Keeshan
• What ex-governor of Georgia and owner of Pickrick Restaurants there, once used an axe handle to chase 3 blacks from his cafe in 1964?	Lester Maddox
• While he was president, Franklin Roosevelt always slept with what tucked under his pillow?	A gun
• After agreeing to resettlement of his people, and then seeing the treaty violated, who led his Northern Sioux tribe to victory over Custer's troops? Afterward, where did this chief and his tribe take refuge? Who was his "right-hand man"?	Sitting Bull; Canada; Crazy Horse
• For how long did Mark Twain serve in the Confederate Army before deserting?	One week
• Pocahontas' body is buried along what river?	The Thames in England
• What occupation did the gangster Al Capone's business card claim for him?	A second-hand furniture dealer
• What 13th-century world traveler introduced pasta to Italy? Where did he learn of pasta's many uses?	Marco Polo; at the court of Kublai Khan
• For what 1939 film did a black performer first win an Academy Award? Who was this "best supporting actress"?	"Gone With The Wind"; Hattie McDaniel
• What famous brothers' given names are repsectively Julian, Arthur, Leonard, Milton and Herbert?	Groucho, Harpo, Chico, Gummo, and Zeppo Marx
• Who did the first "peeping Tom" take a peek at?	Lady Godiva
• Who received the only wooden Oscar ever awarded by the Academy of Performing Arts?	The ventriloquist Edgar Bergen (with his dummy Charlie McCarthy)
• What two U.S. Presidents served as both high-school and college student-body presidents?	Richard Nixon and Ronald Reagan
• What boy – reportedly told by his father, "You care for nothing but shooting, dogs, and rat-catching, and will be a disgrace to yourself and all your family" – grew up to study medicine and make a round-the-world voyage that later led to his formulation of a revolutionary scientific theory?	Charles Darwin
• One signer of the Declaration of Independence didn't get around to signing the document until 1781, five years after it was written. Who was he?	Thomas McKean
• "Lord, His Exalted, Lordship, Excellent, Magnificent, Illustrious . . . " was the lengthy title used by what sea captain in signing documents?	Christopher Columbus
• Heiress Patricia Hearst was kidnapped by what group?	The Symbionese Liberation Army
• Alfred Nobel, the Swede whose will established annual cash awards to great writers, statesmen and scientists, was the inventor of what destructive medium?	Dynamite
• In 1914, the Mexican revolutionary Pancho Villa postponed his attack on the city Ojinago for what reason?	He had sold film-coverage rights for his battles to an American company, and was waiting for the camera operators to arrive

4

- Who originated the 19th-century motto "Nature will castigate those who don't masticate" (espousing the health virtues of chewing food until it is "ready to swallow itself"), that was a favorite of such luminaries as Thomas Edison and John D. Rockefeller?

Horace Fletcher

- What two women, both named Miss America (1955 and 1971), later found their niches in television? What 1975 Miss USA became a TV superhero?

Lee Meriwether and Phillis George; Lynda Carter (TV's "Wonder Woman")

- What do Knute Rockne, Will Rogers, Carol Lombard, Buddy Holly, Ritchie Valens (and almost Walon Jennings), Patsie Cline, Otis Redding, Rocky Marciano, Audie Murphy and Jim Croce have in common?

They all died in plane crashes

- Several significant events in the life of Moses occurred on mountaintops. Name the mountains where he received the Ten Commandments, from which he viewed the Promised Land, and on which he died.

Sinai, Nebo, and Pisgah

- What incredible-but-true tale concerns Lieutenant Hiroo Onoda, a Japanese soldier during World War II?

He hid in a Philippine jungle for 29 years, not knowing the war was over

- What five brothers (Henry, Clement, John, Peter, and Jacob), starting with assets of $68, specialized in chuck wagons to become the world's largest producer of wagons and carriages, and built their first electric "horseless carriage" in 1902?

The Studebakers

- Who was Alexander the Great's (356-323 B.C.) famed tutor?

Aristotle

- What was Audie Murphy's claim to fame in World War II?

He was the United States' most decorated soldier

- When the Romans overtook the Sicilian city of Syracuse in 212 B.C., soldiers were ordered to spare the great mathematician and physicist Archimedes. But a Roman soldier ran the 75-year-old man through with his sword when Archimedes did what?

Complained that the soldier was in his light as he drew geometric diagrams in the sand

- Who was the first U.S. president to drive an automobile?

Warren G. Harding

- Television's Lone Ranger was played by whom? From what piece of clothing was the famed mask said to be made?

Clayton Moore; the vest of John Reid's dead brother, who was killed along with four other real-life lawmen, making Reid the "Lone" Ranger

- Whose mother, while still pregnant, hung engravings of famous cathedrals on the walls of the soon-to-be nursery with her baby's future occupation in mind?

Frank Lloyd Wright's

- What operation did Daniel Hale Williams, a black physician at Chicago's Provident Hospital, first successfully perform in 1893?

The world's first heart operation

- J. Edgar Hoover had the curious habit of not allowing anyone to walk on what?

His shadow

- The chair occupied by the infamous – and first – "public enemy number one" was painted silver after he was gunned down by G-men outside the Biograph Theatre in 1934. Who was this criminal?

John Dillinger

- How many states did Richard Nixon carry in his 1972 Presidential victory? What Democratic candidate did he beat in that race? What states did the Democrat carry?

49; George McGovern; only Massachusetts

- What mythical General-Mills character was concocted as a homey reminder of the cookery's wholesomeness?

Betty Crocker

- Singer and actor Ricky Nelson's real first name was what? — Eric

- Captured in Argentina in 1960 by Israeli agents, who was hanged in 1962, after earlier boasting that he, with the deaths of 5 million people on his conscience, would "leap into my grave laughing [with an] extraordinary satisfaction"? — Karl Adolf Eichmann

- What distasteful act did Ethelred the Unready perform in his baptismal font? — He urinated in it

- Following Watergate and Nixon's resignation, what African leader wished him "a speedy recovery"? — Idi Amin

- What two archeologists discovered the boy-king Tutankhamen's elaborate tomb in 1922? — Howard Carter and Lord Carnarvon

- Leslie Townes used the ring name "Packy East" when he fought. Townes is better known as what renowned comedian? — Bob Hope

- What language did Jesus speak? — Aramaic

- Only one woman has won two Nobel prizes. Who was she? — Marie Curie

- Desi Arnaz and Lucille Ball were a famous pair of married entertainers. Give the equally famous partner who is or was linked to each of the following:

– Christie Brinkley	Billy Joel
– Jayne Wyman	Ronald Reagan
– Paul Newman	Joanne Woodward
– Farrah Fawcett	Lee Majors
– Burt Bacharach	Angie Dickinson
– Carole Lombard	William Powell & Clark Gable
– Loni Anderson & Karen Valentine	Burt Reynolds
– Mel Ferrer	Audrey Hepburn
– Jayne Meadows	Steve Allen
– Laurence Olivier	Vivian Leigh
– Fernando Lamas	Arlene Dahl & Esther Williams
– Gracie Allen	George Burns
– Barbara Streisand	Elliot Gould
– Robert Wagner	Natalie Wood
– Grace Kelly	Prince Rainier
– Douglas Fairbanks	Mary Pickford
– Douglas Fairbanks, Jr.	Joan Crawford
– Sophia Loren	Carlo Ponti
– Steve McQueen	Ali MacGraw
– Eydie Gorme	Steve Lawrence
– Rita Heyworth	Orson Welles
– Eddie Fisher	Elizabeth Taylor & Debbie Reynolds
– Penny Marshall	Rob Reiner
– Artie Shaw	Ava Gardner & Lana Turner
– Clair Bloom	Rod Steiger
– Dale Evans	Roy Rogers

– Mel Brooks	Anne Bancroft
– Marilyn Monroe	Arthur Miller & Joe DiMaggio
– Mickey Rooney	Ava Gardner
– Elizabeth Taylor	Richard Burton

• Distant cousins, Theodore and Franklin Roosevelt pronounced their common last name differently. Teddy said it how? Franklin how? — Teddy rhymed it with "goose" (Ruse-a-velt) and Franklin, Rose-a-velt (as in "rose")

• What world leader was given an unsuccessful tryout by the Washington Senators (now the Minnesota Twins) baseball team? What university did he play ball for? — Fidel Castro; Havana University

• What U.S. President was first to receive any kind of pension, three years after leaving the White House? — Harry Truman

• Julius Caesar was assassinated on what date of 44 B.C.? What were his alleged last words? — On the Ides of March (March 15); "Et tu, Brute?"

• Who fashioned the first steel plow blade from a discarded sawmill blade in 1837? — John Deere

• What early nineteenth-century Tuskegee University botanist and former slave made hundreds of new products from sweet potatoes and peanuts, including peanut butter? — George Washington Carver

• Who was the first woman (in 1893) and the first American woman (in 1902) to appear on a U.S. postage stamp? — Spain's Queen Isabella; Martha Washington

• Who created Miss Piggy, Kermit, and Fozzy Bear? — Jim Henson

• What writer (Paper Lion and Out of My League) has, among other things: practiced as an NFL quarterback; boxed 3 rounds with Archie Moore; pitched a pre-season game in Yankee stadium; performed as a circus trapeze artist, as a comedian in Caesar's palace, and as a percussionist with the New York Philharmonic; driven a race car in an actual auto race; acted as a guard at Buckingham Palace and acted with John Wayne in "Rio Lobo"; ridden in a steeplechase; and gone on an African Safari? — George Plimpton

• How did David Moniac – the first American Indian to be admitted to West Point, rising to the rank of major – die? — Fighting Seminole Indians in the Battle of Wahoo Swamp (Florida, 1836)

• What was Elvis Presley's middle name? — Aaron

• Who designed the Volkswagen ("people's car") for Adolf Hitler? After the war, the British offered what magnate the Volkswagen plant for free (he refused to take it)? — Ferdinand Porsche; Henry Ford II

• Who received 135,000 presents for her eighth birthday in 1936? — Shirley Temple

• Civil rights was furthered by the efforts of Gandhi and by Thoreau's Civil Disobedience. What 1942 organization sprang from Floyd McKissick's similar beliefs? — CORE (Congress of Racial Equality)

• With his body buried in Westminster Abbey, whose decapitated head was embalmed and put on public display by his widow? — Sir Walter Raleigh's (the head was later lost)

• When Clark Gable removed his shirt in a 1934 scene of "It Happened One Night," what was startling; and what was the economic effect on the country? — He wore no undershirt; undershirt retail sales plummeted

• What does George Washington's family motto, "Exitus acta probat," mean? — "The end justifies the means"

• Marcel Duchamp, an artist and master chess player, spent his honeymoon contemplating chess moves until his bride did what? — Glued the chess pieces to the board (they divorced 3 weeks later)

- To what food was Jimmy Carter's brother, Billy, allergic?

- German Field Marshal Ersin Rommel chose death by cyanide over a court hearing and reprisals against his family for his attempted bombing-assassination of who?

- The Reverend Sun Myung Moon founded what?

- What distinction does Pedro Alonso Nino, a navigator and crewman of Columbus's 1492 voyage, hold?

- In Edward Kennedy's 1969 Chappaquiddick accident, who drowned? On what charge was Kennedy convicted?

- What two people did Mark Twain consider the 19th century's most interesting characters?

- One noted author's favorite pastime is reading mail-order catalogues. He says: "I love ordering gadgets. If you need a left-handed monkey wrench, I'm the man to see." Who is he?

- What nickname was given to Napoleon?

- Fred Waring, conductor of The Pennsylvanians, the first band to appear on TV, invented what appliance?

- As a boy, Cary Grant – before running away at age 14 to join a troop of traveling acrobats, and then becoming a song-and-dance man – was expelled from school for what action?

- Who fashioned George Washington's false teeth?

- Frank Sinatra presented Marilyn Monroe with a gift he had named "Mafia." What was Mafia?

- Frank and Cole were the only (and eldest) brothers of what two outlaw families to survive and ultimately go on tour with a wild west show?

- What running mate, "backed 1,000 percent" in his bid for the Presidency, was later dropped by George McGovern?

Peanuts

Adolf Hitler

The Unification Church

He was the first black man to visit the New World

Mary Jo Kopechne; leaving the scene of an accident

Helen Keller and Napoleon

Alex Haley

"The Little Corporal"

The Waring Blender

Trying to sneak into the girls' bathroom

Paul Revere

A white poodle

The James and the Younger brothers

Thomas Eagleton

QUOTES

Trivia to Learn By

• She, more than most, could appreciate the pictures brought to the mind by books. "Literature is my Utopia," she said. Who was she?	Helen Keller
• "When the going gets tough, the tough get going," was the motto of what well-known coach?	Knute Rockne
• What is the architect Buckminster Fuller describing in this definition: "A self-balancing, 28-jointed adapter-base biped . . . the whole complex mechanism guided with exquisite precision from a turret in which are located telescopic and microscopic self-registering and recording range-finders, a spectroscope, etc., the turret control being closely allied with an air conditioning intake-and-exhaust, and a main fuel intake . . . "?	A human being
• "No matter how thin you slice it, it's still baloney," was a famous quip by what colorful politician of the 1920's and 30's?	Al Smith
• Complete Ambrose Bierce's statement from The Devil's Dictionary: "Speak when you are angry and you will make the best speech you will ever _____."	"regret"
• What organization has each of its members pledge, "My Head to clearer thinking, my Heart to greater loyalty, my Hands to larger services, and my Health to better living"? What is this organization's motto?	The 4-H Club; "We learn to do by doing."
• Who lamented, "I shall never rest my head on my pillow in peace and quiet as long as I remember the loss of my American colonies"?	George III of Great Britain
• Who said, "If you want to know the value of money, try to borrow some"?	Benjamin Franklin
• What famed buffalo hunter, army scout, gambler and lawman penned the following just before he suffered a fatal heart attack: " . . . we all get about the same amount of ice. The rich get it in the summertime, and the poor get it in the winter"?	Bartholomew "Bat" Masterson
• Whose last words before being beheaded by the guillotine, were, "I beg your pardon. I did not do it on purpose"?	Marie Antoinette's, spoken to her executioner, on whose foot she had accidentally stepped
• "When I hear anyone talk of culture, I reach for my revolver," was said by whom?	Hermann Goering
• "What hath God wrought?" were the first words transmitted by whom over what device?	Samuel F. B. Morse; sent out from his telegraph in a demonstration to Congress
• What Russian ruler said, "We will in my lifetime rule the world by invitation"?	Nikita Khrushchev
• "Don't give up the ship," was uttered repeatedly by the dying James Lawrence. What ship was Lawrence captaining?	"The Chesapeake"
• An inventor and businessman insisted: "It isn't the incompetent who destroy an organization. The incompetent never get into a position to destroy it. It is those who have achieved something and want to rest on their achievements who are forever clogging things up." Who was he?	Henry Ford
• What U.S. President said, "There's nothing so good for the inside of a man as an outside of a horse"?	Ronald Reagan

1

- "Less is more" is the Robert Browning philosophy shared by what famous architect?

  Mies Van Der Rohe

- What humorist quipped: "You can't say civilization don't advance . . . . Every day they kill you in a new way"?

  Will Rogers

- Who told reporters after losing California's 1962 gubernatorial race, "You won't have [me] to kick around anymore, because, gentlemen, this is my last press conference"?

  Richard Nixon

- He explained: "We're doing a little diversifying. But we have to live or die by cars and trucks." Who is this man?

  Lee Iacocca

- What famous line by Thomas Paine precedes this exerpt: " . . . The summer soldier and the sunshine patriot will, in this crisis, shrink from the service of their country"?

  "These are the times that try men's souls."

- He often said: "I will gladly pay you Tuesday for a hamburger today." Who is this cartoon character?

  Wimpey (from Popeye)

- Walt Kelly (Pogo) took Oliver Perry's Battle of Lake Erie line, "We have met the enemy, and they are ours," and ended it differently. What was Kelly's ending?

  " . . . and it is us."

- What legendary baseball player once asked, "How old would you be if you didn't know how old you was?"

  Satchel Paige

- What is the moral of Benjamin Franklin's statement, " . . . for the want of a nail the shoe was lost; for the want of a horse the rider was lost . . . "?

  "A little neglect may breed great mischief."

- "America is not like a blanket – one piece of unbroken cloth. America is more like a quilt – many patches, many pieces, many colors, many sizes all woven together by a common thread." Who offered this description?

  Rev. Jesse Jackson

- What actor/actress said it?
    - "I want to be alone."

      Greta Garbo
    - "Now cut that out!"

      Jack Benny
    - "I don't get no respect."

      Rodney Dangerfield
    - "When I'm good, I'm very good. But when I'm bad, I'm better."

      Mae West
    - "Here's looking at you, kid."

      Humphrey Bogart

- Samuel Butler made what well quoted comment affirming the need of corporal punishment?

  "Spare the rod and spoil the child."

- "As long as I am mayor, there will be law and order in Chicago," was what politician's response to crime?

  Richard Daley's

- What author is remembered for these last words: "Turn up the lights. I don't want to go home in the dark"?

  O. Henry

- Name the actor and TV character who warned, "One of these days, Alice, pow, right in the kisser"?

  Jackie Gleason, acting as "Ralph Kramden"

- What great physicist-astronomer maintained: "The Bible shows the way to go to heaven, not the way the heavens go"?

  Galileo

- What was Harry S Truman's four-word motto?

  "The Buck Stops Here"

- Who said: "It 's not the men in my life, its the life in my men"?

  Mae West

- What are the first words U.S. astronauts spoke after landing on the moon's surface?

  "Tranquility Base. The Eagle has landed."

- "I'm going to fight hard. I'm going to give them hell." Who said it?

  Harry Truman

- Israel Zangwill coined an enduring two-word term in his statement "America is God's crucible, the great_____ _____."

  "melting pot"

• "I only regret that I have but one life to give for my country," was proclaimed by what American patriot in 1776 before being hanged by the British for spying?	Nathan Hale
• What radical American cautioned: "Never trust anyone over thirty"?	Abbie Hoffman
• What was Samuel Adams referring to when he announced, "What a glorious morning for America!"?	The battle at Lexington, 1775
• The philosopher-writer Bertrand Russell said, "To be _____ (what?) some of the things you want is an indispensable part of happiness."	"without"
• What Shakespearean lines precede these?	
– From *Hamlet:* " . . . and it must follow, as the night the day, thou canst not then be false to any man."	"This above all: to thine own self be true . . . "
– From *Julius Caesar:* " . . . I come to bury Caesar, not to praise him. The evil that men do lives after them. The good is oft interred with their bones."	"Friends, Romans, Countrymen, lend me your ears . . . "
– From *The Merchant of Venice:* " . . . It droppeth as the gentle rain from heaven Upon the place beneath. It is twice blest . . . "	"The quality of mercy is not strain'd . . . "
– From *Romeo and Juliet:* "Deny thy father and refuse thy name, or, if thou will not, be but sworn my love And I'll no longer be a Capulet."	"O Romeo, Romeo, wherefore art thou Romeo . . . "
• Who warned with these words against non-monetary taxes: "We are taxed twice as much by our idleness, three times as much by our pride, and four times as much by our folly; and from these taxes the commissioners cannot ease or deliver us . . . "?	Benjamin Franklin
• What ancient philosopher held the opinion that "The nature of men is always the same; it is their habits that separate them"?	Confucius
• Name the late politician who complained: "Politicians are the same all over. They promise to build bridges, even where there are no rivers."	Nikita Khrushchev
• "Slow and steady wins the race" is the theme of what enduring tale?	Aesop's "The Hare and the Tortoise"
• The well-known phrase "the handwriting on the wall" is a Biblical reference to the prophetic writing that appeared on the walls of what city just before its destruction?	Babylon (Daniel 5:25)
• What aged philosopher, when asked by a young soldier what favor he could grant, replied, "Stand out of my sunlight"? What was the result of this blunt reply?	Diogenes; the soldier, from the army of conquering Alexander the Great, slew him
• Who adamantly proclaimed: "Segregation now, segregation tomorrow, segregation forever"?	Former Alabama governor George Wallace
• "You may fool all of the people some of the time . . . you can even fool some of the people all of the time; but you can't fool all the people all of the time," is attributed to what U.S. statesman?	Abraham Lincoln
• "You ain't heard nothin' yet, folks," was spoken by who and in what broadway play?	Al Jolson; "The Jazz Singer"
• Mother Teresa stated: "It is by forgiving that one is _____(what?)"	"forgiven"
• What comic announced: "I don't want to belong to any club that would accept me as a member"?	Groucho Marx
• What world leader often talked about creating "The Great Society"?	Lyndon B. Johnson

• Who, back in approximately 450 B.C., created the pledge now used by the U.S. Postal Service: "Neither snow, nor rain, nor heat, Nor gloom of night stays these Couriers from the swift completion of their appointed rounds"?	Herodotus
• A famous cartoonist describes life as being "like a ten-speed bike. Most of us have gears we never use." Who is he?	Charles M. Schulz, creator of "Peanuts"
• As Vice President, Spiro Agnew once spouted: "Some newspapers dispose of their garbage by _____ ____(what?)."	"printing it"
• To what was Winston Churchill referring when he called this world region "a riddle, wrapped in a mystery, inside an enigma"?	Russia
• Who wrote to Henry Ford: " . . . I will tell you what a dandy car you make. I have drove Fords exclusively when I could get away with one."	Clyde Barrow (of Bonnie and Clyde fame)
• What sports announcer voiced the well-known words, "Do you believe in miracles? Yes!" when the 1980 U.S. Olympic Hockey Team upset the Soviet Union Team?	Al Michaels
• What creed ends, " . . . the most important thing in life is not the triumph but the struggle. The essential thing is not to have conquered but to have fought well"? Who authored it?	The Olympic Creed; Baron Pierre de Coubertin, founder of the modern Olympic Games, 1896
• Name the prominent figures who first uttered or wrote the following poignant quotes:	
– "O Lord, thou givest us everything, At the price of effort."	Leonardo da Vinci
– "The graveyards are full of indispensable men."	Charles de Gaulle
– "Two roads diverged in a wood, and I – I took the one less traveled by, And that has made all the difference."	Robert Frost
– "Don't find a fault. Find a remedy."	Henry Ford
– "Our scientific power has outrun our spiritual power. We have guided missiles and misguided men."	Martin Luther King, Jr.
– "I have been driven to my knees many times because there was no place else to go."	Abraham Lincoln
– "We cannot do everything, at once, but we can do something at once."	Calvin Coolidge
– "I think and think for months and years. Ninety-nine times, the conclusion is false. The hundredth time I am right."	Albert Einstein
• Who wrote, "Manifest plainness, Embrace simplicity, Reduce selfishness, Have few desires"?	Lao-Tzu (Tao Te Ching)
• What equation-loving thinker said: "If A equals success, then the formula is A = X + Y + Z. X is work. Y is play. Z is keep your mouth shut"?	Albert Einstein
• Fill in the blank in Frank S. Pepper's observation: "Professionals built the _____ – amateurs the ark."	*Titanic*
• In the movie "What's Up Doc," how does Howard Bannister (Ryan O'Neal) respond to Judy Maxwell (Barbara Streisand) when she says the line, "Love is never having to say you're sorry."	"That's the dumbest thing I've ever heard."
• What ancient Roman foresaw immanent treachery and stated: "A snake lurks in the grass"?	*Virgil*
• "An army marches on its stomach," was one of the memorable sayings of what general?	Napoleon Bonaparte

4

- What poet wrote these lines?

  Lo, all our pomp of yesterday
  Is one with Nineveh and Tyre!
  Judge of the nations spare us yet,
  Lest we forget – lest we forget!

  Rudyard Kipling ("Recessional")

- Douglas MacArthur promised, "I shall return." Where was he at the time?

  In a plane, after leaving the Philippines

- What general lamented: "The world has achieved brilliance without conscience. Ours is a world of nuclear giants and ethical infants"?

  Omar Bradley

- Complete Leo Tolstoy's trenchant statement on power: "In order to obtain and hold power a man must_____ ____."

  "love it."

- Who quipped: "Get your facts first, and then you can distort them as much as you please"?

  Mark Twain

- Of whom was Henry Lee speaking when he pronounced: "First in war, first in peace, first in the hearts of his countrymen"?

  George Washington

- What begins with: "I swear by Apollo, the Physician . . . "?

  The Hippocratic oath

- Who said, "I'm not kidding myself. My voice alone is just an ordinary voice. What people come to see is how I use it. If I stand still while I'm singing, I'm dead, man. I might as well go back to driving a truck"?

  Elvis Presley

- Of whom was Adlai Stevenson speaking when he gave this moving eulogy: "She would rather light a candle than curse the darkness"?

  Eleanor Roosevelt

- Who made famous, when hearing a ribald joke, the cold statement "We are not amused"?

  Queen Victoria of England

- What U.S. journalist said, "Go West, young man!"

  Horace Greeley

- What U.S. President said, "He ought to be grateful to us. He gave us a kick in the ass and it made him stronger than ever"? Who was this President referring to?

  John F. Kennedy; Fidel Castro, after the Bay of Pigs

- What movie/TV character said it?

  – "Please Sir, may I have some more?"

  Oliver Twist

  – "Frankly, my dear, I don't give a damn."

  Rhett Butler

  – "The children of the night, what music they make."

  Count Dracula (Bela Lugosi)

  – "Sorry about that, Chief."

  Maxwell Smart

- What author uttered these last words: "God will pardon me; it's his trade"?

  Heinrich Heine

- What nineteenth-century black abolitionist boldly wrote in his paper, *The Liberator:* "On this subject I do not want to think, or speak or write with moderation. No! . . . I am in earnest – I will not equivocate – I will not excuse – I will not retreat a single inch – AND I WILL BE HEARD"?

  William Lloyd Garrison

- How did Porfirio Diaz (1830 - 1915), President of Mexico, complete this statement: "Alas, poor Mexico, so far from God, so near _____."?

  "to the USA"

- What American writer penned the maxim: "All you need in this life is ignorance and confidence, and then success is sure"?

  Mark Twain

- Who would have said – and did say, "I believe the power to make money is a gift of God"?

  John D. Rockefeller

- To what offer was Daniel Webster commenting when he said, "No, thank you. I do not propose to be buried until I am really dead and in my coffin"?

  The opportunity to run for Vice-President

• A history book reads: "The king found her so different from her picture – that he swore they had brought him a Flanders mare." Who was the monarch and who was the lady?	Henry VIII; Anne of Cleves
• Krishnamurti remarked that "the constant assertion of belief is an indication of _____(what?)."	"fear"
• What towering literary figure observed, "I missed my calling. I should have been an interior decorator"?	Victor Hugo (1802 - 1885)
• "The young man who has not wept is a savage, and the old man who will not laugh is a fool," was written by what American philosopher?	George Santayana
• What gracious scientist recorded near the end of his life: "If I have seen further [than other men] it is by standing upon the shoulders of giants"?	Isaac Newton
• "Workers of all lands unite . . . " is the epitaph on whose grave?	Karl Marx's
• Who publicized this motto (which included his name): "Secure knots secure not _____."?	Harry Houdini
• Machiavelli gave much advice about being a strong prince. What man, 2000 years earlier, wisely stated in his *Analects:* "When a prince's personal conduct is correct, his government is effective without the issuing of orders. If his personal conduct is not correct, he may issue orders but they will not be followed"?	Confucius
• "Remember the Maine" was the popular 1898 battle cry in pushing the U.S. into war with what country (indicated by the phrase's second line)?	Spain ("To hell with Spain!")
• How did Ronald Reagan first greet first lady Nancy after his near-fatal assassination attempt? What did he say to the doctors before they operated?	"Honey, I forgot to duck"; "I hope you doctors are all Republicans"
• Fill in the blanks to Albert Einstein's argument that "Science without religion is_____; religion without science is_____." Finish his later statement: "God does not _____ _____ with the universe."	lame; blind; play dice
• After critics lambasted his musicianship, what line did Liberace coin as a rebuttal?	"I cried all the way to the bank."
• The first line of Shakespeare's "Sonnet 18" is completed with what two words? "Shall I compare thee to a _____ _____? Thou art more lovely and more temperate."	"summer's day"
• What was Calvin Coolidge's reply when asked why he agreed to speak at parties, even though he didn't enjoy attending social gatherings?	"Got to eat somewhere."
• Who said: "There is nothing in the Bible that says I must wear rags"?	Rev. Billy Graham
• Goethe commented that "A useless life is an early death." Complete Thomas Fuller's similar sentiment: "_____ _____ are dead all their life long"; also Eleanor Roosevelt's: "When you cease to make a contribution, you begin to _____."	"Idle men"; "die"
• What was Benjamin Franklin's response to a Parisian who, upon witnessing the first test of an unmanned balloon flight, asked, "What good is it?"	"What good is a new-born baby?"
• What mastermind insisted, "Common sense is the deposit of prejudice laid down in the mind before the age of 18"?	Albert Einstein
• Who remarked, "Ah, Mr. President, I see you are teaching your dog to chew the rug"?	Henry Kissinger (to Richard Nixon)

6

• What clergyman humorously observed: "When the missionaries first came to Africa they had the Bible and we had the land. They said, 'let us pray'. We closed our eyes. When we opened them, the tables had been turned: We had the Bible and they had the land."?	Bishop Desmond Tutu
• What beloved character proclaimed: "You have to believe in yourself, that's the secret. Even when I was in the orphanage, when I was roaming the street trying to find enough to eat, even then I thought of myself as the greatest actor in the world. I had to feel the exuberance that comes from utter confidence in yourself. Without it, you go down to defeat"?	Charlie Chaplin
• Who declared: "A man can't ride your back unless it's bent"? What was his most famous phrase?	Martin Luther King, Jr.; "I have a dream..."
• "It is not the neutrals or the lukewarms who make history." What world history-maker articulated this sentiment?	Adolf Hitler
• What phrase describes how the month of March begins and ends?	"March comes in like a lion, goes out like a lamb."
• What word was John F. Kennedy referring to when he said: "When written in Chinese, the word _____ is composed of two characters. One represents danger and the other represents opportunity"?	"crisis"
• How did Napoleon Bonaparte end this sentence: "A leader is a dealer in _____."?	"hope"
• He said: "I am a passenger on spaceship earth." Who was he?	R. Buckminster Fuller
• Who lambasted the U.S Government, noting that it is "basically controlled by the industries which it purports to regulate"?	Ralph Nader
• What opera singer complained: "First I lost my weight. Then I lost my voice. Now I've lost Onassis"?	Maria Callas
• "By the time I reached the second grade, I got tired of spelling all that out and had it shortened to Thurgood." Who said this, and what is his claim to fame?	Thurgood (changed from Thuroughgood) Marshall; the first black American appointed to the Supreme Court
• Herodotus wrote, "You may have observed how the thunderbolt of heaven chastises the insolence of the more enormous animals." What similar expression did Bob Fitzimmons coin before a boxing match with the much larger Jim Jeffries in 1902?	"The bigger they come, the harder they fall."
• What English playwright penned, "Mad dogs and Englishmen go out in the mid-day sun"?	Noel Coward
• "Older men declare war. But it is the youth that must fight and die," was recited by what U.S. President?	Herbert Hoover
• What did General William Tecumseh Sherman have to say about war in an 1880 speech?	"War is hell."
• "I'm the straw that stirs the drink," he once said about himself and his (then) Yankee team. Who is he?	Reggie Jackson
• What British writer put these words into the mouth of a domestic pig: "All animals are equal, but some animals are more equal than others"?	George Orwell in *Animal Farm*
• Who said: A journey of a thousand miles must begin with a single step"?	Lao-Tzu
• Name the preacher who first used the phrase, "Cleanliness is indeed next to godliness."	John Wesley
• Who shouted, "Join the union, girls, and together say, 'Equal Pay for Equal Work'"?	Susan B. Anthony

- In a 1940 speech he declared, "Never in the field of human conflict was so much owed by so many to so few." Who said this, and to whom?

  Winston Churchill; to the Royal Air Force

- Emerson finished this sentence with what word: "Nothing great was ever achieved without _____"?

  "enthusiasm"

- "The first thing we do, let's kill all the lawyers," was the suggestion of what mythical monarch?

  Henry VI (Shakespeare)

- Two legendary football coaches had opposing views on winning. One said: "For when the One Great Scorer comes to mark against your name,/ He writes – not that you won or lost/ – but how you played the game." The other declared: "Show me a good and gracious loser, and I'll show you a failure." Name these two men.

  Grantland Rice and Knute Rockne

- What group has as its slogan: "The difficult we do immediately. The impossible takes a little longer"?

  U.S. Army Corps of Engineers

- "We must, indeed, all hang together or, most assuredly, we shall all hang separately," were the words of what patriot?

  Benjamin Franklin

- Sophie Tucker's key to longevity was, "Keep _____ (what?)."

  "breathing"

SPORTS
Trivia to Learn By

• What is the full name of the first golfing resort, founded in 1754?	The Royal and Ancient Golf Club of St. Andrews, Scotland
• What female runner set world marks in both the 100- and 200-meter dashes in 1988?	Florence Griffith Joyner
• What two baseball expansion teams joined the American League in 1977?	The Toronto Blue Jays and the Seattle Mariners
• What was Kareem Abdul-Jabbar's name before he became a practicing Muslim?	Lew Alcindor
• What language is the source of the terms "tennis," "set," and "love" – meaning, respectively, "look here!", "seven" (originally it took 7 instead of 6 games to win a set) and "egg" (signifying zero)?	French
• Name the two boxers involved in the "long-count bout" of 1927.	Jack Dempsey and Gene Tunney
• Changing directions while yachting is called what?	Tacking
• In football, a halfback's jersey will normally have one of what ten numbers on it? A fullback's? A center's or linebacker's?	20 to 29; 30 to 39; 50 to 59
• The 1960 Summer Olympics was held in what country?	Rome
• Who was the first black heavyweight boxing champion?	Jack Johnson
• Who was the first man to win three consecutive Wimbledon tennis championships since Fred Perry's record in the 1930's?	Bjorn Borg won five in a row
• In baseball, the pitcher and catcher are known jointly as what?	The battery
• What do you call prize money given out at a boxing match or horse race?	The purse
• By far the leader in lifetime passing attempts (6467), completions (3686), yards (47,003), and touchdowns (342), what professional football quarterback was (and still is) the "passingest" of all time?	Fran Tarkenton
• Since the Boston Celtics won their eighth consecutive pro-basketball crown in 1966, only three teams have won back-to-back titles. Who were these "dynasties"?	Boston Celtics (again in 1968-69), L.A. Lakers (1987-88) and Detroit Pistons (1989-90)
• Who said each of these poignant lines? (Some hints are given.)	
– "The Good Lord allows just so much profanity on a team, and I use up our entire quota." (football coach)	Lou Holtz
– "... I started the 'I am the greatest' thing. I began with the poetry and predicting rounds. And it worked. They started coming in with their ten- and twenty-dollar bills to see the braggin' nigger."	Muhammad Ali
– "I could stand up here all night talking about the whole team. But I'm getting sick and tired of talking about myself." (basketball star)	Larry Bird
– "One thing you learn as a Cubs fan: When you bought your ticket, you could bank on seeing the bottom of the ninth." (former catcher-turned-broadcaster)	Joe Garagiola
– "My family was so poor they couldn't afford any kids. The lady next door had me." (a current seniors golfer)	Lee Trevino

– "I went to a fight the other night, and a hockey game broke out." (comedian)	Rodney Dangerfield
– "My biggest thrill was the night Elgin Baylor and I combined for 73 points in Madison Square Garden. Elgin had 71 of them." (basketball all-star-turned-broadcaster)	Hot Rod Hundley
– "I don't want to be a hero; I don't want to be a star. It just works out that way." (former baseball slugger)	Reggie Jackson
– Speaking to the 42-year-old Stan Musial, who had been voted to play in another All-Star game, he said, "A couple of years ago they told me I was too young to be President and you were too old to be playing baseball. But we fooled them."	John F. Kennedy
– "I wouldn't ever set out to hurt anybody deliberately unless it was, you know, important – like a league game or something." (Football Hall of Fame linebacker-turned actor)	Dick Butkus
– "The way to catch a knuckleball is to wait until it stops rolling and then pick it up." (former catcher-turned-broadcaster and television actor)	Bob Uecker
– "You drive the car, you don't carry it." (race-car driver)	Janet Guthrie
– "An athiest is a guy who watches a Notre Dame - S.M.U. football game and doesn't care who wins."	Dwight D. Eisenhower
– "One of my goals in life was to be surrounded by unpretentious, rich young men. Then I bought the Braves and I was surrounded by 25 of them."	Ted Turner
– What coach's wife, in response to a heckler who said, "Your husband is a fathead!" came back: "What husband isn't?" (he coached college football)	Woody Hayes' wife, Anne
– After being struck out on three consecutive called strikes, balls that were thrown right past him, he asked the umpire if he'd seen any of the pitches. The ump said no. He replied, "Neither did I, but that last one sounded kinda high to me."	Babe Ruth
– "It's good sportsmanship not to pick up lost golf balls while they're still rolling." (American humorist)	Mark Twain
– "I never wanted them to forget Babe Ruth. I just wanted them to remember _____ (his own name)." (all-time homerun king)	Henry Aaron
– Asked if he could indeed walk on water, this early riser said, "Well, I won't say I can or I can't; but if I do, I do it before most people get up in the morning." (late-great football coach)	Bear Bryant
– "Nobody ever said, 'Work ball!' They say, 'Play ball!' To me, that means having fun." (Hall-of-Fame Pittsburgh Pirates baseball player)	Willie Stargell
• Name the two black athletes who first raised their fists at the 1968 Mexico City Summer Olympics, to protest U.S. racial inequality.	Tommie Smith and John Carlos
• Illie Nastase, former tennis "bad boy," hailed from what country?	Romania
• When a relief pitcher enters a baseball game, how many warm-up pitches is he allowed?	Eight
• What was the type of automobile that won the first auto race?	An Oshkosh Steamer

- American baseball is a combination of what two English sports?

    Cricket and rounders

- Who was the "Pride of the Yankees"?

    Lou Gehrig

- What team won the first Super Bowl in 1966? Who won the next pro football championship, Super Bowl II?

    The Green Bay Packers; also the Packers

- One professional baseball pitcher has walked more men in his career (over 2500) than any other. But it just so happens that this same pitcher has recorded more strikeouts than anyone in history (over 5,000) and has pitched the most no-hitters (6), the last coming on May 1, 1991 at age 44. Who is this man?

    Nolan Ryan

- "Pacing" and "trotting" are categories of what sport?

    Harness racing

- The record for losses in a single major league baseball season is 117. What team holds this distinction?

    The 1962 New York Mets

- Assuming a boxing match goes 15 rounds, what is the overall length of time between the opening bell and its ending?

    59 minutes (fifteen 3-minute rounds with fourteen 1-minute breaks)

- Acknowledged as the greatest hockey player to ever play the game, what active player continues to smash nearly every NHL scoring record? Also, what is his nickname?

    Wayne Gretsky; "The Great Gretsky"

- A "bomb" may be thrown in what sport?

    Football (it's a long, arching throw downfield)

- Mint julep is the traditional drink at what sporting event?

    The Kentucky Derby

- What two Baseball Hall-of-Fame catchers grew up across the street from each other (on St. Louis' Elizabeth Ave.) and had fathers who worked together at the same clay products company?

    Joe Garagiola and Lawrence "Yogi" Berra

- After an absence of 40 years, what country returned to take part in the 1952 Summer Olympics?

    The Soviet Union

- A volleyball team may strike the ball how many times before it must pass over the net? What is the one exception to this rule?

    Three; if the first strike is from a block at the net, it does not count as a strike

- Who was the first jockey to ride two Triple Crown winners?

    Eddie Arcaro

- What track athlete has won the most Olympic medals?

    Paavo Nurmi won 9 gold and 3 silver medals in the 1920, '24 and '28 Games

- What Los Angeles Ram football lineman was voted to the Pro Bowl eleven times?

    Merlin Olsen

- The Indianapolis 500 is a car race consisting of how many laps around the track?

    200

- With a record number 2056 "credits" in this category, which baseball player walked the most times in his career?

    Babe Ruth

- Identify the sluggers who hold these other professional baseball records:

    - Most home runs in a 162-game season

        Roger Marris (61)

    - Most home runs in a 154-game season

        Babe Ruth (60)

    - Most career home runs

        Henry Aaron (755)

    - Most career hits

        Pete Rose (4,256)

    - Most career runs batted in

        Henry Aaron (2,297)

    - Most career grand slams (home runs with the bases filled)

        Lou Gehrig (23)

    - Most total World Series home runs

        Mickey Mantle (18)

    - Most games played

        Pete Rose (3,562)

    - Most runs scored

        Ty Cobb (2,245)

– Most consecutive games with at least one hit in each	Joe DiMaggio (56)
– Most consecutive games played	Lou Gehrig (2,130)
– Most career stolen bases	Rickey Henderson (broke Lou Brock's record of 938 steals on May 1, 1991)
– Most career strikeouts	Reggie Jackson (2,597)
– Highest career batting average	Ty Cobb (.366)
• Aspiring Spanish bullfighters traditionally learn what trade?	Bricklaying
• Who were the final two opponents to go up against the 1980 Olympic gold-medal winning U.S. Hockey Team?	The Soviet Union and Finland
• Who won five world Grand Prix auto racing crowns?	Juan Fangio
• What was Oscar Robinson's basketball nickname?	The "Big O"
• What baseball team was the first to pay its players?	The Cincinnati Redstockings
• What Japanese skier skied down Mt. Everest, starting at an altitude of 26,200 feet? What film was made of his exploit?	Yuichiro Miura; "The Man Who Skied Down Everest"
• "The Fight of the Century," held March 8, 1971, was fought by what two opponents?	Joe Frazier and Muhammad Ali
• Name the Kansas City Chief quarterback who led his team to a 27-7 victory over the "Purple People Eaters" of Minnesota in Super Bowl IV.	Len Dawson
• When baseball's "Senators" moved from Washington, they became known by what name?	The Minnesota Twins
• "Bulldogging" is a competition in what sport?	Rodeo
• Coined by Mary, Queen of Scots in 1561, from what word was golf's "caddie" obtained?	The French "cadet"
• The highest point-total ever scored by one player in an NBA game was on March 2, 1962. How many points were scored, and by whom?	100 points; Wilt Chamberlain
• To win tennis' Grand Slam, one must win what 4 titles consecutively?	Australian Open, U.S. Open, French Open, and Wimbledon
• Who played pro football for an unsurpassed 26 years, and still holds the records for career points scored (2002), field goal attempts (638), and point after touchdown attempts and number made (959 and 943)?	George Blanda, quarterback and kicker
• In an astonishing jump that broke the then world record by nearly two feet, what long jumper flew 29 feet 2 1/2 inches in the 1968 Olympic Games?	Bob Beamon
• Who held the record for consecutive shut-out innings before Orel Hersheiser broke it in the 1989 season? What is Hersheiser's new record?	Don Drysdale (59 innings); 60 innings
• What player made the most NBA career points? Which retired player averaged the most points per game in his career? (Michael Jordan actively sports an average of around 33 points per game.)	Kareem Abdul-Jabbar (38,387 points); Wilt Chamberlain (30.1 points per game)
• Who was the baseball player known as "The Pride of St. Louis"?	Dizzy Dean
• Identify the missing sports terms in each definition:	
– A _____ is an inept, inexperienced boxer.	Palooka
– Two skiers (or other one-on-one contestants) who are in direct competition with each other (rather than going against the clock) are said to be skiing ____ to ____.	Head to head

– In golf, a sharp bend in the fairway is called a _____.	Dogleg
– _____ is when a hunter hunts game illegally or out of season.	Poaching
– When a batter in baseball strides away from the plate in his swing, instead of towards the pitcher, he is said to be stepping ___ ___ _____.	In the bucket
– When playing informally, a golfer might take a free shot called a _____ when his last shot was poorly played.	Mulligan
– A fox hunter will yell "_____" upon seeing a fox break from cover.	Tallyho!
• What New York Yankee player appeared in the most games for his team – 2400?	Mickey Mantle
• Name the only heavyweight boxing champion to win his title 3 separate times.	Muhammad Ali (1964 to 1979)
• What is the maximum number of clubs a golfer may carry in his bag in tournament play?	Fourteen
• Babe Ruth broke whose season home-run record of 59 in 1927?	His own (he hit 60 that year)
• In what city is the All-American Soap Box Derby held?	Akron, Ohio
• What fighter won the world featherweight championship twice – in 1942 and 1949?	Willie Pep
• What is an illegal move by a baseball pitcher called?	A balk
• In order to achieve golfing's Grand Slam, a player must win which four events consecutively? How many players have done it?	The Masters, the PGA Tournament, the U.S. Open and the British Open; zero
• In inches, what is the diameter of a basketball hoop?	18
• What is the most heavily attended spectator sport in the U.S.?	Horse racing
• Name baseball's three famous Alou brothers.	Felipe, Jesus and Matty
• Jack Dempsey, heavyweight boxing champ, was nicknamed what?	"The Manassa Mauler"
• What is the name of the mountain range, located in British Columbia, considered by skiers as offering the most dangerous and challenging slopes?	The Bugaboos
• To avoid a boycott by Arab states in the 1948 Summer Olympics, what action was taken?	Israeli athletes were excluded
• Who was the inventor of basketball, a sport designed to fill the gap between fall football and spring baseball?	James Naismith
• Who was the last white heavyweight boxing champion?	Sweden's Ingemar Johansson
• The "scissors" can be used in what track and field event? What other sport uses a scissors hold?	The high jump; wrestling
• A race horse that runs well in the rain is called a what?	A "mudder"
• "Sculls" and "sweeps" are used in what sport?	Rowing (A skull is a 9' oar used in pairs; a sweep is a single 12' oar)
• The "Davis Cup" of women's tennis, which pits a team from each country against those of other countries, is known by what name?	The Federation Cup
• The Kentucky Derby is run at what distance?	A mile and a quarter
• Which is considered the world's most expensive sport?	Yacht racing
• Edson Arantes do Nascimento is more popularly known by what name?	Pelé

• What is the distance of a marathon race?	26 miles, 385 yards
• Who was the first player elected to the Baseball Hall of Fame?	Ty Cobb
• In 1989, a Cuban track star became the first person to have ever high jumped eight feet. Who performed this feat?	Javier Sotomayor
• Only one player has been named both the NBA's Most Valuable Player and Rookie of the Year in the same year. What was the player's name?	Wes Unseld (1969)
• If a player hits a single, a double, a triple and a home run in the same game, what is it called?	Hitting for the cycle
• Who wore the first baseball glove in a game?	Charles Waite
• What ailment ended Sandy Koufax's baseball career in 1966?	Arthritis
• What were Babe Ruth's two best known nicknames, and what was his name at birth?	"The Sultan of Swat" and "Bambino"; George Herman Ruth
• The five rings in the Olympic flag represent what?	Continents
• Name the most valuable player of Super Bowls I and II.	Bart Starr (Green Bay Packers)
• "Walking the Dog," "Tick Tack" and "Tie Hop" are maneuvers performed in what sports activity?	Skateboarding
• What is the only NFL team that doesn't have a symbol on its players' helmets?	The Cleveland Browns
• Name the coach of the 1969 Super Bowl champion New York Jets. Who was the team's brash quarterback-leader?	Weeb Ewbank; Joe Namath
• The cancelled 1940 Summer Olympics were scheduled to be held in what city?	Tokyo, Japan
• The world's highest golf course is situated in what country?	Peru
• What track star had his name entered in the record book the most times in a single day?	Jesse Owens set or equalled six records on May 25, 1935
• In bronco riding, a cowboy must stay aboard for how many seconds?	Eight
• What country won the 1960 Olympic gold medal in hockey?	The United States
• Who was the first black pitcher in the Major Leagues?	Satchel Paige
• What is the oldest trophy competed for by pro athletes in North America?	Hockey's Stanley Cup
• What Laker pro-basketball player was known as "Mr. Clutch"?	Jerry West
• In horseracing, a furlong (the approximate length of one plowed furrow) consists of what distance?	1/8 mile
• Who was baseball's "Iron Horse"? How did he earn this nickname?	Lou Gehrig; by playing in a record 2,130 straight games
• At what age is a horse first allowed to race in the Kentucky Derby?	Three years
• The first four-minute mile was run by whom? In which country did he accomplish the feat?	Roger Bannister (3:59.4, 1954); England
• With by far the most total innings pitched (7,356) and games won (511), who is still considered by many the best pitcher in major-league baseball history?	Cy Young
• What is the traditional drink sipped by the champion in the Winner's Circle at the Indianapolis 500?	Milk
• How many Olympic Games were cancelled in all because of World War II?	Four
• According to statistical experts, what are the odds against a golfer sinking a hole-in-one?	300,000 to 1

• Who was the first woman to race in the Indianapolis 500? Who was the first woman licensed to run Top-Fuel dragsters in the U.S.?	Janet Guthric (1976); Shirley Muldowney
• Name the two NFL stars suspended for the entire 1963 season for gambling.	Paul Hornung and Alex Karras
• Who was the first American to take a medal in any international gymnastics competition, winning a 1970 World Games silver?	Cathy Rigby (Mason)
• Which two teams played in the first World series in 1903?	The Boston Red Sox beat the Pittsburgh Pirates 5 games to 3
• The "Miracle Mets" defeated what team in the 1969 World Series?	The Baltimore Orioles
• Who was the first black to captain a major league baseball squad? Who was first to manage a major league team?	Willie Mays; Frank Robinson
• Identify the female figure-skater who has held the most world titles.	Sonja Henie
• Who is the only man to be named twice to the Basketball Hall of Fame, once as a player and once as a coach?	John Wooden
• What renown horse race takes place in Maryland?	The Preakness Stakes
• Prior to 1963, when it was renamed the "Jets," what was New York's football team known as?	The New York Titans
• Henry Aaron broke Babe Ruth's career home run record in 1971. What was the previous record, and how man HR's did Aaron end his career with?	714; 755
• Who supposedly coined the phrase, "When the going gets tough, the tough get going"?	Knute Rockne, Notre Dame football coach
• Who originated these other classic quotes? (Hints are offered here, too.)	
– "The game's not over till it's over." (baseball Hall of Fame catcher, and manager)	Yogi Berra
– "You could look it up." (former major league baseball manager)	Casey Stengel
– "Who's on first, What's on second, I Don't Know is on third."	Bud Abbott and Lou Costello
– "He can run, but he can't hide." (late great professional boxer)	Joe Louis
– "Nice guys finish last." (late Brooklyn Dodgers manager)	Leo Durocher
– "Win one for the Gipper." (former Notre Dame football coach)	Knute Rockne
– "I can lick any man in the house." (former heavyweight boxing champ)	John L. Sullivan
• What football player was known as "The Galloping Ghost"?	Red Grange of Illinois University
• If a baseball player hits the ball, which then hits the foul pole, what happens?	The batter is credited with a home run
• Who coached the most pro-basketball victories? What college basketball coach ended his career with the most wins?	Red Auerbach (1,037); Adolph Rupp (875)
• What four heavyweight boxing champs retired undefeated?	James Jeffries, Gene Tunney, Joe Louis and Rocky Marciano
• Canadian football teams field how many players at a time?	Twelve

- Now considered the greatest speed skater ever, who won all five speed-skating events in the 1980 Lake Placid Olympics?

  Eric Heiden of the U.S.

- Nadia Comaneci received how many perfect scores in gymnastics at the 1976 Montreal Olympics?

  Seven

- A calf-roper must tie together how many of the animal's legs?

  Three

- What is a thoroughbred horse called that has never won a race?

  A maiden

- In 1966, baseball's Braves transferred from what city to Atlanta?

  Milwaukee

- In hockey, how many statistical points may be awarded to a player who assists a teammate (usually by a pass) in scoring a goal?

  Two

- What was the final score of the controversial 1972 Munich Olympics U.S. vs. Soviet basketball final where the Russians broke the U.S. team's streak of 63 straight Olympic wins?

  51 to 50

- Who wrote the lyrics to "Take Me Out to the Ball Game"?

  Jack Norworth

- What is the height of the crossbar on a football goal post? What other sport's "goal" is also placed at this height?

  Ten feet; basketball's hoop

- If a baseball game is forfeited, what is the official recorded score? What is the official score of a forfeited football game?

  9 to 0; 1 to 0

- Red Auerbach's trademark when he felt certain his Boston Celtics had won the game, was to do what? Also, what is Red's given name?

  Light up a cigar; Arnold

WORDS and PHRASES

Trivia to Learn By

• St. Mary's Bethlehem Hospital for the insane in London gave rise to a word, approximating the word "Bethlehem," meaning "a madhouse; place of noisy confusion." What is it?	Bedlam
• What word, has two distinct etymologies and two quite opposite meanings: "to adhere, to cling to," and "to divide or cut asunder"?	Cleave
• The Welsh "one, two, three, four," and "eight, nine, ten," are the roots of what two children's rhymes?	"Eeny, meeney, miney, moe" and "Hickory, dickory, dock"
• In the 1920's what "animal's cry" was slang for the latest in style?	Cat's meow
• "Flotsam" refers to items lost by accident or through the sinking of a ship; "jetsam" denotes material deliberately thrown overboard. What is the word for something thrown overboard, but attached perhaps to a buoy for later retrieval?	Lagan
• What Hebrew word means "so be it"?	Amen
• What does a "funambulist" do?	Walks a tight-rope
• What are the only two English words to end in the letters -gry?	Angry and hungry
• The following definitions describe words taken from names of ancient Greek cities. What is the adjective for someone who is:	
– Hardy, undaunted, frugal, or severe?	Spartan (Sparta)
– Sparing of words; terse?	Laconic (Laconia)
– Luxurious, voluptuous, or pleasure-loving?	Sybartic (Sybaris)
• Meaning "to drop sharply," what word comes from the same root as the chemical symbol for lead?	Plummet (Pb)
• As a blend of "fly" and "vaunt," what term means "to show off"?	Flaunt
• A word was derived from an ancient northern European custom of drinking mead (honeyed wine) as an aphrodisiac during the first month of marriage. What is the word?	Honeymoon
• An unintentional transposing of words and thoughts (i.e. "I remember your name, but I just can't think of your face.") is called a what?	Spoonerism
• Texas Representative Maurice Maverick (1895 - 1954) coined what term to describe his disgust for F.D. Roosevelt's "liberal" New Deal economic program?	Gobbledygook
• Give the word for a type of ship that fits each of these definitions:	
– A device to get a party going.	Ice breaker
– A sharply hit baseball with a low trajectory.	Liner
– A hard pull.	Tug
– A person with nihilistic tendencies.	Destroyer
• What word – in French, two words meaning "rotten pot" – actually refers to a sweet-smelling mixture?	Potpourri
• What word for certain legumes is slang for "an insignificant amount of money"?	Peanuts
• What means "20 of something," "to gain points in a game," or "to scratch"?	Score
• What fabric literally means "cord of the kings"?	Corduroy
• The Arawak Indians were exterminated by Columbus and other explorers, leaving only one known word from their vocabulary. The word named a device used for sleeping, which was soon adopted on European ships. What is the device called?	A hammock
• When deer or horses are in a group, we call them a "herd." Sheep travel in a "flock." What is the group name for these animals?	
– Whale	School, pod, or gam

– Dog	Kennel or pack
– Lion	Pride
– Rhinoceros	Crash
– Duck	Team or flock
– Fish	School or draught
– Kangaroo	Mob or troop
– Bee	Grist or swarm
– Gnat	Cloud or horde
– Frog	Army
– Ferret	Business
– Rabbit	Warren
– Fox	Skulk
– Goose	Gaggle or skein
– Pig	Drove
– Cat	Cluster or clowder
– Bear	Sleuth
– Lark	Exaltation
– Leopard	Leap
– Crow	Murder
– Monkey	Tribe
– Clams or Oysters	Bed

- Each of us suffers from ergophobia sometime in life. What is the affliction? — Fear of or aversion to work; laziness

- What is a golf term whose latin definition is "equal"? — Par

- What is a "bissextile" year? — A leap year

- What would you call a person whose occupation it is to shoe horses? — A farrier

- What root word might follow the prefixes *out*– and *down*–, and mean, respectively, "an outsider; derelict" and "forlorn, depressed"? — Cast

- Name the Armenian-originated dish consisting of seasoned meats and vegetables on a skewer. — Shish kebob

- An outward burst is called an "explosion." What is the term for an inward burst? — Implosion

- What is the English word that, when all its letters are capitalized, comes out the same backward, forward, and upside down? — NOON

- Very few English-language words were borrowed from Chinese. By their definitions, identify these that were.

    - An orange-colored, plum-sized fruit. — Kumquat

    - To show great deference or respect. — Kowtow

    - A "great wind." — Typhoon

    - A popular 1920's game played with tiles. — Mah-jong

- Supply the euphemisms to the following definitions:

    - To sweat. — Perspire

    - To drink alcohol. — Imbibe

    - A prison. — Correctional facility

    - Bad breath. — Halitosis

    - Guts (nerve). — Intestinal fortitude or pluck

    - A dead person. — The late, the deceased, or the departed

2

– Used (as in a "used" car).	Previously owned
– Drunk, soused.	Inebriated or intoxicated
– A war (specifically, the Korean War).	Police action

• Come up with the shortest English word that contains each of the first six letters of the alphabet. — Feedback

• What word means both "swift of foot" and "a group of ships or trucks under one command"? — Fleet

• A derisive name was given to the adherent of the great Middle Ages philosopher and theologian John Duns Scotus after his teachings came under attack. What were his followers called, and what English term meaning "stupid person" is rooted from this? — Dunsmen; dunce

• In order to collect honey, farmers build homes for their bees. What are these artificial hives called? — Apiaries

• "Gnaw" and "gnash" are words that begin with a silent g followed by an n. What are other "gn" words for these definitions?

– To bite or chew.	Gnaw
– A tiny dipterous insect.	Gnat
– A type of African antelope.	Gnu
– A mythical scandinavian race of diminutive, underground beings.	Gnomes
– A philosophical religious movement.	Gnosticism
– A protruding knot on a tree.	Gnarl

• When you lie on your back, you are not "prone." What are you? — Supine

• As in the example, "Madam, I'm Adam," what do you call a phrase or word that reads the same – letterwise – read either forward or backward. — A palindrome

• Give the meanings for these common Latin terms:

– E Pluribus Unim (on U.S. coinage).	"Out of many, one"
– Pro tempore.	"For the first time"
– Alma mater.	"Fostering mother"
– Ipso facto.	"By the very fact"
– Caveat emptor	"Let the buyer beware"
– Annuit coeptis (on the U.S. seal).	"He hath smiled on our undertakings"
– Cum laude	"With praise"

• The letters P.S. written at the end of a card or letter stand for what? — Post script

• What word, taken from the spotless white togas worn by campaigning Roman politicians, now means "one who seeks nomination"? — Candidate (from the white garment, "candidatus")

• One legal term refers to oral defamation while another refers to written defamation. Identify these two terms. — Slander and libel

• In writing, it is the sign used to signify a footnote; in Greek it means "star." What is it? — An asterisk (*)

• These words – lullaby, melody, dawn, amaryllis, gossamer, hush, murmuring, chimes – among others, were thought by Dr. Wilfred Funk to be the most what? — The most beautiful words of the English language

• What multi-spelled word means "a lunch meat" or "nonsense; rubbish"? — Boloney, bologna, bolony, baloney

• What term for "good-bye" literally means "go in health"? — Farewell (or Salud)

• What word, when used as a verb, means "to eat greedily or gluttonously," and, used as a noun, means "a deep, narrow pass between steep heights"? — Gorge

- The French "mouche" ("fly" – as in the insect) became "moucher" ("to fly") which became "mouche" ("run!"). What French-Canadian command finally evolved from this chain of meanings? — Mush!

- A connoisseur of food and drink is called by what name? — An epicure

- What animal word would describe someone who is:

    – A bold and greedy rogue or a rapacious swindler? — Shark

    – Timid, fearful? — Mouse

    – Peevish, grumpy? — Crab

    – Sly? — Fox

    – A docile follower? — Sheep

    - Doublecrossing, despicable? — Rat

    - A speculator who seeks to depress prices? — Bear

    - A dealer who expects high prices? — Bull

    - Little or insignificant? — Shrimp

    - Lazy, indolent? — Sloth (or drone)

- What does a "misogamist" hate? — Marriage

- What is the word for a person who pretends to do or believe something he or she really doesn't do or believe"? In Greek this word means, "I who plays a part." — Hypocrite

- A baby pig is called by what two names? — Shoat or piglet

- Name the Scottish word for the cloth design known in its native India as "kairi," representing the "trivatna" (or "three jewels of Buddha." — Paisley

- What two-word term refers to "a total withdrawal from smoking" or "a type of meat sandwich"? — Cold turkey

- What common word uses each of the five vowels, plus *y*, in their proper order? — Facetiously

- What's the longest word that can be written without using *a,e,i,o,* or *u*? — Rhythm

- What's the longest English word that uses only one vowel? — Strengths

- "Nanook" is the Eskimo word for what? — Polar bear

- Name the "fruit" slang term that might describe:

    – A defective car. — Lemon

    – A beautiful, desirable auto. — Plum

    – A well-liked person. — Peach

    – A hand grenade. — Pineapple

    – Bright red. — Cherry

- What word is taken from the Greek "kismos" and means "something that beautifies or preserves"? — Cosmetics

- The gods and goddess Cupid, Aphrodite (Venus) and Eros all play some part in what human emotion? — Love

- What word has become part of the English language from U.S. Army slang for "Situation Normal, All Fouled Up"? — Snafu

- According to the *Guiness Book of World Records,* what word has the most definitions, with 58 noun uses, 126 verb uses, and 10 uses as a participle adjective? — Set

- What word, pertaining to "the side," is often preceded by "uni," "bi" or quadri"? — Lateral

- An atheist is one who denies or disbelieves the existence of God. What is a person called who believes that the universe, as a whole, *is* God? — A pantheist

• Slang for "prison," what word also indicates the sound made when drinking glasses bump together in a toast?	Clink
• What word means the opposite of "zenith"?	Nadir
• Identify the term signifying a type of divination practice in which the oracle used is an egg.	Oomancy
• From Old French for "to bat back and forth," what word means "to exchange angry words"?	Bandy
• What Italian word, used as both a greeting and as a farewell, was originally "schiavo vosotro" ("I am your slave")?	Ciao
• In John Milton's classic *Paradise Lost*, what word did he coin to reflect the "Capital of Satan"?	Pandemonium
• If a halo encircles the entire body of a person, it would be called a what?	Mandorla
• "Strafe" means to fire at ground targets from the air, or to shoot at close range. The word came from the World War I German slogan, "Gott (God) strafe England." What did it then mean?	Punish
• What word means "a small broom," "a kitchen utensil," and "to brush away or carry off with a brisk, sweeping motion"?	Whisk
• What military weapons, developed in England during World War I, were first called "water carriers," in order to maintain secrecy?	Tanks
• From this list of breakfast foods – ham, eggs, cereal, milk, oranges, toast, rolls, coffee, and chocolate – which Arab-extracted word came to us from the Turkish language?	Coffee
– Which three are derived from Old English?	Ham, milk, eggs
– Which three are of Latin origin, either directly or through French?	Cereal, toast, rolls
– Which is taken from an American Indian name?	Chocolate
– Which came from Sanskrit Persian?	Orange
• "Veto" means, literally, what?	I forbid
• What is the best-known artificial international language?	Esperanto
• Name the word for a period of merrymaking that precedes Lent and which translated means "the putting away of meat."	Carnival
• Give the much simpler synonym for "sanguineous," "winsome," and "eupeptic."	Happy
• Give a two-word term that means "to neck," "to see with some difficulty," and "to write a check."	Make out
• Grizzly bears are not "grizzly" but derived their name from this term. What does "grizzly" mean?	Gray
• "Utopia" is the ancient Greek word meaning what?	Nowhere
• What Chinese army motto, popularized by Evans F. Carlson in his U.S. Marine unit, meant "work together," and now signifies someone who is "extremely dedicated or enthusiastic"?	Gung-ho
• What word means "children," "a question to be decided," and "a copy of a magazine"?	Issue
• This word, taken from the twelfth-century crusades, later described tournaments in which knights rode a circular course, while trying to spear a target ring. Meaning "little war," the word was also used to name a machine run by steam power. By what name do we now know these "little war" machines?	Carousels ("garosello"), or "merry-go-rounds"
• A clumsey dancer might be described as having what two appendages?	Two left feet
• What is the proper title, as used in the Bible, of the dot over an "*i*"?	A tittle
• If you suffer from narcolepsy, what do you keep doing at all hours of the day?	Falling asleep

5

- What means "to choke or strangle" and also "to reduce the fuel intake of a car"?

  Throttle

- The term "robot" came from "robotnik," first used in Czech playwright Karel Capek's 1923 play "R.U.R." What did the word really refer to?

  "Slave"

- Give the plural for these words:

    – Thesis

      Theses

    – Notary public

      Notaries public

    – Judge advocate

      Judge advocates

    – Son-in-law

      Sons-in-law

    – Moose

      Moose

    – Ox

      Oxen

- Ancient moneychangers transacted their business over a portable bench or table. When a moneychanger became insolvent (from the Latin "solvens," meaning "to loosen") his bench was broken (or "rupta"). What do we call this transaction or condition today?

  Bankrupt or bankruptcy

- The Persian "shah mat" (meaning "the king is dead") produced what word denoting finality, and commonly used in an ancient – and still popular – game?

  Checkmate

- Meaning "to abstain from eating," what word also could mean "soundly," and might precede "asleep"?

  Fast

- What term is used to identify any four-sided polygon?

  Quadrilateral

- A "Mae West" on a World War II battleship was the term for what device?

  A life jacket

- The word "science" (meaning "beautiful" in Anglo-Saxon) evolved into what word that describes the appearance of lustrous, healthy hair?

  Sheen

- Give the word that signifies "the best cut of meat," "to make ready," and "the most opportune period"?

  Prime

- What word, taken from the Latin for "one who loves," now refers to a "nonprofessional"?

  Amateur

- *Tri-*, of course, means "three." Name the "tri" words for each of these definitions:

    – The study of the relations between the angles and sides of a triangle.

      Trigonometry

    – A group of three related artistic works.

      Trilogy

    – Neptune's three-pronged spear.

      Trident

    – To divide into three equal parts.

      Trisect

    – The medieval name for the single-course study of grammar, rhetoric, and logic (and also the name of the place where 3 roads meet and friends collect to share gossip and information).

      Trivium (trivia)

    – A period of three months.

      Trimester

MISCELLANEOUS FACTS
Trivia to Learn By

• The Great Seal of the United States (as pictured on the back of a dollar bill) includes three Latin sayings: "E pluribus unum," "Annuit coeptis," and "Novus ordo seclorum." What do they mean?

"Out of many, one," "He has smiled on our undertakings," and "A new order of the ages."

• It takes only two seconds for what animal to accelerate from a standing start to 45 mph?

The cheetah

• As many as 300 individual U.S. flags are flown alternately over what building on a given day?

The U.S. Capitol (to be used as souvenirs)

• What does "c." (circa), written before a date, mean?

"About"

• At birth, a baby has about 305 of these; due to fusion, an adult has only about 206. What are they?

Bones

• What is the highest policy-making bureau of the Soviet Communist Party?

The Politburo

• Before 1883, each city and town in the U.S. kept its own local time. Name the four "time zones" established by Charles Dowd and adopted in that year by the federal government.

Eastern, Central, Mountain and Pacific

• Many eighteenth-century sailors had an image tatooed on their backs in hopes of deterring their ship's captain from punishing infractions with the lash. What was this image?

A crucifix

• Which month was named for:
    – An ancient deity who presided over doors and gates?

January

    – The Roman God of War?

March

    – The Latin word for "to open"?

April

• Which U.S. city, in 1897, was first to have a subway?

Boston

• What is the elevation (in feet above sea level) of Mt. Everest? It rises on the border between what two countries?

29, 028 feet, Nepal and Tibet

• If you removed all of the arteries, veins and capillaries from an average-size man, how far would they stretch if placed end to end?

62,000 miles

• How many sheets of paper are there in a ream?

500

• What is the Hebrew name for the annual Jewish Day of Atonement, a holiday in which a 24-hour fast is observed to symbolize penitence and cleansing?

Yom Kippur

• What is the only even prime number?

Two

• Acupuncture (a Chinese yin cure) is now popular in the West. Ignipuncture (the yang cure) never caught on. What is ignipuncture?

A small cone of crushed, dried leaves is lit and allowed to burn on the patient

• What is the code name for Coca Cola's secret ingredient?

7X

• What two dog stars needed to "come home" in their separate movie features?

Lassie and Snoopy

• According to Greek legend, what monster has the body of a lion, a woman's head, and eats all creatures unable to answer its questions?

The sphinx

• The doctrine that pleasure and happiness are to be sought out, and that their attainment constitutes man's ultimate goal, is known by what name? What Greek school taught the contrasting philosophy that all appetites and passions were to be strictly subdued and governed?

Hedonism; the Stoics

• In what country lives the world's smallest monkey ("tarsius") and one of the largest eagles ("monkeyeater")?

The Philippines

• In the United States, on what day of the week do most fatal car accidents occur?

Saturday

- It was once believed that at the occurance of a particularly common event that one's soul was expelled, and that at that moment a demon could enter and take control of the body. What is this natural event, which still evokes a "blessing" from those nearby?

  A sneeze ("God bless you")

- What is the mathematical definition of a "perfect" number? Hint: 6 (with the factors 3, 2 and 1) and 28 (14, 7, 4, 2, 1) are the two simplest examples.

  A number whose factors, when added together, equal the number itself

- In the nursery rhyme beginning "Rub a dub, dub," what are the occupations of the three men in the tub?

  Butcher, baker, and candle-stick maker

- What is a titmouse? Is it bigger or smaller than a regular mouse?

  It is a bird (not a rodent) about the size of a chickadee (slightly bigger than a mouse)

- What radioactive materials were found some distance from the Three-Mile Island nuclear accident?

  Cat feces (apparently, contaminated mice were still deemed palatable by roving felines)

- In palmistry, what are the four main lines on the hand?

  Life, heart, fate and head

- If your palm begins itching, according to superstition, what will happen?

  You will soon receive unexpected money

- Bird-nest soup is made from the nests of what species of bird?

  The swift

- If you divide the Roman numeral "M" by the numeral "XX", what answer do you get?

  "L" or 50 (1000 divided by 20)

- Why is it especially difficult for foreign visitors to count their change in the United States?

  U.S. coins have no numerical markings

- Who came up with the idea for the "Ten Most Wanted" criminals list – inspired by a fashion survey entitled "Ten Best-Dressed Women"?

  J. Edgar Hoover

- What are the "Three Cardinal Virtues"? What other four characteristics are added to these to make up the "Seven Virtues"?

  Faith, Hope, Charity (Love); Fortitude, Justice, Prudence, Temperance

- What company product had the honor of appearing on the first nationally broadcast television commercial in 1941?

  The Bulova watch

- What are the "four C's" of a diamond?

  Cut, carat, clarity, color

- With hundreds of bird species in the U.S., six states (Illinois, Indiana, North Carolina, Ohio, Virginia, West Virginia) have adopted the same bird as their state bird, and five states (Arkansas, Florida, Mississippi, Tennessee and Texas) have adopted another. What are these two most popular birds?

  The cardinal and the mockingbird

- Many 19th-century British denture-wearers took pride in knowing their teeth were extracted from the dead of what great battle?

  Waterloo ("Waterloo teeth")

- What part of the body has the greatest capacity to cool itself, giving off up to 63.5 Btu's of heat per hour? (The head radiates only about 15.9 Btu/hour.)

  The hands

- The calendar officially in use throughout the world at present – except in a few nations that adhere to the Moslem or Buddhist calendars – is known by what name?

  The Gregorian

- What is the only species of cat that lives and hunts in groups?

  The lion (prides)

- A white substance once sold in China for tongue ailments, and thought to be dragons' brains mixed with the earth, was really what material?

  Asbestos

- Tofu is a curd made from what?

  Soybeans

- How many crosses are permitted on a Catholic bishop's tomb? on a priest's? on an ordinary member's?

  7; 5; 1

- It has 13 stars, 13 stripes, 13 clouds, 13 arrows, 13 laurel leaves, 13 berries, 13 feathers in each wing, 13 tail feathers and 13 pyramid rows. What is it, and where can it most easily be found?

  The Great Seal of the United States; on the back of a dollar bill

- Sight, hearing, touch, taste, and smell are the five basic senses. What is often referred to as the "sixth sense"? — Intuition
- What kind of animals are the following breeds?
    - Poland China, Berkshire, Cheshire — Pigs
    - Clydesdale, Hackney, Percheron — Horses
    - Brahma, Leghorn, Bantam — Chickens
    - Bronze, White Holland, Narraganset — Turkey
    - Brown Swiss, Red Polled, Aberdeen Angus — Cows
    - Peking, Rouen, Muscovy — Ducks
- What San Francisco intersection was considered the center of the 1960's "Hippie" ("flower child") community? — Haight and Ashbury
- Who was the only "last stand" survivor from Custer's regiment? — A horse – some insist it was Custer's mount – whom the Indians named "Comanche"
- What game uses only tiles made of Bavarian maple wood from Germany's Black Forest – used because the close grain of the wood prevents scratches? — *Scrabble*
- Who are the Hindu trinity – the Creator, the Destroyer and Restorer, and the Savior? — Brahma, Shiva, and Vishnu
- In radio operations during World War II, what were the first 3 alphabetically (A, B, and C) ordered "code" words used to test for correct transmission? — Able, Baker, Charlie
- What is the line called that divides a circle into two semicircles? — The diameter
- During the Vietnam War the Pentagon commissioned a playing card company to send 3 million duplicates of a particular card to G.I.'s. The cards were placed on buildings and tanks to help ward off attack; the Vietcong had a morbid fear of this "death card." What was the card? — The Ace of Spades
- What humidifies and filters approximately 500 cubic feet of air each day? — Your nose
- In Ireland, why would one want to kiss the Blarney Stone? — To be blessed with the power of persuasion
- What is the oldest American college fraternity (dating from 1752 at William and Mary)? the oldest sorority (inaugurated in 1852 at Wesleyan College)? — Sigma Pi and Phi Mu
- Using Roman numerals, what is the difference between C and LXIX? — XXXI (100 - 69 = 31)
- In the old English ditty "Pop Goes the Weasel," the "weasel" refers to what family item commonly pawned ("popped") by factory workers to get Saturday night drinking money? — An iron
- Why do many Eskimos buy refrigerators? — To keep food from freezing
- What was the original name for the Ku Klux Klan's leader, the "Imperial Wizard"? — The "Grand Cyclops"
- The name "Philadelphia" is a compound from classical Greek meaning what? — "City of Brotherly Love"
- What cities are identified by these other nicknames?
    - The Eternal City — Rome, Italy
    - Gateway to the West — St. Louis, Missouri
    - Beantown — Boston, Massachusetts
    - Music City U.S.A. — Nashville, Tennessee
    - The Windy City — Chicago, Illinois
    - Big D — Dallas, Texas
    - Biggest Little City in the World — Reno, Nevada

- In what century will we be on January 1, 2000?

  Still in the 20th (the 21st begins January 1, 2001)

- In the army, at what time is "Taps" blown?

  10:00 p.m.

- What name is given the number "1" followed by a hundred zeros?

  "Googol"

- How many tablespoons equal one cup?

  16

- In the comic strip "Blondie," what's the full name of Dagwood Bumstead's boss?

  Julius Ceasar Dithers

- Name the sport or game in which the following moves or plays are made:
    - A lay-up — Basketball
    - Sweeping — Curling
    - The scissors — Wrestling
    - Castling — Chess
    - Veronica — Bull Fighting
    - Trolling — Fishing
    - A flea-flicker — Football

- How many feet make up a mile? How many yards?

  5,280; 1,760

- In the event of a nuclear catastrophe, what creature, able to withstand up to 60,000 roentgens of radiation, could likely take over the earth? (Humans can safely absorb no more than 200 roentgens.)

  The cockroach

- In Ian Fleming's *James Bond* series, what does the "00" prefix signify?

  That the agent has the license to kill

- What is the one animal that has four knees?

  The elephant

- What was the first ship to use the distress signal SOS? What was the signal before that time?

  The *Titanic*, on the night it sank; CQD ("come quickly ... ")

- The three Wise Men of the nativity story, though not named in the Bible, are traditionally known by what names?

  Gaspar, Melchior and Balthazar

- Name the largest museum in the world.

  The Louvre

- About how many pints of blood are in the average adult human body?

  Twelve

- During the Civil War, Union soldiers dined on pork and beans and condensed milk prepared by what two canned food processors of today?

  Van Camp's and Borden's

- "Catgut," used for centuries on stringed instruments, is made from what material?

  Sheep intestines

- Name the 6 fields of contribution in which Nobel Prizes are given each year.

  Physics, chemistry, economics, physiology or medicine, literature, and peace

- At Cincinnati Zoological Park on September 1, 1914, at 1:00 p.m., what last-of-a-species animal died?

  A passenger pigeon

- In order to have a Friday-the-13th, a month must start on what day of the week?

  A Sunday

- What is the White House telephone number?

  (202) 456-1414

- Known in Russia as NENCN-KONA, what is Hugh Hefner's – and the late Elvis Presley's – favorite drink? What cult star made his first-ever TV appearance in a 1950 commercial to endorse this product?

  Pepsi Cola; James Dean

- American colonists turned to drinking what beverage when English tea prices rose, relations soured with the mother country, and other foreign supplies were found to be tainted?

  Coffee

- What would be good advice if you were running away from an alligator? (Alligators run much faster than humans.)

  Zig-zag

- The sum of a dozen, a score and a gross is what?

  176 (12 + 20 + 144)

4

• In the U.S., how many years must a person be missing before he can be declared legally dead?	Seven
• What is the highest valued poker hand? What is the lowest hand that could possibly win?	A Royal Flush in hearts; one-of-a-kind (highest card)
• What is the world's oldest national flag?	The Danish (Dannebrog)
• What travel restriction is put on the President and Vice-President of the U.S.?	They can not travel together
• London's famous "Big Ben" is neither a tower nor a clock. What is it?	The largest and heaviest (13 tons) of the clock's bells
• What letter is on the left end of the upper row of letters on a standard typewriter?	Q
• What color does a Chinese bride traditionally wear?	Red
• Who was Walt Disney's first cartoon character? (He later became the property of Walter Lanz.)	Oswald the Lucky Rabbit
• What is the minimum number of merit badges a Boy Scout must earn to become an Eagle?	21
• What brief inscription is carved onto the tablet held by the Statue of Liberty?	"July 4, 1776"
• What are the mascots of the Army Cadets, the Navy Midshipmen, and the Air Force football teams?	A mule, a goat, and a falcon
• "Little neck" and "Cherrystone" are two types of what seafood?	Clams
• About how many pounds of coffee beans does it take to yield one pound of ground, roasted coffee?	Six
• Alphabetically, which of the U.S. states comes last?	Wyoming
• What German award, equivalent to the Oscar, is annually given to the country's most popular motion picture actor?	The Otto
• What day of the year is Bastille Day (France's Independence Day)?	July 14
• The guardsmen of the British royal palace are known by what name?	Beefeaters
• U.S. coins with no mint mark are minted where? Where are coins marked "D" or "S" minted?	Philadelphia; Denver or San Francisco
• Whose picture is on a two-dollar-bill?	Alexander Hamilton's
• What was the first ready-to-eat breakfast cereal to come on the market?	Shredded Wheat
• What is the number of the CB radio channel generally allocated for emergency use?	Nine
• What is 500% of the square of 2?	20 (5x2x2)
• By what two names is the 10-armed Hindu goddess known?	Parvati or Doorga
• What Egyptian city is nearest King Tut's tomb?	Luxor
• What temperature (in fahrenheit) is considered "room temperature"?	68 degrees
• The American Kennel Club puts dogs into six classifications. What are they?	Working dogs, sporting dogs, non-sporting dogs, hounds, terriers and toys
• The famous Titanic had a sister ship by what name? What was the sister ship of the British liner Lusitania, sunk by Germany in World War I?	*The Olympic; Mauritania*
• What is the name for Islam's ninth month – the month of fasting?	Ramadan
• Name the legal process that advises an individual of any criminal charges and allows a plea to be given.	Arraignment
• A U.S. patent is in force for how many years?	17
• What name was given to the bread once carried on ships to feed the passengers?	Hardtack

5

- Name the two Greek Thespian masks.

  Tragedy and Comedy

- An "alligator pear" is the other name for what fruit?

  The avocado

- Name the respective leaders of West Side Story's two rival gangs, the Jets and the Sharks.

  Riff and Bernardo

- As the source of the world's most expensive spice, what flower requires 70,000 to 80,000 hand-pressed orange-red blossoms to make one pound of spice?

  Saffro

- Traditionally, on what day of the year is a new President of the United States sworn into office?

  January 20

- What punctuation mark separates both Biblical chapter and verse and the two numbers expressing a ratio?

  The colon (:)

- Disney's Mickey Mouse originally went by what name? What are the names of Mickey's two nephews?

  Mortimer Mouse; Ferdy and Morty

- What is a round revolving tray on a dining table called?

  A Lazy Susan

- In value, how many quarters would you need to equal 75 dimes?

  Thirty

- Which two letters are missing from a phone's dialing chart?

  Q and Z

- The bulk of what classic movie is shot in color, but begins and ends in black and white?

  "The Wizard of Oz"

- What is the word for a spotted American Indian pony?

  Pinto

- The first midair collision between two passenger aircraft occurred in 1956 over what popular U.S. tourist attraction?

  The Grand Canyon

- What U.S. colony was given the Latin name for King Charles, who "inaugurated" the land in 1663?

  Carolina

- Name the four U.S. states that have active volcanoes.

  Alaska, California, Hawaii and Washington

- Born in 1932, what is the name of Borden Milk's mascot cow? Who is her mate? Hint: He gave his name to a glue company.

  Elsie; Elmer

- How many upper-case typewritten letters in the English alphabet would be identical to their mirror image?

  Eleven

6

NOTES

NOTES

NOTES

NOTES

COMPACT

C

Classics™

■ WE WOULD LIKE TO HEAR FROM YOU

❑ I am a new customer. Please put me on your mailing list.
❑ I am on your present mailing list. Please note my
   address change.
❑ I have a comment or idea. (See below.)

Name _____
　　　　　　　LAST　　　　　　　　FIRST　　　　　　MIDDLE INITIAL

Street Address _____

City _____ State _____ Zip _____

Phone:
　Day (　　) _____ Evening (　　) _____

Compact Classics makes a great and original gift! Call toll free
1 (800) 755-9777 for current price information.

— · — · — · — · — · — · FOLD · — · — · — · — · — · — ·

■ SHARE YOUR GREAT IDEAS

　Your ideas and suggestions will make a difference. In fact, we'll
pay you $10.00 if you're the first to suggest a popular book or topic
used in a future edition.
　Below, please give us your suggestions or briefly describe
favorite books or topics you'd like to see included in up-coming
Compact Classics.

_____

_____

_____

_____

_____

_____

_____

　　　　　　　　　　Date Mailed _____/_____/_____

TAPE CLOSED

FROM: _____

_____

_____

_____

COMPACT CLASSICS INC.

P.O. BOX 526145
SALT LAKE CITY, UTAH 84152–6145